D1250794

Antislavery
Newspapers and Periodicals

Reference Publications in Afro-American Studies

Professor Charles T. Davis, Editor
Director of Afro-American Studies, Yale University

Professor Henry-Louis Gates, Jr., Assistant Editor
Department of Afro-American Studies, Yale University

Advisory Board

Professor Anthony Appiah, Clare College, University of Cambridge (England)
Professor Christopher Bigsby, University of East Anglia (England)
Professor John W. Blassingame, Yale University
Professor Michael Cooke, Yale University
Dr. St. Clair Drake, Stanford University
Professor Alan Dundes, University of California, Berkeley
Professor Donald Harris, Stanford University
Professor Louis Martz, Yale University
Professors Emmanuel Obiechina, University of Nsukka (Nigeria)
Professor Wole Soyinka, University of Ife (Nigeria)
Professor Robert F. Thompson, Yale University
Professor Victor Turner, University of Virginia

Antislavery
Newspapers and Periodicals

Volume I
(1817–1845)

Annotated Index of Letters in the *Philanthropist,*
Emancipator, Genius of Universal Emancipation,
Abolition Intelligencer, African Observer, and
the *Liberator.*

Edited by
John W. Blassingame and Mae G. Henderson

Withdrawn
Withdrawn
University of Waterloo
University of Waterloo

G.K. HALL & CO. BOSTON, MASSACHUSETTS

The preparation of this volume of the Antislavery Newspapers and Periodicals: Annotated Index of Letters was made possible through grants from the Research Tools Program of the National Endowment for the Humanities and Yale University.

Copyright © 1980 by John Blassingame and Mae G. Henderson

Library of Congress Cataloging in Publication Data
Main entry under title:
Antislavery newspapers and periodicals.
    (Reference publications in Afro-American studies)
    CONTENTS: v. 1. Annotated index of letters in the Philanthropist, Emancipator, Genius of universal emancipation, Abolition intelligencer, African observer, and the Liberator, 1817–1845.
    1. Afro-American newspapers—Indexes. 2. Afro-American periodicals—Indexes. 3. American newspapers—Indexes. 4. American periodicals—Indexes. 5. Newspapers—Sections, columns, etc.—Letters to the editor. 6. Social problems—Indexes. I. Blassingame, John W., 1940–   II. Henderson, Mae. III. Series.
AI3.B55   016.05   79-20230
ISBN 0-8161-8163-2 (v. 1)

This publication is printed on permanent/durable acid-free paper
MANUFACTURED IN THE UNITED STATES OF AMERICA

To the Antislavery Editors

The trials incident to the editorship of a newspaper are many and peculiar, and can be adequately known only to those who have been made acquainted with them by experience. And these trials will be abundantly enhanced in the case of every Editor who ventures to maintain his independence at the risk of his popularity. Of all guides the most uncertain, perhaps, and variable is popular opinion. He who trims his sail to catch the popular breeze, may have a pleasant voyage, perhaps, for a season, that is, supposing him to have thrown conscience and principle overboard. But he will quickly find his bark veering about to every possible point of the compass, and when the tempest—which sooner or later is sure to arise—shall come upon him, he will then find himself destitute of the only pilot that could have safely guided his vessel to land. Look back upon the shores of past time, and behold the innumerable wrecks that testify to the truth of this observation. Principle—Eternal Truth—alone can guide erring man through the straits and over the shallows and quicksands of mortal life, and bring him at last to rest, unharmed, to the haven of endless bliss.

Shall the press dare to speak out freely, or shall it be muzzled? We make it our request that all who feel an interest in this subject, in any way, would communicate with the Editor, with as little delay as possible. We ask that those who approve, as well as those who disapprove of our course, would inform us of their sentiments.--

Elijah P. Lovejoy

Contents

Illustrations

Preface

Most scholars agree that Charles Sainte-Beuve stated the obvious when he observed: "The details of history, in truth, can only be gathered from a study of the immense and varied surface which the literature of newspapers presents." At the same time, most scholars view newspapers and magazines, especially those from the nineteenth century, as labyrinths without a clue because there are no comprehensive journal indexes. We set out in the fall of 1977 to provide some clues to an extensive body of newspaper literature by establishing the Black and Reform Newspaper Indexing Project.

Funded by the National Endowment for the Humanities, the objective of the Project was the preparation of a multivolumed annotated list of letters appearing in selected nineteenth-century abolitionist, black, and reform journals. Unfortunately, we were only able to complete work on abolitionist newspapers and magazines. We chose to concentrate on letters because we felt they contained more of the personal details of history than did editorials, signed articles, book reviews, advertisements, and the like.

The letters in the journals reflect the spirit of the times, the fluctuating interests of blacks, reformers, and others, and represent a valuable tool in reconstructing the past. Until the first decades of the twentieth century Americans were addicted to writing letters to newspapers and magazines. As a result, nineteenth-century black and reform-oriented journals generally filled one-fifth of their columns with letters. Reports of conventions and social affairs, extended debates and discussions of controversial issues, accounts of foreign travel, and narratives of political campaigns were frequent. The body of the letters constitute an incomparable source for genealogists, historians, and students of nineteenth-century American literature, black life and culture, the abolitionist movement, women's rights, music, education, social problems, urbanization, folklore, health and science, social mobility, alcoholism and temperance, pacifism, electoral politics, religion, migration, marriage and family life, immigration, slavery, the Civil War and Reconstruction, interracial violence, prisons and prison reform, emigration, drama, journalism, Indian life and culture, labor, agriculture, and diplomacy.

This published list of letters in newspapers and magazines gives scholars a key to the correspondence of individuals needed for writing biographies. It elucidates many of the intellectual, social, and political currents of the nineteenth century and expands the data available for studying local communities. A surprisingly large number of nineteenth-century journals contained correspondence from all parts of the United States. Often, the only extant letters either written by antebellum blacks or containing descriptions of Afro-Americans in widely scattered cities in the United States were printed in abolitionist newspapers.

Although focussing primarily on their own constituencies, abolitionist journals reprinted letters of correspondents catholic in their interests. Abolitionist newspapers frequently contained letters from Greece, Great Britain, Haiti, Russia, France, Latin America, Africa, and other parts of the world. Famous politicians, stung by editorial attacks, published letters on various topics in the journals. Generally not found in manuscript collections, but often published in abolitionist journals, the letters of such individuals become more accessible to their biographers through the publication of this annotated list.

An overwhelming majority of the correspondents are obscure individuals. Collectively, however, their letters provide a perspective on an almost unlimited range of topics and simplify the task of writing collective sketches, compiling biographical encyclopedias and directories of such groups as nineteenth-century women, abolitionists, Southern and Northern black politicians, novelists, poets, musicians, educators, and others.

Nineteenth-century abolitionist journals are among the most elusive of sources. Standard bibliographies and general histories of American journalism furnish few clues to either the number of journals published or the location of extant copies. There are no central repositories for the journals. Consequently, systematic research is required even to compile a list of nineteenth-century abolitionist periodicals. While some of the titles we discovered have been more elusive than others, we made a concerted effort to locate all of the extant issues of the journals we indexed. Because of the large number and historical dispersion of abolitionist and reform journals published in the nineteenth century, we were unable to locate all of the potential titles. We did, however, search systematically for them. Given limited resources, we tried to index all of the key abolitionist journals, while attempting to ensure geographical and ideological representativeness.

As important as abolitionist journals were during the nineteenth century, contemporary Americans know little about their editors, the financial struggles involved in keeping the journals afloat, or how frequently mobs destroyed them. The story of these journals is an exciting but neglected chapter of American journalism. Although their combined circulation figure was higher than that of such better known contemporaries as the *New York Times* in the nineteenth century, it is the *Times* which has attracted historians and students of journalism. Dozens of histories of the *Times* have been published; there is not only no book-length study of an abolitionist newspaper, but even articles on them are rare. Because so little is known about these journals, it is necessary for us to explain briefly why we concentrated on certain categories of newspapers and magazines.

We were interested in compiling an index of abolitionist newspapers and periodicals because in few general interest journals can the black and reform angle of vision on the nineteenth century be found. All too often when Afro-Americans and reformers sent letters to metropolitan newspapers they were rejected. Willis Hodges, a New York black, narrated a typical experience in the 1840's when he objected to an article in the New York *Sun* attacking Afro-Americans:

> I prepared a reply to this article and took it to the editor of the *Sun*, but he would not publish it unless I paid him $15. He then put my article away down in the corner out of the sight of nine out of ten of the readers. I went to him and demanded to know why? He said because it was "a paid advertisement." I then said, "Well, you told me that you would not put it in unless I paid you, and I, therefore, expected to see it in some other part of the paper. You are only giving light on one side of the case, and your paper says that it 'shines for all.'"
>
> [The editor replied:] "The *Sun* shines for all white men, not black men. You must get up a paper of your own if you want to tell your side of the story to the public. Good morning."

The editors of practically all other nineteenth-century abolitionist journals included a "Correspondents" section in their papers to insure that the sun would also shine on the oppressed, black and white.

Even the most liberal papers carried relatively few communications from blacks because their letters often lacked literary polish. In contrast, black and reform journals often published the letters of the semiliterate in an effort to encourage the development of literary skills in the black community. One correspondent in *Frederick Douglass' Paper*, for instance, observed in 1851 that "it should not be forgotten, that *Frederick Douglass' Paper* has afforded the most extensive opportunity for a free and full expression of sentiments by the illiterate as well as the learned." A year later, Douglass stated an editorial position on publishing letters which was typical of nineteenth-century black and reform editors:

> We sometimes publish letters, which, when viewed apart from the writers, do very little credit to the literary character of our paper. The motive for such publication is to

encourage those for whose special development and elevation this paper was established. Our readers must bear with them and give *our people* a chance to be great as well as themselves.

Open to a much broader spectrum of the reading public than general interest journals edited by whites, abolitionist periodicals contain an indispensable record of nineteenth-century Afro-American life and culture. Many blacks who rarely sent missives to general interest newspapers published dozens of letters in abolitionist newspapers and periodicals.

The early reform journals have been included in the index because they differed in many ways from those published after 1830. Abolitionist editors in the 1820's, for instance, were far more tolerant and less militant than their successors. Published in Tennessee, Missouri, Kentucky, and Maryland, the early journals reflected the gradualist antislavery stance of many Southern abolitionists. John Finley Crowe's 1822 editorial declaration in the Shelbyville (Ky.) *Abolition Intelligencer* that the aim of the paper was "to *prepare* the public mind for taking the necessary *preparatory* measures for the *gradual* abolition of slavery," contrasted sharply with the objectives of William Lloyd Garrison's *Liberator*. Writing in his first issue in 1831, Garrison asserted:

> I shall strenuously contend for the immediate enfranchisement of our slave population. . . . I am aware that many object to the severity of my language; but is there not cause for severity? I *will* be as harsh as truth, and as uncompromising as justice. On this subject, I do not wish to think or speak, or write, with moderation. No! no! Tell a man whose house is on fire to give a moderate alarm; tell him to moderately rescue his wife from the hands of the ravisher; tell the mother to gradually extricate her babe from the fire into which it has fallen;—but urge me not to use moderation in a cause like the present.

Slaveholders appeared in the *Liberator* as sinners; in the earlier journals they were often depicted as ordinary men saddled with a complex social problem by their forefathers. The *Liberator* rejected African colonization; many of the earlier abolitionist journals contended that the only way blacks could obtain equality was by leaving the United States.

Because many of the early abolitionist journals were more moderate in tone than the later ones and were published in the South and Southwest (Tennessee, Missouri, Maryland, and Kentucky) they contain many letters from Southern reformers, colonizationists, and slaveholders. Confronting slavery as a reality rather than an abstraction, Southern correspondents publishing letters in periodicals between 1817 and 1830 present a portrait of the peculiar institution differing in many ways from that drawn by many historians. Southern planters appeared, for instance, quite ready to acknowledge guilt over holding slaves. Southern interest in temperance and other reforms also emerges in letters published in such journals as the *Genius of Universal Emancipation* and the *Abolition Intelligencer*.

We begin by publishing indexes of the letters in abolitionist and reform journals which started publication between 1817 and 1831. The newspapers and magazines indexed in Volume One were published in Tennessee, Maryland, Kentucky, Washington, D.C., Pennsylvania, Ohio, Illinois, and Massachusetts and include the Mount Pleasant (Oh.) *Philanthropist*, 1817–18; Tennessee *Emancipator*, 1820; Shelbyville (Ky.) *Abolition Intelligencer*, 1822–23; *Genius of Universal Emancipation*, 1821–39; *African Observer*, 1827-28 and the Boston (Ma.) *Liberator*, 1831–65. The index of each journal is presented in its entirety with the exception of the long-running *Liberator*. Volume one includes the first fifteen years of the *Liberator* (1831–45). Volume Two will include the second part of the *Liberator* (1846-65).

The annotated list of letters is presented chronologically by date of appearance in each journal and the entries are numbered consecutively throughout the volume. The list of letters in each journal is published in its entirety before beginning those appearing in another. A journal data sheet appears before the list of letters in each journal and presents its history in capsule form: including places where issues are located, whether or not there is a microform, names of editor(s), and place(s) of publication. Whenever they could be located, we have reprinted prospectuses of the journals to give readers some sense of their purpose. For the same reasons, we have included short biographical sketches, autobiographical statements, and reminiscences of the editors, the people who inevitably put their stamp on the journals. We have drawn these sketches, whenever posssible, from nineeteenth-century newspapers, books, pamphlets, and periodicals because biographies written by contemporaries and associates frequently include little known and especially revealing personal anecdotes and facts.

As a general rule, we attempted to present a rough characterization of the letters in as brief a form as was consistent with clarity and utility. Though we would have liked to publish a more detailed précis of each letter, we had to be realistic about the economics of research and printing. Consequently, we sought entries of manageable compactness and clarity. When the material being summarized is from an extract of a letter, this fact is noted. Boldface type is used to denote senders and recipients, dates and places of letters. Each entry has been assigned a number to facilitate indexing.

The entries vary in character and detail and partially reflect the different styles of several dozen graduate and undergraduate students who did the basic research. We tried throughout the project to have researchers write précis of between fifteen and twenty-five words. But as researchers became more familiar with the topics explored by correspondents (or bored with their repetitiveness), they began writing extremely short summaries. In some instances, they were originally so cryptic that we had to expand them during our proof-reading and copyediting. Often a cryptic entry will appear because the annotated letter was part of a series in which the earlier entries give fuller detail. On the other hand, some of our researchers consistently wrote such long "abstracts" that we spent a great deal of time at the copyediting stage trying to reduce them to manageable size. Undoubtedly we have not always succeeded in our search for uniformity.

Despite our best efforts, we occasionally ended up with microfilm of journals where issues were illegible. We have indicated in our summaries those letters which were partially illegible. Illegible issues were much easier for us to handle than thoses rare instances when we began annotating a journal only to find months later that an entire reel of microfilm was illegible. In such cases we first explored the possibility of a second photocopying of the run. Secondly, when the original newspaper was so faded that we could not obtain a readable microfilm, we tried to locate other repositories having runs that we could photo-copy. Finally, when we had exhausted all of the possibilities without being able to obtain complete runs, we decided to include the index of the partial run of such journals. We will note those journals with incomplete runs.

While perfection is perhaps more devoutly to be wished for in a reference tool than in any other work a scholar does, it is also the most difficult of tasks. In the final analysis, we can only tell readers how we tried to ensure accuracy and comprehensiveness and beg their indulgence for any errors of commission or omission.

People indexing newspapers and magazines eventually reach the point where they feel they are the object of the "error conspiracy." Nineteenth-century printers were notorious for mutilating names; inevitably their errors are replicated by researchers. Even with a minimum of errors in the journals being indexed, our typists sometimes fought a losing battle in trying to decipher the script of dozens of researchers. The frequent resort to pseudonyms and initials by nineteenth-century correspondents and the idiosyncratic re-cording of place names made it impossible to verify certain items by turning to other sources.

Generally, we have recorded personal and place names as they appeared in the journals rather than trying to standardize or to modernize them. However strange such spellings as "Porto Rico" and "Mohamet" may appear to contemporary readers, they were ac-ceptable according to nineteenth-century usage. Since we generally recorded names as they appeared in the newspapers and magazines, we have rarely used "*sic*" in our entries.

Occasionally newspapers and magazines committed errors in dating issues and enumerating pages. To indicate such errors, we have normally cited the dates and page numbers as they appeared in the journal and then added the correct information in brackets.

Many of the letters we have annotated covered two or more columns or pages in a journal. Our entries indicate only where each letter begins. Some letters were so long that they were printed in part in one issue of a journal and concluded in another one. We have usually noted when a letter continues from one issue to another.

In a number of cases, correspondents wrote long letters themselves while enclosing other letters which they suggested that an editor also publish. The editors did not always follow such suggestions. Consequently, some of our entries may indicate that a correspondent enclosed a letter while we have no précis of the enclosure.

Nineteenth-century newspapers and magazines were inconsistent in how they defined and treated letters. Letters often appeared in columns labelled "Correspondence," "Exchanges," or with headlines, with and without salutations, and were frequently clipped from other journals. Many editors favored the use of initials by correspondents while others adopted such typographic practices that it was often difficult to separate letters from signed articles. Whatever the practices of the editors, we tried to err on the side of generosity in our annotation of the newspapers and magazines by adopting a broad definition of what constituted a "letter."

In an effort to ensure as high a degree of accuracy as possible, we first proofread the typescripts against the notecards and secondly against the journals. Systematically proofreading our original entries against the newspapers and magazines, we verified the names of correspondents and places, dates, page and column numbers, and the completeness and adequacy of annotations.

The entries are most reliable and useful as guides to the public letters written by individuals to the newspapers and magazines included in these volumes. Although we were unable to expand all of the cryptic entries, they can still often provide useful clues to the creative researcher. For example, it is frequently the case that entries preceding and following a cryptic one will provide enough detail to shed light on it. Thus, an entry on "nonresistance" might be followed by others indicating correspondents' reactions to a recent meeting of the New England Non-Resistance Society. In other words, those readers interested in specific subjects rather than individuals would be well served by checking those cryptic entries indicating larger categories under which their more limited topic might have been subsumed.

In order to avoid confusion, we should say a word about the index. Different correspondents who used the same initials and psuedonyms or who had identical names are included in the same entries in the index. It was, unfortunately, impossible to separate them with any confidence solely on the basis of data appearing in the journals.

The Black and Reform Newspaper Indexing Project was singularly fortunate in being able to build upon the work done by the staff of the Frederick Douglass Papers project between 1973 and 1977. By the latter date, the Douglass staff had compiled more than 60,000 notecards in the course of their search for Douglass letters and speeches published in nineteenth-century journals. Between 1973 and 1977, Yale undergraduates Donald Woodall, Mitchell Crusto, Wendy Jones, Marcia Finkelstein, James Singleton, Peter Bollier, Bart Steinfeld, Teresa McAlpine, Michelle Anderson, Ruth Good, Devon Miller, Carter Eskew, Marsha Moseley, Joanne Payton, Bruce Piersawl, Brent Raulerson, Kenneth Noble, Judith Hall, Phyllis Eckhaus, Christine Eng, Mark Gallego, Elizabeth Hillyer, Nan Helm, and Klara Glowczewski set the tone for dedication and accuracy. Patricia Bates of Spelman College and Yale graduate students Harold Cooke, Glenn May, Carla Carr, Julie Jones, Horace Porter, and Barbara Riley also spent part of their summers annotating letters in nineteenth-century journals. In October 1977 the voluminous periodical files of the Douglass staff were turned over to the Black and Reform Newspaper Indexing Project. It was the work of these researchers which created the foundation upon which the Black and Reform Newspaper Indexing Project was built.

We were blessed throughout the life of the Black and Reform Newspaper Indexing Project with a remarkably talented and committed group of researchers. Jennifer Pruett of the University of New Mexico, David Curtis of Harvard University, Joan Reiss of New Haven, and Kurt Kaboth of Yale were the quintessential researchers during the first year of the project. Our Assistants in Research during the latter stages of the project, Amy Mantell, David Barnett, Richard Kramer, Lois Jameson, Carolyn Cott, Diane Peterson, John Caulfield, Jessica Dunn, Joel Cornwell, Roy Nirschel, LaTanya Bailey, Michael Betz, Delgra Childs, and Ronald Matz, proofed, copyedited, and indexed the volumes. Their work substantially improved the accuracy and consistency of the entries. Our undergraduate researchers spent several months helping us to complete the research begun by the

Douglass staff. The work of Stephen Schwanauer, Amy Wierczorowski, Maria Celichowski, Neeka Harris, Joseph Liken, Daryl Warder, Ruth Copeland, Patricia Granger, Eric Koranteng, Peter Eckerstrom, Michael Cutler, Carlos McDade, Peter Borten, Steven Morris, Jefferson Morley, Cephas Ocloo, and Dorothy Trench helped to make the project more comprehensive than it was originally.

We owe special thanks to Dorothy Trench and Jessica Dunn for translating and proofing French-language newspapers and magazines.

Carl Mallard of Philadelphia contributed greatly to the project with his fine reproductions of our photographs of editors.

The penetrating questions raised by the staff of the Research Tools Division of the National Endowment for the Humanities, especially George Farr, Cathy Fuller, and Maben Herring, forced us to entertain alternative perspectives and to examine our priorities in a more systematic fashion than we otherwise would have. We gained much from critiques of the project by Arthur Link of Princeton University and Joel Myerson of the University of South Carolina. Our editors at G. K. Hall encouraged our efforts to make the project comprehensive, and utilitarian. Ultimately, they saved us from making many mistakes in design and execution of our research.

Our typists, Eileen Bell, Sharon Adams, Delgra Childs, Robert Reilly, Ruth Krigbaum, Anne Granger, Pamela Y. Price, Fabienne Moore, Katherine Harris, Kim Caron, and Jacqueline Shea did yeoman service in standardizing the entries and maintaining a remarkably high level of accuracy in transcribing thousands of notecards. Janet Soresino's cheerfulness as she kept track of all of our drafts and addenda and in the face of our impossible demands inspired all of us.

No large-scale newspaper project can achieve even minimal success without the cooperation of thousands of librarians. We gratefully acknowledge all of those who graciously answered our letters seeking information on nineteenth-century journals, suggested unlikely repositories we might contact, and cheered us on by their enthusiasm for our project. Susan Steinberg of the Yale University Library deserves much of the credit for the success of the project. Suggesting research strategies, warning us of pitfalls in our attempts to locate elusive journals, and acquiring many obscure periodicals, Susan was our best critic, friend, and booster.

Because of the large commitment of time and energy which such projects demand, we must give the greatest credit to our friends and families for their patience and understanding in the face of the long hours we had to devote to the Black and Reform Newspaper Indexing Project. We hope that their sacrifice has helped to provide scholars with some clues to the details of history in nineteenth-century abolitionist newspapers and magazines.

JOHN W. BLASSINGAME
MAE G. HENDERSON
New Haven
May 1979

List of Symbols

AA	Anti-Slavery Association
AAS	American Anti-Slavery Society
ACS	American Colonization Society
AS	Anti-Slavery Society
ASS	Anti-Slavery Societies
CS	Colonization Society
CSS	Colonization Societies
n.p.	no place
n.n.	no name
n.d.	no date
(*)	Whenever printing errors which are not self-correcting result in a repeated page number, an asterisk (*) is placed next to the misleading pagination. The asterisk is used both for a single repeating page number and throughout a series.

State Abbreviations

Alabama—Al.	Montana—Mt.
Alaska—Ak.	Nebraska—Ne.
Arizona—Az.	Nevada—Nv.
Arkansas—Ar.	New Hampshire—N. H.
California—Ca.	New Jersey—N. J.
Colorado—Co.	New Mexico—N. M.
Connecticut—Ct.	New York—N. Y.
Delaware—De.	North Carolina—N. C.
Florida—Fl.	North Dakota—N. D.
Georgia—Ga.	Ohio—Oh.
Hawaii—Hi.	Oklahoma—Ok.
Idaho—Id.	Oregon—Or.
Illinois—Il.	Pennsylvania—Pa.
Indiana—In.	Rhode Island—R. I.
Iowa—Ia.	South Carolina—S. C.
Kansas—Ks.	South Dakota—S. D.
Kentucky—Ky.	Tennessee—Tn.
Louisiana—La.	Texas—Tx.
Maine—Me.	Utah—Ut.
Maryland—Md.	Vermont—Vt.
Massachusetts—Ma.	Virginia—Va.
Michigan—Mi.	Washington—Wa.
Minnesota—Mn.	West Virginia—W. V.
Mississippi—Ms.	Wisconsin—Wi.
Missouri—Mo.	Wyoming—Wy.

Mt. Pleasant (Oh.)
Philanthropist

The
PHILANTHROPIST.

I shall never envy the honours which wit and learning obtain in any other cause, if I can be numbered among those who have given ardour to virtue, and confidence to truth.—Dr. Johnson.

Vol. I.   THIRD MONTH 7th 1818.   No. 26.

FROM THE PORT FOLIO.

Observations on Earthquakes.

[Concluded.]

At a very early period in the history of science, philosophers began to speculate and frame conjectures as to the cause of earthquakes. The subject being such as to afford great scope for the exercise of the imagination, hypothesis after hypothesis sprang up in relation to it with unbounded luxuriance. A hasty view of a few of these may contribute to the momentary amusement of our readers.

By Anaxagoras and his followers, the body of the earth was supposed to be filled with vast caverns, similar in their form to what we denominate, in common language, the "vault of heaven" and not much less extensive in their dimensions. Within these subterranean cavities he believed that clouds were formed analogous to those that glide through the atmosphere. The bursting of the lightning from these clouds beneath our feet, he regarded as the immediate cause of earthquakes.

Another sect of philosophers contended, that the caverns in question contained vast bodies of subterraneous fire. These fires, by their constant action, weakened the walls of the caverns enclosing them, which ultimately fell in, and thus produced the concussions of an earthquake.

Epicurus and other philosophers of the peripatetic school attributed earthquakes to explosions produced by the ignition of certain inflammable gases, imprisoned or engendered in the bowels of the earth.

The sudden conversion of water into steam by the violent action of subterranean fires, has been long regarded as the cause of earthquakes. This hypothesis has numbered a-

mong its advocates some of the most distinguished characters of modern times. Gassendus, Kircher, Schottus, Varenius, Des Cartes, Du Hamel, and Honorius gave it all the support of their talents and authority. Fabri, Dr. Woodward, and the late Dr. Darwin were zealous in defence of different modifications of the same hypothesis.

The stupendous machinery by which these philosophers contrived to bring large bodies of fire and water together in the bowels of the earth—orbes large enough to propagate concussions throughout a great portion of the globe, the limits of credible will not suffer us to describe. The whole apparatus appears to be nothing but a mere creature of the imagination. As far as we now recollect, subterranean geography furnishes not a single fact in favour of its existence. On the other hand, the whole amount of our knowledge in that science, is unfavourable to the notion of deep-seated caverns and central fires. Artificial excavations have been carried nearly two thousand feet into the bowels of the earth—a distance, perhaps, as deep as the seat of earthquakes—yet none of these subterranean caverns have been found. Nor have any discoveries been made which do not tend to a refutation rather than a confirmation of our belief in the existence of internal fires. After descending to the distance of a few hundred feet beneath the surface of the earth, the temperature begins gradually to decline as you advance towards the centre. It is scarcely necessary to add, that the reverse of this would be true, were you still approaching nearer to vast masses of ignited materials. It is, moreover, a well known fact, that the water at the bottom of the ocean, where the

depth extends to several hundred fathoms, is much colder than it is either at the surface, or at any intermediate depth between the two extremes. This circumstance tends also, we think, to prove, that there is no general source of heat situated deep in the bowels of the earth. The existence of subterranean fires in some regions is no less certain, whatever on the main question, as that there are portions of the globe into which fire does occasionally exist, are in lands where they are not produced only by compary direction, and are kindled as it is sometimes by the action of electricity in combustible materials. We regret that without trespassing greatly on the limits assigned us, we cannot discuss this subject at large. Were we as other subjects, it would be most and difficult to reconcile many of them together or to answer the questions, hypotheses which derive their origin quakes from the action of subterranean fire and water. Were these phenomena produced by the mere impetus of imprisoned steam, that agent would, on the opening of the earth, rush out in such enormous quantities and so visible a form, as to establish the fact to the entire satisfaction of every beholder.

The last hypothesis to which we shall invite the attention of our readers, is that which attributes earthquakes to the influence of electricity. Nor shall we attempt to conceal the fact that this is the opinion to which we are ourselves most strongly inclined.

Our inability to point out the precise mode of operation by which the electric fluid gives rise to earthquakes, constitutes no argument whatever against the validity of the doctrine. We are equally ignorant of the mode of opinion of this fluid in the production of water-spouts, hurricanes, and

Figure 1

Charles Osborn

[Editor, *The Philanthropist*]

The Anti-slavery movement of this country may properly be divided into two dispensations. The first had its beginning soon after the introduction of slavery into the colonies, and ended, with only partial results, near the close of the last century. The second began early in the present century, just as slavery was entering upon its baleful career of domination, and closed with its destruction by the power of war, for which the nation had been prepared by the moral and political agitation which preceded the final conflict. Each of these dispensations has its history, and should be studied in the light of its distinguishing facts. . . .

Our accepted histories and manuals agree in according to William Lloyd Garrison the honor of first proclaiming, on this side of the Atlantic, the doctrine of "immediate and unconditional emancipation." They also agree in awarding to Benjamin Lundy the credit of publishing the first anti-slavery newspaper of this century, and of being the pioneer abolitionist of the United States. These statements are now received without question, and supported by Johnson's "Life of Garrison," Greeley's "History of the American Conflict," Wilson's "History of the Rise and Fall of the Slave Power," Von Holst's "Constitutional and Political History of the United States," and various other authorities. It is the chief purpose of this article to controvert these alleged facts, and to show that Charles Osborn, an eminent minister in the Society of Friends, proclaimed the doctrine of immediate and unconditional emancipation when William Lloyd Garrison was only nine years old, and nearly a dozen years before that doctrine was announced by Elizabeth Heyrick, in England; and that Mr. Osborn also edited and published the first anti-slavery newspaper in the United States, and is thus entitled to take rank as the real pioneer of American abolitionism. These statements may appear surprising, but, if true, they should be so recognized. If the current of history has been diverted into a false channel, it should be turned into the true one. The story of the great conflict should be made thoroughly accurate and trustworthy. When a great victory has been won, every general should have his due share in the honor of its achievement, and, if the heroism of any brave man has been slighted, and the fact can be shown by newly-discovered evidence, the record of the battle should be made to conform to the truth. It can scarcely be necessary to say that I have no desire whatever to do the slightest injustice to Garrison and Lundy. Their exalted place as heroes in the grand army of human progress is irreversibly established; and Garrison and Lundy themselves, if living, would be the last to deny to a fellow-laborer in the great cause the share of honor he had fairly earned in its service.

Before proceeding with my task, let me rapidly sketch the principal facts of the life of Charles Osborn. It appears, from the published journal of his travels, that he was born in North Carolina, on the 21st of August, 1775. In his nineteenth year he removed to Tennessee, where he made his first appearance in the ministry about the year 1806.

He soon took rank as a preacher of considerable gifts, and traveled and preached extensively in North Carolina and Tennessee, taking an active part in the anti-slavery societies of these States. He removed to Mount Pleasant, Ohio, in 1816, where he published a religious and reformatory newspaper, and continued his work in the ministry. In 1819 he settled in Indiana. He took an active and leading part, as an orthodox Friend, in the movement against Elias Hicks and his followers, and after this made a religious visit to Great Britain and a part of the continent. He sat at the head of the yearly meetings of this country for about the third of a century, and the like honor was accorded him, though unsought, by Friends on the other side of the Atlantic during his sojourn among them. From his earliest years he was known as a thorough-going abolitionist, and an abstainer from the use of slave-grown produce; and, in his later life, he became involved in a controversy with his society on the slavery question, which resulted in his separation from it in testimony of his unflinching devotion to the slave. . . .

In enumerating these proofs I ought to make more special and emphatic mention of Mr. Osborn's hostility to African colonization. He avowed this in his youth, and never afterward faltered. The fact is as honorable to him as it is remarkable that, while the leading abolitionists of England and the United States were caught in this snare, he was never for a moment deluded by any of its plausibilities. His moral vision detected its character from the beginning. "Emancipation," as he used to declare, "was thrown into the cradle of colonization, there to be rocked and kept quiet until the last slaveholder should become willing to send his human chattels to the colony." Benjamin Lundy and other anti-slavery men discussed it as a scheme of gradual emancipation, and as such Mr. Osborn always understood it. He opposed it because it postponed the freedom of the slaves and placed conditions in its way, and if he did not, in so many words, demand immediate and unconditional emancipation, this was always the ground on which he stood, and was necessarily implied in his action; and he never uttered a sentiment inconsistent with it. No one, certainly, will insist that he favored gradualism, without a syllable of proof, and in the face of positive and overwhelming evidence to the contrary.

It is not pretended, of course, that Mr. Osborn expected the slaveholders would immediately emancipate their slaves. Without the intervention of a miracle this was impossible. The work of emancipation could only go forward under the inevitable conditions by which it was complicated. It had to become an educational process before it could be realized in fact. What he preached to the slaveholder was the gospel of immediate repentance, and that he had no right to put off that repentance to a more convenient season. That was his well-known position in 1830, when the anti-slavery agitation began seriously to disturb the peace of the country; and the Indiana yearly meeting, which could not endure this doctrine in 1842, never disputed the fact that he had at all times avowed it. If it be said that it was well known that the honor of first proclaiming this doctrine in this country was ascribed to Mr. Garrison by his friends, and that Mr. Osborn would have contested this claim if he had felt himself entitled to make it, I reply that he was a traveling minister among Friends, engrossed in his peculiar work, and may have known nothing of the matter. It is quite as reasonable to suppose him ignorant of the claim made by the friends of Mr. Garrison as to suppose the latter ignorant of Mr. Osborn's well-known record as an immediate emancipationist. In justice to him it should also be said that he was too modest to blow his own trumpet, and too much absorbed in his work to concern himself about its honors; and that if this had been otherwise he had no motive to enter into any strife over the question. The champions of immediate emancipation, when it first began to stir the country, and during the life of Mr. Osborn, were obliged to make themselves of no reputation. They were cast out of all the synagogues of respectability, and little dreamed of the honors with which they were finally to be crowned. Mr. Osborn, therefore, could have had no selfish inducement to contest the claim of Mr. Garrison, while either of them would doubtless have been glad to know that the other had avowed this sound and saving principle.

I now come to the proof of my statement that Mr. Osborn edited and published the first anti-slavery newspaper in the United States, and is thus entitled to the honor of being counted the pioneer of latter-day abolitionism. My task will not be difficult, and it will supply some corroborative proof of his anti-slavery position. We have seen that he removed to Mount Pleasant, Ohio, in 1816. In that year he issued his prospectus for a weekly newspaper to be called the *Philanthropist*, and published at that place; and on the twenty-ninth of August, 1817, the first number was issued. Its publication was continued till the eighth of October, 1818. The tone of the paper was earnestly moral and religious. He devoted its columns considerably to the interests of Temperance and Peace, but the burden and travail of his heart was slavery. I speak by authority, having the bound volumes of the paper before me. It was just such a newspaper as Elijah P. Lovejoy was murdered for publishing in Illinois twenty years later. Benjamin Lundy, then residing at St. Clairsville, was one of its agents, as the paper shows. The subject of slavery is discussed from eighty to ninety times, making an average of nearly twice in each weekly number. It was in the beginning of this year that the American Colonization Society was organized with its headquarters at Washington, and the several anti-slavery societies then existing in this region of Ohio were all in favor of colonization as a scheme of gradual emancipation, as were those throughout the country generally; but Mr. Osborn disagreed with them. He opposed the scheme in repeated editorials, but allowed both sides of the question to be heard.

Various articles were admitted favoring the policy of gradual emancipation, but not a line was written by himself in its approval. The limits of this article will not permit numerous or lengthy quotations from the paper, but I offer a few as specimens of its general character, beginning with the editorials. On page 44 of the first volume is the following on colonization:

> Without in anywise wishing to forestall public opinion, or give a bias against the intentions of the American Colonization Society, the editor has great doubts of the justice of the plans proposed. It appears to him calculated to rivet closer the chains that already gall the sons of Africa, and to insure to the miserable objects of American cruelty a perpetuity of bondage. The free persons of color in the city of Philadelphia have protested against being sent back to a soil which separation and habit have combined to render disagreeable to them. The communication which follows is inserted because the author's intention is believed to be good, and because every investigation of the subject will tend to open the eyes of the public to the situation of this people. Those who have traveled through the Southern States, and observed the ignorance and vice with which slavery has enveloped the children of Africa, can hardly be persuaded that they are now fit instruments for propagating the Gospel.

On page 37 is the following:

A correspondent says the coast of Africa has been robbed of its natives, who have with their sweat and blood manured and fertilized the soil of America. If their descendants are now (by way of reparation) to be forced back to that country, whose customs and whose soil are equally repugnant to them—query, are the thieves or the restorers most justifiable?

In the second volume, on page 69, is a strong editorial on the slave trade and slavery. After referring to the action of England and Spain in dealing with this subject, it concludes:

> But much remains to be done. The system of slavery is acknowledged on all hands to be an evil of the greatest magnitude; and it will require a degree of energy commensurate with the effects it has upon society to counteract its baleful influence, and now is the time for the advocates of freedom to exert themselves to overthrow that colossal fabric of despotism. Let the enlightened philanthropists of either hemisphere continue to carry on the benevolent work until they have finally accomplished the same, and receive the just reward of their labors, the grateful acknowledgements of millions of their fellow-mortals, whom they behold emerging from the gloomy caverns of despair and assuming the rank among the sons and daughters of men to which they are entitled by the laws of Nature. In the language of one of the greatest orators of the present day, they will then have the satisfaction to know that through this instrumentaility a large portion of their fellow-creatures are, politically speaking, "redeemed, regenerated, and disenthralled by the Genius of Universal Emancipation."

It will occur to the reader as altogether probable that the name of Lundy's paper, which was started several years afterward, was suggested to him by this editorial. . . .

Mr. Osborn was one of the very first men of this country to oppose the use of slave-grown produce, and he continued personally faithful to this principle during his life; while the *Philanthropist* is believed to be the first newspaper in the United States which espoused this duty. From an article copied from the Westchester *Recorder*, on page 174, I quote the following in reference to the slave trade:

> This great fountain of human blood that hath been flowing on the continent of Africa for ages, whose streams have stained the shores of America and the West Indies, is kept in motion and supported by the consumers of the proceeds of slavery. They are the subscribers that furnish the fund by which the whole business is carried on. A merchant who loads his vessel in the West Indies with the proceeds of slavery does nearly as much at helping forward the slave trade as he that loads his vessel in Africa with slaves. They are both twisting the rope at different ends. *** It is something paradoxical that a man will refuse to buy a stolen sheep, or to eat a piece of one that is stolen, and should not have the same scruples respecting a stolen man.

But I need not multiply these extracts, which I have given merely as illustrations of the spirit and make-up of the paper. I must not fail to mention, however, a very able and eloquent oration on slavery, by Thomas H. Genin, delivered at Mount Pleasant, Ohio, on the eighteenth of May, 1818, which is printed in the second volume, beginning on page 77. Mr. Genin came from New York to Ohio the year before, and was the intimate friend of Mr. Osborn. He also shared the friendship of Charles Hammond, Benjamin Lundy, and De Witt Clinton. He had considerable literary gifts, and was the correspondent of Henry Clay and John Quincy Adams; and, although the rhetoric of his oration is a little florid, he discusses the slavery question with great thoroughness, and evinces a surprising insight into the nature and working of the institution. All the arguments and sophisms of the slave-holders with which the country has been made familiar in later times are taken up and disposed of in this effort sixty-four years ago as if he had been in the midst of the great conflict which so long afterward stirred the blood of both sections of the Union. The speech is prophetic, and deserves to be preserved as a choice relic of the literature of abolitionism in its pioneer days. Let me add, that I find scattered through the pages of the *Philanthropist* frequent selections of anti-slavery poems from Cowper, Shenstone, Montgomery, and others, and I entertain no doubt whatever that its anti-slavery character is quite as clearly defined and uncompromising in tone as Lundy's *Genius of Universal Emancipation*, or James G. Birney's *Philanthropist*, published in Cincinnati in later years.

The priority of Mr. Osborn in the establishment of this paper has already been shown. He sold his establishment to Elisha Bates, and not to Elihu Embree, as Mr. Greeley states in his "Conflict"; and Lundy, not liking the anti-slavery character of the paper under his management, as he declares in his account of these matters, began the publication, at Mount Pleasant, of the *Genius of Universal Emancipation,* in January, 1821, being three years and a half after the issue of the first number of the *Philanthropist*. These facts are given in "The Life of Benjamin Lundy," compiled by Thomas Earle, and published in 1847. . . .

The year after Mr. Osborn sold his newspaper establishment, he removed to Indiana. Several considerations induced him to abandon the publication of his paper. He desired to go further west, where his small resources would enable him to procure land for his children. He also felt that the influence of his paper was seriously thwarted by the mischievous and unmanageable scheme of colonization; while he believed he could more effectively serve the cause of freedom in the wider field of the traveling ministry, in which Woolman had labored with such remarkable results. In 1832, when the anti-slavery agitation had reached its fervent heat under the inspiration and leadership of Garrison, Mr. Osborn gave his heart to the work with renewed zeal. While in England in that year he met Elliott Cresson, an agent of the American Colonization Society, who begged him not to say anything that would hinder the raising of funds in aid of its work; but Mr. Osborn replied that he would not cease to expose its evil designs at home and abroad, and he made

Cresson's mission a failure. His anti-slavery zeal fully kept pace with the multiplying ag-gressions of slavery, and, in the winter of 1839, he visited the Eastern States, where he found the dominating influences among Friends decidedly opposed to his testimonies, and inclined to keep him silent; but he would not be fettered, and spoke out his whole mind freely. Some of his sermons were reported for the anti-slavery newspapers, and these lines of Whittier, inspired by a similar circumstance, were quoted as fitly applying to this in-trepid assertion of the right of free speech:

Thank God for the token! one lip is still free--
One spirit untrammeled, unbending one knee;
Like the oak of the mountain, deep-rooted and firm,
Erect when the multitude bend to the storm;
When traitors to freedom, and honor, and God,
Are bowed at an idol polluted with blood;
When the recreant North has forgotten her trust,
And the lip of her honor is low in the dust--
Thank God that one arm from the shackles has broken!
Thank God that one man as a *free-man* has spoken!

On his return to the West he found the ruling spirits in the Indiana Yearly Meeting had also taken a very decided stand against the abolitionists. The colonization members of the Society, by some strange and unaccountable means, had gained the ascendancy over its anti-slavery members, and he was greatly troubled in mind respecting the situation in which he found himself placed. In the year 1841 the Indiana Yearly Meeting sanctioned a letter of advice which had been previously issued by the Meeting for Sufferings to its monthly and quarterly meetings, forbidding the use of their meeting-houses for anti-slavery lectures, and the joining in anti-slavery organizations "with those who do not profess to wait for Divine direction in such important concerns." The Meeting also advised against anti-slavery publications by Friends without first submitting them to "the examination of a Meeting for Sufferings." This advice was unauthorized by the discipline of the Society, and directly opposed to the well-known practice of Friends on both sides of the Atlantic. It showed that the power of slavery, which had taken captive other religious denominations throughout the country, had at last crept into the Society, and was dictating its action. Charles Osborn was then a member of the Meeting for Sufferings, which is a delegated body in the Society acting under appointment, like a committee, to transact important business in the interim of the regular sessions of the Yearly Meeting; and he and seven other anti-slavery members occupying the same position declined to obey this prohibitory advice. In doing so they justified themselves by the discipline and usages of the Society and its own well-known testimonies against slavery. They felt imperatively bound by their con-sciences to take this course, and that to do otherwise would be to recognize the infallibility of the Yearly Meeting and its right to bind them in all cases whatsoever. For this action these eight members were summarily removed from their positions as "disqualified," and their places filled by those who were willing to become the instruments of the Yearly Meeting in its warfare against the abolitionists.

What was to be done? These men had not violated the discipline of the Society, or gone counter to any of its recognized practices and testimonies. They were not accused of any unsoundness in doctrine; and yet, without any formal charges of misconduct in any par-ticular, and by an act of wanton usurpation, they were degraded from the places they had held. They begged that the reasons for this action might be spread upon the minutes as a matter of simple justice to themselves, and in order that they might not stand recorded as transgressors, and Mr. Osborn pleaded for this in a speech of much power and full of pathos and tenderness; but this petition was disregarded, and the perfectly unprecedented and arbitrary proceeding was carried out. If they submitted to this act of despotism they would be sharers in the apostacy of the Society from its testimonies, and fellow-laborers with it against the slave. If they persisted in their disobedience they would, of course, be disowned for thus obeying their own consciences. They saw but one honorable or decent alternative. As lovers of the Society of Friends, and sincere believers in its doctrines and discipline, they could go out of the body which had cast them off for their anti-slavery principles and violated its discipline for that purpose, and organize a Society of their own, with its machinery of monthly, quarterly and yearly meetings, and free from all pro-slavery domination. This they did, styling themselves the Society of Anti-Slavery Friends. They were driven out of the old body for their abolitionism, and Charles Osborn was spoken of as "gone, fallen, and out of the life," for no other cause. This occurred in 1842, at the yearly meeting which gave Henry Clay, the owner of fifty slaves and President of the American Colonization Society, a seat among the ruling Elders, and who, in a pubic speech the day before, had declared that "the slaves must be prepared for freedom before they can receive that great boon," and that "the Society of Friends take the right stand in relation to this subject."

History was thus repeating the old story of "Pilate and Herod friends," and illustrating the desire of the Society, as expressed by its meeting for sufferings in 1841, to "retain the place and influence" which it had "heretofore had with the rulers of our land." There was a peculiar sting in the saying of Mr. Osborn afterward that these Friends "deemed it a departure from the well-known principles of the Society to do anything in the anti-slavery cause without a divine impulse and clear opening in the light of truth leading thereto; but for their opposition to the abolitionists they had no impulse, no opening, to wait for."

It will probably be news to thousands that the Quakers thus succumbed to the power of slavery; but such is the melancholy fact, and they have no right to "escape history." Among the rank and file of the body in Indiana there were doubtless very many true anti-slavery men; but at the time of which I speak the chief rulers believed in colonization and gradual emancipation. They took special pains, in dealing with legislative bodies, slave-holders and the public, to inform them that they had no connection, in any way, with abolitionism. They so assured Henry Clay while in Richmond. Leading members frequently reiterated the charge that abolitionists had "put back the cause of emancipation;" and some of them insisted that aiding slaves on their way to Canada involved men in the crime of man-stealing. Many of the rulers of the denomination in the Eastern, as well as the Western, States had "their ears filled with cotton." They discoursed very piously about the attempt of abolitionists "to abolish slavery in their own strength," and argued that paying men for anti-slavery lectures was opposed to the Quaker testimony against a "hireling ministry."

Ministers, elders and overseers, took the lead in these reactionary proceedings; and it was one of the curiosities of human nature to find the followers of John Woolman and Anthony Benezett laboring with their brethren for attending anti-slavery meetings, closing the doors of their churches against anti-slavery lectures, and setting up a system of espionage over the publication of anti-slavery articles by members of the Society. Such men as Isaac T. Hopper, among the Hicksite Friends, and Arnold Buffum, among the Orthodox, were disowned for their fidelity to the slave. This work of proscription was generally based upon some false pretense, as was the fact in the case of Mr. Buffum. In dealing with Mr. Osborn and his associates the Indiana yearly meeting did its best to cover up the ugly fact that they were degraded on account of their anti-slavery principles. With great dexterity in the use of Scripture, much circumlocution, and a cunning and tergiversation that would have won the heart of Talleyrand or Loyola, they played their game of ecclesiastical tyranny; but the facts of the transaction, as now seen in the clear perspective of history, leave them perfectly unmasked. I have carefully examined the documents and papers pertaining to the controversy on both sides, and speak from the record. Strange as it may seem, the claims of justice were so completely subordinated to the peace and unity of the Society that even a deputation of English Friends, who came over as mediators in this trouble, utterly refused to look into the merits of the controversy, and insisted upon the unconditional return of the seceding members to the body which had so flagrantly trampled upon their rights. Humanity was forgotten in the service of a sect, and Quakerism itself disowned by its priesthood.

But the anti-slavery movement took an unexpected turn. The annexation of Texas and the war with Mexico roused the country, and poured a flood of light on the character and designs of the slaveholding interest. The anti-slavery agitation of 1848 and the passage of the Fugitive Slave act of 1850 brought large reinforcements to the cause of freedom. The repeal of the Missouri Compromise and the struggle to make Kansas a slave state still further enlightened the people. The dullest scholars began to get their lessons. Slaveholding madness so anointed the eyes of the people that the cloven feet of abolitionism disappeared, and the Quakers, like other religious bodies, began to take a new view of their duties. "The world," on which they turned their backs in 1841 to avoid its "contamination," had at last taught them more wisdom than any "divine impulse" had ever been able to impart. They became themselves abolitionists, and gloried in the very cause which provoked their contempt during the ugly apostacy they had parenthesized into the beautiful anti-slavery record of the sect.

But did they do justice to the men they had persecuted for righteousness sake? Did they make any official acknowledgement of the wrong they had done, as did other religious denominations in like cases? No. Individual members solicited the seceders to return to the fold. They said to them, "Come back to us! No questions will be asked, and no conditions exacted. Make no disturbance, but come and go with us." Most of the seceders finally returned, but some of them demanded an amendment of the minutes of the society which should recognize the injustice done them for their anti-slavery fidelity. This was denied in all such cases, and they stand on the records as "disqualified" members. Charles Osborn died in 1850, a grieved and heartbroken old man, and his grief would not have been assuaged if he could have foreseen the action of the Society in refusing to correct its records after it had espoused the very principles for the advocacy of which he had been exiled from its bosom. Harshly and unjustly as he had been treated, he would scarcely have believed this possible. But the Society was handicapped by its record. Much as it owed Mr. Osborn, morally and spiritually, its love of consistency and the cravenness of human nature triumphed over its conscience. It could not do him justice without condemning itself. It could not espouse his cause as a faithful minister of the Gospel and an anti-slavery prophet without advertising its recreancy to humanity and its injustice to a greathearted and brave man.

But the friends of humanity, irrespective of sect or party, should join in fitly honoring him. During his life abolitionism was a despised thing. He did not live to see the glory which was so soon to come, nor anticipate its coming. As to his reputation, he took no thought for the morrow. The newspaper which proves his right to be ranked as the first of our anti-slavery pioneers seems only to have been preserved by an accident. The memory of other faithful pioneers has been carefully and lovingly guarded; but history has slighted his record, and Liberty, in searching for her jewels, has strangely overlooked his name. Touched by these facts, and believing that "no power can die that ever wrought for truth," I have felt commanded to do my part in the work of adding a new star to the galaxy of freedom, a new name to the roll-call of reformers. If I have succeeded in any degree in this labor of love, I shall rejoice; but, in any event, I shall share the satisfaction which attends a sincere endeavor to serve the truth.

George W. Julian, *International Review* XII
(June, 1882), 533–55
[Some paragraph indentions added.]

Journal Data

TITLE: *Philanthropist*

MOTTO: "I shall never envy the honours which wit and learning obtain in any other cause, if I can be numbered among those who have given ardour to virtue and confidence to truth"—Dr. Johnson (29 Aug. 1817–14 Mar. 1818) "They shall beat their swords into plough-shares, and their spears into pruning hooks: nation shall not lift up sword against nation, neither shall they learn war any more."—Isaiah (14 Mar. 1818–Oct. 1818)* See also "miscellaneous data."

INCLUSIVE DATES OF PUBLICATION: 29 Aug. 1817–8 Oct. 1818; Under Elisha Bates, with same title, 8 Oct. 1818–1822?

PLACE OF PUBLICATION: Mount Pleasant, Ohio

FREQUENCY OF PUBLICATION: Weekly

DAY OF WEEK WHEN PUBLISHED: "every 6th day" of week (29 Aug. 1817–7 Mar. 1818); "every 7th day" (17 Mar. 1818–7 May 1818); "every 5th day" (7 May 1818–8 Oct. 1818)

AVERAGE NUMBER OF PAGES PER ISSUE: 8

SIZE: Small folio size

NUMBER OF COLUMNS PER PAGE: 3

EDITOR(s): Charles Osborn, Editor (29 Aug. 1817 until 8 Oct. 1818) and Benjamin Lundy, Associate Editor (14 Mar. 1818 until 8 Oct. 1818); Elisha Bates, Editor (8 Oct. 1818–1822?)

PUBLISHER: Charles Osborn (29 Aug. 1817 to 8 Oct. 1818)

REPORTER WHO CONTRIBUTED MOST FREQUENTLY: Benjamin Lundy

SPECIAL FEATURES: Advertisements

PRICE: Annual Subscription $3.00

PERSPECTIVE: Anti-slavery, Pacifist, temperance, anti-colonization, boycott of slave produce.

MISCELLANEOUS DATA: A secondary motto, placed halfway through the issue above the editorial column, begins to appear in Vol. II. It is: "Why will men forget that they are brethren." Also, Osborn was absent from issue I.15 (19 Dec. 1817) to I.18 (10 Jan. 1818), when the business was conducted by the printer. Announcement in I.14 (12 Dec. 1817), but announcement dated 6 Dec.

REPOSITORY: Ohio Historical Society. Aug. 1817–8 Oct. 1818.

Prospectus

In the proposals for the publication of this paper, but little was said of the plan it was in contemplation to pursue. The first number is now before the public, and may be taken as a fair specimen of the Editor's view, and intentions. It has been, and will continue to be, a primary object to present a weekly sheet, free from the rancour of party spirit, containing such religious, moral, agricultural and manufacturing information, as may tend to the great aim of giving "ardour to virtue and confidence to truth."

That all will be pleased, the Editor is not sanguine enough to believe, nor indeed is it to be wished, until the character of things shall so far change, that "the lion may lie down with the lamb."

"And boys in flow'ry bands the tiger lead."

Philanthropist, Mt. Pleasant, Ohio, 6
June 1817, (vol. I, No. 1)

[1817]

1 P. R. LUSHINGTON *to* **GENTLEMEN. 11 June 1817. Treasury Chambers.** Reports the Lordship's authority permitting the importation of corn, grain and meal on any ship and from any country until 14 November 1817. 29 August 1817 (vol. I, no. 1) p.8, c1.

2 WILLIAM DILLWORTH CREWDSON, CLERK *to* **FRIENDS. n.d. n.p.** Advocates Christian education and the turning away from worldly goods; affirms "our Heavenly Father's Love." 19 September 1817 (vol. I, no. 2) p.11, c1.

3 ANTHONY BENEZET *to* **CHARLOTTE, QUEEN OF GREAT BRITAIN. 25 August 1783. Philadelphia.** Discusses his reasons for publishing certain tracts and expositions. 26 September 1817 (vol. I, no. 3) p.18, c3.

4 BENJAMIN BATES *to* **A MEMBER OF THE LEGISLATURE OF VIRGINIA. n.d. n.p.** Advocates legislation to allow the freedom of thought and religion; believes one should be allowed to pay a tax toward education in lieu of performing military duty against one's conscience. 3 October 1817 (vol. I, no. 4) p.26, c3.

5 JOSEPH DODDRIDGE *to* **SIR. 8 December 1816. Wellsburgh.** Approves of the communication sent him on slavery; believes the existence of slavery in America "is a flagrant contradiction to all our professions of liberty, equality, and justice." 10 October 1817 (vol. I, no. 5) p.38, c2.

6 PHILANTHROPOS *to* **FRIEND OSBORN. 15 October. St. Clairsville, Oh.** Believes that a correspondent, whom he quotes, does not fairly understand the purposes of the CS, which does not propose that anyone be *forced* back to Africa; justifies the well-organized system of colonization. 17 October 1817 (vol. I, no. 6) p.45, c2.

7 A GENTLEMAN IN PENNSYLVANIA *to* **n.n. [extract] n.d. n.p.** Describes his recent encounter with a German figure who lived through many dramatic and exciting times in Europe. 24 October 1817 (vol. I, no. 7) p.53, c1.

8 ROWE, A NOBLEMAN *to* **PHILARIO, AN INTIMATE COMPANION. n.d. n.p.** Ponders his mis-spent life; wonders whether he will be judged favorably or unfavorably. 31 October 1817 (vol. I, no. 8) p.58, c2.

9 A CONSTANT READER *to* **THE EDITORS OF THE** *NEW YORK GAZETTE.* **n.d. n.p.** Notices that frequently at this season, the clothes of females catch fire, and that should this happen, the sufferer should fall flat on the floor, so as most easily to extinguish the flames, and avoid a painful, untimely death. 7 November 1817 (vol. I, no. 9) p.71, c2.

10 D. *to* **FRIEND OSBORN. n.d. Pennsylvania.** Suggests that the *Philanthropist* include an article on "different parts of that new and fertile region," western Pennsylvania; suggests other topics on the western regions. 28 November 1817 (vol. I, no. 12) p.94, c1.

11 D. C. *to* **FRIEND OSBORN. 22 November 1817. Free Port.** Quotes a correspondent of the *Philanthropist* who defended colonization; claims that his defenses aim "to silence rather than to *satisfy* the enquiring mind"; questions the policy and goals of colonization. 28 November 1817 (vol. I, no. 12) p.94, c3.

12 D. *to* **FRIEND OSBORN. n.d. n.p.** Relates the conversion of Thomas Dick, an Indian in the state of New York; also tells the story of Jesus, the Disciples, and the Great Spirit. 5 December 1817 (vol. I, no. 13) p.97, c2.

13 PHILADELPHUS *to* **CALEB STRONG, LATE GOVERNOR OF MASSA-CHUSETTS. [extract] n.d. n.p.** Notes "collisions of passion, pride, and revenge," in war and society; points out that "Revenge . . . is sweet to the taste, but it is poison to the soul"; proposes alternative methods of dealing with wrongs and violence. 5 December 1817 (vol. I, no. 13) p.100, c1.

14 [CZAR] ALEXANDER *to* **INDIVIDUALS OF THE SOCIETY OF FRIENDS. 4 July 1817. St. Petersburg, Russia.** Thanks them for the volume of essays on peace, and for the expressions of Christian regard in their accompanying letter; wishes them success in the virtuous promotion of peace. 5 December 1817 (vol. I, no. 13) p.101, c2.

15 PHILANTHROPOS *to* **FRIEND OSBORN. n.d. n.p.** Declares he will support colonization as far as it will serve the cause of emancipation; believes that *some* colonization is necessary to show the practicability and safety of emancipation. 12 December 1817 (vol. I, no. 14) p.110, c3.

16 n.n. *to* **n.n. [extract] 14 September 1817. Paris.** Notes that "religion here is at a low ebb"; it is new to the French, the clergy are favored by the monarch, and the Sabbath in Paris "can only be considered as a day of dissipation to the gay." 19 December 1817 (vol. I, no. 15) p.115, c3.

17 M. F. *to* **n.n. June 1812. n.p.** Relates an account of Comfort Collins, who, at the age of one hundred and one years and eight months, cannot remember certain things, but remembers Scripture and her love of God. 25 December 1817 (vol. I, no. 16) p.123, c1.

18 PRESIDENT OF GERMAN BANK IN WOOSTER *to* **A GENTLEMAN IN CHILLICOTHE. [extract] 21 November 1817. Wooster.** Answers affirmatively to his inquirer regarding his credit and the acceptance of German bank notes in Wooster. 25 December 1817 (vol. I, no. 16) p.125, c3.

[1818]

19 n.n. *to* **FRIEND OSBORN. n.d. n.p.** Points out the "inconsistency and irreconcilability" of those who condemn suicide by arguing that man has no right to take that life which the Creator gave him, yet sanction governments which make war. 24 January 1818. p.157, c2.

20 XYLOPHILAX *to* **FRIEND OSBORN. n.d. n.p.** Discusses the relationship of laws of nature, blind chance, and intelligence. 31 January 1818 (vol. I, no. 21) p.168, c2.

21 n.n. *to* **THE EDITOR OF THE** *WEST CHESTER RECORDER***. 18 December 1817. Philadelphia.** Forwards article entitled "Prize goods examined," which he feels will "strike immediately at the root of Slavery." 7 February 1818 (vol. I, no. 22) p.173, c1.

22 GEN. JOHN H. COKE *to* **PETER MINOR, ESQ., SECRETARY OF THE AGRICULTURAL SOCIETY OF ALBEMARLE. October 1817. Bremo.** Discusses the natural history and reproductive process of the Hessian fly. 7 February 1818 (vol. I, no. 22) p.176, c1.

23 A FRIEND IN TENNESSEE *to* **n.n. [extract] 8 January 1818. Tennessee.** States that "the cause of the poor degraded African race still claims the attention of many in these parts"; notes that the subject was recently discussed in the General Assembly, but none of the proposed anti-slavery bills were passed. 14 February 1818 (vol. I, no. 14) p.181, c3.

24 AN OFFICER OF THE AMERICAN SQUADRON AT AMELIA BLAND *to* **SOMEONE IN PROVIDENCE, R.I. [extract] 12 February 1818. Savannah.** Gives an account of "ten of the most miserable days" of his life, when he was among a party ordered on board the *Patriot* to sail under convoy to land; on board were numerous miserable slaves exposed to the elements, many of whom died. 7 March 1818 (vol. I, no. 26) p.207, c1.

25 AN INDIAN CHIEF *to* **HIS FRIEND IN THE STATE OF NEW YORK. n.d. n.p.** Relates that he was born and grew up among Indians, and though he later went to a white school and lived with white people, he still favors his own people and their way of life; believes that in civilized government, "the happiness of the people is constantly sacrificed to the splendor of empire"; also criticizes white prisons. 14 March 1818 (vol. II, no. 1) p.4, c1.

26 n.n. *to* **MR. EDITOR. [from the *Christian Disciple*] n.d. n.p.** Notes that he has enjoyed the articles on the evils of war and the blessings of peace; corrects the false statements on the subject of "national honor," which, according to prevailing opinion, is founded upon military conquests and courage; counters that it should be founded upon *peace*. 21 March 1818 (vol. II, no. 2) p.9, c1.

27 XENO *to* **THE EDITOR. n.d. n.p.** Declares he is satisfied with what nature has done for him, and makes no pretensions to special privileges in religion or friendship; hopes for "future felicity." 21 March 1818 (vol. II, no. 2) p.16, c2.

28 B. F. STICKNEY *to* **NATHAN GUILFORD, CORRESPONDING SECRETARY OF THE WESTERN EMIGRANT SOCIETY. [extract] 20 January 1818. Indian Agency Office, near Ft. Wayne.** Describes the land south of Lake Michigan to near the River Ohio, and surrounding area; reports average temperatures, navigable rivers, and soil quality. 28 March 1818 (vol. II, no. 3) p.20, c1.

29 B. F. STICKNEY *to* **NATHAN GUILFORD, CORRESPONDING SECRETARY OF THE WESTERN EMIGRANT SOCIETY. [extract continued from 28 March] 20 January 1818. Indian Agency Office, near Ft. Wayne.** Describes the Washash River, the Illinois River, the Grand River, other smaller rivers, and Fort Wayne, noting tributaries, fisheries, and types of forest trees. 4 April 1818 (vol. II, no. 4) p.27, c1.

30 B. F. STICKNEY *to* **NATHAN GUILFORD, CORRESPONDING SECRETARY OF THE WESTERN EMIGRANT SOCIETY. 20 January 1818. Indian Agency Office, near Ft. Wayne.** Describes animals and birds in the area, noting the remains of the mammoth, which are plentiful. 11 April 1818 (vol. II, no. 5) p.35, c1.

31 JOSEPH BRINGHURST, ESQ. *to* **H. N. 20 March 1818. Wilmington, De.** Describes the awful explosion of E. L. Dupont's powder mill, started by a fire which killed thirty and wounded twelve. 11 April 1818 (vol. II, no. 5) p.36, c1.

32 n.n. *to* **n.n. [extract] 1818. [date and month unclear] Wilmington, De.** Describes tremendous explosion. [mostly illegible] 11 April 1818 (vol. II, no. 5) p.36, c3.

33 SAMUEL HERRICK, ESQ. *to* **THE EDITOR OF THE *WESTERN HERALD*. [extract] 14 March 1818. Washington.** Forwards reply from the Treasury Department to his inquiry concerning the instructions the Secretary of the Treasury gave to collectors in the state of Ohio. 11 April 1818 (vol. II, no. 5) p.37, c3.

34 WM. H. CRAWFORD *to* **SAMUEL HERRICK. 12 March 1818. n.p.** Discusses instructions given to collector of customs to receive only gold and silver coins and bills of the United States. 11 April 1818 (vol. II, no. 5) p.38, c1.

35 HARD SCRABBLE *to* **THE EDITORS OF THE** *PHILANTHROPIST.* **n.d. n.p.**
Warns others, from personal experience, about the debilitation and evil behavior resulting
from the excessive consumption of liquor; prays to the Lord that he can learn to control
this problem. 11 April 1818 (vol. II, no. 5) p.38, c3.

36 A GENTLEMAN IN LONDON *to* **A CORRESPONDENT IN PHILADELPHIA. [extract] n.d. n.p.** Reports that Mr. Mills and Mr. Burgess are greatly encouraged in their efforts in behalf of colonization; notes that their visit to England has been profitable and
successful. 18 April 1818 (vol. II, no. 6) p.44, c2.

37 MONITOR *to* **n.n. [extract] 22 February 1818. St. Louis.** Reports problems which
caused the Bank of St. Louis to close for a few days. 18 April 1818 (vol. II, no. 6) p.44, c3.

38 THOMAS JEFFERSON *to* **n.n. 26 November 1817. n.p.** States that "You have not
been mistaken in supposing my views and feelings in favour of the abolition of war"; dares
not hope for perpetual peace, but hopes present situation of war will become intolerable.
28 May 1818 (vol. II, no. 11) p.86, c3.

39 THE REV. J. PATTERSON *to* **n.n. [extract] 31 May 1816. St. Petersburgh.** Reports
His Majesty [the Czar] rejected the petition of the Russian Bible Society to import less expensive paper from Holland, but presented them with 15,000 rubles. 28 May 1818 (vol. II,
no. 11) p.87, c3.

40 n.n. *to* **n.n. 28 January 1818. London.** States that contrary to opinions in the United
States, the colony at Sierra Leone is flourishing, its government is secure, and there are no
fears of assault from natives. 28 May 1818 (vol. II, no. 11) p.87, c2.

41 PATRICK HENRY *to* **ANTHONY BENEZET. 18 January 1773. Hanover.** Thanks
Benezet for his book condemning the slave trade; expresses shock that this "abominable
practice" persists and began in one of "the most enlightened ages"; discusses methods for
ending slavery. 4 June 1818 (vol. II, no. 12) p.91, c3.

42 n.n. *to* **CALEB STRONG, ESQ., LATE GOVERNOR OF MASSACHUSETTS. [extract] n.d. n.p.** Demonstrates that war is contrary to the laws of Christ; discusses the two
moral opposites of love and hatred, the social needs of intelligent beings, and principles
derived from the grand law of love. 11 June 1818 (vol. II, no. 13) p.97, c1.

43 n.n. *to* **CALEB STRONG, ESQ., LATE GOVERNOR OF MASSACHUSETTS. [extract continued from 11 June 1818] n.d. n.p.** Demonstrates that war is contrary to the laws
of Christ; examines concepts of property, revenge, acquisition of wealth; discusses inequality, financial and otherwise, between Christians. 25 June 1818 (vol. II, no. 14)
p.105, c1.

44 n.n. *to* **CALEB STRONG, ESQ., LATE GOVERNOR OF MASSACHUSETTS. [extract continued from 25 June 1818] n.d. n.p.** Proves that war is contrary to the laws of
Christ; discusses the strong ambition to gain wealth; asserts that the taking of a fellow
creature's life is unnecessary. 2 July 1818 (vol. II, no. 15) p.113, c1.

45 THE GENERAL ASSEMBLY OF THE PRESBYTERIAN CHURCH *to* **[THE
CLERGY]. n.d. n.p.** Declares that "The aspect of the Church (and its many successful
labors), has probably never been so promising as at the present time"; discusses the change
of times and the vices of drunkenness, gambling, theatrical exhibitions, and dancing. 2 July
1818 (vol. II, no. 15) p.114, c2.

46 n.n. *to* **CALEB STRONG, LATE GOVERNOR OF MASSACHUSETTS. [extract]
n.d. n.p.** Discusses the folly of man's desire for retaliation, noting its evil consequences. 6
July 1818 (vol. II, no. 16) p.121, c1.

47 n.n. *to* **CALEB STRONG, ESQ., LATE GOVERNOR OF MASSACHUSETTS. [extract continued from 6 July 1818] n.d. n.p.** Shows that the law of retaliation is selfish, depraved, and cruel; declares that retaliation was repealed by Christ, who commanded his disciples neither to repel injury with injury nor resist evil with violence. 16 July 1818 (vol. II, no. 17) p.129, c1.

48 AN INQUIRER *to* **FRIEND OSBORN. n.d. n.p.** Mentions grazing, clover, and disease. [mostly illegible] 23 July 1818 [vol. II, no. 18] p.141, c1.

49 n.n. *to* **n.n. [extract] 6 June 1818. Richmond, Va.** Relates story demonstrating the horrors of slavery. 23 July 1818 (vol. II, no. 18) p.141, c2.

50 A MISSIONARY *to* **HIS UNCLE IN THE NORTHERN LIBERTIES (PHILADELPHIA). [extract] 6 May 1818. Chickamaugah.** Reports that the establishment is very well supplied with temporal things, especially lodgings and provisions; tells how the mission is conducted; describes its services. 30 July 1818 (vol. II, no. 19) p.148, c1.

51 A FRIEND ON A TOUR TO THE WEST-WARD *to* **L. [extract] Last Winter. n.p.** Describes the road from the Susquehanna to Huntingdon, especially the banks of the Juniata; briefly recounts the story of Pocahantas and John Smith. 13 August 1818 (vol. II, no. 21) p.163, c1.

52 A FARMER *to* **FRIEND OSBORN. 30 July 1818. Harmony Hill.** Replies to a request for information on "Horse Slobbering"; discusses the various opinions on what causes this distemper, and the best remedy for it. 13 August 1818 (vol. II, no. 21) p.165, c3.

53 D. *to* **FRIEND OSBORN. n.d. n.p.** Reports he has found a manuscript containing some remarkable experiences in the life of David Sands; tells of his escape during the American Revolution from a camp of five hundred men. 13 August 1818 (vol. II, no. 21) p.166, c1.

54 F. BATES, ESQ. *to* **n.n. [extract] n.d. n.p.** Reports the amounts and types of lead and shot exported from his factory and warehouse. 27 August 1818 (vol. II, no. 23) p.183, c2.

55 MONEYSHADOW *to* **[illegible]. n.d. n.p.** Tells of the advantages of banking: the security, the widely-recognized currency, and the ease of saving. 3 September 1818 (vol. II, no. 24) p.187, c1.

56 [illegible] *to* **FRIEND OSBORN. n.d. n.p.** Explains why he believes that a paper medium, in the nature of bank notes, will prove chiefly beneficial to the community. 24 September 1818 (vol. II, no. 25) p.195, c3.

57 S. TROTT *to* **FRIENDS. n.d. n.p.** Tells how the Kentucky Baptist Mission Society has worked among the American Indians; relates that they have now adopted a plan to teach every Indian the Bible, which he may read in a language he has been taught; appeals for funds. 24 September 1818 (vol. II, no. 25) p.196, c3.

58 A TRAVELLER *to* **THE EDITOR OF THE** *PITTSBURGH GAZETTE.* **n.d. n.p.** Writes to prove that the trade of the western country must unavoidably center at New York, not Pennsylvania; suggests ways to improve New York roads and canals. 8 October 1818 (vol. II, no. 26) p.203, c2.

Jonesborough (Tn.)
Emancipator

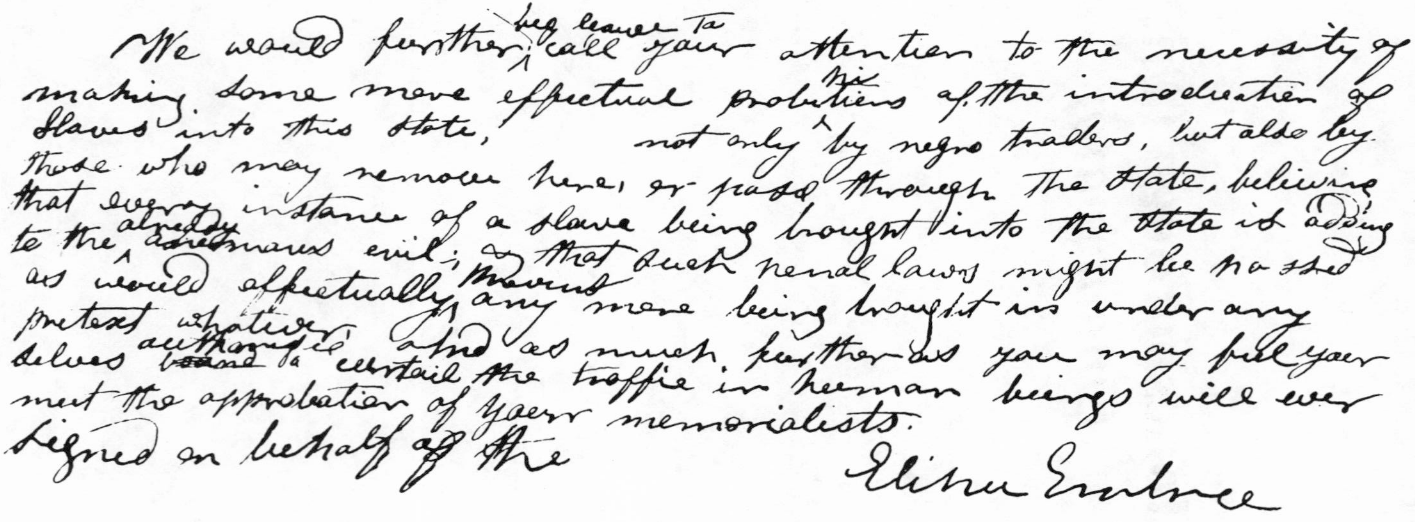

We would further beg leave to call your attention to the necessity of making some more effectual prohibitions of the introduction of slaves into this State, not only by negro traders, but also by those who may remove here, or pass through the State, believing that every instance of a slave being brought into the State is adding to the already enormous evil; and that such penal laws might be passed as would effectually prevent any more being brought in under any pretext whatever. And as much further as you may feel yourselves authorized to curtail the traffic in human beings will ever meet the approbation of your memorialists.

Signed on behalf of the

Elihu Embree

Figure 2. Memorial written by Elihu Embree

Elihu Embree

[Editor, *The Emancipator*]

Friend G. M. & others whom it may concern. In answer to . . . [your inquiry] I will just observe, that, to my shame be it said, I have owned slaves. To my shame be it also said, I have denied for years the truth of the christian religion; and during these years I became possessed of slaves. I always believed slavery to be wrong, but deism had a tendency to make me not very scrupulous in adhering to what I believed to be right, as respected much of my moral conduct. During this time I married a woman [Elizabeth Worley] who had several slaves, and afterwards purchased a man his wife & their only child. During the time I kept those last mentioned slaves, the woman had a 2d child, and not being able to pay for them, I soon had to let the man from whom I bought them, have the woman and her children in part payment, who at the same time transfered them over to a man that I sold the husband to in part pay of another slave I had bought, by which means they were all kept together. This last mentioned slave (who cost me $1000) together with 7 or 8 others, I let go free about 6 or 7 years ago, soon after I became convinced of the reality of the christian religion, and have not claimed them, nor exacted any of their labor since, without compensation. Two are dead.

One circumstance, over which I have not yet had controul, prevents their legal emancipation; but I have arranged that matter to the satisfaction of the society of Friends, of which I am a member, whose well known principles, as well as practice, are so decisive on this point, that I could not retain my membership amongst them, much less become a member, unless I stood fair in this respect.

This is the true history of all my dealing in slaves, by which I have lost in cash not less than $4000. Not so much on account of the loss, as on account of the deviation from rectitude, I repent that I ever owned one. And indeed the crime is of such a hue, that the time may yet come, that a man who has, in a single instance, gone astray thus far, may never be able in his life time to regain public confidence: and should this change of public sentiment take place in my day, and render me disqualified to act in the promotion of this glorious cause, I hope to acquiesce in, and be resigned to suffer the just judgment, and be more humbled under a sense of my past misconduct: meanwhile I shall doubtless have the pleasure of rejoicing at seeing this stigma on our religious professions, and stain upon our national escutcheon, eradicated by men of clean hands.

But in as much as I have not set up even the best part of my life as a criterian, it is to be hoped that the worst acts of the worst part of it cannot be applied in such a way as to render even doubtful this self evident truth, "*That all men are created equally free and independent,*" and are entitled to their liberty, whatever may be the misconduct of others.

Men who plead the crimes of one man against the just claims of another, evince to the world that they either do not believe themselves, or are not reasonable creatures, and deserve in the one case our pity, and in the other our indignation.

E[lihu] E[mbree]. *The Emancipator*,
Jonesborough, [Tn.], 31 August 1820

THE EMANCIPATOR.

VOL. I.]   JONESBOROUGH, 8th Mo. 31, 1820.   [No. 5.

EDITED AND PUBLISHED MONTHLY BY ELIHU EMBREE, AT $1 PER ANN.—IN ADVANCE.

THE OBJECTION
TO THE USE OF PRIZE GOODS
EXAMINED.

(Concluded from page 64.)

There is but right and wrong, good and evil, in the world; yet their grades are many. To refuse purchasing acknowledged prize goods, is to refuse being a party in violence and injustice; also, to bear a testimony against it. Where are cruelty and injustice carried to the same extent that they are in the slave trade? Where is the testimony that the purchasers and consumers of the fruit of slavery do bear against it? To answer in truth, we must say they are all parties in the business, and their testimony is for it. The beginners of the slave trade are the merchants who send their ships to Africa, to carry them across the ocean; and the finishers, are the consumers of their labor; they are the Alpha and the Omega of the business. The people employed in the Guinea ships, who drag them from their homes, the planters in the islands who purchase them, the merchants who import the produce of the slave's labor, the retailers and consumers thereof, are all accessaries in the business: they all assist in turning a wheel in that vast and complicated machine of iniquity. This great engine of destruction, is formed of the parts above described: they are the machine, and contain in themselves the cause of its motion; they constitute a complete whole. Take from it the consumers, and the whole machine must stop.

The merchant will not import an article for which there is no demand: the slave holder in the islands, will have no disposition to buy slaves, when the fruits of their labour will not sell. The Guinea ships will cease to haunt the coast of Africa in quest of slaves, when there is no demand for them in the islands.— Then that fountain of human blood which hath been flowing in Africa so long, would be dried up; and the carnage and misery attending the traffic in human flesh would cease.

This great fountain of human blood that hath been flowing on the continent of Africa for ages, whose streams have stained the shores of America, and the West Indies, is kept in motion, and supported by the consumers of the proceeds of slavery. They are the subscribers that furnish the fund by which the whole business is carried on. A merchant who loads his vessel in the West Indies with the proceeds of slavery, does nearly as much at helping forward the slave trade, as he that loads his vessel in Africa with slaves; they are both twisting the same rope at different ends.

The feasts of the luxurious may be called banquets of human flesh and blood; and the partakers thereof considered as cannibals devouring their own species; if we take into consideration the great distruction in Africa, by the warfare carried on in taking slaves; secondly, in transporting them to the islands in the Guinea ships; and lastly, in seasoning them; which is seasoning them to cruel whipping, hunger and hard labour, which they undergo in the culture of the cane, and the manufacture of sugar, where they are in a few years destroyed.

How is this vast destruction of the rational creation of God, to be accounted for, to him whose justice is infinite; who will not behold iniquity with approbation? On whom will the guilt of this great sacrifice to avarice and luxury fall? Certainly on the whole co-partnership who are parties in the business.

Having demonstrated that the West India produce is prize goods, and the sale of those goods to be the support of the slave trade, and of consequence, the purchasers to be parties in the business; it may not be amiss to observe, that the receiver of stolen goods is said to be equal to the thief. It is something paradoxical that a man should refuse to buy a stolen sheep, or to eat a piece of one that is stolen, and should not have the same scruples respecting a stolen man.

The Apostle Paul, in endeavoring to remove the strong Jewish prejudices for the Mosiac Law, said "Whatsoever is

F

Figure 3

Journal Data

TITLE: *The Emancipator*

INCLUSIVE DATES OF PUBLICATION: (Apr.–Oct. 1820)

SUPERSEDES: *Manumission Intelligencer*

PLACE OF PUBLICATION: Jonesborough, Tennessee

FREQUENCY OF PUBLICATION: Monthly

AVERAGE NUMBER OF PAGES PER ISSUE: 16

SIZE: 10″ x 6 1/2″ (size of reprint pages)

NUMBER OF COLUMNS PER PAGE: 2

EDITOR: Elihu Embree

PUBLISHER: Elihu Embree

PRINTER: J. Howard

PRICE: Annual Subscription $1.00

PERSPECTIVE: Anti-slavery

MISCELLANEOUS DATA: Available bound copy is a *reprint* of *The Emancipator*—includes a biographical sketch of Elihu Embree and two articles written by Embree.

REPOSITORY: Sterling Memorial Library, Yale University. 30 Apr. 1820–31 Oct. 1820. Reprint by B. H. Murphy, Nashville, Tennessee, 1932.

Prospectus

The *Emancipator* will be published monthly in Jonesborough, Ten. by ELIHU EMBREE, on a fine superroyal sheet of paper, in octava form, at One Dollar per annum, payable on receipt of the first number.

This paper is especially designed by the editor to advocate the abolition of slavery, and to be a repository of tracts on that interesting and important subject. It will contain all the necessary information that the editor can obtain of the progress of the abolition of the slavery of the descendants of Africa; together with a concise history of their introduction into slavery, collected from the best authorities.

The constitutions and proceedings of the several benevolent societies in the United States and elsewhere who have had this grand object in view, will be carefully selected and published in the *Emancipator*.

A correspondence between those soci[e]ties, and between individuals in different parts of the nation on the subject of emancipation, will be kept up through the medium of this paper by inserting in its pages all interesting communication, letters, &c. that may come to the knowledge of the editor.

The speeches of those have been and are eminently advocating this glorious cause, either in the congress of the U. S. the state legislatures, or in the parliaments and courts of other nations, will be strictly attended to.

Biographical sketches of the lives of those who have been eminent in this cause, will also occasionally find a place in this work.

A portion of this paper is intended to be devoted as a history of the abolition of the African slave trade, in every part of the world, from its first dawn, down to the present times.

In the prosecution of this work the editor professes that he expects (like other periodical editors) to live much upon the borrow; and to make use of such materials as he may find in his way, suited to his object, without being very particular to take up much time or room in acknowledging a loan, unless he may think it necessary, willing that others should use the same freedom with him, & hoping that by offering such a fair exchange, such borrowing will be thought no robbery.

Communications on the subject, and materials for the work are solicited and will be thankfully received both from societies and individuals friendly to the abolition of slavery. Such communications, if approved of by the editor, will find a hearty welcome in the *Emancipator*.

The Manumission Society of Tenn. in particular, it is expected will afford many tracts on the subject of slavery, which the editor assures them he will feel inclined to respect; and where his judgement should not otherwise dictate, will give them an early and gratuitous insertion. They will find in the *Emancipator* a true chronicle of the proceedings of that benevolent society as far as the editor is enabled—And for this purpose the clerks of the conventions, and of each branch of the society are requested to forward from time to time true copies of all their minutes, which may not be really improper to publish (and it is hoped there will be none such) together with the names of their members, their places of residence, &c. all which particulars we are of opinion will not be unprofitable to the cause of abolition to be published.

Letters from one individual to another, with the names of both, we think will be often beneficial to be published. If they do nothing more they will shew that all are not asleep nor dumb to the cries of suffering humanity.

Those who have had, or may have law suits on hand for the freedom of such as are unlawfully held in bondage, are desired to forward the true history of the facts, their progress, final decision, &c. with the places of residence and names of plaintiff's and defendant's, with every interesting particular, and they shall find in the *Emancipator* a true repository.

Altho the editor is as far from being a man of leisure as any in his acquaintance and not the owner of the office where this paper will be printed, and therefore shall have to hire the printing of it; and altho he has spent several thousand dollars already in some small degree abolishing, and in endeavoring to facilitate the general abolition of Slavery—yet he feels not satisfied without still continuing to throw in his mite, hoping that if the weight of it should not at present be felt, that when the scale comes nearly to a preponderancy, it will more sensibly be perceived, and in some small degree hasten an even balance of equal rights to the now neglected sons of Africa—

And as it will be at considerable trouble and expence [*sic*] that this work will be published, agreeably to the editor's intentions, it is hoped that none who have any love for African liberty, will think hard of paying $1 annually to the support of the only paper of this kind in the United States. And as the sum is too small and the income by no means expected to be sufficient to warrant the editor in travailing [*sic*] over the country to procure subscribers, he takes the liberty of sending the *Emancipator* to a good many whose names and places of residence he has become acquainted with, without their having subscribed. And he requests, and from the nature of the work, he will expect that those to whom they are sent, will, on receiving the first number, and having time to peruse it, remit to the editor, by mail or otherwise, One Dollar in some good current bank paper; or if they do not wish it continued, will carefully wrap it up in a separate paper to preserve it from being injured, and direct it to the editor at Embree's Ironworks.

All communications by mail to the editor must be directed as follows—Elihu Embree, post-master, Embree's Ironworks, Sullivan County, Tennessee—By this mean the postage will be free, both to and from the editor; the government bearing the expence [*sic*], as it righteously ought, of distributing these communications through the country, for the purpose of preparing the public mind for a practical reform from imposing unconditional slavery on a portion of its subjects.—

It is intended that each number bear date the last day of each month.

Those who procure 12 subscribers and pay for them shall be entitled to one gratis.

> Elihu Embree. *The Emancipator*,
> Jonesborough, [Tn.],
> April 30, 1820, (vol. I)

[1820]

59 MODERN LISTNER *to* **CORRESPONDENT. n.d. n.p.** Believes general opinion holds slavery to be wrong, but that what should be done about it is a subject of much discussion; declares that slavery will end when people deny themselves the gains of oppression. 30 April 1820 (vol. I) p.2, c2.

60 CORRESPONDENT *to* **MODERN LISTNER n.d. n.p.** Condemns hypocrisy of religion-professing slaveholders; comments on practice of dying slaveholders freeing slaves; also questions consistency of Southern interest in foreign missions and barbarity at home. 30 April 1820 (vol. I) p.5, c1.

61 ELIHU EMBREE *to* **MANUMISSION SOCIETY OF TENNESSEE AND OTHERS WHOM IT MAY CONCERN. n.d. n.p.** Withdraws from society since publication of newspaper may be violation of their constitution; believes he can be more useful if he does not remain a member, though he will rejoin if constitution is changed. 30 April 1820 (vol. I) p.9, c1.

62 A FRIEND *to* *EMANCIPATOR.* **[extract] 2 March 1820. Philadelphia.** Describes white man of Indian descent who was kidnapped, brutalized, and sold into slavery by his half-brother. 30 April 1820 (vol. I) p.16, c1.

63 CORRESPONDENT *to* **A GENTLEMAN IN THIS CITY [JONESBOROUGH, TN.]. [extract] 2 March 1820. Richmond, Va.** Describes the arrest of a white married couple in Richmond for teaching slave children; reports that the couple was released, but the children were whipped and a ten o'clock curfew for colored citizens was established. 31 May 1820 (vol. I) p.28, c1.

64 GENERAL STOKES *to* **A FRIEND. [extract] n.d. North Carolina.** Declares that the only way the South can hold a considerable portion of Louisiana Territory is to consent to prohibition of slavery in northern part; believes such a provision would not violate the Constitution. 31 May 1820 (vol. I) p.28, c2.

65 ELIHU EMBREE *to* **SENATE AND HOUSE OF REPRESENTATIVES, SECOND SESSION, THIRTEENTH GENERAL ASSEMBLY, STATE OF TENNESSEE. n.d. n.p.** Declares slavery is at odds with founding principles of American government; urges them to select best means of preparing for and effecting abolition. 30 June 1820 (vol. I) p.33, c2.

66 SAMUEL HODGES, JR. *to* **EDITORS OF THE** *BOSTON PATRIOT.* **31 March 1820. Villa de Phaya, St. Jago.** Sends several issues of *Sierra Leone Gazette* which report captured slave ships arriving daily. 31 July 1820 (vol. I) p.51, c1.

67 MODERN LISTNER *to* **THE PRESIDENT OF THE MANUMISSION SOCIETY OF TENNESSEE. n.d. n.p.** Encloses his creed on the subject of slavery; states that any person who can accept it, or even first five articles of it, cannot accept the Negro as a slave. 31 July 1820 (vol. I) p.54, c1.

68 THE RAMBLER *to* **MODERN LISTNER'S CORRESPONDENT. [from the** *Patriot***] n.d. n.p.** Relates a conversation with a group of religious people who favored slavery, as a result of which he became confused by their conflict between profession and practice. 31 July 1820 (vol. I) p.59, c1.

69 ELIHU EMBREE *to* **POSTMASTERS. n.d. n.p.** Suggests that the postal service has been sabotaging copies of the *Emancipator* within the post office and threatens censure of postal employees. 31 July 1820 (vol. I) p.64, c2.

70 G. M. *to* **MR. EMBREE. n.d. n.p.** Provides a solution to the problem of the Jews' permission to have servants and the lack of an explicit scriptural prohibition of slavery: declares no Gentile nation has the same right as the Jews had to hold slaves; maintains that the best policy for the United States would be to please God by freeing slaves. 31 August 1820 (vol. I) p.66, c1.

71 A CORRESPONDENT *to* **THE RAMBLER. n.d. n.p.** Questions the morality of branding justice and humanity as enthusiasm and fanaticism; declares that to use Old Testament custom as justification of slavery is absurd; presents example of Pietas. 31 August 1820 (vol. I) p.70, c1.

72 A CORRESPONDENT *to* **THE RAMBLER. n.d. n.p.** Provides a character sketch of Serena, as a contrast to Pietas whom he described in his last letter: Serena is a practicing Christian who opposes the holding of her fellow man in bondage; if she is a "fanatic," or "enthusiast," it is because she conforms to the spirit and practice of primitive, rather than popular, Christianity. 31 August 1820 (vol. I) p.72, c2.

73 G. M. *to* **FRIEND EDITOR [ELIHU EMBREE]. [extract] 17 August 1820. Nashville.**Informs him of a rumor that he was once a slaveholder, sold his slaves, and then tried to persuade their new owner to free them. 31 August 1820 (vol. I) p.80, c1.

74 E[LIHU] E[MBREE] *to* **G. M. AND OTHERS WHOM IT MAY CONCERN. 31 August 1820. Jonesborough, Tn.** Admits that he was once a slave owner before discovering "the truth of the Christian religion"; relates that he has since sold his slaves at a $4000 loss, and regrets having ever owned them. 31 August 1820 (vol. I) p.80, c1.

75 A CORRESPONDENT *to* **THE EDITOR OF THE** *EMANCIPATOR* **[ELIHU EMBREE]. [extract] 27 August 1820. Norfolk, Va.** Reports new state law which prohibits schools for colored people; discusses his wife's school; compares Virginia with the most despotic governments. 30 September 1820 (vol. I) p.89, c2.

76 GEORGE POINDEXTER *to* **THE EDITOR OF THE** *EMANCIPATOR* **[ELIHU EMBREE]. 31 July 1820. Ashwood Place, Ms.** Notes he has received several unsolicited copies of the *Emancipator*; views subscription price as evidence that others finance Embree's work, which he views as detrimental to social harmony; claims true Christians will wait for emancipation. 30 September 1820 (vol. I) p.91, c1.

77 n.n. *to* **THE EDITOR OF THE** *EMANCIPATOR* **[ELIHU EMBREE]. [extract] 8 August 1820. Rowan County, N.C.** Discusses hired slave who hanged himself rather than be rehired by a cruel master. 30 September 1820 (vol. I) p.93, c1.

78 THE AUTHOR *to* **FRIEND EMBREE. 5 May 1820. Knoxville.** Expresses surprise to see a poem he had written but not intended for publication appear in the *Emancipator*; requests that piece be reprinted with note that it is a quotation from a larger work. 30 September 1820 (vol. I) p.93, c2.

Genius of Universal Emancipation

Figure 4. Benjamin Lundy

Benjamin Lundy

[Editor, *Genius of Universal Emancipation*]

Benjamin Lundy deserves the high honor of ranking as the pioneer of direct and distinctive anti-slavery in America. Many who lived before and contemporary with him were Abolitionists; but he was the first of our countrymen who devoted his life and all his power exclusively to the cause of the slaves. Born in Sussex County, New Jersey, January 4, 1789, of Quaker parents, whose ancestors for several generations had lived and died in this country, he injured himself, while still a mere boy, by excessive labor on his father's farm, incurring thereby a partial loss of hearing, from which he never recovered. Slight in frame and below the common height, unassuming in manner and gentle in spirit, he gave to the cause of Emancipation neither wealth, nor eloquence, nor lofty abilities, for he had them not; but his courage, perseverance, and devotion were unsurpassed; and these combined to render him a formidable, though disregarded if not despised, antagonist to our national crime. Leaving his father's farm at nineteen years of age, he wandered westward at Wheeling, Virginia, where, during the next four years, he learned the trade of a saddler, and gained an insight into the cruelties and villanies of slaveholding—Wheeling being at the time a great thoroughfare for negro-traders and their prey on their route from Maryland and Virginia to the lower Mississippi. Before he made Wheeling his home, he had spent some time at Mount Pleasant, Ohio, whither he returned after learning his trade, and remained there two years, during which he married a young woman of like spirit to his own. He then, after a long visit to his father in New Jersey, settled at St. Clairsville, Ohio, near Wheeling, and opened a shop, by which in four years he made about three thousand dollars above his expenses, and, with a loving wife and two children, he was happy and contented with his lot as any man need be.

But the impression made on his mind by his experience of slavery in Wheeling could not be shaken off nor resisted. In the year 1815, when twenty-six years of age, he organized an anti-slavery association known as the "Union Humane Society," whereof the first meeting was held at his own house, and consisted of but five or six persons. Within a few months, its numbers were swelled to four or five hundred, and included the best and most prominent citizens of Belmont and the adjacent counties. Lundy wrote an appeal to philanthropists on the subject of slavery, which was first printed on the 4th of January, 1816, being his twenty-seventh birthday. Short and simple as it was, it contained the germ of the entire anti-slavery movement. A weekly journal entitled the *Philanthropist* was soon started at Mount Pleasant by Charles Osborne; and Lundy, at the editor's invitation, contributed to its columns, mainly by selections. In a few months he was urged by Osborne to join him in the newspaper enterprise, and finally consented to do so, removing to Mount Pleasant. Meantime he made a voyage to St. Louis in a flat-boat to dispose of his stock of saddlery. Arriving at that city in the fall of 1819, when the whole region was convulsed by the Missouri Question, he was impelled to write on the side then unpopular in the journals of the day. His speculation proved unfortunate—the whole west, and, indeed, the whole country, being then involved in a commercial convulsion, with trade stagnant and almost everyone bankrupt. He returned to his home on foot during the ensuing winter, having been absent nearly two years, and lost all he was worth.

Meantime, Osborne, tired of his thankless and profitless vocation, had sold out his establishment, and it had been removed to Jonesborough, Tennessee, where his newspaper took the title of the *Emancipator*. Lundy removed as he had proposed to Mount Pleasant, and then started, in January, 1821, a monthly entitled the *Genius of Universal Emancipation*. He commenced it with six subscribers, himself ignorant of printing and without materials, having his work done at Steubenville, twenty miles distant; traveling thither frequently on foot, and returning with his edition on his back. Four months later, he had a very considerable subscription list. About this time, Elihu Embree, who had started the *Emancipator* in Tennessee, died, and Lundy was urged to go thither, unite the two journals, and print them himself from the materials of the *Emancipator*. He consented, and made the journey of eight hundred miles, one half on foot and the rest by water. At Jonesborough he learnt the art of printing, and soon issued a weekly newspaper besides the *Genius*, and a monthly agricultural work. He removed his family a few months later, and East Tennessee was thenceforward his home for nearly three years, during which the *Genius of Universal Emancipation* was the only distinctively and exclusively anti-slavery periodical issued in the United States, constantly increasing in circulation and influence. And, though often threatened with personal assault, and once shut up in a private room with two ruffians, who undertook to bully him into some concession by a flourish of deadly weapons, he was at no time subject to mob violence or legal prosecution.

In the winter of 1823-4, the American Convention for the Abolition of Slavery was held in Philadelphia; and Lundy made the journey of six hundred miles and back on purpose to attend it. During his tour he decided on transferring his establishment to Baltimore; and in the summer of 1823, knapsack on shoulder, he set out on foot for that city. On the way he delivered, at Deep Creek, North Carolina, his first public address against slavery. He spoke in a beautiful grove, near the Friends' meeting-house at that place, directly after divine worship; and the audience were so well satisfied that they invited him to speak again in their place of worship. Before the second meeting adjourned, an anti-slavery society was formed; and he proceeded to hold fifteen or twenty similar meetings at other places within that State. In one instance, he spoke at a house-raising; in another, at a militia muster. Here an anti-slavery society of fourteen members was thereupon formed, with the captain of the militia company for its President. One of his meetings was held at Raleigh, the capital. Before he had left the State, he had organized twelve or fourteen Abolition Societies. He continued his journey through Virginia, holding several meetings, and organizing societies—of course, not very numerous, nor composed of the most influential persons. It is probable that his Quaker brethren supplied him with introductions from place to place, and that his meetings were held at the points where violent opposition was least likely to be offered.

He reached Baltimore about the first of October, and issued on the 10th, No. 1 of Volume IV. of *The Genius*, which continued to be well supported, though receiving little encouragement from Baltimore itself. A year afterward, it began to be issued weekly.

Lundy visited Hayti in the latter part of 1825, in order to make arrangements there for the reception of a number of slaves, whose masters were willing to emancipate them on condition of their removal from the country—in fact, were not allowed by the laws of their respective States to free them otherwise. Being detained longer than he had expected, he was met on his return to Baltimore with tidings of the death of his wife, after giving birth to twins, and hastened to his dwelling to find it entirely deserted, his five children having been distributed among his friends. In that hour of intense affliction, he renewed his solemn vow to devote his entire energies to the cause of the slave, and to efforts designed to awaken his countrymen to a sense of their responsibility and their danger. In 1828 he traveled eastward, lecturing and soliciting subscribers to his *Genius*, and calling, in New York, on Arthur Tappan, William Goodell, and other anti-slavery men. At Boston he could hear of no Abolitionists, but made the acquaintance, at his boarding-house, of William Lloyd Garrison, a fellow-boarder, whose attention had not previously been drawn to the slavery question, but who readily embraced his views. He visited successively most of the clergymen of Boston, and induced eight of them, belonging to various sects, to meet him. All of them on explanation approved his labors, and subscribed for his periodical; and, in the course of a few days, they aided him to hold an anti-slavery meeting, which was largely attended. At the close of his remarks, several clergymen expressed a general concurrence in his views. He extended his journey to New Hampshire and Maine, lecturing where he could, and obtaining some encouragement. He spoke also in the principal towns of Massachusetts, Rhode Island and Connecticut: and on his homeward route, traversed the State of New York, speaking at Poughkeepsie, Albany, Lockport, Utica and Buffalo, reaching Baltimore late in October.

Lundy made at least one other visit to Hayti, to colonize emancipated slaves; was beaten nearly to death in Baltimore by a slave-trader, on whose conduct he had commented in terms which seemed disrespectful to the profession; was flattered by the judge's assurance, when the trader came to be tried for the assault, that he (Lundy) had got nothing more than he deserved. He made two long journeys through Texas, to the Mexican departments across the Rio Grande, in quest of a suitable location on which to plant a colony of freed blacks from the United States, but without success. He traveled in good part on foot, observing the strictest economy, and supporting himself by working at saddlery and harness-mending from place to place, as circumstances required. Meantime, he had been compelled to remove his paper from Baltimore to Washington; and finally (in 1836) to Philadelphia, where it was entitled the *National Inquirer*, and at last merged into the *Pennsylvania Freeman*. His colonizing enterprise took him to Monclova, Comargo, Monterey, Matamoras, and Victoria, in Mexico, and consumed the better part of several years, closing in 1834. He also made a visit to the settlements in Canada of fugitives from American slavery, to inquire into the welfare of their inhabitants. On the 17th of May, 1838, at the burning by a mob of Pennsylvania Hall—built by Abolitionists, because they could be heard in no other—his little property, consisting mainly of papers, books, clothes, etc., which had been collected in one of the rooms of that Hall, with a view to his migration westward, was totally destroyed. In July, he started for Illinois, where his children then resided, and reached them in the September following. He planted himself at Lowell, in La Salle country, gathered his offspring about him, purchased a printing office, and renewed the issue of his *Genius*. But in August, 1839, he was attacked by a prevailing fever, of which he died on the 22nd of that month, in the 51st year of his age. Thus closed the record of one of the most heroic, devoted, unselfish, courageous lives that have ever lived on this continent.

Horace Greeley. *Liberator*,
Boston [Ma.], 1 April 1864, p.1, c3

GENIUS OF UNIVERSAL EMANCIPATION.

EDITED AND PUBLISHED BY BENJAMIN LUNDY, BALTIMORE, MD.

"We hold these truths to be self-evident, that all men are created equal, and endowed by their Creator with certain unalienable rights; that among these are life, liberty, and the pursuit of happiness."—*Dec. Independence U. S.*

No. 2. Vol. IV.   NOVEMBER, 1824.   WHOLE No. 45.

EMIGRATION TO HAYTI—No II.

We perceive, by the census taken in the year 1790, that there were, at that time, 757,178 coloured persons in the different States and Territories of the Union. According to the enumeration made in the year 1820, the number amounted to 1,764,832; which shews an increase of 1,007,654 during a period of thirty years. In the year 1810, the number of coloured people was 1,377,810; which deducted from 1,764,832, the amount given in the census of 1820, leaves 387,022 as the increase of that period. This shews that the medium annual increase, for the time just stated, was 38,702 1-5. Probably, in the last year of that time, it fell little short of 42,000.—At present, therefore, making sufficient allowance, and without calculating particularly the geometrical ratio of increase, the yearly augmentation of their number may, perhaps, be estimated at 45,000; and, hence, it may be supposed that there are now, about 1,980,000 persons of that class, in the United States.

It will be seen from the above, that the coloured population of this country more than doubled between the years 1790 and 1820.—But as the importation of slaves was freely permitted prior to the year 1808, and many have, doubtless, since been smuggled into the country, in consequence of the impossibility of enforcing the laws enacted to prevent it, in some particular places, it is probable that the natural increase will vary but little from the estimates of those who have heretofore adopted the opinion, that this population would double every thirty years. Taking this as the basis of our calculation, we shall find that, if nothing is done to check that increase, and admitting that there are, at present, 1,980,000 coloured persons among us, their number will amount, in little more than a century, to upwards of 30,000,000. We must bear in mind, that this estimate is founded on the supposition that *no more slaves shall be introduced from abroad*—that effectual measures shall be taken to prevent the smuggling them into any part of the country—Should any increase be effected by other means than the regular operations of nature, it will, of course, swell the gross amount.

After taking this view of the subject, the question naturally arises: Do we possess the competent means of reducing the vast and rapidly increasing amount of our coloured population? I answer: It is fully believed that we have the means, fairly within our reach, for the attainment of this important object, and that nothing is wanting, but the disposition to undertake it, to ensure the final, and most complete, success of the measure. This, I hope, I shall be able to prove to the satisfaction of every unprejudiced and intelligent reader.

It is now supposed, that between four and five thousand coloured persons have already embarked for Hayti, or will have done so before the end of this month, under the direction of citizen Granville, whose arrival in New York was announced on the 13th day of June last. It is also estimated, that the price of passage, and subsistence during the voyage, from our Atlantic sea ports to that Island, will not exceed fourteen dollars, for grown persons, and half that sum for children, when the proper arrangements shall be made. Admitting, however, that it will average twelve dollars, a head, it would be an easy matter, if proper exertions were now made by the government of the United States, those of individual States, and Societies formed for the purpose, to send out from fifty to sixty thousand, annually. The cost of transporting the latter number, at the price above stated, would be 720,000 dollars; and the whole of the increase for the preceding year, together with 15,000 of the old stock, would be thus removed. It will be observed that, by this mode of proceeding, the number of those persons would be lessened upon the same geometrical principle that it is now augmented. Instead of increasing, it would regularly diminish, without any addition to the annual expense of transportation. Probably all those who were previously free, together with such as should be emancipated, on the condition of their leaving the country, would by this means, be taken away as fast as they could be prepared for removal. If an annual appropriation of 500,000 dollars[*]

* It will be perceived that this sum would not, according to the foregoing calculation, be sufficient, of itself, to draw off the coloured population, as fast as would be requisite, to effect the desired object; but, in all probability, the additions to it from private contributions, together with the aid afforded by the state governments, benevolent societies, &c. would supply the deficiency. We may also calculate that many coloured persons would transport themselves at their own expense; especially if the Haytien government should still consent to advance a part of it, on the condition of their refunding the same at a future period. It may, further, be observed, that if a large proportion of the emigrants should consist of heads of families, and females, between the ages of 14 and 45 years, the ratio of increase, among those remaining, would be far less than if they were taken, indiscriminately, from the mass of population. Hence, it would be advisable to hold out every

Figure 5

Journal Data

TITLES AND SUBTITLES: *Genius of Universal Emancipation* (July 1821–23 June 1827); *Genius of Universal Emancipation or American Anti-Slavery Journal, and Register of News* (4 July 1827–?); *Genius of Universal Emancipation* (2 Sept. 1829–Dec. 1836); *Genius of Universal Emancipation and Quarterly Anti-Slavery Review* (July 1837–Jan. 1838); *Genius of Universal Emancipation* (1839–?)

MOTTO: "We hold these truths to be self evident: that all men are created equal, and endowed by their Creator with certain inalienable rights, that among these are life, liberty, and the pursuit of happiness." (July 1821–Dec. 1836)

INCLUSIVE DATES OF PUBLICATION: July 1821–Sept. 1825 (V. 1–4); ?–31 Dec. 1825 (new ser., V. 1, Nos. 1–18)–1839; Suspended: July–Sept. 1824; Apr. 1831; June–Oct. 1832; July 1833, Nov.–Dec. 1833; Jan.–June 1837

SUPERSEDED BY: *Genius of Liberty*

PLACES OF PUBLICATION: Mt. Pleasant, Ohio (21 Apr.–Mar. 1822); Greeneville, Tennessee (Apr. 1822–June 1824); Baltimore, Maryland (Oct. 1824–Sept. 1830); Washington and Baltimore (Oct. 1830–May 1832); Washington, D.C. (Oct. 1830–Oct. 1833); Philadelphia (Jan. 1834–Jan. 1838); Hennepin, Illinois (1839?–?)

FREQUENCY OF PUBLICATION: Monthly (July 1821–Feb. 1823); Semi-monthly (Mar. 1823–15 Aug. 1823); Monthly (Sept. 1823–Sept. 1825); Weekly (16 Sept. 1826?–5 Mar. 1830); Monthly (Apr. 1830–Dec. 1836); Quarterly (July 1837–Jan. 1838); Weekly (1839 ?–?)

DAY OF WEEK WHEN PUBLISHED: Saturday (19 May 1827–?); Friday (2 Sept. 1829–5 Mar. 1830); (1839?–?)

AVERAGE NUMBER OF PAGES PER ISSUE: 16–56

SIZE: Varies

NUMBER OF COLUMNS PER PAGE: 2–4

EDITOR(s): Benjamin Lundy (1821–1833); W. L. Garrison (1829–?); Evan Lewis (Jan.–Mar. 1834); Edwin Augustus Atlee (Apr. 1834–June 1834); Benjamin Lundy (July 1834–1839?)

PUBLISHER(s): Benjamin Lundy (July 1822–1839?); William Lloyd Garrison (2 Sept. 1829–5 Mar. 1830)

PRINTER(s): Wm. Wooddy (Oct. 1824–Feb. 1825); Benjamin Lundy (Mar. 1825–?)

SPECIAL FEATURES: Advertisements; Illustrations; Supplements; Annual Indexes

PRICE: Per Volume $1.00 Annual Subscription $1.00 Changed in 1826 to: $3.00 Annual Subscription Changed in 1830 to: $1.00 Annual Subscription Changed in 1839 to: $1.50

LANGUAGE(s): English; occasional letters in French

PERSPECTIVE: Anti-slavery

MISCELLANEOUS DATA: Published simultaneously with the *Genius of Universal Emancipation and Baltimore Courier* during 1825–6

REPOSITORY: Columbia Library, University of Missouri. 1821–1839.

Prospectus

The subject of African Slavery has assumed a degree of importance that demands the attention of every citizen of the United States. The question of extending and perpetuating it, has been so critically examined, and so ably discussed of late, that a powerful excitement has been produced, even from Maine to New Orleans, and from the shores of the Atlantic to the savage wilds of the west. The principles and maxims adopted by those sages who laid the foundation for this great and flourishing Empire, are beginning to develope [sic] themselves more fully to the view of the American people, and to attract the admiration of millions of the human race. Thousands are daily becoming more and more enlightened, the prejudice of education is vanishing before the luminous orb of truth, and the gloom of superstition is partially dispelled by the effulgent rays of reason and Christian philosophy. That this abomination of abominations, the system of slavery, *must* be abolished, is as clear as the shining of the sun at noon-day; the very nature of our government forbids its continuance, and the voice of the ETERNAL hath often pleased the ALL WISE to make use of human agency as the means whereby the foulest corruptions have been rooted out, and the most glorious reformations have been effected in the Societies of men, it may fairly be presumed that the present generation will have much to do towards eradicating the noxious plant from the soil of Columbia. Happy will it be for our country, happy will it be for the countless thousands that are to succeed us, and to inhabit the vast and fertile regions of America, if this hydra of iniquity can be vanished, ere the arm of vengeance is raised, and the destroying angel, the gory fiend of *Intestine War*, is permitted to lay waste our cities, our villages, and our fields, and to consign their possessors to the sword. That this will one day be done, there is not a shadow of doubt, unless the sons of liberty be fairly roused from their lethargy, unless they be induced to act consistently with their professions, and remove the evils without the borders of their wide domain.

Nothing is more true than that domestic Slavery is the hot bed of tyran[n]y, and those districts in which it is tolerated are the nurseries of aristocracy and despotism. Hear what that eminent Statesman and profound philosopher, Thomas Jefferson, says upon the subject. In his *Notes on Virginia*, he observes:

"There must doubtless be an unhappy influence on the manners of our people produced by the existence of slavery among us. The whole commerce between master and slave is a perpetual exercise of the most boisterous passions, the most unremitting *despotism* on the one part, and the most degrading submission on the other. Our children see this, and learn to imitate it, for man is an imitative animal! This is the germ of education in him. The parent storms, the child looks on, catches the lineaments of wrath, puts on the same airs in the circle of smaller slaves, and thus nursed, educated, & daily exercised in *tyranny*, cannot but be stamped by it with odious peculiarities. The man must be a prodigy who can retain his manners and morals undepraved by such circumstances. And with what execration should the statesman be loaded, who permitting *one half of the citizens thus to trample on the rights of the other, transforms those into despots*, and these into enemies, destroying the morals of the one part, and the amor patria of the other."

This is a highly finished picture, but who will doubt the truth of it when coming from such a source? Again, speaking on the same subject, he says: "I tremble for my country, when I reflect that God is just, that his justice cannot sleep forever; that considering numbers, nature & natural means only, a revolution of the wheel of fortune, an exchange of situation, is among possible events; that it may become probable by supernatural interference! The Almighty has no attribute which can take side with us in such a contest. But it is impossible to be temperate and to pursue this subject through the various considerations of policy, of morals, of history, natural and civil; we must be contented and they will force their way into every one's mind. I think a change is already perceptible since the origin of the present revolution. The spirit of the master is abating, that of the slave is rising from the dust, his condition mollifying, a way of hope preparing, under the auspices of heaven, *for a total emancipation*, and this is disposed, in the order of events, to be with the consent of the masters, rather than by their extirpation."

Such is the language of one of our wisest Statesmen, and who may, politically speaking, be emphatically termed the brightest star in the constellation of sages that formed the plan of our excellent government. To a mind like his, the hypocritical villainy of the unprincipled advocate of slavery is clearly discernable; and he can readily perceive the germs of aristocracy and tyranny which are thus enwoven with his frame." Admitting the truth of all this, how necessary will it appear for the American people to purge the land of this foul corruption, to expel the insiduous reptile which, by its siren charm, decoys the unwary, and tempts them to turn from the path of honest rectitude.

The republicanism of American Slaveholders, as practically demonstrated, is much of a piece with the politics of the old English Barons: enthusiastically attached to liberty as far as it respects themselves, and those they please to denominate their equals, they are at the same time, in most cases actuated by the most relentless and unfeeling cruelty, and often exercise the most ferocious barbarity in the treatment of those whom cold, calculating Avarice and Despotic Power united, hath made their vassals.

—The same spirit that actuated the king of Egypt when he refused the Israelites their freedom, now actuates them, and would prompt them to reduce to an ignominious bondage their white skin'd brethren, if they had the power, and conceived it to be their interest to do so. The color would be considered as nothing, were Avarice clothed with authority to lengthen the chain of oppresssion. Hence it becomes the duty of the advocates of free government, to observe the signs of the times, to guard with unwearied vigilance the temple of liberty, and cling to the great charter of our national rights, as the ark of political safety; to trace the despotic spirit through all its ramifications in society, to watch, with a lynx eye, its intricate movements, its various evolutions, and to sound the tocsin of alarm when necessary.

For the purpose of aiding in the great & important work of Emancipation, and in order to contribute his mite towards lessening the amount of human woe, the undersigned has commenced the publication of this paper. As it is his intention to devote its pages almost exclusively to the subject under consideration, and as he will carefully select the most important matter connected therewith, expecting at the same time to have the assistance of men of first rate talents, and literary acquirements, he hopes it will be found worthy the patronage of persons of the highest standing in the nation.— If it be urged as an objection, that it is published in a state where slavery is not tolerated, he will observe, that it is by no means to be considered a local publication; but on the contrary, mere local matter will be excluded from its columns, that it may be calculated for general circulation. And as one great object will be to point out the inconsistencies, and overcome the prejudices in the free, as well as the slave holding states, that the individuals in favour of the work of emancipation, throughout the great American family, may be brought to cooperate together, it is desired that it may be read in every part of the Union.

The Genius of Universal Emancipation is designed to rise, like a Phenix, [*sic*] from the ashes of the late *"Emancipator,"* published at Jonesborough, in Tennessee, by Elihu Embree. Had that worthy man still lived to extend his useful labours, it is not likely that this paper would have appeared at this time; but as it hath pleased the Almighty Disposer of events to call him from works to rewards, and as there does not appear to be a prospect of a continuance of the *Emancipator*, it is hoped that this work may supply its place.

Important information from every part of the country, contained in numerous publications, will be collected for this paper, and presented to its readers. Well written essays and communications from societies and individuals, tending to subserve the cause of emancipation will be gratuitously inserted; and the editor requests those who may have it in their power, to furnish him with such miscellaneous or documentary articles as may comport with his plan, to lend him their aid. Short biographical and historical sketches, will occasionally find a place in this work; reports of important law cases, and details of cases of unusual barbarity, when forwarded, will be duly attended to; the constitutions, orations, reports, and proceedings of the various abolition, and other societies, established for the purpose of restoring to the Africans and their descendants, their natural rights, are solicited for publication; amusing and interesting anecdotes will often be welcomed to vary the scene, and the productions of the muses, at all times acceptable, will be thankfully received, and conspicuously placed in the apartment dedicated to the Nine.

In short, the editor intends that this work shall be a true record of passing events, and of the various transactions relative to the enslavement of the Africans; and he hopes it may eventually prove a faithful history of their final Emancipation. He solicits the patronage of an enlightened public, and promises to spare no pains to make it worth the price demanded for it. The philanthropist and the man of leisure are requested to encourage it, as it may be profitable to the one, and amusing to the other. It is hoped the wealthy man will favour it, as a small portion of his riches may be thus devoted to a good purpose: the emancipator will find in it much that will tend to his gratification; and it is even recommended to the perusal of the openly avowed advocate of Slavery,—as he may occasionly [sic] see in it a full length portrait of himself!

Twelve numbers will constitute a volume. A title page and index will be furnished for each volume gratis, and the printing will be neatly executed, that it may be an object to file the numbers and have them bound. The price to Subscribers will be one Dollar *per annum*, payable annually in advance. The difficulty in collecting small sums scattered over so great extent of country, as this work will be, renders a strict adherence to this rule indispensably necessary: any subscriber, however, that may be dissatisfied with it, after perusing two or three of the first numbers, may return them to the editor, and the money shall be refunded: provided, in all cases, the papers are kept clean and whole, and are sent back free of expense.

The paper will be carefully and securely wrapped, and forwarded to subscribers, by mail, or otherwise, agreeable to their directions, to any part of the U. States. And for the accommodation of persons at a distance, who may be willing to patronise [sic] the work, the bills of any specie paying bank in the different states, that may be located near their respective places of residence, will be received for subscriptions. The editor will guaranty the safety of the mails for the transmission of money that may be sent to him, provided the persons who may deposit it in the post office take care to have sufficient proof for the purpose of identifying the different bills, in case they do not come regularly to hand.

Subscribers must begin and end with a volume.

The postage on all letters, communications &c. to the editor must be paid, or they cannot be attended to: persons, however, who are authorised [sic] to act as agents, may keep back the amount of postage, when they make remittances through that channel.

Any person that will procure six subscribers, and forward the money to the editor, shall be furnished with one year's papers gratis.

This number will be presented to divers persons who have not ordered it, that they may have an opportunity of acquainting themselves with the plan of the work. If it should meet their approbation, and they wish to become subscribers, they will please to signify it to the editor; otherwise it will not continue to be sent to them.

B. Lundy. *Genius of Universal
Emancipation,* July, 1821,
(vol. I, no. 1)

[1821]

79 FRANKLIN *to* **THE EDITOR [B. LUNDY]. 1821. Jefferson County, Oh.** Reports that the prospectus for the newspaper provoked discussion of slavery issues in his neighborhood; refutes arguments for slavery and prays for a new generation of abolitionists. July 1821 (vol. I, no. 1) p.4, c2.

80 ENQUIRER *to* **THE EDITOR [B. LUNDY]. n.d. n.p.** Suggests three questions for readers: Why do slaveholders denounce the Austrian emperor? How can they claim that the slave's position has improved? How can free state residents justify excluding free people of color? August 1821 (vol. I, no. 2) p.21, c2.

81 AMICUS LIBERTATI *to* **THE EDITOR OF THE** *BALTIMORE MORNING CHRONICLE.* **n.d n.p.** Provides information about slaveholding and slave trading activities of Supreme Court Justice Bushrod Washington; claims Washington is president of the ACS. August 1821 (vol. I, no. 2) p.25, c2.

82 G.W.B. *to* **HIS BROTHER IN NEW JERSEY. [extract from the** *National Gazette***] 1 June 1821. n.p.** An American gentleman describes a discussion of United States slave trade during a visit to Vienna; reports that he was embarrassed and claimed that the article provoking their talk exaggerated. September 1821 (vol. I, no. 3) p.44, c1.

83 n.n. *to* **THE EDITOR [B. LUNDY]. [extract] n.d. Philadelphia.** Expresses pleasure upon seeing first issue of newspaper. October 1821 (vol. I, no. 4) p.50, c1.

84 n.n. *to* **THE EDITOR [B. LUNDY]. n.d. Kentucky.** Reports satisfaction with second issue of newspaper; hopes sufficient support will be forthcoming; identifies three new subscribers and encourages Lundy, declaring that the abolitionist cause is sanctioned by God. October 1821 (vol. I, no. 4) p.50, c2.

85 n.n. *to* **THE EDITOR [B. LUNDY]. n.d. Illinois.** Wishes Lundy success with his work. October 1821 (vol. I, no. 4) p.50, c2.

86 BUSHROD WASHINGTON *to* **FREDERICK G. SCHAEFFER. [extract] 18 September 1821. Jefferson County, Va.** Defends his recent sale of fifty-four slaves; protests interference by those who question his legal or moral right to dispose of property. October 1821 (vol. I, no. 4) p.52, c1.

87 n.n. *to* **THE EDITOR [B. LUNDY]. n.d. n.p.** Supports the paper's goals, but believes personal reflections should be excluded; proposes a constitutional amendment to abolish slavery by freeing those persons of color born after its ratification. October 1821 (vol. I, no. 4) p.57, c1.

88 HAWLEY *to* **THE EDITOR [B. LUNDY]. n.d. n.p.** Encloses article he authored on slavery and the Constitution. October 1821 (vol. I, no. 6) p.89, c1.

89 TRUMBULL *to* **THE EDITOR [B. LUNDY]. n.d. n.p.** Encloses slave's epitaph found in a Concord, Massachusetts graveyard. December 1821 (vol. I, no. 6) p.90, c1.

[1822]

90 n.n. *to* **n.n. n.d. n.p.** Declares that the world looks to the United States to abolish slavery. January 1822 (vol. I, no. 7) p.104, c2.

91 GENTLEMAN IN INTERIOR OF STATE OF NEW YORK *to* **n.n. n.d. New York.** Expresses pleasure with the newspaper; explains that he has tried to procure new subscribers but has encountered much apathy. January 1822 (vol. I, no. 7) p.105, c1.

92 A CAROLINIAN *to* **THE EDITOR [B. LUNDY]. December 1821. North Carolina.** After reading several issues of the newspaper, concludes that too much party feeling and sectional policy exists; asserts that the best abolition scheme originated in the South with colonization. January 1822 (vol. I, no. 7) p.109, c2.

93 S. C. *to* **THE EDITOR [B. LUNDY]. n.d. n.p.** Wonders how Christians, who are commanded to reprove a sinner, can witness oppression without reprimanding the oppressor. February 1822 (vol. I, no. 8) p.123, c2.

94 INDEPENDENCE *to* **THE EDITOR [B. LUNDY]. n.d. n.p.** Describes his abrupt departure from an inn after seeing two Negro boys brutally whipped for stealing corn. February 1822 (vol. I, no. 8) p.124, c1.

95 A MARYLANDER *to* **THE EDITOR [B. LUNDY]. n.d. n.p.** Approves of Lundy's zeal, but believes various emancipation plans to be unjust; feels that slaves are entitled to complete compensation for their servitude. March 1822 (vol. I, no. 9) p.140, c1.

96 JUSTICE *to* **MESSRS. EDITORS. [from the *Baltimore American*] n.d. n.p.** Inveighs against kidnapping and the internal slave trade; proposes petitioning the state legislature to outlaw interstate transport of slaves. March 1822 (vol. I, no. 9) p.141, c1.

97 JOHN JAY *to* **ELIAS BOUDINOT. 17 November 1819. Bedford, N.Y.** Declares that slavery should be prohibited in new states and gradually abolished in all; upholds constitutional authority to prohibit migration and importation of slaves. April 1822 (vol. I, no. 10) p.160, c1.

98 NARRATOR *to* **THE EDITOR [B. LUNDY]. n.d. n.p.** Relates tale of a minister who prayed for a slaveholder's salvation; the slaveholder later repented and became a preacher of the gospel. May 1822 (vol. I, no. 11) p.166, c1.

99 SOPHRONIA *to* **THE EDITOR [B. LUNDY]. 6 May 1822. n.p.** Encloses several of her letters from Ireneus. May 1822 (vol. I, no. 11) p.166, c2.

100 IRENEUS *to* **SOPHRONIA. November 1821. n.p.** Declares himself convinced of the depravity of human nature; notes man's prejudice and preoccupation with physical beauty; describes his first confrontation with slavery. May 1822 (vol. I, no. 11) p.166, c2.

101 IRENEUS *to* **SOPHRONIA. December 1821. n.p.** Identifies man's violation of primeval law as the cause for slavery; calls slavery the creation of idleness; questions religiousness of slaveholders. May 1822 (vol. I, no. 11) p.168, c1.

102 COMMON SENSE *to* **THE EDITOR [B. LUNDY]. n.d. n.p.** Considers the abolition plan of "A Marylander" inconsistent and designed to increase human suffering; feels that an attempt to exile slaveholders would lead to secession. May 1822 (vol. I, no. 11) p.170, c2.

103 OBSERVATOR *to* **THE EDITOR [B. LUNDY]. n.d. n.p.** Encloses copy of a letter written by a European gentleman to his brother on the subject of American government and slavery. May 1822 (vol. I, no. 11) p.176, c1.

104 W. *to* **JOHN. n.d. n.p.** Argues that characterization of America as a land of liberty is hypocritical because of slavery; describes his visit with a slaveholder's family and the treatment of Negroes on their plantation. May 1822 (vol. I, no. 11) p.176, c2.

105 IRENEUS *to* **SOPHRONIA. January 1822. n.p.** Describes conversation between Tyrannus and Humanitas on the subject of slavery and its legality under the Constitution. June 1822 (vol. I, no. 12) p.187, c1.

106 IRENEUS *to* **SOPHRONIA. January 1822. n.p.** Labels contemporary "Christian" religion false because it tolerates the existence of slavery; interprets the Church's acceptance of slaveholders as a justification of slavery. July 1822 (vol. II, no. 13) p.5, c2.

107 THE FARMER *to* **THE PEOPLE OF TENNESSEE. n.d. n.p.** Claims that slavery is responsible for all social oppression; declares slavery a moral evil; urges that no slaveholder be elected to public office. July 1822 (vol. II, no. 13) p.11, c1.

108 A FRIEND TO TRUTH *to* **THE EDITOR [B. LUNDY]. n.d. n.p.** Encloses article on conditions in Haiti. July 1822 (vol. II, no. 13) p.13, c1.

109 IRENEUS *to* **SOPHRONIA. February 1822. n.p.** Describes a revival meeting at which Tyrannus Clericus inveighed against every crime but slavery, being himself a slaveholder; mentions debate between Ireneus, this clergyman, and Clericus Justitia. August 1822 (vol. II, no. 13) p.18, c1.

110 COMMON SENSE *to* **THE EDITOR [B. LUNDY]. n.d. n.p.** Expresses concern that all consequences be considered when proposing plans for abolition; criticizes the plans suggested by "Howard" and the *Philanthropist*. August 1822 (vol. II, no. 13) p.20, c2.

111 A. *to* **THE EDITOR [B. LUNDY]. n.d. n.p.** Says he has always deprecated domestic slavery; describes incident in which a nursing black mother was knocked down with a shovel by her mistress and then beaten by her master. August 1822 (vol. II, no. 13) p.21, c1.

112 MODERN LISTENER *to* **SIR. n.d. n.p.** Discusses slavery and temperance. [partially illegible] August 1822 (vol. II, no. 13) p.24, c2.

113 JUDGE TOULMIN *to* **n.n. [extract from the *London Monthly Magazine*] n.d. n.p.** Appears to deal with a halfbreed Negro who could speak Indian languages, leading the author to speculate on common ancestry of Negroes and Indians. [partially illegible] August 1822 (vol. II, no. 13) p.26, c1.

114 IRENEUS *to* **SOPHRONIA. April 1822. n.p.** Notes that the spirits of religion and the world have become intermixed; compares Moslems to slaveholding Christians; divides mankind into three classes: the good, the indifferent, and the evil. September 1822 (vol. II, no. 14) p.33, c1.

115 MODERN LISTENER *to* **SIR. 1 September 1821. n.p.** Discusses meetings of the Manumission Society of Tennessee and the origins and present significance of the words "Whig" and "Tory" for slavery; describes opponents of abolition; adds that Manumission Society members object to laws which deprive others of their rights. September 1822 (vol. II, no. 14) p.35, c2.

116 THOMAS BENNETT *to* **SIR. 10 August 1822. Charleston, S.C.** The governor of South Carolina discusses a recent abortive slave uprising in South Carolina led by Denmark Vesey. September 1822 (vol. II, no. 14) p.42, c1.

117 GENTLEMAN IN GEORGIA *to* **FRIEND IN NEWARK. [extract] July 1805. n.p.** Describes reunion of a slave woman with her husband who had been separated from her two years earlier in Africa. September 1822 (vol. II, no. 14) p.48, c1.

118 IRENEUS *to* **SOPHRONIA. May 1822. n.p.** Reports that he has become acquainted with professed Christians of different character like Ecclesiasticus Injustitia, a slaveholder who admits his sin but will not cease sinning; discusses the doctrine of sin and its application to slavery. October 1822 (vol. II, no. 16) p.53, c1.

119 PHILANTHROPIST *to* **MR. LYLE. [from the** *Western Citizen***] n.d. n.p.** Condemns "slave peddling" in Kentucky. October 1822 (vol. II, no. 16) p.59, c1.

120 A. *to* **MR. LUNDY. n.d. n.p.** Advises that the information concerning a female slave assaulted by her master and mistress, which he believed to be true, is, in fact, false. November 1822 (vol. II, no. 17) p.69, c1.

121 IRENEUS *to* **SOPHRONIA. June 1822. n.p.** Identifies man as the only species that destroys its own kind, calling slavery a higher form of cannibalism; hopes slavery will soon be abolished. November 1822 (vol. II, no. 17) p.69, c1.

122 E. H. *to* **BENJAMIN LUNDY. 29 October 1822. n.p.** Encloses copy of a letter to someone in England on African slavery. November 1822 (vol. II, no. 17) p.72, c1.

123 E. H. *to* **ESTEEMED FRIEND. n.d. n.p.** Thanks him for his letters; doubts that the abolition of slave trade will ease the condition of Negroes; addresses the questions whether slavery is contrary to law and Christian doctrine, and whether to continue holding slaves because they are believed unfit for freedom is justifiable. November 1822 (vol. II, no. 17) p.72, c1.

124 S. *to* **FRIEND ALLEN. [from the** *Morning Chronicle***] n.d. n.p.** Condemns celebrations of American freedom as farcical while slavery exists; wonders how men who love their wives can consent to separation of slave couples. November 1822 (vol. II, no. 17) p.76, c2.

125 L. S. *to* **BENJAMIN LUNDY. n.d. New Jersey.** Explains that she had avoided speaking out on abolition, fearing that it was unworthy of attention; condemns those who profess to be Christians yet hold slaves. December 1822 (vol. II, no. 18) p.84, c2.

126 A GENTLEMAN OF HIGH STANDING *to* **THE EDITOR [B. LUNDY]. [extract] 21 November 1822. South Carolina.** Suggests that abolitionist sentiment will require stimulus to give it strength; stresses the importance of effecting emancipation with safety for whites and profit for Negroes. December 1822 (vol. II, no. 18) p.85, c2.

127 IRENEUS *to* **SOPHRONIA. July 1822. n.p.** Describes Gripus, a sentimental slave owner who aims to be wealthy and to enjoy heaven when he dies, but who mistreats his slaves; condemns those who betray their professed Christianity by attachment to worldly goods. December 1822 (vol. II, no. 18) p.85, c2.

128 IRENEUS *to* **SOPHRONIA. August 1822. n.p.** Gives impassioned impressionistic account of the evils of slavery; warns that the sins of slaveholding fathers will be visited upon future generations. December 1822 (vol. II, no. 18) p.88, c1.

[1823]

129 IRENEUS *to* **SOPHRONIA. 1823. n.p.** Observes that a variety of dispositions pervades the human family; discusses Antihumanitas and his convictions about slavery and its abolition. January 1823 (vol. II, no. 19) p.106, c1.

130 A FRIEND *to* **THE EDITOR [B. LUNDY]. [extract] n.d. North Carolina.** Reports having circulated copies of the newspaper among friends in an attempt to procure new subscriptions; finds that its sentiments are generally accepted despite some opposition. February 1823 (vol. II, no. 20) p.115, c1.

131 A GENTLEMAN *to* **THE EDITOR [B. LUNDY]. [extract] n.d. North Carolina.** Promises to attempt to aid the paper's circulation; advocates withdrawal from religious group that accepts slaveholders; offers ideas for the treatment and emancipation of slaves. February 1823 (vol. II, no. 20) p.115, c1.

132 A SUBSCRIBER *to* **THE EDITOR [B. LUNDY]. [extract] n.d. Lower part of Virginia.** Believes that emancipation is gaining ground; hopes true Christians will realize the impropriety of slaveholding; shares his paper frequently. February 1823 (vol. II, no. 20) p.115, c2.

133 ANOTHER EDITORIAL CORRESPONDENT *to* **THE EDITOR [B. LUNDY]. [extract] n.d. n.p.** Hopes Lundy will be as great an apostle of universal liberty as Saint Paul. February 1823 (vol. II, no. 20) p.116, c1.

134 FABIUS *to* **MR. EDITOR [B. LUNDY]. n.d. n.p.** Requests information about a case of attempted manumission in Greene County. February 1823 (vol. II, no. 20) p.119, c1.

135 IRENEUS *to* **SOPHRONIA. 1823. n.p.** Envies her isolation, observing that the world is in a state of continual fermentation; describes the division of a slaveowner's estate. February 1823 (vol. II, no. 20) p.120, c2.

136 MODERN LISTENER *to* **SIR. n.d. n.p.** Tells of a minister who preached an anti-slavery sermon, and was rebuffed by a slaveholding parishioner who refused to believe slavery was a sin and attempted to justify salveholding by citing the biblical example of Abraham. February 1823 (vol. II, no. 20) p.122, c2.

137 A FRIEND OF THE DISTRESSED *to* **THE EDITOR [B. LUNDY]. n.d. n.p.** Comments on a letter which attempts to justify slavery by citing the New Testament. [partly illegible] March 1823 (vol. II, no. 21) p.130, c1.

138 IRENEUS *to* **SOPHRONIA. n.d. n.p.** Considers slaveholding by so-called Christians to be the devil's way of maintaining the curse of slavery; invokes the character of Tyrannus Clericus as an illustration; wonders how religious non-slaveholders can accept slaveholders. March 1823 (vol. II, no. 21) p.132, c2.

139 FREDONIA *to* **THE EDITOR [B. LUNDY]. n.d. n.p.** Believes slaveowners will be punished for their sins on Judgement Day; expresses surprise that no proponent of slavery has written a defense and suggests that they are either ashamed or afraid. March 1823 (vol. II, no. 21) p.135, c1.

140 MODERN LISTENER *to* **SIR. n.d. n.p.** Attempts to disprove the denunciation of the sons of Ham by Noah, arguing that one cannot prove they were black, inhabited Africa, and were condemned to servitude comparable to American Negro slavery. 10 April 1823 (vol. II, no. 22) p.138, c2.

141 D. A. *to* **MODERN LISTENER. n.d. n.p.** Calls for missionaries to be sent to the Negroes. 10 April 1823 (vol. II, no. 22) p.140, c1.

142 HIGHLY ESTEEMED FRIEND *to* **THE EDITOR [B. LUNDY]. n.d. North Carolina.** Perceives that people are becoming enlightened and many appear willing to read this newspaper which is so openly anti-slavery. 30 April 1823 (vol. II, no. 23) p.147, c2.

143 IRENEUS *to* **SOPHRONIA. n.d. n.p.** Discusses the waste of time and money by slaveholders; raises the issues of racial miscegenation and the selling of black offspring. 30 April 1823 (vol. II, no. 23) p.148, c1.

144 MODERN LISTENER *to* **SIR. n.d. n.p.** Compares the situation of biblical servants of the Jews with that of the American slaves, concluding that the analogy slaveholders use to justify their actions is invalid. 23 May 1823 (vol. II, no. 25) p.165, c2.

145 A FRIEND TO MANKIND *to* **THE EDITOR [B. LUNDY]. n.d. n.p.** Describes the case of a slaveowner who sold four slaves, some of whom were apparently his own children. 8 June 1823 (vol. II, no. 26) p.171, c2.

146 A. C. *to* **THE EDITOR [B. LUNDY]. n.d. n.p.** Fears new slave revolts; supports gradual emancipation if slaves receive preparation for freedom; suggests that part of the United States be set aside for freed Negroes or that they be sent to Mexico or Haiti; comments on South Carolina law regarding taxation of free Negroes. 8 June 1823 (vol. II, no. 26) p.172, c1.

147 IRENEUS *to* **SOPHRONIA. n.d. n.p.** Comments on the disposition to oppress when pride overcomes the mind; believes that men were created equal and therefore no man has a right to dominate another; warns that the destruction of past slaveholding empires is prophetic for the United States. 19 June 1823 (vol. II, no. 27) p.180, c1.

148 n.n. *to* **[B. LUNDY]. [extract] 4 June 1823. Illinois.** Reports resolution in Illinois legislature to recognize slavery; warns of potential violent struggle in August 1824 election; urges every friend of liberty to become active or slave interests could win. 19 June 1823 (vol. II, no. 27) p.185, c1.

149 IRENEUS *to* **SOPHRONIA. n.d. n.p.** Relates dialogue between a missionary and a foreigner; the foreigner calls America a land of idolators because its Christian principles are corrupted in application, particularly with regard to slavery; the missionary attempts to defend his country. 19 June 1823 (vol. II, no. 27) p.186, c1.

150 GEORGE EATON AND OWEN EVANS *to* **SIR. 7 June 1823. Athens, Oh.** Thank him for donating a newspaper subscription to the Philomathian Society; express interest in and approval of the newspaper; promise to expose the pernicious effects of slavery. 4 July 1823 (vol. III, no. 29) p.3, c2.

151 A. C. *to* **THE EDITOR [B. LUNDY]. n.d. n.p.** Agrees with Lundy; asserts that slavery is inconsistent with American principles; describes two encounters with heavily chained slaves. 4 July 1823 (vol. III, no. 29) p.4, c1.

152 PHILO HUMANITAS *to* **THE EDITOR [B. LUNDY]. n.d. n.p.** Illustrates the process of action and reaction in morality of the slave trade; states that slave trade was conceived by greedy minds; inveighs against those who call themselves Christians and Republicans, but who accept slavery. 4 July 1823 (vol. III, no. 29) p.5, c2.

153 AGED MEMBER OF THE ABOLITION SOCIETY *to* **THE EDITOR [B. LUNDY]. [extract] 24 April 1823. Pennsylvania.** Reports encounter with a slaveholder in summer of 1787; describes the successful effort to outlaw slavery in Pennsylvania shortly thereafter. 18 July 1823 (vol. III, no. 30) p.9, c2.

154 ANOTHER AGED MEMBER OF THE ABOLITION SOCIETY *to* **THE EDITOR [B. LUNDY]. 27 May 1823. Kentucky.** Feels dejected after considering the status of slave trade and its ramifications; realizes that much remains to be done. 18 July 1823 (vol. III, no. 30) p.10, c2.

155 MODERN LISTENER *to* **SIR. n.d. n.p.** Intends to show that the principle and practice of slavery cannot be supported by Noah's prophecy because prophecy must end and no analogy exists between biblical servitude and American slavery; hopes that biblical justification of slavery will cease. 18 July 1823 (vol. III, no. 30) p.12, c1.

156 PHILO HUMANITAS *to* **THE EDITOR [B. LUNDY]. n.d. n.p.** Believes that the spirit of liberty inspires slaves to revolt; draws an analogy between European monarchies and American slavery. 1 August 1823 (vol. III, no. 31) p.18, c1.

157 n.n. *to* **n.n. [extract from the** *New York Statesman***] n.d. Norfolk, Va.** Relates account of a black freeman, America Walker, who sold his son to a slave trader. 1 August 1823 (vol. III, no. 31) p.22, c2.

158 A VERY RESPECTABLE GENTLEMAN *to* **THE EDITOR [B. LUNDY]. [extract] 9 June 1823. Maryland.** Wishes Lundy success in ending slavery; believes that colonization would be a proper and just compensation to slaves for their oppression. September 1823 (vol. III, no. 33) p.33, c1.

159 Z. *to* **THE EDITOR [B. LUNDY]. n.d. n.p.** Describes the dilemma of a Negro woman who had been working to buy her freedom and that of her child; when the owner died, his sons, one a minister and the other a deacon, would not allow her emancipation. September 1823 (vol. III, no. 33) p.41, c1.

160 T. *to* **THE EDITOR [B. LUNDY]. n.d. n.p.** Reports establishment of a new academy at Port-au-Prince, Haiti; finds it particularly gratifying to see liberty and scientific knowledge flourish among a once degraded race. September 1823 (vol. III, no. 33) p.41, c1.

161 PHILO HUMANITAS *to* **THE EDITOR [B. LUNDY]. n.d. n.p.** Comments on the growth of abolitionist activities; interprets the increasing number of mulattoes as a sign that color prejudice is abating; says that blacks are "whitening out." September 1823 (vol. III, no. 33) p.41, c2.

162 MODERN LISTENER *to* **INNUENDO. n.d. n.p.** Examines barriers against missionary activity in Africa; advocates hanging captured slave traders along the coast of Africa as a sign of good faith and splitting missionary funds between home and foreign missions; suggests administrative techniques for home missions. September 1823 (vol. III, no. 33) p.43, c2.

163 A FRIEND TO HONESTY *to* **THE EDITOR [B. LUNDY]. n.d. n.p.** Discusses proposed boycott of slave-produced goods. September 1823 (vol. III, no. 33) p.45, c2.

164 J. W. OSBORN *to* **THE EDITOR OF THE** *CINCINNATI INDEPENDENT PRESS.* **[extract] 9 September 1823. Vincennes.** Editor of the *Vincennes Journal* tells of a free black man, William Hunter, who sought his help; Hunter was captured by slave hunters, by order of a justice of the peace, and must produce evidence of employment to prove he is emancipated. October 1823 (vol. III, no. 34) p.56, c2.

165 n.n. *to* **SIR. [from the** *Abolition Intelligencer***] n.d. n.p.** Forwards copy of a moving, articulate speech given by a "pious young man of color" about his passage from Africa, eventual enslavement, and ultimate liberation. October 1823 (vol. III, no. 34) p.60, c1.

166 GEO. W. ST. JOHN MILDMAY *to* **EARL BATHURST. [extract from the** *Niles' Weekly Register***] n.d. n.p.** Lieutenant of H. M. S. *Iphigenia* tells of efforts to suppress slave trade on the African coast. October 1823 (vol. III, no. 34) p.62, c1.

167 RECENT SUBSCRIBER *to* **THE EDITOR [B. LUNDY]. n.d. West Tennessee.** Praises the newspaper; suggests it should emphasize the contradiction between slavery and the law, Christianity and Republicanism. November 1823 (vol. III, no. 35) p.68, c2.

168 A VERY INTELLIGENT GENTLEMAN *to* **THE EDITOR [B. LUNDY]. [extract] 14 November 1823. Lower North Carolina.** Praises the newspaper, saying that slaveholders believe such papers should be suppressed as dangerous and the letter-writers arrested as agitators; intends to try still harder to circulate copies. November 1823 (vol. III, no. 35) p.69, c1.

169 A GENTLEMAN OF HIGH STANDING *to* **THE EDITOR [B. LUNDY]. n.d. Ohio.** Cautions against voting for any presidential candidate who supports slavery. November 1823 (vol. III, no. 35) p.69, c2.

170 A SUBSCRIBER *to* **THE EDITOR [B. LUNDY]. [extract] n.d. Virginia.** Expresses his concern for the newspaper's continued success; fears many will not subscribe because the truth hurts. November 1823 (vol. III, no. 35) p.69, c2.

171 NORTH CAROLINA CORRESPONDENT *to* **THE EDITOR [B. LUNDY]. n.d. n.p.** Reports that slaveowners are agitated and unwilling to accept views which do not agree with their own. November 1823 (vol. III, no. 35) p.70, c1.

172 FELLOW TRAVELLER *to* **CHRISTIAN PROFESSING SLAVEHOLDERS. n.d. n.p.** Finds slaveholders to be as just as nonslaveholders save in their treatment of slaves; suggests that if blacks should be emancipated, it would be expedient for our government to secure land in the South, an area "congenial to their natural constitution," on which to settle them. November 1823 (vol. III, no. 35) p.72, c2.

173 A GENTLEMAN *to* **THE EDITOR OF THE** *SCIOTO GAZETTE.* **[extract] n.d. Illinois.** Predicts that if slavery continues after the presidential election, its most objectionable features will be removed and gradual emancipation and colonization will commence. November 1823 (vol. III, no. 35) p.78, c1.

174 A SUBSCRIBER *to* **THE EDITOR [B. LUNDY]. [extract] n.d. Interior Louisiana.** Believes that no reasoning could convince Louisianians of the evils of slavery; fears that Louisiana may become the new St. Domingo; describes a fugitive slave who attempted suicide after his recapture. November 1823 (vol. III, no. 35) p.78, c2.

175 QUERIST *to* **SLAVEHOLDERS. n.d. n.p.** Ridicules the "wisdom and discernment" of slaveholders; concludes they must believe the soul is in the skin. December 1823 (vol. III, no. 36) p.87, c1.

176 A FREDERICK COUNTY FREEHOLDER *to* **PEOPLE OF FREDERICK COUNTY. [from the** *Maryland Political Examiner***] n.d. Maryland.** Argues that the presence of blacks retards the growth of white population and the improvement and rising value of the land; advocates African colonization of free blacks. December 1823 (vol. III, no. 36) p.89, c2.

[1824]

177 A FREDERICK COUNTY FREEHOLDER *to* **PEOPLE OF FREDERICK COUNTY. [from the** *Maryland Political Examiner***] n.d. n.p.** Claims that the employment of large numbers of slaves leads to ownership of large tracts of land and poor cultivation; therefore, the removal of slavery would equalize land prices. January 1824 (vol. III, no. 37) p.106, c1.

178 n.n. *to* **THE EDITOR OF THE** *BALTIMORE AMERICAN.* **[extract] 24 December 1823. Richmond, Va.** Reports increasing military activity in Richmond due to rumors of a general massacre of whites. January 1824 (vol. III, no. 37) p.107, c2.

179 THOMAS JEFFERSON *to* **SIR. 21 January 1811. Monticello.** Considers colonization the best scheme for drawing off the colored population; declares himself willing to defend the colony. February 1824 (vol. III, no. 38) p.116, c1.

180 CITIZEN OF THIS TOWN *to* **THE** *EDWARDVILLE SPECTATOR.* **[extract] 8 November 1823. Fayette County, Ky.** Declares that Kentuckians oppose the extension of slavery into Illinois. February 1824 (vol. III, no. 38) p.116, c2.

181 OLD-FASHIONED *to* **THE EDITOR [B. LUNDY]. n.d. n.p.** Identifies contradictions between South Carolina's support for the Greek struggle against Turkish bondage and its refusal to aid slaves; suggests that the state keep at least one-half of its charity at home. February 1823 (vol. III, no. 38) p.124, c1.

182 n.n. *to* **THE EDITOR [B. LUNDY]. [extract] 23 February 1824. Washington.** A member of Congress comments on the recent CS meeting he attended; claims the CS intends to transport free blacks to Africa without inquiring into ulterior considerations. March 1824 (vol. III, no. 39) p.132, c2.

183 A VERY INTELLIGENT GENTLEMAN *to* **THE EDITOR [B. LUNDY]. [extract] n.d. St. Clair County, Il.** Offers warm wishes for success; warns that the legislature has ordered that a vote be taken for a convention which, he believes, would introduce slavery. March 1824 (vol. III, no. 39) p.133, c1.

184 n.n. *to* **THE EDITOR [B. LUNDY]. n.d. Madison County, Il.** Believes that there would be a majority against slavery if the issue were put before voters now. March 1824 (vol. III, no. 39) p.134, c2.

185 GENTLEMAN HOLDING IMPORTANT OFFICE *to* **THE EDITOR [B. LUNDY]. [extract] n.d. n.p.** Praises Lundy's efforts: "Little strokes fell great oaks." April 1824 (vol. III, no. 40) p.149, c1.

186 A FRIEND AND CORRESPONDENT *to* **THE EDITOR [B. LUNDY]. n.d. n.p.** Expresses confidence that the citizens of the United States possess sufficient wealth to support the emancipation cause and missionary work; acknowledges that Africans have been too long neglected. April 1824 (vol. III, no. 40) p.149, c1.

187 n.n. *to* **BENJAMIN LUNDY. 26 January 1824. Bellville, Il.** Encloses circular address of his society, the Friends of Humanity, noting that the number of members has grown from 16 to 25. April 1824 (vol. III, no. 40) p.155, c2.

188 A MEMBER OF THE SOCIETY OF FRIENDS *to* **THE** *LONDON CHRISTIAN OBSERVER.* **n.d. n.p.** Relates anecdote about an immoral Episcopalian minister who called upon his slave to preach and became pious again as a result. April 1824 (vol. III, no. 40) p.159, c2.

189 VERITAS *to* **THE EDITOR [B. LUNDY]. n.d. n.p.** Claims that a slaveholding preacher is an anomaly. April 1824 (vol. III, no. 40) p.160, c1.

190 ISAAC SMITH *to* **FELLOW CITIZENS OF THE STATE OF TENNESSEE. n.d. n.p.** Urges the use of constitutional means to end slavery; applies the golden rule to slaves. May 1824 (vol. III, no. 41) p.168, c1.

191 JOHN KENRICK, ESQ. *to* **HIS EXCELLENCY JEAN PIERRE BOYER, PRESIDENT OF THE HAYTIAN REPUBLIC. 12 November 1823. Brighton, Ma.** Encloses copies of Lundy's newspaper; desires the United States to recognize Haiti's independence and to form commercial ties. June 1824 (vol. III, no. 42) p.177, c2.

192 B. INGINAC, GENERAL OF BRIGADE *to* **JOHN KENRICK. 20 January 1824. Port-au-Prince, Hayti.** Reports that President Boyer appreciates his lively interest in his country, and assures them that "the unfortunate descendants of Africans" who should be able to come to Haiti will be given land and welcomed as brothers. June 1824 (vol. III, no. 42) p.178, c1.

193 AMERICAN MERCHANT *to* **n.n. [extract] 2 October 1823. Cape Haytien.** Describes the climate as "warm, but not uncomfortable." June 1824 (vol. III, no. 42) p.178, c2.

194 A FREE BLACK MAN *to* **FRIEND IN NEW YORK CITY. [extract] 5 November 1823. Hayti.** Announces that the president has supplied him with everything necessary for farming and has promised to provide for ten families until they become self-sufficient. June 1824 (vol. III, no. 42) p.178, c2.

195 n.n. *to* **SIR. n.d. Illinois.** Believes that slavery would benefit Illinois; considers efforts of the abolition society surprising since he doubts that free men of color want to return to Africa. June 1824 (vol. III, no. 42) p.179, c2.

196 MEMBER OF CONGRESS *to* **THE EDITOR [B. LUNDY]. [extract] 3 May 1824. n.p.** States that he has no plan to deal with the abolition of slavery in District of Columbia but recommends a cautious approach; reports that one important Congressman is likely to prosecute the issue successfully. June 1824 (vol. III, no. 42) p.181, c2.

197 SOUTH CAROLINIAN *to* **THE EDITOR [B. LUNDY]. n.d. n.p.** Refers to the alleged massacre planned by British Admiral Cockburn with the assistance of slaves in March 1815. June 1824 (vol. III, no. 42) p.187, c1.

198 REV. LORING D. DEWEY *to* **PRESIDENT BOYER. n.d. n.p.** Requests information on policies regarding the reception of colored Americans because the CS is contemplating the purchase of land for a colony in Haiti. 1824 (vol. III, Supplement) p.193, c2.

199 JEAN PIERRE BOYER, PRESIDENT OF HAYTI *to* **M. LORING D. DEWEY, GENERAL AGENT FOR THE ACS OF NEW YORK. 30 April 1824. Port-au-Prince.** Thanks Dewey for his interest and replies that he is sending a confidential agent to New York to enter into an agreement with the CS to facilitate emigration. 1824 (vol. III, Supplement) p.194, c1.

200 GEORGE FLOWER *to* **THE EDITOR [B. LUNDY]. [extract] 23 July 1824. Albion, Il.** Encloses a letter from two colored men who had once lived in his neighborhood but have since resettled in Haiti. October 1824 (vol. IV, no. 44) p.9, c2.

201 ARTHUR J. JONES AND GEORGE JANN *to* **GEORGE FLOWER. 26 June 1821. Port-au-Prince.** Express their satisfaction with Haiti, adding that prospects appear better than expected; reports that President Boyer visits frequently. October 1824 (vol. IV, no. 44) p.10, c1.

202 CAPTAIN BARSTOW *to* **SIR [AGENT OF THE EMIGRATION SOCIETY]. [extract] 9 October 1824. Port-au-Prince.** Informs him of his ship's safe arrival after a twenty-three day voyage. November 1824 (vol. IV, no. 45) p.23, c2.

203 W. M. *to* **MR. EDITOR [B. LUNDY]. n.d. n.p.** Describes an encounter with an acquaintance similar to that portrayed in the article "Reason and Truth Against Delusion and Error," published February 1824. November 1824 (vol. IV, no. 45) p.24, c1.

204 n.n. *to* **MR. RICHARD FLOWER. [from the** *National Gazette***] 26 October 1824. Albion, Il.** Reports attack on home of Gilbert Burres by five armed men, presumably slave dealers, in an attempt to take possession of Sally, a Negro woman whose right to freedom was disputed. December 1824 (vol. IV, no. 46) p.35, c1.

205 THOMAS JEFFERSON *to* **EDWARD COLES.** **[from the** *Illinois Intelligencer***]** **25 August 1814. Monticello.** Admits that he had hoped that the first generation born in liberty would free the slaves; believes that the hour of emancipation will come; favors the proposal for emancipating those born after a given day. December 1824 (vol. IV, no. 46) p.46, c1.

[1825]

206 A VERY RESPECTABLE COLORED MAN *to* **n.n. [extract] 18 October 1824. St. Domingo.** Reports sailing on a ship carrying counterfeit money. January 1825 (vol. IV, no. 47) p.50, c1.

207 n.n. *to* **FATHER. [extract from the** *Saturday Evening Post***] 16 November. Port-au-Prince.** Reports that Mr. Winmore and about fifty friends are moving ten miles out of town; having seen the land, he intends to go with them. January 1825 (vol. IV, no. 47) p.58, c1.

208 A COLORED MAN *to* **n.n. [from the** *Saturday Evening Post***] 5 December 1824. Jeremie, Hayti.** Describes the voyage to Haiti and his warm reception; promises to send coffee and fruit as they are plentiful. January 1825 (vol. IV, no. 47) p.58, c1.

209 n.n. *to* **REV. SIR. [extract from the** *Saturday Evening Post***] 6 December 1824. Jeremie, Hayti.** Reports safe arrival of himself and his family; expresses satisfaction with Haiti. January 1825 (vol. IV, no. 47) p.58, c2.

210 REV. WILLIAM DICKEY *to* **n.n. [extract] 8 October 1824. Bloomingsburgh, Ky.** Reports the dismembering of a slave in the presence of other slaves to discourage disobedience and running away. January 1825 (vol. IV, no. 47) p.60, c1.

211 JAMES JONES, PRESIDENT OF THE MANUMISSION SOCIETY OF TENNESSEE *to* **THE EDITOR [B. LUNDY]. [extract] 5 January 1825. n.p.** Reports on activities of their recent convention; expresses pleasure with the propositions of Haitian President Boyer; suggests petitioning legislators to improve conditions for slaves. February 1825 (vol. IV, no. 48) p.66, c1.

212 BENEVOLUS *to* **THE EDITOR [B. LUNDY]. n.d. n.p.** Accuses a writer to the paper of prejudicing readers against the ACS; explains that the society does not oppose emigration to Haiti, but continues to support African colonization, believing that colonization will help to end slave trade. February 1825 (vol. IV, no. 48) p.70, c1.

213 REV. LORING D. DEWEY *to* **DANIEL RAYMOND. 3 February 1825. Hayti.** Reports that 700 colored Americans have resettled in Haiti and received everything promised by the government; advises American blacks, particularly young ones, to come; denies rumors that emigrants cannot leave. March 1825 (vol. IV, no. 49) p.88, c1.

214 GEORGE MAYES *to* **SIR. 6 February 1825. Santo Domingo.** Reports prospects of cultivating good fruit on the land; requests shipment of young fruit trees. March 1825 (vol. IV, no. 49) p.91, c2.

215 MARGARET PATTERSON *to* **MR. B. LUNDY. 12 April 1825. Port-au-Prince.** Reports that they arrived safely and are living on President Boyer's plantation. April 1825 (vol. IV, no. 50) p.99, c1.

216 AFRICANUS *to* **THE EDITOR [B. LUNDY]. n.d. Maryland.** Reports satisfaction with the newspaper; wonders why more of his colored brethren do not emigrate; specifically encourages emigration to Haiti. April 1825 (vol. IV, no. 50) p.103, c2.

217 B. INGINAC *to* **MR. J. C. BLISS. n.d. Hayti.** Thanks him for tracts which will be distributed in the schools. April 1825 (vol. IV, no. 50) p.111, c1.

218 REV. LORING D. DEWEY *to* **MR. WILLIAM MCKENNY. 20 May 1825. Baltimore.** Fears that the CS cannot succeed at its current rate of progress; welcomes Haiti's assistance and recommends colonization there; demands McKenny's reasons for opposing the "Haitian scheme." May 1825 (vol. IV, no. 51) p.122, c1.

219 REV. LORING D. DEWEY *to* **REV. WILLIAM MCKENNY. 20 May 1825. Baltimore.** Believes colored Haitians to be far superior to American blacks and equal to any people; refutes rumors of restrictions placed on emigrants; discusses religious freedom; supports the "Haitian scheme" and its co-worker, the ACS. June 1825 (vol. IV, no. 52) p.138, c1.

220 HARRISON AND STERETT *to* **MR. BENJAMIN LUNDY. 23 July 1825. n.p.** Refute allegation that they are owners of the ships *Statira* and *Orbit*. July 1825 (vol. IV, no. 53) p.149, c1.

221 n.n. *to* **THE EDITOR [B. LUNDY]. [extract] 8 July 1825. Randolph County, N.C.** Expresses pleasure with the newspaper; reports that emigration, colonization and emancipation societies have been formed in North Carolina during the last six months. July 1825 (vol. IV, no. 53) p.151, c1.

222 CHARLES W. FISHER *to* **HIS FATHER. [extract] 13 February 1825. Cape Haytien.** Reports having received a plantation from the government; states that vegetables are plentiful but meat is scarce, causing some complaints among emigrants. July 1825 (vol. IV, no. 53) p.152, c1.

223 CHARLES W. FISHER *to* **HIS FATHER. [extract] 16 April 1825. Cape Haytien.** Reports that he is in good health and that his crops are good; invites others to come. July 1825 (vol. IV, no. 53) p.152, c1.

224 X *to* **MR. EDITOR [B. LUNDY]. n.d. n.p.** Believes that the Fourth of July should not be celebrated while slaves and freemen are denied essential rights. July 1825 (vol. IV, no. 53) p.152, c2.

225 DANIEL COPELAND *to* **REV. R. ALLEN. [from the** *United States Gazette***] 10 May 1825. Samana.** Refutes slanderous reports about Haiti; reports his purchase of 147 acres in addition to the land given him by the government; urges people of color to come to Haiti. August 1825 (vol. IV, no. 54) p.175, c1.

226 n.n. *to* **SIR. n.d. n.p.** Declares that he has decided to emancipate forty-three slaves, believing slavery to be against God's will; requests help in securing their passage to Haiti since he is not wealthy. September 1825 (vol. IV, no. 55) p.178, c1.

227 P. THORNTON, P.M. *to* **MR. LUNDY. 29 September 1825. Camden, S.C.** Informs Lundy that Mr. Adamson, a subscriber, has been shot. September 1825 (vol. IV, no. 55) p.178, c2.

228 PHILO HUMANITAS *to* **THE EDITOR [B. LUNDY]. n.d. Tennessee.** Bemoans the day that a slaveholder was accepted into any religious community; condemns slaveholding preachers, and states his conviction that the admission of slaveholders into Christianity has contributed ten-fold to slavery's perpetuation. September 1825 (vol. IV, no. 55) p.182, c1.

229 PATRICK HENRY *to* **SIR. [extract] n.d. n.p.** Thanks writer for sending book denouncing slave trade; finds it amazing that slavery exists in a country that so prizes liberty. September 1825 (vol. IV, no. 55) p.189, c2.

230 D. *to* **DANIEL WEBSTER. n.d. n.p.** Asks why he has failed to realize his pledge not to rest until the country is purged of slavery; wonders why he did not excoriate slavery during the speech at Bunker Hill. 12 September 1825 (vol. V, no. 3) p.17, c3.

231 PHILO HUMANITAS *to* **THE EDITOR [B. LUNDY]. n.d. Tennessee.** Condemns the admission of slaveholders into Christian communities. 17 September 1825 (vol. V, no. 4) p.26, c2.

232 A CORRESPONDENT *to* **THE EDITOR [B. LUNDY]. 26 April 1825. n.p.** Describes the treatment of three Negro slaves witnessed while on a business trip to Charlotte, North Carolina. 24 September 1825 (vol. V, no. 5) p.33, c3.

233 PETER PIMP *to* **THE EDITOR [B. LUNDY]. n.d. n.p.** Satirizes reformers of the day. [mostly illegible] 24 September 1825 (vol. V, no. 5) p.34, c2.

234 n.n. *to* **n.n. [extract] 31 May 1821. Vienna.** A gentleman travelling through Europe writes to his friend in America about his mortification at being American; reports that he cannot explain slavery when Europeans question him. 24 September 1825 (vol. V, no. 5) p.34, c3.

235 D. RAYMOND *to* **VOTERS OF BALTIMORE CITY. 21 September 1825. Baltimore.** Reports that the evils of slavery are rapidly increasing; supports emancipation of slaves born after 4 July 1826. 24 September 1825 (vol. V, no. 5) p.36, c3.

236 THOMAS JEFFERSON *to* **MR. BLATCHLY. 22 October 1824. Monticello.** Thanks Blatchly for the pamphlet on commonwealths although he doubts that the principle could work in a large society; looks to education as a means of improving man's condition. 1 October 1825 (vol. V, no. 6) p.46, c3.

237 n.n. *to* **SIR. n.d. n.p.** Reports his decision to follow David Minge's example by freeing his forty-three slaves; seeks information on procuring their passage to Haiti since he is not wealthy. 15 October 1825 (vol. V, no. 8) p.57, c3.

238 P. THORNTON, P.M. *to* **MR. LUNDY. 29 September 1825. Camden, S.C.** Informs Lundy that Mr. Adamson, a subscriber, was shot and killed. 15 October 1825 (vol. V, no. 8) p.61, c1.

239 J. ASHMUN *to* **SIR. 22 August 1825. Monrovia.** Reports no dangerous illness in the colony and only two deaths; informs that he has employed a carpenter to build several homes. 22 October 1825 (vol. V, no. 9) p.68, c2.

240 A FRIEND TO NATIVE GENIUS *to* **THE EDITOR [B. LUNDY]. n.d. n.p.** Criticizes an educational book currently in use, and praises the *American System of English Grammar* by James Brown. 22 October 1825 (vol. V, no. 9) p.69, c2.

241 ACACIUS *to* **DANIEL WEBSTER. n.d. n.p.** Complains that Webster omitted any expression of concern for slaves from his Bunker Hill address; contrasts the plight of Greeks to that of Negroes; praises the successes of the Haitian Republic. 12 November 1825 (vol. V, no. 12) p.92, c3.

242 DAVID BROWN *to* **THE EDITOR OF THE** *FAMILY VISITOR***. 2 September 1825. Willstown, Cherokee Nation.** Discusses Indian removal and his efforts to translate the New Testament; describes the land of Cherokee Nation, its conditions and the activities of its people. 12 November 1825 (vol. V, no. 12) p.94, c2.

243 SIDNEY *to* **JAMES BARBOUR, SECRETARY OF WAR. n.d. n.p.** Criticizes Barbour's recent address as too sympathetic to slavery. 26 November 1825 (vol. V, no. 14) p.109, c2.

244 ROBERT OWENS *to* **AMERICANS. October 1825. At sea, New York packet.** Remarks that Americans have retained advantages derived from their European ancestry, but have also continued Old World errors and prejudices; points out the false notion that man may believe or disbelieve at will, which religions are based upon. 26 November 1825 (vol. V, no. 14) p.110, c1.

245 SIDNEY *to* **JAMES BARBOUR, SECRETARY OF WAR. n.d. n.p.** Condemns Barbour's plan for slave treatment as contrary to every law of man and nature; predicts that free states will not consent to the continuance of slavery; counters the accusation that the North dictates to the South by arguing that the South attempts to gag dissent. 10 December 1825 (vol. V, no. 15) p.113, c1.

246 OBSERVER *to* **MR. EDITOR [B. LUNDY]. n.d. n.p.** Expresses gratitude upon learning of a stenography teacher in the city, and recommends shorthand to all young men. 10 December 1825 (vol. V, no. 15) p.118, c1.

247 SIDNEY *to* **JAMES BARBOUR, SECRETARY OF WAR. n.d. n.p.** Criticizes new Southern doctrine claiming that only slaveholders have the right to speak about slavery; admonishes Barbour to begin eliminating slavery. 17 December 1825 (vol. V, no. 16) p.121, c1.

248 EDITOR OF THE *FRIEND OF PEACE to* **THE EDITOR [B. LUNDY]. November 1825. Brighton.** Commends Lundy's newspaper and the work of abolition societies; understands why many slaveowners fear emancipation; suggests that all emancipation societies should be peace societies as well. 17 December 1825 (vol. V, no. 16) p.124, c1.

249 PHILOS *to* **THE EDITOR [B. LUNDY]. n.d. n.p.** Regrets that slaves must be removed in order to enjoy human rights; suggests that a memorial be presented to Congress requesting funding for free colored people who wish to emigrate to Africa or Haiti. 17 December 1825 (vol. V, no. 16) p.124, c2.

250 n.n. *to* **BENJAMIN LUNDY. 27 November 1825. Brighton.** Sends ten dollars to assist in transporting sixty slaves to a land of freedom. 17 December 1825 (vol. V, no. 16) p.125, c3.

251 FRANCES WRIGHT *to* **THE EDITOR [B. LUNDY]. [extract] 7 November 1825. Jackson, West Tennessee.** Discusses plans for a school to prepare slaves for freedom. 17 December 1825 (vol. V, no. 16) p.126, c1.

252 SIDNEY *to* **JAMES BARBOUR. n.d. n.p.** Believes that the open avowal by slaveholders of their determination to continue slavery is new; predicts that the North, having heard this, will work harder to abolish slavery; states that the perpetuation of slavery must never be a condition for the perpetuation of the Union. 24 December 1825 (vol. V, no. 17) p.129, c1.

253 Q IN A CORNER *to* **THE EDITOR [B. LUNDY]. n.d. n.p.** Encloses copy of an advertisement entitled "Cash! Cash! For Whites!", offering "a great bargain" for white boys and girls whom he would sell as slaves in Algiers; the advertisement was previously refused by the *National Intelligencer*. 24 December 1825 (vol. V, no. 17) p.132, c2.

254 n.n. *to* **THE EDITOR [B. LUNDY]. [extract] 10 December 1825. Yorkville, S.C.** Believes that the cause of emancipation will eventually succeed. 24 December 1825 (vol. V, no. 17) p.134, c1.

255 AN OFFICER IN THE COLUMBIAN NAVY *to* **HIS BROTHER. [extract] 23 October 1825. Carthagena.** Tells of planned invasion of Cuba. 24 December 1825 (vol. V, no. 17) p.135, c1.

256 SIDNEY *to* **HIS EXCELLENCY LEVI LINCOLN, GOVERNOR OF MASSACHUSETTS. n.d. n.p.** Admonishes Lincoln for not mentioning slaves in his Thanksgiving proclamation. 31 December 1825 (vol. V, no. 18) p.137, c1.

257 C. *to* **MR. EDITOR [B. LUNDY]. [from the** *Christian Monitor*] **n.d. n.p.** Relates story of a Scottish surgeon's son who, as governor of a West Indian island, freed two shiploads of slaves. 31 December 1825 (vol. V, no. 18) p.140, c3.

[1826]

258 FRANCES WRIGHT *to* **ESTEEMED FRIEND [B. LUNDY]. 10 January 1826. Memphis, Tn.** Charges that the article about her is false. January 1826 (vol. IV, no. 56) p.1, c2.

259 A VERY INTELLIGENT GENTLEMAN *to* **HIS FRIEND IN BALTIMORE. [extract] 24 December 1825. Fredericksburg, Va.** Thinks that Virginia will not be a slave state in fifteen to twenty years; wishes success to manumission societies; reports some fear of slave revolts. January 1826 (vol. IV, no. 56) p.4, c1.

260 HIRAM *to* **MR. EDITOR [B. LUNDY]. n.d. n.p.** Denies that slavery is upheld by Masons; argues that slavery is as consistent with Masonry as piracy with Christianity. January 1826 (vol. IV, no. 56) p.6, c2.

261 HENRY STIER, ABNER M. PLUMMER, T. G. PLUMMER *to* **SIR. n.d. n.p.** Report changes in Newmarket AS. January 1826 (vol. IV, no. 56) p.6, c2.

262 PHILADELPHUS *to* **THE PEOPLE OF MARYLAND. n.d. n.p.** Discusses oppression and revolts in various countries. January 1826 (vol. IV, no. 56) p.7, c1.

263 PHILO PUBLIUS *to* **MEMBERS OF BOTH HOUSES OF THE MARYLAND LEGISLATURE. 24 January 1826. Newmarket, Md.** Desires to awaken a greater sympathy toward the colored population. January 1826 (vol. IV, no. 56) p.8, c1.

264 n.n. *to* **n.n. [extract] 4 February. Harrisburg, Pa.** Reports proceedings on a fugitive slave law. January 1826 (vol. IV, no. 56) p.12, c2.

265 SIDNEY *to* **HIS EXCELLENCY LEVI LINCOLN, GOVERNOR OF MASSACHUSETTS. n.d. n.p.** Asks pardon for not mentioning slaves in his Thanksgiving address; calls Massachusetts an honored part of the great Union; asks whether Massachusetts continues to tolerate slavery and slave trade. 7 January 1826 (vol. V, no. 19) p.145, c1.

266 SIDNEY *to* **JAMES BARBOUR, SECRETARY OF WAR. n.d. n.p.** Believes that kind slaveowners take undeserved credit; holds that Barbour referred to the slave as a kind of brute and that any man who believes slaves are well-treated, even by Barbour's standards, is a fool. 7 January 1826 (vol. V, no. 19) p.146, c1.

267 SIDNEY *to* **JAMES BARBOUR. n.d. n.p.** Condemns Barbour for insisting that the system of slavery should not be touched; calls him a fool for believing he can convince others that slaves are happy. 14 January 1826 (vol. V, no. 20) p.153, c1.

268 VINDICATOR *to* **MR. EDITOR [B. LUNDY]. n.d. n.p.** Applauds members of a Newmarket benevolent society for each offering one dollar to every person who will emigrate; castigates Lundy for failing to acknowledge the plan's merit. 21 January 1826 (vol. V, no. 21) p.165, c1.

269 ANDREW STEWART *to* **JUDGE SHRIVER. 13 December 1825. Washington City.** Reports the discovery of a new summit level in the Chesapeake and Ohio Canal. 21 January 1826 (vol. V, no. 21) p.167, c2.

270 SIDNEY *to* **JAMES BARBOUR. n.d. n.p.** Considers Barbour's sentiments inconsistent with republicanism; attacks his insinuations that a servile laboring class must exist and that God approves slavery. 28 January 1826 (vol. V, no. 22) p.169, c1.

271 n.n. *to* **EDITOR OF THE** *WATCHMAN*. **[extract] 17 January. Dover, De.** Reports the arrival of Maryland commissioners to confer with other state legislators on the subject of Negro runaways. 28 January 1826 (vol. V, no. 22) p.172, c2.

272 A VERY INTELLIGENT MAN *to* **HIS FRIEND IN BALTIMORE. [extract] 24 December 1825. Fredericksburg, Va.** Predicts that Virginia will not be a slave state in fifteen to twenty years; wishes good luck to manumission societies; reports fears of a slave uprising among the people. 28 January 1826 (vol. V, no. 22) p.173, c1.

273 HENRY STIER, ABNER M. PLUMMER, T. G. PLUMMER *to* **THE EDITOR [B. LUNDY]. n.d. n.p.** Report that Newmarket AS has been revived with the election of new officers. 4 February 1826 (vol. V, no. 23) p.177, c1.

274 PHILADELPHUS *to* **THE PEOPLE OF MARYLAND. n.d. n.p.** Reports the introduction of a bill into the Maryland House of Delegates that would worsen the condition of slaves. 4 February 1826 (vol. V, no. 23) p.177, c1.

275 HIRAM *to* **MR. EDITOR [B. LUNDY]. n.d. n.p.** Denies that Masons condone slavery; argues that slavery is as consistent with Masonry as piracy with Christianity. 4 February 1826 (vol. V, no. 23) p.177, c3.

276 PHILO PUBLIUS *to* **BOTH HOUSES OF THE LEGISLATURE OF MARYLAND. 24 January 1826. New-Market, Md.** Considers slavery a moral evil and political disorder that must be eradicated; prays for consistency between the legislators' professed Christianity and their actions; seeks to awaken greater sympathy toward the slaves. 4 February 1826 (vol. V, no. 23) p.178, c1.

277 n.n. *to* **n.n. [extract] 4 February. Harrisburg, Pa.** Reports introduction of a bill regarding fugitive slaves in the Pennsylvania House of Representatives. 11 February 1826 (vol. V, no. 23) p.188, c1.

278 FRANCES WRIGHT *to* **THE EDITOR [B. LUNDY]. 10 January 1826. Memphis, Tn.** Complains that her school to prepare slaves for freedom has received very few contributions. 11 February 1826 (vol. V, no. 23) p.188, c2.

279 A VERY RESPECTABLE LADY IN NORTH CAROLINA *to* **THE EDITOR [B. LUNDY]. [extract] n.d. n.p.** Disagrees with the governor; believes that no man in North Carolina is free and that the master-slave bond is indissoluble; charges that colored citizens are taxed every hour of their lives, but the governor does nothing to assist them. 11 February 1826 (vol. V, no. 24) p.189, c1.

280 JOHN, BISHOP OF CHARLESTON *to* **JOHN S. TYSON, ESQ. 23 January 1826. Norfolk, Va.** Commends Tyson for his support of the Jew Bill. 18 February 1826 (vol. V, no. 25) p.197, c2.

281 JUNIUS BRUTUS *to* **MR. EDITOR [B. LUNDY]. n.d. n.p.** Supports reapportionment in Maryland. 18 February 1826 (vol. V, no. 25) p.197, c3.

282 n.n. *to* **MR. LUTHER M. SCOTT. [extract from the** *Cambridge Chronicle***] 6 February 1826. Federalsburg, Md.** Reports kidnapping of two young Negro boys. 25 February 1826 (vol. V, no. 26) p.203, c2.

283 ONE OF THE OUTER COURT *to* **HIRAM. n.d. n.p.** Concludes that Hiram is a Mason; asks why it is more consistent to name a friend of slavery as "Grand Master" than to name a friend of piracy as leader of a Christian community. 25 February 1826 (vol. V, no. 26) p.204, c1.

284 n.n. *to* **EDITOR OF THE** *WILMINGTONIAN***. [extract] 15 December 1825. Buenos Ayres.** Reports on preparations for war with Brazil. 26 February 1826 (vol. V, no. 26) p.204, c1.

285 RICHARD H. LEE *to* **MEMBERS OF THE CS OF LOUDEN. 14 February 1826. n.p.** Reports the adoption by the New Jersey and Connecticut legislatures of resolutions recommending government support for colonization; describes a Pennsylvania resolution proposing that all states should help pay for the removal of colored people. 4 March 1826 (vol. V, no. 27) p.211, c2.

286 n.n. *to* **n.n. [extract] 19 February 1826. Stokes County, N.C.** Observes that the state legislature is growing more embittered against emancipation; reports that the bill against free colored people passed in the senate but lost in commons; discusses the effectiveness of manumission societies in slave states. 4 March 1826 (vol. V, no. 27) p.211, c2.

287 JERH. EVARTS *to* **REV. R. R. GURLEY. 13 January 1826. Boston, Ma.** Encloses copies of two letters he has received. 11 March 1826 (vol. V, no. 28) p.217, c2.

288 DR. THEOPHILUS BLUMBARDT *to* **DIRECTORS OF THE ACS. 18 October 1826. Basle, Switzerland.** Inquires about the possibility of establishing a mission in the vicinity of Montserado settlement; adds that he has also written to Mr. Ashmun. 11 March 1826 (vol. V, no. 28) p.217, c2.

289 DR. THEOPHILUS BLUMBARDT *to* **J. ASHMUN, ESQ. 18 October 1826. Basle, Switzerland.** Expresses interest in establishing missions in Africa; requests further information and advice for his board of directors; suggests that Ashmun include any other information he thinks important. 11 March 1826 (vol. V, no. 28) p.218, c1.

290 AN AGENT OF THE NEWMARKET ANTI-SLAVERY LIBRARY *to* **MR. EDITOR [B. LUNDY]. n.d. n.p.** Thanks those who have donated to the library. 11 March 1826 (vol. V, no. 28) p.219, c1.

291 A MEMBER *to* **MR. EDITOR [B. LUNDY]. 3 March 1826. n.p.** Asks for an abstract of the 7 December 1825 meeting of the Newmarket AS. 11 March 1826 (vol. V, no. 28) p.221, c3.

292 COKE *to* **GENTLEMEN. [from the** *Georgia Journal***] n.d. n.p.** Defends the necessity of colonizing free Negroes in Africa through the ACS. 18 March 1826 (vol. V, no. 29) p.225, c1.

293 REV. JONAS KING *to* **SENIOR EDITOR OF THE** *NEW YORK OBSERVER*. **16 April 1826. Jerusalem.** Describes the situation in Jerusalem during a visit by the Pasha of Damascus. 18 March 1826 (vol. V, no. 29) p.230, c3.

294 n.n. *to* **MR. EDITOR [B. LUNDY]. n.d. n.p.** Discusses biblical slavery as a sin which Israelites witnessed and imitated; declares that the New Testament neither ignores nor condones slavery; interprets biblical slavery as the servitude of hired slaves or apprentices. 25 March 1826 (vol. V, no. 30) p.233, c1.

295 CEPHAS *to* **SIR. n.d. n.p.** Challenges his objections to sending delegates to the Congress of Panama; declares that protestation against Americans mixing with people of African descent is un-Christian; recommends that he pay less attention to color; questions the effect of his reasoning on Panama. 25 March 1826 (vol. V, no. 30) p.234, c1.

296 PATRICK HENRY *to* **SIR. n.d. n.p.** Acknowledges receipt of a book opposing slave trade; regards living without slaves as an inconvenience, but hopes for an opportunity to abolish slavery or at least to transmit pity for their lot to his descendants. 25 March 1826 (vol. V, no. 30) p.235, c1.

297 L. *to* **MR. EDITOR [B. LUNDY]. n.d. n.p.** Contrasts American and biblical slavery. 1 April 1826 (vol. V, no. 31) p.241, c1.

298 CEPHAS *to* **SIR. n.d. n.p.** Refutes argument that to send delegates to the Congress of Panama would endanger our country, as South American governments oppose slavery; believes that to decline to send delegates would offend the Spanish provinces, and that if they should then conquer Cuba, the danger to the Southern states would be greater. 1 April 1826 (vol. V, no. 31) p.242, c2.

299 FRANCES WRIGHT *to* **A GENTLEMAN IN THIS CITY. [extract from the** *Boston Christian Register***]** 2 December 1825. Memphis, Tn. Reports plans to begin a farming experiment; describes Mr. Flower's role in her plans. 1 April 1826 (vol. V, no. 31) p.243, c1.

300 JAMES BRYAN *to* **THE EDITOR OF THE** *RELIGIOUS MESSENGER*. **5 March 1826. Cambridge.** Reports the adoption of anti-slavery resolutions at the quarterly conference meeting in his circuit, urging the necessity of protest in the interests of humanity and religion. 8 April 1826 (vol. V, no. 32) p.254, c2.

301 n.n. *to* **THE EDITOR [B. LUNDY]. [extract] 8 March 1826. Stokes County, N.C.** Believes that ending slavery in Maryland and Virginia would have a powerful effect on the South; criticizes John Randolph's Senate speech of 2 March. 15 April 1826 (vol. V, no. 33) p.258, c2.

302 n.n. *to* **THE EDITOR [B. LUNDY]. 12 March 1826. Newbury Court House, S.C.** Enjoys the reaction of slavery's advocates to talk of emancipation because it demonstrates their fears. 15 April 1826 (vol. V, no. 33) p.258, c3.

303 n.n. *to* **THE EDITOR [B. LUNDY]. [extract] n.d. Jamestown, N.C.** States that each year an unnecessary number of Negroes are sent from Maryland to Georgia; proposes that they be sent to Haiti as indentured servants; enumerates benefits which would result. [mostly illegible] 15 April 1826 (vol. V, no. 33) p.258, c3.

304 LIBER HOMO *to* **THE EDITOR [B. LUNDY]. n.d. n.p.** Discusses American interest in Ireland; encloses remarks by Daniel O'Connell on slavery in the United States. 22 April 1826 (vol. V, no. 34) p.268, c2.

305 n.n. *to* **THE EDITOR [B. LUNDY]. [extract] 11 April 1826. London Grove, Chester County, Pa.** Submits that the only way to avoid the impending storm over slavery is to communicate a feeling of oppressed humanity; requests information about obtaining free cotton. 22 April 1826 (vol. V, no. 34) p.269, c1.

306 n.n. *to* **THE EDITOR [B. LUNDY]. [extract] 6 April 1826. Chester District, S.C.** Discusses the case of a black family taken to West Tennessee. 29 April 1826 (vol. V, no. 35) p.275, c2.

307 CHARLES W. DABNEY, VICE CONSUL OF THE UNITED STATES FOR THE AZORES *to* **S. W. POMEROY, ESQ. [extract] 19 March 1826. Fayal.** Describes a fire aboard the ship *Hiram.* 29 April 1826 (vol. V, no. 35) p.278, c2.

308 SIDNEY *to* **THE REPRESENTATIVES OF MASSACHUSETTS. n.d. n.p.** Argues that Massachusetts must bear most of the reproach for the continuation of slavery because of its role in framing the Constitution; declares that Northern states asked for no guarantees, believing that each state would abolish slavery. 6 May 1826 (vol. V, no. 36) p.281, c1.

309 WILLIAM HUGHES *to* **MEMBERS OF THE AS. 21 January 1826. Newmarket, Frederick County, Md.** Urges friends of emancipation to contemplate past oppression and how God dealt with it in order to renew their faith. 6 May 1826 (vol. V, no. 36) p.282, c1.

310 VERITAS *to* **MR. EDITOR [B. LUNDY]. n.d. n.p.** Affirms the inalienable right of liberty, which no man has the right to take from another. 6 May 1826 (vol. V, no. 36) p.282, c3.

311 SIDNEY *to* **THEODORE SEDGEWICK, ESQ. n.d. n.p.** Expresses pleasure at seeing his name connected with humanitarian legislation; insists that Massachusetts share the blame for slavery and the obligation to work for its abolition. 13 May 1826 (vol. V, no. 37) p.289, c1.

312 SIDNEY *to* **THEODORE SEDGEWICK, ESQ. n.d. n.p.** Warns that guilt about slavery will continue until the state acts against the continuation of slavery; urges Sedgewick to bring this subject before the legislature. 20 May 1826 (vol. V, no. 38) p.297, c1.

313 LITT W. TAZEWELL *to* **HIS EXCELLENCY JOHN TYLER. 24 April 1826. Washington, D.C.** Encloses a document pertaining to a property compensation case involving a slave; relates that the House of Representatives concluded that slaves are not property and can be taken as soldiers. 20 May 1826 (vol. V, no. 38) p.300, c3.

314 JOHN TYLER *to* **SIR. 2 May 1826. Richmond.** Thanks him for the information relayed and declares that the nation has reached point of frightful apprehension; believes that politicians went too far in trying to make blacks equal. 20 May 1826 (vol. V, no. 38) p.301, c1.

315 J. W. *to* **THE EDITOR [B. LUNDY]. 4 May 1826. Philadelphia.** Objects to an anonymous letter which slandered the character of Frances Wright. 20 May 1826 (vol. V, no. 38) p.301, c2.

316 SIDNEY *to* **THEODORE SEDGEWICK, ESQ. n.d. n.p.** Fears that the country's stability is threatened by slaves' willingness to join the enemy and by the Northern states' bearing an unequal share of the burden of defense; believes history shows that slavery has been responsible for the destruction of great empires. 27 May 1826 (vol. V, no. 39) p.305, c1.

317 JUNIUS *to* **MR. EDITOR [B. LUNDY]. n.d. n.p.** Desires to see a speech by Mr. Livingston of Louisiana in the newspaper, and expresses wish that he could be enlisted as an anti-slavery man; contrasts his conduct with that of other Southerners. 27 May 1826 (vol. V, no. 39) p.307, c1.

318 TYRO *to* **MR. EDITOR [B. LUNDY]. n.d. n.p.** Questions how those who call themselves Christians can engage in the slave trade. 27 May 1826 (vol. V, no. 39), p.309, c3.

319 A KNIGHT TEMPLAR *to* **MR. EDITOR [B. LUNDY]. n.d. n.p.** Encloses a poem which he has copied and praises the author. 27 May 1826 (vol. V, no. 39) p.311, c1.

320 BENJAMIN LUNDY *to* **B. INGINAC. 17 March 1826. Port-au-Prince.** Praises Inginac's efforts to encourage emigration to Haiti; credits him with arousing the interest of those who never thought about slavery and with paving the way for the gradual abolition of slavery; offers a plan for future operations. 3 June 1826 (vol. V, no. 40) p.313, c1.

321 B. INGINAC *to* **LUNDY. 5 May 1826. Port-au-Prince.** Reports the presentation of Lundy's proposal to the Philanthropic Society; explains why the Haitian government ceased its support of emigration; adds that several philanthropic societies are willing to try again; praises Lundy for his work. 3 June 1826 (vol. V, no. 40) p.315, c1.

322 B. LUNDY *to* **B. INGINAC. 5 May 1826. Port-au-Prince.** Expresses gratitude for the cordiality with which his proposal was received; notes that there are a few points on which he must request more information. 3 June 1826 (vol. V, no. 40) p.316, c1.

323 B. INGINAC *to* **LUNDY. 9 May 1826. Port-au-Prince.** Answers Lundy's questions concerning emancipated slaves interested in emigration; promises to send several copies of the new agricultural code as soon as it is published. 3 June 1826 (vol. V, no. 40) p.316, c2.

324 FRANCES WRIGHT *to* **REV. HUGH MC MILLAN. 3 May 1826. Nashoba, Tn.** Discusses the slave family she is training; describes her farm and its inhabitants; reports receipt of a $580.00 donation from a New York Quaker. 10 June 1826 (vol. V, no. 42) p.325, c1.

325 LOTT CARY *to* **WILLIAM CRANE, COR. SEC. AFRICAN MISSIONARY SOCIETY. 23 April 1826. Monrovia.** Regrets he cannot leave yet as an additional 150 people have fever; reports the destruction of the slave factory at Trade Town, and the formation of a missionary society. 10 June 1826 (vol. V, no. 42) p.325, c3.

326 K. TEMPLAR *to* **MR. LUNDY. n.d. n.p.** Encloses poem which he thinks Lundy may find trifling, but hopes that Lundy will nevertheless print it. 17 June 1826 (vol. V, no. 43) p.335, c1.

327 n.n. *to* **FRIEND LUNDY. 15 June 1826. Beaufort, N.C.** Reports the emancipation and departure for Haiti of a large number of slaves; describes their appearance. 24 June 1826 (vol. V, no. 43) p.340, c3.

328 ARCHIBALD JOHNSON *to* **HIS FRIEND IN WASHINGTON CITY. [extract] 1 May 1826. n.p.** Considers himself Haitian, so bids farewell to America. 24 June 1826 (vol. V, no. 43) p.341, c3.

329 n.n. *to* **n.n. [extract] 27 May. Havana.** Reports arrivals and departures of several ships. 24 June 1826 (vol. V, no. 43) p.342, c1.

330 JOHN MCLEAN *to* **SIR. 27 May 1826. Post Office Department.** Reports complaints of loss and delay in the mailing of newspapers; gives directions for proper handling. 24 June 1826 (vol. V, no. 43) p.342, c1.

331 SIDNEY *to* **HIS EXCELLENCY, LEVI LINCOLN, GOVERNOR OF MASSACHUSETTS. n.d. n.p.** Calls his attention to an oversight in the governor's latest message; believes much cause for gratitude exists, notwithstanding the treatment of slaves; fails to understand Lincoln's satisfaction, given the dangers of slavery. 8 July 1826 (vol. V, no. 45) p.353, c1.

332 THEOPHILIS *to* **MR. EDITOR [B. LUNDY]. June 1826. Randolph County, N.C.** Likes Mr. Everett's speech less and less; calls it a perversion of the Scriptures and a slander of religion; asserts that Everett has no claim to popular distinction; claims that even slave states do not accept his doctrine. 8 July 1826 (vol. V, no. 45) p.353, c2.

333 n.n. *to* **FRIEND B. LUNDY. 7 July 1826. Jamestown, N.C.** Sends copy of Nathaniel Jones' will providing for the gradual emancipation of his slaves when state law so permits, and justifying his actions; describes legal litigation arising from the will. 15 July 1826 (vol. V, no. 46) p.362, c1.

334 W. *to* **THE PEOPLE OF THE UNITED STATES. n.d. n.p.** Reminds readers that fifty years have passed since national independence and the establishment of slavery; urges that slavery be abolished soon. 15 July 1826 (vol. V, no. 46) p.362, c3.

335 WILLIAM *to* **MR. EDITOR [B. LUNDY]. n.d. n.p.** Encloses for publication a piece found in the *Juvenile Portfolio*; hopes it will induce slaveholder to liberate his slaves. 15 July 1826 (vol. V, no. 46) p.363, c1.

336 n.n. *to* **SIR. 26 June 1826. New York.** Hopes that new emigrants to Haiti will not land at Port-au-Prince where they might encounter those who thought their needs could be met without work; regards new emigrants as gullible; claims that conditions in Haiti are misrepresented in the United States press. 15 July 1826 (vol. V, no. 46) p.365, c2.

337 GEORGE FLOWER *to* **SIR. 12 June 1826. Nashoba, Tn.** Refuses to accept slaveholders' excuses; discusses avenues of emancipation and colonization; describes the philosophy and practice of the Emancipating Labor Society in Shelby County, Tennessee. 15 July 1826 (vol. V, no. 46) p.366, c1.

338 LIBER *to* **MR. EDITOR [B. LUNDY]. [from the *Norfolk Herald*] n.d. n.p.** Rejoices that the fiftieth anniversary of independence will be marked by collections for the ACS; calls slavery a stain on the honor of our freedom; believes that colonization removes a portion of the evil and offers hope for extinguishing the rest. 22 July 1826 (vol. V, no. 47) p.369, c1.

339 C. A. WICKLIFFE *to* **HENRY CLAY. 12 April 1826. Washington.** Recalls a resolution of the Kentucky state legislature alerting representatives to the Canadian government's reception and protection of fugitive slaves; asks what action the president has taken. 22 July 1826 (vol. V, no. 47) p.372, c1.

340 HENRY CLAY *to* **C. A. WICKLIFFE. 12 April 1826. Department of State.** Reports that the problem of slaves' escaping and taking refuge in foreign countries has been brought to presidential attention, but that relevant negotiations have not progressed. 22 July 1826 (vol. V, no. 47) p.372, c2.

341 L'AMI DES BLANCS *to* **THE EDITOR OF THE *NORFOLK HERALD*. n.d. n.p.** Charges that a recent letter from "Liber," which appealed for funds for the CS, and discussed the inalienable rights of man, served to incite insubordination among slaves. 29 July 1826 (vol. V, no. 48) p.377, c1.

342 ANTIQUARIOUS *to* **LUNDY. n.d. n.p.** Encloses translation of an old African song received from a friend in Sierra Leone. 29 July 1826 (vol. I, no. 48) p.380, c3.

343 LIBER *to* **EDITOR OF THE** *NORFOLK HERALD.* **n.d. n.p.** Argues that any mischief resulting from his remarks will occur because others perverted them; denies that there is any dangerous sentiment in his piece; insists that his sole object was to aid the ACS and that his sentiments are consistent with policy and peace. 5 August 1826 (vol. I, no. 49) p.385, c1.

344 MICHAEL LAMB AND BENJAMIN LUNDY *to* **FARMERS, PLANTERS AND OTHERS, IN THE UNITED STATES AND ELSEWHERE. 5 August 1826. Baltimore.** Announce a boycott of slave-labor produce; report opening of a mercantile house in Baltimore for the purchase and sale of free goods on commission. 5 August 1826 (vol. I, no. 49) p.388, c2.

345 PHILADELPHUS *to* **FRIENDS OF THE ANTI-SLAVERY CAUSE. n.d. n.p.** Reminds that no great reformation is effected without opposition; declares that reformation must occur in the system of slavery and that failure is impossible when God favors the cause; warns against apathy. 5 August 1826 (vol. I, no. 49) p.389, c1.

346 B. LUNDY *to* **THE SLAVEHOLDERS OF THE UNITED STATES. 5 August 1826. Baltimore.** Reports an arrangement with the Philanthropic Society of Haiti whereby all slaves permitted to emigrate will have their passage paid and wants supplied until they are self-sufficient. 5 August 1826 (vol. V, no. 49) p.390, c3.

347 LIBER *to* **THE EDITOR OF THE** *NORFOLK HERALD.* **[continued from 5 August 1826] n.d. n.p.** Explains that he intended his letter for freemen only; discredits his critics' fear of discussing slavery, asserting that "there is nothing really dangerous to man or people, but a willful neglect of duty." 12 August 1826 (vol. V, no. 50) p.393, c1.

348 n.n. *to* **A MEMBER OF THE LATE GENERAL ASSEMBLY OF NORTH CAROLINA. 27 July 1826. n.p.** Asserts that slavery cannot be reconciled with our system of government; urges more benevolent treatment of slaves. 26 August 1826 (vol. V, no. 51) p.401, c1.

349 LABASTILLE *to* **MR. PHINEAS NIXON. 15 July 1826. Aux Cayes.** Needs thirty good farmers for a plantation; offers to provide for them until they can support themselves and to divide the produce of the estate equally with them; requests advance notice of their departure. 26 August 1826 (vol. V, no. 51) p.406, c2.

350 LITTLE WILLIAM *to* **CITIZENS OF NORTH CAROLINA AND THOSE OF HER DARK COMPLECTED SISTERS. 1 August 1826. Guilford County, N.C.** Urges the formation of female emancipation societies to influence others, and promote the abolition of slavery. 2 September 1826 (vol. V, no. 52) p.409, c3.

351 DANIEL RAYMOND *to* **VOTERS OF THE CITY OF BALTIMORE. 12 September 1826. Baltimore.** Reports that if he is elected anti-slavery representative to the legislature, he will present a proposal that all children hereafter born in Maryland be free; reviews the history and effect of slavery in Maryland. 16 September 1826 (vol. VI, no. 53) p.1, c1.

352 SIDNEY *to* **FRIENDS AND FELLOW CITIZENS. 4 July 1826. United States.** Reminds that the country has undergone a biblical jubilee period; asks what has been done to remove oppressions and redress grievances; acknowledges that slave importation has been outlawed, slave trade declared piracy, and a colony established. 16 September 1826 (vol. VI, no. 53) p.2, c2.

353 A CAROLINIAN *to* **GENTLEMEN. [from the** *Recorder and Telegraph***] 9 September 1825. n.p.** Opposes the immediate and entire abolition of slavery; believes that the liberation of two million ignorant slaves would reduce citizens from affluence to poverty and destroy the South. 16 September 1826 (vol. VI, no. 53) p.3, c1.

354 n.n. *to* **FRIEND LUNDY. [from the** *Christian Inquirer***] n.d. n.p.** Explains how the person Lundy labelled an "honorable gentleman man-stealer" obtained the office from which he recently resigned. 16 September 1826 (vol. VI, no. 53) p.6, c2.

355 A SUBSCRIBER *to* **MR. EDITOR [B. LUNDY]. 28 August 1826. Baltimore.** Encloses a biblical quotation for Lundy's comment. 23 September 1826 (vol. VI, no. 54) p.9, c2.

356 A GENTLEMAN OF HIGH RESPECTABILITY *to* **THE EDITOR [B. LUNDY]. [extract] 27 August 1826. North Carolina.** Reports severe food shortages in South Carolina; declares that free states are not happy at the prospect of receiving colored people. 23 September 1826 (vol. VI, no. 54) p.9, c3.

357 A FRIEND IN NORTH CAROLINA *to* **n.n. [extract] n.d. n.p.** Announces election to the Senate of Gen. Alexander Gray, a member of the Manumission Society. 23 September 1826 (vol. VI, no. 54) p.13, c1.

358 X. *to* **MR. LUNDY. 5 August 1826. North Carolina.** Discusses the subscriber who cancelled because of cruelties described in the newspaper; assumes that he either thought the descriptions shocking or was too naive to believe them; promises to submit reports of unusual cruelty, and includes five. 23 September 1826 (vol. VI, no. 54) p.13, c2.

359 JOSE MARIA MICHELENA AND JOSE DOMINGUES *to* **HIS EXCELLENCY THE MINISTER OF STATE AND DOMESTIC AND FOREIGN AFFAIRS. 15 August 1826. Acapulco.** Report ratification of a Treaty of Alliance and Perpetual Amity between the new American states. 23 September 1826 (vol. VI, no. 54) p.14, c2.

360 HIERONYMUS *to* **MESSRS. EDITORS. [from the** *Recorder and Telegraph***] n.d. n.p.** Asserts that Northern writers should realize that neither emancipation nor the amelioration of the suffering of blacks can occur without Southern cooperation. [partially illegible] 30 September 1826 (vol. VI, no. 55) p.17, c3.

361 ANTI-SLAVITE *to* **MECHANICS OF BALTIMORE. n.d. n.p.** Argues that a free society can employ more mechanics than a slave society and therefore, that every mechanic should be interested in abolition; endorses Daniel Raymond for legislature. 30 September 1826 (vol. VI, no. 55) p.20, c1.

362 GEORGE FLOWER *to* **THE EDITOR [B. LUNDY]. 25 August 1826. Nashoba, Tn.** Discusses farm run by Frances Wright, who bought a slave family and, in exchange for fifteen years' labor, fed, clothed, and educated them, then sent them to a foreign country to be free; believes the establishment of many such institutions would soon end slavery. 30 September 1826 (vol. VI, no. 55) p.21, c2.

363 WILLIAM SWAIN *to* **MR. EDITOR [B. LUNDY] n.d. n.p.** Reports on the proceedings of a recent meeting of the General Association of the North Carolina Manumission Society. 7 October 1826 (vol. VI, no. 56) p.25, c1.

364 W. *to* **MR. EDITOR [B. LUNDY] n.d. n.p.** Claims that "slavites," aware that they are losing ground, are reduced to using abstractions and circumstantial evidence to justify their position; cites examples. 7 October 1826 (vol. VI, no. 56) p.27, c1.

365 A PLUMPER [*sic***]** *to* **MR. EDITOR [B. LUNDY] n.d. n.p.** Asks Lundy to discuss the proposition that there would be greater demand for mechanics if the slaves were free. 14 October 1826 (vol. VI, no. 57) p.33, c1.

366 G. H. STEWART *to* **THE EDITORS OF THE** *AMERICAN.* **10 October 1826. n.p.** Denies rumors that he would contest the recent election; expresses astonishment that anyone knowing his character would say such a thing. 14 October 1826 (vol. VI, no. 57) p.37, c3.

367 DE WITT CLINTON *to* **PRESIDENT OF THE UNITED STATES. 4 September 1826. Albany.** Encloses proof that Gilbert Horton, a man of color imprisoned in Washington, is a free man; applies for his release. 14 October 1826 (vol. VI, no. 57) p.38, c1.

368 DANIEL BRENT *to* **DE WITT CLINTON. 14 September 1826. Washington.** Reports that Gilbert Horton has already been freed. 14 October 1826 (vol. VI, no. 57) p.38, c1.

369 JAMES H. DICKEY *to* **n.n. 30 September 1826. n.p.** Reports seeing a large number of slaves chained together with one slave holding the American flag at the head of the line. 27 October 1826 (vol. VI, no. 58) p.45, c1.

370 HARRISON *to* **MR. EDITOR [B. LUNDY]. n.d. n.p.** Asserts that biblical slavery was not divinely sanctioned. 4 November 1826 (vol. VI, no. 59) p.52, c2.

371 A CITIZEN OF HAYTI *to* **n.n. [extract] 19 September 1826. Cape Haytien.** Reports cessation of trade with France, and adds that without a few American adventurers, people would starve. 4 November 1826 (vol. VI, no. 59) p.53, c1.

372 LITTLE WILLIAM *to* **MR. EDITOR [B. LUNDY]. October 1826. Guilford County, N.C.** Discusses the history and plan of operation of the North Carolina Manumission Society; contrasts Northern and Southern lifestyles; explains that the Manumission Society seeks to collect information and communicate it to the body politic. 11 November 1826 (vol. VI, no. 60) p.57, c1.

373 WILLIAM H. FITZHUGH, ESQ. *to* **A GENTLEMAN OF NEW YORK. [extract] 11 August 1826. Ravensworth, Va.** Discusses the rationale behind African colonization and ways of funding it. 11 November 1826 (vol. VI, no. 60) p.59, c1.

374 n.n. *to* **MR. B. LUNDY. 30 October 1826. n.p.** Announces that he must cancel his subscription as he dare not receive the paper; reports that several issues have fallen into hands of others, causing great excitement. 11 November 1826 (vol. VI, no. 60) p.61, c2.

375 JOSEPH ALLEN *to* **EDITOR OF THE** *LEXINGTON INTELLIGENCER.* **n.d. n.p.** Claims that he offered his four slaves their freedom, but that they preferred to remain as sharecroppers; discusses the possible sale of one man's wife and children; expresses willingness to help send them to Africa. 11 November 1826 (vol. VI, no. 60) p.61, c3.

376 A GENTLEMAN IN SANDWICH *to* **HIS FRIEND IN MONTREAL. [extract] n.d. n.p.** Discusses tobacco grown by some escaped slaves who are farming his land. 18 November 1826 (vol. VI, no. 61) p.68, c1.

377 n.n. *to* **SIR. 28 August 1826. Williams College.** Reports that to send delegates to the American convention would be impractical; announces the formation of an AS at Williams College; discusses theories of abolitionism and colonization. 2 December 1826 (vol. VI, no. 63) p.82, c1.

378 DAVID GREENE *to* **MR. EDITOR [B. LUNDY]. n.d. n.p.** Discusses the condition of slaves and his plans to publish a book examining slavery as it exists in law and fact. 2 December 1826 (vol. VI, no. 63) p.83, c1.

379 MANY-SUCH-IN-THE-SOUTH *to* **MR. EDITOR [B. LUNDY]. October 1826. Guilford County, N.C.** Insists that there is ample power on earth to abolish slavery and that abolition would not destroy the civil and political significance of half the United States; denies that American slaves are incapable of self-government. 2 December 1826 (vol. VI, no. 63) p.84, c1.

[1827]

380 HOWARD *to* **THE EDITOR OF THE** *TELESCOPE.* **n.d. n.p.** Describes an encounter in New Haven, Connecticut, with a West Indian Negro who stowed away, was caught, jailed and returned to slavery; believes the man became free as soon as he landed in the United States. 8 January 1827 (vol. VI, no. 67) p.116, c2.

381 VERUS *to* **THE EDITOR OF THE** *BALTIMORE GAZETTE.* **n.d. n.p.** Discusses a memorial in the *Gazette* about a petition to Congress concerning slavery in Washington; argues that slavery is incompatible with Christianity and contrary to the law. 8 January 1827 (vol. VI, no. 67) p.117, c3.

382 A REAL DEMOCRAT *to* **THE PEOPLE OF HERFORD COUNTY. [from the** *Bond of Union***] n.d. n.p.** Observes that people are begining to understand that they must abolish slavery in order to be consistent Republicans and Christians; urges the formation of ASS. 8 January 1827 (vol. VI, no. 67) p. 118, c2.

383 CIVIS *to* **THE EDITOR [B. LUNDY]. n.d. n.p.** Commends the AS of Williams College; notes plans for an annual anti-slavery oration on Independence Day. 27 January 1827 (vol. VI, no. 69) p.129, c2.

384 JUSTICE *to* **THE AGRICULTURAL SOCIETIES OF MARYLAND AND STATES TO THE SOUTH. n.d. n.p.** Excoriates the societies for excluding slavery from their stated purpose of improving the conditions of man through more effective farming techniques; calls this omission criminal. 27 January 1827 (vol. VI, no. 69) p.129, c3.

385 n.n. *to* **MR. LUNDY. January 1827. Baltimore County.** Relates the story of a man who had provided for the emancipation of his slaves in his will, but his heirs destroyed the will prior to his death and have now put the slaves up for sale. 27 January 1827 (vol. VI, no. 69) p.132, cl.

386 PHILO VERUS *to* **EDITORS OF THE** *BALTIMORE GAZETTE.* **6 January 1827. n.p.** Berates those who claim to oppose slavery, but who refuse to discuss any plan to abolish it; argues that slavery is contrary to Christianity; accuses the editors of manipulating language for their own benefit. 24 February 1827 (vol. VI, no. 70) p.137, c2.

387 AFRICANUS *to* **MR. EDITOR [B. LUNDY]. n.d. n.p.** [illegible] 24 February 1827 (vol. VI, no. 70) p.143, c2.

388 SAMUEL BLANY *to* **MR. EDITOR [B. LUNDY]. 7 February 1827. Franklin Township, Pa.** Reports that the number of advocates of slavery is decreasing in Franklin Township; discusses the formation and constitution of the Franklin Township AS. 3 March 1827 (vol. VI, no. 71) p.145, c3.

389 G. M. TROUP *to* **JAMES BARBOUR, SECRETARY OF WAR. 17 February 1827. Georgia.** Warns that he will resist any military attack by the United States government on Georgia. 3 March 1827 (vol. VI, no. 71) p.146, c2.

390 A COLORED BALTIMOREAN *to* **MR. EDITOR [B. LUNDY]. n.d. n.p.** Explains that the intention of the memorial to the white population of Baltimore was to solicit aid for those colored people wishing to emigrate, but not to imply that the majority wished to go; many hope to share equal rights in America, and see little reason to leave what is their home. 3 March 1827 (vol. VI, no. 71) p.149, c2.

391 n.n. *to* **n.n. [extract] 12 December 1826. Nagadoches, Tx.** Considers the affairs of the government to be in desperate condition; predicts an open rupture between American settlers and the Mexican government; reports that slave importation is prohibited. 3 March 1827 (vol. VI, no. 71) p.150, c3.

392 n.n. *to* **THE EDITOR OF THE** *NEW YORK TIMES.* **[extract] 6 November 1826. Rio de Janeiro.** Describes the city: miserable hotels, mixed population, slave vessels arriving every day from Africa. 3 March 1827 (vol. VI, no. 71) p.151, c1.

393 S. D. *to* **MESSRS. EDITORS. [from the** *Courier and Telegraph***] n.d. n.p.** Declares that the time is at hand for the Christian Church to act against intemperance; asserts that professing Christians must abandon the use of alcohol completely or side with the drunkard. 15 March 1827 (vol. VI, no. 72) p.157, c1.

394 HOUSE OF DELEGATES *to* **THE EDITORS OF THE** *AMERICAN.* **10 March 1827. Annapolis.** Discusses bill concerning internal improvements. 15 March 1827 (vol. VI, no. 72) p.159, c1.

395 JUSTICE *to* **MR. EDITOR [B. LUNDY]. n.d. n.p.** Approves of the ACS in principle, but disagrees with its projected course of action; asks several questions. 24 March 1827 (vol. VI, no. 73) p.161, c1.

396 A GENTLEMAN *to* **HIS FRIEND IN NEVILLE, OHIO. [extract] 8 December 1826. Harrisburg, La.** Discusses a case in which a white child was kidnapped and allegedly sold as a slave. 24 March 1827 (vol. VI, no. 73) p.162, c3.

397 A NORTH CAROLINIAN *to* **MR. EDITOR [B. LUNDY]. 12 January 1827. Orange County.** Praises the sentiments of the governor except for his desire to whip criminals; wishes the governor would let Africans go home so that whites could find jobs. 31 March 1827 (vol. VI, no. 74) p.169, c1.

398 *GENIUS OF UNIVERSAL EMANCIPATION to* **"FREE" PEOPLE SOUTH OF THE GREENE RIVER. n.d. n.p.** Reproves them on the issue of slavery; asserts that free states continue to encourage the existence of slavery by purchasing slave produce; appeals to residents of this area because theirs is the only slaveholding section of Kentucky. 14 April 1827 (vol. VI, no. 75) p.181, c1.

399 *GENIUS OF UNIVERSAL EMANCIPATION to* **"FREE" PEOPLE SOUTH OF THE GREENE RIVER. n.d. n.p.** Discusses some of the effects of slavery; argues that greater personal security is found in the laws and government of free states; claims that slavery creates an oppressive aristocracy; denies that slaves are inferior and demands justification for man-stealing. 21 April 1827 (vol. VI, no. 76) p. 185, c1.

400 G. *to* **THE EDITOR [B. LUNDY]. 2 February 1827. Virginia.** Needs to hire slaves; asks Lundy to discuss the differences between hiring and purchasing; finds new hope in the discovery of so many anti-slavery Southerners; reproves those who have become involved in foreign affairs but ignore slaves' needs. 21 April 1827 (vol. VI, no. 76) p.188, c1.

401 JUDGE A. CALDWELL *to* **SIR. 20 April 1826. Washington.** Compliments his plan for preventing forgery of bank bills. 21 April 1827 (vol. VI, no. 76) p.190, c2.

402 A. CALDWELL *to* **SIR. [extract] 12 December 1826. n.p.** Hopes that his trip to Europe serves the purpose of perfecting his engraving invention. 21 April 1827 (vol. VI, no. 76) p.190, c3.

403 AMICUS *to* **MR. EDITOR [B. LUNDY]. February 1827. Guilford County, N.C.** Discusses freedom of the press, particularly with regard to slavery and emancipation; attributes the lack of prosperity to an increase in slave population and its effect on the moral and physical energies of the people. 28 April 1827 (vol. VI, no. 77) p.193, c1.

404 n.n. *to* **MR. EDITOR [B. LUNDY]. 1827. South Carolina.** Wishes he could do more for emancipation, but living in slavery's stronghold prevents him; reports that his acquaintances believe slavery to be a necessary evil; believes that opposition to emancipation is in vain. 28 April 1827 (vol. VI, no. 77) p.194, c1.

405 n.n. *to* **THE EDITOR [B. LUNDY]. [extract] 28 December 1826. Kentucky.** Praises Lundy's work. 28 April 1827 (vol. VI, no. 77) p.194, c2.

406 *GENIUS OF UNIVERSAL EMANCIPATION to* **FELLOW CITIZENS. [from the** *Russellville* **(Ky.)** *Messenger]* **n.d. n.p.** Presents a plan to rid the state of slavery; recommends emigration of blacks to Haiti, which is willing to bear the expenses; argues that slavery cannot be abolished through legislation without full compensation to slaveowners. 28 April 1827 (vol. VI, no. 77) p.194, c2.

407 JOSEPH WATSON, MAYOR *to* **DAVID HOLMES AND J. E. DAVIS. 20 January 1827. Philadelphia.** Thanks Holmes and Davis for their role in unearthing a conspiracy to kidnap freeborn black children and sell them into slavery. 28 April 1827 (vol. VI, no. 77) p.197, c1.

408 JOSEPH WATSON *to* **D. S. WALKER. 24 January 1827. Philadelphia.** Encloses Peter Hook's narrative; explains that he was referred to Walker for legal assistance in returning kidnapped blacks to their homes; asks if he might send depositions instead of people since money is scarce for travel. 28 April 1827 (vol. VI, no. 77) p.197, c1.

409 D. S. WALKER *to* **JOSEPH WATSON, 25 February 1827. Natchez.** Refuses any compensation for his work; describes his progress to date; responds that depositions are legal. 28 April 1827 (vol. VI, no. 77) p.197, c2.

410 AMICUS *to* **MR. EDITOR [B. LUNDY]. February 1827. Guilford County, N.C.** Observes that free states believe they must warn other states of danger, adding that the South does not appreciate this; claims that Northern financial interests would not benefit by the abolition of slavery; urges the governor to recommend gradual emancipation. 5 May 1827 (vol. VI no.78) p.201, c1.

411 GOULD JOHNSON *to* **THE EDITOR [B. LUNDY]. n.d. n.p.** Encloses a copy of the constitution and proceedings of the AS of Brucetown, Virginia, for publication. 5 May 1827 (vol. VI, no. 78) p.202, c2.

412 *GENIUS OF UNIVERSAL EMANCIPATION to* **FELLOW CITIZENS. [from the** *Russellville Messenger]* **n.d. n.p.** Urges passage of a law emancipating all children born after March 1828; believes that the legislature must provide for both their support and adequate compensation; claims that the plan would cost the state nothing. 5 May 1827 (vol. VI, no. 78) p.203, c2.

413 JOHN BLAIR *to* **HIS CONSTITUENTS. [extract] 1826. Virginia.** Reports an $800 appropriation to the Richmond and Manchester CS; explains that he has recently begun to appreciate the beneficial impact of a colony on African civilization; discusses Jefferson's views on slavery. 5 May 1827 (vol. VI, no. 78) p.204, c1.

414 A GENTLEMAN IN ARKANSAS *to* **THE EDITOR [B. LUNDY]. [extract] 27 February 1827. n.p.** Expresses pleasure upon learning that support for emancipation is spreading; reports that he has heard the sounds of slavery and knows many professed Christians who still own slaves. 5 May 1827 (vol. VI, no. 78) p.204, c3.

415 n.n. *to* **n.n. [extract] n.d. West Tennessee.** Feels thankful that he can assist slaves; sends ten dollars for subscription; assumes the newspaper cannot have much circulation because pro-slavery sentiment is so entrenched. 5 May 1827 (vol. VI, no. 78) p.205, c1.

416 n.n. *to* **A GENTLEMAN IN BALTIMORE. 15 February 1827. France.** Reports that the Haitian government has adopted the financial plan of Mr. Lafitte and appointed him banker for the country. 5 May 1827 (vol. VI, no. 78) p.207, c1.

417 n.n. *to* **MEMBERS OF THE GUNPOWDER BRANCH OF THE AS OF MARYLAND. 20 April 1827. Baltimore.** Stresses that past injustices may be amended, but that the government awaits the expressed will of the people; calls for action. 12 May 1827 (vol. VI, no. 78) p.209, c1.

418 WILBERFORCE *to* **MR. POLK. [from the** *Danville* **(Ky.)** *Olive Branch***] n.d. n.p.** Compares American slavery to European tyranny; concludes that African slave trade cannot be explained by accepted principles of involuntary servitude, and that Americans have no right to hold slaves in perpetuity. 12 May 1827 (vol. VI, no. 78) p.210, c1.

419 SUB UMBRA *to* **MR. EDITOR [B. LUNDY]. [from the** *Western Luminary***] n.d. n.p.** Owns several slaves without feeling guilty; doubts the wisdom of partial emancipation without first educating the slave; yet believes that the existence of slavery is a national curse and that its end approaches. 12 May 1827 (vol. VI, no. 78) p.210, c3.

420 THOMAS JEFFERSON *to* **n.n. [extract] 22 April 1820. Monticello.** States that he considered the Missouri question to be the death knell of the Union; calls the compromise a temporary reprieve; argues that the passage of slaves from one state to another would not increase the total number of slaves, and would facilitate emancipation by "dividing the burden on a greater number of coadjutors." 19 May 1827 (vol. VI, no. 80) p.221, c1.

421 JOHN AND THOMAS L. BERRY *to* **MR. S. R. BAKEWELL. 1 May 1827. Baltimore.** Praise the brick firing kiln which they built according to Bakewell's new plan. 19 May 1827 (vol. VI, no. 80) p.224, c2.

422 W. WINCHESTER *to* **MR. BAKEWELL. 17 February 1827. Baltimore.** Commends Bakewell's stoneware pipes. 19 May 1827 (vol. VI, no. 80) p.224, c3.

423 RICHARD HENDERSON *to* **THE EDITOR OF THE** *LONDON COURIER***. 1 February 1827. Cornhill, London.** Refutes alleged governmental proclamation as a forgery and an attempt to imply that Haiti has a labor system of rigid and severe exactitude. 26 May 1827 (vol. VI, no. 81) p.227, c2.

424 W. *to* **MR. EDITOR [B. LUNDY]. n.d. n.p.** Demonstrates through statistical analysis that slaves will soon outnumber whites in the Southern states. 16 June 1827 (vol. VI, no. 84) p.251, c3.

425 GEN. INGINAC *to* **THE EDITOR [B. LUNDY]. [extract] 11 April 1826. Port-au-Prince.** Forwards a series of resolutions by the Philanthropic Society pertaining to slave emigration to Haiti. 16 June 1827 (vol. VI, no. 84) p.254, c1.

426 GEN. INGINAC *to* **THE EDITOR [B. LUNDY]. [extract] 9 May 1826. Port-au-Prince.** Discusses the terms under which colored people may emigrate to and become citizens of Hayti. 16 June 1827. (vol. VI, no. 84) p.254, c2.

427 W. *to* **MR. LUNDY. n.d. n.p.** Discusses population growth in nine new states and two territories; compares New York and Maryland, in order to demonstrate the detrimental effects of slavery. 4 July 1827 (vol. VII, no. 141) p.2, c1.

428 E. P. ATLEE *to* **ESTEEMED FRIEND [B. LUNDY]. 18 June 1827. Philadelphia.** Reports decision to form a society to promote the consumption of free goods; encloses the constitution of the Pennsylvania Free Produce Society. 4 July 1827 (vol. VII, no. 141) p.2, c3.

429 C. *to* **MESSRS. EDITORS. [from the** *Village Record***] n.d. n.p.** Praises the *American Farmer* for discussing the relative value of slave and free labor. 4 July 1827 (vol. VII, no. 141) p.3, c2.

430 W. *to* **MR. LUNDY. n.d. n.p.** Claims that free states are not receiving their due in the distribution of electoral votes. 11 July 1827 (vol. VII, no. 142) p.10, c2.

431 WILBERFORCE *to* **MR. EDITOR [B. LUNDY]. 1827. Baltimore.** Believes much has been done unwittingly to damage the cause of emancipation; claims that a majority of the total white population is pro-slavery; considers slavery inconsistent with Christianity, and that policy, justice, morality and religion require its abolition. 11 July 1827 (vol. VII, no. 142) p.10, c2.

432 AMICUS *to* **MR. EDITOR [B. LUNDY]. 19 May 1827. Guilford County.** Warns that the economic system cannot reach maturity with an indolent aristocracy and an oppressed slave class; reports that those who emigrate with slaves go to other slave states, while farmers and mechanics move North; discusses the probability of slave insurrection. 21 July 1827 (vol. VII, no. 143) p.18, c1.

433 ANDREW JACKSON *to* **CARTER BEVERLY. 6 June 1827. Hermitage.** Discusses the corrupt bargain by which Clay became secretary of state under Adams. 21 July 1827 (vol. VII, no. 143) p.22, c2.

434 PHILANTHROPOS *to* **MR. LUNDY. 15 June 1827. Berlin.** Warns that slaves will not accept the treatment they now receive unless their powers of reason are removed; claims that God will soon punish the country. 28 July 1827 (vol. VII, no. 144) p.26, c1.

435 JAMES RICHARDSON *to* **MR. LUNDY. 25 June 1827. Nashoba.** Encloses a few extracts of Frances Wright's records which he thinks may be of interest. 28 July 1827 (vol. VII, no. 144) p.29, c3.

436 WILBERFORCE *to* **MR. LUNDY. n.d. n.p.** Discusses Martin Luther, arguing that intemperate language is not becoming to reformers; states that he hesitates to judge a man's character solely on the grounds that he holds slaves; cites examples of charitable masters. 18 August 1827 (vol. VII, no. 147) p.50, c2.

437 MENTOR *to* **MR. LUNDY. 8 August 1827. Philadelphia.** Condemns Frances Wright for allegedly condoning illicit sexual activity without the benefit of marriage; claims that such conduct demonstrates the guilt of slavery itself, as Wright's students are purchased slaves, subject to new masters. 18 August 1827 (vol. VII, no. 147) p.54, c1.

438 A WAVERING MAN *to* **SIR. [from the** *Telescope***] 8 July 1827. Utica.** Discusses racial discrimination, particularly in admission to church; accuses those who discriminate of judging God's work and demonstrating a holier-than-thou attitude. 18 August 1827 (vol. VII, no. 147) p.54, c3.

439 COL. AUGUSTUS STORRS *to* **SIR. 13 May 1827. Santa Fe Trace, 120 miles west of Franklin.** Describes progress of the Santa Fe Company whose 105 men and fifty-three wagons he feels would appear formidable to any Indians who observed them; lists officers appointed to govern the company. 25 August 1827 (vol. VII, no. 148) p.59, c2.

440 SHARPE *to* **MR. EDITOR [B. LUNDY]. n.d. n.p.** Encloses biographical sketch of Thomas Clarkson. 2 September 1827 (vol. VII, no. 149) p.66, c2.

441 OBSERVER *to* **MR. EDITOR [B. LUNDY]. n.d. n.p.** Rejoices that God is rapidly bringing emancipation closer. 2 September 1827 (vol. VII, no. 149) p.66, c3.

442 JOHN FOSTER *to* **FRIENDS. May 1827. London.** Fears that sin and transgression are keeping people from God; advises those who are saved to make constant witness to Christ; condemns slave trade, but believes that the cause of the oppressed is gaining ground. 2 September 1827 (vol. VII, no. 149) p.68, c3.

443 ARGUS *to* **MR. EDITOR [B. LUNDY]. 10 August 1827. Randolph County, NC.** Reports new form of slave punishment: stripping the victim, whipping him cruelly and driving him into the woods without clothing. 2 September 1827 (vol. VII, no. 149) p.71, c2.

444 W. *to* **MR. EDITOR [B. LUNDY]. n.d. n.p.** Asserts that the cause suffers from the inactivity of many of its supporters; urges those opposed to slavery to vote for anti-slavery candidates. 8 September 1827 (vol. VII, no. 150) p.74, c2.

445 J. *to* **MR. LUNDY. n.d. n.p.** Expresses dismay that slavery still exists despite democratic revolutions; wonders if men have become so inured to slavery that they are callous to better judgement; calls the ballot box the best remedy for slavery. 8 September 1827 (vol. VII, no. 150) p.78, c1.

446 W. *to* **MR. EDITOR [B. LUNDY]. n.d. n.p.** Finds no evidence of love, mercy and justice in daily life, particularly with regard to slavery; believes that Christianity is in a dreadful state; claims American Protestants are put to shame by Latin-American Catholics who have abolished slavery. 15 September 1827 (vol. VII, no. 151) p.82, c3.

447 D. RAYMOND *to* **VOTERS OF BALTIMORE. n.d. n.p.** Regrets the influence of the presidential election on state elections; declares he will work for Adams' re-election and gives his reasons; defends Clay's support of Adams in the previous election, adding that Clay is qualified to be secretary of state. 15 September 1827 (vol. VII, no. 151) p.84, c3.

448 HARPER *to* **MR. SKILLMAN. [from the** *Western Luminary***] n.d. n.p.** Praises recent series on slavery; discusses internal slave trade within the South; believes that slaves are ruining the country and should be returned to Africa. 15 September 1827 (vol. VII, no. 151) p.86, c2.

449 n.n. *to* **MR. EDITOR. [from the** *New Jersey Eagle***] n.d. n.p.** Discusses benefits of rising early. 15 September 1827 (vol. VII, no. 151) p.87, c2.

450 JAY *to* **MR. LUNDY. n.d. n.p.** Apologizes for his apparent misrepresentation of Wilberforce's sentiment; questions whether slavery can be practiced with impunity; explains that the greater the value of slave to owner, the less prepared the slave is for freedom, and the greater the need for abolition. 22 September 1827 (vol. VII, no. 152) p.90, c3.

451 MOSES *to* **MR. EDITOR [B. LUNDY]. n.d. n.p.** Criticizes the writings of Jay and Wilberforce; declares that to enslave a man is worse than to kill him, because a slave is "robbed of himself." 22 September 1827 (vol. VII, no. 152) p.91, c2.

452 BENJAMIN F. TAYLOR *to* **B. LUNDY. 23 August 1827. Loudoun County, Va.** Reports on meeting of the first Virginia convention for the abolition of slavery and on the decision to establish a permanent annual convention. 29 September 1827 (vol. VII, no. 153) p.102, c2.

453 n.n. *to* **THE EDITOR [B. LUNDY]. 12 June 1827. Liverpool.** Claims that the government cannot convince colonists to improve the condition of slaves, so that talk of removing slaves by emigration is futile; depicts the internal slave trade as extensive and horrible. 29 September 1827 (vol. VII, no. 153) p.102, c2.

454 TOUSSAINT L'OUVERTURE *to* **CITIZEN DEMUGE. n.d. n.p.** Reports activity of the French military against Haitian rebels; instructs Demuge to defend his position at Jeremie and not to trust whites; reports that he has ordered towns and plains around Cayes burned if they cannot be held. 6 October 1827 (vol. VII, no. 154) p.105, c3.

455 Z. *to* **MR. EDITOR [B. LUNDY]. n.d. n.p.** Believes that the duty of every literate man is to write about the evils of slavery; wants the decline of slave population to result from manumission. 6 October 1827 (vol. VII, no. 154) p.106, c2.

456 n.n. *to* **MR. EDITOR. [from the** *Richmond Family Visitor***] n.d. n.p.** Counsels his readers not to assume that the Scriptures authorize every practice for which their imprimatur is invoked; concludes from an examination of the biblical system of servitude that slavery is contrary to the biblical spirit. 6 October 1827 (vol. VII, no. 154) p.107, c1.

457 BONAPARTE *to* **TOUSSAINT L'OUVERTURE. n.d. n.p.** Warns that he is sending General LeClerc as magistrate of the island, and hopes L'Ouverture will cooperate; asks L'Ouverture what he wishes, and assures him that Haitians will have liberty, but as citizens of France. 14 October 1827 (vol. VII, no. 155) p.113, c2.

458 PHILANTHROPOS *to* **MR. LUNDY. 5 September 1827. Berlin.** Realizes that much cruel opposition to educating slaves exists; claims education would make slaves more obedient. 14 October 1827 (vol. VII, no. 155) p.114, c2.

459 INVESTIGATOR *to* **MESSRS. EDITORS. [from the** *Freedom's Journal***] n.d. n.p.** Finds that advocates of colonization are stirred by popular motives and use popular arguments; views as enemies those who claim that the colored population is inferior and unable to achieve respectable status in this country. 14 October 1827 (vol. VII, no. 155) p.119, c2.

460 Z. *to* **MR. EDITOR [B. LUNDY]. n.d. n.p.** Argues that true Christians are not obliged to obey laws protecting slavery; condemns judges who enforce these laws. 20 October 1827 (vol. VII, no. 156) p.122, c2.

461 FRIEND OF MAN *to* **MR. EDITOR [B. LUNDY]. n.d. n.p.** Denounces the argument that Negroes are better off as slaves; brands it a last resort by those who have not a shadow of justice on their side to vindicate themselves. 20 October 1827 (vol. VII, no. 156) p.122, c3.

462 Z. *to* **MR. EDITOR [B. LUNDY]. n.d. n.p.** Urges that slaveholders be treated as enemies to the community. [partially illegible] 27 October 1827 (vol. VII, no. 157) p.131, c1.

463 AFRICUS *to* **MR. SKILLMAN. [from the** *Western Luminary***] n.d. n.p.** States that much can be done to promote the final goal of emancipation and, in the interim, to improve slaves' mental and moral condition; claims that the moral and religious condition of the slave population is little above heathenism. 27 October 1827 (vol. VII, no. 157) p.132, c1.

464 LITTLE WILLIAM *to* **FREEMEN OF NORTH CAROLINA. September 1827. Guilford County, N.C.** Demands an explanation of the difference between African and internal slave trade; declares that the former can never be abolished until the latter is destroyed; asks why slave trade has not been driven from North Carolina. 3 November 1827 (vol. VII, no. 158) p.138, c2.

465 AFRICUS *to* **THE SYNOD OF KENTUCKY. [from the** *Western Luminary***] n.d. n.p.** Believes that the Church is responsible for the "intellectual, moral, and religious degradation" of the slave population; believes it should educate slaves. 3 November 1827 (vol. VII, no. 158) p.140, c1.

466 n.n. *to* **THE EDITOR [B. LUNDY]. [extract] n.d. Remote part of Southern slaveholding country.** Praises Lundy's newspaper; encloses fifteen dollars for subscriptions. 10 November 1827 (vol. VII, no. 159) p.149, c2.

467 W. *to* **MR. EDITOR [B. LUNDY]. n.d. n.p.** Predicts that the harvest from work toward emancipation will be great; asks why slavery is so deeply rooted; observes that zealous workers are rare. 17 November 1827 (vol. VII, no. 160) p.154, c1.

468 Z. *to* **MR. EDITOR [B. LUNDY]. n.d. n.p.** Reminds that Toussaint and other prominent figures in the Haitian Revolution were slaves; predicts that soon the West Indies will be governed by that population thought by Southerners to be "deficient of . . . a capacity of self-organization." 17 November 1827 (vol. VII, no. 160) p.154, c2.

469 A. B. *to* **FARMERS, EMIGRANTS, AND OTHER SETTLERS. n.d. n.p.** Discusses aspects of Maryland which make it attractive for settlement; emphasizes the decline of slave population and need for free labor. 17 November 1827 (vol. VII, no. 160) p.155, c2.

470 Z. *to* **MR. EDITOR [B. LUNDY]. n.d. n.p.** Believes that slavery creates rift between the United States and South American republics. 25 November 1827 (vol. VII, no. 161) p.162, c2.

471 JOHN THOMPSON KILBY *to* **THOMAS MASSEY. [from the** *American Farmer***] 23 October 1827. Suffolk, Va.** Computes cost of slave labor. 25 November 1827 (vol. VII, no. 161) p.165, c3.

472 [illegible] *to* **THE EDITOR [B. LUNDY]. n.d. n.p.** Believes it self-evident to an impartial investigator that slavery can not be condoned or practiced by any Christian. 15 December 1827 (vol. VII, no. 164) p.186, c2.

473 n.n. *to* **MESSRS. EDITORS OF THE** *SATURDAY EVENING CHRONICLE***. n.d. n.p.** Reviews "An inquiry concerning the intellectual and moral faculties and literature of Negroes; followed with an account of the life and works of fifteen Negroes and mulattoes, distinguished in science, literature, and the arts," written by H. Gregoire in 1810. 15 December 1827 (vol. VII, no. 164) p.188, c1.

474 AFRICUS *to* **MR. SKILLMAN. [from the** *Western Luminary***] n.d. n.p.** [illegible] 22 December 1827 (vol. VII, no. 165) p.195, c1.

475 TH. PRINGLE *to* **SIR [B. LUNDY]. 9 September 1827. London.** Reports that he has received several issues of the newspaper through James Cropper of Liverpool and has shown them to the London AS; sends a set of the society's publications and asks for Lundy's publications on Negro slavery. 29 December 1827 (vol. VII, no. 166) p.204, c1.

476 JUSTICE *to* **AGRICULTURAL SOCIETY OF MARYLAND. n.d. n.p.** Asks why the society has not done anything to end slavery; declares that no agricultural improvement is possible in a system of slave labor; enumerates the evils of slavery. 5 January 1828 (vol. VIII, no. 167) p.10, c1.

477 A SUBSCRIBER *to* **MR. EDITOR [B. LUNDY]. 31 December 1827. Philadelphia.** Encloses proceedings of a recent meeting of the Pennsylvania Abolition Society. 12 January 1828 (vol. VIII, no. 168) p.11, c1.

478 A GENTLEMAN RESIDING NEAR LONDONGROVE *to* **THE EDITOR [B. LUNDY]. [extract] n.d. Chester County, Pa.** Encloses an account of a small manufacturing concern with which he is involved; aims to produce cotton goods without slave labor. 26 January 1828 (vol. VIII, no. 169) p.22, c3.

479 n.n. *to* **n.n. [from the** *National Advocate***] 24 January 1828. Washington, D.C.** Reports end of debate over a claim by D. Auterive for compensation for an injury received by his slave during the Battle of New Orleans; believes that the sanctioning of the doctrine of property in slaves would not have been accepted without the aid of Northern votes. 9 February 1828 (vol. VIII, no. 171) p.35, c1.

480 D. HARRYMAN *to* **THE AMERICAN CONVENTION FOR PROMOTING THE ABOLITION OF SLAVERY, AND IMPROVING THE CONDITION OF THE AFRICAN RACE. 21 September 1827. Baltimore.** Discusses legal status of slaves in Maryland; mentions a petition to Congress to abolish slavery in Washington; suggests initiating correspondence with the ACS. 23 February 1828 (vol. VIII, no. 172) p.44, c1.

481 PHILO-AFRICUS *to* **MR. SKILLMAN. [from the** *Western* **(Ky.)** *Luminary***] n.d. n.p.** Discusses recent attendance at a religious meeting for people of color; advocates giving greater attention to the religious instruction of blacks. 23 February 1828 (vol. VIII, no. 172) p.47, c1.

482 n.n. *to* **n.n. [extract from the** *National Advocate***] n.d. Richmond.** Believes that practices and ways of life must change in Virginia; discusses the effect of slave labor on agriculture and the balance of trade. 23 February 1828 (vol. VIII, no. 172) p.47, c1.

483 PHILO-AFRICUS *to* **MR. SKILLMAN. [from the** *Western Luminary***] n.d. n.p.** Discusses recent evening of religious instruction, "holden *specially* for the blacks"; adds that there are now twelve black persons who wish to join the congregation. 1 March 1828 (vol. VIII, no. 173) p.51, c2.

484 SAMUEL JANNEY *to* **THE AMERICAN CONVENTION FOR PROMOTING THE ABOLITION OF SLAVERY AND IMPROVING THE CONDITION OF THE AFRICAN RACE. 28 September 1827. Alexandria, Va.** Regrets his inability to send delegates to the meeting; discusses the history of the society and its accomplishments. 1 March 1828 (vol. VIII, no. 173) p.52, c1.

485 JUDGE BRICE *to* **THE GOVERNOR OF MARYLAND. [extract] 11 December 1827. Baltimore.** Believes penal laws require thorough revision; discusses Penitentiary Law; claims that many of the black population are jailed because they are unprepared for freedom and reduced to theft; argues that manumission contingent on certain terms is unfair, as it places the Negroes in a sort of middle class which is neither slave nor free. 1 March 1828 (vol. VIII, no. 173) p.54, c1.

486 A FREE CONSCIENCE *to* **n.n. [from the** *Baltimore Patriot***] 14 February 1828. Eastern Shore, Md.** Declares himself unimpressed by Judge Brice's desire to restrict manumissions. 1 March 1828 (vol. VIII, no. 173) p.54, c2.

487 A SOUTHERN MAN *to* **THE EDITOR [B. LUNDY]. n.d. n.p.** Cancels his subscription because he feels that Lundy prints too many articles giving rise to fears of insurrection; disagrees with colonizationists and others who fear the presence of free Negroes incites slave insurrection. 8 March 1828 (vol. VIII, no. 174) p.63, c2.

488 CORRESPONDING COMMITTEE OF THE MANUMISSION SOCIETY OF NEW YORK *to* **SIR. n.d. n.p.** Reports decision to correspond with distinguished persons interested in the emancipation of slaves and the abolition of slavery in Washington, D.C.; adds that the society is circulating a memorial to be sent to both houses of Congress on the subject of abolition. 15 March 1828 (vol. VIII, no. 175) p.68, c1.

489 n.n. *to* **EDITORS OF THE** *NEW YORK GAZETTE.* **[extract] 19 January. Washington.** Cautions that issues recently under debate in Congress are being affected by extraneous feelings; reports that the presidential question is alluded to in every discussion. 15 March 1828 (vol. VIII, no. 175) p.70, c3.

490 A GENTLEMAN IN LOUDON COUNTY *to* **n.n. [extract] 10 March 1828. Virginia.** Describes recent incident in which a slave woman poisoned herself rather than be sold. 29 March 1828 (vol. VIII, no. 176) p.75, c3.

491 REV. STEPHEN TAYLOR *to* **GENTLEMEN. [from the** *Visitor and Telegraph***] n.d. n.p.** Reports thirty dollar donation for the religious education of slaves. 29 March 1828 (vol. VIII, no. 176) p.79, c1.

492 INCOGNITO *to* **MESSRS. EDITORS OF THE** *VISITOR AND TELEGRAPH.* **n.d. n.p.** Asks fellow Presbyterians why they do not give their slaves religious education; suggests joint construction of a special church; sends thirty dollars to Rev. Taylor. 29 March 1828 (vol. VIII, no. 176) p.79, c1.

493 n.n. *to* **THE EDITOR OF THE** *MASSACHUSETTS JOURNAL.* **[extract] 8 February 1828. Washington.** Reports consternation in House of Representatives at request to propose a resolution involving the multiplication of postal routes. 29 March 1828 (vol. VIII, no. 176) p.80, c2.

494 n.n. *to* **SIR. 13 December 1827. Natchez, Ms.** Requests intercession of the Department of State on behalf of Abduhl Rahhahman, nephew of the former King of Timbuktu, who has been held as a slave in this country for thirty-nine years. 12 April 1828 (vol. VIII, no. 177) p.84, c1.

495 SPIRIT OF '28 *to* **MR. EDITOR. [from the** *Ithaca Chronicle***] n.d. n.p.** Describes being rudely awaken by inexplicable sounds of gunfire and ringing bells; adds that upon discovering that they were commemorating the Battle of New Orleans, he considers General Jackson a lucky man. 12 April 1828 (vol. VIII, no. 177) p.88, c2.

496 A COLORED AMERICAN *to* **MESSRS. EDITORS OF THE** *BOSTON AMERICAN.* **n.d. n.p.** Criticizes recent article signed by "an American Citizen"; declares that his statement that marriages between free blacks are illegal in Maryland was completely unfounded. 3 May 1828 (vol. VIII, no. 197) p.99, c1.

497 THOMAS B. RUTTER AND WILLIAM L. GILL *to* **FELLOW CITIZENS AND FELLOW CHRISTIANS. January 1828. Baltimore.** Report resolution of Young Men's Bible Society of Baltimore to provide every poor family in Maryland with a Bible in a year's time; discuss reasons for this campaign and detail a plan of action. 3 May 1828 (vol. VIII, no. 197) p.101, c3.

498 LINDLEY *to* **MR. EDITOR [B. LUNDY]. December 1827. Randolph, N.C.** Examines the validity of American claims to be a land of liberty, and concludes that they are ill-founded; brands American slavery a "most unhallowed system of superlative oppression, violence and barbarity"; charges that the United States has never offered an asylum to the oppressed. 10 May 1828 (vol. VIII, no. 198) p.109, c1.

499 CLARKSON *to* **MR. EDITOR [B. LUNDY]. n.d. n.p.** Discusses the possibility of blacks driving cabs and carts; hopes blacks will not be deprived of means to earn a living; claims that common justice dictates that Negroes be allowed to make themselves useful. 10 May 1828 (vol. VIII, no. 198) p.109, c3.

500 S. W. C. *to* **MR. EDITOR [B. LUNDY]. n.d. n.p.** Defends blacks against charges that they are an inferior race; encourages blacks to obtain an education; rejoices in the appearance of new abolitionist societies. 24 May 1828 (vol. VIII, no. 199) p.115, c1.

501 THEO. FRELINGHUYSEN *to* **REV. R. R. GURLEY. 15 March 1828. Newark.** Acknowledges receipt of a letter concerning Gerrit Smith's proposition to raise funds for the CS, which he considers the best hope for Africa's "unhappy children"; agrees to donate one hundred dollars a year for ten years. 24 May 1828 (vol. VIII, no. 199) p.115, c3.

502 LINDLEY *to* **MR. EDITOR [B. LUNDY]. December 1827. Randolph, N. C.** Poses a series of rhetorical questions concerning the status of the African race in America; concludes that free Negroes are only one step removed from the status of slaves. 24 May 1828 (vol. VIII, no. 199) p.116, c1.

503 JAMES CROPPER *to* **THE EDITORS OF THE** *LIVERPOOL MERCURY.* **n.d. n.p.** Argues that a reduction in the value of labor will not abolish slavery; discusses the profitability of slavery compared to that of free labor. 7 June 1828 (vol. VIII, no. 200) p.122, c2.

504 CONSTITUENT *to* **REPRESENTATIVE IN THE LAST CONGRESS. [extract] n.d. n.p.** Admits the necessity of linking emancipation and colonization, but does not believe that freeing slaves without plans for colonization will result in danger. 7 June 1828 (vol. VIII, no. 200) p.125, c1.

505 A HOG REEVE *to* **MR. EDITOR. [from the** *Newburyport Herald*] **n.d. n.p.** Announces his election as a Hog Reeve and details his plans for carrying out the job. 14 June 1828 (vol. VIII, no. 201) p.136, c2.

506 A. M'ILHENNY *to* **SIR. [from the** *Political Examiner*] **28 May 1828. Union Town.** Fails to understand why people wish to replace President Adams with a man about whom they know very little; relates 1811 incident in which Jackson behaved abusively toward an agent of the Choctaw nation when asked to show his passport. 21 June 1828 (vol. VIII, no. 202) p.139, c2.

507 R. *to* **MR. EDITOR [from the** *Vermont Chronicle*] **n.d. n.p.** Describes an encounter with two young boys driving an ox sled across which sprawled their drunken father. 21 June 1828 (vol. VIII, no. 202) p.144, c2.

508 A COLORED BALTIMOREAN *to* **MR. EDITOR [B. LUNDY]. n.d. n.p.** Derides the ACS for presenting itself as the representative of free people of color; challenges them to call public meetings of his people and learn their true opinions of colonization. 28 June 1828 (vol. VIII, no. 203) p.146, c2.

509 AN OBSERVER *to* **MR. EDITOR [B. LUNDY]. 4 JUNE 1828. North Carolina.** Ridicules Fourth of July celebrations; declares that the time has come to admit that the despotism of slavery is worse than that practiced by any European government; claims that the promises of the Declaration of Independence are withheld from Negroes. 28 June 1828 (vol. VIII, no. 203) p.148, c1.

510 WANDERER *to* **MESSRS. EDITORS OF THE** *GEORGIA COURIER*. **n.d. n.p.** Describes a public oration delivered by a bear hunter in the mountains. 4 July 1828 (vol. VIII, no. 204) p.160, c1.

511 W. L. *to* **MR. EDITOR [B. LUNDY]. n.d. n.p.** Declares that if we extend the blessings of liberty to all within our boundaries, we will be doing more to promote the principles of liberty than has ever been done; rejoices that the CS is growing, and believes it to be the only plan by which slavery can be abolished. 12 July 1828 (vol. VIII, no. 205) p.164, c1.

512 S. *to* **MR. EDITOR [B. LUNDY]. n.d. n.p.** Encloses an extract from a speech by Sir William Joneson on slavery. 26 July 1828 (vol. VIII, no. 207) p.179, c3.

513 NESTOR *to* **MR. EDITOR [B. LUNDY]. n.d. n.p.** Charges South with bribing legislators; condemns "white slaves" in the North—representatives who are slaves to money and power, whom the South has been able to buy. 26 July 1828 (vol. VIII, no. 207) p.182, c3.

514 JOHN VANBLARIOUM *to* **THE FREEMEN OF INDIANA. n.d. n.p.** Discusses his intention of running for governor. 26 July 1828 (vol. VIII, no. 207) p.184, c2.

515 A FRIEND TO JUSTICE *to* **MR. EDITOR [B. LUNDY]. n.d. n.p.** Chastizes "A Friend to Civility" for instructing colored population to be careful not to push or press against anyone; asks if he is advising colored people to walk in the gutters. 23 August 1828 (vol. VIII, no. 210) p.194, c3.

516 J. A. H. *to* **MR. EDITOR [B. LUNDY]. 1828. Arkansas Territory.** Describes a case in which a man freed his slaves in a will executed prior to his death; following his death, the man's sons were attempting to break the will when a newly freed slave shot one of them. 23 August 1828 (vol. VIII, no. 210) p.195, c3.

517 A FRENCH DOCTOR WHO HAS LIVED IN CONSTANTINOPLE FOR THIRTY YEARS *to* **n.n. [extract from the** *Smyrna Courier*] **n.d. n.p.** Describes the successful vaccination of the young children of the Turkish sultan; before Turkey accepted Western ideas, no Christian was allowed for any reason to lay hands on an Ottoman prince. [original in French] 16 September 1828 (vol. X, no. 223) p.16, c2.

518 n.n. *to* **n.n. [extract from the** *Augsbourg Gazette*] **3 November. London.** Reports on the continuation of the conference on Greek affairs: if the Divan accepts limits on power of the Greek state and renounces his rights to tribute and suzerainty, Greece will be accepted as a European Power; if not, it will be placed under the protection of France, England and Russia; asserts that many princes are already intriguing for the Greek monarchy in spite of the limits on its independence. [original in French] 16 September 1828 (vol. X, no. 243) p.136, c3.

[1829]

519 WM. LLOYD GARRISON *to* **THE PUBLIC. n.d. n.p.** Declares that, despite his devotion to slave emancipation, he has not forgotten other reform causes; states his views on abolition and emancipation; considers colonization an inadequate remedy, but prefers Haiti to Liberia. 2 September 1829 (vol. X, no. 227) p.5, c3.

520 AN OBSERVER *to* **MESSRS. EDITORS [BENJAMIN LUNDY AND W. L. GARRISON]. n.d. n.p.** Describes fourteenth of July celebration by blacks, observing that there was moderate drinking, no swearing and no rowdy behavior; reports poorly-received oration by local clergyman who claimed that the liberation of the slaves would not be to their benefit. 2 September 1829 (vol. X, no. 227) p.7, c1.

521 SIMPLET *to* **ADOLPHE. 3 August 1829. New York.** Describes New York City and the ethnic diversity of its inhabitants; sends his friend a book of caricatures, *Life in Philadelphia.* [original in French] 16 September 1829 (vol. X, no. 223) p.16, c2.

522 A FRIEND TO THE CAUSE *to* **THE EDITORS OF THE** *GENIUS OF UNIVERSAL EMANCIPATION* **[B. LUNDY AND W. L. GARRISON]. n.d. n.p.** Criticizes the report of blacks celebrating the fourteenth of July; questions the means by which Garrison and Lundy are pursuing the goal of emancipation; charges that Lundy tacitly approved the conduct of a Negro who stabbed a policeman. 16 September 1829 (vol. X, no. 228) p.14, c4.

523 SIMPLET *to* **n.n. August 1829. New York.** Gives his impressions of New York. [original in French] 16 September 1829 (vol. X, no. 228) p.16, c2.

524 GEORGE COLE *to* **THE EDITORS OF THE** *GENIUS OF UNIVERSAL EMANCIPATION* **[BENJAMIN LUNDY AND W. L. GARRISON]. n.d. Port-au-Prince.** Learns that many slaveholders are willing to set their slaves free upon the condition that they leave the United States; recommends Haiti because it has rich soil and pays good wages. 25 September 1829 (vol. X, no. 229) p.18, c1.

525 n.n. *to* **n.n. [from the** *Plymouth Journal***] 18 April 1818. Havana.** Reports witnessing the cruelty and hardships slaves endure on the Spanish schooner *Josepha* sailing from the coast of Africa. 25 September 1829 (vol. X, no. 229) p.19, c3.

526 G. *to* **MESSRS. EDITORS [BENJAMIN LUNDY AND W. L. GARRISON]. n.d. n.p.** Encloses ten year-old poem which he believes relates to the objectives of the newspaper. 9 October 1829 (vol. X, no. 231) p.35, c4.

527 D. RAYMOND *to* **VOTERS OF THE CITY OF BALTIMORE. 25 September 1829. n.p.** Claims that his friends announced him as a candidate for the legislature without his knowledge; consents to allow his name to remain on the ballot, but will not actively campaign; explains his conception of the duties of a representative. 9 October 1829 (vol. X, no. 231) p.38, c1.

528 n.n. *to* **THE EDITORS OF THE** *GENIUS OF UNIVERSAL EMANCIPATION* **[B. LUNDY AND W. L. GARRISON]. [extract] 8 September 1829. Port-au-Prince.** Reports high prices of staple goods due to a lack of shipments; complains that times are dull. 9 October 1829 (vol. X, no. 231) p.38, c4.

529 n.n. *to* **EDITORS [BENJAMIN LUNDY AND W. L. GARRISON]. 6 October 1829. Salisbury, Pa.** Expresses his pleasure with the editors' principles; believes no danger exists in emancipating slaves. 16 October 1829 (vol. X, no. 232) p.41, c1.

530 THOMAS JEFFERSON *to* **EDWARD COLES. 25 August 1814. Monticello.** States that he hoped that the first generation of free Americans would emancipate the slaves; believes that the time of emancipation is fast approaching; advocates the emancipation of those born after a certain date. 22 October 1829 (vol. X, no. 233) p.49, c1.

531 LUTHER *to* **MR. CONVERSE. [from the** *Richmond Visitor and Telegraph***] n.d. n.p.** Rejoices at the growing interest in temperance; complains that the sin of adultery is ignored. 22 October 1829 (vol. X, no. 233) p.49, c4.

532 n.n. *to* **n.n. [extract] n.d. Pennsylvania.** Praises Garrison's views, but questions immediate emancipation; insists that education must accompany emancipation. 30 October 1829 (vol. X, no. 234) p.57, c3.

533 JAMES L. PIERCE *to* **THE COMMITTEE OF THE FREE PRODUCE SOCIETY. 28 September 1829. Philadelphia.** Details difficulties involved in obtaining free goods. 30 October 1829 (vol. X, no. 234) p.58, c3.

534 n.n. *to* **n.n. [extract] n.d. Massachusetts.** Suggests they use a less strident tone in order to gain more sympathy for the cause and to make their statements less liable to charges of extravagance. 30 October 1829 (vol. X, no. 234) p.59, c2.

535 AGNES *to* **ISABEL. n.d. n.p.** Fails to understand Isabel's lack of interest in the issue of slavery. 30 October 1829 (vol. X, no. 234) p.60, c2.

536 ROBERT LEEKE *to* **ALL WHOM IT MAY CONCERN. 4 April 1829. Washington.** Requests information about Adam Smith, who is claimed by two slave traders as a slave, but who maintains that he is a free white. 6 November 1829 (vol. X, no. 235) p.67, c4.

537 LADIES' SOCIETY FOR THE ENCOURAGEMENT OF FREE LABOR *to* **FRIEND. 31 April [sic] 1829. Philadelphia.** Attempts to introduce and promote the use of cotton goods produced by free labor. 6 November 1829 (vol. X, no. 235) p.68, c2.

538 AGNES *to* **ISABEL. n.d. n.p.** Dismisses Isabel's claim that to become an opponent of slavery at this time is inconvenient; rejects the excuse that others with stronger religious convictions are uninvolved; argues that slavery is either positively right or wrong. 6 November 1829 (vol. X, no. 235) p.68, c4.

539 DANIEL O'CONNELL *to* **SIR. [from the** *Cork Mercantile Chronicle***] 13 September 1829. Derrynane Abbey.** States that the vices of great men are doubly enormous as they contradict the tenor of their lives; declares that slavery is a crime and should be abolished; insists upon immediate freedom for every slave; regrets that he had to attack one flaw in George Washington's character. 13 November 1829 (vol. X, no. 236) p.74, c2.

540 n.n. *to* **n.n. n.d. Coast of Africa.** Reports that yellow fever is killing many people, but that Liberia remains a healthy place to live. 13 November 1829 (vol. X, no. 236) p.75, c3.

541 AGNES *to* **ISABEL. n.d. n.p.** Criticizes silent disapproval of injustice as insufficient; questions Isabel's devotion to justice if she is unwilling to sacrifice luxuries. 13 November 1829 (vol. X, no. 236) p.76, c2.

542 AN ENGLISHMAN *to* **THE EDITORS OF THE** *GENIUS OF UNIVERSAL EMAN-CIPATION* **[B. LUNDY AND W. L. GARRISON]. n.d. n.p.** Complains about American ignorance on the subject of monarchial governments; feels obliged to call attention to the subject of slavery; declares that Americans cannot boast of their country's freedom until people are equally free. 20 November 1829 (vol. X, no. 237) p.81, c1.

543 B. INGINAC *to* **MESSRS. LUNDY AND GARRISON. 19 October 1829. Port-au-Prince.** Acknowledges receipt of Lundy's letter and repeats its contents. 20 November 1829 (vol. X, no. 237) p.86, c3.

544 B. INGINAC *to* **MESSRS. LUNDY AND GARRISON. 19 October 1829. Port-au-Prince.** Acknowledges receipt of Lundy's letters. [original in French] 20 November 1829 (vol. X, no. 237) p.88, c1.

545 B. INGINAC *to* **MR. LUNDY AND MR. GARRISON. 13 October 1829. Port-au-Prince.** Acknowledges receipt of Mr. Lundy's letter to the Haitian President; promises to welcome former slaves as brothers and friends, and expresses delight with the project of Miss Frances Wright to send twenty or thirty imigrants to Haiti; compliments the three first issues of the new series of the *Genius of Universal Emancipation*. 20 November 1829 (vol. X, no. 237) p.88, c1.

546 A COLORED BALTIMOREAN *to* **MESSRS. EDITORS [BENJAMIN LUNDY AND W. L. GARRISON]. n.d. n.p.** Doubts that American people of color can be prevailed upon to leave country; questions the notion that emigration will prove that color is not a barrier to progress; ridicules the idea that blacks are uniquely suited to act as missionaries. 27 November 1829 (vol. X, no. 238) p.89, c1.

547 A BYSTANDER *to* **THE EDITOR OF THE** *GREENBOROUGH* **(N.C.)** *PATRIOT*. **n.d. n.p.** Reports the Randolph Superior Court decision that a master cannot be punished for slave abuse. 27 November 1829 (vol. X, no. 238) p.91, c4.

548 AGNES *to* **ISABEL. n.d. n.p.** Applauds Isabel's newly-adopted resolution; defends herself against the accusation that she exaggerates the problem of slavery, and urges Isabel to convert others to the cause. 27 November 1829 (vol. X, no. 238) p.92, c2.

549 AFRICANUS *to* **GENTLEMEN OF THE** *GENIUS OF UNIVERSAL EMANCIPATION*. **26 November 1829. Washington City.** Argues on the basis of Scripture that education improves the morals of blacks. 4 December 1829 (vol. X, no. 239) p.98, c2.

550 JOHN WHEATLEY [MASTER OF PHYLLIS WHEATLEY] *to* **n.n. [PUBLISHER OF PHYLLIS' WORKS]. 14 November 1772. Boston.** Declares that Phyllis learns quickly and has an exceptional aptitude for learning foreign languages. 4 December 1829 (vol. X, no. 239) p.100, c1.

551 AGNES *to* **ISABEL. n.d. n.p.** Argues that even if a slave has a good master, to hold him in bondage is wrong; adds that to claim Negroes are not educable is to compound the sin of slavery. 4 December 1829 (vol. X, no. 239) p.100, c2.

552 H. G. WARD *to* **RIGHT HONORABLE G. CANNING. 13 March 1826. Mexico.** Describes the free labor system in Mexico; explains that the difficulty of obtaining slaves encouraged land owners to liberate them and allow them to intermarry with Indians, thus propagating a race of free laborers; pronounces the use of free labor successful. 11 December 1829 (vol. X, no. 240) p.105, c3.

553 H. *to* **THE EDITOR. [from the** *Columbia* **(S.C.)** *Telescope*] **n.d. n.p.** Hears that people are teaching slaves to read and write, an act which he brands impolitic, if not criminal; hopes that the new legislative session will pass a law against educating slaves. 11 December 1829 (vol. X, no. 240) p.107, c4.

554 A COLORED OBSERVER *to* **MESSRS. EDITORS [BENJAMIN LUNDY AND W. L. GARRISON]. n.d. n.p.** Criticizes lecture by Rev. Hewitt, who claimed that free people of color suffer greatly from intemperance; reminds that this is an argument used by slaveholders against emancipation; denies that existence of degraded free people of color could justify the perpetuation of slavery. 18 December 1829 (vol. X, no. 241) p.114, c1.

555 A COLORED BALTIMOREAN *to* **MESSRS. EDITORS [BENJAMIN LUNDY AND W. L. GARRISON]. n.d. n.p.** Declares that he is tired of the subject of African colonization and of the public's unwillingness to hear opposition to the CS; proposes to let the burden of collecting funds for colonization fall on those who want people of color out of the country. 18 December 1829 (vol. X, no. 241) p.114, c2.

556 AGNES *to* **ISABEL. n.d. n.p.** Discusses her feelings after reading about 3,000 slaves kept in the hold of a single ship. 18 December 1829 (vol. X, no. 241) p.116, c2.

[1830]

557 T. *to* **MESSRS. EDITORS [BENJAMIN LUNDY AND W. L. GARRISON]. n.d. n.p.** Examines class and reproduction patterns in the South. 1 January 1830 (vol. X, no. 243) p.129, c1.

558 W. *to* **FELLOW CITIZENS. n.d. n.p.** Examines the original thirteen states to show their comparative rates of progress; argues that slavery prevents the South from enjoying prosperity and that the replacement of the slave population by a free population would create more demand for manufactured goods. 1 January 1830 (vol. X, no. 243) p.130, c3.

559 ANOTHER LOW-LANDER *to* **THE EDITORS OF THE** *CONSTITUTIONAL WHIG.* **n.d. n.p.** Complains that while slavery is acknowledged as a curse, every effort appears to be aimed at imposing it on succeeding generations; asks why slaves cannot gradually be emancipated. 8 January 1830 (vol. X, no. 244) p.139, c1.

560 I AM THY FRIEND *to* **ESTEEMED FRIEND. n.d. n.p.** Discusses boycott of goods produced by slave labor; reports that a group is forming to ease the procurement of free goods; refutes the theory that conditions for free laborers may be worse than for slaves by claiming that our trade does not directly affect foreign workers. 8 January 1830 (vol. X, no. 244) p.140, c2.

561 T. B. *to* **MESSRS. EDITORS [BENJAMIN LUNDY AND W. L. GARRISON]. n.d. n.p.** Continues discussion of the marital and reproductive patterns of the Southern classes; proposes to transfer slave ownership to the public by means of a tax. 15 January 1830 (vol. X, no. 245) p.145, c1.

562 W. *to* **MESSRS. EDITORS [BENJAMIN LUNDY AND W. L. GARRISON]. n.d. n.p.** Reports that more free people of color than whites or slaves have passed age forty-five; challenges pro-slavery advocates to explain the discrepancy. 15 January 1830 (vol. X, no. 245) p.145, c4.

563 AGNES *to* **ISABEL. n.d. n.p.** Urges her friend not to despair that slavery will be soon abolished; believes that a reasonable hope exists for emancipation in the near future. 15 January 1830 (vol. X, no. 245) p.148, c2.

564 B[ENJAMIN] FRANKLIN *to* **MR. STRAHAN. 5 July 1775. Philadelphia.** Charges that Strahan is one of that majority of the Parliament which has doomed America to destruction. 15 January 1830 (vol. X, n. 245) p.150, c1.

565 A COLORED BALTIMOREAN *to* **MESSRS. EDITORS [BENJAMIN LUNDY AND W. L. GARRISON]. n.d. n.p.** Accuses Mr. Hepburn of distorting his words; denies that the persistence of slavery is sufficient cause to abandon America, which is the strongest argument Hepburn puts forth in favor of colonization. 29 January 1830 (vol. X, no. 247) p.163, c1.

566 A. G. *to* **MESSRS. EDITORS [BENJAMIN LUNDY AND W. L. GARRISON]. 15 January 1830. Pennsylvania.** Concludes that the division of men into religious sects and political parties is the result of fate rather than conviction; describes his experience collecting signatures on a petition to Congress for the abolition of slavery in Washington, D.C. 5 February 1830 (vol. X, no. 248) p.170, c3.

567 JAMES C. BROWN *to* **n.n. n.d. Canada.** Reports that he and his family have found desirable land and are in good health; requests tobacco and hemp seeds, garden and corn seeds; discusses plans for his house, a school, a church and other buildings. 5 February 1830 (vol. X, no. 248) p.171, c2.

568 HON. R. M. JOHNSON *to* **THE EDITORS OF THE** *JOURNAL OF COMMERCE.* **17 January 1830. City of Washington.** Believes debtors' prisons should be abolished. 5 February 1830 (vol. X, no. 248) p.173, c4.

569 WASHINGTON CORRESPONDENT OF THE *NEW YORK COMMERCIAL ADVERTISER to* **n.n. [extract] n.d. n.p.** Describes a dynamic speech by Daniel Webster concerning powers of federal government. 5 February 1830 (vol. X, no. 248) p.174, c1.

570 n.n. *to* **MESSRS. EDITORS [from the** *Boston Philanthropist and Investigator]* **n.d. n.p.** Describes how she resolved to work toward improving the condition of slaves; tells how her family raised $500 for the CS. 12 February 1830 (vol. X, no. 249) p.180, c3.

571 n.n. *to* **n.n. [extract from the** *Courrier des Etats-Unis***] 7 January 1830. Caracas.** Reports that Generals Bermudas and Monaga and their troops stand ready at the border for Venezuela's defense; morale is excellent, and only friends and relatives of Bolivar have voiced opposition. [original in French] 26 February 1830 (vol. X, no. 251) p.200, c3.

572 n.n. *to* **n.n. [extract] n.d. Salem, Oh.** Applauds their work; reports strong prejudice against blacks, who he claims are illiterate, but moral and industrious; feels that advocates for emancipation were hurting the cause by working for gradual emancipation. 5 March 1830 (vol. X, no. 252) p.202, c2.

573 AGNES *to* **ISABEL. n.d. n.p.** Urges Isabel to continue her efforts in behalf of the slave. 5 March 1830 (vol. X, no. 252) p.204, c1.

574 CIVIS *to* **THE PUBLIC n.d. n.p.** Encourages boycott of slave produce; compares domestic and foreign slave trade; believes that slaveholders would be better served if they used free labor which is cheaper than slave labor. April 1830 (vol. XI, no. 253) p.7, c2.

575 n.n. *to* **THE EDITOR OF THE** *GENIUS OF UNIVERSAL EMANCIPATION.* **[extract] 7 March 1830. Port-au-Prince.** Reports arrival of Frances Wright and twenty freed slaves; informs that they have been settled on the president's land. April 1830 (vol. XI, no. 253) p.16, c2.

576 JOHN N. COSTE *to* **JOHN NOEL. [extract] 21 January 1830. Port-au-Prince.** Reports on the condition of emigrants brought by Lundy. April 1830 (vol. XI, no. 253) p.16, c2.

577 JUSTICE *to* **THE EDITOR OF THE** *GENIUS OF UNIVERSAL EMANCIPATION.* **n.d. n.p.** Praises him for his stand against the "intolerable abuse" of the Constitution by legislators who enacted Louisiana's *Codes Noirs.* [original in French] May 1830 (vol. XI, no. 254) p.29, c1.

578 R. KING, JR. *to* **WILLIAM WASHINGTON. 13 September 1828. Hampton.** Discusses management of the Butler Estate and the cultivation of sugar cane. May 1830 (vol. XI, no. 254) p.30, c1.

579 G. B. *to* **EDITORS. [from the** *United States Gazette***] n.d. n.p.** Expresses pleasure upon learning that the colonization committee intends to send a ship to Liberia in September; states intention of sending one hundred dollar donation to the committee. June 1830 (vol. XI, no. 255) p.36, c2.

580 BENJAMIN LUNDY *to* **THE EDITOR OF THE** *MINERVA.* **24 June 1830. Baltimore.** Charges the editor with misquoting him and drawing the unfounded conclusion that Garrison "suffered voluntary imprisonment" in the Todd case; explains that Garrison did not have money to pay the fine, and thus had no choice but to go to prison. July 1830 (vol. XI, no. 256) p.51, c2.

581 WM. LLOYD GARRISON *to* **NICHOLAS BRICE, JUDGE OF BALTIMORE CITY COURT. 13 May 1830. Baltimore Jail.** Intends to write a series of articles about Brice's treatment of his case. July 1830 (vol. XI, no. 256) p.54, c1.

582 WM. LLOYD GARRISON *to* **RICHARD W. GILL, DEPUTY ATTORNEY FOR THE STATE. 13 May 1830. Baltimore Jail.** Informs Gill of his intention to write a sketch of his trial with an unflattering portrait of Gill; criticizes him for his remarks on slavery during the trial. July 1830 (vol. XI, no. 256) p.54, c2.

583 WM. LLOYD GARRISON *to* **MR. HENRY THOMPSON. 13 May 1830. Baltimore Jail.** Declares that he does not begrudge Thompson the pleasure he is getting from his imprisonment. July 1830 (vol. XI, no. 256) p.54, c2.

584 n.n. *to* **EDITOR [BENJAMIN LUNDY]. [extract] n.d. Tennessee.** Observes that Southerners are concerned about their future because they realize that slavery cannot continue, and that something must be done with the black population once they are free; proposes colonization utilizing the Navy's ships, and sharecropping as solutions. August 1830 (vol. XI, no. 257) p.65, c2.

585 n.n. *to* **THE EDITOR [BENJAMIN LUNDY]. [extract] 5 July 1830. Hayti.** Reports that the emigrants whom Lundy helped to settle at l'Arcahai are well and happy. August 1830 (vol. XI, no. 257) p.68, c1.

586 JEFFERSON *to* **MR. EDITOR [BENJAMIN LUNDY]. August 1830. Baltimore.** Reminds citizens to renew their petitions to the state legislature on the subject of gradual abolition of slavery. August 1830 (vol. XI, no. 257) p.70, c2.

587 MUSHULATUBA, CHIEF OF THE CHOCTAW NATION *to* **THE VOTERS OF MISSISSIPPI. [from the** *Courrier des Etas Unis***] 1 April 1830. The Choctaw Nation.** Asserts his devotion to the country, the Republic, and her laws; wishes to fulfill his duties as an American citizen by representing them in Congress; asks their support. [original in French] August 1830 (vol. XI, no. 257) p.77, c2.

588 CONSISTENCY *to* **EDITOR [BENJAMIN LUNDY]. 8 June 1830. Minot, Me.** A former slaveholder argues that political liberty is essential neither for happiness nor for our form of government, but that personal liberty is essential; its loss is the "greatest calamity which can befall an innocent man"; denies nevertheless that Scripture permits man to secure either by violent means. September 1830 (vol. XI, no. 258) p.84, c2.

589 S. R. J. *to* **MR. LUNDY. 1830. Western Virginia.** Encloses correspondence for Lundy's use. September 1830 (vol. XI, no. 258) p.85, c2.

590 A FRIEND *to* **n.n. [extract] n.d. n.p.** Declares that he does not believe that the individual can do anything about slavery, and that the American people are neither interested nor willing to act against it. September 1830 (vol. XI, no. 258) p.85, c2.

591 S. R. J. *to* **SIR. n.d. n.p.** Notes that the greatest reforms are achieved by combining the efforts of a few; believes that a remedy can be found for every barrier to emancipation. September 1830 (vol. XI, no. 258) p.86, c1.

592 THOMAS CRUSE *to* **THE PUBLICK. 29 September 1830. Baltimore.** Reports he has received no answer to his offer to buy all female slaves of a certain age in Baltimore; laments demise of his plan to prevent the birth of any more slaves in his fair city. September 1830 (vol. XI, no. 258) p.86, c2.

593 n.n. *to* **EDITOR [BENJAMIN LUNDY]. n.d. n.p.** Encloses poem inspired by an engraving of female slave in chains which appeared in the *Genius* of the previous May. September 1830 (vol. XI, no. 258) p.91, c1.

594 n.n. *to* **MR. LUNDY. [extract] n.d. n.p.** Protests sentencing of Garrison. October 1830 (vol. XI, no. 259) p.104, c2.

595 A. B. *to* **FRIEND B. LUNDY. [extract] n.d. n.p.** Encloses extract of a letter questioning the proposition that, had the Society of Friends remained faithful to their opposition to slavery, they would have addressed themselves to the use of slave produce. November 1830 (vol. XI, no. 260) p.117, c2.

596 THY ASSURED FRIEND *to* **BELOVED FRIEND. 4 May 1824. n.p.** Declares that only blindness to "new creation" explains the continuation of slavery; discusses boycott of slave produce. November 1830 (vol. XI, no. 260) p.117, c2.

597 JACOB W. PROUT *to* **THE EDITOR [BENJAMIN LUNDY]. [extract] 22 September 1830. Monrovia, Africa.** Reports travel up the St. Paul River by Captain W. F. Martin of the schooner *Zembina*. November 1830 (vol. XI, no. 260) p.119, c1.

[1831]

598 n.n. *to* **n.n. [extract] 16 December 1830. n.p.** Believes that the cause of emancipation deserves the sympathy and assistance of every man; encloses money for one year's subscription. January 1831 (vol. XI, no. 262) p.150, c1.

599 n.n. *to* **n.n. 18 December 1830. n.p.** Forwards donation to the *Genius* from several colored individuals. January 1831 (vol. XI, no. 262) p.150, c1.

600 A FRIEND IN PHILADELPHIA *to* **n.n. [extract] 4 November 1830. Philadelphia.** Reports on meeting of colored people to discuss means of promoting the use of free produce; notes the establishment of two free schools for colored adults. January 1831 (vol. XI, no. 262) p.150, c2.

601 ANTHONY BENEZET *to* **ABBE RAYNAL. [extract] 16 July 1781. n.p.** Condemns Guinea slave trade and the encouragement of natives to kidnap each other for slave trade. January 1831 (vol. XI, no. 262) p.151, c2.

602 PATRICK HENRY *to* **n.n. 18 January 1776. Hanover.** Acknowledges receipt of Anthony Benezet's book on the slave trade; finds it surprising that Christians should encourage slave trade in enlightened times; regrets that he himself owns slaves; believes that the time for abolition is approaching. January 1831 (vol. XI, no. 262) p.151, c2.

603 PRESBYTERY OF CHILICOTHE *to* **CHURCHES UNDER THEIR CARE. [extract] n.d. n.p.** Forwards an anti-slavery resolution, along with an explanation of its meaning. January 1831 (vol. XI, no. 262) p.158, c2.

604 n.n. *to* **THE EDITOR [BENJAMIN LUNDY]. [extract] 22 December 1830. Alexandria.** Reports departure on 18 December of brig *Comet*, carrying 170 slaves; informs that the brig *United States* is expected to sail soon with more slaves. January 1831 (vol. XI, no. 262) p.160, c1.

605 WILLIAM LLOYD GARRISON *to* **THE PUBLIC. 1 January 1831. Boston.** Explains his decision to publish his newspaper in Boston; declares that he will not speak moderately or defensively on the subject of slavery. February 1831 (vol. XI, no. 263) p.162, c2.

606 PRESBYTERY OF CHILICOTHE *to* **CHURCHES UNDER THEIR CARE. [extract continued from January 1831] n.d. n.p.** Discusses the apostolic teachings on slavery; insist that it is incredible that apostles would preach against every sin but slavery. February 1831 (vol. XI, no. 263) p.165, c2.

607 n.n. *to* **n.n. [extract] 17 March 1831. Havana.** Reports that planters are doing poorly because sugar and coffee prices are low; informs that nearly 2,000 Negroes landed at ports in Cuba worth only $250.00 each. April 1831 (supplement to vol. XI) p.200, c2.

608 G. *to* **MR. LUNDY. n.d. n.p.** Believes that a great injustice is done the colored population overlooking their accomplishments and causing discouragement; discusses the meeting of a free produce association attended by the writer. June 1831 (vol. XII, no. 266) p.23, c1.

609 n.n. *to* **MR. LUNDY. n.d. n.p.** Favors preventing slavery, but cannot support more than this; refuses to discuss the right to hold slaves as property; states his willingness to reinvest in more profitable capital, but doubts that anything can be done for present generation. June 1831 (vol. XII, no. 266) p.26, c1.

610 A COLORED BALTIMOREAN *to* **MR. EDITOR [BENJAMIN LUNDY]. 4 July 1831. Baltimore.** Asserts that nothing past or present supports the doctrine that people of color should share equally the rights of free men; argues that the Declaration of Independence will not permit the perpetuation of black degradation. July 1831 (vol. XII, no. 267) p.46, c2.

611 A GENTLEMAN IN NORTH CAROLINA *to* **THE EDITOR [BENJAMIN LUNDY]. [extract] 3 June 1831. North Carolina.** Deplores slavery and wishes that its abolition were already underway; contends that slavery was never abolished out of justice or humanity, but because the interests of those in power were better suited by abolition. August 1831 (vol. XII, no. 268) p.50, c2.

612 A FRIEND IN LOWER VIRGINIA *to* **n.n. [extract] 15 May 1831. Virginia.** Discusses his attempts to open discussion on the subject of slavery. August 1831 (vol. XII, no. 268) p.51, c1.

613 A GENTLEMAN RESIDING IN DISTRICT OF COLUMBIA *to* **SIR. n.d. Washington.** Requests that his name be added to list of subscribers; believes that in 150 years blacks will completely possess the Southern states because the laboring classes will have emigrated; warns that slaveowners believe they can defeat liberty by dissolving the Union. August 1831 (vol. XII, no. 268) p.51, c1.

614 EDITOR OF THE *NORFOLK* **(Va.)** *HERALD to* **n.n. 24 August 1831. Virginia.** Reports slave insurrection in upper Southampton County during which forty or fifty people were killed; includes list of victims. August 1831 (vol. XII, no. 268) p.62, c1.

615 n.n. *to* **n.n. [extract from the** *Richmond Whig***] 23 August 1831. n.p.** Describes slave revolt in Southampton County. August 1831 (vol. XII, no. 268) p.63, c1.

616 AUSTIN STEWARD AND BENJAMIN PAUL *to* **MR. EDITOR [BENJAMIN LUNDY]. n.d. Wilberforce Settlement, Upper Canada.** Describe progress of the settlement. September 1831 (vol. XII, no. 269) p.79, c2.

617 HUMANITAS *to* **MESSRS. EDITORS OF THE** *NEW YORK GENIUS OF TEMPERANCE***. n.d. n.p.** Proposes "total abstinence" from the use of slave produce as a means of abolishing slavery; suggests organizing ASS along the lines of temperance societies. December 1831 (vol. XII, no. 271) p.112, c1.

[1832]

618 AN OFFICER ON BOARD THE *POTOMAC to* **A GENTLEMAN IN NEW YORK. 23 October 1831. Rio de Janeiro Harbor.** Reports insurrection of the blacks on the island Cobras; rebels intended to capture Rio, but the disturbance was quelled. January 1832 (vol. XII, no. 272) p.125, c1.

619 n.n. *to* **n.n. [extract] 9 October 1831. Rio de Janeiro.** Reports excitement over the discovery of a cache of arms; states that authorities were informed of an attempt by mulattoes to overthrow the government. January 1832 (vol. XII, no. 272) p.125, c2.

620 n.n. *to* **n.n. 16 November 1831. Macon, Ga.** Reports violence against John Lamb for receiving the newspaper; warns that mob is preparing editor's effigy for burning. January 1832 (vol. XII, no. 272) p.127, c1.

621 B. LUNDY *to* **THE AMERICAN CONVENTION. 11 December 1829. Washington.** Encloses committee report on the cultivation of sugar, cotton and other crops by free labor. February 1832 (vol. XII, no. 273) p.146, c2.

622 MR. WARD *to* **HON. GEORGE CANNING. [extract] 13 March 1826. n.p.** Reports that the possibility of introducing a free labor system into the West Indies is under discussion in England; cites results of an experiment in Mexico with free labor. February 1832 (vol. XII, no. 273) p.146, c2.

623 NAT FIELD *to* **GENTLEMEN. [from the** *Liberator***] 4 February 1832. Jeffersonville, In.** Believes that his suspicion that freedom of the press is being curtailed in South Carolina has been confirmed; denies that his pamphlet is incendiary. May 1832 (vol. XII, no. 276) p.193, c2.

624 n.n. *to* **n.n. n.d. Gloucester, Sierra Leone.** Believes that with equal opportunity, Africans can develop in the same manner as other members of society; denies that their minds are inferior. May 1832 (vol. XII, no. 276) p.197, c1.

625 A COLORED CITIZEN OF BROOKLYN *to* **MR. GARRISON. [from the** *Liberator***] n.d. New York.** Declares that the Wilberforce settlement has exceeded the expectations of many, and contrasts it to Liberia. May 1832 (vol. XII, no. 276) p.199, c2.

626 HENRY DRAYTON AND HENRY JOHNSON *to* **MR. EDITOR [BENJAMIN LUNDY]. 28 June 1832. Hartford.** Report their mistreatment by officers of the steamboat *McDonough* during a recent trip from New York to Hartford, adding that they believe the CS to be responsible. 1832 (vol. XII supplement) p.202, c1.

627 THOMAS JEFFERSON *to* **SIR. 25 August 1814. Monticello.** Admits that he had hoped that the first generation born in liberty would free the slaves; believes that the hour of emancipation will come; favors the proposal for emancipating those born after a given day. 1832 (vol. XII supplement) p.203, c1.

628 GODERICH *to* **GOVERNOR, SIR J. C. SMYTH, BAHAMAS. 29 May 1832. Downing Street.** Informs Smyth that a condition must be inserted in future land grants by the Crown providing for the forfeiture of the land if it is cultivated by slaves. November 1832 (vol. XIII, no. 277) p.10, c2.

629 DAVID G. BURNETT *to* **ANTHONY DEY, WM. H. SUMNER, AND GEORGE CURTIS. [extract] November 1830. n.p.** Receives grant of land in Texas; describes the land. December 1832 (vol. XIII, no. 278) p.21, c1.

630 A WORTHY CLERGYMAN *to* **THE EDITOR [BENJAMIN LUNDY]. n.d. n.p.** Laments selfishness and inconsistency of elected officials who do nothing about slavery; wishes to know why no money is appropriated for slave emancipation or education; calls efforts of the CS only slightly helpful. December 1832 (vol. XIII, no. 278) p.24, c1.

631 n.n. *to* **FRIEND. 7 December 1832. Wilberforce, Canada.** Prays for success of Lundy's trip to Mexico because the establishment of a Southern colony would open new possibilities for emancipation; reports that the settlement is doing well. December 1832 (vol. XIII, no. 278) p.25, c2.

[1833]

632 CHARLES STEWART *to* **THE EDITOR [BENJAMIN LUNDY]. 30 July 1831. London.** Praises the ACS for its efforts to civilize Africa; protests failure to attack prejudice against free people of color; believes that substitution of colonization for emancipation is a bane for all people of color. January 1833 (vol. XIII, no. 279, p.34, c2.

633 DAVID G. BURNETT *to* **ANTHONY DEY, WM. H. SUMNER, AND GEORGE CURTIS. [extract continued from December 1832] November 1830. n.p.** Continues glowing description of his land in Texas. January 1833 (vol. XIII, no. 279) p.36, c1.

634 THOMAS JEFFERSON *to* **T. J. RANDOLPH. 25 August 1814. Monticello.** Declares the plight of slaves a disgrace; proposes gradual emancipation. January 1833 (vol. XIII, no. 279) p.38, c2.

635 A COLORED FEMALE OF PHILADELPHIA *to* **THE *LIBERATOR*. 2 January 1832. Pennsylvania.** Feels that emigrants must become part of established society; reminds that other governments offer equal rights to men, including colored citizens; believes that Mexico is the best country for emigration. January 1833 (vol. XIII, no. 279) p.46, c1.

636 JAMES CROPPER *to* **FRIEND. 2 October 1832. Liverpool.** Regrets seeing him listed as a supporter of the ACS; claims that society arose from prejudice against free blacks; believes that slaveowners fear competition from free black labor; argues that the colonization of all blacks is not feasible. February 1833 (vol. XIII, no. 280) p.53, c2.

637 CORRESPONDING COMMITTEE OF THE FREE PRODUCE ASSOCIATION AT GREEN PLAINS, OHIO *to* **THE LADIES' FREE PRODUCE SOCIETY IN PHILADELPHIA. 24 December 1832. Ohio.** Appreciates knowing that others are interested in the acquisition of free goods. March 1833 (vol. XIII, no. 281) p.77, c1.

638 n.n. *to* **LYDIA WHITE. [extract] 10 March 1833. Harrisville, Oh.** Requests information on obtaining free dry goods for a new AS. March 1833 (vol. XIII, no. 281) p.77, c1.

639 F. D. *to* **SIR. [from** *Le Courrier des Etats Unis***] 1 November 1832. Vera Cruz.** Reports on archaeological work of M. J. F. Valdeck in the ruins of Pelenque. April 1833 (vol. XIII, no. 282) p.89, c2.

640 A SUBSCRIBER *to* **THE EDITOR [BENJAMIN LUNDY]. n.d. n.p.** Relates two instances in which giving hired slaves money for personal use increased their output. April 1833 (vol. XIII, no. 282) p.92, c2.

641 SECRETARY OF THE LADIES' NEGRO'S FRIEND SOCIETY *to* **MARQUIS LAFAYETTE. 16 August 1831. n.p.** Asks him to intercede with the new king on behalf of slaves in French colonies. April 1833 (vol. XIII, no. 282) p.93, c1.

642 THOMAS HAMBLETON AND MARTHA LAMBORN *to* **ESTEEMED FRIENDS. 6 April 1833. Oxford, Pa.** Believe that correspondence between different ASS is good; suggest several propositions on the subject of free produce for their consideration; ask for a response. May 1833 (vol. XIII, no. 283) p.110, c1.

643 BENJAMIN LUNDY *to* **THE ANNUAL CONVENTION OF THE FREE PEOPLE OF COLOR. 28 May 1833. Nashville, Tn.** Believes a favorable change in the conditions for people of African descent is at hand; reviews accomplishments of past fifty years with respect to slavery; asks them to consider a provision for an asylum for free Negroes; restates his views on this subject. June 1833 (vol. XIII, no. 284) p.118, c1.

644 A CITIZEN OF TEXAS *to* **SIR. [from the** *Louisiana Advertiser***] n.d. n.p.** Warns not to buy land without first seeing it; discusses land acquisition, and describes Texas. June 1833 (vol. XIII, no. 284) p.120, c1.

645 J. S. P. *to* **MR. EDITOR [BENJAMIN LUNDY]. n.d. n.p.** Praises Garrison's work; maintains that Northerners have the right to interfere in the question of slavery; thinks Southerners do not have a comprehensive view of the issue; declares that it is time to confront the issue of slavery. August 1833 (vol. XIII, no. 286) p.149, c1.

646 A GENTLEMAN IN LOWER VIRGINIA *to* **GEN. GREEN. [extract from the** *Washington Telegraph***] 7 August 1833. Virginia.** Attributes to Northern fanatics the responsibility for creating discontent among the slaves. August 1833 (vol. XIII, no. 286) p.150, c2.

647 BENJAMIN LUNDY *to* **SIR. 8 September 1833. St. Antonio de Bexar, Tx.** Reports cholera at Nashville and Brazoria; describes future travel plans. October 1833 (vol. XIII, no. 288) p.182, c1.

648 T. F. BUXTON *to* **W. L. GARRISON. 12 July 1833. 54 Devonshire Street.** Apologizes for his inability to attend meetings; agrees that the CS is diabolical. October 1833 (vol. XIII, no. 288) p.183, c2.

[1834]

649 CORRESPONDING COMMITTEE OF THE GREEN PLAIN FREE PRODUCE SOCIETY *to* **FRIENDS. 28 May 1833. Green Plain, Oh.** Reports that they have accomplished little as a society, but that the awareness of having done their duty is ample reward. January 1834 (vol. XIV, no. 289) p.13, c2.

650 n.n. *to* **MR. EDITOR, THE** *PRESBYTERIAN.* **n.d. n.p.** Acknowledges having received the proceedings of a recent anti-slavery convention; feels that their actions are unwise and imprudent; asks for an editorial comment which would enlighten deluded men. February 1834 (vol. XIV, no. 290) p.21, c1.

651 n.n. *to* **BENJAMIN LUNDY. 23 November 1833. Washington County, Pa.** Regrets the division among abolitionists over the best means to achieve their goals because it encourages supporters of slavery; advocates emancipation and colonization; suggests that the government provide financial assistance. February 1834 (vol. XIV, no. 290) p.23, c1.

652 B. LUNDY *to* **FRIEND. 23 October 1833. Monclova.** Still hopes for the success of his mission; describes the weather and the landscape. March 1834 (vol. XIV, no. 291) p.37, c1.

653 H. LYMAN *to* **THE EDITOR OF THE** *EMANCIPATOR.* **4 March 1834. Lane Seminary, Walnut Hills, Oh.** Describes the history of anti-slavery feeling at the school and the outcome of a debate on the abolition of slavery and the CS. April 1834 (vol. XIV, no. 292) p.61, c1.

654 EDWIN P. ATLEE *to* **WILLIAM LLOYD GARRISON. 25 March 1834. Philadelphia.** Describes Evan Lewis' illness and death. April 1834 (vol. XIV, no. 292) p.64, c2.

655 T. D. WELD *to* **LEWIS TAPPAN. [from the** *New York Evangelist***] 18 March 1834. Lane Seminary, Oh.** Reports changes in thought regarding slavery; states that students believe faith without works is dead and have formed an organization to aid colored people; requests assistance. May 1834 (vol. XIV, no. 293) p.69, c1.

656 JOSHUA COFFIN *to* **SIR. 23 April 1834. Philadelphia.** Encloses extracts of several letters commenting on conditions in Liberia. May 1834 (vol. XIV, no. 293) p.74, c1.

657 JAMES TEMPLE *to* **JACOB RHODES. [extract] n.d. n.p.** Claims that Liberia is good only for the natives; calls it murder to send people there. May 1834 (vol. XIV, no. 293) p.74, c1.

658 JAMES TEMPLE *to* **REV. THOMAS P. HUNT. [extract] n.d. n.p.** Warns Hunt not to bring his family to Liberia unless they are well equipped; reports that missionaries are needed, and the twenty-five ministers there do nothing; recommends to Hunt that he remain in Philadelphia. May 1834 (vol. XIV, no. 293) p.74, c2.

659 JAMES TEMPLE *to* **THOMAS BLACK. [extract] n.d. n.p.** Expresses disappointment with Africa, but intends to make the best of a bad situation; longs to return home, but fears it would ruin his reputation. May 1834 (vol. XIV, no. 293) p.74, c2.

660 JAMES TEMPLE *to* **THOMAS BLACK. [extract] n.d. n.p.** Calls Africa a land of banishment and misery; cautions that slaves sent to Africa become slaves to the CS; charges the organization with murdering more slaves than have slaveholders during the last twenty years. May 1834 (vol. XIV, no. 293) p.75, c1.

661 JAMES TEMPLE *to* **MR. A. WILLIAMS. 1834. Africa.** Declares Africa unfit for colonization; reports seeing nothing but death and destruction since the first ship arrived; compares the colony to a gloomy prison. May 1834 (vol. XIV, no. 293) p.75, c2.

662 AUGUSTUS WATTLES *to* **EDITORS OF THE** *WESTERN RECORDER.* **6 March 1834. Lane Seminary, Oh.** Describes a recent anti-slavery debate at Lane Seminary; renounces all connections with the CS of Oneida Institute. May 1834 (vol. XIV, no. 293) p.76, c1.

663 A SUBSCRIBER *to* **REV. J. LEAVITT. 7 April 1834. New York.** Describes his response to an account in the *Evangelist* of a colored boy's removal from school on charges of being a slave; encloses a contribution, praying he may not be sent back into slavery. May 1834 (vol. XIV, no. 293) p.78, c1.

664 WILLIAM JAY *to* **SIR. [from the** *New York Evangelist***] 12 February 1834. Bedford.** Questions the expediency of measures adopted by the CS and the soundness of some of its principles; counters the belief that the CS exerts moral influence in favor of emancipation; condemns the society as anti-abolitionist. May 1834 (vol. XIV, no. 293) p.79, c1.

665 BALAAM'S ASS *to* **MR. EDITOR [BENJAMIN LUNDY]. n.d. n.p.** Discusses the treatment of Negroes in Christian churches. June 1834 (vol. XIV, no. 294) p.87, c2.

666 BENJAMIN LUNDY *to* **n.n. [extract] 9 May 1834. Nashville, Tn.** Rejoices to see a change in public sentiment; urges those interested in emancipation onward. June 1834 (vol. XIV, no. 294) p.99, c1.

667 D. I. FISHER *to* **MR. EDITOR [BENJAMIN LUNDY]. n.d. n.p.** Believes the time of emancipation is fast approaching; discusses inconsistencies of pride in American liberty and the existence of slavery; appeals to the Irish, whom he describes as the most prejudiced against the manumission of colored people. July 1834 (vol. XIV, no. 295) p.102, c1.

668 B. LUNDY *to* **PATRONS OF THE** *GENIUS OF UNIVERSAL EMANCIPATION.* **18 June 1831. New Orleans.** Apologizes for his lengthy absence; describes his travels; laments the death of Evan Lewis; requests continued support for the newspaper. July 1834 (vol. XIV, no. 295) p.110, c1.

[1836]

669 STEPHEN F. AUSTIN *to* **THE** *AYUNTAMIENTO* **OF SAN FELIPE DE AUSTIN. 17 January 1834.** Monterrey. Reports his arrest, but does not blame the government; claims that he followed the general wish of those who sent him to promote the forming of Texas into a state of the Union; states that the events in Texas grew out of the revolution of Jalapa. October 1836 (vol. XIV, no. 300) p.169, c2.

670 S. F. AUSTIN *to* **SIR. 4 August 1836. Columbia.** Refuses to decline the nomination for the presidency of Texas; favors the annexation of Texas to the United States, and promises to do everything in his power to effect it with the least delay. October 1836 (vol. XIV, no. 300) p.182, c2.

671 LUCY TOWNSEND *to* **THE** *GENIUS OF UNIVERSAL EMANCIPATION.* **[extract] 21 March 1836. Birmingham, England.** Laments the loss of Miss Chandler. December 1836 (vol. XIV, no. 300) p.185, c2.

[1837]

672 n.n. *to* **FRIEND. 24 July 1837. n.p.** Explains that he was not aware of being behind in his subscription; thinks it ironic that a professed abolitionist should be in debt to an anti-slavery newspaper. July 1837 (vol. XV, no. 301) p.8, c1.

673 A FRIEND *to* **THE** *GENIUS OF UNIVERSAL EMANCIPATION.* **[extract] n.d. n.p.** Describes the spirit of unity and generosity displayed at the anniversary of the Ohio AS; states that slavery must fall because abolitionists cannot be resisted. July 1837 (vol. XV, no. 301) p.9, c2.

674 EDWARD C. DELAVAN *to* **GERRIT SMITH. 10 May 1837. Ballston Centre, N.Y.** Reports that he joined the AS; explains that he hesitated to join earlier because he was afraid of harming the temperance cause with which he is associated; believes that the AS is the only hope for achieving emancipation. July 1837 (vol. XV, no. 301) p.19, c2.

675 ANNA WARREN WESTON, ABBY ANN COX, AND MARY GREW *to* **THE ANTI-SLAVERY WOMEN OF GREAT BRITAIN. 12 May 1837. New York.** Thank them for their sympathy and example; ask them to continue their efforts until slavery is abolished throughout the world; invite them to join the boycott of slave produce; describe their convention. July 1837 (vol. XV, no. 301) p.20, c2.

676 COLORED ABOLITIONISTS OF ST. PIERRE *to* **GENTLEMEN. 25 November 1836. St. Pierre.** Observe that the French government is determined to put an end to colonial slavery; promise their united assistance, but recommend that the government adopt measures to increase colonial industry. July 1837 (vol. XV, no. 301) p.25, c2.

677 H. C. WRIGHT *to* **BROTHER. [from the** *Friend of Man***] 11 May 1837. Boston.** Describes a city near New York which went bankrupt because Southern debtors failed to pay their creditors; reports that banks in Boston and New York have suspended specie payments. July 1837 (vol. XV, no. 301) p.28, c1.

678 C. C. BURLEIGH *to* **n.n. n.d. n.p.** Relates events at the New England AS Convention; reports that abolition appears to be thriving in Massachusetts and New England. July 1837 (vol. XV, no. 301) p.31, c1.

679 MARY S. PARKER AND MARIA WESTON CHAPMAN *to* **FEMALE ASS THROUGHOUT NEW ENGLAND. 7 June 1837. Boston.** Request that the societies aid Sarah and Angelina Grimke in their work; urge them to realize their position and responsibilities to this and coming generations. July 1837 (vol. XV, no. 301) p.38, c1.

680 n.n. *to* **HON. JOHN C. CALHOUN. [from the** *Christian Register and Observer***] 26 April 1837. n.p.** Agrees with Calhoun's statement that a man ought to try to eliminate what he perceives to be a moral evil [slavery]; hopes the statement will encourage open discussion. July 1837 (vol. XV, no. 301) p.39, c2.

681 A SPECTATOR *to* **MR. EDITOR [BENJAMIN LUNDY]. n.d. n.p.** Discusses the debate on whether to emigrate to the southwestern United States would be advantageous to people of color. July 1837 (vol. XV, no. 301) p.41, c2.

682 n.n. *to* **MR. LUNDY. n.d. n.p.** Encloses a poem which Lundy may publish or destroy. July 1837 (vol. XV, no. 301) p.51, c1.

683 VOX POPULI *to* **THE EDITOR OF THE** *QUINCY PATRIOT.* **n.d. n.p.** Commends Adams for his work in the last Congress. July 1837 (vol. XV, no. 301) p.52, c2.

684 MARY S. PARKER AND ANGELINA GRIMKE *to* **THE SOCIETIES OF ANTI-SLAVERY WOMEN IN THE UNITED STATES. n.d. n.p.** Urge the societies to petition for the abolition of slavery in Washington and Florida and for an end to internal slave trade; declare that the influence of women is a dreaded power, and urge women not to be submissive. July 1837 (vol. XV, no. 301) p.53, c1.

685 WILLIAM H. PRITCHARD *to* **THE EDITOR OF THE** *CONSTITUTIONALIST*. **20 December 1836. Aiken S.C.** Describes a recent coroner's inquest concerning the body of a runaway slave who refused to be taken alive. July 1837 (vol. XV, no. 301) p.57, c1.

686 JOSEPH KINGSBURY *to* **SECRETARY OF THE SALISBURY AND AMESBURY AS. [from the** *New England Spectator***] n.d. n.p.** Believes that it is time to join the anti-slavery cause; declares that he had hesitated earlier only because he thought the abolitionists were going too far too fast. July 1837 (vol. XV, no. 301) p.58, c1.

687 JOHN EDGAR, D. D. *to* **MEMBERS OF THE AMERICAN CHURCHES. [from the** *New York Evangelist***] n.d. Belfast.** Comments that while the world rejoices in American liberty, their hearts sink at the thought of American slavery; beseeches them to end slavery. July 1837 (vol. XV, no. 301) p.59, c1.

688 LINDLEY COATES *to* **ESTEEMED FRIEND. [from the** *Liberator***] 17 October 1837. Harrisburg, Pa.** Declares his dissatisfaction with Garrison's stance on the Sabbath; says that the signers of "Clerical Appeal and Protest" were not abolitionists; urges Garrison to continue his work. October 1837 (vol. XV, no. 302) p.64, c2.

689 A CITIZEN OF BUCKS COUNTY *to* **FRIEND. [from the** *National Enquirer***] n.d. n.p.** Discusses a recent election in Bucks County, following which the pro-Van Buren ticket contested the outcome on grounds that voting by people of color is illegal. October 1837 (vol. XV, no. 302) p.66, c2.

690 A GENTLEMAN IN NEW ENGLAND *to* **THE EDITOR [BENJAMIN LUNDY]. [extract] 10 August 1837. n.p.** Denounces resolution offered by a Pennsylvania legislator to the United States House of Representatives declaring that the House could not be petitioned by a slave without debasing its dignity; urges the Friends of Pennsylvania to unseat him. October 1837 (vol. XV, no. 302) p.69, c1.

691 A GENTLEMAN IN NEW YORK *to* **n.n. [extract] 18 August 1837. New York.** Lauds Pennsylvania's response to the question of admitting Texas into the Union; expresses gratification that Lundy occasionally presents political views, because even abolitionists have to vote. October 1837 (vol. XV, no. 302) p.69, c1.

692 W. H. BURLEIGH *to* **FRIEND LUNDY. 22 August 1837. Warwick Furnace, E. Nantmeal.** Discusses the progress of his lecture tour; reports that opposition to abolitionism is melting away. October 1837 (vol. XV, no. 302) p.69, c2.

693 J.P. JR. *to* **BENJAMIN LUNDY. 8 September 1837. Burlington, N.J.** Reports on a recent Burlington County Anti-Slavery meeting. October 1837. (vol. XV, no. 302) p.79, c2.

694 H. C. W. *to* **FRIEND LUNDY. 4 September 1837. Lower Makefield, Yardleyville.** Relates that in course of his speech discussing the claim of the CS to civilize and Christianize Africa, it was asked where their missionaries would come from; he replied that they would be found in jails, bars, houses of ill repute, and other such places to which the CS claims all free blacks find their way. October 1837 (vol. XV, no. 302) p.86, c2.

695 E. N. *to* **FRIEND LUNDY. n.d. n.p.** Reports that his wife had originally decided not to join the anti-slavery movement, but recently wrote a poem indicating that she had changed her mind. October 1837 (vol. XV, no. 302) p.87, c1.

696 MARY JOHNSON *to* **RESPECTED FRIENDS. 4 August 1837. Buckingham.** Reports renewed interest in the use of free produce; asserts that abstention from slave goods is the duty of every abolitionist and that its neglect justifies a charge of inconsistency; requests Lundy's opinion on the boycott and advice on obtaining free goods. October 1837 (vol. XV, no. 302) p.91, c2.

697 MARY GREW *to* **RESPECTED FRIEND. 12 September 1837. Philadelphia.** Rejoices over their interest in free goods. Agrees all anti-slavery groups must be alerted to the subject; informs them where free goods can be obtained; encourages them to write again. October 1837 (vol. XV, no. 302) p.92, c1.

698 A FREE WOMAN OF AMESBURY *to* **MR. PAGE. n.d. n.p.** Demands proof of Page's assertion that the condition of Southern slaves is no worse than that of Northern free laborers; calls Page a slanderer. October 1837 (vol. XV, no. 302) p.94, c2.

699 A MEMBER OF THE UNITED STATES SENATE *to* **A GENTLEMAN OF THIS CITY. [extract] 29 September 1837. Washington.** Promises to present a memorial against the annexation of Texas; adds that he will not worry about the financial outcome unless it becomes a question of party politics. October 1837 (vol. XV, no. 302) p.96, c2.

700 A MEMBER OF CONGRESS *to* **HIS FRIEND IN THIS CITY. [extract]   30 September 1837. Washington.** Acknowledges receipt of a memorial against the annexation of Texas, and adds that he has presented it to the House; urges that the stream of memorials not be interrupted. October 1837 (vol. XV, no. 302) p.97, c1.

701 J. BLANCHARD *to* **FRIEND LUNDY. [from the** *National Enquirer***] 8 September 1837. Canal Boat Lehman, above Dauphin.** Describes his visit to Perry County; believes that churches which countenance slavery will soon be reviled as "dens of slavery," and that the Methodist Church will be forced to take a stand against slavery or lose members. October 1837 (vol. XV, no. 302) p.97, c2.

702 MEMBER OF THE MEETING OF THE DELEGATES OF THE ASS OF BEL-MONT COUNTY, OHIO *to* **n.n. [extract] n.d. n.p.** Describes the proceedings of a recent meeting; discusses sentiments on the admission of Texas. October 1837 (vol. XV, no. 302) p.106, c2.

703 n.n. *to* **FRIEND. 22 September 1837. Schoolcraft, Mi.** Reports the success of the anti-Texas annexation memorial; supports a policy of trading numbers for political influence. October 1837 (vol. XV, no. 302) p.108, c2.

704 A LADY IN THE COUNTRY *to* **HER FRIEND IN PHILADELPHIA. [extract] 4 July 1837. Chester County, Pa.** Calls it a mockery to shout the word "liberty" in our country; feels discouraged by the apathy which prevails on the subject of abolition; argues that the boycott of slave goods makes no difference to the slave under present circumstances. October 1837 (vol. XV, no. 302) p.112, c2.

705 ALEXANDER CAMPBELL *to* **JAMES G. BIRNEY [extract] 15 September 1837. Bethany, Va.** States that he is not an abolitionist but has always opposed slavery; explains that he hoped to provide for the gradual emancipation of slaves when the Virginia constitution was revised, but did not succeed; denies that slaveholders are worse than other men. October 1837 (vol. XV, no. 302) p.115, c2.

706 JOSEPH PARRISH *to* **JOHN SERGEANT. n.d. n.p.** Criticizes Sergeant's resolution to prohibit the emigration of free people of color and fugitive slaves into Pennsylvania; asks how he can reconcile this resolution with the spirit of the state constitution and the Christian religion. October 1837 (vol. XV, no. 302) p.117, c2.

707 H. C. WRIGHT *to* **FRIEND LUNDY. 24 October 1837. n.p.** Discusses a recent lecture on Thomas Shipley, citing Shipley's aid to those on trial as runaway slaves; brands Pennsylvania a hunting ground for fugitive slaves; wishes Shipley had published his book, and notes that the Pennsylvania Abolition Society has the power to do so. October 1837 (vol. XV, no. 302) p.121, c2.

[1838]

708 OBSERVER *to* **MR. LUNDY. n.d. n.p.** Encloses a commentary on colonization from the *Commercial Herald.* January 1838 (vol. XV, no. 303) p.126, c1.

709 L. G. HAMILTON *to* **BENJAMIN LUNDY. 17 January 1838. Port-au-Prince.** Expresses pleasure upon learning that twenty years of labor have not dimmed Lundy's zeal; reports that Messrs. Burleigh and Gunn have arrived and are well received. January 1838 (vol. XV, no. 303) p.127, c1.

710 n.n. *to* **MR. BENJAMIN LUNDY. 20 January 1838. n.p.** Acknowledges receipt of several copies of the *Extra Enquirer,* and praises its contents; encloses a contribution to help defray expenses. January 1838 (vol. XV, no. 303) p.143, c1.

711 J.G.W.W. *to* **PEOPLE OF PENNSYLVANIA. [from the** *National Enquirer***] n.d. n.p.** Protests a recent decision to deprive free people of color of their right to vote in Pennsylvania; claims that the convention is crushing colored citizens even lower and that colonization forces them out of the country. January 1838 (vol. XV, no. 303) p.143, c2.

712 AN ENGLISHMAN *to* **A GENTLEMAN IN AMERICA. [extract] n.d. n.p.** States that law will keep Negroes in order after their apprenticeship, but that moral improvement is the best safeguard; predicts that even if equal rights of suffrage are given, there will be no danger of amalgamation. January 1838 (vol. XV, no. 303) p.146, c2.

713 MARY S. WILSON *to* **WILLIAM GOODELL. 27 December 1837. Macedon.** Hopes to see more written to discourage the use of slave produce; declares that slave goods are blood-stained, and suggests the formation of cooperatives for free goods. January 1838 (vol. XV, no. 303) p.151, c2.

714 HON. CHIEF JUSTICE WARD *to* **A COMMITTEE OF GENTLEMEN AGAINST ANNEXATION OF TEXAS TO THE UNION. [extract from the** *Boston Courier***] n.d. n.p.** Expresses strong opposition to the admission of Texas into the Union. January 1838 (vol. XV, no. 303) p.153, c2.

715 n.n. *to* **n.n. [extract] n.d. Albany.** Reports that memorials on human rights come in daily; notes that several laws and resolutions will pass in the lower House only to be killed in the Senate; feels that the cause of benevolence and human rights is moving forward. January 1838 (vol. XV, no. 303) p.156, c1.

716 A CITIZEN OF HAYTI *to* **THE** *GENIUS OF UNIVERSAL EMANCIPATION.* **15 January 1838. Port-au-Prince.** Reports that the French fleet has not yet arrived, but that the English are watching their movements. January 1838 (vol. XV, no. 303) p.156, c2.

[1839]

717 AN ABOLITIONIST IN PHILADELPHIA *to* **THE EDITOR [BENJAMIN LUNDY]. n.d. n.p.** Observes that the abolitionist cause is advancing; believes that the recent violations of the law at Harrisburg have opened the eyes of the people to the danger of mobs; describes his activities as a lecturer. 8 March 1839 (vol. XVI, no. 307) p.10, c1.

718 A GENTLEMAN IN EDGER COUNTY *to* **THE EDITOR [BENJAMIN LUNDY].** **n.d. Illinois.** Thinks that a lack of information exists on abolition; finds that the clergy is the most opposed to emancipation; reports the circulation of a petition to abolish the internal slave trade and slavery in the District of Columbia and the Territory of Florida. 8 March 1839 (vol. XVI, no. 307) p.10, c2.

719 A FRIEND AT JACKSONVILLE *to* **n.n. [extract] 22 January 1839. Illinois.** Reports an attempt to organize a chapter of the CS. 8 March 1839 (vol. XVI, no. 307) p.10, c2.

720 A FRIEND IN MORRIS COUNTY *to* **n.n. [extract] 11 February 1839. New Jersey.** [illegible] 8 March 1839 (vol. XVI, no. 307) p.10, c2.

721 W. R. HAYES *to* **REV. H. G. LUDLOW. 26 December 1838. Barbadoes.** Describes period of celebration and profound peace since emancipation; discredits earlier fears that former slaves would "relapse into barbarism"; discusses increasing land value and high wages paid to the new class of free laborers to prevent emigration. 8 March 1839 (vol. XVI, no. 307) p.10, c4.

722 B. J. CONRALD *to* **J. Q. ADAMS. 19 December 1839. Montgomery, Al.** Accuses Adams of impeaching the honor of his cousin, the minister to England; threatens to shoot Adams if he makes any further remarks. 8 March 1839 (vol. XVI, no. 307) p.11, c1.

Shelbyville (Ky.)
Abolition Intelligencer

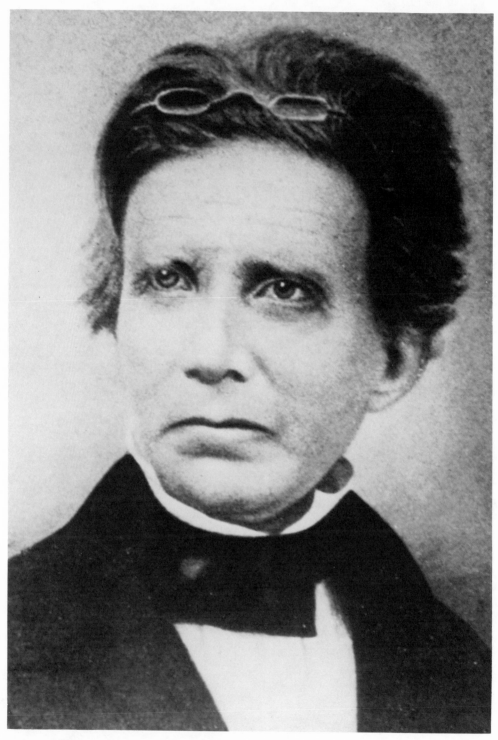

Figure 6. Rev. John Finley Crow

Journal Data

TITLE: *Abolition Intelligencer and Missionary Magazine*

INCLUSIVE DATES OF PUBLICATION: 7 May 1822–Apr. 1823 (Vol. I, Nos. 1–12)

PLACE OF PUBLICATION: Shelbyville, Kentucky

FREQUENCY OF PUBLICATION: Monthly (See "Miscellaneous Data")

AVERAGE NUMBER OF PAGES PER ISSUE: 16

NUMBER OF COLUMNS PER PAGE: 2

EDITOR: John Finley Crow

PUBLISHER: John Finley Crow

PRICE: Annual Subscription $1.50
Changed June 1822 to: $1.00 Annual Subscription

PERSPECTIVE: Anti-slavery

MISCELLANEOUS DATA: The first issue proposed an "every other week" scheme, but the second issue declared a "monthly" publication.

REPOSITORY: Wisconsin Historical Society. 7 May 1822–Mar. 1823.

ABOLITION INTELLIGENCER,
AND
MISSIONARY MAGAZINE.

EDITED AND PUBLISHED BY JOHN FINLEY CROW.

Vol. I.]   SHELBYVILLE, Ky. MARCH, 1823.   [No. 11.

TO OUR PATRONS.

One No. more will complete the 1st volume of the Abolition Intelligencer and Missionary Magazine, and also probably close the work.—Not because we apprehend there is no necessity for its continuance, nor because we dispair of effecting any good by its publication, but because we feel unable longer to bear the expenses necessarily incurred by its prosecution.

Between five and six hundred copies have been regularly stricken off and distributed, but a great number of them have been sent to gentlemen, in different parts of the country, who were supposed to be the friends of science, and the friends of humanity, on whom consequently we have no legal claim for a compensation.

The first number contained a respectful request that, should it not meet the approbation of those to whom it was sent, so far as to secure their patronage and support, they would have the goodness to return it to the Editor by mail. Very few of the first numbers were returned, but we are sorry to say that not a few, after having taken the work for two, and in some instances for three quarters of the year, have ungenerously declined' receiving it longer, without making any compensation for our trouble and expense.

We feel, however, a degree of confidence, that those gentlemen, who have continued through the year to receive the work, will promptly, on reception of the last number, either pay to our agents in their neighbourhood, or transmit by mail to us the small trifle which according to our terms is due for our labours, and which is absolutely necessary to enable us, without serious embarrasment, to close our accounts.

Those who did not commence with the year, are not considered bound for the full price of the volume.—Twelve and a half cents, per No. for those numbers received, is all that is required.

The following gentlemen are respectfully solicited to act as our Agents in receiving and transmitting to us by mail monies due for the Abolition Intelligencer & Missionary Magazine.

William Wright—Columbia, Penn.
Joseph Bingherst—Wilmington, Del.

EDUCATION OF THE BLACKS.

In a former No. we attempted to shew the *policy* of extending to our slave population the advantages of education—The *propriety* of the measure remains to be attended to.

"Nothing" says Dr. Rush, "can be politically right, which is morally wrong." This proposition must recommend itself to every honest and enlightened mind as "next kin" to self-evident. And the converse must be equally true, viz nothing can be morally wrong which is politically right—For "right wrongs no man." According to this view of the subject, policy and propriety may be regarded as synonomous terms. But multitudes, by *policy*, understand a kind of political cunning which has little or nothing to do with

Figure 7

Prospectus

As the patronage of an enlightened and generous public is now solicited in behalf of this work, it is but reasonable that a more full and explicit enunciation of its design should be given, than that which is contained in the prospectus.

The great object of the society under whose patronage it appears, and of the editor who has the immediate direction of its course is to aid, so far as they may have it in their power, the cause of suffering humanity.

They would never forget the important and interesting fact announced by the pen of inspiration that "God has made of one blood all the nations that dwell upon the earth." Under a conviction of the verity of this declaration, they are constrained to regard all men as their brethren, members of the same great family, and consequently as having a legitimate claim on their sympathies and on their benevolence. But they have not so far forgotten the duties they owe to that civil society of which they are members, as to violate any of its claims in the exercise of their charities. They regard "the powers that be as ordained of God" and therefore feel a disposition to render unto them all due subjection.

This declaration may be necessary in order to allay the apprehensions of some timerous [sic] persons, who suppose that the object of the Abolition Society is to rob them of their property (their Slaves) either by force or intrigue. Such persons are surely not aware that the possession of their property, is secured to them by the constitution of this Commonwealth; and that no law can be enacted to bring about even a gradual emancipation, without first calling a convention and revising the constitution.

All therefore that the society can hope to effect is, to meliorate, as they may have opportunity the situation of free people of colour, by giving them proper aid and encouragement in the discharge of the great duties of morality and religion—to defend the rights of those who are legally free, but are likely to be still kept in bondage, and to prepare the public mind for taking the necessary preparatory measures for the future introduction of a system of laws, for the gradual abolition of slavery, as those degraded people may be prepared for the enjoyment of civil liberty.

In the prosecution of these objects they hope ever to exercise candour and forbearance. "Letting their moderation be known to all men." Being fully aware that an opposite course might increase, but could never lessen the evils they would remedy. Such is their confidence in the candour, the benevolence and the good sense of the great mass of their fellow citizens, that, they feel convinced that nothing more is necessary, in order to secure their approbation and support, in any measure that may be conducive to the interests of our country, the happiness of individuals or to the cause of humanity, than merely to convince them, that those measures are good and necessary. And they are no less confident, that a system of absolute, involuntary & hereditary slavery, may be demonstrated to be a national, an individual and a moral evil—Hostile to the spirit of our government, ruinous to the prosperity of the nation, destructive of social happiness and subversive of the great principles of morality. These are objects however, on which there exists diversity of opinion. Hence the necessity of inquiry and investigation. And hence their columns will always be open for the insertion of candid, liberal and temperate communications on both sides of the question.

There is evidently a want of light on the subject. We find multitudes of Slave holders in the western and southern States, who could not without a flagrant violation of charity, be regarded in any other light than as the children of God, born of his spirit and heirs of his grace, who nevertheless in their treatment of their slaves, are led by the example of the multitude around them who have no fear of God before their eyes.

From their infancy have they been accustomed to see the blacks held in bondage, without any attention being paid to their spiritual interests—without any effort to teach them to read the word of God, which is able to make them wise unto salvation, and they have perhaps never heard the propriety of such a course of treatment called into question. If they feed and clothe their servants well, they seem disposed to take some merit to themselves, as using them so much better than they are used by multitudes of others.

The Christian world, at this moment, teems with publications devoted to the advancement of the Redeemers kingdom among the heathen in heathen lands. Bible and Missionary Societies "Those two great instruments" as they have been called, "in the hand of the Head of the Church by which the work of enlightening the dark corners of the earth is to be effected," receive ample attention. We are informed of all the minutia of their operations, and of the happy effects, which in many instances, have been produced through their instrumentality.

Our hearts are also often cheered by accounts of the out pouring of the Spirit in our own happy land; and Christians are exhorted and encouraged to rally around the Standard of the cross—to become fellow labourers in the great and splendid work of evangelizing the world and bringing about the glorious millennial era when "Righteousness shall cover the earth as the waters do the sea."

Almost every part of Christian duty, comprehended under the general heads of piety of God, and benevolence to man, has been explained, illustrated and enforced. Yet strange as it may seem, scarcely a word is ever heard about the degraded, oppressed and perishing condition of TWO MILLIONS of our fellow creatures, who are found scattered through our country, our neighbourhoods and in our houses. No one seems to care for their Souls. No one condescends to plead their cause and to call the attention to Christains [sic] and others, to the duties which they owe to the sable sons of Africa.

Is it so, that the tender charities of our nature are all exhausted in caring for the heathen whom we have never seen, so that we can with the most perfect apathy, behold those immortal beings, invelloped [sic] in the darkness of ignorance, sinking under the weight of their guilt down to the bottomless pit?

No, we are pursuaded [sic] that such is not the fact, and that nothing more is necessary in order to excite a proper solicitude, and corresponding exertions on this subject, than simply to state it in all its length and breadth. Because such is the constitution of our nature, that we mechanically fall into habits and practices from the influence of example, without investigating or even thinking of their propriety or impropriety.

Such is the prejudice that exists in the minds of multitudes against the indiscriminate emancipation of slaves, that it would be very difficult, if not impossible, in the ordinary way, to secure patronage to a work professedly devoted to the interests of liberty.

This must form the editor's apology, for sending his paper to so many of his friends, and the friends of humanity without first soliciting their patronage. He feels a strong confidence that the name of his paper would not unfrequently, excite opposition, when the thing itself, if examined, would secure decided approbation. Affectionately therefore, does he invite all those to whom it is directed, to give in so far as they may have opportunity, an impartial reading. If they approve the object, they will doubtless not fail to patronize and encourage it. If, on the contrary, it should not meet their approbation, they will have the goodness to enclose the number in a piece of paper as they found it, and direct it back to the editor.

We close our remarks by observing that judicious and well written pieces for publication in the *Intelligencer* will at all times be gratefully received, as will also the minutes and other important documents of Abolition and Manumission Societies.

Abolition Intelligencer, and Missionary Magazine, Shelbyville, [Ky.], May 7, 1832, (vol. I, no. 1)

[1822]

723 ELDER ISAAC MC COY *to* **A GENTLEMAN IN KENTUCKY. [extract] 19 February 1822. Fort Wayne.** Describes the progress of the Indians, including the Miamies, the Potawatamies, and the Ottawas; states that the Secretary of War is disposed to aid them, and is now preparing to move the mission's seat to the midst of the Potawatamies. June 1822. p.27, c1.

724 ELIJAH BOARDMAN *to* **THE EDITOR OF THE** *METHODIST MAGAZINE.* **[extract] 21 January 1822. n.p.** Describes his visit with Rev. Mr. Crane, Presbyterian missionary to the Tuscarora tribe in Lewistown; notes the size of the tribe, the quality of its singing school, and the devout, pious attitude of many tribe members. June 1822. p.28, c1.

725 J. SOULE *to* **THE EDITORS OF THE** *METHODIST MAGAZINE.* **29 November 1821. New York.** Sends extract of a letter from Rev. James B. Finley, missionary to the Wyandott and other Indians. June 1822. p.29, c1.

726 REV. JAMES B. FINLEY *to* **BROTHER. [extract] 4 November 1821. Upper Sandusky.** The missionary to the Wyandott Indians states that he arrived in Upper Sandusky recently, and finds that the "children of the forest" are prepared to receive religious instruction, and learn quickly; requests financial aid and two additional teachers in order to reach other Indian nations. June 1822. p.29, c1.

727 WILLIAM MCKENDREE *to* **THE CORRESPONDING SECRETARY OF THE MISSIONARY SOCIETY OF THE METHODIST EPISCOPAL CHURCH. 28 February 1822. Augusta.** Notes the good disposition of the Creek Indians, and the near completion of a schoolhouse for the tribe; informs the society that Rev. Isaac and Mrs. Smith are in charge of the mission, aided by Brother Andrew Hammill, and that Gideon Mason and John J. Triggs are missionaries in the west of Georgia. July 1822. p.45, c2.

728 CLEMENTIA *to* **MR. EDITOR. [from the** *Christian Herald*] **n.d. n.p.** Discredits Northern extremism toward abolition, which he views as the cause of the entire nation; claims that slaves are "in no means" prepared for emancipation, but must first be converted to Christianity; calls on Christian planters to allow religious instruction for slaves. August 1822. p.50, c1.

729 n.n. *to* **THE EDITOR OF THE** *GENIUS OF UNIVERSAL EMANCIPATION.* **n.d. n.p.** Forwards correspondence between L. Sterne and Ignatius Sancho. August 1822. p.56, c2.

730 IGNATIUS SANCHO *to* **REV. L. STERNE. n.d. n.p.** A colored man compares his early life in the service of a family who "judged ignorance the best and only security for obedience," with his later years spent with a benevolent family; expresses his love of books and his appreciation of Sterne's sermons, which have made others aware of the horrors of slavery. August 1822. p.56, c2.

731 L. STERNE *to* **IGNATIUS SANCHO. 27 July 1766. Coxwold.** Notes that in the natural world, complexions change by the most insensible gradations, and that one knows not how far blood ties extend, but that it is not uncommon for half of mankind to use the other half as brutes; asserts his respect for those "bound in chains of darkness." August 1822. p.57, c1.

732 PLINY FISK *to* **COR. SECRETARY. 10 February 1822. Alexandria.** Describes the illness, death, and funeral of Brother Parsons in Alexandria. August 1822. p.63, c2.

733 WILLIAM M'KENDREE *to* **n.n. n.d. n.p.** Reports on Creek Indians in South Carolina who are almost finished building and are ready to open a school; reports that Rev. Isaac Smith and Brother Andrew Hammill have offered themselves as missionaries to the Indians, and that Gideon Mason and John J. Triggs are missionaries in the west of Georgia. September 1822. p.73, c2.

734 MR. L. S. WILLIAMS *to* **n.n. [extract] 18 June 1822. n.p.** Reports the success of a recent revival at the Choctaw Mission, at which ten of the "notoriously wicked" adults evinced a change of heart; notes that most of the natives are unaffected, but are beginning to attend meetings. September 1822. p.75, c1.

735 ALFRED WRIGHT *to* **SIR. n.d. n.p.** Reports he has visited the "consecrated spot" several times since Brother and Sister Williams commenced their work; adds that conversions have had "very distinctive marks of genuineness," and that relief has been obtained in prayer. September 1822. p.77, c1.

736 REV. AHAB JINKS *to* **FRIEND IN CINCINNATI. 24 June 1822. n.p.** Observes the power of God's grace in the town; feels conversion of a sinner brought many people closer to God. September 1822. p.78, c1.

737 AN UNKNOWN FRIEND IN THE STATE OF MISSOURI *to* **SIR. [extract] 6 July 1822. Washington County, Mo.** Discusses the "lamentable declention of religion" in the western regions, essentially caused by slavery; proposes questions to challenge professors who hold slaves and claim slavery is not a moral evil. November 1822. p.100, c1.

[1823]

738 IRENEUS *to* **SOPHRONIA. May 1822. n.p.** Reports that she has become acquainted with professing Christians and their defense of slavery; discusses her own views of Christian morality and the evil of slavery, hoping others will reflect on the subject. February 1823. p.150, c1.

739 PHILANTHROPIST *to* **MR. LYLE. [from the** *Western Citizen***] n.d. n.p.** Discusses the growth of commercial traffic and trade in Kentucky, particularly the alarming growth of "soulpeddling," or slave-trafficking; describes pitiful scene of slaves being driven, wrenched from their homes. February 1823. p.152, c2.

740 REV. WM. GOODELL *to* **n.n. [extract] n.d. n.p.** Recounts his pleasant trip to the Tuscaroras, during which he visited several families, smoked the calumet of peace with one household, and sang with others. February 1823. p.160, c1.

741 MR. MACK *to* **DR. RAYLAND. [extract] 28 January 1822. Serampore.** Notes he arrived in time to join a prayer meeting, and that he finds the natives in this area less heathen than those in other places; comments on visits to native schools in Calcutta, where little has been done toward converting the masses. March 1823. p.171, c2.

742 REV. P. FISK *to* **CORRESPONDENT IN STURBRIDGE, MA. [extract] 25 August 1822. Malta.** Reports his days are spent studying Arabic and Italian and talking with Brother and Sister Temple, who also preach in several languages. March 1823. p.173, c2.

743 JOHN RIDGE *to* **DAVID BROWN. [from the** *Evangelical Monitor***] 13 December 1822. Springplace, Cherokee Nation.** A native Cherokee tells of the advances of his people and describes their system of government; notes that white men continue to sell them whiskey, but that the use of intoxicating liquors is regulated. March 1823. p.175, c2.

Philadelphia
African Observer

Figure 8. Enoch Lewis

Journal Data

TITLE: *African Observer, A Monthly Journal, Containing Essays and Documents Illustrative of the General Character, and Moral and Political Effects, of Negro Slavery.*

INCLUSIVE DATES OF PUBLICATION: Apr. 1827–Mar. 1828 (V. I)

PLACE OF PUBLICATION: Philadelphia, Pennsylvania

FREQUENCY OF PUBLICATION: Monthly

AVERAGE NUMBER OF PAGES PER ISSUE: 32

SIZE: 8¾'' x 5½'' (size of reprint pages)

NUMBER OF COLUMNS PER PAGE: 2

EDITOR: Enoch Lewis

SPECIAL FEATURES: Annual Indexes; Statistical Charts

PRICE: Annual Subscription $2.00

PERSPECTIVE: Anti-slavery

MISCELLANEOUS DATA: Issues are not numbered

REPOSITORY: Sterling Memorial Library, Yale University. Apr. 1827–Mar. 1828. Reprint by Negro Universities Press, Westport, Connecticut, 1970.

THE

African Observer.

FIFTH MONTH, 1827.

NEGRO SLAVERY.

(*Continued from page* 9.)

It has been frequently asserted by the advocates of slavery that a large part of the Africans are slaves in their own country, and that their transportation across the Atlantic, though they are still subjected to the servile yoke, is an important melioration of their state.

B. Edwards observes, when speaking of the slave trade, which he admits to be incapable of general defence, "A good mind may honestly derive some degree of consolation in considering that all such of the wretched victims as were slaves in Africa, are by being sold to the whites, removed to a situation infinitely more desirable, even in its worst state, than that of the best and most favoured slaves in their native country. It is, on all hands, admitted, that the condition of these poor people, under their own governments, is the most deplorable that we can conceive a human creature to be subject to. They have no security for property, nor protection for their persons; they exist at the will and caprice of a master, who is not amenable to any law for his ill treatment of them, and who may slaughter them at his pleasure. He has in truth, very little interest in their preservation, having no means of employing them in profitable labour, and when provisions are scarce, he has even a strong inducement to destroy them."[*]

For these sweeping declarations, no authorities are cited,[†] but from whatever source he derived his information, he must have been unhappy in his se-

[*] Hist. W. Indies, vol. 2, p. 99.

[†] Unless the anonymous witness cited in a former part of the chapter, and the witnesses examined by the Privy Council, and the House of Commons, are to be considered as such. If they are, the conclusion is certainly much too broad for the premises. The *paraphrase* owes more of its fulness and generality to the genius of the writer, than to the facts established by the original. It may be proper here to remark, that the writer of these essays has no desire to impeach the veracity of the eminent historian, from whose work the above extract is taken. We have here an instance, not by any means a novel one, of the readiness, even of a powerful mind, to consider a conclusion, which corresponds with a favourite hypothesis, as fairly proved by testimony, which to an understanding, not similarly biassed, would appear totally inadequate to its support.

Figure 9

Prospectus

It is our privilege to live in an age of surpassing improvement. The sciences and the arts are deeply indebted to the genius and enterprise of our co-temporaries; and schemes, of extensive utility, are now in successful operation, which, half a century ago, would have been considered as fit only to supply a void in the brain of a maniac, or to exercise the idle ingenuity of a visionary projector. By new and efficacious experiments, principles in natural science, unknown to our fathers, have been developed, and new avenues opened to the enjoyment of man.

Of those improvements in physical and political science, which have stamped their character on the last and the passing age, the inhabitants of the western world claim a distinguished share—There ingenuity has displayed its inventions to the gaze and imitation of the world, and there the principles of government have been traced to their source, and the laws of immutable justice solemnly proclaimed as the proper basis and support of political institutions.

If we review the periods of our national growth, and mark our unparalleled progress in the march of nations, we must subscribe to the sentiment, that no people have greater cause reverently to commemorate the goodness of a beneficent Creator than the people of these United States. No where have the choicest blessings of the all-bountiful Parent been spread with a more unsparing hand. To no other people, ancient or modern, has the cup of felicity been presented, with fewer bitter ingredients, or more completely purified from the lees of political thraldom.

If, judging of the future from the past, we endeavour to delineate our course through ages yet to come, a series of pleasing anticipations warms the reflecting mind. With a fertile soil, extending through every desirable variety of climate, and capable of affording all that luxury could demand to supply the wants, or promote the comfort of man; with a population enlightened and free; with a government over which the laws are supreme, and the people the arbiters of the law; the way appears open to that national greatness which ambition could not wish to enhance, and to individual prosperity, in which discontent might blush to complain.

Are these the delusive prospects of a feverish patriotism, the visions of poetry; or are they the anticipations of sober reflection? Is there no ill boding omen to dim the light that glitters on our future course? Alas! one portentous cloud is impending over some of the fairest portions of our favoured land. One dire disease, deeply infixed in our national system, has "grown with our growth, and strengthened with our strength." The light of freedom, which we so highly prize, shines on a part of our population only by reflection, and to them is rather "darkness visible" than light.

This appalling subject is forced upon us, however reluctant we may feel to investigate its character, or contemplate its rugged and forbidding aspect. A population of more than a million and a half, familiar with all the privacies of our domestic life; accustomed to hear liberty extolled as the highest and noblest of enjoyments; and yet, finding the bitter draught of hereditary servitude its own hopeless portion; incapable, from its degraded condition, of appreciating the blessing of the government under which we live, and having little to dread from any change or convulsions of the political world—presents to our view a prospect too awful to be contemplated with stoic indifference. The cloud is thickening with the progress of time; and prudence admonishes, that, if it cannot be dissipated, it should, if possible, be disarmed of its lightning.

Whether slavery is, or is not, a political evil; or whether a free or a slave population is most conducive to national prosperity, can scarcely, in this age, and in this country, require a serious discussion.

If slavery has, in all ages, and among all nations, been considered as among the greatest of evils; if liberty is always the highest wish and ultimate aim of the slave; how repulsive must that condition appear to an observant eye, when contrasted with the civil and religious freedom, by which, in the United States, it is every where surrounded.

But, however we may commiserate the condition of those who are doomed to hereditary servitude, the zeal which this feeling excites may sometimes warm without enlightening the philanthropic mind. The slave, sunk and degraded below the proper level of humanity, may find, in the lethargic insensibility resulting from his situation, a retreat from mental suffering; yet, though bent to the yoke, he still possesses the stamina of the human character—the aspiring tendency of his nature, though suppressed and concealed, is not destroyed—his dormant passions are not extinct. The tranquility which prevails, may be suddenly disturbed—for the slumbering volcano retains its fires, and those who occupy its smoking verge may themselves become the victims of the devouring element.

The slave is not the only object that demands our consideration. The introduction of negro slavery into the United States was not the work of the present generation. The system was entailed upon them by their ancestors; and justice demands the admission, that evils, both moral and political, are more easily discovered than removed; and that those who are subjected, by the circumstances of their birth, to the hard alternative, either to new model the habits which have grown with their years, or to maintain a system which their sober judgments cannot approve, are objects of sympathy with the truly christian mind.

The jealousies and antipathies which the distinction between slave-holding and non slave-holding states has engendered and fed, may be safely classed among the disastrous concomitants of the system; especially as they oppose a stubborn obstacle to any general effort for the removal of the other acknowledged evils of slavery. Unhappily for the cause of humanity, the advocate of the slave has been too often identified with the antagonist of his owner. The interests of these opposite classes have been considered as incompatible, and friendship for the one as synonymous with enmity for the other.

To soften or remove those antipathies, and promote, between the inhabitants of the different sections of our country, a community of feeling on this momentous subject, is an object of vital importance, worthy of the efforts of those who seek alike the good of all. This cause, though critical and arduous, is not desperate. Happily the purblind philosophy, which taught mankind to believe that one part of the community could rise only by the depression of another, has passed away with the ages that are gone, and a more enlightened era has dawned. Man is a social being, and finds his own particular advantage in the promotion of the general good. Party strifes and sectional jealousies result from erroneous and limited views of private interest; and often from imperfect acquaintance with the motives by which others are actuated: The people of the United States are bound together by one great federal interest; and however the inhabitants of the north may disapprove and abhor the system of servitude which prevails in the south, and however they may compassionate its victims, there must, from their common interests, as well as common origin, always exist, in the prejudices and sympathies of the former, a strong preponderance in favour of the superior class.

There is probably no subject more deeply interesting to every section of the Union than negro slavery, and none which has stronger claims on the clearest heads and purest hearts among us. To open a way, equally safe and salutary, for the master and the slave to escape from the evils in which they are involved, and thus to clear ourselves from the reproach of having disavowed, by our practice, the noble principles on which we assumed a rank among the nations of the earth, is the great political problem, which this or some succeeding generation must solve.

Animated by a desire to contribute towards the attainment of this momentous object, and supported by the encouragement of his friends, the subscriber has concluded to offer to public acceptance, a monthly periodical journal, with the title prefixed to this article, designed to include an extensive range of inquiries connected with this subject. To combat the prejudices which this system has produced, and which have varied their shades according to the points from which the condition has been viewed—to trace the moral influence of slavery on those who breathe its atmosphere—and to point out the best means for its peaceful extinction, will be among the prominent objects of discussion.

The work will comprise the following general divisions.

1. Sketches of the history, ancient and modern, of Africa—of the progress of geographical discovery therein—of its productions, commerce, and future prospects; and of the manners, government, and arts of the negro race.

2. The history, character, and incidents of slavery among the ancients, with its decline and extinction among the moderns.

3. The African slave trade. Its history, character, and extent—Efforts that have been used for its abolition—Its present state; with its effect on the inhabitants of Africa.

4. The nature and character of negro slavery in the islands and on the continent of America—The internal slave trade within the United States—Laws and usages in relation to slavery, including those enacted for its extinction or melioration.

5. Principles of political economy, in relation to slave labour and consumption compared with free.

6. Biographical notices of negroes who have been distinguished for their virtue or abilities.

7. Plans for improving the condition of the slaves in the United States, with an account of experiments, on this subject, made by the holders of slaves.

8. View of the situation, character, and future prospects of the free coloured population of the United States.

In the collections which shall be made on these various topics, the works of the ablest writers among the ancients and moderns will be consulted; the narratives of travellers carefully examined; and such extracts made from the periodical works of the day, as shall appear properly calculated to illustrate the subjects embraced by the plan. Measures are taken to establish an extensive correspondence with persons of intelligence and veracity, in this country and in Europe, from whose communications considerable assistance is anticipated.

The editor being anxious so to conduct his investigations, that such as differ from him in opinion may not be repelled by any appearance of severity or rudeness, from a calm and patient attention to the facts or arguments adduced, every thing of a vindictive character will be carefully excluded from his columns.

It may be added that a rigid adherence to the order above exhibited in the arrangement of his subjects, is not intended, and that several of those topics will be brought into view in each of the successive numbers. In the 12th number an index to the volume will be given.

CONDITIONS.

The work will be published in Philadelphia, on the first of each month, beginning with the Fourth month next, each number containing 32 pages printed in double columns.

The price two dollars per annum, payable *in advance.*

Such of the patrons of the work as may choose to withdraw their subscriptions at the expiration of the year, will be expected to give notice to the editor or his agent, two months previously; those who omit forwarding this notice will be considered as continuing their subscriptions, and their bills presented accordingly.

12th mo. 23d, 1826.   Enoch Lewis. *The African Observer*, Philadelphia, [Pa.],
                                               Fourth Month [April], 1827

[1827]

744 RICHARD STOCKTON *to* **HON. JOSEPH WATSON. 26 May 1826. Natchez.** Writes on behalf of John W. Hamilton, the buyer and subsequent liberator of ex-slaves and freemen kidnapped from Philadelphia; states that Hamilton will send the Negroes to Watson so they can testify against their kidnappers but requests their return if their freedom is not established by 1 January. May 1827. p.41, c1.

745 DAVID HOLMES AND J. E. DAVIS *to* **HON. JOSEPH WATSON. 23 December 1826. Natchez.** Bring to the attention of Watson the kidnapping case of Peter Hook; ask the mayor to take measures to punish the aggressors; also refer the mayor to Duncan S. Walker, the lawyer-recorder of the Peter Hook narrative, for legal assistance. May 1827. p.43, c2.

746 JOSEPH WATSON AND J. E. DAVIS *to* **DAVID HOLMES. 20 January 1827. Philadelphia.** Extend thanks to Holmes for information concerning the abduction of free coloreds from Philadelphia; inform him that Governor Shulze has issued warrants for the arrest of the kidnappers, although none has yet been apprehended; affirm his resolve that the matter will be settled. May 1827. p.45, c1.

747 JOSEPH WATSON, MAYOR OF PHILADELPHIA *to* **DUNCAN S. WALKER. 24 January 1827. Philadelphia.** Thanks Walker, who recorded the abduction of Peter Hook, for his information about a subject which deeply concerns him in the interest of his citizens; encourages Walker in his investigation of the kidnapping case. May 1827. p.45, c2.

748 D. S. WALKER *to* **HON. JOSEPH WATSON. 25 February 1827. Natchez.** Answers Mayor Watson's letter supporting Walker's investigations into the rash of kidnappings in the Philadelphia area in the spring of 1825; responds to what he believes was an intimation of an offer by declaring that he cannot compensate in such a case; also includes the narrative of Lydia Smith. May 1827. p.46, c2.

749 A NAVAL OFFICER OF RANK *to* **n.n. 10 April 1827. Bight of Biafra.** Tells of his ship's capture of a Brazilian brig carrying a cargo of 309 slaves; states purpose of letter is to make (his friend) aware of the miseries of slavery; calculates that this capture brings the total number of slaves emancipated by his ship to 2,497. October 1827. p.202, c2.

750 A NAVAL OFFICER OF RANK *to* **A FRIEND. 22 May 1872. Sierra Leone.** Informs of the arrival of surgeons and assistants on the *Orestes*; reports the deaths of several within the month, as well as the prevalence of fever and dysentery. October 1827. p.203, c2.

751 A GENTLEMAN IN ILLINOIS *to* **HIS FRIEND IN PHILADELPHIA. [extract] 23 August 1827. Illinois.** Writes with pleasure of a recent judicial decision of the Supreme Court of Missouri concerning gradual emancipation of slaves in the territory northwest of the Ohio; notes he has tried to convince slave-owners that such an act would lull the Negroes for a while, preventing their pressing for a higher court decision which might instantly free them; cites as example a case of a Negro who successfully instituted a suit for his freedom. October 1827. p.204, c2.

752 L. E. *to* **THE EDITOR OF THE *AFRICAN OBSERVER* [ENOCH LEWIS]. 21 September 1827. Philadelphia.** Supports the *African Observer*'s writings concerning the exclusion of Negro testimony from the Southern tribunals, and calls editor's attention to its effect on the recovery of kidnapped freemen; relates that in some instances, the kidnapped victim cannot provide a white witness to prove his identity and his family's word cannot satisfy the courts; discusses the Maryland law facilitating the recovery of fugitive slaves and suggests a similar law for the recovery of kidnapped freemen. October 1827. p.219, c1.

753 J. ASHMUN, *AFRICAN REPOSITORY to* **GENTLEMEN. 20 May 1827. Caldwell.**
Writes of the colonies set up in Africa on land protected from the slave trade; relates difficulty in trading between Liberia and Sierra Leone since British restrictions on trading with the United States were imposed; discusses the health problem among the colonists and various remedies being used to treat disorders. December 1827. p.282, c1.

754 J. ASHMUN, *AFRICAN REPOSITORY to* **GENTLEMEN. 27 August 1827. n.p.**
Discusses landing of French slave ship on the shores near the colony, despite official warnings concerning liberation of its cargo; notes that action was taken. December 1827. p.284, c1.

THE LIBERATOR.

VOL. I.] WILLIAM LLOYD GARRISON AND ISAAC KNAPP, PUBLISHERS. [NO. 6.

BOSTON, MASSACHUSETTS.] OUR COUNTRY IS THE WORLD—OUR COUNTRYMEN ARE MANKIND. [SATURDAY, FEBRUARY 5, 1831.

THE LIBERATOR
IS PUBLISHED WEEKLY
AT NO. 11, MERCHANTS' HALL.

WM. LLOYD GARRISON, EDITOR.

TERMS.

☞ Two Dollars per annum, payable in advance.
☞ Agents allowed every sixth copy.
☞ No subscription will be received for a shorter period than six months.
☞ All letters and communications must be post paid.

THE LIBERATOR.

'By the law of God, unchangeable and eternal, while men despise fraud, and loathe rapine, and abhor blood, they shall reject with indignation the wild and guilty fantasy, that man can hold property in man!'—BROUGHAM.

PRISON ANECDOTE.

I will give the public an anecdote, showing in what manner a slaveholder can reason.

During my late incarceration in Baltimore prison, four men came to obtain a runaway slave. He was brought out of his cell to confront his master, but pretended not to know him—did not know that he had ever seen him before—could not recollect his name. Of course, the master was exceedingly irritated. 'Don't you remember,' said he, 'when I gave you, not long since, thirty-nine lashes under the apple-tree? Another time, when I gave you a sound flogging in the barn? Another time, when you was scourged for giving me the lie, by saying that the horse was in a good condition?'

'Yes,' replied the slave whose memory was thus quickened, 'I do recollect. You have beaten me cruelly without a cause; you have not given me enough to eat and drink; and I don't want to go back again. I wish you to sell me to another master—I had rather even go to Georgia, than to return home.'

'I'll let you know, you villain,' said the master, 'that my wishes, and not yours, are to be consulted. I'll learn you how to run away again.'

The other men advised him to take the black home, and cut him up in inch pieces for his impudence, obstinacy and desertion—swearing tremendously all the while. The slave was ordered back to his cell.

I had stood speechless during this singular dialogue, my blood boiling in my veins, and my limbs trembling with emotion. I now walked up to the gang, and addressing the master as calmly as possible, said—

'Sir, what right have you to that poor creature?'

He looked up in my face very innocently, and replied—

'My father left him to me.'

'Suppose,' said I, 'your father had broken into a bank, and stolen ten thousand dollars, and safely bequeathed the sum as a legacy: could you conscientiously keep the money? For myself, I had rather rob any bank to an indefinite amount, than kidnap a fellow being, or hold him in bondage: the crime would be less injurious to society, and less sinful in the sight of God.'

The man and his crew were confounded. What! to hear such sentiments in Maryland,—and in jail, too! Looking them full in the face, and getting no reply, I walked a few steps to the door. After a brief consultation, the master came up to me and said—

'Perhaps you would like to buy the slave, and *give him his liberty?*'

'Sir, I am a poor man; and were I ever so opulent, it would be necessary, on your part, to make out a clear title to the services of the slave, before I could conscientiously make a bargain.'

After a pause, he said—

'Well, sir, I can prove from the bible that slavery is right.'

'Ah!' replied I, 'that is a precious book—the rule of conduct. I have always supposed that its spirit was directly opposed to every thing in the shape of fraud and oppression. However, sir, I should be glad to hear your text.'

He somewhat hesitatingly muttered out—

'Ham—Noah's curse, you know?'

'O, sir, you build on a very slender foundation. Granting, even—what remains to be proved—that the Africans are the descendants of Ham, Noah's curse was a *prediction* of future servitude, and not an injunction to oppress. Pray, sir, is it a merciful desire to fulfil the scriptures, or to make money, that induces you to hold your fellow men in bondage?'

'Why, sir,' exclaimed the slavite, with unmingled astonishment, 'do you really think that the slaves are beings like ourselves?—that is, I mean do you believe that they possess the same faculties and capacities as the whites?'

'Certainly, sir,' I responded; 'I do not know that there is any moral or intellectual quality in the curl of the hair, or the color of the skin. I cannot conceive why a black man may not as reasonably object to my color, as I to his. *Sir, it is not a black face that I detest, but a black heart—and I find it very often under a white skin.*'

'Well, sir,' said my querist, 'how should you like to see a black man President of the United States?'

'As to that, sir, I am a true republican, and bow to the will of the majority. If the people prefer a black President, I shall cheerfully submit; and if he be qualified for the station, may peradventure give him my vote.'

'How should you like to have a black man marry your daughter?'

'I am not married—I have no daughter. Sir, I am not familiar with *your* practices; but allow me to say, that slaveholders generally should be the last persons to affect fastidiousness on that point; for they seem to be enamored with *amalgamation*.'

Thus ended the dialogue. Here you have the notions of a Maryland slaveholder.

SPIRIT OF VERMONT.

The editor of the 'Horn of the Green Mountains'—a spirited paper published in Manchester, Vermont—in acknowledging the receipt of our first number, uses the following energetic language on the subject of slavery:

'It is devoted to the cause of emancipation—to the exposure of that vicious traffic which revels in the price of human flesh—which darkens like a nightfall over our otherwise free institutions—which tramples under foot the first great principle of moral liberty, and exposes the revered declaration that 'all men are created equal,' as a mere tumor of fictitious dignity—a mere thief-like guise to cover the emptiness and hollow-heartedness of republican justice, where it stands opposed to human power and human frailty.

The curse of *slavery* is upon us. It is a foul, a deepening, a heaven-daring stain upon the land.—What avails the show of liberty when the reality is wanting?—What avails the spirit that glows in our bosoms at the bare mention of our nation's birth-day, when the clank of chains is heard beneath the very walls of our capitol?—and when oppression, rank, inordinate, cruel oppression, lords it with iron hand over some of our fairest fields and smiling vallies? This then is not a fancy sketch;—it is not the ideal working of a mind grown vapid; it is not the mere indulgence of a mawkish taste. No—*it is real.*—It tells of a national sin; it bespeaks a national calamity. Justice cannot always sleep in quiet on the hill-tomb of the slave. Mercy may avert for a time the doom that justice demands; but our country must be ridden from the curse of slavery, or her southern plains will one day swell and dilate with the tide of human blood.

It may be urged that New-England has nothing to do with slavery,—that the breath of oppression cannot pollute her air, or the footsteps of human ignominy contaminate her soil. But this opinion obtains only in the reckless imbecility of the human heart. It is the same feeling which prompts the slave to live on in toil and in bondage, rather than risk his life in an honorable struggle for emancipation. New England is a part of the great federal compact; the same laws govern, the same power protects. Her influence is felt throughout the Union; and if the oppressed shall rise, and the spirit of Ruin shall sweep along in its desolating track, will *her* arms be folded in despair—will she stand a silent and unconcerned spectator, while the blood of southern myrmidons is smoking upon the plains, and going up a sacrifice to the avenger, to heal the wrongs of centuries? No. Whatever may befal those states—whatever judgment may await them when the spirit which now quails beneath the task-master's lash, is roused to concert and energy of action,—New-England must bear her part. In New-England, then—proud spirited, intelligent, patriotic New-England—let the torch of emancipation be lighted, to avert the doom that otherwise sooner or later awaits this now prosperous and happy republic.'

The following extract from the Diary of Judge Sewall, of this State, shows an early friend to the cause of emancipation and the rights of the blacks. It seems, however, that he was as little successful in his benevolent attempt, as are philanthropists at the present day.

'1716—June 22. I essayed to prevent negroes and Indians being rated with horses and hogs, but could not prevail.'

☞ We are informed, from a credible source, that the late Judge Lowell, who was born in Newburyport, was the first individual in Massachusetts who freed a slave. This fact is peculiarly gratifying to us, being ourselves natives of the same place.

SLAVERY IN MISSISSIPPI.

The following extract of a letter from a lady in Mississippi, (favorably known in Massachusetts, it is said, as the 'Maid of the Grove,') to her Nephew in this State, we find in the New-Bedford Weekly Register. The writer, it seems, does not find the condition of the slave so wretched as she had imagined; and she is 'now reconciled to the expediency of continuing slavery, (!) until emancipation can be effected by a gradual process.' Whether this lady be the wife of a slaveholder, or, if single, whether she expect to wed one for a husband, that has thus altered her opinion of the slave system, we are not informed. In what state of servitude she expected to find the slaves more terrible and heart-rending than their present, we are at a loss to conceive.—They are neither so well treated, as a body, by their masters, nor so efficiently protected by the laws, as cattle: chains are upon their bodies and thick darkness upon their souls. But so it is. Our New-England men and women go to reside in the slave states, and there they 'first endure, then pity, then embrace' the horrid monster, and send home palliatives in behalf of soul-buyers and soul-destroyers. The Lord, in his mercy, save the poor blacks from the dominion of Yankee task-masters!

We are not surprised to learn, that 'very many extensive slaveholders in Mississippi are friendly to the American Colonization Society.' Our wonder is, that this Society, which, in our opinion, is so well adapted to perpetuate slavery and to protect masters, should find any opposition among that class at the south.

'Gladly would I complete this outline of the character of my adopted State, without recurring to a subject which must be revolting to your feelings as a man, a patriot, and a Christian. But alas, the foul blot upon the character of our State is too conspicuous for concealment; and though we share it in common with all the states south of the Potomac, our shame is not lessened. This, however, is an hereditary evil, and has been much ameliorated in its character; but, 'disguise thyself, SLAVERY, as thou wilt, still thou art a bitter draught.' Bitter indeed to all who are concerned in it, not less to the owner than to the slave. Yet the condition of the degraded descendants of Africa is much less deplorable here, than I had imagined before I came to reside among them. After nearly five years' residence in a slaveholding State, and having visited many plantations, and become familiar with the details of slave management, I do not hesitate to say that I would far rather be a slave in Mississippi, than a free black in any of the Northern States. To be called a free man, and yet to feel that there is an impassible barrier between him and other free men, to possess rights in the abstract without being capable of enjoying them, appears to be a far more deplorable condition than that of absolute slavery. That there are men so brutalized that they can extort the sweat and blood of a fellow creature, without considering that nature has bestowed on him any right but the right to suffer, is undeniably true; but such instances are rare. Slavery, in general, is considered an evil which all lament; and I have never met but one person who has justified it on principle. This gentleman is one of the most kind and benevolent men I have ever met, and an uncommonly mild and gentle master. He deduces the practice of slaveholding from scriptural authority, and argues that it is right, because it was permitted to the patriarchs, and was never forbidden by the Saviour of mankind. Though as much as ever opposed to slavery in *principle*, I am reconciled to the *expediency* of continuing the practice, until emancipation can be effected by a gradual process. God speed the Colonization Society, is a wish which I am certain is heartily responded by very many extensive slave holders in Mississippi.'

OUR FREE COUNTRY!

We copy the concluding verse of a poetical effusion from the pen of Mrs. Hale, recently published in her Magazine, which is travelling through the country, and will doubtless be inserted with great complacency in our southern periodicals. How so intelligent and accomplished a lady could deal in such unfortunate glorification, and so outrageously violate truth, we cannot imagine. Do no tyrants reign in this country? Look at the South! Are there not two millions of our countrymen—ay, and *countrywomen*, Mrs Hale—who are trodden under feet, and deprived of all sources of knowledge?

'My country, yes, thy sons are proud,
True heirs of Freedom's glorious dower,
For never here has knee been bowed,
In homage to a mortal power:
No, never here has tyrant reigned,
And never here has thought been chained.
Then who would follow Europe's sickly light,
When here the soul may put forth all her might,
And show the nations as they gaze in awe,
That wisdom dwells with Liberty and Law?
O when will Time his holiest triumph bring—
"Freedom o'er all the earth, and God alone reigns king."'

☞ There is something inexpressibly touching in the following lines, which, one would suppose, must thrill through every nerve even of an iron-hearted slaveholder. They are copied from the last number of the *Genius of Universal Emancipation*, and were written by the young lady who so often enriches its pages with her productions.

THE KING-FISHER.

A newspaper paragraph, of last summer, gives an account of the instance of maternal affection in a bird, which has been made the subject of the following lines:—

The king-fisher sat on her hidden nest,
Shielding her young with a downy breast;
She had built her home where the wave went by,
Soothing her ear with its melody;
And the wild bright blossoms bent to dip
In the rushing waves their thirsty lip.

Pleasant it was while the skies were fair,
And perfume flung on the sunny air,
While the wind in a low sweet whisper died,
Ere it could ruffle the flowing tide;
And the arching skies o'er the waters threw
The deep clear tint of their own pure blue.

But what that is bright, on earth may last?
Soon were the days of her sunshine past:
On came the storm-winds muttering loud,
Sweeping before them the thunder cloud;
And faster, as flashed the lightning's flame,
Dashing to earth the sky-torrents came.

Yet, with her cold wet wing unstirred,
On her shaken nest sat the mother-bird;
Still 'midst danger and death, she clung
With faithful love to her lifeless young,
Till high around her hath risen the tide,
And with her pinion stretched o'er them she died.

Oh! if affection like this hath part
In the warm depths of a wood-bird's heart—
That e'en to die, is a better fate
Than to leave her dear ones desolate;—
What is the love of a mother's breast,
With the seal of a deathless nature prest?

Yet there are men who will rudely tear
The dearest chords that are cherished there;
Wrench from its mother's frantic hold,
Her weeping babes, to be pawn'd for gold;
And scourge her amidst that living death
If she dares but give her wo to breath!

Know ye the land where such deeds are done,
In the broad light of the blessed sun?
Where the spoiler bursts, with savage hand,
The holy links of the household band;
And the ties of nature's love are cast,
With a daring hand, to the idle blast?

CONSTANCE.

SLAVES IN KENTUCKY.

The Legislature of Kentucky have before them two bills designed to afford relief, in some degree, to the slave population. One of them has been ordered to a third reading in the Senate—23 to 11. It prohibits jailors from receiving slaves into jail, unless committed by due process of law, under pain of being removed, and fined $50—the object being to prevent slave traders from using the county jails to facilitate their operations. There may be some efficacy in this bill. The other amounts to nothing. It declares that none shall be slaves in Kentucky, except those that may be such on the 1st of June next, and their descendants, or those which may be introduced by emigrants for other purposes than those of merchandize, or who shall fall to citizens of the State by descent, devise or marriage, together with the descendants of each. Slaves belonging to travellers passing through the State are also excepted from the operation of the bill.

Until the testimony of persons of color against white criminals be admissible in our southern courts of justice, all laws enacted for their benefit will be comparatively nugatory. Without the evidence of white witnesses, they can have no redress for the most cruel treatment. Slaveholders are totally incapacitated to legislate humanely and wisely in behalf of their slaves. ''Trust not,' said the late Secretary Canning of England, in 1799, in speaking of Colonial Slavery—and an experience of thirty years has proved the truth of his words—'trust not the masters of slaves in what concerns legislation for slavery. However specious their laws may appear, depend upon it, they must be ineffectual in their operation. It is in the nature of things that they should be so. Let then the British House of Commons do their part themselves. Let them not delegate the trust of doing it to those who cannot execute that trust fairly. Let the evil be remedied by

Figure 10

Boston
Liberator
1831-1845

Figure 11. William Lloyd Garrison

William Lloyd Garrison

[Editor, *The Liberator*]

William Lloyd Garrison, an American Abolitionist, born in Newburyport, Mass., Dec. 10, 1805. His parents were natives of the province of New Brunswick. His father, Abijah Garrison, was master of a vessel engaged in the West India trade, and a man of some literary ability and taste; but he became intemperate, and, under the influence of that vicious habit, went away from his family while his children were young, and never returned. The mother, left in utter poverty, became a professional nurse, and in 1814 went to Lynn, taking William with her, and placing him with Gamaliel Oliver, a Quaker, to learn the trade of a shoemaker. He was extremely small for his age, and his knees trembled under the weight of the lapstone. His mother, finding that the business did not suit him, sent him back to Newburyport at the end or three of four months, placing him under the care of Deacon Esekiel Bartlett. In order to relieve his mother from the necessity of paying his board, he employed himself when out of school in assisting the deacon in his occupation as a wood-sawyer, going with him from house to house. At school he was taught reading, writing, ciphering, and a smattering of grammar. In 1815 he went with his mother to Baltimore, where he remained a year, in the capacity of a chore boy, and then returned to Newburyport.

In 1818 he was apprenticed to Moses Short, a cabinet-maker, in Haverhill; but, as he strongly disliked the trade, he persuaded Mr. Short to release him. In October of the same year he was indentured to Ephraim W. Allen, editor of the *Newburyport Herald,* to learn the art of printing. This occupation suited his tastes; he quickly became an adept at the mechanical part of the business, and when only 16 or 17 years of age began to write upon political and other topics for the *Herald,* carefully preserving his incognito. It was a long time before Mr. Allen learned that the correspondent whose communications he eagerly sought and commended was his own apprentice, who often had the satisfaction of putting his own articles into type, and once received through the post-office a letter of thanks from his master, with a request that he would continue to write. He soon commenced writing also for the *Haverhill Gazette,* the *Salem Gazette* and the *Boston Commercial Gazette,* all of which received his contributions with favor. The editor of the journal last named, Samuel L. Knapp, Esq., appreciated his articles very highly. A series of papers which he wrote for the *Salem Gazette,* under the signature of "Aristides," attracted much attention in political circles, being commended by Robert Walsh, at that time editor of the Philadelphia *National Gazette,* who attributed them to the venerable Timothy Pickering. In 1824, during the somewhat protracted absence of Mr. Allen, he edited the *Herald,* superintending the printing at the same time. The struggle of the Greeks for freedom fired his youthful zeal, insomuch that at one time he seriously contemplated entering the academy at West Point, to qualify himself for a military career.

In 1826, his apprenticeship being honorably closed, he became the proprietor and editor of a journal in his native town, called the *Free Press.* He toiled hard, generally putting his editorial articles in type without committing them to paper, but the enterprise proved unsuccessful. He then went to Boston, where he worked for a time as a journeyman. In 1827 he became the editor of the *National Philanthropist* in that city, the first journal ever established to advocate the cause of "total abstinence"; but before the end of the year the proprietorship changed, and he was induced, early in 1828, to join a friend in the publication of the *Journal of the Times* at Bennington, Vt. This journal supported John Quincy Adams for the Presidency, and was in part devoted to peace, temperance, anti-slavery, and other reforms; but it failed to receive an adequate support. During his residence in Bennington, he produced considerable excitement upon the subject of slavery, not only in that place, but throughout the State, in consequence of which there was transmitted to Congress an anti-slavery memorial more numerously signed than any similar paper previously submitted to that body.

Benjamin Lundy, an advocate of the gradual abolition of slavery, was then engaged in publishing the *Genius of Universal Emancipation* at Baltimore. He had met Mr. Garrison during the previous year in Boston, and received from him timely assistance in bringing his cause to the notice of the people of that city. Admiring his talents and zeal, and wishing for a coadjutor, he went to Bennington, and engaged Mr. Garrison to join him in the editorship of his journal. On July 4, 1829, Mr. Garrison delivered in Park street Church, Boston, at a religious and philanthropic celebration of the day, an address which excited general attention by the boldness and vigor of its assault upon slavery. In the autumn of that year he began his labors in Baltimore as joint editor with Mr. Lundy of the *Genius of Universal Emancipation,* and in the first number issued under his supervision he made a distinct avowal of the doctrine of immediate emancipation as the right of the slave and the duty of the master. Mr. Lundy did not concur with him in this doctrine, but as each of them appended his initials to his articles, the difference interposed no barrier to hearty cooperation.

The journal, by its bold and uncompromising tone, produced considerable excitement among the supporters of slavery, while Mr. Garrison's denunciation of the Colonization Society aroused the hostility of some who, upon other grounds, were inclined to sympathize with him. An event soon occurred which resulted in a dissolution of his connection with the paper. The ship *Francis,* owned by Francis Todd of Newburyport, having taken a cargo of slaves from Baltimore to Louisiana, Mr. Garrison denounced the act as a "domestic piracy," and declared his purpose to "cover with thick infamy" all those implicated therein. Baltimore being then the seat of an extensive domestic traffic in slaves, his denunciation produced a great deal of feeling, and he was in consequence indicted and convicted, in the City Court, May term, 1830, for "a gross and malicious libel" against the owner and master of the *Francis,* though it was proved by the custom-house records that the number of slaves transported was much greater than he had alleged. He was sentenced to pay a fine of $50 and costs of Court. He was defended by Charles Mitchell, who held a position at the Baltimore bar second only to that of William Wirt. Being unable to discharge the judgement, he was committed to jail. Mr. Todd, in a civil suit for damages, subsequently obtained a verdict against him for $1,000; but the judgement, probably on account of his well-known poverty, was never enforced.

During his incarceration, he occupied a cell just vacated by a man who had been hanged for murder. He was, however, treated very kindly by the jailer. He at once interested himself in the cause of some of his fellow-prisoners, and was instrumental in procuring the release of some who were deserving of merciful consideration, by writing petitions in their behalf to the Governor. He eagerly embraced the opportunity afforded him for conversing with speculators to slaves, who came to the prison to purchase recaptured slaves, always urging his anti-slavery opinions upon them. His friend Lundy and a few other Quakers were the only persons who visited him to express their sympathy. The press at the North generally condemned his imprisonment as unjust. His letters to different newspapers excited a deep interest, and several sonnets which he inscribed on the walls of his cell were spoken of in influential quarters as worthy of an honorable place in literature. The Manumission Society of North Carolina protested against his imprisonment as an infraction of the liberty of the press.

He remained in jail forty-nine days, when Arthur Tappan, a merchant of New York, paid the fine and costs, and he was set at liberty. It subsequently appeared that Mr. Tappan had, in this act, anticipated by a few days the generous purpose of Henry Clay, whose interposition had been invoked by a mutual friend. Daniel Webster, soon after his release, gave him willing audience, and addressed him in words of sympathy and encouragement. His next step was to issue a prospectus for an anti-slavery journal, to be published in Washington; and with a view to excite a deeper interest in his enterprise, he prepared a course of lectures on slavery, which he subsequently delivered in Philadelphia, New York, New Haven, Hartford and Boston. In Baltimore, his attempts to obtain a hearing were unsuccessful. Private efforts to procure a suitable place for the delivery of his lectures in Boston having been made in vain, he advertised in one of the daily journals that, if a meeting-house or hall were not offered before a certain day, he would address the people on the Common. An association of persons calling themselves Infidels thereupon proffered him the gratuitous use of a hall under their control, and, no other offer being made, he delivered his lectures in the place thus opened; taking care, at the same time, to avow his faith in Christianity as the power which alone could break the bonds of the slaves.

His lectures were attended by large audiences, and awakened in some minds a permanent interest in the anti-slavery cause. His experiences as a lecturer, however, convinced him that Boston rather than Washington was the best location for an anti-slavery journal, and that a revolution of public sentiment at the North must precede emancipation at the South. He accordingly issued the first number of *The Liberator* in Boston, Jan. 1, 1831, taking for his motto, "My Country is the World, my Countrymen are all Mankind"; and declaring, in the face of the almost universal apathy upon the subject of slavery, "I am in earnest, I will not equivocate, I will not excuse, I will not retreat a single inch, and I will be heard." Mr. Isaac Knapp was his partner in the printing and publishing department. As they were without capital or promise of support from any quarter, they were unable to open an office on their own account.

The foreman in the office of the *Christian Examiner,* being a warm personal friend of Mr. Garrison, generously employed him and his partner as journeymen, taking their labor as compensation in part for the use of his types. Mr. Garrison, after working mechanically in the daytime, spent a large portion of the night in editorial labor. Having issued one number, they waited anxiously to see whether they would find encouragement to proceed.

The receipt of $50 from James Forten, a wealthy colored citizen of Philadelphia, with the names of twenty-five subscribers, was the first cheering incentive to perseverance, and the journal was issued without interruption from that day. At the end of three weeks they opened an office for themselves; but for nearly two years their resources were so restricted that they made the office their only domicile. Their bed was made on the floor, and they subsisted upon the humblest fare.

The Liberator attracted general attention, not only at the North, but at the South. In some quarters it found sympathy, in others it was denounced as fanatical and incendiary. The Mayor of Boston, Harrison Gray Otis, having been appealed to by a Southern magistrate to suppress it, if possible, by law, wrote in reply that his officers had "ferreted out the paper and its editor, whose office was an obscure hole, his only visible auxiliary a negro boy, his supporters a very few insignificant persons of all colors." Almost every mail, at this period, brought letters threatening Mr. Garrison with assassination if he did not discontinue his journal; and in December, 1831, the Legislature of Georgia passed an act, offering a reward of $5,000 to any person who should arrest, bring to trial, and prosecute to conviction, under the laws of that State, the editor or the publisher. Many of Mr. Garrison's friends, deeming his life seriously imperilled, besought him to arm himself for defence; but, being a non-resistant, he was conscientiously restrained from following their advice.

On January 1, 1832, he secured the cooperation of eleven others with himself in organizing the New England (afterward Massachusetts) Anti-Slavery Society, upon the principle of immediate emancipation. This was the parent of those numerous affiliated associations by which the anti-slavery agitation was for many years maintained. In the spring of 1832 he published a work entitled "Thoughts on African Colonization," &c., in which he set forth at length the grounds of his opposition to that scheme. He went immediately afterward to England, as an agent of the New England Anti-Slavery Society, to solicit the cooperation of the people of that country in measures designed to promote emancipation in the United States, and to lay before them his views of the colonization project. He was warmly received by Wilberforce, Brougham, and their associates. In consequence of statements made by Mr. Garrison, Wilberforce and eleven of his most prominent coad-jutors issued a protest against the American Colonization Society, pronouncing its plans delusive, and its influence an obstruction to the abolition of slavery. He also succeeded in inducing Mr. George Thompson, one of the most prominent champions of the anti-slavery cause in Great Britain, to come to the United States as an anti-slavery lecturer. Soon after Mr. Garrison's return, the American Anti-Slavery Society was organized at Philadelphia, upon the principles of which he was the champion. The "Declaration of Sentiments" issued by the association—an elaborate paper, setting forth its principles, aims and methods—was prepared by him.

The agitation previously excited was now greatly intensified, and at length awakened a resistance which manifested itself in a mobocratic spirit, insomuch that for two or three years the holding of an anti-slavery meeting almost anywhere in the free States was a signal for riotous demonstrations, imperilling property and life. Mr. Thompson's arrival from England in 1834 inflamed the public mind to such a degree that at length, by the advice of his friends, he was induced to desist from his labors and return to his native land.

In October, 1835, a meeting of the Female Anti-Slavery Society of Boston was riotously broken up by a collection of persons, described in the journals of the day as "gentlemen of property and standing." Mr. Garrison, who went to the meeting to deliver an address, after attempting to conceal himself from the fury of the mob in a carpenter's shop in the rear of the hall, was violently seized, let down by a rope from the window to the ground, and, partly denuded of his clothing, dragged through the streets to the City Hall; whence, as the only means of saving his life, he was taken to jail by order of the Mayor, upon the nominal charge that he was "a disturber of the peace." He was released on the following day, and, under protection of the city authorities, escorted to a place of safety in the country.

These scenes of violence were followed by a discussion of the Peace question, in which he took an earnest part as a champion of non-resistance; and in 1838 he led the way in the organization of the New England Non-Resistance Society. The "Declaration of Sentiments" issued by that body was prepared by him. About this time, the question of the rights of women as members of the Anti-Slavery Societies began to be mooted, Mr. Garrison contending that, so far as they wished to do so, they should be permitted to vote, serve on committees, and take part in discussion, on equal terms with men. Upon this question there was a division of the American Anti-Slavery Society in 1840; and in the "World's Anti-Slavery Convention," held that year in London, Mr. Garrison, being a delegate from that Society, refused to take a seat because the female delegates from the United States were excluded. . . .

He was ever earnestly opposed to the formation of a political party by the Abolitionists, from a conviction that such a measure would inevitably corrupt the purity of the movement and postpone the day when emancipation might be secured. He never sought or contemplated the abolition of slavery in the States by Congress, or any other branch of the National government, his views as to the powers of that government over the subject being the same that were generally held by statesmen of all parties at the North, as well as by many at the South. His first idea was, that slavery might be abolished by moral influence, with such incidental aid as the National government could constitutionally afford, and without disturbing the Union of the States; but upon this point he at length changed his opinions, his observation of the movements of political parties and his reflections upon the provisions of the Constitution relating to the subject leading him to the settled conclusion that some of the conditions of compact between the free and the slave States were immoral, and that a dissolution of the Union was necessary to the freedom of the North and the emancipation of the slaves. In 1846 he made his third visit, for anti-slavery purposes, to Great Britain. In 1843 a small volume of his "Sonnets and other Poems" was published; and in 1852 appeared a volume of "Selections" from his "Writings and Speeches" (12 mo., Boston). . . .

During his life, Mr. Garrison made four or five visits to England for antislavery purposes, and was received with much distinction. On one of these occasions the Duchess of Sutherland, the Mistress of the Robes—a kind of female prime minister—invited him to sit for his portrait, and subsequently placed it among the pictures of nobles and statemen that adorn the walls of Stafford House. While abroad in 1867 the Duke of Argyll, John Bright, John Stuart Mill, Earl Russell, and other prominent persons, gave him a banquet in London; while the Lord Provost of Edinburgh, in obedience to a vote of the civil authorities, conferred upon him the freedom of the metropolis of Scotland.

In 1843 Mr. Garrison was chosen President of the American Antislavery Society. He held the position till the anniversary meeting in May, 1865, when, the war being over and the negroes free, he counseled the dissolution of the Society on the ground that its work was done, insisting that an American antislavery society was a misnomer after American slavery had ceased to exist. He failed to carry his point, and thereupon he resigned the office of President. On the same grounds he suspended the publication of the *"Liberator"* at the close of the war. Its work was done. [He died in New York City on 24 May 1879.]

National Anti-Slavery Standard, [N.Y.],
24 December 1859, p.5, c6 and
Appleton's Annual Cyclopaedia,
n.s. IV (1879), 396–98. [Some paragraph indentions added.]

Journal Data

TITLE: *The Liberator*

MOTTO: "Our Country is the World—Our Countrymen are Mankind"

INCLUSIVE DATES OF PUBLICATION: 1 Jan. 1831–29 Dec. 1865 (Vol. I-35)

PLACE OF PUBLICATION: Boston, Massachusetts

FREQUENCY OF PUBLICATION: Weekly

DAY OF WEEK WHEN PUBLISHED: Sat. (1 Jan. 1831–18 Mar. 1837); Friday (24 Mar. 1837–?)

AVERAGE NUMBER OF PAGES PER ISSUE: 4

NUMBER OF COLUMNS PER PAGE: 4

EDITOR: William Lloyd Garrison

PUBLISHER(s): William Lloyd Garrison (1 Jan. 1831–2 Jan. 183?); Isaac Knapp (1 Jan. 1831–?)

PRINTER(s): Stephen Foster (1 Jan. 1831–?); Isaac Knapp (4 Jan. 1839–27 Dec. 1839); Oliver Johnson (3 Jan. 1840–4 June 1841); J. Brown Yerrington (11 June 1841–29 Dec. 1848)

SPECIAL FEATURES: Advertisements; Illustrations; Annual Indexes; Cartoons

PRICE: Annual Subscription $2.00; changed 8 December 1837 to: $2.50 Annual Subscription

PERSPECTIVE: Anti-slavery

REPOSITORY: Sterling Memorial Library, Yale University. 1 Jan. 1831-29 Dec. 1865. See also Beinecke Rare Book and Manuscript Library.

Prospectus

In the month of August, I issued proposals for publishing '*The Liberator*' in Washington City; but the enterprise, though hailed in different sections of the country, was palsied by public indifference. Since that time, the removal of the *Genius of Universal Emancipation* to the Seat of Government has rendered less imperious the establishment of a similar periodical in that quarter.

During my recent tour for the purpose of exciting the minds of the people by a series of discourses on the subject of slavery, every place that I visited gave fresh evidence of the fact, that a greater revolution in public sentiment was to be effected in the free states—and particularly in New England—than at the South. I found contempt more bitter, opposition more active, detraction more relentless, prejudice more stubborn, and apathy more frozen than among slave owners themselves. Of course there were individual exceptions to the contrary. This state of things afflicted, but did not dishearten me. I determined, at every hazard, to lift up the standard of emancipation in the eyes of the nation, within sight of Bunker Hill and in the birth place of liberty. That standard is now unfurled: and long may it float, unhurt by the spoliations of time or the missiles of a desperate foe—yea, till every chain be broken, and every bondman set free. Let southern oppressors tremble—let their secret abettors tremble—let their northern apologists tremble—let all the enemies of the presecuted blacks tremble.

I deem the publication of my original Prospectus* unnecessary, as it has obtained a wide circulation. The principles therein inculcated will be steadily pursued in this paper, excepting that I shall not array myself as the political partisan of any man. In defending the great cause of human rights, I wish to derive the assistance of all religions and of all parties.

Assenting to the 'self-evident truth' maintained in the American Declaration of Independence, 'that all men are created equal, and endowed by their Creator with certain inalienable rights—among which are life, liberty, and the pursuit of happiness,' I shall strenuously contend for the immediate enfranchisement of our slave population. In Parkstreet Church, on the Fourth of July, 1829, in an address on slavery, I unreflectingly assented to the popular but pernicious doctrine of gradual abolition. I seize this opportunity to make a full and unequivocal recantation, and thus publicly to ask pardon of my God, of my country, and of brethren the poor slaves for having uttered a sentiment so full of timidity, injustice, and absurdity. A similar recantation from my pen was published in the *Genius of Universal Emancipation* at Baltimore, in September, 1829. My conscience is now satisfied.

I am aware, that many object to the severity of my language; but is there not cause for severity; I will be as harsh as truth, and as uncompromising as justice. On this subject I do not wish to think, or speak, or write, with moderation. No! no! Tell a man whose house is on fire, to give a moderate alarm; tell him to moderately rescue his wife from the hands of

---

*I would here offer my grateful acknowledgement to those editors who so promptly and generously inserted my Proposals. They must give me an available opportunity to repay their liberality.

the ravisher; tell the mother to gradually extricate her babe from the fire into which it has fallen;—but urge me not to use moderation in a cause like the present. I am in earnest—I will not equivocate—I will not excuse—I will not retreat a single inch—and I will be heard. The apathy of the people is enough to make every statue leap from its pedestal, and to hasten the resurrection of the dead.

It is pretended that I am retarding the cause of emancipation by the coarseness of my invective, and the precipitancy of my measures. The charge is not true. On this question my influence,—humble as it is—is felt at this moment to a considerable extent, and shall be felt in coming years—not perniciously, but beneficially—not as a curse, but as a blessing; and posterity will bear testimony that I was right. I desire to thank God, that he enables me to disregard 'the fear of man which bringeth a snare,' and to speak his truth in its simplicity and power. And here I close with this fresh dedication:

'Oppression! I have seen thee, face to face,
And meet thy cruel eye and cloudy brow;
But thy soul-withering glance I fear not now—
For dread to prouder feelings doth give place,
Of deep abhorrence! Scorning the disgrace
Of slavish knees that at thy footstool bow,
I also kneel—but with far other vow
Do hail thee and thy herd of hirelings base—
I swear, while life-blood warms my throbbing veins,
Still to oppose and thwart, with heart and hand,
Thy brutalising sway—till Afric's chains
Are burst, and Freedom rules the rescued land,—
Trampling Oppression and his iron rod;
Such is the vow I take—SO HELP ME GOD!'

WILLIAM LLOYD GARRISON
Boston, January 1, 1831.

The Liberator, Boston, [Mass.], January 1, 1831

[1831]

755 ONE OF THE MOST DISTINGUISHED REFORMERS OF THE AGE *to* **n.n.** [extract] **n.d. n.p.** Urges abolition of slavery; proposes examination of the subject rather than fear of discovering the crime of slavery. 1 January 1831. p.3, c1.

756 GENTLEMAN IN VERMONT *to* **SIR. [W. L. GARRISON].** [extract] **n.d. n.p.** Applauds beginning of Garrison's paper, the *Liberator;* encourages Garrison's enthusiasm; affirms that moral uprightness is on the side of the abolitionists. 1 January 1831. p.3, c1.

757 GENTLEMAN IN MOUNT VERNON (N. H.) *to* **SIR [W. L. GARRISON].** [extract] **n.d. n.p.** Wishes publisher "godspeed"; asks to be added to list of subscribers. 1 January 1831. p.3, c2.

758 A COLORED MAN IN A DISTANT CITY *to* **SIR [W. L. GARRISON]. n.d. n.p.** Rejoices to hear that the *Liberator* has been established and is working for equality and justice. 8 January 1831. p.7, c2.

759 WM. CORBETT *to* **THE KING. 17 November 1830. Bolt Court.** Proposes to stop the burnings which are disrupting the country. 15 January 1831. p.11, c3.

760 n.n. *to* **THE EDITOR [W. L. GARRISON]. n.d. n.p.** Suggests that the government buy Texas and reserve part of it for free colored people. 22 January 1831. p.13, c1.

761 U. I. E. *to* **THE EDITOR [W. L. GARRISON]. 4 January 1831. n.p.** Suggests creation of a juvenile department in his paper to teach children the evils of slavery while they are young. 22 January 1831. p.13, c2.

762 A MAN OF COLOR *to* **THE EDITOR [W. L. GARRISON].** Thanks editor for educating people on the oppression of slavery. 22 January 1831. p.14, c3.

763 A COLORED BOSTONIAN *to* **THE EDITOR [W. L. GARRISON]. n.d. Boston.** Describes suspicious death of "Walker," author of a flagitious pamphlet. 22 January 1831. p.14, c4.

764 JAMES G. BARBADOES *to* **THE EDITOR [W. L. GARRISON]. 20 January 1831. Brattle Street.** Asks editor to call upon African Humane and Abolition Societies to persevere for liberation. 22 January 1831. p.14, c4.

765 A GENTLEMAN IN PHILADELPHIA *to* **A FRIEND. 13 January 1831. Philadelphia.** Discusses first issue of *Liberator* and foolishness of colonizing people of color in Liberia. 22 January 1831. p.15, c1.

766 A. L. *to* **THE EDITOR [W. L. GARRISON]. n.d. n.p.** Suggests creation of a column, "Slavery Record," to record evil occurrences of slavery such as murders, atrocities, etc. 29 January 1831. p.17, c3.

767 R. *to* **THE EDITOR [W. L. GARRISON]. 20 January 1831. Philadelphia.** Presents short essay on Liberty and its joys and privileges. 29 January 1831. p.17, c3.

768 LEO *to* **THE EDITOR [W. L. GARRISON]. 21 January 1831. Philadelphia.** States his opposition to pamphlet, "Walker's Appeal." [notes from Garrison follow] 29 January 1831. p.17, c4.

769 n.n. *to* **THE EDITOR [W. L. GARRISON]. n.d. n.p.** States that law prohibiting whites from marrying blacks and mulattoes is unjust and unfair. 29 January 1831. p.18, c1.

770 W. *to* **THE EDITOR [W. L. GARRISON]. n.d. n.p.** Compares working for the rights of slaves to working for the rights of the working class. 29 January 1831. p.19, c3.

771 "THE MAID OF THE GROVE," A LADY IN MISSISSIPPI *to* **HER NEPHEW IN MASSACHUSETTS. [extract] n.d. Mississippi.** Opposes the principle of slavery, but reconciles herself to its expediency until slavery can be gradually abolished. 5 February 1831. p.21, c3.

772 J. I. W. *to* **THE EDITOR [W. L. GARRISON]. n.d. n.p.** Discusses a letter on *Walker's Appeal* from "Leo," published in 29 January *Liberator.* 5 February 1831. p.22, c2.

773 W. *to* **THE EDITOR [W. L. GARRISON]. n.d. n.p.** Questions the necessity of an unequal distribution of luxury in the United States. 5 February 1831. p.23, c3.

774 A COLORED PHILADELPHIAN *to* **THE EDITOR [W. L. GARRISON].   3 February 1831. Philadelphia, Pa.** Believes emigration to Africa is absurd; advocates that ACS spend money promoting education and equality of colored people, not on forcing them back to Africa. 12 February 1831. p.25, c3.

775 PAUL CUFFEE *to* **THE PEOPLE OF COLOR. n.d. Philadelphia, Pa.** Urges colored people to put shoulders to the wheel and stop being passive; wants them to gain the power of knowledge, not expect "benevolent white friends" to do all the work. 12 February 1831. p.25, c4.

776 JAMES G. BARBADOES *to* **THE EDITOR [W. L. GARRISON]. n.d. n.p.** Commends editor on his fine paper; urges abolition of slavery to ensure true liberty and justice in America. 12 February 1831. p.26, c1.

777 S. T. U. *to* **THE EDITOR [W. L. GARRISON]. 12 February 1831. n.p.** Calls for a thorough investigation and free discussion of abstinence from slave labor products; includes twelve questions of fact and opinion for readers. 19 February 1831. p.29, c3.

778 A. *to* **n.n. 9 February 1831. Philadelphia.** Urges those who are opposed to the oppression of slavery not to "touch" the products of slave labor. 19 February 1831. p.29, c3.

779 A MAN OF COLOR *to* **THE EDITOR [W. L. GARRISON]. n.d. n.p.** Declares that attainment of just rights for colored people depends on education and supplication to God. 19 February 1831. p.29, c4.

780 A COLORED BALTIMOREAN *to* **THE EDITOR [W. L. GARRISON]. 12 February 1831. Baltimore.** Criticizes ministers who protect slaveholders by not speaking out against slavery; urges them to "cry aloud and spare not: lift up thy voice like a trumpet." 19 February 1831. p.30, c1.

781 LEO *to* **THE EDITOR [W. L. GARRISON]. 9 February 1831. Philadelphia.** In response to "J. I. W.'"s letter in 5 February *Liberator,* states he supports neither Gordon nor Walker. 19 February 1831. p.30, c2.

782 T. *to* **THE EDITOR [W. L. GARRISON]. n.d. n.p.** Excerpts from a diary written while he was travelling in the South; includes story of a slave beaten to death, accounts of starvation, and lack of sleeping facilities for the slaves. 19 February 1831. p.30, c3.

783 n.n. *to* **THE EDITOR [W. L. GARRISON]. [extract] n.d. Connecticut.** Prophesies there will never be peace within the country's border as long as slavery exists. 26 February 1831. p.33, c1.

784 n.n. *to* **THE EDITOR [W. L. GARRISON]. [extract] n.d. Connecticut.** Declares that nation must do justice to people of color to avert "the vengeance of Jehovah." 26 February 1831. p.33, c1.

785 n.n. *to* **THE EDITOR [W. L. GARRISON]. [extract] n.d. District of Columbia.** Thanks editor for giving nation "moral energy." 26 February 1831. p.33, c1.

786 n.n. *to* **THE EDITOR [W. L. GARRISON]. [extract] n.d. Indiana.** Encourages editor to persevere; promises aid and encouragement. 26 February 1831. p.33, c2.

787 n.n. *to* **THE EDITOR [W. L. GARRISON]. [extract] n.d. Vermont.** Expresses hope that *Liberator* will pour light upon New England. 26 February 1831. p.33, c2.

788 n.n. *to* **THE EDITOR [W. L. GARRISON]. [extract] n.d. New York.** Cites universal emancipation, not colonization, as only method of redeeming nation from evil of slavery. 26 February 1831. p.33, c2.

789 n.n. *to* **THE EDITOR [W. L. GARRISON]. [extract] 18 February 1831. Hartford.** Praises the *Liberator,* and wishes for freedom of colored people in United States; thinks the CS is a good thing insofar as it is conducted properly. 26 February 1831. p.33, c4.

790 JOHN WESLEY *to* **n.n. [extract] n.d. n.p.** Urges friend to keep fighting American slavery, "the vilest that ever saw the sun." 4 March 1831. p.37, c1.

791 n.n. *to* **THE EDITOR OF THE** *CHRISTIAN REGISTER.* **n.d. n.p.** Suggests that the ACS use its funds for educating free colored people instead of exporting them. 4 March 1831. p.38, c1.

792 CATO *to* **THE EDITOR [W. L. GARRISON]. 23 February 1831. Philadelphia.** Colored man writes to denounce emigration to Africa. 12 March 1831. p.41, c2.

793 S. T. U. *to* **THE EDITOR [W. L. GARRISON]. n.d. n.p.** Comments on childish and un-Christian prejudice against colored citizens in the North. 12 March 1831. p.41, c3.

794 HANNIBAL *to* **COLONIZATIONISTS. n.d. Philadelphia.** Derides colonizations for their "unrighteous schemes" and "fruitless attempts" at justice and humanity. 12 March 1831. p.42, c2.

795 F. *to* **THE EDITOR [W. L. GARRISON]. 28 February 1831. Philadelphia.** Cries for an end to the tyranny of slavery. 19 March 1831. p.46.

796 A COLORED PHILADELPHIAN *to* **THE EDITOR [W. L. GARRISON]. 28 February 1831. Philadelphia.** Asserts that colored people want schools, trades, businesses, not deportation. 19 March 1831. p.46, c2.

797 C. D. P. *to* **THE EDITOR [W. L. GARRISON]. 3 March 1831. Philadelphia.** Questions why Philadelphia is the only place in the state where colored people cannot vote. 19 March 1831. p.46, c4.

798 A. B. *to* **MR. EDITOR [W. L. GARRISON]. 6 March 1831. Philadelphia.** Describes meeting of young men of color; makes enthusiastic promise of patronage to the *Liberator.* 19 March 1831. p.46, c4.

799 T. *to* **MR. EDITOR [W. L. GARRISON]. n.d. n.p.** Expresses interest in the *Liberator;* includes extracts from "A Journal written from the South in 1813." 19 March 1831. p.47, c1.

800 SAMUEL K. SNEAD *to* **MR. T. T. SKILLMAN. 26 February 1831. n.p.** Asks to be included in the fifty supporters of Essay No. Six. 19 March 1831. p.50, c1.

801 MAGAWISCA *to* **THE EDITOR [W. L. GARRISON]. 14 March 1831. Philadelphia.** Condemns white American slaveholders for their inhumanity and abuse of liberty. 26 March 1831. p.50, c2.

802 A. B. *to* **MR. EDITOR [W. L. GARRISON]. n.d. n.p.** Encloses an article from the *Boston Recorder* suggesting that white children contribute a penny to Sunday school to send "children whose skins are a little darker" to Africa. 26 March 1831. p.50, c2.

803 n.n. *to* **MR. EDITOR [W. L. GARRISON]. 13 March 1831. Hartford.** Comments on the potential ability of slaves to overthrow their masters. 26 March 1831. p.50, c3.

804 A MEMBER OF THE SOCIETY OF FRIENDS IN THE STATE OF NEW YORK *to* **n.n. [extract] n.d. New York.** Urges freedom; condemns colonization. 26 March 1831. p.50, c3.

805 n.n. *to* **MESSRS. EDITORS OF THE** *NEW YORK OBSERVER.* **21 February 1831. Washington City.** Discusses Cherokee problems and Indian oppression. 26 March 1831. p.52, c2.

806 n.n. *to* **THE EDITOR [W. L. GARRISON]. n.d. n.p.** Replies to S. T. V.'s letter in 19 February *Liberator;* cites reasons for not buying slave labor products. 2 April 1831. p.54, c1.

807 MRS. SARAH SKINNER *to* **COUSIN IN HARTFORD. [extract] 21 March 1831. Ashford.** Laments the deaths of her son, his wife, and their children in Africa. 2 April 1831. p.56, c2.

808 n.n. *to* **THE EDITOR [W. L. GARRISON]. n.d. Hudson, N.Y.** Discusses Quakers' negative attitudes toward slavery. 9 April 1831. p.57, c3.

809 A COLORED LADY *to* **THE EDITOR [W. L. GARRISON]. n.d. Medford.** Points out hypocrisy of slavery in the "land of liberty"; criticizes so-called "Christian" slaveowners. 9 April 1831. p.57, c3.

810 ONEAS *to* **MR. EDITOR. n.d. Philadelphia.** Believes that colored people must actively protest against the CS. 9 April 1831. p.57, c4.

811 ADRIAN *to* **THE EDITOR [W. L. GARRISON]. n.d. Philadelphia.** Questions why intelligent men have not actively defended colored people. 9 April 1831. p.57, c4.

812 n.n. *to* **THE EDITOR [W. L. GARRISON]. n.d. Hartford, Ct.** Compliments editor on his courage and morals. 9 April 1831. p.58, c1.

813 PAUL CUFFEE *to* **THE EDITOR OF THE** *LIBERATOR* **[W. L. GARRISON]. 27 March 1831. Philadelphia.** States that man is his own worst foe but that the "Great Arbiter" will punish the wicked and aid the oppressed. 9 April 1831. p.58, c1.

814 R. *to* **THE EDITOR [W. L. GARRISON]. 8 April 1831. Philadelphia.** Attacks editor of *Liberia Herald;* desires to remain in America. 16 April 1831. p.62, c2.

815 A FRIEND TO EMANCIPATION *to* **THE EDITOR [W. L. GARRISON]. n.d. n.p.** Suggests establishment of missions and schools among slaves to aid emancipation. 16 April 1831. p.62, c3.

816 A. O. *to* **THE EDITOR [W. L. GARRISON]. n.d. n.p.** Supports emancipation, but not sure whether gradual or immediate. 23 April 1831. p.65, c3.

817 S. *to* **THE EDITOR [W. L. GARRISON]. 22 March 1831. Philadelphia.** Compliments editor on fine and humane paper. 23 April 1831. p.66, c2.

818 V. *to* **THE EDITOR [W. L. GARRISON]. n.d. n.p.** Gives detailed critique of *Walker's Appeal.* 30 April 1831. p.69, c1.

819 C. D. T. *to* **THE EDITOR [W. L. GARRISON]. n.d. Philadelphia.** Discusses negative effects of CS. 30 April 1831. p.70, c3.

820 AMERICAN GENTLEMAN *to* **HIS CORRESPONDENT IN NEW HAVEN. [extract] 24 March 1831. Antigua.** Reports that island is in state of insurrection but martial law may soon restore order. 30 April 1831. p.71, c4.

821 n.n. *to* **n.n. [extract] 17 March 1831. Havana.** Reports on low price of sugar, condition of Negroes. 30 April 1831. p.71, c4.

822 JOHN P. BIGELOW *to* **THE EDITOR OF THE** *COURIER.* **n.d. n.p.** Writes letter to exonerate himself, after being accused of supporting intermarriage between people of different colors; explains that he opposed a restrictive marriage law as weak and unfair, particularly in its prohibition of Indian-white marriages; expresses disapproval of black-white unions. 30 April 1831. p.72, c2.

823 n.n. *to* **n.n. [extract] 13 April 1831. Norfolk.** Relates account of a Negro who saved the life of a white man; the latter subsequently wanted to buy the slave and set him free. 30 April 1831. p.72, c3.

824 A COLORED AMERICAN *to* **THE COLORED CITIZENS OF NEW YORK. 22 April 1831. New York.** Remarks sarcastically on advertisement by CS of New York for passage to Africa. 7 May 1831. p.73, c2.

825 ADAM ARATOR *to* **THE EDITOR [W. L. GARRISON]. n.d. n.p.** Farmer explains how his wife and children convinced him to change from slave to free articles, even though they are more expensive. 7 May 1831. p.74, c1.

826 Y. L. *to* **THE EDITOR [W. L. GARRISON]. n.d. n.p.** Relates account of how household servants overcame their prejudice against a black servant and learned to treat her as an equal; discusses the excellent qualities of this woman, and urges others who know intelligent, kind black people to tell about them. 7 May 1831. p.74, c2.

827 NO "WHITE SLAVE" *to* **THE EDITOR [W. L. GARRISON]. n.d. n.p.** Tells of evil young man in a Southern state, who inherited a plantation and slaves and beat a pregnant slave woman to death while she was tied to a pole; laments that the public censure was expressed in dislike and avoidance, but no legal recourse or punishment was forced upon him. 7 May 1831. p.74, c3.

828 n.n. *to* **NEW YORK COMMERCIAL ADVERTISER. [extract] 21 March 1831. London.** Discusses the excitement over the Reform Bill; notes interesting speeches and debates by Robert Peel, Sir Charles Wetherell, Tom Macanley, and Shelley. 7 May 1831. p.76, c2.

829 J. E. *to* **THE EDITOR [W. L. GARRISON]. n.d. n.p.** Urges readers to use free articles rather than those produced by slaves; believes that everyone has a duty to do anything that might help and that such an action would bring together those supporting the cause. 14 May 1831. p.78, cl.

830 O. L. *to* **THE EDITOR [W. L. GARRISON]. n.d. n.p.** Hopes that Bible Society will distribute Bibles to both black and white people in the South; feels that the principles of the gospel will lead to abolition of slavery. 14 May 1831. p.78, c3.

831 N. *to* **THE** *CHRISTIAN REGISTER.* **n.d. n.p.** Objects to CS because it abuses and depresses free blacks and retards emancipation of slaves. 14 May 1831. p.79, c1.

832 n.n. *to* **THE** *LIBERATOR.* **n.d. Boston.** Attacks lotteries for stealing from the poor; hopes that Rhode Island will outlaw them so tickets will stop coming into Boston. 14 May 1831. p.80, c4.

833 COLORED GENTLEMAN *to* **n.n. [extract] 30 April 1831. New York.** Criticizes Col. Stone of CS; tells of Rev. Benjamin Paul and sixty others who emigrated to Canada. 21 May 1831. p.81, c1.

834 n.n. *to* **n.n. [extract] n.d. Maine.** Announces plans to open a school for blacks in Maine. 21 May 1831. p.81, c1.

835 NO "WHITE SLAVE" *to* **THE EDITOR [W. L. GARRISON]. n.d. n.p.** Discusses the evils of slavery, with a reminder that whites started slavery; claims that even now Boston men are involved in slave trade; notes that Massachusetts representatives just voted in Congress to extend slavery to Missouri. 21 May 1831. p.81, c4.

836 J. C. *to* **MR. EDITOR [W. L. GARRISON]. n.d. n.p.** Asks to present to the public a petition from John Eliot, written during the time of Philip's War, against selling Indians as slaves [petition follows]. 21 May 1831. p.82, c1.

837 n.n. *to* **n.n. [extract] 21 February 1831. Charleston.** Gives account of a slave auction. 21 May 1831. p.82, c2.

838 Q. *to* **MR. EDITOR [W. L. GARRISON]. 12 May 1831. Theological Seminary, Princeton, Pa.** Discusses the seminary's "Society of Inquiry on the State of Africans"; wonders if its purpose is just to appease conscience and gather knowledge, or to act. 21 May 1831. p.83, c2.

839 LYDIA WHITE *to* **THE** *LIBERATOR.* **[extract] n.d. Philadelphia.** States that she is an owner of a free dry goods store; notes growing concern to bear testimony against slavery by abstinence from buying slave products; receives more orders from all over. 28 May 1831. p.87, c2.

840 n.n. *to* **JOHN R. PETERS. [from the** *New York Standard***] 14 April 1831. n.p.** A thief sends fifty dollars which is principal and interest of what he stole a few years ago. 28 May 1831. p.88, c4.

841 A COLORED BALTIMOREAN *to* **MR. EDITOR [W. L. GARRISON]. n.d. n.p.** Replies to a column in the *Baltimore American* discussing colonization; charges that the arguments in support of colonization are actually evidence of fear and prejudice; claims that colonizers use the increase of people of color as a warning, yet declare at the same time that people of color will never live freely in this country. 4 June 1831. p.89, c1.

842 U. I. E. *to* **THE EDITOR [W. L. GARRISON]. n.d. n.p.** Engages in philosophical discussion on whether slaveholders can claim to be morally innocent. 4 June 1831. p.89, c3.

843 ELLA *to* **THE EDITOR [W. L. GARRISON]. 25 May 1831. Philadelphia.** Wonders why her people are called "Negroe," which she considers to be a degrading term; also questions the practice of forcing people of color to sit behind whites in church; feels they are equally able to pray to God. 4 June 1831. p.90, c2.

844 J. K. *to* **THE EDITOR [W. L. GARRISON]. 30 May 1831. Hartford.** Describes recent race riots in Hartford by men of color incensed over the exploitation of black women and the denial of equal rights to the black community. 4 June 1831. p.90, c3.

845 JAMES L. PEIRCE, PETER WRIGHT, AND JOSEPH PARKER *to* **ESTEEMED FRIEND [W. L. GARRISON]. 12 May 1831. Philadelphia.** Discuss free-labor produce in the United States, the supply and demand, and prospects for an increased supply. 11 June 1831. p.93, c3.

846 JUNIUS *to* **THE EDITOR [W. L. GARRISON]. n.d. Philadelphia.** Wonders how Americans can profess belief in their Declaration of Independence, which asserts that all men are created equal, when thousands of their fellow men are in chains; prophesies that the time will come when they will be free. 11 June 1831. p.94, c2.

847 n.n. *to* **THE EDITORS OF THE** *PHILADELPHIA GAZETTE.* **[extract] 29 May 1821. Fayetteville, N.C.** Describes devastating fire that caused one million dollars of damage in Fayetteville. 11 June 1831. p.95, c2.

848 A GENTLEMAN IN LIBERIA *to* **A FRIEND IN BOSTON. [extract] 1 November 1830. Liberia.** Discusses life in Liberia, including mortality rate among emigrants; asserts that Americans must pay passage as well as provide support for emigrants, even through inevitable illness; reports that slave trade continues in western Africa. 18 June 1831. p.97, c3.

849 W. L. GARRISON *to* **READERS. [extract] 10 June 1831. Philadelphia.** Describes his trip to New Haven where he heard speech by Mr. Jocelyn, a long-time abolitionist; reports that the site for a college for colored people in New Haven is in the planning stage only. 18 June 1831. p.98, c4.

850 PHILELEUTHEROS *to* **MR. EDITOR [W. L. GARRISON]. n.d. n.p.** Gives critique of article from the *Christian Spectator* called "Review on African Colonization"; quotes to demonstrate what the CS does not accomplish. 2 July 1831. p.106, c3.

851 CONSISTENCY *to* **THE EDITOR [W. L. GARRISON]. n.d. n.p.** Discusses "The Non-Resistance Doctrine"; questions the morality of the Americans' struggle against the British and other wars of independence; suggests that when the slaves fight back under oppression they can take their place with others who fought for liberation. 9 July 1831. p.109, c2.

852 AN ANONYMOUS PHILANTHROPIST IN CONNECTICUT *to* **SIR [W. L. GARRISON]. n.d. Connecticut.** Discusses project to build a college for colored men and Arthur Tappan's offer to contribute $1,000; urges courses in religion, mechanic arts, agriculture, and horticulture. 9 July 1831. p.111, cl.

853 PHILELEUTHEROS *to* **MR. EDITOR [W. L. GARRISON]. n.d. n.p.** Reviews the "Review on African Colonization"; discusses morality of slavery; declares that man who buys the slave is as guilty as the man who actually steals and chains him; quotes Bible to demonstrate that slavery is wrong. 16 July 1831. p.114, cl.

854 A SUBSCRIBER *to* **THE EDITOR [W. L. GARRISON]. n.d. n.p.** Suggests new term "Africamerican" to designate colored citizens of African descent in the United States, yet stresses American citizenship; finds terms "Negro" and "colored" offensive. 16 July 1831. p.114, c4.

855 C. C. DEAN AND OLIVER JOHNSON *to* **W. L. GARRISON. n.d. n.p.** Write about Sabbath school for colored children, connected with the Boston Sabbath School Union; wish to dispel any notion that the school is associated with the CS. 16 July 1831. p.115, c2.

856 n.n. *to* **n.n. [extract] n.d. England.** Briefly discusses London anti-slavery meeting; reports that at least half of 2,500 people attending were women. 23 July 1831. p.117, cl.

857 INTELLIGENT COLORED FRIEND *to* **SIR. [extract] 14 July 1831. Baltimore.** Sends nine subscriptions to *Liberator;* commends the excellent quality of the paper. 23 July 1831. p.117, c3.

858 LEO *to* **MR. EDITOR [W. L. GARRISON]. n.d. n.p.** Protests against colonization; asserts that colored people want to be free in this country. 23 July 1831. p.118, cl.

859 A FRIEND TO YOU AND JUSTICE *to* **W. L. GARRISON. 4 July 1831. St. Thomas.** Translates a decree from the King of Sweden and Norway permitting equal rights to colored people in St. Baris to vote, hold property; chides "independent" Americans for slavery. 30 July 1831. p.121, c3.

860 NEW YORK *to* **MR. EDITOR [W. L. GARRISON]. n.d. n.p.** Reports that the Presbyterian church followed Garrison's advice that free people of color pray rather than celebrate the Fourth of July; reports that they did celebrate the abolition of slavery in New York on the fifth of July; also relates that they are patronizing each other and supporting the sympathetic presses, as Garrison suggested. 30 July 1831. p.121, c4.

861 n.n. *to* **W. L. GARRISON. n.d. Portland Me.** Describes the sociable, intelligent side of colored people; urges that more people give money to help educate black people, rather than to deport them by colonization; suspects that colonizationists misrepresent the truth, in order to promote their scheme; urges Garrison to come to address them. 30 July 1831. p.122, c2.

862 PHILELEUTHEROS *to* **MR. EDITOR [W. L. GARRISON]. n.d. n.p.** Responds to question, "What shall be done about slavery?" Proposes emancipating slaves between the ages of twenty-one and fifty, and setting up a system of education for them. 6 August 1831. p.125, cl.

863 H. C. P. *to* **THE EDITOR OF THE** *PETERSBURG TIMES.* **n.d. Port-au-Prince, Hayti.** Rebukes what he regards as Garrison's ignorant statements about Haiti and suggests he should visit before making such claims; describes Haitian revolution for independence as heroic and claims that Haiti was only modern country to revolt without foreign help because all other nations possessed slaves; prophesies that some day slaves of America will demand rights and the "land of liberty will quake." 6 August 1831. p.126, cl.

864 n.n. *to* **THE EDITOR [W. L. GARRISON]. 1 August 1831. Lowell.** Describes personal change of sentiment on anti-slavery issue; relates that he supported CS as the best and fastest way to abolish slavery before he realized that it was based on prejudice and fear; now supports Garrison and others against colonization. 6 August 1831. p.126, c2.

865 MENTOR *to* **FRIEND GARRISON. n.d. n.p.** Points out that the CS was organized to help stop the evils of the slave trade, but that now the work must be extended to the task of abolishing all slavery; feels that colonization arose from good intentions and has done some good. 6 August 1831. p.126, c2.

866 PHILO-AFRICAMERICANUS *to* **THE EDITOR [W. L. GARRISON]. n.d. n.p.** Finds it difficult to attack Southern inequality when Northerners refuse to allow blacks to vote, to hold office, or even to sit in church with whites; suggests that North's faults are worse, as North claims to be more educated, more free. 6 August 1831. p.126, c4.

867 JOHN B. HEPBURN *to* **THE EDITOR [W. L. GARRISON]. 19 July 1831. Alexandria.** A colored Texan defends colonization as the fastest and most efficient way to emancipate slaves, until Garrison proposes a better plan; believes that emancipation without colonization is unlikely, as it would ruin South's economy; compares Liberian colony's problems to those of early American colonies. 13 August 1831. p.130, cl.

868 HENRY BERRIAN, CHAIRMAN AND HENRY N. MERRIMAN, SECRETARY *to* **THE EDITOR [W. L. GARRISON]. 8 August 1831. New Haven.** Report resolves of the Peace and Benevolent Society of Afric-Americans, which are mostly against colonization; regard America as home. 13 August 1831. p.130, c3.

869 P. *to* **MR. EDITOR [W. L. GARRISON]. 28 July 1831. Brooklyn, N.Y.** Thanks *Liberator* for supporting the Afric-American cause; believes that the press is the best weapon against slavery; expresses his personal satisfaction that W. L. Garrison verbally attacked Mr. Gurley, a pro-colonization speaker. 13 August 1831. p.130, c4.

870 J. TELEMACHUS HILTON, ROBERT WOOD, AND J. H. HOW *to* **W. L. GARRISON. 7 August 1831. Boston.** Thank Garrison for excellent job supporting the cause of descendants of Africans; forward donation to the *Liberator*. 20 August 1831. p.133, c1.

871 JAMES SCOTT, GARDNER JONES, AND WILLIAM L. JEFFERS *to* **W. L. GARRISON. 27 July 1831. New York.** Thank Garrison for supporting emancipation of colored people; express their gratification that he has the courage to fight the slander and hatred he frequently encounters. 20 August 1831. p.133, c3.

872 A COLORED PHILADELPHIAN *to* **THE EDITOR [W. L. GARRISON]. 28 July 1831. Philadelphia.** States that in Fayetteville, North Carolina, a free colored man was viciously whipped in public for joking with a white neighbor; warns that colored people will not always willingly submit, but will soon revolt for liberty. 20 August 1831. p.133, c3.

873 n.n. *to* **MR. EDITOR [W. L. GARRISON]. 1 August 1831. Middletown.** Preaches on the goodness of God; quotes Scriptures to show that God does not favor any nation, neither Gentile nor Jew. 20 August 1831. p.133, c4.

874 AN ADVOCATE FOR CONSISTENCY *to* **THE EDITOR [W. L. GARRISON]. 1 August 1831. Providence.** Deduces that if those who buy slaves are as guilty as those who kidnap them from Africa, then those who use slave goods are as guilty as those who run plantations producing them. 27 August 1831. p.138, c1.

875 EUTHYMUS *to* **THE EDITOR [W. L. GARRISON]. 11 August 1831. Columbia, Pa.** Quotes Scripture to challenge allegations of white superiority. 27 August 1831. p.138, c3.

876 W. L. GARRISON *to* **MESSRS. J. TELEMACHUS HILTON, ROBERT WOOD, AND J. H. HOW. 13 August 1831. Boston.** Thanks them for kind letter supporting him; recognizes that his path is full of thorns, yet he must carry on the cause. 27 August 1831. p.139, c3.

877 REV. S. A. WORCESTER *to* **A SECRETARY OF THE AMERICAN BOARD OF FOREIGN MISSIONS. [extract from the** *Boston Recorder***)** **18 July 1831. Jail at Camp Gilmer.** Describes his arrest and brutal journey to prison. 27 August 1831. p.140, c2.

878 JOHN B. HEPBURN *to* **THE EDITOR [W. L. GARRISON]. 19 August 1831. Alexandria.** Replies to Garrison's attack on Hepburn's first article; charges that Garrison's attacks were insubstantial and poorly documented; dislikes the idea of sending colored people to another clime, but feels it is their only hope for obtaining liberty and equality. 3 September 1831. p.141, c1.

879 S. L. A. *to* **THE EDITOR [W. L. GARRISON]. 16 August 1831. Middletown.** Expresses amazement to find an Afric-American, J. B. Hepburn, defending colonization in last issue; feels Hepburn must be under influence of whites and colonizationists; regards him as uninformed and speaking contrary to the Declaration of Independence. 3 September 1831. p.141, c3.

880 HOPE *to* **THE EDITOR [W. L. GARRISON]. 23 August 1831. Boston.** Commends letter from "A Colored Philadelphian" in last issue; urges better treatment of colored people instead of schemes to send them to Liberia; hopes for their cause of liberty. 3 September 1831. p.142, c1.

881 A GENTLEMAN *to* **FRIEND IN BALTIMORE. [extract] 23 August 1831. Richmond.** Reports insurrection in Southampton in which seventy whites were massacred; describes militia's retreat before six or eight hundred blacks. 3 September 1831. p.142, c2.

882 EDITORS OF THE *NORFOLK HERALD to* **LYFORD. [extract] 24 August 1831. Norfolk.** Relay information about slave insurrection in Southampton County; reports that forty or fifty people were slain and that the militia is growing in power. 3 September 1831. p.142, c2.

883 n.n. *to* **LYFORD. [extract] n.d. Norfolk.** Confirm prior reports; estimate that insurgent force consists of 300 Negroes well mounted and armed. 3 September 1831. p.142, c3.

884 n.n. *to* **n.n. 24 August 1831. Belfield.** Reports that between twenty-five and thirty-five white families have been destroyed but that Negroes cannot cross bridge and will probably perish in a few days. 3 September 1831. p.142, c3.

885 JOHN WHEELER *to* **n.n. 25 August 1831. Murfreesborough, N.C.** Reports a black insurrection in Southhampton; describes massacres and attempts at protection. 3 September 1831. p.142, c3.

886 n.n. *to* **W. L. GARRISON. 4 August 1831. Princeton, N.J.** Curses, insults, and threatens Garrison for editing such a "silly" and "hellish" newspaper. 10 September 1831. p.145, c2.

887 A FREEMAN *to* **W. L. GARRISON. 26 August 1831. Washington City.** Southern slaveholder, who despises Garrison and his work, warns that *Liberator* will not be tolerated much longer; tells Garrison to go to Africa if he wants equality with Negroes. 10 September 1831. p.145, c2.

888 A CLERGYMAN *to* **THE EDITOR [W. L. GARRISON]. n.d. n.p.** Reports that his fellow passengers in stagecoach discussed recent insurrection and expressed belief that Garrison was partly responsible and that he would be killed quickly if he ever went to the South. 10 September 1831. p.145, c3.

889 R. R. GURLEY *to* **THE EDITOR [W. L. GARRISON]. 26 August 1831. Washington.** Corrects some mistakes charged by Garrison's writers; avows that he never quoted Garrison or his paper out of context nor did he speak to a colored audience in Brooklyn. 10 September 1831. p.146, c3.

890 AUSTIN STEWARD AND BENJAMIN PAUL *to* **MR. EDITOR [W. L. GARRISON]. n.d. Wilberforce Settlement, Upper Canada.** Describe settlement in Canada, its churches, crops, and buildings; also report recent election of board to raise funds in order to continue the project and enable others to join them. 17 September 1831. p.150, c1.

891 n.n. *to* **MR. EDITOR [W. L. GARRISON]. n.d. n.p.** Forwards extract of letter from Arthur Singleton, alias Rev. Henry C. Knight; mentions the recent publication of Knight's *Lectures* and *Sermons,* which received high praise. 17 September 1831. p.150, c2.

892 ARTHUR SINGLETON, ESQ., ALIAS REV. HENRY C. KNIGHT *to* **n.n. [extract] n.d. n.p.** Discusses slavery in Louisiana; describes plantation mansion, slaves' tasks, food, and punishments. 17 September 1831. p.150, c2.

893 O. L. *to* **THE EDITOR [W. L. GARRISON]. n.d. n.p.** Discusses causes of the recent slave insurrection; charges that the wrongs and oppressions that the Negroes suffer make them rebel, not inflammatory writing in the *Liberator;* believes that the Americans' claim that theirs is a land of freedom also causes the slaves to rebel. 17 September 1831. p.150, c2.

894 A SUBSCRIBER AND CITIZEN OF THE UNITED STATES *to* **MR. EDITOR [W. L. GARRISON]. 1 September 1831. Philadelphia.** Replies to suggestion of use of term "Afric-American"; finds the term unwieldly and silly; comments on "men of color" as a common term, but prefers simply "Americans" as a designation connoting no distinction. 24 September 1831. p.153, c4.

895 ZELMIRE *to* **MR. EDITOR [W. L. GARRISON]. n.d. n.p.** Forwards story for the Juvenile Department about a young girl, Emily, returning home from boarding school and hearing of the horrors of slavery. 24 September 1831. p.155, c1.

896 S. B. EMMONS *to* **MR. GREENE [EDITOR OF THE** *BOSTON CHRISTIAN HERALD***]. 24 September 1831. Waltham.** Describes insurrection in Virginia and horrible mutilation of black prisoners; believes that whites there are sick of slaves, but are still unwilling to liberate them; describes Virginia huts where slaves live. 1 October 1831. p.159, c2.

897 J. E. *to* **THE EDITOR [W. L. GARRISON]. n.d. n.p.** Lauds the sermons of Rev. Mr. May and hopes to see them printed in the *Liberator,* or published in cheap form soon; commends sermon particularly in its position that Northerners are not guiltless so long as slavery exists. 8 October 1831. p.161, c1.

898 n.n. *to* **THE EDITORS OF THE** *NEW YORK JOURNAL OF COMMERCE.* **29 September 1831. New York.** Gives eye-witness account of the action taken by blacks in Maryland and Delaware since the insurrection. 8 October 1831. p.162, c3.

899 A WITNESS *to* **THE EDITOR [W. L. GARRISON]. n.d. n.p.** Describes services held by descendants of Africans to pray for peace and emancipation rather than bloodshed between slaves and masters in the South. 8 October 1831. p.163, c3.

900 W. L. GARRISON *to* **THE EDITORS OF THE** *NATIONAL INTELLIGENCER* **[MESSRS. GALES AND SEATON]. n.d. n.p.** Attacks their harsh judgment of him and *Liberator;* accuses them of appealing to New England to sustain slavery, but asserts that he will never desert the cause. 15 October 1831. p.165, c1.

901 A GENTLEMAN *to* **THE EDITOR [W. L. GARRISON]. [extract] 1 October 1831. Georgia.** Gives account of slave who died from whipping by overseer, who remains unmolested, uncharged. 22 October 1831. p.170, c3.

902 n.n. *to* **THE** *LIBERATOR.* **[extract] n.d. Baltimore.** Reports that constables are searching houses of colored families for guns. 29 October 1831. p.173, c1.

903 SIMEON S. JOCELYN *to* **W. L. GARRISON. 12 October 1831. New Haven.** Admonishes that a "lying spirit" and persecution of those who fight for the oppressed have prevailed in our land; urges that we should go forth and crush oppression. 29 October 1831. p.173, c2.

904 n.n. *to* **W. L. GARRISON. 8 October 1831. Georgia.** Informs of several Negroes who were awakened in the night and tortured in an attempt to make them confess to a rumored insurrection; adds that the incident provoked an uprising the following day, which was quickly suppressed by the militia. 29 October 1831. p.174, c1.

905 J. CLAY *to* **GEN. SOWELL WOOLFOLK. 3 October 1831. Fort Mitchell, Al.** Warns of possible insurrection of Negroes; speculates that if the slaves were to riot, the Indians could join in and there could really be trouble. 29 October 1831. p.174, c3.

906 GENTLEMAN *to* **n.n. [extract] n.d. Providence.** Censures Mr. Orr's account of Capt. Stuart's "Voice from England." 29 October 1831. p.175, c4.

907 L'AMI DES NOIRS ET DU *LIBERATEUR to* **MR. EDITOR [W. L. GARRISON]. n.d. n.p.** Rejoices that Garrison publishes the truth about the horrible cruelty toward the Negro people, which he feels is the only way to begin to promote needed reforms. 5 November 1831. p.178, c1.

908 n.n. *to* **THE EDITOR [W. L. GARRISON]. n.d. Georgia.** Writes that his conscience has been silenced by the familiarity of cruelty and injustice to slaves in South; but seeing *Liberator* has reawakened his moral sensibilities; describes some practices such as lack of medical care for slaves, and separation of families, etc. 5 November 1831. p.178, c2.

909 A LADY IN VIRGINIA *to* **n.n. [extract] 13 October 1831. Virginia.** Describes fear and distress of whites after insurrection. 5 November 1831. p.178, c3.

910 n.n. *to* **THE EDITOR [W. L. GARRISON]. n.d. Georgia.** Reports that the situation of the blacks in the South is such that something must change soon; tells of Negro who was flogged to death with a handsaw, without comment from local papers. 12 November 1831. p.182, c1.

911 F. *to* **THE EDITOR OF PAULSON'S** *PHILADELPHIA AMERICAN DAILY ADVERTISER.* **25 October 1831. Philadelphia.** Discusses various statements about the true mortality rate in Liberia; wants to inform public of information he has received from a reliable source. 12 November 1831. p.184, c3.

912 CAP'T. CHARLES STUART *to* **THE EDITOR [W. L. GARRISON]. 30 July 1831. London.** Dislikes the ACS's prejudice against colored people; believes that they should not be persecuted just because God gave them dark skin. 19 November 1831. p.185, c2.

913 JOSEPH PHILLIPS *to* **W. L. GARRISON. 25 July 1831. London.** Defends his sentiments as coming not from books, but from living in Antigua 28 years; reports on the state of anti-slavery legislation in England: crown has manumitted all 2,000 of its slaves. 19 November 1831. p.185, c3.

914 T. TREZVANT, POSTMASTER AT JERUSALEM, VA. *to* **THE EDITOR OF THE** *NORFOLK BEACON.* **31 October 1831. Jerusalem, Va.** Gives the details of the capture of Nat Turner, leader of recent slave revolt; relates Nat has now changed his mind and regrets his action. 19 November 1831. p.186, c3.

915 n.n. *to* **n.n. [extract from the** *Richmond Whig***] 31 October 1831. Southampton County, Va.** Conveys impressions he received from talking with Nat Turner; feels that Nat is humble, intelligent, but in a state of fanatical delusion. 19 November 1831. p.186, c3.

916 HUMANITAS *to* **MESSRS. EDITORS OF THE** *GENIUS OF TEMPERANCE.* **n.d. n.p.** Proposes total abstinence from slave products as means to end slavery. 26 November 1831. p.190, c4.

917 C. *to* **MR. EDITOR [W. L. GARRISON]. n.d. n.p.** Anecdotal letter about gentleman cursing the *Liberator,* although he has never read an issue. 26 November 1831. p.191, c2.

918 n.n. *to* **THE *LIBERATOR*. 17 November 1831. Philadelphia.** On the rate of mortality in Liberia; reports that one-third of emigrants die from fever and from climate. 3 December 1831. p.191, c2.

919 n.n. *to* **SIR [W. L. GARRISON]. 16 November 1831. Macon, Ga.** Reports that a friend, Mr. John Lamb, was mobbed, tarred and feathered, and ducked in the river for receiving the *Liberator.* 3 December 1831. p.194, c4.

920 GOWDEY *to* **MR. LUMMUS. 5 November 1831. Gowdeysville, S.C.** Contends that the slaves in his part of the country are content and that papers like the *Liberator* and the *Lynn Mirror* only serve to make them unhappy. 3 December 1831. p.195, c3.

921 A SPECTATOR *to* **MR. EDITOR [W. L. GARRISON]. 29 November 1831. New York.** Speaks highly of the Philomathean Society of New York which was formed by young colored men for their improvement. 10 December 1831. p.197, c3.

922 FIAT JUSTITIA *to* **MR. EDITOR [W. L. GARRISON]. 3 December 1831. Philadelphia.** Condemns recent meeting to expel all colored people; believes that the men at the meeting are disgraceful elements of society. 10 December 1831. p.198, c2.

923 NESTOR *to* **MR. EDITOR [W. L. GARRISON]. n.d. Vermont.** A highly esteemed clergyman wonders why the *Boston Recorder* and other papers say nothing in favor of abolition. 10 December 1831. p.198, c3.

924 A. B. *to* **THE *NATIONAL JOURNAL*. n.d. n.p.** Wants Freemasonry abolished because he is afraid that the free Negroes who have joined will start another insurrection. 10 December 1831. p.200, c2.

925 R. B. H. *to* **MR. EDITOR [W. L. GARRISON]. n.d. n.p.** Calls for action against colonization; believes the removal of slavery by sending away free-born American citizens is impossible. 17 December 1831. p.201, c3.

[1832]

926 GARDNER JONES *to* **REV. ISAAC ORR. 23 December 1831. New York.** Raises questions about the financial practicality of colonization; also believes that to deport Americans against their will is wrong. 7 January 1832. p.3, c1.

927 A WHITE LADY *to* **n.n. n.d. Salem.** Describes society formed in 1818 for the benefit and education of colored people. 7 January 1832. p.3, c2.

928 A GENTLEMAN *to* **THE EDITOR [W. L. GARRISON]. [extract] n.d. Indiana.** Asks for newspaper; states his opposition to slavery. 7 January 1832. p.3, c2.

929 n.n. *to* **THE EDITOR [W. L. GARRISON]. n.d. New York.** States that he no longer supports CS because its members are slaveholders. 7 January 1832. p.3, c3.

930 A SLAVITE IN VIRGINIA *to* **THE EDITORS OF THE *NEW YORK COURIER AND ENQUIRER*. [extract] n.d. Virginia.** Expresses pride that so few slaves joined the revolt in Southampton; argues that this minority demonstrates that the majority of slaves are happy. 7 January 1832. p.4, c3.

931 D. W. E. *to* **MR. EDITOR [W. L. GARRISON]. n.d. n.p.** Argues for the necessity of freedom and education for the slaves. 14 January 1832. p.5, c3.

932 R. *to* **MR. EDITOR [W. L. GARRISON]. n.d. n.p.** Asks editor to announce to the public that on 31 December, Rev. Nathaniel Paul, of Wilberforce, Upper Canada, departed for Liverpool; explains that his purpose is to seek patronage of the Crown and to convey details of the founding of the settlement. 14 January 1832. p.5, c5.

933 n.n. *to* **THE EDITOR [W. L. GARRISON]. n.d. n.p.** Worries that the frequent intercourse between white males and female slaves will produce so many mulattoes that distinguishing who should and should not be free will be difficult. Wonders if this area belongs to the discipline of any churches. 14 January 1832. p.6, c1.

934 n.n. *to* **THE EDITOR [W. L. GARRISON]. 2 December 1831. Georgia.** Describes two slaves who are condemned to death for attacking a white man who tried to separate them in a fight over a woman they both love. 14 January 1832. p.6, c2.

935 COLORED GENTLEMAN *to* **n.n. [extract] n.d. Maryland.** Quotes from Bible and praises the *Liberator* for continuing to "thunder and lighten." 21 January 1832. p.9, c1.

936 A CLERGYMAN *to* **THE EDITOR [W. L. GARRISON]. [extract] n.d. Connecticut.** Expresses pleasure with pictures in previous issue and disappointment with his fellow Christians. 21 January 1832. p.9, c2.

937 S. T. U. *to* **THE EDITOR [W. L. GARRISON]. n.d. n.p.** Advocates the use of free goods; draws comparison between the evils of using sugar and using spirits; asks about Free Produce Societies in America. 21 January 1832. p.10, c2.

938 RHODE ISLAND *to* **THE EDITOR [W. L. GARRISON]. n.d. n.p.** Urges people not to buy slave goods, for as long as the slave-owners can make money through the use of slaves, they will continue with that system; quotes extensively from Bible to illustrate how wrong slavery is. 21 January 1832. p.10, c3.

939 AGNES *to* **ISABEL. [from the** *Genius of Universal Emancipation*] **n.d. n.p.** Warns Isabel that if she does not support abolition, she will be guilty in the eyes of God. 21 January 1832. p.10, c5.

940 W. L. GARRISON *to* **JOHN QUINCY ADAMS. n.d. n.p.** Asks Adams why he did not support the petition to remove slavery from the District of Columbia; discusses reasons why ex-President Adams was elected to Congress; declares respect and admiration for Adams. 21 January 1832. p.11, c1.

941 L'AMI *to* **THE SUBSCRIBERS OF THE "FIFTEEN PETITIONS" OF INHABITANTS OF PENNSYLVANIA. [from the** *Massachusetts Journal*]. Supports their fight against slavery but wonders why Quakers ever sent their petitions to J. Q. Adams, who supports abolishing the slave trade in the District of Columbia, but not slavery itself; author believes that where slavery exists, there will be a market, a trade. 28 January 1832. p.13, c4.

942 A COLORED FEMALE OF PHILADELPHIA *to* **MR. EDITOR [W. L. GARRISON]. 2 January 1832. Philadelphia.** Favors colored emigration to Canada and Mexico, but strongly opposes colonization, or separation of colored people; feels they should settle among others and not isolate themselves; regards Mexico as excellent future home for colored people, where they can be free and equal. 28 January 1832. p.14, c2.

943 AGNES *to* **ISABEL. [from the** *Genius of Universal Emancipation***] n.d. n.p.** Urges her friend to examine her conscience on the subject of slavery; argues that slavery must either be right or wrong, with no middle ground; and that since slavery cannot possibly be consistent with Christian principles, we are all guilty with that knowledge, unless we work against slavery. 28 January 1832. p.14, c3.

944 A SLAVEHOLDER *to* **THE EDITOR [W. L. GARRISON]. 10 January 1832. Athens, Ga.** Accuses Garrison of unholy, illegal, unjustifiable motives, prompted by personal gain or desire to disrupt the peace and harmony of the country; accuses Garrison of making conditions worse for slaves; challenges him to mortal combat. 28 January 1832. p.14, c4.

945 PAUL CUFFEE *to* **THE EDITOR [W. L. GARRISON]. 19 January 1832. Philadelphia.** Discusses a pamphlet by Matthew Carey on colonization; feels Carey is quite limited in his knowledge of colored people or he would certainly know how opposed they are to colonization; advises Carey to aid colored people in their home, America, or to leave them alone. 28 January 1832. p.15, c2.

946 CHARLESTOWN *to* **MR. EDITOR [W. L. GARRISON]. n.d. n.p.** Believes that the CS seeks to carry away free persons of color, not liberate slaves; feels that such a cause will only serve to make the slave more miserable. 28 January 1832. p.15, c2.

947 A PENNSYLVANIAN *to* **THE POULSON'S** *AMERICAN DAILY ADVERTISER.* **14 January 1832. Philadelphia.** Expresses shock at the comments he read in article on the trial of John Cisco and wife; relates that his observations of people of color in Pennsylvania show them to be "scrupulously exact" in the legality of their marriages, as well as honest and good citizens. 28 January 1832. p.15, c5.

948 MELVILLE *to* **THE** *NEW ENGLAND CHRISTIAN HERALD.* **26 December 1831. North Carolina.** Describes fate of slave who saved his master in the late insurrection in Virginia by tricking the insurgents; the slave then found his master and gave him a gun to shoot him, swearing he would never strike another blow for a man as a slave; he had hoped to be freed, but was shot instead. 4 February 1832. p.18, c3.

949 AGNES *to* **ISABEL. n.d. n.p.** Informs her friend that to disapprove of slavery in silence is not enough, one must openly avow the cause to benefit and educate others; argues that if one is truly dedicated to a cause, one can make a few sacrifices. 4 February 1832. p.18, c4.

950 D. W. E. *to* **MR. EDITOR [W. L. GARRISON]. n.d. n.p.** Believes that the South is headed for certain destruction if it does not modify or abolish its slavery system; argues that if whites could be taught not to hate colored people, and if blacks could be taught religion, then colored people could be safely integrated into white society. 11 February 1832. p.21, c5.

951 A COLORED RESIDENT OF GEORGIA *to* **THE EDITOR [W. L. GARRISON]. 20 January 1832. Georgia.** Informs editor that he is one of the few whites whom colored people will trust and hopes he goes on with his good work; argues that if black people eat same food as whites, suffer from same diseases, are harmed by same weapons, should not they also get same revenge against wrongs? 11 February 1832. p.22, c1.

952 A YANKEE *to* **THE EDITOR [W. L. GARRISON]. n.d. n.p.** Proposes new colonization scheme to send back all Dutchmen on Hudson River to Holland, which would be easier than sending blacks to Africa; argues that they speak improper English, they swear uncouthly, they do not live like their neighbors, and they have settled on the best, most fertile lands. 11 February 1832. p.22, c2.

953 AGNES *to* **ISABEL. [from the** *Genius of Universal Emancipation]* **n.d. n.p.** Supports her friend's decision to take an open stand on the abolition of slavery; regards even the mildest form of slavery, where the slave is kindly treated, as no guarantee that he will remain that way. 11 February 1832. p.23, c1.

954 AGNES *to* **ISABEL. [from the** *Genius of Universal Emancipation]* **n.d. n.p.** Contends that even if all American slaves are well-treated, well-fed, and attended to, we would still have no right to keep them in bondage; and that a well-kept state may ease oppression of the body, but not of the mind, which is worse. 18 February 1832. p.26, c5.

955 GARDNER JONES *to* **REV. ISAAC ORR. 6 February 1832. New York.** Chides Orr for his silence; since six weeks have passed since Jones' article was published on the colonization controversy, wonders if Orr's silence indicates that he is now against colonization? 18 February 1832. p.27, c3.

956 THOMAS JEFFERSON *to* **SIR. [from the** *Portland Advertiser]* **25 August 1814. Monticello.** Supports abolition of slavery, despite his belief that Negroes are inferior; objects to immediate abolition, but suggests emancipation of those born after a certain day; advocates education and expatriation for Negroes. 25 February 1832. p.29, c3.

957 O. *to* **THE EDITOR [W. L. GARRISON]. 20 January 1832. Portland.** Forwards letter from the editor of the *Portland Advertiser* with hopes that it will be printed. 25 February 1832. p.29, c5.

958 B. [MR. BROOKS, EDITOR OF THE *PORTLAND ADVERTISER]to* **n.n. [extract] 12 January 1832. Washington.** Warns that slaves are gaining in numbers in slaveholding states; believes that the masters want them to increase so they will have more workers, yet are afraid of the growth in slave population; urges abolition of slavery in the District of Columbia. 25 February 1832. p.29, c5.

959 D. W. E. *to* **THE** *LIBERATOR.* **n.d. n.p.** Questions how many of the United States should be left to an African population; some Southern states may be so hot and unhealthy that only blacks can work in them; believes whites can accomplish more on Southern lands than blacks. 25 February 1832. p.30, c2.

960 AMERICUS *to* **THE EDITORS OF THE** *NEW ENGLAND CHRISTIAN HERALD.* **12 January 1832. North Carolina.** Northern man contends that a storm is gathering in the South and has little hope that it will be diverted by God; discusses bill in North Carolina legislature requiring free Africans to put up a security, or be sold into slavery. 25 February 1832. p.30, c4.

961 AGNES *to* **ISABEL. [from the** *Genius of Universal Emancipation]* **n.d. n.p.** Describes the horrors of a slave ship, the shock and misery of being wrenched from a familiar home, the suffering in a ship's dark hold, and worst of all, the fate of the slave at the hands of his master. 25 February 1832. p.30, c5.

962 NAT. FIELD *to* **THE VIGILANCE SOCIETY OF COLUMBIA, S. C. 4 February 1832. Jeffersonville, In.** Suspects that a "Junta" has been formed in South Carolina to abridge the liberty of the press; charges that the *Telescope,* a reputedly philanthropic paper, refused to publish his pamphlet on emancipation, and that the *Telescope* accused him of inciting slaves. 3 March 1832. p.33, c2.

963 W. *to* **MR. PAINTER. [from the** *West Chester Register]* **n.d. n.p.** Describes the *Liberator,* its history and purpose; discusses unqualified emancipation; urges reader to unite with others to unshackle the African from the miseries of slavery. 3 March 1832. p.35, c4.

964 S. S. *to* **MR. EDITOR [W. L. GARRISON]. [from the** *New Hampshire Observer***] n.d. n.p.** Favors immediate abolition and emancipation, as slavery is truly an evil blot on the conscience of our republic. 10 March 1832. p.37, c2.

965 G. X. *to* **MR. EDITOR [W. L. GARRISON]. n.d. n.p.** Forwards article entitled "Dialogue between Toussaint L'Ouverture and Washington." 10 March 1832. p.37, c5.

966 CANDOR *to* **MR. EDITOR [W. L. GARRISON]. n.d. n.p.** Wonders how anyone can justify biblically the practice of slavery; questions whether God's law in any way allows it; urges immediate emancipation. 10 March 1832. p.37, c5.

967 Z. *to* **SIR. n.d. n.p.** Remarks on the condition of slaves in the South; reminds owners that if they free the slaves and employ freemen, the value of their land and the productivity of labor will increase, and they will enjoy greater personal safety. 10 March 1832. p.37, c5.

968 R. T. *to* **MR. EDITOR [W. L. GARRISON]. n.d. n.p.** Notes past *Liberator* articles urging colored people to learn to read and write; relates the story of a young woman who learns to read as solace after the deaths of her husband and child; illustrates that one is not too old to learn to read if one really desires to learn. 10 March 1832. p.38, c2.

969 SIMEON S. JOCELYN *to* **THE EDITOR [W. L. GARRISON]. [from the** *New Haven Advertiser***] 1 March 1832. New Haven.** Sends copy of letter Jocelyn had written to Rev. R. R. Gurley of the ACS in Washington, D.C., who declined to publish the letter, and returned it. 17 March 1832. p.41, c3.

970 SIMEON S. JOCELYN *to* **REV. R. R. GURLEY, COR. SEC. OF THE ACS, WASHINGTON CITY. 31 December 1831. New Haven.** Describes the evils of slavery; wonders how Virginians can be allowed to expatriate freemen of color who are charged with no crime; wonders how the CS can, in good conscience, promote the forcible removal of men from their homeland. 17 March 1832. p.41, c3.

971 n.n. *to* **FRIEND. 8 September 1831. n.p.** Feels that one of the true evils of slavery is not allowing slaves to read; describes family's colored servant, whose wisdom and kindness they all respected. 17 March 1832. p.42, c3.

972 WILLIAM LADD *to* **W. L. GARRISON. 10 March 1832. Minot.** Corrects a misunderstanding; Garrison had quoted him incorrectly as saying he did not believe that slaves should be taught to read; concludes that they differ on feelings toward colonization, but both support emancipation. 17 March 1832. p.43, c1.

973 R. R. GURLEY *to* **SIMEON S. JOCELYN. 15 February 1832. Washington.** Returns Jocelyn's letter and explains that he did not publish it because of its non-conciliatory, anti-colonizationist nature; feels that the letter is uncalled for, as a change is occurring in the South. 24 March 1832. p.45, c1.

974 SIMEON S. JOCELYN *to* **REV. R. R. GURLEY. 6 March 1832. New Haven.** Defends his letter and criticizes Gurley for declining to publish it; examines works from other papers discussing colonization; hopes that indeed a change is occurring in the South, and that it will result in better conditions for the people of color. 24 March 1832. p.45, c2.

975 S. S. *to* **THE** *NEW HAMPSHIRE OBSERVER***. n.d. n.p.** Defines liberty in civil and political terms; objects to slavery as a deprivation of the African's natural liberty; believes that the slave could become a "civilized and enlightened being" without endangering the South. 24 March 1832. p.46, c2.

976 WILLIAM LADD *to* **W. L. GARRISON. 14 March 1832. Minot.** Clarifies story he had told, which was published in a previous *Liberator;* an unordained preacher struck a Negro and believed he had died instantly; ordered other slaves to burn the body in order to avoid burial, not to torture him. 24 March 1832. p.46, c3.

977 ELLA *to* **BROTHER. n.d. Philadelphia.** Urges brother to be virtuous and hard-working; if tempted to stray, think of family love and childhood; rise above white scorn and make something of himself. 24 March 1832. p.46, c5.

978 B. K. *to* **THE EDITORS OF THE** *NEW YORK OBSERVER.* **9 March 1832. Boston.** Objects to a letter printed in the *Observer*, probably by a Southerner, urging emancipation and immediate deportation to Liberia; refutes writer's statement that the plan is a matter of policy, not of principle. 24 March 1832. p.47, c3.

979 ALARM *to* **W. L. GARRISON. n.d. n.p.** Begs Garrison to stop his work; suggests metaphor of caged tiger being released to devour neighbors and imagines thousands of "tigers" (slaves) in the South being released to destroy enlightened and civilized whites. 24 March 1832. p.47, c4.

980 A COLORED FEMALE *to* **BROTHER IN CHRIST. [extract] n.d. n.p.** Prays for the freedom of her brothers and sisters in slavery; proclaims that God has spoken and He will carry through. 24 March 1832. p.48, c5.

981 ADAM ARATOR *to* **THE EDITOR [W. L. GARRISON]. n.d. n.p.** Confirms that he now supports his wife's and daughter's belief that the use of any item produced by slaves is a prolongation of the existence of slavery; tells of conversation between his wife and a squire who disagreed on the issue of slavery in the abstract. 31 March 1832. p.49, c1.

982 J. B. VASHON *to* **MESSRS. GARRISON AND KNAPP. 16 March 1832. Pittsburgh.** Reports that he enjoys the *Liberator,* especially the attacks on CSS, which he feels are un-just and morally evil. 31 March 1832. p.49, c3.

983 n.n. *to* **THE EDITOR OF THE** *NEW YORK GAZETTE.* **[extract] 2 March. Kingston, Jamaica.** Reports the rebellion is over but slaves are sulky and ready to revolt again; informs that Mr. Beaumont supports the English Ministry. 31 March 1832. p.50, c2.

984 HOTSPUR *to* **W. L. GARRISON. 13 March 1832. Aldie, Va.** Attacks Garrison and *Liberator* for being anti-colonization; declares that the free Negro population is "univer-sally lazy" and "vicious in the extreme"; believes that whites and Negroes who intermarry should be hanged. 31 March 1832. p.51, c1.

985 A. S. *to* **MR. EDITOR [W. L. GARRISON]. 20 March 1832. Wilbraham.** Replies to a request that he state his views on colonization; although he feels it has some defects and errors, on the whole he is in favor of it. 31 March 1832. p.51, c4.

986 J. R. McDOWELL *to* **THE EDITORS OF THE** *GENIUS OF TEMPERANCE.* **n.d. n.p.** Discusses his feelings toward the Methodist church; does not agree with what they teach, but did not reproach or attack them in his previous article. 31 March 1832. p.52, c5.

987 A COLORED CITIZEN OF BROOKLYN *to* **W. L. GARRISON. n.d. n.p.** Tells of the success of the Wilberforce colony in Canada, which is thriving with about 2,000 souls; contrasts it with the colony in Liberia, where half or two thirds of the emigrants die before they become acclimatized; claims that Canada receives colored people as brothers and sub-jects under the King, not like the oppressive Americans. 7 April 1832. p.55, c5.

988 GARDNER JONES *to* **THE PUBLIC. 5 April 1832. New York.** Attacks the Rev. Isaac Orr in relation to the colonization controversy; calls him ungentlemanly and cowardly; accuses Mr. Orr of skulking from his questions on colonization. 14 April 1832. p.59, c5.

989 S. S. *to* **THE EDITOR OF THE** *NEW HAMPSHIRE OBSERVER.* **n.d. n.p.** Disagrees with the objection to immediate emancipation that slaves are not ready for freedom; notes that if emancipation is gradual, the slave would be frustrated and likely to do harm; yet does not advocate giving slave privileges like voting immediately. 21 April 1832. p.62, c1.

990 ADAM ARATOR *to* **THE EDITOR [W. L. GARRISON]. n.d. n.p.** Notes that if other farmers would not trade with him because they thought he had come by his produce dishonestly, he would learn very quickly what he had done wrong; such, he feels, would be the case with the slaveholders if customers would refuse to buy their slave-produced goods. 21 April 1832. p.62, c2.

991 n.n. *to* **THE LADIES OF THE UNITED STATES. n.d. n.p.** Informs her sisters that slavery is "sapping the foundations" of civil and religious privileges. 21 April 1832. p.63, c1.

992 A COLORED FREEMAN *to* **W. L. GARRISON. 14 April 1832. Brooklyn, N.Y.** Informs public of convention against colored expatriation. 21 April 1832. p.63, c5.

993 A MEMBER OF THE HOUSE *to* **THE EDITORS OF THE** *BOSTON SENTINEL.* **25 February 1832. State House.** Informs the people of Massachusetts of the unfairness in their state government; states that no amendment can be passed to change state constitution without a majority in the House two years in a row; charges this is the tyranny of an aristocratic minority. 21 April 1832. p.64, c3.

994 WALKER *to* **THE EDITOR [W. L. GARRISON]. n.d. Philadelphia.** Replies to "Carpe Diem's" letter in the *U. S. Gazette* of September 1831, which calls for immediate deportation of the colored population, willing or unwilling; attacks this view, especially the use of force. 28 April 1832. p.65, c2.

995 GARDNER JONES *to* **REV. ISAAC ORR. 15 April 1832. New York.** Asks Orr how all black people could be removed from our shores, with their own consent, if they are almost universally opposed to colonization; asks why the condition of black people cannot be ameliorated here; asks if Orr considers prejudice good or bad. 28 April 1832. p.65, c5.

996 COLORED GENTLEMAN *to* **n.n. [extract] n.d. A distant city.** Comments on bad reports from Liberia; feels that American press should show both sides of colonization. 28 April 1832. p.67, c2.

997 n.n. *to* **n.n. [extract] n.d. New York.** Reports on enthusiastic applause for speakers from CS; adds that when it came time for donations, 400 people dwindled to twenty. 28 April 1832. p.67, c2.

998 REV. ISAAC ORR *to* **GARDNER JONES. 20 April 1832. Washington.** Replies to Jones's attack; refuses to answer questions that Mr. Jones asked; claims he is not seeking controversy. 28 April 1832. p.67, c3.

999 H. R. P. *to* **THE EDITORS OF THE** *RICHMOND WHIG.* **23 March 1832. Goochland.** Describes slave boy who wrung the necks of two birds locked in violent struggle, only to find that they were bald eagles; sees this as a prediction that while North and South are engaged in struggle, the black race will conquer them both. 28 April 1832. p.68, c3.

1000 S. S. *to* **THE EDITOR OF THE** *NEW HAMPSHIRE OBSERVER.* **n.d. n.p.** Disagrees with Southerners who say that immediate abolition is dangerous and insists that the slaves must be enlightened and educated first; asserts that if slaves are not liberated immediately, they will never be freed; reports on immediate emancipation in St. Domingo, which quickly brought about great improvements in the Negroes' conditions without harming resident whites. 5 May 1832. p.69, c3.

1001 GARDNER JONES *to* **REV. ISAAC ORR. 20 April 1832. New York.** Charges that Orr has avoided some of the questions in his letters; replies to the statement that colored people will not be happy here because of the great prejudice against them, urges that we fight this evil, not give in to it; asks how colored people will gain by going to Africa since they will not receive any land. 5 May 1832. p.69, c4.

1002 n.n. *to* **n.n. [extract from the** *New York Daily Advertiser***] 12 April 1832. Washington.** Describes differences between Northern freemen and Southern slaveholders; the former think carefully and take responsibility for their mistakes, the latter blame misfortunes on everyone else. 5 May 1832. p.72, c2.

1003 A. C. M. *to* **THE EDITOR OF THE** *NEW YORK EVANGELIST.* **n.d. n.p.** Relates conversation with a colored man who told him that he "never drank to success"; extends this infelicity literally, concluding that only temperance can bring one success, and that no one, not even great intellects or clergymen, can drink to success. 5 May 1832. p.72, c4.

1004 EUTHYMUS *to* **SIR [W. L. GARRISON]. n.d. n.p.** Congratulates editor on excellence of paper; encourages all men of color to buy paper, and to help support it; calls upon slaveholders to look into themselves to see if they are fully convinced that they are not committing a grave injustice. 12 May 1832. p.73, c4.

1005 GARDNER JONES *to* **REV. ISAAC ORR. 1 May 1832. New York.** Asks what will keep the colored people colonized in Africa from destroying natives there, the way whites did to the red man here, why uncivilized Africa is the only place fit for the degraded colored Americans, and how will they ever become educated there. 12 May 1832. p.74, c1.

1006 J. R. C. *to* **MR. EDITOR [W. L. GARRISON]. n.d. n.p.** Describes effects of the *Liberator* in New Hampshire, where it had never been seen before; blames complete silence of other public journals for keeping the people ignorant; explains that black and white men can flourish together and that they are indistinguishable in some parts of the South. 12 May 1832. p.74, c3.

1007 S. S. *to* **THE EDITOR OF THE** *NEW HAMPSHIRE OBSERVER.* **n.d. n.p.** Asks to whom the slaves can look for the recovery of their liberties; replies that it is not to their owners, as long as wealth, power, and influence are so dear to them, nor to the legislature; concludes that they must look to New England, which must shake off its apathy and raise its voice to help them. 12 May 1832. p.74, c3.

1008 n.n. *to* **PRES. HUMPHREY. 1829. Greensboro', Al.** Describes New England and contemplates some of the causes which produce great differences between the character of the North and South; concludes that climate and scenery have influence, but slavery makes the difference; discusses moral and intellectual influences of slavery and hopes it will be abolished. 12 May 1832. p.76, c2.

1009 A. S. *to* **THE** *LIBERATOR.* **n.d. Wilbraham.** Replies to Garrison's criticism of the CS; reports that the funding of colonization will come from general and state governments; explains that the CS does not expect to deport the whole colored population, because it will not use force; declares that most others will want to follow, though. 19 May 1832. p.77, c1.

1010 A . . . ILA [illegible] *to* **THE EDITOR [W. L. GARRISON]. n.d. n.p.** Advises the colored population how to help better their position in society; tells them to get an education, support merchants and mechanics of their own, help to get workshops and farm schools started, and create schools where they may learn together. 19 May 1832. p.77, c3.

1011 TEMPLETON *to* **SIR [W. L. GARRISON]. n.d. n.p.** Points out a shameful contradiction in America which consists of securing tracts of land for distressed Poles who seek asylum while shipping people of color off to Africa; believes that provisions should be made for blacks who have fought for the independence and prosperity of America. 19 May 1832. p.77, c4.

1012 BRUTUS *to* **MR. EDITOR [W. L. GARRISON]. 1832. Philadelphia.** Appeals to patriotism, consistency, and the heroes of American Revolution to forbid the cruel propositions of colonization. 19 May 1832. p.77, c4.

1013 L. *to* **n.n. [extract from the** *Boston Sentinel***] n.d. Portugal.** Reports the complete abolition of slavery in the dominions under the government of Donna Maria, with no compensation to masters; regrets that many Portuguese ships still make huge profit selling slaves from Africa to Brazil. 19 May 1832. p.78, c4.

1014 AUNT MARGERY *to* **THE YOUNG FOLKS. n.d. n.p.** Sends letter for the Juvenile Department, reminding children of her past articles on the unfairness of slavery; tells of talented mathematician who could have succeeded if only he had not been a slave. 19 May 1832. p.79, c1.

1015 RICHARD MORAN *to* **THE EDITOR [W. L. GARRISON]. 8 May 1832. Lawrenceburgh, In.** Former slave, held in bondage until the age of twenty-two, claims that the exertions colored people make to educate and better themselves are futile, especially when they are told by colonizationists that they must leave; prefers asylums such as Canada and Mexico to Africa, but does not want to leave America. 26 May 1832. p.81, c5.

1016 A GENTLEMAN AT WASHINGTON *to* **A FRIEND IN BOSTON. [extract from the** *Salem Register***] 21 May 1832. Washington.** Discusses the Houston outrage concerning the fight between Arnold of Tennessee and Major Heard on the steps of the Capitol; reports that Heard was saved by Arnold's friends, although Heard started the fight. 26 May 1832. p.83, c3.

1017 n.n. *to* **n.n. [extract from the** *U. S. Gazette***] 22 March 1832. Port-au-Prince, Hayti.** Reports that there are no beggars in Haiti, the tropical climate makes food abundant, and the country is more charming than the city; notes friendly feelings towards the United States, and suggests that Haiti could be useful to commerce and manufacturers of the United States. 26 May 1832. p.84, c2.

1018 GARDNER JONES *to* **REV. ISAAC ORR. 15 May 1832. New York.** Counters the charge that blacks are inferior to whites; shows that at one time blacks were vastly superior in point of civilization and high degree of scientific knowledge; quotes extensively to support points. 2 June 1832. p.85, c2.

1019 A PHILANTHROPIST IN THE STATE OF NEW YORK *to* **n.n. [extract] n.d. New York.** Attacks the premise that slaves are treated well when they are robbed of their earnings, not given enough to eat or wear; urges that slaveholders cease their evil ways immediately. 2 June 1832. p.87, c3.

1020 J. *to* **THE EDITOR OF THE** *CATSKILL RECORDER***. n.d. n.p.** Discusses free school education for colored children; comments on school which has faithful teacher, thirty students; asks for contributions, as most parents are too poor to sustain the school. 2 June 1832. p.88, c3.

1021 BEN FRANKLIN *to* **THOMAS PAINE. n.d. n.p.** Comments on Paine's pamphlet attacking religion; informs Paine that he cannot succeed, he will only make himself disliked; states that some people need the assistance of religion to lead a virtuous life. 2 June 1832. p.88, c4.

1022 GARDNER JONES *to* **REV. ISAAC ORR. 24 May 1832. New York.** Objects to CS because it is hostile to the abolition of slavery; finds this an anomaly, as it claims benevolence, yet accepts a system it admits is wrong; quotes from CS papers and concludes that colonizationists must not know the real condition of blacks in the South. 9 June 1832. p.89, c3.

1023 GARDNER JONES *to* **REV. ISAAC ORR. 1 June 1832. New York.** Disagrees with CS claims that their scheme will end the slave trade; argues that since Liberia has no protection, colored people can be stolen into slavery again; denies that colonization scheme is benevolent. 23 June 1832. p.98, c1.

1024 n.n. *to* **n.n. 26 September 1831. Liberia, Africa.** Begs secrecy, as CS treats with contempt those who write to America against them; writes to help protect colored brethren against the deceit of colonizationists; states that colonizationists send colored people to miserable conditions, and do not help them once they are there. 30 June 1832. p.102, c2.

1025 n.n. *to* **n.n. 24 February 1828. St. Paul, Africa.** Recounts tragic tale of life in Liberia; laments difficulty in procuring items like coffee and rice, dependence on natives' whimsy for foodstuffs, and the high price of provisions; declares that most reports sent to America, especially those published in the *African Repository,* do not tell the truth about the sufferings of the colonists. 30 June 1832. p.102, c3.

1026 H. *to* **SIR [W. L. GARRISON]. 23 June 1832. Providence.** Encloses an article; confesses having ridiculed *Liberator*'s beliefs and endeavors and supported colonization; declares he has been converted to anti-colonization, and supports Garrison in his noble cause. 30 June 1832. p.102, c4.

1027 A CLERGYMAN IN A NEIGHBORING STATE *to* **n.n. [extract] n.d. n.p.** Praises Garrison's work on CS, showing falsity of its intent; argues against the ability of colony to advance Christianity; longs for the establishment of a missionary station in Africa, not the colonization of colored people there. 30 June 1832. p.103, c2.

1028 A GENTLEMAN IN NEW YORK *to* **n.n. n.d. New York.** Describes iniquities of CS and looks forward to the time when it will stop meeting. 30 June 1832. p.103, c3.

1029 A METHODIST MINISTER *to* **MR. EDITOR [W. L. GARRISON]. 15 June 1832. Philadelphia.** Reports that many of the white sufferers in the Virginia rebellion were Methodists, most of whom have now converted to colonizationism; urges those Methodists not to handle the evil, unclean slavery. 7 July 1832. p.105, c2.

1030 H. C. P. *to* **MR. EDITOR [W. L. GARRISON]. 18 May 1832. Port-au-Prince.** Refutes earlier article on Haiti; claims there is no difference between colored emigrants and native Haitians; denies that natives look on colored emigrants as inferiors. 7 July 1832. p.105, c3.

1031 GARDNER JONES *to* **REV. ISAAC ORR. 8 June 1832. New York.** Tries to elucidate the true meaning of prejudice in its relation to the free people of color; explains that prejudice means refraining from associating with respectable people simply because of the color of their darker skin; attacks colonizationists for claiming superior blood and skin color. 7 July 1832. p.105, c4.

1032 BEATRICE *to* **FRIENDS. n.d. Philadelphia.** Urges the cultivation of women's minds; claims that although women do not have the physical strength nor the moral courage and ambition of men, they do have the wide field of the domestic circle. 7 July 1832. p.106, c3.

1033 G. W. S. *to* **W. L. GARRISON. 6 July 1832. Boston.** Wonders how the just and desperate struggle against slavery can possibly want for support; curses the man who says he loves God, yet supports slavery; congratulates Garrison on his efforts and reminds him his cause is noble. 7 July 1832. p.106, c5.

1034 HENRY DRAYTON AND HENRY JOHNSON *to* **MR. EDITOR [W. L. GAR-RISON]. 28 June 1832. Hartford.** Two respected colored gentlemen describe taking passage from New York to Hartford; report that they had to keep to upper deck, stay outside half of the night and amongst the kitchen pots the other half; ask what their fathers had done to warrant such oppression. 7 July 1832. p.107, c1.

1035 J. K. *to* **SIR. 3 July 1832. Newton.** Expresses joy that Congress has finally decided to compensate Revolutionary War veterans; notes that there are more black vets than white vets alive, due to their temperate habits; wonders if blacks will actually get their pay or be robbed of it by white masters. 7 July 1832. p.107, c2.

1036 H. *to* **THE EDITOR [W. L. GARRISON]. n.d. n.p.** Defends colonization and stresses its connection with the general government; addresses the question of whether the federal government will ever appropriate the necessary money to the CS; believes colonizationism has national support and will therefore receive federal funding. 14 July 1832. p.109, c1.

1037 SOPHANISBA *to* **n.n. [extract] n.d. n.p.** Reports on inspiring speech by abolitionist; urges friend to support the oppressed. 14 July 1832. p.110, c5.

1038 K. *to* **MR. EDITOR [W. L. GARRISON]. n.d. n.p.** Since Congress has requested the President to appoint a fast day, he explains biblical references to, and practices of, fasts; notes that fasting averted destruction of the Ninevites. 14 July 1832. p.111, c4.

1039 ELISHA B. NYE AND HOLDEN DWIGHT *to* **MR. EDITOR [W. L. GARRISON]. 4 July 1832. Middletown.** Request that the editor stop sending his paper, since members do not approve principles. 21 July 1832. p.113, c2.

1040 n.n. *to* **SIR. [W. L. GARRISON]. 7 July 1832. Providence.** A professor of religion involved in many benevolent groups states that he had been a strong advocate of colonization and had contributed much money, especially to itinerant collectors of the society; claims that he had only heard one side, a lecture made him see the other, and he is now against colonization. 21 July 1832. p.113, c2.

1041 n.n. *to* **W. L. GARRISON. 12 July 1832. Providence.** Declares that Garrison's book against colonization has convinced him of the wrongs of CS; states that he previously heard a speaker for colonization and donated money, although he was uneasy about it, but now he knows better. 21 July 1832. p.113, c3.

1042 GARDNER JONES *to* **REV. ISAAC ORR. 26 June 1832. New York.** Discusses the climate of Africa; points out that colored people in America have become habituated to our climate, and like the whites, will die if they move too close to the equator; charges that this lie of the colonizationists is another manifestation of their wickedness. 21 July 1832. p.113, c.4.

1043 ZILLAH *to* **A FRIEND. [extract] 23 February 1832. n.p.** Tries to convince her friend that colonization is wrong and that her people are happiest in America, which is their home; states that there are too many wicked people in Haiti or Mexico while Great Britain has too many of her own starving. 21 July 1832. p.115, c1.

1044 n.n. *to* **THE EDITORS OF THE** *COURIER.* **n.d. n.p.** Attacks Rev. Mr. Danforth for his pro-colonization speech; challenges him to a debate at the New England AS. 21 July 1832. p.115, c2.

1045 J. *to* **THE EDITORS OF THE** *COURIER.* **n.d. n.p.** Reports that Rev. Mr. Danforth has left town and cannot reply to the AS's proposal of a debate. 21 July 1832. p.115, c2.

1046 A COLORED GENTLEMAN *to* **n.n. [extract] n.d. Poughkeepsie, N.Y.** Reports kidnapping of small free colored boy and attempt to sell him in Virginia; explains that town committee rescued boy, imprisoned man who sold him. 28 July 1832. p.118, c5.

1047 A METHODIST OF THE OLD EPISCOPAL CHURCH *to* **MR. EDITOR [W. L. GARRISON]. 12 July 1832. Hartford.** Notes his pleasure at seeing people of color worshipping together; tells of church conflict which is dividing the congregation and weakening them; hopes Garrison can influence them to stay together. 28 July 1832. p.119, c2.

1048 GARDNER JONES *to* **REV. ISAAC ORR. 12 July 1832. New York.** Accuses CS of subordinating the interests of the colored people to those of the whites; sums up all his past arguments; quotes passages from the colonizationists, showing them to be intolerant and prejudiced; warns them of their future. 4 August 1832. p.121, c1.

1049 GARDNER JONES *to* **THE READERS OF THE** *LIBERATOR.* **12 July 1832. New York.** Declares that he neither cares about nor hates Rev. Isaac Orr, only attacks him as a colonizationist; urges readers to continue their worthy, noble cause by working against slavery. 4 August 1832. p.121, c1.

1050 PAUL CUFFEE *to* **MR. EDITOR [W. L. GARRISON]. 25 July 1832. Philadelphia.** Reports with great satisfaction that, in spite of much publicity, only $355.14 was raised in Philadelphia for the ACS; hopes that he hears the society strangling for lack of funds. 4 August 1832. p.123, c1.

1051 REV. GEORGE WHITEFIELD *to* **THE INHABITANTS OF MARYLAND, VIRGINIA, NORTH AND SOUTH CAROLINA. 23 January 1740. Savannah.** Informs them he believes that God has a quarrel with them, because they hold slaves, which no Christian may do, and especially becaue they keep their Negroes ignorant of Christianity. 11 August 1832. p.125, c2.

1052 A FRIEND OF LIGHT *to* **W. L. GARRISON. n.d. Ohio.** Discusses a former pupil of his who went to college but was persecuted and insulted because of his dark skin and bushy black hair; tutor explained to an offended student that it was all right to eat with him because he was really white, instead of telling student it was all right to eat with Negroes. 11 August 1832. p.125, c4.

1053 BERA *to* **ZOE. 1832. Westphila, Philadelphia County.** Discusses education and its contribution to the perfection of art, science, progress of civilization, extension of Christianity; believes that parents and guardians must choose and guide the knowledge of juveniles. 11 August 1832. p.127, c1.

1054 ZOE *to* **BERA. 27 July 1832. Philadelphia.** Finds faults in both the system and practice of education; feels that children rarely get enough education, which is fault of parents, not system; desires that teachers take into consideration which students get help at home and which do not. 11 August 1832. p.127, c1.

1055 REV. JEHIEL C. BEMAN *to* **THE EDITOR [W. L. GARRISON]. 4 August 1832. Middletown, Ct.** Refutes charges against him; explains that he did not refuse a mandate, but was offered a missionary position by his church which he respectfully declined; denies attempting to divide the congregation; expresses pleasure that so many people of color in Middletown regularly attend services. 11 August 1832. p. 127, c3.

1056 WILLIAM SAUNDERS *to* **MR. EDITOR [W. L. GARRISON]. 3 August 1832. New York.** Recounts wretched treatment on steamboat from New York to Hartford; explains he was treated well until evening, then told that colored people could not enter cabins to rest; after protesting, he was landed on a desolate part of Long Island with wild cattle; wife received same treatment at another time. 11 August 1832. p. 127, c4.

1057 BENJAMIN LUNDY *to* **n.n. [extract] n.d. n.p.** Describes Northern trip in the Lake Erie area, and the deplorable conditions of the roads; in several places he had to cross deep icy streams. 18 August 1832. p.129, c2.

1058 n.n. *to* **THE EDITOR [W. L. GARRISON]. July 1832. Providence.** Rejoices that the supporters of emancipation are growing and that those who looked to the CS as a cause are now realizing that they must look elsewhere; calls upon fellow citizens to work for immediate emancipation and abolition of slavery forever. 18 August 1832. p.129, c5.

1059 WOODBY *to* **ZILLAH. n.d. Philadelphia.** Feels that Zillah misunderstood the meaning of the colored woman last week; explains that the woman was totally against colonization, but if the United States enacted compulsory laws forcing them to leave, she hoped a place of refuge would be found. 18 August 1832. p.131, c1.

1060 ZILLAH *to* **WOODBY. n.d. Philadelphia.** Feels Woodby has misinterpreted her; urges Woodby to read Garrison on emigration, as he willingly and bravely pleads their cause in an inspiring way; states that she never wants to leave her native land, America. 18 August 1832. p.131, c1.

1061 CHARLES W. GARDNER *to* **FRIEND [W. L. GARRISON]. 23 July 1832. Philadelphia.** Reports that he had been in Baltimore, where colored people are not allowed to stay more than ten days, under penalty; CS there knew he opposed it, so arranged to have him arrested; tried to escape but was arrested on departing boat, brought to trial, and acquitted. 18 August 1832. p.131, c3.

1062 A CLERGYMAN IN A NEIGHBORING TOWN *to* **W. L. GARRISON. [extract] n.d. n.p.** Bemoans slavery and traffic in human flesh; states that slavery is a national sin which can no longer be excused by ignorance; declares that he used to support colonization, but now supports only immediate abolition. 25 August 1832. p.134, c1.

1063 A COLORED VISITOR *to* **THE EDITOR [W. L. GARRISON]. 20 August 1832. Boston.** Discusses the oppression of free persons of color in Charleston, S. C., where they treat dogs better than colored people and deny colored people justice or trials; wonders if South Carolinians read the Bible or if they are heathen. 25 August 1832. p.134, c1.

1064 R. B. H. *to* **MR. EDITOR [W. L. GARRISON]. 22 August 1832. Boston.** Reports he had attended a meeting to organize an association to help the poor and sick in case of a cholera epidemic; relates doctor's stories of those dying because they had no place to go in Rhode Island. 25 August 1832. p.134, c2.

1065 NATHANIEL PAUL *to* **W. L. GARRISON. 3 July 1832. London.** Comments on the zeal of the English AS, and the long petition sent to United States Congress; reports on beginnings of cholera outbreak. 25 August 1832. p.135, c2.

1066 JOS. R. DAILEY *to* **REV. S. S. JOCELYN. 15 April 1832. Liberia.** Reports he has been frequently attacked by natives who were angrv at the suspension of the slave traffic in which they formerly participated; states that natives were subdued by citizens armed with modern weapons. 25 August 1832. p.136, c2.

1067 JOHN RANKIN *to* **MR. THOMAS RANKIN. n.d. Ohio.** Demonstrates that the African was not created for slavery; argues that God does not create without design, and since the Africans do have the capacity for freedom, God did not create them for slavery; wonders how his brother would feel if his own wife or daughter were being cruelly lashed; declares every man desires to be free. 1 September 1832. p.137, c4.

1068 S. P.D. *to* **THE EDITOR [W. L. GARRISON]. n.d. n.p.** States that he had not really looked favorably on the CS, but since reading Garrison's works, has become strongly in favor of that position; adds that very few people in New England get both sides of the colonization question; encourages Garrison in his holy cause and asks about the state of education of blacks in Boston. 1 September 1832. p.138, c4.

1069 ARNOLD BUFFUM *to* **n.n. 25 August 1832. Northampton.** Discusses meeting at which Rev. J. N. Danforth of the ACS tried to discredit the New England AS. 1 September 1832. p.138, c5.

1070 ARNOLD BUFFUM *to* **n.n. [extract] 9 July 1832. New Bedford.** Reports that he made two speeches in this town on the heels of speeches for colonization; states he changed several people's minds and hopes to attend meeting of colored people at New Bedford. 1 September 1832. p.139, c2.

1071 ARNOLD BUFFUM *to* **n.n. [extract] 16 July 1832. Providence.** Reports that he attended meeting of colored people in New Bedford and spoke on education and temperance; took collections at Newport and Bristol, a slave-trading town. 1 September 1832. p.139, c3.

1072 ARNOLD BUFFUM *to* **n.n. 18 July 1832. Fall River.** Requests a paper by J. N. Danforth in order to convince every honest man that colonizationists are un-Christian; discusses future travel plans. 1 September 1832. p.139, c3.

1073 ARNOLD BUFFUM *to* **n.n. 20 July 1832. Taunton.** Reports that his audience in Fall River was not very large; describes interesting interview with Rev. B. C. Grafton, Baptist minister, and William Sproat, Esq., attorney. 1 September 1832. p.139, c4.

1074 ARNOLD BUFFUM *to* **n.n. 25 July 1832. Smithfield.** Reports on visit to Pawtucket and Providence where he gave speeches, took collections; feels encouraged at his good receptions, but does run into some that are so prejudiced against "Niggers" that he feels it useless to argue. 8 September 1832. p.141, c1.

1075 ARNOLD BUFFUM *to* **n.n. 30 July 1832. Uxbridge.** Explains that whenever encouraged, he thinks of his friends and writes them so that they too can share that hope and inspiration; reports on speeches at Blackstone, Woonsocket Falls, and Slaterville; realizes he must make clear that CS is not an AS. 8 September 1832. p.141, c2.

1076 ARNOLD BUFFUM *to* **n.n. 7 August 1832. Worcester.** Reports that he remained at Uxbridge two days, then went to Gratton where he delived good speeches and obtained some subscriptions for the *Liberator;* proceeded to Worcester and Leicester; returned to Worcester to attempt to lecture despite opposition from colonizationists. 8 September 1832. p.141, c2.

1077 ARNOLD BUFFUM *to* **n.n. 13 August 1832. Ware.** Rejoices that he was finally allowed to speak in Worcester to crowd of about 300; laments that minister who announced next speech at Ware disapproved of his work and credited the AS with causing the insurrection at Southampton. 8 September 1832. p.141, c3.

1078 ARNOLD BUFFUM *to* **n.n. 19 August 1832. Springfield.** Informs that he spoke in Belchertown where the minister had given such a negative notice that only thirty to forty men and not one woman attended; adds that he gave another lecture, by request, to a much fuller house; proceeded to Springfield and gave three lectures. 8 September 1832. p.141, c3.

1079 ARNOLD BUFFUM *to* **n.n. 22 August 1832. Amherst.** Reports that several ministers in Springfield acknowledged their firm opposition to colonization cause before he left; adds that his opponents are still speaking against him, but did not influence converts to his just and noble cause. 8 September1832. p.141, c4.

1080 JOHN RANKIN *to* **MR. THOMAS RANKIN. n.d. Ohio.** Argues that the first evil resulting from slavery is gross ignorance; points out that education would mean loss of labor and expense to the slaveholder, so it is forbidden; also notes that if the oppressed knew their rights, they might become dangerous; declares that the system of slavery becomes more difficult to maintain as slaves' numbers increase. 8 September 1832. p.141, c5.

1081 A CORRESPONDENT *to* **THE EDITOR OF THE** *EMANCIPATOR.* **[extract] 27 August 1820. Norfolk, Va.** Reports new law which prohibits even Sabbath schools from staying open to teach colored people. 8 September 1832. p.142, c1.

1082 R. B. H. *to* **THE EDITOR [W. L. GARRISON]. n.d. n.p.** Describes the double-talk of the CS; explains that to Southerners, it appears as a way to hold slaves more securely, while to Northerners, it seems like a way to abolish slavery; gives many quotes to show that the society does not want to "meddle" with emancipation at all. 8 September 1832. p.142, c5.

1083 BERA *to* **ZOE. 1832. Westphila, Philadelphia County.** Feels that the problem with present forms of education lies not with parents and teachers, but with the age of schooling; believes the child starts too early and suggests letting mother school child for first ten years. 8 September 1832. p.143, c2.

1084 E. W. *to* **MR. ISHAM. [from the** *Hudson Observer***] n.d. n.p.** Asks moral questions about distinctions between right and wrong, the existence of a conscience, and differences between men and brutes. 8 September 1832. p.144, c5.

1085 JOHN RANKIN *to* **MR. THOMAS RANKIN. n.d. n.p.** Asserts that slave populations were always kept in gross ignorance, yet many Africans have fine minds; describes many amiable, intelligent, and wealthy inhabitants who were once in bondage; refuses to discuss whether Africans are better off in the United States than in native land because enslaving them is still wrong. 15 September 1832. p.145, c1.

1086 O. S. M. *to* **MR. EDITOR [W. L. GARRISON]. August 1832. Philadelphia.** Comments on colored friend who wrote many books and suggests that a state on outskirts of United States be given to colored people as their state; tells of his own suffering in Africa's intolerable climate and attacks colonization. 15 September 1832. p.146, c1.

1087 ZOE *to* **BERA. 1832. Philadelphia.** Agrees that children should be taught to read before going to school; agrees that children might benefit from education at home for ten years, but notes that most parents are not interested; discusses problems parents create in children's schooling. 15 September 1832. p.147, c1.

1088 Z. *to* **MR. GARRISON. n.d. n.p.** Describes the colored population of New Bedford, their church, and their employment; shows them to be upright and hardworking. 22 September 1832. p.149, c1.

1089 JOHN RANKIN *to* **MR. THOMAS RANKIN. n.d. Ohio.** Curses the evil of involuntary slavery and the tyranny of slaveholders who prostitute female slaves and enslave their own children. 22 September 1832. p.149, c4.

1090 JOHN RANKIN *to* **MR. THOMAS RANKIN. n.d. n.p.** Concludes that the very best of men are disqualified from the proper exercise of power regarding slavery; shows how the worst of men are unqualified because of the immense degree to which that power extends. 22 September 1832. p.149, c4.

1091 ARNOLD BUFFUM *to* **FRIEND [W. L. GARRISON]. 17 September 1832. Taunton.** Reports on speaking tour, the various towns where he spoke, the size of his audience, and how he was received; notes the conversion of another minister from supporting colonization to attacking it. 22 September 1832. p.150, c1.

1092 ALMIRA *to* **FRIENDS. n.d. n.p.** A colored woman, age fifteen, and a member of the Society of Colored Ladies in Providence for Improvement in Morals and Literature, discusses the beauty and omnipresence of Christianity. 22 September 1832. p.150, c4.

1093 DESTOUCHES *to* **FRIENDS. n.d. n.p.** A colored woman, member of the Society of Colored Ladies in Providence for Improvement in Morals and Literature, notes the goodness and pleasure she receives from being in the society. 22 September 1832. p.150, c4.

1094 JOHN RANKIN *to* **MR. THOMAS RANKIN. n.d. Ohio.** Asserts that slaveholders hold powers over their slaves' eating, work, chastity, marriage, sale, and removal; decries the evils of slavery in Kentucky and the disregard of liberty manifested at slave auctions. 29 September 1832. p.153, c1.

1095 O. S. M. *to* **THE EDITOR OF THE** *VERMONT TELEGRAPH.* **n.d. n.p.** Argues with the editors of the *Telegraph* about where his letters should be published; charges the editors with shrinking from the subject of immediate abolition. 29 September 1832. p.153, c5.

1096 JOHN RANKIN *to* **MR. THOMAS RANKIN. n.d. n.p.** Continues to tell of the slaveholder's power over his slaves; explains that a wicked master may prevent his slaves from worshipping God and may tyrannize their conscience; tells of cruel master in Georgia who demanded such excessive labor from six girls that they hanged themselves. 6 October 1832. p.157, c1.

1097 W. L. GARRISON *to* **n.n. 7 September 1832. Worcester, Ma.** Declares that since his enemies have been growing confident, it is time to give them their just retribution; wants to do justice to himself, correct his "madman" image, and further organize abolitionists, or the cause will be lost; tells of anti-Masonic state convention and supports the total abolition of freemasonry. 6 October 1832. p.158, c3.

1098 BERA *to* **ZOE. 1832. Westphila, Philadelphia County.** Contends that parents are much more successful in educating their children than are teachers; explains that parents watch their children's dispositions form and spend two-thirds more time with them; calls for more and better education of females' minds. 6 October 1832. p.158, c5.

1099 E. H. *to* **MR. EDITOR [W. L. GARRISON]. 30 August 1832. U. Oxford, Chester County, Pa.** Questions whether Garrison thinks intemperance is more evil than slavery; quotes Garrison as saying he would rather be a slaveholder than sell spirits to his fellow man; reminds him that intemperance is voluntary, and enslavement is not voluntary. 6 October 1832. p.159, c2.

1100 NATHAN EVANS *to* **THE EDITOR [W. L. GARRISON]. 6 September 1832. Willistown, Chester County, Pa.** Although Pennsylvania is clear of the sin of slavery, he wishes there were a copy of the *Liberator* in every home, because there exists a mountain of prejudice against blacks; compliments Garrison on the value and honesty of the paper. 13 October 1832. p.161, c2.

1101 JOHN RANKIN *to* **MR. THOMAS RANKIN. n.d. Ohio.** Remarks upon the extent of the slaveholder's power in relation to the infliction of corporal punishment; states that slaveholders can punish slaves in any way they want and tells of vicious, vengeful punishments; quotes part of essay by Rev. William Dickey giving an example of this terrible abuse of power. 13 October 1832. p.161, c3.

1102 W. L. GARRISON *to* **L. 13 September 1832. Providence.** Complains about the miseries of stage-riding; describes countryside and factories en route from Worcester to Providence; describes wonderful Providence Arcade, City Hotel, and visit with Moses Brown, patriarch of the Society of Friends; gives account of his speeches and various receptions. 13 October 1832. p.162, c1.

1103 ZOE *to* **BERA. 1832. Philadelphia.** Continues discussion on education; agrees with Bera that parents have a great influence on children, but reminds her that teachers do, too; tells story of boy who refused to love infant brother until teacher told him that he should and must. 13 October 1832. p.163, c1.

1104 n.n. *to* **THE EDITOR OF THE *REL. HERALD*. 5 July 1832. Buckingham County.** Describes shocking exhibition of intemperance; relates that as Mr. A. became more intemperate, he became more brutal to his family and finally killed himself. 13 October 1832. p.164, c3.

1105 JOHN RANKIN *to* **MR. THOMAS RANKIN. n.d. Ohio.** Discusses the effects of slavery on the enslaved; criticizes lack of domestic peace for slaves, idleness and vice among free inhabitants of slaveholding states, and debilitation in constitution of slaveholders; believes that ignorance is a result of slavery, and that slavery weakens the state by cultivating cruelty and tyranny. 20 October 1832. p.165, c1.

1106 W. L. GARRISON *to* **n.n. 24 September 1832. Portland.** Describes perfect weather during trip from Boston to Portland; discusses article on the ACS in which the writer tries to prove that the CS was conceived by a gang of Negro thieves in Virginia; describes Portland and gives account of interviews and speeches. 20 October 1832. p.165, c5.

1107 W. L. GARRISON *to* **n.n. 28 September 1832. Hallowell.** Praises Maine countryside, villages, and White Mountains; describes Hallowell, and reports on conversations with preachers and AS supporters; discusses several quotes from various works he has been reading. 20 October 1832. p.166, c2.

1108 L'AMI *to* **MR. EDITOR [W. L. GARRISON]. n.d. n.p.** Discusses the mental capacity of blacks, and asserts that even slaveholders admit them to be sagacious and clever; stresses that whatever their mental capacity may be, there is no excuse for their oppression. 20 October 1832. p.167, c4.

1109 ARNOLD BUFFUM *to* **n.n. 23 October 1832. Lowell.** Reports that he went to New Haven to speak with S. S. Jocelyn, with whom he was very impressed; discusses temperance meetings and the School for Colored Children; describes speech at Providence wherein he tried to correct the deceptions afloat about the CS. 27 October 1832. p.170, c2.

1110 W. L. GARRISON *to* **L. 2 October 1832. Bangor.** Describes Bangor; discusses funding for the AS and makes several suggestions on how to collect money; laments inhumanity of an ad for runaway slaves. 27 October 1832. p.170, c4.

1111 JOHN RANKIN *to* **MR. THOMAS RANKIN. n.d. Ohio.** Discusses the beginning of slavery; argues that since the Negroes' ancestors were originally free, the nation has sinned by enslaving them. 27 October 1832. p.171, c1.

1112 MARY *to* **W. L. GARRISON. 9 September 1832. n.p.** Stresses that love is life; discusses how to fight slavery philosophically; believes colonization is only a partial step since slavery itself must be stopped. 27 October 1832. p.171, c1.

1113 n.n. *to* **SIR [W. L. GARRISON]. 4 September 1832. Hudson, Oh.** Expresses desire to subscribe to *Liberator;* asks about future plans of New England AS; denounces CS. 3 November 1832. p.172, c2.

1114 JOHN RANKIN *to* **MR. THOMAS RANKIN. n.d. Ohio.** Argues that modern slavery is prohibited by the Bible; discusses Noah's curse, Abraham's alleged slaves, and the Mosaic institutions; concludes by stating that the attempt to justify slavery through the Bible is absurd. 3 November 1832. p.173, c1.

1115 n.n. *to* **MR. EDITOR [W. L. GARRISON]. n.d. n.p.** Reveals he has reached decision that the CS cannot contribute to the good of either the whites or the colored people of America; believes that colored people must work together in a separate place, perhaps a Western territory; feels that if CS is destroyed, a substitute is needed. 3 November 1832. p.174, c1.

1116 GLOSTER SIMPSON AND ARCHY MOORE *to* **REV. R. R. GURLEY. 27 September 1832. Washington.** Describe their trip to Liberia; report that the people there possess a spirit of independence and liberty, have schools, churches, fertile soil, and good health. 3 November 1832. p.174, c3.

1117 ARNOLD BUFFUM *to* **n.n. 31 October 1832. Salem.** Describes talk in Lowell where the congregation was satisfied with his views; reports that lectures in Newbury, Newburyport, and Ipswich changed several minds. 3 November 1832. p.175, c1.

1118 n.n. *to* **SIR [W. L. GARRISON]. 24 September 1832. New York.** Congratulates those engaged in noble cause; suggests changing name of New England AS to AS of the United States; asks questions about the society. 10 November 1832. p.177, c2.

1119 W. L. GARRISON *to* **n.n. 8 October 1832. Waterville.** Describes village of Waterville and weather; summarizes his speeches against colonization and in defense of the principles and purposes of the AS. 10 November 1832. p.177, c2.

1120 JOHN RANKIN *to* **MR. THOMAS RANKIN. n.d. Ohio.** Disagrees with Rev. Archibald Cameron, who misinterprets a translation of "servant" to "slave" in Greek; states that Cameron tries to use New Testament to prove Christians are allowed to have slaves when the original text refers to servants. 10 November 1832. p.177, c3.

1121 JOSIAH GREEN *to* **MR. EDITOR [W. L. GARRISON]. n.d. Rochester, N.Y.** Discusses Rochester's treatment of colored people; relates that five years ago an African Sunday school, a school, and finally a state school district were established with the help of state funds. 10 November 1832. p.178, c1.

1122 ARNOLD BUFFUM *to* **n.n. 5 November 1832. Woburn, Ma.** Reports on his second visit to Lowell where he changed the opinion of an editor of the *Telegraph* who had given him bad reviews; states that in Woburn he gave speech to well-satisfied audience. 10 November 1832. p.178, c3.

1123 ELIZABETH WALBRIDGE *to* **n.n. 3 March 1797. n.p.** Delivers a lecture on morality to brother. 10 November 1832. p.180, c4.

1124 JOHN RANKIN *to* **MR. THOMAS RANKIN. n.d. Ohio.** Quotes several passages of Scripture which he believes to be decidedly opposed to slavery's existence; considers some of the excuses made for slavery. 17 November 1832. p.181, c1.

1125 n.n. *to* **W. L. GARRISON. 8 November 1832. Salem.** Informs Garrison of a female AS that was established in February 1832; regrets that Garrison's visit was so short. 17 November 1832. p.183, c2.

1126 ARNOLD BUFFUM *to* **n.n. 19 November 1832. Boston.** Reports on lectures in Boston and Salem where he spoke only on slavery; plans to give another talk since citizens later requested to hear about colonization. 24 November 1832. p.187, c2.

1127 ARNOLD BUFFUM *to* **n.n. 26 November 1832. Lynn.** Reports that minister in Salem finally agreed to a public discussion of their differences but never showed up; states he is still willing to take him on whenever possible; feels encouragement and hope. 1 December 1832. p.190, c1.

1128 P. *to* **MR. EDITOR [W. L. GARRISON]. 17 November 1832. New Bedford.** Gives account of travel from North Bridgewater to New Bedford; finds it difficult to find refreshment or a place to stay; adds that hotel keepers will cater only to whites, not colored people. 1 December 1832. p.190, c2.

1129 JAMES CROPPER *to* **W. L. GARRISON. 31 August 1832. Buxton, England.** Agrees with Garrison's work and hopes to stop the ACS, which he feels is an abomination; supports immediate abolition; sends extract of his letter on immediate emancipation to Arnold Buffum. 15 December 1832. p.197, c3.

1130 JAMES CROPPER *to* **ARNOLD BUFFUM. [extract] n.d. n.p.** Condemns colonization as an act of national suicide; extols immediate emancipation. 15 December 1832. p.197, c3.

1131 JOSEPH PHILLIPS *to* **SIR [W. L. GARRISON]. 16 September 1832. Dingle Park, Liverpool.** Hopes to save slaves from the wilds of Liberia and plans to form an anti-colonization group; proposes newspaper exchanges with West Indians; calls for immediate emancipation. 15 December 1832. p.197, c4.

1132 n.n. *to* **A MEMBER OF ONE OF OUR NEW ENGLAND COLLEGES. [from the** *Christian Soldier***] n.d. Georgia.** Recounts to his brother the story of a runaway slave who was hanged for trying to kill his master. 15 December 1832. p.198, c4.

1133 WILLIAM C. SAPSLEY *to* **SIRS [THE EDITORS OF THE** *LIBERATOR***]. 5 November 1832. Tuskaloosa, Al.** Calls them "d--ned fools" and asserts that they, too, would have slaves but are too poor, so they have to sell newspapers; threatens to lash them if they ever come South and entreats them to quit printing. 15 December 1832. p.199, c2.

1134 JOSIAH QUINCY *to* **n.n. 28 November 1832. Cambridge.** Reports that he received a letter from General Lafayette seeking information about a recently deceased French gentleman who lived in Boston and left a large estate. 15 December 1832. p.200, c4.

1135 E. *to* **FRIEND PAINTER OF THE** *WEST CHESTER REGISTER***. n.d. n.p.** Declares his conviction that the public must oppose colonization; questions a few of the doctrines of the CS; urges the paper and free men of color to save their slave brothers. 22 December 1832. p.201, c3.

1136 J. MECHLIN, COLONIAL AGENT *to* **REV. R. R. GURLEY. [extract] September 1832. Liberia.** Describes latest shipload of immigrants as the lowest and most abandoned of their class; reports that the majority are women and children who have no male to provide for them; asserts that some suffering exists because there are lazy individuals. 22 December 1832. p.201, c5.

1137 FRANCIS DEVANY *to* **SIR. 28 September 1832. Monrovia, Liberia.** Acknowledges that he received the *Liberator,* which completely disagrees with his positive report on conditions in Liberia; accuses Garrison of being the worst enemy of the people in Liberia; admits he does not want to ingratiate himself with the CS. 22 December 1832. p.202, c2.

1138 W. P. P. *to* **MR. EDITOR [W. L. GARRISON]. 10 December 1832. New Bedford.** Discusses the marriage of a white man and mulatto woman in Kentucky; asserts that the honorable man has not erred according to the laws of God. 22 December 1832. p.202, c3.

1139 J. P. H. *to* **THE EDITOR [W. L. GARRISON]. 15 March 1832. Port-au-Prince, Hayti.** Approves of the *Liberator* and its patriotic sentiments in regard to slavery; calls for liberty for everyone in United States, but does not support the Southampton violence. 22 December 1832. p.202, c4.

1140 A. F. *to* **THE COLORED CITIZENS OF BOSTON. n.d. Geneva, N.Y.** Praises colored citizens for their meeting to abolish slavery in the District of Columbia; calls upon brethren all over the United States to support the cause. 22 December 1832. p.202, c4.

1141 K. *to* **W. L. GARRISON. n.d. n.p.** Discusses the murder of a female slave by a justice of the peace in North Carolina last June. 22 December 1832. p.202, c5.

1142 n.n. *to* **TRULY RESPECTED FRIEND. 17 December 1830. n.p.** Reassures friend she has nothing to fear if she believes in God and puts her trust in Him; urges her to remain simple and humble. 22 December 1832. p.203, c2.

1143 EDWARD PAYSON *to* **SISTER. [from the** *Albany Daily Advertisement***] n.d. n.p.** Informs sister that he feels very close to the celestial city and looks forward to land of peace; hopes to meet her in heaven. 22 December 1832. p.204, c4.

1144 HOPE *to* **MR. EDITOR [W. L. GARRISON]. 25 December 1832. Boston.** Informs Garrison of newly formed society, Colored Female Charitable Society, which visits widows and orphans; hopes for the society's success. 29 December 1832. p.207, c5.

[1833]

1145 ELIZUR WRIGHT, JR. *to* **W. L. GARRISON. 11 December 1832. Hudson, Oh.** Asserts that after reading Garrison's pamphlet, his doubts on Garrison's views are gone; reports that the meeting of ministers to discuss demolition of the CS kindled opposition to the society. 5 January 1833. p.1, c3.

1146 E. W. *to* **MR. ISHAM. [from the** *Hudson Observer and Telegraph***] n.d. n.p.** Believes that the high proportion of crime among free blacks is the result of the degradation of slavery; asserts that if the expense of colonization were put to education, this would be stopped. 5 January 1833. p.1, c5.

1147 ALEXANDER PLUMLEY *to* **REV. BERIAH GREEN. 15 December 1832. Hudson, Oh.** Forwards a copy of objections to the CS. 5 January 1833. p.2, c2.

1148 ELIZUR WRIGHT *to* **EDITOR [W. L. GARRISON]. n.d. n.p.** Explains how Alexander Plumley, an agent of the ACS, became offended at the suggestion that he read a list of objections to the ACS before audience. 5 January 1833. p.2, c2.

1149 BERIAH GREEN *to* **REV. S. S. JOCELYN. [extract] 5 November 1832. Hudson, Port County, Oh.** A professor of sacred literature in Western Reserve College reports that recently the students and professors have come to feel that abolitionism is a cause most worthy of their support; adds that many had previously been supporters of the CS. 5 January 1833. p.2, c3.

1150 L'AMIE *to* **W. L. GARRISON. n.d. n.p.** Charges that Southerners and Republicans are only interested in taking power from the free states, so as not to endanger their slave system; declares that the Southerners support whichever side of the tariff and commerce question is most injurious to the North; warns of increasing determination among Northerners to keep the South in line. 5 January 1833. p.3, c2.

1151 THOMAS S. GRIMKE, ESQ. *to* **FELLOW CITIZENS OF SOUTH CAROLINA. [extract from the** *Charleston Courier***] 1 December 1832. Charleston.** Informs fellow citizens that the ordinance they passed at the convention at Columbia will be the grave of liberty; accuses them of directly violating the United States Constitution, which still binds them, by assembling troops; states that they are foolish to refuse to pay harbor tax since United States can blockade them and prevent them from leaving the Union. 5 January 1833. p.4, c2.

1152 EDWARD RUSHTON *to* **GEORGE WASHINGTON. 20 February 1797. Liverpool.** Reproaches Washington for holding slaves; considers it ironic that a man who fought the British for freedom and became president of the land of liberty holds slaves; charges that Washington is violating his beliefs. 12 January 1833. p.5, c2.

1153 O. L. S. *to* **FRIEND D---. 8 December 1832. Middletown.** Explains the departure of Mr. Ray, a colored gentleman, from Wesleyan University; reports that students opposed to him, mostly from the South, organized a meeting when most of his supporters were not there; although they passed a resolution for his dismissal, Ray decided to leave of his own accord; adds supporting extract from friend. 12 January 1833. p.7, c2.

1154 L. A. R. *to* **THE** *BOSTON TRAVELLER***. n.d. n.p.** Discusses lecture given by Mr. Pearl at Roxbury; defends CS from attacks by AS. 19 January 1833. p.9, c1.

1155 ARNOLD BUFFUM *to* **THE EDITOR OF THE** *BOSTON TRAVELLER***. n.d. n.p.** Repeats "shameless charges" he made against CS, including claims that the CS originated with slaveholders, and wants to banish free people of color. 19 January 1833. p.9, c2.

1156 L. A. R. *to* **THE EDITOR OF THE** *BOSTON TRAVELLER***. n.d. n.p.** Argues that Buffum's charges against CS are entirely unfounded, but declines to discuss subject since "the tediousness . . . would infallibly disgust the public." 19 January 1833. p.9, c2.

1157 ARNOLD BUFFUM *to* **THE EDITOR OF THE** *BOSTON TRAVELLER***. n.d. n.p.** Replies to L. A. R.'s letter; offers to organize a public discussion of colonization in Roxbury. 19 January 1833. p.9, c3.

1158 R. N. *to* **THE EDITOR OF THE** *BOSTON TRAVELLER***. [from the** *Boston Daily Advocate***] n.d. n.p.** Defends himself against accusation that he garbled a sentence from the *African Repository*. 19 January 1833. p.9, c3.

1159 ROCKCASTLEAN *to* **MR. SKILLMAN. [from the** *Western* **(Ky.)** *Luminary***] n.d. n.p.** Argues that slavery is more expensive than free labor; hopes his fellow Kentuckians will realize this and liberate their slaves. 19 January 1833. p.10, c3.

1160 n.n. *to* **n.n. [extract] 18 December. New Orleans.** Relates gathering of 200 armed slaves, ready to join the insurrection in South Carolina. 19 January 1833. p.10, c4.

1161 WILLIAM COWPER *to* **REV. J. NEWTON. 12 July 1781. n.p.** Declares that he has written for charity in order to do good, not to reap popularity; writes farewell jingle at end. 26 January 1833. p.16, c3.

1162 C. W. [CHARLES WALKER, AGENT OF CS] *to* **MR. EDITOR. [from the** *Brandon Telegraph***] n.d. n.p.** States that personal engagements and the spirit of O. S. M.'s letter prevent him from replying to questions on colonization; informs that many other articles, including some by Danforth, have been published recently and give plenty of explanation. 9 February 1833. p.22, c3.

1163 RAY POTTER *to* **W. L. GARRISON. 19 January 1833. Pawtucket.** Declares he has long been an advocate of immediate abolition but has just awakened to the awful truth about the CS; believes that New England should incur guilt for its indirect support of slavery. 9 February 1833. p.22, c4.

1164 E. W. [PROFESSOR WRIGHT OF HUDSON COLLEGE] *to* **SIR. 26 January 1833. Hudson, Oh.** Comments on Garrison's being accused of abusing the Christian ministry; wonders if one is supposed to respect a minister because of his office or because he holds the principles of God; asserts that if ministers take sides with slaveholders, they must expect to be criticized. 9 February 1833. p.22, c5.

1165 A GENTLEMAN IN NEW JERSEY *to* **W. L. GARRISON. n.d. New Jersey.** Declares that ever since he knew anything of the CS, he had been a warm supporter of it, but only believed its assertions because everyone around him believed them; confides that Garrison's pamphlet opened his eyes to the truth and that he now works against colonization. 16 February 1833. p.25, c3.

1166 A CLERGYMAN IN MAINE *to* **THE EDITOR [W. L. GARRISON]. n.d. n.p.** Decries the horrible system of slavery and advocates immediate abolition; points out that the CS has transported 2000 souls to Africa, but only 388 of them had been slaves; argues that if slaveholders support the CS, it cannot truly be working for emancipation. 16 February 1833. p.25, c4.

1167 A CLERGYMAN IN MAINE *to* **SIR [W. L. GARRISON]. n.d. n.p.** Subscribes to the *Liberator;* tells of many individuals who have changed their minds about colonization in the past months. 16 February 1833. p.25, c5.

1168 A CLERGYMAN IN CONNECTICUT *to* **SIR [W. L. GARRISON]. n.d. n.p.** Reports he has read and enthusiastically supports the resolutions, addresses, and reports of the New England AS. 16 February 1833. p.25, c5.

1169 O. J. *to* **W. L. GARRISON. n.d. n.p.** A supporter of emancipation is cheered to see the bad motives of the CS finally coming to light; sends extract of letter from clergyman friend who was converted from pro-colonization to pro-immediate emancipation by Garrison's works. 16 February 1833. p.25, c5.

1170 JAMES CROPPER *to* **THOMAS CLARKSON. 2 October 1832. Liverpool.** Regrets that his friend Clarkson supports colonization; asserts that slaveholders want to send away free blacks to get rid of slave competition; predicts that Southern legislators will either compel free blacks to leave legally, or make their situation intolerable. 16 February 1833. p.26, c1.

1171 JOHN REMOND *to* **MR. EDITOR [W. L. GARRISON]. 7 February 1833. Salem.** Reports that he invited Arnold Buffum of AS to speak to colored people in Salem so the people could hear both sides of the story; adds that Rev. Danforth of the CS would not speak because Buffum was in the audience. 16 February 1833. p.27, c3.

1172 ARNOLD BUFFUM *to* **FRIEND GARRISON. 13 February 1833. Boston.** Denies he made remarks attributed to him in Salem on his last visit; refutes other slanderous charges. 16 February 1833. p.27, c4.

1173 ELIZUR WRIGHT, JR. *to* **THE EDITORS OF THE** *GENIUS OF TEMPERANCE.* **23 January 1833. Hudson, Oh.** Puts forward what he considers to be the most salient questions on slavery and discusses every man's duty concerning its abolition; declares that although some people, particularly colonizationists, take fright at his questions, God urges them to be answered. 23 February 1833. p.29, c1.

1174 X. *to* **SIR [W. L. GARRISON]. 8 February 1832. Washington City.** Reports he attended a meeting of the CS where the recently elected officers favored turning from colonization to abolition, which resulted in the board's recommending that the officers resign their seats; expresses conviction that the CS can never reconcile abolition and colonization. 23 February 1833. p.29, c4.

1175 ISRAEL LEWIS *to* **FRIEND GARRISON. 11 February 1833. Schenectady.** Criticizes Garrison for printing slanderous letters written about his moral and public character regarding his duties at the Wilberforce Settlement; hopes Garrison will examine matters before printing them in the future. 23 February 1833. p.30, c1.

1176 EDWARD PALMER *to* **REV. RUSSELL. 12 February 1833. Woodstock, Ct.** Rejoices at the boldness of speech in the *Liberator;* declares there is no danger of too much zeal in so just a cause and proclaims abolitionists as the servants of Christ. 23 February 1833. p.31, c2.

1177 n.n. *to* **n.n. [extract] 8 January 1833. Washington.** Explains that when Southern states blocked Northern commerce and a tariff ensued, the North suffered, but never considered nullification; believes that labor is honorable in the North, but not in the South; condemns slavery as the root of all evil. 23 February 1833. p.32, c2.

1178 ESTWICK EVANS, ESQ. *to* **THE EDITOR [W. L. GARRISON]. [extract] 12 February 1833. Washington.** Expresses concern over the movements in South Carolina; discusses nullification, noting that even before the revolution, the colonies were united and dependent on each other; declares he is not against states' rights, but believes states have contracts and obligations. 2 March 1833. p.33, c1.

1179 AMERICANUS *to* **MR. PALFIA. [from the** *Salem Register***]** **n.d. n.p.** Forwards extract from the *African Repository* confining the scope of the CS to the colonization of freemen and not the emancipation of slaves. 2 March 1833. p.34, c3.

1180 ARNOLD BUFFUM *to* **THE PUBLIC. 2 February 1833. Boston.** Gives public explanation of his debate with J. N. Danforth, agent for the CS. 2 March 1833. p.34, c3.

1181 AN AMERICAN *to* **n.n. [extract] 2 February 1833. Porto Rico.** Reports preparations in Puerto Rico for a slave insurrection that turned out to be a false alarm. 2 March 1833. p.34, c5.

1182 W. L. GARRISON *to* **THE EDITOR OF THE** *REGISTER.* **23 February 1833. Boston.** Writes to obviate any misapprehension due to discussion between him and Rev. Dr. Flint; confesses he was ignorant of Flint's name and profession at the time and intended no personal disrespect. 2 March 1833. p.35, c2.

1183 n.n. *to* **THE EDITORS OF THE** *AMERICAN SENTINEL.* **[extract] 16 February. Washington.** Describes intellectual pleasure derived from the debate between Calhoun and Webster. 2 March 1833. p.35, c3.

1184 O. J. *to* **THE EDITOR [W. L. GARRISON]. n.d. n.p.** Replies on behalf of the *Boston Recorder;* affirms that the *Recorder* allowed abolitionists to state their objections to the CS. 2 March 1833. p.35, c4.

1185 B. *to* **THE EDITORS OF THE** *PORTLAND ADVERTISER.* **[extract] 4 February 1833. Washington.** Discusses the differences between Northern Yankees and Southerners; asserts that Northerners love common sense, practicality, and business; believes that in the South, the white man is ashamed to labor. 2 March 1833. p.36, c2.

1186 ONE WHO HAS RIGHTS *to* **THE EDITORS OF THE** *BOSTON TELEGRAPH.* **n.d. n.p.** Disagrees with two passages from the *African Repository* on the origin of slavery and the rights of kidnappers; upholds the right of the slave to be free. 9 March 1833. p.37, c1.

1187 O. S. M. *to* **THE EDITOR OF THE** *BRANDON TELEGRAPH.* **n.d. n.p.** Wonders why Charles Walker cannot reply to his charges if he is able to work and write for the CS; quotes extracts from other papers supporting himself and his candor; challenges Charles Walker to expose O. S. M.'s errors, if he truly can. 9 March 1833. p.37, c4.

1188 SPECTATOR *to* **MR. EDITOR [W. L. GARRISON]. n.d. n.p.** Describes speech by Mr. McLane of the CS, who asserted that every benevolent group has opponents; states that McLane told audience that a line of distinction had been drawn by the Creator between colored people and whites, which is why they cannot live together equally and why the colored population should be deported. 9 March 1833. p.39, c1.

1189 INQUIRER *to* **THE EDITOR [W. L. GARRISON]. n.d. n.p.** Wishes to know exactly how many colored people have been deported to Liberia, how many recaptured Africans were sent there, and how many of the emigrants are still living? 9 March 1833. p.39, c2.

1190 GEORGE W. BENSON *to* **FRIEND [W. L. GARRISON]. n.d. Providence.** Describes Prudence Crandall's efforts to start a high school for colored girls in Canterbury, Connecticut; reports that the prejudiced citizens are trying to stop her because they are afraid their property value will be depreciated if blacks go to school. 9 March 1833. p.39, c4.

1191 DAVID HUDSON, CALEB PITKIN, AND HARVEY COE *to* **MR. ISHAM. 4 February 1833. Hudson.** Remark on comments of Elizur Wright; suggest that slavery in England and its dependencies is different than in the United States and that discussions on slavery have also been very different in the two countries; do not believe that harsh preaching against colonization is appropriate in church. 16 March 1833. p.41, c1.

1192 D. *to* **THE EDITOR OF THE** *MARBLEHEAD REGISTER.* **n.d. n.p.** Feels that if the people in New England could see colonization the way Southerners do, they would reject it; discusses Salem debate between Arnold Buffum and Rev. Mr. Danforth. 16 March 1833. p.42, c2.

1193 HENRY E. BENSON *to* **W. L. GARRISON. 12 March 1833. Providence, R.I.** Account of town meeting in Canterbury, Connecticut which tried to prevent Prudence Crandall from opening her school for colored females; relates that the character and motives of Miss Crandall were attacked and the concept of educating blacks was refused; reports that Miss Crandall, unmoved, is still trying. 16 March 1833. p.42, c3.

1194 LEWIS T. LAINE *to* **W. L. GARRISON. 4 March 1833. Theological Seminary, Andover.** Forwards request of AS to publish four resolutions, which follow letter. 16 March 1833. p.42, c4.

1195 n.n. *to* **MR. FINLEY. 10 March 1833. New York.** Requests answers to questions on the CS's intentions to abolish slavery. 16 March 1833. p.42, c5.

1196 n.n. *to* **THE** *NEW YORK OBSERVER.* **n.d. Washington.** Gives account of CS meetings; states that funds are lacking to send more colored people to Liberia; describes Mr. Garrison's principles as "fiery." 23 March 1833. p.45, c1.

1197 ELIZUR WRIGHT, JR. *to* **FRIEND GARRISON. 27 February 1833. Hudson, Oh.** Suggests that a colonization scheme would be practical for extremely apathetic people; urges sending them to Europe where king and pope could handle all their political and moral decisions; concludes that this will benefit the country as well as stop the slave trade. 23 March 1833. p.46, c1.

1198 BERIAH GREEN *to* **W. L. GARRISON. March 1833. Western Reserve College.** States that he does not know who the editor of the *Boston Telegraph* is, but takes him to task for his slanderous statements and his mistaken views of slavery, tyranny, and property. 23 March 1833. p.46, c2.

1199 I. B. *to* **MR. ISHAM. n.d. n.p.** Addresses whether a man's duty is ever modified by circumstances; argues that since God has made man's duties clear, one should not dare to disobey God's laws. 23 March 1833. p.46, c4.

1200 C. S. W. E. *to* **MR. ISHAM. n.d. n.p.** Explains that the doctrine of the devil is that if a man's circumstances render his duty inconvenient, he is under no obligation; refuses to accept duty as convenience and declares one must always follow only God's laws and doctrines. 23 March 1833. p.46, c5.

1201 A COLORED BALTIMOREAN *to* **THE EDITOR [W. L. GARRISON]. 7 March 1833. Baltimore.** Replies to address on colonization by Rev. Mr. Hammett, a Methodist minister; disagrees with Hammett that colored and white citizens can never live together in America; notes that Hammett admits the biggest problem is prejudice of whites. 23 March 1833. p.47, c1.

1202 ARNOLD BUFFUM *to* **FRIEND. 18 March 1833. New Haven.** Describes good reception at Providence and small audience at Norwich; recalls visit to try to help Prudence Crandall in Canterbury, where she was not allowed to speak; reports on speeches in New London, Hartford, and New Haven. 30 March 1833. p.49, c1.

1203 A FRIEND OF THE BLACKS *to* **THE EDITOR [W. L. GARRISON]. n.d. n.p.** Describes the 13 March meeting of the Young Men's CS; attacks reasoning that free blacks must live in degradation here, and charges that the guilt for this lies in the prejudice of whites, not in the blacks' morals. 30 March 1833. p.49, c3.

1204 EMANCIPATION *to* **THE EDITOR [W. L. GARRISON]. 12 March 1833. New Haven.** Expresses disappointment after reading a sarcastic, poorly written review of Garrison's "Thoughts on African Colonization" in the *Christian Spectator;* as a new convert to immediate and entire emancipation, he urges Garrison to continue educating and converting. 30 March 1833. p.49, c5.

1205 CHARLES STUART *to* **BROTHER [W. L. GARRISON]. n.d. n.p.** Urges Garrison to go forth with the noble cause of anti-slavery; sends English anti-slavery pamphlets; asks about several American abolitionists, and how they have been treated. 30 March 1833. p.51, c4.

1206 n.n. *to* **W. L. GARRISON [extract] n.d. n.p.** Informs Garrison he will be among kindred spirits in London. 30 March 1833. p.51, c4.

1207 ENOCH STALLAD, NESTOR FREEMAN, AND WILLIAM C. NELL *to* **MR. GARRISON. n.d. n.p.** Present Garrison with a silver medal on behalf of the Juvenile Garrison Independent Society. 30 March 1833. p.51, c5.

1208 BERIAH GREEN *to* **MESSRS. GOODELL AND HINES. 22 February 1833. Western Reserve College.** Wonders why American editors are so silent on the topic of Britain since she has just emancipated her slaves; believes this could be a great demonstration to Americans that social order would not fall apart if slaves were freed. 6 April 1833. p.53, c1.

1209 A FRIEND TO THE COLONIZATION CAUSE *to* **THE EDITOR OF THE** *NORWICH REPUBLICAN.* **n.d. n.p.** Discusses Prudence Crandall's school for colored females; charges that it inflames sectional hostilities and that it would encourage interracial marriages; reports that the people of Canterbury are angry at the interference at their town meeting from outsiders. 6 April 1833. p.54, c3.

1210 LIET. COM. JAMES MCINTOSH *to* **n.n. [extract] 19 February 1833. U. S. Schr.** *Porpoise,* **Island of St. Thomas.** Reports that recently emancipated slaves do not know how to provide for themselves at Liberia and often starve or stay paupers. 6 April 1833. p.55, c1.

1211 ARTHUR TAPPAN *to* **MR. LEWIS LANE. 26 March 1833. New York.** Describes his conversion from pro- to anti-colonization; claims one of the things which changed his mind was the society's sanction of selling liquor in Liberia; now believes the society will never abolish slavery. 6 April 1833. p.55, c2.

1212 ARNOLD BUFFUM *to* **SAMUEL E. SEWELL, ESQ. [extract] 21 March 1833. New Haven.** Comments on a speech he delivered in New Haven before a restless congregation, and notes that he later delivered speeches at several religious ceremonies. 6 April 1833. p.55, c2.

1213 AUSTIN STEWARD *to* **MESSRS. GARRISON AND KNAPP. 12 March 1833. Wilberforce.** Relates story of his calamitous relations with Israel Lewis. 13 April 1833. p.57, c1.

1214 AUSTIN STEWARD, JOSEPH TAYLOR, PHILLIP HARRIS, JNO. WHITEHEAD, WM. BELL, PETER BUTLER, AND SAMUEL PETERSON *to* **FRIEND GARRISON. March 1833. Wilberforce.** State that Israel Lewis is no longer connected with the Wilberforce Colony because he collected and embezzled money; condemn Israel Lewis for cheating his colored brethren. 13 April 1833. p.57, c3.

1215 FRANCIS W. SMITH *to* **FRIEND GARRISON. 11 March 1833. Wilberforce, Upper Canada.** Asserts that the quarrel at Wilberforce between Lewis and Steward is purely personal; charges that most of the men at the meeting to eject Lewis were so ignorant that they could not write their own names. 13 April 1833. p.57, c5.

1216 W. L. GARRISON *to* **S. SNOWDEN, P. HALL, G. PUTNAM, P. HOWARD, C. CAPLES, W. BROWN, J. B. PERO, J. T. HILTON, G. W. THOMPSON, J. SILVER, L. YORK, J. LENNOX, F. STANDING, T. COLE, C. L. REMOND, E. F. B. MUNDRUEU, AND H. THACKER. 4 April 1833. Boston.** Thanks them for silver cup sent to him; hopes all New Yorkers can unite to conquer slavery. 13 April 1833. p.58, c5.

1217 ELIZUR WRIGHT, JR. *to* **THE EDITORS OF THE** *GENIUS OF TEMPERANCE.* **10 March 1833. Hudson, Oh.** Urges immediate abolition; declares that if men are not abolitionists, they might as well be slaveholders; hopes to see free colored Americans educated and elevated, man to man. 20 April 1833. p.61, c4.

1218 VIATOR *to* **THE EDITORS OF THE** *BOSTON TELEGRAPH.* **n.d. n.p.** Forwards the diary of a Christian slaveholder that he found. 20 April 1833. p.61, c5.

1219 LIBERTY *to* **MR. EATON. [from the** *North Star***] n.d. n.p.** Attacks colonization in Liberia; sends extract of letter from Mechlin, agent of the CS, claiming that most of the people sent are vagrant no-goods. 20 April 1833. p.62, c2.

1220 J. MECHLIN *to* **n.n. September 1832. Liberia.** Comments on "great number of ignorant and abandoned characters" arriving from America. 20 April 1833. p.62, c2.

1221 THOMAS FOWELL BUXTON *to* **W. L. GARRISON. 12 November 1832. Northrupp's Hall, Cromer.** Feels that although Liberia is an interesting and useful undertaking, the thought that it may abolish slavery is ridiculous; reports that the English government is favorably disposed toward emancipation. 20 April 1833. p.62, c5.

1222 CORRESPONDENT *to* **MR. GARRISON. 10 March 1833. New Orleans.** Describes CS meeting in Louisiana with speaker, Mr. Binney. 20 April 1833. p.63, c1.

1223 JAMES CROPPER *to* **W. L. GARRISON. 15 February 1833. Liverpool.** Laments that Elliott Cresson is still in England; hopes he will be thrown out soon; looks forward to the immediate emancipation of England's slaves in the West India colonies; believes emancipation would set a good example for the United States. 20 April 1833. p.63, c1.

1224 D. R. *to* **THE EDITORS OF THE** *GENIUS OF TEMPERANCE***. 21 March 1833. New York.** Questions Mr. R. S. Finley about his latest address praising the CS. 20 April 1833. p.64, c3.

1225 PHILO *to* **MR. EDITOR [W. L. GARRISON]. n.d. n.p.** Attacks nonsensical objections to Negroes enjoying the same rights as whites; asserts that the objectors only depend on what their neighbors say. 27 April 1833. p.65, c5.

1226 P. CRANDALL *to* **THE EDITORS OF THE** *GENIUS OF TEMPERANCE***. n.d. n.p.** Sarcastically suggests the creation of an "Anti-American Society" to make sure that those trying to educate and better the conditions of blacks do not succeed. 27 April 1833. p.66, c3.

1227 VIRGINIUS *to* **n.n. n.d. n.p.** Describes the horrors of slavery; believes the sensibilities of Southerners have been dulled by the constant presence of cruelty. 27 April 1833. p.66, c4.

1228 P. B. FISK *to* **MR. EDITOR [W. L. GARRISON]. 17 April 1833. Jamaica, Vt.** Informs Garrison that his arguments are finally seeping into Vermont; tells of meeting where resolution supporting colonization was voted down. 27 April 1833. p.67, c3.

1229 Z. *to* **MR. EDITOR [W. L. GARRISON]. 2 April 1833. Andover.** Sends extract from writer in Cornwall, Vermont. 27 April 1833. p.67, c3.

1230 A WORTHY CITIZEN *to* **n.n. [extract] n.d. Cornwall, Vt.** Reports on meeting of Young Gentlemen's Society where resolution not to support the CS was just passed. 27 April 1833. p.67, c3.

1231 J. N. DANFORTH, GEN. AGENT ACS *to* **COL. WILLIAM L. STONE, CHAIRMAN OF THE EXECUTIVE COMMITTEE OF THE NEW YORK CITY CS. 28 March 1833. Boston.** Draws line between colonization with gradual emancipation and immediate emancipation; discusses Garrison's "venomous pen" and work against the CS; asserts that colonization encourages Southerners to emancipate slaves. 4 May 1833. p.69, c4.

1232 REV. CHESTER WRIGHT *to* **MR. EDITOR [W. L. GARRISON]. 17 April 1833. Montpelier.** Reports that he invited colored youth to express their desire for education to him; explains that he is not starting a school, just wants to know if the general desire exists; encourages colored men to attend the Manual Labor School of the New England AS. 4 May 1833. p.71, c3.

1233 B. K., JR. *to* **MR. EDITOR [W. L. GARRISON]. 8 May 1833. Boston.** Disapproves of recent article, signed "The Firebrand," which attacked the Methodist Church for being as secretive as the Masons; feels Methodists do many valuable things. 11 May 1833. p.74, c1.

1234 OBSERVER *to* **MR. EDITOR [W. L. GARRISON]. n.d. n.p.** Recounts attending recent "Mental Feast" of a society of young ladies; states that universal taste for literature pervades the society, which hopes to correct bad impressions of females' intelligent minds. 11 May 1833. p.74, c5.

1235 W. L. GARRISON *to* **SIR. [from the** *Moral Daily Advertiser***] 2 May 1833. On board ship,** *Hibernia.* Bids adieu to city and nation; expresses anxiety over abolition's future; sends sonnet he has written on board. 11 May 1833. p.75, c1.

1236 ARNOLD BUFFUM *to* **FRIENDS. 6 May 1833. New York.** Feels concerned about terrible lethargy in the public mind on the subject of slavery, but remains encouraged that the colored people seem to be waking up to the problem; reports on speeches and a meeting with Garrison. 11 May 1833. p.75, c2.

1237 ELIZUR WRIGHT, JR. *to* **THE EDITORS OF THE** *GENIUS OF TEMPERANCE.* **10 April 1833. Hudson, Oh.** Attacks recent article which he feels is a defense of slavery; discusses the practicality of the doctrine of universal emancipation and "preparation" for liberty. 18 May 1833. p.77, c3.

1238 JUSTITIA *to* **THE EDITOR OF THE** *NEW ENGLAND GALAXY.* **n.d. n.p.** Questions the justice of the penal system, which places white boys in House of Reformation and black boys in Leverett Street Jail; condemns sending blacks to a place considered ruinous for white boys. 18 May 1833. p.78, c2.

1239 n.n. *to* **THE EDITOR [W. L. GARRISON]. 2 May 1833. Providence.** Recounts story of a slave whose master died suddenly, leaving him with no free papers; describes unsuccessful attempts to sell him back into slavery. 18 May 1833. p.79, c2.

1240 APOLLO *to* **MR. EDITOR [W. L. GARRISON]. n.d. n.p.** Review of recent concert in St. Phillip's Church in New York; comments on full church, good performance, admirable solo by Miss Jennett Miller. 18 May 1833. p.79, c4.

1241 ONESIMUS *to* **THE EDITOR [W. L. GARRISON]. n.d. n.p.** Clarifies the fact that he did not mean to attack all Methodists, only Methodist slaveholders. 25 May 1833. p.82, c4.

1242 PRUDENCE CRANDALL *to* **MR. HOLBROOK. [from the** *Brooklyn Advertiser***] 7 May 1833. Canterbury.** Makes a public statement of her intentions; explains that she started by taking one colored girl into her school who had a deep desire for learning; consequently recognized the extreme prejudice against blacks; desires to teach blacks so their moral and intellectual wants may be supplied. 25 May 1833. p.82, c5.

1243 C. STUART *to* **THE EDITOR OF THE** *LIVERPOOL MERCURY.* **n.d. n.p.** Replies to charges of Mr. Elliott Cresson that wise Americans are not to be doubted if they support colonization; answers that only angels make perfect judgments; asserts that he speaks for Negroes, not himself, when he says that they do not want to go to Liberia. 25 May 1833. p.83, c1.

1244 A TEACHER *to* **MR. EDITOR [W. L. GARRISON]. n.d. n.p.** Replies to comment by Mr. Finley that there was but one teacher in the African Sabbath schools in Boston who opposed colonization; affirms that he and many others oppose colonization; criticizes colonization very strongly. 1 June 1833. p.87, c1.

1245 JOSHUA COFFIN *to* **MR. EDITOR [W. L. GARRISON]. n.d. n.p.** Forwards letter from an anti-colonizationist in England. 1 June 1833. p.87, c1.

1246 A DISTINGUISHED GENTLEMAN IN STAFFORDSHIRE, ENGLAND *to* **JOSHUA COFFIN. 19 March 1833. Staffordshire, England.** Rejoices that Great Britain's participation in evil and unjust slavery is about to end; hopes to be able to give Americans a helping hand to the same end; deplores CS. 1 June 1833. p.87, c1.

1247 B. K., JR. *to* **ONESIMUS. n.d. n.p.** Contends that his assertions about the Methodist Church were not valid arguments; feels that the church should not be held up to public scorn. 1 June 1833. p.87, c2.

1248 JEAN PIERRE BOYER, PRESIDENT OF HAYTI *to* **MR. KENDRICK. 9 June 1818. Port-au-Prince.** Congratulates Kendrick on his philanthropic work; thanks him for copy of *Horrors of Slavery.* 8 June 1833. p.89, c2.

1249 n.n. *to* **n.n. [from the** *New York Observer***] 6 April 1833. London.** Recounts enthusiasm of the 1 April anti-slavery meeting in London; feels that the extinction of slavery in all parts of British Empire is near. 8 June 1833. p.90, c3.

1250 WILLIAM BURLEIGH *to* **THE EDITOR OF THE** *ADVERTISER.* **3 May 1833. Plainfield, Ct.** Complains that the supposedly free press will only discuss one side of every issue; comments on a few articles against Prudence Crandall; feels they were written with malignity and hate; corrects false impression that Prudence Crandall seeks to amalgamate the two races. 8 June 1833. p.90, c5.

1251 LA ROY SUNDERLAND *to* **MR. EDITOR [W. L. GARRISON]. 3 June 1833. Andover, Ma.** Corrects eight mistakes made by correspondent "Onesimus" on the Methodist Church and slaveholders; quotes the general rules of the church and discusses its doctrines to prove that the Methodist Church does not support slavery. 15 June 1833. p.94, c4.

1252 JUSTITIA *to* **MR. EDITOR [W. L. GARRISON]. 10 June 1833. Andover.** Discusses lectures of Mr. Finley, agent of the CS; hoped he would refute and answer charges against the society; disappointed that all he did was boldly assert their plan while claiming no time for proof; feels Finley was trying to twist colonization to suit Northerners. 15 June 1833. p.95, c1.

1253 GEORGE W. BENSON *to* **MR. EDITOR [W. L. GARRISON]. 11 June 1833. Providence.** Reports that Prudence Crandall's school has eighteen to twenty students, needs more; states that she wants to fill school to show how colored people value educational opportunity. 15 June 1833. p.95, c2.

1254 Q IN THE CORNER *to* **THE EDITOR OF THE** *MERCANTILE JOURNAL.* **n.d. n.p.** Answers charge of colonizationists that abolitionists have zeal but no plans; states that abolitionists plan to preach the gospel and the truth, like Christ's plan for the conversion of the world. 22 June 1833. p.98, c2.

1255 A. B. AND J. B. *to* **THE EDITOR OF THE** *REVIVALIST.* **n.d. n.p.** Suggest, as celebration of anniversary of American freedom, that several churches get together to pray for immediate emancipation, and for God's forgiveness, as the sinful slave system persists. 22 June 1833. p.98, c2.

1256 UNCLE SIMON'S EASY CHAIR NO. I *to* **MR. EDITOR [W. L. GARRISON]. n.d. Boston.** Discusses difficulty of finding complete issues of the *African Repository* which he believes is evidence of the apathy people feel on the subject; takes Mr. Danforth to task for his statements about temperance in Liberia; believes, personally, that more Africans are killed as a result of drinking liquor than are taken by slave traders. 22 June 1833. p.98, c3.

1257 N. S. H. *to* **MR. EDITOR [W. L. GARRISON]. n.d. n.p.** Congratulates editor on success of the glorious cause in which he is engaged; reports that after debate between Prof. Wright and Mr. Finley, he met many people who turned anti-slavery because Wright spoke like a Christian and a gentleman, while Finley spoke like a blackguard. 22 June 1833. p.98, c5.

1258 B. K., JR. *to* **MR. EDITOR [W. L. GARRISON]. n.d. n.p.** Reports that Onesimus has backed out of his dispute with B. K., Jr. and that Onesimus acknowledges the Northern conferences of Methodists as exceptions to his charge; hopes Onesimus will, in the future, study the basis of his assertions more closely. 22 June 1833. p.98, c5.

1259 REV. NATHANIEL PAUL *to* **FRIEND GARRISON. 10 April 1833. Bristol, England.** Informs him that slavery in the West Indies is soon to be abolished and there will be no half-way measures; states that people in England support Garrison's point of view; saddened by difference between the way people of color are treated in England and in America. 22 June 1833. p.99, c1.

1260 N. O. P. *to* **MR. EDITOR [W. L. GARRISON]. 14 June 1833. Philadelphia.** Describes the colored convention, its president, Mr. Shadd, and its formation of a conventional temperance society. 22 June 1833. p.99, c4.

1261 ONE OF THE PEOPLE *to* **THE EDITOR OF THE** *ESSEX GAZETTE.* **n.d. n.p.** Reports on plan in Essex to get the people to support the CS; relates that theological students announce at church that a slave will be liberated in Kentucky and sent to Liberia for every thirty dollars they donate; notes that the people have begun to see through the CS and warns others not to fall for this trick. 29 June 1833. p.101, c5.

1262 UNCLE SIMON'S EASY CHAIR NO. II *to* **MR. EDITOR [W. L. GARRISON]. n.d. n.p.** Discusses the large amounts of whiskey and rum being exported to the colony at Liberia; wonders how Mr. Gurley can believe that the natives of Africa will stop drinking spirits if their demand is constantly supplied; charges the colony with a corrupt existence. 29 June 1833. p.102, c1.

1263 E. WRIGHT, JR. *to* **FRIEND [W. L. GARRISON]. 9 June 1833. Albany.** Reports on his debates in New Haven and New York; describes speeches at meeting of colonizationists, whom he terms "misguided fanatics." 29 June 1833. p.102, c2.

1264 n.n. *to* **THE EDITOR [W. L. GARRISON]. [extract] 17 June 1833. New Haven.** Describes recently formed society to advance the cause of emancipation; supports immediate emancipation; wants to spread the truth; asks Garrison's support. 29 June 1833. p.102, c3.

1265 A SUBSCRIBER *to* **MR. EDITOR [W. L. GARRISON]. n.d. n.p.** Wonders how men of Christian principles, like ministers and editors of religious papers, differ with Garrison on holding men in involuntary and perpetual servitude. 29 June 1833. p.102, c3.

1266 n.n. *to* **MR. EDITOR [W. L. GARRISON]. 18 June 1833. Troy, N.Y.** Informs Garrison of formation of an "African Female Benevolent Society"; lists officers. 29 June 1833. p.102, c4.

1267 WILLIAM JAY *to* **MR. DENISON. [from the** *New York Emancipator*] **1 May 1833. Bedford, Westchester County.** Reminds Denison that the "patient waiters" for gradual emancipation must be brought to support immediate emancipation; states that CS does have some value, but it will not stop slavery. 29 June 1833. p.102, c5.

1268 A LOVER OF TRUTH *to* **MR. SNELLING. [from the** *New England Galaxy*] **n.d. n.p.** Believes that the issues of colonization and abolition are becoming very important to United States citizens and that Southern slavery, not Northern manufacturing, would be responsible for any separation of the states; tells of discussion with Mr. Finley and reports that Finley presents very different cases to Northern and Southern audiences. 6 July 1833. p.106, c3.

1269 A. T. *to* **MR. WHITING. [from the** *Religious Intelligencer*] **n.d. n.p.** Forwards speech by one of Miss Crandall's scholars on prejudice. 6 July 1833. p.106, c5.

1270 A STUDENT AT MISS CRANDALL'S SCHOOL FOR COLORED YOUNG LADIES *to* **FRIENDS. n.d. n.p.** Rejoices that she may finally enjoy the enlightenment of education; worries that the school might be closed; deplores prejudice in America. 6 July 1833. p.106, c5.

1271 UNCLE SIMON'S EASY CHAIR NO. III *to* **MR. EDITOR [W. L. GARRISON]. n.d. n.p.** Argues that since even defenders and vindicators of the colony in Liberia admit there is a traffic in spirits there, we must believe it and work to stop it; gives anecdotes and examples of people refusing to see things they do not want to see. 6 July 1833. p.107, c1.

1272 A PASSER-BY *to* **MR. EDITOR [W. L. GARRISON]. n.d. n.p.** Describes visit to Miss Prudence Crandall's School for Colored Females; reports that the students are as well behaved and interesting as any in Connecticut and their minds are deeply concerned with religion; urges more students to attend the school; reports recent imprisonment of Miss Crandall. 6 July 1833. p.107, c2.

1273 W. L. GARRISON *to* **n.n. 23 May 1833. Liverpool.** Reports fatigue upon his arrival; feels at home with people whose cry is universal freedom; states that his object for visiting is to collect funds for a manual labor school for educating American colored youth. 6 July 1833. p.107, c3.

1274 ARTHUR TAPPAN *to* **REV. R. R. GURLEY, SEC. OF THE ACS. n.d. n.p.** Replies to charges in the *African Repository* against him; asserts that he does have information from an agent of the CS that proves the sale of spirits in Liberia. 6 July 1833. p.107, c4.

1275 ARTHUR TAPPAN, GEORGE BOURNE, WILLIAM GOODELL, JOSHUA LEAVITT, LEWIS TAPPAN, S. P. HINES, HENRY R. PIERCY, CHARLES W. DENISON, REV. L. D. DEWEY, THEODORE D. WELD, REV. C. G. FINNEY AND G. R. BARKER *to* **THE SECRETARY AND BOARD OF MANAGERS OF THE ACS. 7 March 1833. New York.** Seek to learn what exactly is the policy of the CS; inquire of representatives of the society whether the purpose and aim of the society is to eliminate slavery completely in the United States, and whether the principles of the society condone expatriation of free people of color if state governments deny them continual residence. 13 July 1833. p.109, c1.

1276 R. R. GURLEY *to* **MESSRS. TAPPAN, BOURNE, GOODELL, LEAVITT, TAPPAN, HINES, PIERCY, DENISON, DEWEY, WELD, FINNEY, AND BARKER. 28 March 1833. Washington.** Admits that more could be done for free people of color in this country, but thinks it would be more beneficial if done in Africa; answers the questions put to the society; declares that society is not for abolition, if it involves tampering with government or individual rights. 13 July 1833. p.109, c1.

1277 MESSRS. TAPPAN, BOURNE, GOODELL, BARKER, TAPPAN, HINES, PIERCY, DENISON, AND WELD *to* **REV. R. R. GURLEY. June 1833. New York.** Rejoice that Gurley replied and find his answers definite, if not always satisfactory; feel that the society was talking around some of the questions, particularly those on the abolition of slavery. 13 July 1833. p.109, c3.

1278 UNCLE SIMON'S EASY CHAIR NO. IV *to* **MR. EDITOR [W. L. GARRISON]. n.d. n.p.** Quotes from Mr. Finley on first expedition to Liberia; comments on and criticizes the ambiguities and hypocrisy of Finley's reasoning; wonders why so many blacks are urged to go to Liberia from the North when the society could buy slaves with the money. 13 July 1833. p.110, c3.

1279 W. L. GARRISON *to* **n.n. 24 May 1833. Liverpool.** Describes debate in all English newspapers about abolition; feels planters should be compensated like felons, by punishment; describes plans of various lords for emancipation. 13 July 1833. p.110, c5.

1280 Q. *to* **MR. EDITOR [W. L. GARRISON]. n.d. n.p.** Notes instances in Mississippi when female slaves have been tracked by bloodhounds and whipped to death. 20 July 1833. p.114, c5.

1281 SPECTATOR *to* **MR. EDITOR [W. L. GARRISON]. n.d. n.p.** Describes July fourth meeting of Windham County, Connecticut CS which denounced anti-slavery doctrines and elected agents, including one Andrew Judson, notorious in relation to oppression of Prudence Crandall. 20 July 1833. p.114, c5.

1282 n.n. *to* **A FRIEND. n.d. n.p.** Pleads that slavery, as well as other evils, should be publicly censured by the clergy. 20 July 1833. p.115, c1.

1283 A. M. R. *to* **W. L. GARRISON. n.d. n.p.** Rejoices on reading the *Liberator,* which has furnished him with a cause for which to work. 20 July 1833. p.115, c2.

1284 n.n. *to* **n.n. n.d. Baltimore.** Approves of the *Liberator* and its stand on colonization; comments on vice president of CS, who became incensed when his son inpregnated a slave, and sold mother and his grandchild to a Southern trader; quotes English poem on freedom. 27 July 1833. p.118, c5.

1285 WILLIAM LADD, ESQ. *to* **THE EDITOR [W. L. GARRISON]. n.d. n.p.** Asserts that he has never spoken a word against the New England AS; states he is in favor of colonization, but only with colored people's consent. 27 July 1833. p.119, c1.

1286 ONE OF THE SUFFERERS *to* **FRIEND. 8 July 1833. Philadelphia.** Reports the return of some settlers from Liberia who say rum-selling is the best trade and religion is at low ebb; account of sick and dead. 27 July 1833. p.119, c4.

1287 GOV. MECHLIN [OF LIBERIA] *to* **n.n. [extract] n.d. n.p.** States he is unable to write much since he has been sick; comments on unhealthy season, lack of doctors. 27 July 1833. p.119, c4.

1288 ONE OF MISS CRANDALL'S SCHOLARS *to* **n.n. n.d. n.p.** Urges forgiveness and meekness, no retaliation; affirms that she and her schoolmates are subject to trials and struggles; deplores prejudice but does not urge retaliation against the white people. 3 August 1833. p.122, c3.

1289 UNCLE SIMON'S EASY CHAIR NO. VI *to* **MR. EDITOR [W. L. GARRISON]. n.d. n.p.** Declares it is easier for writers to make things up than to research the truth; gives many examples of anti-slavery pro-colonization articles and statements, which he then proves are false. 3 August 1833. p.122, c4.

1290 VERITAS *to* **MR. EDITOR [W. L. GARRISON]. 30 July 1833. Providence.** Describes colonization meeting where Rev. R. R. Gurley was to answer any objections to colonization; notes that it was declared that only those friendly to colonization could speak. 3 August 1833. p.122, c5.

1291 JOHN G. WHITTIER *to* **THE EDITORS OF THE** *JEFFERSONIAN AND TIMES.* **RICHMOND, VA. 22 July 1833. Haverhill, Ma.** Notes that now the tariff question is solved, the South gripes about abolition; refuses to be quoted as the "Voice of New England"; gives outline of why he is working to abolish slavery. 10 August 1833. p.125, c1.

1292 BENJAMIN FRANKLIN *to* **HIS SISTER. [extract] n.d. Philadelphia.** Refutes a letter from Benny, his nephew, who claims he was poorly treated by Mr. Parker, a friend whom Franklin knows to be sober and pious. 10 August 1833. p.128, c2.

1293 A FRIEND OF THE OPPRESSED *to* **MR. EDITOR [W. L. GARRISON]. n.d. n.p.** Suggests the last Monday evening in every month as an occasion for a national concert of prayer for the abolition of slavery. 10 August 1833. p.128, c5.

1294 JOHN G. WHITTIER *to* **THE EDITORS OF THE** *JEFFERSONIAN AND TIMES,* **RICHMOND, VA. [from the** *Essex Register***] 29 July 1833. Haverhill, Ma.** Discusses misrepresentation of Northern abolitionists; asserts that they have never sought to incite rebellion or violence among the slaves and are opposed to "political interposition" of the government. 17 August 1833. p.129, c1.

1295 BERIAH GREEN *to* **BROTHER CUMMINGS. 12 April 1833. Western Reserve College, Oh.** Dogmatically discusses abstract doctrines requiring one to act on one's beliefs, instead of merely talking about them. 17 August 1833. p.129, c5.

1296 UNCLE SIMON'S EASY CHAIR NO. VII *to* **MR. EDITOR [W. L. GARRISON]. n.d. n.p.** Describes two sorts of historians: those who investigate facts and draw conclusions and those who bend the facts to what they wish to be true; gives examples from politicians and colonizationists. 17 August 1833. p.130, c5.

1297 R. W. P. *to* **THE EDITOR [W. L. GARRISON]. 2 July 1833. Putnam County, Oh.** Expresses conviction that if the principles of abolitionists were fully disseminated and explained, the cause would soon have numbers of advocates; reports on AS in Ohio and anti-colonization. 17 August 1833. p.131, c2.

1298 A COLORED MAN *to* **MR. EDITOR [W. L. GARRISON]. n.d. n.p.** Announces Mrs. Jasper's new school for colored children to improve their minds in reading, spelling, and sewing; urges parents to send their children and to support the school. 17 August 1833. p.131, c3.

1299 UNCLE SIMON'S EASY CHAIR NO. VIII *to* **MR. EDITOR [W. L. GARRISON]. n.d. n.p.** Compares Polonius (in *Hamlet*) to submissive obsequious agents of CS; looks forward to a time when the support of colonization would be illegal; notes that colonization tries to look like abolition in the North and like slavery in the South. 24 August 1833. p.134, c5.

1300 ARNOLD BUFFUM *to* **S. E. SEWALL, ESQ. 12 August 1833. Fall River.** Describes his attempt to procure subscriptions and contributions to a manual labor school for people of color; reports on speeches in Nantucket and New Bedford. 24 August 1833. p.135, c2.

1301 C. R. *to* **MR. EDITOR [W. L. GARRISON]. 20 August 1833. Newburyport.** Praises Rev. Mr. Levington's speech with the remark "no one had expected anything half so good from a man of color"; believes it will strengthen the abolitionist cause. 24 August 1833. p.135, c2.

1302 A SPECTATOR *to* **MR. EDITOR [W. L. GARRISON]. 14 August 1833. Andover.** Reports that the annual exhibition at Phillip's Academy sponsored attempts in dialogue to caricature those who oppose slavery; feels it was calculated to increase prejudice; objects to indecent allusions and vulgar representations unbecoming of the institution. 24 August 1833. p.135, c3.

1303 n.n. *to* **THE EDITOR [W. L. GARRISON]. 14 August 1833. Portland.** Reports on complaint filed against Captain Thomas and Captain Turner for importing slaves. 24 August 1833. p.135, c3.

1304 ARNOLD BUFFUM *to* **S. E. SEWALL. 17 August 1833. Smithfield, R.I.** Notes that his father had been member of Rhode Island Abolition Society until he died; states that he gave speech to benefit the school fund; hopes former spirit will revive and that an AS will be started soon. 31 August 1833. p.138, c1.

1305 Z. *to* **MR. EDITOR [W. L. GARRISON]. 22 August 1833. Theol. Sem., Andover.** Includes letter that states Andover abolitionists are driving prejudice, gradualism, exile, and slavery into close quarters; also tells of Dr. Porter's opinion that slavery is a great national evil. 31 August 1833. p.138, c2.

1306 W. L. GARRISON *to* **THE BOARD OF MANAGERS OF THE NEW ENGLAND AS. 20 June 1833. London.** Feels it providential that he is in England during their great debate on abolition of slavery; enjoys discussions daily with abolitionists; gives lectures against colonization. 31 August 1833. p.139, c1.

1307 CHARLES STUART *to* **ARNOLD BUFFUM. 29 June 1833. London.** Expresses concern that England's measures will not immediately abolish slavery; praises Garrison, attacks Cresson (agent of CS). 31 August 1833. p.139, c2.

1308 M. B. *to* **MR. EDITOR [W. L. GARRISON]. n.d. n.p.** Urges everyone to read *Mrs. Child's Appeal;* hopes particularly that the book will appeal to women, as the fairer sex has been shamefully apathetic about working for abolition and emancipation. 7 September 1833. p.142, c5.

1309 ARNOLD BUFFUM *to* **THE BOARD OF MANAGERS OF THE NEW ENGLAND AS. 19 August 1833. Uxbridge.** Remembers former visit to Uxbridge; attended funeral sermon for someone he loved, meditated and prayed at her empty home; discusses death and loss. 7 September 1833. p.143, c1.

1310 JOSHUA WOODROW *to* **MR. EDITOR [W. L. GARRISON]. 10 August 1833. Brown County, Oh.** Asks opinion on idea presented at abolition meeting regarding petition to Congress to appropriate lands for the education of colored children and for a college. 7 September 1833. p.143, c1.

1311 W. L. GARRISON *to* **THE BOARD OF MANAGERS OF THE AS. 1 July 1833. London.** Summarizes the significance of his trip; reports on latest successes in British fight to abolish slavery in colonies; gives account of his lectures against agent Cresson and the CS. 7 September 1833. p.143, c2.

1312 ARNOLD BUFFUM *to* **THE BOARD OF MANAGERS OF THE NEW ENGLAND AS. 24 August 1833. Amherst.** Reports that he spoke at Amherst to approximately 250 young men; calls it a good opportunity to spread knowledge about the cause to other people. 14 September 1833. p.146, c5.

1313 SAMUEL N. SWEET *to* **THE EDITOR [W. L. GARRISON]. 6 September 1833. Adams, Jefferson County, N.Y.** Congratulates editor on fine paper which has "liberated" his mind from any positive belief in colonization; believes that immediate emancipation is the only way to prevent a catastrophic slave revolt. 14 September 1833. p.147, c1.

1314 ARTHUR TAPPAN *to* **n.n.** [from the *Genius of Temperance*] **n.d. n.p.** Relates Col. Stone's charges against Prudence Crandall, impugning her motives for starting school and criticizing her character. 14 September 1833. p.147, c5.

1315 JOHN B. PINNEY *to* **MR. EDITOR [W. L. GARRISON]. 27 August 1833. Columbia.** Replies to a resolution from the citizens of Columbia, South Carolina; reminds them that he is a Southerner by birth and denies charges of being a "foreigner"; also denies any connection between himself and the CS; questions how a public body in the land of freedom can dare to threaten violence. 21 September 1833. p.149, c4.

1316 ABOLITIONIST *to* **MR. SMITH.** [from the *Portland Courier*] **n.d. n.p.** Sends an extract from the *Portsmouth Journal* of 1824, questioning the CS about why it is so zealously supported by slaveholders. 21 September 1833. p.150, c2.

1317 UNCLE SIMON'S EASY CHAIR NO. IX *to* **MR. EDITOR [W. L. GARRISON]. n.d. n.p.** Credits the Virginia legislature with the original suggestion to colonize colored people in 1800; presents their resolution and reveals that after sixteen years of secret debate, resolution was abandoned; also charges that when the CS was formed, everyone who spoke at its formation was a slaveholder. 21 September 1833. p.150, c4.

1318 ARNOLD BUFFUM *to* **THE CORRESPONDING SECRETARY OF THE NEW ENGLAND AS. 6 September 1833. Albany.** Relates that he was given a meetinghouse for a speech in Northampton, but since many important Southerners were in town, this offer was withdrawn; declares that too many of our leaders are interested in careers in general government, and consequently conciliate the South. 21 September 1833. p.150, c5.

1319 M. B. *to* **MR. EDITOR [W. L. GARRISON]. n.d. n.p.** Questions how much choice the CS really allows colored people on the question of emigration; charges that the society's true purpose is to encourage prejudice against the colored population. 21 September 1833. p.151, c1.

1320 ELIZUR WRIGHT, JR. *to* **THE EDITOR OF THE** *BOSTON RECORDER.* **28 July 1833. Hudson, Oh.** Attacks the editor of the *Boston Recorder;* informs him that abolitionists are working for the slave to be immediately raised to the same status as whites; asserts that voting should be determined by reading and writing, not skin color. 28 September 1833. p.154, c3.

1321 UNCLE SIMON'S EASY CHAIR NO. X *to* **MR.EDITOR [W. L. GARRISON]. n.d. n.p.** Attacks the *Boston Recorder* and the CS; looks forward to a time when the CS will have to close in New England for lack of support. 28 September 1833. p.154, c4.

1322 SAMUEL J. MAY *to* **MR. HOLBROOK.** [from the *Brooklyn* (Ct.) *Advertiser*] **n.d. n.p.** Answers questions put to him by Holbrook; supports total abolition, immediate extension of all rights to blacks, and intermarriage of the races. 28 September 1833. p.155, c2.

1323 STAND FAST *to* **THE EDITORS OF THE** *VERMONT CHRONICLE.* **n.d. n.p.** Accuses editors of misrepresentation and chicanery; offers to write them a series of letters on his point of view, but only if they will publish them exactly as written. 28 September 1833. p.155, c4.

1324 n.n. *to* **MR. EDITOR [W. L. GARRISON]. n.d. n.p.** Quotes extracts from Luther Martin, Daniel Webster, and others on slavery; relates the history of government discussion on the slave trade; relates attempts to introduce Pierpont's book into South Carolina schools; deplores "mensellers" and kidnappers; believes that American slave trade is just as bad as that of Africa. 5 October 1833. p.157, c1.

1325 ARNOLD BUFFUM *to* **THE BOARD OF MANAGERS OF THE AS. 24 September 1833. Catskill.** Reports he was unable to obtain meetinghouse to speak at Troy; managed to speak to a small group in Albany, although colonization has a stronghold in that city; received money at Hudson even though he did not take up a collection; notes a warm reception at Catskill. 5 October 1833. p.158, c2.

1326 ARNOLD BUFFUM *to* **THE BOARD OF MANAGERS OF THE AS. 30 September 1833. New York.** Discovers a striking liberality in Poughkeepsie, large audiences, good collection, and interesting colored school; reports that Newburgh did not have a meeting hall, and neither did Fishkill. 5 October 1833. p.158, c2.

1327 UNCLE SIMON'S EASY CHAIR NO. XI *to* **MR. EDITOR [W. L. GARRISON]. n.d. n.p.** Discusses Mr. Danforth's letters in the *African Repository;* agrees with the part of Mr. Danforth's speech that discussed the degradation and oppression of the colored race; but feels that his claim about Africa as an asylum to which people of color must flee for liberty and equal rights is contrary to the nature of the American republic. 5 October 1833. p.158, c4.

1328 W. L. GARRISON *to* **THE EDITOR OF THE** *LONDON CHRISTIAN ADVOCATE.* **10 August 1833. 18, Aldermanbury.** Supports abolition, attacks CS and Cresson, agent for CS; asks editor to insert protest and to hang millstone around neck of that society. 12 October 1833. p.162, c5.

1329 CHARLES STUART *to* **ARTHUR TAPPAN. 5 August 1833. London.** Discusses pamphlet, "Remarks on African Colonization and the Abolition of Slavery By a Citizen of New England"; asserts that he did not turn against colonization because of the AS, but as a result of listening to Elliot Cresson, a pro-colonizationist. 12 October 1833. p.163, c3.

1330 A MEMBER OF THE NEW ENGLAND AS *to* **MR. EDITOR [W. L. GARRISON]. n.d. n.p.** Describes disgraceful scene in New York: while AS met to write constitution, a huge mob collected to stop them; chides narrow-minded prejudice of New York citizens. 19 October 1833. p.167, c4.

1331 W. L. GARRISON *to* **THE EDITOR OF THE** *PATRIOT.* **22 July 1833. Aldermanbury.** Requests the publication of two letters he has received; informs that he will be helping to free two million slaves in United States and preventing a benevolent and well-meaning person from giving money to the CS. 26 October 1833. p.169, c2.

1332 ZACHARY MACAULAY *to* **W. L. GARRISON, ESQ. 14 July 1833. Conway, North Wales.** Regrets that he missed Garrison's meeting; would like to see CS denounced and opposed by all; believes that the society works through feelings of hate and prejudice for the Negro race, not love. 26 October 1833. p.169, c2.

1333 W. ALLEN *to* **W. L. GARRISON. 15 July 1833. Paradise Row, Stoke, Newington.** States that he had supported the CS and believed the settlement in Africa would protect the coast from slave traders, but became convinced by speeches and pamphlets that the platform of the CS is influenced by prejudice, condescension, and hate. 26 October 1833. p.169, c3.

1334 SAMUEL J. MAY *to* **THE EDITOR OF THE** *BROOKLYN* **(CT.)** *UNIONIST.* **n.d. n.p.** Believes Judge Daggett has sanctioned an erroneous notion which will cause difficulties; sends opinions of others whom he feels have made more correct decisions. 26 October 1833. p.170, c3.

1335 WILLIAM JAY *to* **REV. S. J. MAY. 30 September 1833. Bedford.** States that Miss Crandall's opponents found it expedient to deprive the whole free colored population of the protection of the Constitution by denying that they were citizens; encloses documentation which might be useful if the case is reopened. 26 October 1833. p.170, c3.

1336 DE WITT CLINTON, GOV. OF NEW YORK *to* **PRESIDENT ADAMS. 4 September 1826. Albany.** Pleads for release of Gilbert Horton, a free citizen of New York, from the Washington jail. 26 October 1833. p.170, c4.

1337 n.n. *to* **THE EDITOR OF THE** *U. S. GAZETTE.* **20 June 1833. Brazil.** Believes that the extensive slave trade in Brazil will soon be a curse to it; law forbade slave trade in 1831, but smuggling prevails; believes that the entire Christian world should work to stop this evil. 26 October 1833. p.170, c5.

1338 ARNOLD BUFFUM *to* **THE BOARD OF MANAGERS OF THE NEW ENGLAND AS. 12 October 1833. Philadelphia.** Describes a journey to the slaveholding state where he gave a particularly severe speech; describes the very liberal audience who listened patiently, contributed, supported him; still mourns the existence of the CS; wonders if it will ever be stopped. 26 October 1833. p.171, c1.

1339 EXAMINER *to* **MR. EDITOR [W. L. GARRISON]. n.d. n.p.** Attacks an article from the *New York Observer* on the Wilberforce protest of United States slavery; attacks *Observer* for supporting colonization; calls for more eloquent anti-slavery brethren to discover the truth. 26 October 1833. p.171, c2.

1340 UNCLE SIMON'S EASY CHAIR NO. XII *to* **MR. EDITOR [W. L. GARRISON]. n.d. n.p.** States that if anyone wants to see the intellect and uprightness of blacks, he need only peruse the *African Repository,* published by the CS; believes that while blacks are inferior here, when they get to Liberia they "transform" to intelligent, Christian, good people. 26 October 1833. p.171, c4.

1341 DARK COLOR *to* **THE EDITOR OF THE** *RHODE ISLAND PHILAN-THROPIST.* **n.d. n.p.** Discusses the Rev. Mr. Levington, a regularly ordained and highly recommended Episcopal clergyman from Baltimore, who was refused admission into the churches of Rhode Island because of his color. 26 October 1833. p.172, c2.

1342 EMERY BROWN AND LOUIS O. COWAN *to* **W. L. GARRISON. 21 October 1833. Augusta, Me.** Support immediate abolition of a bondage which is cruel, unjust, and contrary to principles of morality and Christianity; inform that during Garrison's absence, an agent of the CS made another speech in Augusta; state that even without Garrison's defense, the agent failed to convince listeners. 2 November 1833. p.173, c4.

1343 B. C. B. *to* **FRIEND GARRISON. n.d. n.p.** Sends him an article from *Jefferson* (N.Y.) *Reporter* on Garrison and the *Liberator;* expresses satisfaction that the *Reporter* is finally discussing the subject of abolition. 2 November 1833. p.173, c5.

1344 THOMAS PRICE *to* **THE EDITOR OF THE** *BAPTIST MAGAZINE.* **14 June 1833. Lower St., Islington.** Revokes his earlier support of the ACS; states that if free colored population is as debased as colonizationists say, then sending them to Africa is a crime to that continent; conveys British admiration for Garrison. 2 November 1833. p.174, c4.

1345 TRUTH *to* **THE EDITOR [W. L. GARRISON]. September 1833. Middletown, Ct.** Sends letter from students at Wesleyan University warning colored people not to speak there and threatening violence; "Truth" points out spelling mistakes, gives history, and points out problems and inconsistencies. 2 November 1833. p.175, c4.

1346 TWELVE OF US *to* **YOUNG BEMAN. n.d. Wesleyan University.** Warn Beman not to speak at Wesleyan; threaten violence. 2 November 1833. p.175, c4.

1347 J. P. GAZZAM *to* **W. L. GARRISON. 12 October 1833. Pittsburgh, Pa.** Reports formation of Pittsburgh AS; congratulates Garrison on return to United States. 2 November 1833. p.175, c5.

1348 DR. E. MACK *to* **MR. GOODELL. 7 October 1833. Plainville, Luzerne County, Pa.** Informs Goodell how much he admires and enjoys the *Genius;* shocked that people in this part of Pennsylvania support the present system of slavery; encourages all editors to continue supporting emancipation until the fight is won. 9 November 1833. p.177, c1.

1349 n.n. *to* **W. L. GARRISON. September 1833. London.** Describes recent discussion he had in Ipswich where he convinced several people that colonization was an evil idea supporting slavery; tried unsuccessfully to get a public interview with Cresson, a CS agent. 9 November 1833. p.177, c3.

1350 LEO *to* **W. L. GARRISON. 19 October 1833. Philadelphia.** Congratulates him on safe return; discusses the bill presented to Great Britain's House of Commons, its opponents, and its eventual passage; reports attending meeting of colored missionaries about to leave for Africa. 9 November 1833. p.177, c3.

1351 CLARKSON *to* **MR. POULSON [EDITOR OF POULSON'S** *AMERICAN DAILY ADVERTISER*]. **n.d. n.p.** Questions if there had been a law passed some years since in Louisiana making it a penal offense to remove slaves from one state to sell them in Louisiana. 9 November 1833. p.177, c5.

1352 PRESIDENT B. GREEN *to* **MR. GOODELL. [from the** *Genius of Temperance*] **12 October 1833. Whitesboro'.** Reminds pro-slavery supporters that they are likely to encounter contempt and hatred for refusing to admit that they and their church are poisoned by Negro-hatred; informs that the press, too, has softened public outrage at pro-slavers; urges the abolitionists to continue their struggle. 16 November 1833. p.181, c5.

1353 W. L. GARRISON *to* **ELLIOTT CRESSON [EX-AGENT OF THE ACS]. n.d. n.p.** Informs that he has heard that Cresson was given a handsome inscribed plate at a recent CS meeting in Philadelphia; mocks Cresson, his reception in England, and his cursed colonization plans. 16 November 1833. p.182, c3.

1354 n.n. *to* **W. L. GARRISON. 17 October 1833. Plymouth, N.H.** Informs that citizens in this area supported colonization because it was the first and only defense they heard on behalf of the Negro; states that Garrison and his anti-colonization, immediate emancipation ideas are beginning to be realized. 16 November 1833. p.182, c5.

1355 PRESIDENT GREEN *to* **THE** *LIBERATOR*. **[extract] n.d. n.p.** Rejoices that Garrison is "safe home again." 16 November 1833. p.182, c5.

1356 n.n. *to* **n.n. [extract] 21 October 1833. Waterville.** Congratulates Garrison on his return to the United States; discusses CS's wickedness in opposing Garrison and the *Liberator;* hopes the CS is in desperation. 16 November 1833. p.182, c5.

1357 n.n. *to* **n.n. [extract] 5 October 1833. Hudson, Oh.** Informs that the community supports abolitionists, except for their hostility to the CS; the people must be convinced that colonization is wrong; supports Garrison and his glorious cause. 16 November 1833. p.183, c1.

1358 LINDLEY COATES *to* **ESTEEMED FRIEND [W. L. GARRISON]. 21 October 1833. Sadsbury, Pa.** Alludes to article in Vol. III, no. 37; worries that editor claims that slaveholders can be Christians; believes that slaveholders break the laws of God and are not Christians. 16 November 1833. p.183, c1.

1359 ARNOLD BUFFUM *to* **THE BOARD OF MANAGERS OF THE NEW ENGLAND AS. 31 October 1833. Providence.** Describes speeches in Burlington and Bristol; details speeches in Philadelphia on education of free colored people, and in Newark; relates that he engaged in discussion with Southern slaveholders on the boat to Providence; adds that mariners were gentlemanly, but did not accept religious scruples as a reason to stop slavery. 16 November 1833. p.183, c3.

1360 N. M. *to* **MR. EDITOR [W. L. GARRISON]. n.d. n.p.** Relates a story concerning a mother cat who takes in a black kitten, rejects it at first, then helps and feeds it; suggests this as a moral lesson. 23 November 1833. p.185, c2.

1361 NATHANIEL PAUL *to* **ANDREW T. JUDSON, ESQ. 29 August 1833. London, England.** Sarcastically commends Judson for his "patriotic, Christian behavior" in preventing Prudence Crandall from opening her school for young ladies of color. 23 November 1833. p.185, c3.

1362 A COLORED GENTLEMAN *to* **FRIEND [W. L. GARRISON]. 28 October 1833. Baltimore.** Sympathizes with Garrison on the severity of his lot; grieves that colonizationists apparently deliberately misrepresent abolitionists. 23 November 1833. p.185, c3.

1363 W. L. GARRISON *to* **NATHANIEL PAUL. 17 August 1833. London.** Informs that Wilberforce Settlement, which Paul represents, displays human fortitude and heroism; believes that the longer the settlement lasts, the less secure the system of slavery is because the settlement provides necessary asylum for slaves; commends Paul's integrity and moral worth. 23 November 1833. p.187, c1.

1364 CLARKSON *to* **W. L. GARRISON. n.d. n.p.** Informs that he wrote two articles for the *Mercantile Journal* on the condition of slaves, stating that the editor refused to publish them, even though the publishers were not opposed. 30 November 1833. p.189, c2.

1365 CLARKSON *to* **THE EDITOR OF THE** *MERCANTILE JOURNAL.* **n.d. n.p.** Refutes all logic that denies that slaves are less comfortable than their white masters. 30 November 1833. p.189, c2.

1366 CLARKSON *to* **THE EDITOR OF THE** *MERCANTILE JOURNAL.* **n.d. n.p.** Attacks his reasoning that because slaves reproduce faster than free blacks, they are more comfortable; asserts that if they were dogs or horses, such logic might apply, but that they are living men who thirst for freedom. 30 November 1833. p.189, c2.

1367 CLARKSON *to* **THE EDITOR OF THE** *MERCANTILE JOURNAL.* **n.d. n.p.** Charges that the editor, a colonizationist, is a hypocrite for not printing his previous two letters. 30 November 1833. p.189, c3.

1368 n.n. *to* **THE TREASURER OF NEW ENGLAND AS. 14 November 1833. P---, N.H.** Transfers a donation from the Bible Society to AS because former supplies Bibles to destitute families, but not slaves; believes that slaves are shamefully passed over by almost every benevolent society; adds that teaching slaves Sabbath instruction leads to death and questions if this is a Christian land. 30 November 1833. p.191, c4.

1369 M. *to* **SIR [W. L. GARRISON]. n.d. n.p.** Reports that intended slave insurrection at Wilmington, North Carolina was to be concurrent with insurrection at Southampton; leaders of proposed insurrection were hanged; believes that rebellion is natural for oppressed, and that as long as slavery exists, the South is in danger of violence. 7 December 1833. p.194, c4.

1370 WILBERFORCE *to* **MR. EDITOR [W. L. GARRISON]. n.d. n.p.** Reminds him that colored populations in the North live in cities and seaports, where there is more vice and crime than in the country, which partially explains the higher proportion of crime among free colored people compared to that among whites; believes that slavery is wrong. 7 December 1833. p.195, c2.

1371 J. *to* **MR. EDITOR [W. L. GARRISON]. n.d. n.p.** Condones action of the public meeting of the people of Albany who voted to appropriate money to free some slaves if they want to go to Liberia; informs that Albany citizens recognize the poorness of the present colony, its intemperance, and will send only those people of color who are willing to Africa. 14 December 1833. p.198, c5.

1372 H. B. B. *to* **MR. GARRISON. 4 December 1833. Providence.** Forwards letter from a Baptist. 14 December 1833. p.199, c1.

1373 A BAPTIST *to* **MR. EDITOR [W. L. GARRISON]. n.d. n.p.** Informs that a portion of the Baptist ministers and churches in Kentucky withdrew from the main body in 1805 and termed themselves "Emancipators", believing the possession of men as property to be wrong and inconsistent with Christian beliefs. 14 December 1833. p.199, c1.

1374 AN ABOLITIONIST *to* **THE EDITOR OF THE** *NEW YORK EVANGELIST.* **n.d. n.p.** Discusses colonization controversy; states that for the colonizationists and abolitionists to get along, the colonizationists must modify their views; lists three points that all abolitionists subscribe to in an effort to clarify the divisions between the two benevolent groups. 14 December 1833. p.199, c3.

1375 W. L. GARRISON *to* **THE EDITOR OF THE** *PATRIOT.* **6 August 1833. Aldermanbury.** Replies to Elliott Cresson, agent of the CS; disagrees both with Cresson's figures and with his ideology; begs the British to support anti-slavery, not colonization. 21 December 1833. p.201, c1.

1376 JONATHAN A. SARGEANT AND BENJAMIN BRIERLY *to* **W. L. GARRISON. 23 December 1833. Amesbury, Ma.** Discuss the prevalence of ignorance and darkness on the subject of slavery in New England; note recent formation of anti-slavery group in Amesbury. 28 December 1833. p.207, c3.

1377 n.n. *to* **MESSRS. GARRISON AND KNAPP. 23 December 1833. Salem, Ma.** Believes that humanity and justice are spreading, and hopes the white and black man can love each other before God; notes that many people are now saying that they have been deceived by the CS. 28 December 1833. p.207, c3.

1378 A DELIGHTED LISTENER *to* **MR. EDITOR [W. L. GARRISON]. n.d. n.p.** Expresses pleasure upon hearing concert by the Garrison Juvenile Choir; credits instructresses for their zeal and perseverance. 28 December 1833. p.207, c5.

[1834]

1379 CHARLES STUART *to* **W. L. GARRISON. 16 October 1833. Liverpool.** States that he delayed writing because he is spending the winter in England, but will soon travel to the United States; hopes to be present at the formation of the National AS. 4 January 1834. p.1, c1.

1380 CHARLES STUART *to* **THE EDITOR OF THE** *LONDON PATRIOT.* **16 September 1833. Moneymore, Tyrone, Ireland.** Refutes article by Beta, who is a thorough colonizationist; discusses the conditions of the races in the United States, the state of society in the United States, and the relation of CS to conditions in the United States and other countries; beseeches countrymen not to be deluded. 4 January 1834. p.1, c1.

1381 O'CONNELL *to* **MR. EDITOR [W. L. GARRISON]. n.d. n.p.** Criticizes recent article in the *African Repository* by Mr. Pearl, who classifies his opponents; charges that the CS has not answered the questions of any opposing group. 4 January 1834. p.1, c1.

1382 C. F. *to* **MR. EDITOR [W. L. GARRISON]. n.d. Portland.** Believes abstinence from slave products may retard the cause of abolition and hurt the slaves. 4 January 1834. p.2, c2.

1383 A JACKSON MAN *to* **MR. THAYER [EDITOR OF THE** *ESSEX GAZETTE***]. n.d. n.p.** Declares that he previously respected sectional differences, but can no longer be silent; declares that Northerners, too, are guilty in the existence of slavery and that the North must speak up and put a stop to slavery. 11 January 1834. p.5, c2.

1384 A FREEMAN *to* **THE EDITOR OF THE** *ZION'S HERALD***. n.d. n.p.** Proclaims the inconsistency of slavery in a land of liberty; adds that inconsistency is enlarged when Christian ministers support slavery; sends extract from Wesley's opinions on slavery. 11 January 1834. p.5, c2.

1385 W. D. *to* **SIR [W. L. GARRISON]. n.d. n.p.** Rejoices that men of color will now have some hope in this land of liberty with national anti-slavery conventions; hopes they can break the band of ruffians who profit from slavery. 11 January 1834. p.6, c5.

1386 ORSON S. MURRAY *to* **MR. EDITOR [W. L. GARRISON]. 25 December 1833. Bennington.** Reports that after colonizationists engaged Murray to speak on slavery they voted and cancelled his appearance; considers colonization supporters to be a close-minded mob. 11 January 1834. p.6, c6.

1387 GEORGE THOMPSON, ESQ. *to* **W. L. GARRISON, ESQ. 5 October 1833. Edinburgh.** Describes tour of Scotland; lectures on Haiti and England; sends copy of Scottish newspaper which was formerly pro-colonizationist; criticizes E. Cresson (CS Agent) whose friends are falling away daily. 11 January 1834. p.7, c1.

1388 n.n. *to* **n.n. [extract] August 1833. Portland, United States.** Informs friend in England of two groups who will be sending representatives to England: colonizationists and anti-slavery workers; asks him not to prejudge either group, but depicts colonizationists much more favorably. 11 January 1834. p.7, c2.

1389 JOSEPH COOPER *to* **W. L. GARRISON. 16 October 1833. Southwalk.** Describes conditions in the West Indies; wonders how the slaves will accept British gradual emancipation; hopes that American immediate abolitionists are not discouraged; considers haters of slavery in the abstract to be the most effective supporters of the system. 18 January 1834. p.10, c1.

1390 ARNOLD BUFFUM *to* **THE ANNUAL MEETING OF THE NEW ENGLAND AS. 9 JANUARY 1834. Philadelphia.** Wishes he could be at the meeting; impressed with the society's accomplishments in only two years; urges them to be strong and continue fighting. 18 January 1834. p.10, c2.

1391 SAMUEL J. MAY *to* **MR. BENJAMIN C. BACON. 14 January 1834. Brooklyn.** Regrets that he cannot attend the second anniversary meeting of the AS; believes that rapidly changing public opinion in his area shows that people are beginning to appreciate the importance of the anti-slavery cause. 18 January 1834. p.10, c2.

1392 JOHN G. WHITTIER *to* **SAMUEL E. SEWALL, SECRETARY OF THE NEW ENGLAND AS. 10 January 1834. Haverhill.** Regrets he cannot attend the second anniversary meeting of the New England AS, but vows to support them and the cause of abolition heart and soul; urges people of the free states to work for moral reform and criticizes the evil silence of those who do not work against slavery. 18 January 1834. p.10, c3.

1393 n.n. *to* **W. L. GARRISON. 13 January 1834. Portland.** Tells of the formation of an AS in Portland; reports that the preamble and constitution were drawn up with depth of feeling and profound sense of duty. 18 January 1834. p.11, c4.

1394 A NEIGHBOR *to* **W. L. GARRISON. 14 January 1834. Portland.** Reports new AS in Bath, Maine, established and continued under opposition, whose members remain vigorous and not discouraged. 18 January 1834. p.11, c4.

1395 n.n. *to* **W. L. GARRISON. 2 December 1833. Hebron, N.Y.** Encourages Garrison to continue his work, in spite of the prejudice and preconceived opinions with which he must contend; reports that Garison's principles are gaining support. 18 January 1834. p.11, c4.

1396 A FRIEND TO THE COLORED MAN *to* **W. L. GARRISON. 18 December 1833. Geneva, Ontario County, N.Y.** Explains he never supported colonization and believed emancipation to be too impractical; tells of his discussions with colonizationists which made him realize that they are fools and speak against common sense. 18 January 1834. p.11, c4.

1397 MOTT *to* **THE EDITOR [W. L. GARRISON]. n.d. Portland.** Discusses the duty of refusing to partake of the productions of slave labor; states that any consideration of national or personal finances must be ignored; this is a question of moral right or wrong. 18 January 1834. p.11, c5.

1398 HON. JOSEPH SOUTHWICK, DEA. JOHN EVELETH, EMERY BROWN, RICHARD H. VOSE, AND HENRY A. JONES *to* **MR. EDITOR [W. L. GARRISON]. 4 January 1834. Augusta Me.** Report that the anti-slavery cause is progressing; many former colonizationists have realized their error and now support anti-slavery. 18 January 1834. p.11, c5.

1399 n.n. *to* **THE EDITORS OF THE** *VERMONT CHRONICLE.* **n.d. n.p.** Accepts the divine sentiment that Christian men should be meek and charitable; questions whether the leaders of the anti-slavery convention can quiet the slaves into a peaceful wait for redress of their wrongs; states that the anti-slavery proponents want to free slaves immediately, but do not want them to inflict violence on ex-masters. 25 January 1834. p.13, c1.

1400 REV. JOHN SCOBLE *to* **n.n. [extract] 25 September 1833. Bexler Heath, near London.** Reports visits to several towns in Kent, sowing the seeds of opposition to the CS; urges Garrison to continue his work until he achieves succes. 25 January 1834. p.13, c3.

1401 MOTT *to* **THE EDITOR [W. L. GARRISON]. n.d. n.p.** States that public opinion is what sustains slavery, silence is consent, inactivity is accession; urges action, not just thinking, to further the anti-slavery cause. 25 January 1834. p.13, c6.

1402 A COLORED BALTIMOREAN *to* **MR. EDITOR [W. L. GARRISON]. n.d. n.p.** Disapproves of the method of making Maryland a free state by the expatriation of more than 100,000 to Africa; attacks and criticizes the CS on several points. 25 January 1834. p.14, c1.

1403 ARNOLD BUFFUM *to* **FRIEND. 18 January 1834. Philadelphia.** Rejoices that the *Liberator* is helping the anti-slavery cause to expand; informs of excellent speech by Friend Coffin to colored people, after which many subscribed to *Liberator*; believes colored people must be encouraged to work for their own improvement and rights. 25 January 1834. p.14, c2.

1404 A FRIEND OF THE OPPRESSED *to* **FRIEND GARRISON. n.d. n.p.** Criticizes the person in last *Gazette* who undertook to defend slavery in the free state of Massachusetts; protests that anyone north of the Potomac still subscribes to those unenlightened ideas. 25 January 1834. p.14, c2.

1405 N. LORD *to* **THE EDITORS OF THE** *NEW HAMPSHIRE OBSERVER.* **n.d. n.p.** Informs that he has recently read an extract of a letter which was not authorized by him in that form; but agrees with some of the ideas; encloses a letter which more clearly gives his views. 25 January 1834. p.14, c6.

1406 N. LORD *to* **SIR. 7 January 1834. Dartmouth College.** Declares his position on slavery and emancipation. 25 January 1834. p.14, c6.

1407 A COLORED FRIEND IN UTICA *to* **W. L. GARRISON. 6 January 1834. Utica.** Describes interesting discussion between President Green and J. N. Danforth; states there is an increase in Utica of converts to the doctrine of immediate emancipation; Green has routed the colonizationists. 25 January 1834. p.15, c4.

1408 MR. JOSEPH PHILLIPS *to* **n.n. [extract] 22 August 1833. London.** Declares that God has followed [Garrison] with a particular providence and that his visit has done a great deal of good in England and the United States; hopes the monster slavery will soon be exterminated. 1 February 1834. p.17, c2.

1409 N. SOUTHARD *to* **W. L. GARRISON. n.d. n.p.** Reports on a trip to his home state of New Hampshire, where he was greeted with a mixed reaction; reports that he converted many from pro-colonization to anti-slavery. 1 February 1834. p.19, c3.

1410 MOTT *to* **THE EDITOR [W. L. GARRISON]. n.d. n.p.** Argues that every man who partakes of the fruits of slave labor contributes in some degree directly towards the support and the existence of slavery. 1 February 1834. p.19, c4.

1411 A RECENT RESIDENT OF LOWELL *to* **MR. CASE [from the** *Lowell Mercury***] 11 January 1834. Portsmouth.** Congratulates citizens of Lowell for rejecting the "absurd idea" of forming an AS. 8 February 1834. p.21, c1.

1412 ELIZABETH DUDLEY *to* **THE LADIES FORMING THE AA IN READING, MASSACHUSETTS. 18 July 1833. Peckham, England.** Declares that she was always taught that slavery is wrong; rejoices they are finally standing up and preaching against slavery; reports that district visiting may be used to diffuse knowledge and collect funds; notes much commiseration among the poor and the working class; observes much ignorance on the subject of slavery. 15 February 1834. p.26, c6.

1413 n.n. *to* **THE EDITORS OF THE** *RICHMOND ENQUIRER.* **[extract] 16 January 1834. Utica, N.Y.** States that the North is sound on the question of abolition and will let the South take care of its own problem; reports on a public meeting which condemned abolitionists, collected contributions toward colonization, and burned Mr. Green in effigy. 22 February 1834. p.29, c1.

1414 MOTT *to* **THE EDITOR [W. L. GARRISON] n.d. n.p.** Declares that one cannot expect recompense for doing his duty by not using slave produce; argues that slave produce is not really more expedient because slaveholders are wasting the land and the Southern white is becoming indolent. 22 February 1834. p.30, c4.

1415 A FRIEND AT THE EASTWARD *to* **W. L. GARRISON. 13 February 1831. Portland.** Describes the address he gave to the AS of Bath, Maine; recommends that other societies engage speakers to increase membership. 22 February 1834. p.30, c5.

1416 LOVER OF FACTS *to* **MR. EDITOR [W. L. GARRISON]. n.d. n.p.** Suggests that anyone who doubts the accuracy of attacks on conditions in Liberia should listen to the testimony at the ACS; claims that too many women and children are sent to Liberia with no men to take care of them; claims that most die from an attack of fever, and that others cannot find employment. 22 February 1834. p.31, c6.

1417 n.n. *to* **EDITOR OF THE** *APALACHICOLA ADVERTISER.* **n.d. n.p.** Criticizes Gen. Jones of Washington City, who offered his plantation for the purpose of educating African youth; refuses to believe that one can raise the character of blacks in any part of the South. 1 March 1834. p.33, c1.

1418 THOMAS A HOLCOMBE *to* **THE EDITOR OF THE** *NEW YORK EVANGELIST.* **28 December 1833. Lynchburg.** Lists names to be removed as subscribers to the *New York Evangelist;* explains that they live in a slaveholding state and must preserve harmony, but that they support emancipation and colonization. 1 March 1834. p.33, c1.

1419 n.n. *to* **W. L. GARRISON. n.n. Philadelphia.** Believes that intellectual inferiority is not necessarily linked to colored skin; entreats the colored population, for their own sake, to repress their resentment and desire for revenge; argues that indulgence of angry feelings will not bring peace; claims that if they try to love their enemies as God instructed, He will reward them. 1 March 1834. p.33, c4.

1420 PLYMOUTH *to* **MR. EDITOR [W. L. GARRISON]. n.d. n.p.** Defines the term "Excited Journalists" as those who have moral courage enough to do a cause more good than harm; adds that they are often treated with ingratitude by less efficient coadjutors. 1 March 1834. p.33, c5.

1421 n.n. *to* **MR. EDITOR [W. L. GARRISON]. n.d. n.p.** Reports that many local preachers encourage the immediate repentance of sin, yet oppose the anti-slavery cause; charges that they claim to be abolitionists, yet support colonization in Liberia; calls on these men to put aside their prejudices and examine these inconsistencies. 1 March 1834. p.33, c5.

1422 n.n. *to* **MR. EDITOR [W. L. GARRISON]. [extract] n.d. Northampton, Ma.** Reports that he has become a firm abolitionist by reading the *Liberator;* believes that Northern men are deceived in supporting colonization; hopes that this ignorance will be eradicated soon. 1 March 1834. p.33, c6.

1423 n.n. *to* **MR. EDITOR [W. L. GARRISON]. n.d. n.p.** Points out that colonizers must send lumber, shingles, and nails to Africa to build houses for the colonists; regards these as trifling items of expense which colonization agents ignore in their public addresses. 1 March 1834. p.33, c6.

1424 n.n. *to* **MR. EDITOR [W. L. GARRISON]. n.d. n.p.** Sends a paragraph from the *Atlas* by a Yankee captain who complained about the delays in Jamaica and blamed them on a black judge's administration of the law; explains that the delays were in fact due to a holiday. 1 March 1834. p.33, c6.

1425 ABSTINENCE *to* **W. L. GARRISON. 1 February 1834. Lampeter, Pa.** Criticizes a recent letter in the *Liberator;* explains the effect that total universal abstinence from slave-produce would have on the system of slavery; argues that the free people only tolerate slave-produce because they are habituated to the system. 1 March 1834. p.34, c2.

1426 O. S. M. *to* **MR. EDITOR [W. L. GARRISON]. 7 February 1834. Orwell, Vt.** Reminds Garrison that any class of sinners will attempt to find shelter under the Bible; argues that American slaveholders should be the last to claim sanction from that holy book; reasons that the divine direction allowing Jews to have servants extended only to Jews living at that time. 1 March 1834. p.34, c5.

1427 n.n. *to* **THE EDITOR [W. L. GARRISON]. [extract] 6 February 1834. Whitestown, N.Y.** Tells of the Utica, New York debate between Rev. Mr. Danforth, an agent of the CS, and Mr. Green; reports that the debate opened his eyes to the truth; believes that an institution should be built to educate blacks, and that it would not be difficult to raise funds. 1 March 1834. p.34, c6.

1428 LINDLEY COATES *to* **THE EDITOR [W. L. GARRISON]. 24 January 1834. Sadsbury, Pa.** Refers to a recent letter in the *Liberator* in which a man suggests that Garrison be treated with contemptuous silence, yet lambasts him publicly; encourages Garrison not to fear; claims that slaveholders do not follow the Bible's precepts. 1 March 1834. p.34, c6.

1429 n.n. *to* **THE EDITOR [W. L. GARRISON]. [extract] n.d. Vermont.** Criticizes the *Vermont Chronicle* for "chilling and blasting all sympathy for the colored man and the slave." 1 March 1834. p.35, c1.

1430 RAY POTTER *to* **THE EDITOR [W. L. GARRISON]. 28 January 1834. Pawtucket.** Sarcastically informs Garrison that abolitionists are allowed to assemble and "run free" in his area; tells of converting talented, intelligent men in the area to the cause; encloses information on a newly formed AS. 1 March 1834. p.35, c1.

1431 n.n. *to* **THE EDITOR [W. L. GARRISON]. 18 January 1834. Jamaica, Vt.** Describes a meeting to pray for the suffering people of color in America; asks Garrison to forward a petition for abolition to Congress. 1 March 1834. p.35, c1.

1432 n.n. *to* **THE EDITOR [W. L. GARRISON]. 22 January 1834. Middletown.** Sends support and encouragement; congratulates Garrison on his late mission to England; reports that there are still some unshaken ones among them, but that he is working to enlighten them. 1 March 1834. p.35, c1.

1433 n.n. *to* **THE EDITOR [W. L. GARRISON]. [extract] n.d. Neighboring town.** Believes that the anti-slavery cause is both religious and noble; declares that he is glad, not surprised, at the recent problems of the CS. 1 March 1834. p.35, c2.

1434 JOHN M. S. PERRY *to* **THE EDITOR [W. L. GARRISON]. 21 February 1834. Mendon.** Tells of the formation of an AS at Uxbridge; reports that 310 names were subscribed to the constitution; declares that the society's popularity and progress are wholly unexpected, but welcome. 1 March 1834. p.35, c2.

1435 NO PUN-DIT *to* **THE EDITOR [W. L. GARRISON]. n.d. n.p.** Puns on three-quarters of the names of those who signed the anti-slavery declaration while simultaneously advocating immediate emancipation. 1 March 1834. p.35, c2.

1436 ELLIOTT CRESSON *to* **ALEXANDER CRUIKSHANK. 9 September 1833. Adelphi.** Supports colonization; attacks Garrison; maintains that his society has given blacks a home, a country, and hope for a freehold in Africa. 1 March 1834. p.35, c4.

1437 n.n. *to* **THE EDITORS OF THE *OHIO OBSERVER*. n.d. n.p.** Discusses the evil of tobacco; claims that tobacco intoxicates, producing an unnatural excitement like that of the daily moderate drinker. 1 March 1834. p.36, c5.

1438 ORSON S. MURRAY *to* **BROTHER GOODELL. n.d. n.p.** Replies to a charge that identifies colonizationism with mobocracy in Vermont; claims that colonizationism in Vermont is the same as in New York or elsewhere; relates instances in various parts of the northeast when colonizationists have interrupted speeches because they did not wish to allow the spread of "fanaticism." 8 March 1834. p.37, c5.

1439 AN ABOLITIONIST *to* **THE EDITOR [W. L. GARRISON]. n.d. n.p.** Sends encouragement; declares his joy that the paper has enlarged; compares the paper's goals to Brutus' sworn revenge upon tyranny; warns the oppressors in Georgia that they, too, will have to pay for their sins; declares that slavery is at the foundation of our national sins. 8 March 1834. p.38, c2.

1440 E. P. W. *to* **THE EDITOR [W. L. GARRISON]. n.d. Mantua-Ville, near Philadelphia.** Praises Garrison for his indefatigable exertions; reports that six months ago, he supported colonization blindly, thinking that he was helping his colored brothers; after talking to a respectable colored man about the prejudice that the society was causing, he now heartily supports the AS and immediate emancipation. 8 March 1834. p.38, c3.

1441 N. P. ROGERS *to* **FRIEND GARRISON. 20 February 1834. Plymouth, N.H.** Reports the formation of an AS; sends a list of organizers and officers; advocates universal emancipation. 8 March 1834. p.38, c5.

1442 n.n. *to* **THE EDITOR [W. L. GARRISON]. 18 February 1834. Nantucket.** Reports recent formation of a Nantucket AS; quotes from the constitution; lists officers. 8 March 1834. p.38, c5.

1443 A DEVOTED FEMALE ABOLITIONIST *to* **THE EDITOR [W. L. GARRISON]. [extract] 20 February 1834. Fall River.** Rejoices to learn that the circulation of the *Liberator* is so extensive; declares that those fighting for God's will, the abolition of slavery, are blessed. 8 March 1834. p.38, c5.

1444 n.n. *to* **W. L. GARRISON. 19 February 1834. New Garden.** Urges abstention from use of slave-labor produce; encourages abolitionists; gives many biblical quotations to support the anti-slavery cause. 8 March 1834. p.38, c5.

1445 P. M. N. *to* **W. L. GARRISON. 17 February 1834. Portland.** States that he has learned from articles in the *Liberator* that many Quakers are very active in the cause of abolition and advocate immediate emancipation; chides those who are aloof and apathetic; urges all to work for the abolition of slavery. 15 March 1834. p.41, c3.

1446 n.n. *to* **THE EDITOR [W. L. GARRISON]. 15 February 1834. Belchertown.** Feels that colonization is the great demon of slavery; compares colonization to a deadly malady; urges those opposed to colonization not to be silent until slavery is annihilated. 15 March 1834. p.41, c3.

1447 n.n. *to* **W. L. GARRISON. [extract] n.d. Ohio.** Reports that the anti-slavery cause is gaining ground, but that there are still few societies; observes that many halfway emancipationists object to giving colored men the protection of the law; predicts that the time is not far distant when the Church will be divided. 15 March 1834. p.41, c4.

1448 n.n. *to* **MR. EDITOR [W. L. GARRISON]. n.d. n.p.** Reports on a newspaper advertisement inviting all to a colonization meeting; states that he decided to go and passed an anti-slavery meeting on the way. 15 March 1834. p.43, c3.

1449 B. W. *to* **W. L. GARRISON. 28 February 1834. Philadelphia.** Describes a wedding where the cake was not only made of free sugar, but was decorated with mottoes opposing slavery; hopes that this example will be imitated. 15 March 1834. p.43, c4.

1450 A. *to* **THE EDITOR OF THE *MORNING CHRONICLE*. n.d. n.p.** Reports that fifty-nine slaves destined for New Orleans were sold at Mount Vernon by Judge Washington (first president of the ACS, nephew of George Washington); adds that a larger drove of slaves was sold by the same man the following week. 22 March 1834. p.45, c1.

1451 BUSH. WASHINGTON *to* **FREDERICK G. SHAEFFER, ESQ. [from the *Baltimore Telegraph*] 18 September 1821. Jefferson County, Va.** Corrects misrepresentations in papers; enters a protest on behalf of Southern citizens against the questioning of their right, legal or moral, to dispose of their own property; claims that he did not separate children and parents or husbands and wives; attempts to justify his practices. 22 March 1834. p.45, c1.

1452 n.n. *to* **W. L. GARRISON. 8 March 1834. Andover Theological Seminary.** Encourages and praises Garrison; describes slavery in Kentucky; reports that most slaves are ignorant even of the existence of God; quotes letters from a friend in Kentucky telling of extreme religious ignorance; thinks that slaves are treated with more kindness in other states. 22 March 1834. p.45, c4.

1453 X. Y. Z. *to* **MR. EDITOR [W. L. GARRISON]. [continued from 15 March 1834] n.d. n.p.** Gives a brief report of the speeches, proceedings, and resolutions of a recent colonization meeting in Boston; reports some debate over whether they should concentrate on the care or enlargement of the colony. 22 March 1834. p.47, c2.

1454 F. *to* **FRIEND GARRISON. 17 March 1834. Boston.** Corrects Garrison's statement that Green denounced the abolitionists as fanatics; declares that he said nothing bad about them, but that he did recommend the CS; believes that Green is terribly ignorant and misinformed and that he will regret his actions when he sees the light. 22 March 1834. p.47, c5.

1455 TRUTH *to* **W. L. GARRISON. February 1833. Middletown.** States that he just learned from a friend who visited the South, particularly South Carolina, that some slaveholders do not believe blacks to be inferior and that no slaves labor freely; gives some examples; reports that Charles Denison's speech in Middletown was disrupted by mobs. 22 March 1834. p.47, c5.

1456 R. H. S. *to* **W. L. GARRISON. 22 January 1834. Hennepin, Il.** Comments on an editorial in the recent *Presbyterian;* encloses an article entitled "African Colonization"; quotes from an article in the *Presbyterian* on the nature of slavery and on Garrison's trip to England, and then comments on it. 29 March 1834. p.49, c3.

1457 REV. EDWIN W. GARRISON *to* **COUSIN [W. L. GARRISON]. 5 February 1834. Fayette, Me.** Describes the progress of the abolition cause in Maine; reports that he is working to change public sentiment; describes his recent address on slavery, and encloses some introductory remarks: "Slavery is an open and palpable infringement of Divine law," "Slavery permitted by God among the Jews was freedom compared to the condition of slaves in the South." 29 March 1834. p.49, c5.

1458 n.n. *to* **W. L. GARRISON. 6 February 1834. Putnam County, Il.** Gives a short account of the local AS, which started with only eleven members, and quotes its constitution; describes their activities during the year; tells of extreme prejudice against blacks; reminds him that truth is powerful and will prevail. 29 March 1834. p.50, c1.

1459 BENJAMIN PAUL, WILLIAM A. SMITH, AND LEMUEL A. FREEMAN *to* **FRIEND GARRISON. 3 March 1834. Wilberforce.** Discuss a recent resolution at their meeting to publicize the present condition and future prospects of their colony in upper Canada; report that females make their own apparel and that a new school is being built; feel they are truly Americans; hope for support from their friends abroad. 29 March 1834. p.50, c2.

1460 PHILADELPHIA *to* **MR. EDITOR [W. L. GARRISON]. 17 March 1834. Boston.** Encloses a short article for publication called "What Have Ladies to Do With the Subject of Anti-Slavery?"; declares that there are few subjects of importance with which ladies have not something to do; refuses to draw the boundary of women's dominions around their hearts; asserts that women, too, can assume personal responsibility and help ASS. 29 March 1834. p.50, c3.

1461 H. B. STANTON *to* **BROTHER LEAVITT. 10 March 1834. Lane Seminary, Walnut Hills, near Cincinnati, Oh.** Reports that a flourishing CS has existed among them for a long time; states that they held a large public discussion in February with forty-five hours of debate about abolition and colonization; reports that one of the student speakers was an emancipated slave and that almost everyone voted to abolish slavery; adds that there was more diversity of sentiment on colonization, but that it was voted down; announces the recent formation of an AS. 29 March 1834. p.50, c3.

1462 DANIEL R. CONDOLL, JOHN CONDOLL, WILLIAM M. CAMPBELL, WILLIAM CONDOLL, JOHN CONDOLL, AND AMOS M. CAMPBELL *to* **W. L. GARRISON. 10 March 1834. Lyme, Ct.** Report the formation of a temperance society to show colored people's desire to improve themselves morally as well as intellectually; enclose their constitution and a list of elected officers and directors. 29 March 1834. p.50, c6.

1463 JUSTICE *to* **W. L. GARRISON. n.d. n.p.** Describes a huge procession of mechanics and laborers in Philadelphia; proposes the addition of a brigade of slaves hoisting a banner reading, "We hold these truths to be self-evident. . . ," as he feels that the parade should include a protest against oppression. 29 March 1834. p.51, c5.

1464 N. *to* **MR. EDITOR [W. L. GARRISON]. n.d. n.p.** Introduces an article; encourages and praises Garrison; includes "The Honest Lawyer," a story about an ethical lawyer; wishes other lawyers were as upright. 29 March 1834. p.52, c2.

1465 T. H. A. *to* **W. L. GARRISON. 4 March 1834. New Bedford.** Relates a story told him by a young sailor at a Methodist prayer meeting; the sailor had been sick in South Carolina and the doctors had given up when a slave prayed for him and brought about a miraculous recovery; believes that God not only gave slaves souls, but also listens to their prayers. 29 March 1834. p.52, c5.

1466 n.n. *to* **THE EDITOR OF THE** *EMANCIPATOR***. 4 March 1834. Oneida Institute.** Summarizes the history of their CS which was formed in July 1833 and later lost many members to the abolition cause; reports that he offered resolutions against supporting the CS because it worsens the conditions of colored brethren; adds that the resolutions were adopted unanimously. 5 April 1834. p.53, c5.

1467 UNCLE SIMON'S EASY CHAIR NO. XIII *to* **MR. EDITOR [W. L. GARRISON]. n.d. Philadelphia.** Comments on the retirement of Danforth, former agent of the CS; believes that all other colonization agents will have to retire when the truth about their society becomes known. 5 April 1834. p.54, c1.

1468 INVESTIGATOR *to* **THE EDITOR [W. L. GARRISON]. 4 March 1834. Portland.** Replies to and comments on a letter in the *Columbian Sentinel* signed "Washington, Feb. 22"; quotes a long passage from the article upholding slavery in South Carolina; opposes the article's claim that Northerners have no right to interfere with Southern slavery. 5 April 1834. p.54, c4.

1469 SPECTATOR *to* **MR. EDITOR [W. L. GARRISON]. 18 March 1834. Jericho, Vt.** Reports on a discussion of the merits of the CS in Middlebury; states that it was held by a club and that pro-colonizationists spoke longer than the allotted time and harassed the anti-colonization speakers; adds that he does not know how the meeting terminated. 5 April 1834. p.54, c6.

1470 EDWIN P. ATLEE *to* **W. L. GARRISON. 25 March 1834. Philadelphia.** Grieves at the death of their mutual friend, Evan Lewis; reports that he had suffered from a disease of the function of assimilation or digestion which the doctors could not cure; adds that Lewis had been a teacher of the High School for Abolition and an editor of the *Genius of Universal Emancipation*. 5 April 1854. p.55, c3.

1471 A COLORED GENTLEMAN *to* **FRIEND [W. L. GARRISON]. 28 March 1834. Philadelphia.** Mourns the death of Evan Lewis, a devoted abolitionist and a friend of people of color. 5 April 1834. p.55, c3.

1472 MISS S. PAUL *to* **THE EDITOR [W. L. GARRISON]. 1 April 1834. Boston.** Reports the rudeness of coach drivers who refused to take them to Salem because they are colored; states that she does not despair because the cause has made rapid progress. 5 April 1834. p.55, c4.

1473 A FRIEND OF THE COLORED PEOPLE *to* **MR. HALLETT. n.d. n.p.** Congratulates the colored population on the recent appointment of Mr. Abner Forbes as master of the grammar school in Belknap Street; praises Forbes' education and intellect. 5 April 1834. p.55, c5.

1474 THEODORE D. WELD *to* **LEWIS TAPPAN. [from the** *New York Evangelist***] 18 March 1834. Lane Seminary.** Describes the changes in Lane Seminary; reports that many have questioned their consciences and become abolitionists, even some members of slaveholding families; reports that they believe that faith without works is dead and have established a lyceum for the education of colored people; solicits contributions. 12 April 1834. p.57, c5.

1475 C. STUART *to* **THE FRIENDS OF RELIGION AND HUMANITY. 1 November 1833. W. T. Blair's, Bathwick-hill, Bath.** Informs the British people that two million people in America are slaves; describes the insane and cruel prejudice against people of color, including free blacks who are threatened with expatriation; discusses the noble struggles of blacks against these wrongs. 12 April 1834. p.58, c4.

1476 CHARLES STUART *to* **W. L. GARRISON. [extract] n.d. England.** Writes that he will soon come to America to join his friends; feels anxious about Miss Crandall's persecution. 12 April 1834. p.59, c1.

1477 JOSEPH STURGE *to* **FRIEND [W. L. GARRISON]. [extract] n.d. Birmingham, England.** Rejoices that America has established a national AS; reminds him that many English abolitionists want to help; tells of George Stephens' memorial to the American people. 12 April 1834. p.59, c1.

1478 JOSEPH PHILLIPS *to* **W. L. GARRISON. 21 February 1834. London.** Reports on a society for universal emancipation and abolition of slave trade formed by Charles Stuart; explains that the formation of the United States AS gave them renewed enthusiasm and hope; feels anxious about Prudence Crandall; reports difficulty receiving the *Liberator.* 12 April 1834. p.59, c1.

1479 REV. NATHANIEL PAUL *to* **W. L. GARRISON. 22 January 1834. Kensington, near London.** Intended to reply to Elliott Cresson's latest article, but others wrote first; remarks that Cresson has few friends or supporters left; expresses concern about the threats Garrison receives; sends encouragement. 12 April 1834. p.59, c1.

1480 N. P. ROGERS *to* **W. L. GARRISON. 26 March 1834. Plymouth, N.H.** Replies to criticism of the *Vermont Chronicle;* says that the size of the slave must not be answered by a plea in abatement; argues that the situation demands action. 12 April 1834. p.59, c3.

1481 UNCLE SIMON'S EASY CHAIR NO. XIV *to* **MR. EDITOR [W. L. GARRISON]. n.d. Philadelphia.** Corrects his former statement on the number of slaves sent to Liberia in 1833 from 108 to 251; questions the numbers given by the CS, which claims 2769, 2630, and 3123 as the total number; asks which figures are right, if any; realizes that they will use the number which best suits their purposes; criticizes the theory of colonization. 12 April 1834. p.59, c4.

1482 JOHN G. WHITTIER *to* **n.n. [extract] n.d. n.p.** Describes the rise of anti-slavery sentiment; believes that colonization has lost its vitality; pleads for courage; looks forward to the future. 12 April 1834. p.59, c5.

1483 MARY JANE COOK *to* **DAVID L. CHILD OF BOSTON. 9 March 1834. Belfast.** The sister of James Hall, a free man of New Hampshire, who was sold back into slavery, corrects the rumor that her brother was in debt. 12 April 1834. p.59, c5.

1484 HENRY SIPKINS *to* **FELLOW CITIZENS. 25 March 1834. New York.** Announces the Fourth Annual Convention of the Free People of Color to be held in New York on the first Monday of June; reminds freemen of the need to combat prejudice by educating and improving themselves. 12 April 1834. p.59, c6.

1485 ELIA *to* **MR. EDITOR [W. L. GARRISON]. 5 April 1864. South Reading.** Describes a town meeting to form an AS; includes the preamble, the constitution, and the resolutions passed. 19 April 1834. p.63, c1.

1486 CLARKSON *to* **W. L. GARRISON. 1 April 1834. Middletown.** Reports on the second annual meeting of the Middletown Home Temperance Society; presents their resolutions on the unhealthy effect of ardent spirits and wine; lists members of the board of managers. 19 April 1834. p.63, c1.

1487 E. B. D. *to* **W. L. GARRISON. n.d. n.p.** Submits propositions for an instantaneous end to oppression: instant cessation of unjust practices, and immediate emancipation; believes that prejudiced editors are beginning to favor abolition, but admits that truth requires action and action requires time. 19 April 1834. p.63, c2.

1488 JOHN PETERSON, HENRY GARNET, AND THOMAS H. TOMPKINS *to* **W. L. GARRISON. 2 April 1834. New York.** Announce the formation of the Garrison Literary and Benevolent Association for boys aged four to twenty; intend it as a society for mental improvement and as a token of respect for Garrison; assert that the name of Garrison spreads terror and dismay among tyrants and oppressors. 19 April 1834. p.63, c4.

1489 JOHN W. LEWIS, PRINCE LOVERIDGE, AND GEORGE W. FRANCIS *to* **n.n. 26 March 1834.** Report that the New York Committee of the Garrison Literary and Benevolent Association will prepare an abridgement of their constitution for publication. 19 April 1834. p.63, c4.

1490 PLUTARCH *to* **THE EDITOR OF THE** *EMANCIPATOR.* **5 April 1834. New York.** Describes his visit to the Garrison Society; reports that approximately 130 children delivered addresses and read compositions; adds that one trustee was displeased with the name Garrison, but that the consensus was to keep it. 19 April 1834. p.63, c4.

1491 NED BUCKET *to* **W. L. GARRISON. n.d. Macon, Ga.** Threatens Garrison if he dares to enter Georgia; reports that a Georgia planter has grown a patch of hemp to make a rope especially for Garrison; calls him names. 19 April 1834. p.63, c5.

1492 A MEMBER OF CONGRESS *to* **THE EDITOR OF THE** *KENTUCKY OBSERVER.* **25 February 1834. Congress Hall.** Tries to describe how Daniel Webster so interests his audience. 19 April 1834. p.64, c2.

1493 OLD WESTMINSTER *to* **THE EDITOR OF THE** *BROOKLYN UNIONIST.* **8 April 1834. Westminster.** Mocks Andrew T. Judson who opposed Prudence Crandall's Canterbury School for black girls, and the "anti-Negro excitement" which surrounds him. 27 April 1834. p.66, c1.

1494 THE WALTHAM AS *to* **MR. EDITOR [W. L. GARRISON]. n.d. n.p.** Encloses the constitution of the Waltham AS, the preamble, resolutions, and list of officers. 27 April 1864. p.66, c2.

1495 PHILEMON R. RUSSELL *to* **W. L. GARRISON. 14 April 1834. West Boylston.** Describes the anti-slavery movement in West Boylston, Holden, and vicinity; reports that there was almost no interest until he wrote many articles under the name "The Spy" and gave many lectures; states that he created many ASS. 27 April 1834. p.66, c3.

1496 EQUITY *to* **THE LADIES OF BOSTON. n.d. n.p.** Reminds them to think of the slave, even in their most happy and contented moments; urges them to take God's will into their own hands; declares that apathy enrages her. 27 April 1834. p.67, c3.

1497 n.n. *to* **n.n. [extract] 1 April 1834. Lane Seminary.** Describes the AS at Lane Seminary; argues that Northerners and travellers do not really see the South, that one can comprehend the horror of slavery only by living in the South; tells of a woman in Cincinnati who bought freedom for herself and all but one of her children; the master sold the remaining child to a new master in New Orleans. 27 April 1834. p.67, c3.

1498 HENRY SIPKIN *to* **FELLOW CITIZENS. 25 March 1834. New York.** Announces the fourth annual convention of the Free People of Color to be held in June in New York; encloses extracts from the minutes. 27 April 1834. p.67, c5.

1499 H. J. *to* **MR. EDITOR [W. L. GARRISON]. n.d. n.p.** Believes that all, even defensive, wars are wrong; urges others to form peace societies. 27 April 1834. p.68, c4.

1500 REV. DR. COX *to* **THE EDITOR OF THE** *NEW YORK EVANGELIST.* **n.d. n.p.** Gives an unchronological account of his visit to Europe; discusses "Slavery as related to our own country and England"; after arguing in England, he completely reversed his views and decided that if the free colored population opposes colonization, it is wrong to encourage it. 3 May 1834. p.69, c2.

1501 COLUMBUS *to* **MESSRS. CHADWICK AND LITTLE. n.d. n.p.** Reminds all of the Christian obligation to pray for the slaves. 3 May 1834. p.70, c3.

1502 UNCLE SIMON'S EASY CHAIR NO. XV. *to* **MR. EDITOR [W. L. GARRISON]. n.d. Philadelphia.** Constructs an analogy between Liberia and a troubled wife; states that the patience and purse strings of the husband, the United States, have been exhausted because the wife, Liberia, is intemperate, slovenly, and unsuccessful. 3 May 1834. p.70, c5.

1503 LA ROY SUNDERLAND *to* **W. L. GARRISON. 20 April 1834. Andover.** Relates recent news from Liberia; reports that Rev. Mr. Wright, a thorough-going colonizationist, was utterly disappointed by his visit to Liberia; adds that Wright was so harsh in his criticisms that he decided not to publish his letters; feels that this is a crime against truth. 3 May 1864. p.71, c1.

1504 CALVIN TEMPLE *to* **W. L. GARRISON. 23 April 1834. Reading.** The treasurer of the Reading AS encloses two dollars for Garrison to use to buy Bibles for poor colored persons. 3 May 1834. p.71, c6.

1505 LA ROY SUNDERLAND *to* **MR. EDITOR [W. L. GARRISON]. 5 May 1834. Andover.** States that he did not intend the letter to Garrison for publication; declares that he has learned that Mr. Wright wrote to missionary board members privately, not officially, asking them not to publish his negative impressions of Liberia; adds that the board is going to publish the letters in their entirety. 10 May 1834. p.73, c4.

1506 HUMANITUS *to* **W. L. GARRISON. n.d. Philadelphia.** Suggests that all the colored people sent "back" to Africa be returned to the United States since the colony cannot support them and the society is running out of money. 10 May 1834. p.73, c4.

1507 n.n. THE EDITOR [W. L. GARRISON]. n.d. n.p. Encourages Garrison; believes that Garrison is on God's path, even though he must be encountering many barriers. 10 May 1834. p.73, c5.

1508 GEORGE L. LEROW *to* **W. L. GARRISON. 19 April 1834. Waterville.** Announces the recent formation of the Waterville AS; reports that they number eighty-two, after less than three weeks, and that they aim to enlighten public opinion by presenting the facts; hopes to see the slave unchained and protected by the law. 10 May 1834. p.73, c5.

1509 J. B. HEADLEY *to* **THE EDITOR OF THE** *WESTERN RESERVE.* **10 April 1834. Oneida Institute.** Sends a unanimous resolution of the AS of the Oneida Institute that prejudice against colored citizens is contrary to the spirit of freedom and Christianity in America. 10 May 1834. p.73, c6.

1510 GEORGE BENSON *to* **BENJAMIN C. BACON, ESQ. 17 April 1834. Brooklyn, Ct.** The 82-year-old President of the New England AS will be unable to attend Bacon's meeting; gives some quotes from the debate in the British Parliament on slavery. 10 May 1834. p.74, c2.

1511 JUSTICE *to* **MR. EDITOR [W. L. GARRISON]. 22 February 1834. Philadelphia.** Criticizes white citizens of Connecticut for a recent memorial. 10 May 1834. p.74, c3.

1512 n.n. *to* **W. L. GARRISON, ESQ. 31 March 1834. Millbury.** Reports that the anti-slavery cause is gaining strength in his area and that people are beginning to lose their illusions about colonization; believes that the Declaration of Rights published by the AS converted many from colonization to abolition; adds that they will soon form a society. 10 May 1834. p.74, c3.

1513 ZORAH *to* **THEOPHILUS. n.d. n.p.** Describes a ride in the country during which he saw a company of slaves being moved by white "gentlemen"; sympathizes with the Negro men; describes the chains and clubs of the masters. 10 May 1834. p.74, c6.

1514 n.n. *to* **n.n. [extract] 24 March 1834. Port-au-Prince.** Reports that Chambers of Commerce in Havre and Bordeaux inquired about the relations between France and Haiti; learned that commerce between the two countries could be carried on without risk. 10 May 1834. p.75, c4.

1515 THOMAS MARSHALL *to* **MR. BARBER. 29 April 1834. Arlington.** Sends regrets that he cannot attend the Vermont anti-slavery convention; offers his cooperation and encouragement. 17 May 1834. p.77, c2.

1516 HENRY B. STANTON *to* **BROTHER LEAVITT. 22 April 1834. Lane Seminary, Walnut Hills, Oh.** Describes the internal slave trade as carried on in the Mississippi Valley; observes that the trade is brisker now than ever before; explains the reasons for the current high demand for slaves; describes emigration downriver and the resulting deprivations. 17 May 1834. p.77, c3.

1517 n.n. *to* **THE EDITOR [W. L. GARRISON]. 13 May 1834. Boston.** Describes the annual celebration of the Garrison Juvenile Society, including prayers and speeches on slavery and religion; reports on donations. 17 May 1834. p.79, c4.

1518 HENRY SIPKINS *to* **FELLOW CITIZENS. 25 March 1834. New York.** Reports on a convention of the Free People of Color to be held in New York in June; quotes extracts from the minutes. 17 May 1834. p.79, c6.

1519 n.n. *to* **THE EDITORS OF THE** *NEW YORK DAILY ADVERTISER.* **n.d. n.p.** Relates an anecdote about Daniel Webster. 17 May 1834. p.80, c4.

1520 T. S. R. *to* **RESPECTED FRIENDS. n.d. n.p.** Preaches that those who can observe the pleasures and privileges of Sabbath must remember and pray for those who have not their own freedom. 17 May 1834. p.80, c4.

1521 HENRY B. STANTON *to* **BROTHER LEAVITT. 22 April 1834. Lane Seminary, Walnut Hills, Oh.** [continued from 17 May 1834] Discusses the internal slave trade; describes the unspeakable cruelty of separation of families, physical mistreatment, and the lies and tricks used to sell slaves farther South. 24 May 1834. p.81, c3.

1522 WILLIAM JAY *to* **ELIZUR WRIGHT, JR. 19 April 1834. Bedford, N.Y.** Forwards a paper on slavery in the District of Columbia with a very short introductory note. 24 May 1834. p.81, c5.

1523 n.n. *to* **W. L. GARRISON. n.d. n.p.** Discusses letter from Rev. J. B. Pinney, colonial agent, to R. R. Gurley, secretary of the ACS; feels that the offense of the CS is in the adherence to error, rather than in the original commision of it; quotes extensively from the *African Repository* and criticizes it. 24 May 1834. p.83, c2.

1524 W. P. POWELL *to* **W. L. GARRISON. 13 May 1834. New Bedford.** Declares that it is a right and a duty to fellow brethren for those who believe that slavery and colonization tend to tyranny and anti-republicanism to speak against them; announces that the New Bedford Union Society has chosen Richard Johnson as its representative to the fourth annual convention of colored people. 24 May 1834. p.83, c4.

1525 C. PHELPS *to* **n.n. 12 May 1834. Wrentham.** Reports that Mrs. A. A. Phelps expresses gratitude for the memento from the Boston Female AS; donates fifteen dollars. 24 May 1834. p.83, c5.

1526 PHILO-BIBLOS *to* **THE EDITOR OF THE** *NEW ENGLAND TELEGRAPH.* **n.d. n.p.** Explains that the professed object of the American Bible Society is to give every destitute family a Bible, unless they refuse it, but that slaves are prevented by law from having a Bible; reports that the AS has offered five thousand dollars to help them give slaves Bibles; wonders what the Bible Society will decide to do. 31 May 1834. p.85, c3.

1527 JOEL BATTEY *to* **W. L. GARRISON. 13 May 1834. Starksborough.** Sends the preamble, the constitution, and a list of officers and counselors of the newly formed AS in Starksburg, Addison County, Vermont. 31 May 1834. p.85, c4.

1528 T. D. L. *to* **MR. EDITOR [W. L. GARRISON]. n.d. n.p.** Describes the recent meeting of the Connecticut CS; exposes the different purposes of the society in different parts of the country; paraphrases various speeches and reports; feels that if more of the society's secrets were revealed, it would collapse. 31 May 1834. p.86, c1.

1529 JOSHUA COFFIN *to* **THE EDITOR OF THE** *GENIUS OF UNIVERSAL EMANCIPATION.* **22 April 1834. Philadelphia.** Includes extracts from five or six letters by James Temple on the conditions in Liberia; Temple reports that Liberia is no place for anyone except the financially secure. 31 May 1834. p.87, c3.

1530 JAMES TEMPLE *to* **JACOB RHODES. [extract] n.d. Africa.** Reports that there are healthy natives, but claims that it is murder to send slaves to Liberia since even horses and dogs from America die with fever. 31 May 1834. p.87, c3.

1531 JAMES TEMPLE *to* **REV. THOMAS P. HUNT. [extract] n.d. Liberia.** Advises Hunt to remain in Philadephia; reports that there are too many preachers in Liberia and that it is expensive to live there. 31 May 1834. p.87, c3.

1532 JAMES TEMPLE *to* **THOMAS BLACK. [extract] n.d. Liberia.** Desires to return to the United States, but does not want to ruin his reputation. 31 May 1834. p.87, c3.

1533 JAMES TEMPLE *to* **THOMAS BLACK. [extract] n.d. Liberia.** Declares that Liberia is a place of misery; believes that the CS commits a greater sin than do slaveholders because the CS is murdering colored people by bringing them to Liberia. 31 May 1834. p.87, c3.

1534 JAMES TEMPLE *to* **n.n. [extract] n.d. Liberia.** Gives description of Africa; reports the presence of lawlessness, unrest, leopards, insects, and death "all around us." 31 May 1834. p.87, c3.

1535 JAMES TEMPLE *to* **MR. WILLIAMS. [extract] 1834. Liberia.** Complains that there are no comforts in Liberia; describes it as a "gloomy prison." 31 May 1834. p.87, c4.

1536 THOMAS W. JENKYN *to* **THE EDITOR OF THE** *NEW YORK EVANGELIST.* **[extract] n.d. Owestrey, Shropshire, England.** Wishes that the editor would introduce an anti-slavery department into his otherwise varied newspaper; reports that Liberia plans have failed in England; gives "A Parable for the Carolinas," a comparison between slavery in ancient Egypt and in the Southern United States. 31 May 1834. p.87, c4.

1537 ARCHIBALD BLACKLOCK *to* **n.n. [extract] 1 April 1834. Dumfries.** Describes the exhumation and examination of the poet Burns' skull; reports that they made a plaster cast of it. 31 May 1834. p.88, c2.

1538 J. M'COSH *to* **n.n. [extract] n.d. n.p.** Reports the loss of the *Lady Monroe,* a ship sunk off an island en route from Calcutta; adds that seventy-eight drowned and twenty-one survived. 31 May 1834. p.88, c3.

1539 A CORRESPONDENT AT THE WEST *to* **n.n. [extract] 12 December 1833. n.p.** Describes passage on a steamboat downriver from Cincinnati; reports that a slave driver brought four slaves on board and treated them cruelly; wonders how long the sin of slavery will exist in this land. 7 June 1834. p.89, c3.

1540 ROBERT B. HALL *to* **SAMUEL E. SEWALL. 22 May 1834. New Haven.** Regrets that he cannot attend the New England AS convention; supports them wholeheartedly; asserts that the meeting bears the responsibility of determining New England sentiment on slavery; stresses the importance of the monthly concert of prayer for colored people. 7 June 1834. p.89, c4.

1541 REV. SIMEON S. JOCELYN *to* **B. C. BACON, ESQ. 24 May 1834. New Haven.** Regrets his inability to attend the New England AS convention; rejoices at the spread of the Gospel and the growth of supporters of abolition; urges the watchword of immediate emancipation. 7 June 1834. p.89, c4.

1542 N. EMMONS *to* **MR. B. C. BACON. 25 April 1834. Franklin.** Regrets that he cannot attend the New England AS convention, but his extreme age prevents him from travelling long distances; sends his encouragement and prayers. 7 June 1834. p.89, c5.

1543 PLUTARCH *to* **MR. EDITOR [W. L. GARRISON]. 3 June 1834. New York.** Writes from the Convention of the Free People of Color as it is in session; tells who has given speeches and which resolutions have been passed. 7 June 1834. p.91, c6.

1544 THEODORE D. WELD *to* **JAMES HALL, EDITOR OF THE** *WESTERN MONTHLY MAGAZINE.* **n.d. n.p.** Replies to an article by Hall in the *Western Monthly Magazine* on the slavery discussions at Lane Seminary; rebukes Hall for misrepresentation and narrow-minded prejudice; counters each vague point with impressive statistics and a well-thought-out argument. 14 June 1834. p.93, c2.

1545 OBSERVER *to* **W. L. GARRISON. n.d. n.p.** Quotes from the *African Repository* a speech by Elliott Cresson in which he tries to show that the late Wilberforce was pro-colonizationist despite the protest against colonization which he signed on his deathbed; attacks this statement, believing that Wilberforce knew exactly what he was doing. 14 June 1834. p.93, c6.

1546 n.n. *to* **THE EDITOR [W. L. GARRISON]. 27 May 1834. New Haven.** Reports on speeches by Rev. Mr. Phelps and Mr. Thome; adds that, after a few disturbances, Mr. Bacon, a colonizationist, rose, agreed with most of the statements made by the abolitionists, and severely criticized the "Southern youngsters" for making the disturbances; feels that Bacon showed open-mindedness and courtesy. 14 June 1834. p.93, c6.

1547 ILLINOIS WINTER *to* **W. L. GARRISON. 15 May 1834. Andover.** Replies to Rev. P. R. Russell's claim that an overwhelming majority at his recent speech before the Lyceum voted with him against colonization; asserts that the voting was about even, possibly a bit higher for Russell. 14 June 1834. p.93, c6.

1548 JOSEPH A DUGDALE AND BENJAMIN B. DAVIS *to* **THE EDITOR [W. L. GARRISON]. May 1834. New Garden, Oh.** Report on a visit to the settlement of blacks in Lexington Township, Stark County; found them amazingly well off, comfortable, and industrious; report that they were glad they had not long been deceived by colonizationists. 14 June 1834. p.94, c2.

1549 JAMES HAMBLETON *to* **W. L. GARRISON. 9 April 1834. Spruce Vale, Oh.** Reports that the county is so removed from the scenes of slavery's oppression that apathy, forgetfulness, and ignorance prevail; states that many support colonization, but some ASS have been formed; encourages their correspondence. 14 June 1834. p.94, c3.

1550 M. B. *to* **MR. EDITOR [W. L. GARRISON]. n.d. n.p.** Believes that slaveholders are daily and hourly transgressing the natural laws of God; predicts that natural punishment will be inflicted on slaveholders and on the nation as long as they disobey those laws. 14 June 1834. p.94, c3.

1551 JOHN RANKIN, L. TAPPAN, AND E. WRIGHT, JR. *to* **W. L. GARRISON. 28 May 1834. Anti-Slavery Office, New York.** Claim that truth is the instrument by which the world will be renewed; ask Garrison to help them collect money on the Fourth of July and on the last Monday of every month. 14 June 1834. p.94, c4.

1552 n.n. *to* **THE EDITOR [W. L. GARRISON]. [extract] 14 May 1834. Philadelphia.** Reports that he went to hear a publicly announced colonization lecture, but that they would not allow spectators; longs to see apathy to the slave's condition shaken. 14 June 1834. p.95, c1.

1553 EDWIN P. ATLEE, ROBERT PURVIS, ISAAC PARRISH, JOSHUA COFFIN, W. L. GARRISON, H. B. STANTON, JAMES A. THOME, AND AMOS A. PHELPS *to* **CAPT. LEWIS DAVIS. 5 May 1834. Philadelphia.** Inform Capt. Davis that the undersigned were induced to patronize his boat because of his friendly disposition to the black; hope he will continue to act according to the individual's merit rather than his skin color. 14 June 1834. p.95, c3.

1554 BENJAMIN LUNDY *to* **n.n. [extract] n.d. n.p.** Rejoices at the change of public sentiment in the United States, slow though it is; urges anti-slavery workers on. 14 June 1834. p.95, c4.

1555 C. STUART *to* **MESSRS. GARRISON AND KNAPP. 13 June 1834. Boston.** Vindicates William Wilberforce, who he insists did not sign the "Protest" in the feebleness of illness, as charged; argues that he signed it after much inquiry and thought, while in perfect health. 14 June 1834. p.95, c5.

1556 PAR[?]NS *to* **THE EDITOR OF THE** *LONDON PATRIOT*. **n.d. n.p.** Asks if the information in "Sprague on Revivals" and the *Quarterly Review* is correct as to conditions in Liberia and the number of slaves in the United States. 21 June 1834. p.97, c2.

1557 CHARLES STUART *to* **THE EDITOR OF THE** *VERMONT CHRONICLE*. **3 June 1834. Concord, N.H.** Corrects the impression of him created by the *Vermont Chronicle;* reveals that the *Chronicle* had published only his few broad-minded compliments to the CS while omitting his more important accusations and criticisms. 21 June 1834. p.97, c5.

1558 A SPECTATOR *to* **SIR [W. L. GARRISON]. 24 May 1834. Middletown, Ct.** Reports that all meetinghouses are closed to anti-slavery groups; describes how mobs attacked the meeting to form an AS, insulted speakers, threw eggs, and chased one speaker who luckily escaped. 21 June 1834. p.97, c6.

1559 T. D. L. *to* **MR. EDITOR [W. L. GARRISON]. n.d. n.p.** Discusses the adjourned meeting of the Connecticut CS; describes Rev. Dr. Hewitt's speech supporting the CS and countering the main objections to it. 21 June 1834. p.98, c1.

1560 J. H. LEROY *to* **W. L. GARRISON. 13 June 1834. Concord.** Reports that the "fanatics" have been among them, wonderfully disturbing the peace of their community by calling for equal rights; tells of a speech by Capt. Charles Stuart, resolutions, and a debate. 21 June 1834. p.98, c5.

1561 GEO. L. LEROW *to* **MESSRS. GARRISON AND KNAPP. 22 May 1834. Waterville.** Reports on the number of members in the new Waterville AS; includes their resolutions. 21 June 1834. p.98, c6.

1562 JAMES TEMPLE *to* **A PHYSICIAN IN BOSTON. [from the** *Philadelphian***] 21 March 1834. Africa.** Reports that white as well as black men live in Africa; observes that school children are smarter there and that some in the colony live in luxury while others suffer. 21 June 1834. p.99, c2.

1563 n.n. *to* **THE EDITOR [W. L. GARRISON]. n.d. n.p.** Feels provoked and ashamed that Garrison notices the *Vermont Chronicle;* accuses the editor of that paper of splitting hairs on clear-cut questions. 21 June 1834. p.99, c5.

1564 W. L. GARRISON *to* **THE EDITOR OF THE** *BOSTON COURIER*. **n.d. n.p.** Writes because of an erroneous letter in the *Courier,* purportedly by a defender of the anti-slavery cause; believes that no compensation is due any slaveholder for liberating his slaves; quotes the Anti-Slavery Convention Declaration as supporting evidence. 21 June 1834. p.99, c6.

1565 JOHN G. WHITTIER *to* **E. WRIGHT, JR. 3 June 1834. Haverhill.** Reports that he just returned from the New England AS convention; presents cheering evidence of the growing strength of the cause; tells of inspiring people at the convention and of the emotional intensity of some of the speeches. 21 June 1834. p.100, c2.

1566 n.n. *to* **n.n. 9 June 1834. Washington.** States that he just left Mr. Ewing of the Senate reading the report on post office affairs; admits that he is embarrassed for his countrymen; asserts that the post office is corrupt and deficient; wonders how much longer Americans will submit to this outrage. 21 June 1834. p.100, c4.

1567 J. COFFIN *to* **W. L. GARRISON. 17 June 1834. Philadelphia.** Account of recent colonization meetings; reports that no speakers explained how American ignorance, pollution, and crime will be transformed into Christianity and civilization by a mere change of location for the Negroes; states that they recognize that either anti-slavery or colonization efforts can be successful, but not both. 28 June 1834. p.102, c1.

1568 ARNOLD BUFFUM *to* **FRIENDS. 20 June 1834. Philadelphia.** Regrets that colonization meetings are held so frequently in an attempt to choke abolitionism to death; charges colonizationists with working in ignorance of the truth; urges abolitionists not to be meek or modest, but to fight. 28 June 1834. p.102, c1.

1569 GEORGE W. LIGHT *to* **THE EDITOR [W. L. GARRISON]. n.d. n.p.** Favors the colony of Liberia; believes that the CS is made up of men who err; states that he does not believe that the colony has anything to do with slavery; supports total and immediate abolition. 28 June 1834. p.102, c2.

1570 P. R. RUSSELL *to* **W. L. GARRISON. 20 June 1834. West Boylston.** Defends himself against the charges of "Illinois Winter" that he reported the results of a public debate incorrectly; forwards a statement signed by ten people asserting that Russell's report was correct. 28 June 1834. p.102, c3.

1571 E. B. *to* **MR. EDITOR [W. L. GARRISON]. n.d. n.p.** Condemns the influential gentlemen of the anti-slavery meeting in Cambridge who sanctioned the doctrine of compensation to slaveholders; feels that compensation means recognizing that a wrong has been committed, but believes that the slaveholder is wrong to have slaves, and is not wronged in giving them freedom. 28 June 1834. p.102, c3.

1572 JEMES DINNEY *to* **n.n. 16 April 1834. Muckleburgh, Oh.** Inarticulate, possibly farcical, account of a meeting and debate between abolitionists and colonizationists; states that colonizationists spoke first and so disrupted the meeting that the abolitionists quit; adds that he and most area residents support colonization. 28 June 1834. p.102, c4.

1573 LUCIUS KINGMAN *to* **W. L. GARRISON. 23 June 1834. North Bridgewater.** Announces an anti-slavery address on the Fourth of July; reports that the Fourth of July speech has always suported colonization, but that the people are catching on and the colonizationists only collected two dollars last year. 28 June 1834. p.103, c3.

1574 n.n. *to* **MEN AND BRETHREN. 23 June 1834. Albany.** Anticipates the approaching day of liberty; feels sad that Americans are misguided by colonizationists. 28 June 1834. p.103, c3.

1575 n.n. *to* **SIR [W. L. GARRISON]. 24 June 1834. Cambridge.** Replies to an article in the *Courier* on the last Cambridge AS meeting; denies that they disclaimed connection with Garrison and Buffum. 28 June 1834. p.103, c5.

1576 X *to* **MR. EDITOR [W. L. GARRISON]. n.d. n.p.** Expresses outrage that the wax representation of the Lord's Supper on display at the Masonic Temple is now open on Sunday evening. 28 June 1834. p.104, c4.

1577 A TRAVELLER *to* **MR. PRINTERS. [from the** *New York Commercial Advertiser***] 6 May 1834. New York.** Describes his travels last year in Britain, frequently following the path where Dr. C---- had been giving his "Anti-Christian, Anti-Scriptural, Anti-Orthodox language and opinions"; reports that most British supported universal abolition and thought that Dr. C---- was mad; adds that Dr. C---- has since revised his views. 5 July 1834. p.105, c1.

1578 N. *to* **MR. EDITOR [W. L. GARRISON]. n.d. n.p.** Replies to an article by the editor of the *Ohio Observer;* argues that just because papers insert occasional articles on slavery, they are not therefore abolition presses; says that no compromise is being reached, but that colonizationists are switching to anti-slavery. 5 July 1834. p.105, c2.

1579 A CONSTANT READER *to* **MR. EDITOR [W. L. GARRISON]. 25 June 1834. North Berwick.** Expresses shock that the philanthropic cause of anti-slavery should meet with opposition; trusts that things will improve; urges hope in God. 5 July 1834. p.107. c1.

1580 A TRUE-HEARTED AND DEVOTED ABOLITIONIST IN OHIO *to* **W. L. GARRISON. n.d. Ohio.** Sends encouragement and love; reports that he has pleaded the cause for the past ten years and has gained many adversaries; assumes that most other supporters are too timid to come out in public; lectures to black people to help them elevate themselves; encourages other abolitionists to persevere. 5 July 1834. p.107, c2.

1581 n.n. *to* **THE EDITOR OF THE** *NEW YORK EVANGELIST.* **13 June 1834. Washington, D.C.** Reports that several bills on slavery in the District of Columbia were postponed; announces that finally one has been passed 106 to 47 with 80 abstaining; adds that the House of Representatives has directly sanctioned the introduction and existence of slavery in the District of Columbia. 5 July 1834. p.107, c4.

1582 W. E. *to* **MR. EDITOR [W. L. GARRISON]. n.d. n.p.** Describes a town in Middlesex where a non-religious tavern keeper banished rum and spirits from the bar; reports that he later sold the tavern to members of the Orthodox Church who refurnished the bar with spirits; questions the consistency of such men. 5 July 1834. p.108, c5.

1583 UNION *to* **MESSRS. MILLER AND BREWSTER. n.d. n.p.** Believes that there is no wise plan for the emancipation of slaves because setting them free would mean leaving them to starve or to become paupers and thieves. 12 July 1834. p.109, c1.

1584 F. *to* **MR. EDITOR [W. L. GARRISON]. 3 July 1834. n.p.** Believes that when the public and the law have sanctioned the investiture of any kind of property, they cannot then destroy that sytem without some indemnity; counters arguments frequently advanced by abolitionists against compensation. 12 July 1834. p.109, c2.

1585 CHARLES W. DENISON *to* **W. L. GARRISON. 20 June 1834. New York.** Tells of attending the nineteenth anniversary of the Hudson River Baptist Association; reports that the resolution for a committee to investigate giving Bibles to every colored family was rejected this year, but that it raised important moral questions. 12 July 1834. p.109, c4.

1586 J. H. LEROY *to* **W. L. GARRISON. 20 June 1834. Concord.** Recounts a discussion he had with colonizationists; reports that some colonizationists realize that the society will not end slavery or send all blacks to Africa, but support it because it is the only group working to help blacks; feels that such candid gentlemen will soon be abolitionists; adds that other colonizationists refused to answer questions or debate. 12 July 1834. p.109, c5.

1587 S. C. *to* **W. L. GARRISON n.d. n.p.** Believes that it is now accepted that slavery is wrong and that the only debate is how best to remedy the evil; observes that most editors support gradual abolition and fear immediate abolition without expatriation; proposes as an amendment to gradual emancipation that slaveholders exchange places with slaves until universal emancipation can be safely and justly effected. 12 July 1834. p.110, c1.

1588 A FRIEND IN AUGUSTA, MAINE *to* **n.n. [extract] n.d. Augusta, Me.** Congratulates him on the success of the cause in the past year; regretfully reports that abolition is not very important to people in his area; hopes a powerful lecturer will come to inspire thought on the subject and to create more friends of human liberty. 12 July 1834. p.110, c2.

1589 CHARLES W. DENISON *to* **n.n. 6 July 1834. Temperance House.** Believes editors should state that the abolitionists present at the Chatham Street church oppose any resort to violence. 12 July 1834. p.111, c6.

1590 ARTHUR TAPPAN AND JOHN RANKIN *to* **n.n. 14 July 1834. n.p.** Disclaim the desire to encourage interracial marriage; enclose a hand-bill encouraging resistance to laws and intentions to dissolve the Union. 19 July 1834. p.114, c6.

1591 BISHOP BENJ. T. ONDERDONKE *to* **REV. PETER WILLIAMS. 12 July 1834. College Place.** Regrets that Williams had to close his church; urges him to disclaim all connections with the AS and to make public his resignation. 19 July 1834. p.115, c1.

1592 REV. PETER WILLIAMS *to* **THE CITIZENS OF NEW YORK. 14 July 1834. New York.** As directed by his bishop, he renounces his membership on the board of directors of the AAS; gives reasons for not supporting colonization. 19 July 1834. p.115, cl.

1593 LIBERTAS *to* **THE EDITOR OF THE** *COURIER.* **n.d. n.p.** Reports that none of the prominent abolitionists in New England favor intermarriage between blacks and whites. 26 July 1834. p.117, c2.

1594 W. M. RICHARDS *to* **W. L. GARRISON. 24 June 1834. Auburn Theological Seminary.** Sends the preamble and constitution of the AS lately formed in the Auburn Theological Seminary. 26 July 1834. p.117, c3.

1595 AMOS A. PHELPS *to* **W. L. GARRISON. 17 July 1834. Boston.** Corrects the report of a riot at Norwich, Connecticut; forwards the constitution of the Ladies AS formed recently; charges that not one of the facts presented on the mob is true; claims that there was no lecture, no riot, and no mob that evening. 26 July 1834. p.117, c5.

1596 AN ESTEEMED COLORED FRIEND IN NEW BEDFORD *to* **n.n. [extract] n.d. New Bedford.** Notes that a planter, who just arrived from Georgia, intends to liberate and educate his slaves. 26 July 1834. p.117, c6.

1597 CHARLES W. DENISON *to* **W. L. GARRISON. 27 June 1834. New York.** Reports that he is presently confined to his tasks in the city; tells of his own lectures in "The Five Points"; states that he is compiling a history of free people of color in the United States and writing a book opposing theaters. 26 July 1834. p.117, c6.

1598 ARTHUR TAPPAN, JOHN RANKIN, E. WRIGHT, JR., JOSHUA LEAVITT, W. GOODELL, LEWIS TAPPAN, AND SAMUEL E. CORNISH *to* **THE HON. CORNELIUS W. LAWRENCE [MAYOR OF NEW YORK CITY]. 17 July 1834. New York.** As members of the executive committee of the AS, they wish to demonstrate that they have done nothing inconsistent with their duties as patriots, citizens, and Christians; defend anti-slavery; attack colonization. 26 July 1834. p.119, cl.

1599 REV. MR. FROST *to* **W. L. GARRISON n.d. n.p.** Supplements remarks on his speech at the New England AS convention; replies to slaveholders' charges that anti-slavery men never define their terms and indiscriminately condemn slaveholders; defines slavery, slaveholder, and slave. 2 August 1834. p.122, cl.

1600 B. *to* **MR. EDITOR [W. L. GARRISON]. n.d. n.p.** Replies to a criticism of his article against compensation for slaveholders; believes that slaves have value because they are the cheapest mode of labor available to the Southern planter; adds that slaves are valuable also as breeders for a market. 2 August 1834. p.122, c3.

1601 J. H. LEROY *to* **THE EDITOR OF THE** *BOSTON COMMERCIAL GAZETTE.* **19 July 1834. Concord, N.H.** Disapproves of the editor's description of the late riots in New York; does not believe they should be termed "anti-slavery riots"; argues that the abolitionists were exercising their right to freedom of speech and that abolitionists never condone violence or riots. 2 August 1834. p.122, c4.

1602 A COLORED FRIEND IN BALTIMORE *to* **FRIEND [W. L. GARRISON]. [extract] n.d. Baltimore.** Sympathizes with abolitionists more than ever because their houses and lives are endangered by mobs; expresses surprise and contempt for the courts in New York; prays that abolitionists may be preserved. 2 August 1834. p.122, c5.

1603 n.n. *to* **W. L. GARRISON. 23 July 1834. New Haven.** States that his opinions on slavery have completely turned around since visiting the North; requests a subscription to the *Liberator* in order to learn still more. 2 August 1834. p.122, c6.

1604 CHARLES GREENE *to* **W. L. GARRISON. 18 July 1834. Hartford.** Encloses a letter which was written to the editors of the *Christian Adovcate and Journal,* but refused by them. 2 August 1834. p.122, c6.

1605 A METHODIST *to* **THE EDITORS OF THE** *CHRISTIAN ADVOCATE AND JOURNAL.* **30 June 1834. Hartford.** Disagrees with the *Advocate*'s reports of the New York riots: criticizes a paragraph from one of the *Advocate*'s issues. 2 August 1834. p.122, c6.

1606 H. G. LUDLOW *to* **THE EDITORS OF THE** *NEW YORK JOURNAL OF COMMERCE.* **25 July 1834. n.p.** Insists that he opposes the amalgamation of white and black people, that he has never attended an interracial marriage ceremony, and that he never wishes to; also apologizes for his remark to an AS meeting. 9 August 1834. p.125, c6.

1607 EFFINGHAM L. CAPRON *to* **THE EDITOR OF THE** *MASSACHUSETTS SPY.* **19 July 1831. Uxbridge.** Endorses "Disclaimer" published in New York; opposes marriages between colored and white people; considers this subject distinct from abolition; states that the AS is based on principles of non-resistance. 9 August 1834. p.126, c3.

1608 n.n. *to* **W. L. GARRISON. n.d. n.p.** Sends five advertisements taken from a recent *Washington Globe* so that more people will know and fight the slave-trade existing in the seat of our government. 9 August 1834. p.126, c4.

1609 S. C. *to* **W. L. GARRISON. n.d. n.p.** Announces another decisive reason for rejecting immediate abolition; discusses the general indolence of slaveholders who are used to being waited on; suggests that these slaveholders be forced to work awhile, so they will not starve to death when their slaves are gone. 9 August 1834. p.126, c5.

1610 BROTHERLY LOVE *to* **MR. EDITOR [W. L. GARRISON]. n.d. n.p.** Reports on a colonization meeting in New Hampshire; relates what was said about anti-slavery. 9 August 1834. p.126, c6.

1611 JAMES FISKE *to* **MR. EDITOR [W. L. GARRISON]. [extract] 4 August 1834. West Boylston.** Asserts that Rev. Mr. Russell and he did not agree on the statement although R. claims that they did. 9 August 1834. p.127, cl.

1612 A HEARER *to* **MR. EDITOR [W. L. GARRISON]. n.d n.p.** Criticizes Mr. Blagden's conduct at the Salem Street Church last Sabbath; examines the reasoning behind Blagden's sermons defending colonization; charges that Blagden refuses to fill public appointment and retires to his own pulpit to speak. 9 August 1834. p.127, cl.

1613 JAMES G. BIRNEY *to* **REV. THORNTON J. MILLS. 15 July 1834. Mercer County.** Resigns from the post of vice-president of the Kentucky CS because his feelings about colonization have changed; explains that he does not impugn the motives of colonizationists. 16 August 1834. p.129, cl.

1614 J. COFFIN *to* **FRIENDS. 21 July 1834. Philadelphia.** Believes that persecution always strengthens the cause it was designed to crush, and that selfishness, like that of the New York mobsters, always defeats its own purpose; gives examples of persecution leading to new ideas and new countries. 16 August 1834. p.132, c4.

1615 n.n. *to* **SIR [W. L. GARRISON]. 7 August 1834. Groton.** Describes a meeting held by Mr. Breckinridge; reports that the turnout was very small and Breckinridge spoke well but, as it was for a bad cause, the effect was minimal; charges that his speech was calculated to incite the crowd to repeat the New York riots against abolition. 16 August 1834. p.132, c5.

1616 X. *to* **W. L. GARRISON. n.d. n.p.** Includes a quote from the *Alabama Advertiser* illustrating the abuse and slander suffered by abolitionists; claims that such language can only help the cause. 23 August 1834. p.133, cl.

1617 B. F. *to* **W. L. GARRISON. 18 August 1834. Boston.** Strongly admires Hon. J. G. Birney's letter, published in the last issue of the *Liberator*; sends money for copies of Birney's letter to be sent to all clergymen in Boston. 23 August 1834. p.133, c2.

1618 VERITAS *to* **MR. EDITOR [W. L. GARRISON]. n.d. n.p.** Quotes Mr. Beecher on colonization as a form of redress for the wrongs of Africa; criticizes the inconsistencies in Beecher's views; quotes the governor of the colony, who says that, as yet, nothing has been done for the natives; argues that gunpowder and rum have not encouraged peace and a Christian influence. 23 August 1834. p.133, c2.

1619 A CONSTANT READER *to* **MR. EDITOR [W. L. GARRISON]. 5 August 1834. North Berwick, Me.** Wonders whether the recent riots indicate that the country is headed toward despotism or anarchy; believes that opposition to abolition, an enterprise so obviously in accordance with Christian principles, is untenable. 23 August 1834. p.133, c3.

1620 n.n. *to* **W. L. GARRISON. 16 August 1834. Academical and Theological Institution, New Hampton, N.H.** Reports success in the institution; believes that no one there still supports the ACS; adds that the town meetinghouse was refused them, but that they met elsewhere and formed an AS. 23 August 1834. p.135, cl.

1621 P. R. RUSSELL *to* **MR. EDITOR [W. L. GARRISON]. 14 August 1834. West Boylston.** Counters the report of Illinois Winter on a debate between the AS and the CS; reminds Garrison that he presented an affidavit supporting himself with several signatures while Winter's was signed by only one. 23 August 1834. p.135, cl.

1622 ROBERT PURVIS *to* **W. L. GARRISON. 13 July 1834. London.** Reports that black skin is favored in Britain and that abolitionists there are shocked at the CS's charge that Wilberforce was not in possession of his mental faculties when he signed the protest; describes a discussion with Daniel O'Connell. 23 August 1834. p.135, c2.

1623 A HIGHLY RESPECTABLE MEMBER OF THE BAR IN NEW HAMPSHIRE *to* **n.n. [extract] n.d. n.p.** Hopes that Mr. Birney's letter will finally kill colonization; feels impatient that colonization still has some power; believes that Garrison is reproached for harshness of expression, when he is really too tame and gentle. 23 August 1834. p.135, c5.

1624 n.n. *to* **THE EDITORS OF THE** *RICHMOND WHIG.* **15 August 1834. Boydton, Mecklenburg.** Reports a rumored insurrection among the slaves in the Boydton area and in Georgia; suspects it of being a mere abolitionist trick since both dates reported are the same. 30 August 1834. p.139, cl.

1625 S. H. *to* **W. L. GARRISON. 15 August 1834. Boston.** Corrects the statement that the Rev. Breckinridge supports blasphemy; reports that he is an anti-slavery man and regrets the charge because it cannot be proved and because some colonizationists are benevolently motivated. 30 August 1834. p.139, c4.

1626 J. C. B. *to* **THE EDITOR [W. L. GARRISON]. n.d. n.p.** Describes the female literary societies of color in Philadelphia; reports that there are two and that both have increased in number and popularity, and have improved their mental faculties; praises the presidents. 30 August 1834. p.139, c5.

1627 THE LATE SIR JAMES MACKINTOSH *to* **n.n. n.d. n.p.** Eulogizes his late wife, and praises her influence on him. 30 August 1834. p.140, c4.

1628 GEORGE SHEPERD *to* **MR. LEWIS TAPPAN. 21 June 1834. Hallowell.** Explains that he cannot remember who is treasurer of the AAS; submits contributions totaling eighty dollars; reports that no money went to the CS that season. 6 September 1834. p.141, c2.

1629 C. V. CAPLES *to* **MR. EDITOR [W. L. GARRISON]. n.d. n.p.** Wonders by what rule the Rev. A. Stevens referred to Boston Colored Infant School pupils as "little Africans"; argues that, by the same logic, white children in New England are little Englishmen, Scotchmen, and Swiss. 6 September 1834. p.143, c4.

1630 H. *to* **THE EDITOR OF THE** *NEW YORK TRUTH.* **n.d. n.p.** Questions certain "insults" whites have received at the hands of colored people; mentions colored men passing by the inside of the curb, instead of the outside, as an example. 6 September 1834. p.144, c3.

1631 TRUTH *to* **MR. EDITOR [W. L. GARRISON]. n.d. n.p.** Warns that whoever attempts to correct the errors of his race attempts a thankless, discouraging, Herculean task; adds that he will get no reward, but must return curses with kindnesses. 6 September 1834. p.144, c5.

1632 LINDLEY COATES *to* **THE EDITOR [W. L. GARRISON]. 1 September 1834. Sadsbury, Pa.** Reports that an AS formed by residents of Lancaster and Chester counties has been operating for two years; encloses the preamble and constitution. 13 September 1834. p.145, c3.

1633 A CORRESPONDENT OF THE *NEW YORK OBSERVER* *to* **MESSRS. EDITORS. 8 August 1834. St. George, Bermuda.** Characterizes the First of August in Bermuda; describes early morning celebration and prayer, public thanksgiving, and prayer meetings; believes that the peacefulness can be attributed to the influence of Sunday schools; previously feared that the day might provoke over-excitement among liberated slaves. 13 September 1834. p.145, c5.

1634 ANTI-SLAVERY *to* **THE EDITOR OF THE** *NORTH STAR.* **n.d. n.p.** Describes Mrs. Malcom, whose department at Sunday school is comprised of Negroes; reports that she sought them throughout the city because she believes that they have an intellectual energy which needs release from oppression; urges all Christian women to empathize with oppressed Africans. 13 September 1834. p.146, c3.

1635 BALAAM'S ASS *to* **THE EDITOR OF THE** *GENIUS OF UNIVERSAL EMANCIPATION.* **n.d. n.p.** Wonders at the hypocrisy of professed Christians who will not accept colored people in their churches; tells of a congregation which insisted that a colored man either move to the back corner or leave in the middle of a service. 13 September 1834. p. 146, c3.

1636 G. THOMPSON *to* **PRUDENCE CRANDALL. 27 March 1834. Aldermanbury, London.** Writes that he has witnessed a deep sympathy for her, because of the persecution she has suffered, and an admiration for her ideals and courage; forwards some books and a plate as a testimonial from the women of Britain. 13 September 1834. p.146, c4.

1637 MARY W. MOLINE *to* **PRUDENCE CRANDALL. 11 March 1834. London.** Declares that she and her English sisters sympathize with and support Crandall; they send Crandall a small book. 13 September 1834. p.146, c4.

1638 LYDIA MOLINE *to* **PRUDENCE CRANDALL. 6 March 1834. London.** Wonders why the citizens of Canterbury are not ashamed to stop Crandall from teaching brethren of color; wishes she could help her; adds that she and her sister Mary send her the *Life of Miss Graham*. 13 September 1834. p.146, c5.

1639 MARY ANNE ERSKINE *to* **PRUDENCE CRANDALL. 5 March 1834. Edinburgh.** Hopes that Crandall will honor the ladies of Edinburgh by accepting a Bible and concordance as a testimony of their admiration; sends sympathy and support. 13 September 1834. p. 146, c5.

1640 MARY ANNE ERSKINE *to* **MISS CRANDALL. 7 March 1835. Edinburgh.** Writes for members of the committee of the Edinburgh Ladies' Emancipation Society who admire Crandall's conduct in teaching colored females; reports that they sympathize with Crandall's sufferings and rejoice in her perseverance. 13 September 1834. p.146, c6.

1641 A. AND E. BLAIR *to* **MISS CRANDALL. 27 February 1834. Wilbeck St.** Send a pincushion as a small token of Christian regard and admiration for her noble exertion in the cause of humanity. 13 September 1834. p.146, c6.

1642 REBECCA WATERHOUSE *to* **MISS CRANDALL. 25 March 1834. Liverpool.** Sends a small work bag, suggesting that its contents and other trifles be distributed among Crandall's young pupils; adds that it was prepared by Waterhouse and her children, who admire Crandall and her brave work. 13 September 1834, p. 146, c6.

1643 JANE AND CAROLINE BLAIR *to* **MISS CRANDALL. 7 March 1834. Bathwick Hill.** Send her a pen-wiper and pincushion which they made; hope that she will accept them. 13 September 1834. p. 146, c6.

1644 A DEVOTED ABOLITIONIST IN ENGLAND *to* **n.n. [extract] n.d. England.** Commends the National Anti-Slavery Declaration as eloquent, impressive, and convincing; expresses astonishment that Elliott Cresson is persevering; intends to acquire a written refutation of Cresson's statement on the Wilberforce protest from men who knew Wilberforce well at that time. 13 September 1834. p.147, c2.

1645 S. MORSE *to* **THE EDITOR [W. L. GARRISON]. 8 September 1834. New Hampton Institution.** Corrects statements by an anonymous writer; claims that the parson is not a staunch colonizationist and did not impel the trustees of the town meetinghouse to refuse it to abolitionists; contends that the new AS is much smaller than the anonymous writer had indicated. 20 September 1834. p.149, c3.

1646 F. *to* **THE EDITOR OF THE** *NEW YORK JOURNAL OF COMMERCE.* **n.d. n.p.** Believes that the ''late excitement'' was caused partly by the society of abolitionists and partly by Abner Kneeland, the infidel; states that the former struck at the prejudices and the latter at the root of the social system; criticizes the editor of the paper for exploiting the passions of the mob. 20 September 1834. p.149, c6.

1647 J. *to* **THE** *NEW YORK JOURNAL OF COMMERCE.* **18 August 1834. New York.** Censures the recent riots; poses questions on the preservation of public peace and suggests measures to help counteract the recent apathy of many citizens. 20 September 1834. p.150, c2.

1648 A DEVOTED FEMALE PHILANTHROPIST IN THIS STATE *to* **FRIEND [W. L. GARRISON]. [extract] 30 August 1834. Massachusetts.** Sends clothing for destitute children; describes the charitable meetings and projects of her family; wishes that colonization speakers would do something besides preach in order to earn their support. 20 September 1834. p.150, c6.

1649 C. F. DURANT *to* **THE EDITORS OF THE MORNING PAPERS. 14 September 1834. Tremont House, Boston.** Describes his twelfth aerial voyage. 20 September 1834. p.151, c5.

1650 A CONSTANT READER *to* **MR. EDITOR [W. L. GARRISON]. 17 September 1834. North Berwick, Me.** Counters several assumptions made by opponents of immediate emancipation; declares that most opposition is founded on "gross, palpable error." 27 September 1834. p.155, cl.

1651 MEDICUS *to* **MR. EDITOR [W. L. GARRISON]. n.d. n.p.** Quotes a passage from Dr. Smith's *Anatomical Class Book* which clearly shows Smith to be a racist because he claims that all pictures of Negroes look alike and that their features cannot display dignity or intelligence. 27 September 1834. p.155, c2.

1652 WESTERN GRAVES *to* **W. L. GARRISON. 4 September 1834. Toronto, Upper Canada.** Declares that he has reached British soil, and that he has no desire to return; reports that no people in Canada are classified by their color. 27 September 1834. p.155, c2.

1653 REV. JOHN SCOBLE *to* **ARNOLD BUFFUM. 6 June 1834. London.** Initiates correspondence with Buffum, and forwards abolitionist newspapers to him; declares that slavery is a crime, and that the English cannot comprehend the cruelty of Americans; sends his support and encouragement. 27 September 1834. p.155, c4.

1654 JAMES G. BIRNEY *to* **THE MINISTERS AND ELDERS OF THE PRESBYTERIAN CHURCH IN KENTUCKY. 2 September 1834. Mercer County.** Discusses characteristics of slavery; criticizes the Church's excuses for not urging abolition; discusses the consequences of immediate emancipation. 4 October 1834. p.157, c2.

1655 JAMES G. BIRNEY *to* **MR. WILLIAM GOODELL [EDITOR OF THE *EMANCIPATOR*]. 7 September 1834. Danville, Ky.** Corrects some mistakes in Goodell's preface to one of Birney's letters; states that he was never solicitor general in Alabama, or seated on the bench of the Supreme Court in that state, or formally offered a professorship at Centre College. 4 October 1834. p.158, c5.

1656 CHRISTIAN PHILANTHROPIST *to* **W. L. GARRISON. 2 September 1834. A-----.** Discusses the evangelization of Africa from an anti-slavery point of view; encourages pious missionaries and true Christian colonies in Africa to spread the Gospel. 4 October 1834. p.159, cl.

1657 SEWALL HARDING *to* **THE ANTI-SLAVERY CONVENTION, CONVENED AT GROTON. 30 September 1834. Waltham.** Regrets that he cannot attend; sends sympathy to the cause and prayers for success. 11 October 1834. p. 162, c6.

1658 JOHN G. WHITTIER *to* **AMOS FARNSWORTH. 27 September 1834. Haverhill.** Fears that he will not be able to attend the anti-slavery convention at Middlesex; rejoices to see the movement growing in the county; discusses the present stance of Massachusetts on the subject of slavery. 11 October 1834. p.162, c6.

1659 A CORRESPONDENT *to* **THE** *NEW YORK OBSERVER*. **1 August 1834. London.** Declares this is a proud day for Britain, but a humiliating one for America; announces that 800,000 former British slaves are slaves no more, proving to the world that Africans, wherever found, have a right to be free; believes this should be a warning to America. 11 October 1834. p.163, c2.

1660 SAMUEL J. MAY *to* **THE EDITORS OF THE** *CHRISTIAN EXAMINER*. **10 August 1834. Brooklyn.** Criticizes reviewer of Prof. Palfrey's sermon respecting abolitionists; discusses the "real sentiments and purposes of abolitionists," admitting that some measures used by abolitionists are ill-advised; poses questions to reviewer. 18 October 1834. p.165, cl.

1661 REV. O. S. MURRAY *to* **THE EDITORS OF THE** *VERMONT STATE JOURNAL*. **22 September 1834. Burlington.** Relates harassing experience he endured while attempting to deliver an anti-slavery speech; questions freedom of speech in Vermont. 18 October 1834. p.166, cl.

1662 OMICRON *to* **THE EDITOR OF THE** *CHRISTIAN MIRROR*. **n.d. n.p.** Relates anecdote concerning a man who thought that slavery did not exist in America; decries public ignorance concerning slavery; calls for public education on the subject. 18 October 1834. p.166, c2.

1663 BEZA *to* **THE EDITOR OF THE** *NEW ENGLAND TELEGRAPH*. **n.d. n.p.** Informs that many believe that if slavery is a sin, then immediate emancipation is a duty; asserts that it is always safe to stop sinning, so emancipation must be safe. 18 October 1834. p.166, c3.

1664 C. STUART *to* **THE EDITOR OF THE** *ROCHESTER LITERARY ENQUIRER*. **30 September 1834. Buffalo.** States that he heard that the trustees of the church where he was to speak had been threatened by a mob, so the trustees had decided to close the church; reminds him that outrage and persecution only encourage and strengthen the cause. 18 October 1834. p.166, c4.

1665 DR. JOHN BOWRING *to* **ONE OF HIS FRIENDS IN THIS COUNTRY. [extract] 9 August 1834. Paris.** Believes the slavery question is the opprobrium of the United States, and that one must labor in order to rid the commonwealth of infirmities. 18 October 1834. p.166, c6.

1666 BETA SIGMA *to* **THE EDITORS OF THE** *METHODIST ADVOCATE AND JOURNAL*. **n.d. n.p.** A Methodist preacher for twenty-six years affirms his love of liberty and equal rights grieves that their pages are shut to the discussion of slavery; declares that slavery is not just evil, but that is a sin; hopes all will work to "hunt this dragon from our shores." 18 October 1834. p.166, c6.

1667 AMOS A. PHELPS *to* **W. L. GARRISON. 13 October 1834. Portland.** Describes George Thompson's arrival and visit in Portland; gives an account of his eloquent speech and the audience's reaction. 18 October 1834. p.167, c2.

1668 L. *to* **THE EDITOR OF THE** *BOSTON WHIG*. **n.d. n.p.** States that proceedings of the past year were marked by violence and outrage, and showed no regard for the supremacy of the law; asks what happened to the boasted land of freedom; blames the present administration as the primary cause. 18 October 1834. p.168, c2.

1669 CYRUS PITT GROSVENOR *to* **THE SECOND BAPTIST CHURCH IN SALEM. 12 September 1834. Salem.** Believes it his duty to resign the pastoral office of the Baptist church in Salem because of his health and because he feels that many are alienated and angered by his strong anti-slavery sentiments. 18 October 1834. p.168, c4.

1670 THE TRUSTEES OF THE NOYES ACADEMY *to* **THE AMERICAN PUBLIC. 11 September 1834. Canaan, N.H.** State that they have decided to admit colored students also; justify the change according to the law; announce that it is their wish to remove unnatural pressure from "the colored portion of our fellow citizens." 25 October 1834. p.169, c2.

1671 BROTHERS AND ALLIES [BRITISH ABOLITIONISTS] *to* **PRESIDENT, SENATE, REPRESENTATIVES, AND THE PEOPLE OF AMERICA GENERALLY. n.d. n.p.** Exalt in their principles of liberty and equal rights in the common heritage between Britain and America; remind them that slavery is a crime before God; discuss their own realization of the sin and the measures used to redress it. 25 October 1834. p.169, c3.

1672 AMOS. A. PHELPS *to* **W. L. GARRISON. 17 October 1834. Hallowell.** Corrects his statement concerning a resolution passed by a body of clergymen in Portland; explains that the resolution opposed preaching by foreign agents, whether colonizationists or abolitionists, in Maine. 25 October 1834. p.170, c3.

1673 Z. *to* **MR. EDITOR [W. L. GARRISON]. n.d. n.p.** Wonders if the only method for direct abolition is to enlighten the minds of the oppressed victims; theorizes that a free mind will throw off the chains of the body. 25 October 1834. p.170, c3.

1674 GEORGE THOMPSON *to* **W. L. GARRISON. 28 October 1834. Portland, Me.** Sketches his eastern tour, providing a description of his impressions of New England and a very brief itinerary of the past sixteen days; urges the cause onward. 1 November 1834. p.175, c2.

1675 n.n. *to* **GARRISON AND KNAPP. 27 October 1834. Newton.** Encloses one dollar; wishes he could send more, but is in "untoward circumstances"; hopes other delinquent subscribers will follow suit. 1 November 1834. p.175, c5.

1676 JAMES APPLETON, JR. *to* **n.n. 22 October 1834. Portland.** Announces the formation of a young men's AS in Portland; lists the officers. 1 November 1834. p.175, c5.

1677 D. L. CHILD *to* **MR. GILBERT NOURSE. 9 October 1834. Boston.** Withdraws from the Masonic Institution, not because he opposes the order, but because he is convinced that it will do no good. 1 November 1834. p.175, c6.

1678 E. M. P. WELLS, JAMES LORING, S. E. SEWALL, ELLIS GRAY LORING, A. BRONSON ALCOTT, JOHN S. WILLIAMS, CHAS. T. HILDRETH, THOMAS R. SEWELL, D. L. CHILD, T. BULFINCH, S. G. SHIPLEY, DRURY FAIRBANKS, EDWIN PRONK, JOHN GULLIVER, AND FRANCIS JACKSON *to* **ABOTT LAWRENCE, ESQ. 28 October 1834. Boston.** Announce Lawrence's nomination as candidate for representative in Congress; wish to discuss slavery and the slave trade in the District of Columbia with him, as Congress has the right to legislate for the District of Columbia which it does not have in the case of the States; quote from notices of the trade and sale of Negroes, urging Lawrence to right this wrong. 8 November 1834. p.178, c3.

1679 ABBOTT LAWRENCE *to* **GENTLEMEN. 31 October 1834. Boston.** Acknowledges receipt of their letter; agrees that slavery is the greatest moral question America has ever faced, but feels that he should be elected into office unpledged and untrammelled on every question. 8 November 1834. p.178, c6.

1680 BOSTON *to* **W. L. GARRISON. n.d. n.p.** Commends the students leaving Lane Seminary; agrees that the action of the trustees has been reprehensible and unjustified; declares that as a subscriber to the fund supporting the institution, he no longer wishes to contribute. 8 November 1834. p.179, c1.

1681 A STUDENT *to* **W. L. GARRISON. 28 October 1834. Petersboro, N.Y.** Describes manual labor school established by Gerrit Smith for colored youth as pleasant and healthy; informs that the colonization scene is rapidly changing in the area; reports on visit and speeches of Beriah Green. 8 November 1834. p.179, c1.

1682 ONE OF THE STUDENTS AT WATERVILLE COLLEGE *to* **GEORGE THOMP-SON. 18 October 1834. Waterville College.** Admires Thompson and states that he supports the same cause; reminds him that he is protected by God. 8 November 1834. p. 179, c2.

1683 SOMEONE IN BARBADOES *to* **A COMMERCIAL HOUSE. [extract from the** *Alexandria Gazette*]. **n.d n.p.** Believes that the great measure of emancipation is working better than the warmest friends of that law could have anticipated. 8 November 1834. p.179, c6.

1684 A. *to* **MR. EDITOR. [from the** *Zion's Advocate*] **n.d. n.p.** Queries why no calls have been made for Bibles for Southern slaves; quotes gospel supporting this doctrine. 8 November 1834. p.180, c5.

1685 W. H. PEARCE *to* **MR. BRAINERD. 20 August 1834. Natchez, Ms.** Believes that no man in his senses will emancipate his slaves unless he knows their situation will be no worse; states that schools and missions among slaves have been planned to insure this; points out that slaveholders wish to be compensated for emancipated slaves. 15 November 1834. p.181, c1.

1686 ANTI-SLAVERY *to* **THE EDITORS OF THE** *VERMONT STATE JOURNAL*. **n.d n.p.** Argues against the reasoning that people of color can be elevated in Africa, but not in this country; asserts that only weak, ignorant wicked men are the slaves of prejudice and that this prevents blacks from being elevated here. 15 November 1834. p.181, c5.

1687 A CONSTANT READER *to* **MR. EDITOR [W. L. GARRISON]. n.d. North Berwick, Me.** Informs that many respectable people object to abolitionists because of their "disorganizing tendency"and because they are subversive to the national compact; argues that the nation's laws are not perfect but God's law is, and that slavery is against God's law. 15 November 1834. p.182, c4.

1688 A MEMBER OF THE ASSOCIATION *to* **MR. EDITOR [W. L. GARRISON]. n.d n.p.** Gives preamble and resolutions recently reported by the Old Colony Baptist Associa-tion; reports that resolutions state that slavery is a sin against God, it is every citizen's duty to promote immediate manumission. 15 November 1834. p.182, c5.

1689 T. FOWELL BUXTON *to* **W. L. GARRISON. 30 September 1834. London.** Disagrees with CS report claiming Wilberforce signed the protest when not in control of his mind; informs that Wilberforce was in good health at the time and that he wrote Buxton a letter endorsing it; criticizes United States' inconsistency of slavery in "free" states. 15 November 1834. p.183, c1.

1690 B. C. BACON *to* **W. L. GARRISON. 12 November 1834. Concord, N.H.** Gives the resolutions passed at the New Hampshire convention; reports on speeches made and the discussion of resolutions. 15 November 1834. p.183, c4.

1691 SAMUEL FESSENDEN *to* **THE EDITOR OF THE** *NEW YORK EVANGELIST*. **n.d. n.p.** Reports that he attended most of George Thompson's lectures at the state AS meeting in Maine; praises Thompson; describes the audience's reaction. 22 November 1834. p.185, c1.

1692 A LAYMAN *to* **W. L. GARRISON. n.d. n.p.** Sends article from the *Christian Register* showing the neglect of the colored people of Boston due to criminal effects of prejudice. 22 November 1834. p.186, c3.

1693 CORRESPONDENT *to* **THE** *CHRISTIAN WATCHMAN*. **n.d. Philadelphia.** Describes the evening he spent with a doctor who was the medical attendant to John Randolph when he died; depicts Randolph's deathbed scene. 22 November 1834. p.188, c2.

1694 n.n. *to* **n.n. [extract] 11 May 1834. Beyrout.** Describes catastrophe in the Church of the Sepulchre in Jerusalem; states that 15,000 to 20,000 were packed in the church, and that during the panic some fainted and were trampled to death. 22 November 1834. p.188, c3.

1695 SAMUEL H. COX *to* **BROTHER LEAVITT. 17 November 1834. n.p.** Explains why he no longer writes for the public; states that he still believes slavery is a sin; sends letter from Dr. Raffles. 29 November 1834. p.189, c5.

1696 THOMAS RAFFLES *to* **SAMUEL H. COX. 14 October 1834. New Brighton, near Liverpool.** Sympathizes with sufferings endured in the cause of emancipation; doubts that there will be colonization to Liberia when the millennium comes. 29 November 1834. p.189, c6.

1697 H. A. WOODMAN *to* **MR. EDITOR [W. L. GARRISON]. 25 November 1834. Woburn.** Comments that the abolition cause has taken deep root in Woburn; gives an account of the preamble, constitution, and officers elected of the newly formed AS. 29 November 1834. p.190, c4.

1698 JAMES HAMBLETON *to* **W. L. GARRISON. 16 November 1834. Spruce Vale, Oh.** Announces the formation of county AS; quotes preamble, constitution, resolutions. 29 November 1834. p.190, c4.

1699 THOMAS CHANDLER *to* **W. L. GARRISON. 4 November 1834. Near Adrian, Michigan Territory.** Announces the death of Elizabeth Margaret Chandler on 2 November at age twenty-seven; praises her character and abolition work. 29 November 1834. p.191, c2.

1700 H. C. H. *to* **GEORGE THOMPSON. 12 November 1834. Putnam, Oh.** Welcomes his arrival into the country; informs that his cause is advancing in his area, but that it will never succeed without the help of females; blesses Thompson and wishes him well. 29 November 1834. p.191, c4.

1701 n.n. *to* **BROTHER. 13 November 1834. n.p.** Acknowledges receipt of letter from Elizur Wright; hopes to have brother's company at anti-slavery state convention. 29 November 1834. p.191, c4.

1702 n.n. *to* **W. L. GARRISON. 24 November 1834. Providence.** Describes George Thompson's three lectures there; informs that Thompson argued that there was no such thing as property in men and that immediate and entire emancipation is the only righteous and efficient remedy. 29 November 1834. p.191, c4.

1703 n.n. *to* **SIR [W. L. GARRISON]. 17 November 1834. Portland.** Believes that if one is aware of the atrocities of slavery, to keep quiet is a violation of the laws of God; supports Garrison's idea of questioning congressional candidates about their stands on slavery. 29 November 1834. p.191, c5.

1704 REV. WILLIAM INNES *to* **n.n. [extract] n.d. Edinburgh, Scotland.** Sends regards to Dr. Cox; expresses sorrow to hear of mob attacking Cox's house and insulting him; hopes this conduct stops. 29 November 1834. p.191, c6.

1705 REV. JAMES T. WOODBURY *to* **JOHN FARMER, ESQ. 30 October 1834. Acton.** States that he is pleased that he can attend the New Hampshire anti-slavery convention; claims that the people of New Hampshire have a keen quick sense of wrong; informs that he is an abolitionist, and urges Farmer on in the cause. 6 December 1834. p.193, c2.

1706 F. *to* **MR. EDITOR [W. L. GARRISON]. n.d. n.p.** Gives an account of two man-stealers in Cincinnati who seized two blacks but were caught at the last minute; states that one escaped, and one was taken to jail. 6 December 1834. p.193, c6.

1707 N. P. ROGERS *to* **W. L. GARRISON. 17 November 1834. Plymouth, N.H.** Reports arrival of Messrs. Thompson, Grosvenor, and Phelps from the convention at Concord; reports on public auditory on slavery at which some speakers were abolitionists, but all were against the evils of prejudice; gives an account of Thompson's speech; informs that the resolution against slavery passed. 6 December 1834. p.194, c1.

1708 RAY POTTER *to* **W. L. GARRISON. 28 November 1834. Pawtucket.** Reports on George Thompson's speech in Providence, Rhode Island and states that he attended his speech in Pawtucket, Rhode Island; reports that Thompson was well-received. 6 December 1834. p194, c2.

1709 A. RAND *to* **W. L. GARRISON. 3 December 1834. n.p.** Gives an account of Thompson's anti-slavery speeches in Lowell. 6 December 1834. p.194, c3.

1710 A FEMALE FRIEND *to* **W. L. GARRISON. 25 November 1834. Uxbridge.** Quotes several members of the Society of Friends on slavery; points out that the Society of Friends speaks the same language with regard to slavery as other Christian religions. 6 December 1834. p.194, c4.

1711 B. F. R. *to* **MR. EDITOR [W. L. GARRISON]. November 1834. n.p.** Discusses article on the difficulties of colored people in trying to enter a trade; states that he came to the city with a good recommendation from a shoemaking apprenticeship and was refused work, probably because of dark skin; informs that the number of black tradesmen is small; asks for sympathy and encouragement. 6 December 1834. p.194, c5.

1712 A CONSTANT READER *to* **MR. EDITOR [W. L. GARRISON]. n.d. n.p.** Discusses a reply to his former article; admits the Portland correspondent was right in correcting him stating that slavery is not approved or encouraged by the Constitution. 6 December 1834. p.194, c5.

1713 n.n. *to* **W.L. GARRISON. 13 November 1834. Waltham.** Asks whether he has a lawful right to assist runaway slaves to retain freedom, or if he will be liable for the monetary value of the slave. 6 December 1834. p.194, c6.

1714 A CITIZEN OF THEAS UNITED STATES OF AMMERICA [sic] *to* **REV. DR. THOMPSON. 2 December 1834. Lowell.** As a friend, he recommends that Thompson leave the area, as there is a plot to immerse him in a vat of indelible ink. 6 December 1834. p.195, c3.

1715 GEORGE COOKE *to* **PHILLIP E. THOMAS. 25 November 1834. Anne Arundel County.** Reports that the company has not been able to find and arrest the murderers of Washington Railroad superintendents; informs that citizens nearby are threatening to drive out all Irishmen in the county; suggests that if ringleaders cannot be found, the whole work force should be dismissed and a new set hired. 6 December 1834. p.195, c4.

1716 M. GEROULD *to* **THE EDITORS OF THE** *NEW HAMPSHIRE OBSERVER.* **5 November 1834. New Alstead.** Announces that the Monadnock Association does not believe the paper should print discussion of colonization and abolition principles because it injures the religious influence of the paper. 13 December 1834. p.197, c2.

1717 M. G[EROULD] *to* **GENTLEMEN. 5 November 1834. New Alstead.** Gives an extended version of an earlier letter explaining why a discussion of colonization and abolition injures the religious influence of the paper. 13 December 1834. p.197, c2.

1718 n.n. *to* **SIR [W. L. GARRISON]. [extract] n.d. New Hampshire.** Discusses the mandate recently issued by the Monadnock Association to the editors of the *New Hampshire Observer*, telling them to exclude colonization and abolition discussion from their paper; wonders how any moral cause will advance if no discussion is allowed. 13 December 1834. p.197, c3.

1719 M. S. CUSHMAN *to* **MR. EDITOR [W. L. GARRISON]. 6 December 1834. Kingston, Ma.** Describes formation of Kingston AS; reports preamble, constitution, and committees; states that the cause is progressing. 13 December 1834. p.197, c5.

1720 n.n. *to* **W. L. GARRISON. 1 December 1834. Whitingham, Vt.** Writes from remote areas of Vermont; states that the biggest difficulty is the want of correct information on the causes of truth; believes that many cling to colonization because they do not know its true character. 13 December 1834. p.197, c6.

1721 AN ABOLITIONIST *to* **W. L. GARRISON. 6 December 1834. South Reading.** Discusses George Thompson's lecture at a Baptist meetinghouse in South Reading; states that the topics and arguments are so profound that he will not attempt to paraphrase Thompson's speech. 13 December 1834. p198, c1.

1722 n.n. *to* **THE EDITOR [W. L. GARRISON]. n.d. n.p.** Discusses the mob at Concord which allowed a peaceful meeting of men to hear George Thompson speak, but disrupted the meeting of the ladies of the town; states that he knows the names of several members of the mob, and plans to reveal them. 13 December 1834. p.198, c2.

1723 n.n. *to* **W. L. GARRISON. 19 November 1834. Weybridge, Vt.** Reports formation of female AS in Weybridge two months ago; sends preamble and constitution of the society. 13 December 1834. p.198, c3.

1724 ESTHER KINGMAN *to* **n.n. 10 December 1834. Reading.** Briefly reports progress of the ladies' AS since the last annual meeting; states that eighty have paid subscriptions; quotes from the Bible on "the glorious cause." 13 December 1834. p.198, c4.

1725 P. H. G. *to* **n.n. n.d. Portland.** Discloses that the issue on the National Compact has been resolved between himself and the correspondent; finds the correspondent's argument worth listening to. 13 December 1834. p.198, c4.

1726 G. M. *to* **THE EDITORS OF THE** *NEW HAMPSHIRE OBSERVER.* **1 December 1834. White Hills.** A resident of the region of Agiocohook informs that they had just begun to learn about the evils of slavery when they discovered the mandate silencing the *Observer*. 13 December 1834. p.198, c4.

1727 ARNOLD BUFFUM *to* **THE BOARD OF MANAGERS OF THE NEW ENGLAND AS. 30 November 1834. Philadelphia.** Appeals for permanent and legitimate support for the *Liberator*; believes that the *Liberator* was established to enlighten whites and most colored people cannot afford to subscribe to it. 13 December 1834. p.199, c1.

1728 P. H. *to* **MR. EDITOR [W. L. GARRISON]. n.d. n.p.** Expresses shock at finding an advertisement in *Richmond Enquirer* for the legal services of Fontaine H. Pettis, who offers to help Southerners find runaway slaves. 13 December 1834. p.199, c2.

1729 W. COBBETT *to* **JOHN MARSHALL, LABORER. 22 September 1834. Normandy Tithing, Parish of Ash, County of Surrey, Dublin.** Describes trip to Ireland; informs that over one thousand workers must lodge and eat in a huge house; compares land in Normandy to land in Ireland; points out consequences of the lack of poor laws. 13 December 1834. p.200, c2.

1730 MAINE *to* **THE EDITOR OF THE** *EMANCIPATOR*. **n.d. n.p.** Notices objections to organizing state AS, believing that it would imply endorsing the sin of "Garrisonism"; wonders if this sin is anything other than a phantom of the imagination; agrees that Garrison is human and prone to err, yet believes he is activated by a truly philanthropic spirit. 20 December 1834. p.201, c4.

1731 GERRIT SMITH *to* **REV. LEONARD BACON. 24 November 1834. Peterboro, N.Y.** Sends three essays which he thought might interest Bacon. 20 December 1834. p.202, c1.

1732 T----- OF L----- *to* **THE EDITOR OF THE** *NEW ENGLAND SPECTATOR*. **n.d. n.p.** Discusses a statement by a correspondent who claims to be an anti-slavery man, but not a "Garrisonite"; believes that this attitude only diverts public attention from the cause. 20 December 1834. p.202, c4.

1733 A CONSTANT READER AND SUBSCRIBER *to* **W. L. GARRISON. 10 December 1834. Lowell.** Claims that it was not foreigners who persecuted Thompson's speech, insisting that he knows no foreigner who is not an enemy of riots and mobs; discusses the resolutions passed at meeting after Thompson's speech. 20 December 1834. p.203, c1.

1734 A CONSTANT READER *to* **MR. EDITOR [W. L. GARRISON]. n.d. n.p.** Believes that P. H. misunderstood his article; explains that his implication that P. H. might be wrong was intended merely to elicit an elaboration of P.H.'s views and sentiments. 20 December 1834. p.203, c2.

1735 W. T. S. *to* **MR. EDITOR [W. L. GARRISON]. n.d. n.p.** Mentions that an address by Dr. A. L. Cox to the New York citizens has just been published by the New York AS; states that the address discusses slavery among the Jews and in America; urges public to buy and read it. 20 December 1834. p.203, c2.

1736 Z. *to* **MR. EDITOR [W. L. GARRISON]. n.d. n.p.** Discusses difficulty of instructing slaves; reminds that when the Union was formed, the free states made a compact not to interfere with slavery; concludes, therefore, that instruction cannot be carried out by the government without committing a breach of trust. 20 December 1834. p.203, c2.

1737 L'AMIE DES ENFANTS *to* **MADAM. n.d. n.p.** A "jeu d'esprit" on the care of uniting ease and strength while knitting a pair of stockings. 20 December 1834. p.204, c2.

1738 H. A. H. *to* **THE EDITOR OF THE** *LANDMARK*. **n.d. n.p.** Objects to character of the *New England Spectator*; points out strong differences between the first issue and consequent issues; states that apparently the editor has disavowed the idea of making the paper an anti-slavery paper. 27 December 1834. p.205, c1.

1739 A CONSTANT READER AND SUBSCRIBER *to* **W. L. GARRISON. 13 December 1834. Lowell.** Sends encouragement to those working to overthrow slavery and oppression; states that it is unfortunate that the cause elicits malice, but believes it must if it is to succeed. 27 December 1834. p.205, c5.

1740 M. HALE WILDER *to* **W. L. GARRISON. 20 December 1834. Boston.** Refutes correspondent who claimed that there were few schools in the West and that they were taught by drunken Scotchmen; charges that any missionary making that statement is not worthy of confidence. 27 December 1834. p.205, c6.

1741 INQUIRER *to* **MR. EDITOR [W. L. GARRISON]. 25 December 1834. Boston.** Inquires what George Thompson meant when he asserted in his speech the previous night "the master is always more degraded than the slave." 27 December 1834. p.206, c5.

1742 A LOVER OF TRUTH AND PEACE *to* **FRIEND GARRISON. 22 December 1834. Boston.** Replies to a correspondent; argues that errors of Garrison should not deter any from working to free oppressed slaves; criticizes Garrison for too much bitter and unkind language. 27 December 1834. p.207, c1.

1835

1743 ONESIMUS *to* **MR. EDITOR. [from the *Landmark*] n.d. n.p.** Reports on speech by George Thompson; explains Thompson's argument against slavery based on both the Old and New Testaments; asserts that Thompson treated the subject as a religious, not a political issue. 3 January 1835. p.1, c2.

1744 CHARLES STUART *to* **FRIEND. [from the *Emancipator*] 11 December 1834. Utica.** Reports on his travels and speeches from Buffalo to Utica; notes that he met Theodore Weld at Lane Seminary. 3 January 1835. p.1, c4.

1745 JOSHUA COFFIN *to* **MR. EDITOR. [from the *Emancipator*] 13 December 1834. Philadelphia.** Declares that the information furnished by a former slave to the Rev. Stephen C. King is true; a woman, lately arrived from Georgia, corroborates the story. 3 January 1835. p.1, c6.

1746 n.n. *to* **MR. GARRISON. 25 December 1834. Kingston.** Charges that greater liberty is found under a king than in a republic; expresses his shock at the opposition and violence aroused by Thompson's efforts for the oppressed; tells of Thompson's visit and speeches in Plymouth. 3 January 1835. p.2, c1.

1747 A. T. *to* **WM. L. GARRISON. 23 December 1834. North Yarmouth, Me.** Rejoices that Garrison must no longer labor alone; tells of the formation of an AS of forty members at North Yarmouth, and of speeches delivered to them by Dr. Phelps. 3 January 1834. p.2, c2.

1748 ANTI-SLAVERY *to* **MR. GARRISON. 21 December 1834. Lowell.** Wonders how people can admire in some men traits and characteristics which in others they deem coarse and ungentlemanly; questions the charge of foreign interference in reference to Lowell mobs. 3 January 1835. p.2, c2.

1749 A CITIZEN OF THE WORLD *to* **SIR. n.d. n.p.** Discusses the Irish as another poor, weak, and unpopular people who are subjected to prejudice for their willingness to work for low wages; urges help and education rather than restricted privileges. 3 January 1835. p.2, c3.

1750 NATHANIEL SWASY *to* **MR. GARRISON. 15 December 1834. Bath.** Asks if Mr. Thompson could visit them this winter; believes that theirs was the first AS formed in Maine; notes that there still exists much prejudice, which good speakers might overcome. 3 January 1835. p.2, c4.

1751 M. EDDY *to* **MR. GARRISON. 26 December 1834. Bridgewater.** Declares that the churches and presses of Bridgewater are all free, and able to undertake discussion of the fiery subject of slavery; reports that Mr. Thompson has been attentively received and has won the respect of many. 3 January 1835. p.2, c5.

1752 A GENTLEMAN IN CAMPTON, N.H. *to* **HIS FRIEND IN CONCORD. [extract] n.d. Concord.** Writes of approaching anti-slavery convention; believes that the notice of the convention may offend some, but will do them good; states that those who support colonization do not wish blacks to have the same rights and privileges as whites. 3 January 1835. p.2, c6.

1753 O. *to* **FRIEND. 22 December 1834. Portland.** Explains why he enjoys the *Liberator* so much; reviews the articles in the previous issue; discusses Garrison's latest editorial concerning colored voters. 3 January 1835. p.2, c6.

1754 A GENTLEMAN OF THE CITY OF NEW YORK *to* **n.n. [extract] 10 December 1834. Fort Mitchell, Al.** Describes fire on steamboat *Van Buren* travelling from Columbus to Apalachicola; notes that most passengers survived but all baggage was lost. 3 January 1835. p.6, c5.

1755 n.n. *to* **n.n. 5 May 1831. Cape Palmas.** Writes to his mother that he is willing to sell himself into slavery in order to get back to Maryland. 10 January 1835. p.7, c1.

1756 A COLORED BALTIMOREAN *to* **FRIEND GARRISON. 1 January 1834.[*sic*] Baltimore.** Criticizes Maryland colonization scheme; finds it unjust and cruel. 10 January 1835. p.7, c1.

1757 ONE OF THE SIXTY-TWO *to* **FRIEND GARRISON. n.d. n.p.** Replies to charge of many philanthropists that they cannot work under the leaders of the AS; declares that the officers would give up their posts gladly to help the cause; asks that the disgruntled come forward, to speak and lead. 10 January 1835. p.7, c1.

1758 O. SCOTT *to* **MR. EDITOR. [from the *Zion's Herald*] 30 December 1834. n.p.** Furnishes several communications on slavery for the columns of the *Herald*; declares he is no longer willing to slumber over an evil of such magnitude, and that he is willing to be unpopular in defense of his sentiments. 17 January 1835. p.9, c5.

1759 W. T. ALLEN *to* **RESPECTED FACULTY OF LANE SEMINARY. n.d. n.p.** Presents the report of the Lane Seminary AS, which was unanimously adopted. 17 January 1835. p.10, c3.

1760 JOSIAH L. THOMAS *to* **FRIEND GARRISON. 8 January 1835. Portland.** Supports Garrison's unceasing efforts for immediate emancipation; feels that if Garrison and others sometimes lack a "strict regard to methodical language," friends should pardon them, as they act in the spirit of liberty and their work is destined to succeed. 17 January 1835. p.11, c1.

1761 A CONSTANT READER AND SUBSCRIBER *to* **MR. GARRISON. 25 December 1834. Lowell.** Praises the noble cause and good work Garrison has done for it; criticizes the *Mercury*'s and others' attacks on Thompson and abolition; includes anecdote about John Wesley and the truth of the Bible. 17 January 1835. p.11, c1.

1762 F. *to* **MR. GARRISON. n.d. n.p.** Congratulates him for resisting censorship of the press; declares that an abolitionist is like one who sees a neighbor's house burning—he should not act meekly, but shout "fire!" Hopes Garrison will continue to call things by their right names. 17 January 1835. p.11, c2.

1763 GERRIT SMITH *to* **REV. LEONARD BACON. n.d. n.p.** Details the founding of the ACS, its good effects, and its relation to the AAS; discusses Mr. Birney's ideas on colonization; criticizes various opponents of the CS. 24 January 1835. p.13, c1.

1764 H. B. B. *to* **MR. GARRISON. n.d. n.p.** Describes the American Union Convention; condemns the narrow-minded restrictions put on the speakers; states that the leaders, especially those on the Executive Committee, were extremely partial and refused to discuss improvement of the condition of the people of color. 31 January 1835. p.17, c4.

1765 A CONSTANT READER *to* **MR. GARRISON. 7 January 1835. Lowell.** Comments on the *Nashville Western Methodist*, published by Rev. J. N. Maffitt and Rev. L. Garritt; charges that since they are not against slavery, they are for it. 31 January 1835. p. 17, c5.

1766 AMICUS LIBERTATIS *to* **MR. EDITOR [W. L. GARRISON]. n.d. n.p.** Calls for another petition drive to abolish slavery in the District of Columbia; charges that to allow slavery in the seat of government is to sanction slavery itself, and that it is every citizen's duty to put a speedy end to this outrage; demands renewed protest of this bloody system of oppression in the "land of the free." 31 January 1835. p.18, c2.

1767 A BROTHER TO ALL MANKIND *to* **THE** *LIBERATOR*. **n.d. n.p.** Reports that he attended recent meeting of AS which he enjoyed immensely; wishes that eveyone in America could have heard the addresses given there. 31 January 1835. p.18, c4.

1768 JOSEPH TRACY *to* **THE** *LIBERATOR*. **26 January 1835.** *Recorder* **office.** Corrects reports of his remark at the American Union Convention: he had addressed the moderator, not Mr. Thompson, and had asked foreigners to question their consciences and to remain if they felt welcome. 31 January 1835. p.18, c4.

1769 WM. LLOYD GARRISON *to* **GERRIT SMITH. n.d. n.p.** Reviews Smith's three letters to Rev. Leonard Bacon, which praised the AAS, the doctrine of immediate emancipation, and ACS; accuses Smith of fallacies and contradictions. 31 January 1835. p.18, c5.

1770 ARTHUR TAPPAN *to* **THE** *RECORDER*. **17 January 1835. New Haven.** Believes that the New Society for Benefitting the Colored Race and the AS hold the same sentiments on emancipation, and that neither society should impugn the other's motives if they adopt different measures. 31 January 1835. p.19, c3.

1771 LEWIS TAPPAN *to* **W. L. GARRISON. 26 January 1835. New York.** Urges Garrison on against oppression; agrees with Garrison's remarks concerning the recent convention in Boston, which he feels may be called an "Anti-Garrison Society." 31 January 1835. p.19, c4.

1772 A. T. *to* **W. L. GARRISON. 17 January 1835. North Yarmouth, Me.** Recommends holding district meetings to consider the subject of slavery in the United States; feels much encouraged by one such meeting held recently in North Yarmouth; urges anti-slavery supporters on. 7 February 1835. p.21, c2.

1773 D. H. *to* **MR. EDITOR [W. L. GARRISON]. n.d. n.p.** Replies to assumption that Mr. Thompson's object is to convert slaveholders to a sense of the moral guilt of slavery; points out that Northerners are also to blame as they use and support the system, and that Northerners are not all in favor of the idea of immediate emancipation. 7 February 1835. p.21, c3.

1774 J. *to* **FRIEND GARRISON. n.d. n.p.** Believes that indifference to the wrongs of the oppressed is an outrage to humanity; hopes all unenlightened minds, particularly those of ministers, will soon be educated so that the great work will be accomplished. 7 February 1835. p.21, c4.

1775 n.n. *to* **WM. LLOYD GARRISON. 8 January 1835. Union Bridge, Md.** Former colonizationist supports immediate emancipation and equal treatment of blacks; finds that opportunities are few to do good for the poor slaves, as he resides in a slave state; tells of censorship of the press. 7 February 1835. p.21, c4.

1776 n.n. *to* **WILLIAM LLOYD GARRISON. 17 January 1835. Philadelphia.** Sends copy of the *Pennsylvania Inquirer and Courier* containing a fiery anti-slavery article from the Abbe de la Mennais; describes the editor of the *Inquirer* as an "unflinching advocate of universal freedom." 7 February 1835. p.21, c6.

1777 O. SCOTT *to* **MEMBERS OF THE NEW ENGLAND ANNUAL CONFERENCE OF THE METHODIST EPISCOPAL CHURCH. 30 January 1835. n.p.** Reports that he has purchased 100 copies of the *Liberator* for them in the hope that they will reflect on the subject of slavery, a momentous issue which they can no longer innocently neglect; does not ask that they believe everything, but feels their duties as ministers demand they examine the subject. 7 February 1835. p.21, c6.

1778 GOTHAM *to* **THE EDITORS OF THE** *LIBERATOR* **[W. L. GARRISON]. n.d. n.p.** Responds to the account of the American Union proceedings; criticizes them, pointing out that mildness and conciliation in clergymen will never rid the world of sin or evil. 7 February 1835. p.22, c1.

1779 F. *to* **MR. GARRISON. n.d. n.p.** Reports that he attended the convention of the American Union; criticizes them for setting themselves up as "benefactors of mankind"; feels that the spirit of freedom was lacking; condemns abuse of members and "Hang Garrison" spirit of leaders. 7 February 1835. p.22, c2.

1780 n.n. *to* **FRIEND GARRISON. 28 January 1835. Weston.** Announces formation of AS; outlines constitution and lists officers. 7 February 1835. p.22, c4.

1781 n.n. *to* **n.n. [extract] 19 January 1835. Andover.** Describes three lectures by Mr. Thompson, which defended the Bible from the charge of sanctioning slavery and insisted on the duty and safety of immediate emancipation; notes that one result of the lectures was the formation of an AS. 7 February 1835. p.22, c4.

1782 THE SECRETARY OF THE EDINBURGH AS *to* **GEORGE THOMPSON. [extract] n.d. n.p.** Asserts that there is "no prejudice about the color of a man's skin" in Edinburgh, reports that Rev. Mr. Paul, a black man, has raised much money for the Wilberforce Settlement and received unanimous support and sympathy there. 7 February 1835. p.22, c5.

1783 CHARLES WHITE *to* **MR. EDITOR. [from the** *Massachusetts Spy*] **n.d. n.p.** Forwards the report of the Board of Directors of the Holden AS which urges immediate emancipation. 7 February 1835. p.22, c5.

1784 WM. LLOYD GARRISON *to* **GERRIT SMITH. n.d. n.p.** Reviews Smith's second letter; charges him with "startling inconsistencies," and "glaring contradictions"; compares Smith's hard and soft language. 7 February 1835. p.23, c1.

1785 n.n. *to* **FRIEND [AGENT FOR THE** *LIBERATOR* **IN PROVIDENCE]. n.d. n.p.** Sends an extra thirty cents with his subscription order as a tiny effort to help sustain the *Liberator*; hopes others will take the hint, so the paper can remain financially solvent. 7 February 1835. p.23, c5.

1786 D. RUGGLES *to* **MR. EDITOR [W. L. GARRISON]. 15 January 1835. New York.** Mentions that all communications addressed to him must be postpaid. 7 February 1835. p.23, c5.

1787 n.n. *to* **n.n. [extract] 4 January 1835. Natchez.** Reports that Foster, the murderer of his wife, was acquitted by the jury but whipped, tarred, and feathered by a mob of the "most respectable citizens." 7 February 1835. p.24, c2.

1788 JOHN T. HILTON *to* **FELLOW CITIZENS AND BRETHREN. n.d. n.p.** Appeals to the free colored citizens of the United States to support the *Liberator*. 14 February 1835. p.26, c1.

1789 ONE WHO WISHES TO KNOW *to* **MR. GARRISON. n.d. n.p.** Asks who takes sides with the rioters of the present day and pursues a course to encourage the spirit of mobocracy. 14 February 1835. p.26, c3.

1790 B. *to* **FRIEND GARRISON. n.d. n.p.** Composes parable mocking the American Union and its "puerile proceedings." 14 February 1835. p.26, c3.

1791 P. *to* **MR. PORTER. [extract from the** *New England Spectator*] **29 January 1835. H---.** Mocks the late Convention for the Colored Race, charging that participants are still sympathetic to colonization and only beginning to wake up; adds that the convention furthered the cause of colonization, not anti-slavery. 14 February 1835. p.26, c3.

1792 GEORGE THOMPSON *to* **BROTHER. 10 February 1835. Portland, Me.** Describes itinerary, speeches given, and receptions attended on recent trip; attributes his success to the goodness of the cause and the cooperation of the ministers of religion. 14 February 1835. p.27, c1.

1793 O. *to* **THE EDITOR. [from the** *Christian Mirror*] **n.d. n.p.** Questions whether premiums should be offered for best essays on religious subjects; feels authors should be motivated by virtue. 14 February 1835. p.28, c6.

1794 J. E. EDWARDS, A. R. BAKER, JAS. L. THOMPSON, WM. S. TYLER, AND SAM'L. WALCOTT *to* **THE EDITOR OF THE** *BOSTON RECORDER*. **2 February 1835. Andover Theological Seminary.** Assert that both CS and AS exist at the institution, and that from the large attendance at George Thompson's lectures, one should not infer that all support him; believe that duties as theological students are most important, and disapprove of future discussions on slavery. 21 February 1835. p.29, c1.

1795 LEONARD WOODS *to* **REV. JOSEPH TRACY OF THE** *BOSTON RECORDER*. **3 February 1835. Theological Seminary, Andover.** Speaks for the faculty, rejoicing that the students realized that they could not form societies and agitate on the subject of slavery without endangering the spirit of brotherly love and piety which was the object of the institution. 21 February 1835. p.29, c1.

1796 A MEMBER OF CONGRESS *to* **HIS FRIEND IN MASSACHUSETTS. [extract] 19 January 1835. n.p.** Declares that Congress does little else but debate the choice of the next president; feels that leaders of both parties have united to put a stop to free inquiry and free discussion of slavery. 21 February 1835. p.29, c4.

1797 D. D. WHEDON *to* **n.n. [from** *Zion's Herald*] **3 February 1835. Wesleyan University.** Condemns efforts of popery; expresses pro-slavery sentiments. 28 February 1835. p.33, c1.

1798 A CONSTANT READER *to* **MR. GARRISON. 5 February 1835. Lowell.** Criticizes ingenuous articles in recent *Western Methodist;* forwards one entitled "Slavery in Tennessee." 28 February 1835. p.33, c3.

1799 n.n. *to* **n.n. [extract] n.d. Cincinnati.** Contends that times are changing in the West; people are becoming undeceived; Weld and Birney have risen and stripped off the false covering. 28 February 1835. p.33, c4.

1800 GEO. THOMPSON *to* **W. L. GARRISON. 17 February 1835. Brighton St.** Sends Garrison the constitution, the address, and resolutions passed by the Cumberland County AS; recommends the *Liberator* to the abolitionists, praising its adherence to the principles of liberty and equality. 28 February 1835. p.33, c5.

1801 SAMUEL FESSENDEN, SAMUEL F. HUSSEY, JAMES APPLETON, NATHAN WINSLOW, SAMUEL EDWARDS, AND PITT GREENLEAF *to* **W. L. GARRISON. 23 January 1835. Portland.** Invite all interested to attend convention to form a county AS. 28 February 1835. p.33, c6.

1802 A LISTENER *to* **FRIEND GARRISON. n.d. n.p.** Reports on meeting of Boston Young Men's AA to debate whether those who support immediate abolition can be members of the American Union; some agreed on grounds of compromise, but the majority viewed the two as inconsistent. 28 February 1835. p.34, c2.

1803 ELIJAH DEMOND *to* **MR. EDITOR [W. L. GARRISON]. 14 February 1835. Holliston.** Sends preamble and constitution of the Holliston AS. 28 February 1835. p.34, c4.

1804 REV. JOSHUA V. HIMES *to* **CAPT. J. BATES. 16 February 1835. Boston.** Rejoices that his friend realizes that Garrison is persecuted for no fault other than speaking out against an immoral system. 28 February 1835. p.34, c4.

1805 SAMUEL BARRY *to* **W. L. GARRISON. 29 January 1835. Jamaica, Vt.** Hopes a great effort is made toward collecting signers of the petition for the abolition of slavery in the District of Columbia; recounts his experience of collecting several hundred signatures for a similar petition the previous year. 28 February 1835. p.34, c5.

1806 DELTA *to* **FRIEND GARRISON. 18 February 1835. Boston.** Quotes portions of an article from the *Southern Literary Messenger;* stresses that friends of immediate emancipation must study the opinions of the South, which are "founded in the most revolting selfishness." 28 February 1835. p.34, c6.

1807 O. S. MURRAY *to* **THE EXECUTIVE COMMITTEE OF THE VERMONT AS.** [from the *Middlebury Free Press*] **n.d. n.p.** Describes his latest anti-slavery tour; spent four weeks travelling in Randolph, Woodstock, and Windsor, Vermont; gave sixteen lectures, but was prevented by violence from giving four others; formed some societies; describes the great deception surrounding colonization. 28 February 1835. p.35, c1.

1808 WM. LLOYD GARRISON *to* **GERRIT SMITH n.d. n.p.** Criticizes Smith's confused logic in recent letters on slavery and colonization. 28 February 1835. p.35, c3.

1809 DAVID RUGGLES *to* **THE *LIBERATOR*. 5 February 1835. New York.** Thanks committee for efforts in extending subscription of paper. 28 February 1835. p.35, c6.

1810 n.n. *to* **n.n. [extract] 16 February 1834. Washington.** Reports the presentation of another petition for the abolition of slavery in the District of Columbia by Mr. Dickson; describes "animated and somewhat tart" discussion; states that South now attempts to prevent the North from presenting such petitions. 7 March 1835. p.37, c1.

1811 JAMES G. BIRNEY *to* **n.n. [extract] 6 January 1835. Kentucky.** Describes changes since his father's agreement gradually to emancipate all slaves on his farm; reports that the slaves receive wages and are supervised by an emancipated former slave who replaced the overseer. 7 March 1835. p.37, c2.

1812 n.n. *to* **n.n. [from the *Hudson Observer*] 18 December 1834. Louisville, Ky.** Discusses apathy of public on slavery and its remedy; feels most are ignorant of the principles of the CS and AS; tells of Southern slaveholding preacher who sold a slave down river away from his wife, then lied to her about it. 7 March 1835. p.37, c4.

1813 EUPHEMIA JOHNSTON, SARAH BROWN, AND JANE SMEAL *to* **THE LADIES OF THE PHILADELPHIA FEMALE AS. 3 September 1834. Glasgow.** Acknowledge communications and literature on behalf of the Glasgow Female AS; rejoice that both societies work for the same cause; urge them to increase their efforts for the slaves. 7 March 1835. p.38, c1.

1814 VERMONT *to* **BROTHER GARRISON. 20 February 1835. Whereabout.** Expresses shame and anger at the behavior at Wesleyan University, where mobs prevented George Thompson from speaking; attacks Prof. Whedon for his letter supporting the behavior. 7 March 1835. p.38, c1.

1815 A. W. *to* **FRIEND GARRISON. 23 February 1835. Philadelphia.** Describes discussion of slavery he had with George Thompson while travelling by stage from Boston to Providence; praises Mrs. Child, whom he met on a boat to New York; believes abolition prospects are cheering. 7 March 1835. p.38, c3.

1816 GEO. THOMPSON *to* **W. L. GARRISON. 24 February 1835. Brooklyn, N.Y.** Describes pleasant journey by land and water to New York, during which he engaged in many discussions of slavery; discusses his speech at the monthly concert of prayer in Rev. Dr. Lansing's church. 7 March 1835. p.38, c4.

1817 A CONSTANT READER *to* **MR. GARRISON. 14 February 1835. Lowell.** Discusses the relation of the Constitution to slavery. 7 March 1835. p.38, c5.

1818 B. F. R. *to* **MR. EDITOR [W. L. GARRISON]. n.d. n.p.** Relates story of a man born in Africa, then stolen, separated from his mother, and sold into slavery, who endured hard toil under extreme heat but finally escaped; decries the unjust, evil nature of slavery. 7 March 1835. p.39, c1.

1819 WM. LLOYD GARRISON *to* **GERRIT SMITH. n.d. n.p.** Reviews Smith's fourth letter; claims that Smith is not persecuted for his beliefs because he is willing to waver, while Garrison upholds all of his convictions; accuses Smith of being pro-colonization. 7 March 1835. p.39, c2.

1820 GEORGE THOMPSON *to* **THE EDITOR OF** *ZION'S HERALD.* **18 February 1835. n.p.** Forwards a dignified reply to the violent letter of Prof. Whedon, in which the latter lambasts anti-slavery views of religion. 14 March 1835. p.41, c3.

1821 W. H. MURCH FOR THE BOARD OF BAPTIST MINISTERS IN AND NEAR LONDON *to* **THE BAPTIST CHURCHES IN AMERICA. [from the** *London Baptist Magazine***] 31 December 1833. London.** Describes slave insurrection at their mission in Jamaica in 1832, which caused them to re-examine their views of the slave system; urges Americans to re-examine their views, and to liberate their slaves as did the English. 14 March 1835. p.41, c4.

1822 LUCIUS BOLLES FOR THE BAPTIST BOARD OF FOREIGN MISSIONS IN AMERICA *to* **BOARD OF BAPTIST MINISTERS IN AND NEAR LONDON. [from the** *London Baptist Magazine***] 1 September 1834. n.p.** Explains that differences between English and American political organization and slave populations necessitates differences in the two countries' treatment of the problems of slavery. 14 March 1835. p.41, c6.

1823 E. P. ATLEE *to* **W. L. GARRISON. 10 March 1835. Philadelphia.** Reports on visit of George Thompson and the charming, eloquent, and powerful arguments employed in his speeches; notes that Philadelphia is at last free from mobocracy. 14 March 1835. p.43, c1.

1824 CHARLES T. TORREY *to* **MR. EDITOR [W. L. GARRISON]. 3 March 1835. Andover.** Reports that he recently organized AS of fifty members; includes extracts from the constitution and list of officers; declares that light and education are all that is needed to render Andover the most energetic anti-slavery town in New England. 14 March 1835. p.43, c1.

1825 M. S. CUSHMAN *to* **MR. EDITOR [W. L. GARRISON]. 5 March 1835. Kingston.** Sends resolution passed by Kingston AS commending the work of those trying to abolish slavery in the District of Columbia. 14 March 1835. p.43, c2.

1826 BARON STOW AND JOHN G. WHITTIER *to* **THE** *CHRISTIAN MIRROR.* **31 January 1835. Boston.** Deny claim that they supported the American Union. 14 March 1835. p.43, c4.

1827 PROF. W. FISK OF WESLEYAN UNIVERSITY *to* *ZION'S HERALD.* **[extract] n.d. n.p.** Protests Northern abolitionist tactics; contends that if abolitionists go South and try to implement their ideals, they will realize their impracticality; charges that public opinion on slavery was "abundantly better" before abolitionists touched it, and that prejudice has since increased. 21 March 1835. p.45, c1.

1828 A. W. *to* **THE EDITOR OF THE** *LIBERATOR* **[W. L. GARRISON]. 4 March 1835. Philadelphia.** Finds the spirit in his area encouraging, although the number of active abolitionists is small; hopes sentiments are turning away from colonization and toward abolition; believes speech by George Thompson helped enlighten many. 21 March 1835. p.45, c4.

1829 ARNOLD BUFFUM *to* **FRIEND GARRISON. 5 March 1835. Philadelphia.** Reports that a powerful speech by George Thompson converted many to the spirit of "immediate abolitionism"; forwards resolution of the AS thanking Thompson; notes recent speech by Amasa Walker. 21 March 1835. p.45, c5.

1830 N. C. *to* **THE** *LIBERATOR.* **[extract] 10 March 1835. Amesbury.** Describes lecture by Mr. Grosvenor; believes that the cause of the colored man need only be understood and felt to be triumphant. 21 March 1835. p.45, c6.

1831 A CLERGYMAN *to* **MR. THOMPSON. [extract] 15 February 1835. Oh.** Worries about Thompson's health; approves Eastern delegates' attendance at religious meetings in London; hopes discussion of slavery converts many to immediate abolition; quotes letter from Weld. 21 March 1835. p.45, c6.

1832 A SUBSCRIBER *to* **MR. GARRISON. n.d. n.p.** Sends letter from P. J. 21 March 1835. p.46, c1.

1833 P. J. *to* **MR. EDITOR [W. L. GARRISON]. n.d. n.p.** Believes that the colonizing or expatriating scheme is wholly inconsistent with abolition; believes that to remove all the people of color to Africa is "preposterous in the extreme"; dissents with Gerrit Smith. 21 March 1835. p.46, c1.

1834 P. J. *to* **n.n. [extract] 1 February 1835. Charleston, S.C.** Describes departure of slave boat from South Carolina to New Orleans; tells of weeping woman forced to part with her husband. 21 March 1835. p.46, c2.

1835 O. SCOTT *to* **MR. GARRISON. 16 March 1835. n.p.** Refers to disturbances in New York during the previous July, charging that mobs originate with the higher classes, which use the lower classes as tools; criticizes article in *Christian Advocate* by D. M. Reese which attacks George Thompson. 21 March 1835. p.46, c3.

1836 ORSON S. MURRAY *to* **MESSRS. EDITORS.** [from the *Middlebury Free Press*] **n.d. n.p.** Holds these editors "pre-eminently responsible" for recent outrages and mob violence in Vermont; charges that they circulate gross misrepresentations of the sentiments and purposes of abolitionists. 21 March 1835. p.46, c4.

1837 D. D. WHEDON *to* **MR. EDITOR.** [from the *Zion's Herald*] **4 March 1835. Wesleyan University.** Refutes allegation by George Thompson that Whedon accuses him of foreign interference; affirms presence of foreigners, supported by the Garrison party, seeking to agitate in the United States. 28 March 1835. p.49, c1.

1838 C. C. BURLEIGH *to* **BROTHER GARRISON. 17 March 1835. Groton.** Describes his anti-slavery tours; reports warm receptions at Boston and Sudbury, the blocking of his speech at Townsend by a minister who supports the American Union. 28 March 1835. p.50, c4.

1839 A. W. *to* **THE** *LIBERATOR.* **6 March 1835. Philadelphia.** Contends that prejudice toward colored people is greatly strengthened by the mistaken belief that they cannot be elevated; wishes that disbelievers could see those in Philadelphia who have acquired wealth, education, and respectability. 28 March 1835. p.50, c5.

1840 QUISQUIS *to* **MR. GARRISON. 23 March 1835. Andover Theological Seminary.** Describes the favorable impression produced by George Thompson's address on the subject of slavery and his discussion with students; notes that soon after, an attempt was made to reorganize the AS. 28 March 1835. p.50, c6.

1841 ELISHA FAXON *to* **MR. EDITOR [W. L. GARRISON]. 19 March 1835. Abington.** Reports that the citizens of Abington also sent a petition to Congress to abolish slavery in the District of Columbia; notes that many in the town are in favor of forming an AS, but are waiting for Mr. Thompson to come and lecture. 28 March 1835. p.51, c2.

1842 n.n. *to* **MR. EDITOR.** [from the *Salem Landmark*] **16 March 1835. Topsfield.** Describes speech, given the previous evening by Rev. Mr. Grosvenor on emancipation, which did not excite prejudice, but stirred love and good feelings toward the whole human family. 4 April 1835. p.53, c6.

1843 W. *to* **MR. GARRISON. 1 April 1835. Boston.** Responds to communication from "Quisquis," expressing shock at the report that Andover and Lane Theological Seminaries have forbidden conversation or public prayer on the subject of slavery; hopes public sentiment will force a change if the seminaries have descended to such low measures. 4 April 1835. p.54, c2.

1844 E. A. B. *to* **MR. EDITOR [W. L. GARRISON]. 30 March 1835. n.p.** Criticizes a "shocking" article in *Zion's Herald* on "Foreign Intervention," declaring that its author was "under the influence of heated brain"; hails the "foreign messenger," Thompson. 4 April 1835. p.54, c2.

1845 ARNOLD BUFFUM *to* **GARRISON AND KNAPP. 27 March 1835. Philadelphia.** Describes second visit of George Thompson, who gave two lectures; reports many meetinghouses denied them; warns that the oppressed slaves must be helped and freed or "their blood be required at our hands." 4 April 1835. p.54, c4.

1846 JOSEPH BRACKETT *to* **W. L. GARRISON. 23 March 1835. Limington, Me.** Reports that an AS was just formed in Limington; lists officers and quotes extracts from constitution; looks to the future when the evil of slavery will be eradicated. 4 April 1835. p.54, c4.

1847 C. P. GROSVENOR *to* **THE** *NEW ENGLAND SPECTATOR.* **24 March 1835. Salem.** Quotes the Epistle of Paul to the Corinthians; feels dishonored by letter from the Baptist Board of Foreign Ministers and angry that the British letter was suppressed for a year; declares it is time the rights of the churches be re-examined and maintained. 4 April 1835. p.54, c6.

1848 JAMES G. BIRNEY *to* **MR. LEWIS TAPPAN. 3 February 1835. Danville, Ky.** Believes that Danville citizens favor some form of emancipation; hopes the legislature will take up the question and terminate slavery; discredits the American Union. 4 April 1835. p.55, c1.

1849 THEODORE D. WELD *to* **BROTHER WRIGHT. [extract] 2 March 1835. Putnam, Oh.** Declares there has been a change in public sentiment since his speeches at Concord, Oldtown, Bloomingburg, and Circleville; feels that the character of those places is now decidedly abolitionist. 4 April 1835. p.55, c3.

1850 J. S. *to* **GARRISON AND KNAPP. n.d. Providence.** Questions veracity of the "tale of distress" of an African man, appearing in recent *Liberator,* as the story has been retold in varied and embellished forms. 11 April 1835. p.58, c3.

1851 A. *to* **MR. EDITOR [W. L. GARRISON]. 1 April 1835. New Hampshire.** Relates disagreement between Dr. Fisk and Rev. G. Storrs who adapted one of Fisk's lectures on temperance to a lecture on abolition, with an explanatory introduction giving Fisk credit; reports that Fisk nevertheless published a scathing criticism of Storrs. 11 April 1835. p.58, c4.

1852 NAUMKEAG *to* **FRIEND GARRISON. 6 April 1835. Salem.** Believes that the Monthly Concert of Prayer for the Slaves is one of the best methods to ensure the success of abolition; reports that three ministers of Salem refused to read the notices concerning the meetings; adds that two of them were members and the third served on the Executive Committee of the American Union. 11 April 1835. p.58, c5.

1853 JAMES B. WHITCOMB *to* **MR. GARRISON. 31 March 1835. Brooklyn.** Announces the formation of the Brooklyn AS; quotes its preamble and constitution; lists officers. 11 April 1835. p.58, c6.

1854 WM. SCALES *to* **GARRISON AND KNAPP. 28 March 1835. Canaan, N.H.** Quotes extracts from a letter by Rev. D. T. Kimball and comments on them; claims abolitionists seek to break the barriers which prevent self-elevation of the colored race; believes colored persons should be educated. 11 April 1835. p.58, c6.

1855 REV. D. T. KIMBALL *to* **THE PRINCIPAL OF NOYES' ACADEMY. [extract] n.d. n.p.** Inquires, on behalf of his colored friends, whether they could be admitted despite their lack of previous education; asks what are the necessary expenses. 11 April 1835. p.58, c6.

1856 n.n. *to* **THE EDITORS OF RELIGIOUS NEWSPAPERS. [from the** *Cincinnati Journal***]** **n.d. n.p.** Criticizes their practice of referring to people as "a very worthy brother" or "one of the most respectable members," claiming that the practice is bad for the character and reputation of the newspapers, the editors, and all parties concerned. 11 April 1835. p.60, c2.

1857 REV. MR. MAY *to* **MR. B. C. BACON. [extract] 13 April 1835. Fall River.** Reports that he received a hearty welcome at Fall River, where he stayed with the family of Nathaniel Borden; also preached on 12 April at Unitarian and Baptist meetinghouses. 18 April 1835. p.62, c4.

1858 S. J. MAY *to* **W. L. GARRISON. 14 April 1835. Fall River.** Describes meeting of the managers of the Fall River AS, and his recent lectures; notes he is to meet with some members of the Society of Friends. 18 April 1835. p.62, c4.

1859 VERMONT, A METHODIST *to* **BROTHER GARRISON. n.d. n.p.** Attacks Prof. Whedon of Wesleyan University; charges that Whedon is trying to buy up the pupils and patronage of Southern planters and menstealers by misrepresenting George Thompson and by attacking and discrediting the *Liberator* and Garrison. 18 April 1835. p.62, c5.

1860 n.n. *to* **MR. EDITOR [W. L. GARRISON]. n.d. n.p.** Describes meeting in Boston to form an auxiliary to the American Union for the Relief and Improvement of the Colored Race; reports that although about twenty abolitionists arrived, the attendance dwindled, as it seemed that the abolition of slavery was not one of the society's objectives. 18 April 1835. p.63, c4.

1861. F. *to* **MR. GARRISON n.d. n.p.** Noticed in a previous article that only six individuals in the entire city of Boston attended a meeting to form an auxiliary to the American Union; notes, however, that the Monthly Concert of Prayer was attended by 900; believes the American Union to be inefficient. 18 April 1835. p.63, c4.

1862 W. M. C. *to* **W. L. GARRISON. 15 April 1835. Providence.** Describes George Thompson's speech in Providence to the ladies of the city, and the subsequent formation of a female AS; reports the constitution was signed by 106 ladies; hopes ladies elsewhere will follow their example. 18 April 1835. p.63, c5.

1863 A GENTLEMAN TRAVELLING SOUTH *to* **FRIEND IN NEWBURYPORT. [extract] 19 March 1835. Charleston, S.C.** Notices the many colored people thronging the streets, who, in their crouching and retreating, seem to be in perpetual awe of the whites. 18 April 1835. p.64, c4.

1864 H. F. STEARNS *to* **REV. J. P. ATKINSON. [from the** *Concord* **(N.H.)** *Star and Universalist***] 20 January 1835. Maj. Woods' Plantation, Alabama.** Finds that Northern zealots have misrepresented the moral condition of the slaves; while Stearns does not want to be accused of advocating slavery, he points out that it is not as bad as many charge; details slaves, conditions and living arrangements. 25 April 1835. p.65, c1.

1865 G. *to* **HIS BROTHER IN MASSACHUSETTS. 28 March 1835. Georgia.** Relates that slaves are not taught to read or write, nor are they taught religious principles; declares that masters who treat their slaves well do not fear universal emancipation, but cruel masters do; asserts that slavery has a ruinous effect on the moral and religious character of Southern whites. 25 April 1835. p.65, c3.

1866 R. N. A. *to* **MR. EDITOR [W. L. GARRISON]. n.d. n.p.** Discusses the doom of the slaveholders who ignore repeated reproval by God and their fellow men; believes that moral reasoning with slaveholders is useless, but that God will redress the wrongs of the slave. 25 April 1835. p.65, c6.

1867 NATHANIEL SOUTHARD *to* **REV. A. STEVENS. 9 April 1835. Boston.** Congratulates him on a recent speech, most of which Southard is in agreement with; denies, however, that slaveholders keep slaves ignorant out of necessity; hopes all laborers for the cause will aim their attacks at the opposition, and not at each other. 25 April 1836. p.66, c2.

1868 n.n. *to* **THE** *LIBERATOR.* **17 April 1835. Reading.** Describes readings, sermons, and prayers which comprised the services in Reading on the fast day. 25 April 1835. p.66, c3.

1869 A METHODIST MINISTER *to* **MR. GARRISON. 14 April 1835. n.p.** Criticizes the "Counter Appeal" in the *Zion's Herald Extra*; notes that only eight ministers signed it, most of whom were at least forty miles from Boston, indicating that abolitionism is strong in the area. 25 April 1835. p.66, c3.

1870 C. V. CAPLES *to* **MR. EDITOR [W. L. GARRISON]. 1 April 1835. Boston.** Criticizes Rev. Louis Jansen's article in *Zion's Herald*; challenges Jansen's belief that colonization is the only efficient way to free the slaves, hoping that others like him will not obstruct the work of abolitionists. 25 April 1835. p.66, c4.

1871 S. J. MAY *to* **FRIEND. 16 April 1835. Taunton.** Describes meeting with members of the Society of Friends, at which he insisted that quiet testimony is not enough, and that the abolition cause demands action; mentions several recent speeches which stressed the need to abolish slavery in the District of Columbia. 25 April 1835. p.66, c5.

1872 SAMUEL J. MAY *to* **FRIEND. 20 April 1835. New Bedford.** Reports that he spoke with ministers of many denominations in Taunton, most of whom were interested in discussing slavery; notes that over 1,000 attended his speech in New Bedford. 25 April 1835. p.66, c5.

1873 GEO. THOMPSON *to* **W. L. GARRISON. 16 April 1835. New York.** Sends two copies of most recent *London Abolitionist,* the editor of which concurs in the belief that slavery degrades the oppressor as much as the slave; recounts fatiguing journey to Providence and the cheering reception given his speech there. 25 April 1835. p.66, c6.

1874 HENRY VANMETER *to* **W. L. GARRISON. 3 April 1835. New Bedford.** Tells of a fraud by the CS, which convinced him to sell his farm in Maine at a loss in order to go to Liberia; reports that upon his arrival at Boston, he was told that he was too old and that the change in climate would kill him; adds that the society has not helped him get his money or property back, and he is now in danger of having to go to the almshouse. 25 April 1835. p.66, c6.

1875 GEORGE STACY *to* **THE SEVERAL MEETINGS FOR SUFFERINGS IN AMERICA. n.d. n.p.** Encourages them to take action to right the wrongs suffered by oppressed Africans in America; tells of the measures taken in Britain, where there is a deep and lively interest in the termination of slavery. 25 April 1835. p.67, c1.

1876 S. *to* **FRIEND BACON. 15 April 1835. Winthrop.** Forwards list of delegates to the AAS from Maine in order to warn their opponents that they are not a small and feeble group. 25 April 1835. p.67, c5.

1877 J. W. *to* **MR. GARRISON. n.d. n.p.** Sends poem entitled "The Word 'Wrong' substituted for 'Sin' ''; praises Garrison's work in abolition cause. 25 April 1835. p.68, c1.

1878 ARNOLD BUFFUM *to* **SAMUEL J. MAY. 17 April 1835. Philadelphia.** Encourages him in his duties as corresponding secretary and general agent of the Massachusetts AS; recounts positive effects of speeches by George Thompson; describes debate at Young Men's Debating Society concerning the AS. 2 May 1835. p.70, c3.

1879 GEORGE THOMPSON *to* **W. L. GARRISON. 20 April 1835. Temperance Hotel, Albany, N.Y.** Declares that his trip up the Hudson reminded him of Scotland; reports that a recent meeting of colored people decided it was best not to send children to Canada for education, nor to encourage emigration there, but rather to stay and fight prejudice; Thompson agrees with this decision. 2 May 1835. p.70, c4.

1880 S. J. MAY *to* **W. L. GARRISON. 24 April 1835. New Bedford.** Continues description of his tour; discusses his lectures and meetings with other abolitionists in New Bedford and Fairhaven. 2 May 1835. p.70, c5.

1881 SAMUEL L. GOULD *to* **W. L. GARRISON. 27 April 1835. Westerly, R.I.** Recounts his tour of Rhode Island, speaking and campaigning for the anti-slavery cause; notes that he has encountered much apathy and little interest in the slavery question, but has frequently been able to change minds and open eyes to the importance of the slavery problem. 2 May 1835. p.70, c6.

1882 VERMONT *to* **BROTHER GARRISON. n.d. n.p.** Replies to "Counter Appeal" in *Zion's Herald* by Dr. Fisk and others; attacks Fisk's attempt to find justification of slavery in the Bible; affirms that slavery is a sin against man and God. 2 May 1835. p.71, c1.

1883 E. A. B. *to* **MR. EDITOR [W. L. GARRISON]. 7 April 1835. n.p.** Discusses his attempts to dissuade bitter opponents of the anti-slavery cause; calls for an end to resistance to the laws of God, which demand an end to slavery. 2 May 1835. p.71, c3.

1884 THOMAS PAUL *to* **W. L. GARRISON. 9 April 1835. Canaan.** Describes abolition, the activities taking place on the day of fast, and the local school in Canaan. 2 May 1835. p.71, c4.

1885 WILLIAM WHIPPER *to* **THE FREE COLORED POPULATION OF THE UNITED STATES. 22 April 1835. Philadelphia.** Announces the Fifth Annual Convention of the Free People of Color for improving their condition in the United States, to be held in Philadelphia on 1 June; calls on the "phalanx of Piety, Philanthropy, and Patriotism" to plead their cause. 2 May 1835. p.71, c4.

1886 MARTIN VAN BUREN *to* **A GENTLEMAN IN MISSISSIPPI. 11 July 1834. Washington.** Believes the slavery question belongs under the jurisdiction of the individual states, not Congress; denies the right of the general government to interfere. 2 May 1835. p.72, c2.

1887 THE REV. JAMES THOMPSON *to* **THE REV. A. BRANDRAM. [extract] 5 November 1834. Spanish Town, Jamaica.** Hopes to establish a Bible society in each parish of the island; notes that some have already been established; forwards several extracts of letters from Negroes in the country. 9 May 1835. p.73, c2.

1888 n.n. *to* **n.n. [extract] n.d. n.p.** Attests that Negroes in Jamaica are anxious to receive Bibles and religious instruction. 9 May 1835. p.73, c3.

1889 n.n. *to* **MR. EDITOR [W. L. GARRISON]. n.d. n.p.** Observes with great pleasure the advance of the anti-slavery cause; reports on new agents of the AS. 9 May 1835. p.73, c6.

1890 E. A. ATLEE *to* **WM. GOODELL. 23 April 1835. Philadelphia.** Reports that he received a letter from Lundy, proving he is not dead. 9 May 1835. p.74, c2.

1891 BENJAMIN LUNDY *to* **E. A. ATLEE. 21 March 1835. Matamoras.** Discusses results of his recent visit to the interior of the country; failed to obtain a land grant in Coahuila or Texas, but succeeded in getting one north of Texas country for 250 settlers; will furnish additional details later. 9 May 1835. p.74, c2.

1892 ALPHONSO *to* **MR. GARRISON. February 1835. Sedgwick, Me.** Claims that it is the duty of the ministers of the gospel to engage in the anti-slavery cause; believes slavery is a great moral evil. 9 May 1835. p.74, c3.

1893 n.n. *to* **THE OWNERS AND HOLDERS OF SLAVES. n.d. n.p.** Feels they are wrong to hold a human being in bondage; declares that his obligations to God, to them, to their slaves, and to himself force him to speak; warns them to absolve themselves of the evil of slaveholding. 9 May 1835. p.74, c4.

1894 n.n. *to* **FRIEND BACON. n.d. Maryland.** Declares that he would like to obtain a copy of the "Oasis" by Mrs. Child; notes there are a few true abolitionists in Maryland; believes that the law forbidding the abolition of slavery in Maryland is unconstitutional as well as unjust. 9 May 1835. p.74, c5.

1895 HENRY B. STANTON *to* **BROTHER GARRISON. 27 April 1835. Putnam, Oh.** Describes convention for forming state AS, attended by representatives from every section of the state; reports on speeches and committees; describes great harmony of spirit. 9 May 1835. p.74, c5.

1896 G. L. C. *to* **MR. GARRISON. 22 April 1835. Taunton.** Describes lecture of S. J. May on slavery, and the town's reaction; states that plans have been made to form an AS, but debates and arguments from colonizationists have delayed the formation of the society. 9 May 1835. p.74, c6.

1897 GEORGE THOMPSON *to* **W. L. GARRISON. 29 April 1835. Albany.** Reports on anti-slavery progress in Albany; adds that he has given several successful speeches, and a new AS is forming; notes also good reception in Greenbush. 9 May 1835. p.75, c2.

1898 GERRIT SMITH *to* **THE** *EMANCIPATOR.* **n.d. n.p.** Criticizes the *Liberator* and W. L. Garrison. 9 May 1835. p.75, c3.

1899 SEBRIED DODGE, PRINCIPAL ENGINEER ON THE WABASH AND ERIE CANAL *to* **SAMUEL FORRER. [extract] 10 April 1835. Maumee.** Describes conflict in Ohio and Michigan; reports on armed resistance in Michigan to the running of the line through their territory; adds that Ohio gives no protection to the disputed territory. 9 May 1835. p.75, c5.

1900 W. FISK *to* **THE EDITOR. [from the** *Zion's Herald*] **9 March 1835. Wesleyan University.** Quotes article by Prof. Whedon in *Liberator* to demonstrate "to what a pitch of acrimony and gall the modern spirit of abolitionism" has turned; attacks the *Liberator* for supporting George Thompson. 16 May 1835. p.77, c1.

1901 SIMON GOVE *to* **THE** *LIBERATOR.* **5 May 1835. Weare, N.H.** Relates anti-slavery progress in New Hampshire; reports that a better spirit prevails, an AS was recently formed, and zeal has been awakened. 16 May 1835. p.77, c4.

1902 AMOS POLLARD, M.D. *to* **W. L. GARRISON. 15 February 1835. Columbia, Texas, Mexico.** Claims that Texas is settling fast; communicates this information only to Northern and Eastern states in order that they may settle Texas before the Southerners and prevent slavery from gaining a foothold there. 16 May 1835. p.77, c5.

1903 JOSEPH A. DUGDALE *to* **W. L. GARRISON. 22 April 1835. Zanesville, Oh.** Relates the progress of the abolition cause near Ohio; describes his own tour and lectures to promote the cause; believes he awakened some from slumbering apathy. 16 May 1835. p.77, c5.

1904 A HIGHLY RESPECTABLE SOUTHERN LADY *to* **W. L. GARRISON. 15 April 1835. Philadelphia.** Recounts sufferings of slaves in the Charleston Work House; quotes description of horrible conditions and cruel labor from friend in Charleston in order to show Northerners that they make a great mistake when they suppose that house Negroes are not cruelly treated. 16 May 1835. p.78, c3.

1905 VERMONT *to* **BROTHER GARRISON. n.d. n.p.** Attacks Dr. Fisk and supporters of his "scripture argument" for slavery; examines the specific texts used and criticizes their interpretation; believes they pervert the word of the Lord. 16 May 1835. p.78, c4.

1906 ARNOLD BUFFUM *to* **GARRISON AND KNAPP. 9 May 1835. Philadelphia.** Feels encouraged by the progress of their good cause; describes speeches by Birney and Stanton; announces formation of a young men's AS; wishes to see a discussion of the moral rectitude of colonization. 16 May 1835. p.78, c6.

1907 THOMAS PAUL *to* **W. L. GARRISON. 4 May 1835. Canaan.** Describes anti-slavery speech by Rev. Storrs of New Hampshire, as a result of which many of those present became abolitionists and a society was organized. 16 May 1835. p.79, c1.

1908 n.n. *to* **n.n. [extract] n.d. New Hampshire.** Praises *Liberator* for its straightforward course; wishes every American family in the United States could have a copy. 16 May 1835. p.79, c1.

1909 n.n. *to* **THE *LIBERATOR*. 7 May 1835. Boston.** Requests donations for the Boston Samaritan Asylum for indigent colored children; reports that, organized almost a year ago, it has provided for nine children. 16 May 1835. p.79, c1.

1910 W. L. GARRISON *to* **MY PARTNER, KNAPP. 9 May 1835. New York.** Reports that he has just arrived and has held discussions with many abolitionists; forwards the declaration of sentiments adopted by Ohio State Anti-Slavery Convention. 16 May 1835. p.79, c2.

1911 CYRUS P. GROSVENOR *to* **BRO. BACON. 18 May 1835. Worcester Co.** Declares he has finally come to believe that he must plead the cause by writing for the public eye; gives brief itinerary of a recent trip, decribing his speeches and future lecture plans. 23 May 1835. p.81, c2.

1912 C. C. BURLEIGH *to* **BROTHER GARRISON. 6 April 1835. Sudbury.** Discusses his lectures in the Groton-Western area; reports that in some towns, he received very warm and hearty approval and welcome, but he frequently received small audiences in towns where the minister opposed anti-slavery efforts and would not publicly announce his speech. 23 May 1835. p.81, c3.

1913 DR. F. A. COX *to* **n.n. 12 May 1835. n.p.** Notes declining attendance at the anti-slavery meeting. 23 May 1835. p.82, c4.

1914 RHODE ISLAND *to* **MR. EDITOR [W. L. GARRISON]. 6 May 1835. Abouthere.** Conveys his respects to "Vermont," whose pieces are read with interest by the local Methodist community; hopes for deliverance from the influence of slaveholding ministers. 23 May 1835. p.83, c5.

1915 n.n. *to* **MESSRS. EDITORS. [from the *New York Journal of Commerce*] n.d. n.p.** Replies to comment, "Was there ever such a Spring?"; sends extracts of weather from other years when it was unseasonably cold in spring or summer. 23 May 1835. p.84, c3.

1916 F. A. COX *to* **THE MANAGERS OF THE AS. 12 May 1835. n.p.** Declines their invitation to address their meeting, but asserts his neutrality toward their principles. 30 May 1835. p.85, c1.

1917 n.n. *to* **MR. J. W. WEBB n.d. n.p.** Invites Webb to listen to addresses by Thompson and Cox, who are in favor of immediate emancipation. 30 May 1835. p.85, c1.

1918 J. S. *to* **THE *JOURNAL OF COMMERCE*. n.d. n.p.** Corrects their article on the freeing of American slaves by the civil authorities in Bermuda; discusses whether slave owners have the right to complain of their losses; proves that the act was agreeable to the Law of Nations. 30 May 1835. p.85, c4.

1919 RHODE ISLAND *to* **MR. EDITOR [W. L. GARRISON]. 7 May 1835. Abouthere.** Quotes from *Christian Advocate and Journal* on the "wretched snarl of abolitionism"; attacks columns by Nathan Bangs, D.D.; charges that no anti-slavery lecture or paper has used language as "uncourteous, unchristian and severe" as that in anti-abolition papers. 30 May 1835. p.85, c6.

1920 n.n. *to* **W. L. GARRISON. 20 April 1835. Freedom Hall, Va.** Forwards extract of letter from citizen in Georgia. 20 May 1835. p.85, c6.

1921 n.n. *to* **n.n. [extract] n.d. n.p.** Declares that to feed, clothe, and force African slaves to work is "the best mercy we can safely extend to them." 30 May 1835. p.85, c6.

1922 SAMUEL H. COX *to* **REV. AND DEAR SIR. 5 May 1835. Auburn, Cayuga County, N.Y.** Explains that he was unable to leave his position to travel to the New England Anti-Slavery Convention; salutes all the friends of God and man. 30 May 1835. p.86, c1.

1923 ZADOC HUMPHREY *to* **THE NEW ENGLAND ANTI-SLAVERY CONVENTION. 23 May 1835. Boston.** Regrets he cannot attend the convention; describes their society, organized last October, and relays other news from abolitionists in the Boston area. 30 May 1835. p.86, c2.

1924 DAVID THURSTON *to* **MR. S. E. SEWALL. 21 May 1835. Winthrop.** Regrets he cannot attend the anti-slavery convention; celebrates the cause; calls for the justice of God to end the nation's crime of slavery. 30 May 1835. p.86, c2.

1925 J. COFFIN *to* **MR. EDITOR [W. L. GARRISON]. 23 May 1835. Philadelphia.** Sends communication from Henry Parsons, captain of the *Ninus,* which brought emancipated slaves to Liberia. 30 May 1835. p.87, c1.

1926 HENRY PARSONS *to* **n.n. [extract] n.d. n.p.** Relates disappointment of his passengers, the emancipated slaves, upon arriving at Liberia and finding they were not to have their own houses as had been promised; reports on their health, activities, and education. 30 May 1835. p.87, c1.

1927 A HEARER *to* **W. L. GARRISON. 18 May 1835. Reading.** Describes excellent speech by C. C. Burleigh which corrected public sentiment on many issues. 30 May 1835. p.87, c2.

1928 n.n. *to* **W. L. GARRISON. 29 May 1835. Boston.** Member of Yale's sophomore class, currently teaching in Boston, discusses his attendance at a recent anti-slavery convention; rejoices at the untiring perseverance of friends of the cause; feels inspired now to travel and spread word of the cause. 30 May 1835. p.87, c2.

1929 HENRY TATEM *to* **GEORGE JAS. ADAMS. 24 May 1835. Warwick.** Discusses resolutions passed at Phenix Meetinghouse which deal with the evil of slavery and the need for its abolition. 30 May 1835. p.87, c3.

1930 THOS. FOWELL BUXTON *to* **PROF. WRIGHT. 10 April 1835. London.** Takes deep, heartfelt interest in the question of abolition of slavery in America; believes that slavery is a crime which must therefore be abolished. 30 May 1835. p.87, c5.

1931 STEPHEN THURSTON *to* **COL. JOSEPH AMES. [extract from the *Portland Mirror*] 27 September 1834. West Prospect, Me.** Declines commission from late governor of Maine because Thurston is a Christian and opposes war. 30 May 1835. p.88, c4.

1932 AN ABOLITIONIST OF THE OLD SCHOOL *to* **THE** *PRESBYTERIAN.* **n.d. n.p.** Quotes from the British and Foreign Society for the Abolition of Slavery, which claims that "foreign emissaries" uniting with Garrison have retarded by a generation the cause of African freedom in the United States, and that Garrison is an agitator who declares war on social relations. 6 June 1835. p.89, c2.

1933 JUNIUS *to* **MR. CLARK. n.d. n.p.** Regrets hearing of mob resistance to Mr. Thompson, whom he finds an intelligent and noble man; argues that Thompson's claim that slaves have the "privileges and dignity of an immortal being" would convict slaveholders of a "damning sin"; hopes the truth about slavery continues to be unveiled. 6 June 1835. p.90, c2.

1934 JOS. WARREN CROSS *to* **SIR. 3 June 1835. Boxborough.** Announces recent formation of male and female ASS; describes choice of constitution models and lists officers. 6 June 1835. p.90, c5.

1935 n.n. *to* **W. L. GARRISON. 3 May 1835. Mount Desert, Me.** Tells of the formation of the Mount Desert AS; lists officers and directors. 6 June 1835. p.90, c6.

1936 DANIEL O'CONNELL, JR. *to* **MR. ATWILL. [from the** *Concord Freeman***] 25 May 1835. Townsend.** Describes early incident which increased his interest in the cause; reports that the trustees of a church refused the building to S. J. May for a speech, saying it would cause too much "excitement"; calls for free discussion as the quickest way to dispose of the controversy. 13 June 1835. p.93, c6.

1937 A. JOHNSON *to* **W. L. GARRISON. 19 May 1835. Rupert, Vt.** Forwards an essay concerning claims by the CS that it is a benevolent institution. 13 June 1835. p.94, c1.

1938 VERMONT *to* **BROTHER GARRISON. 20 May 1835. Whereabout.** Feels he must expose the wickedness of the faculty of Wesleyan University who attempt to justify slavery with Scripture; quotes pertinent texts; attacks the logic of the faculty's reasoning. 13 June 1835. p.94, c3.

1939 RHODE ISLAND *to* **MR. EDITOR [W. L. GARRISON]. 10 May 1835. Abouthere.** Criticizes Nathan Bangs, D.D., editor of the *Christian Advocate and Journal,* who has called abolitionists "injudicious, anti-republican, jacobinacal, speculative, and hotheaded," and who refuses to publish any opinions disagreeing with his own; writer claims that no abolitionist has ever employed such practices. 13 June 1835. p.94, c5.

1940 GRANITE STATE *to* **FRIEND GARRISON. 2 June 1835. Allabout.** Expresses gratitude to Mr. "Vermont" for his articles on Wesleyan University; feels that "Southern Benevolence" explains the outcry at Wesleyan University. 13 June 1835. p.94, c5.

1941 LIBERTAS *to* **MR. EDITOR [W. L. GARRISON]. n.d. n.p.** Hopes that the coming Fourth of July will be celebrated appropriately by friends of immediate emancipation; hopes to hear many orators and lecturers. 13 June 1835. p.94, c6.

1942 JOHN PRENTICE *to* **W. L. GARRISON. 8 June 1835. Providence.** Corrects a statement by Rev. R. R. Gurley, who quoted Prentice as saying he would rather dissolve the Union of the United States than have slavery exist one year; explains that Prentice actually said he would rather dissolve the Union than perpetuate this system of iniquity and blood. 13 June 1835. p.94, c6.

1943 BENJAMIN LUNDY *to* **AMERICAN PHILANTHROPISTS. 11 May 1835. Nashville.** Reports he has just explored the eastern parts of the Republic of Mexico and obtained a land grant to establish a colony; invites public attention to it, especially that of enterprising planters, agriculturalists, manufacturers, mechanics, and laborers; intends to have a free system of labor and no slavery. 13 June 1835. p.96, c2.

1944 L. W. *to* **MESSRS. GARRISON AND KNAPP. 25 May 1835. Pittsburgh, Pa.** Describes the great spirit of moral improvement, particularly among the colored population; notes improvements in education, temperance, and religious training. 13 June 1835. p.96, c5.

1945 REV. J. W. NEVIN *to* **SIR. 2 June 1835. Allegheny.** Declines to address anti-slavery meeting that night, although he had previously agreed to do so; believes he would injure the seminary with which he is connected if he lectured on such an unpopular cause; attempts to justify his actions. 20 June 1835. p.97, c1.

1946 ARISTIDES *to* **FRIEND GARRISON. 4 June 1835. Boston.** Reports on a Methodist missionary meeting he attended, held to raise funds for their missions in Africa; describes speeches and debates by Rev. Seys, Dr. Bangs, and Dr. Fisk; concludes that they are unfair to the slave in upholding his rights and blessings by telling him to find them in Africa. 20 June 1835. p.99, c1.

1947 RHODE ISLAND *to* **MR. EDITOR [W. L. GARRISON]. 12 May 1835. Abouthere.** Asserts he must publicly reprove Dr. N. Bangs for meddling with the "anti-republican Abolitionists"; criticizes Bangs' offensive language, particularly since many whom he attacked were his "ministering brethren." 20 June 1835. p.99, c1.

1948 LA ROY SUNDERLAND *to* **MR. EDITOR [W. L. GARRISON]. 13 June 1835. n.p.** Declares that the recent letter in the *Liberator* from "L. W." did an injustice by making unqualified remarks about the members and ministry of the Methodist Church. 20 June 1835. p.99, c2.

1949 A. W. *to* **FRIEND GARRISON. n.d. n.p.** Sends letter from "highly respected correspondent" in Philadelphia. 20 June 1835. p.99, c2.

1950 n. n. *to* **A. W. [extract] n.d. Philadelphia.** Believes nothing would advance the cause of abolition as much as a declaration of the peace principles by abolitionists and free people of color. 20 June 1835. p.99, c2.

1951 ANNA PURINTON *to* **MR. GEORGE THOMPSON. 17 June 1835. Lynn.** Presents a copy of a resolution of thanks from the Female AS of Lynn, which respects and encourages his cause. 20 June 1835. p.99, c5.

1952 MR. WILLIAM SMEAL, JR. *to* **GEORGE THOMPSON. [extract] 26 March 1835. Glasgow.** Discusses recent successful meeting of Glasgow Emancipation Society; notes that many excellent speeches were delivered, and that members were gratified by accounts of Mr. Thompson's labors in the United States. 27 June 1835. p.101, c6.

1953 S. PERKINS *to* **MR. EDITOR [W. L. GARRISON]. 7 May 1835. Hebron.** Reports the organization of a town AS of about thirty members; prays for freedom for slaves. 27 June 1835. p.102, c6.

1954 BEVERLY R. WILSON *to* **THE** *NORFOLK BEACON.* **[extract] n.d. n.p.** Describes differences between the African fever and other types of fevers. 27 June 1835. p.103, c3.

1955 OLD GOVERNOR WINSLOW *to* **W. L. GARRISON. n.d. n.p.** Comments on presidential candidates Judge White and Richard M. Johnson. 27 June 1835. p.103, c4.

1956 AN INQUIRER *to* **W. L. GARRISON. n.d. n.p.** Explains that he committed himself to a donation to Lane Seminary, but has since realized that the seminary is anti-abolitionist and that he would prefer to donate to the Oberlin Institute; seeks Garrison's advice. 27 June 1835. p.103, c5.

1957 n.n. *to* **MR. EDITOR [W. L. GARRISON] 21 June 1835. Boston.** Upon hearing a sermon delivered on the topic of cruelty to animals, notes the irony that the same minister was not equally moved by the subject of cruelty to men, namely slavery. 27 June 1835. p.103, c5.

1958 AN OLD FRIEND *to* **MR. EDITOR [W. L. GARRISON] 18 June 1835. Boston.** Requests information about the Massachusetts CS and its officers; ridicules the society and its officers. 27 June 1835. p.103, c5.

1959 JOHN WINSLOW, EFFINGHAM L. CAPRON, JOSEPH HEALY, JOHN G. WHITTIER, AND MOSES A. CARTLAND *to* **JAMES G. BIRNEY. 28 May 1835. n.p.** Residents of slaveholding states wish to know about plans for emancipation, their effect on slaveholders, and Birney's opinion of the ACS. 4 July 1835. p.105, c2.

1960 JAMES G. BIRNEY *to* **JOHN WINSLOW, EFFINGHAM L. CAPRON, JOSEPH HEALY, JOHN G. WHITTIER, AND MOSES A. CARTLAND. 29 May 1835. Boston.** Replies to their questions, declaring that the best way to preserve tranquility among the slaves is to inform them of the peaceful efforts being made in their behalf; declares that he supports neither gradual emancipation nor colonization. 4 July 1835. p.105, c3.

1961 O. P. *to* **THE** *NEW YORK EVANGELIST.* **n.d. n.p.** Quotes letter from a friend who found Dr. Reese's answer to Mr. Jay's book a "silly, pointless argument." 4 July 1835. p.105, c4.

1962 W. C. C. *to* **BROTHER GARRISON. n.d. Montgomery County, N.Y.** Wonders how best to encourage people to act; observes that urging people to hear his cause and question themselves only incurs their wrath and rudeness; finds encouragement in the *Liberator.* 4 July 1835. p.105, c5.

1963 VERMONT *to* **BROTHER GARRISON. 20 May 1835. Whereabout.** Attacks the "Scripture Argument" by which Dr. Fisk tries to justify slavery; asserts that Christianity arose with the Golden Rule and a spirit of equality which is inconsistent with slavery. 4 July 1835. p.106, c1.

1964 A COLORED BALTIMOREAN *to* **FRIEND. 24 June 1835. Baltimore.** Observes that abolitionists still suffer from persecution; reports that they are portrayed by colonizationists as alarming and evil; concludes with amusing anecdotes. 4 July 1835. p.106, c3.

1965 NATHANIEL SWASEY *to* **W. L. GARRISON. 10 May 1835. Bath.** Defends abolitionists in response to a letter from H. F. Stearns, who opposed slavery until he went South; challenges Stearns' observations and conclusions regarding the South. 4 July 1835. p.106, c4.

1966 ORSON S. MURRAY *to* **MR. EDITOR [W. L. GARRISON]. 22 June 1835. Fairfield, Vt.** Reports on controversy between himself and the *American Baptist*'s editor over the reporting of an anti-slavery meeting; feels that the editor misrepresents several speakers. 4 July 1835. p.106, c5.

1967 n.n. *to* **THE** *FALL RIVER RECORDER.* **n.d. n.p.** Discusses plight of members of a ship's crew who are imprisoned on charges of secreting a runaway slave on board, and face the death penalty if convicted; questions society's toleration of such injustice. 11 July 1835. p.109, c3.

1968 DAVID STOWELL *to* **MR. EDITOR. [from the** *Herald of Freedom***] 18 June 1835. Goffstown.** Discusses resolutions against slavery adopted at a meeting of the Congregational Church; notes that most members favor immediate emancipation. 11 July 1835. p.109, c5.

1969 OLIVER JOHNSON *to* **FRIEND GARRISON. 6 July 1835. Middlebury, Vt.** Gives account of a recent convention to form a county AS, listing resolutions and officers; encloses letter read to the convention from Rev. Dr. Beman; declares he is cheered by the course and success of the cause in the past three years. 11 July 1835. p.110, c6.

1970 NATHAN S. S. BEMAN *to* **THE GENTLEMEN OF THE COMMITTEE TO FORM A VERMONT AS. 26 June 1835. Troy.** Declines invitation to attend their convention, as he has just returned to his parish and cannot leave again; expresses his feelings towards their goals; urges efforts toward immediate emancipation. 11 July 1835. p.111, c1.

1971 RHODE ISLAND *to* **MR. EDITOR [W. L. GARRISON]. 29 June 1835. Abouthere.** Criticizes N. Bangs, D.D. for accusing abolitionists of inciting mob violence; points out that New York mobs cited Bangs' articles as justification for their acts. 11 July 1835. p.111, c2.

1972 W. *to* **MR. EDITOR [W. L. GARRISON]. n.d. n.p.** Replies to "Inquirer" that he was also a friend of Lane Seminary, but in view of its anti-abolitionist stand, he has withdrawn his pledge and doubled the amount in favor of Oberlin College. 11 July 1835. p.111, c3.

1973 C. P. GROSVENOR *to* **W. L. GARRISON. 30 June 1835. Salem.** Describes insulting and threatening letter received from an anonymous writer; urges the writer not to hide in a cowardly manner, but to come forward. 11 July 1835. p.111, c4.

1974 R. *to* **MR. GARRISON. n.d. n.p.** Recounts day of fasting and prayer recently observed at the Evangelical Congregation Church in Kingston, Massachusetts. 11 July 1835. p.111, c4.

1975 n.n. *to* **SIR. 26 June 1835. New York.** Describes anti-slavery meeting of the previous day; reports that no colonizationists attended, and that speeches were given calling for an end to prejudice and encouraging prayers for the slaveholders. 11 July 1835. p.111, c5.

1976 EGO *to* **BROTHER GARRISON. 30 June 1835. Andover Theological Seminary.** Criticizes recent speech of Mr. Gurley, the champion of colonization; finds his eloquence "windy," his arguments sophistical, and his assertions of the impracticality of abolitionist principles unsupported. 18 July 1835. p.113, c2.

1977 RHODE ISLAND *to* **MR. EDITOR [W. L. GARRISON]. 30 June 1835. Abouthere.** Reminds him that the paper which Dr. Bangs edits is not supposed to be a sectional paper, but one belonging to the entire Church; argues that by opposing abolitionists and defending slavery, Dr. Bangs is a slaveholder in practice. 18 July 1835. p.113, c4.

1978 REV. JAMES HARGREAVES *to* **REV. SAMUEL J. MAY. [extract] 31 March 1835. Waltham Abbey, England.** Believes slavery is a foul blot on America; rejoices that May is working for emancipation, but hopes that he will continue to devote efforts to the cause of peace; reminds that war has killed more than slavery has and is more abominable. 18 July 1835. p.113, c6.

1979 SAMUEL G. HOWE *to* **THE** *LIBERATOR.* **6 July 1835. New England Institution for the Education of the Blind.** Corrects implications of a poem in the *Liberator* which pictured a blind black boy being refused admission; explains that blacks are admitted, as well as children of any color. 18 July 1835. p.113, c6.

1980 RAY POTTER *to* **FRIEND GARRISON. 6 July 1835. Pawtucket.** Reports recent uncommon interest in the subject of slavery; gives brief summaries of various speeches and debates, including an address from George Thompson which was received "gloriously." 18 July 1835. p.114, c2.

1981 R. T. ROBINSON *to* **W. L. GARRISON. 25 June 1835. North Ferrisburgh, Vt.** Praises Garrison's doctrine of "utter denial of *everything* which had a tendency to sustain or encourage iniquity"; applies this doctrine to the slaves' cause by refusing to use any article produced by slave labor. 18 July 1835. p.114, c3.

1982 EGOMET *to* **SIR. 30 June 1835. Here.** Points out inconsistency of preacher who supports the cause of peace, but advises his parish to stay away from the anti-slavery cause, as it is "so exciting." 18 July 1835. p.114, c3.

1983 TRUTH *to* **MR. EDITOR [W. L. GARRISON]. n.d. n.p.** Details his conversion from colonization to abolition when he realized that "Old Lady [colonization] and her pale faced children don't like the Niggers," and that they were primarily responsible for the sufferings of free blacks. 18 July 1835. p.114, c4.

1984 R. N. A. *to* **MR. EDITOR [W. L. GARRISON]. n.d. n.p.** Remarks upon the irony of holding Fourth of July celebrations of liberty and equality amid the sufferings of a slave population. 18 July 1835. p.114, c4.

1985 E. L. A. *to* **MR. EDITOR [W. L. GARRISON]. 10 July 1835. n.p.** Exposes fraud about practices of the CS, which purported to collect money to send 125 emigrants to Liberia, but in fact sent only 81; criticizes similar "mistakes" of colonizationists. 18 July 1835. p.114, c5.

1986 C. *to* **W. L. GARRISON. n.d. n.p.** Furnishes information on Jamaica reported by John Wood: the new system is working well, the apprentices are a bit discontented but behave peaceably, and schools and churches are being erected for the colored population. 18 July 1835. p.114, c5.

1987 A YOUNG FRIEND *to* **W. L. GARRISON. n.d. n.p.** Declares that the "grand-child of Madam Colonization" seems to have been "still-born" in his city; notes attempts at founding a CS seem to have failed. 18 July 1835. p.114, c6.

1988 WILLIAM COE *to* **FRIEND GARRISON. 9 July 1835. Portland.** Sends copies of resolutions adopted at the Conference of Ministers and Delegates of Christians in Maine, which condemn slavery and call for its abolition in the District of Columbia. 18 July 1835. p.114, c6.

1989 S. G. WILSON *to* **MR. EDITOR [W. L. GARRISON]. n.d. n.p.** Forwards transcript of meeting at which a mob attempted to prevent him from giving an anti-slavery speech; complains that free speech in church is no longer sacred. 18 July 1835. p.115, c1.

1990 R. REED *to* **BROTHER GARRISON. 15 July 1835. Andover.** Describes speeches delivered by Rev. Mr. Phelps and George Thompson, both of which exposed the "monster" of the CS; admonishes the public to judge the arguments for themselves. 18 July 1835. p.115, c2.

1991 J. W. A. *to* **MR. BRAINARD. 11 May 1835. Cincinnati.** Recounts abuse suffered by a kidnapped woman, Lydia Howard, and her three small children, before she was able to show her free papers and escape. 18 July 1835. p.115, c3.

1992 DANIEL O'CONNELL *to* **THE** *LONDON MORNING CHRONICLE.* **16 May 1835. 9 Clarges Street.** Corrects their report of his speech: his reference to Americans as "the basest and vilest of mankind" was not made to all Americans, but only to slaveholders. 18 July 1835. p.115, c5.

1993 C. *to* **W. L. GARRISON. n.d. n.p.** Encloses extracts from the will of Samuel Gist, which provided for the emancipation of his slaves after his death and the sharing of profits and surpluses from his plantation among them; Virginia law prohibited the execution of the will, and after Gist's death, his agents sent away his former slaves and retained the land for themselves. 25 July 1835. p.117, c5.

1994 N. P. ROGERS *to* **W. L. GARRISON. 8 July 1835. Plymouth.** Believes there is too much "abstract" abolition and too little concrete action against prejudice and poverty; reports on speeches by four young colored men from Noyes Academy to an anti-slavery meeting. 25 July 1835. p.118, c1.

1995 MRS. D. L. CHILD *to* **EDITOR OF THE** *LIBERATOR* **[W. L. GARRISON]. n.d. n.p.** Forwards letters from L. M. Child and Benjamin Davenport concerning the Institution for the Blind, in order to convince a critic that the reference made to the institution in a poem about a "Little Blind Boy" was based on truth. 25 July 1835. p.118, c2.

1996 L. M. CHILD *to* **DR. HOWE. n.d. n.p.** States that she cannot trace the author of the poem about a "little blind boy"; provides evidence that Dr. Howe refused to admit colored children to the Institution for the Blind, in order not to offend Southern patrons; criticizes this weak excuse for prejudice on the part of a benevolent institution. 25 July 1835. p.118, c2.

1997 BENJAMIN DAVENPORT *to* **MR. EFFINGHAM L. CAPRON. 13 January 1834. Mendon.** Reports that the legislature awarded sufficient funds to the Institution for the Blind to provide for twenty students, and that although only twelve or thirteen applications had been received, the trustees refused that of a young colored boy because of his race. 25 July 1835. p.118, c2.

1998 AN OFFICER ON BOARD THE U.S. FRIGATE *POTOMAC* *to* **THE** *LIBERATOR.* **[extract] 29 April 1835. Gibraltar.** Reports deaths of William Johnson, Basil Edwards, Gordon Taylor, and others aboard the ship, in order to inform their families and friends. 25 July 1835. p.118, c4.

1999 A FRIEND OF THE BIBLE *to* **MR. EDITOR [W. L. GARRISON]. n.d. n.p.** Declares that Mr. Gurley misquoted the Bible for his own purposes. 25 July 1835. p.119, c5.

2000 STRONG AND GERRY *to* **MESSRS. EDITORS. [from the** *Boston Commercial Gazette*] **n.d. n.p.** Report on a discussion he attended between Mr. Gurley, a colonizationist, and Mr. May, an abolitionist; feel that Mr. May made a gross and abusive attack on the noble CS, but that Mr. Gurley was gifted, eloquent and gentlemanly; protest against such future public discussions. 1 August 1835. p.121, c1.

2001 A CLERGYMAN OF BOSTON *to* **FRIEND IN NEW YORK. [extract from the** *New York Journal of Commerce*] **18 July 1835. Boston.** Advocate of colonization describes discussion between Gurley and May, at which Gurley presented intelligent, eloquent, and logical arguments, while May's presentation was weak and unconvincing. 1 August 1835. p.121, c2.

2002 JAMES FORTEN *to* **REV. W. S. PORTER. 10 June 1835. Philadelphia.** Expresses surprise that Gurley and the colonizationists have forgotten about the meeting held in 1817 by the people of color in Philadelphia, at which their response to the Liberia project was a tremendous, unanimous "No." 1 August 1835. p.121, c3.

2003 n.n. *to* **W. L. GARRISON. 17 July 1835. Philadelphia.** Provides full report of the trial of Mary Gilmore, a white girl claimed by a man as his mulatto slave; describes "disgraceful" riots in Philadelphia, and condemns attacks on defenseless victims. 1 August 1835. p.121, c4.

2004 ONE WHOSE HEART HAS BEEN WARMED WITH THE SIMPLE STORY OF LITTLE JAMES *to* **FRIEND GARRISON. n.d. n.p.** Discusses the *Memoir of James Jackson,* the tale of an attentive and obedient scholar who died at the age of six years and eleven months; finds it a moving and morally instructive book, and hopes many others will buy copies. 1 August 1835. p.122, c3.

2005 JAMES BALLARD *to* **FRIEND GARRISON. 4 July 1835. Bennington.** Describes Fourth of July meeting and anti-colonization speeches delivered at the school AS; reports subsequent formation of a town AS; includes constitution and list of officers. 1 August 1835. p.122, c3.

2006 SAMUEL G. HOWE *to* **EDITOR OF THE** *LIBERATOR* **[W. L. GARRISON]. 27 July 1835. New England Institution for the Education of the Blind.** Refutes charges by Mrs. Child that his institution denied admission to students because of color; quotes his previous letter to her. 1 August 1835. p.122, c4.

2007 SAMUEL G. HOWE *to* **MRS. CHILD. 23 July 1835. Cohasset.** Replies to her charges, claiming that the case is not "fairly or fully" stated, particularly in reference to charges from Benjamin Davenport; denies that the conversations she quotes took place. 1 August 1835. p.122, c4.

2008 OBSERVATOR *to* **MR. EDITOR [W. L. GARRISON]. 27 July 1835. Andover Theological Seminary.** Claims that letters from C. published in the *Boston Courier* misrepresented the debates there between Messrs. Thompson and Phelps; notes that majority of those in the seminary favor anti-slavery and immediate emancipation. 1 August 1835. p.122, c5.

2009 H. C. W. *to* **MR. EDITOR. [from the** *New England Spectator***] n.d. n.p.** Criticizes Rev. Joseph Tracy's article in the *Recorder* on talks between Gurley and May; claims that Tracy's charges are unfounded and unsupported, and that he misrepresented the spirit of the audience which was decidedly in favor of abolition, not colonization. 1 August 1835. p.123, c1.

2010 INDIVIDUALS RESIDING IN MISSISSIPPI *to* **n.n. [extract] n.d. n.p.** Describe plans for slave insurrection which was discovered and prevented. 1 August 1835. p.123, c1.

2011 CYRUS FOSTER *to* **W. L. GARRISON. n.d. n.p.** Recommends Mr. Hannibal Lewis, a colored man who makes boots and shoes. 1 August 1835. p.123, c5.

2012 n.n. *to* **n.n. [extract] 3 July 1835. Canton, Ms.** Reports that the Negroes are about to rise upon the whites again; several whites have been arrested as conspirators. 1 August 1835. p.124, c4.

2013 R. REED *to* **MR. EDITOR [W. L. GARRISON]. n.d. n.p.** Describes anti-slavery meetings at Andover; quotes from Mr. Thompson's speeches concerning his application of ancient history lessons to slavery in America; notes that Thompson remained in control of his Christian dignity and calmness, even during abusive question and answer period. 8 August 1835. p.125, c3.

2014 WILLIAM H. HILLIARD, DAVID JONES, AND PAUL BLOUNT *to* **THE EDITOR OF THE** *LIBERATOR* **[W. L. GARRISON]. 30 July 1835. Princeton, N.J.** Report formation of Princeton, New Jersey Young Men's AS; lists resolutions and officers. 8 August 1835. p.126, c4.

2015 n.n. *to* **n.n. [extract] 8 July 1835. Jackson, Ms.** Reports that a company of white men and Negroes was detected and subdued before they did any mischief; describes hanging of trouble-makers; claims that the whole county is armed for protection. 8 August 1835. p.126, c5.

2016 T. H. PURKETT *to* **W. L. GARRISON. n.d. n.p.** Replies to Mr. Phelps; admits they did not publish the book *Memoir of James Jackson,* but they do carry the book for sale, contrary to Phelps' charge. 8 August 1835. p.127, c5.

2017 L. W. *to* **THE** *LIBERATOR.* **27 June 1835. Pittsburgh, Pa.** Responds to unfounded charges against letter he wrote; claims there was no mention of the Methodist Episcopal church in Pennsylvania. 8 August 1835. p.128, c5.

2018 H. *to* **MR. EDITOR. [from the** *New England Spectator]* **n.d. n.p.** Quotes from Mr. Gurley's speech in support of the ACS; asks what the society is doing for the abolition of slavery, and what are the slaveholders doing to emancipate their slaves. 15 August 1835. p.129, c3.

2019 n.n. *to* **MR. FARMER. n.d. n.p.** Discusses two components of anti-slavery action: the principle prompting action, and the measures proposed for accomplishing the undertaking; believes the measures proposed by AS are pacific in the extreme. 15 August 1835. p.129, c3.

2020 CIVIS *to* **MESSRS. GARRISON AND KNAPP. 27 July 1835. Boston.** Discusses the necessity of a daily paper devoted principally to the cause of immediate emancipation; believes the abolition cause is fast approaching a crisis and opponents are becoming more malignant. 15 August 1835. p.129, c5.

2021 AGITATOR *to* **W. L. GARRISON. n.d. n.p.** Reminds him that the Constitution of the United States was formed with the doors tightly closed, and that the proceedings remained secret; wonders why the document is considered so sacred, when it was the work of a "secret conclave." 15 August 1835. p.129, c5.

2022 D. L. CHILD *to* **EFFINGHAM L. CAPRON. 27 July 1835. Boston.** Requests further information on the controversy between Mrs. Child and Dr. Howe over the admission of colored students to the Institution for the Education of the Blind. 15 August 1835. p.131, c3.

2023 EFFINGHAM L. CAPRON *to* **DAVID L. CHILD. 4 August 1835. Uxbridge.** Concurs with report of Benjamin Davenport that a colored boy was refused admission at the Institution for the Blind. 15 August 1835. p.131, c3.

2024 BENJAMIN DAVENPORT *to* **D. L. CHILD, ESQ. 4 August 1835. Mendon.** Provides information on the rejection of a colored boy from the Institution for the Blind, solely because of his race. 15 August 1835. p.131, c3.

2025 COMMODORE PORTER *to* **n.n. [extract] n.d. Constantinople.** Relates anecdotes and descriptions of life in Turkey. 15 August 1835. p.132. c2.

2026 n.n. *to* **n.n. [extract] 27 July 1835. Havana.** Reports uprising of forty Negroes who were waiting to be emancipated; most were caught and face execution. 15 August 1835. p.132, c4.

2027 A BOSTONIAN *to* **W. L. GARRISON. n.d. n.p.** Curses Garrison and his "detestable," "nefarious" causes; threatens him with a just reward. 22 August 1835. p.135, c1.

2028 n.n. *to* **W. L. GARRISON. 7 August 1835. Montgomery.** Swears at Garrison and his "set of damned rascals"; tells him not to interfere in matters which are not his own. 22 August 1835. p.135, c1.

2029 AMOS KENDALL *to* **EDMUND ANDERSON, POST MASTER GENERAL. n.d. n.p.** Sends copy of letter explaining his views. 22 August 1835. p.135, c3.

2030 AMOS KENDALL *to* **THE POSTMASTER AT CHARLESTON, S.C. [extract] 4 August 1835. Post Office Department.** States that the post office has no legal right to detain mail, but in view of the "incendiary" nature of the slavery pamphlets and the good of the community, he will not condemn the Postmaster's refusal to send them in the mail. 22 August 1835. p.135, c3.

2031 POST OFFICE DEPARTMENT *to* **POSTMASTER, CHARLESTON, S.C. 4 August 1835. n.p.** Replies to question of whether the postmaster has the power to detain papers if they are insurrectionary and incendiary: states that the post office cannot legally sanction such behavior, but will not condemn it, in view of higher laws of communities. 22 August 1835. p.135, c3.

2032 A SUBSCRIBER *to* **MESSRS. EDITORS. [from the** *Journal of Commerce***] n.d. n.p.** Inquires by what authority a postmaster can open mail or papers directed to an individual. 22 August 1835. p.135, c3.

2033 POSTMASTER AT NEW YORK *to* **EXECUTIVE COMMITTEE. [extract] n.d. New York.** Explains that he assumes responsibility, and has decided to refuse to send pamphlets of the AS in the mail. 22 August 1835. p.135, c3.

2034 CORRESPONDENT *to* **n.n. 4 August 1835. Bermuda.** Describes church service and celebration of first anniversary of emancipation of slaves throughout British colonies. 22 August 1835. p.135, c4.

2035 A RECENT EMIGRANT TO THE STATE OF MISSISSIPPI *to* **n.n. n.d. Mississippi.** Discusses recent "apprehension and excitement"; details recent slave insurrection, the executions and whippings of those who incited it, and the search for others still at large. 22 August 1835. p.136, c2.

2036 n.n. *to* **n.n. [extract] 12 August 1835. Washington.** Reports that the city is "in a ferment"—an abolitionist was imprisoned, and a mob demands his execution. 29 August 1835. p.137, c2.

2037 ANNA PURINTON *to* **MRS. CHILD. 8 August 1835. Lynn.** Ladies of Lynn and Salem present her with a watch in commemoration of her efforts and their support. 29 August 1835. p.137, c3.

2038 L. MARIA CHILD *to* **n.n. 11 August 1835. Boston.** Acknowledges watch and thanks the women of Lynn and Salem; trusts to God for the success of their cause. 29 August 1835. p.137, c3.

2039 n.n. *to* **W. L. GARRISON. 16 April 1835. Putnam County, Il.** Encourages him; finds that slaveholders are exasperated by the *Liberator,* which proves that the *Liberator* is a threat to their vile prejudice. 29 August 1835. p.137, c3.

2040 JHO. H. PLEASANTS *to* **W. L. GARRISON. 8 August 1835. Richmond, Va.** Asserts that Mr. Wickham has vindicated his conduct and that *Liberator*'s correspondent C. has done him wrong. 29 August 1835. p.137, c4.

2041 JNO. WICKHAM *to* **SIR. 31 July 1835. Richmond, Va.** Defends his behavior in relation to the will of Samuel Gist; declares that he was not the acting executor and that he never had the care or direction of the Negroes; attests that Gist's property was sold and the proceeds given to the Negroes. 29 August 1835. p.137, c4.

2042 MOSES THACHER *to* **THE EDITOR OF THE** *LIBERATOR* **[W. L. GARRISON]. 19 August 1835. North Wrentham.** Expresses surprise that the editor has not received his letter posted at Valley Falls, Rhode Island, which he saw delivered into the postmaster's hands; feels that the selectivity of postal service threatens freedom of speech. 29 August 1835. p.137, c5.

2043 RAY POTTER *to* **FRIEND GARRISON. n.d. n.p.** Declares that "Our hope is alone in God"; urges all abolitionists to pray daily together. 29 August 1835. p.138, c3.

2044 CHAS. LENOX REMOND *to* **FRIENDS GARRISON AND KNAPP. 11 August 1835. Salem.** Reports meeting of colored citizens of Salem to express their disapproval of the "selfish, corrupt, unjust, cruel and hypocritical" principles and doctrines of the ACS. 29 August 1835. p.138, c4.

2045 HOWARD MALCOLM *to* **THE EDITOR OF THE** *LIBERATOR* **[W. L. GARRISON]. 25 August 1835. Boston.** Corrects editor concerning discussion he had with Mr. Lundy; Malcolm had argued that the border states Kentucky, Virginia, and Maryland would gradually become free, followed by the border states Tennessee and North Carolina; in this way, slavery would gradually disappear. 29 August 1835. p.138, c4.

2046 JAMES ARVEN, WILLIAM MARDEN, AND SYLVANUS B. MORGAN *to* **THE** *REGISTER AND OBSERVER.* **3 August 1835. Canaan.** Report town resolution opposing a colored school there; declare citizens will take effectual measures to remove it. 5 September 1835. p.141, c4.

2047 A FRIEND OF HUMAN RIGHTS *to* **MR. EDITOR. [from the** *New England Spectator***] n.d. n.p.** Finds it amusing that abolitionists are accused of being "intemperate, fanatical, incendiary"; quotes from a Charleston newspaper and from the *Christian Observer,* reporting outrageous whippings and cruelty to which blacks are subjected. 5 September 1835. p.141, c5.

2048 A NEW ENGLANDER *to* **THE EDITOR OF THE** *LIBERATOR* **[W. L. GARRISON]. 26 August 1835. n.p.** Reports that he attended the Faneuil Hall Meeting for the purpose of denouncing abolitionists; refutes arguments which anti-abolitionists put forth; asserts that abolitionists dread and object to war to free slaves. 5 September 1835. p.142, c1.

2049 CHARLES V. CAPLES *to* **MR. EDITOR [W. L. GARRISON]. n.d. n.p.** Gives brief description of prayers and business of the Fourteenth Anniversary Meeting of the Humane Society. 5 September 1835. p.142, c2.

2050 W. L. GARRISON *to* **HON. PELEG SPRAGUE. n.d. n.p.** Reviews Sprague's last speech at Faneuil Hall; declares that he has lost any respect he had for Sprague's character; dares him to justify his behavior and support his statements against abolition. 5 September 1835. p.142, c2.

2051 W. L. GARRISON *to* **HON. HARRISON GRAY OTIS. n.d. n.p.** After reading Otis's speech against abolitionists, wonders what has become of the wise scribe he used to know as Otis; calls on him to study the Bible, and recognize the blot of slavery. 5 September 1835. p.142, c5.

2052 n.n. *to* **n.n. [extract] 7 August 1835. Charlestown, Md.** Reports that the town is in an uproar and is being patrolled; notes that a suspicious person from New Orleans was found conversing with Negroes, and is now in jail awaiting trial. 5 September 1835. p.144, c5.

2053 TRUTH *to* **MESSRS. EDITORS [W. L. GARRISON] n.d. n.p.** States that he enjoyed the recent article drawing a parallel between Lafayette and George Thompson; defends Thompson and abolitionists in general from the charge that they are interfering in domestic matters of the South, citing freedom of speech and press. 12 September 1835. p.146, c1.

2054 n.n. *to* **n.n. [extract] n.d. North Carolina.** Discusses the case of the crew of the schooner *Butler* of Bath, who have been imprisoned since 20 May for trying to help a Negro escape. 12 September 1835. p.146, c3.

2055 W. L. GARRISON *to* **HON. PELEG SPRAGUE. n.d. n.p.** States that he rebuked Sprague in his last letter because he feels it is better not to hide one's feelings; points out how close Sprague's feelings are to the abolitionists' on the evils of slavery; adds that they differ, however, in regard to what course of action to take. 12 September 1835. p.146, c4.

2056 A BOSTONIAN *to* **MR. EDITOR [W. L. GARRISON]. n.d. n.p.** Curses the editor for his insolence. 12 September 1835. p.147, c3.

2057 A MARYLANDER AND A RESIDENT OF PHILADELPHIA *to* **W. L. GARRISON. 17 August 1835. n.p.** Warns him of plots on his life and rewards offered for his murder. 12 September 1835. p.147, c3.

2058 SAMUEL J. MAY *to* **W. L. GARRISON. n.d. n.p.** Gives account of his work for the anti-slavery cause in the past ten days, during which he delivered speeches, held discussions with ministers, visited Haverhill, Bradford, Amesbury, West Newbury, and returned to Boston. 12 September 1835. p.147, c4.

2059 n.n. *to* **THE** *NEW YORK SUN.* **n.d. n.p.** Asks the editors to discontinue subscription since they have come out in favor of abolitionists. 12 September 1835. p.147, c5.

2060 SELECT COMMITTEE *to* **OWNER OF DRY GOODS STORE. n.d. Charleston, S.C.** Warns that if he is seen going into any abolitionist's establishment, his business will be harmed. 12 September 1835. p.148, c4.

2061 AMOS KENDALL *to* **SAMUEL L. GOUVERNEUR, ESQ. n.d. n.p.** States that the postmaster general has no legal authority to exclude from the mails any species of newspaper or magazine, but that only legal power deters him from excluding all abolitionist publications from the South; declares that if he were situated as Gouverneur is, he would do as Gouverneur has done. 19 September 1835. p.149, c3.

2062 W. L. GARRISON *to* **HON. HARRISON GRAY OTIS. n.d. n.p.** Contends that Otis' knowledge of abolitionists and their writings is imperfect; quotes Otis' misrepresentations and corrects him. 19 September 1835. p.150, c1.

2063 A. E. GRIMKE *to* **RESPECTED FRIEND. 30 August 1835. Philadelphia.** Declares she is glad that abolitionists have not retreated from their principles, in spite of increased persecution and mob violence; calls for willingness to suffer. 19 September 1835. p.150, c3.

2064 n.n. *to* **W. L. GARRISON. 2 September 1835. Haverhill.** Argues that slavery cannot withstand discussion; the oppressors have dragged it out to be talked about, and its doom is therefore sealed. 19 September 1835. p.150, c4.

2065 A FLORIDA SLAVE HOLDER *to* **W. L. GARRISON. 10 August 1835. New York.** Declares that flames of persecution are being constantly fanned in New York by colonizationists; sees violence and lawlessness growing, with only a small portion of community supporting immediate abolition of slavery, despite general acknowledgment of its cruelty and injustice. 19 September 1835. p.151, c4.

2066 n.n. *to* **THE** *UNITED STATES GAZETTE.* **n.d. n.p.** Reports that the promised history of Mary Gilmore is almost finished. 19 September 1835. p.152, c4.

2067 ROBERT N. ANDERSON *to* **THE** *ENQUIRER.* **3 September 1835. Physic Spring, Buckingham, Va.** Calls for the ferreting out and silencing of any Presbyterian ministers tainted by support of abolition. 26 September 1835. p.153, c2.

2068 MOSES THACHER *to* **EDITOR OF THE** *LIBERATOR* **[W. L. GARRISON]. 31 August 1835. North Wrentham.** Quotes article in *Rhode Island County Journal* telling of meeting against immediate emancipation; believes abolitionists are alone in upholding seventh commandment, yet are always accused of amalgamation; criticizes resolutions passed at the meeting. 26 September 1835. p.153, c3.

2069 M. M. F. *to* **MR. EDITOR [W. L. GARRISON]. 11 September 1835. Franklin.** Approves recent address by S. J. May, who vindicated everyone's right and duty to discuss the subject of slavery in the North, and proved slavery against natural justice and revealed religions; reports that the AS is large and flourishing. 26 September 1835. p.154, c1.

2070 ACTION *to* **MESSRS. EDITORS [W. L. GARRISON]. 1 September 1835. Boston.** Agrees with recent proposal in *Liberator* to begin a daily abolition newspaper; believes that abolitionists have been misrepresented too long, and that the paper would be well supported. 26 September 1835. p.154, c3.

2071 n.n. *to* **SOMEONE IN BIRMINGHAM. 11 June 1835. New York.** Reports that Dr. Cox refused to give a speech on the anniversary of AS, claiming that he could not enter into a political controversy. 26 September 1835. p.155, c1.

2072 n.n. *to* **n.n. [extract from the** *Cazenovia Monitor***] n.d. n.p.** Claims that no civil law exists in South; Mr. Birney was forced to flee Kentucky because he is against slavery. 26 September 1835. p.155, c3.

2073 n.n. *to* **n.n. [extract] 6 September 1835. Manawha Salines.** Describes arrest and trial of four white men for endeavoring to persuade several slaves to leave their masters; reports that they received lashes and banishment when convicted; author considers this to be a striking illustration of the work of those "devilish philanthropists, Garrison, Tappan and Co." 26 September 1835. p.155, c4.

2074 RESIDENT OF NASHVILLE *to* **HIS BROTHER IN BOSTON. [extract from the** *Salem Register***] 9 August 1835. Nashville.** Claims that since the disturbances in Mississippi, large committees have been appointed in every town to protect and guard the country; reports that an abolitionist who was caught selling Bibles, abolitionist tracts, and the *Emancipator* was lashed and almost lynched. 3 October 1835. p.157, c1.

2075 JOHN G. WHITTIER *to* **FRIEND. [from the** *Haverhill Gazette***] 9 September 1835. Boston.** Corrects the mistakes of Boston papers in their reports of disturbances in Concord, New Hampshire; believes that the mob violence was not the result of abstract hatred of abolition principles, but was used for political effect. 3 October 1835. p.157, c3.

2076 A SUBSCRIBER *to* **MR. EDITOR [W. L. GARRISON]. 18 September 1835. South Reading.** Decries "disgraceful" resolutions passed at meeting of twenty citizens opposed to ASS; believes the cause of abolition is gaining ground. 3 October 1835. p.157, c5.

2077 CLERICUS *to* **REV. MOSES STUART. n.d. n.p.** Attacks the logic of Stuart's recent theology class lecture at Andover in which he tried to sustain or palliate slavery with arguments drawn from Scripture; counters with scriptural quotes showing slavery to be wrong and sinful. 3 October 1835. p.158, c1.

2078 OLD ITINERANT *to* **MR. EDITOR [W. L. GARRISON]. 21 September 1835. New England.** Attacks article in the *Christian Advocate and Journal* written in opposition to the friends of universal emancipation; counters the author's charges, and claims that abolitionists are not the first to be persecuted for preaching against the sins of church members. 3 October 1835. p.158, c2.

2079 LAW *to* **MR. EDITOR [W. L. GARRISON]. n.d. n.p.** Accuses the *Boston Recorder* of indirectly supporting slavery, and apologizing for mobs and outrages committed against unoffending men. 3 October 1835. p.158, c4.

2080 GEO. THOMPSON *to* **THE** *DAILY ATLAS.* **30 September 1835. Boston.** Denies having said that every slaveholder in the United States ought to have his throat cut, and that every slave should be taught to cut his master's throat; declares he abhors the shedding of blood. 3 October 1835. p.159, c3.

2081 REV. DR. W. FISK *to* **BROTHER KINGSBURY. [from the** *Zion's Herald***] 31 August 1835. Middletown, Ct.** Sends farewell before embarking on a distant voyage; declares he is not favorable to a public agitation of the abolition question, as it threatens to divide the Methodist Episcopal church and the United States; feels North must leave South alone. 10 October 1835. p.161, c1.

2082 MOSES THACHER *to* **THE EDITOR OF THE** *LIBERATOR* **[W. L. GARRISON]. 1 September 1835. North Wrentham.** Discusses resolution of meeting at Woonsocket which remarked that the Constitution was the result of a compromise between the North and the South; states that the original compromise imposes no serious obstacle to the manumission of slaves. 10 October 1835. p.162, c1.

2083 ONE WHO DOES NOT AND NEVER WILL BELONG TO A SLAVERY SOCIETY *to* **W. L. GARRISON. [extract] n.d. n.p.** Urges Southerners to stop interfering with the mails before we become a nation of slaves, oppressed by tyrants. 10 October 1835. p.162, c2.

2084 n.n. *to* **W. L. GARRISON. n.d. n.p.** Encloses article by C. N. entitled "How Children May Promote the Cause of Abolition," which tells of an eight-year-old boy who prays for masters to free their slaves. 10 October 1835. p.162, c2.

2085 WOOLMAN *to* **THE EDITOR OF THE** *LIBERATOR* **[W. L. GARRISON]. 12 September 1835. Providence.** Recounts actions of Jeptha White, a member of Friends School at Providence, whose home is in North Carolina; White recently freed a mother and her children, and defrayed their expenses to Indiana. 10 October 1835. p.162, c2.

2086 WICKLIFFE *to* **MR. EDITOR [W. L. GARRISON]. n.d. n.p.** Discusses whether slaveholders deserve to have their throats cut, as abolitionists are reported by New York and Boston newspapers and by Southerners to believe; author denies this, as the abolition motto is "Non-Resistance." 10 October 1835. p.162, c3.

2087 J. V. HIMES *to* **MR. EDITOR [W. L. GARRISON]. 20 September 1835. Boston.** Responds to letter from a Georgian who wants his paper stopped; notes hypocrisy of Southerners who claim Garrison is a hot-headed, deluded fanatic, yet offer $5,000 reward for his death. 10 October 1835. p.162, c4.

2088 n.n. *to* **n.n. [extract] 14 September 1835. Canaan.** Describes outrages committed against abolitionists; yet believes a time will come when all countrymen will be converted to abolition. 10 October 1835. p.162, c4.

2089 W. L. WEAVER *to* **NATHANIEL BRANDER, ESQ. 11 June 1835. Edina.** Discusses dreadful circumstance of previous night; Joe Harris took an armed force to Port Cresson and killed or wounded about eighteen settlers; the colonists have declared war on the natives. 10 October 1835. p.162, c5.

2090 B. F. *to* **FRIEND GARRISON. n.d. n.p.** Asserts that the threats of Southerners to dissolve the Union remind him of a stagecoach ride he took seven years ago, when an old maid yelled and threatened to walk if the driver did not slow down; when given the chance to carry out her threat she refused and finally kept quiet. 17 October 1835. p.165, c4.

2091 S. *to* **MR. EDITOR [W. L. GARRISON]. n.d. n.p.** Reminds him that now, especially when thousands crave knowledge of their glorious cause, it is the right and duty of abolitionists to distribute pamphlets and papers advancing their cause. 17 October 1835. p.165, c5.

2092 OBSERVER *to* **W. L. GARRISON. n.d. n.p.** Recounts proceedings of the 26–27 August meeting of Cumberland Baptist Association where a resolution advocating immediate emancipation was rejected in a close vote; notes that there was less discussion of the question of slavery than of whether the North should interfere. 17 October 1835. p.166, c1.

2093 UTI IN SPECULUM *to* **MR. EDITOR [W. L. GARRISON]. n.d. n.p.** Compares parable of a rich man, who refuses to pay a poor man and is backed by the court because of his influence, to the situation of slavery. 17 October 1835. p.166, c2.

2094 PHILOS *to* **MESSRS. GARRISON AND KNAPP. October 1835. Boston.** Suggests that the *Liberator* expand again as interest and support for the abolition cause has grown; suggests the removal of the engraving logo which the writer believes is false and offensive to some who might otherwise read the paper. 17 October 1835. p.166, c2.

2095 CATO *to* **MR. EDITOR [W. L. GARRISON]. n.d. n.p.** Charges Homer and Palmer, editors of the *Boston Commercial Gazette,* with inciting mobs against abolitionists; quotes from the *Gazette* to show the false criticisms and accusations they level at abolitionists. 17 October 1835. p.166, c4.

2096 R. *to* **W. L. GARRISON. 15 October 1835. East Abington.** Describes recent address by Mr. Thompson, attended by a large audience; charges that opponents of abolition are trampling upon the Constitution, and Yankee farmers will not consent to this. 17 October 1835. p.166, c4.

2097 WILLIAM LYNCH *to* **AMOS KENDALL, UNITED STATES POSTMASTER GENERAL. 2 September 1835. Lynchtown.** Explains the changes which have occurred in his job; he now not only must receive and forward mail, but he must censor periodicals; he cannot always tell what is "incendiary." 17 October 1835. p.168, c2.

2098 A MEMBER OF THE BOSTON FEMALE ANTI-SLAVERY SOCIETY *to* **THE COURIER. n.d. n.p.** Declares that it is their right to hold meetings and employ such lecturers as they feel will advance the cause of human rights; wonders at the inconsistency of those who champion the Constitution yet stifle the ideals it stands for; tells of gentlemen who put up false notices claiming the society's meetings were cancelled. 24 October 1835. p.169, c2.

2099 n.n. *to* **MR. LEAVITT. [from the** *New York Evangelist***]** **n.d. n.p.** Sends a prayer for "all the female friends of Christ, everywhere"; urges them to unite in a sunrise concert of prayer for peace, freedom, knowledge and salvation. 24 October 1835. p.169, c3.

2100 S. *to* **MR. EDITOR [W. L. GARRISON]. n.d. n.p.** Describes the annual meeting of the Vermont CS; found the meeting was neither well-attended nor generously supported by members; briefly summarizes speeches and prayers given. 24 October 1835. p.170, c2.

2101 ZEDEKIA H. DOWNING *to* **MR.** *LIBERATOR.* **15 September 1835. Portland.** Comments on the recent Whig meeting to put down abolitionists; reports that in certain circumstances it is patriotic to disregard the laws, particularly in the case of the mails. 24 October 1835. p.170, c4.

2102 E. G. HOWE *to* **THE EDITOR OF THE** *LIBERATOR* **[W. L. GARRISON]. 15 October 1835. Halifax, Plymouth County, Ma.** Claims recent lecture of Samuel May persuaded many former opponents to join the AS; holds lectures of this sort necessary to educate people on the true evils of slavery. 24 October 1835. p.171, c1.

2103 A SOUTHERN SLAVE HOLDER *to* **MR. GEO. H. EVANS. [from the** *New York Workingman's Advocate***] 13 September 1835. Puerto de Plata, Hayti.** Describes his travels in Haiti; gives detailed descriptions of country, towns, fertile land, and hospitable and friendly people; claims government "approaches nearer to pure republicanism than any other now in use or on record." 24 October 1835. p.172, c2.

2104 n.n. *to* **A COMMERCIAL HOUSE IN NEW YORK. [extract] 15 September 1835. Port-au-Platt, Hayti.** Describes inhabitants as holding no jealousy of caste and free of crime; declares all religions are equally protected. 24 October 1835. p.172, c3.

2105 JOHN RANKIN *to* **MR. BRAINARD. [from** *Cincinnati Journal***] n.d. Ripley, Brown County, Oh.** Reports that Kentucky Sabbath school for slaves was broken up by magistrate; declares the only argument for gradual emancipation is the avarice of the master, and that currently no preparation or education for freedom is allowed. 24 October 1835. p.172, c5.

2106 A HIGHLY RESPECTABLE GENTLEMAN IN UTICA *to* **n.n. 21 October 1835. Utica.** Gives description of abolitionist convention held in Utica: disruption by anti-abolitionists; yelling and hissing which prevented listening to the speaker; adjournment forced by disorder; supportive delegates more numerous than expected. 31 October 1835. p.174, c1.

2107 TIMOTHY HUBBARD, S. B. FLINT, HUGH GOURLEY, J. T. MARSTON, GEO. W. HILL, D. P. RUSSELL AND MOSES E. HALE *to* **SAMUEL MAY. 23 October 1835. Montpelier.** Order him out of town without any further attempt at spreading "the absurd doctrine of anti-slavery." 31 October 1835. p.174, c4.

2108 A CITIZEN *to* **MR. EDITOR [W. L. GARRISON] n.d. n.p.** Describes Whig mob which sought out and almost hanged an abolitionist; author has been a Whig and thought they stood for liberty and freedom; is loath to discover how narrow-minded and oppressive they really are. 31 October 1835. p.174, c5.

2109 GEO. THOMPSON *to* **BROTHER GARRISON. 22 October 1835. n.p.** Rejoices that Garrison escaped the mob in Boston; encourages him to go on because no mob or enemy has yet shaken the principles of abolitionists nor their faith that their cause is just. 31 October 1835. p.175, c1.

2110 A VOICE FROM THE INTERIOR *to* **MESSRS. GARRISON AND KNAPP. n.d. n.p.** Suggests that the abolitionists nominate candidates for the legislature; encourages those working for the cause as it is progressing. 31 October 1835. p.175, c5.

2111 RAY POTTER *to* **MESSRS. GARRISON AND KNAPP. n.d. n.p.** Calls for more letters from those who would like to convene together to remember the anti-slavery cause daily; hopes all abolitionists will pray frequently for the slaves and their freedom. 7 November 1835. p.177, c2.

2112 OLD ITINERANT *to* **MR. EDITOR [W. L. GARRISON]. n.d. n.p.** Continues examination of several charges against the New England conference made by fourteen New Yorkers, which range from being influenced chiefly by abolitionists to making abolition a prerequisite for candidacy. 7 November 1835. p.177, c3.

2113 GEORGE THOMPSON *to* **FRIEND GARRISON. 22 October 1835. n.p.** Feels much sympathy for Garrison during his trials and persecutions; criticizes the opponents of the cause of emancipation, particularly in their resorting to mob violence. 7 November 1835. p.178, c1.

2114 HANCOCK *to* **MR. EDITOR [W. L. GARRISON]. n.d. n.p.** Discusses the recent Boston mob which was called by Homer and Palmer, editors of the *Gazette;* charges that Theodore Lyman, Mayor of Boston, cooperated with the mob. 14 November 1835. p.182, c4.

2115 WILLIAM COMSTOCK *to* **W. L. GARRISON. n.d. n.p.** Decries the behavior of the recent Boston mob which disrupted one man and thirty women during a lecture; declares that such violent opposition to liberty has been characterized by baseness and turpitude; praises George Thompson, and is confident that the abolition cause will be successful. 14 November 1835. p.183, c2.

2116 EMANCIPATION *to* **W. L. GARRISON. n.d. n.p.** Denies that George Thompson urged every slave to cut his master's throat; criticizes A. Kaufman, Jr. for charging Thompson with the statement. 14 November 1835. p.183, c3.

2117 A DEMOCRAT *to* **MR. EDITOR. [from the** *Daily Reformer***] n.d. n.p.** Declares that he is thankful he is not a citizen of Boston, a city where mobs are sanctioned and incited by "gentlemen of the first respectability." 14 November 1835. p.184, c2.

2118 WICKLIFFE *to* **THE** *NEW ENGLAND SPECTATOR.* **n.d. n.p.** Criticizes the behavior of the editor of the *Recorder* regarding the recent violence connected with an abolition meeting; regrets that the *Recorder* claims to be a Christian paper; quotes from articles and editorials to show its support of oppression. 14 November 1835. p.184, c2.

2119 A BOSTON BOY *to* **W. L. GARRISON. n.d. n.p.** Recounts the story of a boy whose father was challenged to a fight by a man who criticized Garrison; the father had no desire to fight, but the son later reminded him that even if he had been whipped, it would have been for a good cause. 21 November 1835. p.185, c3.

2120 C. C. BURLEIGH *to* **BROTHER GARRISON. 5 November 1835. Reading.** Contends that the notice of an anti-slavery meeting does not inspire rioting everywhere in New England; describes an uninterrupted, pleasant speech he gave at a meeting in Reading; expresses dismay at the recent shameful mobs in Boston. 21 November 1835. p.185, c3.

2121 A NEAR ECCLESIASTICAL RELATIVE, BUT ONE WHO IS ASHAMED OF HIS RELATION *to* **MR. EDITOR [W. L. GARRISON]. n.d. n.p.** Criticizes justification of the Boston mob by the editor of the *Christian Watchman;* wonders what was obnoxious to God or man in the principles of the female AS. 21 November 1835. p.185, c4.

2122 S. J. M. *to* **MR. EDITOR [W. L. GARRISON]. 10 November 1835. n.p.** Attacks letter he received from L. Holbrook which criticizes abolitionists and their interference in Southern domestic concerns. 21 November 1835. p.185, c5.

2123 L. HOLBROOK *to* **SAMUEL J. MAY. 12 September 1835. Danville, Va.** Believes the Union is endangered by the conduct of the abolitionists in non-slaveholding states; the South was flourishing and happy until lately flooded with incendiary papers, but now is in a state of feverish excitement; Southerners will never be told how to run their domestic concerns. 21 November 1835. p.185, c5.

2124 J. COFFIN *to* **W. L. GARRISON. 11 November 1835. Philadelphia.** Condemns the degradation and disgrace of Boston by the mobbing of the Female AS meeting. 21 November 1835. p.186, c4.

2125 AN ABOLITIONIST *to* **W. L. GARRISON. n.d. n.p.** Attacks letter in *Liberator* signed Hancock, which charged Mr. Lyman, the mayor of Boston, with cooperating with the recent mob there; believes Lyman was sincere in trying to restore peace. 21 November 1835. p.186, c5.

2126 WILLIAM COMSTOCK *to* **W. L. GARRISON. n.d. n.p.** Supports Garrison and Thompson and their struggle; believes abolitionists have the right to interfere with the "domestic concerns" of the slaveholders; praises the honesty of abolitionists, who have "no smooth words to pave their way to popularity," but only a determination to extinguish slavery. 21 November 1835. p.187, c2.

2127 J. CABLE *to* **SIR. [extract] 19 October 1835. Nacogdoches, Tx.** Gives latest news from Texas; the success of Americans at Goliad, and arrival of more troops. 21 November 1835. p.188, c5.

2128 I. M. ALLEN *to* **BRETHREN. 28 October 1835. Philadelphia.** Explains that the Baptist Tract Society has no connections to abolition groups, whom they feel are interfering in the rights of the South; hopes that his explanations of official policy relieve all subscribing brethren, especially those in the South. 28 November 1835. p.189, c1.

2129 n.n. *to* **n.n. [extract] n.d. Virginia.** Declares that "We must secede from the Whigs and cut off all intercourse with the North"; all abolitionists must be hunted out. 28 November 1835. p.189, c1.

2130 MOSES *to* **W. L. GARRISON. n.d. n.p.** Mocks the Boston mob which was so "brave" that it "hissed, hooted, cursed, and insulted a few praying females" and seized Garrison, who is well known for his principles of non-resistance; criticizes the Synod of Virginia, which claims abolition is contrary to common sense, humanity and the gospel. 28 November 1835. p.189, c3.

2131 J. S. *to* **MR. EDITOR [W. L. GARRISON]. 2 November 1835. Newburyport.** Believes that the CS plans are but "an idle dream"; points out that the colored population has doubled since the society's formation; praises the abolitionists and their humanitarian principles, wishing success to the *Liberator*. 28 November 1835. p.189, c4.

2132 A BAPTIST *to* **MESSRS. GARRISON AND KNAPP. n.d. n.p.** Inquires of the Baptists whether they are satisfied with the *Christian Watchman* as their religious journal; believes it is "a sickly journal"; prefers one which would speak out on all moral questions. 28 November 1835. p.189, c4.

2133 ANOTHER ABOLITIONIST *to* **THE *LIBERATOR*. n.d. n.p.** Counters previous letters in the *Liberator*; defends the mayor's actions during the recent mob violence; believes he acted to protect Garrison and others from the mob. 28 November 1835. p.192 [190], cl.

2134 PETER PARKER *to* **MOSES P. ATWOOD. 19 November 1835. Bradford.** Relates resolutions adopted at a recent meeting of the Young Men's Association for Mutual Improvement, concerning the unparalleled success of the anti-slavery cause and admiration for Garrison, Tappan, and May. 28 November 1835. p.192 [190], c3.

2135 n.n. *to* **MR. EDITOR [W. L. GARRISON]. n.d. n.p.** Encloses character sketch of William Wilberforce. 28 November 1835. p.192 [190], c4.

2136 GERRIT SMITH *to* **ABRAHAM L. COX. 12 November 1835. Peterboro.** Decides to join the AAS; criticizes mobsters and those who deny free speech; urges immediate cessation of slavery, the "giant wickedness." 28 November 1835. p.192 [190], c5.

2137 SAMUEL J. MAY *to* **FRANCIS JACKSON, ESQ. 21 November 1835. Boston.** Thanks Jackson, on behalf of the Massachusetts AS, for offering his house to the Boston Female AS; decries the recent outrages against these women by mobs; upholds the principle of free speech. 28 November 1835. p.191, c1.

2138 FRANCIS JACKSON *to* **REV. S. J. MAY. 25 November 1835. Boston.** Declares that in offering his home to the Boston Female AS meeting, he not only enjoyed giving shelter to those working for a noble cause but also meant to uphold the principle of free speech, without which liberty cannot exist. 28 November 1835. p.191, c1.

2139 n.n. *to* **MR. GEO. H. EVANS. 29 September 1835. Cape Haytien.** Describes the countryside of Haiti, the inland valleys and mountains, and the city Cape Haytien; comments also on the inhabitants. 28 November 1835. p.192, c3.

2140 DUKE W. HULLUM *to* **HIS EXCELLENCY HIRAM G. RUNNELS. 25 September 1835. Hardeman County, Tn.** Asks that members of the mob who killed his son at Vicksburg on 6 July be brought to justice. 28 November 1835. p.192, c5.

2141 LA ROY SUNDERLAND *to* **EDITOR [W. L. GARRISON]. 24 October 1835. Bolton.** Expresses his astonishment at the alleged quote from George Thompson that slaves ought to cut their masters' throats, as he was present during the conversation and heard Thompson deny the right of slaves to spill blood. 5 December 1835. p.194, c4.

2142 JARVIS GREGG *to* **MR. THOMPSON. 27 October 1835. Hudson, Oh.** States that he understood Thompson to say, in discussion with Mr. Kaufman, that slaves should be taught "passive submission to wrong," and that it was not the duty of slaves to murder their masters. 5 December 1835. p.194, c5.

2143 AMOS A. PHELPS *to* **THOMPSON. 2 November 1835. Farmington.** Refutes Mr. Kaufman's charge that Thompson said slaves ought to cut their masters' throats; paraphrases his recollection of the actual discussion. 5 December 1835. p.194, c5.

2144 GEO. THOMPSON *to* **W. L. GARRISON. 27 November 1835. St. John, New Brunswick.** Gives account of his journey since he bade Garrison farewell, relating discussions of slavery on board the ship; writes of his love of America and prays for her release from slavery as well as the abolition of slavery all over the world. 5 December 1835. p.195, c2.

2145 n.n. *to* **RECIPIENT IN WASHINGTON CITY. 6 November 1835. Vera Cruz.** Reports that the port of Vera Cruz has been shut; they have sent ammunition and are collecting troops to go to Texas; North Americans are very much disliked. 5 December 1835. p.195, c5.

2146 VICOMTE DE CHATEAUBRIAND *to* **THE FRENCH CHAMBER OF DEPUTIES. [extract] n.d. n.p.** States that while he proposed laws in lieu of censorship, they suggest laws in exchange for liberty; discusses freedom of the press and censorship of ideas. 5 December 1835. p.196, c3.

2147 WILLIAM JAY *to* **REV. OLIVER WETMORE. [from the** *New York Standard and Democrat*] **17 November 1835. New York.** Gratefully acknowledges the honor done to him in his election as president of the New York State AS; warns that those who employ use of mobs frequently suffer from their own instruments; declares abolitionists' opponents are afraid to let people hear the truth. 12 December 1835. p.199, c1.

2148 ONE OF THE SLANDERED *to* **THE** *NEW ENGLAND SPECTATOR***. n.d. n.p.** Questions whether Mr. Tracy, editor of the *Boston Recorder*, lies deliberately or out of ignorance in stating that abolitionists choose instances of extraordinary cruelty by slaveholders, and portray them as the norm. 19 December 1835. p.201, c3.

2149 GENIUS OF AFRICA *to* **MR. EDITOR [W. L. GARRISON]. n.d. n.p.** Reviews Dr. Channing's recently published book on slavery. 19 December 1835. p.202, c1.

2150 ANOTHER ABOLITIONIST *to* **W. L. GARRISON. n.d. n.p.** Wishes to correct Garrison's interpretation of his previous letter; he had wished to say that when a mob is triumphant, the authorities must pursue the best course, be it dispersion or imprisonment, for the protection of the individuals being attacked; believes the mayor of Boston acted without malicious intentions. 19 December 1835. p.202, c2.

2151 SIMEON S. JOCELYN *to* **BROTHER GARRISON. 14 November 1835. New Haven.** Sympathizes with Garrison in his persecution; declares that as sufferers they may more deeply sympathize with the oppressed; sends contribution to the *Liberator*. 19 December 1835. p.202, c3.

2152 S. PERKINS AND WILLIAM H. DEERING *to* **SIR. 2 November 1835. Hebron, Oxford County, Me.** Send congratulations and respects from the Hebron AS; wish for an end to persecutions of those supporting the cause; remind him that God is just and the work for the slaves must go on. 19 December 1835. p.202, c3.

2153 ANOTHER BAPTIST *to* **W. L. GARRISON. n.d. n.p.** Replies to inquiries about starting a new Baptist paper, stating that it would be bad policy to start a new paper and thereby create division in Baptist ranks; also opposes a new paper as "too proscriptive" a course, which might reduce the independence of the press. 19 December 1835. p.202, c4.

2154 JAMES BALLARD *to* **W. L. GARRISON. 24 November 1835. Bennington.** Describes cordial reception given the Rev. Mr. May in Vermont recently; rejoices that at least one part of New England encourages free speech and discussion. 19 December 1835. p.202, c4.

2155 ALBERT G. SWEETSER *to* **W. L. GARRISON. 14 December 1835. South Reading.** Reports resolutions recently passed in his town AS praising the work of George Thompson and the work of the *Liberator*. 19 December 1835. p.202, c5.

2156 A MEMBER OF THE PROVIDENCE LADIES AS *to* **n.n. [extract] n.d. n.p.** Looks with pity and contempt at men who assembled at the door to disturb their meeting; declares that rather than hinder their efforts, men should lend a helping hand. 19 December 1835. p.203, c2.

2157 A DISTINGUISHED UNITARIAN CLERGYMAN IN THE INTERIOR OF MASSACHUSETTS *to* **n.n. [extract] 7 November 1835. n.p.** Praises various people engaged in promoting the abolition cause; describes recent anti-slavery meeting which he attended. 19 December 1835. p.203, c3.

2158 n.n. *to* **n.n. [extract] n.d. n.p.** Humorously describes the zeal, confidence, and activity of "incendiary abolitionists." 19 December 1835. p.203, c4.

2159 A CITIZEN OF MONROVIA *to* **n.n. [extract] 25 September 1835. n.p.** Describes people who wish to go to Sierra Leone, especially the suffering poorer class; reports loss of Mr. Johnston's schooner at Sagaree and the scarcity of provisions. 19 December 1835. p.204, c4.

2160 C. *to* **W. L. GARRISON. 19 December 1835. Providence, R.I.** Sends report of the Providence Juvenile AS; discusses its organization, the election of officers, and the character of the meeting. 26 December 1835. p.205, c4.

2161 DANIEL *to* **MR. EDITOR [W. L. GARRISON]. n.d. n.p.** Discusses Rev. Hubbard Winslow who advocates following laws of man rather than law of God, and whose doctrine he finds atheistic and "fraught with deep and dreadful consequences to man", upholds God's law above all others. 26 December 1835. p.206, c1.

2162 GENIUS OF AFRICA *to* **MR. EDITOR [W. L. GARRISON]. n.d. n.p.** Criticizes Rev. Dr. Channing's charges against Garrison and abolitionists; doubts that Channing is truly a friend of the oppressed. 26 December 1835. p.206, c2.

[1836]

2163 JUSTICE *to* **BROTHER GARRISON. December 1835. New England.** Points out that although abolitionists are charged with encouraging amalgamation, Southerners are actually responsible for it, as they have already fathered half a million mulattoes and whites frequently live openly with black mistresses. 2 January 1836. p.2, c4.

2164 GENIUS OF AFRICA *to* **MR. EDITOR [W. L. GARRISON]. n.d. n.p.** An African slave charges that the American slave system, which denies legal marriage to slaves, is "a system of sacrilege, of concubinage, of plunder, of piracy and murder." 2 January 1836. p.2, c4.

2165 E. D. CULVER *to* **BROTHER MURRAY. 19 November 1834. Fort-Ann, Washington County, N.Y.** Describes recent meeting to form a county AS, which was disturbed by mobs; claims that the cause moves forward nevertheless, and urges perseverance. 2 January 1836. p.3, c5.

2166 STEPHEN SEWALL *to* **BROTHER GARRISON. n.d. n.p.** Describes recent meetings of the Winthrop AS; lists resolutions adopted. 9 January 1836. p.6, c1.

2167 WILLIAM COMSTOCK *to* **W. L. GARRISON. n.d. n.p.** Argues that Channing is wrong to urge cool and dispassionate behavior; believes this is not a time for tameness and lethargy, and that only by expressing shame and indignation can one effect a change. 9 January 1836. p.6, c2.

2168 H. B. S. *to* **SIR. 31 December 1836. Hopkinton.** Gives quotation from biblical commentary on the mark of Cain. 9 January 1836. p.6, c2.

2169 CHARLES MARRIOTT *to* **W. L. GARRISON. 23 November 1835. Hudson, N.Y.** Condemns recent outrage against Garrison; points out that by torturing and putting to death Northern citizens, whose only crime is their support of abolition, Southerners may actually be working against themselves and the slavery system; encourages Garrison to continue his work. 9 January 1836. p.6, c3.

2170 A BLACK IN NEW YORK *to* **THE** *LIBERATOR.* **[extract] n.d. n.p.** Encourages Garrison in spite of the persecutions he has had to bear; reminds him that the cause must prevail. 9 January 1836. p.6, c3.

2171 JAMES G. BIRNEY *to* **GENTLEMEN. 9 December 1835. Cincinnati.** Replies to the unjust charges of the committee against himself and the character of abolitionists; explains and justifies the abolition cause. 16 January 1836. p.9, c1.

2172 SAMUEL J. MAY *to* **SIR. 8 January 1836. Boston.** Announces fourth annual meeting of Massachusetts AS; requests societies to appoint delegates. 16 January 1836. p.10, c4.

2173 W. *to* **MR. EDITOR [W. L. GARRISON]. n.d. n.p.** Refutes argument of Baptist ministers who say that if separated, slaves may marry again, because their old union is thereby dissolved as if by death. 16 January 1836. p.10, c4.

2174 OLD FRIEND *to* **PRESIDENT JACKSON. n.d. n.p.** Asserts that he read Jackson's late message to Congress with emotions of great pain; asks what in the conduct of abolitionists is so obnoxious; declares that Jackson's friends in the free states can neither support him nor submit to a "gag" law. 16 January 1836. p.10, c5.

2175 n.n. *to* **THE SECRETARY OF THE MASSACHUSETTS AS. 4 January 1836. Pawtucket.** Lists officers of newly formed Hebronville AS; tells of its creation after Mr. Goodell's speech. 16 January 1836. p.11, c1.

2176 M. S. P. TEMPLE *to* **W. L. GARRISON. 29 December 1835. Reading.** Reports on officers recently elected by the Reading Female AS meeting. 16 January 1836. p.11, c1.

2177 CHARLES STUART *to* **n.n. [extract] n.d. n.p.** Describes interruption of his speech by a mob. 16 January 1836. p.11, c5.

2178 W. L. MARCY *to* **JOHN GAYLE, THE GOVERNOR OF ALABAMA. 8 December 1835. Executive Department, Albany, N.Y.** Acknowledges receipt of the requisition for the arrest and delivery of Robert G. Williams, stating that he does not believe the demand holds up to legal and constitutional scrutiny, and that he must decline to comply with the requisition. 23 January 1836. p.13, c3.

2179 W. L. GARRISON *to* **REV. SAMUEL J. MAY. 17 January 1836. Brooklyn, Ct.** Regrets he could not attend the Massachusetts AS meeting; urges the delegates to "Be Bold for God"; reminds them that the battle is the Lord's and not theirs. 27 January 1836. p.15, c3.

2180 TATTER *to* **MR. CUMMINGS. [from the** *Christian Mirror*] **n.d. n.p.** Condemns actions of mob in Denmark, Maine, which forced a discussion on slavery to adjourn by covering every pew and desk "with the vilest and most filthy materials." 23 January 1836. p.16, c3.

2181 O. SCOTT *to* **MR. EDITOR [W. L. GARRISON]. 29 December 1835. Holliston.** Laments departure of George Thompson, whose influence will still be felt despite his absence. 30 January 1836. p.18, c1.

2182 GEORGE BOURNE *to* **A FRIEND IN OHIO. n.d. n.p.** Asserts that after being brought up in the midst of the institution, he finally sees the sin of slavery as it is practiced under our government. 30 January 1836. p.18, c3.

2183 A. W. *to* **W. L. GARRISON. 20 January 1836. Boston.** Believes we must overcome evil with good; notes his surprise at an appeal in the *Boston Recorder* to stop circulation of the *Liberator*; sends names of three friends to whom he donates subscriptions. 30 January 1836. p.18, c4.

2184 ELISHA BASS AND R. B. DICKIE *to* **MR. EDITOR [W. L. GARRISON]. 30 December 1835. Hanover, Ma.** Report recent formation of town AS; quote its declaration of principles, its constitution, and resolutions adopted. 30 January 1836. p.18, c5.

2185 W. DROWN *to* **W. L. GARRISON. December 1835. Foster, R.I.** Rejoices at the progress of the anti-slavery cause; reports that while visiting slave states, he had been told that many abolitionists, including Garrison, had left the country. 30 January 1836. p.19, c1.

2186 CIVIS *to* **MR. EDITOR [W. L. GARRISON]. n.d. n.p** Asserts that the South stifles humanitarian poetry because it criticizes their slavery system; quotes from the English poet Moore, whose poetry "breathes a deeper detestation of American slavery" than most others. 6 February 1836. p.21, c2.

2187 Z. Y. Z. *to* **MR. EDITOR [W. L. GARRISON]. n.d. n.p.** Quotes from Hon. Tristam Burgess of Rhode Island, who apologizes for slaveholders and maintains that they are Christians; finds it notorious that the followers of Christ could support slavery. 6 February 1836. p.21, c2.

2188 W. L. GARRISON *to* **KNAPP. 3 February 1836. Providence.** Discusses the Rhode Island State Anti-Slavery Convention, attended by 400 individuals; describes the meetinghouse and the character of the audience. 6 February 1836. p.22, c1.

2189 W. L. GARRISON *to* **THE PRESIDENT OF THE ANTI-SLAVERY CONVENTION IN PROVIDENCE. 30 January 1836. Brooklyn, Ct.** Regrets he cannot attend convention; congratulates little Rhode Island, which attracted more people to its convention than did the much larger state of New York; discusses the object of the convention; supports their spirit of immediate emancipation. 6 February 1836. p.22, c1.

2190 JAMES G. BIRNEY *to* **WILLIAM M. CHASE. 22 January 1836. Cincinnati.** Gives reasons why he cannot attend the convention, which include his wife's illness and a threat on his life by a gentleman from Kentucky; prays that abolitionists increase and remain strong. 6 February 1836. p.22, c3.

2191 GEORGE BOURNE *to* **THE RHODE ISLAND ANTI-SLAVERY CONVENTION. 1 February 1836. New York.** States that inclement weather prevents his attendance; declares that slavery would long have been erased had it not been supported by the Christian Church and the women of the South; encourages the convention's work. 6 February 1836. p.22, c3.

2192 LEWIS TAPPAN *to* **WILLIAM M. CHASE. 29 January 1836. New York.** Regrets he cannot attend the Rhode Island Anti-Slavery Convention; sends prayers and encouragement. 6 February 1836. p.22, c4.

2193 JOHN RANKIN *to* **W. A. CHASE. 13 January 1836. New York.** Hopes he can attend the Rhode Island Anti-Slavery Convention; sends his thanks for the money pledged to the Providence Ladies' AS. 6 February 1836. p.22, c4.

2194 HOXSIE PERRY AND JOSEPH STANTON *to* **THE PRESIDENT OF THE RHODE ISLAND ANTI-SLAVERY CONVENTION. 26 January 1836. Charlestown, R.I.** Regret they cannot attend convention, although they are decidedly against slavery; send their encouragement. 6 February 1836. p.22, c4.

2195 BERIAH GREEN *to* **THE PRESIDENT OF THE ANTI-SLAVERY CONVENTION IN RHODE ISLAND. 26 January 1836. Whitesboro, N.Y.** Looks forward to attending the convention; feels that the exertions of the friends of humanity have come a long way, but that they still must struggle against evil and slavery; looks to God for wisdom and strength. 6 February 1836. p.22, c4.

2196 WILLIAM PECKHAM, BENJAMIN CARY, HEZEKIAH BABCOCK, AMOS C. WILBUR, N. C. ARMSTRONG, ROBERT C. BROWN, JOB W. WATSON, JOHN SMITH, THOMAS B. CHURCH, WILLIAM FRENCH, HENRY ELDRED, JR., P. HELME, THOMAS R. WELLS, PELEG JOHNSON, WELCOME C. BURDICK, CHRISTOPHER COMSTOCK AND JOHN ALDRICH *to* **THE PRESIDENT OF THE ANTI-SLAVERY CONVENTION IN PROVIDENCE-SOUTH KINGSTON, RHODE ISLAND. 2 February 1836. n.p.** Regret they cannot attend the convention; declare that they support the doctrine that all men are created equal, and will not interfere with the constitutional rights of the South; add that they will not allow their own rights of free speech to be invaded. 6 February 1836. p.22, c5.

2197 GERRIT SMITH *to* **REV. R. R. GURLEY. 24 November 1835. Peterboro, N.Y.** Reports that he cannot attend the anniversary of the ACS; regrets that one is now charged with inconsistency if he supports both colonization and anti-slavery; states that his interest in the AAS as the last hope for the slave is increasing. 6 February 1836. p.23, c2.

2198 n.n. *to* **n.n. [extract] n.d. Boston.** Describes the Boston riot, defending the "justifiable anger" and "most orderly manner" of the citizens who interrupted the "abolition maniacs." 6 February 1836. p.23, c3.

2199 REV. J. HAWES *to* **THE COMMITTEE OF THE ANTI-SLAVERY CONVENTION IN NORTHAMPTON. 8 January 1836. Hartford.** Regrets he cannot attend the meeting; prays that God will guide their work. 13 February 1836. p.26, c1.

2200 W. LADD *to* **W. L. GARRISON. n.d. n.p.** Contends that most every anti-slavery man he has known has also been a peace man; describes tracts he has imported from the London Peace Society, explaining the need to buy and circulate them. 13 February 1836. p.26, c3.

2201 n.n. *to* **n.n. [extract] n.d. Virginia.** Describes the slave trade in Virginia, which is being carried out to a far greater extent than ever; great numbers of the wealthiest citizens are leaving with their slaves. 13 February 1836. p.26, c3.

2202 JAMES W. WIER AND SAMUEL CROSS *to* **SAMUEL L. GOULD. 8 January 1836. Harrisburg.** Express surprise that Gould's speech was interpreted as an effort to excite the bad passions of the slaves; writers did not come away with that impression. 13 February 1836. p.27, c4.

2203 JOHN G. WHITTIER *to* **EDWARD EVERETT, GOVERNOR OF MASSACHUSETTS. n.d. n.p.** Comments on the governor's recent message on slavery; discusses sentiments of the people of Massachusetts concerning the right of the Constitution to allow or abolish slavery, as well as the writing of the Constitution and free discussion. 20 February 1836. p.29, c2.

2204 GEORGE THOMPSON *to* **W. L. GARRISON. 6 January 1836. Liverpool.** Reports that he landed on Monday the fourth after full share of rough weather, and that many enquire after Garrison; informs that many are horrified and astonished at Governor M'Duffie's speech. 20 February 1836. p.30, c3.

2205 THEODORE DWIGHT WELD *to* **THE RHODE ISLAND STATE ANTI-SLAVERY CONVENTION. 25 January 1836. Ithaca, N.Y.** Declares that he cannot attend their convention to form another AS; discusses Rhode Island heritage in the cause of human liberty and urges solidarity in the crisis. 20 February 1836. p.30, c4.

2206 OBSERVATOR *to* **W. L. GARRISON. n.d. n.p.** Looks back at the treatment of young men attached to Lane Seminary by the leaders of that institution; many have left, and now Lane has only thirty students. 20 February 1836. p.30, c5.

2207 JOSIAH GIFFORD *to* **HENRY G. CHAPMAN, ESQ. 10 February 1836. Sandwich.** Sends money to the Massachusetts AS; although a poor man, wants to do something to help the society aid the oppressed; wishes them success in their glorious cause. 20 February 1836. p.30, c5.

2208 L. *to* **W. L. GARRISON. n.d. n.p.** Describes in detail the proceedings of the anniversary of the American Union for the Relief and Improvement of the Colored Race; charges that they have accomplished nothing, will continue to accomplish nothing until they admit that slaveholding is a sin. 20 February 1836. p.30, c5.

2209 WILLIAM GOODELL *to* **BROTHER GARRISON. 16 February 1836. Providence, R.I.** Asserts that he was privileged to attend a meeting to form an AS; briefly describes the proceedings; tells of his work and tour of the past week; declares he has been heartened and encouraged on the whole. 20 February 1836. p.31, c1.

2210 J. H. M. *to* **MESSRS. GARRISON AND KNAPP. n.d. n.p.** Praises them and their work for the benefit of humankind; reports on their last monthly concert; reminds that prayer is the weapon which the oppressors of God's will find difficult to parry. 20 February 1836. p.32, c4.

2211 F. *to* **MR. EDITOR [W. L. GARRISON]. n.d. n.p.** Mocks and criticizes Mr. Tracy and his 5 February article in the *Boston Recorder*. 27 February 1836. p.34, c1.

2212 n.n. *to* **REV. MR. MAY. n.d. Connecticut.** Sends thanks for book, *Right and Wrong in Boston*; congratulates all those who participated in recent meetings in Northampton, Boston, and Providence; wishes convention had made a general motion in favor of abolition. 27 February 1836. p.34, c1.

2213 C. WRIGHT *to* **THE** *VERMONT CHRONICLE.* **2 January 1836. Montpelier.** Declares his "utter abhorrence" of language used by the *Liberator* respecting Rev. R. W. Bailey; although Wright has joined the AS, he also supports the CS. 27 February 1836. p.35, c1.

2214 W. L. GARRISON *to* **OLIVER JOHNSON. 10 February 1836. Brooklyn, Ct.** Believes abolitionism is indigenous to the soil of Vermont, noting that almost all his first efforts in the cause of universal emancipation were made there; criticizes the Southern claim to compensation; tells of London anti-slavery meeting he attended in 1833. 5 March 1836. p.37, c3.

2215 SAM'L COX *to* **DR. JONA A. ALLEN. 10 February 1836. Auburn, N.Y.** Explains that even if some slaves are treated well, slavery is still a system which is "utterly and awfully wrong"; believes that the moral sin of slavery is of great criminality. 5 March 1836. p.37, c5.

2216 MOSES *to* **BROTHER GARRISON. 10 December 1835. Cincinnati.** Criticizes Dr. Beecher's recent speech, which flattered government and institutions of America but remained silent on the enslavement of two million black Americans. 12 March 1836. p.41, c2.

2217 H. B. STANTON *to* **BROTHER GARRISON. 2 March 1836. Utica, N.Y.** Discusses the principles and success of Brother Weld's recent speeches, which were attended by large, well-mannered audiences; reports that nearly 1200 have signed petitions to Congress. 12 March 1836. p.42, c1.

2218 GEORGE THOMPSON *to* **MR. EDITOR [W. L. GARRISON]. 14 January 1836. Liverpool.** Reports that he has been reunited with wife and children; notes that he finds the work of Dr. Channing on slavery rather simplistic. 12 March 1836. p.42, c3.

2219 AMOS A. PHELPS *to* **BROTHER THOMPSON. 2 November 1835. Farmington.** Describes conversation between Mr. Kaufman and Mr. Thompson at Andover; refutes Kaufman's allegation that Thompson advised that slaves be told to cut their masters' throats. 12 March 1836. p.42, c4.

2220 H. *to* **W. L. GARRISON. n.d. n.p.** Criticizes the "supercilious and tyrannical conduct" of the chairman of the legislative committee, the Hon. Mr. Lunt of Essex, who interrupted speakers and prevented them from answering questions; declares that such "outrageous" occurrences exemplify the muzzling and gagging principle pressed on the North by the South. 12 March 1836. p.43, c3.

2221 n.n. *to* **THE** *SALEM LANDMARK.* **n.d. n.p.** Declares the wicked mob and its instigators hardly expected that the iron shutters they forced Mr. Tappan to put on his windows would be such good protection against many other things. 19 March 1836. p.48, c4.

2222 JOSEPH SOUTHWICK AND HENRY E. BENSON *to* **HON. SENATE OF THE COMMONWEALTH OF MASSACHUSETTS. 9 March 1836. Boston.** State that the memorial of the Massachusetts AS declares that the joint committee of the legislature will not grant them a full hearing; assert their desire for an opportunity to present their defense. 26 March 1836. p.51, c2.

2223 W. S. JENNINGS, PREFECT *to* **THE FRIENDS OF MENTAL CULTURE AMONG THE PEOPLE OF COLOR. 26 March 1836. Boston.** Reports the formation of the Boston Philomathean Society for the promotion of literature and the establishment of a library; solicits donations. 26 March 1836. p.51, c5.

2224 L. M. CHILD *to* **DR. CHANNING. n.d. n.p.** Criticizes his recent work on slavery and thanks him for many plain truths, eloquently spoken; disagrees with assertion that masters who hold their slaves from disinterested considerations deserve praise, and refutes his arguments against immediate emancipation. 2 April 1836. p.53, c2.

2225 CHARLOTTE JONES *to* **WALKER HAWES. 10 September 1835. Monrovia.** Reports that she is well, but that times are very hard and she does not like the place; promises to serve him the rest of her life if he will send for her. 2 April 1836. p.54, c1.

2226 ELIZABETH BROCK *to* **WALKER HAWES. 10 September 1835. Monrovia.** Reports that she is well, and asks him to send for her and her three children; states that no way to make a living exists in her country. 2 April 1836. p.54, c1.

2227 SIMEON S. JOCELYN *to* **BROTHER GARRISON. 29 February 1836. New Haven, Ct.** Sends obituary of Harriet Rosette Lanson, who had been committed to his guardianship; describes her parents, her early life, and his sadness at losing her. 2 April 1836. p.56, c4.

2228 JUSTICE *to* **THE** *CHRISTIAN WATCHMAN*. **n.d. n.p.** Replies to their request that he give his name; states that he prefers not to give it as his information would neither be helped nor hindered by identifying himself. 9 April 1836. p.58, c2.

2229 J. G. PIKE *to* **BROTHER. 14 November 1835. Derby, England.** Praises the Foreign Mission Society and its progress; rejoices that the *Morning Star* is a decidely anti-slavery paper; declares Christians must exert every power against slavery's continuance. 9 April 1836. p.58, c4.

2230 JUNIUS *to* **MR. EDITOR [W. L. GARRISON]. 20 February 1836. Acton, Me.** Declares that he must take his stand for immediate emancipation when he hears of the slanderous charges directed against abolitionists and government support of mobs. 9 April 1836. p.58, c4.

2231 E. L. A. *to* **BROTHER GARRISON. n.d. n.p.** Describes the destruction of the colony at Port Cresson in Liberia; quotes the report of the CS which implies that the natives were fired upon and their village burned before they made any assault on the colony; also quotes the society's comments on the efficacy of their system. 9 April 1836. p.58, c5.

2232 CLAUDIUS B. FARNSWORTH *to* **THE EDITOR [W. L. GARRISON]. 22 February 1836. Groton.** Presents the preamble of the Ladies AS of Groton; hopes the principles it embodies will inspire others. 9 April 1836. p.59, c1.

2233 M. R. *to* **JOSEPH R. CHANDLER. [from the** *United States Gazette***] 16 February 1836. n.p.** Wonders if the Pennsylvania Legislature will pass a law allowing the Postmaster General to determine what kind of communications can be sent through the mail; believes this would display "consummate ignorance of the feelings of freemen." 16 April 1836. p.61, c3.

2234 A FRIEND TO ALL MANKIND *to* **MY BELOVED PASTOR. 8 April 1836. Dorchester.** Wonders why the pastor has instructed him that slavery is one of the greatest evils in their beloved country, but that the subject must be left alone. 16 April 1836. p.62, c1.

2235 H. B. STANTON *to* **BROTHER GARRISON. 6 April 1836. Rochester, N.Y.** Describes Theodore D. Weld's recent lectures in Rochester, due to which between 800 and 900 new members joined the AS; hopes his triumphant work continues. 16 April 1836. p.62, c1.

2236 THINE *to* **n.n. n.d. n.p.** Wonders why no voices have been raised against the provision of the proposed constitution of Arkansas which would prevent any legislation from abolishing slavery; hopes men will awaken before slavery is sanctioned for eternity in Arkansas. 16 April 1836. p.64, c3.

2237 n.n. *to* **THE** *NEW YORK AMERICAN*. **n.d. n.p.** Quotes letter from friend in Philadelphia opposing the proposed constitution in Arkansas, because it "immortalizes slavery in Arkansas." 16 April 1836. p.64. c3.

2238 J. B. MALLORY *to* **THE HON. MARTIN VAN BUREN, VICE PRESIDENT. [from the** *Richmond Enquirer***] 5 March 1836. Richmond.** Inquires whether Van Buren believes that Congress is endowed by the Constitution with authority to interfere with the slave question or to abolish slavery in the District of Columbia. 23 April 1836. p.65, c1.

2239 M. VAN BUREN *to* **SIR. 11 March 1836. Washington.** Forwards his correspondence with citizens of North Carolina, in response to questions about his opinion on the constitutional power of Congress to interfere with slavery. 23 April 1836. p.65, c1.

2240 JUNIUS AMIS, ISAAC HALL, JOHN WALL, C. YELLOWBY, SAM'L B. SPIR-RILL AND JAS. W. PUIZINN *to* **HIS EXCELLENCY MARTIN VAN BUREN. 23 February 1836. Jackson, N.C.** Ask Van Buren if he believes Congress has the constitutional power to interfere with or abolish slavery in the District of Columbia. 23 April 1836. p.65, c1.

2241 M. VAN BUREN *to* **MESSRS. JUNIUS AMIS, ISAAC HALL, JOHN WALL, C. YELLOWBY, SAM'L B. SPIRRILL AND JAMES W. PUIZINN. 6 March 1836. Washington.** Replies that Congress has no right to interfere on the subject of slavery; Congress should not agitate for the abolition of slavery in the District of Columbia; slavery is a matter for each state to decide. 23 April 1836. p.65, c1.

2242 HU. L. WHITE *to* **JOHN B. D. SMITH, ESQ. 17 March 1836. Washington.** Believes Congress has no power to abolish slavery in the District of Columbia; if Congress did possess that power, he thinks that its exercise would be "the very worst of policy." 23 April 1836. p.65, c4.

2243 GEORGE LUNT *to* **SIR. 19 March 1836. Boston.** Charges that the paper is determined to misrepresent him; claims that the language they attributed to him in relation to the abolition committee was attributed falsely. 23 April 1836. p.66, c3.

2244 BENJ. F. HALLETT *to* **GEORGE LUNT. 21 March 1836. Boston.** Asks Lunt to specify and prove his claims that Hallett misquoted him; Hallett is not an abolitionist, and is not trying to do Lunt injustice; believes Lunt dishonors the state of Massachusetts by suggesting gag laws. 23 April 1836. p.66, c3.

2245 ABRAHAM BAER, JR. *to* **BROTHER. 5 March 1836. Osnaburg, Oh.** Relates history of county AS, which started with very few supporters but has recently grown; feels heartened by their progress despite the persecutions they suffer. 23 April 1836. p.66, c5.

2246 A SUBSCRIBER *to* **W. L. GARRISON. 13 April 1836. n.p.** Remembers many happy hours with his intelligent friend, Mr. Cummings, now editor of the *Portland Mirror*; feels saddened that Cummings has changed so radically that he now defends slavery. 23 April 1836. p.67, c1.

2247 S. B. *to* **REV. 25 November 1835. Boston.** Reports that some of the answers on the subject of slavery from his pastor have grieved him; explains that he supports immediate emancipation on the basis of his reading of the Bible. 23 April 1836. p.67, c1.

2248 JOHN ALDEN *to* **FRIEND GARRISON. 18 March 1836. Plaistow.** Quotes from George Mason, Patrick Henry, John Smith and other true patriots who opposed slavery. 23 April 1836. p.67, c2.

2249 MARY S. PARKER AND MARIA W. CHAPMAN *to* **THE WOMEN OF GREAT BRITAIN. n.d. n.p.** Praise George Thompson; describe the horrors of slavery; believe the abolitionists to be true patriots. 30 April 1836. p.69, c4.

2250 n.n. *to* **EDITOR [W. L. GARRISON]. April 1836. Providence.** A young man, who rescued a child as its mother was left in a burning building, reminds that children of slaves are also in danger of being separated from their parents, a cruel practice which is sanctioned by law. 30 April 1836. p.70, c5.

2251 n.n. *to* **MR. EDITOR [W. L. GARRISON]. n.d. Norfolk County.** Notes that recent newspapers give no news; declares that editors must not suppress even offensive truths; quotes from British papers. 30 April 1836. p.70, c5.

2252 HARPER AND BROTHERS *to* **THE** *COLUMBIA TELESCOPE*. **31 December 1835. New York.** Publishers of Reed and Matheson's narrative did not find the book offensive, and regret that the editor did; note that they have in many other cases refused to publish abolition material. 30 April 1836. p.71, c1.

2253 GEORGE THOMPSON *to* **W. L. GARRISON. 5 March 1836. Liverpool.** States that his reception in Scotland has been overwhelmingly enthusiastic; he has given about sixteen lectures, at which many resolutions supportive of Americans were adopted. 30 April 1836. p.71, c1.

2254 SAMUEL J. MAY *to* **MR. ISAAC KNAPP. n.d. n.p.** Gives account of his recent public labors in the anti-slavery cause: upon returning from Vermont, visited Boston; began traveling in February; has been met everywhere by willing listeners. 30 April 1836. p.71, c1.

2255 ELIZA T. LOUD *to* **W. L. GARRISON. 23 April 1836. South Weymouth.** Relates information of South Weymouth Female AS meeting on 19 November 1835; lists present officers. 30 April 1836. p.71, c2.

2256 M. VAN BUREN *to* **MR. CICOGNANI, TO BE SHOWN TO THE POPE. 20 July 1830. Washington.** Reciprocates the friendly and liberal sentiments conveyed by the Pope; reminds him that all United States citizens enjoy freedom of religion and suffer no persecution, and that there exists a "unity of faith" in the United States. 30 April 1836. p.72, c3.

2257 NATH'L SOUTHARD *to* **W. L. GARRISON. 23 April 1836. Boston.** Reports that he delivered an address on the evils of slavery to a Worcester County meeting, at which an AS was formed and a petition against the admission of Arkansas as a slave state was signed. 7 May 1836. p.74, c4.

2258 W. L. GARRISON *to* **KNAPP. 11 May 1836. New York.** Describes his distinguished company on the boat from Providence to New York; Mr. Ladd addressed the passengers on the subject of peace, but was urged by a preacher not to continue, as it would create bitter feelings and disagreements. 14 May 1836. p.78, c3.

2259 SAMUEL J. MAY *to* **FRIEND. 11 May 1836. New York.** Comments on cheering meeting of the AAS; lists speeches and reports; describes proceedings. 14 May 1836. p.78, c4.

2260 N. SOUTHARD *to* **KNAPP. 10 May 1836. New York.** Describes the annual meeting of the AAS; reports speeches by Wm. Jay, Gerrit Smith and others; large audiences were quiet and attentive. 14 May 1836. p.78, c4.

2261 W. *to* **BROTHER. 10 May 1836. New York.** Compares the participants of a CS meeting and their attitude concerning the relationship between colored and white men unfavorably with the attitude of those attending an AAS meeting. 14 May 1836. p.78, c4.

2262 n.n. *to* **n.n. [extract] 7 April 1836. Clinton. Parish of East Felicianna, La.** Describes recent court case which awarded $350 to a master because other slaveholders beat and punished his slaves. 14 May 1836. p.79, c4.

2263 AUGUSTUS WATTLES *to* **BROTHER GARRISON. 28 April 1836. Granville, Oh.** Reports anniversary meeting, held in a barn, which raised $10,000 for anti-slavery purposes. 14 May 1836. p.79, c5.

2264 ABNER G. KIRK *to* **W. L. GARRISON. 5 March 1836. Salem, Oh.** Refutes objections to anti-slavery work; believes the principal objection to immediate emancipation is the self-interest of slaveholders; affirms the work will go on, despite opposition. 21 May 1836. p.81, c5.

2265 JOSEPH A. DUGDALE *to* **W. L. GARRISON. [extract] 11 January 1836. Green Plain, Clark County, Oh.** Reports on abolitionists in the area, where the brethren and sisterhood compose one society; describes their proceedings, his visit to Cincinnati, and his discussions with Brother Wattles. 21 May 1836. p.82, c1.

2266 J. M. B. *to* **MR. EDITOR [W. L. GARRISON]. 9 May 1836. Limington, Me.** Argues that Garrison is not alone in the cause; describes large meetings in his town for the formation of an AS; nearby towns progressing equally well. 21 May 1836. p.82, c2.

2267 THOS. J. RUSH, SECRETARY OF WAR, TEXAS *to* **THE PEOPLE TOWARDS NACOGDOCHES. 23 April 1836. Army.** Describes victory over Santa Anna, who is now their prisoner. 21 May 1836. p.82, c5.

2268 n.n. *to* **THE** *ZION'S HERALD.* **[extract] n.d. n.p.** Discusses the Wesleyan conference and motions made by Dr. Bangs; summarizes Dr. Bangs' report and those of other committees. 21 May 1836. p.83, c2.

2269 M. C. *to* **n.n. 28 April 1836. St. Louis, Mo.** Relates the murder of Deputy Sheriff Hammond by escaping prisoner; a mob then took the prisoner from the jail, chained him to a tree, and slowly burned him to death. 21 May 1836. p.83, c3.

2270 n.n. *to* **THE** *RELIGIOUS HERALD.* **n.d. n.p.** Recommends that other societies follow the simplicity of the Baptist Tract Society, which has decided to discountenance popular titles given to preachers, such as Rev., D.D., A.M., in order to exemplify meekness and humility. 21 May 1836. p.84, c4.

2271 GEORGE THOMPSON *to* **W. L. GARRISON. 13 April 1836. Glasgow.** Describes speeches and travels of the past fortnight, through which he strove to do "full justice to America"; notes that the women of Great Britain are very active in the cause. 28 May 1836. p.85, c4.

2272 GEORGE THOMPSON *to* **HENRY E. BENSON. [extract] 13 April 1836. n.p.** Relates that his reception has been flattering and enthusiastic; notes his discussion with Dr. Cox, the activities of the ultra-abolitionists in England, and other European anti-slavery news. 28 May 1836. p.86, c1.

2273 GEORGE THOMPSON *to* **W. L. GARRISON. 29 April 1836. Glasgow.** Notes important movement in the Synod, an ecclesiastical court, of the United Secession Church of Scotland, which appointed a committee to draft letter to United States clergy, stressing the evils of slavery and the need for emancipation; quotes their resolutions. 4 June 1836. p.91, c4.

2274 W. L. GARRISON *to* **W. H. SCOTT. 20 April 1836. Boston.** Reports that he must appear by proxy at the meeting of the Young Men's AS of Philadelphia; recounts his early work for the cause, and how his later work has changed; declares he does not despair of his country. 4 June 1836. p.92, c2.

2275 H. *to* **MR. EDITOR [W. L. GARRISON]. n.d. n.p.** Recommends to the AS the celebration of the anniversary of American independence by speeches and addresses. 11 June 1836. p.94, c5.

2276 A GENTLEMAN IN MARION COUNTY, MO. *to* **n.n. 24 May 1836. Palmyra, Mo.** Reports that anti-abolitionists are burning books and papers and tarring and feathering people; W. Muldrow stabbed Dr. Bosley, who attempted to stop him from reading an abolition petition in church. Muldrow is now in jail awaiting trial. 18 June 1836. p.98, c2.

2277 A GENTLEMAN IN MISSOURI *to* **n.n. [extract] 27 May 1836. Near Palmyra, Mo.** Reports that Col. Muldrow proposed to give $10,000, and urged others to give for the indemnity of slaveholders, in the event that the government freed the slaves; Dr. Bosley rose in opposition, drew his pistol, then was stabbed. 18 June 1836. p.98, c4.

2278 WILLIAM JAY *to* **MR. EDITOR [W. L. GARRISON]. 4 June 1836. Bedford.** Protests a resolution against the everyday use of products of slave labor; believes the choice is up to the individual, and it is not the role of the AAS to dictate behavior. 18 June 1836. p.98, c4.

2279 A FRIEND OF THE AMERICAN UNION *to* **MR. EDITOR [W. L. GARRISON]. 13 June 1836. n.p.** Compares early Christian idolators who ate the meat sacrificed to the gods, to Americans who consume products of slave labor. 18 June 1836. p.98, c5.

2280 n.n. *to* **W. L. GARRISON. n.d. n.p.** Explains his statements concerning the admission of Arkansas into the Union as a slave state; discusses states' rights, federal rights, and the Constitution's powers. 18 June 1836. p.98, c5.

2281 n.n. *to* **THE** *NEW YORK JOURNAL OF COMMERCE.* **3 June 1836. Washington.** Reports on hostilities of Creek Indians and the prospect of a general Indian war which may also include the Cherokees; discloses that United States agents were sent to steal Seminole children as slaves. 18 June 1836. p.100, c5.

2282 H. W. *to* **THE** *ZION'S HERALD.* **n.d. n.p.** Expresses his rage at a mob's recent burning of a man by slow fire at St. Louis; declares all citizens are guaranteed trial by jury, and such atrocities must not be allowed to be perpetrated with impunity. 25 June 1836. p.101, c3.

2283 THEODORE D. WELD *to* **BROTHER POTTER. [from the** *Free Discussion Advocate***] 11 June 1836. Troy.** Regrets he cannot be there with Potter; reports that since Weld's last letter they have been mobbed again in the day time and that the anti-abolition fury is breaking out anew. 26 June 1836. p.102, c2.

2284 J. COFFIN *to* **W. L. GARRISON. 11 June 1836. Pittsburgh, Pa.** Discusses the appearance of sixty-five emigrants to Liberia; declares that his sensibilities have been awakened to the wretchedness of the system of colonization; criticizes enclosed letter from McElroy, an agent of CS. 26 June 1836. p.102, c3.

2285 G. W. M'ELROY *to* **J. COFFIN. 10 June 1836. n.p.** Reports his arrival with sixty-five emigrants destined for Africa; discusses his labors for their emancipation and preparations for their trip; notes that he had worried that some would refuse to go and be taken back by their masters. 26 June 1836. p.102, c3.

2286 A BENEVOLENT LADY *to* **W. L. GARRISON. 9 June 1836. Boston.** Sends a small sum to aid the glorious cause; praises the New England AS convention. 26 June 1836. p.103, c4.

2287 n.n. *to* **n.n. [extract] 2 June 1836. New Orleans.** Informs that Gen. Houston is in bad health and fears death. 26 June 1836. p.103, c4.

2288 A BOSTON BOY *to* **FRIEND GARRISON. n.d. n.p.** Quotes from Mr. Pinckney's report; mocks the colonizationists and the American Union. 2 July 1836. p.105, c4.

2289 Z. *to* **MR. EDITOR [W. L. GARRISON]. n.d. n.p.** Rebukes speech made by Mr. Tracy, editor of the *Boston Recorder*, at the recent anniversary meeting of the American Union; wonders how long the Christian community will patronize his wretched paper. 2 July 1836. p.105, c5.

2290 JOSEPH BRACKETT *to* **W. L. GARRISON. 1 June 1836. Limington, Me.** Contradicts report by J. M. B. on the progress of anti-slavery sentiment in the town; states that meetings were held during the summer but disturbances began in November and actually killed the society for a time, but it is growing again. 2 July 1836. p.106, c2.

2291 n.n. *to* **W. L. GARRISON. 12 June 1836. Williams College.** Encourages Garrison; reports the formation of a college AS at Williams, whose motto is immediate and total abolition. 2 July 1836. p.106, c2.

2292 GERRIT SMITH *to* **W. L. GARRISON. 24 June 1836. Peterboro.** Explains his conduct concerning the resolution criticized by Judge Jay; claims that he did not speak out much at that meeting, as he was afraid others still doubted his recent adoption of abolition principles; stresses his personal belief in the importance of abstinence from slave products. 2 July 1836. p.106, c2.

2293 DAVID NELSON *to* **THOSE OF MARION COUNTY WHO THREATEN ME.** **[from the** *Illinois Courier***] n.d. n.p.** Declares that he will not threaten in return or flatter them, nor will he renounce his sentiments; states that he has read a pro-colonization paper; asks whether his opponents actually question the truth of the matters they charge him with. 2 July 1836. p.106, c5.

2294 W. L. GARRISON *to* **KNAPP. 22 June 1836. Newport, R.I.** States that he and others are in Newport to defend themselves from a gag-law bill introduced by Benjamin Hazard to silence abolitionists; finds that Hazard and others have backed out of the discussion. 2 July 1836. p.107, c3.

2295 W. APESS *to* **W. L. GARRISON. n.d. n.p.** Asserts that the situation of the Marshpee Indians is improving and the new government is working well; forwards a public notice of future camp meeting. 2 July 1836. p.107, c5.

2296 n.n. *to* **EDITOR. [from the** *Woonsocket Patriot***] n.d. n.p.** Wonders why the news of the capture of Santa Anna was so "great and glorious," and why he was called a tyrant and a despot; feels the nation should not have fought a war not declared by Congress. 9 July 1836. p.109, c5.

2297 THE EMPEROR OF RUSSIA *to* **GOV. M'DUFFIE OF SOUTH CAROLINA. n.d. Palace of the Czars, St. Petersburgh, Russia.** States that slavery is also the foundation of Russian despotism; congratulates him on the "delightful affinity" between the two countries. 9 July 1836. p.110, c5.

2298 GEORGE M'DUFFIE *to* **THE EMPEROR OF RUSSIA. n.d. Council Room, Charleston, S.C.** Rejoices in the return of America to the principles of despotism; hopes the Czar will come to live permanently in America. 9 July 1836. p.110, c5.

2299 SAMUEL KEESE *to* **FRIEND GARRISON. 25 June 1836. Peru, Clinton County, N.Y.** Hopes Judge Jay has realized his error in protesting a boycott of slave labor products; fails to see how a boycott can be considered unconstitutional. 9 July 1836. p.110, c5.

2300 W. L. GARRISON *to* **KNAPP. 5 July 1836. Providence.** Discusses his visit to Fall River, and the Fourth of July celebration at which he spoke; wonders when this will finally be a free country. 9 July 1836. p.111, c3.

2301 A. C. GARRETT *to* **BROTHER LEAVITT. 21 May 1836. Quincy, Il.** Describes his narrow escape from harm at Marion College in Missouri; states that he arrived there with two free colored boys who wished to be educated before going to Africa; he was searched for anti-slavery books, and told to leave the state or receive 150 lashes; barely escaped. 9 July 1836. p.112, c2.

2302 WILLIAM SLADE *to* **DR. ISAAC PARISH [from the** *Philadelphia Independent Press***] 18 March 1836. Washington.** Expresses appreciation for compliments on his work in Congress; declares that theirs is a noble cause and friends of emancipation occupy a difficult position in America; gives encouragement and love to Parish and the Young Men's AS of Philadelphia. 16 July 1836. p.114, c1.

2303 JOHN SMITH AND S. HOPKINS EMERY *to* **MR. EDITOR [W. L. GARRISON]. 11 July 1836. Andover.** Give an account of the annual meeting of the Andover AS; list exercises, summarize discourse, and list officers. 16 July 1836. p.115, c1.

2304 JOSIAH GIFFORD *to* **W. L. GARRISON. 6 July 1836. Sandwich.** Describes the Third Annual Meeting of the Sandwich AS; gives history of the society; lists new officers. 16 July 1836. p.115, c1.

2305 CHARLES O. LIBBY *to* **W. L. GARRISON. 6 July 1836. Gorham, Me.** Regrets the present spirit of "liberty," favoring admission of Arkansas as slave state, and rule of lynch law in South; gives history of town's AS; hopes for the victory of abolitionism. 16 July 1836. p.115, c2.

2306 A PROTESTANT CLERGYMAN *to* **MR. SLEEPER. [from the** *Mercantile Journal***] n.d. n.p.** Reports that he saw a picture of a Roman Catholic priest being used for target practice at the engine house at South Boston; regrets such occurrences in this country of freedom. 16 July 1836. p.115, c2.

2307 A REAL BORN BOSTONIAN *to* **EDITOR OF THE** *LIBERATOR* **[W. L. GARRISON]. 7 July 1836. n.p.** Replies to article from "A Protestant Clergyman," noting he found that the same engine also shot at a Protestant priest's picture, and a sign painted "Thompson, Foreign Emissary"; feels this engine company is a disgrace to the city. 16 July 1836. p.115, c2.

2308 B. B. DAVIS *to* **n.n. [extract] 14 June 1836. New Garden, Oh.** Reports that after having difficulty in arranging for a meetinghouse, five or six ASS met together; gives brief summary of events. 16 July 1836. p.115, c3.

2309 A. M. HUNT *to* **THE** *LIBERATOR*. **3 June 1836. Ohio City, Oh.** Reports formation of Ohio City AS; presently their numbers are small but they are confident they will grow. 16 July 1836. p.115, c3.

2310 n.n. *to* **n.n. [extract] n.d. Chester Cross Roads, Geauga County, Oh.** Announces that their AS numbers 136; reports they are growing fast. 16 July 1836. p.115, c4.

2311 C. *to* **MR. EDITOR [W. L. GARRISON]. n.d. n.p.** Finds Paulding's work on slavery full of "miserable sophistries, and the gross perversion of Scripture." 23 July 1836. p.117, c4.

2312 P. SNYDER *to* **W. L. GARRISON. 13 July 1836. Union College, Schenectady, N.Y.** Reports the founding of another college AS; quotes its preamble on the evil and injustice of involuntary servitude. 23 July 1836. p.117, c5.

2313 GERRIT SMITH *to* **REV. DR. BEECHER. [from** *Friend of Man***] 29 June 1836. Peterboro.** Believes Beecher is truly the colored man's friend, but criticizes Beecher's hope for future, rather than immediate, emancipation; discusses Beecher's recent speech to a colonization meeting; hopes his noble sentiments are transferred soon to the side of the oppressed. 23 July 1836. p.118, c2.

2314 W. L. GARRISON *to* **KNAPP. 19 July 1836. Brooklyn.** Writes that he has been sick, but is now somewhat better; sends an article criticizing Dr. Beecher's speech in Pittsburgh. 23 July 1836. p.118, c4.

2315 M. S. S. *to* **MR. EDITOR [W. L. GARRISON]. n.d. n.p.** Believes the church is "too much assimilated to the world" these days, and that church leaders give too much consideration to people's reaction to their projects; feels they should only be following God's directions; applies this doctrine to the slavery question. 30 July 1836. p.122, c1.

2316 WOOLMAN *to* **THE PROFESSORS OF CHRISTIANITY. n.d. n.p.** Asserts that slavery is almost universally acknowledged as an evil; questions why so many are disposed to palliate, to compromise, to excuse it, urging them to rise out of indifference. 30 July 1836. p.122, c3.

2317 A HIGHLY INTELLIGENT FEMALE FRIEND *to* **n.n. [extract] 26 June 1836. Philadelphia.** Replies to William Jay's severe criticism of the AAS resolution relative to the use of slave labor products; refers Jay to the constitutions of many anti-slavery societies which have similar articles. 30 July 1836. p.122, c5.

2318 n.n. *to* **BROTHER. n.d. n.p.** Reports that in a recent contest held in Alton, Illinois for the purpose of designing the best architectural plan for a new hotel, the choice was the plan of a colored man, which mortified them; thus demonstrates that whites do not have superior intellects. 30 July 1836. p.122, c5.

2319 A NORTHERN LADY, NOW RESIDING IN THE SOUTH *to* **n.n. [extract] n.d. n.p.** Claims that domestic life in the south is different; the climate slows everyone down, and Southern ladies are accustomed to being inactive and having others do things for them; believes the discipline of the slaves is "not necessarily oppressive." 6 August 1836. p.125, c3.

2320 AN AMERICAN LADY *to* **THE** *AMERICAN LADIES' MAGAZINE.* **n.d. n.p.** Replies to Northern lady now living in South; denies that slaveholders can be highminded or honorable; discredits the former Northerner's statement that the slaves are happy and contented. 6 August 1836. p.125, c3.

2321 W. S. A. *to* **MR. EDITOR [W. L. GARRISON]. n.d. n.p.** Considers the arguments justifying Mr. Calhoun's incendiary bill unsound; says that slaveholding states have no right to pass any laws restricting liberty of the press; believes the bill is entirely unconstitutional. 6 August 1836. p.125, c5.

2322 W. DROWN *to* **W. L. GARRISON. 7 July 1836. Providence.** Claims that it is painful to witness an unwillingness to boycott slave products, as it is so important that everything possible be done for the liberation of the slaves. 6 August 1836. p.126, c1.

2323 C. P. SUMNER *to* **THE** *EVENING TRANSCRIPT.* **n.d. n.p.** Explains his conduct in the rescue of two colored women, alleged to be slaves; he had gone to his usual post that day, and only later did he hear of the trouble. 6 August 1836. p.127, c4.

2324 JOHN REED *to* **THE LADIES OF NEW BEDFORD WHO SENT A MEMORIAL TO CONGRESS. 22 June 1836. Washington City.** Reports that he presented their memorial to Congress, but that Arkansas has been received into the Union as a slave state, nevertheless; respects the ladies' spirit of benevolence. 13 August 1836. p.129, c4.

2325 JOHN REED *to* **GENTLEMEN. 22 June 1836. Washington City.** Reports that he received their memorial and presented it to Congress, but nevertheless Arkansas was admitted to the Union as a slave state; relates the astonishing conduct of Congress relative to slavery in the District of Columbia. 13 August 1836. p.129, c4.

2326 L. MARIA CHILD *to* **W. L. GARRISON. 5 August 1836. South Natick.** Describes pleasant chat with Mr. Southard, a fellow abolitionist; reports that clergyman protested Southard's use of hall for incendiary speech. 13 August 1836. p.130, c2.

2327 n.n. *to* **W. L. GARRISON. 8 August 1836. West Boylston.** Expresses amazement at the president's unauthorized order sending regiments to Mexico; feels that if the report is true, the president ought to be impeached, as he is aiming to propagate slavery. 13 August 1836. p.130, c3.

2328 D. L. CHILD *to* **SIR. 15 September 1835. New Rochelle.** Declares that some "slaveholding and insatiable countrymen" are trying to wrest from Mexico the "noble and beautiful province of Texas"; urges the preservation of the integrity of the Mexican Republic by the prevention of slavery in a country now free. 13 August 1836. p.130, c4.

2329 THE SCHOLARS OF THE UNION EVANGELICAL SCHOOL *to* **THE COL-ORED CHILDREN OF MISS PAUL'S SCHOOL. 4 July 1836. Amesbury and Salisbury.** Express pity for the slaves; rejoice that the colored children are in school, and donate their Fourth of July candy money for the use of the colored children. 13 August 1836. p.130, c5.

2330 S. PAUL *to* **THE CHILDREN OF THE UNION EVANGELICAL SABBATH SCHOOL OF AMESBURY AND SALISBURY. 30 July 1836. Boston.** Sends thanks for letter and money. 13 August 1836. p.130, c5.

2331 CONSISTENCY *to* **THE** *OHIO FREE PRESS.* **n.d. n.p.** Wonders if it is consistent with the feelings of the American people as republicans to allow the Fourth of July, our national day, to be "degraded and polluted with such party spirit." 20 August 1836. p.134, c4.

2332 C. P. SUMNER *to* **THE** *SENTINEL AND GAZETTE.* **13 August 1836. n.p.** Denies he had any knowledge or belief of any other process of the writ of Habeas Corpus; believed the women would be peaceably discharged. 20 August 1836. p.134, c5.

2333 JOHN MURRAY *to* **W. L. GARRISON. 14 June 1836. Glasgow.** Recounts debate between George Thompson and Mr. Breckenridge; lists regulations they agreed upon; reports that Breckenridge charged that Garrison printed a placard urging a Boston mob to attack him. 20 August 1836. p.135, c1.

2334 A BAPTIST *to* **REV. DR. L. BOLLES. n.d. n.p.** Feels he cannot continue to contribute to the aid of foreign missions until the board retracts its letter apologizing for and cooperating with a system of slavery. 20 August 1836. p.135, c1.

2335 J. J. THOMAS *to* **EDITOR OF THE** *LIBERATOR* **[W. L. GARRISON]. 23 July 1836. Ledyard, Cayuga County, N.Y.** Criticizes former letters to the *Liberator* on the use of slave products; asks what right we have to use those products and what right a master has to the unrequited work of the slave. 20 August 1836. p.135, c2.

2336 W. H. JOHNSON *to* **W. L. GARRISON. 27 July 1836. Buckingham, Bucks County, Pa.** Reports formation of AS which works for immediate emancipation; lists officers. 20 August 1836. p.135, c3.

2337 G. *to* **THE** *LIBERATOR.* **26 July 1836. Portland, Me.** Relates that a while ago, an AS which was formed was disturbed by mob; thirteen of the mob were later selected for prosecution and were punished. 20 August 1836. p.135, c3.

2338 A. W. *to* **W. L. GARRISON. 6 August 1836. Saratoga Springs.** Discusses Temperance Convention; describes Chancellor Walworth, the president, and the proceedings, which included much anti-slavery discussion as well. 20 August 1836. p.135, c4.

2339 JOHN RANDOLPH *to* **n.n. [extract] n.d. Roanoke.** Describes the evils of avarice and slavery as one result. 20 August 1836. p.135, c4.

2340 JOHN W. LEWIS, JR., WINDSOR GARDNER, JAMES W. JOHNSON, AND CHARLES K. COOK *to* **THE PEOPLE OF COLOR THROUGHOUT NEW ENGLAND. n.d. n.p.** Invite them to send delegates to a convention to discuss formation of a New England temperance society for people of color. 20 August 1836. p.135, c5.

2341 F. A. COX *to* **THE** *LONDON PATRIOT.* **31 May 1836. Hackney.** Declares that some consider George Thompson's work impertinent interference, while others respect and encourage it. 27 August 1836. p.138, c2.

2342 JAMES HOBY *to* **THE** *LONDON PATRIOT.* **25 May 1836. Coleford.** Replies to Mr. Thompson's charge that Hoby's concluding remarks at New York Abolition Meeting were misrepresentations. 27 August 1836. p.138, c2.

2343 JOSEPH BELCHER *to* **THE** *LONDON PATRIOT.* **30 May 1836. Paternoster-row.** Challenges Mr. Thompson to specify the meeting at which Cox allegedly pledged himself to a plan of conduct regarding slavery. 27 August 1836. p.138, c2.

2344 THO. PRICE *to* **THE** *LONDON PATRIOT.* **28 May 1836. Finchley Common.** Reacts to allusion made to himself in Dr. Cox's reply to Mr. Thompson. 27 August 1836. p138, c3.

2345 ELIZABETH EMERY AND MARY P. ABBOTT *to* **MR. EDITOR [W. L. GARRISON]. 22 August 1836. Andover, Ma.** Describe formation of Female AS in the belief that women have a right and a duty to work against the evil of slavery; quote constitution of the society and list officers. 27 August 1836. p.138, c4.

2346 n.n. *to* **n.n. [extract] 1 and 2 August 1836. Hillsboro, Highland County, Oh.** Reports commotion over Birney's anticipated speech on abolition and fears of mobs; declares that the strength of abolition made opponents afraid to stir up trouble. 27 August 1836. p.139, c4.

2347 n.n. *to* **n.n. [from the** *New York Sun***] 2 August. Cincinnati.** Claims lawlessness reigns; colored people are attacked and driven from homes. 27 August 1836. p.139, c4.

2348 THE UXBRIDGE FEMALE ANTI-SLAVERY SOCIETY *to* **PROFESSING CHRISTIAN WOMEN OF KENTUCKY. [from the** *Philanthropist***] n.d. n.p.** Sympathize with them in view of their connection with slavery; for the happiness of the master and mistress, as well as that of the slave, plead for them to give it up. 27 August 1836. p.140, c2.

2349 S. J. C. *to* **THE** *HAMPSHIRE REPUBLICAN.* **n.d. n.p.** Discusses recent resolutions passed by the General Association of Connecticut; claims the purpose of these resolutions is to check the present effort for reform and to put a stop to "revivals"; for example, listening to abolition lectures without the permission of a priest is forbidden. 3 September 1836. p.141, c2.

2350 n.n. *to* **THE** *NEW YORK EVANGELIST.* **n.d. n.p.** Points out that the General Association of Connecticut was a collection of sixteen self-appointed ministers and therefore has no relation to the Congregational church in Connecticut; discusses and criticizes their resolutions. 3 September 1836. p.141, c4.

2351 AN ABOLITIONIST *to* **W. L. GARRISON. 5 August 1836. New York.** Wonders why abolitionists cannot sacrifice their peculiar Christian customs, such as the observance of the Sabbath, to unite and fight slavery; if abolitionists divide over minor characteristics, they will not be able to fight slavery effectively. 3 September 1836. p.141, c5.

2352 n.n. *to* **MR. EDITOR [W. L. GARRISON]. n.d. n.p.** Announces the pupils of the Smith School who received prizes at the last annual exhibition. 3 September 1836. p.142, c1.

2353 C. *to* **MR. EDITOR [W. L. GARRISON]. n.d. n.p.** Replies to those who consider slavery a sin in the abstract, but wish not to stir up excitement about it; compares them to passers-by who watch a priest fall in mud, and who object to the mud, but will not help him get out. 3 September 1836. p.142, c1.

2354 GEORGE THOMPSON *to* **FRIEND GARRISON. 11 July 1836. London.** Sends a packet of papers and pamphlets concerning English actions and views on the subject of American slavery; sends encouragement. 3 September 1836. p.142, c2.

2355 JOHN SCOBLE *to* **THE** *PATRIOT.* **1 July 1836. London.** Discusses the resolution published by the Baptist Union in favor of Drs. Cox and Hoby, and opposing the conduct of George Thompson; declares that the union had no right to condemn Thompson. 3 September 1836. p.142, c2.

2356 MR. BROOKS *to* **n.n. [extract] n.d. n.p.** Claims that newspapers in Europe are scarce; the journals of Italy rejoice to report that the American Union is collapsing. 3 September 1836. p. 144, c3.

2357 CLERICUS *to* **THE EXECUTIVE COMMITTEE OF THE AMERICAN BOARD OF COMMISSIONERS FOR FOREIGN MISSIONS. 26 August 1836. n.p.** Declares that he used to give his surplus income to aid their foreign missions, but his scruples now forbid him to, as they favor slavery; declines to put his money where the Lord will not bless and make prosper. 10 September 1836. p.145, c1.

2358 JAMES G. BIRNEY *to* **BROTHER. [from the** *New York Evangelist***] 10 August 1836. Cincinnati.** Describes assault on the *Philanthropist* office while he was out of town; reports anti-slavery friends in Ohio roused to a virtuous indignation. 10 September 1836. p.148, c2.

2359 MARY ANN GAGE *to* **THE SOUTH READING FEMALE AS. 29 July 1836. Concord, Ross County, Oh.** Rejoices at news of their society; writes to encourage them, as the poor slave has few to plead for him; tells of her family's recent visit to a small colored community in Ohio. 17 September 1836. p.150, c1.

2360 A LADY IN CINCINNATI *to* **A RELATIVE IN THE VICINITY. [extract] 31 August 1836. Cincinnati.** Reports on her recent visit with the Birneys; Mr. Birney is planning to resume publication of the *Philanthropist*; the spirit of slavery is violent and outrageous in the region. 17 September 1836. p.150, c3.

2361 ELIZABETH B. CHACE AND SARAH G. BUFFUM *to* **W. L. GARRISON. 6 September 1836. Fall River.** Describe the formation of the Fall River Anti-Slavery Sewing Society; quote resolutions, preamble; list officers. 17 September 1836. p.150, c3.

2362 MR. KENNEDY, SECRETARY TO THE AUXILIARY SOCIETY OF PEOPLE *to* **THE SECRETARY OF THE BRITISH AND FOREIGN BIBLE SOCIETY. [extract] 26 February 1836. Barbadoes.** Gratefully acknowledges their letter and the interest taken by the parent society and friends of humanity in England. 17 September 1836. p.151, c1.

2363 J. CROSS *to* **BROTHER GOODELL. [from the** *Friend of Man***] 25 August 1836. Camden.** Sends an unsigned letter containing a threat from an anti-abolitionist. 17 September 1836. p.151, c3.

2364 n.n. *to* **SIR. n.d. n.p.** Threatens that his days will be numbered unless he ceases his abolition activity. 17 September 1836. p.151, c3.

2365 MANY SOUTHERNERS *to* **THE** *NEW YORK EVANGELIST.* **n.d. n.p.** Suggest that a benevolent individual offer a premium for the best essay on the slavery question, in order that the most correct answer can immediately be applied. 17 September 1836. p.151, c5.

2366 n.n. *to* **n.n. [extract] 23 March 1836. n.p.** Describes Thomas Jefferson's residence at Monticello, including the room in which he died; believes Monticello is "rapidly fulfilling its destiny as a naked, forgotten desolation." 17 September 1836. p.152, c3.

2367 n.n. *to* **THE** *EMANCIPATOR*. **n.d. n.p.** Asserts that Rev. R. J. Breckenridge has lost his temper and said foolish things because of George Thompson's provocations. 24 September 1836. p.155, c2.

2368 ROBERT PURVIS *to* **THE** *LIBERATOR*. **19 September 1836. Bucks County, Pa.** Announces death of Thomas Shipley; gives obituary and poem written in his memory. 24 September 1836. p.155, c5.

2369 JOHN SCOBLE *to* **REV. ELIZUR WRIGHT. [from the** *Emancipator***] 19 August 1836. London.** Discusses recent interesting and important public meeting at which he heard address by George Thompson on American slavery; discusses resolutions passed; commends Thompson's performance in his recent debate against Breckenridge. 1 October 1836. p.158, c3.

2370 n.n. *to* **n.n. [extract] 17 August 1836. Cincinnati.** Denounces the recent city riots, causing violence unsurpassed by any other mob; declares that to pursue a man with bloodhounds is not the way to change his views. 1 October 1836. p.158, c4.

2371 C. *to* **W. L. GARRISON. 19 September 1836. Philadelphia.** Describes funeral of Thomas Shipley and the reactions to his death; eulogizes Shipley and his benevolent work. 1 October 1836. p.159, c2.

2372 LA ROCHEFOUCAULT LIANCOURT, AL LABORDE AND ISAMBERT *to* **W. L. GARRISON. 23 July 1836. Paris.** Report they have elected Garrison a corresponding member of The French Society for the Abolition of Slavery; convey their high consideration. 1 October 1836. p.159, c3.

2373 JAMAICAN *to* **THE** *WATCHMAN*. **29 May 1836. New York.** Wishes to advise his countrymen of the treatment of colored people in "this boasting, tyrannical, and hypocritical land" which claims free institutions; declares America will certainly fall under God's displeasure for her sins. 1 October 1836. p.160, c3.

2374 A FRIEND OF TRUTH AND HUMANITY *to* **THE** *BUFFALO JOURNAL*. **29 August 1836. Buffalo.** Describes the Holland Purchase Baptist Association, its organization, proceedings, and its resolutions passed against slavery. 1 October 1836. p.160, c5.

2375 n.n. *to* **n.n. n.d. n.p.** Forwards resolutions from the committee in his church appointed to prepare a report on slavery. 8 October 1836. p.162, c4.

2376 ISAAC SAWYER, JR. *to* **THE** *LIBERATOR*. **26 September 1836. South Reading.** Contends that the Church of Christ has slumbered too long over the sin of slavery; condemns the "false zeal" of those who wish to convert Burma and Siam but ignore their own country; declares the churches can no longer be innocent in "supine indifference." 8 October 1836. p.162, c4.

2377 GILBERT PILLSBURY *to* **W. L. GARRISON. 21 September 1836. Derby, N.H.** Discusses speakers at the recent meeting of the New Hampshire Association; most chose careful, unexciting topics, except Mr. Root, who spoke on the inflammatory subject of anti-slavery; reports abolitionists were not allowed to speak at the convention, but lobbied outside. 8 October 1836. p.162, c5.

2378 J. P. W. *to* **THE** *HAMPSHIRE REPUBLICAN*. **n.d. n.p.** Quotes from Southern papers on the high prices of cotton, rice, Negroes, and other goods; declares that this combination makes the South the garden of America, and that Negro labor keeps everything going, from Maine to the Mississippi. 8 October 1836. p.164, c4.

2379 SAMUEL SLATER *to* **THE** *BOSTON COMMERCIAL GAZETTE*. **n.d. n.p.** Criticizes abolitionists for taking a slave child from him to "freedom"; charges that the abolitionists have broken up the family, and that they only want the child's services, not her freedom. 15 October 1836. p.165, c1.

2380 AN OLD MAN *to* **THE** *VERMONT STATE JOURNAL*. **n.d. n.p.** Urges all to fight the annexation of Texas, because this would force America's involvement in a war with Mexico, and because Texas is to be a slave state. 15 October 1836. p.165, c3.

2381 AN ORTHODOX MINISTER OF THE GOSPEL IN THE STATE OF PENN-SYLVANIA *to* **n.n. [extract] 8 August 1836. n.p.** Reports that he enjoyed the work on Dr. Beecher; comments on the "momentary triumph of the demon slavery at Cincinnati," and the destruction of Mr. Birney's press; reports that hearings are going on, and the citizens will not remain quiet for long. 15 October 1836. p.165, c4.

2382 LAURA LEE *to* **W. L. GARRISON. n.d. n.p.** Sends report of recent anti-abolition meetings; asks Garrison whether he realized the existence of the alliance between church, legislation, and anti-abolition. 15 October 1836. p.165, c5.

2383 ARNOLD BUFFUM *to* **W. L. GARRISON. 30 September 1836. Philadelphia.** Mourns the loss of Thomas Shipley and his untiring benevolent work; reports on recent speech by Lucretia Mott; argues that mere abstinence from evil does not guarantee acceptance into heaven, adding that one must actively fight evil. 15 October 1836. p.165, c5.

2384 JOSEPH BOWERS AND M. GRAY *to* **W. L. GARRISON. n.d. London or Chelmsford.** Report that Garrison's name and work are beloved in England; criticize Cox and Hoby for urging interest in the slavery problem while striving to avoid agitation; draw biblical analogies. 15 October 1836. p.166, c1.

2385 X. *to* **W. L. GARRISON. 5 September 1836. North Yarmouth, Me.** Discusses young man who spoke for immediate emancipation at his graduation from Waterville College three years ago; since then he has moved to Kentucky, renounced his principles, and become a slaveholder. 15 October 1836. p.166, c2.

2386 TRUTH TELLER *to* **MR. EDITOR [W. L. GARRISON]. 10 May 1836. Abington, Ma.** Criticizes Mr. Van Buren's letter; states that he had known that Van Buren was not an abolitionist, but had thought he would at least favor free discussion; discusses pecuniary influence on slaveholders. 15 October 1836. p.166, c3.

2387 ELLEN B. LADD *to* **W. L. GARRISON. 12 October 1836. East Bradford, Ma.** Reports formation of new female AS; answers the charge that women have little to do with this subject; looks to a future when love will fill every breast. 15 October 1836. p.167, c1.

2388 NATHANIEL SOUTHARD *to* **BROTHER KNAPP. 21 September 1836. Boston.** Forwards extracts describing his convictions and life in prison from letters written to his father; as a pacifist, he had refused training in the militia, refused to pay fine, and was therefore imprisoned. 15 October 1836. p.167, c1.

2389 NATHANIEL SOUTHARD *to* **n.n. [extract] 23 August 1836. Boston.** Describes conditions in prison. 15 October 1836. p.167, c2.

2390 ADELPHOS *to* **MR. PORTER. n.d. n.p.** Declares he is a long-standing anti-slavery man, and that "wisdom and discretion" counsel him to control his exhibitions of opinion; criticizes the individual whose "indiscriminate and sweeping denunciations of those who differ" are hurting the cause. 15 October 1836. p.167, c2.

2391 W. S. A. *to* **RICHARD FLETCHER, ESQ. n.d. n.p.** Asks Fletcher, who has been nominated by the Whig Party to Congress, about his opinions on the slave question; refers to his speech a year ago at Faneuil Hall, which criticized the conduct of abolitionists; realizes that he could have changed his mind or have been under false impression. 22 October 1836. p.170, c5.

2392 A. W. *to* **W. L. GARRISON. n.d. n.p.** Reacts to "Miss Grimke's Appeal"; declares that "no great improvement was ever made in the condition of the human race without assistance of the gentler race"; hopes "Miss Grimke's Appeal" will inspire many women in the country. 22 October 1836. p.170, c5.

2393 AN EYE WITNESS *to* **n.n.** [from the *Taunton Gazette*] **12 October 1836. Mansfield.** Describes disruption of speech at Mansfield where several gentlemen with drums and bugles prevented Mr. Burleigh from speaking and resisted ejection by constable; claims that the mob "has made more abolitionists than Mr. Burleigh could have done if he lectured." 22 October 1836. p.171, c3.

2394 A GENTLEMAN IN MANSFIELD *to* **MR. BURLEIGH.** [extract] **18 October 1836. n.p.** Reports that the disruption of his speech on Monday did the work of twelve lectures; all present believed that the laws must be supported, and that through perseverance he will yet lecture in peace in Mansfield. 22 October 1836. p.171, c4.

2395 SOUTHERN SUBSCRIBER *to* **THE** *BOSTON COURIER.* **18 September 1836. Buford's Bridge, S.C.** Supports most of the paper's positions, but believes its stand against abolitionists is not strong enough; while the editor asserts that abolition is "inexpedient," the author believes it to be unlawful, unrighteous, foul, and sinful as well. 29 October 1836. p.173, c1.

2396 MR. GOULD *to* **BROTHER PHELPS. n.d. n.p** Reports on meetings of French Creek Baptist Association, which comprises eighteen churches; summarizes his own speech, and quotes resolutions formally adopted. 29 October 1836. p.173, c3.

2397 H. C. W. *to* **THE** *NEW ENGLAND SPECTATOR.* **n.d. n.p.** Discusses resolution passed at recent meeting of the Newburyport AS; believes that Christians in the North must let Southerners know of their disapproval of the system of slavery. 29 October 1836. p.173, c4.

2398 B., A GENTLEMAN IN GEORGIA *to* **HIS BROTHER IN NEW ENGLAND. 11 July 1836. Lexington.** Claims he does not believe that slavery is a sin, quoting from the Bible as proof; admits that there are some cruel slaveholders, but charges that there are cruel men in the North also. 29 October 1836. p.174, c1.

2399 TRUTH SEEKER *to* **W. L. GARRISON. 18 October 1836. Boston.** Discusses the four candidates for the office of President: Van Buren, White, Harrison and Webster; believes that no consistent abolitionist would vote for any of them. 29 October 1836. p.174, c5.

2400 Z. *to* **SIR. n.d. n.p** Asks for whom a consistent abolitionist can vote, if not for Mr. Van Buren. 29 October 1836. p.174, c5.

2401 A. *to* **MR. EDITOR [W. L. GARRISON]. 18 October 1836. Newburyport.** Hopes that Mr. Garrison will continue his work, both for the sake of the slave as well as the country; charges that the guilt of slavery is not local or partial, but strictly national; we must confess as a nation that we are disgraced. 29 October 1836. p.174, c5.

2402 REV. H. C. WRIGHT *to* **W. L. GARRISON. 25 October 1836. Bristol, R.I.** Reports that he went to Bristol to lecture on immediate abolition; although placards protesting his speech were circulated, the citizens prevented any mobbing or disruption; they favored free discussion of the subject, whether they supported abolition or not. 29 October 1836. p.175, c1.

2403 GAUIS *to* **MR. THACHER. n.d. n.p.** Discusses a maxim from Mark, "he followeth not us," which he claims is the doctrine of expediency and justification of the doings of the general association. 29 October 1836. p.176, c2.

2404 WILLIAM JAY *to* **THE REV. OLIVER WETMORE. 26 September 1836. Bedford.** Submits his letter of resignation as president of the New York AS because he cannot discharge his duties when his residence is so far away; comments on the character of the struggle in which they are involved. 5 November 1836. p.178, c4.

2405 H. G. CHAPMAN *to* **W. L. GARRISON. 3 November 1836. Boston.** Acknowledges receipt of gift from Squire Shove of Danvers in aid of the anti-slavery cause. 5 November 1836. p.179, c5.

2406 TRUTH SEEKER *to* **W. L. GARRISON. 21 October 1836. Boston.** Replies to charge that he "writes more like a politician than an abolitionist"; affirms devotion to the cause of the oppressed slave; justifies his discussion of political candidates. 5 November 1836. p.179, c5.

2407 THEODORE S. WRIGHT *to* **REV. ARCHIBALD ALEXANDER, D.D. 11 October 1836. New York.** Declares that he is innocent of the alleged impudence of which a former college student accused him; describes the incident in which he was kicked and almost thrown out of a meeting. 5 November 1836. p.180, c2.

2408 n.n *to* **RECIPIENT IN NEW YORK. [extract] 19 October 1836. Rice Hope, North Santee.** Describes misery, human suffering, and great loss of property, expecially of Negroes who have a very high mortality rate. 5 November 1836. p.180, c5.

2409 THOMAS VAN RENSALAER *to* **HON. RICHARD RIKER. n.d. n.p.** Charges that he did a great injustice to the colored people of the city of New York; claims that Riker is mistaken in his conclusion that emancipation confers a curse rather than a blessing. 12 November 1836. p.181, c3.

2410 TRUTH TELLER *to* **W. L. GARRISON. 4 November 1836. Abington, Ma.** Charges that "Truth Seeker" unfairly accused "Truth Teller" of willfully departing from the truth; declares he cannot uphold the conduct of candidates White and Harrison; claims he did not single out the conduct of Van Buren for attack. 12 November 1836. p.182, c1.

2411 A COLORED METHODIST BROTHER IN A SLAVE HOLDING STATE *to* **THE EDITOR [W. L. GARRISON]. [extract] n.d. n.p.** Blushes at his denomination, which should be ashamed of itself; asserts that the eagerness of Methodists to conciliate public sentiment and their concentration on the political aspect of the anti-slavery cause is no justification for the timorous course they pursue. 12 November 1836. p.182, c3.

2412 J. V. HIMES *to* **BROTHER. n.d. n.p** Relates the proceedings of the annual session of the Massachusetts Christian Conference on Slavery; describes resolutions and discussions, most of which condemned the idea of palliating or apologizing for slavery. 12 November 1836. p.182, c3.

2413 NEUTRALITY *to* **THE** *NEW YORK COMMERCIAL ADVERTISER.* **14 September 1836. Nacogdoches, Tx.** A "first-rate Texan" recounts his arrival in Texas and questions the neutrality of American troops which cross the Sabine to fight Mexico, a friendly country. 12 November 1836. p.184, c2.

2414 JOHN W. YARBOROUGH *to* **MR. S. C. ATKINSON. 11 August 1836. Hamburg, S.C.** Declares that if his "breath smells of foul, darkened dissension," and if he has become "a degraded and inhuman abolitionist," then farewell to his Southern interest. 19 November 1836. p.185, c1.

2415 SAMUEL STILLMAN *to* **MOSES BROWN, ESQ. 14 February 1836. Boston.** Sends thanks for pamphlets; declares he has long lamented the "awful business of enslaving mankind" and will ever bear testimony against it. 19 November 1836. p.187, c4.

2416 C. L. KNAPP, ESQ. *to* **n.n. 31 October 1836. Montpelier, Vt.** Describes Brother Stanton's recent lectures; reports that resolutions on slavery in the District of Columbia have been introduced into each branch of legislature. 19 November 1836. p.187, c4.

2417 MR. CROCKER *to* **n.n. [extract] 21 June 1836. Edina.** Discusses conditions in the Liberia colony, where living conditions are crude, provisions very scarce, and inhabitants starving in places; finds great apathy among the natives regarding school and education. 19 November 1836. p.188, c2.

2418 REV. DR. CHANNING *to* **n.n. [extract] n.d. n.p.** Opposes popery, but admits that most Protestant sects are built on the papal foundation; affirms his "profound respect" for individuals in all communions of Christianity, although he looks on some sects with "grief, shame and pity." 19 November 1836. p.188, c3.

2419 n.n. *to* **W. L. GARRISON. n.d. n.p.** Sends extract from letter he received from gentleman in Maine who had been a secretary of a prominent AS there. 26 November 1836. p.189, c5.

2420 n.n. *to* **n.n. [extract] n.d. n.p.** The former secretary of an AS in Maine describes his dedication to the cause despite his advanced age and poor health. 26 November 1836. p.189, c5.

2421 R. J. BRECKINRIDGE *to* **THE REV. RALPH WARDLAW, D.D. OF GLASGOW. 20 August 1836. Paris.** Disagrees with Wardlaw's judgements on American slavery and American opinions on slavery; wonders if it was ignorance, national vanity, or both which caused the abolition party in Britain to misunderstand Americans. 26 November 1836. p.190, c1.

2422 C. STUART *to* **THE** *FRIEND OF MAN.* **24 October 1836. Whitesboro.** Comments on letter from Breckinridge to Wardlaw; as a personal friend to Wardlaw and Thompson, a British subject, and an uncompromising enemy to slavery, he attacks Breckinridge and his four propositions in detail. 26 November 1836. p.190, c3.

2423 JAMES G. BIRNEY *to* **THE** *EMANCIPATOR.* **[extract] n.d. n.p.** Every day he sees fresh evidence that the cause of emancipation is soon to be predominant; believes that the crisis of their cause is near. 26 November 1836. p.191, c3.

2424 ROBERT BERNARD HALL *to* **THE** *LONDON PATRIOT*. **25 July 1836. London.** Indignantly repels charges made and insinuated against him in a letter from R. J. Breckinridge; declares his love for America, but he pities her weaknesses and abhors her crimes; refutes many of Breckinridge's charges as completely false. 26 November 1836. p.192, c2.

2425 RICHARD MORAN *to* **AMOS DRESSER. [from the** *Friend of Man***] 5 September 1835. Near Lawrenceburg, In.** Thanks God for the fortitude with which Dresser bore the recent outrages against him; hopes that wicked acts will convert some Presbyterian elders to the cause of immediate emancipation; prays to do what is right, that God will sustain him. 5 December 1836. p.193, c2.

2426 REV. THOMAS WILLCOCKS *to* **THE REV. DRS. COX AND HOBY. 1836. London.** Reports that their conduct in America relative to the slavery question has led to disapprobation and censure by some brothers at home; outlines their trip to America; criticizes their speeches. 5 December 1836. p.194, c1.

2427 GEORGE S. BULL *to* **ARTHUR TAPPAN. [from the** *Emancipator***] 7 September 1836. Yorkshire, England.** Reports that recent public meeting in Bradford, England voted to protest American slavery and conveys its sympathy and encouragement to abolitionists. 5 December 1836. p.194, c4.

2428 AN ACCREDITED CORRESPONDENT OF THE *AMERICAN PRESBYTERIAN* *to* **BROTHER EDGAR. 13 August 1836. Alabama.** Discusses three great hindrances to the progress of the gospel in southern Alabama: the roving disposition of the people, the secular engagements of the clergy, and the almost universally neglected condition of the slaves. 5 December 1836. p.195, c1.

2429 MATTHEW FORSTER *to* **W. L. GARRISON. 21 September 1836. Newcastle-upon-Tyne.** Sends information on their AS; tells of their love of America, their hatred of slavery, and their satisfaction with the *Liberator*. 5 December 1836. p.195, c2.

2430 H. C. W. *to* **THE** *EMANCIPATOR*. **n.d. n.p.** Sends epitaphs from tombstones of men who were engaged in the slave trade; criticizes the eulogies given to men who were pirates and robbers of human freedom and dignity. 5 December 1836. p.196, c2.

2431 J. HORTON *to* **THE** *ZION'S HERALD*. **14 November 1836. Boston.** Criticizes the *Christian Advocate and Journal* for publishing Rev. Mr. Breckenridge's half of a debate without also including the address of Dr. Wardlaw; believes that American Christians should be aware of the feelings of their British brethren. 10 December 1836. p.197, c2.

2432 B. WILLIAMS *to* **BROTHER SUNDERLAND. [from the** *Zion's Watchman***] 11 November 1836. West Mendon, N.Y.** Fails to see why the editors of the *Christian Advocate and Journal* consider the letter of Breckinridge to Wardlaw "a valuable production"; rejoices that most members of the Genessee conference are abolitionists. 10 December 1836. p.197, c3.

2433 n.n. *to* **SAMUEL CROTHERS. n.d. Ross County, Oh.** Describes incidents of July 1835 in Yazoo County, Mississippi, when stranger named Hunter, accused of inciting a slave rebellion, was whipped and hanged. 10 December 1836. p.197, c3.

2434 A LADY NOW RESIDING IN A SLAVE STATE *to* **HER FRIEND IN THE EAST.** **[extract from the** *New York Evangelist***] n.d. n.p.** Comments on the great evils of slavery and heathenism in the state; declares she has become more of an abolitionist than ever. 10 December 1836. p.197, c5.

2435 ISAIAH HUNTLEY *to* **BROTHER MURRAY. [from the** *Brandon Telegraph*] **11 November 1836. Westford.** Reports the organization of an AS of 320 members. 10 December 1836. p.197, c5.

2436 THOMAS WILLCOCKS *to* **THE REV. DRS. COX AND HOBY. [continued from 5 December 1836] 1836. London.** Criticizes their behavior in relation to the slave question and their speeches which oppose abolition on grounds of political expediency. 10 December 1836. p.198, c1.

2437 THOS. WILLCOCKS *to* **THE BAPTIST CHURCHES OF ENGLAND. June 1836. Devonport.** Calls upon them to disavow the compact with the triennial convention that Drs. Cox and Hoby have entered into; charges it would compromise their principles as the friends of Negro emancipation. 10 December 1836. p.198, c3.

2438 n.n. *to* **GENTLEMEN. 12 November 1836. Ann Arbor.** Reports on the anti-slavery convention held at Ann Arbor to form the Michigan State AS; lists resolutions passed and officers elected. 10 December 1836. p.198, c5.

2439 S. L. POMROY AND GEORGE SHEPARD *to* **THE MEMBERS OF THE MAINE AS. n.d. n.p.** Regret they cannot be there, but send assurances of their interest and support; expect that the year will witness great progress in their righteous cause. 10 December 1836. p.199, c1.

2440 SAMUEL FESSENDEN AND DAVID THURSTON *to* **THE MAINE AS. 27 October 1836. n.p.** Report that the mayor replied to the committee which requested protection from the city government that he knew no way to give them efficient protection. 10 December 1836. p.199, c2.

2441 JOHN G. WHITTIER *to* **W. L. GARRISON. 2 December 1836. Haverhill.** Fears that their petition for the abolition of slavery in the District of Columbia will be tabled again; suggests how to ensure that their representatives understand the firm and widespread support for the petition. 10 December 1836. p.199, c3.

2442 N. SOUTHARD *to* **W. L. GARRISON. 8 December 1836. n.p.** Reports on his discussion with other passengers aboard a steamboat from New York to Boston on the subject of abolition and the use of slave products; also reports scuffle between captain and young colored waiter. 17 December 1836. p.201, c4.

2443 GILMAN JONES *to* **W. L. GARRISON. 29 November 1836. Ashburnham.** Forwards citizens' petition for abolition of slavery and slave trade in District of Columbia; urges other towns to make similar efforts; urges the freemen of Massachusetts to speak out. 17 December 1836. p.201, c5.

2444 EQUALITY *to* **THE** *LIBERATOR.* **n.d. n.p.** Discusses female influence and the duty of patriotic females, especially in the North, to fight slavery; declares that the only reason a large majority of females are not involved is that they are ignorant. 17 December 1836. p.202, c1.

2445 S. S. JOCELYN *to* **MESSRS. EDITORS [W. L. GARRISON]. 6 December 1836. New Haven.** Furnishes account of the riot which took place after Rev. Mr. Rand's speech; a mob followed Rand and Mr. and Mrs. Jocelyn to the Jocelyns' house and began to throw objects at the house and break windows. 17 December 1836. p.203, c4.

2446 A. S. *to* **n.n. [extract] 21 November 1836. Lyme.** Reports formation of a town AS, which has encountered little opposition other than a bit of drumming and sounding of horns during the meeting. 24 December 1836. p.205, c5.

2447 n.n. *to* **n.n. 19 December 1836. Boston.** Comments on the Temperance Society formed in Lyme, New Hampshire ten years earlier, and opposition to it. 24 December 1836. p.205, c5.

2448 ELIAS SHARPE *to* **W. L. GARRISON. 11 December 1836. Natchaug.** Reports the actions of the Rhode Island and Connecticut Christian Conference on the subject of slavery; discusses resolution recommending the abolition of slavery, which was approved by all members. 24 December 1836. p.206, c1.

2449 ROYAL REED *to* **W. L. GARRISON. 12 December 1836. Theological Institute, East Windsor.** Urges immediatism, not gradualism, and in order to practice what he preaches, he immediately settles his debt with the paper. 24 December 1836. p.206, c2.

2450 TRUTH *to* **MR. EDITOR [W. L. GARRISON]. 8 December 1836. Gettysburg, Pa.** Relates history of the anti-slavery movement in Gettysburg; during the previous fall an attempt to start an AS failed, but a very recent attempt succeeded in spite of opposition. 24 December 1836. p.206, c3.

2451 W. M. REYNOLDS *to* **n.n. 21 November 1836. Gettysburg, Pa.** Reports arrangements made for county AS; asserts his amazement at the changes which have taken place, and the decrease in anti-slavery opponents in the last two years; believes that Pennsylvania will be one of the most energetic laborers in the anti-slavery cause. 24 December 1836. p.206, c4.

2452 GERRIT SMITH *to* **W. L. GARRISON. 13 December 1836. New York.** Declares that although he has sometimes found fault with "the temper and taste of passages in the *Liberator*," he now recognizes its importance to the cause; encloses fifty dollars as a donation. 24 December 1836. p.206, c5.

2453 H. C. W. *to* **W. L. GARRISON. 15 December 1836. New York.** Describes the funeral of John R. McDowall, held at the tabernacle and attended by a multitude, many of whom were colored. 24 December 1836. p.207, c1.

2454 HENRY C. WRIGHT *to* **W. L. GARRISON. 15 December 1836. New York.** Announces his appointment by the AAS as children's AS agent; his heart is drawn to children and he looks forward to communicating and working with them. 24 December 1836. p.207, c2.

2455 AN AMERICAN NOW IN ENGLAND *to* **n.n. [extract] 8 October 1836. London.** Discusses work of Dr. Cox in England; believes he has lost his strength and influence among the Baptists. 24 December 1836. p.207, c5.

[1837]

2456 WILLIAM E. CHANNING *to* **JAMES G. BIRNEY. [from the** *Philanthropist***] 1 November 1836. Boston.** Asserts that abolitionists are not only champions of the colored race, but also sufferers for the liberty of thought, speech and press; discusses and refutes charges against abolitionists. 2 January 1837. p.1, c1.

2457 A FRIEND IN PHILADELPHIA *to* **n.n. [extract] n.d. n.p.** Describes speech given by C. C. Burleigh in a school room; reports that colonizationists present declined to meet the AS in a public discussion; discusses a document from Gov. McDuffie and from the governor of Pennsylvania. 2 January 1837. p.3, c1.

2458 MATTHEW FORSTER *to* **W. L. GARRISON. 3 November 1836. Newcastle-upon-Tyne.** Briefly summarizes Mr. Thompson's twelve or thirteen lectures in the area surrounding Newcastle-upon-Tyne, which inspired the creation of several new societies. 2 January 1837. p3, c2.

2459 B. LUNDY *to* **W. L. GARRISON. 25 December 1836. Philadelphia.** Mourns the death of Dr. Edwin P. Atlee, another signer of the declaration of sentiments at the anti-slavery convention in 1833. 2 January 1837. p.3, c5.

2460 O. SCOTT *to* **BROTHER BROWN. [from the** *Zion's Herald***] 16 December 1836. Lowell.** Describes his lecture at Harvard, which could barely be heard above constant interruptions; summarizes his main points. 2 January 1837. p.4, c4.

2461 GEN. EATON *to* **HIS WIFE. [extract from the** *Herald of Freedom***] 6 April 1799. Tunis.** Writes that Christian slaves in Tunis remind him of his sorrow for the situation of slavery in his native country. 7 January 1837. p.5, c5.

2462 H. C. W. *to* **W. L. GARRISON. 28 December 1836. New York.** Denounces hypocrisy of participants in a meeting held in the tabernacle on behalf of the tailoresses and seamstresses of New York; claims that they also support slavery. 7 January 1837. p.6, c1.

2463 W. H. BURLEIGH *to* **W. L. GARRISON. 10 December 1836. Plainfield, Ct.** Recounts his recent trip to the southern part of the state where he lectured on slavery, despite threats of violence. 7 January 1837. p.6, c2.

2464 N. SOUTHARD *to* **W. L. GARRISON. 27 December 1836. Holmes Hole.** Reports on his recent lectures, additional signatures gathered for the petition, and a false fire alarm which went off harmlessly during his speech. 7 January 1837. p.6, c2.

2465 ZEDEKIAH DOWNING *to* **MR.** *LIBERATOR.* **31 October 1836. Portland.** Reports on the great Whig "meetin" in town "agin the abolitionists"; explains purpose and proceedings of the meeting; describes Mr. Randolph Codman's speech urging suppression of abolition discussions. 7 January 1837. p.6, c3.

2466 F. *to* **W. L. GARRISON. n.d. n.p.** Quotes letter accusing the *Boston Recorder* of supporting abolition; discredits the charge, as it was made by a slaveholder. 7 January 1837. p.6, c5.

2467 D. P. M. *to* **THE** *BOSTON RECORDER.* **24 October 1836. n.p.** Notices an article in the *Recorder* which seems to favor abolition, a doctrine he considers irreligious; returns the paper and cancels subscription. 7 January 1837. p.6, c5.

2468 H. B. STANTON *to* **W. L. GARRISON. 2 January 1837. Boston.** Recounts his travels and lectures with Amos Dresser in Worcester County, Massachusetts the past three weeks; finds that men in the county need only to know the truth to embrace it. 7 January 1837. p.7, c2.

2469 H. B. S. *to* **W. L. GARRISON. n.d. n.p.** Announces next quarterly meeting of the Middlesex County AS, at which Amos Dresser and others will speak. 7 January 1837. p.7, c5.

2470 BIDFORD GINRESS *to* **LA ROY SUNDERLAND. 13 August 1836. Mount Meigs, Montgomery, Al.** Informs Sunderland of $50,000 offered for his capture; encloses notices of rewards offered by citizens' meeting for the apprehension of abolitionists. 14 January 1837. p.9, c1.

2471 SAMUEL TUKE *to* **THE YEARLY MEETING OF FRIENDS OF INDIANA. n.d. n.p.** A member of the London Yearly Meeting of Friends sympathizes with the oppressed slave; regrets that the abolition of slavery in Britain was delayed by the requirement of a term of apprenticeship; encourages them in their work, but suggests, on behalf of the London meeting, that they not join the AS, as this would divide their loyalties. 14 January 1837. p.9, c1.

2472 JOHN G. WHITTIER *to* **W. L. GARRISON. n.d. n.p.** Reports on recent meeting of Essex County AS; quotes resolutions passed, describes two and a half-hour speech by Rev. J. H. Towne; declares that the cause of emancipation moves onward. 14 January 1837. p.10, c1.

2473 H. C. WRIGHT *to* **W. L. GARRISON. 4 January 1837. New York.** Discusses the sentiments of children, who are opposed to slavery because they shrink instinctively from all horror; urges abolitionists to teach children the horrors of slavery so they will not grow up excusing it. 14 January 1837. p.10, c1.

2474 n.n. *to* **W. L. GARRISON. 5 January 1837. Philadelphia.** Criticizes inconsistencies in Channing's letter to Birney; looks to the dawn of immediate emancipation, although "the grand battle is yet to be fought." 14 January 1837. p.10, c3.

2475 CHARLES O. LIBBEY *to* **RESPECTED FRIEND. 29 December 1836. Gorham, Me.** Sends the first annual report of the Gorham AS; includes list of officers and a short account of the meeting. 14 January 1837. p.10, c3.

2476 J. E. FULLER *to* **W. L. GARRISON. 4 January 1837. No. 1, Pitts Street.** Encloses letter from George Thompson for publication. 14 January 1837. p.10, c5.

2477 GEORGE THOMPSON *to* **FRIEND. 11 November 1836. Manchester.** Thanks him for his letter; informs that he is attempting to rouse the Christians in England to a sense of duty in regard to slavery. 14 January 1837. p.10, c5.

2478 CHARLES E. WILSON *to* **ADAM SLEMMER, ESQ., JOSIAH W. EVANS, ESQ., AND OTHERS. 26 December 1836. Norristown.** Explains why he will not form an auxiliary CS: he used to support colonization because he felt it would end the African slave trade and Christianize Africa, but as he no longer believes that, he now supports immediate emancipation. 21 January 1837, p.13, c5.

2479 AMOS DRESSER *to* **STANTON. 14 January 1837. Mulberry Grove, Leicester.** Reports on his speeches in Northbridge and his conversations with Bro. Ebenezer Cadwell; adds that in Leicester he stayed with Patience Earle, the sister of Arnold Buffum, and that he also spoke and saw a new AS formed. 21 January 1837. p.15, c1.

2480 J. V. HINES *to* **W. L. GARRISON. 7 January 1837. Boston.** Corrects *Liberator* article; declares that the First Christian Society must be exonerated from all blame in his recent "dismission." 21 January 1837. p.15, c4.

2481 H. CLAY *to* **REV. R. R. GURLEY. 22 December 1836. Washington.** Sends note to secretary of the ACS, accepting the presidency. 21 January 1837. p.16, c4.

2482 D. C. JEWETT *to* **W. L. GARRISON. 5 December 1836. Londonderry, N.H.** Claims that the Lord has taught him, as a freedman, "to scorn the thought of being in bondage"; declares his heart is pained at the wrongs inflicted on helpless captives, and he will labor until every yoke is broken. 28 January 1837. p.17, c3.

2483 WILBUR FISK *to* **REV. TIMOTHY MERRITT. [extract from the** *Zion's Herald*] **n.d. n.p.** Replies to letter from Merritt which was favorable to abolitionists; points out that Merritt omitted an important abolitionist principle: the belief that it is a sin for any man to sustain the relation of master to slave. 28 January 1837. p.17, c4.

2484 ELLIS GRAY LORING *to* **MR. GREEN. [from the** *Morning Post*] **26 January 1837. n.p.** Corrects possibly erroneous interpretations of his statements in the *Morning Post;* opposes a resort to physical force in order to abolish slavery. 28 January 1837, p.19, c5.

2485 O. SCOTT *to* **W. L. GARRISON. 16 January 1837. Lowell.** Discusses speech of Amos Dresser, at which a good collection was taken and 518 names were added to a petition to Congress. 4 February 1837. p.24, c2.

2486 CHARLES DICKSON *to* **REV. ORANGE SCOTT. 7 January 1837. Natick.** Reports on constitution, resolutions, and officers of the newly formed Natick AS. 4 February 1837. p.24, c2.

2487 W. H. BURLEIGH *to* **n.n. [extract] n.d. n.p.** Reports having met a gentleman from Hartford County, Maryland, who stated there is considerable anti-slavery sentiment in his area. 4 February 1837. p.24, c4.

2488 J. G. WHITTIER *to* **W. L. GARRISON. 2 February 1837. Harrisburg.** Gives brief account of the proceedings of the Pennsylvania Anti-Slavery Convention held at Harrisburg; reports financial concerns of AAS; states he has never been present at a "more united and harmonious meeting." 11 February 1837. p.26, c5.

2489 A MEMBER OF THE NEW ENGLAND YEARLY MEETING *to* **W. L. GARRISON. n.d. n.p.** Agrees with Garrison that it is the right use of language, not the abuse of it, which annoys the opponents of abolitionists; tells of the different behavior of Friends in America and Friends in England respecting abolition. 18 February 1837. p.29, c2.

2490 W. T. B. *to* **MR. EDITOR [W. L. GARRISON]. n.d. n.p.** Regrets that even in Boston, the metropolis of New England, abolitionists of the purest motives are forced to meet in a stable; condemns attempts of Boston citizens to put down free discussion; asserts that the truth has gone forth nevertheless. 18 February 1837. p.29, c3.

2491 A UNIVERSALIST *to* **MR. EDITOR [W. L. GARRISON]. n.d. n.p.** Criticizes the *Trumpet*, the new Universalist newspaper, which contains no discussion of slavery despite having nearly 6,000 subscribers; urges the *Trumpet* to support free discussion and open its pages to sympathy for the slave. 18 February 1837. p.29, c4.

2492 S. B. *to* **W. L. GARRISON. January 1837. Dorchester.** Describes discussion with friend who criticized and objected to abolitionists; when he read from the Bible, his friend accused him of choosing only pro-abolition chapters. 18 February 1837. p.29, c4.

2493 Q. *to* **MR. EDITOR [W. L. GARRISON]. n.d. n.p.** Reports the departure of a young gentleman from a church when two well-dressed women, "a shade darker in their complexions than the majority of the congregation," sat next to him. 18 February 1837. p.29, c4.

2494 JOHN G. WHITTIER *to* **BROTHER LEAVITT. 30 January 1837. n.p.** Describes the arrival of crowds of anti-slavery convention delegates; tells of the success of anti-slavery agents in the state of Pennsylvania; reports on debates and resolutions of the convention. 18 February 1837. p.31, c1.

2495 JOHN G. WHITTIER *to* **BROTHER LEAVITT. 1 February 1837. Harrisburg.** Describes the arrival of crowds of anti-slavery convention delegates; tells of the success of anti-slavery agents in the state of Pennsylvania; describes proceedings of the convention. 18 February 1837. p.31, c1.

2496 TRUTH TELLER *to* **MR. EDITOR [W. L. GARRISON]. 27 December 1836. Abington, Ma.** Criticizes message from Gov. M'Duffie of South Carolina, which attacked the North for not penalizing abolitionists, and which suggested a Southern convention to dissolve the Union; adds that he speaks partly from fear of violence from the slaves. 18 February 1837. p.31, c3.

2497 MARY CLARK *to* **ANGELINA E. GRIMKE. November 1835. Concord, N.H.** Praises Grimke and Garrison on behalf of the Female AS in Concord, New Hampshire; hopes that these times of persecution will help strengthen their cause and the Church. 25 February 1837. p.33, c1.

2498 A. E. GRIMKE *to* **THE LADIES' AS OF CONCORD. 16 March 1836. n.p.** Thanks them for their letter and encourages their efforts; states that the Church must now fear the sins of the world; suggests formation of a female peace society. 25 February 1837. p.33, c2.

2499 H. C. WRIGHT *to* **W. L. GARRISON. 24 January 1837. New York.** Declares he has long believed that in order to regenerate and save the world, one must direct his efforts to children; quotes lecture on anti-slavery; hopes that every yoke imposed by man on his brother will soon be broken. 25 February 1837. p.35, c1.

2500 ALANSON ST. CLAIR *to* **W. L. GARRISON. 8 February 1837. West Boylston.** Describes the rise and progress of abolition in his town since the formation of an AS the previous year; notes that AS has faced great opposition until recently; reports that a lecture by Stanton captivated many former opponents. 25 February 1837. p.35, c2.

2501 RICHARD THAYER *to* **THE** *LIBERATOR.* **11 February 1837. Mansfield.** Reports formation of an AS of 133 members after meeting in the Methodist meetinghouse; lists officers elected. 25 February 1837. p.35, c2.

2502 MRS. D. L. GILL AND MRS. LEONARD BATTIS *to* **THE** *LIBERATOR.* **3 February 1837. Fitchburg, Ma.** Describe recent formation of Men's and Ladies' ASS; quote the ladies' preamble and resolutions; ask for advice or suggestions from sister societies. 25 February 1837. p.35, c3.

2503 n.n. *to* **W. L. GARRISON. 23 January 1837. East Bradford.** Criticizes speculators who take advantage of the poor for personal profit; refers to those who withhold grain until prices rise, warning that these men are breaking God's law; also encourages those working for the cause of the oppressed African. 25 February 1837. p.35, c3.

2504 JOHN QUINCY ADAMS *to* **THE** *PATRIOT.* **1 February 1837. Washington.** Sends letter to the petitioners for abolition of slavery in the District of Columbia. 25 February 1837. p.36, c2.

2505 JOHN QUINCY ADAMS *to* **THE PETITIONERS FOR THE ABOLITION OF SLAVERY IN THE DISTRICT OF COLUMBIA. 31 January 1837. Washington.** Lists the towns and states from which he has received petitions; finds male petitioners from his district have been comparatively few; cites instances of dictatorial behavior by speaker in preventing discussion of slavery. 25 February 1837. p.36, c2.

2506 n.n. *to* **n.n. [extract] 1 February 1837. New Orleans.** Expresses his surprise that the Northern press has come out in favor of Texas, as the great aim of the South is to have Texas admitted into Union; predicts that if Texas' independence is recognized, New Orleans will become the great slave market of the South. 4 March 1837. p.47 [38], c5.

2507 SAMUEL J. MAY *to* **W. L. GARRISON. 21 February 1837. South Scituate.** Expresses dissatisfaction with the report of his speeches at the Massachusetts AS; provides his own account of the essential parts of his speech. 4 March 1837. p.47 [38], c4.

2508 W. H. BURLEIGH *to* **W. L. GARRISON. 7 February 1837. Plainfield, Ct.** States that he is often discouraged by the apathy that he finds toward human rights, exemplified by the Connecticut black law and clerical gag-laws, which demonstrate the state's sympathy toward slaveholders. 4 March 1837. p.47 [38], c5.

2509 O. C. FELTON *to* **W. L. GARRISON. 23 January 1837. South Brookfield, Ma.** Reports formation of South Brookfield AS; lists officers, quotes resolutions; reports fifty-two members thus far, and very little opposition. 4 March 1837. p.39, c1.

2510 A FRIEND WHO KNEW HENRY BENSON WELL *to* **n.n. [extract] n.d. n.p.** Rejoices for the late Henry Benson, who is now in heaven with his Father, working harder and more successfully for the cause. 4 March 1837. p.39, c3.

2511 ALGERNON SIDNEY *to* **REV. WILLIAM E. CHANNING, D.D. [from the** *Boston Courier***] 16 January 1837. Boston.** Replies to Channing's letter to Mr. Birney on abolition, which he feels is erroneous and injurious to the cause; criticizes Channing's claim of "moral necessity" in writing, and refutes his charge that abolitionist literature is incendiary and fierce. 4 March 1837. p.40, c2.

2512 W. L. GARRISON *to* **THE** *BOSTON COURIER.* **n.d. 5 Hayward Place.** Criticizes *Courier* correspondent who borrows the name of Algernon Sidney; applauds the lynch law, and complains about abolitionists. 4 March 1837. p.40, c3.

2513 ALGERNON SIDNEY *to* **THE REV. W. E. CHANNING, D.D. [from the** *Boston Courier***] 20 January 1837. Boston.** Discusses Channing's communication to Mr. Birney; argues that abolitionists are cowards, noting that they hid from their assailants, but believes that there is some courage among the women. 11 March 1837. p.41, c2.

2514 W. L. GARRISON *to* **THE** *COURIER.* **n.d. 5 Hayward Place.** Ridicules Algernon Sidney; asserts that he does not intend to vindicate Dr. Channing, but only to correct false accusations; shows that Gov. M'Duffie and slaveholders are the real incendiaries, not abolitionists. 11 March 1837. p.41, c4.

2515 EVENING SPECTATOR *to* **THE** *DETROIT EVENING SPECTATOR.* **n.d. n.p.** Reports that a speech by Mrs. Cole, concerning the sanctioning of slavery by the Bible, was interrupted by a man who carried a knife and others who threw objects through the church windows. 11 March 1837. p.43, c1.

2516 CRISPIN *to* **MR. EDITOR [W. L. GARRISON]. February 1837. Sandwich.** Criticizes correspondent Algernon Sidney's letters to Dr. Channing; charges that Sidney's idea of moral courage means total ignorance of personal safety; refutes charge that abolitionists have no moral courage. 11 March 1837. p.43, c2.

2517 A FRIEND *to* **SAMUEL J. MAY. [extract] n.d. n.p.** Discloses that the writer who signed himself "Algernon Sidney" in the *Boston Courier* was Walter Colton; summarizes Colton's life and education. 11 March 1837. p.43, c3.

2518 THE REPORTER *to* **W. L. GARRISON. 4 March 1837. Boston.** Noted in a recent *Liberator* that the Rev. Samuel May was aggrieved by the report of his recent speeches; declares he did not use shorthand, nor attempt to repeat speeches verbatim; disavows any feelings of hostility to May or other speakers. 11 March 1837. p.43, c3.

2519 ALGERNON SIDNEY *to* **REV. W. E. CHANNING, D.D. [from the** *Boston Courier***] 27 January 1837. Boston.** Accuses him of praising disingenuousness at the cost of honesty; charges that abolitionists have intentionally produced false impressions; asserts that abolitionists are without moral honesty. 18 March 1837. p.45, c1.

2520 W. L. GARRISON *to* **THE** *COURIER.* **n.d. 5 Hayward Place.** Provides further evidence that Southern slaveholders and their Northern abettors are instigating violence among the slaves by whipping, starving, plundering, and brutalizing them; admonishes abolitionists to hold to the doctrine of "non-resistance." 18 March 1837. p.45, c3.

2521 VERBUM SAT. *to* **THE** *PLYMOUTH COUNTY REPUBLICAN.* **n.d. n.p.** Agrees with editor's comment on the conduct of John Quincy Adams; believes Adams has acted for the rights of all; hopes and encourages all to express to Adams their approbation of his conduct. 18 March 1837. p.45, c6.

2522 L. MARIA CHILD *to* **W. L. GARRISON. n.d. n.p.** Inquires whether he has read *Archy Moore,* as it is a wonderful book; believes that the book shows intimate knowledge of all the peculiarities of the South; compares Archy Moore to Charles Ball. 18 March 1837. p.47, c2.

2523 H. C. WRIGHT *to* **W. L. GARRISON. 1 March 1837. New York.** Reports on activities in New York: outrages committed by kidnappers, revivals in many of the churches, and meetings of colored people to petition for suffrage and the abolition of slavery in New York. 18 March 1837. p.47, c2.

2524 GEORGE THOMPSON *to* **W. L. GARRISON. [extract] 21 January 1837. Edinburgh.** Relates personal news; takes courage from his past year's work in England; encourages efforts in America, and invites Garrison to visit. 18 March 1837. p.47, c3.

2525 CANDOR *to* **W. L. GARRISON. n.d. n.p.** Declares that Mr. Graham's lecture was "a rich intellectual treat" on the peculiar situation of colored people. 18 March 1837. p.47, c6.

2526 ADAMS *to* **MR. EDITOR [W. L. GARRISON]. n.d. n.p.** Foresees little chance that slavery will be abolished in the District of Columbia under present circumstances, as the President has said he would never sign such a bill; regrets that the President's first message declared his hatred for anti-slavery. 24 March 1837. p.50, c1.

2527 EDMUND CAPRON *to* **THE** *OLIVE BRANCH.* **15 March 1837. Millville.** Compliments editor on his fine work and on his paper's stress on religious freedom, but disagrees with his praise of Van Buren's support of human rights and free speech; finds that Van Buren, an anti-abolitionist, fails to uphold these rights. 24 March 1837. p.50, c1.

2528 J. E. HOOD, B. F. S. GRIFFIN AND J. W. WIGGIN *to* **W. L. GARRISON. 20 March 1837. Hampton Falls, N.H.** Report discussion of slavery at the Lyceum, and formation of an AS; quote constitution and resolutions of society. 24 March 1837. p.50, c2.

2529 THOMAS HASKELL *to* **W. L. GARRISON. 26 February 1837. Gloucester.** Agrees with suggestion to begin a Universalist paper; suggests also that some portion of it be devoted to the cause of peace; considers himself a Universalist. 24 March 1837. p.50, c2.

2530 THE AUTHOR *to* **W. L. GARRISON. n.d. n.p.** Explains his opinion of the "Negro Pew" controversy; argues that colored people are entitled to absolutely equal privileges in society. 24 March 1837. p.50, c3.

2531 ALGERNON SIDNEY *to* **REV. W. E. CHANNING, D.D. 1 February 1837. Boston.** Accuses him of errors, weaknesses and inconsistencies in attempting to defend a bad cause; wonders if the multitude may not control the right of speech. 24 March 1837. p.50, c6.

2532 W. L. GARRISON *to* **THE** *COURIER.* **n.d. 5 Hayward Place.** Replies to the letters of Algernon Sidney; defends abolitionists against Sidney's charge of unchristian censures and abusive language. 24 March 1837. p.51, c1.

2533 A DEMOCRAT *to* **MR. HUNTRESS. [from the** *Lowell Courier***] n.d. n.p.** Believes Mr. Van Buren's position on the slave question "is a disgrace to patriotism, philanthropy and Christianity"; predicts that Van Buren will only last one term. 24 March 1837. p.52, c3.

2534 OLIVER JOHNSON *to* **n.n. [extract] n.d. Harrisburg, Pa.** Reports on Rev. Mr. Nourse, formerly an agent of the CS, who claimed he was instructed by the society to depict its aims in the South as beneficial to the security and value of slave property. 24 March 1837. p.52, c3.

2535 CLERICUS *to* **MR. EDITOR [W. L. GARRISON]. n.d. n.p.** Discusses use of the Greek word *"douloi,"* which Southerners translate as "slave" in the biblical use; argues that this word is more frequently used to mean "servant." 31 March 1837. p.53, c3.

2536 CHARLES FITCH *to* **W. L. GARRISON. 22 March 1837. Boston.** Reports he was invited to lecture to the people of Stoneham on the subject of slavery, where his speech was well-received; during his second visit a mob interrupted his speech, but this only served to convert many to the abolition cause. 31 March 1837. p.53, c4.

2537 AMBROSE KINGMAN *to* **MR. EDITOR [W. L. GARRISON]. n.d. n.p.** Sends preamble and resolutions passed by the Orthodox Church in Reading, South Parish. 31 March 1837. p.53, c5.

2538 TRUTH TELLER *to* **MR. EDITOR [W. L. GARRISON]. n.d. n.p.** Criticizes Henry F. Harrington's political and economical excuses for slavery, and his reasoning that slavery is a sin "entailed upon the Southern people without any act or consent of theirs." 31 March 1837. p.53, c5.

2539 ALGERNON SIDNEY *to* **REV. W. E. CHANNING, D.D. [from the** *Boston Courier***] 6 February 1837. Boston.** Composes a hypothetical discussion between Rev. Mr. May and a Southern slave about the justifiable killing of a master by slave; accuses May of inciting slaves to murder masters. 31 March 1837. p.53, c6.

2540 GEN. SANTA ANNA *to* **THE MINISTER OF WAR AND MARINE. 20 February 1837. Vera Cruz.** Having obtained his liberty, he is on his way to his plantation and family at Manga du Clavo; rejoices at returning to native soil. 31 March 1837. p.54, c1.

2541 JUAN N. ALMONTE *to* **GEN. DON JOSE MARIA TORNEL. 20 February 1837. Vera Cruz.** Reports that he has escaped "the claws of the banditti of Texas." 31 March 1837. p.54, c2.

2542 AMERICAN GENTLEMAN *to* **n.n. [extract] 29 December 1836. St. Johns.** Reports that people in Antigua prefer emancipation to apprenticeship; wishes all Americans could visit and witness this. 31 March 1837. p.54, c4.

2543 GEO. THOMPSON *to* **W. L. GARRISON. 13 February 1837. Edinburgh.** Sends sympathy to Garrison and wife for the loss of their father, Mr. George Benson, and brother, Henry E. Benson; tells of Thompson's associations with the Bensons. 31 March 1837. p.54, c6.

2544 CAUTION *to* **THE COLORED CITIZENS OF PHILADELPHIA, NEW YORK AND BOSTON. n.d. n.p.** Warns them to beware of the religious anniversaries, as they may be attended by many Southerners who may have other objects in mind, namely, kidnapping. 31 March 1837. p.54, c6.

2545 WILLIAM WHITING *to* **W. L. GARRISON. 22 March 1837. East Abington.** A preacher of the Universalist order feels it his duty to express his approbation of the suggestion to start a new Universalist paper; adds he is astonished by apathy toward the subject of slavery. 31 March 1837. p.55, c1.

2546 J. COFFIN *to* **MR. EDITOR [W. L. GARRISON]. n.d. n.p.** Discusses discourse of Rev. Jonathan Edwards in 1791, denouncing the injustice of the slave trade and urging its abolition. 31 March 1837. p.55, c2.

2547 n.n. *to* **MR. EDITOR [W. L. GARRISON]. 27 March 1837. Lynn.** Describes incident between abolitionist shoe dealer and a Southerner who refused to patronize him because of his beliefs; the shoe seller refused to be gagged or deprived of his free speech for the sake of selling shoes. 31 March 1837. p.55, c2.

2548 n.n. *to* **n.n. [extract] 16 February 1837. Utica, N.Y.** Reports that he has just heard Gerrit Smith speak for the first time; believes Smith "one of the most eloquent men in the United States," and wishes he could have a seat in the Senate. 31 March 1837. p.55, c2.

2549 HENRY T. CORNETT *to* **W. L. GARRISON. 23 March 1837. Providence.** Forwards resolution recently passed by the Providence AS, declaring that anyone who helped recapture an escaped slave violates the laws of God and man. 31 March 1837. p.55, c2.

2550 AN ACCOMPLISHED LADY IN WORCESTER COUNTY *to* **n.n. [extract] n.d. n.p.** Hopes that when another edition of *The Slave* is published, the title will be changed to *Archy Moore.* 31 March 1837. p.55, c2.

2551 AN ABOLITIONIST *to* **W. L. GARRISON. 23 March 1837. North Andover.** Approves the decision of Universalists to discuss the propriety of starting a new abolitionist paper. 31 March 1837. p.55, c3.

2552 n.n. *to* **n.n. [extract] 10 February 1837. Fall River.** Asserts that people are awakening from the death-like sleep of colonization; believes New England will soon come forth in her strength and support anti-slavery. 31 March 1837. p.55, c3.

2553 JOSIAH GIFFORD *to* **HENRY G. CHAPMAN, ESQ. 10 February 1837. Sandwich.** Sends five dollars for the Massachusetts AS; hopes the disciples of God soon awaken to the cause of the slaves. 31 March 1837. p.55, c3.

2554 A GENTLEMAN IN MATTHEWS COUNTY, VIRGINIA *to* **THE *NORFOLK HERALD.* 7 March 1837. East River.** Describes imprisonment of three Negroes who deserted from a vessel. 31 March 1837. p.55, c5.

2555 E. WRIGHT, JR. *to* **ASS. 3 March 1837. New York.** Requests information for the secretary of domestic correspondence of the AAS. 31 March 1837. p.55, c6.

2556 HAMPDEN *to* **THE *HERALD OF FREEDOM.* n.d. n.p.** Urges all to read *Archy Moore,* which has exposed the secret of the Southern prison house; believes the reading of *Archy Moore* "will transform the age." 31 March 1837. p.56, c3.

2557 D. A. *to* **W. L. GARRISON. n.d. n.p.** Quotes conversation between Mr. Dresser and a young lad on Dresser's proposed speech for the Stoneham AS; discusses argument won by Dresser against anti-abolitionists. 7 April 1837. p.58, c2.

2558 OLIVER JOHNSON *to* **W. L. GARRISON. n.d. n.p.** Describes false fire alarm in Marblehead which sounded during his speech; after the commotion ended, most of the audience resumed their seats. 7 April 1837. p.58, c3.

2559 H. C. WRIGHT *to* **W. L. GARRISON. 28 March 1837. Lynn.** Briefly reports on Massachusetts AS meeting, on his conversation with a former slaveholder who declared slaves were brutes, and on his speech to the children of Lynn. 7 April 1837. p.58, c3.

2560 H. C. WRIGHT *to* **W. L. GARRISON. 25 March 1837. Boston.** Reports on his meeting with Boston Juvenile AS; declares that children everywhere are his most attentive and sympathetic listeners. 7 April 1837. p.58, c4.

2561 STEPHENS BAKER, P.M. *to* **W. L. GARRISON. 1 April 1837. Post Office, Beverly, Essex County, Ma.** Discusses charges against his office: in the case of Dr. Kittredge, the sender sealed mail and was charged letter postage; had it not been sealed he would have paid the cheaper pamphlet postage. 7 April 1837. p.58, c4.

2562 H. C. WRIGHT *to* **W. L. GARRISON. n.d. n.p.** Quotes extracts from the journal of Mr. Perkins, a missionary to Persia, from the February issue of the *Missionary Herald*; accuses Perkins of hypocrisy in calling the United States a land of "wholesome laws" with "humane administration." 7 April 1837. p.58, c5.

2563 ADAMS *to* **MR. EDITOR [W. L. GARRISON]. n.d. n.p.** Asserts that he is very pleased with the legislature's recent resolves relative to slavery, which upheld principles over the time-serving policy of the day; regrets that certain editors are impugning the motives of those who voted for the resolves. 7 April 1837. p.59, c2.

2564 GEORGE W. KILTON *to* **W. L. GARRISON. 28 March 1837. Brooklyn, Ct.** Sends resolutions passed at the last quarterly session of the Connecticut Christian Conference. 7 April 1837. p.59, c6.

2565 LONDON CORRESPONDENT *to* **n.n. [extract] 27 February. n.p.** Discloses that the British cabinet is secretly negotiating for possession of Cuba. 7 April 1837. p.60, c4.

2566 J. H. KIMBALL, ESQ. *to* **n.n. n.d. New Hampshire.** Reports on the Wesleyan conference, composed of twenty-four missionaries from ten islands; notes their unanimous resolutions. 7 April 1837. p.60, c4.

2567 JOHN QUINCY ADAMS *to* **THE** *PATRIOT.* **18 March 1837. Washington.** Explains his stand on abolition petitions; desires to protect the right of petition from being suppressed, rather than to support the specific objectives of the petitions themselves. 14 April 1837. p.61, c1.

2568 n.n. *to* **MR. EDITOR [W. L. GARRISON]. n.d. n.p.** Discusses the objection that abolitionists work in the North when they are really needed in the South; claims that the pro-slavery sentiment in the North must be eradicated before the South can be changed; notes that slaves are still found in the North, even in Pennsylvania. 14 April 1837. p.62, c1.

2569 P. H. SWEETSER *to* **W. L. GARRISON. n.d. n.p.** Describes the recent meeting of the Universalists of Boston and vicinity, who voted unanimously to form an association to start a paper. 14 April 1837. p.62, c2.

2570 J. G. W. *to* **W. L. GARRISON. n.d. n.p.** Reports that he has just read a speech of Hon. Francis James of the Pennsylvania Senate, supporting a bill granting a jury trial for alleged runaway slaves; adds that the speech was eloquent and well-reasoned, but the bill was defeated because of party feeling. 14 April 1837. p.62, c3.

2571 A. E. GRIMKE *to* **L. L. DODGE. 14 July 1836. Shrewsbury, N.J.** Expresses appreciation of esteem of the Essex County Olive Branch Society; adds that she supports it because she has great faith in its importance, and is interested that it is made up of women; praises the moral consciences and goodness of women. 14 April 1837. p.62, c3.

2572 L. MARIA CHILD *to* **THE LADIES OF THE OLIVE BRANCH CIRCLE. 22 June 1836. Boston.** Supports the cause of peace and the propriety of women's influence; encourages them to continue their work. 14 April 1837. p.62, c4.

2573 ADAMS *to* **MR. EDITOR [W. L. GARRISON]. n.d. n.p.** States that actions of the legislature have shown that his confidence in their patriotism and firmness was somewhat misplaced, as the House voted to "non-concur" in the Senate amendments; relates this to guide abolitionist voting. 14 April 1837. p.62, c4.

2574 JOHN E. FULLER *to* **MR. EDITOR [W. L. GARRISON]. n.d. n.p.** Sends note from John Henderson as evidence of Scotland's high regard for George Thompson, as well as its abhorrence of slavery. 14 April 1837. p.62, c4.

2575 JOHN HENDERSON *to* **JOHN E. FULLER. 16 February 1837. Paisley.** Sends copies of speeches delivered in honor of George Thompson, representing all classes of the community throughout Scotland. 14 April 1837. p.62, c4.

2576 JOHN PHILIP *to* **SIR. 22 February 1837. 9 Wells Street, Hackney.** Regrets, for his and Professor Stowe's sakes, that Stowe so misapprehended Philip's sentiments; states that "impudence" should have read "imprudence." 14 April 1837. p.63, c2.

2577 GEORGE THOMPSON *to* **REV. AMOS D. PHELPS AND REV. DR. PHILIP. 25 February 1837. Edinburgh.** Sends quote from *Boston Recorder* which suggests that Philip opposes the policy and propriety of sending men such as Thompson to the United States, and wishes to know if Philip actually said this; believes Philip is dodging the issue in claiming misapprehension. 14 April 1837. p.63, c2.

2578 MR. CHILD *to* **n.n. [extract] n.d. n.p.** Reports that when dining near London recently, a gentleman well acquainted with the West Indies informed him that four years of an apprentice's time was actually valued at more than his entire body and soul before emancipation; elaborates details. 14 April 1837. p.63, c5.

2579 A MEMBER OF THE SOCIETY OF FRIENDS *to* **THE POPE. n.d. n.p.** Asserts that the Pope and his Cardinals are very unlike the Apostles and disciples of Christ; accuses them of vanities and hypocrisies; declares that unless they make a thorough reformation, they shall never enter Heaven. 14 April 1837. p.64, c3.

2580 n.n. *to* **ORSON MURRAY. 17 January 1837. Cambridge.** Angry that the paper has changed from a religious to an anti-slavery paper; supports anti-slavery, but expects to receive a religious paper when he orders one. 14 April 1837. p.64, c4.

2581 JOHN QUINCY ADAMS *to* **THE *QUINCY PATRIOT*. 14 January 1837. n.p.** Sends to editors of district papers copies of public documents which they might find interesting; states that when he first presented petitions for abolition in the District of Columbia, he did not support them, but now he believes they must be discussed to preserve the right of petition. 21 April 1837. p.66, c2.

2582 L. MARIA CHILD *to* **W. L. GARRISON. n.d. n.p.** Reports that her husband is in Europe learning the process of manufacturing beet sugar; sends extracts from his last letter. 21 April 1837. p.66, c4.

2583 D. L. CHILD *to* **n.n. n.d. n.p.** Describes visit to France, the countryside, the people, and their mode of doing business; stresses the crucial part women play in the economy and the society. 21 April 1837. p.66, c4.

2584 C. C. BURLEIGH *to* **W. L. GARRISON. 10 April 1837. Blockley, Philadelphia County, Pa.** Reports that the cause is advancing but that the Pennsylvania legislature is not nearly as enlightened as New England's; looks forward to conventions. 21 April 1837. p.66, c5.

2585 H. C. WRIGHT *to* **W. L. GARRISON. n.d. n.p.** Deplores arrest and trial of Wm. Dixon, who was alleged to be a runaway slave; the judge refused to declare him free despite statements by witnesses that Dixon had worked in New York since 1830. 21 April 1837. p.66, c5.

2586 H. C. WRIGHT *to* **W. L. GARRISON. 13 April 1837. Patterson.** Continues to discuss trial of Wm. Dixon, who is accused of being a runaway slave; declares the system is built on the unjust assumption that every colored person is a slave unless proved a freedman, placing burden of proof on the accused colored citizen. 21 April 1837. p.67, c1.

2587 E. G. *to* **SISTER. 3 April 1837. Fitchburg.** Acknowledges letter telling of death of Miss A. G. Chapman; praises Miss Chapman and her devotion to the anti-slavery cause; sends her sympathies. 21 April 1837. p.67, c4.

2588 n.n. *to* **n.n. [extract] n.d. Vermont.** Reports that the cause of the slave is advancing; notes that several large societies have been formed; adds that mobs are out of fashion; wonders why papers are suppressing news from the West Indies. 21 April 1837. p.67, c5.

2589 ADAM HUNTSMAN *to* **WILLIAM GOODELL. [from the** *Friend of Man***] 6 January 1837. Washington.** Charges Goodell with mail fraud for sending him the paper contrary to his wishes; explains laws of Tennessee, stating that sending his paper there would inflict "infamous punishment" upon the receiver. 28 April 1837. p.69, c1.

2590 D. I. ROBINSON *to* **BROTHER. [from the** *Herald of Freedom***] 4 April 1837. Plymouth.** Reports he has just had a long talk with a member of Congress who believes abolition petitions will be rejected; believes that new territories are excellent areas for abolition work, and hopes Texas can be persuaded not to be a slave state. 28 April 1837. p.69, c5.

2591 F. A. COX *to* **BROTHER GOING. 28 January 1837. Hackney.** Protests the "malignity of mind" displayed against him, both in article in the *Emancipator* and in letter from Garrison; contradicts the reports that he is out of favor. 28 April 1837. p.69, c6.

2592 HAMPDEN *to* **MR. EDITOR. [from the** *Herald of Freedom***] n.d. n.p.** Reports that it will take a long time to awaken New Hampshire to the evils of slavery; urges the "Lane Seminary boys" to go there and teach them the truth; calls for Weld and Stanton, who would quickly educate and convert the state. 28 April 1837. p.70, c3.

2593 AN ABOLITION UNIVERSALIST *to* **W. L. GARRISON. n.d. n.p.** Disapproves the idea of establishing a Universalist-abolition paper; believes there are already several very good papers, and that funds should be used to support existing papers, especially the *Liberator*. 28 April 1837. p.71, c1.

2594 NATHANIEL SWASEY *to* **W. L. GARRISON. 6 April 1837. Bath.** Rejoices at the idea of a Universalist anti-slavery paper; has been hoping for one for some time; hopes this idea is more than talk. 28 April 1837. p.71, c1.

2595 H. C. WRIGHT *to* **W. L. GARRISON. n.d. n.p.** Quotes the constitution of Virginia and the Declaration of Independence, whose principles are discredited by the case of Wm. Dixon, a New York man accused of being a runaway slave. 28 April 1837. p.71, c3.

2596 H. B. STANTON *to* **W. L. GARRISON. 24 April 1837. Boston.** Describes his recent anti-slavery labors, including lectures at Danvers, Salem, Lynn, Boston, East Bradford, and Andover; summarizes topics; relates outcomes of meetings he attended. 28 April 1837. p.71, c3.

2597 H. C. WRIGHT *to* **W. L. GARRISON. n.d. n.p.** Reports that Rev. Flavel S. Mines, pastor of the Leight Street Church in New York City, forced the resignation of the superintendent of the Sunday school and the disbanding of the school because the superintendent introduced principles of anti-slavery and total abstinence. 5 May 1837. p.75, c3.

2598 J. E. F. *to* **W. L. GARRISON. n.d. 1 Pitts Street.** Describes anti-abolition gentlemen who go to England and find themselves surrounded by abolitionists; believes that in order to combat their discomfort, they deal in "slanderous misrepresentation." 5 May 1837. p.75, c3.

2599 n.n. *to* **THE** *PENNSYLVANIA SENTINEL.* **[extract] 2 May 1837. Harrisburg.** Reports on the convention of the "Friends of the Integrity of the Union"; sends copy of the preamble and resolutions passed. 12 May 1837. p.77, c4.

2600 CHARLES THOMPSON *to* **THE** *EMANCIPATOR.* **21 February 1837. Manse of the Scotch Church. North Shields.** Transmits extract from the committee of North Shields and Tynemouth AS; blesses his labors and work in the anti-slavery cause. 12 May 1837. p.77, c5.

2601 MINISTERS AND DEACONS IN ENGLISH CHURCHES *to* **CONGREGA-TIONAL BAPTISTS IN AMERICA. n.d. n.p.** Comment on the unchristian principles of slavery and the sin and evil of a slave system; urge Americans to do all in their power to end slavery. 12 May 1837. p.77, c6.

2602 P. H. SWEETSER *to* **W. L. GARRISON. n.d. n.p.** Criticizes and mocks "An Abolitionist Universalist"; refutes his arguments against a Baptist Universalist paper, which he believes must be established and sustained. 12 May 1837. p.79, c2.

2603 C. CUSHING *to* **W. L. GARRISON. 4 April 1837. Chesterfield, N.H.** Believes the *Liberator* supports a noble cause; subscribes because he seeks information on slavery. 12 May 1837. p.79, c2.

2604 H. C. WRIGHT *to* **W. L. GARRISON. 10 May 1837. New York.** Reports on fourth anniversary of the AAS; quotes resolutions adopted; summarizes discussions; describes Ladies' Convention meeting. 12 May 1837. p.79, c4.

2605 J. W. DAVIS *to* **PHELPS. 18 April 1837. Macedon, Wayne County, N.Y.** Obtains information from students at Oberlin that the American Board of Commissioners for Foreign Missions holds slaves and justifies the practice; reports that several committees have been set up to investigate the issue. 19 May 1837. p.81, c2.

2606 DAVID S. INGRAHAM *to* **REV. W. J. ARMSTRONG, SEC. AMERICAN BOARD OF COMMISSIONERS FOR FOREIGN MISSIONS. 18 December 1835. Oberlin.** States that he has followed the history of the American Board of Commissioners for Foreign Missions; claims he heard that they own a slave at Choctaw station; questions whether this is true and whether they justify the situation. 19 May 1837. p.81, c2.

2607 W. J. ARMSTRONG, SEC. AMERICAN BOARD OF COMMISSIONERS FOR FOREIGN MISSIONS *to* **D. S. INGRAHAM. 30 December 1835. Missionary Rooms, Boston.** Replies that at times the Board has hired slave laborers, and sometimes even purchased them; states that in no case is this done against slave's will. 19 May 1837. p.81, c2.

2608 E. P. INGERSOLL AND C. STUART RENSHAW *to* **THE SECRETARIES OF THE AMERICAN BOARD OF COMMISSIONERS FOR FOREIGN MISSIONS. 7 February 1836. Oberlin College, Inst. Loraine County, Oh.** Comment on reply of Rev. Wm. Armstrong, admitting the Board's ownership of slaves; point out the sin of this practice and urge abolition of slavery. 19 May 1837. p.81, c3.

2609 W. J. ARMSTRONG *to* **E. P. INGERSOLL. 26 February 1836. Missionary Rooms, Boston.** Defends the American Board of Commissioners for Foreign Missions' use of slave labor; states that there were a few contracts made many years ago, and that with the exception of a few cases, those contracts have all been completed. 19 May 1837. p.81, c4.

2610 JAMES T. WOODBURY *to* **COR. COM. OF THE AMERICAN BOARD OF COMMISSIONERS FOR FOREIGN MISSIONS. 10 January 1837. Acton, Ma.** Life member of the board and annual contributor requests information about the board's alleged holding of slaves. 19 May 1837. p.81, c4.

2611 DAVID GREENE, SEC. AMERICAN BOARD OF COMMISSIONERS FOR FOREIGN MISSIONS *to* **REV. J. T. WOODBURY. 25 January 1837. Missionary Rooms, Boston.** Replies to letter questioning their slavery policy; reminds Woodbury that neither the Board nor the presidential committee has ever expressed the belief that slavery is a sin; adds that a slave's contract is always agreed to by slave who is paid an annual sum for his labors and can eventually buy his freedom. 19 May 1837. p.81, c5.

2612 O. SCOTT *to* **BROTHER BROWN. 8 May 1837. Lowell.** Reports resolutions adopted in the quarterly conference of the Lowell station; considers the suggestion of memorializing the annual conference to be of great importance. 19 May 1837. p.82, c5.

2613 A FREEDMAN *to* **W. L. GARRISON. 28 April 1837. New York.** Quotes handbill, found posted in many places in New York, accusing abolitionists of mobbing and of undermining the Constitution. 19 May 1837. p.83, c1.

2614 H. C. WRIGHT *to* **W. L. GARRISON. n.d. n.p.** Calls for God's truth and light to bring the nation to repentance for slavery; notes concern caused by business failures; believes that slavery will be the ruin of the South. 19 May 1837. p.83, c2.

2615 H. C. WRIGHT *to* **W. L. GARRISON. n.d. n.p.** Makes predictions of topics to be discussed by the ministers assembling in the city; hopes the pulpits will no longer be held by advocates of slavery and sin. 19 May 1837. p.83, c2.

2616 F. M. T. *to* **FELLOW CITIZENS. n.d. n.p.** Comments on the appeal of John Hopper, who was insulted in Savannah; condemns the lack of respect of his countrymen, the depravity of mobs, and the "popular jury." 19 May 1837. p.83, c3.

2617 JOSHUA COFFIN *to* **THE COR. SEC. OF THE MASSACHUSETTS AS. n.d. n.p.** Recounts story of Mr. Johnson, who was kidnapped from Africa; tells how his master slit the throat of a young female slave for having spilled gravy on guest's gown; describes his own escape and legal manumission. 19 May 1837. p.83, c3.

2618 H. C. WRIGHT *to* **W. L. GARRISON. n.d. n.p.** Asserts that God is on the side of the slave, progress is being made in the cause; urges slaves to look to God and rejoice; urges abolitionists to come forth and fight. 26 May 1837. p.85, c4.

2619 J. SEXTON *to* **W. L. GARRISON. 21 April 1837. Adamsville.** Announces formation of AS in Adamsville of thirty-one members; reports on declaration of sentiments and elected officers. 26 May 1837. p.85, c5.

2620 ALETHIA *to* **W. L. GARRISON. n.d. n.p.** Comments on Mr. Wright's lecture to children; questions one passage which may have led children to think that God gave man dominion over man. 26 May 1837. p.85, c5.

2621 F. W. T. *to* **W. L. GARRISON. n.d. n.p.** Hopes that the coming convention will adopt resolutions approving the position of many young men on the subject of slavery; states that he belongs to an AS in his New England college; encourages emancipationists to look to young men. 26 May 1837. p.85, c6.

2622 JUVENILE ABOLITIONISTS *to* **W. L. GARRISON. 8 May 1837. Williamstown.** Notice anti-slavery agents in all parts of Berkshire County except in the northwest; hope that a speaker can come to enlighten them soon. 26 May 1837. p.85, c6.

2623 HORACE MOULTON *to* **W. L. GARRISON. 8 May 1837. East Granville.** Acknowledges, with gratitude, the lively interest of the Female AS of Boston; praises the *Liberator* and encourages Garrison's work. 26 May 1837. p.85, c6.

2624 JOSEPH S. ELLIS *to* **MR. EDITOR [W. L. GARRISON]. 18 May 1837. Fitchburg.** Asks which slave states forbid the emancipation of slaves by law, and how many slaves exist in those states. 26 May 1837. p.85, c6.

2625 GERRIT SMITH *to* **THE** *NEW YORK EVANGELIST.* **n.d. n.p.** Sends correspondence between Smith and Edward C. Delavan for publication. 26 May 1837. p.86, c1.

2626 GERRIT SMITH *to* **EDWARD C. DELAVAN, ESQ. 10 April 1837. Peterboro.** Reports that he enrolled Delavan's name in the AS; enumerates and refutes Delavan's possible objections to the society and the cause. 26 May 1837. p.86, c1.

2627 EDWARD C. DELAVAN *to* **GERRIT SMITH. 10 May 1837. Ballston Center, Saratoga County, N.Y.** Replies that he has already joined the AS, which he has long felt was his duty, but which he feared might have interfered with his temperance work; believes the AS is the most effective means of stopping slavery. 26 May 1837. p.86, c2.

2628 E. M. P. WELLS *to* **SIR. 24 April 1837. Boston.** States that the church must be used only for sacred or religious purposes, concluding that it is doubtful that an AS meeting could be held there. 26 May 1837. p.86, c4.

2629 WM. E. CHANNING *to* **FRANCIS JACKSON, ESQ. 22 April 1837. n.p.** Informs that he will send a letter regarding use of their Federal Street Church for an AS meeting to the standing committee of the church. 26 May 1837. p.86, c4.

2630 GEO. S. HILLARD *to* **FRANCIS JACKSON, ESQ. 29 April 1837. Boston.** Reports that the standing committee of Federal Street Church denies the AS the use of their church for their convention. 26 May 1837. p.86, c4.

2631 SAMUEL BARRETT *to* **FRANCIS JACKSON. 24 April 1837. Boston.** States he will send a letter to the Chambers Street Church requesting its use for AS meeting. 26 May 1837. p.86, c4.

2632 GEO. LANE *to* **FRANCIS JACKSON, ESQ. 28 April 1837. Boston.** States that the standing committee of Twelfth Congregational Church has denied the request of the AS to hold a convention in their church. 26 May 1837. p.86, c5.

2633 JOHN PIERPONT *to* **FRANCIS JACKSON, ESQ. 22 April 1837. Boston.** Reports that he has sent letter regarding use of Hollis Street Church for the AS meeting to the standing committee of the church. 26 May 1837. p.86, c5.

2634 JAMES BOYD, MOSES EVERETT, ISAAC PARKER *to* **REV. JOHN PIERPONT. 22 April 1837. Boston.** State that the standing committee of Hollis Street Church is not qualified to make a decision regarding use of church for AS convention; inform that there will be a meeting Monday evening and application may be renewed. 26 May 1837. p.86, c5.

2635 ALEXANDER YOUNG *to* **FRANCIS JACKSON. 21 April 1837. Boston.** Informs that the AS must apply to standing committee of church for permission to use the church for AS convention. 26 May 1837. p.86, c5.

2636 FRANCIS OLIVER *to* **FRANCIS JACKSON. 1 May 1837. Boston.** Declines permission to use King's Chapel for an AS convention, stating that the chapel can only be used for public purposes during Sunday exercises. 26 May 1837. p.86, c5.

2637 SAMUEL HUNT *to* **FRANCIS JACKSON. 22 May 1837. Boston.** States that the standing committee of West Church has denied request of the AS to hold a convention in their church. 26 May 1837. p.86, c5.

2638 GEORGE RIPLEY *to* **FRANCIS JACKSON, ESQ. 21 April 1837. Boston.** Declares that he has no authority to determine who may use their church. 26 May 1837. p.86, c5.

2639 DANIEL GIBBENS *to* **FRANCIS JACKSON, ESQ. 24 April 1837. Boston.** States that the standing committee of First Church denies the request of the AS to use their church for a convention. 26 May 1837. p.86, c5.

2640 CHARLES UPHAM *to* **FRANCIS JACKSON. 24 April 1837. Boston.** Claims that church laws forbid its use by groups other than its own society; therefore the AS convention cannot be held there. 26 May 1837. p.86, c5.

2641 FRANCIS PARKMAN *to* **FRANCIS JACKSON. 21 April 1837. Boston.** Informs that applications for use of North Church have always been denied; states that if AS still desires to apply for use of church, he will send letter to the standing committee. 26 May 1837. p.86, c5.

2642 IVERS J. AUSTIN *to* **n.n. n.d. n.p.** Reports that the standing committee of the church in Brattle Square has denied request of the AS to hold convention there. 26 May 1837. p.86, c5.

2643 G. W. CROCKETT *to* **REV. CHARLES FITCH. 20 April 1837. Boston.** Reports that the prudential committee of Bowdoin Street Congregational Society has denied request to use the church for the AS convention. 26 May 1837. p.86, c6.

2644 HIRAM BOSWORTH *to* **REV. CHARLES FITCH. 19 April 1937. Boston.** States that the prudential committee of Pine Street Meetinghouse denies request of the AS to hold a convention there. 26 May 1837. p.86, c6.

2645 CHARLES PRATT *to* **n.n. 28 April 1837. Boston.** Reports that the standing committee of Congregational Church and Society of Green Street denied request to hold an AS meeting in church. 26 May 1837. p.86, c6.

2646 JAMES MEARS *to* **CHARLES FITCH. 15 April 1837. Boston.** Denies permission to use Old South Church for AS convention. 26 May 1837. p.86, c6.

2647 GEORGE VINTON *to* **CHARLES FITCH. 22 April 1837. Boston.** States that the examining committee of Union Church denies request of the AS to use the church for its convention. 26 May 1837. p.86, c6.

2648 CHARLES COOK *to* **B. B. MUZZY, D. B. HARRIS, P. H. SWEETSER. 8 May 1837. n.p.** Informs that the Universalist Society denies request of the AS to hold a convention in their church. 26 May 1837. p.86, c6.

2649 SAMUEL SMITH *to* **MESSRS. MUZZY, HARRIS AND SWEETSER. 21 May 1837. Boston.** Reports that the Second Society of Universalists denies request of the AS to hold its convention there. 26 May 1837. p.86, c6.

2650 AARON BRIGHAM *to* **JOHN SULLIVAN, ESQ. 16 May 1837. Boston.** Reports that the standing committee of Charles Street Baptist Society denies request of the AS to hold its convention there. 26 May 1837. p.86, c6.

2651 LEVI CONANT *to* **MR. JOHN SULLIVAN. n.d. n.p.** Informs that the Second Baptist Society denies request of the AS to hold its convention in their church. 26 May 1837. p.86, c6.

2652 S. EVELETH *to* **n.n. 18 April 1837. Boston.** States that the Federal Street Baptist Meetinghouse is already in use during week of the AS convention, and is therefore not available. 26 May 1837. p.86, c6.

2653 E. W. WHITING *to* **MR. NATH'L SOUTHARD. 20 May 1837. Boston.** Informs that the Church Street Church Board unanimously approved the use of the church for an AS meeting. 26 May 1837. p.86, c6.

2654 C. W. GOOCH *to* **SIR. 26 April 1837. Post Office, Richmond, Va.** Reports that Rev. Mr. Converse, editor of the *Southern Religious Telegraph,* does not want the *Liberator* sent to him as he finds it "pernicious in its tendencies." 26 May 1837. p.87, c2.

2655 A LAYMAN *to* **THE** *CHRISTIAN WATCHMAN.* **n.d. n.p.** Replies to article in the 26 February issue discussing church laws in relation to the pastor's duty; believes the writer misread scriptural meaning and instructions. 26 May 1837. p.88, c5.

2656 A LAYMAN *to* **REV. E. THRESHER. n.d. n.p.** Wonders why Thresher refuses to publish his letter as promised; queries whether Thresher thinks he can shield slavery, an "important evil," from discussion. 26 May 1837. p.88, c5.

2657 WILLIAM GOODELL *to* **LEONARD BACON. [extract] n.d. n.p.** Urges Bacon to see the Norfolk resolutions in their true light; insists that they will lead to nothing short of the suppression of freedom of the press. 2 June 1837. p.89, c2.

2658 WILLIAM H. PRITCHARD, CORONER (EX OFFICIO), BARNWELL DISTRICT, SOUTH CAROLINA *to* **THE** *CONSTITUTIONALIST.* **20 December 1836. Aiken, S.C.** Reports on inquest concerning the body of a deceased Negro man who was a runaway. 2 June 1837. p.89, c4.

2659 H. C. WRIGHT *to* **BROTHER. [from a** *Friend of Man***] n.d. n.p.** Discusses his visit to a city in the vicinity of New York; reports that the city had gone bankrupt, and that the South owes the city five million dollars; declares that this is happening all over the North, and that slavery is the cause. 2 June 1837. p.90, c6.

2660 n.n. *to* **THE HON. J. C. CALHOUN, UNITED STATES SENATOR FROM SOUTH CAROLINA. [from the** *Christian Register and Observer***] 26 April 1837. n.p.** Quotes Calhoun's comment to a senator from Virginia that if he believed slavery was evil, then it was his duty to work to end it; hopes that this attitude will encourage free discussion. 2 June 1837. p.91, c1.

2661 J. LEAVITT, EDITOR OF THE *NEW YORK EVANGELIST* *to* **n.n. n.d. Philadelphia.** Describes his visit to the colored Presbyterian church as a very moving and inspiring experience; hopes that those in the area where large droves of slaves pass will continue to voice their disapproval. 2 June 1837. p.91, c2.

2662 REV. M. STUART *to* **REVEREND SIR. 10 April 1837. Andover.** Quotes New Testament to prove that slavery is not a violation of Christian faith; claims that Paul expected that Christianity would ultimately destroy slavery, monarchy, and aristocracy, but that this could not happen immediately. 9 June 1837. p.93, c1.

2663 W. FISK *to* **REV. MR. MERRITT. n.d. n.p.** Vindicates slavery; shows that it is not a violation of the Christian faith; calls upon Dr. Stuart for support. 9 June 1837. p.93, c1.

2664 E. W. J. *to* **W. L. GARRISON. n.d. n.p.** Laments lack of practical abolition; believes that too many are satisfied with being labeled abolitionists but are passive in the cause; urges abolitionists to take an active stand. 9 June 1837. p.94, c6.

2665 H. C. WRIGHT *to* **W. L. GARRISON. n.d. n.p.** Replies to "Alethea's" questions concerning his lecture to children; asserts his belief that the will of God is the only code that a Christian must follow; adds that he teaches this doctrine to children and that he also supports God's law of peace; regrets that "Alethea" does not support his doctrines. 9 June 1837. p.95, c1.

2666 ANNA BLACKWELL, SECRETARY *to* **THE HON. JOHN Q. ADAMS. n.d. n.p.** Thanks him for championing the rights of women to speak in legislative halls and for maintaining the right of petition; regrets that he does not support abolition in the District of Columbia. 9 June 1837. p.95, c2.

2667 MARY S. PARKER AND MARIA WESTON CHAPMAN OF THE BOSTON FEMALE AS *to* **FEMALE ASS THROUGHOUT NEW ENGLAND. 7 June 1837. Boston.** Urge them to support Sarah M. and Angelina Grimke in their labors; declare that they work strenuously for the lives and fortunes of others. 9 June 1837. p.95, c4.

2668 n.n. *to* **n.n. [extract] 13 May 1837. Jamaica.** Thanks God for present tranquility; informs that the apprenticeship is working; believes that Jamaica will be more prosperous when the slaves are emancipated. 9 June 1837. p.96, c4.

2669 C. *to* **n.n. [extract] 6 June 1837. Andover.** Describes speech of Mr. Birney from Ohio; finds him a calm, intelligent, and eloquent speaker, but criticizes his "reckless" reasoning on the Constitution question. 16 June 1837. p.97, c1.

2670 H. WAINWRIGHT *to* **W. L. GARRISON. 14 April 1837. Port-au-Prince.** Contends that he, like Garrison, is the "most strenuous and undeviating advocate" of equal rights to all men; praises and encourages Garrison's paper; states that he would like to be a coadjutor or agent for the paper; calls for immediate emancipation. 16 June 1837. p.97, c2.

2671 WILLIAM GOODELL *to* **n.n. [extract from the** *Friend of Man***] n.d. n.p.** Reports on speech of James G. Birney in Hartford which was disrupted by a crowd; laments that a Southerner was forced to plead with New Englanders for the right of free speech. 16 June 1837. p.97, c5.

2672 W. L. GARRISON *to* **JOHN FARMER. 6 June 1837. Boston.** Explains that he cannot attend their state AS meeting; urges them not to waste time discussing points which are not of vital importance, but to concentrate on the crucial question of Texas, which must not be admitted as a slave state. 16 June 1837. p.98, c1.

2673 JOHN G. WHITTIER *to* **JOHN FARMER. 6 June 1837. Boston.** Sends his sympathies to those present at the New Hampshire AS meeting; stresses the necessity and duty of immediate action on the Texas annexation question, declaring that they must not support a state peopled by exiled ruffians who want only to extend slavery. 16 June 1837. p.98, c1.

2674 J. J. DANIEL *to* **n.n. 9 March 1837. Halifax, N.C.** Returns copy of George Washington's letter on slavery; asserts that his slaves are better fed and clothed than nine-tenths of the white people of Massachusetts; asks to be let alone on the subject of slavery. 16 June 1837. p.98, c5.

2675 MR. S. H. WEED *to* **HON. SIR. 21 March 1837. New Bedford.** Declares that he is glad Daniel treats his slaves well, but he is still guilty of an act of injustice in reducing them to property for the sake of gain; states that abolitionists do not wish to harm him. 16 June 1837. p.98, c5.

2676 H. C. WRIGHT *to* **W. L. GARRISON. 8 June 1837. Boston.** Describes his recent meetings with the children and juvenile societies of Boston, who were deeply affected by the sight of a whip used on slaves; reports that many more children wish to join but are forbidden by their parents to do so. 16 June 1837. p.98, c6.

2677 WILLIAM GOODELL *to* **MR. EDITOR [W. L. GARRISON]. 12 June 1837. No. 7 Hollis Street.** Discusses the "Enemies of the Constitution Discovered," a small pamphlet showing anti-abolitionists to be unpatriotic; criticizes most abolition books as too specific and localized. 16 June 1837. p.99, c1.

2678 E PLURIBUS UNUM *to* **SIR. 25 January 1837. n.p.** Reports that on the previous Fourth of July, she wondered whether she should go to services of abolitionists, for she had no money to give; states that she has worked and saved, now contributes and will continue to do so. 16 June 1837. p.99, c3.

2679 S. *to* **MR. ANTHONY. [from the** *Bristol County Democrat***] n.d. n.p.** Describes the Graham Boarding House in Boston, noting conduct of boarders, quality of food, and the prohibition of intoxicants from the premises. 16 June 1837. p.100, c2.

2680 THOS. PAINE, COMMANDER UNITED STATES NAVY *to* **THE** *GEORGIAN***. 22 May 1837. U.S. Ship** *St. Louis***, Pensacola Bay.** Replies to charges in the paper that his men forcibly abducted a Negro man from Haiti; claims that this is untrue, but that they took back a Negro midshipman who had deserted. 16 June 1837. p.100, c4.

2681 EZRA STILES ELY *to* **A GENTLEMAN IN BOSTON. [extract from the** *New Bedford Gazette***] n.d. n.p.** Describes his contract with his slave, Ambrose, under which Ambrose can work to earn his freedom; declares that Ambrose is cared for better than he would be if he were free; supports only colonization, not immediate emancipation. 23 June 1837. p.101, c1.

2682 SAMUEL LOCKWOOD *to* **BROTHER POWERS. [from the** *Zion's Watchman***] 13 March 1837. Kempville, N.Y.** Informs him that an abolitionist has twice been prevented from speaking; states that Powers would be welcome to come there to teach a school, and that he will be well-received if he does not take sides with abolitionists. 23 June 1837. p.101, c5.

2683 PHILANDER POWERS *to* **BROTHER LOCKWOOD. 30 April 1837. Middleport.** Replies that he would like to teach at their school, but he will not be forced to join anti-abolitionists, whom he equates with slaveholders and their abettors; explains that he cannot, as a Christian, join these anti-abolitionists, nor can he remain silent and uninvolved. 23 June 1837. p.101, c5.

2684 W. H. C. *to* **W. L. GARRISON. n.d. n.p.** Charges that the reason slavery, drunkenness, licentiousness and other vice is tolerated by the church is that its ministers are frequently bribed by food or hospitality; gives example of lavish treatment given ministers visiting the South. 23 June 1837. p.101, c6.

2685 n.n. *to* **n.n. [extract] n.d. Columbus, Ga.** Attempts to prove the dishonesty of Northern abolitionists by showing that they refer to Southerners and slaveholders as "dear brethren." 23 June 1837. p.102, c3.

2686 S. B. *to* **W. L. GARRISON. 21 June 1837. Dorchester.** Shows that many use the excuse "What Good Can I Do?" to do nothing to promote emancipation; states that everyone has talents they can use to work for the cause. 23 June 1837. p.102, c5.

2687 A MEMBER *to* **MR. EDITOR [W. L. GARRISON]. 13 June 1837. Boston.** Relates motions adopted in the Free Will Baptist Church in Boston refusing to admit to the pulpit any pro-slavery or anti-temperance person. 23 June 1837. p.102, c5.

2688 ANGELINA E. GRIMKE *to* **CATHERINE E. BEECHER. 12 June 1837. Brookline, Ma.** Quotes from Beecher's book; questions and criticizes her arguments; summarizes abolition principles, especially those stressing that slavery is a national sin. 23 June 1837. p.102, c6.

2689 W. H. TAYLOR *to* **THE NEW ENGLAND CHRISTIAN CONVENTION. 5 May 1837. Fairhaven.** Regrets he cannot attend the convention; states that he supports it and believes the country's conflict over slavery is the work of God; affirms that there is no justification of slavery in the Bible. 30 June 1837. p.105, c6.

2690 W. H. TAYLOR *to* **J. V. HINES. 5 May 1837. Fairhaven.** Solicits Hines' opinion of Dr. Clough's appeal. 30 June 1837. p.105, c6.

2691 J. V. HINES *to* **W. H. TAYLOR. 16 June 1837. Tremont Street, Boston.** Believes Taylor criticized Clough very strongly, but that he sees no other way to treat him, because Clough attempts to prove that abolitionists act against the teachings of the Bible. 30 June 1837. p.106, c1.

2692 H. C. WRIGHT *to* **W. L. GARRISON. n.d. n.p.** Condemns reply of Professor Moses Stuart of Andover Seminary; believes Stuart has shown himself to be a true advocate of slavery by arguing that slavery is not a violation of Christian faith; questions Stuart's honesty as an interpreter of the word of God. 30 June 1837. p.106, c2.

2693 ADAMS *to* **MR. EDITOR [W. L. GARRISON]. n.d. n.p.** Dismisses abolitionists' apprehensions about political involvement; feels it would not endanger the cause, but make men in office more free to show and exercise their abolitionist feelings; notes that the recent anti-slavery convention acted nobly on this question. 30 June 1837. p.106, c3.

2694 A WOBURNITE *to* **MR. EDITOR [W. L. GARRISON]. n.d. n.p.** Corrects *Liberator* report of recent proceedings; informs that it was Wm. Beard, not Bradley Richardson, who was involved in the trial for rioting and was recently jailed for drunkenness and abuse toward his parents; notes that anti-temperance men and pro-slavery men are united against truth. 30 June 1837. p.106, c4.

2695 R. *to* **MR. EDITOR [W. L. GARRISON]. n.d. n.p.** Quotes from Professor Stuart and Dr. Payson; reminds that emancipation of our "nation" of slaves could happen over-night. 30 June 1837. p.106, c4.

2696 A. E. GRIMKE *to* **CATHERINE BEECHER. 17 June 1837. Brookline, Ma.** Corrects Beecher's understanding of what abolitionists mean by immediate emancipation; explains why slaveholding is against morality and against the principles of the Constitution; urges immediatism, not gradualism. 30 June 1837. p.106, c5.

2697 EDWARD R. TYLER *to* **THE** *EMANCIPATOR.* **19 June 1837. Middletown.** Reports on landmark case involving Nancy Jackson, a Georgia slave, whose master lived in Connecticut; Judge Williams granted her freedom, ruling that slaves brought into Connecticut could go free. 7 July 1837. p.109, c3.

2698 H. C. WRIGHT *to* **BROTHER. n.d. n.p.** Forwards letter from Barbados showing that treatment of slaves in West Indies is as bad under the system of apprenticeship as it was under slavery. 7 July 1837. p.110, c4.

2699 n.n. *to* **JOSEPH STURGE. [extract] December 1836. Bridgetown, Barbadoes.** Describes treadmill run by Negroes who are frequently flogged, men and women alike; reports disgusting, intolerable conditions of jails. 7 July 1837. p.110, c4.

2700 H. C. WRIGHT *to* **ALETHEA. 24 June 1837. Salem.** Argues that human govern-ment is founded on man's laws, not God's, and for this reason refutes its authority; affirms that violence of any kind is a sin against God. 7 July 1837. p.110, c5.

2701 H. C. WRIGHT *to* **W. L. GARRISON. 27 June 1837. Salem.** Comments on speeches by Sarah M. and Angelina E. Grimke in Lynn, South Danvers, and Salem; states that in some places they were refused meetinghouses and ministers refused to give notice of their speeches, but they nevertheless moved and convinced many listeners. 7 July 1837. p.110, c6.

2702 P. H. SWEETSER *to* **MR. EDITOR [W. L. GARRISON]. 26 June 1837. Boston.** Relates proceedings of the recent Universalist State Convention, at which a resolution deprecating slavery was voted down; states that many believed slavery is a political affair and has no place in religious conventions. 7 July 1837. p.111, c1.

2703 A. E. GRIMKE *to* **CATHERINE E. BEECHER. 23 June 1837. Lynn.** Explains the main principles of her society, based upon God's holy command; contrasts American abolition to British; believes there is no middle path. 7 July 1837. p.111, c2.

2704 A GENTLEMAN IN ABERDEEN, SCOTLAND *to* **THE REV. DR. PROUDFIT, SECRETARY OF NEW YORK CS. [from the** *New York Journal of Commerce***] 17 April 1837. Aberdeen.** Reports progress of their five-year-old CS; criticizes "rancorous" speech by George Thompson; inquires about progress of ACS. 14 July 1837. p.113, c1.

2705 THE ASSOCIATION OF CONGREGATIONAL CHURCHES IN ABERDEEN *to* **THE CONGREGATIONAL BRETHREN IN THE UNITED STATES OF AMERICA. n.d. n.p.** Rejoices in the rapid progress of religion in America; grieves at the extent to which slavery exists; urges them to let the oppressed go free. 14 July 1837. p.113, c2.

2706 n.n. *to* **BROTHER MURRAY. [from the** *Vermont Telegraph***] n.d. n.p.** Quotes four resolutions passed at the fifty-seventh anniversary meeting of the Shaftsbury Baptist Association declaring the sin and evil of slavery and the duties of Christians to work to end slavery. 14 July 1837. p.113, c6.

2707 N. P. ROGERS *to* **THE** *HERALD OF FREEDOM.* **5 July 1837. Plymouth.** Describes Fourth of July observance at Campton, which comprised a morning discussion of temperance, and an afternoon discussion of anti-slavery. 14 July 1837. p.114, c1.

2708 OUR COUNTRY *to* **THE** *BELMONT CHRONICLE.* **n.d. n.p.** Begs citizens to protest admission of Texas to the Union, which he believes would strengthen slavery; affirms citizens' duties to the slave; argues that if Texas remains with Mexico, Texans may be forced to give up slavery, as the Mexicans did. 14 July 1837. p.114, c3.

2709 B. *to* **W. L. GARRISON. 6 July 1837. Holliston, Ma.** Describes Fourth of July observance in Holliston, which included a meeting, prayers, songs, and a speech on immediate emancipation given by Rev. Jacob Ide. 14 July 1837. p.115, c2.

2710 BIRNEY *to* **A FRIEND. [extract from the** *Philanthropist*] **11 June 1837. Hanover.** Reports on his New England tour, during which he gave speeches at Andover Theological Seminary and at Dartmouth; declares he has received kindness and hospitality everywhere. 14 July 1837. p.115, c3.

2711 A. A. PHELPS *to* **THE ABOLITIONISTS IN MASSACHUSETTS. n.d. n.p.** Reminds them where to send pledges to the Massachusetts AS and to the AAS; urges their generosity. 14 July 1837. p.115, c6.

2712 REV. R. W. BAILEY *to* **PROFESSOR SMYTH OF BOWDOIN COLLEGE. [extract] n.d. n.p.** Predicts that if Smyth accomplishes his scheme, they will see slavery perpetuated in the South. 21 July 1837, p.117, c1.

2713 MARIUS R. ROBINSON *to* **MR. FROST. [from the** *Free Discussion*] **n.d. n.p.** Describes his troubles in the town of Berlin; after he made a date to give his second abolition speech, he was jailed without writ, and testimonies were entered against him; however, the magistrate found no evidence against him and released him. 21 July 1837. p.117, c2.

2714 J. N. BUFFUM *to* **FRIEND HENSHAW. [from the** *Lynn Record*] **n.d. n.p.** Condemns demoralizing effects of slavery; cites story of a lawyer from Maine who received mail which implicated him as an abolitionist while he was in Georgia; even Quakers were found among the party which set out to lynch him. 21 July 1837. p.117, c3.

2715 H. C. WRIGHT *to* **W. L. GARRISON. 12 July 1837. Newburyport.** Praises the Domestic Institution, which "educates man for two worlds: for time and for eternity"; describes Sabbath discussion between S. M. and A. E. Grimke; states that he has decided that God alone has right of dominion over man. 21 July 1837. p.118, c5.

2716 ADOLESCENCE *to* **MR. EDITOR [W. L. GARRISON]. n.d. n.p.** Reports on Sabbath meeting at Bowdoin Street Church; summarizes the sermon and adds his own conclusions; proposes a new edition of the Bible, as the sermon quoted from the Bible to show that it allows slavery. 21 July 1837. p.119, c1.

2717 A MEMBER OF THE CONVENTION *to* **MR. EDITOR [W. L. GARRISON]. n.d. n.p.** Replies to comments of R. H. Sweetser on the Universalist convention; states that the resolution condemning slavery as an evil was not rejected as Sweetser charged, but was deemed inexpedient; points out that protesting the introduction of the slavery question into the convention is not the same as opposing slavery. 21 July 1837. p.119, c1.

2718 A FRIEND *to* **n.n. n.d. West Brookfield.** Reports formation of West Brookfield AS; states that most people are uninformed but that all that is wanting is information. 21 July 1837. p.119, c2.

2719 A. E. GRIMKE *to* **CATHERINE E. BEECHER. July 1837. Danvers, Ma.** Asks why all the rage on the part of slaveholders, if abolitionists are as ineffective as charged? 21 July 1837. p.119, c2.

2720 H. C. WRIGHT *to* **W. L. GARRISON. 20 July 1837. Newburyport.** Gives account of speeches of S. M. and A. E. Grimke in the Newburyport-Ipswich area; reports they tried to speak at the Ladies' Seminary but had no audience; discusses public debates on biblical sanction of slavery. 28 July 1837. p.122, c3.

2721 DELTA *to* **W. L. GARRISON. n.d. n.p.** Reports on the Fourth of July festivities in Pepperhill, which included guns, drums, rum, marching, and the absence of talk of slavery. 28 July 1837. p.122, c4.

2722 A MEMBER OF NEW YORK YEARLY MEETING *to* **W. L. GARRISON. n.d. n.p.** Asserts that the attention of the Friends within the Yearly Meeting has been increasingly drawn to the sufferings of slaves; notes that abolition is growing and gaining support; states that he is grieved and shamed at the course of the meeting, but encourages the abolition spirit. 28 July 1837. p.122, c5.

2723 P. H. SWEETSER *to* **MR. EDITOR [W. L. GARRISON]. 24 July 1837. Boston.** Replies to correspondent who accused Sweetser of falsifying his report of the Universalist convention; criticizes the excuse of "inexperience" for not adopting anti-slavery resolutions. 28 July 1837. p.122, c5.

2724 W. BASSETT *to* **W. L. GARRISON. 19 July 1837. Lynn.** Corrects a misunderstanding regarding his previous statement concerning the Philadelphia Yearly Meeting and regarding Thomas Evans, who was the distributor of the address, not a signer. 28 July 1837. p.122, c6.

2725 A. E. GRIMKE *to* **CATHERINE E. BEECHER. 8 July 1837. Newburyport.** Challenges the principle which allows a distinction between the men who constitute an association and the measures which it advocates; grieves at her friend's unkind insinuation about William Lloyd Garrison. 28 July 1837. p.122, c6.

2726 C. C. BURLEIGH *to* **W. L. GARRISON. 10 July 1837. Philadelphia.** Reports on his recent lectures and his debate in Bucks County with a lawyer named Titus, who attempted to use Scripture to prove that slavery is not a sin. 4 August 1837. p.125, c3.

2727 A. A. FOLSOM *to* **MR. EDITOR [W. L. GARRISON]. 20 July 1837. Hingham.** Replies to P. H. Sweetser, asking why he troubles himself with business which does not concern him, and in what way he considers himself a Universalist; criticizes his "ungentlemanly remarks" and his argument. 4 August 1837. p.125, c4.

2728 W. M. G. CROCKER *to* **REV. BARON STOW. 24 March 1837. Edina, Africa.** Asserts that Africa has suffered much, and that its problems are not sufficiently regarded by his denomination; regrets that few missionaries choose to go to Africa. 4 August 1837. p.125, c5.

2729 F. *to* **W. L. GARRISON. 11 July 1837. Albany, N.Y.** Reports that on his recent travels in New York he has found considerable anti-slavery sentiment in the smaller towns, and has learned that most of the religious denominations have heard petitions on behalf of the slave. 4 August 1837. p.125, c6.

2730 H. C. WRIGHT *to* **W. L. GARRISON. 17 July 1837. Newburyport.** Denounces document issued by Orthodox Congregational ministers of Massachusetts, which complains of lack of deference to the pastoral office and chastises ministers who force exciting subjects on their congregations. 4 August 1837. p.126, c1.

2731 SAMUEL L. GOULD *to* **REV. AMOS A. PHELPS. 22 July 1837. Sandwich, Barnstable County, Ma.** Forwards abstracts of his journal describing visits to Abington, Martha's Vineyard, and Falmouth, where he encountered objections and disturbances; reports that he spoke primarily on anti-slavery, but also on the question of Texas. 4 August 1837. p.126, c2.

2732 SAMUEL L. GOULD *to* **REV. AMOS A. PHELPS. 27 July 1837. Boston.** Reports he has just returned from a tour of the southeastern part of the state; discusses his lectures in Sandwich, which were well attended despite a pastor's lack of support; tells of a white mariner with tanned skin, who was almost jailed in the South as a runaway slave. 4 August 1837. p.126, c3.

2733 n.n. *to* **W. L. GARRISON. 28 July 1837. Boston.** Discusses his speeches in Haverhill, one of which was prohibited by the committee in charge of the meetinghouse; conveys news, obtained from an unreliable source, of bad conditions and trouble among slaves in Trinidad. 4 August 1837. p.126, c4.

2734 H. C. WRIGHT *to* **W. L. GARRISON. 27 July 1837. Andover.** Informs that the Grimke sisters receive no remuneration for their services and that they are not under the direction of any society; also reports on their recent speeches. 4 August 1837. p.126, c5.

2735 A. E. GRIMKE *to* **CATHERINE BEECHER. 20 July 1837. Amesbury.** Approves the aggressive spirit of anti-slavery papers; refutes charges against abolitionists of offensive language; discusses abolitionists' attack on a benevolent society and the CS. 4 August 1837. p.126, c6.

2736 ELIZABETH POND *to* **W. L. GARRISON. 17 July 1837. Franklin.** Reports the formation of a Female Auxiliary AS after a speech given by Rev. Elam Smalley; believes females ought to involve themselves in moral questions. 4 August 1837. p.127, c1.

2737 MATTHEW FORSTER *to* **W. L. GARRISON. 29 May 1837. Newcastle-upon-Tyne.** Believes that Garrison's cause is making progress among the English, but that they need to be shown further evidence of the cruelties and horror of American slavery. 4 August 1837. p.127, c4.

2738 A FRIEND *to* **n.n. [extract] n.d. Europe.** Compares anecdote about the Merino buck to the present financial crisis in New York. 4 August 1837. p.128, c3.

2739 JAMES S. KEMPER *to* **P. H. KEMPER, HIS FATHER. [extract from the** *Cincinnati Gazette***] 6 July 1837. South Hanover.** Describes tornado which has left South Hanover in ruins. 4 August 1837. p.128, c5.

2740 THE GENERAL ASSOCIATION OF MASSACHUSETTS *to* **THE CHURCHES UNDER THEIR CARE. n.d. n.p.** Reminds them that agitating subjects must not be forced on churches; stresses the importance of maintaining the respect and deference of the pastoral office; warns of dangers to the character of women who must not assume the role and character of men as public reformers. 11 August 1837. p.129, c1.

2741 W. M. CHACE, SECRETARY OF RHODE ISLAND AS *to* **n.n. 18 July 1837. Providence.** Wishes to know recipient's opinion concerning the abolition of slavery in the District of Columbia, and the annexation of Texas. 11 August 1837. p.129, c2.

2742 DUTEE J. PEARCE *to* **W. M. M. CHACE. 20 July 1837. Newport.** Replies to inquiry that he opposes slavery and believes Congress has the right to abolish slavery in the District of Columbia; states that he would never vote to admit Texas as a slave state. 11 August 1837. p.129, c2.

2743 JESSE HOWARD *to* **W. M. M. CHACE. 25 July 1837. Cranston.** Believes Congress has the right to abolish slavery in the District of Columbia, but that this right should not be exercised against the wishes of residents of the District; opposes the annexation of Texas. 11 August 1837. p.129, c2.

2744 JOSEPH L. TILLINGHAST *to* **W. M. CHACE. 19 July 1837. Providence.** Replies to Chace's question: believes Congress has the right to abolish slavery in the District of Columbia; supports the unabridged right to petition; opposes annexation of Texas. 11 August 1837. p.129, c3.

2745 R. B. CRANSTON *to* **W. M. CHACE. 25 July 1837. Newport.** Replies to his inquiry that he believes Congress has no right to annex Texas and that he supports the right to petition. 11 August 1837. p.129, c3.

2746 THOMAS W. DORR *to* **W. M. CHACE. 27 July 1837. Providence.** Replies to his inquiry that he believes Congress has the right to abolish slavery in the District of Columbia, that he supports the right to petition, and that he opposes the annexation of Texas. 11 August 1837. p.129, c4.

2747 DAN KING *to* **W. M. CHACE. 25 July 1837. Charlestown.** Replies to his inquiry: believes Congress has the right to abolish slavery in the District of Columbia; he supports the right to petition; opposes the annexation of Texas. 11 August 1837. p.129, c5.

2748 ABRAHAM SHRINER *to* **EMMON KIMBER. [from the** *National Enquirer***] 30 June 1837. Little Ripe Creek.** Writes that he has been informed that his runaway slave is residing with Kimber; asks that Kimber encourage him to return. 11 August 1837. p.129, c5.

2749 EMMON KIMBER *to* **ABRAHAM SHRINER. 7 July 1837. n.p.** Replies that Shriner's runaway slave is not living at Kimber's house, and that if he were, Kimber would not advise him to go back. 11 August 1837. p.129, c5.

2750 A. E. GRIMKE *to* **CATHERINE E. BEECHER. 23 July 1837. Haverhill.** Detects persistence of prejudice in her friend's comments, which colonization principles have not erased; urges her to join in the anti-slavery cause. 11 August 1837. p.130, c4.

2751 THE EDITOR PRO TEM. OF THE *LIBERATOR* **to THE** *SPECTATOR***. 7 August 1837. Boston.** Refutes charges against the *Liberator* made by Mr. Fitch and others; asks why the complaints were published in the *Spectator* and not the *Liberator*. 11 August 1837. p.131, c1.

2752 L. MARIA CHILD *to* **THE** *LIBERATOR***. n.d. n.p.** Believes petitions by children absurd, as they do not possess the understanding necessary to the responsibilities of citizenship. 11 August 1837. p.131, c4.

2753 LEONARD WOODS *to* **THE** *NEW YORK EVANGELIST***. 22 July 1837. Andover.** Corrects the *Liberator*: he did not preside over the AS, as it reported; apologizes for praying with the society. 11 August 1837. p.131, c4.

2754 JOSEPH WARREN CROSS *to* **W. L. GARRISON. 7 August 1837. Boxborough.** Quotes resolution, approved unanimously by his church, which defined slavery as a sin. 11 August 1837. p.131, c5.

2755 A MEMBER OF THE CHURCH *to* **THE** *LIBERATOR***. 8 August 1837. Cambridgeport.** Corrects the *Liberator*: Mr. Wm. Farwell spoke at a recent AS meeting, but he is not a deacon, as was reported. 11 August 1837. p.131, c5.

2756 A. A. PHELPS *to* **MESSRS. FITCH, SANFORD, CORNELL, PERKINS AND TOWNE. n.d. n.p.** Replies to their appeal: disagrees with their view of ministers' duties; declares that priests must address the moral questions of the day. 18 August 1837. p.134, c2.

2757 L. PHILLIPS *to* **THE EDITOR OF THE** *LIBERATOR*. **6 August 1837. Marshfield.** Informs that an extract from a young lady's journal which was published in the *Liberator* was not sent from Marshfield. 18 August 1837. p.135, c5.

2758 A CITIZEN OF MISSOURI *to* **THE** *ALTON OBSERVER*. **28 June 1837. Southern Missouri.** Declares that many Missourians oppose slavery, but feel that individual effort is useless; urges Northerners to flood Missouri and turn popular opinion against slavery. 18 August 1837. p.136, c2.

2759 S. *to* **MR. EDITOR. n.d. n.p.** Reports an unusual response to the escape of a slave: Mr. Stockton forwarded emancipation papers and a recommendation of excellent work to his former coachman, in order that he could visit his wife and children safely. 25 August 1837. p.137, c3.

2760 JOHN ROBERTS *to* **MR. R. C. STOCKTON. 8 July 1837. Toronto, Upper Canada.** Declares he will not forfeit his freedom for anything, not even to see his wife and children; chides his former master for suspecting the motives of the friend who helped him escape. 25 August 1837. p.137, c4.

2761 JOSHUA COFFIN *to* **MR. EDITOR. 11 July 1837. Philadelphia.** Quotes from a book published in 1798 entitled *An Historical Account of the Incorporated Society for the Propagation of the Gospel in Foreign Parts*. 25 August 1837. p.138, c3.

2762 P. H. SWEETSER *to* **MR. EDITOR. 7 August 1837. Boston.** Replies to comments by Rev. A. A. Folsom: affirms his respect for all ministers except those who support a system of oppression; hopes the anti-slavery cause will advance among the Universalists despite Folsom's influence. 25 August 1837. p.138, c4.

2763 A GARRISON ABOLITIONIST *to* **MR. EDITOR. 10 August 1837. Newburyport.** Criticizes clerical hypocrisy in relation to abolition; hopes people of all denominations unite to fight slavery. 25 August 1837. p.138, c4.

2764 DAMON *to* **MR. EDITOR. n.d. n.p.** Notes that at the recent meeting of the Essex South Conference of Congregational Churches, many prayers were heard for the oppressed abroad, but none for slaves in America. 25 August 1837. p.138, c5.

2765 GILMAN JONES *to* **W. L. GARRISON. 5 August 1837. Ashburnham.** Reports on annual meeting of Ashburnham AS; lists officers. 25 August 1837. p.138, c6.

2766 A. A. PHELPS *to* **FRIEND PORTER. n.d. n.p.** Comments on the appeal of students at Andover, signed contrary to the desires of the faculty; the students wish the question of abolition to be separated from all other questions. 25 August 1837. p.139, c3.

2767 A. E. GRIMKE *to* **CATHERINE E. BEECHER. 8 July 1837. Groton.** Counters her friend's charge that abolitionists are accountable for the outrages committed against them, asking if Christ tempted those who committed outrages against him; also argues that the North is implicated in the crime of American slavery. 25 August 1837. p.139, c4.

2768 W. L. GARRISON *to* **FRIEND. 14 August 1837. Brooklyn.** Forwards a religious poem entitled "True Rest." 25 August 1837. p.140, c1.

2769 H. WILSON *to* **BROTHER ISHAM. 26 July 1837. Amherstburgh, Upper Canada.** Discusses progress of colored American emigrants to Canada; refutes whites' prediction that colored people would not be able to care for themselves if freed. 25 August 1837. p.140, c2.

2770 CHARLES FITCH AND JOSEPH H. TOWNE *to* **MR. PORTER. [from the** *New England Spectator***] 18 August 1837. Boston.** Declare that their appeal was both appropriate and well-timed, and that they will speak further, if in doing so they can aid the cause. 1 September 1837. p.141, c2.

2771 J. T. WOODBURY *to* **BROTHERS FITCH AND TOWNE. 17 August 1837. Acton.** A fellow abolitionist commends their appeal, but does not support Garrison, who he feels is working for the overthrow of the Sabbath and the Christian ministry. 1 September 1837. p.141, c2.

2772 S. H. HODGES AND HENRY B. HOLMES *to* **THE** *VERMONT CHRONICLE.* **10 August 1837. n.p.** Urge a county meeting and the adoption of resolutions opposing slavery as an evil and affirming the need to work against it; believe the tone of such resolutions would allow many to unite in their support. 1 September 1837. p.141, c3.

2773 WM. SMITH *to* **BROTHER COMMINGS. n.d. n.p.** Contrasts his and Garrison's use of language and views of religion; admires Garrison's self-denying dedication to the cause. 1 September 1837. p.141, c6.

2774 n.n. *to* **THE** *HAVERHILL GAZETTE.* **n.d. n.p.** Challenges his correspondent to furnish proofs of his charges of slander against the *Liberator*; states that he has learned a great deal from the *Liberator*, but if these charges prove true he will renounce the paper. 1 September 1837. p.142, c1.

2775 J. B. *to* **W. L. GARRISON. 28 August 1837. West Bradford.** Reports that sentiments in West Bradford favor abolition and "immediate repentance"; J. B. sees no need for change or a new organization. 1 September 1837. p.142, c2.

2776 O. Z. *to* **W. L. GARRISON. n.d. n.p.** Remarks on the recent "shout of triumph and approbation" which the enemies of abolition sent up on reading the "Appeal." 1 September 1837. p.142, c2.

2777 E. P. D. *to* **W. L. GARRISON. 28 August 1837. Abington.** Supports the "Layman's Reply to the Clerical Appeal," along with many other abolitionists near Abington. 1 September 1837. p.142, c2.

2778 W. L. GARRISON *to* **J. H. KIMBALL. 16 August 1837. Brooklyn, Ct.** Regrets he cannot attend the Young Men's State Anti-Slavery Convention; affirms the importance of the meeting, and the need for the support of the young. 1 September 1837. p.142, c6.

2779 W. L. GARRISON *to* **JAMES T. WOODBURY. 28 August 1837. Boston.** Replies to Woodbury's criticisms, labelling his disclaimer a "piece of superfluous folly." 1 September 1837. p.143, c2.

2780 A. A. PHELPS *to* **W. L. GARRISON. n.d. n.p.** Reports that the editor of the *Boston Recorder* refused to publish his reply to the Appeal of Messrs. Fitch and Towne. 1 September 1837. p.143, c5.

2781 SAMUEL BENJAMIN *to* **MR. CUMMINGS. [from the** *Portland Mirror***] 24 July 1837. Winthrop.** Requests publication of the resolutions passed at the anniversary meeting of the Winthrop AS. 1 September 1837. p.144, c5.

2782 CHARLES FITCH AND JOSEPH H. TOWNE *to* **THE** *NEW ENGLAND SPEC-TATOR*. **n.d. n.p.** Discuss their previous article, which was intended to draw attention to some of the evils connected with abolition; also explain why it was not published in the *Liberator*. 8 September 1837. p.145, c4.

2783 C. *to* **W. L. GARRISON. 23 August 1837. Providence.** Reports on anti-slavery meeting in Newport, held in the state house; declares that times have changed since Newport citizens attempted to make it illegal to hold anti-slavery discussions, and that they now view slavery as piracy and murder. 8 September 1837. p.146, c4.

2784 W. L. GARRISON *to* **ORSON S. MURRAY. 11 August 1837. Brooklyn, Ct.** States that he would be happy to attend the convention on peace; although he is dedicated to abolition, he also promotes the cause of peace. 8 September 1837. p.146, c5.

2785 A. E. GRIMKE *to* **CATHERINE E. BEECHER. 17 August 1837. Brookline.** Discusses biblical passages; argues that ultimate effect of measures prove their expediency; declares that abolition is beginning to affect the South and will eventually succeed. 8 September 1837. p.147, c1.

2786 n.n. *to* **W. L. GARRISON. 2 September 1837. Lowell.** Challenges the letter from Messrs. Fitch and Towne; believes that their feelings do not meet with the general approbation of abolitionists. 8 September 1837. p.147, c2.

2787 ELISHA FAXON *to* **W. L. GARRISON. 1 September 1837 Abington.** Replies to letter of Messrs. Fitch and Towne, stating he does not believe Rev. White has been too severely criticized; forwards his correspondence with the latter. 8 September 1837. p.147, c3.

2788 ELISHA FAXON *to* **REV. ELIPHALET WHITE. 10 August 1835. Abington.** Criticizes him for preaching the word of God while keeping slaves. 8 September 1837. p.147, c3.

2789 E. WHITE *to* **ELISHA FAXON. 11 August 1835. East Randolph.** Thanks him for his concern, but assures him that his own situation is anything but unpleasant and that his conscience is undisturbed. 8 September 1837. p.147, c3.

2790 O. P. B. *to* **SIR. 4 September 1837. Dorchester.** Denies charge that the signers of the "clerical appeal" belong to anti-slavery groups, noting that Mr. Cornell, of Quincy, has never been a member of an AS. 8 September 1837. p.147, c3.

2791 DR. CHANNING *to* **MR. CLAY. [extract] n.d. n.p.** Discusses the Texas revolution; charges that Texas was not won by its colonists, but by Americans seeking excitement, trouble and land; questions whether we really want Texas as a state. 8 September 1837. p.148, c2.

2792 HANCOCK *to* **THE** *SALEM REGISTER*. **n.d. n.p.** Urges a public meeting to discuss the question of Texas; calls upon citizens of Salem to speak out "against annexing those refugees from justice, those assassins and slaveholders." 8 September 1837. p.148, c3.

2793 A MOTHER *to* **MR. EDITOR. 20 July 1837. Fitchburg.** Insists that women consider themselves quite as capable of judging moral causes as men; draws inferences from sermon by Hubbard Winslow, who preached against moral reform. 8 September 1837. p.148, c4.

2794 VIATOR *to* **MR. SLEEPER. n.d. n.p.** Describes his recent trip from New York to Providence, during which cigar-smoking clergymen drove ladies away; urges temperance in all things, including wine, beer, cider, smoking and chewing. 8 September 1837. p.148, c4.

2795 DANIEL C. BAGLEY *to* **JAMES WATSON. 5 September 1837. Amesbury Mills.** Reports that members of the Amesbury and Salisbury AS do not approve of the "Clerical Appeal" by Messrs. Fitch and Towne and disagree with its charges against the *Liberator*. 15 September 1837. p.150, c5.

2796 ALBERT G. SWEETSER *to* **MR. EDITOR. 8 September 1837. South Reading.** Reports resolutions against the "Clerical Appeal" of Messrs. Fitch, Towne, and others; affirms his confidence in Garrison and his paper. 15 September 1837. p.150, c5.

2797 W. H. BURLEIGH *to* **W. L. GARRISON. 7 September 1837. Lampeter, Lancaster County, Pa.** Finds that the "Appeal" by Messrs. Towne, Fitch, and others is hailed by colonizationists and supporters of slavery, but despaired of by all abolitionists he has met. 15 September 1837. p.150, c6.

2798 S. *to* **W. L. GARRISON. 8 September 1837. Newburyport.** Affirms support of abolitionists from Garrison's home town. 15 September 1837. p.151, c1.

2799 GROTON *to* **W. L. GARRISON. 11 September 1837. Groton.** One who has read the "Clerical Appeal" wonders if Messrs. Fitch, Towne and others are interested particularly in the *Spectator;* hopes these men will rally to the abolition cause and become its true supporters. 15 September 1837. p.151, c1.

2800 PHILO. *to* **THE *LIBERATOR*. 22 August 1837. Lowell.** Supports Garrison and the *Liberator*, arguing that Messrs. Fitch and others have destroyed their influence among abolitionists; also advises on finding meetinghouses for anti-slavery lectures. 15 September 1837. p.151, c1.

2801 W. ADAMS *to* **W. L. GARRISON. 3 September 1837. Pawtucket, R.I.** Encourages Garrison, and challenges Fitch and Towne to produce evidence supporting their "Appeal." 15 September 1837. p.151, c2.

2802 A CONGREGATIONALIST *to* **MR. EDITOR. 12 September 1837. Amesbury.** States that the "Appeal" has been received there and is passing on with no divisions in the ranks; believes ulterior motives influenced Towne in publishing the article. 15 September 1837. p.151, c2.

2803 MARY CLARK *to* **W. L. GARRISON. 1 September 1837. Concord.** Forwards, on behalf of the Ladies' AS of Concord, a copy of "Word from a Petitioner to Congress," as a token of their continued respect and esteem. 15 September 1837. p.151, c4.

2804 P. R. RUSSELL *to* **W. L. GARRISON. 11 September 1837. Lynn.** Reports that he has just been appointed a local agent of the AS; states that he is ready to serve anti-slavery friends as a lecturer. 15 September 1837. p.151, c5.

2805 KIAH BAILEY *to* **MR. N. SOUTHARD. 25 August 1837. Hardwick, Vt.** Writes that he is pleased with the Almanac; recommends it to every family. 15 September 1837. p.151, c5.

2806 P. R. RUSSELL *to* **BROTHER. [from the *Christian*] 12 August 1837. Lynn.** Reports on his lectures near Lynn and the formation of an AS at Essex. 22 September 1837. p.153, c2.

2807 GERRIT SMITH *to* **REV. D. R. GILLMER. [from the *Friend of Man*] 4 September 1837. Peterboro.** Replies to Gillmer's charge of insincerity; accepts proposition to take over the slaves of Hon. Carter Braxton and free them; charges that greed prompts clergy and slaveholders to keep their free labor. 22 September 1837. p.153, c4.

2808 A CHRISTIAN *to* **THE** *PHILANTHROPIST.* **29 August 1837. Upper Alton.**
Reports that a mob destroyed the *Alton Observer*'s press and attacked its editor, Mr. Lovejoy, and that Mr. Lovejoy has been prevented from preaching; believes that ultimately these events will only serve to advance the cause of the slave. 22 September 1837. p.154, c1.

2809 n.n. *to* **THE** *COLORED AMERICAN.* **23 August 1837. Alton.** Reports on "mob law" in Alton where he witnessed the destruction of the *Alton Observer*'s press, and was also struck in the head by stone hurled through a window. 22 September 1837. p.154, c1.

2810 Z. Y. *to* **MR. EDITOR. n.d. n.p.** Discusses Mr. Codding's lecture on slavery in North Bridgewater; declares that slavery, as a moral wrong, requires removal by moral, not physical means. 22 September 1837. p.154, c2.

2811 AUSTIN BEARSE *to* **THE MAYOR OF BOSTON. 29 August 1837. Boston.**
Criticizes tyrannical actions of the mayor, who stopped a preacher from giving a sermon on the Commons. 22 September 1837. p.154, c2.

2812 WILLIAM COMSTOCK *to* **W. L. GARRISON. n.d. n.p.** Criticizes "Appeal" by Messrs. Towne and Fitch; declares he fears neither them nor Satan, for he knows his cause is right. 22 September 1837. p.154, c3.

2813 C. C. BURLEIGH *to* **BROTHER GARRISON. 15 September 1837. Philadelphia.**
Finds that the latest attacks on the *Liberator* have only convinced him of the paper's value and success; informs that all the abolitionists he has talked with support the *Liberator*. 22 September 1837. p.154, c3.

2814 JOHN G. WHITTIER *to* **BROTHER GARRISON. 16 September 1837. Amesbury.**
Worries that the appeals, counterappeals, and disagreements among abolitionists will divide them, yet maintains his belief in the ultimate triumph of the cause. 22 September 1837. p.154, c5.

2815 ABBY KELLEY *to* **W. L. GARRISON. 21 September 1837. Lynn.** Informs that the Lynn Female AS approves of the course of the *Liberator* and regrets criticisms from abolitionists; sends money to help the paper. 22 September 1837. p.155, c1.

2816 LUCRETIA MOTT AND MARY GREW *to* **W. L. GARRISON. 15 September 1837. Philadelphia.** Send resolutions of the Philadelphia Female AS criticizing the "Clerical Appeal" and supporting Garrison and the *Liberator*. 22 September 1837. p.155, c1.

2817 S. B. AND E. B. CHACE *to* **FRIEND GARRISON. 18 September 1837. Fall River.**
Convey their sympathy in times of hardship; express support of Garrison and belief that setbacks will not impede the cause for long. 22 September 1837. p.155, c1.

2818 A JAY (NOT A GARRISON) ABOLITIONIST *to* **THE ABOLITIONISTS. n.d. n.p.** Believes they give too much consequence to the "Clerical Appeal" and risk ascribing too much importance to its authors. 22 September 1837. p.155, c1.

2819 SIMPLE VERITY *to* **FRIEND GARRISON. n.d. n.p.** Asserts that his confidence in the ministers of the Gospel has been lessened by the Church's behavior regarding the anti-slavery movement. 22 September 1837. p.155, c2.

2820 A. E. GRIMKE *to* **CATHERINE E. BEECHER. n.d. n.p.** Believes that despite attacks against abolition, the tendencies of the age are toward emancipation; challenges the claim that the North has no right to rebuke the South; argues that the South was never prepared for emancipation. 22 September 1837. p.155, c2.

2821 ALVAN STEWART *to* **THE** *NEW YORK EVANGELIST.* **[extract] n.d. n.p.** Recounts extraordinary coincidences in the escape of a runaway slave from South Carolina. 22 September 1837. p.156, c4.

2822 CHARLES FITCH AND J. H. TOWNE *to* **THE** *NEW ENGLAND SPECTATOR.* **n.d. n.p.** Clarify their protest regarding the duty of a minister in his own pulpit; regard the present controversy as proof of their charges against Garrison. 29 September 1837. p.157, c1.

2823 HAMPDEN *to* **THE** *HERALD OF FREEDOM.* **n.d. n.p.** Feels that the anti-slavery movement is fighting itself rather than its opponents; hopes abolitionists will soon unite against slavery; defends Garrison against the charges of Fitch and Towne. 29 September 1837. p.158, c4.

2824 WILLIAM COMSTOCK *to* **W. L. GARRISON. n.d. n.p.** Affirms Garrison abolitionism, which employs stronger weapons than silent contempt for the slaveholder; urges strength and unity. 29 September 1837. p.159, c2.

2825 H. *to* **W. L. GARRISON. 18 September 1837. Lowell.** Declares that those who recently attacked Garrison lacked his commitment to the cause of humanity; asserts that truth and justice must and will prevail. 29 September 1837. p.159, c2.

2826 N.Y. *to* **BROTHER GARRISON. 23 September 1837. West Amesbury.** Contends that even the apathetic abolitionists of West Amesbury did not swallow the "Appeal" of Fitch and Towne; admires the course pursued by Garrison and the *Liberator*. 29 September 1837. p.159, c3.

2827 ALANSON ST. CLAIR *to* **MR. JOHN PARKER. 15 September 1837. Boston.** Forwards copy of the *Liberator* and invites Parker to furnish the paper with proof of his charges against Rev. Samuel Gould. 29 September 1837. p.159, c3.

2828 A. E. GRIMKE *to* **CATHERINE E. BEECHER. 28 August 1837. Brookline.** Discusses the position of women; argues that women must not be defenseless and dependent; believes women have the right to petition. 29 September 1837. p.159, c4.

2829 DR. CHANNING *to* **HENRY CLAY. [extract] n.d. n.p.** Asserts that the cause of liberty forbids the annexation of Texas; believes we must strengthen confidence in our free nation. 29 September 1837. p.160, c2.

2830 JOHN S. EBAUGH *to* **n.n. 5 September 1837. Washington City.** Informs that he has been nominated chaplain of the House of Representatives; describes his experience and solicits their patronage. 29 September 1837. p.160, c4.

2831 DANIEL THOMAS *to* **n.n. [extract from the** *Friend of Man*] **22 July 1837. Greatfield, near Aurora.** Corrects *Liberator* account concerning Nathaniel Crenshaw; quotes from friend's letter on John Randolph's will. 29 September 1837. p.160, c5.

2832 MILLS BARRETT *to* **MR. HIMES. [from the** *Christian*] **1 September 1837. Norfolk, Va.** Criticizes Himes' paper, the *Christian*; desires no communication from abolitionists, whom he views no differently than murderers. 6 October 1837. p.161, c1.

2833 SARAH M. GRIMKE *to* **A FRIEND. July 1837. Haverhill.** Compares the pastoral letter of the general association to the opinions of Cotton Mather on witchcraft; believes the rights of women need only to be investigated to be asserted, and that women have no more intellectual or moral weaknesses than men. 6 October 1837. p.161, c2.

2834 D. I. ROBINSON *to* **THE** *HERALD OF FREEDOM.* **31 August 1837. Wells, Me.** Adds to the report of the mob at Meredith that the people of Bridge also threatened to prevent any discussion of anti-slavery in neighboring villages. 6 October 1837. p.161, c3.

2835 J. BLANCHARD *to* **REV. J. LEAVITT. [from the** *Emancipator***] 18 September 1837. Waynesboro, Franklin County, Pa.** Informs that Thaddeus Stevens, nominee for state legislature, supports jury trial in questions of liberty and opposes annexation of Texas; includes quotes from Stevens' speeches; also reports that a law student named Johnson was lynched at Carlisle. 6 October 1837. p.161, c5.

2836 NATHANIEL BUDD AND JAMES C. WHITE *to* **MR. PORTER. [from the** *New England Spectator***] n.d. n.p.** Representatives from the Salem Street AS express the society's decided approval of Mr. Towne's actions. 6 October 1837. p.161, c5.

2837 SOPHIA L. LITTLE *to* **BROTHER. 20 August 1837. Newport.** Criticizes those ministers, particularly Mr. Fitch, who believe they will hasten the coming of the Lord by refusing to read anti-slavery notices. 6 October 1837. p.162, c1.

2838 ELIZA KELLY, FOR THE PAWTUCKET FEMALE JUVENILE EMANCIPATION SOCIETY *to* **THE** *LIBERATOR.* **25 September 1837. Pawtucket.** Sends donation as an expression of the society's confidence in him; hopes his work is not impeded by his enemies. 6 October 1837. p.162, c1.

2839 SILVA W. JONES *to* **W. L. GARRISON. 4 August 1837. Ashburnham.** Reports on the first annual meeting of the female AS in Ashburnham and lists officers; believes that their most effective tool is prayer. 6 October 1837. p.162, c2.

2840 E. W. JACKSON *to* **BROTHER GARRISON. 8 August 1837. Portland.** Reports on the formation and membership of a female AS in Winthrop, Maine; encloses preamble and list of officers. 6 October 1837. p.162, c2.

2841 EDWARD R. DIKE AND GEORGE O. HARMON *to* **W. L. GARRISON. 27 September 1837. Haverhill.** State that the Haverhill AS spends the last Monday evening of the month in prayer for the slaves; report their resolutions disapproving the "Clerical Appeal" and supporting Garrison and the *Liberator*. 6 October 1837. p.162, c2.

2842 OREN SPENCER AND ALBERT ANTHONY *to* **FRIEND GARRISON. 27 September 1837. Coventry.** Send copy of preamble and resolutions adopted at the annual meeting of the Kent County Young Men's AS. 6 October 1837. p.162, c2.

2843 OREN SPENCER, THOMAS TEW, JOHN W. DANA, WALTER O. PEARL, AND PETER T. W. MITCHELL *to* **THE** *LIBERATOR.* **2 October 1837. Coventry, R.I.** Criticize resolutions adopted by the Kent County Young Men's AS; oppose taking sides in a newspaper quarrel; urge united effort to fight slavery. 6 October 1837. p.162, c3.

2844 CHARLES GREEN AND WILLIAM HENRY ANTHONY *to* **FRIEND GARRISON. 25 September 1837. Coventry, R.I.** Forward resolutions of the Coventry AS denouncing division in the ranks of abolitionists, criticizing the "Clerical Appeal," and supporting the editor of the *Liberator*. 6 October 1837. p.162, c3.

2845 B. F. *to* **FRIEND GARRISON. 30 September 1837. Boston.** Reports he found no one during his tour of four New Hampshire counties who did not condemn "Clerical Appeal." 6 October 1837. p.162, c4.

2846 SUSAN B. ANTHONY AND MARY ANN PECK *to* **FRIEND GARRISON. 2 October 1837. Coventry.** Report resolutions of Kent County Female AS criticizing the "Clerical Appeal" and supporting the *Liberator*. 6 October 1837. p.162, c4.

2847 SARAH M. DOUGLAS *to* **BROTHER GARRISON. 30 September 1837. Philadelphia.** Expresses the sympathy of the Philadelphia Female Literary Association for Garrison's late trials, and declares that they heartily support the course he has followed. 6 October 1837. p.162, c4.

2848 J. B. CUTLER AND J. T. HILTON *to* **THE COLORED CITIZENS OF BOSTON. n.d. n.p.** Report that the *Colored American* refused to print a response to the "Clerical Appeal" made by citizens at a public meeting; praise Garrison and his work. 6 October 1837. p.163, c5.

2849 HENRY CARRELL, P. GAMBIEL, JOSEPH TAYLOR, JOHN MARSHALL AND H. SMITH *to* **W. L. GARRISON. 27 September. Boston.** Correct report that John Debois is the agent for the Bethel Society in West Centre street; inform that he has been replaced in the past year. 6 October 1837. p.163, c5.

2850 W. *to* **MR. EDITOR. [from the** *United States Gazette***] 25 September 1837. Philadelphia.** Quotes extracts from the *New York Journal of Commerce*, which presents a false view of the creed of Garrisonians; contends that truth is mighty and will prevail. 13 October 1837. p.165, c2.

2851 DAVID RUGGLES *to* **MR. EDITOR. [from** *Zion's Watchman***] n.d. New York.** Reports that he has witnessed eleven slaves brought into the reputedly free state of New York during the past month. 13 October 1837. p.165, c3.

2852 H. C. WRIGHT *to* **BROTHER GARRISON. n.d. Newton, Bucks County, Pa.** Grieves at the "Appeal" endorsed by men whom he once supported and respected; refutes their charges; affirms his faith in the cause and his support of Garrison. 13 October 1837. p.166, c2.

2853 H. C. WRIGHT *to* **BROTHER GARRISON. n.d. n.p.** Praises the Bucks County AS for supporting the *Liberator*; conveys his encouragement and support to the Grimkes. 13 October 1837. p.166, c3.

2854 n.n. *to* **BROTHER GARRISON. 22 March 1837. Newark, N.J.** States that he has signed a declaration renouncing allegiance to the government of the United States and asserting the authority of Jesus Christ; declares that the United States disregards the Bible, its own Constitution, and its treaties with the Indians. 13 October 1837, p.166, c4.

2855 E. W. JACKSON *to* **W. L. GARRISON. 30 September 1837. Kent's Hill, Me.** Believes that a crisis has come to their cause, yet is cheered that the views of Fitch, Towne and others have gained little acceptance; believes that abolitionists must learn from trials that their strength is in God. 13 October 1837. p.166, c5.

2856 WYLLYS AMES *to* **W. L. GARRISON. 6 October 1837. Providence.** Reports he knows very few abolitionists in the city who support the "Appeal" of Fitch and Towne; expresses his support for the *Liberator*; urges a united effort against slavery. 13 October 1837. p.166, c6.

2857 J. G. W. *to* **W. L. GARRISON. n.d. n.p.** Quotes from Leitch Ritchie's letter to the editor of *Slavery in America*, which charges that slaveholders violate God's law and should therefore be cut off from the Church; urges Northern abolitionists to forget sectarian differences and to purify their churches. 13 October 1837. p.166, c6.

2858 JOHN G. WHITTIER *to* **BRO. GARRISON. 7 October 1837. Amesbury.** Discusses the annual meeting of the Esssex County AS, which ill health prevented him from attending. 13 October 1837. p.167, c1.

2859 A. E. GRIMKE *to* **C. E. BEECHER. 2 October 1837. East Boylston.** Relates that her work in the anti-slavery cause has necessitated an investigation of human rights in general; discusses the place of women in sectarian controversy and political intrigue; refutes the charge that women sign petitions only to contribute to political agitation. 13 October 1837. p.167, c2.

2860 CHARLES FITCH *to* **MR. PORTER. [from the** *New England Spectator*] **3 October 1837. Boston.** States that the recent articles he published in the paper reflect his own views, and not those of his church; explains that while he supports the principles of abolitionists, he dissents from their errors in practice. 13 October 1837. p.167, c4.

2861 JOHN FORSYTH, SECRETARY OF STATE *to* **THE GENERAL MEMUCAN HUNT, AND CO. 25 August 1837. Department of State, Washington.** Declares that the United States bears no unfriendly spirit towards the government or people of Texas, and acknowledges Texas' independence; adds that the annexation of Texas would involve the United States in a war, and as long as Texas is at war and the United States at peace with Mexico, the United States intends to respect its treaty obligations. 13 October 1837. p.167, c5.

2862 THE MINISTER OF TEXAS *to* **JOHN FORSYTH, SECRETARY OF STATE. [extract] n.d. n.p.** States that the United States' rejection of the annexation of Texas will not be imputed to an unfriendly spirit toward the government and people of Texas. 13 October 1837. p.167, c5.

2863 JOHN GULLIVER *to* **W. L. GARRISON. 10 October 1837. Boston.** Contends that Garrison has done him a great injustice; requests that Garrison copy Gulliver's remarks from the *Spectator* and let readers judge for themselves. 13 October 1837. p.167, c6.

2864 CAPTAIN GEORGE H. JENNINGS *to* **n.n. [extract] 3 September 1837. Ship** *Susan*, **St. Thomas.** Describes hurricane which dismasted his ship and six others during the past four days. 13 October 1837. p.168, c3.

2865 AMATOTE *to* **MR. CUMMINGS. [from the** *Christian Mirror*] **n.d. n.p.** Discusses controversy between the *Liberator*, that incendiary and unchristian paper, and the *Boston Spectator*; wonders why only one person in the Maine AS has spoken out; believes Garrison is in error. 20 October 1837. p.169, c1.

2866 P. *to* **MR. PORTER. [from the** *New England Spectator*] **7 October 1837. Boston.** Urges the New England clergy to cooperate with existing organizations to overthrow slavery; explains that the clergy once supported colonization, from pure although mistaken motives, and that many who have withdrawn have yet to take further action. 20 October 1837. p.169, c2.

2867 ZETA *to* **THE** *CHRISTIAN WITNESS.* **4 October 1837. n.p.** Reports resolution of Pittsburgh and Allegheny Ladies' AS supporting Garrison in his work to liberate the millions of enslaved Americans. 20 October 1837. p.170, c3.

2868 E. B. K. *to* **FRIEND GARRISON. n.d. n.p.** Supports freedom of speech for women, particularly on the subject of slavery, which is not only political, but moral and religious as well; cites scriptural passages concerning the attributes of women. 20 October 1837. p.170, c4.

2869 H. C. H. *to* **W. L. GARRISON. 9 October 1837. Pittsburgh.** Rejoices that the odium once attached to the name "abolitionist" is now imputed to opponents of abolition; observes that these enemies often act in hypocrisy, rather than honesty. 20 October 1837. p.170, c4.

2870 JONATHAN P. MAGILL *to* **FRIEND GARRISON. 27 September 1837. Solebury, Bucks County, Pa.** Declares that he is astonished and pained by the "Clerical Appeal," and advises men to forsake the clergy for a higher and holier leader, God; urges Garrison on in the cause of peace. 20 October 1837. p.170, c5.

2871 JAMES RHOADS *to* **FRIEND GARRISON. 9 October 1837. Blackley, Philadelphia County, Pa.** Forwards resolutions of the AS of Delaware County, Pennsylvania, expressing their confidence in Garrison and his work; criticizes the "Clerical Appeal," which most Pennsylvania abolitionists oppose. 20 October 1837. p.170, c5.

2872 H. C. WRIGHT *to* **BROTHER GARRISON. 14 October 1837. Schuylkill, Pa.** Forwards resolutions of the Kimberton AS; rejoices to see evidence of high regard for Garrison. 20 October 1837. p.170, c6.

2873 JOHN BUTLER *to* **BROTHER GARRISON. 6 October 1837. North Yarmouth.** Reports resolutions adopted by the Maine Baptist Convention condemning slavery as a sin and criticizing ministers who believe the Bible supports slavery; foresees victory in the just struggle for emancipation. 20 October 1837. p.171, c1.

2874 O. SCOTT *to* **THE SIGNERS OF THE CALL AND OTHER BRETHREN IN NEW ENGLAND. [from** *Zion's Watchman***] 9 October 1837. Lowell.** Announces convention of the Methodist Episcopal Church to be held at Lynn, Massachusetts; urges their attendance at this most important meeting. 20 October 1837. p.171, c1.

2875 WYLLYS AMES AND ELIAS SMITH *to* **W. L. GARRISON. 18 October 1837. Providence.** Send preamble and resolutions of Providence AS, which criticize "clerical-abolitionist protests" as attempts to lower the standard of emancipation. 20 October 1837. p.171, c2.

2876 BENJ. FROST *to* **FRIEND GARRISON. 14 October 1837. Boston.** Corrects error in report of abolitionist meeting of the Free Church; criticizes the base and inaccurate comments of the editor of the *Spectator*. 20 October 1837. p.171, c5.

2877 WILLIAM BASSETT *to* **W. L. GARRISON. 13 October 1837. Lynn.** States he is happy to find that his remarks on the Society of Friends' objection to joining anti-slavery societies were incorrect. 20 October 1837. p.171, c5.

2878 A FEMALE ABOLITIONIST *to* **THE** *LYNN RECORD***. n.d. n.p.** Expresses approbation of Wm. Bassett's reply to a friend who inquired why he joined an aboliton society. 20 October 1837. p.171, c5.

2879 G. B. *to* **THE EDITOR OF THE** *LIBERATOR* **[W. L. GARRISON]. 5 October 1837. New York.** Criticizes both Mr. Stone and Mr. Tracy for their misrepresentations of him in the *New York Observer*; condemns both for their defense of slavery. 20 October 1837. p.172, c5.

2880 W. L. GARRISON *to* **THE** *SPECTATOR***. 20 October 1837. Boston.** Charges that for three years the editor of the *Spectator* has professed a brotherly love for Garrison, but now attacks him; defends himself, charging that the editor has betrayed humanity and bears personal hostility against him. 27 October 1837. p.173, c1.

2881 EDWARD DAVIS, WILLIAM JONES AND WILLIAM WILLIAMSON *to* **FELLOW COUNTRYMEN AND FELLOW CHRISTIANS. n.d. n.p.** Appeal to Welshmen in America to use all available means to remove the curse of slavery; add that they have been working for the same object in the British dominions, and hope soon to hear of the glorious triumph of American emancipation. 27 October 1837. p.173, c4.

2882 W. BASSETT *to* **THE SOCIETY OF FRIENDS. [extract] n.d. n.p.** Replies to their objections to joining the AS, inquiring whether they are supportive of the CS, which is at variance with their principles, and whether they believe that sin should be abandoned immediately; urges them to join the AS and work for immediate emancipation. 27 October 1837. p.173, c6.

2883 AN ABOLITIONIST *to* **THE** *CONNEAUT, OHIO GAZETTE.* **n.d. n.p.** Demands proof of the charge that abolitionists are trying to organize a political party; states that abolitionists question candidates for the legislature out of a sense of duty, and to avoid voting contrary to abolition principles. 27 October 1837. p.174, c1.

2884 CONSISTENCY *to* **BRO. GARRISON. n.d. n.p.** Reports that Mr. Grosvenor, the Calvinist clergyman in Uxbridge and reputedly an anti-slavery man, refused to read a notice of an anti-slavery meeting in his own town on the grounds that no meetings should be held on the Sabbath that are not of a religious nature. 27 October 1837. p.174, c3.

2885 WILLIAM COMSTOCK *to* **W. L. GARRISON. n.d. n.p.** Reports that a Methodist who chartered a vessel for the camp meeting refused the passage of an elderly, well-respected woman because she was colored. 27 October 1837. p.174, c3.

2886 A. E. G. *to* **BRO. GARRISON. n.d. n.p.** Argues that the greatest sufferings of the slave is not under the lash, but in the daily condition of being under the control of another man. 27 October 1837. p.174, c3.

2887 CLERICUS *to* **W. L. GARRISON. n.d. n.p.** Defends Garrison from clerical attacks, reminding that true and faithful preachers of righteousness have always been persecuted; calls upon all churches to fulfill their responsibilities of philanthropy and general reform. 27 October 1837. p.174, c4.

2888 E. T. LOUD AND LYDIA PRATT *to* **W. L. GARRISON. 21 October 1837. South Weymouth.** Forward resolutions adopted at the annual meeting of the South Weymouth Female AS supporting the good work of the Misses Grimke, criticizing the "Clerical Appeal," and praising the *Liberator.* 27 October 1837. p.174, c5.

2889 D. C. COLESWORTHY *to* **W. L. GARRISON. 16 October 1837. Portland.** An abolitionist refuses to bow to an unfaithful priesthood; criticizes the course Messrs. Fitch and Towne and others have taken; declares he remains a faithful follower of Garrison. 27 October 1837. p.174, c6.

2890 LINDLEY COATES *to* **W. L. GARRISON. 17 October 1837. Harrisburg, Pa.** Esteems Garrison, a consistent advocate of the rights of all men; believes every man should endeavor to propagate his own religious views; discredits signers of the "Clerical Appeal" as true abolitionists. 27 October 1837. p.174, c6.

2891 JOHN G. WHITTIER *to* **BRO. GARRISON. n.d. n.p.** Believes that abolitionists in Massachusetts should sustain the *Liberator,* yet considers the decision of the state AS to assume pecuniary responsibility for the paper an unfortunate one. 27 October 1837. p.175, c1.

2892 MAINE *to* **MR. EDITOR [W. L. GARRISON]. n.d. n.p.** Wonders about the consistency of the editor of the *Christian Mirror,* who attacks Garrison's harsh language while describing him as "malignant and dangerous"; notes recent abusiveness of the *Mirror* toward the abolition cause. 27 October 1837. p.175, c1.

2893 H. C. WRIGHT *to* **BROTHER GARRISON. 14 October 1837. Schuylkill, Pa.** Questions whether slavery or murder is the greater evil, according to the gospel; weighs the relative importance of the causes of peace and abolition. 27 October 1837. p.175, c3.

2894 ADAMS *to* **MR. EDITOR [W. L. GARRISON]. n.d. n.p.** Rejoices that abolitionists have avowed their determination to maintain their principles at the polls; believes they are bound to exercise their franchise for the good of humanity. 27 October 1837. p.175, c3.

2895 W. *to* **THE EDITOR OF THE** *LIBERATOR* **[W. L. GARRISON]. n.d. n.p.** Urges questioning of candidates for state offices regarding their views on topics related to slavery; remarks that the sentiments of Morton and Foster are not generally known. 27 October 1837. p.175, c4.

2896 H. L. TRUESDALL *to* **W. L. GARRISON. 14 September 1837. Providence, R.I.** Reports formation of Providence Female AS of sixty-five members; lists officers. 27 October 1837. p.175, c4.

2897 N. B. *to* **MR. EDITOR [W. L. GARRISON]. 30 September 1837. Rhode Island.** States that he hoped that the different religious denominations of New England could cooperate; regrets senseless attacks by clergy on the editor of the *Liberator*. 27 October 1837. p.175, c4.

2898 W. S. HASTINGS *to* **REV. A. A. PHELPS. 14 October 1837. Washington.** Concurs with several remonstrances, signed by citizens of Dedham, Roxbury, and others, against the annexation of Texas. 27 October 1837. p.175, c6.

2899 GEORGE STORRS *to* **BROTHER SUNDERLAND. [from** *Zion's Watchman***] 23 September 1837. Perry, Genesee County, N.Y.** Refutes the charge of clergymen that abolitionists slander their brethren; discusses the nature of the Sabbath, arguing that in a sense the Sabbath belongs to the slave; urges the cause onward. 3 November 1837. p.177, c4.

2900 A SOUTHERNER *to* **J. G. BIRNEY, ESQ. n.d. n.p.** States that he used to be opposed to abolition, but God has shown him that abolitionists are not fanatics; they are the only men who have heart and soul enough to act for the rights of others. 3 November 1837. p.177, c6.

2901 W. G. OUSELEY *to* **MY LORD, VISCOUNT PALMERSTON. 10 May 1837. Rio de Janeiro.** Reports that more vessels are fitted out now for carrying on the slave trade than ever before; a company has been formed to escape the vigilance of His Majesty's cruisers, and both the United States and England are selling them boats. 3 November 1837. p.177, c6.

2902 OLIVER JOHNSON *to* **FRIEND GARRISON. 23 October 1837. Coventry, R.I.** Believes the words of Charles Fitch are like firebrands compared to the language of the abolitionists; believes the time has come for abolitionists to reveal the corruptions of the ministry; urges rebuke, rather than patient silence. 3 November 1837. p.178, c2.

2903 MARY PEISLEY *to* **n.n. [extract] 1755. Philadelphia.** Believes God uses all men in his plan for reformation, not only those such as clergymen who have been designated leaders. 3 November 1837. p.178, c3.

2904 G. J. ADAMS AND ALBERT ANTHONY *to* **FRIEND GARRISON. 27 October 1837. Coventry, R.I.** Give sketch of meeting of Kent County Young Men's AS, at which the right of the minority to publish its dissenting opinion was discussed. 3 November 1837. p.178, c3.

2905 ROBERT PURVIS *to* **W. L. GARRISON. 23 October 1837. Bridgewater, Bucks County, Pa.** States that he is sure that the oppressed and degraded would support Garrison in the controversy with his clerical opponents; forwards extract of a letter from George Thompson. 3 November 1837. p.178, c4.

2906 GEORGE THOMPSON *to* **ROBERT PURVIS. [extract] n.d. n.p** Condemns soldiers who desert their regiments; urges support for the *Liberator*. 3 November 1837. p.178, c4.

2907 JAMES FORTEN, JR., JACOB C. WHITE AND JAMES MCCRUMMILL *to* **W. L. GARRISON. 23 October 1837. Philadelphia.** Applaud his "fearlessness of purpose" and excellent work; present resolutions from the colored citizens of Philadelphia affirming their unshaken confidence in Garrison. 3 November 1837. p.178, c4.

2908 AMOS FARNSWORTH *to* **SIR. 23 October 1837. Groton.** Solicits opinions of political candidates on the right of petition, the power of Congress to prohibit slave trade or abolition, and other subjects. 3 November 1837. p.178, c5.

2909 L. M. PARKER *to* **AMOS FARNSWORTH. 30 October 1837. Shirley.** Replies to Farnsworth's inquiry, referring him to his report to the Senate on petition; adds that he is opposed to slavery in any form. 2 November 1837. p.178, c5.

2910 LEVI FARWELL *to* **AMOS FARNSWORTH. 26 October 1837. Cambridge.** Replies to questions: supports the right of petition; believes Congress has the power to abolish slavery and slave trade in District of Columbia; opposes annexation of states supporting slavery. 3 November 1837. p.178, c5.

2911 WM. LIVINGSTON *to* **MR. FARNSWORTH. 30 October 1837. Lowell.** Replies to questions posed by Farnsworth: supports freedom of the press and of speech; questions Congress' right to abolish slavery in the District of Columbia, but feels that if it has the right, it should be exercised; supports right to petition. 3 November 1837. p.178, c5.

2912 N. BROOKS *to* **AMOS FARNSWORTH. 25 October 1837. Concord.** Declines to answer Farnsworth's questions; believes that asking political candidates' opinions invites corruption and usurps Congress' role as a deliberative body. 3 November 1837. p.178, c5.

2913 WEYMOUTH *to* **THE *PATRIOT*. n.d. n.p.** Reports that the Massachusetts legislature protested the national House of Representatives' policy of laying on the table petitions on slavery, calling the policy illegal and a denial of the right to petition; discloses that Abel Cushing of Dorchester opposed these resolutions. 3 November 1837. p.178, c6.

2914 E. W. *to* **W. L. GARRISON. n.d. n.p** Urges abolitionists to make sure they do not cast their vote for candidates who uphold slavery in any way; believes that Morton, Foster, and Everett would not favor the cause. 3 November 1837. p.179, c1.

2915 A. A. PHELPS *to* **FRIEND GARRISON. n.d. n.p.** Reports that memorials against annexation of Texas have been received by Messrs. Fletcher, Cushing, Parmenter, and Lincoln. 3 November 1837. p.179, c1.

2916 W. A. GIBBS *to* **MR. EDITOR. [from the *Colored American*] 20 September 1837. Matanzas.** Cautions all persons of color to beware of the island of Cuba; reports execution of black man found with abolition pamphlets, and the persecution of whites, for abolitionism. 3 November 1837. p.179, c1.

2917 A. E. GRIMKE *to* **C. E. BEECHER. 23 October 1837. Holliston.** Wonders why Beecher thinks women are more suited than men to the drudgery of teaching children; believes that men will soon view teaching as an honorable position; asserts that women can be both abolitionists and teachers at the same time. 3 November 1837. p.179, c2.

2918 W. S. PORTER *to* **W. L. GARRISON. 27 October 1837. n.p.** Corrects erroneous report of meeting. 3 November 1837. p.179, c6.

2919 ELIJAH P. LOVEJOY *to* **THE** *PHILANTHROPIST***. 7 October 1837. Alton.** Reports the second destruction of his press by a mob; informs of other assaults upon him. 3 November 1837. p.180, c2.

2920 ELIJAH P. LOVEJOY *to* **THE** *TELEGRAPH***. n.d. n.p** Describes assault on him in St. Charles, Missouri, where a mob entered his house, drew a knife on his wife, threatened him, and finally forced him to leave his house. 3 November 1837. p.180, c2.

2921 A FRIEND TO THE SLAVE *to* **MR. CUMMINGS. [from the** *Christian Mirror***] n.d. n.p.** Expresses surprise that so many clergymen in England are aloof toward both the temperance and the anti-slavery causes; believes that ultimately neither will succeed without the aid of the clergy. 3 November 1837. p.180, c4.

2922 JOSEPH WOLFF, MISSIONARY *to* **MY AMERICAN FRIENDS IN GENERAL. 21 October 1837. Philadelphia.** Wishes to promote the salvation of all mankind, but feels he cannot take part in an AS, as he is a stranger and a foreigner. 10 November 1837. p.181, c1.

2923 n.n. *to* **THE MEXICAN MINISTER AT PHILADELPHIA OR WASHINGTON. [from the** *Boston Morning News***] n.d. n.p.** Describes the division between the North and South on the annexation of Texas; feels it is clear that the Mexican government has no stability or strength, and has lost Texas; believes Mexico's only hope is to enlist foreign aid if she is to keep the rest of her territory. 10 November 1837. p.181, c2.

2924 AN EYE WITNESS *to* **THE** *EMANCIPATOR***. n.d. n.p.** Reports that Rev. Mr. Ludlow was giving an anti-slavery lecture in Meriden, Connecticut when a company of rioters entered the church and threw eggs at the speaker and the audience; informs that lawsuits have been brought against members of the mob. 10 November 1837. p.181, c6.

2925 NICHOLAS GUINDON AND ROW'D T. ROBINSON *to* **O. S. MURRAY [from the** *Brandon* **(Vt.)** *Telegraph***] 12 October 1837. North Ferrisburgh.** Send resolutions adopted at a Ferrisburgh AS meeting, criticizing documents such as the "Clerical Appeal" which evince a sectarian spirit, and expressing support of Garrison. 10 November 1837. p.182, c1.

2926 WINTHROP ATWILL *to* **HON. EDWARD EVERETT. [from the** *Northampton Courier***] 26 October 1837. Northampton.** Asks whether he still opposes slavery. 10 November 1837. p.182, c2.

2927 EDWARD EVERETT *to* **MR. WINTHROP ATWILL. 28 October 1837. Boston.** Declares he is not friendly to slavery; believes it is a social, political, and moral evil. 10 November 1837. p.182, c2.

2928 WILLIAM JACKSON *to* **EDWARD EVERETT. [from the** *Boston Daily Advertiser***] 14 October 1837. Newton.** Solicits Everett's opinions on emancipation, abolition of slavery in the District of Columbia, and the annexation of Texas, explains why he thinks it is pertinent and proper to ask. 10 November 1837. p.182, c2.

2929 EDWARD EVERETT *to* **HON. WILLIAM JACKSON. 31 October 1837. Boston.** Asserts that since slavery is universally admitted to be a moral, social and political evil, he supports emancipation, especially in the District of Columbia; opposes the annexation of Texas, which would extend slavery territory. 10 November 1837. p.182, c3.

2930 H. WILLIAMS *to* **ANDREW ROBESON. 28 October 1837. New Bedford.** Supports right of petition and freedom of speech and press; believes that Congress has the right to abolish slavery in the District of Columbia, and that it should exercise this right. 10 November 1837. p.182, c4.

2931 C. H. WARREN *to* **ANDREW ROBESON, ESQ. 30 October 1837. New Bedford.** Condemns slavery as a "gross moral offense," and a "deplorable political evil"; believes Congress has the right to abolish slavery in the District of Columbia; opposes admission of any new slave state; believes legislature should act according to these views. 10 November 1837. p.182, c5.

2932 JOHN EDDY *to* **A. ROBESON, ESQ. 31 October 1837. Fall River.** Asserts that slavery is an evil; believes the right of petition is sacred and inalienable, as is the right to free speech and free press; contends that Congress has the right to abolish slavery in District of Columbia and territories, and that this right should be exercised. 10 November 1837. p.182, c5.

2933 STUART J. PARK *to* **A. FARNSWORTH. 3 November 1837. Groton.** States that if elected, he would wish to be free from pledges to any party; he does not wish to answer questions on slavery, which he believes are irrelevant to his work in the state legislature. 10 November 1837. p.182, c6.

2934 REUBEN BACON *to* **AMOS FARNSWORTH, ESQ. 28 October 1837. Bedford.** Refers him to the resolutions of the previous winter's session as an explanation of his views on slavery. 10 November 1837. p.182, c6.

2935 JOEL FULLER *to* **AMOS FARNSWORTH. 31 October 1837. Newton.** Replies to questions concerning his opinions regarding slavery, slave trade, right to petition, and the admission of new slave states. 10 November 1837. p.182, c6.

2936 LILLEY EATON *to* **AMOS FARNSWORTH. 1 November 1837. South Reading.** Offers his opinions regarding slavery, the slave trade, the right to petition, and the admission of new slave states. 10 November 1837. p.183, c1.

2937 FRANCIS BOWMAN *to* **DR. FARNSWORTH. 1 November 1837. Cambridgeport.** Replies to inquiry: supports the right to petition and freedom of speech and press; discusses Congress' right to abolish slave trade in the District of Columbia and the admission of new slave states. 10 November 1837. p.183, c1.

2938 S. G. GOODRICH *to* **ELIAS RICHARDS, ESQ. [from the *Quincy Patriot*] 30 October 1837. Jamaica Plains.** Replies to Richards' inquiries on behalf of voters: supports right to petition; believes that Congress has the right to abolish slavery in the District of Columbia and the territories; opposes the admission of new slave states. 10 November 1837. p.183, c1.

2939 A. SANGER *to* **W. L. GARRISON. 7 November 1837. Danvers.** Forwards letter from Wm. Foster, in answer to questions put to him. 10 November 1837. p.183, c2.

2940 WM. FOSTER *to* **MESSRS. JOSEPH Q. OSGOOD, ALFRED PORTER, W. EN-DICOT, E. W. UPTON AND ABNER SANGER. 6 November 1837. Boston.** Replies to their questions on freedom of speech, freedom of press and the right of petition, the right of Congress to abolish slavery and the slave trade, and the admission of new slave states. 10 November 1837. p.183, c2.

2941 A. H. EVERETT *to* **ORIN P. BACON, ESQ. 3 November 1837. Roxbury.** Replies to questions on Congress' constitutional right to abolish slavery in the District of Columbia and the territories and to abolish the slave trade; discusses the right to petition and freedom of speech and press. 10 November 1837. p.183, c3.

2942 A NORTHERN FREEMAN *to* **THE *PROVIDENCE JOURNAL*. n.d. n.p.** Reports on discussion of the Texas question on board the steamboat *Providence*; comments on speeches by Birney, Lewis Tappan, Hall and Stanton; informs of resolution adopted against annexation. 17 November 1837. p.186. c3.

2943 MARCUS MORTON *to* **MORTON EDDY, ESQ. 28 September 1837. Northampton.** Replies to questions on his opinions on topics related to slavery and the rights of petition, free speech, and free press. 17 November 1837. p.186. c4.

2944 NATHANIEL SHERRILL *to* **A. BLAIR, ESQ., PRESIDENT O.C.A.S.S. 25 October 1837. Hampton.** Believes slavery is a heavy curse which should be abolished immediately; supports right of petition; opposes annexation of slaveholding Texas. 17 November 1837. p.186. c4.

2945 GERRIT SMITH *to* **MR. GOODELL. [from the** *Friend of Man***] 20 October 1837. Peterboro.** Accepts offer of all of Hon. Carter Braxton's slaves, made by Braxton through the *Friend of Man*; instructs Braxton to make arrangements and send the slaves to him with warm clothes, for which Smith will reimburse him. 17 November 1837. p.186, c4.

2946 I. CODDING *to* **BROTHER PORTER. 2 November 1837. Kingston.** Informs that in their article on the concert of prayer for the slaves observed by the Free Church, the paper inadvertently replaced his name with that of Mr. Cook, who has no connection with abolition. 17 November 1837. p.187, c1.

2947 SAMUEL J. MAY *to* **W. L. GARRISON. 4 November 1837. South Scituate.** Reports that the Grimke sisters have been staying with his family for the past week; informs of their many speeches in the neighborhood, giving his opinions on the right of females to speak in public; criticizes the "Clerical Appeal." 17 November 1837. p.187, c1.

2948 WEYMOUTH *to* **MR. EDITOR [W. L. GARRISON]. n.d. Weymouth.** Corrects article in the *New England Spectator*; reports that the committee of the Union AS which presented resolutions concerning the "Clerical Appeal" supported them unanimously, and that nearly all the resolutions were adopted unanimously. 17 November 1837. p.187, c1.

2949 G. C. CHANDLER *to* **W. L. GARRISON. 6 November 1837. Boston.** Sends extract of a letter from a lady in Vermont who had lately visited Connecticut. 17 November 1837. p.187, c1.

2950 A LADY *to* **n.n. [extract] n.d. Vermont.** Describes attempt by a mob to prevent an anti-slavery conference in Meriden, Connecticut. 24 November 1837. p.190, c2.

2951 S. L. POMROY *to* **THE** *CHRISTIAN MIRROR***. 7 November 1837. Bangor, Me.** Reports that the conference of Christian ministers and churches in Lincoln County, Maine denied a minister permission to speak for the slaves. 24 November 1837. p.190, c2.

2952 J. SISSON, JR. AND R. KENT *to* **W. L. GARRISON. 7 November 1837. Pawtucket.** Send resolutions passed at quarterly meeting of Pawtucket AS criticizing the "Clerical Appeal" and supporting Garrison and the *Liberator*. 24 November 1837. p.190, c4.

2953 BENJAMIN C. BACON *to* **BROTHER GARRISON. 4 November 1837. Philadelphia.** Affirms the dedication of those who pledged themselves as co-workers at the formation of the New England AS; states that his own dedication has grown and strengthened. 24 November 1837. p.190, c4.

2954 W. *to* **BROTHER CHESTER. 8 November 1878 [sic]. Alton.** Reports that a mob attacked the *Alton Observer*'s warehouse, destroyed its presses, and murdered its editor, Rev. Elijah P. Lovejoy. 24 November 1837. p.190, c5.

2955 LIBERTY *to* **n.n. n.d. n.p.** States that the friends of law and liberty wish to hold a public meeting to express their opinions on the murder of Rev. Mr. Lovejoy. 24 November 1837. p.191, c6.

2956 SAMUEL H. PECKHAM *to* **THE** *NEW ENGLAND SPECTATOR.* **7 September 1837. Haverhill.** Disapproves of Garrison and the "insufferable" tone of the *Liberator*; thanks Brother Towne and others for speaking out against them in their appeal. 1 December 1837. p.193, c1.

2957 TRUTH TELLER *to* **THE FREE LABORING MEN AND WOMEN OF THE UNITED STATES. n.d. n.p.** Compares the free laborer to the slave; claims that there is a wide and irreconcilable difference between them. 1 December 1837. p.193, c2.

2958 J. C. PARKER *to* **ALANSON ST. CLAIR. 10 October 1837. Wood's Hole.** Forwards statement of the secretary of the anti-aboliton meeting at Falmouth, responding to St. Clair's inquiry about the meeting. 1 December 1837. p.193, c4.

2959 A. ST. CLAIR *to* **MR. J. C. PARKER. 17 October 1837. Ipswich.** Apologizes for his delinquency in responding to his letter; believes that Parker has misunderstood his object; asks for better proof that Gould's charges against Hooker were incorrect. 1 December 1837. p.193, c4.

2960 WM. BASSETT *to* **W. L. GARRISON. 31 October 1837. Lynn.** Discusses whether those who are indirectly involved in slavery share the guilt of those directly involved; views slavery as robbery, as the laborer is given no pay. 1 December 1837. p.193, c6.

2961 H. C. WRIGHT *to* **BROTHER GARRISON. 16 November 1837. Newburyport.** Views the institution of the family as created by God to mold the character of man; charges that one of the most appalling features of slavery is that it annihilates the family system. 1 December 1837. p.194, c1.

2962 H. C. WRIGHT *to* **W. L. GARRISON. 23 November 1837. Newburyport.** States that he has just heard of the unjust death of Brother Lovejoy; criticizes the Church, presses, statesmen, and citizens who remain silent at the outrageous, unlawful behavior of the mob; urges non-resistance. 1 December 1837. p.194, c2.

2963 PEACE *to* **THE** *SALEM REGISTER.* **n.d. n.p.** A "Garrison abolitionist" condemns the lawless spirit which threatens freedom of the press and martyred Lovejoy, but regrets that they defended themselves against the mob with weapons; declares the teachings of Christ oppose violent resistance to evil. 1 December 1837. p.195, c2.

2964 E. CARPENTER *to* **W. L. GARRISON. 21 November 1837. New York.** Believes that abolitionists should not mourn Lovejoy, as this will not restore him, but should organize anti-slavery meetings to discuss this tragedy and take up collections for his family; urges them to help Lovejoy's widow re-establish the *Alton Observer*. 1 December 1837. p.195, c4.

2965 H. C. WRIGHT *to* **n.n. [extract] n.d n.p.** Reports astonishing misconception of *Liberator*'s religious sentiments by editor of the *Friend of Man*, Brother Goodell. 1 December 1837. p.195, c5.

2966 H. C. WRIGHT *to* **BROTHER GARRISON. 25 November 1837. Newburyport.** Rejoices that Garrison spoke out against the violent behavior of Lovejoy and his friends in killing one of the mob; believes that it is foul murder to slaughter a man, whether in offense or defense. 8 December 1837. p.197, c2.

2967 WEYMOUTH *to* **MR. EDITOR [W. L. GARRISON]. n.d. n.p.** Charges the *New England Spectator* with misrepresentation of the sentiments of the society toward its adopted resolutions. 8 December 1837. p.198, c2.

2968 WM. E. CHANNING *to* **THE CITIZENS OF BOSTON. n.d. n.p.** Reports that a petition for the use of Faneuil Hall, to hold a public discussion of freedom of press and the recent murder in Alton, was denied by city officials; fails to understand why city officials do not support freedom of the press and criticism of mobs. 8 December 1837. p.198, c3.

2969 FRANCIS JACKSON, ELLIS GRAY LORING, AND EDMUND QUINCY *to* **THE PUBLIC. 2 December 1837. n.p.** Present brief statement regarding W. E. Channing's request for use of Faneuil Hall to discuss death of Lovejoy; state that the meeting was not meant to be a party movement, but to express the sentiments of whole community. 8 December 1837. p.198, c4.

2970 ONE OF THE MANY *to* **THE** *BOSTON MORNING POST*. **n.d. n.p** Thanks him for his criticisms of city officials who refused the use of Faneuil Hall to certain petitioners; suggests meeting to discuss measures against this spirit of the city board. 8 December 1837. p.199, c1.

2971 JOSIAH GIFFORD *to* **MR. HENRY G. CHAPMAN. 28 November 1837. Sandwich.** Forwards money collected at a monthly concert for the widow of Rev. Elijah P. Lovejoy as a token of their sympathy. 8 December 1837. p.199, c6.

2972 n.n. *to* **THE** *FALL RIVER PATRIOT*. **28 November 1837. Saybrook.** Reports on his travels from Fall River to New York; the captain sailed out of Newport in the midst of a fog, a storm came up and the boat barely made it to Saybrook without sinking. 8 December 1837. p.200, c2.

2973 n.n. *to* **W. L. GARRISON. n.d. n.p.** Asserts that the murder of Lovejoy has once again revealed the ugliness and sinfulness of slavery, and that the *Alton Observer* must be published again in Alton; offers his services as printer. 15 December 1837. p.201, c6.

2974 DANIEL C. COLESWORTHY *to* **BROTHER GARRISON. n.d. n.p.** Charges that the public men of Alton were more responsible than the mob for Lovejoy's murder; believes that the editors of papers who criticize workers for the enslaved and oppressed are also guilty; assails the persecuting spirit of the church. [partially illegible] 15 December 1837. p.201, c6.

2975 W. *to* **THE** *BOSTON MERCANTILE JOURNAL*. **10 November 1837. Havana.** Speculates that the reason behind Gov. Tacon's order to imprison all American blacks arriving in the harbor is the treaty between English and Spanish governments. 15 December 1837. p.204, c2.

2976 W. *to* **THE** *CINCINNATI JOURNAL*. **25 November 1837. Alton.** Reports that ministers in Alton are threatened if they speak out against the mob, and that the press is unwilling to address the issue; declares this is not a matter of abolition, but of free press; discusses public address made by Lovejoy shortly before his murder. 22 December 1837. p.205, c1.

2977 W. E. CHANNING *to* **ABOLITIONISTS. 14 December 1837. Boston.** Regrets hearing that one of their respected brethren fell with arms in his hands; believes that Christian philanthropy may not be carried out with force; conveys his opinions concerning abolitionist principles and behavior. 22 December 1837. p.206, c1.

2978 A. E. GRIMKE *to* **BROTHER GARRISON. 10 December 1837. Brookline.** States that she is shocked at the death of Lovejoy, not because an abolitionist fell victim to popular fury against freedom of the press, but because he did not fall the unresisting victim to that fury; discusses doctrines of peace and non-resistance, and their adoption by abolitionists. 22 December 1837. p.207, c1.

2979 H. C. WRIGHT *to* **BROTHER GARRISON. n.d. n.p.** Quotes notices of Lovejoy's death from three Boston and New York papers; points out the hypocrisy of those who regret that Lovejoy fought in self-defense, yet eulogize our forefathers of the revolution for acting on the same principles. 22 December 1837. p.207, c2.

2980 O. SCOTT *to* **BROTHER PORTER. 24 November 1837. Lowell.** Explains that the Methodist Episcopal Church has never formed any New England state, county or town AS. 22 December 1837. p.207, c3.

2981 E. G. L. *to* **DR. CHANNING. 17 December 1837. Boston.** Wishes to suggest to Channing that theology, not abolition, dictates whether slaveholding is grounds for exclusion from the communion table; affirms that violence must be discouraged. 22 December 1837. p.207, c3.

2982 EDMUND QUINCY *to* **HENRY G. CHAPMAN. 23 November 1837. Boston.** Sends fifteen dollars for life subscription to Massachusetts AS; retracts his criticisms of Garrison's course concerning "Clerical Appeal"; sees now the justice of Garrison's motives. 22 December 1837. p.207, c4.

2983 HENRY G. CHAPMAN *to* **EDMUND QUINCY, ESQ. 25 November 1837. Boston.** Acknowledges receipt of Quincy's money; requests permission to publish Quincy's letter as an example of a candid mind following its own convictions. 22 December 1837. p.207, c4.

2984 EDMUND QUINCY *to* **HENRY G. CHAPMAN, ESQ. 27 November 1837. Boston.** Expresses surprise that anyone would receive support or encouragement from his letters, but he gives Chapman permission to publish them; states that he has admired abolitionists from the first. 22 December 1837. p.207, c5.

2985 CHARLES C. BURLEIGH *to* **n.n. [extract] n.d. n.p.** Laments Lovejoy's death and his departure from peace principles in defending himself; feels certain that had he not resisted, he probably would not have been killed, or that if he had been killed unresisting, he would have brought favorable reaction to the cause. 22 December 1837. p.207, c5.

2986 REV. JOHN J. MITOR *to* **BROTHER STANTON. [extract] 30 October 1837. Alton.** Reports on the convention held for the formation of state AS in Upper Alton; describes meetings, speakers, proceedings, and resolutions. 22 December 1837. p.208, c2.

2987 n.n. *to* **THE** *CINCINNATI JOURNAL***. [extract] 8 November 1837. Alton.** Quotes from the *First Intelligencer* on the murder in Alton. 22 December 1837. p. 208, c4.

2988 REV. MR. GRAVES *to* **THE** *NEW YORK EVANGELIST***. [extract] n.d. n.p.** Reports fall of Lovejoy in defense of the anti-slavery cause and freedom of the press. 22 December 1837. p.208, c6.

2989 REV. JOEL W. PARKER *to* **THE** *NEW YORK OBSERVER***. n.d. n.p.** Believes mob members and killer of Lovejoy are well-known names, but they will not be brought to justice because the law is prostrate, and violence rules. 22 December 1837. p.208, c6.

2990 CARTER BRAXTON *to* **THE** *RICHMOND ENQUIRER***. 28 November 1837. Middlesex.** States he has observed notice in many papers that Carter Braxton has offered all his slaves to Gerrit Smith; declares to the public that the letter is a complete fraud. 29 December 1837. p.209, c1.

2991 A SUBSCRIBER *to* **MR. SPEAR. [from the** *Norfolk Argus***] 6 December 1837. n.p.** Objects to speech of J. T. Austin at Faneuil Hall meeting; concurs with criticisms of him. 29 December 1837. p.209, c6.

2992 A FRIEND *to* **THE** *LIBERATOR* **[W. L. GARRISON]. [extract] n.d. n.p.** Criticizes speech by Mr. Austin at Faneuil Hall meeting; believes the procedure of city government on this issue has revealed its corruption. 29 December 1837. p.209, c6.

2993 P. TILLINGHAST *to* **MRS. LOVEJOY. n.d. n.p.** Writes for Providence Female AS, expressing their sorrow and sympathy for her husband's death; forwards the society's resolutions respecting the incident. 29 December 1837. p.210, c2.

[1838]

2994 G. B. *to* **REV. DR. CHANNING. n.d. n.p.** Criticizes Channing's address on abolitionists, addressing Channing's objection to the abolitionists' use of severe language and his objection to the exclusion of slaveholders from the privileges of the Christian church. 5 January 1838. p.2, c3.

2995 S. M. G. *to* **BROTHER GARRISON. December 1837. Brookline.** Believes Lovejoy's death fulfilled Christ's prophecy, "Those who take the sword shall perish by the sword"; points out the hypocrisy of praising Lovejoy's defense of freedom of the press even until martyrdom, while criticizing his taking up of arms. 5 January 1838. p.2, c5.

2996 LEWIS TAPPAN *to* **W. L. GARRISON. 15 December 1837. New York.** Wishes to explain that the declaration of sentiments of the AAS, which advocates non-resistance, applies only to its signers, while the constitution of the society does not demand non-resistance; also gives further detail of Lovejoy's death. 5 January 1838. p.2, c6.

2997 SAMUEL J. MAY *to* **REV. BERIAH GREEN. [from the** *Emancipator***] 11 December 1837. South Scituate.** Points to the inconsistency of Green and others on the executive committee of the AAS who signed the declaration of sentiments rejecting the use of violence, who call Lovejoy a martyr; mourns Lovejoy's death, but criticizes his use of violence. 5 January 1838. p.3, c1.

2998 BLAND *to* **THE LEGISLATURE OF VIRGINIA. [from the** *Richmond Enquirer***] n.d. n.p.** Urges them to reorganize their militia, look to the public arsenals, and not waste time in debate on federal relations. 5 January 1838. p.3, c2.

2999 SARAH M. GRIMKE *to* **FRIEND. 11 July 1837. Amesbury.** Gives her opinions on the province of women, depending solely on the Bible to designate that role; believes God created man and woman in perfect equality, and that man has no dominion over his wife. 5 January 1838. p.4, c2.

3000 SARAH M. GRIMKE *to* **SISTER. 17 July 1837. Newburyport.** Asks men to "take their feet from off our necks" and let women occupy their rightful, equal place; quotes from Bible to demonstrate that no supremacy was granted to man; shows how women were turned into a kind of property by the cupidity of man. 5 January 1838. p.4, c3.

3001 W. SMYTH *to* **MR. PORTER. [from the** *New England Spectator***] 27 December 1837. Brunswick.** Believes the bitter and denunciatory style of Mr. Garrison is wrong, especially his universal attack on ministers of the gospel; sees no hope of change in Mr. Garrison, and believes abolitionists should proceed with the plans for the new organization; criticizes Brother Phelps' latest letter. 12 January 1838. p.5, c1.

3002 DANIEL PALMER *to* **MR. EDITOR [W. L. GARRISON]. 6 December 1837. New Rowley.** Secretary of the New Rowley AS writes of their resolutions which mourn Lovejoy's death yet rejoice that he was willing to sacrifice his life. 12 January 1838. p.6, c1.

3003 CHARLES A. EASTMAN, SECRETARY *to* **BROTHER GARRISON. 15 December 1837. Mason Village, N.H.** Reports resolutions adopted by the Mason AS criticizing appeals in New England, disapproving of the course of the *New England Spectator*, and praising Lovejoy and others. 12 January 1838. p.6, c2.

3004 BOARD OF MANAGERS EAST FALLOWFIELD AS *to* **FRIEND. 18 November 1837. East Fallowfield, Pa.** Criticizes "Clerical Appeal" and those referring to themselves as "clerical abolitionists"; refutes complaints against the *Liberator*; praises Garrison for his "straightforward course." 12 January 1838. p.6, c2.

3005 JAMES FULTON, JR., RECORDING SECRETARY *to* **FRIEND GARRISON. 4 December 1837. East Fallowfield, Chester County, Pa.** Forwards resolutions which were unanimously adopted at the last meeting of the East Fallowfield AS, which criticize "Clerical Appeal," praise and support Garrison, denounce actions of Alton mob, and mourn Lovejoy. 12 January 1838. p.6, c3.

3006 JOHN PARKHURST *to* **W. L. GARRISON. 7 December 1837. Chelmsford.** Sends copy of salutation, preamble, and resolutions of the Baptist church in Chelmsford condemning slavery as an evil sin, upholding the duty of all Christians to work in the cause of slavery, and affirming the error of slaveholding ministers and Christians. 12 January 1838. p.6, c3.

3007 SALISBURY *to* **W. L. GARRISON. 20 December 1837. n.p.** Tells of minister in nearby Newburyport who turned "town-crier" by announcing a lost purse at the end of sermon. 12 January 1838. p.6, c4.

3008 J. C. W. *to* **FRIEND GARRISON. n.d. n.p.** Criticizes T. C. Cook's behavior in a recent interview concerning Rev. Mr. Towne; believes Cook's charges are false; inquires about the actual conversation. 12 January 1838. p.6, c5.

3009 JOSEPH A. WHITMARSH *to* **BROTHER GARRISON. 2 January 1838. Boston.** Writes from the Leverett Street Jail, where he is incarcerated for libel; affirms that the soul is free in Jesus, even in jail; sends notice to the subscribers of the *Illuminator* that while he is in jail he will arrange to send them some other moral reform paper. 12 January 1838. p.6, c5.

3010 JOHN QUINCY ADAMS *to* **FRIEND. [from the** *National Enquirer***] 29 December 1837. Washington.** Reports he was called to order and silenced for daring to pronounce the name of Lovejoy and the word murder in the House of Representatives; expresses his concern about the cause of peace and about war with Mexico. 12 January 1838. p.7, c4.

3011 SARAH M. GRIMKE *to* **FRIEND. July 1837. Haverhill.** Criticizes the pastoral letter of the General Association of Congregational Ministers of Massachusetts; believes that if women only examine their rights, they will come to a different conclusion than that of the association; women may and should lead moral reform. 12 January 1838. p.8, c2.

3012 SARAH M. GRIMKE *to* **FRIEND. 27 July 1837. Andover.** Believes that the social intercourse of man and woman is degrading to both as moral and intellectual beings, because it focuses on their differences; maintains that relations must be purified by forgetfulness of sex. 12 January 1838. p.8, c3.

3013 SARAH M. GRIMKE *to* **SISTER. 4 August 1837. Groton.** Examines the condition of women in Asia and Africa, where men either dress women like dolls or sell and make slaves of them, giving the husband complete dominion. 12 January 1838. p.8, c4.

3014 SARAH M. GRIMKE *to* **FRIEND. 15 August 1837. Groton.** Discusses condition of women in Asia and Africa; gives example of women in history who filled thrones, to refute the theory of women's inferiority; contrasts Hindu and other cultures in which the women are treated like animals. 12 January 1838. p.8, c5.

3015 A. A. PHELPS *to* **THE ABOLITIONISTS OF NEW ENGLAND. n.d. n.p.** Replies to Professor Smyth's criticism of Phelps' earlier letter; criticizes the call for a convention to form a new AS; disapproves of the proceedings thus far; refutes the attacks on Garrison and the Massachusetts society. 19 January 1838. p.9, c1.

3016 A FRIEND OF WOMAN *to* **BROTHER GARRISON. n.d. n.p** Rejoices that the *Liberator*'s prospectus of Vol. VIII declares its columns open to discussion of women's rights, asserting that men would also gain by the proposed change in society; reports on the meeting at the Lyceum to discuss male and female equality in civil rights and duties. 19 January 1838. p.10, c2.

3017 P. *to* **W. L. GARRISON. 30 December 1837. North Marshfield.** Stresses that "the doctrine of non-resistance is the very bulwark of the anti-slavery enterprise"; summarizes Rev. Mr. May's sermon criticizing the mob for murder and Lovejoy for resorting to violence. 19 January 1838. p.10, c3.

3018 TRUTH AND CANDOR *to* **FRIEND GARRISON. n.d. n.p.** Supports the peace principle, but thinks Wright and the Grimkes go too far in calling Lovejoy a murderer, believes it is all right to take life, if so directed by God; believes Lovejoy's behavior was wicked, but not murderous. 19 January 1838. p.10, c3.

3019 FREDERICK BAGLEY *to* **FRIEND GARRISON. 27 November 1837. Salisbury.** Reports resolutions adopted unanimously by the Amesbury Baptist Church speaking out against Lovejoy's murder, criticizing the *Christian Watchman* for so little reference to this terrible event, and sympathizing with Mrs. Lovejoy. 19 January 1838. p.10, c5.

3020 NATH. SWASEY *to* **W. L. GARRISON. 6 January 1838. Bath.** Reports that residents of Bath have resolved to speak out boldly in defense of their right to a free discussion of slavery; reports difficulties in obtaining a meeting place, and of formation of ladies' AS. January 1838. p.10, c6.

3021 M. V. BALL *to* **THE EDITOR OF THE** *LIBERATOR* **[W. L. GARRISON]. 16 January 1838. Boston.** Sends resolutions from Boston Female AS recommending the *Liberator* and renewing subscription of fifty copies. 19 January 1838. p.11, c6.

3022 ORIN P. BACON *to* **FRIEND GARRISON. December 1837. Dorchester.** Sends resolutions from Dorchester AS asserting their confidence in Garrison, praising his editorial work, and urging support of the *Liberator*. 19 January 1838. p.11, c6.

3023 SARAH M. GRIMKE *to* **SISTER. 22 August 1837. Brookline.** Discusses the condition of women in Europe; feels that they have not been as uniformly or as deeply debased as in the eastern countries, but finds their history to be unsatisfactory; gives examples in Greece, ancient Rome, Poland, Russia, and France. 19 January 1838. p12, c2.

3024 SARAH M. GRIMKE *to* **SISTER. 1837. Brookline.** Discusses condition of women in the United States, criticizing the deficiency of education among the "fashionable"; discusses the deplorable condition of female slaves; urges equality of the sexes. 19 January 1838. p.12, c3.

3025 O. SCOTT *to* **BRETHREN. 21 December 1837. Lowell.** Reports on his "sayings and doings" of the past few weeks; gave lectures in various towns in Massachusetts, collected money, and helped form new societies; urges that the Alton press be set up again in Alton. 26 January 1838. p.13, c2.

3026 J. G. W. *to* **THE** *EMANCIPATOR.* **[extract] n.d. n.p.** Reports on lecture by Brother Stanton on the right and duty of free discussion; tells of attending convention at Farmington, Connecticut to form Hartford County AS; summarizes speeches given there. 26 January 1838. p.13, c3.

3027 DR. J. HAWES *to* **THE SECRETARY OF THE AAS. 7 December 1837. Hartford.** States that he has supported the principles and aims of the AAS for nearly three years, although he does not agree with the sentiments of all its members. 26 January 1838. p.13, c3.

3028 A DEMOCRAT *to* **THE** *WASHINGTON SENTINEL AND FREE PRESS.* **5 January 1838. Hebron.** Urges abolitionists and all others opposed to gag laws and in favor of freedom of the press and speech to take courage; shows that opinions in Congress are beginning to turn to their side. 26 January 1838. p.13, c6.

3029 C. CUSHING *to* **THE** *LOWELL COURIER.* **13 January 1838. House of Representatives.** Corrects *Courier*'s report of Mr. Patton's resolution to lay petitions relating to abolition of slavery on the table; also corrects earlier article on petition rights. 26 January 1838. p.15, c1.

3030 BENJAMIN FROST *to* **THE BOSTON FEMALE AS. 8 January 1838. Boston.** Disagrees with society's last annual report; claims that the *New England Spectator* never was the organ of the Free Church, as the society reports; corrects resolutions respecting the Free Church, charging that the *New England Spectator* was "poor authority to found assertions upon." 26 January 1838. p.15, c3.

3031 MARIA W. CHAPMAN, CORRESPONDING SECRETARY, BRITISH AND FOREIGN AS *to* **MR. BENJAMIN FROST. n.d. n.p.** Writer of the annual report declares she is obliged to him for his criticism of statements he feels are incorrect; replies that certain of their assertions, however, are true; believes the society lives up to its good reputation, and that its report was fair. 26 January 1838. p.15, c3.

3032 AUGUSTUS WILLIAM HANSON *to* **W. L. GARRISON, ESQ. 15 January 1838. No. 8 High Street, Salem.** A native African of English descent and educated in England, Hanson claims that he was tricked into coming to the United States to work; finds to his amazement that blacks are treated very differently here; asks for help. 26 January 1838. p.15, c4.

3033 WM. WHIPPER *to* **THE** *COLORED AMERICAN.* **1 January 1838. Columbia.** Wonders why the editor refused Whipper's offer to discuss their differences; considers it "unfair and illiberal" that the editor continues to publish old articles he no longer supports. 26 January 1838. p.15, c5.

3034 SARAH M. GRIMKE *to* **SISTER. 25 August 1837. Brookline.** Discusses the heroism and courage of women who behave as well as, and sometimes better than, men in positions of authority. 26 January 1838. p.16, c2.

3035 SARAH M. GRIMKE *to* **SISTER. August 1837. Brookline.** Argues that men do not desire the improvement of women; gives examples of the intellectual powers of women; charges that women, even in the supposedly "free United States," do not enjoy all advantages given men. 26 January 1838. p.16, c3.

3036 SARAH M. GRIMKE *to* **SISTER. September 1837. Brookline.** Discusses women's dress; admits she has yielded to the pressure of her circumstances by allowing herself to be frivolously ornamented; declares women must study improvement of the mind, not fashion. 26 January 1838. p.16, c3.

3037 AMOS A. PHELPS *to* **MR. PORTER. [from the** *Spectator***] n.d. n.p.** Replies to Professor Smyth's criticism of his articles; explains that the convention was originally called to discuss the formation of a new society, but not to form it, as Smyth contends; adds that only those wanting a new society should attend. 2 February 1838. p.17, c2.

3038 CHARLES F. MITCHELL *to* **THE** *NEW YORK AMERICAN***. 1 January 1838. Washington.** States that he opposed Mr. Patton's resolution "abolishing" the right of petition, but was not present to vote against it, as he was out of the city and confined due to "severe indisposition." 2 February 1838. p.18, c1.

3039 L. T. *to* **W. L. GARRISON. 23 January 1838. New York.** Reports on new book in press, *The Narrative of James Williams—alias W. Jones*, written "from the lips of the hero of the story" by J. G. Whittier; adds that Williams is a fugitive slave who seeks freedom in Great Britain. 2 February 1838. p.18, c3.

3040 EDMUND C. JENKINS, SECRETARY *to* **W. L. GARRISON. 24 January 1838. West Amesbury.** Lists officers of West Amesbury AS; quotes resolutions passed supporting right of petition, denouncing the outrage at Alton, and mourning Lovejoy's death. 2 February 1838. p.18, c4.

3041 L. WAKEFIELD *to* **W. L. GARRISON. 23 December 1837. Reading.** Reports officers elected at 13 December meeting. 2 February 1838. p.18, c4.

3042 S. M. STANLEY *to* **W. L. GARRISON. 23 January 1838. West Attleborough.** Reports formation of West Attleborough AS with seventeen members; lists officers; declares their membership is increasing rapidly. 2 February 1838. p.18, c4.

3043 ETHAN DAVIS *to* **MR. EDITOR [W. L. GARRISON]. 23 January 1838. Holden.** Lists officers of Holden AS elected at annual meeting. 2 February 1838. p.18, c4.

3044 X. *to* **W. L. GARRISON. n.d. n.p.** Reports that a friend who recently attended concert of prayer for the enslaved at Marlboro Chapel was shocked at the irreverent conduct of the audience, which applauded the speaker. 2 February 1838. p.18, c4.

3045 SARAH M. GRIMKE *to* **SISTER. 6 September 1837. Concord.** Discusses the legal disabilities of woman, which rob her of her independence and essential rights; argues women have no political existence; discusses differences in property laws for men and women, comparing laws relating to women to those relating to slaves. 2 February 1838. p.20, c2.

3046 SARAH M. GRIMKE *to* **SISTER. 6 September 1837. Brookline.** Discusses relationship of husband and wife, expressing astonishment at the servitude of women; finds somewhat less bondage of mind among poorer classes; asserts the Bible supports equality between the sexes. 2 February 1838. p.20, c4.

3047 HON. CHIEF JUSTICE WARD *to* **A COMMITTEE OF GENTLEMEN. [extract from the** *Boston Courier***] n.d. n.p.** Declares he is "firmly and inflexibly, in all events, opposed to the admission of Texas into the Union" as a slave state; the doctrine of slavery is one against which "religion, justice and the feelings of humanity revolt"; discusses relation between states, adoption of constitution, and its effect on slavery. 9 February 1838. p.22, c3.

3048 OLIVER JOHNSON *to* **FRIEND GARRISON. n.d. n.p.** Calls attention of abolitionists to a most valuable pamphlet, "A Discourse," by Adin Ballou; states that its chief virtue is that it gives, in compact form, conclusive answers to most common objections to anti-slavery principles and measures. 9 February 1838. p.23, c2.

3049 H. C. WRIGHT *to* **BROTHER GARRISON. 2 February 1838. Providence.** Gives brief sketch of his labors of the past two months; visited Lynn in December, held discussions of the peace principle, then went to Pawtucket, Attleborough, and Seekonk. 9 February 1838. p.23, c2.

3050 n.n. *to* **n.n. [extract] 1 January 1838. Amherst College.** Reports discussions at Amherst College between president, students, and faculty, which resulted in the faculty's approval of an AS and free discussion. 9 February 1838. p.23, c4.

3051 L. G. HAMILTON *to* **W. L. GARRISON. 17 October 1837. Port-au-Prince.** Reports for the Haitian Abolition Society, whose managers and members praise his devotion to the cause of the colored American; believes Garrison will succeed. 9 February 1838. p.23, c5.

3052 MR. ROBERT DOUGLASS, JR. *to* **n.n. [extract] n.d. n.p.** Describes speeches and spectacles at Haitian Independence celebration. 9 February 1838. p.23, c5.

3053 ONE YOUNG MAN OF BOSTON *to* **MR. EDITOR [W. L. GARRISON]. n.d. n.p.** Declares that young men of Boston await a call from Garrison to assemble to protest the congressional gag law. 9 February 1838. p.23, c6.

3054 SARAH M. GRIMKE *to* **SISTER. September 1837. Brookline.** Argues that if man and woman were created equal and with same intellectual powers, they have the same moral duties to preach the riches of Christ; quotes from Bible and history to show that women may preach. 9 February 1838. p.24, c2.

3055 A SUBSCRIBER *to* **MESSRS. HALE AND HALLOCK. 5 January 1838. Humphreysville.** Sends extract from a private letter from Galveston, Texas. 9 February 1838. p.24, c6.

3056 A PASSENGER ON BOARD THE SCHOONER *MOBILE* *to* **n.n. [extract] 18 November 1837. Galveston, Tx.** Describes destruction caused by tornado in Galveston; reports vessels wrecked, crews unable to leave, and food scarce; also reports widespread sickness in Houston, generally among the dissipated. 9 February 1838. p.24, c6.

3057 A PETITIONER *to* **JOHN Q. ADAMS. n.d. n.p.** Writes on the inalienable and sacred right of petition, as slavery is undeniably a "pestiferous disease in our republic"; discusses the question of Congress' power to abolish slavery in the District of Columbia. 16 February 1838. p.25, c2.

3058 A. A. PHELPS *to* **BROTHER LEAVITT. [from the** *Emancipator*] **3 February 1838. Boston.** Discusses recent article in the *Emancipator* on the "Boston Schism," the division of opinion on new anti-slavery organization; clarifies the difference between the "Boston Schism" and the "New Organization"; summarizes arguments and their outcome. 16 February 1838. p.26, c6.

3059 D. C. COLESWORTHY *to* **W. L. GARRISON. 10 February 1838. Portland.** Writes of Mr. Birney's visit there and his speeches; notes much less opposition than the year before. 16 February 1838. p.26, c6.

3060 W. H. BURLEIGH *to* **BROTHER GARRISON. 15 January 1838. Penn's Grove, Chester County, Pa.** Reports he has been welcomed with profound interest, although some places still suffer from "icy apathy"; discusses public debate on colonization in Oxford Village, summarizing arguments. 16 February 1838. p.27, c1.

3061 J. K. BRAGG *to* **W. L. GARRISON. 15 January 1838. Amherst College.** Reports recent formation of AS with fifty to sixty members; relays their resolutions denouncing the system of slavery and supporting immediate emancipation. 16 February 1838. p.27, c3.

3062 H. C. WRIGHT *to* **BROTHER GARRISON. 9 February 1838. Providence.** Reports on debate before the Providence AS on the use of discretionary force and its relation to Christian teachings. 16 February 1838. p.27, c3.

3063 SARAH M. GRIMKE *to* **SISTER. 20 October 1837. Uxbridge.** Believes man and woman are equally guilty for the fall; urges women to investigate equality in the Bible; believes that what is morally right for a man is also morally right for a woman. 16 February 1838. p.28, c2.

3064 A PETITIONER *to* **HON. JOHN Q. ADAMS. n.d. n.p.** Grieves that the petitions against slavery are not heard in Congress; charges that slavery is not a political question, as is shown by the differences of petitioners urging abolition; deprecates the position of women and the family under slavery; claims that Southerners fear that Christian women will unmask their wrongs, therefore they subjugate them. 23 February 1838. p.29, c2.

3065 HAMPDEN *to* **THE HON. DANIEL WEBSTER. [From the** *Herald of Freedom***]** **n.d. n.p.** Hears that W. C. Preston of South Carolina threatened that if an abolitionist came within the borders of the state he would be hanged; wonders why Webster and others remain silent on this unjust, unchristian threat to their constituents. 23 February 1838. p.29, c4.

3066 AN ABOLITIONIST *to* **THE REV. DR. CHANNING. [from the** *Hampshire Republican***] 1 February 1838. Northampton.** Responds to Channing's letter to abolitionists; believes that the remarks in the letter are predicated upon wrong assumptions; charges that Channing makes no discrimination between Lovejoy's acts as an abolitionist and as a defender of Illinois government. 23 February 1838. p.29, c5.

3067 DAVID LEE CHILD *to* **MESSRS. GARRISON AND PHELPS, COMMITTEE OF ARRANGEMENTS. 23 January 1838. Boston.** Regrets he cannot attend the anniversary meeting of the Massachusetts AS; discusses the change which has taken place in Europeans' views of America; the Europeans deplore mobs, slavery, and unfair treatment of abolitionists. 23 February 1838. p.30, c1.

3068 OLIVER JOHNSON *to* **FRIEND GARRISON. 11 February 1838. Providence.** Forwards letter of Gerrit Smith for publication. 23 February 1838. p.30, c2.

3069 GERRIT SMITH *to* **OLIVER JOHNSON. 26 October 1837. Peterboro.** Believes that many men object to the work of the Grimke sisters simply because of vanity and egotism; criticizes attacks on Garrison; believes ministers should not support slavery. 23 February 1838. p.30, c2.

3070 P. H. S. *to* **W. L. GARRISON. 17 February 1838. Boston.** Reports on the meeting of the "Evangelical AS," whose main objection to the present anti-slavery organization is its public denunciation of men who will not grant the use of a house for an anti-slavery meeting; notes that no members joined. 23 February 1838. p.31, c3.

3071 G. BECKLEY *to* **W. L. GARRISON. 8 February 1838. Northfield, Vt.** Praises Garrison and announces that the cause of the oppressed is advancing in every part of Vermont; notes the opposition is not as violent or as large as it formerly was and the "New Organization" has not one friend there. 23 February 1838. p.31, c3.

3072 WILLIAM JACKSON *to* **FRANCIS JACKSON. 11 April 1836. Washington.** Announces Dr. Crandall's acquittal; declares he was very impressed by Dr. Crandall; believes that his alleged crime, distributing abolition tracts, is no violation of the law; reports Crandall was forced to flee capital, however, because of threats on his life. 23 February 1838. p.31, c4.

3073 HENRY GREW *to* **W. L. GARRISON. 5 January 1838. Philadelphia.** Sends article originally designed for publication in the *Spectator*; believes the editor of the *Spectator* grossly misrepresents Garrison's views. 23 February 1838. p.32, c3.

3074 HENRY GREW *to* **BROTHER PORTER. n.d. n.p.** Criticizes the *Spectator*'s attacks on Mr. Garrison; charges that the *Spectator* misrepresents Garrison's views; also discusses the Sinai law. 23 February 1838. p.32, c3.

3075 A PURITAN *to* **MR. EDITOR [W. L. GARRISON]. n.d. n.p.** Discusses objections to the pamphlet "Slavery Illustrated in its Effects Upon Woman and Domestic Society"; explains that the pamphlet does not apply to every individual, as the character and effects of slavery vary widely, but that there is still much evidence to support its charges. 23 February 1838. p.32, c6.

3076 SAMUEL FESSENDEN *to* **W. L. GARRISON. 13 February 1838. Portland.** Points out error in the *Liberator*; explains that the advertisement involved in a libel suit was not printed in the *Liberator*, and that its editor, therefore, is not charged with even inadvertently publishing anything libellous. 2 March 1838. p.35, c3.

3077 M. W. C. *to* **W. L. GARRISON. n.d. n.p.** Grieves that Garrison is ill and confined to his chamber this week; forwards his letter to a friend. 2 March 1838. p.35, c5.

3078 M. W. C. *to* **FRIEND. n.d. n.p.** Describes the pleadings of A. E. Grimke before the legislative committee on slavery; quotes from her discussion of the Florida war; describes the extraordinary effect she had on the audience. 2 March 1838. p.35, c5.

3079 A PETITIONER *to* **JOHN Q. ADAMS. January 1838. Castle of Good Hope.** Argues that if every individual in the republic has the right to petition, as Adams has stated, then surely slaves are entitled to this right; suggests meetings all over the country for slaves and free blacks to petition to end slavery in the District of Columbia. 9 March 1838. p.37, c6.

3080 JOHN FARMER, CORRESPONDING SECRETARY OF NEW HAMPSHIRE AS *to* **ISAAC HILL, GOVERNOR OF NEW HAMPSHIRE. [from the** *Herald of Freedom***] 1 January 1838. Concord.** Inquires, on behalf of the New Hampshire AS, about Hill's views on various questions relating to slavery in the District of Columbia, the right of citizens to petition, the annexation of Texas, and right to jury trial of fugitive slaves. 9 March 1838. p.38, c2.

3081 ISAAC HILL *to* **JOHN FARMER, ESQ. 10 January 1838. Concord.** Replies to Farmer's inquiry concerning various issues related to slavery. 9 March 1838. p.38, c2.

3082 JAMES WILSON, JR. *to* **JOHN FARMER, ESQ. 3 February 1838. Keene.** Replies to Farmer's questions concerning slavery in the District of Columbia, freedom of speech, press, and petition, the annexation of Texas, and the right to jury trial of fugitive slaves. 9 March 1838. p.38, c3.

3083 AN ABOLITIONIST *to* **W. L. GARRISON. 28 February 1838. Hallowell.** Reports that Mr. Codding is lecturing in Maine and collecting many converts to the cause; adds that Codding spoke twice before a joint committee of both branches of the House against the annexation of Texas and the abolition of slavery in the District of Columbia; reports that he is not sure of the reaction to Codding's addresses. 9 March 1838. p.38, c6.

3084 n.n. *to* **W. L. GARRISON. n.d. n.p.** Considers both duelers, Cilley and Graves, to be disgraceful murderers; suggests citizens send a memorial to their congressmen and senators denouncing dueling as a way to uphold honor. 9 March 1838. p.39, c3.

3085 A HEARER *to* **W. L. GARRISON. 28 February 1838. n.p.** Praises Mr. Wendell Phillips' lecture on witchcraft, demonology, and apparitions; believes Mr. Phillips is a philanthropist and an emancipationist in the strictest sense of the words. 9 March 1838. p.39, c3.

3086 n.n *to* **W. L. GARRISON. 28 February 1838. Hartford.** Reports on Connecticut State Anti-Slavery Convention, called to order by Philip Pearl and attended by about 200 delegates; describes disturbance by mob and city council vote to adjourn to another building. 9 March 1838. p.39, c5.

3087 OLIVER JOHNSON *to* **THE ABOLITIONISTS OF RHODE ISLAND. 7 March 1838. Providence.** Announces special meeting of Rhode Island AS at which Ballou and St. Claire will be speakers. 9 March 1838. p.39, c6.

3088 H. C. WRIGHT *to* **W. L. GARRISON. 17 February 1838. Pawtucket.** Reports discussion before a biblical society in Providence of whether men can be justified by Christian principles in sustaining civil laws which might involve physical force in their execution. 9 March 1838. p.40, c2.

3089 H. C. WRIGHT *to* **BROTHER GARRISON. 2 November 1837. Philadelphia.** Discusses moral means by which parents may bring the souls of children into perfect submission to divine will. 9 March 1838. p.40, c3.

3090 GERRIT SMITH *to* **REUBEN PALMER. 12 January 1838. Peterboro.** Regrets that the doors of the meetinghouse were closed to Palmer and his friends for their religious meeting; disagrees with some of their views, but believes nevertheless they have the right to meet. 9 March 1838. p.40, c5.

3091 S. H. WEED *to* **BROTHER GARRISON. 1 January 1838. Philadelphia.** Reports that recently his life was in jeopardy in Maryland; states that he was arrested because a slaveholding Methodist minister, who had feigned abolitionist sympathies, charged Weed with inciting discontent among slaves; adds that he was acquitted and escaped. 16 March 1838. p.42, c4.

3092 MARIA W. CHAPMAN *to* **BROTHER GARRISON. n.d. n.p.** Sends article from the *London True Sun,* which she believes will strengthen and encourage women in America; reminds of the Philadelphia convention coming in May. 16 March 1838. p.42, c4.

3093 H. BOWLAND *to* **W. L. GARRISON. 9 February 1838. Norway Village, Me.** Expresses his acknowledgment and thanks to the Salem Golden Rule Association for making him a life member of the New York Moral Reform Society. 16 March 1838. p.43, c3.

3094 JAMES BOYLE *to* **W. L. GARRISON. n.d. Rome, Ashtabula County, Oh.** Praises Garrison and his devotion to the cause of humanity; expresses surprise that the "clerical abolitionists" object to Garrison's opinions on the Sabbath; compares justifications of slavery to justifications of sin and objections to spiritual freedom. 23 March 1838. p.45, c1.

3095 H. C. WRIGHT *to* **BROTHER GARRISON. 13 March 1838. North Marshfield.** Discusses the duel in which Graves killed Cilley; charges that all who countenance duelling countenance murder, as duelling takes life without commission from God, the author of life; urges more to speak up for peace and abolition. 23 March 1838. p.46, c2.

3096 OLIVER JOHNSON *to* **W. L. GARRISON. 18 March 1838. Providence.** Discusses President Wayland's late work, "The Limitations of Human Responsibility," addressing the sections on voluntary and ecclesiastical associations; shows that Wayland's arguments against voluntary associations apply "with ten-fold force" to the Church. 23 March 1838. p.46, c3.

3097 HAMPDEN *to* **MR. EDITOR [W. L. GARRISON]. n.d. n.p.** Urges abolitionists to steer clear of all political parties; declares all benefit of mingling with them is temporary and delusive, and that they must work only with truth and win the support of the people; praises the narrative of James Williams, a true illustration of slavery. 23 March 1838. p.46, c4.

3098 W. H. BURLEIGH *to* **W. L. GARRISON. 2 March 1837. Penn's Grove, Chester County, Pa.** Reports many believe he is presumptuous and wicked because he criticized two colonization clergymen; deplores the coarse, crude, extremely vulgar language which these ministers used against him, and the wicked spirit of colonization. 23 March 1838. p.46, c4.

3099 O. P. BACON *to* **BROTHER GARRISON. n.d. n.p.** Refutes assertion found in last *New England Spectator*, concerning Garrison's remarks about the Norfolk County AS. 23 March 1838. p.46, c6.

3100 E. A., AN INTELLIGENT AND PHILANTHROPIC LADY *to* **A MEMBER OF THE LEGISLATURE. [extract] 10 March 1838. Westfield.** Suggests purchase of Miss Sarah M. Grimke's pamphlet containing her letters on the rights of women; hopes the world is being enlightened on this important subject; feels women have been regarded as inferior beings for too long. 23 March 1838. p.46, c6.

3101 A FRIEND TO THE SLAVE *to* **MISS GRIMKE. 13 March 1838. Boston.** Relates that, although he was born on a plantation and educated to believe the colored person his slave, he hesitated to accept this doctrine; believes that not only are those who take slaves sinners, but also those who keep them; reports he has freed all his slaves. 23 March 1838. p.47, c1.

3102 n.n. *to* **n.n. [extract] n.d. Providence.** Reports the cause is progressing in Providence; notes the good response to Friend Johnson's address as proof that a spirit of inquiry has awakened in the public mind. 23 March 1838. p47, c1.

3103 W. L. GARRISON *to* **FRIEND. 14 August 1837. Brooklyn.** Affirms there is a better life, and God is preparing it. 23 March 1838. p.48, c1.

3104 CHARLES L. *to* **BROTHER GOODELL. [from the** *Friend of Man***] n.d. n.p.** Describes an interview he attended between John Q. Adams and an abolitionist woman; quotes the "noble words" of Adams, who believes elected leaders must be men of prayer and piety, and who oppose the annexation of Texas; reports other occurrences in his trip to the capital. 30 March 1838. p.50, c4.

3105 S. B. *to* **BROTHER GARRISON. n.d. n.p.** Sends copy of letter she wrote to a gentleman on the rights of women; notes she has often had to quit her work for the slave to contend for the rights of herself and other females. 30 March 1838. p.51, c1.

3106 S. B. *to* **A GENTLEMAN. n.d. n.p.** Replies to his inquiries on her views on the rights of women; believes women were created to help men, but not to be ruled over against their consent; believes God gave no intimation that woman is man's inferior; believes women have the right and the duty to lecture and preach moral reform. 30 March 1838. p.51, c1.

3107 THOMAS CLARKSON *to* **P. T. LONG, ESQ. [from the** *British Emancipator***]** **12 January 1838. Playford Hall.** Regrets he cannot attend their meeting; explains his unfit physical condition which has confined him to home for two years; believes Parliament should shorten the contract time of apprentices because masters are still grossly mistreating their former slaves. 30 March 1838. p.51, c3.

3108 ANTI-SLAVERY FRIEND *to* **n.n. [extract] n.d. Worcester.** Reports outrage committed against the brother of the late Lovejoy, who had been at Alton to settle his brother's business; passengers on steamboat from Illinois threatened to throw him overboard and commandeer the boat; captain was forced to put Lovejoy ashore. 30 March 1838. p.51, c6.

3109 HUBBARD WINSLOW *to* **MR. SLEEPER. [from the** *Boston Mercantile Journal***]** **n.d. n.p.** States that his sermon, published in the *Journal*, was well-received by all except abolitionists, who he believes misapprehend and misrepresent him; writes not to defend his views, but simply to state them: he is completely against slavery, but does not believe Northerners have the right to meddle with peculiar institutions of the South. 6 April 1838. p.53, c1.

3110 n.n. *to* **THE** *NEW HAMPSHIRE OBSERVER***. n.d. n.p.** Complains that although public opinion has been excited by the death of a member of Congress in a duel, and the public presses speak freely of the tragedy, few of them have commented on the murder of Lovejoy; discusses the "folly and inconsistency" of these responses, and the corruption of the press. 6 April 1838. p.53, c6.

3111 n.n. *to* **n.n. [extract] 20 March 1838. Washington City.** Reports that they received several remonstrances from the ladies against duelling; ladies are alive to the interests and honor of the male sex, and without them the world would be dreary, anguished. 6 April 1838. p.54, c1.

3112 I. *to* **MR. EDITOR [W. L. GARRISON]. 31 March 1838. Hingham.** Notes that great obstacles to the cause of abolition in Hingham are ignorance and prejudice; citizens do not want to believe that they are also responsible for slavery; reports on Mr. Phillips' two visits in Hingham. 6 April 1838. p.54, c6.

3113 H. C. WRIGHT *to* **BROTHER GARRISON. 13 March 1838. North Marshfield.** Relates dialogue between Dr. Johnson and Mrs. W. Knowles; remarks on Johnson's views of women, the responsibilities of nations, and Quakers. 6 April 1838. p.55, c1.

3114 C. *to* **W. L. GARRISON. n.d. n.p.** Forwards article which was sent to the office of the *Times* but not printed. 6 April 1838. p.55, c2.

3115 COSMOPOLITE *to* **THE** *TIMES***. 5 March 1838. Boston.** Asserts that the famous petition from the "females in Rehoboth" was not a burlesque; the ladies believe that in non-slaveholding states, people are denied civil rights because of color. 6 April 1838. p.55, c2.

3116 PRESIDENTS OF THE NEW ENGLAND AS *to* **n.n. n.d. n.p.** Urge attendance at the society's convention. 6 April 1838. p.55, c6.

3117 GERRIT SMITH *to* **ELDER RAY POTTER. 5 March 1837. Peterboro.** Reminds that Christ loves best not he who has erred least, but he who has the most penitent heart. 6 April 1838. p.56, c3.

3118 THOMAS SHORE, P. M. *to* **GENERAL PEGRAM. 8 February 1838. Post Office. Petersburgh.** Asks Pegram to peruse the article "A Presbyterian, on Bible Slavery"; believes it is an incendiary publication and ought to be suppressed; solicits Pegram's opinion. 13 April 1838. p.57, c1.

3119 J. W. PEGRAM *to* **T. SHORE, P.M. 9 February 1838. Petersburgh.** Reports he has carefully examined the article sent to him by Shore; explains the act of assembly in reference to material inciting persons of color to insurrection; in his opinion, the article is clearly of that incendiary nature and should be suppressed. 13 April 1838. p.57, c1.

3120 C. W. *to* **MR. EDITOR [W. L. GARRISON]. n.d. n.p.** Relates a dialogue which he lately heard between Miss M. and Mr. W. on abolitionists. 13 April 1838. p.58, c4.

3121 NEWBURY *to* **MR. EDITOR [W. L. GARRISON]. n.d. n.p.** Describes speech of H. C. Wright explaining that no slaveholders can be Christians, and that the essential sin of slavery was in making a man into property; reports on abortive attempts to break up the meeting with loud speakers. 13 April 1838. p.58, c4.

3122 RHO. *to* **MR. EDITOR [W. L. GARRISON]. 8 March 1838. Foxboro.** Declares he has for many years been opposed to all types of war except defensive; this kind is justifiable, as it maintains good order and individuals' just rights, and is not fought in a spirit of revenge. 13 April 1838. p.58, c6.

3123 JESPER BEMENT *to* **W. L. GARRISON. 10 January 1838. Ashfield.** Criticizes Miss Grimke's letter; disagrees with the doctrine of non-resistance, which Grimke upholds in criticizing Mrs. Lovejoy for striking men who attacked her husband. 13 April 1838. p.59, c1.

3124 C. C. NICHOLS *to* **W. L. GARRISON. 2 April 1838. Assonett Village, Freetown.** Reports formation of Freetown AS; lists officers. 13 April 1838. p.59, c1.

3125 H. C. WRIGHT *to* **BROTHER GARRISON. n.d. n.p.** Refutes charges that the causes of peace and abolition oppose family, civil governments, and the Church. 13 April 1838. p.60, c2.

3126 J. M. MCKIM *to* **n.n. [from the** *Emancipator***] 6 February 1838. Washington, D.C.** Describes rude and profane Southern "gentleman"; reports sad scene of slave purchases; describes slave factory. 13 April 1838. p.60, c3.

3127 HENRY W. DUCACHET *to* **MESSRS. W. H. SCOTT, ISAAC PARRISH, W. HARNED, DANIEL NEAL, AND PETER WRIGHT, EASTERN EXECUTIVE COMMITTEE. 2 April 1838. Philadelphia.** Returns their "Address of the AS to the Ministers of the Gospel in the State of Pennsylvania"; believes they have no right to issue such a paper; believes they perverted the Scriptures; criticizes and refutes their arguments. 20 April 1838. p.61, c1.

3128 N. CANNON, GOVERNOR OF TENNESSEE *to* **MR. JAS. G. BIRNEY. 12 December 1837. Nashville.** Declares that his own opinions are "fix'd and settled"; seldom examines the vague notions of others, so he will not examine Birney's anti-slavery material; declares slaves enjoy better care than some in the North. 20 April 1838. p.61, c2.

3129 J. M. MCKIM *to* **REV. JOSHUA LEAVITT. 14 February 1838. Pittsburgh, Pa.** Discusses his visit to the capital city and the slave prison; relates his conversation with the jail keeper; feels a strengthened conviction that no man can fully understand the horrors of slavery. 20 April 1838. p.61, c3.

3130 C. C. *to* **H. C. WRIGHT. n.d. n.p.** Questions Wright's application of the peace principle in the following case; if two boys are earnestly fighting, may the father separate them by physical force? 20 April 1838. p.63, c3.

3131 A LADY IN CONCORD *to* **HER FRIEND IN BOSTON. 12 April 1838. Concord.** Discusses the final days of Joseph Kimball, who died the previous day; declares he was dedicated to the cause of the oppressed until the end. 20 April 1838. p.63, c4.

3132 n.n. *to* **MESSRS. EDITORS. [from the** *Newburyport Herald*] **n.d. n.p.** Disagrees with article entitled "Mob in West Newbury" which appeared in their paper. 27 April 1838. p.65, c1.

3133 JOHN Q. ADAMS, JOHN REED, LEVI LINCOLN, C. CUSHING, W.B. CALHOUN, RICHARD FLETCHER, S. C. PHILLIPS, GEO. GRENNELL, JR., AND W. S. HASTINGS *to* **HON. JAMES C. ALVORD. 22 March 1838. Washington.** Report that the House has effectually enjoined silence upon interdicted topics and has refused to remove the injunction by a large and resolute majority; signers protest this breach of freedom. 27 April 1838. p.65, c2.

3134 J. W. HINTON, W. H. MURCH, JOSEPH BELCHER, AND EDWARD STEANE *to* **THE MINISTERS AND MEMBERS OF BAPTIST CHURCHES IN THE UNITED STATES. 19 January 1838. London.** Members of the Baptist Union of Great Britain discuss the horrors of slavery, urging the Americans to emancipate the slaves; suggest that the church's power be consecrated to "this noble and godlike service." 27 April 1838. p.65, c4.

3135 n.n. *to* **n.n. 16 April 1838. Hingham.** Sends report on the speeches of Dr. Poyen on animal magnetism and slavery; Dr. Poyen is opposed to immediate emancipation and describes Africans in their homeland as more like brutes than men; he also charges that the abolition movement is not a philanthropic, but a party movement. 27 April 1838. p.65, c6.

3136 H. C. WRIGHT *to* **C. C. n.d. n.p.** Replies to C. C.'s questions of whether the application of the non-enforcing principle would allow a father to separate two fighting sons; fails to see how the non-enforcing principle has anything to do with it, as it relates only to what is discretionary power over liberty and life. 27 April 1838. p.66, c1.

3137 DAVID CAMPBELL *to* **FRIEND GARRISON. 23 April 1838. Leverett Street Jail, Boston.** Reports he is in jail again for the neglect of military duty; compares his unfair incarceration to that of the slave; believes that we must renounce war, or renounce Christianity. 27 April 1838. p.66, c2.

3138 W. HARLOW *to* **W. L. GARRISON. 18 April 1836. Wrentham.** Forwards resolutions passed at last meeting of Wrentham AS for publication. 27 April 1838. p.66, c3.

3139 CELIA *to* **W. L. GARRISON. 7 April 1838. Haverhill.** Reports her discussion with a friend who believes that New Englanders who receive money from slave products must either renounce them or be as guilty as Southerners. 27 April 1838. p.66, c3.

3140 n.n. *to* **W. L. GARRISON. n.d. n.p.** Finds publication, "Mr. Allen's speech before the Convention of Ministers of Worcester County," an "eloquent and timely production"; recommends it to every minister and citizen. 27 April 1838. p.67, c5.

3141 A LADY IN MAINE *to* **n.n. [extract] n.d. n.p.** Reports that the labors of Messrs. Birney and Codding have awakened interest in Maine, which she trusts "will never subside until our work is done." 27 April 1838. p.67, c5.

3142 OLIVER JOHNSON, CORRES. SEC., RHODE ISLAND AS *to* **MR. EDITOR [W. L. GARRISON]. 9 April 1838. Providence.** Sends correspondence between the secretary of the Rhode Island AS and the Hon. Messrs. Sprague and Childs. 27 April 1838. p.68, c2.

3143 W. SPRAGUE *to* **OLIVER JOHNSON. 28 March 1838. Warwick.** Replies to questions; believes Congress has the right to abolish slavery in the District of Columbia, and to suppress the slave trade between the the states; supports the right to petition and freedom of press and speech; opposes annexation of Texas. 27 April 1838. p.68, c2.

3144 JOSEPH CHILDS *to* **OLIVER JOHNSON. 26 March 1838. Portsmouth.** Replies to questions: believes Congress has the right to abolish slavery in the District of Columbia and to stop the slave trade between the states; opposes annexing Texas; supports right to petition and freedom of press and speech. 27 April 1838. p.68, c2.

3145 JOSEPH CHILDS *to* **OLIVER JOHNSON. 5 April 1838. Portsmouth.** Replies to another question; as citizens of one state are not permitted to hold a human being in slavery, he sees no excuse for allowing citizens of another state to violate that principle of natural right. 27 April 1838. p.68, c3.

3146 AN ENGLISH CORRESPONDENT *to* **THE** *NEW YORK EVANGELIST.* **[extract] n.d. n.p.** Argues that the scene in the American Congress in December was "unworthy of them as a Christian and a free People"; to declare that petitions related to abolition of slavery should be laid on the table is evidence of the "corrupting and debasing influence" of slavery. 4 May 1838. p.70, c3.

3147 P. NOYES *to* **W. L. GARRISON. 27 April 1838. Putney, Vt.** As many women used to earn money braiding the palm leaf for men's hats, suggests its use in ladies' hats also; feels women need the work, and some of the money would certainly go to charity; urges industry, not idleness. 4 May 1838. p.71, c1.

3148 N. *to* **n.n. 23 April 1838. New Haven.** Replies that he knew James Boyle well while he lived in New Haven, and refutes charges that Boyle had several wives; also discusses H. C. Wright and non-resistance. 4 May 1838. p.71, c2.

3149 A. ST. CLAIR *to* **BROTHER GARRISON. n.d. n.p.** Inquires about the truth of a report that Garrison was once defeated in election for secretary of the ACS, after which he abandoned colonization and became opposed to the society. 4 May 1838. p.71, c2.

3150 A FRIEND *to* **W. L. GARRISON. 4 January 1838. n.p.** Praises the latest prospectus of the *Liberator* and the course it will follow; reports he once followed the CS, but realized it would never end slavery; supports the rights of women and immediate emancipation. 4 May 1838. p.71, c2.

3151 A SEEKER AFTER TRUTH *to* **MR. EDITOR [W. L. GARRISON]. n.d. n.p.** Reports he attended the anti-duelling lecture and was disappointed by so many who mocked the discussion; notes that the pro-slavists used arguments to defend duelling very similar to their defense of slavery. 4 May 1838. p.71, c4.

3152 EDWARD EVERETT *to* **EDMUND QUINCY, ESQ. [from the** *Boston Daily Advertiser***] 26 April 1838. Boston.** Found the narrative of Messrs. Thome and Kimball describing their tour of the West Indies very interesting and informative; believes the success of abolition there gives hope that a similar project would bless the United States. 4 May 1838. p.71, c5.

3153 A. F. MANN *to* **LA ROY SUNDERLAND. [from the** *Zion's Watchman***] 19 March 1838. Dusplin, N.C.** Urges Sunderland to tend to the objects of charity in the North, for if abolitionists refuse to let Southern institutions alone, all communication between North and South will soon stop. 11 May 1838. p.73, c1.

3154 O. A. BROWNSON *to* **W. L. GARRISON. [from the** *Boston Reformer***] 14 April 1838. Mount Bellingham.** Complains of the injustice that Garrison has done to him and the *Boston Quarterly Review*; claims that Garrison has denounced him harshly without specific charges; believes himself a tireless worker for reform and emancipation. 11 May 1838. p.73, c2.

3155 W. B. SHEAD *to* **THE** *ZION'S WATCHMAN*. **n.d. n.p.** Hopes the Union will be dissolved, so that they can be free of the burden of the North. 11 May 1838. p.74, c4.

3156 HANSON L. KNOWLES AND W. A. CLAPP *to* **MR. EDITOR [W. L. GARRISON]. n.d. n.p.** Announce formation of AS in Saxonville; list officers. 11 May 1838. p.74, c6.

3157 C. P. GROSVENOR *to* **BROTHER GARRISON. 1 May 1838. Rutland, Ma.** Reports that the Rutland AS condemns the course pursued by the House of Representatives in laying all abolition petitions on the table, and praises several men who spoke against the resolution. 11 May 1838. p.74, c6.

3158 FRANCIS PIZARRO MARTINEZ *to* **THE HON. JOHN FORSYTH, SECRETARY OF STATE OF THE UNITED STATES. 20 April 1838. New Orleans.** Sends official statement regarding Mexican behavior toward the steamboat *Columbia*, and her passengers' charges against the Mexican brig of war, *Iturbide*. 11 May 1838. p.75, c2.

3159 n.n. *to* **THE** *LOUISVILLE JOURNAL*. **n.d. n.p.** Reports on explosion of the steamer *Oronko*, which burst one of her boilers after leaving Princeton, Mississippi; many passengers were killed or very badly scalded; the *Peru*, the *North Albany*, and the *Independence* promptly answered the distress call. 11 May 1838. p.75, c3.

3160 G. *to* **KNAPP. n.d. New York.** Describes anniversary meeting of the AAS in New York; the meeting was opened with prayer; Scriptures were read; speeches and reports were given. 11 May 1838. p.75, c4.

3161 H. R. HITCHCOCK *to* **THE** *EMANCIPATOR*. **18 November 1837. Kaluaaha, Sandwich Islands.** Writes not to encourage, but because he believes all should take a stand in favor of those working to crush slavery; describes work of his mission on the island of Molohai; declares he supports immediate emancipation. 18 May 1838. p.78, c6.

3162 THOS. P. RYDER *to* **BRO. GARRISON. 23 April 1838. East Bridgewater.** Reports formation of female AS of twenty-five members; lists officers. 18 May 1838. p.79, c5.

3163 C. C. *to* **THE** *PROVIDENCE JOURNAL*. **n.d. n.p.** Describes usually painful surgical operation, performed on Mrs. Carr while she was under the influence of animal magnetism; she withstood the operation in a composed and painless state, although she said she was conscious of everything happening. 18 May 1838. p.80, c3.

3164 n.n. *to* **MR. HOWE. 28 March 1838. Her Majesty's Ship,** *Hercules,* **Halifax Harbor.** Tells of noble conduct of American ship *Commerce,* commanded by Capt. Perry, which rescued the entire crew of the wrecked ship *Elizabeth Caroline.* 18 May 1838. p.80, c5.

3165 FRANKLIN *to* **THE SENATOR WHO THREATENED ABOLITIONISTS WITH HANGING. [from the** *Herald of Freedom*] **n.d. n.p.** Declares the senator could not have done anything more effectually to advance the cause of equal rights or the abolition of slavery; his threat betrays the devil's inspiration of slavery and its complete defiance of law and order. 25 May 1838. p.81, c3.

3166 A LADY OF BOSTON, NOW IN PHILADELPHIA *to* **n.n. [extract] 18 May 1838. Philadelphia.** Describes mob attack on Philadelphia Hall during women's convention, after which the mob burned the hall. 25 May 1838. p.82, c5.

3167 H. C. WRIGHT *to* **BROTHER GARRISON. 18 May 1838. Philadelphia.** Condemns mob which burned Philadephia Hall; declares the cause is a deep-rooted hatred of the oppressed brethren, fostered by the ACS. 25 May 1838. p.83, c4.

3168 H. C. WRIGHT *to* **BROTHER GARRISON. 18 May 1838. n.p.** Reports infamous conduct of John Swift, mayor of Philadelphia; declares his speech spurred the mob on; calls Swift the "Cowardly King of Mobocrats." 25 May 1838. p.83, c4.

3169 E. BEECHER *to* **THE CHAIRMAN OF THE COMMITTEE OF ARRANGEMENTS. [extract] 11 March 1838. Illinois College.** Regrets that his duties will not allow him to come East to the convention; hopes the nation arises from its lethargy on the subject. 1 June 1838. p.85, c1.

3170 F. JULIUS LEMOYNE *to* **LEWIS TAPPAN. 27 February 1838. Washington, Pa.** Regrets he must decline the invitation to attend the anti-slavery convention; sends his sincere desires and prayers for a successful meeting. 1 June 1838. p.85, c1.

3171 JOHN Q. ADAMS *to* **LEWIS TAPPAN. 7 April 1838. Washington.** Expresses appreciation of the invitation to the AAS convention, but reports he is not free to leave while Congress is in session. 1 June 1838. p.85, c2.

3172 n.n. *to* **THE** *PENNSYLVANIA FREEMAN.* **20 May 1838. Washington, D.C.** Sends congratulations upon the late outrage of the Philadelphia mob, which has done more for the cause of freedom in one day than has been done in ages. 1 June 1838. p.86, c4.

3173 JEFFERSON *to* **THE EDITOR OF THE** *LIBERATOR* **[W. L. GARRISON]. n.d. n.p.** Notices that there are to be no meetings of the New England AS convention at night; hopes this is not due to fear of mobs. 1 June 1838. p.87, c2.

3174 FRANCIS JACKSON, AMASA WALKER, SAMUEL E. SEWALL, EDMUND JACKSON, EDMUND QUINCY, W. L. GARRISON, ELLIS GRAY LORING, GEO. JACKSON, JAMES C. WHITE, WENDELL PHILLIPS, GAMALIEL BRADFORD, AND PEREZ GILL *to* **THE MAYOR AND ALDERMEN. 25 May 1838. Boston.** Write on behalf of committee of 124 legal voters; protest refusal of the use of Faneuil Hall for anti-slavery meeting. 1 June 1838. p.87, c3.

3175 H. C. WRIGHT *to* **BROTHER GARRISON. 19 May 1838. Philadelphia.** Declares Philadelphia is still under control of the mob, which has stoned several buildings and burned the new shelter for colored orphans; charges the civil authorities "may be termed the mob." 1 June 1838. p.87, c4.

3176 H. C. WRIGHT *to* **BROTHER GARRISON. 20 May 1838. Philadelphia.** Reports the city is still in the hands of the mob, although threats have been more numerous and bloody than deeds; criticizes the mayor, who has not, in four days of rioting, called out the military and restored order. 1 June 1838. p.87, c4.

3177 BARBADOES *to* **A COMMERCIAL HOUSE IN NEW HAVEN. 30 April 1838. n.p.** Reports that the prospect that the apprenticed slaves will be made free on 1 August is now definite, over which the apprentices have expressed joy and congratulations. 1 June 1838. p.87, c6.

3178 FRANCIS JAMES *to* **SAMUEL WEBB AND W. H. SCOTT. 22 December 1837. Harrisburg.** Declines the invitation from the managers of the Pennsylvania Hall Association, although he has kind feelings for their objects; affirms his support of freedom of speech. 1 June 1838. p.88, c2.

3179 GERRIT SMITH *to* **MESSRS. S. WEBB AND W. H. SCOTT. 26 December 1837. Peterboro.** Rejoices in the noble enterprise of the stockholders and builders of Pennsylvania Hall; hopes it stands long to testify to human rights; regrets he cannot be present to deliver an address on its opening. 1 June 1838. p.88, c2.

3180 THADDEUS STEVENS *to* **SAMUEL WEBB AND OTHERS, COMMITTEE. 4 May 1838. Gettysburg.** Regrets he cannot be with them at the opening of Pennsylvania Hall, although he fully and joyously supports its stand for free discussion. 1 June 1838. p.88, c2.

3181 THEODORE D. WELD *to* **MESSRS. S. WEBB AND W. H SCOTT. 3 January 1838. New York.** Thanks them for their invitation to address the opening of Pennsylvania Hall, but states he cannot speak in public due to an affliction of the throat. 1 June 1838. p.88, c2.

3182 JOHN Q. ADAMS *to* **SAMUEL WEBB AND W. H. SCOTT. 19 January 1838. Washington.** Lauds the building of Pennsylvania Hall as a place where liberty and civil rights can be discussed; rejoices that Philadelphia supports freedom of speech. 1 June 1838. p.88, c3.

3183 NATHAN S. S. BEMAN *to* **FRIENDS. 8 January 1838. Troy, N.Y.** Supports the erection of Pennsylvania Hall for free discussion of liberty and civil rights; accepts their kind invitation to speak at its opening. 1 June 1838. p.88, c3.

3184 NATHAN S. S. BEMAN *to* **FRIENDS. 12 April 1838. Troy, N.Y.** Reports his health has been impaired since February, and he will not be able to speak at the opening of Pennsylvania Hall after all; sends his encouragement. 1 June 1838. p.88, c3.

3185 DAVID PAUL BROWN *to* **S. WEBB AND W. H. SCOTT. 25 December 1837. n.p.** Accepts their invitation to give a dedication address at the opening of Pennsylvania Hall. 1 June 1838. p.88, c4.

3186 X. *to* **THE** *PHILADELPHIA DAILY FOCUS.* **n.d. n.p.** Declares that a mob is "a natural and indispensable portion of the machinery of a republic"; wonders why those "pernicious fanatics," abolitionists, have the right to disturb the tranquility of the country; feels abolitionists threaten the peace and the very existence of the Union, and that mobocracy is better than abolitionism. 8 June 1838. p.89, c1.

3187 JOHN FORSYTH *to* **THE PRESIDENT OF THE UNITED STATES. 31 May 1838. Washington.** Requests that the president communicate to the House of Representatives any correspondence between the government and the Republic of Texas, relating to the annexation of Texas. 8 June 1838. p.91, c4.

3188 G. W. B. *to* **J. G. BIRNEY, ESQ. 29 May 1838. New Haven.** States that the General Assembly has adopted resolutions protesting Patton's gag order in Congress and vindicating right of petition. 8 June 1838. p.91, c4.

3189 T. D. PEURIFOY [SUPERINTENDENT OF THE ALACHUA MISSION, ON THE TALLAHASSEE DISTRICT] *to* **BR. CAPERS. n.d. n.p.** Describes the murder of his family by Florida Indians. 8 June 1838. p.92, c4.

3190 A. *to* **SIR. 17 May 1838. Philadelphia.** Discusses abolition and the Pennsylvania Hall, the temple erected to the cause of amalgamation; describes whites and blacks walking arm in arm from the meetings there; criticizes the people of Philadelphia for allowing this. 15 June 1838. p.93, c1.

3191 A. *to* **MR. JONES. 17 May 1838. Philadelphia.** Retracts his criticism of the people of Philadelphia; reports he joined in the burning of Pennsylvania Hall, the abolitionists' "castle of iniquity." 15 June 1838. p.93, c1.

3192 H. C. WRIGHT *to* **BROTHER GARRSON. 7 June 1838. Reading.** Reports discussions in Reading on the use of violence and self-defense; favors abolition of the military, a "legalized ruffian and assasin"; declares military spirit is at a low ebb in Reading. 15 June 1838. p.94, c3.

3193 AMASA WALKER *to* **GARRISON. n.d. n.p.** Explains that he withdrew his resolution praising George Thompson at the New England Anti-Slavery Convention because a gentleman vigorously protested, and Walker wished to uphold the harmony and peace of the convention. 15 June 1838. p.94, c3.

3194 C. C. B. *to* **BROTHER GARRISON. n.d. n.p.** Forwards "dying testimony" to James Nayler, from Sewell's *History of the Quakers,* to Garrison and his readers. 15 June 1838. p.94, c4.

3195 WM. GOODELL *to* **REV. A. A. PHELPS. 26 May 1838. Utica.** Regrets he cannot attend the Fifth New England Anti-Slavery Convention; rejoices in the progress they have made so far; yet reminds that the lash still falls on the slaves' backs. 15 June 1838. p.94, c5.

3196 A FRIEND OF TRUTH *to* **THE EDITOR OF THE [ELLSWORTH, ME.]** *NORTHERN STATESMAN.* **n.d. n.p.** Objects to editor's treatment of the Mount Desert AS, which has exerted a good influence in behalf of the oppressed. 15 June 1838. p.94, c6.

3197 RALPH WALDO EMERSON *to* **MARTIN VAN BUREN, PRESIDENT OF THE UNITED STATES. 23 April 1838. Concord, Ma.** Calls his attention to the plight of the Cherokee Indians and their efforts at self-improvement; asks for correct information on December 1835 treaty giving up Cherokee land, as the papers claim that the Indian deputies did not represent the will of the nation. 22 June 1838. p.98, c1.

3198 PHEBE *to* **AMOS A. PHELPS. n.d. n.p.** Asks Phelps about the propriety of attendance by men and women at the same meetings and of speeches by women at meetings. 22 June 1838. p.98, c5.

3199 LEWIS TAPPAN *to* **MR. EDITOR [W. L. GARRISON]. 15 June 1838. New York.** Corrects report of an interview between himself and the vice-president: the latter wished to get a fugitive slave back at any cost, and therefore offered to emancipate him, but refused to accept the emancipation deed Tappan prepared. 22 June 1838. p.98, c5.

3200 A SLAVEHOLDER *to* **A LADY IN WORCESTER. 18 January 1838. Macon.** Suggests that she and the others of her "fair body" send a delegation to examine the slave trade as it now exists in the South before they transcend the limits of their domestic duties and meddle with slavery. 22 June 1838. p.98, c6.

3201 WILLIAM SLADE *to* **FRANCIS JACKSON, ESQ. n.d. n.p.** Apologizes for the delay in replying to Jackson; explains that health and duties prevent his commenting on the resolutions of the Massachusetts AS; he will work to advance their cause. 22 June 1838. p.99, c1.

3202 A. W. HANSON *to* **MR. EDITOR. 15 June 1838. Boston.** Corrects an error in the recording of the salary paid him by Mr. Brookhouse. 22 June 1838. p.99, c6.

3203 SIMPLEX VERITAS *to* **BROTHER JOHNSON. 18 June 1838. Brunswick, Me.** Reports "invidious remarks" about abolitionism made in a speech by Rev. N.H. Harding of North Carolina; criticizes Harding, a former abolitionist, for his inconstant support. 29 June 1838. p.102, c4.

3204 STEPHEN NICHOLS, WARREN DUREN, AND SETH WYMAN *to* **MESSRS. BROWN, RICHARD, AND EAGER. 8 June 1838. Woburn.** Representatives from a Universalist meetinghouse refuse its use to anti-slavery members, declaring they would rather see it burn. 29 June 1838. p.103, c3.

3205 A.A.P. *to* **ABOLITIONISTS OF MASSACHUSETTS. n.d. n.p.** Suggests they complete their subscriptions and make donations to benefit anti-slavery work by the Fourth of July. 29 June 1838. p.103, c4.

3206 LOUISA WAKEFIELD [SECRETARY] *to* **THE EDITOR. 20 June 1838. Reading.** Forwards a resolution of the Reading Female AS which lamented the death of Mrs. Esther Kingman. 29 June 1838. p.103, c6.

3207 H. C. W[RIGHT] *to* **BROTHER [W. L. GARRISON]. 22 June 1838. Pawtucket.** Reports on public discussion which considered whether any circumstances could justify the taking of a man's life on Christian grounds; Wright finds the penal and military codes of the United States hypocritical and inconsistent with Christian beliefs. 6 July 1838. p.105, c5.

3208 A FRIEND *to* **FRIEND. n.d. n.p.** Pleads the cause of the Cherokee Indians; condemns American aggression against "the rightful inheritors of our soil." 6 July 1838. p.105, c6.

3209 PHILANTHROPOS *to* **MR. GARRISON. n.d. n.p.** Declares he hates slavery "in the abstract," but that "such evil times" condone the enslavement of some for the benefit of all; believes that if Garrison would renounce his faith in "such invisible things as truth and justice" and consider expediency, then he would favor Philanthropos' proposal of slavery as a solution to the Irish problem. 6 July 1838. p.106, c1.

3210 FRATER *to* **GARRISON. 2 June 1838. Dartmouth College, N.H.** Decries tyranny and oppression; praises the "noble and independent stand" of Dartmouth College, which accepted both a colored man and an Indian as students. 6 July 1838. p.106, c3.

3211 A CONSERVATIVE *to* **MR. EDITOR [W. L. GARRISON]. n.d. n.p.** Criticizes the doctrines of Henry C. Wright as contrary to both the New Testament and the dictates of "Natural Religion." 6 July 1838. p.106, c5.

3212 L. W. *to* **MR. GARRISON. n.d. n.p.** Criticizes H. C. Wright's and A. E. Grimke's literal exposition of Christ's precept, "Resist not evil," as it fails to consider Christ's having driven the money-changers from the temple. 6 July 1838. p.106, c6.

3213 GOVERNOR W. W. ELLSWORTH *to* **A. F. WILLIAMS. 19 May 1838. New Haven.** Thanks him for sending the *Journal of Thome and Kimball;* feels that its exposition of benefits of emancipation in the West Indies could be instrumental in ending slavery in the States. 6 July 1838. p.107, c5.

3214 J. EDWARDS [PRESIDENT OF ANDOVER THEOLOGICAL SEMINARY] *to* **MR. BIRNEY. 16 June 1838. Andover.** Thanks him for forwarding the *Journal of Thome and Kimball;* feels that the experience of emancipation in the West Indies described therein is undeniable proof that "Negroes are *men*." 6 July 1838. p.107, c5.

3215 H. C. WRIGHT *to* **BROTHER [W. L. GARRISON]. 25 June 1838. Providence.** Replies to queries from "Peace" in previous *Liberator*; discusses his own views of John the Baptist's behavior in relation to the peace principle and war; reiterates that soldiers are by profession ruffians and butchers of men. 13 July 1838. p.110, c5.

3216 G. W. B. *to* **BROTHER GARRISON. n.d. n.p.** Believes we are approaching a crisis in moral reform; does not support following expediency rather than God's law. 13 July 1838. p.110, c6.

3217 WM. COMSTOCK *to* **MR. GARRISON. n.d. n.p.** Quotes from one of Bulwer's novels, which shows that slaves' laughter and dancing does not mean they are happy and satisfied. 13 July 1838. p.110, c6.

3218 A. H. BROWN *to* **MR. EDITOR [W. L. GARRISON]. 6 July 1838. Andover.** Announces new officers of the Andover AS; gives brief summary of annual meeting. 13 July 1838. p.111, c1.

3219 A FRIEND IN MISSISSIPPI *to* **A MEMBER OF CONGRESS. [from the** *Globe***] n.d. n.p.** Warns that times are alarming; many plantations are stripped of Negroes and horses by the sheriff; banks are in trouble; suits in the courts are multiplying. 13 July 1838. p.111, c2.

3220 GERRIT SMITH *to* **MR. TAPPAN. 24 May 1838. Peterboro'.** Discusses the moral duty of the Board regarding acceptance of money from slaveholders. 13 July 1838. p.112, c1.

3221 HIRAM WILSON *to* **BROTHER JOHNSON. 29 June 1838. Canal Boat, near Palmyra, N.Y.** Corrects gross misrepresentations of his speech as reported in the *Boston Morning Post*; states he is utterly opposed to war, whether aggressive or defensive. 20 July 1838. p.114, c5.

3222 A FRIEND OF LIBERTY AND EQUAL RIGHTS *to* **MR. EDITOR [W. L. GARRISON]. 2 July 1838. Woburn.** Criticizes letter by committee of Woburn Universalist Society which refused the use of the Universalist meetinghouse for an anti-slavery meeting; he and many other Universalists have no personal objection to the use of the meetinghouse for that purpose. 20 July 1838. p.114, c6.

3223 T. COLE *to* **MR. JOHNSON. 7 July 1838. Boston.** Reports that he has just received a cheering letter from his friend Remond, a black AS agent; letter shows that prejudice is diminishing. 20 July 1838. p.114, c6.

3224 C. LENOX REMOND *to* **T. COLE. 3 July 1838. Winthrop.** Reports that his lectures in Maine have elicited marked attention and aroused good feeling for the cause; in one place a society was formed after his lecture; also attended conference of Congregationalists and spoke to Baptists; warns that slavery is trembling, and hopes it will soon be buried. 20 July 1838. p.114, c6.

3225 A. A. PHELPS *to* **MR. JOHNSON. n.d. n.p.** Criticizes and corrects the *Liberator*; asserts differences in his opinions of the case of Abner Kneeland, Rev. Elipha White, and the use of the word "evangelical." 27 July 1838. p.118, c6.

3226 HENRY B. STANTON *to* **THE** *EMANCIPATOR.* **[extract] n.d. n.p.** Reports on uproar caused at a Utica meeting of the New York Young Men's Whig Convention by the announcement of an AS meeting to be held at Bleeker Street Church the following evening. 27 July 1838. p.119, c2.

3227 FORTY [BLACK] MEMBERS OF THE BOSTON FIRST METHODIST EPISCOPAL ZION'S CHURCH *to* **WHOM IT MAY CONCERN. 13 June 1838. Boston.** Resolve to withdraw from the church and re-convene as an African Methodist Episcopal Zion's church, since black ministers are not allowed to preach in their present congregation. 27 July 1838. p.119, c5.

3228 J. Q. ADAMS *to* **EDMUND QUINCY, ESQ. 28 July 1838. Quincy.** Pleads poor health and the privilege of his years in declining the invitation to address the Massachusetts AS meeting; rejoices that the defense of the cause of human freedom has fallen into younger hands, and cheers them on. 3 August 1838. p.122, c4.

3229 H. C. W. *to* **BROTHER [W. L. GARRISON]. 13 July 1838. Fall River.** Reports on the public discussion of peace in Fall River, which addressed the incompatibility of military systems and peace principles; compliments participants' willingness to engage in free discussion. 3 August 1838. p.123, c5.

3230 H. C. WRIGHT *to* **BROTHER [W. L. GARRISON]. 5 July 1838. Freetown.** Reports that he has lectured in Freetown on slavery, human rights, the peace principle, and on the cruelty and injustice of military systems; also spoke to a group of children on total abstinence. 3 August 1838. p.123, c5.

3231 H. C. WRIGHT *to* **BROTHER [W. L. GARRISON]. 10 July 1838. Fall River.** Explains the passage John 2:15 to L. W. who wrote to him through the *Liberator*; claims that no proof exists that Christ whipped men; argues that the above passage does not justify resistance. 3 August 1838. p.124, c2.

3232 H. C. WRIGHT *to* **BROTHER [W. L. GARRISON]. 12 July 1838. Fall River.** Replies to letter in the *Liberator* critricizing Wright's frequent use of the phrase "discretionary power"; asserts all men have a right to self-defense; men defend peace by nonresistance and the conquest of evil. 3 August 1838. p.124, c2.

3233 DR. MAYO *to* **GEN. ANDREW JACKSON. 2 December 1830. n.p.** Sends document in secret alphabet; resided in the same hotel as Samuel Houston; discusses Houston's history; tells of Houston's "romantic projections" for Texas. 10 August 1838. p.125, c6.

3234 ANDREW JACKSON *to* **WILLIAM FULTON, ESQ. [SECRETARY OF THE TERRITORY OF ARKANSAS]. 10 December 1830. Washington.** Reports rumors of extensive expedition against Texas being organized in the United States, to be led by Samuel Houston; hopes this information is erroneous; asks Fulton to keep Jackson advised of the real situation. 10 August 1838. p.126, c1.

3235 WM. HARLOW *to* **MR. JOHNSON. 2 August 1838. Wrentham.** Sends resolutions recently adopted by the Wrentham AS regarding emancipation in the British West Indies, slavery, and the right of petition. 10 August 1838. p.127, c1.

3236 CONSISTENCY *to* **MR. EDITOR [W. L. GARRISON]. n.d. n.p.** Wonders how societies which "are as much opposed to slavery as you are" can refuse the use of their meetinghouse for anti-slavery meetings; considers possible explanations. 10 August 1838. p.127, c1.

3237 JOSEPH RITNER *to* **MR. HENRY HANNEN. [from the** *Christian Witness***] 5 April 1838. Harrisburg.** Replies to questions on his opinions of the abolition of slavery in the District of Columbia, Congress' power to abolish the slave trade, the annexation of Texas, and jury trials for runaway slaves. 10 August 1838. p.128, c2.

3238 J. R. JOHNSON *to* **THE** *PENNSYLVANIA FREEMAN.* **n.d. Cincinnatus, N. Y.** Declares that a speech by Rev. Wilbur Fisk convinced him to turn from the colonizationist to the abolitionist cause. 10 August 1838. p.128, c3.

3239 J. Q. ADAMS *to* **A. BRONSON, ESQ. 30 July 1838. Quincy.** Explains that he cannot take part in any public meetings, due to infirm health and an enfeebled voice; regrets that he must decline invitation to Fall River AS. 10 August 1838. p.128, c5.

3240 R. F. W. *to* **SIR. n.d. n.p.** Reports he has just read the twenty-first annual report of the ACS with feelings of "unutterable disgust"; criticizes their motives, principles, and hypocrisy; quotes from report. 17 August 1838. p.130, c3.

3241 B. *to* **MR. JOHNSON. n.d. n.p.** Recommends that invitation to visit the United States be extended to another British philanthropist, Joseph Sturge, who has collected information in the West Indies and has been an efficient, devoted, indefatigable laborer for the cause. 17 August 1838. p.130, c4.

3242 MARY ANN PECK *to* **JOHNSON. 13 August 1838. Coventry, R. I.** Reports resolution of the Kent County Female AS concurring with Johnson's proposal to invite British philanthropists Stuart and Thompson to return to this country. 17 August 1838. p.130, c4.

3243 WM. S. FULTON *to* **HON. BEN. C. HOWARD. 7 July 1838. Senate Chamber.** Discusses the whereabouts of a copy of a letter from Gen. Jackson to Wm. S. Fulton. 17 August 1838. p.131, c1.

3244 JOHN QUINCY ADAMS *to* **MESSRS. PRITCHETT AND STUART. [extract] n.d. n.p.** Expresses repugnance at speaking in public on every subject connected with slavery or its abolition; finds public opinion of North and South so inharmonious that he is reluctant to disturb it further, but prays for the success of their cause. 17 August 1838. p.131, c3.

3245 ROBERT F. WALCUTT *to* **SIR. n.d. n.p.** Reminds that emancipation in Santo Domingo and the British West Indies occurred under very different circumstances; elaborates on these differences, explaining that the example of the West Indies illustrates the expediency of emancipation. 24 August 1838. p.133, c4.

3246 H. C. WRIGHT *to* **BROTHER [W. L. GARRISON]. 26 July 1838. Newport.** Reports on public lectures on the subject of peace in all its bearings, and summarizes the discussion of the resolutions brought forth; describes the colored population of Newport. 24 August 1838. p.133, c5.

3247 CHARLES SIMMONS *to* **FRIEND JOHNSON. n.d. n.p.** Writes to encourage abolitionists; feels their cause is that of the common people who carry a great responsibility to work for the oppressed; quotes Scripture to demonstrate that a life of active benevolence and self-denial is the road to temporal and spiritual prosperity. 24 August 1838. p.134, c1.

3248 JOHN QUINCY ADAMS *to* **THE INHABITANTS OF THE TWELFTH CONGRESSIONAL DISTRICT OF MASSACHUSETTS. [from the** *Quincy Patriot***] 13 August 1838. Quincy.** Discusses concerns of the country and government: the plight of the Cherokees, Treasury disputes, questions of the right to petition, the annexation of Texas; relates his own opinions and behavior on these subjects. 24 August 1838. p.134, c3.

3249 ELEAZER COBURN, JOSIAH PEET, ARTHUR DRINKWATER, GEORGE W. HATHAWAY, DANIEL B. RANDALL *to* **HON. EDWARD KENT, ESQ., GOVERNOR OF THE STATE. [from the** *Advocate of Freedom***] 23 July 1838. Norridgwock.** Inform Kent that he has been nominated as chief magistrate for the state; state views, as executive committee of the Somerset County AS, on slavery and their right to petition for its end; solicit his views on the subject. 24 August 1838. p.135, c1.

3250 EDWARD KENT *to* **THE EXECUTIVE COMMITTEE OF THE ANTI-SLAVERY SOCIETY OF SOMERSET COUNTY. [from the** *Advocate of Freedom***] 27 July 1838. Bangor.** Cheerfully acknowledges citizens' right to ask candidates' opinions; regards slavery as a great moral and political evil; rejects right to interfere with the domestic institutions of sister states; believes the right to petition is sacred and regrets that it has been invaded. 24 August 1838. p.135, c1.

3251 WM. LLOYD GARRISON *to* **OLIVER JOHNSON. 14 August 1838. Brooklyn.** Discusses his journey from Brooklyn to New York and his visit with Messrs. Treat and Johnson; adds that he spoke in New York at commemoration of the emancipation of blacks in the West Indies, and that he has been ill since his return home. 24 August 1838. p.135, c3.

3252 G. H. DURFEE *to* **BROTHER PHELPS. 20 August 1838. Fall River.** Discusses favorable response to Phelps' plan for state and county meetings; tells of arrangements for county meeting at Taunton. 24 August 1838. p.135, c5.

3253 ASA BRONSON *to* **FRIEND AND BROTHER. 20 August 1838. Fall River.** Suggests that county meeting at Taunton initiate a series of county meetings; Messrs. Smith, Birney, and Stanton can begin there and proceed to other meetings. 24 August 1838. p.135, c5.

3254 J. HORTON *to* **BROTHER PHELPS. 20 August 1838. Worcester.** Approves of the plan for a Young Men's State Convention which he believes will be very helpful to the cause; however, his friends believe Northampton or Springfield would be a better site for a convention than Worcester. 24 August 1838. p.135, c5.

3255 MAYNARD KING *to* **BROTHER JOHNSON. 20 August 1838. West Boylston.** Expresses satisfaction to hear the call for a Young Men's State Convention; suggests where to hold it and whom to invite. 24 August 1838. p.135, c5.

3256 REV. O. SCOTT *to* **BROTHER JOHNSON. 17 August 1838. Lowell.** Heartily approves of the idea of a Young Men's State Convention; believes time is right to tap latent and potentially valuable source of revenue and energy; hopes, too, that the call for George Thompson and others to visit America will be answered. 24 August 1838. p.135, c5.

3257 J. H. *to* **MR. MURRAY. [from the *Vermont Telegraph*] n.d. n.p.** Reports that many in the past year have come to support the anti-slavery cause and would join the AS were it not for the presence of "hotheads" like Mr. Garrison; believes that many will join and contribute to the cause if Garrison is turned out. 24 August 1838. p.136, c3.

3258 n.n. *to* **n.n. [extract from a London paper] 15 February 1838. Port-au-Prince.** Correspondence on President Boyer of Haiti and his distinguishing characteristics of good faith and clemency. 24 August 1838. p.136, c4.

3259 THOMAS JONES *to* **MR. EDITOR. [from the *Philanthropist*] 20 June 1838. Smockville, Ia.** Relates conversation on Mississippi River with a slave whose wife and children were going to Texas, but whose master, a Presbyterian minister, would not sell him to the man taking away his family. 31 August 1838. p.137, c5.

3260 H. C. WRIGHT *to* **BROTHER [W. L. GARRISON]. 16 July 1838. Fall River.** He has just returned from lecture on women's rights, examining the right or duty of women to act in the anti-slavery cause; believes that women receive "brutal and inhuman treatment" from churches and benevolent associations, and that women deserve human rights. 31 August 1838. p.138, c3.

3261 G. EVANS *to* **MR. EDITOR [W. L. GARRISON]. 24 August 1838. Worcester.** Strongly supports the idea of a Young Men's Anti-Slavery Convention; believes many young men will work hard for the cause; suggests Worcester as best place to hold the convention. 31 August 1838. p.139, c1.

3262 SAMUEL SHOVE, 2D. *to* **BROTHER JOHNSON. 25 August 1838. North Attleborough.** Favors a Young Men's Anti-Slavery Convention; believes that to get the spirit moving, the convention should be held in several places, and that Birney, Stuart, Stanton, and Smith should speak. 31 August 1838. p.139, c1.

3263 T. P. RYDER *to* **BROTHER JOHNSON. 27 August 1838. East Bridgewater.** Glad to see the call for a Young Men's State Convention; wishes to convince congressional representatives that all citizens and future citizens in Massachusetts must be heard. 31 August 1838. p.139, c1.

3264 J. W. ALDEN *to* **BROTHER JOHNSON. 25 August 1838. Cambridgeport.** Reports that Board of Managers of Cambridgeport AS passed a resolution supporting the Young Men's Anti-Slavery Convention; suggests that it be held in Worcester. 31 August 1838. p.139, c1.

3265 GEO. W. WEISSENGER *to* **MR. J. CLARK. 6 July 1838. Louisville, Ky.** Reports that the latest state effort to call a convention to discuss the gradual abolition of slavery was supported by the Van Buren party and opposed by most of the Whig members; Mr. Clay opposed to a convention. 31 August 1838. p.139, c2.

3266 CALEB BELCHER *to* **SIR. 30 August 1838. Falmouth.** Reports that the AS formed after Samuel Gould's speech last autumn has grown to sixty or seventy members; lists officers. 7 September 1838. p.142, c2.

3267 T. A. MERRILL *to* **MR. JOHNSON. 1 September 1838. Georgetown.** Reports that Georgetown AS responded very favorably to the suggestion of a Young Men's State Anti-Slavery Convention; expresses indifference about site. 7 September 1838. p.142, c2.

3268 H. B. STANTON *to* **BROTHER JOHNSON. 1 September 1838. Anti-Slavery Rooms, N. Y.** Encourages the call for a Young Men's Convention; suggests various parts of the state where energy and conviction could be roused for the anti-slavery cause. 7 September 1838. p.143, c5.

3269 WILLIAM SLADE *to* **REV. J. LEAVITT. [from the** *Emancipator***] 7 August 1838. Middlebury, Vt.** Reports that he has copy of Thome and Kimball's *Journal* which Leavitt sent him "with a deep and thrilling interest"; believes it shows that immediate emancipation is practical; requests one hundred copies. 7 September 1838. p.144, c2.

3270 n.n. *to* **THE** *CINCINNATI JOURNAL.* **[extract] n.d. Kentucky.** Believes a great many Southerners will be indignant at sneers and flouts at abolitionists from Mr. Breckenridge (of the *Western Presbyterian Herald*); declares that principles of abolition are taking root in the South. 7 September 1838. p.144, c5.

3271 HARRIET MARTINEAU *to* **THE FORMER CORRESPONDING SECRETARY OF THE WOMEN'S ANTI-SLAVERY SOCIETY IN LYNN. [from the** *Lynn Record***] 20 June 1838. Fludyer St., Westminister.** Accepts "with high gratification" the gift and certificate of membership in the Massachusetts AS; thanks her American sisters, praises their spirit and kindness; cautions against oppression and urges vigilance over the recently emancipated West Indies slaves. 14 September 1838. p.145, c1.

3272 A NEW YORK ABOLITIONIST *to* **MR. EDITOR [W. L. GARRISON]. 8 August 1838. Boston.** Expresses his disappointment at seeing Bostonians make such a political question of slavery; believes the most successful method uses moral means to persuade slaveholders of their wrong. 14 September 1838. p.146, c4.

3273 A NEW YORK ABOLITIONIST *to* **MR. EDITOR [W. L. GARRISON]. 13 August 1838. Boston.** Discusses the address of the Board of Managers of the Massachusetts AS to the abolitionists in the state; both agrees and disagrees with their points; believes abolitionists should ask candidates' opinions and vote accordingly. 14 September 1838. p.146, c4.

3274 JOHN W. LEWIS *to* **THE COLORED PEOPLE IN NEW ENGLAND. n.d. n.p.** Sends reminder that the time for the third annual meeting of the New England Temperance Society is fast approaching, and encourages attendance; also expounds on the virtues of temperance. 14 September 1838. p.146, c5.

3275 D. HART *to* **THE** *JAMAICA JOURNAL*. **[extract] 19 July 1838. Kingston.** Corrects malicious report that his workmen have struck and are holding out for double wages; asserts that all his workers are working happily, even though they do not know what their salary will be. 14 September 1838. p.147, c4.

3276 A. A. PHELPS *to* **FRIENDS OF FREEDOM. n.d. n.p.** Writes for the Board of Managers of the Massachusetts AS to request donations, announce conventions, and promote the circulation of more petitions; urges efforts in behalf of the slave. 21 September 1838. p.150, c3.

3277 CHARLES K. TRUE *to* **HON. JAMES G. BIRNEY. 28 August 1838. Lynn Common.** Requests that his name be withdrawn from the constitution of the AAS in compliance with the decisions of the New York Annual Conference; promises always to work against involuntary servitude, but will act as minister of the Methodist Episcopal Church. 21 September 1838. p.151, c3.

3278 LEVI GAYLORD *to* **MR. GOODELL. 13 August 1838. Sodus.** Relates discussion with Mr. Otis Reynolds, a gentleman from St. Louis, Missouri who claimed that he witnessed the sale of a daughter of Thomas Jefferson in New Orleans for one thousand dollars; quotes Jefferson on slavery. 21 September 1838. p.152, c5.

3279 Entry number not used.

3280 JOHN FAIRFIELD *to* **MESSRS. E. COBURN, &C., COMMITTEE OF THE SOMERSET ANTI-SLAVERY SOCIETY. 15 August 1838. Saco.** Replies to their questions on various subjects; he believes slavery to be a moral and political evil, but objects to abolitionist methods for removing it; supports the right to petition. 28 September 1838. p.153, c1.

3281 H. C. WRIGHT *to* **BROTHER [W. L. GARRISON]. 20 September 1838. Boston.** Tells of Peace Convention and the subsequent formation of the New England Non-Resistance Society; discusses the peace principle and its application to both ancient and modern life. 28 September 1838. p.155, c1.

3282 A. A. PHELPS *to* **FRIEND JOHNSON. n.d. n.p.** Sends extract of a letter from Mr. Stanton. 28 September 1838. p.155, c2.

3283 MR. STANTON *to* **A. A. PHELPS. [extract] n.d. n.p.** Briefly reports on "mighty meeting" in Utica, attended by 700–800 men who were delegates, and 400–500 women who were not delegates; resolved to start a monthly paper edited by William Goodell. 28 September 1838. p.155, c2.

3284 W. *to* **MR. EDITOR [W. L. GARRISON]. 24 September 1838. Bradford.** Advocates visit by George Thompson, who has freed the slave in England. 28 September 1838. p.155, c2.

3285 DANIEL WISE *to* **MR. EDITOR [W. L. GARRISON]. n.d. Quincy.** Lists officers of new Quincy AS, founded after series of lectures by Rev. Alanson St. Clair; expects to send delegation to the Worcester convention. 28 September 1838. p.155, c2.

3286 A. STEVENSON *to* **DANIEL O'CONNELL, ESQ. 9 August 1838. 23 Portland Place.** Criticizes the language O'Connell used in referring to him in a speech reported in the *Spectator*; asks if article, which claimed O'Connell called him "a disgrace to human nature," was correct. 28 September 1838. p.155, c5.

3287 DANIEL O'CONNELL *to* **A. STEVENSON. 10 August 1838. 16 Pall-Mall.** Replies to Stevenson that the *Spectator* did not quote him correctly. 28 September 1838. p.155, c5.

3288 A. STEVENSON *to* **DANIEL O'CONNELL. 11 August 1838. 23 Portland Place.** Acknowledges receipt of O'Connell's letter; expresses satisfaction with O'Connell's disavowal of offensive criticism of Stevenson. 28 September 1838. p.155, c5.

3289 n.n. *to* **BROTHER. [from the** *Bangor Journal***] 10 March 1838. n.p.** Hopes to see a time when the marriage contract between slaves is inviolable; thinks the state law forbidding slaves to read is unnecessary, as many can and do read; claims that the best informed Negroes are the best servants, and that Southerners do not live in constant terror of the slaves. 5 October 1838. p.157, c1.

3290 ONE OF YOUR CONSTANT READERS *to* **MR. EDITOR [W. L. GARRISON]. 13 September 1838. Newburyport.** Encloses article on Christianity and the anti-slavery cause previously sent to the *Watch Tower*, a religious paper, which refused to print it. 5 October 1838. p.158, c2.

3291 H. W. DAVISON *to* **FRIEND GARRISON. 27 September 1838. New York.** Reports the arrival of Rev. Joel Parker from New Orleans, an apologist for slavery; reports changing of ministers in the First Free Church after Parker's arrival and disputes between colonizationists and abolitionists. 5 October 1838. p.158, c3.

3292 M. W. C. *to* **THE EDITOR OF THE** *LIBERATOR* **[W. L. GARRISON]. n.d. n.p.** Defines civil government, the Church, voluntary associations, creed, and declaration of sentiments; debates at the Peace Convention show these definitions to be much in need. 5 October 1838. p.158, c4.

3293 WM. E. CHANNING *to* **EDMUND QUINCY, ESQ. 10 August 1838. Newport.** States that if he is in Boston, he would be pleased to attend the Peace Convention, as he abhors violence, and peace is a subject in which he is deeply interested. 5 October 1838. p.158, c4.

3294 HEMAN ALLEN *to* **E. L. JONES, ESQ., SEC'RY. ST. ALBANS AS. [from the** *Vermont Watchman***] 17 September 1838. Burlington.** Regrets he cannot attend anti-slavery convention at St. Albans; has always held the principles of that society in high respect; believes Congress has a right and a duty to abolish slavery in the District of Columbia; regrets the right to petition has been stilled. 5 October 1838. p.159, c1.

3295 J. Z. *to* **MR. EDITOR [W. L. GARRISON]. 25 August 1838. Boston.** Expresses surprise that Rev. Theodore Clapp from New Orleans was recently admitted to preach in Mr. Pierpont's pulpit, as Clapp is a slaveholder, and has preached that the Bible supports slavery. 5 October 1838. p.159, c3.

3296 OLIVER JOHNSON *to* **FRIEND KNAPP. 2 October 1838. Worcester.** Reports on first day's proceedings of the Young Men's Anti-Slavery Convention; views participants as men of great talent and moral energy; gives account of letters read, and resolutions discussed concerning Great Britain's sympathy for philanthropic efforts. 5 October 1838. p.159, c4.

3297 A FRIEND IN JAMAICA *to* **REV. JOHN CLARKE. [extract] 7 August 1838. Brown's Town.** Relates advent of emancipation on the first of August passed with no rioting or drunkenness; gives account of the watch night on 31 July and huge celebratory dinner the following day; notes that people are ready to work, but some masters plot a "mad scheme or arrogant folly." 5 October 1838. p.159, c4.

3298 A COLORED GENTLEMAN *to* **REV. JOHN CLARKE. 7 August 1838. Jericho, St. Thomas in the Vale [Jamaica].** Relates that the day of freedom passed with the greatest quietness; tells of prayer meetings held; warns people that to work without an agreement will lead to further encroachment of their rights. 5 October 1838. p.159, c4.

3299 THOMAS W. DORR *to* **SIR. 29 September 1838. Providence, R. I.** Regrets he will be detained by business and unable to attend the Young Men's Anti-Slavery Convention; believes the younger generation will "come upon the stage of action with better feelings, sounder principles," and more courage to act according to them. 12 October 1838. p.161, c4.

3300 JAMES C. ALVORD *to* **EDMUND QUINCY, ESQ. 29 September 1838. Greenfield.** Expresses thanks for invitation to Young Men's Convention, but regrets his duties prevent him from attending; cannot accept the credit and praise attributed to him. 12 October 1838. p.161, c4.

3301 WILLIAM SLADE *to* **MR. OLIVER JOHNSON. 20 September 1838. Middlebury, Vt.** Thanks him for the invitation to the Young Men's Anti-Slavery Convention; declares that these young men will see the day when the slave is free, and that he believes they will respond to the call of liberty. 12 October 1838. p.161, c4.

3302 E. D. BARBER *to* **MR. OLIVER JOHNSON. 29 September 1838. Middlebury, Vt.** Regrets he cannot attend the Young Men's Anti-Slavery Convention; examines Dr. Wayland's works and suggests reading them to see how the opponents of abolition are driven to the wall; urges abolition in the District of Columbia. 12 October 1838. p.161, c5.

3303 N. P. ROGERS *to* **BROTHER PHELPS. 28 September 1838. Plymouth, N.H.** Regrets he cannot attend the Young Men's Convention but is there in spirit; urges the assertion of their great and all-conquering principles; hopes that the young men of Massachusetts can shake off the "death-spell" of slavery. 12 October 1838. p.162, c2.

3304 O. S. MURRAY *to* **W. L. GARRISON. 1 October 1838. Brandon, Vt.** Regrets he cannot attend the Peace Convention, but cannot neglect his editing of the *Telegraph*; heartily supports them, and asks that his name be affixed to their Declaration of Sentiments. 12 October 1838. p.163, c3.

3305 CONSISTENCY *to* **MR. EDITOR [W. L. GARRISON]. n.d. n.p.** States that he was surprised to hear Rev. Elipha White preach in a Boston church, as White is from South Carolina, and reputed to be a slaveholder; discusses hypocrisy of a slaveholder's preaching Christian principles. 12 October 1838. p.163, c3.

3306 VERITAS *to* **DR. BAILEY. 18 September 1838. Ripley.** Recounts arrest of Rev. Mr. Mahan of Sardinia, as a fugitive from justice in Kentucky; describes the matter as "highly mysterious," since Mahan has not been in Kentucky for nineteen years; worries that no one is safe from perjury and injustice. 12 October 1838. p.163, c4.

3307 J. HAMILTON [LATE GOVERNOR OF SOUTH CAROLINA] *to* **THE *RICHMOND ENQUIRER*. 15 August 1838. London.** Reports on discussion of Mr. O'Connell's character, writings, and harsh language; criticizes O'Connell sharply on each count. 12 October 1838. p.164, c5.

3308 DANIEL O'CONNELL *to* **THE EDITOR OF THE** *MORNING CHRONICLE.* **13 September 1838. Derrynane Abbey.** Objects to the publication of one-sided correspondence between himself and Mr. Stevenson; charges that Mr. Stevenson sent him inaccurate reports, misrepresented information, and made "gratuitous assumptions"; claims that the sole object was to rouse attention to the cruel and criminal in the American slave system. 19 October 1838. p.166, c3.

3309 UP TO THE MARK *to* **BROTHER. n.d. n.p.** Urges Massachusetts voters to discard both parties' candidates in the coming district elections, and vote for "true men"; if they scatter their votes and no one is chosen, then hopefully the elections will be repeated until there is a good candidate. 19 October 1838. p.166, c4.

3310 LEWIS TAPPAN *to* **THE EDITOR OF THE** *LIBERATOR* **[W. L. GARRISON]. 10 October 1838. New York.** Writes to correct letter from H. W. Davison on the call of Rev. Joel Parker to the Tabernacle Church; explains the true complications involved in uniting the two churches under one minister; points out the inconsistency in Parker's preaching before and since his residence in New Orleans. 19 October 1838. p.166, c4.

3311 E. C. P. *to* **MR. EDITOR [W. L. GARRISON]. n.d. n.p.** Sends extract of a letter from a friend living in Massachusetts. 19 October 1838. p.166, c4.

3312 n.n. *to* **n.n. [extract] n.d. n.p.** Relates the story of the transportation of twelve fugitive slaves to the Canadian border. 19 October 1838. p.166, c4.

3313 J. L. *to* **MR. EDITOR [W. L. GARRISON]. 13 October 1838. Hingham.** Tells of the course of lectures given by Rev. Daniel Wise in Hingham; thanks Wise for his faithful work among them, although many in the town "are determined that they will not become Abolitionists." 19 October 1838. p.166, c5.

3314 SILAS BRUCE *to* **MR. EDITOR [W. L. GARRISON]. 13 October 1838. Leominster.** Reports proceedings of the Worcester North District AS quarterly meeting. 19 October 1838. p.166, c5.

3315 JOHN PIERPONT *to* **THE EDITOR OF THE** *LIBERATOR* **[W. L. GARRISON]. n.d. n.p.** Replies to article on his having admitted Rev. Mr. Clapp of New Orleans into his pulpit; supports freedom of speech, press, and therefore, free pulpit, knowing that people have the right to accept or reject for themselves what they have heard. 19 October 1838. p.166, c6.

3316 WILLIAM LADD *to* **n.n. [from the** *Christian Mirror***] 22 September 1838. Boston.** Discusses the Peace Convention; reports that some delegates and committee members formally withdrew, that he found the constitution too "ultra" and did not vote for it, and that he did not join the new Non-Resistance Society; feels that the convention was "highly auspicious to the cause of peace." 19 October 1838. p.168, c2.

3317 C. *to* **THE EDITORS OF THE** *ADVOCATE OF FREEDOM.* **n.d. n.p.** Condemns editors of the *Christian Mirror* for their inconsistency in paying lip service to Mr. Garrison while publishing pro-slavery material. 26 October 1838. p.169, c2.

3318 SAMUEL PHILLIPS *to* **BROTHER BROWN. n.d. Sandwich, Ct.** Tells of speech on American slavery given by the Rev. Joseph Marsh in Wareham, which was interrupted by a mob which hooted and threw stones through windows. 26 October 1838. p.169, c4.

3319 WM. LLOYD GARRISON *to* **E. D. HUDSON. [from the** *Hartford Charter Oak***] 8 September 1838. Brooklyn, Ct.** Regrets cannot attend the meeting of the Litchfield County AS; feels he no longer stands alone as there are now many able speakers on the subject; admits to prior self-doubt but determination in working for the cause. 26 October 1838. p.169, c6.

3320 n.n. *to* **SIR [W. L. GARRISON]. 20 October 1838. Rowley.** Reports that Mr. Philo C. Pettibone just completed a series of lectures in Rowley in a citizen's house since the congregation prevented him from speaking in the church; believes the formation of an AS in Rowley proves "The ice is broken, and the way prepared for great results." 26 October 1838. p.171, c1.

3321 O. SCOTT *to* **FRIEND GARRISON. 20 October 1838. n.p.** Expresses surprise that the *Liberator* passed judgement on his article before publishing it, asking why the article was not allowed to stand on its own; advocates belief that human governments may exist without taking life. 26 October 1838. p.171, c5.

3322 W. B. S. *to* **BRO. GARRISON. 20 October 1838. Hardwick.** Forwards money collected from the outer districts of Hardwick for a year's subscription to the *Liberator*, which he believes to be one of the best assets of the cause. 26 October 1838. p.171, c5.

3323 THOMAS E. VALENTINE *to* **SIR [W. L. GARRISON]. 18 October 1838. Northborough.** Sends corrections of anti-slavery pledge and donation list: he is the treasurer of the Northborough AS, not Gill Valentine, and has pledged fifty dollars, not twelve dollars and eighty-nine cents. 26 October 1838. p.171, c5.

3324 O. SCOTT *to* **FRIEND GARRISON. 13 October 1838. Lowell.** Discusses his reservations about the manner in which the Non-Resistance Society was organized; expresses disappointment to see the Society limp in upon the crutches of "peace" and "abolition"; believes in human government and thinks government should be reformed, not destroyed. 26 October 1838. p.172, c2.

3325 H. C. WRIGHT *to* **BROTHER [W. L. GARRISON]. 15 October 1838. Newburyport.** Sends passage on non-resistance explaining that one's duty is to submit, rather than resist; explains that the passage refers to Christians, not to rulers; discovers nothing in the passage forcing Christians to hold office or take part in military systems. 26 October 1838. p.172, c4.

3326 ORIN P. BACON *to* **FRIEND GARRISON. 22 October 1838. Dorchester.** Sends correspondence of Mr. A. H. Everett; hopes to prove to *Liberator* correspondent, Mr. "Up to the Mark", that Everett's views need not be doubted. 2 November 1838. p.173, c4.

3327 A. H. EVERETT *to* **SIR. 3 November 1837. Roxbury.** Replies to a request that he state his opinion on slavery; believes Congress has the right to abolish slavery in the District of Columbia, and finds no reason why this right should not be exercised immediately; supports the right of petition and feels Congress' behavior relating to this is a disgrace. 2 November 1838. p.173, c4.

3328 STANDFAST *to* **THE AUTHOR OF "THE TOCSEN." n.d. n.p.** States his opinion that the author's letter in the *Liberator* did not address the true questions involved in Mr. Clapp's officiating in a house of worship; asserts that this is not a case of free discussion, and that slavery can be reconciled neither with justice and humanity, nor with Christianity. 2 November 1838. p.174, c3.

3329 PHILO C. PETTIBONE *to* **WM. LLOYD GARRISON. 12 October 1838. Georgetown.** Reports on the state of the cause in Essex County and his lectures which have been very well received, particularly by children; remarks that four ASS have been formed and lists their officers. 2 November 1838. p.174, c4.

3330 A. FARNSWORTH *to* **SIR [W. L. GARRISON]. 10 October 1838. Groton.** Addresses candidates for state secretary, asking their opinions on abolition of slavery in the District of Columbia and on the Massachusetts legislature's protest of the admission of new states into the Union. 2 November 1838. p.175, c1.

3331 SIDNEY WILLARD *to* **AMOS FARNSWORTH, ESQ. 15 October 1838. Cambridge.** As a candidate for state secretary, he answers questions on the abolition of slavery, but avoids specific details; refuses to go into office "fettered and hand-cuffed." 2 November 1838. p.175, c1.

3332 THOMAS J. GREENWOOD *to* **AMOS FARNSWORTH, ESQ. 15 October 1838. Marlborough.** Replies to Farnsworth's questions addressed to state secretary candidates; maintains that he is neither an advocate nor an apologist of slavery, but votes according to what his constituents want. 2 November 1838. p.175, c1.

3333 BOWEN BUCKMAN *to* **DR. AMOS FARNSWORTH. 17 October 1838. Woburn.** In response to Farnsworth's questions addressed to state secretary candidates, states that he opposes slavery but is "not altogether prepared to answer fully." 2 November 1838. p.175, c2.

3334 J. W. MANSUR *to* **DR. AMOS FARNSWORTH. 23 October 1838. Lowell.** In response to Farnsworth's questions addressed to state secretary candidates, declares that he is opposed to slavery but has not changed opinions which he expressed formerly as a member of the legislature. 2 November 1838. p.175, c2.

3335 WM. PARMENTER *to* **DR. AMOS FARNSWORTH. 16 October 1838. East Cambridge.** In response to Farnsworth's questions addressed to state secretary candidates, states that his stand in Congress on questions of slavery is a matter of public record; believes slavery an evil and discusses abolition in the District of Columbia. 2 November 1838. p.175, c2.

3336 NEW YORK *to* **FRIEND GARRISON. n.d. New York.** Comments that minorities can have more effect in Massachusetts because of majority system; hopes that abolitionists do not throw away their votes on negative men. 2 November 1838. p.175, c2.

3337 A SUBSCRIBER *to* **MR. EDITOR [W. L. GARRISON]. n.d. n.p.** Suggests that candidates for representative positions in Congress should be asked how they would vote if called upon to select a president. 2 November 1838. p.175, c5.

3338 A WHIG BUT NO ABOLITIONIST *to* **MR. EDITOR [W. L. GARRISON]. [from the** *New York Gazette*] **n.d. n.p.** Contrasts letters published in the *New York Gazette* by Mr. Seward and Mr. Bradish; praises and supports the tone and ideas of Seward but strongly criticizes those of Bradish, an abolitionist; considers abolitionists an "infatuated and seditious conclave of disorganizers." 9 November 1838. p.177, c2.

3339 n.n. *to* **MR. EDITOR. [from the** *Meadville* **(Pa.)** *Statesman*] **n.d. n.p.** Sends extract from a letter written by a young man of his village to a friend. 9 November 1838. p.177, c4.

3340 n.n. *to* **n.n. [extract from the** *Meadville* **(Pa.)** *Statesman*] **n.d. n.p.** Relates account of the separation of a husband and wife who were slaves. 9 November 1838. p.177, c4.

3341 EDMUND QUINCY *to* **ABNER SANGER. 22 October 1838. Boston.** Expresses regret that he cannot attend the county convention at Danvers; hopes every man will make an effort to go since now is the time to act for liberty and justice; discusses definition of "abolitionist." 9 November 1838. p.178, c1.

3342 JOHN QUINCY ADAMS *to* **MESSRS. ISAAC L. HEDGE, SETH SPRAGUE, JR. AND ELIHU HOBART. 27 October 1838. Quincy.** Gratefully accepts nomination, especially as it was accompanied by a declared approbation of his past actions; expresses satisfaction with unanimity of spirit among his constituents, and state of foreign affairs, but not with the abuse of freedom of speech, slavery, and other domestic problems. 9 November 1838. p.178, c3.

3343 H. WILLIAMS *to* **REV. P. CRANDALL. 1 November 1838. Taunton.** Answers questions on his opinions by referring to his course in the state senate and to a letter published last year; affirms that he still believes slavery is evil and that no slave states should be admitted to the Union; briefly states his ideas of good, sound legislation. 9 November 1838. p.178, c4.

3344 JOHN EDDY *to* **REV. P. CRANDALL. 1 November 1838. Fall River.** Answers questions on his opinions by referring to several earlier published letters and several resolutions he supported; believes Congress has the power to abolish slavery in the District of Columbia, and should do so without delay. 9 November 1838. p.178, c4.

3345 EPHRAIM KEMPTON *to* **P. CRANDALL, ESQ. 1 November 1838. New Bedford.** In answer to questions regarding his opinions, he refers to several similar resolutions in the House of Representatives for which he voted; declares that he has not changed his opinions. 9 November 1838. p.178, c4.

3346 SAMPSON PERKINS *to* **REV. PHINEAS CRANDALL. 2 November 1838. New Bedford.** Declares he has not changed his opinions; still believes Congress should abolish slavery immediately in the District of Columbia and forbid the admission of any new state into the Union whose constitution tolerates slavery. 9 November 1838. p.178, c4.

3347 A. A. PHELPS *to* **FRIEND GARRISON. n.d. n.p.** Provides account of meeting in Dedham of the friends of emancipation in the District; the seventy or eighty delegates present passed resolutions against slavery, supporting abolition in the District of Columbia and Territory of Florida. 9 November 1838. p.178, c5.

3348 A. H. EVERETT *to* **DR. SIMEON B. CARPENTER AND EDWARD MANN. 29 October 1838. Roxbury, Ma.** In response to their letter containing questions to candidates, refers them to his published letter to Orin P. Bacon, which includes distinct affirmative answers to their inquiries; discusses "the baleful state of public opinion," evinced at Alton, Boston, and Philadelphia. 9 November 1838. p.178, c5.

3349 WM. S. HASTINGS *to* **SIMEON B. CARPENTER AND EDWARD MANN, ESQ. 1 November 1838. Mendon.** Replies in detail to questions put to political candidates: believes Congress has the power to abolish slavery in the District of Columbia as well as in the territories, and favors the immediate exercise of this right; also supports abolition of the slave trade. 9 November 1838. p.178, c6.

3350 FRANCIS JACKSON *to* **HON. RICHARD FLETCHER. 30 October 1838. Boston.** Asks congressional nominee, Fletcher, his opinions on the admission of new states which allow slavery, the abolition of slavery in the District of Columbia, and the abolition of the slave trade. 9 November 1838. p.179, c1.

3351 RICHARD FLETCHER *to* **FRANCIS JACKSON, ESQ. 6 November 1838. Boston.** Responding to Jackson's questions, states his belief that "it is inconsistent with his duty, for a candidate to pledge himself to any particular measure"; feels, however, that Congress ought to abolish slavery in the District of Columbia and exclude new states which allow slavery. 9 November 1838. p.179, c1.

3352 S. G. SHIPLEY *to* **BRADFORD SUMNER, ESQ. 2 November 1838. Boston.** Asks a congressional candidate, Sumner, his opinions on several issues relating to the abolition of slavery. 9 November 1838. p.179, c2.

3353 BRADFORD SUMNER *to* **S. G. SHIPLEY. 5 November 1838. Boston.** Replies to Shipley that he is uncertain whether Congress has the right to abolish slavery in the District of Columbia, but that he would favor its exercise; also opposes the admission of new states which allow slavery. 9 November 1838. p.179, c2.

3354 FENELON *to* **MR. EDITOR [W. L. GARRISON]. n.d. n.p.** Declares that the views of Mr. Nathan Brooks, congressional candidate in the Fourth District, have been misrepresented; believes that Brooks may be wrong for his refusal to answer questions, but that he has consistently supported anti-slavery legislation and the right to petition, and has opposed annexation of Texas and admission of new slave states. 9 November 1838. p.179, c3.

3355 ABOLITION DOCTRINE *to* **MR. EDITOR [W. L. GARRISON]. n.d. n.p.** Discloses that partisans and enemies are making the most of the enclosed circular, endorsed by "a fraction" of the officers and members of the Albany AS; urges readers, irrespective of party, not to support any pro-slavery candidate. 9 November 1838. p.179, c5.

3356 H. C. WRIGHT *to* **BROTHER [W. L. GARRISON]. 13 October 1838. Newburyport.** Discusses the late Peace Convention in Boston; upholds principles of peace and non-resistance, declaring that even those who oppose those principles are not willing to label them unchristian, but feel the time has not yet come to propagate such a doctrine. 9 November 1838. p.180, c2.

3357 GEO. W. CLEAVELAND *to* **n.n. 23 October 1838. Orleans, Ma.** Finds his name appears among members of late Peace Convention in Boston; requests that his name be removed, as he was not present during much of the convention and cannot support its declaration of sentiments. 9 November 1838. p.180, c3.

3358 D. RAYMOND *to* **SIR [W. L. GARRISON]. 8 October 1838. Friendsville, Md.** Sends payment and discontinues subscription to the *Liberator*, as he cannot abide Mr. Garrison's doctrine of non-resistance, and feels Garrison must be "deranged or desperately wicked" if he thinks one is bound by divine law to submit passively to outrages by ruffians. 9 November 1838. p.180, c3.

3359 H. T. *to* **MR. GARRISON. n.d. n.p.** Comments on the meeting of the Plymouth County AS at Hingham; praises the ladies' efforts; notes with satisfaction the formation of the Juvenile AS, as he feels that more encouragement should be given to the young. 16 November 1838. p.181, c2.

3360 AN ABOLITIONIST *to* **MR. EDITOR [W. L. GARRISON]. n.d. n.p.** Stresses the importance of questioning candidates, and regrets it is not done more widely; has decided, after much deliberation, to throw aside party prejudices, and cast his vote to benefit the slave; advises abolitionists to use their vote wisely, and suggests they throw a scattering vote. 16 November 1838. p.181, c3.

3361 SAMUEL WARE *to* **HON. JAMES C. ALVORD. 17 October 1838. South Deerfield.** Asks the opinion of congressional candidate, Alvord, on issues relating to slavery, abolition, and the slave trade. 16 November 1838. p.181, c4.

3362 JAMES C. ALVORD *to* **REV. SAMUEL WARE. 19 October 1838. Greenfield.** Replies to Ware's questions to political candidates: cites his behavior as a member of the Senate, to demonstrate his views; believes Patton's resolution for laying petitions on the table is a violation of freedom of speech and the right to petition, yet states that he voted against its remonstrance because of expediency. 16 November 1838. p.181, c4.

3363 THOMAS NIMS *to* **MR. SAMUEL WARE. [extract] n.d. n.p.** A congressional candidate replies to inquiries concerning his opinions on slavery and abolition: believes that the District of Columbia should be receded and that territories should abolish slavery before admission to the Union; disapproves of Congress' actions regarding petitions. 16 November 1838. p.181, c5.

3364 WILLIAM B. CALHOUN *to* **CHAUNCY CHAPIN, ESQ. 24 October 1838.** **Springfield.** Answers questions posed by the AS on the right of Congress to abolish slavery in the District of Columbia and the right of Congress to end the slave trade. 16 November 1838. p.181, c5.

3365 JOHN W. BROWNE *to* **THE WHIG COUNTY COMMITTEE OF THE COUNTY OF ESSEX. 5 November 1838. Lynn.** Declines Whig Party's unexpected nomination as candidate for the Massachusetts Senate; believes the claim of the Van Buren party to democracy is "wholly unfounded"; discusses the influence of slavery on United States politics. 16 November 1838. p.181, c6.

3366 CALEB CUSHING *to* **JOHN WHITTIER, ESQ. 8 November 1838. Salem.** Favors the abolition of slavery and the slave trade in the District of Columbia; explains that in his last letter he felt he could not stipulate his future course in Congress, but he entertains no disposition to change his views. 16 November 1838. p.182, c1.

3367 JOHN B. MAHAN *to* **A FRIEND. [extract] 26 September 1838. [from prison]** Notes that his health is improved and faith strengthened; entrusts his friend with the care of his wife and family, should he never see them again. 16 November 1838. p.182, c1.

3368 JOHN B. MAHAN *to* **JOSEPH VANCE, GOVERNOR OF OHIO. [extract from the** *Columbus Journal and Register*] **4 October 1838. Washington, Ky.** Denies having authorized anyone to write the letter concerning his arrest appearing in the 17 September issue of *Journal and Register;* reports he is being treated with all due civility; affirms his innocence of any wrongdoing. 16 November 1838. p.182, c2.

3369 JOHN B. MAHAN *to* **HIS WIFE. [extract] 22 September 1838. [from prison]** Informs that he is tolerating prison; feels deprived of the comfort of his family, but is sustained by his faith, and prays for his enemies. 16 November 1838. p.182, c1.

3370 JOHN B. MAHAN *to* **n.n. [extract] n.d. [from prison]** Explains his predicament and affirms "Heaven's will be done." 16 November 1838. p.182, c2.

3371 JOHN B. MAHAN *to* **HIS WIFE. [extract] 2 October 1838. [from prison]** Desires to be with her, but entrusts his fate to God. 16 November 1838. p.182, c2.

3372 JOHN B. MAHAN *to* **n.n. [extract] 1 October 1838. [from prison]** Reports that he has spent two weeks in prison and must wait six more before going to court; hopes to enjoy again the company of family and friends. 16 November 1838. p.182, c2.

3373 JOSEPH STURGE *to* **THE** *BRITISH EMANCIPATOR*. **1 September 1838.** **Birmingham, England.** Encloses extract of letter from a trusted friend in Jamaica. 16 November 1838. p.182, c6.

3374 n.n. *to* **JOSEPH STURGE. [extract from the** *British Emancipator*] **19 June 1838.** **Jamaica.** Relates incidents showing unusual cruelty by Mr. Whitehouse, a minister of the Wesleyan Society, toward his servants. 16 November 1838. p.182, c6.

3375 BENJ. LEAVENS *to* **SIR [W. L. GARRISON]. 30 October 1838. Dudley.** Reports formation of AS in Dudley; lists officers and resolutions; summarizes speeches and discussions. 16 November 1838. p.183, c3.

3376 D. L. CHILD *to* **GARRISON. 7 November 1838. Northampton.** Warns that Texas' withdrawal of application for admission is a dangerous maneuvre, based on a treaty between the United States and Texas which may be quite insulting to Mexico; believes a war between the United States and Mexico may be more imminent now than ever. 16 November 1838. p.183, c3.

3377 S. MILLEKEN *to* **MR. EDITOR [W. L. GARRISON]. 20 October 1838. Seaville, Me.** Reports on Hancock County anti-slavery convention, held in Ellsworth. 16 November 1838. p.183, c3.

3378 DAVID RUGGLES *to* **MR. EDITOR [W. L. GARRISON]. 30 October 1838. New York.** Gratefully acknowledges the aid of patrons and friends in putting the *Mirror of Liberty* on safe ground; states that his doctor believes that the disease affecting his eyes is related to mental anxiety, so he is retiring to Europe for a short time. 16 November 1838. p.183, c4.

3379 O. SCOTT *to* **FRIEND GARRISON. 3 November 1838. Pittsburg, Pa.** Comments briefly on their discussion of non-resistance; provides examples of his earlier objections which he feels Garrison has evaded; believes abolitionists should concentrate on abolition, not non-resistance. 16 November 1838. p.184, c2.

3380 A SIGNER OF THE DECLARATION *to* **MR. EDITOR [W. L. GARRISON]. [from the** *Emancipator*] **n.d. n.p.** Regrets that abolitionists and anti-slavery newspapers are discussing the pros and cons of the Non-Resistance Society, as he feels it is exciting prejudice against their doctrines, and alienating abolitionists. 16 November 1838. p.184, c5.

3381 CALVIN WILLARD, PLINY MERRICK, GEO. T. RICE, BENJ. BUTMAN, AND JOHN WRIGHT *to* **HON. LEVI LINCOLN. 5 November 1838. Worcester.** Request a copy of the correspondence between Lincoln and the Worcester AS; hope Lincoln will allow them to publish it for fellow citizens in the congressional district he represents. 23 November 1838. p.185, c1.

3382 LEVI LINCOLN *to* **MR. EDWARD EARLE. n.d. n.p.** Quotes letter from Earle, president of Worcester AS, asking opinions on topics relating to slavery; states that no interrogatories were posed by the district nominating committee which took evidence of his behavior in the past; declines to answer most of their questions, urging them to study his record. 23 November 1838. p.185, c1.

3383 NATH'L B. BORDEN *to* **REV. S. HOPKINS EMERY. 8 November 1838. Fall River.** Opposes candidates' pledging themselves in advance, as situations may change and the member should be free to change with them; however, details his views on slavery and abolition; encourages anti-slavery workers. 23 November 1838. p.185, c3.

3384 NATHANIEL COLVER *to* **BROTHER COWLES. 12 October 1838. Wolcottville.** Has attended the recent Hartford County AS meeting, and presented resolutions against slavery at the Hartford Baptist Association meeting; discusses Christianity and slavery. 23 November 1838. p.186, c1.

3385 SAMUEL J. MAY *to* **MR. ELIAS RICHARDS. 12 November 1838. South Scituate.** Regrets he cannot attend the County AS meeting at Weymouth; expresses dismay at unfavorable sentiment toward Hon. John Q. Adams; counsels that to withdraw confidence from Adams would be unwise, ungrateful, and unjust. 23 November 1838. p.186, c4.

3386 JOHN L. LORD *to* **BRO. GARRISON. 20 November 1838. Newbury (Belleville).** Reports that Rev. P. R. Russell of Lynn visited and gave three lectures on slavery, after which a society of fifty members was formed; lists officers. 23 November 1838. p.186, c5.

3387 GERRIT SMITH *to* **THE** *FRIEND OF MAN.* **[extract] n.d. n.p.** Suggests that the organization of a new AA for those abolitionists who cannot hold fellowship with those who vote for pro-slavery lawmakers or candidates would be expedient. 23 November 1838. p.186, c5.

3388 JONATHAN P. MAGILL *to* **EDMUND QUINCY AND OTHERS. 12 September 1838. Bucks County, Pa.** Expresses thanks for invitation to the Peace Convention; feels the convention is an entering wedge in the fight between love and organized violence. 23 November 1838. p.188, c2.

3389 WM. LADD *to* **MR. GARRISON. 7 November 1838. Portsmouth, N.H.** Clarifies his views of the Peace Convention; believes that "Woman was formed to persuade, rather than command," and that women should not speak at public assemblies; asserts that *"all war is contrary to the spirit of the Gospel,"* yet disagrees with many points in the Peace Constitution. 23 November 1838. p.188, c2.

3390 THOS. VAN RENSSELAER *to* **REV. JOSHUA LEAVITT. 26 November 1838. Boston.** Complains of poor treatment he received on board the steamboat *J. W. Richmond*, travelling from Boston to Providence; having paid more for his berth than white passengers, he was nevertheless removed by force and made to stay on the deck. 30 November 1838. p.189, c2.

3391 LEVERETT SALTONSTALL *to* **MESSRS. E. HUNT, WM. B. DODGE, AND BENJ. F. NEWHALL. 1 November 1838. Salem.** Replies to questions regarding his opinions on slavery in the District of Columbia, on Congress' authority to abolish slavery there and in the territories, and on its authority to abolish the slave trade. 30 November 1838. p.189, c4.

3392 GERRIT SMITH *to* **BROTHER GOODELL. 8 November 1838. Peterborough.** Hopes that voters will not cast ballot for those who simply call themselves "abolitionists," but for those who gave satisfactory anwers to interrogations; compares candidate Bradish favorably to Seward. 30 November 1838. p.189, c5.

3393 A MEMBER OF THE INDIANA YEARLY MEETING [OF FRIENDS] *to* **WILLIAM BASSETT. [extract] 12 October 1838. n.p.** Reports that only one copy of Bassett's letter is in circulation in the area, due to the Friends' stand on abolitionism; they support immediate emancipation and oppose colonization, yet are not allowed to support the AS. 30 November 1838. p.190, c1.

3394 JOSEPH STURGE *to* **THE EDITOR OF THE** *LONDON SUN.* **4 October 1838. Birmingham.** Challenges those who report that blacks in the West Indies are refusing to work for equitable wages to prove their allegation if this is truly the case; Sturge has only heard evidence to the contrary. 30 November 1838. p.190, c2.

3395 SAMUEL J. MAY *to* **FRIEND [W. L. GARRISON]. 24 November 1838. South Scituate.** Writes to correct published letter to Mr. Richards; discusses views of John Quincy Adams, who he believes is unsure of the limits and duties of his power, yet is very zealous and interested in the cause of the enslaved. 30 November 1838. p.190, c4.

3396 L. *to* **FRIEND GARRISON. 20 November 1838. Salem.** Challenges the *Liberator*'s interpretation of election results; does not find that Saltonstall has won by so huge a majority as reported in the *Liberator*; believes that the abolitionist cause has been retarded rather than advanced by the elections. 30 November 1838. p.190, c4.

3397 J. C. PATTERSON, STANMORE BROOKS, WILLIAM EDDINS, JAMES S. POPE *to* **REV. MR. TURPIN. 14 June 1838. Cambridge.** Inform Turpin, on behalf of members of the community, that his labors as missionary to the black population are quite unpopular in their section of the country. 30 November 1838. p.190, c6.

3398 JAMES S. POPE AND 352 OTHERS *to* **REV. MR. TURPIN. n.d. n.p.** Citizens of Abbeville and Edgefield protest his missionary work among the black population; they prefer the old, safe customs, and regard his teaching of catechism and the Bible as the future cornerstone of abolition. 30 November 1838. p.190, c6.

3399 AMOS FARNSWORTH *to* **FRIENDS OF THE SLAVE. n.d. n.p.** Announces a convention of abolitionists of the Fourth Congressional District to decide how best to vote. 30 November 1838. p.191, c4.

3400 DANIEL HENSON, THOS. BROWN, IRA GRAY, WILLIAM JUNIER AND THOS. DALTON *to* **MR. KNAPP. 6 August 1838. Boston.** Members of the Committee of Colored Friends esteem and praise Knapp's labors in the field of abolition; find their enemy—prejudice—retiring, and the monster—slavery—trembling. 30 November 1838. p.191, c5.

3401 N. P. ROGERS *to* **OLIVER JOHNSON. 17 October 1838. Plymouth, N.H.** Regrets he cannot attend the third anniversary meeting of the Rhode Island AS; notes progress of the cause, despite Dr. Wayland's criticism; compares abolitionists to Roger Williams in his search for freedom. 7 December 1838. p.194, c2.

3402 LOUIS SHERIDAN *to* **LEWIS TAPPAN, ESQ. 16 July 1838. Edina, Liberia.** Details findings of soil study for which he was sent to Africa by the Young Men's CSS of Pennsylvania and New York; also tells of his surprise and indignation at conditions in Liberia and the behavior of the governor. 7 December 1838. p.194, c4.

3403 LEWIS TAPPAN *to* **n.n. [extract] n.d. n.p.** Gives brief biography of Louis Sheridan, who has just been sent by CSS to conduct a soil study in Africa. 7 December 1838. p.194, c5.

3404 A FUGITIVE SLAVE *to* **MR. EDITOR [W. L. GARRISON]. 19 November 1838. New York.** Assails insurrection in Canada as a "sanguinary struggle for what is called Liberty"; discredits "American Liberty," and hopes Canada remains in the Commonwealth to protect colonies of runaway American slaves there. 7 December 1838. p.195, c1.

3405 SILAS S. JOHNSON *to* **MR. EDITOR [W. L. GARRISON]. 5 November 1838. Stoughton.** Reports on anti-slavery events in Stoughton; recent series of lectures by Rev. Wise well-attended; new AS being formed. 7 December 1838. p.195, c1.

3406 P. R. RUSSELL *to* **BRO. GARRISON. n.d. n.p.** Reports that he has recently assisted in the formation of ASS in Wenham, Salisbury Point, and Belleville (Newbury). 7 December 1838. p.195, c2.

3407 HIGHLY RESPECTABLE FRIEND IN THE SOUTH *to* **n.n. [extract] n.d. n.p.** Feels "heartily sick" of people there, who seem "almost void of a moral sense"; denounces behavior of "respected" men, who cheat and use violence to settle disputes. 7 December 1838. p.195, c3.

3408 AMOS FARNSWORTH *to* **FRIENDS OF THE SLAVE. n.d. Massachusetts.** Admonishes them to vote in the 17 December elections; announces abolitionist convention at Middlesex Hotel, Concord, on Tuesday 11 December. 7 December 1838. p.195, c4.

3409 A. ST. CLAIR *to* **BR. GARRISON. n.d. n.p** Reports having heard from Rev. Mr. Towne, formerly of Amesbury, that Garrison once ran for Secretary of ACS, and upon losing, switched his allegiance to immediate emancipation; inquires whether it is true that revenge is his motive. 7 December 1838. p.195, c4.

3410 n.n. *to* **n.n. [extract] n.d. Montpelier, Vt.** Reports that Elliot Cresson is making a hasty tour through their state, lecturing on colonization; affirms continued support for recently passed anti-slavery resolutions; encloses resolutions on Texas and the right of petition. 7 December 1838. p.195, c5.

3411 HENRY GREW *to* **BROTHER [W. L. GARRISON]. 15 November 1838. Philadelphia.** Entreats him to review the principles of his new organization; supports him in advocacy of forbearance, non-resistance, and peace, yet cannot support his disavowal of human government. 7 December 1838. p.196, c2.

3412 H. C. WRIGHT *to* **G. C. BECKWITH, COR. SEC. OF THE AMERICAN PEACE SOCIETY. 27 November 1838. Essex.** Requests that Beckwith state publicly whether he believes that principles of the gospel apply to the relation of individuals to society and of citizens to government; understands that Beckwith believes so, but would like him to explain his views. 7 December 1838. p.196, c4.

3413 WILLIAM A. STEERE *to* **WILLIAM LLOYD GARRISON. 29 November 1838. Smithfield.** Believes that the constitution of the New England Non-Resistance Society must be consistent with Christian law; requests that his name be included among signers; wonders why so many fear abolishing human government. 7 December 1838. p.196, c5.

3414 H. R. HITCHCOCK *to* **THE EDITOR OF THE** *EMANCIPATOR.* **18 November 1837. Kaluaaha.** Reports on abolition in the Sandwich Islands; believes that victory is surely on abolitionist side, and that a neutral response to slavery cannot be justified; describes the state of their mission. 14 December 1838. p.197, c2.

3415 REV. J. S. GREEN *to* **BROTHER LEAVITT. [extract] 29 May 1837. Honolulu, Oahu, Sandwich Islands.** Prays for his efforts for the downtrodden slave; tells of lecture by Dr. Lafon, a former Virginia slaveholder who now speaks against slavery. 14 December 1838. p.197, c3.

3416 REV. PETER GULICK *to* **REV. THEODORE S. WRIGHT. [extract] June 1837. Honolulu.** Relates that he has sympathized with abolitionists ever since he investigated the system of slavery; believes slavery is against the teaching of God, and supports immediate emancipation. 14 December 1838. p.197, c3.

3417 HENRY SCOTT *to* **FELLOW CITIZENS. [from the** *Massachusetts Spy*] **4 December 1838. Worcester, Ma.** Charges that he and his brothers of color are treated as "villains" in Worcester; argues that they uphold the same duties as white men, yet are denied the same privileges. 14 December 1838. p.197, c4.

3418 JOSEPH STURGE *to* **THE EDITOR OF THE** *LONDON PATRIOT.* **9 October 1838. Birmingham.** Sends extracts of letters recently received from Jamaica which testify that his view of the admirable conduct of Negroes in Jamaica is correct. 14 December 1838. p.198, c1.

3419 GEORGE BLYTHE *to* **JOSEPH STURGE. [extract] 21 August 1838. Hampden, Trelawney, Jamaica.** Reports that all are pleased with the behavior of emancipated Negroes after the celebration; most returned to the same labor to which they had been accustomed, many without even knowing their wages. 14 December 1838. p.198, c1.

3420 J. M. PHILLIPPO *to* **JOSEPH STURGE. [extract] 25 August 1838. Sligoville, Jamaica.** Describes the honorable behavior of the newly-emancipated blacks; states that planters' behavior remains unchanged, guided by mercenary and selfish motives; tells of extremely low wages offered by some, and the people's determination to receive just compensation. 14 December 1838. p.198, c2.

3421 H. C. WRIGHT *to* **BROTHER [W. L. GARRISON]. n.d. n.p.** Reports that Elliot Cresson is in New England, "inflaming the prejudices and hatred" of whites against blacks; remembers his attack on New England and Garrison in a speech given the previous year; relates his new plan to plead the cause of African missions. 14 December 1838. p.199, c2.

3422 J. B. *to* **THE** *LIBERATOR*. **10 December 1838. Andover, Ma.** Assails Elliot Cresson, who had given a recent pro-colonization lecture series; criticizes arguments put forth. 14 December 1838. p.199, c3.

3423 P. C. P. *to* **n.n. [extract] n.d. Andover.** Discloses that Elliot Cresson refused to participate in a public discussion of the merits of colonization while at Andover; calls on abolitionists everywhere to defeat the fiendish purpose of colonization. 14 December 1838. p.199, c4.

3424 n.n. *to* **BROTHER GARRISON. [extract] n.d. Plainfield, Ct.** Exhorts Christians to carry out principles of non-resistance. 14 December 1838. p.200, c2.

3425 THOMAS HASKELL *to* **FRIEND GARRISON. 3 December 1838. Gloucester.** Supports principles of the New England Non-Resistance Society; reports that H. C. Wright has given lectures, and principles are taking "strong hold" in Gloucester. 14 December 1838. p.200, c2.

3426 H. C. WRIGHT *to* **G. C. BECKWITH, COR. SEC. OF THE AMERICAN PEACE SOCIETY. 27 November 1838. Essex.** Reviews work of Beckwith, who is currently devoting his efforts to a Congress of Nations; counsels him to attempt plan on a smaller scale. 14 December 1838. p.200, c3.

3427 GERRIT SMITH *to* **MR. EDITOR. [From the** *Union* **(Cazenovia)** *Herald*] **23 November 1838. Peterborough.** Urges abolitionists to elect national and state legislators who will work to repeal laws allowing slavery; states his reasons for advocating the creation of a new Abolition Society. 21 December 1838. p.201, c2.

3428 A. BROWN, JR. *to* **MR. W. H. BURLEIGH. 21 November 1838. Beaver, Pa.** Reports having met Rev. Mr. Babcock on board steamboat from Beaver to Pittsburgh, Pennsylvania; relates that Babcock denounced Rev. O. Scott as a liar upon reading his letter in the *Emancipator*; notes that Scott became known as a liar *after* he became an abolitionist. 21 December 1838. p.201, c4.

3429 THE PUBLISHER OF THE *MEMPHIS GAZETTE to* **THE** *EMANCIPATOR*. **8 March 1838. Memphis, Tn.** Demands that they stop sending their paper; if they wish to disseminate their doctrine, they should come South and distribute the papers themselves, and risk being hanged at Tennesseans' expense. 21 December 1838. p.201, c5.

3430 OLIVER JOHNSON *to* **HON. JOHN QUINCY ADAMS. 27 November 1838. Providence, R.I.** Sends resolution of the Rhode Island AS, praising Adams' work in Congress against oppression. 21 December 1838. p.202, c1.

3431 J. Q. ADAMS *to* **OLIVER JOHNSON. 13 December 1838. Washington.** Feels honored by the resolutions of the Rhode Island AS; discusses the need for the "free" land of America to abolish slavery, as servitude is incompatible with any system of liberty. 21 December 1838. p.202, c1.

3432 P. R. RUSSELL *to* **BRO. GARRISON. 17 December 1838. Lynn.** Tells of his anti-slavery lectures in Chelmsford; the meeting was disrupted by rioters, some of whom he names, but was not forced to adjourn until the end. 21 December 1838. p.203, c1.

3433 M. *to* **MR. GARRISON. n.d. n.p.** Urges that anti-slavery petitions be circulated soon and sent to Congress; wishes to be rid of the sin of slavery; suggests withdrawal of all government troops from Southern states. 21 December 1838. p.203, c1.

3434 NATHAN BROOKS *to* **W. L. GARRISON, ESQ. 15 December 1838. Concord.** Refutes Mr. Stanton's accusation, published in the *Liberator*, that he closed meetinghouses to anti-slavery meetings; wonders if "sinister motives" prompted Stanton's lies. 21 December 1838. p.203, c3.

3435 A. A. PHELPS *to* **FRIEND GARRISON. n.d. n.p.** Sends letter received from Mr. Woodbury for publication. 21 December 1838. p.203, c3.

3436 JAMES T. WOODBURY *to* **A. A. PHELPS. 15 December 1838. Acton.** Expresses appreciation of the resolutions passed at the recent anti-slavery meeting, which convinced him of propriety and necessity of questioning candidates for political office. 21 December 1838. p.203, c3.

3437 A. A. PHELPS *to* **FRIEND GARRISON. n.d. n.p.** Rejoices that the scattering of votes in the last election was not done wholly by Democrats in the fourth district, but by all parties; notes that this shows mutual confidence of abolitionists in all parties. 21 December 1838. p.203, c3.

3438 A YOUNG MECHANIC *to* **n.n. [extract] Brooklyn, Ct.** Asks to become a member of the Non-Resistance Society; sends contribution. 21 December 1838. p.204, c2.

3439 H. C. WRIGHT *to* **G. C. BECKWITH, COR. SEC. OF THE AMERICAN PEACE SOCIETY. 28 November 1838. Essex.** Discusses the great object of the cause of peace, "to ascertain and inculcate the gospel method of adjusting difficulties between men and men," and its application. 21 December 1838. p.204, c2.

3440 DAVID L. DODGE *to* **THE NEW ENGLAND NON-RESISTANCE SOCIETY. 8 October 1838. Cedar Brook, Plainfield, N.J.** Observes the progress of the society with deep interest; agrees with their doctrine of the unlawfulness of war, whether offensive or defensive, but disagrees with several points in their constitution. 21 December 1838. p.204, c3.

3441 H. C. H. *to* **WILLIAM LLOYD GARRISON. 5 December 1838. Spring Dale, Pa.** Requests a copy of the proceedings of the Non-Resistance convention; used to believe such societies were worthless, as they did not adopt strong enough principles, yet realizes that the Non-Resistance Society has done so. 21 December 1838. p.204, c4.

3442 H. *to* **MR. WILLIS. [from the** *Boston Recorder*] **n.d. n.p.** Differs with the *Recorder*'s account of the Peace Convention; feels that the community will eventually "settle down" under the beliefs which it at first found too "ultra." 21 December 1838. p.204, c5.

3443 GERRIT SMITH *to* **THE EDITOR OF THE** *UNION HERALD*. **1 December 1838. Peterborough.** Reports that John Williams and John Williams Scott, the two fugitive slaves of Samuel Ferguson to whom the editor loaned his horse, are making undisturbed progress. 28 December 1838. p.205, c2.

3444 GERRIT SMITH *to* **S. E. CORNISH. 6 December 1838. Peterboro'.** Reports that James G. Birney is detained at Smith's house, recovering from fall off horse; discusses Cornish's idea to send ship to African colony to bring "sufferers home." 28 December 1838. p.205, c6.

3445 HENRY B. STANTON *to* **WM. LLOYD GARRISON. 25 December 1838. Cambridgeport.** Replies to letter from Nathan Brooks which accused Stanton of lying about the anti-slavery convention in Concord; discusses their points of difference; quotes many abolitionists supporting Stanton's report. 28 December 1838. p.206, c4.

3446 GEORGE W. BANCROFT AND LUTHER BOUTELLE *to* **STANTON. 25 December 1838. Groton.** Report on their business at Townsend; agree that Stanton's representation of the meeting at Concord was correct. 28 December 1838. p.206, c5.

3447 FRANCIS JACKSON AND WENDELL PHILLIPS *to* **WM. LLOYD GARRISON. 27 December 1838. Boston.** Declare that they heard all of Mr. Stanton's words at the meeting in Concord, and that he did not lead them to think that Mr. Brooks advised the closing of doors against him. 28 December 1838. p.207, c1.

3448 n.n. *to* **n.n. [extract] 26 December 1838. Carlisle, Middlesex County.** Reports on St. Clair's second lecture at which men turned out to mob them, but did not disrupt the meeting; declares that the mob awakened them, and they are now going to organize a society. 28 December 1838. p.207, c3.

3449 J. P. BLANCHARD *to* **THE EDITOR OF THE** *LIBERATOR* **[W. L. GARRISON]. n.d. n.p.** Believes that Brother Wright's letters attempt to correct an inconsistency of the Executive Committee of the American Peace Society; tries to answer Wright's questions about their interpretation of the gospel. 28 December 1838. p.208, c2.

3450 S. W. *to* **FRIEND GARRISON. 10 December 1838. Lee.** Feels pleased with Garrison's course as an editor and as an abolitionist; fails to see how a man can be a consistent abolitionist without being a "peace man." 28 December 1838. p.208, c3.

3451 CHARLES MARRIOTT *to* **WM. L. GARRISON. 15 December 1838. Hudson, N.Y.** Believes slavery will soon be abolished; discusses the Non-Resistance Society, the doctrine of non-resistance, and the place of females. 28 December 1838. p.208, c4.

[1839]

3452 A. STEVENSON *to* **THE EDITOR OF THE** *LONDON MAIL***. 29 October 1838. 23 Portland Place.** Refers to correspondence between himself and Mr. O'Connell, publicized in the *Chronicle*; denies allegation that he is a slave-breeder. 4 January 1839. p.1, c5.

3453 n.n. *to* **BROTHER [W. L. GARRISON]. 30 November 1838. Philadelphia, Pa.** Thanks him for his last letter; regrets persistence of prejudice, even among abolitionists, toward his people. 4 January 1839. p.1, c6.

3454 H. C. WRIGHT *to* **BROTHER [W. L. GARRISON]. 22 December 1839. Newburyport.** Encloses extract of a letter from one of the "multilated victims of American liberty" expressing his views on America. 4 January 1839. p.1, c6.

3455 n.n. *to* **H. C. WRIGHT. [extract] 30 November 1838. Philadelphia.** Condemns persistence of prejudice; considers Wright a true friend because his actions "do not give the lie" to his words; believes the Declaration of Sentiments of the Peace Convention are sound, but feels unprepared to sign them. 4 January 1839. p.1, c6.

3456 O. SCOTT *to* **FRIEND GARRISON. 28 December 1838. Lowell.** On Gerrit Smith's proposal for the re-organization of the AS. 4 January 1839. p.2, c1.

3457 HENRY B. STANTON *to* **MR. EDITOR [W. L. GARRISON]. 1 January 1839. Cambridgeport.** Annotates extracts of letters from Levi Warren, Abner Brooks, and A. A. Phelps, relating to his being barred from speaking against slavery in Townsend. 4 January 1839. p.3, c3.

3458 LEVI WARREN, LEVI CONANT AND ABNER BROOKS *to* **MR. EDITOR. [from the** *Yeoman's Gazette***] 25 December 1838. Townsend, West Village.** On the refusal to grant Mr. H. B. Stanton the opportunity to speak on abolitionism in Townsend. 4 January 1839. p.3, c3.

3459 A. A. PHELPS *to* **MR. STANTON. 28 December 1838. Boston, Ma.** Reports arrangements made for Stanton to speak in Townsend. 4 January 1839. p.3, c3.

3460 JAMES WILSON, JR. *to* **N. P. ROGERS. 15 November 1838. Keene.** Whig candidate for governor of New Hampshire expresses his views on abolitionism. 11 January 1839. p.6, c2.

3461 B. S. CONWALD *to* **J. A. ADAMS. [from the New York** *Journal of Commerce***] 19 December 1838. Montgomery, Al.** Threatens Adams with assassination for maligning Mr. Stevenson, the Minister to England. 11 January 1839. p.6, c5.

3462 MR. BURKE *to* **NATH'L P. ROGERS. 15 November 1838. Newport.** Expresses opinions on slavery. 11 January 1839. p.6, c3.

3463 MARIA W. CHAPMAN *to* **OLIVER JOHNSON. 4 November 1838. Boston.** Regrets that she and her husband were unable to attend a meeting of the Rhode Island AS. 11 January 1839. p.6, c5.

3464 OLD MIDDLESEX *to* **MR. EDITOR [W. L. GARRISON]. n.d. n.p.** Pleads for help from abolitionists of the Fourth Congressional District in Massachusetts. 11 January 1839. p.6, c6.

3465 JUSTICE *to* **MR. EDITOR [W. L. GARRISON]. n.d. n.p.** Criticizes colonizationists. 11 January 1839. p.6, c6.

3466 A MEMBER OF THE BOSTON FEMALE AS *to* **MR. GARRISON. 4 January 1839. Boston, Ma.** Corrects earlier error by the *Liberator*; the annual meeting of Boston Female AS, not a prayer meeting, was mobbed on 21 October 1835. 11 January 1839. p.7 c1.

3467 G. W. S. *to* **BRO. GARRISON. 2 January 1839. Carlisle.** Reports abolitionists are still working hard in Carlisle despite "mobocratic" attacks. 11 January 1839. p.7, c2.

3468 WENDELL PHILLIPS *to* **MESSRS. JACKSON, QUINCY AND BASSETT. 7 January 1839. Boston.** Wishes continued success to the *Liberator*. 11 January 1839. p.7, c2.

3469 CLERGYMAN *to* **REV. MR. M. OF MASSACHUSETTS. 1 January 1839. New York.** Warns of danger of false "friends of the oppressed" and of using improper means to advance the abolitionist cause; refers to article entitled "Revivals Hindered," from 29 December *New York Observer*. 11 January 1839. p.7, c5.

3470 ORIGEN BACHELER *to* **FRIEND GARRISON. 29 December 1838. New York.** Demands that Garrison substantiate charges that a resolution offered by Bacheler at a recent peace meeting was absurd and contrary to Mr. Ladd's resolution. 11 January 1839, p.8, c5.

3471 AMASA WALKER *to* **FRIEND GARRISON. 31 December 1838. Boston.** A member of the American Peace Society disavows hostility toward Non-Resistance Society alleged by *Liberator*; hopes both groups can cooperate despite differences in doctrines. 11 January 1839. p.8, c6.

3472 J. S. GREEN *to* **THE PRESIDENT OF THE ONEIDA INSTITUTE. 29 January 1838. Maui, Sandwich Isles.** States that he has not forgotten the poor slaves in the United States, yet holds that existence of 3,000,000 slaves does not justify forgetting 500,000,000 "unevangelized" elsewhere. 18 January 1839. p.9, c2.

3473 GROTON *to* **FRIEND GARRISON. n.d. n.p.** Proposes that Fourth District abolitionists should not wait for lecturers to come, but organize now, in order to scatter twelve hundred votes in February. 18 January 1839. p.10, c3.

3474 FOURTH DISTRICT *to* **THE EDITOR [W. L. GARRISON]. n.d. Massachusetts.** Assails Senator Prentiss of Vermont for his non-support of Vermont resolutions; warns that candidates Brooks and Parmenter are similarly inclined. 18 January 1839. p.10, c4.

3475 CAMBRIDGE *to* **ABOLITIONISTS OF THE FOURTH DISTRICT. n.d. Cambridge, Ma.** Urges them to double their vote and defeat pro-slavery congressional candidates, Brooks and Parmenter. 18 January 1839. p.10, c4.

3476 n.n. *to* **THE EDITOR [W. L. GARRISON]. n.d. n.p.** Declares that Fourth District election will determine whether the successive defeat of pro-slavery candidates will force political parties to endorse anti-slavery candidates; if so, the formation of a separate anti-slavery party would be unnecessary. 18 January 1839. p.10, c4.

3477 H. B. STANTON *to* **WM. LLOYD GARRISON. 15 January 1839. Cambridgeport.** Sends extracts from letters relating to the controversy taking place in the Fourth District. 18 January 1839. p.10, c5.

3478 N. P. ROGERS *to* **H. B. STANTON. 10 January 1839. Plymouth, N.H.** Exhorts abolitionists to vote in congressional trial. 18 January 1839. p.10, c5.

3479 JAMES G. BIRNEY *to* **H. B. STANTON. 24 December 1838. New York.** Foresees victory in the Fourth Congressional District. 18 January 1839. p.10, c5.

3480 JOHN G. WHITTIER *to* **BROTHER STANTON. 12 January 1839. Philadelphia, Pa.** Feels encouraged by abolitionist gains in the Fourth District of Massachusetts; urges voters to "be true to the slave." 18 January 1839. p.10, c6.

3481 PRESERVED SMITH *to* **THE EDITOR [W. L. GARRISON]. 8 January 1839. Carlisle.** Refutes charges of having participated in a riot. 18 January 1839. p.11, c1.

3482 n.n. *to* **THE** *LIBERATOR.* **11 January 1839. Amesbury.** Reports remarks of Rev. Mr. Torrey at previous AS meeting in Essex County that those in charge of abolitionist cause were prepared to hand over management to younger members, and that the *Liberator* was being discontinued by many in the Salem area. 18 January 1839. p.11, c3.

3483 n.n. *to* **THE** *LIBERATOR.* **7 January 1839. Amesbury.** Reports rumour circulated at recent Essex County AS meeting that Garrison and other "standard bearers" were prepared to abandon the cause. 18 January 1839. p.11, c3.

3484 FRIEND FROM LYNN *to* **FRIEND GARRISON. 14 January 1839. Fitchburg, Ma.** Reports on Mr. St. Clair's resolution, passed at a recent district society meeting, to circulate a new abolitionist paper among those who subscribe to none; resolution appears as part of scheme to undermine the *Liberator.* 18 January 1839. p.11, c4.

3485 n.n. *to* **THE** *LIBERATOR.* **[extract] n.d. Lynn, Ma.** Encloses copy of the Fitchburg Resolutions [not printed], which ASS are called upon immediately to endorse and support at annual meeting; believes the scheme will fail at Lynn. 18 January 1839. p.11, c4.

3486 PHILIP SCARBOROUGH *to* **BROTHER GARRISON. 11 January 1839. Brooklyn.** Reports that the Windham County AS has unanimously passed an endorsement of the *Liberator*, proposed by Rev. Mr. Coe. 18 January 1839. p.11, c5.

3487 MARIA W. CHAPMAN *to* **MESSRS. JACKSON, QUINCY AND BASSETT. n.d. n.p.** Renews annual subscription for the Boston Female AS; quotes resolution praising the *Liberator*. 18 January 1839. p.11, c6.

3488 LUTHER S. NOYES *to* **BROTHER. 31 December 1838. New Ipswich.** On the Boston Peace Convention. 18 January 1839. p.12, c3.

3489 SETH WHITMORE *to* **THE EDITOR [W. L. GARRISON]. 18 November 1838. Lockport, N.Y.** Announces that he will replace D. Raymond as a subscriber to the *Liberator*. 18 January 1839. p.12, c4.

3490 S. ROBBINS *to* **FRIEND GARRISON. 18 November 1838. Lockport, N.Y.** Reports that many in Lockwood embrace principles of "ultra abolitionism" and non-resistance; however, efforts to these ends remain to be seen. 18 January 1839. p.12, c5.

3491 DISTRICT NUMBER FOUR *to* **THE EDITOR OF THE** *BOSTON COURIER*. **20 December 1838. n.p.** Assails Whig abolitionists of Fourth District for defeating, against the popular will, citizens' efforts to secure representation in Congress. 25 January 1839. p.13, c1.

3492 A UNIVERSALIST ABOLITIONIST *to* **BRO. GARRISON. 10 December 1838. Woburn.** Assails Mr. Whittemore of the *Trumpet* for preaching universalism but practicing prejudice. 25 January 1839. p.14, c1.

3493 HARRIET FOSTER *to* **GARRISON. 5 January 1839, n.p.** Forwards one hundred dollars from the Salem Female AS. 25 January 1839. p.14, c3.

3494 J. W. ALDEN *to* **FRIEND GARRISON. 15 January 1839. Cambridgeport.** Criticizes recent editorial entitled "Watchman, What of the Night?" for the undue alarm it manifested over the prospect of a new political paper in Massachusetts. 25 January 1839. p.14, c3.

3495 GERRIT SMITH *to* **HENRY B. STANTON. 12 January 1839. Peterboro'.** On the Fourth District election. 25 January 1839. p.14, c4.

3496 CHARLES T. TORREY *to* **MR. GARRISON. 18 January 1839. Salem.** Refutes anonymous letter in the previous *Liberator* which attributed false statements to him. 25 January 1839. p.14, c5.

3497 A. ST. CLAIR *to* **BRO. GARRISON. n.d. n.p.** Charges Garrison with making false statements in his editorial entitled, "Watchman, What of the Night?" 25 January 1839. p.14, c6.

3498 A. A. PHELPS *to* **MR. GARRISON. n.d. n.p.** Denies any prior knowledge of the resolutions of the Fitchburg meeting [to publish a new abolitionist paper]. 25 January 1839. p.15, c1.

3499 SAMUEL J. MAY *to* **THE ABOLITIONISTS OF MASSACHUSETTS. 10 January 1839. South Scituate.** Laments the division of abolitionist ranks created by the questions of women's rights and non-resistance. 25 January 1839. p.15, c4.

3500 ICHABOD MORTON *to* **WM. L. GARRISON. 20 January 1839. Plymouth.** Condemns sectarians as "Pharisees" among true abolitionists. 25 January 1839. p.15, c6.

3501 ORIGEN BACHELER *to* **FRIEND GARRISON. 14 January 1839. New York.** Refutes principles of "no-government" [non-resistance]. 25 January 1839. p.16, c4.

3502 n.n. *to* **MR. EDITOR [W. L. GARRISON]. n.d. Essex, Ma.** Urges abolitionists of the Fourth District to do their duty by the slave in forthcoming congressional election. 1 February 1839. p.19, c6.

3503 S. L. *to* **MR. EDITOR [W. L. GARRISON]. 1 January 1839. Theological Seminary, Andover.** On the General Assembly of 1837 and abolition. 8 February 1839. p.21, c6.

3504 JOHN O. BURLEIGH *to* **SIR [W. L. GARRISON]. 15 January 1839. Oxford.** Notes that disastrous consequences would have ensued, had the managerial reins of the AS fallen into the hands of the clergy. 8 February 1839. p.22, c1.

3505 WM. WILBUR *to* **GARRISON. 22 January 1839. Fall River.** Reports on Bristol County anti-slavery proceedings. 8 February 1839. p.22, c2.

3506 A. ST. CLAIR *to* **BR. GARRISON. 28 January 1839. Lynn.** Discusses the Fitchburg resolution controversy. 8 February 1839. p.22, c3.

3507 D. L. CHILD AND L. M. CHILD *to* **THE MASSACHUSETTS AS. 15 January 1839. Northampton.** Having been unable to attend AS meeting, the Childs send a letter to the Society discussing the division in the ranks of abolitionists. 8 February 1839. p.22, c4.

3508 ONE WHO KNOWS *to* **MR. EDITOR [W. L. GARRISON]. n.d. n.p.** Advocates equal rights for women. 8 February 1839. p.22, c4.

3509 O. SCOTT *to* **FRIEND GARRISON. 4 February 1839. n.p.** Corrects minutes of a Massachusetts AS meeting in the *Liberator*. 8 February 1839. p.22, c5.

3510 EZRA R. JOHNSON *to* **FRIEND GARRISON. 25 January 1839. New Bedford.** Remarks on the fourth and fifth resolutions passed by the Bristol County meeting. 8 February 1839. p.22, c5.

3511 GEORGE W. STACY *to* **MR. EDITOR [W. L. GARRISON]. n.d. n.p.** Corrects false charges. 8 February 1839. p.22, c6.

3512 E. DAVIS, PRESIDENT OF THE HOLDEN AS *to* **WILLIAM L. GARRISON. 21 January 1839. Holden.** Reports that the Holden AS did not pass Fitchburg resolutions proposed by A. St. Clair. 8 February 1839. p.22, c6.

3513 TRUTH TELLER *to* **BRO. GARRISON. n.d. Marshfield, Ma.** Discusses clergymen's interest in the cause and the opposition generated to the *Liberator*. 8 February 1839. p.23, c1.

3514 WM. SMITH *to* **BROTHER GARRISON. 18 January 1839. Spring Arbor.** Requests renewal of his subscription. 8 February 1839. p.23, c2.

3515 A BROTHER IN OHIO *to* **THE *LIBERATOR*. n.d. n.p.** Urges the *Liberator* to remain faithful to the principles stated in its prospectus. 8 February 1839. p.23, c2.

3516 A. A. PHELPS *to* **MR. GARRISON. n.d. n.p.** Corrects his own error; states that only Messrs. Colover and St. Clair favored Fitchburg resolutions before the public meeting, but many spoke in favor during the meeting. 8 February 1839. p.23, c2.

3517 WM. LLOYD GARRISON *to* **JOHN QUINCY ADAMS. n.d. n.p.** Questions Adams about his middle-of-the-road stance on slavery. 8 February 1839. p.23, c3.

3518 I. BOUTWELL *to* **MR. GARRISON. 31 December 1838. Theological Seminary, Andover.** Encloses extract of letter from friend relating the history of the Louisville African Sabbath School. 8 February 1839. p.24, c5.

3519 n.n. *to* **I. BOUTWELL. n.d. n.p.** Details the origin, progress, and dissolution of the African Sabbath School in Louisville. 8 February 1839. p.24, c5.

3520 SOUTH *to* **SIR [W. L. GARRISON]. December 1838. Somerton, Va.** Requests that no more copies of the *Liberator* be sent south of the Potomac. 15 February 1839. p.25, c1.

3521 LYNCH CLUB OF CHARLESTON *to* **"YOU SON OF A BITCH." n.d. Charleston, S.C.** Declares that Garrison will be lynched at the state's expense if his papers are sent South again. 15 February 1839. p.25, c1.

3522 STEPHEN C. PHILLIPS *to* **E. G. LORING. [from the** *Boston Atlas***] 25 January 1839. Salem, Ma.** Declines invitation to address a meeting of citizens in favor of abolition in the District of Columbia, as he is not a public speaker, and does not wish to appear an abolitionist. 15 February 1839. p.25, c4.

3523 W. R. HAYES *to* **H. G. LUDLOW. 26 December 1838. Barbadoes.** Discourses on the West Indies. 15 February 1839. p.25, c6.

3524 SETH SPRAGUE *to* **FRIEND GARRISON. 9 February 1839. Duxbury.** Denies rumor that he stated, at Faneuil Hall, that Washington was not a slaveholder. 15 February 1839. p.27, c1.

3525 DANIEL MANSFIELD *to* **MR. EDITOR [W. L. GARRISON]. 28 January 1839. Malden.** On abolition in Malden. 15 February 1839. p.28, c5.

3526 A GENTLEMAN IN BRISTOL *to* **THE** *LIBERATOR***. [extract] n.d. Bristol.** Notes hostility and suspicion from the clergy toward Garrison. 15 February 1839. p.28, c5.

3527 MASSACHUSETTS *to* **THE EDITOR [W. L. GARRISON]. 26 January 1839. Massachusetts.** Refers to advertisement in the *Emancipator* showing Northerners benefiting from slavery; holds that abolitionists and Northerners do not yet realize the pervasiveness of the evils of slavery. 15 February 1839. p.28, c5.

3528 WM. M. CHASE *to* **n.n. [extract from the** *Pennsylvania Freeman***] n.d. n.p.** Tells of mob which prevented C. C. Burleigh from delivering a speech at a public schoolhouse in Bristol. 22 February 1839. p.29, c5.

3529 GERRIT SMITH *to* **WILLIAM L. GARRISON. 9 February 1839. Peterboro'.** Clarifies his plan regarding abolitionism. 22 February 1839. p.31, c2.

3530 A. A. PHELPS *to* **MR. GARRISON. 19 February 1839. Boston.** On the division among the abolitionists. 22 February 1839. p.31, c3.

3531 CONSISTENCY *to* **BROTHER GARRISON. 8 February 1839. n.p.** Relates that St. Clair and Stanton dodged the question of adopting the annual report. 22 February 1839. p.31, c3.

3532 n.n. *to* **BROTHER GARRISON. [extract] n.d. Middlesex Co.** Regrets the work of enemies of the *Liberator*, and the disruptions during the annual meeting at Marlborough Chapel on the twenty-third of the previous month. 22 February 1839. p.31, c3.

3533 A RHODE ISLAND MAN *to* **THE EDITOR OF THE** *PROVIDENCE COURIER***. n.d. Rhode Island.** Expresses dismay at increase in power in the General Assembly gained by the abolitionist party, whose goals he considers to be a threat to the Union. 1 March 1839. p.33, c1.

3534 L. M. CHILD *to* **BROTHER GARRISON. 15 February 1839. Northampton.** On the lectures of Elliot Cresson, a proponent of colonization. 1 March 1839. p.33, c3.

3535 LUCRETIA LAWRENCE *to* **ESTEEMED FRIEND [W. L. GARRISON]. 24 January 1838. Salem.** Writes on behalf of the colored people of Salem; expresses their appreciation of Garrison's paper. 1 March 1839. p.33, c6.

3536 BRYAN MORSE *to* **BROTHER GARRISON. 6 February 1839. Lowell.** Sympathizes with Garrison in his efforts to vindicate the rights of the slave. 1 March 1839. p.34, c1.

3537 DAVID STOWELL *to* **FRIEND GARRISON. 18 February 1839. Townsend.** Favors a new paper. 1 March 1839. p.34, c2.

3538 DANIEL WISE *to* **BROTHER GARRISON. n.d. Quincy, Ma.** Explains need for a new paper. 1 March 1839. p.34, c2.

3539 ORIN P. BACON *to* **FRIEND AND BROTHER GARRISON. 11 February 1839. Dorchester.** Questions views of Daniel Wise of Quincy. 1 March 1839. p.34, c2.

3540 TRUTH TELLER *to* **BRO. GARRISON. 22 February 1839. Marshfield.** Account of Daniel Wise's lecture given at Marshfield. 1 March 1839. p.34, c3.

3541 GEORGE THOMPSON *to* **FRIEND. 5 January 1839. Edinburgh.** Relates personal news and his concern for Garrison; states that he has been working in connection with the London Aborigines Protection Society, founded by Mr. Buxton. 1 March 1839. p.34, c4.

3542 OLIVER JOHNSON *to* **FRIEND GARRISON. 21 February 1839. Middlebury, Vt.** Account of annual meeting of the Vermont AS. 1 March 1839. p.34, c5.

3543 n.n. *to* **THE** *LIBERATOR.* **[extract] n.d. n.p.** Relates disturbing impression left by his visit to the South. 1 March 1839. p.35, c2.

3544 A. ST. CLAIR *to* **CONSISTENCY. n.d. n.p** Declares he will answer question posed in the previous *Liberator* when "Consistency" will "come out like a man" and sign his name. 1 March 1839. p.35, c6.

3545 M. H. B. *to* **WILLIAM LLOYD GARRISON. 14 January 1839. Cape Haytien.** Informs him of the death of Mr. Anthony Potter at age fifty-six. 1 March 1839. p.35, c6.

3546 ORIGEN BACHELER *to* **FRIEND GARRISON. 28 January 1839. New York.** Argues that the non-government principle is contrary to Scripture. 1 March 1839. p.36, c2.

3547 ELKANAH NICKERSON *to* **FRIEND GARRISON. 9 February 1839. Harwich.** Concurs with the principles of the Non-Resistance Society. 1 March 1839. p.36, c3.

3548 THOMAS AND A. E. HAMBLETON *to* **BROTHER GARRISON. 27 January 1839. Pennsgrove, Pa.** Favor the principles of non-resistance. 1 March 1839. p.36, c3.

3549 JOSEPH A. WHITMARSH *to* **BROTHER GARRISON. 31 January 1839. Boston.** States his reasons for opposing the Declaration of Sentiments of the Peace Convention. 1 March 1839. p.36, c4.

3550 H. F. *to* **THE EDITOR OF THE** *FRIEND OF MAN.* **3 February 1839. Lima, N.Y.** Reports on the trial of La Roy Sunderland, at Genesee, in which Mr. Sunderland defended himself and was acquitted of libelous charges made against him. 1 March 1839. p.36, c5.

3551 n.n. *to* **THE** *GUADALOUPE JOURNAL COMMERCIAL.* **[extract] 12 January 1839. St. Pierre, Martinique.** Reports on a "dreadful calamity" at Fort Royal which has levelled the city and killed over 522. 1 March 1839. p.36, c6.

3552 n.n. *to* **n.n. [extract] n.d. Washington, D.C.** Reports that over forty slaves were sold South from Washington on 30 January; describes their condition. 8 March 1839. p.38, c6.

3553 J. G. WHITTIER *to* **GARRISON. 24 February 1839. Amesbury.** Takes exception to the 1 March *Liberator* in which Garrison compared Whittier in Boston to Henry Clay on the Missouri question; clarifies earlier statement on theological differences between Garrison and Phelps. 8 March 1839. p.39, c1.

3554 A. A. PHELPS *to* **THE ABOLITIONISTS OF MASSACHUSETTS. 4 March 1839. Boston.** Urges abolitionists to hear both sides of the issues at stake. 8 March 1839. p.39, c2.

3555 A. A. PHELPS *to* **MR. GARRISON. n.d. n.p.** Corrects Garrison's statement in the 15 February *Liberator* that a prominent abolitionist had turned against the cause; quotes letter from the man in question as proof. 8 March 1839. p.39, c2.

3556 WENDELL PHILLIPS *to* **BROTHER GARRISON. n.d. n.p.** Urges abolitionists to take political action. 8 March 1839. p.39, c3.

3557 H. C. WRIGHT *to* **WILLIAM LADD. n.d. n.p.** Attacks the principles of the American Peace Society. 8 March 1839. p.40, c2.

3558 NATHAN EVANS *to* **WILLIAM LLOYD GARRISON. n.d. Willistown, Pa.** On the topic of peace and goodwill. 8 March 1839. p.40, c3.

3559 H. G. OTIS *to* **JOHN WHITTLE. 1 March 1839. Boston.** On the Atherton Resolutions and agitation over the slave question. 15 March 1839. p.42, c3.

3560 BRYAN MORSE *to* **BROTHER GARRISON. 23 February 1839. Lowell.** Reports that ladies in Lynn petitioned for the abolition of laws prohibiting interracial marriage. 15 March 1839. p.42, c6.

3561 AN EYE WITNESS *to* **BROTHER GARRISON. 27 February 1839. Andover.** Notes that Elliot Cresson had lectured on colonization in Andover. 15 March 1839. p.42, c6.

3562 N. H. WHITING, SECR'Y MASSACHUSETTS AS *to* **BRO. GARRISON. 7 March 1839. Marshfield.** Reports on the annual meeting of the Marshfield AS; lists new officers and includes resolutions passed supporting the *Liberator* and denying the right of an AS to compel its members to vote. 15 March 1839. p.43, c1.

3563 A. ST. CLAIR *to* **BR. GARRISON. n.d. n.p.** Encloses proceedings of meeting of newly-formed AS in Attleborough. 15 March 1839. p.43, c2.

3564 MOSES P. ATWOOD *to* **THE EDITOR [W. L. GARRISON]. 25 February 1839. Bradford.** Lists resolutions adopted by the East Bradford AS calling for the repeal of prejudicial laws in Massachusetts and expressing disapprobation of legislators for disregarding their petitions. 15 March 1839. p.43, c2.

3565 WILLIAM S. BALCH, MOSES P. ATWOOD, AND PETER PARKER, JR. *to* **SIR [W. L. GARRISON]. 5 March 1839. Bradford.** Request the *Liberator* to delay publishing their AS resolutions censuring Mr. Greenwood until he is given a chance to clarify his statements. 15 March 1839. p.43, c2.

3566 MARIA W. CHAPMAN *to* **MR. EDITOR [W. L. GARRISON]. 8 March 1839. n.p.** Calls to abolitionists, especially women, to examine the divisions of the cause. 15 March 1839. p.43, c3.

3567 J. LE BOSQUET *to* **THE EDITOR OF THE** *HERALD OF FREEDOM.* **n.d. n.p.** Criticizes the *Liberator* and Mr. Garrison. 15 March 1839. p.44, c5.

3568 A TRUE BLUE ABOLITIONIST *to* **FRIEND ROGERS. [from the** *Herald of Freedom***] n.d. n.p.** Concurs with letter from Le Bosquet; assails Garrison. 15 March 1839. p.44, c5.

3569 J. N. T. TUCKER *to* **ELDER ABEL BROWN, JR. [from the** *Union Herald***] n.d. n.p.** Opposes the convention of a National Baptist AA. 22 March 1839. p.45, c6.

3570 n.n. *to* **THOMAS HUME. [from the** *Pennsylvania Freeman***] 20 December 1838. Estherton Farm.** Relates the arrest of a free Negro, the nurse to a child in his party, during a visit to Georgia. 22 March 1839. p.46, c1.

3571 O. S. C. *to* **THE EDITOR OF THE** *CHRISTIAN REFLECTOR.* **9 February 1839. Boston, Ma.** Relates that he has freed his slaves; praises the Northern press. 22 March 1839. p.46, c2.

3572 FEMALE SOUTHERN ABOLITIONIST *to* **n.n. n.d. n.p.** Assails "Pharisee" slaveholders; reports misunderstanding, among intelligent Southerners, of Northern abolitionists. 22 March 1839. p.46, c3.

3573 ARATUS *to* **FRIEND GARRISON. n.d. n.p.** Upholds abolitionists' duty to use moral and legal influence to end slavery. 22 March 1839. p.46, c4.

3574 JAMES MOTT *to* **THE** *LIBERATOR.* **[extract] n.d. Philadelphia.** Reports on the near success of a slavehunter in enslaving William Stanbury, a free black man, by obtaining false witnesses to testify that he was a runaway. 22 March 1839. p.46, c5.

3575 JOSHUA COFFIN *to* **BROTHER [W. L. GARRISON]. 12 March 1839. Philadelphia.** Reports on his return after six months' journey to the South and West; feels he is now a real "abolition fanatic." 22 March 1839. p.46, c6.

3576 Entry number not used.

3577 J. G. B. *to* **MR. EDITOR [W. L. GARRISON]. n.d. n.p.** Describes his dreams about a black man in Congress. 22 March 1839. p.46, c6.

3578 MARY GREW, COR. SEC. OF THE PHILADELPHIA FEMALE AS *to* **MR. GARRISON. 11 March 1839. Philadelphia.** Orders thirty copies of the *Liberator*; expresses confidence in the paper and its editor. 22 March 1839. p.47, c6.

3579 A FRIEND *to* **FRIEND GARRISON. 9 March 1839. n.p.** On the crisis among abolitionists. 22 March 1839. p.48, c2.

3580 LAURA S. HAVILAND *to* **BROTHER GARRISON. 25 January 1839. Raisen, Mi.** Comments on the Declaration of Sentiments of the Peace Convention. 22 March 1839. p.48, c2.

3581 JULIUS WAY *to* **SIR [W. L. GARRISON]. 3 March 1839. Meriden, Ct.** Chooses to patronize the *Liberator*. 22 March 1839. p.48, c3.

3582 NATHANIEL BARNEY *to* **WM. L. GARRISON. 4 March 1839. Nantucket.** Expresses his confidence that the *Liberator* would survive the storm of protest. 22 March 1839. p.48, c3.

3583 EDWIN THOMPSON *to* **FRIEND GARRISON. 23 February 1839. Lynn.** Lists new ASS. 22 March 1839. p.48, c4.

3584 P. CRANDALL *to* **MR. GARRISON. 9 March 1839. Fall River.** Disputes the *Liberator*'s statement that the Board of Managers of the Bristol County AS "give *prima facia* evidence of hasty action, and an alienated spirit." 22 March 1839. p.48, c4.

3585 LOUISA S. WILCOX *to* **FRIEND GARRISON. 23 February 1839. Amesbury.** Sends resolutions, adopted by the Amesbury and Salisbury Femals AS, pledging continued support to the *Liberator*, and urging paper and its correspondents to overlook minor differences and unite against the common enemy. 22 March 1839. p.48, c4.

3586 ELIJAH BIRD *to* **REV. S. HOPKINS EMERY. [from the** *Taunton Whig*] **18 March 1839. Taunton.** Questions propriety of resolutions passed by the Bristol AS concerning the Massachusetts AS. 29 March 1839. p.50, c5.

3587 D. H. *to* **MR. EDITOR [W. L. GARRISON]. n.d. Essex Co.** On the political situation in the Fourth District. 29 March 1839. p.51, c1.

3588 H. C. WRIGHT *to* **BROTHER [W. L. GARRISON]. n.d. n.p.** Discusses the meaning of being an abolitionist. 29 March 1839. p.51, c3.

3589 GERRIT SMITH *to* **W. L. GARRISON, M. W. CHAPMAN AND E. QUINCY. 15 March 1839. Peterboro'.** Praises the *Non-Resistant*; encloses a one-hundred dollar contribution. 29 March 1839. p.51, c4.

3590 JAMES BOYLE *to* **WM. LLOYD GARRISON. 24 February 1839. Cincinnati.** Discusses the Sabbath, human governments, and religion in the light of Scripture; praises the *Non-Resistant*. 29 March 1839. p.52, c2.

3591 BENJAMIN OBER *to* **MR. GARRISON. 22 March 1839. Wrentham.** Disputes Mr. William Harlow's claims, published in the *Liberator*, that Ober advocates slavery; includes extracts of speeches as evidence. 5 April 1839. p.54, c3.

3592 O. SCOTT *to* **BROTHER GARRISON. n.d. n.p.** On J. G. Birney, politics, and human government. 5 April 1839. p.54, c4.

3593 J. G. BIRNEY *to* **THE EDITOR [W. L. GARRISON]. 2 April 1839. Andover.** Draws attention to an error in the *Liberator*. 5 April 1839. p.54, c5.

3594 H. B. STANTON *to* **H. C. W., ALIAS HENRY C. WRIGHT. n.d. n.p.** Assails Wright for misrepresenting his position on voting to the *Liberator*; includes extracts of articles and letters in his support. 5 April 1839. p.54, c6.

3595 Z. *to* **BELOVED BROTHER [W. L. GARRISON]. 16 March 1839. Alleghany County, Pa.** Complains abolitionist papers are too "silver-toned"; encloses letter from E. N. of Ohio, which was rejected by the *Christian Witness*. 5 April 1839. p.55, c2.

3596 E. N. *to* **THE** *CHRISTIAN WITNESS*. **17 February 1839. Ohio.** Condemns clerical hypocrisy. 5 April 1839. p.55, c2.

3597 S. B. *to* **FRIEND GARRISON. 30 March 1839. Dorchester.** Suggests measures to alleviate the friction between certain abolitionist factions. 5 April 1839. p.55, c2.

3598 H. C. WRIGHT *to* **BROTHER [W. L. GARRISON]. n.d. n.p.** Advocates doctrine of non-resistance. 5 April 1839. p.56, c2.

3599 LAURA P. BOYLE *to* **BROTHER GARRISON. 4 March 1839. Cincinnati, Oh.** Expresses support for Garrison. 5 April 1839. p.56, c2.

3600 ISRAEL MATTISON *to* **BRO. GARRISON. February 1839. Granby, Oh.** Supports the principles of non-resistance. 5 April 1839. p.56, c3.

3601 A DISTINGUISHED AUTHORESS *to* **THE** *LIBERATOR*. **[extract] n.d. n.p.** Regrets not having attended the Peace Convention of September, 1838; remains convinced of the importance of *Christian Witness* and the principles of the convention. 5 April 1839. p.56, c3.

3602 AMOS DRESSER *to* **GARRISON. n.d. n.p.** Praises Israel Mattison for upholding principles of non-resistance. 5 April 1839. p.56, c3.

3603 WM. WEST *to* **FRIEND GARRISON. 22 March 1839. Boston.** Resents Garrison's implication that atheists are pro-slavery. 5 April 1839. p.56, c4.

3604 n.n. *to* **n.n. [extract from the** *Journal of Commerce***] 11 December 1838. Bridgetown, Barbadoes.** Reports that the colony is in a state of "perfect tranquility"; notes that employment, crime, economy have improved since emancipation. 12 April 1839. p.58, c4.

3605 REV. D. S. INGRAHAM *to* **n.n. [extract from the** *Oberlin Evangelist***] n.d. Jamaica.** Discusses the West Indies. 12 April 1839. p.58, c4.

3606 LEWIS TAPPAN *to* **THE EDITOR [W. L. GARRISON]. n.d. n.p.** Charges Garrison with incorrect reporting of the last meeting of the Massachusetts AS. 12 April 1839. p.58, c5.

3607 J. N., JR. *to* **THE EDITOR [W. L. GARRISON]. 8 April 1839. Abington.** Expresses satisfaction that the AS chose to sustain the board of directors. 12 April 1839. p.59, c1.

3608 Z. *to* **BROTHER GARRISON. n.d. n.p.** Encloses his letter to the *Pittsburgh Christian Witness* on the subject of non-resistance, part of which was rejected by the paper. 12 April 1839. p.60, c3.

3609 Z. *to* **BROTHER BURLEIGH. [extract] n.d. n.p.** Criticizes the *Pittsburgh Christian Witness* for falsifying views of the New England Non-Resistance Society. 12 April 1839. p.60, c3.

3610 AN AGENT OF THE *LIBERATOR to* **THE** *LIBERATOR*. **[extract] n.d. Worcester County.** Decries the many "spurious abolitionists" in Worcester. 12 April 1839. p.60, c3.

3611 EYE WITNESS *to* **BROTHER GARRISON. 1 April 1839. Andover.** Charges the Rev. Mr. Birney with eighteen falsehoods. 12 April 1839. p.60, c4.

3612 UNIVERSALIST ABOLITIONIST *to* **BR. GARRISON. n.d. n.p.** Reports that two Universalist papers are to start publication. 12 April 1839. p.60, c4.

3613 H. C. WRIGHT *to* **J. G. BIRNEY AND H. B. STANTON. n.d. n.p.** Outlines position of the AAS on voting. 19 April 1839. p.62, c6.

3614 NATHANIEL H. WHITING *to* **BRO. GARRISON. 10 April 1839. Hanover.** Reports that he was refused permission to speak at a church in East Bridgewater. 19 April 1839. p.63, c1.

3615 EXPERIENCE BILLINGS *to* **SIR. 28 March 1839. Foxboro'.** Account of the last meeting of the Mansfield and Foxborough Juvenile Society. 19 April 1839. p.63, c2.

3616 JOHN ALLEN *to* **BR. GARRISON. 1 April 1839. Watertown.** Discusses lecture given by Mr. Thompson. 19 April 1839. p.63, c2.

3617 TIMOTHY TITUS *to* **RESPECTED FRIEND [W. L. GARRISON]. 25 March 1839. Wheatly, L.I.** Expresses satisfaction with the non-resistance movement. 19 April 1839. p.64, c3.

3618 H. K. BURKELL *to* **J. G. WHITTIER. 18 March 1839. Jamaica.** On Jamaican emancipation. 26 April 1839. p.66, c1.

3619 n.n. *to* **THE EDITOR OF THE** *NEW BEDFORD REGISTER*. **n.d. New Bedford.** Praises Garrison after having heard his speech in New Bedford. 26 April 1839. p.66, c2.

3620 AN OLD COUNTRY ABOLITIONIST *to* **BRO. GARRISON. n.d. n.p.** Cites statements by Henry Stanton, James Birney, Mr. Tappan, and Brother Leavitt, which he feels have discredited the Executive Committee of the AS at New York. 26 April 1839. p.66, c3.

3621 S. BAKER *to* **FRIEND GARRISON. 15 April 1839. Dorchester.** Refutes the report of Minot Thayer's committee, which investigated the affixing of names to a petition in Dorchester. 26 April 1839. p.66, c5.

3622 A FUGITIVE *to* **WM. LLOYD GARRISON. 29 March 1839. Stanstead, Canada.** Notifies Garrison and others who aided his escape that he has arrived safely in Canada. 26 April 1839. p.66, c6.

3623 D. S. INGRAHAM *to* **BENEDICT. 17 January 1839. Kingston.** On conduct of the natives of Jamaica. 26 April 1839. p.66, c6.

3624 HARRIET FOSTER *to* **MR. GARRISON. 5 January 1839. Salem.** Sends one hundred dollar donation to Garrison from the Salem Female AS. 26 April 1839. p.67, c3.

3625 WM. LLOYD GARRISON *to* **HARRIET FOSTER. n.d. n.p.** Sends thanks for donation from Salem Female AS. 26 April 1839. p.67, c3.

3626 DANIEL WISE *to* **WM. LLOYD GARRISON. 13 April 1839. Quincy.** Corrects a mistake printed in the *Liberator*. 26 April 1839. p.67, c4.

3627 HENRY C. WRIGHT *to* **BROTHER [W. L. GARRISON]. n.d. n.p.** Discusses non-allegiance to human governments. 26 April 1839. p.68, c2.

3628 ABNER KIRK *to* **MR. GARRISON. n.d. Stark County, Oh.** Discusses abolitionists' tendency to deliberate rather than concern themselves with the emancipation of the slaves. 3 May 1839. p.71, c1.

3629 A. A. PHELPS *to* **MR. JACKSON. 29 April 1839. Boston.** Announces resignation from the Board of Managers of the Massachusetts AS. 3 May 1839. p.71, c5.

3630 WILLIAM BARDWELL *to* **THE EDITOR OF THE** *ZION'S WATCHMAN*. **4 March 1839. Sandwich, Ma.** Quotes letter from Thomas C. Perry relating the cruelty of a preacher from South Carolina, William Whitby, toward his slaves. 10 May 1839. p.74, c3.

3631 THOMAS C. PERRY *to* **HIS WIFE. 3 March 1839. n.p.** Account of the cruelty of a Southern minister, William Whitby, toward his slaves. 10 May 1839. p.74, c3.

3632 A. A. PHELPS *to* **MR. J[ACKSON]. n.d. n.p.** Criticizes the Board of Managers of the Massachusetts AS for their resolution calling the charges implied in his letter of resignation "groundless." 10 May 1839. p.74, c6.

3633 HIRAM WILSON *to* **THE REV. CHARLES T. TORREY. 21 February 1839. Toronto.** Appeals for assistance to fugitives in Canada. 17 May 1839. p.77, c6.

3634 GEORGE BRADBURN *to* **MISS SARAH BAKER. 4 May 1839. Nantucket.** Discusses the Massachusetts law forbidding interracial marriage. 17 May 1839. p.79, c2.

3635 H. C. WRIGHT *to* **BROTHER [W. L. GARRISON]. n.d. n.p.** Discusses the protection of human rights in relation to Christianity. 17 May 1839. p.80, c2.

3636 GERRIT SMITH *to* **H. C. WRIGHT. 20 April 1839. Peterboro'.** On violence in relation to Scripture. 17 May 1839. p.80, c3.

3637 JOHN BEMENT *to* **BRO. HIMES. 22 April 1839. Woodstock, Vt.** Discusses non-resistance. 17 May 1839. p80, c4.

3638 GERRIT SMITH *to* **JOSHUA LEAVITT. 11 May 1839. New York.** Account of an anti-slavery meeting in Newburgh. 24 May 1839. p.81, c1.

3639 G. *to* **THE EDITOR OF THE** *BOSTON COURIER.* **n.d. n.p.** Reports on stir caused on board a steamer by colored women who slept in the same berth as the white women whom they were accompanying; notes that their full passage had been paid. 24 May 1839. p.81, c2.

3640 W. B. HOLDREDGE *to* **JOSHUA LEAVITT. 19 January 1839. Kingston, Jamaica.** Favors rumored change in Jamaican government to an executive council; notes appearance of new West Indian journal, the *Colonial Reformer.* 24 May 1839. p.83, c1.

3641 JAMES B. GRAHAM *to* **ARTHUR TAPPAN. 14 April 1839. Kingston, Jamaica.** Reports on good behavior of the emancipated slaves; suggests plan to market Jamaican produce in the United States. 24 May 1839. p.83, c1.

3642 H. C. WRIGHT *to* **ORANGE SCOTT. 18 April 1839. Philadelphia.** Supports non-resistance. 24 May 1839. p.84, c2.

3643 HENRY GREW *to* **H. C. WRIGHT. n.d. n.p.** Debates Wright's views on allegiance to earthly governments. 24 May 1839. p.84, c3.

3644 JAMES G. BIRNEY *to* **BRO. LEAVITT. [from the** *Emancipator***] 17 May 1839. Philadelphia.** Reports on crisis caused by slavery question in the Presbyterian church in Philadelphia. 31 May 1839. p.86, c5.

3645 LEWIS TAPPAN *to* **BRO. LEAVITT. [from the** *Emancipator***] 21 May 1839. Philadelphia.** Reports on discussion of slavery in the general assembly of the Presbyterian church in Philadelphia. 31 May 1839. p.86, c5.

3646 GERRIT SMITH *to* **LEAVITT. 14 May 1839. Farmington, Ct.** Reports that Smith's speech in New Haven was disrupted by a mob. 31 May 1839. p.86, c5.

3647 H. H. *to* **BRO. GARRISON. 13 April 1839. Dudley.** On the anti-slavery cause in Dudley; reports that Brother Thompson had spoken at a town meeting, and a collection was taken up for the Massachusetts AS. 31 May 1839. p.86, c6.

3648 FRANCIS C. WOODWORTH *to* **H. C. WRIGHT. 12 February 1839. New York Theological Seminary.** Maintains his support of non-resistance principles; disagrees with Wright concerning human government. 31 May 1839. p.88, c2.

3649 W. H. JOHNSON *to* **H. C. WRIGHT. 22 February 1839. Buckingham, Pa.** Discusses the Declaration of Sentiments of the Non-Resistance Society. 31 May 1839. p.88, c2.

3650 H. C. WRIGHT *to* **BROTHER [W. L. GARRISON]. 15 May 1839. Boston.** Discusses Mr. Birney's attack on non-resistance. 31 May 1839. p.88, c3.

3651 SARAH C. RUGG *to* **THE** *LIBERATOR.* **[extract] 25 March 1839. Groton.** Praises the *Liberator*; joins Non-Resistance Society. 31 May 1839. p.88, c4.

3652 n.n. *to* **THE** *VERMONT VOICE OF FREEDOM.* **[extract] 3 January 1839. New Brighton.** Proposes development of silk production as economic means to undermine slavery. 31 May 1839. p.88, c5.

3653 WM. C. BUCK *to* **R. R. GURLEY. April 1830. Louisville, Ky.** Discusses his practice of keeping his slaves until they have raised their passage to Liberia or some foreign place, so as to avoid liability for them while free in this country. 31 May 1839. p.88, c5.

3654 ONE OF THE SOCIETY OF FRIENDS *to* **FRIEND GARRISON. 3 June 1839. Lynn.** Reports that the society refused the use of its meetinghouse to a member who wished to speak against slavery. 7 June 1839. p.91, c5.

3655 DANIEL WISE *to* **BRO. BROWN. [from the** *Zion's Herald***] 31 May 1839. Boston.** Reports the forming of a new state AS. 14 June 1839. p.93, c1.

3656 n.n. *to* **THE** *PENNSYLVANIA FREEMAN.* **n.d. Frederick County, Md.** Laments that the abolitionist cause is still unpopular, although persecution of abolitionists has only strengthened their resolve; views the CS as a major threat. 14 June 1839. p.94, c1.

3657 WM. BASSETT *to* **BRO. GARRISON. 31 May 1839. Lynn.** Criticizes the Society of Friends, a pro-emancipation organization, for discouraging their members from mixing with other benevolent associations. 14 June 1839. p.94, c6.

3658 LAMEAH *to* **BRO. GARRISON. 11 June 1839. Andover Theological Seminary.** On abolitionist activity at Andover. 14 June 1839. p.95, c2.

3659 G. F. *to* **FRIEND GARRISON. 5 June 1839. Andover.** Laments "retrograde motion" by the abolitionist movement in Andover. 14 June 1839. p.95, c2.

3660 FRANCIS JACKSON *to* **WENDELL PHILLIPS. 4 June 1839. Boston.** Expresses appreciation for his anti-slavery labors; wishes him well on his travels in Europe. 14 June 1839. p.95, c4.

3661 GRACE AND SARAH M. DOUGLASS *to* **BROTHER GARRISON. 27 May 1839. Philadelphia.** Express sympathy for the attacks on Garrison by his enemies. 21 June 1839. p.98, c2.

3662 SETH SPRAGUE *to* **FRIEND GARRISON. 17 June 1839. Duxbury.** Reports that he wrote A. A. Phelps to stress that a public announcement of his appointment as vice-president of the Massachusetts AS would be a disgrace to him. 21 June 1839. p.98, c2.

3663 PACIFICUS *to* **HENRY GREW. n.d. n.p.** Discusses the constitution of the Non-Resistance Society. 21 June 1839. p.100, c2.

3664 n.n. *to* **THE** *BOSTON ATLAS*. **[extract] n.d. New York.** Condemns Daniel O'Connell. 21 June 1839. p.100, c4.

3665 A MERCHANT *to* **THE** *LIBERATOR*. **[extract] 20 May 1839. Vicksburg.** Describes lawlessness in Vicksburg. 21 June 1839. p.100, c5.

3666 A. *to* **THE EDITOR OF THE** *WORCESTER PALLADIUM*. **31 May 1839. Boston.** Questions Garrison's qualities as a leader. 21 June 1839. p.101, c1.

3667 JOSEPH S. WALL *to* **FRIEND GARRISON. 15 June 1839. Worcester.** Requests a subscription to the *Liberator*. 28 June 1839. p.101, c3.

3668 WM. LLOYD GARRISON *to* **THE EDITOR OF THE** *EMANCIPATOR*. **31 May 1839. Boston.** Replies to James G. Birney regarding the constitution of the AAS and the no-government question. 28 June 1839. p.102, c1.

3669 BETH *to* **FRIEND GARRISON. 22 June 1839. Andover Theological Seminary.** Laments speeches advocating colonization and defending the slave trade which were given at Andover by Governor Pinney and an unnamed Southerner. 28 June 1839. p.103, c3.

3670 PHILOS *to* **GARRISON. 22 June 1839. Andover.** Gives a further report on the abolitionist-colonizationist debate between C. C. Burleigh and Gov. Pinney in Andover. 28 June 1839. p.103, c3.

3671 J. G. BIRNEY *to* **J. LEAVITT. [from the** *Emancipator***] 11 June 1839. Cincinnati.** Reports on his address at an annual meeting in Greensburg, Indiana. 28 June 1839. p.103, c4.

3672 H. C. WRIGHT *to* **BROTHER [W. L. GARRISON]. 6 June 1839. Brookline.** On J. Q. Adams and non-resistance. 28 June 1839. p.104, c2.

3673 H. C. WRIGHT *to* **BROTHER [W. L. GARRISON]. 13 June 1839. Pawtucket.** Comments on a letter from J. G. Birney to F. H. Filmore. 28 June 1839. p.104, c2.

3674 WM. KENRICK *to* **THE EDITOR OF THE** *FARMER'S REGISTER*. **1 April 1839. Portsmouth, Va.** Examines the effect of slavery on the agriculture of Virginia. 5 July 1839. p.106, c2.

3675 ABOLITIONIST *to* **MR. GARRISON. n.d. Kingston, Ma.** Discusses an address on slavery given by the Rev. Cummings of Duxbury. 5 July 1839. p.105, c4.

3676 ONE OF THE MEMBERS *to* **BROTHER GARRISON. n.d. n.p.** States that a Boston Female AS member was charged with making an unauthorized address. 5 July 1839. p.106, c5.

3677 Z. *to* **THE EDITOR [W. L. GARRISON]. n.d. n.p.** Informs that members of the clergy assaulted citizens. 5 July 1839. p.106, c5.

3678 HORACE MOULTON *to* **FRIEND GARRISON. 5 April 1839. Marlborough.** Opposes the *Liberator*'s new no-government cause. 5 July 1839. p.108, c2.

3679 BENJ. W. DYER *to* **BROTHER GARRISON. 23 June 1839. Braintree, Vt.** Supports non-resistance. 5 July 1839. p.108, c2.

3680 CLOTHER GIFFORD *to* **WM. L. GARRISON. n.d. Fairhaven.** Sympathizes with the members of the New England Non-Resistance Society. 5 July 1839. p.108, c3.

3681 WM. GOODELL *to* **JOHN QUINCY ADAMS. 19 June 1839. Utica, N.Y.** Discusses the petition presented to Adams. 12 July 1839. p.109, c1.

3682 SAMUEL PHILBRICK *to* **FRIEND GARRISON. 8 July 1839. Brookline.** Charges that the Society of Friends in New England is not an abolition society. 12 July 1839. p.110, c2.

3683 S *to* **MR. EDITOR [W. L. GARRISON]. 4 July 1839. Newburyport.** On clerical abolitionism in Newburyport. 12 July 1839. p.110, c5.

3684 G. W. STACY *to* **BRO. GARRISON. 4 July 1839. Carlisle.** Describes the "glorious" Fourth of July in Carlisle. 12 July 1839. p.110, c5.

3685 T. P. RYDER *to* **BROTHER GARRISON. 29 June 1839. E. Bridgewater.** Gives an account of his visit to Stoneham. 12 July 1839. p.110, c6.

3686 EQUAL RIGHTS *to* **MR. GARRISON. 15 July 1839. Kingston.** On the danger of allowing the leadership of the anti-slavery cause to fall into the hands of unscrupulous clergymen. 19 July 1839. p.114, c3.

3687 WM. P. POWELL *to* **FRIEND [W. L. GARRISON]. 10 July 1839. Boston.** States that abolition is the cure for slavery. 19 July 1839. p.114, c4.

3688 n.n. *to* **MR. GARRISON. 6 July 1839. Lexington.** Wonders whether one's Christian duty is absolute, or affected by circumstances. 19 July 1839. p.116, c2.

3689 G. D. *to* **THE EDITOR OF THE** *PHILANTHROPIST*. **27 May 1839. n.p.** Relates an incident from school days in which an historical text had been re-edited to omit material unfavorable to slavery. 19 July 1839. p.116, c4.

3690 O. SCOTT *to* **MR. HUNTRESS. [from the** *Lowell Courier*] **n.d. n.p.** Explains circumstances of new Massachusetts AS; favors Lowell AS's becoming auxiliary. 26 July 1839. p.117, c1.

3691 P. SCOTT *to* **BROTHER WRIGHT. [From the** *Massachusetts Abolitionist*] **29 June 1839. Lowell.** Favors formation of new state AS; opposes Garrison's views on political action. 26 July 1839. p.117, c2.

3692 A CHRONICLER *to* **MESSRS. ROBERTS AND GRISWALD. [from the** *Detroit Post and Craftsman*] **5 June 1839. Roxbury, Ma.** Satirizes the Phelps-Garrison dispute. 26 July 1839. p.117, c2.

3693 REV. ZENAS BLISS *to* **MR. TRACY. [from the** *Vermont Chronicler*] **June 1839. Quechee, Vt.** Encloses three letters between himself and Rev. Nathan Lord of Dartmouth College. 26 July 1839. p.117, c4.

3694 REV. ZENAS BLISS *to* **REV. NATHAN LORD. 16 April 1839. Quechee, Vt.** Requests Rev. Lord's views on the duties of lay persons and the authority of the pastor over "itinerant" agitators for the abolitionist cause. 26 July 1839. p.117, c4.

3695 NATHAN LORD *to* **REV. Z. BLISS. 30 May 1839. Dartmouth College.** In response to Bliss's query; does not see the pastor's authority as "paramount" over others who wish to address the community on moral issues. 26 July 1839. p.117, c5.

3696 ZENAS BLISS *to* **REV. NATHAN LORD. n.d. n.p.** Expresses disappointment with Rev. Lord's position on pastoral authority. 26 July 1839. p.117, c6.

3697 n.n. *to* **FRIEND GARRISON. n.d. n.p.** Grieves at the "strife and contention among professed abolitionists." 26 July 1839. p.118, c6.

3698 TRUTH TELLER *to* **FRIEND GARRISON. n.d. n.p.** Reports on train accidents on the Fourth of July. 26 July 1839. p.118, c6.

3699 Q IN A CORNER *to* **FRIEND GARRISON. n.d. n.p.** Bewails laws that make emancipation difficult, if not impossible, and the love of money which makes slavery so desirable to those who profit from it. 26 July 1839. p.119, c1.

3700 JOHN SMITH, JR. *to* **n.n. [extract from the** *New York Evening Post*] **n.d. Arkansas.** Decries the "senseless, and useless, and miserable twaddle" issuing from the Northern press. 26 July 1839. p.119, c4.

3701 A PENNSYLVANIA CLERGYMAN *to* **THE** *HARRISBURG CHRONICLE.* **14 January 1839. Florence, Italy.** Laments mob violence and lynchings in United States, which have gained much attention in Europe. 26 July 1839. p.120, c3.

3702 GEO. STORRS *to* **LEAVITT. 28 June 1839. Hampden, Me.** Reports resolution of the struggle among abolitionists of Maine. 26 July 1839. p.120, c3.

3703 n.n. *to* **THE** *EMANCIPATOR.* **9 July 1839. Kinderhook.** Details favorable results of emancipation in West Indies. 2 August 1839. p.122, c2.

3704 REV. DR. OSGOOD *to* **BROTHER GARRISON. 7 July 1839. Springfield.** Reports on the division among the Massachusetts abolitionists. 2 August 1839. p.122, c3.

3705 WM. LLOYD GARRISON *to* **DR. OSGOOD. n.d. n.p.** Discusses division among the abolitionists of Massachusetts. 2 August 1839. p.122, c5.

3706 BENJ. KINGSBURG *to* **THE** *LIBERATOR.* **27 July 1839. Roxbury.** Denies authorship of satire signed "a chronicler," which appeared 26 July and was attributed to him. 2 August 1839. p.123, c6.

3707 T. E. LONGSHORE *to* **FRIEND GARRISON. 20 July 1839. Attleboro', Pa.** Expresses his approbation of the *Liberator.* 2 August 1839. p.124, c2.

3708 CLOTHER GIFFORD *to* **BROTHER GARRISON. n.d. n.p.** Expresses sympathy for the non-resistants. 2 August 1839. p.124, c3.

3709 ADIN BALLOU *to* **MARIA W. CHAPMAN. 18 March 1839. Mendon.** Declares that he has become a thorough convert to the non-resistance principles. 2 August 1839. p.124, c3.

3710 JOS. TREVOR *to* **FRIEND GARRISON. 15 January 1839. Philadelphia.** States that he is unable to come to a firm decision regarding non-resistance. 2 August 1839. p124, c3.

3711 MESSRS. KEEP AND DODGE *to* **THE** *EMANCIPATOR.* **[extract] 6 July 1839. London.** Reports that George Thompson, Lord Brougham, and Daniel O'Connell spoke at a meeting of the newly-formed British India Society. 9 August 1839. p.125, c3.

3712 N. H. WHITING *to* **COLLINS. 25 July 1839. N. Brookfield.** Reports that he was refused permission by the Rev. Levi Packard to speak in Spencer. 9 August 1839. p.125, c5.

3713 A. A. HASKELL *to* **FRIEND GARRISON. 20 July 1839. Newburyport.** Reports that colonization support is weak in Newburyport. 9 August 1839. p.125, c6.

3714 C. B. E. *to* **MR. EDITOR [W. L. GARRISON]. 14 June 1839. West Millbury.** Believes that Church is presently threatened by lethargy; asks if Garrison concurs. 9 August 1839. p.126, c6.

3715 JAMES G. BARBADOES *to* **FRIEND GARRISON. n.d. n.p.** Details first of August celebration in Boston. 9 August 1839. p.127, c1.

3716 ISAAC T. HOPPER *to* **WILLIAM LLOYD GARRISON. n.d. n.p.** Defends the Society of Friends. 9 August 1839. p.127, c1.

3717 JUSTICE *to* **BRO. GARRISON. 20 June 1839. Andover.** Opposes colonization. 9 August 1839. p.127, c2.

3718 L. *to* **THE EDITOR [W. L. GARRISON]. 18 July 1839. Newburyport.** Describes colonization meeting in Newburyport. 9 August 1839. p.127, c2.

3719 WM. LLOYD GARRISON *to* **JOHNSON. 5 August 1839. Brooklyn, Ct.** Gives an account of the National Anti-Slavery Convention. 9 August 1839. p.127, c3.

3720 HON. THOMAS MORRIS *to* **N. SAFFORD. 22 July 1839. Cincinnati.** Regrets that he was unable to attend the National Convention in Albany. 16 August 1839. p.130, c2.

3721 EDWARD C. DELAVAN *to* **GENTLEMEN. 28 July 1839. Ballston Centre.** Regrets that he was unable to attend the National Convention. 16 August 1839. p.130, c2.

3722 THEODORE SEDGWICK *to* **LEAVITT AND STANTON. 23 July 1839. Stockbridge.** Regrets that he was unable to attend the National Convention. 16 August 1839. p.130, c2.

3723 T. P. RYDER *to* **BRO. GARRISON. 6 August 1839. Providence, R. I.** On anti-slavery progress in Rhode Island. 16 August 1839. p.130, c5.

3724 THOS. P. RICHMOND *to* **W. L. GARRISON. 16 July 1839. Bristol, R.I.** Reports on the anti-slavery cause in Bristol. 16 August 1839. p.130. c5.

3725 MARIA AND HENRY CHAPMAN *to* **T. HILTON. 1 August 1839. n.p.** Regret absence from first of August festivities; commends Hilton celebrating "without the aid of the wine-cup." 16 August 1839. p.131, c2.

3726 TRUTH TELLER *to* **BRO. GARRISON. 12 August 1839. n.p.** Expresses gladness at learning that Mr. Hammond, of the *Cincinnati Gazette*, is not an "infidel," as was supposed. 16 August 1839. p.131, c3.

3727 HENRY GREW *to* **PACIFICUS. 23 July 1835. Philadelphia.** Opposes the Non-Resistance Society's contention that all civil governments are unjust. 16 August 1839. p.132, c2.

3728 H. C. WRIGHT *to* **GEORGE BRADBURN. 10 July 1839. Nantucket.** Denies man's right to kill in self-defense. 16 August 1839. p.132, c3.

3729 JAMES BOWKER *to* **WM. LLOYD GARRISON. 26 July 1839. Richmond.** Assails Garrison for sending paper; returns it unread. 23 August 1839. p.133, c2.

3730 E. S. *to* **FRIEND GARRISON. 24 July 1839. Providence, R.I.** Relates that "a goodly number" of slaves are escaping to Canada, despite the passage of a black law the previous winter. 23 August 1839. p.133, c5.

3731 C. PHELPS *to* **H. B. STANTON. 27 July 1839. West Townsend, Vt.** States that he was unable to attend the convention in Albany. 23 August 1839. p.133, c5.

3732 TRUTH TELLER *to* **BRO. GARRISON. n.d. n.p.** Denounces efforts to divide abolitionists over the questions of women's rights, political action, and non-resistance. 23 August 1839. p.134, c2.

3733 TRUTH *to* **BRO. GARRISON. July 1839. Andover.** Discloses that professors at Andover have avoided or opposed anti-slavery meetings. 23 August 1839. p.134, c4.

3734 HUMANITY *to* **BROTHER GARRISON. n.d. n.p.** Asks Garrison whether one can consistently support the Massachusetts AS if one upholds women's rights and refuses to vote or support the government. 23 August 1839. p.134, c5.

3735 X *to* **BROTHER GARRISON. 1 August 1839. West Amesbury.** Discusses the division in the once peaceful ranks of the abolitionists. 23 August 1839. p.134, c5.

3736 AMICUS *to* **FRIEND GARRISON. 10 August 1839. Wrentham.** Discloses that Rev. Mr. Cummings claimed to have proof that Garrison is an infidel. 23 August 1839. p.134, c5.

3737 FAIR PLAY *to* **MR. GARRISON. 15 August 1839. Franklin.** Cautions Garrison about the tactics of the members of the new organization. 23 August 1839. p.134, c5.

3738 DECENCY *to* **MR. EDITOR [W. L. GARRISON]. n.d. n.p.** Criticizes the improper conduct of a member of the common council from Ward 5. 23 August 1839. p.134, c6.

3739 A FRIEND *to* **GARRISON. 29 July 1839. n.p.** Believes Joseph Gurney's pamphlet, "Free and Friendly Remarks," exemplifies the attitude of Friends, who oppose slavery yet have not overcome color prejudice. 23 August 1839. p.135, c1.

3740 SAMUEL PHILBRICK *to* **FRIEND GARRISON. 12 August 1839. Brookline.** Assails hypocrisy of members of the Society of Friends in North Carolina, who continue to hold slaves. 23 August 1839. p.135, c1.

3741 CHRISTINA F. NEWELL, SARAH ANN ROSIER, CYNTHIA POTTS, MARY ANN KENDALL, AND AMELIA J. PIPER *to* **BROTHER GARRISON. 12 August 1839. New Bedford.** Announce the formation of the New Bedford Female Union Society which will aid the *Liberator* and the Massachusetts AS. 23 August 1839. p.135, c1.

3742 WENDELL PHILLIPS *to* **GARRISON. 31 July 1834. London.** Reports having seen George Thompson and heard much debate of the India question in London. 23 August 1839. p.135, c2.

3743 H. C. WRIGHT *to* **BROTHER [W. L. GARRISON]. 16 August 1839. Barnstable.** Reports on his non-resistance lecturing in Nantucket. 23 August 1839. p.136, c2.

3744 H. C. W. *to* **BROTHER [W. L. GARRISON]. n.d. n.p.** Believes principles of non-resistance unattainable in present society. 23 August 1839. p.136, c3.

3745 T. P. *to* **BROTHER GARRISON. 11 August 1839. Sandwich, Ma.** Gives an account of H. C. Wright's lecture at Sandwich. 23 August 1839. p.136, c4.

3746 S. J. *to* **BROTHER GARRISON. 13 August 1839. Centreville, Ma.** Praises H. C. Wright's lectures in Centreville. 23 August 1839. p.136, c4.

3747 GEO. BRADBURN *to* **ESTEEMED FRIEND. 19 August 1839. Nantucket.** Gives an account of the National Anti-Slavery Convention. 30 August 1839. p.138, c2.

3748 GERRIT SMITH *to* **WILLIAM LLOYD GARRISON. 7 June 1839. Peterboro.** Discusses resolution passed by the National Convention to allow members to abstain from voting on measures which are against their conscience, and also a resolution to support elective franchise. 30 August 1839. p.138, c6.

3749 H. C. WRIGHT *to* **BROTHER [W. L. GARRISON]. 25 August 1839. Duxbury.** Gives an account of his lecture tour. 30 August 1839. p.139, c3.

3750 n.n. *to* **THE** *LONDON SUNDAY TIMES.* **[extract] 27 July 1839. Birmingham, England.** Fears continued violence and destruction of property in Birmingham; middle class antagonized by workers; still no evidence concerning fires on the fifteenth of July. 30 August 1839. p.140, c4.

3751 WARREN FAY *to* **MR. WILLIS. [from the** *Boston Recorder*] **n.d. n.p.** Expresses shock and remorse at the [unexplained] actions of the Council. 30 August 1839. p.140, c4.

3752 CHESIRE *to* **THE EDITOR OF THE** *NEW HAMPSHIRE SENTINEL.* **n.d. n.p.** Comments on a lecture held in New Hampshire which condemns slavery and counts all those who refuse to join new anti-slavery political party as pro-slavery. 6 September 1839. p.141, c1.

3753 H. CLAY *to* **THE WHIGS OF NANSEMON COUNTY, VA. 25 May 1839. Ashland.** In response to a letter of approval on the action taken by Clay on the abolition question. 6 September 1839. p.141, c1.

3754 LUTHER LEE *to* **THE EDITOR OF THE** *ZION'S WATCHMAN.* **10 July 1839. Utica, N.Y.** Refutes Garrison's comments in 28 June *Liberator*, arguing that non-resistance is not a condemnation of our forefathers, that AS constitution does not condemn human governments, and that Mr. Garrison reasons fallaciously concerning political action. 6 September 1839. p.141, c2.

3755 L. MARIA CHILD *to* **FRIEND [W. L. GARRISON]. 2 September 1839. n.p.** Reports on the present state of the Massachusetts AS. 6 September 1839. p.142, c1.

3756 A. K. *to* **ELIZUR WRIGHT, JR. 28 August 1839. Farmington, Ct.** On women's rights activity in Lynn. 6 September 1839. p.142, c3.

3757 DAVID CAMPBELL *to* **FRIEND GARRISON. 3 September 1839. Boston.** Informs that he was imprisoned for refusing to enlist in military. 6 September 1839. p.142, c4.

3758 S. *to* **BROTHER GARRISON. 29 August 1839. Boston.** Criticizes the orator's and poet's speeches at commencement exercises at Cambridge. 6 September 1839. p.142, c5.

3759 OBSERVER *to* **MR. GARRISON. 26 August 1839. Kingston.** Considers non-resistance principles, introduced by H. C. Wright the previous week, an important discovery for citizens of Kingston. 6 September 1839. p.144, c3.

3760 JOSHUA LEAVITT *to* **THE COMMITTEE ON BEHALF OF THE AFRICAN PRISONERS AT NEW HAVEN. 6 September 1839. 143 Nassau St.** Reports on the condition of prisoners of the *Amistad,* who were charged with murder and claimed as property by Spaniards; they are unable to communicate with their captors or other Africans in the area. 13 September 1839. p.146, c1.

3761 J. C. G. *to* **THE EDITOR OF THE** *BOSTON COURIER.* **n.d. n.p.** Laments the predicament of the African captives in New Haven. 13 September 1839. p.146, c1.

3762 AN AMERICAN LAWYER *to* **THE EDITORS OF THE** *NEW YORK COMMERCIAL ADVERTISER.* **n.d. n.p.** Argues that the African prisoners in New Haven were kidnapped and should not be considered slaves. 13 September 1839. p.146, c2.

3763 T. P. RYDER *to* **BRO. GARRISON. 24 August 1839. Westerly, R.I.** Believes that the clergy should not be silent about its political convictions. 13 September 1839. p.146, c6.

3764 WM. COMSTOCK *to* **MR. GARRISON. n.d. n.p.** Praises the strength of Mrs. Child's anti-slavery convictions. 13 September 1839. p.147, c1.

3765 A FREEMAN *to* **MR. GARRISON. 7 September 1839. Salem.** Criticizes Dr. Flint's poem which belittles Garrison. 13 September 1839. p.147, c1.

3766 GERRIT SMITH *to* **WM. LLOYD GARRISON. 1 September 1839. Peterboro.** Notes that Garrison lost one of Smith's letters. 13 September 1839. p.147, c2.

3767 LEWIS TAPPAN *to* **MR. GARRISON. 6 September 1839. New York.** Denies that he urged the *Liberator* to "leave the cause." 13 September 1839. p.147, c5.

3768 E. B. CUNNINGHAM *to* **BROTHER GARRISON. 2 September 1839. Hartford.** Condemns clergy who have what he considers un-Christian views; expresses satisfaction that a pro-colonization speech did not encourage others in this view. 13 September 1839. p.148, c2.

3769 WILLIAM GOODELL *to* **BRO. STANTON. 5 February 1839. Utica.** Regrets tone of "warfare" between Garrison, Torrey, St. Clair, Phelps, and others. 13 September 1839. p.148, c4.

3770 JAMES C. FULLER *to* **WM. L. GARRISON. 28 August 1839. Skaneateles.** Comments on a letter written by Samuel Philbrick. 20 September 1839. p.149, c6.

3771 O. SCOTT *to* **BROTHER LEAVITT. [from the** *Emancipator***] 28 August 1839. Lowell.** Encloses letter from J. Q. Adams to clarify a point of order which arose at the Albany Convention. 20 September 1839. p.150, c3.

3772 J. Q. ADAMS *to* **O. SCOTT. [from the** *Emancipator***] 9 September 1839. Quincy.** On the rules governing a motion to adjourn. 20 September 1839. p.150, c3.

3773 GEO. BRADBURN *to* **LEAVITT. 9 September 1839. Nantucket.** Discusses a letter written by J. Q. Adams. 20 September 1839. p.150, c3.

3774 A. K. *to* **BROTHER GARRISON. September 1839. Torringford, Ct.** Reports on his visit to Hartford to advise a newly formed female society. 20 September 1839. p.150, c3.

3775 WM. JAY *to* **LEWIS TAPPAN. [from the** *Emancipator***] 7 September 1839. Bedford.** Sends a contribution to the committee appointed to defray the legal defense of the *Amistad* captives. 20 September 1839. p.150, c4.

3776 WENDELL PHILLIPS *to* **GEORGE THOMPSON. [extract from the** *Glasgow Argus***] n.d. Great Britain.** Expresses gratitude for support of the English abolitionists and for new movement concerning India, which will "seal the fate" of slavery in America; hopes civilization will approach America from both East and West. 20 September 1839. p.150, c5.

3777 GEORGE THOMPSON *to* **BROTHER [W. L. GARRISON]. 20 August 1839. London.** Looks forward to seeing Garrison at the upcoming convention in London. 20 September 1839. p.151, c5.

3778 GEO. BRADBURN *to* **H. C. WRIGHT. 31 August 1839. Nantucket.** Elaborates his reservations concerning the principles of non-resistance. 20 September 1839. p.152, c2.

3779 REV. J. A. JAMES *to* **THE EDITOR OF THE** *NEW YORK EVANGELIST.* **[extract] n.d. Birmingham, England.** Believes that no justification can allow a minister to support slavery. 20 September 1839. p.152, c5.

3780 P. P. *to* **BROTHER WRIGHT. 12 September 1838. Boston.** Gives an account of Norfolk County meeting at Wrentham. 27 September 1839. p.153, c1.

3781 EDWARD B. BARBER *to* **T. B. WATSON. 26 June 1839. Middlebury, Vt.** Declines an invitation to attend a Fourth of July convention. 27 September 1839. p.153, c4.

3782 ROSINA *to* **FRIEND [W. L. GARRISON]. 13 August 1839. Lexington.** Feels that women's rights are not respected; argues that woman, created as a "help-meet" to man, possesses "capabilities suited to a perfect reciprocity of thought and of feelings." 27 September 1839. p.153, c5.

3783 THOMAS M'CLINTOCK *to* **OLIVER JOHNSON. 12 September 1839. Waterloo, N.Y.** Discusses the past course and present position of Garrison. 27 September 1839. p.153, c6.

3784 W. B. *to* **BRO. GARRISON. n.d. n.p.** Believes that it should be a matter of personal choice whether Quakers join the AS. 27 September 1839. p.154, c1.

3785 S. T. *to* **BRO. GARRISON. n.d. n.p.** Summarizes the West Boylston AS meeting of 13 September: Massachusetts AS and the *Liberator* upheld; Massachusetts Abolition Society condemned; motives of Garrison and Wendell Phillips discussed. 27 September 1839. p.154, c4.

3786 MACCINE *to* **MR. GARRISON. September 1839. Kingston.** Corrects an error in the treasurer's report. 27 September 1839. p.154, c5.

3787 VINDEX *to* **MR. GARRISON. 13 September 1839. Washington, Ct.** Reports hostile reception given to Abby Kelley's anti-slavery lectures in Washington. 27 September 1839. p.154, c5.

3788 SOPHIA L. LITTLE *to* **FRIEND [W. L. GARRISON]. 25 May 1839. Pawtucket.** Upholds doctrines of peace and non-resistance. 27 September 1839. p.156, c3.

3789 WM. P. POWELL *to* **SIR [W. L. GARRISON]. 26 August 1839. New Bedford.** Gives an account of a public meeting held in New Bedford. 27 September 1839. p.156, c4.

3790 D. *to* **BROTHER GARRISON. 28 August 1839. Boston.** On the division of the abolitionists. 27 September 1839. p.156, c4.

3791 A. *to* **BROTHER GARRISON. 14 September 1839. Danvers (New Mills).** Comments on the lecture by Brother Johnson. 27 September 1839. p.156, c4.

3792 OREILLA KENDRICK *to* **MR. GARRISON. 16 September 1839. Millbury.** Reports that the Millbury Female AS passed resolutions in support of efforts of the Massachusetts AS and condemning sectarian efforts to narrow its own membership. 27 September 1839. p.156, c5.

3793 J. C. JACKSON *to* **R. [from the** *Union Herald***] 9 September 1839. Peterboro'.** Discusses the present crisis in the anti-slavery cause. 4 October 1839. p.157, c1.

3794 X. Y. *to* **W. L. GARRISON. n.d. n.p.** Requests that the *Liberator* publish enclosed letters from John Pierpont. 4 October 1839. p.157, c3.

3795 JNO. PIERPONT *to* **THE PROPRIETORS OF THE MEETING HOUSE IN HOLLIS STREET. n.d. n.p.** Comments on the motion to have him removed from office. 4 October 1839. p.157, c3.

3796 A MASSACHUSETTS METHODIST ABOLITIONIST *to* **BRO. SUNDERLAND. [from the** *Zion's Watchman***] 5 August 1839. Massachusetts.** Criticizes the *Watchman* for aggravating the split in abolitionists' ranks. 4 October 1839. p.157, c5.

3797 ORVILLE DEWEY *to* **THE EDITOR OF THE** *EVENING POST***. n.d. n.p.** Quotes from speech of the previous Sunday, in which he likened the African prisoners of the *Amistad* to American forefathers in their fight for freedom. 4 October 1839. p.185 [158], c1.

3798 BENJ. CLARK *to* **THE POSTMASTER OF THE TOWN OF WORCESTER. 19 September 1839. Fredericksburg, Va.** On the kidnapping of a free colored boy. 4 October 1839. p.185[158], c1.

3799 SAMUEL PHILBRICK *to* **FRIEND GARRISON. 24 September 1839. Brookline.** Discusses the course pursued by Joseph John Gurney and James C. Fuller. 4 October 1839. p.185[158], c3.

3800 EDWIN FUSSELL *to* **BROTHER [W. L. GARRISON]. 27 July 1839. Pendleton, In.** Comments on the discord among Eastern abolitionists. 4 October 1839. p.185[158], c4.

3801 TRUTH TELLER *to* **BRO. GARRISON. n.d. n.p.** Decries hypocritical Christian stand of the *Boston Recorder*. 4 October 1839. p.185[158], c5.

3802 THETA *to* **FRIEND GARRISON. n.d. n.p.** Declares that Massachusetts abolitionists plan to flood the next legislature with petitions. 4 October 1839. p.159, c1.

3803 J. C. HATHAWAY, WM. O. DUVALL, DANIEL A. ROBINSON, WM. R. SMITH, AND ESEK WILBUR *to* **FRIEND GARRISON. n.d. n.p.** Dissent from the Albany Convention's decision to exclude woman; hail *Liberator*'s stand. 4 October 1839. p.159, c2.

3804 A. A. PHELPS *to* **MR. GARRISON. 26 September 1839. Boston.** Corrects the *Liberator*: states that Stanton did not write the introductory remarks to William Goodell's recently published letter. 4 October 1839. p.159, c3.

3805 PACIFICUS *to* **HENRY GREW. n.d. n.p.** Continues their debate on non-resistance. 4 October 1839. p.160, c2.

3806 A. H. *to* **THE EDITOR OF THE** *CHRISTIAN REGISTER***. 5 September 1839. Philadelphia.** A Southerner discusses slavery. 11 October 1839. p.161, c1.

3807 HIRAM WILSON *to* **WM. GOODELL. 24 August 1839. Toronto.** Comments on the emigration of fugitives into Canada. 11 October 1839. p.161, c2.

3808 GEORGE BRADBURN *to* **WM. CLARK. [from the** *Boston Courier***] 1 October 1839. Boston.** Gives account of kidnappings in Virginia. 11 October 1839. p.162, c1.

3809 H. C. WRIGHT *to* **BROTHER [W. L. GARRISON]. n.d. n.p.** Discusses slavery and the clergy. 11 October 1839. p.162, c4.

3810 G. B. *to* **MR. GARRISON. n.d. n.p.** Asks Garrison to publish the whole of enclosed letter from himself to Mr. Jenks, which was printed, in part, by the *Nantucket Inquirer*. 11 October 1839. p.162, c6.

3811 G. B. *to* **MR. JENKS. n.d. n.p.** On the emancipated islands of the West Indies. 11 October 1839. p.162, c6.

3812 EDMUND QUINCY *to* **GARRISON. 30 September 1839. Quincy.** Encloses his letter to Edward Everett. 11 October 1839. p.163, c4.

3813 EDMUND QUINCY *to* **EDWARD EVERETT. 28 September 1839. Boston.** Resigns as justice of peace, as he feels he cannot discharge duties which involve his assuming the right to take a man's life. 11 October 1839. p.163, c4.

3814 GEORGE E. DAY *to* **THE EDITORS OF THE** *JOURNAL OF COMMERCE.* **8 October 1839. New Haven.** Feels that the concurring testimonies of the African prisoners in New Haven, concerning their departure from Africa and their cruel treatment by Mr. Pipi Ruiz, have convinced those involved in their examination. 18 October 1839. p.166, c1.

3815 WM. BROWN *to* **THE EDITOR [W. L. GARRISON]. October 1839. Foster.** On the colored people in Rhode Island. 18 October 1839. p.166, c4.

3816 CELIA *to* **MR. GARRISON. n.d. n.p.** Offers definition of "conscience." 18 October 1839. p.166, c5.

3817 H. HUTCHINSON *to* **BROTHER GARRISON. n.d. n.p.** Reports the formation of a new society in Sutton. 18 October 1839. p.166, c6.

3818 REV. SILAS RIPLEY *to* **MR. EDITOR [W. L. GARRISON]. 8 October 1839. Foxborough.** Claims the *Liberator* misrepresented his statements to the Norfolk County AS concerning the exclusion of women. 18 October 1839. p.167, c2.

3819 n.n. *to* **BROTHER GARRISON. 15 October 1839. Lynn.** Describes degrading treatment of a respectable colored citizen who attempted to ride the train from Lynn to Boston. 18 October 1839. p.167, c2.

3820 NATHANIEL A. BORDEN *to* **FRIEND GARRISON. 11 October 1839. New Bedford.** Reports that on 10 October the colored citizens of New Bedford adopted a resolution condemning sectarianism and disorganization as efforts on the part of those trying to obstruct the work of true abolitionists. 18 October 1839. p.167, c2.

3821 A. W. *to* **BROTHER GARRISON. 8 October 1839. Ashburnham.** Reports on speech on slavery given by the Rev. J. D. Lewis, a colored man. 18 October 1839. p.167, c5.

3822 H. C. WRIGHT *to* **HON. J. Q. ADAMS. 4 September 1839. Boston.** Asks Adams' opinion on the nature and extent of the commitment implied by an oath of allegiance to a government. 18 October 1839. p.168, c2.

3823 J. Q. ADAMS *to* **H. C. WRIGHT. 12 September. Quincy.** Replies to Wright's query, stating that an oath of allegiance to a government obliges one to submit to the laws, support the constitution, and defend the country, by arms if necessary. 18 October 1839. p.168, c2.

3824 JOHN R. FRENCH *to* **MR. ROGERS. [extract from the** *Herald of Freedom***] n.d. New Hampshire.** Praises participants of the annual meeting of the Hillsborough County AS, held at Weare. 25 October 1839. p.169, c2.

3825 JAMES DAVENPORT *to* **BRO. GARRISON. 19 October 1839. West Boylston.** Accuses Charles Torrey of lying. 25 October 1839. p.170, c1.

3826 T. P. R. *to* **FRIEND GARRISON. 16 October 1839. Fall River.** Relates details of another case of "color-phobia." 25 October 1839. p.170, c1.

3827 GERRIT SMITH *to* **THE EDITOR [W. L. GARRISON]. 12 October 1839. Peterboro'.** Corrects an error in the *Liberator* regarding resolutions passed at the New York AS meeting. 25 October 1839. p.170, c2.

3828 ONE WHO KNOWS *to* **FRIEND GARRISON. 7 October 1839. Worcester County.** Cautions abolitionists in the use of their funds. 25 October 1839. p.170, c2.

3829 HENRY G. CHAPMAN *to* **W. L. GARRISON. 21 October 1839. Boston.** Regarding the estate of William Williams. 25 October 1839. p.170, c2.

3830 JNO. PIERPONT *to* **THE PROPRIETORS OF THE HOLLIS STREET MEETING HOUSE. 7 October 1839. Boston.** Charges that they have chosen not to uphold the freedom and independence of their pulpit, that they have failed to clarify their accusation that he spoke of "exciting topics," and that his dispute with them can only be satisfactorily settled before an impartial tribunal. 25 October 1839. p.171, c3.

3831 PHINEAS CRANDALL *to* **BRO. GARRISON. n.d. n.p.** Claims that the *Liberator* published an untrue account of his statement. 1 November 1839. p.173, c5.

3832 CHAS. T. TORREY *to* **WM. L. GARRISON. 26 October 1839. Worcester.** Charges the *Liberator* with false reporting. 1 November 1839. p.173, c6.

3833 TRUTH *to* **BROTHER GARRISON. 23 October 1839. Weymouth.** Reports that the annual meeting of the Weymouth AS approved resolution in favor of the Massachusetts AS and the *Liberator*, and opposed to "new organization." 1 November 1839. p.175, c1.

3834 NATHANIEL B. BORDEN *to* **GOVERNOR EDWARD EVERETT. 18 October 1839. Fall River.** Wishes to know Everett's position on abolition and the admission of new slave states to the Union. 1 November 1839. p.175, c3.

3885 GOV. EDWARD EVERETT *to* **HON. NATHANIEL B. BORDEN. 24 October 1839. Watertown.** Replies to Borden's inquiry; favors immediate abolition of slavery in the District of Columbia; opposes admission of new slave states to Union. 1 November 1839. p.175, c3.

3836 SAMUEL CHANDLER *to* **H. COWDREY. 19 October 1839. Sandisfield.** Answers Cowdrey's inquiry; believes that the government should exercise its right to abolish slavery in the District of Columbia, to abolish slave traffic, and to refuse admission to new states whose constitutions allow slavery. 1 November 1839. p.175, c3.

3837 NATHAN HALE *to* **FRANCIS JACKSON. 30 October 1839. Boston.** Fails to see any connection between abolition and the present election. 1 November 1839. p.175, c4.

3838 SAMUEL B. WALCOTT *to* **DR. H. COWDREY. 23 October 1839. Hopkinton.** Replies to Cowdrey's inquiry; opposes slavery, and has supported Legislature's efforts to end it; opposes intermarriages. 1 November 1839. p.175, c4.

3839 THOMAS J. GREENWOOD *to* **DR. H. COWDREY. 18 October 1839. Marlborough.** Replies to queries by Mr. Cowdrey; abhors slavery, but believes that the Representatives are bound to represent the views of the citizens who elect them, and that it is wrong for anyone else to instruct them. 1 November 1839. p.175, c4.

3840 LUTHER FISHER *to* **H. COWDREY. 14 October 1839. Waltham.** Replies to Cowdrey; refers him to resolves of the First and Second Legislatures of 1838, of which he approves; opposes laws which make distinctions based on color. 1 November 1839. p.175, c4.

3841 GEORGE THOMPSON *to* **JOHN E. FULLER. 20 September 1839. Manchester, England.** Feels encouraged by John Scoble's lectures on emancipation in the West Indies; plans anti-slavery lecture tour beginning in Liverpool. 1 November 1839. p.176, c5.

3842 JOHN PIERPONT *to* **MESSRS. JAMES BOYD AND EDMUND JACKSON. 22 October 1839. Boston.** Expresses thanks to the dissenting minority of the committee which relieved him of his duties at the Hollis Street church. 8 November 1839. p.177, c1.

3843 JAMES C. FULLER *to* **W. L. GARRISON. 9 October 1839. Skaneateles.** Defends himself against objections made to one of his letters. 8 November 1839. p.178, c2.

3844 N. H. WHITING *to* **BRO. GARRISON. 30 October 1839. Abington.** Reports on the formation of the Abington society. 8 November 1839. p.178, c4.

3845 GEO. THOMPSON *to* **JOHN LEVY. 17 September 1839. Manchester.** Discusses Bradburn's views of the *Liberator*. 8 November 1839. p.178, c6.

3846 S. G. SHIPLEY *to* **BRADFORD SUMNER. 3 November 1839. Boston.** Discusses the Congress' power to abolish slavery. 8 November 1839. p.179, c3.

3847 BRADFORD SUMNER *to* **S. G. SHIPLEY. 5 November 1839. Boston.** Replies to Shipley's letter; believes that Congress can abolish slavery. 8 November 1839. p.179, c3.

3848 MARCUS MORTON *to* **DANIEL HENSHAW. 28 October 1839. Taunton.** Refuses to reiterate his views on slavery. 8 November 1839. p.179, c3.

3849 NATHAN WILLIS *to* **AMOS FARNSWORTH. 23 October 1839. Pittsfield, Ma.** Responds to Farnsworth's inquiry that he favors means to "diminish" slavery. 8 November 1839. p.179, c3.

3850 SETH SPRAGUE *to* **MESSRS. MICAH POOL ET AL. 4 November 1839. Duxbury.** Responding to their inquiry, states that his actions speak louder than words; cites membership in national, state and local ASS. 8 November 1839. p.179, c4.

3851 DAVID CHOATE *to* **MESSRS. DODGE, HALE, GRAY, UPHAM, AND PUTNAM. 2 November 1839. Essex.** Responds to their circular; takes anti-slavery position on questions concerning the District of Columbia and the admission of new states. 8 November 1839. p.179, c4.

3852 FRANCIS JACKSON, CHARLES T. HILDRETH, THOMAS R. SEWALL, AND ELLIS G. LORING *to* **ABBOTT LAWRENCE. 18 October 1839. Boston.** Wish to know Lawrence's views on slavery. 8 November 1839. p.180, c4.

3853 Entry number not used.

3854 CHARLES LESTER *to* **J. A. COLLINS. 3 October 1839. W. Stockbridge.** On the transgressions of certain abolitionists. 15 November 1839. p.181, c5.

3855 T. P. R. *to* **FRIEND GARRISON. n.d. n.p.** Suggests appropriate Thanksgiving observance for abolitionists. 15 November 1839. p.181, c6.

3856 CHARLES P. BOSSON *to* **BRO. GARRISON. 17 October 1839. Manchester.** Reports on events in England. 15 November 1839. p.182, c1.

3857 J. E. P. *to* **THE EDITOR [W. L. GARRISON]. 5 November 1839. Topsfield.** Discusses the lectures of Mr. St. Clair in Topsfield. 15 November 1839. p.182, c2.

3858 HENRY GREW *to* **PACIFICUS. n.d. n.p.** On the punishment of children. 15 November 1839. p.184, c2.

3859 LEWIS TAPPAN *to* **BRO. LEAVITT. n.d. n.p.** Opposes anti-slavery political party, which Leavitt favors. 22 November 1839. p.186, c2.

3860 SAMUEL J. MAY *to* **WM. M. CHACE. 12 November 1839. South Scituate.** On the formation of an abolitionist political party. 22 November 1839. p.186, c4.

3861 JOSHUA LEAVITT *to* **BROTHER [W. L. GARRISON]. November 1839. New York.** States he is unable to attend the State Anniversary. 22 November 1839. p.186, c4.

3862 THOMAS P. RICHMOND *to* **MESSRS. EAMES, CHACE, AND SMITH. 12 November 1839. Bristol, R.I.** On unity among abolitionists. 22 November 1839. p.186, c5.

3863 H. CUMMINGS *to* **MR. WM. L. GARRISON. 14 November 1839. Boston.** Reprimands one of *Liberator*'s correspondents for incorrect reporting on the Rhode Island AS meeting. 22 November 1839. p.186, c5.

3864 LEWIS C. GUNN *to* **BROTHER [W. L. GARRISON]. 16 November 1839. Philadelphia.** Comments on an address given by the managers of the Massachusetts AS. 22 November 1839. p.186, c6.

3865 A. A. PHELPS *to* **MR. GARRISON. 16 November 1839. Boston.** Discusses the book, *Right and Wrong in Massachusetts*. 22 November 1839. p.186, c6.

3866 C. P. JOHNSON *to* **W. L. GARRISON. 16 November 1839. Farmingham.** Corrects misstatements made in a letter written by H. C. Wright. 22 November 1839. p.187, c1.

3867 O. *to* **FRIEND GARRISON. n.d. n.p.** Reports that students at the Friends' Boarding School in Providence are forbidden to read the *Liberator*. 22 November 1839. p.187, c1.

3868 JOHN CUMMINGS *to* **FRIEND GARRISON. 11 November 1839. N. Dartmouth.** Reports the organization of a new society at North Dartmouth. 22 November 1839. p.187, c1.

3869 WM. B. EARLE *to* **FRIEND GARRISON. 13 November 1839. Leicester.** Corrects an article in the *Liberator* which erroneously signed his name to a speech he did not give. 22 November 1839. p.187, c1.

3870 PHILOS *to* **BROTHER GARRISON. 13 November 1839. Andover.** Reports that two abolitionists were elected to legislature from Andover. 22 November 1839. p.187, c2.

3871 L. M. BALL *to* **MR. GARRISON. n.d. n.p.** Corrects item in the minutes of the Boston Female AS. 22 November 1839. p.187, c2.

3872 GEORGE THOMPSON *to* **GARRISON. 17 September 1839. Manchester.** Longs to be back in the United States. 22 November 1839. p.187, c5.

3873 H. C. WRIGHT *to* **THE ESSEX NORTH ASSOCIATION OF CONGREGA-TIONAL MINISTERS. 6 November 1839. Boston.** Discusses his appearance before the association. 22 November 1839. p.188, c2.

3874 H. C. WRIGHT *to* **MR. EDITOR [W. L. GARRISON]. 14 November 1839. Providence.** Discusses abolition and the clergy. 22 November 1839. p.188, c4.

3875 JONAS EAMES *to* **FRIEND GARRISON. 20 November 1839. Amesbury Mills.** Discusses Mr. Jackson's lectures in Amesbury. 29 November 1839. p.190, c2.

3876 CHARLES LESTER *to* **J. A. COLLINS. 10 October 1839. West Stockbridge.** Discussion of issues concerned with the anti-slavery struggle. 29 November 1839. p.190, c5.

3877 CHARLES T. TORREY *to* **MARIA WESTON CHAPMAN. 12 November 1839. Templeton.** Discusses Mrs. Chapman's book, *Right and Wrong in Massachusetts.* 29 November 1839. p.191, c4.

3878 MARIA WESTON CHAPMAN *to* **CHARLES T. TORREY. 22 November 1839. Boston.** Replies to Torrey's comments on Mrs. Chapman's book, *Right and Wrong in Massachusetts.* 29 November 1839. p.191, c4.

3879 PETER JAQUES *to* **MYRICK. [from the *Union Herald*] 28 October 1839. Temple Grove.** Notes the stubborn strength of convictions of the people in Massachusetts. 29 November 1839. p.192, c2.

3880 SINE QUA NON *to* **MYRICK. [from the *Union Herald*] n.d. n.p.** Gives his impression of the anti-slavery cause in the East. 29 November 1839. p.192, c2.

3881 J. W. LEWIS *to* **BROTHER GARRISON. 20 November 1839. Concord, N.H.** Discusses the state of the anti-slavery cause in New Hampshire. 6 December 1839. p.194, c2.

3882 ANNA GARDNER *to* **WILLIAM LLOYD GARRISON. 5 October 1839. Nantucket.** Reports the formation of a new county AS. 6 December 1839. p.194, c2.

3883 JOHN CHANEY *to* **WM. H. HOUSLEY. 5 October 1839. Conneaut, Oh.** On behalf of Freewill Baptists, notifies Housley that the body cannot recognize him as a minister of Christ because he is a slaveholder. 6 December 1839. p.194, c4.

3884 A. A. PHELPS *to* **MR. GARRISON. 26 November 1839. Boston.** Criticizes Mrs. Chapman's book entitled *Right and Wrong in Massachusetts.* 6 December 1839. p.195, c2.

3885 DAVID STOWELL *to* **H. C. WRIGHT. [from the *Abolitionist*] 26 October 1839. Townsend.** Reports on lectures on slavery by Mr. Hawley and Mr. Jones in Townsend. 6 December 1839. p.195, c2.

3886 S. HAWLEY *to* **THE EDITOR OF THE *ABOLITIONIST*. 14 November 1839. Stoneham.** Corrects misstatements written by Rev. David Stowell. 6 December 1839. p.195, c2.

3887 ANNE WARREN WESTON *to* **MR. GARRISON. 2 December 1839. Weymouth.** Declares herself the author of the communication, published 7 November, signed "a life member of the Boston Female AS." 6 December 1839. p.195, c4.

3888 J. C. JACKSON *to* **MYRICK. [from the *Cazenovia Herald*] n.d. n.p.** On the political tactics of the Whigs. 13 December 1839. p.198, c3.

3889 GERRIT SMITH *to* **MR. GOODELL. 12 November 1839. Peterboro'.** Declares that he no longer opposes the formation of an abolitionist party. 13 December 1839. p.198, c3.

3890 LIEUT. WHALEY ARMITAGE *to* **THE *BRITISH EMANCIPATOR*. 10 June 1839. Aura, coast of Africa.** Describes progress and agreeable conditions at Sierra Leone; writes less favorably of Liberia. 13 December 1839. p.198, c4.

3891 H. C. WRIGHT *to* **BROTHER [W. L. GARRISON]. 3 December 1839. New London.** Maintains that abolition, being a moral question, ought also to be dealt with from the pulpit. 13 December 1839. p.198, c6.

3892 ANTI-CASTE *to* **FRIEND GARRISON. n.d. n.p.** Relates incident in which he was assumed to be a servant because he was seen helping a gentleman from his horse and carrying his baggage; therefore he was not allowed to dine with "gentlemen," despite his being white. 13 December 1839. p.198, c6.

3893 ELIZUR WRIGHT, JR. *to* **H. B. STANTON. 12 October 1839. Dorchester.** Private letter obtained by the *Liberator*: Wright proposes scheme to put forth an Abolitionist Party presidential candidate. 13 December 1839. p.199, c4.

3894 EDWARD ROSSETER, J. HILLMAN, H. RUSSELL, J. MUNRO, W. MARTIN, S. GLOVER, J. MCMURRAY, G. MOORE, AND R. GLOVER *to* **DR. R. R. MADDEN. 22 November 1839. New York.** Express gratitude to Madden for his acts of liberality and humanity while in Havana. 20 December 1839. p.202, c1.

3895 DR. R. R. MADDEN *to* **EDWARD ROSSETER, J. HILLMAN, H. RUSSELL, J. MUNRO, W. MARTIN, S. GLOVER, J. MCMURRAY, G. MOORE, AND R. GLOVER. 22 November 1839. New York.** Acknowledges letter of gratitude for his acts of liberality and humanity while in Havana. 20 December 1839. p.202, c1.

3896 ISAAC STEARNS *to* **FRIEND JOHNSON. 27 November 1839. Marshfield.** Discusses the merits of the new abolitionist organization. 20 December 1839. p.202, c4.

3897 SIMEON MILLIKEN *to* **MR. EDITOR [W. L. GARRISON]. 14 August 1839. Seaville.** Asks the members of the Baptist Home Mission Society if they want the slaveholder to sell his slaves for the purpose of increasing their funds. 20 December 1839. p.202, c5.

3898 H. C. WRIGHT *to* **BROTHER [W. L. GARRISON]. 8 December 1839. Chaplin, Ct.** On the plight of the Africans of the *Amistad*. 20 December 1839. p.202, c5.

3899 JOHN BURDEN, PRESIDENT OF THE GEORGETOWN YOUNG MEN'S AS *to* **MR. EDITOR [W. L. GARRISON]. 12 December 1839. Georgetown.** Details proceedings of their annual meeting. 20 December 1839. p.202, c6.

3900 N. J. *to* **BROTHER GARRISON. 12 December 1839. Alfred, Me.** Reports supposed case of kidnapping in Maine. 20 December 1839. p.202, c6.

3901 E. WRIGHT, JR. *to* **H. B. STANTON. [from the *Massachusetts Abolitionist*] 12 October 1839. n.p.** Proposes a scheme to put forward an Abolitionist Party presidential candidate. [reprint of letter first appearing 13 December 1839] 20 December 1839. p.203, c3.

3902 S. J. M. *to* **THE EDITOR OF THE *MONTHLY MISCELLANY OF RELIGION AND LETTERS*. n.d. n.p.** Discusses non-resistance. 20 December 1839. p.204, c2.

3903 LEWIS TAPPAN *to* **JAMES G. BIRNEY. [extract] n.d. n.p.** Suggest that the formation of an abolitionist political party may be prohibited by the AS constitution. 27 December 1839. p.205, c2.

3904 JAMES G. BIRNEY *to* **LEWIS TAPPAN. [extract] n.d. n.p.** Argues that formation of a third [abolitionist] party is not forbidden by any provision of the AS constitution and is not incompatible with its intent. 27 December 1839. p.205, c2.

3905 ELIZUR WRIGHT, JR. *to* **H. B. STANTON. 12 October 1839. Dorchester.** Proposes a scheme to put forward an Abolitionist Party presidential candidate. [reprint of letter first appearing 13 December 1839] 27 December 1839. p.205, c5.

3906 S. HAWLEY *to* **GERRIT SMITH. 22 November 1839. Groton.** Feels that the points of issue between the two abolition parties are not great enough to keep alive the contention. 27 December 1839. p.206, c1.

3907 A. *to* **THE EDITORS OF THE** *NEW HAVEN DAILY HERALD.* **n.d. n.p.** Denies propriety of rumored presidential decree to send African prisoners of the *Amistad* back to Cubans who claim to be their masters. 27 December 1839. p.206, c2.

3908 GEO. BRADBURN *to* **FRANCIS JACKSON. 16 December 1839. Nantucket.** Discusses factionalism in the anti-slavery cause. 27 December 1839. p.206, c3.

3909 DAVID CAMPBELL *to* **BROTHER GARRISON. 23 December 1839. Boston.** Attacks George Combe. 27 December 1839. p.206, c4.

3910 S. *to* **FRIEND GARRISON. n.d. n.p.** Defends George Combe, in reply to 20 December letter from David Campbell. 27 December 1839. p.206, c5.

3911 H. C. WRIGHT *to* **BROTHER [W. L. GARRISON]. 19 December 1839. Hartford.** Reports that resolutions condemning the formation of an anti-slavery political party were passed by the Connecticut AS. 27 December 1839. p.206, c6.

3912 JONATHAN P. MAGILL *to* **EDMUND QUINCY. n.d. n.p.** Preaches on the law of love and non-resistance. 27 December 1839. p.208, c2.

3913 GEORGE STORRS *to* **BROTHER SUNDERLAND. 27 May 1839. Lebanon, N.H.** Labels the "no civil government" policy a "dangerous heresy." 27 December 1839. p.208, c3.

[1840]

3914 SAMUEL CUSHMAN *to* **THEOPHILUS FISK. 15 May 1838. Washington, D.C.** Expresses surprise and dismay at hearing that Fisk aided abolitionists while in the North. 3 January 1840. p.1, c2.

3915 THEOPHILUS FISK *to* **A NORTHERN ABOLITIONIST. [extract] n.d. n.p.** Claims that the Bible vindicates slavery. 3 January 1840. p.1, c2.

3916 QUINTIUS *to* **MR. EDITOR [from the** *Rochester Freeman***] 2 December 1839. Ontario County.** On independent political action among abolitionists. 3 January 1840. p.1, c3.

3917 JOHN QUINCY ADAMS *to* **THE EDITOR OF THE** *BOSTON COURIER.* **[extract] n.d. n.p.** Laments predicament of African prisoners of the *Amistad.* 3 January 1840. p.1, c4.

3918 REV. DR. NELSON *to* **BROTHER LEAVITT. [from the** *Emancipator***] 22 November 1839. Mission Institute.** Admonishes readers that they will be called on to account for their acts: are they for or against slavery? 3 January 1840. p.1, c6.

3919 DANIEL LANCASTER *to* **MR. EDITOR [from the** *New Hampshire Panoply***] n.d. n.p.** Attacks Brother Cummings' dictatorial attitude as editor. 3 January 1840. p.2, c1.

3920 MARCUS WOODWARD *to* **N. P. ROGERS. [from the** *Herald of Freedom***] 11 November 1839. Stoneham.** Requests that his paper be stopped, as he is "sick of the wrangling and nonsense of the old society." 3 January 1840. p.2, c4.

3921 ELIZUR WRIGHT, JR. *to* **H. B. STANTON. 12 October 1839. Dorchester.** Proposes a scheme to put forward an Abolitionist Party presidential candidate. [reprint of letter first appearing 13 December 1839] 3 January 1840. p.2, c4.

3922 PALMER TANNER *to* **BROTHER [W. L. GARRISON]. n.d. Anterville, R.I.** Encourages Garrison. 3 January 1840. p.3, c3.

3923 HENRY GREW *to* **BROTHER [W. L. GARRISON]. 18 December 1839. Philadelphia.** Objects to Adin Ballou's limited definition of non-resistance. 3 January 1840. p.4, c2.

3924 BETA *to* **MR. PORTER. [from the *New Haven Record*] 24 November 1839. n.p.** On the African captives of the *Amistad*. 3 January 1840. p.4, c5.

3925 JAMES G. BIRNEY *to* **MESSRS. MYRON HOLLEY, JOSHUAH H. DARLING, AND JOSIAH ANDREWS. 17 December 1839. New York.** Replies to a group of abolitionists who nominated him as presidential candidate. 10 January 1840. p.6, c1.

3926 F. JULIUS LEMOYNE *to* **MESSRS. MYRON HOLLEY, JOSHUAH H. DARLING, AND JOSIAH ANDREWS. 10 December 1839. Washington, Pa.** Declines nomination for vice-president of the United States on the anti-slavery ticket. 10 January 1840. p.6, c1.

3927 SPECTATOR *to* **BROTHER [W. L. GARRISON]. 27 December 1839. Hartford.** Commends the Hartford County Anti-Slavery Convention for passing a resolution that censures "the narrow limits of a religious or political party." 10 January 1840. p.6, c5.

3928 EDWIN THOMPSON *to* **BROTHER GARRISON. 6 January 1840. Taunton.** Gives account of his "labors in the cause." 10 January 1840. p.6, c6.

3929 LUTHER LEE *to* **BROTHER GARRISON. 30 December 1839. Barnstable.** Argues that the *Liberator*'s account of his speech at Marlborough Chapel contained unwarranted criticisms. 10 January 1840. p.7, c1.

3930 S. HAWLEY *to* **GERRIT SMITH. 25 November 1839. Groton.** Denounces friends of the "new organization" who have used sectarian means to attain their object. 17 January 1840. p.9, c4.

3931 ELIZUR WRIGHT, JR. *to* **HENRY B. STANTON. 12 October 1839. Dorchester.** Proposes a scheme to put forward an Abolitionist Party presidential candidate. [reprint of letter first appearing 13 December 1839] 17 January 1840. p.9, c6.

3932 LEWIS TAPPAN *to* **THE COMMITTEE ON BEHALF OF THE CAPTURED AFRICANS. 7 January 1840. New Haven.** Discusses the trial of the African captives of the *Amistad*. 17 January 1840. p.10, c4.

3933 AN OLD SCHOOL ABOLITIONIST *to* **FRIEND GARRISON. 1 January 1840. Boston.** States he was surprised to find Charles Tappan presiding at the 24 December meeting at Marlboro Chapel. 17 January 1840. p.10, c6.

3934 H. C. WRIGHT *to* **BROTHER [W. L. GARRISON]. 9 January 1840. Hartford.** Reports on resolutions passed by the AS of Connecticut deprecating the organization of an anti-slavery political party. 17 January 1840. p.11, c1.

3935 WM. B. EARLE *to* **RESPECTED FRIEND GARRISON. 25 November 1839. Leicester.** On the organization of a county AS in South Worcester. 17 January 1840. p.11, c2.

3936 J. CROSS *to* **BROTHER LEAVITT. [from the** *Emancipator***] 14 December 1839. Joliet, Il.** Account of kidnapping cases in Illinois. 24 January 1840. p.14, c2.

3937 WM. RAYMOND *to* **BRO. GARRISON. 1 January 1840. Ashburnham.** On the labors of Hiram Wilson. 24 January 1840. p.15, c1.

3938 CHARLES FITCH *to* **MR. W. L. GARRISON. 9 January 1840. Newark.** Regrets his earlier writings entitled "Clerical Appeal." 24 January 1840. p.15, c3.

3939 CORA *to* **FRIEND GARRISON. 13 January 1840. Kingston.** Refutes statements appearing in the *Abolitionist* which claim that the "new organization" is free of sectarianism. 24 January 1840. p.15, c3.

3940 JOHN SMITH *to* **BROTHER GARRISON. 14 September 1839. Mecca, Oh.** Regrets he cannot attend the anniversary of the New England Non-Resistance Society; requests that his name be affixed to its Declaration of Sentiments and constitution. 24 January 1840. p.16, c2.

3941 GERRIT SMITH *to* **JOSHUA LEAVITT. 24 December 1839. Peterboro'.** Proclaims the right of abolitionists to vote for whomever they please. 31 January 1840. p.17, c2.

3942 J. H. HEWES *to* **MR. GARRISON. 20 January 1840. Haverhill.** Reports events from quarterly meeting of women's anti-slavery conference at Haverhill. 31 January 1840. p.19, c4.

3943 H. C. WRIGHT *to* **n.n. [from the** *Non-Resistant***] 22 December 1839. Willimantic, Ct.** Describes lectures he has given in Connecticut. 31 January 1840. p.20, c2.

3944 S. HAWLEY *to* **GERRIT SMITH. [from the** *Union Herald***] 5 January 1840. Groton.** Discusses false reasons the separatists give for breaking with the original society. 7 February 1840. p.21, c2.

3945 GEO. BRADBURN *to* **THE EDITOR OF THE** *COURIER***. 30 January 1840. Marlboro' Hotel.** Discusses the marriage law. 7 February 1840. p.22, c1.

3946 TRUTH TELLER *to* **THE ABOLITIONISTS OF MASSACHUSETTS. 26 January 1840. n.p.** Details the Massachusetts AS's weekly contribution plan for raising money. 7 February 1840. p.22, c4.

3947 JAMES SAYLES BROWN *to* **COLLINS. 14 January 1840. Hampshire County.** Gives account of previous meeting of the Berkshire County AS. 7 February 1840. p.22, c5.

3948 AN OLD SCHOOL ABOLITIONIST *to* **MR. GARRISON. 25 January 1840. Lowell.** On the humble and magnanimous confession of Mr. Fitch printed in the *Liberator*. 7 February 1840. p.22, c6.

3949 ADIN BALLOU *to* **BROTHER GARRISON. 13 January 1840. Mendon, Ma.** Responds to Henry Grew's criticism of his version of non-resistance. 7 February 1840. p.24, c2.

3950 BOARD OF MANAGERS OF THE MASSACHUSETTS AS *to* **THE EXECUTIVE COMMITTEE OF THE PARENT SOCEITY. 6 December 1839. Boston.** On the pecuniary embarrassments of the parent society, and the relation between the two bodies. 14 February 1840. p.25, c3.

3951 W. L. GARRISON *to* **CHARLES STEARNS. 10 February 1840. Boston.** Debates one's moral obligation to pay a military fine. 14 February 1840. p.27, c1.

3952 J. D. BRIDGE *to* **WM. L. GARRISON. 6 February 1840. Duxbury.** Declines the honor of his nomination as vice-president of the Massachusetts AS. 14 February 1840. p.27, c3.

3953 CHARLES STEARNS *to* **WM. LLOYD GARRISON. 31 January 1840. Hartford County Jail.** Discusses his choice to go to prison rather than pay a military fine. 14 February 1840. p.28, c2.

3954 H. C. WRIGHT *to* **BROTHER [W. L. GARRISON]. 6 February 1840. West Bloomfield, N.Y.** Gives details of abolitionist convention held recently in West Bloomfield. 21 February 1840. p.29, c2.

3955 H. C. H. [HENRY C. HOWELLS] *to* **GERRIT SMITH. 25 December 1839. Allegheny, Pa.** Supports Smith's plan to sustain the foreign missions. 21 February 1840. p.29, c4.

3956 CHARLES WHITE *to* **MR. W. L. GARRISON. 7 February 1840. Holden.** Reports on resolutions adopted by the Holden AS discouraging the formation of an anti-slavery political party. 21 February 1840. p.29, c5.

3957 ABRAHAM WILKINSON *to* **FRIEND WM. L. GARRISON. 15 February 1840. Pawtucket.** States that the Pawtucket AS opposes the formation of an anti-slavery political party. 21 February 1840. p.30, c2.

3958 E. THOMPSON *to* **BROTHER GARRISON. 7 February 1840. West Bridgewater.** Reports that he has formed new AS in West Bridgewater; lists officers. 21 February 1840. p.30, c2.

3959 ELIZABETH NILES *to* **MR. GARRISON. n.d. Abington.** Reports that the Abington Female AS passed resolutions supporting Garrison, condemning slavery, and rebuking ministers who preach about slavery on the Sabbath. 21 February 1840. p.30, c2.

3960 GEORGE C. SHAW *to* **FRIEND GARRISON. 21 January 1840. Newport, R.I.** Reports that the Newport AS praises Judge Johnson for his recent decision concerning the *Amistad* Captives. 21 February 1840. p.30, c2.

3961 A FRIEND TO TRUTH *to* **BROTHER GARRISON. 15 February 1840. Andover.** Corrects misstatements in letter from Luther Lee. 21 February 1840. p.30, c2.

3962 JOSEPH SMITH, JR. *to* **MR. EDITOR. [from the** *West Chester* **(Pennsylvania)** *Register*] **25 January 1840. n.p.** On beliefs of the Latter-Day Saints. 21 February 1840. p.32, c2.

3963 DAVID RUGGLES *to* **THE EDITOR OF THE** *EMANCIPATOR*. **11 January 1840. New York.** Expresses his appreciation to those who formed the committee to investigate the criminal prosecution against him. 21 February 1840. p.32, c3.

3964 J. P. BISHOP *to* **MYRICK. [from the** *Union Herald*] **6 January 1840. New Haven, Ct.** Discusses the division of anti-slavery forces in Massachusetts. 28 February 1840. p.33, c4.

3965 ALVAN STEWART *to* **WEBB. [from the** *Pennsylvania Freeman*] **20 January 1840. Utica.** Denounces the "no system plan"; urges political action on behalf of the slave. 28 February 1840. p.33, c6.

3966 THOMAS BICKNELL *to* **MR. GARRISON. 14 February 1840. Kingston.** States Rev. Cummings' reasons for organizing another anti-slavery group in Kingston. 28 February 1840. p.34, c2.

3967 JOHN W. LEWIS *to* **BROTHER GARRISON. 8 February 1840. Concord, N.H.** On anti-slavery activity in New Hampshire. 28 February 1840. p.34, c2.

3968 S. BRADFORD *to* **BROTHER GARRISON. 6 February 1840. Kingston.** Condemns the *Liberator* for its pro-war stance. 28 February 1840.p.34, c3.

3969 SUSANA AND AUGUSTUS WATTLES *to* **BRO. GARRISON. 6 February 1840. Mercer County, Oh.** Praise the aims of the *Liberator*. 28 February 1840. p.34, c3.

3970 FRANCIS JACKSON *to* **THE ABOLITIONISTS OF THE UNITED STATES. n.d. n.p.** Condemns attempts to divide the abolitionists. 28 February 1840. p.35, c1.

3971 HENRY GREW *to* **BRO. GARRISON. n.d. n.p.** Corrects a misrepresentation about him printed in Ballou's letter. 28 February 1840. p.36, c2.

3972 RAM GOPAUL GHOSE *to* **WILLIAM ADAM. July-August 1839. Calcutta.** Expresses gratitude for the British India Society; relates plans for new vernacular school in connection with the Hindoo College. 6 March 1840. p.37, c5.

3973 A FEMALE OF NEW HAMPSHIRE *to* **THE EDITOR OF THE** *HERALD OF FREEDOM.* **n.d. n.p.** Notes the irony in abolitionists' discrimination against women. 6 March 1840. p.38, c2.

3974 J. C. JACKSON *to* **GARRISON. 24 February 1840. Waterloo, N.Y.** Furnishes copy of letter from Joseph C. Hathaway. 6 March 1840. p.38, c4.

3975 JOSEPH C. HATHAWAY *to* **n.n. [from the** *Friend of Man***] 24 February 1840. Waterloo.** Refutes charges made against him by Gerrit Smith. 6 March 1840. p.38, c4.

3976 JOHN P. PERRY *to* **BROTHER GARRISON. 20 January 1840. Dighton.** Discusses activities of Dighton ASS. 6 March 1840. p.38, c5.

3977 LYDIA MARIA CHILD *to* **THE EDITOR [W. L. GARRISON]. n.d. n.p.** Discusses the "woman question"; upholds women's rights. 6 March 1840. p.38, c6.

3978 LEWIS TAPPAN *to* **THE EDITOR [W. L. GARRISON]. 17 February 1840. New York.** Defends himself against charges published in a letter from the managers of the Massachusetts AS, published 15 February. 6 March 1840. p.39, c1.

3979 EDWARD C. DELAVAN *to* **THE EDITORS OF THE** *ALBANY ARGUS.* **5 February 1840. Ballston Centre.** Reports on temperance reform in Ireland. 6 March 1840. p.40, c2.

3980 CHARLES H. FREEMAN AND THOMAS BUTTILOW *to* **THE EDITOR OF THE** *BARNSTABLE PATRIOT.* **n.d. n.p.** Report on a lecture by Rev. H. Cummings. 13 March 1840. p.41, c6.

3981 SETH SPRAGUE *to* **C. H. FREEMAN. 11 February 1840. Duxbury.** Denounces Hiram Cummings' misrepresentation of the Massachusetts AS; criticizes the narrow platform of the new Massachusetts Abolition Society. 13 March 1840. p.41, c6.

3982 H. C. WRIGHT *to* **BROTHER [W. L. GARRISON]. 26 February 1840. Waterloo.** Reports on several county and local anti-slavery conventions in western New York. 13 March 1840. p.42, c3.

3983 GERRIT SMITH *to* **H. C. WRIGHT. 29 February 1840. Peterboro'.** Challenges statements made by Wright regarding the Bloomfield convention. 13 March 1840. p.42, c4.

3984 SPECTATOR *to* **BRO. GARRISON. 3 March 1840. Danvers.** Reports that Mr. Wise's recent anti-slavery lecture in Danvers closed with criticisms of the Massachusetts AS, the *Liberator*, and Garrison. 13 March 1840. p.42, c5.

3985 HENRY GREW *to* **BROTHER GARRISON. n.d. n.p.** Discusses Adin Ballou's printed misrepresentations of him. 13 March 1840. p.44, c2.

3986 ADIN BALLOU *to* **BROTHER GARRISON. n.d. n.p.** Apologizes to Henry Grew for what was an innocent misunderstanding of his remarks. 13 March 1840. p.44, c3.

3987 SENIOR *to* **THE EDITOR [W. L. GARRISON]. n.d. n.p.** Reports that the annual meeting of the Vermont AS resolved not to support or recognize clergymen who oppose emancipation. 20 March 1840. p.45, c1.

3988 LEWIS TAPPAN *to* **THE EDITOR [W. L. GARRISON]. 10 March 1840. New York.** Refutes Lydia M. Child's criticism of him in her recent letter. 20 March 1840. p.45, c6.

3989 CHARLES P. BOSSON *to* **FRIEND GARRISON. n.d. n.p.** Lists his expenses for recent trip to England, for the benefit of those intending to travel to the London Convention. 20 March 1840. p.46, c2.

3990 n.n. *to* **BRO. GARRISON. 7 March 1840. Utica.** Informs readers that an "economical gentleman" could travel to the London Convention for two hundred dollars; itemizes expenses. 20 March 1840. p.46, c2.

3991 MARIA WESTON CHAPMAN *to* **MR. GARRISON. n.d. n.p.** Encloses letter from E. G. Taber; states that the actions he reports taken on behalf of the Boston Female AS were taken without the body's knowledge or consent. 20 March 1840. p.46, c3.

3992 E. G. TABER *to* **MARIA W. CHAPMAN. 8 March 1840. New Bedford.** Informs her that twenty-five copies of *Massachusetts Abolitionist* were sent to the New Bedford Female AS, purportedly by the Boston Female AS. 20 March 1840. p.46, c3.

3993 JAMES C. JACKSON *to* **BELOVED GARRISON. 6 March 1840. Waterloo.** Praises various articles and letters which had lately appeared in the *Liberator*. 20 March 1840. p.46, c3.

3994 J. J. THOMAS *to* **THE EDITOR OF THE *FRIEND OF MAN*. 28 February 1840. Macedon.** Contradicts Gerrit Smith's letter, which charged H. C. Wright and J. C. Jackson with "thrusting broadly, boldly and repeatedly, the doctrines of non-resistance on the [West Bloomfield Anti-Slavery] Convention." 20 March 1840. p.46, c4.

3995 JOSEPH LUNDY *to* **W. L. GARRISON. 16 January 1840. Rancocas.** Expresses his wish that a narrator other than Garrison undertake the biography of Benjamin Lundy. 20 March 1840. p.46, c6.

3996 J. V. HIMES *to* **BRO. GARRISON. 17 March 1840. Boston.** Relates a conversation he had with Rev. Beman on the old and new abolitionist organizations in Massachusetts. 20 March 1840. p.47, c4.

3997 A FRIEND *to* **FRIEND GARRISON. n.d. n.p.** Submits extract from the epistle of the London Yearly Meeting of Friends giving views of principles of peace. 20 March 1840. p.42[48], c2.

3998 HENRY JACKSON *to* **MR. EDITOR [W. L. GARRISON]. 24 February 1840. New Bedford.** Encloses resolutions, agreed to by a committee of ministers, concerning the announcement of public meetings from the pulpit and the holding of Sabbath evening meetings by societies. 20 March 1840. p.42[48], c4.

3999 GERRIT SMITH *to* **WILLIAM GOODELL. 4 March 1840. Peterboro'.** Expresses his hope for good results from the Albany convention. 27 March 1840. p.49, c5.

4000 N. H. WHITING *to* **BRO. GARRISON. 14 March 1840. Marshfield.** Gives account of a meeting held at Abington. 27 March 1840. p.50, c1.

4001 D. L. CHILD *to* **WM. GOODELL. 21 March 1840. Boston.** Accuses Goodell of making unjust statements regarding the Massachusetts AS. 27 March 1840. p.50, c2.

4002 H. C. WRIGHT *to* **MYRON HOLLEY. 22 February 1840. Port Byron.** Discusses resolution presented at the Bloomfield convention. 27 March 1840. p.50, c4.

4003 H. C. WRIGHT *to* **GERRIT SMITH. n.d. n.p.** Reports on the introduction of non-resistance principles at the West Bloomfield convention. 27 March 1840. p.50, c5.

4004 MYRON HOLLEY *to* **H. C. WRIGHT. 24 February 1840. Rochester.** Explains his defense of human governments. 27 March 1840. p.50, c5.

4005 WM. LLOYD GARRISON *to* **GERRIT SMITH. n.d. n.p.** Explains position of the AAS on the use of the elective franchise. 27 March 1840. p.51, c1.

4006 H. C. WRIGHT *to* **BROTHER. [from the** *Union Herald***] 27 December 1840. Windsor.** Believes that subserviency to the will of man instead of God has weakened society. 27 March 1840. p.52, c3.

4007 DANIEL O'CONNELL *to* **A FRIEND. 13 December 1839. Darrynane Abbey.** Believes that the misery of the Indians is caused by English misgovernment of British India. 3 April 1840. p.53, c3.

4008 G. W. STACY *to* **BRO. GARRISON. n.d. n.p.** Gives an account of the Boylestown AS convention. 3 April 1840. p.53, c6.

4009 AN ABOLITIONIST *to* **BROTHER GARRISON. n.d. n.p.** Offers opinion of how one should observe a fast. 3 April 1840. p.53, c6.

4010 J. P. BISHOP *to* **BRO. GARRISON. 2 March 1840. New Haven, Ct.** On the course followed by the *Emancipator*. 3 April 1840. p.54, c1.

4011 n.n. *to* **BRO. LEAVITT. [from the** *Emancipator***] n.d. n.p.** Debates Leavitt's views on the founding of an anti-slavery political party, as presented in 26 December 1839 *Emancipator*. 3 April 1840. p.54, c1.

4012 R. HARRISON BLACK *to* **THE EDITOR OF THE** *BRITISH EMANCIPATOR***. 16 December 1839. Paris.** Reports that M. de St. Anthoine will represent France at London convention; other countries will also send delegates. 3 April 1840. p.54, c3.

4013 J. Q. ADAMS *to* **A GENTLEMAN IN BROOKLYN. [extract] n.d. n.p.** Declares that he has never belonged to any "partial associations" which try to influence public policy, that he struggles primarily for freedom of speech in Congress, and that he has never advocated immediate uncompensated emancipation. 3 April 1840. p.56, c2.

4014 EDWARD C. DELEVAN *to* **THE EDITORS OF THE** *ALBANY ARGUS.* **21 March 1840. Ballston Centre.** Discusses the temperance cause in Ireland. 3 April 1840. p.56, c2.

4015 ABBY KELLEY *to* **FRIEND GARRISON. 31 March 1840. Millbury.** Laments the "disorganizing scheme" of new organization of friends in Massachusetts; reports that abolition is less popular in Connecticut. 10 April 1840. p.57, c3.

4016 H. C. WRIGHT *to* **BROTHER [W. L. GARRISON]. 18 March 1840. Farmington.** Reports on the anti-slavery cause in western New York. 10 April 1840. p.57, c4.

4017 W. O. DUVALL *to* **FRIEND GARRISON. 19 March 1840. Farmington, Ontario County, N.Y.** Reports on an anti-slavery meeting in western New York. 10 April 1840. p.57, c5.

4018 WM. B. STONE *to* **BRO. GARRISON. 21 February 1840. West Brookfield.** Relays information on the Andover Theological Seminary. 10 April 1840. p.57, c6.

4019 ONE OF ITS MEMBERS *to* **FRIEND GARRISON. 21 March 1840. Lynn.** Comments on the course of the CS and the Society of Friends. 10 April 1840. p.57, c6.

4020 CORA *to* **MR. GARRISON. 30 March 1840. Kingston.** Expresses opinion on the formation of an abolitionist party. 10 April 1840. p.58, c4.

4021 E. MACK *to* **BROTHER GARRISON. 31 March 1840. Dover, N.H.** Discusses the question of the dissolution of the AAS. 10 April 1840. p.58, c4.

4022 EDMUND QUINCY *to* **WM. ELLERY CHANNING. 12 April 1840. Dedham.** Argues that if the Church does not fight against slavery, others will; expresses anger that an abolitionist was denied a church funeral. 17 April 1840. p.63, c2.

4023 GERRIT SMITH *to* **HENRY C. WRIGHT. 1 April 1840. Peterboro'.** Discusses five points debated upon at the West Bloomfield convention. 24 April 1840. p.65, c1.

4024 GERRIT SMITH *to* **W. L. GARRISON. 6 April 1840. Peterboro'.** Discusses the duty of abolitionists to vote. 24 April 1840. p.65, c2.

4025 WM. WALKER *to* **BRO. GARRISON. 11 April 1840. Andover Theological Seminary.** Describes the formation of the Andover Theological Seminary AS. 24 April 1840. p.65, c3.

4026 W. O. DUVALL *to* **FRIEND GARRISON. 7 March 1840. Port Byron.** Gives commentary on a pamphlet entitled, "Speech of Mr. Slade of Vermont on the rights of Petition." 24 April 1840. p.65, c4.

4027 S. GRAHAM *to* **FRIEND GARRISON. 12 April 1840. Northampton.** In defense of George Combe and phrenology. 24 April 1840. p.65, c4.

4028 A PLAIN MAN *to* **THE EDITOR [W. L. GARRISON]. n.d. n.p.** Explains the rights and duties of abolition voters. 24 April 1840. p.65, c5.

4029 SUMNER LINCOLN *to* **BROTHER GARRISON. 4 April 1840. Gardner.** Discusses the formation of an abolitionist party. 24 April 1840. p.65, c6.

4030 WM. M. CHACE *to* **WM. LLOYD GARRISON. 20 April 1840. Boston.** Sends extracts of letter from Charles C. Burleigh. 24 April 1840. p.66, c2.

4031 CHARLES C. BURLEIGH *to* **n.n. [extract] n.d. n.p.** Praises Garrison and the *Liberator*. 24 April 1840. p.66, c2.

4032 JAMES S. GIBBONS *to* **FRIEND LEAVITT. 12 April 1840. n.p.** Observes the split among the abolitionists based on disagreements over AS constitutional amendment. 24 April 1840. p.66, c3.

4033 D. ROOT *to* **BRO. LEAVITT. [from the** *Emancipator***] n.d. n.p.** Discusses proposal to form a national anti-slavery board of commissioners, which he intends to move at next annual AS meeting. 24 April 1840. p.66, c4.

4034 E. N. *to* **W. L. GARRISON. March 1840. Philadelphia.** Defends the Society of Friends. 24 April 1840. p.68, c2.

4035 WILLIAM GOODELL *to* **DAVID LEE CHILD. 6 April 1840. Utica.** Replies to charges made by Child that he attended a Whig meeting and spoke in support of Gen. Harrison. 1 May 1840. p.69, c6.

4036 A PLAIN MAN *to* **THE EDITOR [W. L. GARRISON]. n.d. n.p.** Replies to attacks made by Goodell on his article entitled, "Hints to Abolitionists on Political Action." 1 May 1840. p.70, c2.

4037 C. M. BURLEIGH *to* **BROTHER GARRISON. 22 April 1840. Taunton.** Account of a meeting of the Bristol AS. 1 May 1840. p.70, c2.

4038 W. L. GARRISON *to* **FRIEND. 14 April 1840. Boston.** Regrets he cannot attend meeting in Leominster. 1 May 1840. p.70, c3.

4039 CHARLES T. TORREY *to* **MR. GARRISON. 20 April 1840. Worcester.** Encloses notice of meeting for those who wish to support candidacy of James G. Birney and Thomas Earle for president and vice-president respectively of the United States. 1 May 1840. p.70, c4.

4040 CHARLES T. TORREY *to* **MR. GARRISON. n.d. n.p.** Declares that, being well acquainted with friends of the "new organization," he knows of no one who favors dissolution of the AAS. 1 May 1840. p.70, c4.

4041 A. F. WILLIAMS *to* **THE EXECUTIVE COMMITTEE OF THE AAS. n.d. n.p.** Submits amendments to AS constitution for consideration at next annual meeting. 1 May 1840. p.70, c5.

4042 WM. B. EARLE *to* **THE EXECUTIVE COMMITTEE OF THE AAS. 14 April 1840. Leicester.** Informs them of proposal which will be submitted at the annual meeting. 1 May 1840. p.70, c5.

4043 CHARLES T. TORREY *to* **THE EXECUTIVE COMMITTEE OF THE AAS. 16 April 1840. Worcester.** Submits amendment to AS constitution, to be acted upon at the annual meeting. 1 May 1840. p.70, c5.

4044 JAMES S. GIBBONS *to* **FRIEND GARRISON. 27 April 1840. New York.** Announces that the *Emancipator* will be published thereafter under the auspices of the New York City AS. 1 May 1840. p.71, c3.

4045 A MEMBER OF THE HOUSE *to* **MR. GARRISON. n.d. n.p.** Condemns House members who voted against the marriage bill; lists names. 8 May 1840. p.73, c4,

4046 ELLIS GRAY LORING *to* **THE EDITOR OF THE** *EMANCIPATOR*. **1 May 1840.** **Boston.** Articulates his views on the present controversy in the Massachusetts AS regarding non-resistance. 8 May 1840. p.74, c2.

4047 GARRISON *to* **GERRIT SMITH. n.d. n.p.** Refutes Gerrit's letter concerning the position of the AAS on voting. 8 May 1840. p.75, c1.

4048 JOSEPH STURGE *to* **A MEMBER OF THE AS EXECUTIVE COMMITTEE. 3 March 1840. Birmingham, England.** Stresses importance of attendance at forthcoming London convention. 8 May 1840. p.75, c5.

4049 L. M. BALL *to* **MR. GARRISON. 14 December 1839. Boston.** Replies on behalf of the Boston Female AS to column entitled "Unimpeachable Testimony," appearing in an earlier issue of the *Liberator*. 8 May 1840. p.75, c6.

4050 H. C. WRIGHT *to* **BROTHER [W. L. GARRISON]. 2 May 1840. Philadelphia.** On non-resistance and Wm. Goodell's inconsistency on the topic. 15 May 1840. p.77, c3.

4051 H. C. H. [HENRY C. HOWELLS] *to* **W. L. GARRISON. 24 April 1840. Allegheny, Pa.** Laments the division of abolitionists over the question of one's duty to vote. 15 May 1840. p.77, c3.

4052 AN ORTHODOX MAN *to* **BROTHER GARRISON. 3 April 1840. Danvers.** Account of an inept and equivocal sermon given by the Rev. Milton P. Braman. 15 May 1840. p.77, c5.

4053 CORA *to* **FRIEND GARRISON. 30 April 1840. Kingston.** Discusses the upcoming presidential election. 15 May 1840. p.77, c5.

4054 J. O. BURLEIGH *to* **BROTHER GARRISON. 6 May 1840. Oxford.** Reports on Worcester County Abolition Society proceedings. 15 May 1840. p.78, c3.

4055 W. O. DUVALL *to* **THE EDITOR OF THE** *AMERICAN FARMER*. **7 February 1840. Batavia, N.Y.** Deplores proposed legal action to separate slaves from freemen in Maryland; believes such separation unfortunately already exists. 15 May 1840. p.78, c3.

4056 WM. SLADE *to* **WILLIAM LLOYD GARRISON. 28 April 1840. Washington.** Informs Garrison he was reproached by a correspondent of the *Liberator*. 15 May 1840. p.78, c4.

4057 NATHANIEL P. ROGERS *to* **THE ABOLITIONISTS OF NEW HAMPSHIRE. [from the** *Herald of Freedom*] **n.d. n.p.** Writes in anticipation of London convention, which he will attend; entrusts paper to Parker Pillsbury for remainder of year. 15 May 1840. p.79, c1.

4058 GARRISON *to* **FRIEND. 12 May 1840. New York.** Reports on proceedings of the national convention. 15 May 1840. p.79, c2.

4059 MAJOR THOMAS G. WESTERN *to* **n.n. [extract] 1-5 April 1840. Bexar.** Reports that Mexicans are gaining ground and Bexar is "destroyed and plundered." 15 May 1839. p.79, c3.

4060 ARNOLD BUFFUM *to* **BROTHER [W. L. GARRISON]. 27 April 1840. Wilmington, Oh.** Discusses a resolution adopted at a quarterly meeting of the Essex County AS condemning Quakers as pro-slavery. 22 May 1840. p.81, c4.

4061 MARY T. BURRAGE *to* **MR. GARRISON. 6 May 1840. Fitchburg.** Encloses an extract of a letter against slavery which she had written to one of the deacons of her church. 22 May 1840. p.81, c5.

4062 MARY T. BURRAGE *to* **RESPECTED FATHER IN THE CHURCH. n.d. n.p.** Explains her decision to leave church, which she feels has abrogated the duty to make its influence felt. 22 May 1840. p.81, c5.

4063 H. C. WRIGHT *to* **BROTHER [W. L. GARRISON]. 15 May 1840. New York.** On the new national organization. 22 May 1840. p.83, c3.

4064 SAMUEL E. SEWALL *to* **THE EDITOR [W. L. GARRISON]. 19 May 1840. Boston.** States his position in relation to the Massachusetts AS. 22 May 1840. p.83, c4.

4065 ABIMILECH SNOWDROP *to* **THE** *BAY STATE DEMOCRAT.* **12 May 1840. New York.** Informs that a group of New England abolitionists were denied occupancy at a New York hotel. 29 May 1840. p.85, c2.

4066 ANTI-ABOLITION CONSISTENCY *to* **NATHANIEL P. ROGERS. n.d. n.p.** Notes inconsistency of "abolitionists" who also contribute to unfriendly causes. 29 May 1840. p.85, c5.

4067 H. C. WRIGHT *to* **BROTHER [W. L. GARRISON]. 20 May 1840. New Haven.** Feels that the spirit of slavery has triumphed in Connecticut. 29 May 1840. p.86, c4.

4068 EDWARD C. DELAVAN *to* **THE EDITORS OF THE** *ARGUS.* **24 April 1840. Albany.** Reports on temperance cause in Ireland. 29 May 1840. p.88, c3.

4069 W. H. BURLEIGH *to* **MR. GARRISON. 19 May 1840. Pittsburg.** Replies to charges made by Henry C. Howells that Orange Scott blocked the passage of a "momentous clause" in the Western Pennsylvania AS constitution. 5 June 1840. p.89, c6.

4070 GERRIT SMITH *to* **WILLIAM LLOYD GARRISON. 18 May 1840. Peterboro'.** Asks Garrison to correct misstatements made in the 8 May *Liberator.* 5 June 1840. p.90, c1.

4071 AN ANTI-SLAVERY WOMAN *to* **MR. EDITOR [W. L. GARRISON]. n.d. n.p.** Assails anti-feminism on the part of abolitionists. 5 June 1840. p.90, c3.

4072 J. P. BISHOP *to* **JOHNSON. 30 May 1840. Boston.** Proceedings of the annual meeting of the Massachusetts Abolition Society held 28 May. 5 June 1840. p.90, c3.

4073 JAMES BOYLE *to* **OLIVER JOHNSON [extract] n.d. n.p.** Supports the position of the Massachusetts AS in advocating principles of non-resistance. 5 June 1840. p.92, c2.

4074 E. C. DELAVAN *to* **THE EDITOR OF THE** *ARGUS.* **18 May 1840. Ballston Centre.** Reports on the temperance cause in Ireland. 5 June 1840. p.92, c3.

4075 EDMUND QUINCY *to* **SAMUEL D. HASTINGS. 1 May 1840. Dedham, Ma.** Declines an invitation from East Pennsylvania State Convention to speak on slavery. 12 June 1840. p.93, c3.

4076 N. P. ROGERS *to* **SAMUEL D. HASTINGS. 27 April 1840. Concord, N.H.** Declines invitation to attend the annual meeting of the East Pennsylvania AS. 12 June 1840. p.93, c3.

4077 WM. HENRY BRISBANE *to* **SAMUEL D. HASTINGS. 28 April 1840. Cincinnati, Oh.** Declines invitation to attend a meeting of the East Pennsylvania AS. 12 June 1840. p.93, c3.

4078 N. P. ROGERS *to* **PARKER PILLSBURY. 19 May 1840. New York.** Foresees "stormy" London convention; cites questions of women's rights and the secession of new American and Foreign AS from old society. 12 June 1840. p.93, c4.

4079 WM. GOODELL *to* **MR. EDITOR [W. L. GARRISON]. 2 June 1840. Whitesboro', N.Y.** Refutes remarks about himself printed 15 May in column entitled "Abolition and Non-Resistance." 12 June 1840. p.94, c3.

4080 EDWARD PALMER *to* **FRIEND. 28 May 1840. Worcester.** On the evils of money, the love of which makes slavery almost impossible to eradicate. 12 June 1840. p.95, c2.

4081 H. C. WRIGHT *to* **GERRIT SMITH. 2 April 1840. Aurora.** Supports non-resistance. 12 June 1840. p.96, c2.

4082 J. C. NOTT *to* **THE EDITOR OF THE** *MERCHANTS' AND PLANTERS' JOURNAL.* **n.d. n.p.** Encloses letter from Rev. G. F. Simmons to himself; assails Simmons for his unwelcome abolitionist sermons. 19 June 1840. p.97, c1.

4083 REV. GEORGE F. SIMMONS *to* **J. C. NOTT. 21 May 1840. n.p.** Criticizes his Southern hosts for their unwillingness to hear the truth. 19 June 1840. p.97, c1.

4084 A. F. WILLIAMS *to* **MR. EDITOR [W. L. GARRISON]. 2 June 1840. Farmington.** Corrects misstatements made by H. C. Wright in regard to Connecticut AS's stand on women and Friends. 19 June 1840. p.97, c6.

4085 A.C. *to* **THE EDITOR OF THE** *LIBERATOR* **[W. L. GARRISON]. 11 June 1840. Boston.** Praises Thomas Jennings, a black dentist in Boston. 19 June 1840. p.98, c2.

4086 M. H. GRISELL *to* **BROTHER GARRISON. 4 June 1840. Ohio.** Gives unfavorable commentary on the "new organization" principles which are against women and voting. 19 June 1840. p.98, c2.

4087 SION HARRIS *to* **n.n. [extract from the** *Journal of Commerce***] 16 April 1840. Caldwell, Liberia.** Details natives' attack on Heddington. 19 June 1840. p.100, c3.

4088 n.n. *to* **THE** *PRACTICAL CHRISTIAN.* **n.d. n.p.** Assails "Garrisonism" as threat to church and state. 26 June 1840. p.101, c3.

4089 J. S. GIBBONS *to* **THE EDITOR OF THE** *EMANCIPATOR.* **[from the** *National Anti-Slavery Standard***] 9 June 1840. n.p.** Contradicts 22 May *Emancipator*'s unflattering review of speech given by Garrison before leaving for England. 26 June 1840. p.101, c5.

4090 F. F. MANFORD *to* **THE EDITOR [W. L. GARRISON]. 17 June 1840. Boston.** Account of a case of color-phobia. 26 June 1840. p.101, c6.

4091 WILLIAM GOODELL *to* **H. C. WRIGHT. 2 June 1840. Whitesboro'.** Defends his supposed fickleness with regard to non-resistance. 26 June 1840. p.104, c2.

4092 H. C. HOWELLS *to* **BROTHER [W. L. GARRISON]. 15 June 1840. Allegheny, Pa.** Refutes W. H. Burleigh's statement that O. Scott's influence prompted the Western Pennsylvania AS to omit a clause from its constitution which denied a slave's right to use violence to secure his liberty. 3 July 1840. p.105, c4.

4093 TRUTH TELLER *to* **BRO. JOHNSON. n.d. n.p.** On the resolution against pro-slavery church and clergy at recent New England convention. 3 July 1840. p.105, c5.

4094 J. A. COLLINS *to* **ABOLITIONISTS OF MASSACHUSETTS. n.d. n.p.** Solicits funds to support Massachusetts AS. 3 July 1840. p.106, c6.

4095 D. T. KIMBALL *to* **H. C. WRIGHT n.d. n.p.** Notifies Wright that he has been withdrawn as a member of the Essex North [Congregational] Association for "walking contrary to our rules." 3 July 1840. p.108, c2.

4096 H. C. WRIGHT *to* **THE ESSEX NORTH [CONGREGATIONAL] ASSOCIATION. 4 June 1840. Brookline.** Refuses to reprimand them for withdrawing his membership; asserts he will continue labors for the cause. 3 July 1840. p.108, c2.

4097 ABBY KELLEY *to* **THE EDITOR OF THE** *ANTI-SLAVERY STANDARD.* **19 June 1840. Torrington, Ct.** Deplores divisions caused by non-resistance and women's rights in the Connecticut AS. 10 July 1840. p.110, c3.

4098 D. N. *to* **BROTHER LEAVITT. [from the** *Emancipator***] 5 May 1840. Mission Institute.** Relates "melancholy" incident of encountering young slave who did not know who Jesus Christ was. 10 July 1840. p.110, c5.

4099 A SUBSCRIBER *to* **THE EDITOR [W. L. GARRISON]. n.d. n.p.** Vents opposition to the militia laws of Massachusetts. 10 July 1840. p.112, c2.

4100 WM. GOODELL *to* **THE EDITOR [W. L. GARRISON]. 24 June 1840. Whitesboro'.** Replies to two editorials from the 12 June edition. 17 July 1840. p.113, c2.

4101 A. D. JONES *to* **n.n. [from the** *New York Evangelist***] 8 June 1840. Newark, Choctaw Nation.** Relates continued harassment and eventual murder of a freed mulatto family. 17 July 1840. p.114, c5.

4102 JOHN G. WHITTIER *to* **JOSHUA LEAVITT. 24 June 1840. Amesbury.** Gives an account of the proceedings of the AAS meeting. 17 July 1840. p.115, c2.

4103 H. C. WRIGHT *to* **WM. GOODELL. 29 June 1840. Philadelphia.** Advocates non-resistance principles. 17 July 1840. p.116, c2.

4104 S. G. SHIPLEY *to* **LEWIS JOSSELYN. [from the** *Bay State Democrat***] 13 July 1840. Boston.** States that his nomination by the abolitionist convention for presidential elector was put forth without his knowledge or consent. 24 July 1840. p.117, c4.

4105 SUMNER LINCOLN *to* **THE EDITOR [W. L. GARRISON]. July 1840. Gardner.** Sends a few words in regard to the Massachusetts AS. 24 July 1840. p.117, c5.

4106 H. C. WRIGHT *to* **A. F. WILLIAMS. 11 July 1840. Hampton, Ct.** Condemns him for his belief that women should not vote or speak on politics. 24 July 1840. p.117, c6.

4107 WM. LLOYD GARRISON *to* **JOHNSON. 3 July 1840. London.** Discusses proceedings of the World's Convention. 24 July 1840. p.119, c3.

4108 WENDELL PHILLIPS *to* **JOHNSON. June 1840. London.** Gives an account of anti-slavery meetings in England. 24 July 1840. p.119, c4.

4109 H. C. WRIGHT *to* **AMOS A. PHELPS. 6 June 1840. Boston.** Corrects location given earlier for the Grimke's lectures; comments on women's role. 24 July 1840. p.120, c2.

4110 WM. LLOYD GARRISON *to* **JOHNSON. 3 July 1840. London.** Submits a formal protest against the exclusion of a portion of the American delegates from the Anti-Slavery Convention in London. 31 July 1840. p.121, c3.

4111 GARRISON *to* **n.n. [extract] 28 May 1840. In the Gulf Stream.** En route to the London Convention; writes that he departed from New York on 22 May, weathered dismal storm; finds many "godless" sorts on board. 31 July 1840. p.123, c1.

4112 GARRISON *to* **n.n. [extract] 12 June 1840. At sea.** Gives news of the voyage; has decided he "is no sailor." 31 July 1840. p.123, c1.

4113 GARRISON *to* **n.n. [extract] 14 June 1840. Within sight of land.** Observes that the weather is fine; remarks that passengers of which he complained "most cordially hate" him. 31 July 1840. p.123, c2.

4114 GARRISON *to* **n.n. [extract] 15 June 1840. At sea, approaching Liverpool.** Continues journal of his voyage to London. 31 July 1840. p.123, c2.

4115 GARRISON *to* **n.n. [extract] 29 June-3 July 1840. London.** Notes that the "Woman question" is hotly disputed at the London Convention; reports he has spoken at a *soiree* and met many celebrated figures. 31 July 1840. p.123, c5.

4116 EDMUND QUINCY, WM. BASSETT, H. C. WRIGHT, T. SOUTHWICK, MARIA W. CHAPMAN, J. V. HIMES, C. K. WHIPPLE, O. JOHNSON, AND ANNE W. WESTON *to* **ARTHUR TAPPAN. 1 June 1840. Boston.** Deny charges made by Tappan against the New England Non-Resistance Society. 31 July 1840. p.124, c2.

4117 JOHN G. WHITTIER *to* **CHARLES. 6 July 1840. Amesbury.** Declares that he was charged with heresy by H. C. Wright for having been a member of the American and Foreign AS. 7 August 1840. p.126, c3.

4118 W. H. BURLEIGH *to* **MR. JOHNSON. 18 July 1840. Pittsburgh.** Replies to H. C. Howells' charge that he lied. 7 August 1840. p.126, c5.

4119 H. C. WRIGHT *to* **AMOS A. PHELPS. [continued from 24 July 1840] n.d. n.p.** Believes that "violence will beget violence." 7 August 1840. p.128, c2.

4120 TRUTH TELLER *to* **ABOLITIONISTS OF THE UNITED STATES. [first of a series] n.d. n.p.** Appeals to abolitionists not to vote for William Harrison or Van Buren for president. 14 August 1840. p.129, c1.

4121 C. M. BURLEIGH *to* **BROTHER JOHNSON. 24 July 1840. Plainfield, Ct.** On the spirit of new anti-slavery organization. 14 August 1840. p.129, c2.

4122 H. C. WRIGHT *to* **OLIVER. 29 July 1840. Wethersfield, Ct.** On new organization in Connecticut. 14 August 1840. p.129, c3.

4123 JAMES LYONS *to* **GEN. W. H. HARRISON. 14 April 1840. Richmond.** Discusses Harrison's position on the question of abolition. 14 August 1840. p.129, c5.

4124 GEN. W. H. HARRISON *to* **JAMES LYONS. 1 June 1840. North Bend, Cincinnati.** Addresses Lyons' position on abolition. 14 August 1840. p.129, c5.

4125 W. H. HARRISON *to* **GOVERNOR OWEN. [from the** *Wilmington* **(N.C.)** *Advertiser***] 16 February 1840. Cincinnati.** Declares he has never belonged to an abolitionist society, contrary to his statement to James Lyons. 14 August 1840. p.129, c6.

4126 WM. GOODELL *to* **H. C. WRIGHT. 25 July 1840. Whitesboro', N.Y.** Defends himself against the accusation that he changed his views on non-resistance. 14 August 1840. p.132, c2.

4127 WM. GOODELL *to* **THE EDITOR [W. L. GARRISON]. 25 July 1840. Whitesboro', N.Y.** Thanks him for printing his letter on non-resistance. 21 August 1840. p.133, c1.

4128 TRUTH TELLER *to* **ABOLITIONISTS. [continued from 14 August 1840] n.d. n.p.** Appeals to abolitionists not to vote for William Harrison or Van Buren for president. 21 August 1840. p.135, c1.

4129 GARRISON *to* **ANTI-SLAVERY FRIENDS AND COADJUTORS. 19 August 1840. Boston.** Mentions what transpired at the World's Convention in London. 21 August 1840. p.135, c3.

4130 THOMAS COLE *to* **BRO. JOHNSON. 7 August 1840. Newport, R. I.** Account of his trip to Providence. 21 August 1840. p.135, c4.

4131 N. P. ROGERS *to* **PARKER PILLSBURY. [from the** *Herald of Freedom***] 22 July 1840. Edinburgh.** Sends words of encouragement to the anti-slavery people of New Hampshire. 21 August 1840. p.135, c5.

4132 WM. HOWITT *to* **LUCRETIA MOTT. 27 June 1840. London.** Concerns the exclusion of women from the convention in London. 28 August 1840. p.139, c5.

4133 H. C. WRIGHT *to* **THEODORE D. WELD. n.d. n.p.** Denies man's right to armed resistance of evil. 28 August 1840. p.140, c2.

4134 TRUTH TELLER *to* **ABOLITIONISTS. [continued from 21 August 1840] n.d. n.p.** Appeals to abolitionists not to vote for Harrison or Van Buren for president. 4 September 1840. p.141, c5.

4135 H. C. WRIGHT *to* **BROTHER [W. L. GARRISON]. 20 August 1840. Tolland, Ct.** Condemns the hypocrisy of pro-slavery clergymen. 4 September 1840. p.141, c6.

4136 H. C. WRIGHT *to* **GARRISON. 26 August 1840. Hartford, Ct.** Gives an account of the convention in Connecticut called to hear the report of the delegates to the London Convention. 4 September 1840. p.142, c1.

4137 H. C. HOWELLS *to* **JOHNSON. 18 August 1840. Allegheny.** Replies to charges made by W. H. Burleigh. 4 September 1840. p.142, c2.

4138 LUCRETIA MOTT *to* **DANIEL O'CONNELL. 17 June 1840. London.** Asks his opinion concerning the rejection of women from the General Anti-Slavery Conference in London. 4 September 1840. p.143, c2.

4139 DANIEL O'CONNELL *to* **LUCRETIA MOTT. 20 June 1840. 20 Pall Mall.** Believes that exclusion of women from the London convention was an injustice. 4 September 1840. p.143, c2.

4140 H. C. WRIGHT *to* **THEODORE D. WELD. 27 June 1840. Philadelphia.** Believes that non-resistance will not hinder abolition. 4 September 1840. p.144, c2.

4141 TRUTH TELLER *to* **ABOLITIONISTS. [continued from 4 September 1840] n.d. n.p.** Appeals to abolitionists not to vote for William Henry Harrison or Martin Van Buren for president. 11 September 1840. p.145, c1.

4142 JAMES BOYLE *to* **BROTHER [W. L. GARRISON]. n.d. n.p.** Discusses the great Christian principle, "Thou shalt love thy neighbor as thyself." 11 September 1840. p.145, c2.

4143 CHARLES W. DENISON *to* **FRIEND GARRISON. 8 September 1840. Boston.** Corrects statements regarding his course on the question of women and voting. 11 September 1840. p.146, c3.

4144 GEO. THOMPSON *to* **GARRISON. 2 August 1840. Edinburgh.** Sends a farewell to Garrison and wishes him well in his journey. 11 September 1840. p.147, c1.

4145 JAMES G. BARBADOES, THOMAS COLE, AND J. T. HILTON *to* **WM. LLOYD GARRISON. 18 August 1840. Boston.** Invite Garrison to speak at a meeting of colored citizens of Boston. 11 September 1840. p.147, c2.

4146 WM. LLOYD GARRISON *to* **JAMES G. BARBADOES ET AL. 19 August 1840. Boston.** Accepts invitation to speak at a meeting of colored citizens of Boston. 11 September 1840. p.147, c2.

4147 WM. GOODELL *to* **BRO. JOHNSON. 28 August 1840. Whitesboro', N.Y.** States his views against non-resistance. 11 September 1840. p.148, c2.

4148 JAMES BOYLE *to* **BROTHER [W. L. GARRISON]. July 1840. Ohio.** On the failure of associations for moral, political, and religious reform. 18 September 1840. p.149, c1.

4149 H. C. WRIGHT *to* **SARAH M. GRIMKE AND ANGELINA E. WELD. n.d. n.p.** Ridicules the idea that women should not be equal to men. 18 September 1840. p.149, c3.

4150 TRUTH TELLER *to* **ABOLITIONISTS. [continued from 11 September 1840] n.d. n.p.** Appeals to abolitionists not to vote for William Harrison or Martin Van Buren for president. 18 September 1840. p.150, c4.

4151 A MODERN FANATIC *to* **SIR. 10 September 1840. East Abington.** On the approaching election. 18 September 1840. p.150, c5.

4152 H. H. R. *to* **MR. EDITOR [W. L. GARRISON]. 8 September 1840. Abington.** Reports on the new organization in Abington. 18 September 1840. p.150, c5.

4153 WM. GOODELL *to* **MR. EDITOR [W. L. GARRISON]. 31 August 1840. Whitesboro'.** Believes that non-resistance principles oppose abolition. 18 September 1840. p.152, c2.

4154 TRUTH TELLER *to* **ABOLITIONISTS. 16 September 1840. Marshfield.** Appeals to abolitionists not to vote for William Henry Harrison or Martin Van Buren for president. 25 September 1840. p.153, c2.

4155 H. C. WRIGHT *to* **SARAH M. GRIMKE AND ANGELINA E. WELD. [continued from 18 September 1840] n.d. n.p.** Concerning the "Woman Question" and "new organization." 25 September 1840. p.153, c5.

4156 NEW HAVEN RESIDENTS *to* **MR. EDITOR [W. L. GARRISON]. 30 August 1840. New Haven, Ct.** Refutes article headed "National Convention" appearing in 21 August *Liberator*, which misrepresented the nature of a New Haven public meeting. 25 September 1840. p.153, c6.

4157 THOMAS CLARKSON *to* **WILLIAM LLOYD GARRISON. n.d. n.p.** Repudiates the ACS. 25 September 1840. p.154, c6.

4158 ELIZABETH PEASE *to* **FRIEND [GARRISON]. 3 September 1840. Liverpool.** Sends news of England; encloses above letter from Thomas Clarkson. 25 September 1840. p.155, c2.

4159 GEO. THOMPSON *to* **GARRISON. 4 September 1840. Liverpool.** Bids Garrison farewell. 25 September 1840. p.155, c2.

4160 CHARLES LENOX REMOND *to* **GARRISON. 30 August 1840. Manchester.** Reports on a well-attended meeting at which British India was discussed. 25 September 1840. p.155, c2.

4161 JOSEPH ADSHEAD *to* **GARRISON. 3 September 1839. Manchester.** Discusses East India emancipation meetings. 25 September 1840. p.155, c3.

4162 RICHARD D. WEBB *to* **GARRISON. 7 February 1840. Dublin.** Encloses copy of pamphlet on "Non-Resistant Principles." 25 September 1840. p.155, c3.

4163 RICHARD ALLEN *to* **GARRISON. 1 July 1840. Dublin.** Gives brief discussion of anti-slavery. 25 September 1840. p.155, c4.

4164 ELIZABETH PEASE *to* **WILLIAM BASSETT. [from the** *Worcester Reformer*] 3 **August 1840. Liverpool.** Thanks him for periodicals he has sent; urges abolitionists to persevere against sectarianism. 25 September 1840. p.155, c5.

4165 DAVID BRENT PRICE *to* **DANIEL O'CONNELL. 26 June 1840. Farringdon Street.** Comments on the performance of several prominent American abolitionists in England. 2 October 1840. p.157, c4.

4166 CHARLES RAMSAY *to* **LUCINDA RAMSAY. 3 June 1840. Georgetown, British Guiana.** Gives account of his arrival in Georgetown and informs wife of his good health. 2 October 1840. p.158, c1.

4167 FRANCIS A. CREW *to* **MARY JANE CREW. 3 June 1840. Demarara.** Reports on his arrival in Damarara and informs wife of his good health. 2 October 1840. p.158, c1.

4168 A WHIG ABOLITIONIST *to* **WHIG ABOLITIONISTS. n.d. n.p.** Explains his reasons for deciding to give his vote to Harrison. 2 October 1840. p.158, c5.

4169 J. TELEMACHUS HILTON *to* **MR. EDITOR [W. L. GARRISON]. n.d. n.p.** Refutes charges made against the attendants of a national convention held in New Haven. 2 October 1840. p.158, c6.

4170 JAMES DURPE *to* **MEREDITH. 31 August 1840. Sumterville.** Reports on proceedings of the Baptist Anti-Slavery Convention. 9 October 1840. p.161, c1.

4171 JAMES BOYLE *to* **BROTHER. n.d. n.p.** Argues that Jews are not alone in being God's chosen people. 9 October 1840. p.161, c2.

4172 B. LUNDY *to* **L. MOTT. 19 September 1835. Philadelphia Prison.** Writes during his one-week imprisonment. 9 October 1840. p.161, c4.

4173 n.n. *to* **WILLIAM LLOYD GARRISON. 13 January 1840. White Marsh, Pa.** Forwards note written by Benjamin Lundy, for his biographer. 9 October 1840. p.161, c4.

4174 BENJAMIN LUNDY *to* **n.n. 18 May 1838. Philadelphia, Pa.** Relates loss of valuables in 17 May 1838 destruction of Pennsylvania Hall. 9 October 1840. p.161, c5.

4175 WM. SMEALE ET AL. *to* **THE EDITOR OF THE** *GLASGOW ARGUS.* **12 August 1840. Glasgow.** States that Society of Friends made it publicly known that they held no fellowship with Lucretia Mott. 9 October 1840. p.162, c3.

4176 JAMES MOTT *to* **WM. SMEALE. 24 August 1840. Liverpool.** Explains Lucretia Mott's clash with the Society of Friends. 9 October 1840. p.162, c3.

4177 C. LENOX REMOND *to* **FRIEND JACKSON. 25 August 1840. Liverpool.** Comments on the deliberations of the World's Convention. 9 October 1840. p.162, c6.

4178 WM. LLOYD GARRISON *to* **MY EDITORIAL CHAIR. 6 October 1840. Worcester.** Encloses notes on the state anti-slavery convention. 9 October 1840. p.163, c4.

4179 CHARLES LENOX REMOND *to* **REV. C. B. RAY. 30 June 1840. London.** Decries the exclusion of women from the World's Convention. 16 October 1840. p.165, c5.

4180 n.n. *to* **n.n. 11 August 1840. Mount Freedom, Jamaica.** Elaborates beneficial results of emancipation in the West Indies. 16 October 1840. p.165, c6.

4181 LUTHER MYRICK *to* **JOHN A. COLLINS. 25 September 1840. Cazenovia.** Declines an invitation to attend a meeting of the Massachusetts AS. 16 October 1840. p.166, c6.

4182 J. N. T. TUCKER *to* **JOHN A. COLLINS. 21 September 1840. Apulia, N.Y.** Accepts an invitation to attend the conventions at Worcester and Springfield. 16 October 1840. p.167, c1.

4183 PELEG CLARKE *to* **JOHN A. COLLINS. 25 September 1840. Conventry, R.I.** Declines an invitation to attend the Worcester convention. 16 October 1840. p.167, c1.

4184 J. C. HATHAWAY *to* **JOHN A. COLLINS. 17 September 1840. Farmington, N.Y.** Declines an invitation to attend the Worcester and Springfield conventions. 16 October 1840. p.167, c2.

4185 J. M. MCKIM *to* **JOHN A. COLLINS. 30 September 1840. Philadelphia.** Declines an invitation to attend the Worcester convention. 16 October 1840. p.167, c2.

4186 W. L. GARRISON *to* **MRS. MARIA W. CHAPMAN. 13 October 1840. Boston.** Congratulates the Boston Female AS. 16 October 1840. p.167, c3.

4187 DANIEL S. MILLER, JR. *to* **WILLIAM LLOYD GARRISON. 2 October 1840. Philadelphia.** Invites Garrison to attend a meeting of the Free Produce Association. 16 October 1840. p.167, c4.

4188 T. S. KENDALL *to* **THE EDITOR OF THE** *XENIA FREE PRESS.* **7 September 1840. Monroe County, East Tennessee.** Reports violent disturbance of an anti-slavery sermon in South Carolina. 23 October 1840. p.169, c1.

4189 REV. T. S. KENDALL *to* **THE EDITOR. [from the** *Xenia Free Press***] 7 September 1840. Monroe County, Tn.** Reports that he was denounced as an outlaw in South Carolina for preaching against slavery. 23 October 1840. p.169, c1.

4190 DR. G. BAILEY, JR. *to* **J. A. COLLINS. 28 September 1840. Cincinnati.** Declines an invitation to the Worcester convention. 23 October 1840. p.169, c4.

4191 A. A. PHELPS *to* **MR. GARRISON. 5 October 1840. Boston.** Refutes an article from the *Liberator* which alleged a "friendly understanding" between Phelps and Mr. Winslow, a man known to be unfriendly to the cause. 23 October 1840. p.170, c1.

4192 ANNA BAILEY *to* **BROTHER GARRISON. 4 October 1840. New Bedford.** Reports on the founding of a Juvenile Female AS in New Bedford. 23 October 1840. p.170, c1.

4193 C. LENOX REMOND *to* **FRIEND. 21 September 1840. Edinburgh.** Describes his travels in England. 23 October 1840. p.171, c4.

4194 WM. GOODELL *to* **MR. EDITOR [W. L. GARRISON]. 3 October 1840. Whitesboro', N.Y.** Defends his previous statement that abolitionists must confront and take sides on the question of non-resistance. 23 October 1840. p.172, c2.

4195 M. V. BALL *to* **ELIZABETH PEASE. [extract] 6 May 1840. Boston.** Explains the dissolution of the Boston Female AS. 30 October 1840. p.173, c4.

4196 ELIZABETH PEASE *to* **n.n. n.d. n.p.** Asks further clarification of circumstances surrounding the dissolution of Boston Female AS. 30 October 1840. p.173, c4.

4197 HARRIET MARTINEAU *to* **n.n. [extract] n.d. Tynemouth, Northumberland.** Encourages Boston Female AS in their efforts; sends two pounds as donation. 30 October 1840. p.174, c2.

4198 ANNE KNIGHT *to* **n.n. 4 August 1840. England.** Decries exclusion of women from the struggle. 30 October 1840. p.174, c2.

4199 J. P. B. *to* **BRO. GARRISON. 20 October 1840. Boston.** Reports that Beriah Green, president of the Oneida Institute, has spoken in Boston in favor of "new organization" and a third [abolitionist] political party. 30 October 1840. p.174, c3.

4200 C. LENOX REMOND *to* **MR. THOMAS COLE. 2 October 1840. Edinburgh.** Describes his travels in England. 30 October 1840. p.174, c5.

4201 GEO. BRADBURN *to* **FRIEND GARRISON. 22 October 1840. Nantucket.** Affirms the duty of abolitionists to refuse to vote for any candidate who is not also an abolitionist. 30 October 1840. p.174, c6.

4202 FRANCIS JACKSON *to* **JOHN DAVIS. 26 September 1840. Boston.** Wishes to know Davis' views on slavery. 30 October 1840. p.175, c4.

4203 E. *to* **GEO. BRADBURN. 30 October 1840. North Rochester.** Regrets that Bradburn intends to vote for Gen. Harrison for president. 6 November 1840. p.178, c3.

4204 EQUALITY *to* **FRIEND GARRISON. 21 October 1840. West Newbury.** Condemns reprehensible behavior of "abolitionists" in Newbury. 6 November 1840. p.178, c4.

4205 FAUSTULUS *to* **MR. EDITOR [W. L. GARRISON]. 19 October 1840. Worcester.** Reports on the closing of meetinghouses to abolitionists. 6 November 1840. p.178, c5.

4206 ARTHUR TAPPAN, J. LEAVITT, AND H. DRESSER *to* **WM. HENRY HARRISON. 21 September 1840. New York.** Wish to know Harrison's views on slavery. 13 November 1840. p.181, c1.

4207 WM. HENRY HARRISON *to* **ARTHUR TAPPAN, J. LEAVITT, AND H. DRESSER. 2 October 1840. Cincinnati.** Replies to their inquiry, affirming that he joined an abolition society years ago and has found no reason to change his views since then. 13 November 1840. p.181, c1.

4208 A. A. *to* **n.n. [from the** *New Hampshire Panoply***] October 1840. New Hampshire.** Denies Rev. Alanson St. Clair's right to be called a Christian and a clergyman. 13 November 1840. p.181, c1.

4209 JAMES R. CAMPBELL, M. A. *to* **W. L. GARRISON. 14 October 1840. Montrose, Scotland.** Encloses address to annual meeting of the Congregational Union of Scotland. 13 November 1840. p.181, c2.

4210 E. D. HUDSON *to* **MR. EDITOR. [from the** *Anti-Slavery Standard***] 27 October 1840. New London.** Describes proceedings of a meeting in Mystic. 13 November 1840. p.182, c1.

4211 n.n. *to* **MR. EDITOR. [from the** *New Hampshire Panoply***] n.d. n.p.** Upholds good standing of Rev. Alanson St. Clair in the church, contrary to the *Panoply*'s intimations. 13 November 1840. p.182, c5.

4212 REV. ALANSON ST. CLAIR *to* **REV. J. V. HIMES. 12 October 1840. Dunbarton.** Requests that he be dismissed from Himes' congregation and that a statement of his standing be forwarded to the First Congregational Church in Dunbarton. 13 November 1840. p.182, c5.

4213 CHARLES LENOX REMOND *to* **FRIEND GARRISON. n.d. n.p.** Appends notice of speech to be given by R. R. Gurley; affirms resolve to fight efforts of the ACS. 13 November 1840. p.183, c2.

4214 SARAH SHEARMAN *to* **MR. GARRISON. n.d. London.** Sympathizes with American women who were shut out from the convention in London. 13 November 1840. p.183, c2.

4215 CHAS. J. MCDONALD *to* **S. M. GATES. 10 September 1840. Milledgeville, Ga.** Criticizes Congressman Gates' use of the franking privilege to disseminate resolutions from the World's [Anti-Slavery] Convention in London. 20 November 1840. p.185, c3.

4216 A. P. BAGBY *to* **HON. S. M. GATES. 2 September 1840. Tuscaloosa.** An opponent of abolition questions the propriety of Gates' use of the congressional frank to forward resolutions of a foreign abolition convention to him. 20 November 1840. p.185, c3.

4217 W. PENNINGTON *to* **THOMAS CLARKSON. 30 July 1840. Newark, N.Y.** Thanks him for having forwarded communications of the abolition convention in London. 20 November 1840. p.185, c4.

4218 R. R. MADDEN *to* **THE BRITISH AND FOREIGN AS. 18 August 1840. Alexandria, Egypt.** Reports that he was among a delegation which presented two addresses from the London Anti-Slavery Convention to Mahamet Ali, Pacha of Egypt. 20 November 1840. p.185, c4.

4219 J. RUSSELL *to* **THOMAS CLARKSON. 21 August 1840. Downing Street.** Reports he has delivered Clarkson's address on emancipation to Her Majesty. 20 November 1840. p.185, c5.

4220 W. S. *to* **A FRIEND. n.d. n.p.** Criticizes a speech by Mr. Dana, in which he claimed that women differed from men in intellectual as well as physical capabilities. 20 November 1840. p.186, c1.

4221 JAMES BOYLE *to* **DR. BAILEY. 12 October 1840. n.p.** Notes clever arguments against slavery put forth by Southern Whigs in order to secure votes for Harrison. 20 November 1840. p.186, c3.

4222 THOS. MORRIS *to* **DR. BAILEY. n.d. n.p.** Comments on an Anti-Slavery Congress at Washington. 20 November 1840. p.186, c4.

4223 J. R. DAILY *to* **n.n. [extract from the** *Pennsylvania Freeman***] n.d. Liberia.** Condemns Liberian government; feels blacks have no more liberty there than in the States. 20 November 1840. p.186, c5.

4224 GEORGE BRADBURN *to* **FRIEND GARRISON. 9 November 1840. Nantucket.** Discusses the presidential candidates. 20 November 1840. p.187, c1.

4225 H. C. WRIGHT *to* **WM. GOODELL. 10 September 1840. Philadelphia.** Argues that the government of the United States is a military government, and therefore Christians are obligated not to support it. 20 November 1840. p.188, c2.

4226 JUSTICE *to* **THE EDITOR OF THE** *COURIER***. n.d. n.p.** Differs with men who claim that a woman is only fit for "an appropriate sphere of action." 27 November 1840. p.189, c2.

4227 JOHN G. WHITTIER *to* **n.n. 24 September 1840. Amesbury.** Believes that the exclusion of women does not afford just grounds for a sweeping condemnation of the World's Anti-Slavery Convention. 27 November 1840. p.190, c3.

4228 SARAH M. GRIMKE *to* **HER SISTER [ANGELINA E. GRIMKE]. 22 October 1840. Belleville.** Declines an invitation to speak. 27 November 1840. p.190, c4.

4229 PRO CLERICUS *to* **MR. EDITOR. [from the** *Zion's Herald***] 1840. New England.** Declares that William L. Garrison, Maria W. Chapman, and Henry C. Wright have hindered the progress of emancipation by straying from the question of abolition. 27 November 1840. p.190, c5.

4230 JAMES MCTEAR *to* **SIR [W. L. GARRISON]. 31 October 1840. Glasgow.** Sends his respects to Garrison; notes that R. R. Gurley has had little success in Glasgow. 27 November 1840. p.191, c1.

4231 H. C. WRIGHT *to* **n.n. 13 November 1840. Philadelphia.** Regrets he cannot attend the Sabbath, Church and Ministry Convention; affirms the need for such a convention. 27 November 1840. p.191, c2.

4232 SAMUEL MYERS *to* **E. QUINCY. 1 November 1840. New Lisbon, Oh.** Discusses questions to be considered at the forthcoming religious convention. 27 November 1840. p.191, c2.

4233 THOMAS LONGSHORE *to* **E. QUINCY. 2 November 1840. New Lisbon, Oh.** Looks forward to the coming convention on the Sabbath, Church, and ministry. 27 November 1840. p.191, c3.

4234 J. C. JACKSON *to* **GERRIT SMITH. 3 September 1840. Peterboro'.** Discusses Smith's candidacy for governor. 4 December 1840. p.193, c3.

4235 E. D. HUDSON *to* **THE EDITOR OF THE** *NATIONAL ANTI-SLAVERY STANDARD.* **n.d. n.p.** Reports an instance of "mobocracy" at an anti-slavery lecture. 4 December 1840. p.193, c4.

4236 J. T. [JOSEPH TRACY] *to* **MESSRS. EDITORS. [from the** *New York Observer***]** **23 November 1840. Boston.** Reports on proceedings of the Sabbath Convention. 4 December 1840. p.194, c2.

4237 WM. W. LAMBORN *to* **FROST. 4 November 1840. Knox Township, Oh.** Explains his reasons for refusing to participate in the presidential election. 4 December 1840. p.194, c5.

4238 JUSTICE *to* **THE EDITOR OF THE** *COURIER.* **16 November 1840. Cambridge.** Upholds women's rights. 4 December 1840. p.194, c6.

4239 A CONNECTICUT FARMER *to* **BROTHER GARRISON. December 1840. Plainfield, Ct.** Feels that the time had arrived for another anti-slavery campaign. 4 December 1840. p.195, c4.

4240 n.n. *to* **MR. EDITOR [W. L. GARRISON]. 18 November 1840. n.p.** Informs Garrison that an attack on *Liberator* in 18 November *Zion's Herald* was written by J. D. Bridge of Duxbury. 4 December 1840. p.195, c4.

4241 H. C. WRIGHT *to* **WM. GOODELL. 11 September 1840. Philadelphia.** Refutes Goodell's argument, which attempted to reconcile supporting Birney for president with opposing government by military power. 4 December 1840. p.196, c2.

4242 n.n. *to* **DR. BAILEY. [from the** *Philanthropist***] n.d. Cincinnati.** Describes illegal slave-trafficking incident in Ohio, which went unopposed by apathetic observers. 11 December 1840. p.197, c3.

4243 H. C. WRIGHT *to* **WM. GOODELL. 12 September 1840. Philadelphia.** Opposes allegiance to human government. 11 December 1840. p.200, c2.

4244 P. ATHERTON *to* **MR. EDITOR [W. L. GARRISON]. 12 November 1840. Fitchburg, Ma.** Praises Dr. Watson of Washington Street in Boston for curing his case of scrofula. 11 December 1840. p.200, c5.

4245 HENRY GREW *to* **BROTHER GARRISON. 4 December 1840. Philadelphia.** Gives his reasons for discontinuing his subscription to the *Liberator.* 18 December 1840. p.201, c4.

4246 S. R. *to* **BRO. CARTER. [from the** *Christian Herald***] 8 November 1840. Lynn.** Discusses the proceedings of the recent Sabbath Convention. 18 December 1840. p.202, c4.

4247 THOMAS COLE *to* **n.n. November 1840. Boston.** Discusses political parties. 18 December 1840. p.202, c5.

4248 CHARLES M'EWAN *to* **GARRISON. n.d. n.p.** Gives account of an anti-slavery meeting held in Dr. Wardlaw's chapel. 18 December 1840. p.203, c1.

4249 H. C. WRIGHT *to* **WM. GOODELL. 10 September 1846. Philadelphia.** Replies to Goodell that non-resistants, himself included, do not support abolition of slavery through legislative action because their beliefs prohibit them from supporting the government. 18 December 1840. p.204, c2.

4250 CHARLES SIMMONS *to* **DR. THOMAS ROBBINS. 6 November 1840. Wareham.** Elaborates biblical proof that slavery is sinful. 25 December 1840. p.205, c1.

4251 G. S. S. JERNINGHAM *to* **DON EVARISTO PEREZ DE CASTRO. 5 January 1840. Madrid.** Discusses the case of the African prisoners of the *Amistad.* 25 December 1840. p.206, c3.

4252 JOSEPH STURGE *to* **THE EDITOR OF THE** *PATRIOT.* **November 1840. Birmingham, England.** Relates that he declined an invitation to meet Dr. Wayland, President of Brown University, because the latter is an apologist for slavery. 25 December 1840. p.206, c5.

4253 JOHN BOWRING *to* **WM. LLOYD GARRISON. 9 November 1840. London.** Applauds the movement for women's rights. 25 December 1840. p.207, c2.

4254 HIRAM WILSON *to* **WM. L. GARRISON. 12 December 1840. Toronto.** Encourages abolitionists. 25 December 1840. p.207, c3.

[1841]

4255 B. MANLY *to* **FATHER MERCER. 29 October 1840. University of Alabama.** Prescribes steps which Baptists must take to prevent abolitionists from disrupting the Union of Baptists. 1 January 1841. p.1, c1.

4256 ALVAN STEWART *to* **GOV. JAMES K. POLK OF TENNESSEE. 18 November 1840. Utica, N.Y.** Declares that Polk should not have been outraged, but grateful, to Congressman Gates, who forwarded to him communications of the London Anti-Slavery Convention informing him of the low estimation in which his "peculiar institution" is held by one of the most "remarkable" bodies of men ever assembled. 1 January 1841. p.2, c2.

4257 THOMAS MORRIS *to* **DR. BAILEY. n.d. n.p.** Defends his proposal, submitted to the public through the *Philanthropist,* to send an anti-slavery committee to attend congressional sessions in Washington. 1 January 1841. p.2, c2.

4258 JOHN G. WHITTIER *to* **THE EDITOR OF THE** *NATIONAL ANTI-SLAVERY STANDARD.* **18 December 1840. Amesbury.** Criticizes an editorial in the *Standard* which stated that because he did not favor the use of moral suasion alone to end slavery, he could no longer be considered an abolitionist. 1 January 1841. p.2, c3.

4259 J. P. BISHOP *to* **BRO. GARRISON. 28 December 1840. Boston.** Objects to Garrison's criticizing his letter without publishing it and allowing his readers to judge it. 1 January 1841. p.2, c4.

4260 ANTI-BACCHUS *to* **THE EDITOR. 22 December 1840. Providence, R.I.** Denounces the ministry for lack of attention to their sacred duties. 1 January 1841. p.2, c5.

4261 ORILLA KENDRICK AND A. B. HUMPHREY *to* **MR. EDITOR. 19 December 1840. Millbury.** Forward a resolution supporting Abby Kelley adopted by the Female AS. 1 January 1841. p.2, c5.

4262 WM. GOODELL *to* **H. C. WRIGHT. 19 December 1840. Whitesboro', N.Y.** Denies that he is a "mental reservationist" as Wright charges; elaborates his views of civil government. 1 January 1841. p.4, c2.

4263 X. Y. Z. *to* **THE EDITOR OF THE** *NANTUCKET ISLANDER.* **n.d. n.p.** Defends the Chardon Street Convention, the subject of much ridicule, as a gathering of truth-seekers to discuss the divinity of the Sabbath, the ministry and the Church. 8 January 1841. p.5, c2.

4264 X. *to* **THE EDITOR OF THE** *LONDON TIMES.* **16 November 1840. Colonial Club.** Discusses the civilization of Africa. 8 January 1841. p.5, c4.

4265 ABBY H. FOLSOM *to* **W. L. GARRISON. 2 January 1841. Boston.** Advises how to establish a community based on love. 8 January 1841. p.6, c6.

4266 CLOTHER GIFFORD *to* **WM. L. GARRISON. 28 December 1840. Fairhaven.** Wants to establish an ideal social community. 8 January 1841. p.6, c6.

4267 JAMES HAUGHTON *to* **THE EDITOR OF THE** *DUBLIN EVENING POST.* **4 November 1840. 31 Eccles Street.** Reports on the progress of the temperance movement in Ireland. 8 January 1841. p.8, c2.

4268 GERRIT SMITH *to* **W. L. GARRISON. 31 December 1840. Peterboro'.** Sends ten dollars to the *Liberator*; denounces sectarianism in the cause. 8 January 1841. p.8, c3.

4269 VIRTUE *to* **THE EDITOR OF THE** *QUINCY PATRIOT.* **n.d. n.p.** Advocates recognition of the rights of women. 8 January 1841. p.8, c3.

4270 GEORGE BRADBURN *to* **N. CROSBY. [from the** *Temperance Journal***] December 1840. Nantucket.** Praises Father Mathew, an advocate of Irish temperance. 15 January 1841. p.9, c1.

4271 JOHN W. LEWIS *to* **THE EXECUTIVE COMMITTEE OF THE NEW HAMP-SHIRE AS. 28 December 1840. Concord, N.H.** A colored abolitionist resigns from the society because of its "useless controversy" with the New Hampshire Abolition Society, which he views as detrimental to the anti-slavery cause. 15 January 1841. p.10, c3.

4272 JAMES POTTS *to* **SIR. 5 November 1840. Newcastle-Upon-Tyne, England.** Sends resolution passed by the Tuthill-Stairs Baptist Church condemning religious fellowship with slaveholders. 15 January 1841. p.10, c4.

4273 E. HUGHES *to* **THE EDITOR OF THE** *ANTI-SLAVERY REPORTER.* **n.d. Bryn Lion, Holywell.** Reports that his congregation voted on an AS convention. 15 January 1841. p.10, c4.

4274 JAMES CHURCHILL *to* **SIR. 2 November 1840. Thames Ditton, Surrey, England.** Reports that a church in Surrey adopted anti-slavery resolutions. 15 January 1841. p.10, c4.

4275 JAMES CHURCHILL *to* **THE COMMITTEE OF THE BRITISH AND FOREIGN AS. n.d. n.p.** Reports that his congregation denounces fellowship with slaveholders. 15 January 1841. p.10, c4.

4276 GEORGE EVANS *to* **THE EDITOR OF THE** *ANTI-SLAVERY REPORTER.* **2 November 1840. London.** Forwards a resolution of the Congregational Church of Brunswick Chapel, London condemning fellowship with slaveholders. 15 January 1841. p.10, c4.

4277 JOHN PAIN *to* **n.n. 9 November 1840. Horncastle, England.** Forwards a resolution of the Church of Christ, condemning fellowship with slaveholders. 15 January 1841. p.10, c5.

4278 GERRIT SMITH *to* **REV. W. E. CHANNING. 29 December 1840. Peterboro'.** Commends Channing's book on emancipation in the West Indies; denounces sectarianism. 15 January 1841. p.10, c6.

4279 A MEMBER OF THE MASSACHUSETTS AS *to* **THE EDITOR [W. L. GARRISON]. n.d. n.p.** Denies that the Liberty Party's opposition to congressional candidate Borden was chiefly "an attack of the 'new organization' upon the old." 15 January 1841. p.11, c2.

4280 S. J. M. *to* **FRIEND [W. L. GARRISON]. 9 January 1841. South Scituate.** Encloses extracts of letters from Rev. C. Brooks and Mrs. Adams. 15 January 1841. p.11, c4.

4281 REV. CHARLES BROOKS *to* **S. J. M. [extract] n.d. Paris.** Tells of respect given black men in Paris. 15 January 1841. p.11, c4.

4282 MRS. JOHN ADAMS *to* **JOHN ADAMS. [extract] 22 September 1774. n.p.** Describes slavery to her husband, the elder President Adams, as "the daily robbing and plundering from those who have as good a right to freedom as we have." 15 January 1841. p.11, c4.

4283 J. MARSH *to* **MESSRS. HALE AND HALLOCK. n.d. n.p** Discusses temperance in Ireland. 15 January 1841. p.12, c2.

4284 E. MACK *to* **BROTHER ROGERS. n.d. n.p.** Sends an article reporting the refusal of the New Hampshire legislature to incorporate an abolitionist printing establishment. 22 January 1841. p.14, c1.

4285 SAMUEL WALKER *to* **THE OHIO LEGISLATORS. 22 December 1840. Logan County, Oh.** Believes citizens who own slaves should lose their political rights. 22 January 1841. p.14, c3.

4286 LEVESON *to* **J. H. TREDGOLD. 14 December 1840. Foreign Office.** Informs him that Lord Palmerston does not believe that Britain's refusal to conclude a commercial treaty with Texas would affect slavery in the territory. 22 January 1841. p.14, c3.

4287 M. *to* **MESSRS. EDITORS. [from the *Journal of Commerce*] n.d. n.p.** Discusses the *Amistad* Negroes and legal principles involved in their case. 22 January 1841. p.14, c4.

4288 ABEL BROWN *to* **BRO. GARRISON. 7 January 1841. Northampton.** Condemns political and religious hypocrisy in the Hampshire County AS. 22 January 1841. p.14, c6.

4289 F. J. *to* **W. L. GARRISON. n.d. n.p.** Sends deed to land in Jamaica Plains willed to the AS by John Gore. 22 January 1841. p.15, c1.

4290 JOSHUA V. HIMES *to* **BRO. GARRISON. 18 January 1841. Boston.** Encloses letter discussing lectures by Alanson St. Clair. 22 January 1841. p.15, c2.

4291 n.n. *to* **JOSHUA V. HIMES. [extract] 31 December 1840. New Hampton.** Reports on a speech given by Alanson St. Clair in New Hampton, in which he defended the "new" abolitionist organization against the "old." 22 January 1841. p.15, c2.

4292 THOMAS EARLE *to* **RICHARD M. JOHNSON. 26 December 1840. Philadelphia.** Forwards a petition from citizens of the commonwealth, to be presented to the Senate. 22 January 1841. p.15, c3.

4293 RICHARD M. JOHNSON *to* **THOS. EARLE. 4 January 1841. United States Senate Chamber.** Refuses to submit an anti-slavery petition to the United States Senate. 22 January 1841. p. 15, c3.

4294 RICHARD ALLEN *to* **LORD PALMERSTON. 17 December 1840. Dublin, Ireland.** Denounces England's recognition of Texas. 29 January 1841. p.17, c2.

4295 J. C. JACKSON *to* **BROTHER [W. L. GARRISON]. 11 January 1840. Farmington.** Reports on an anti-slavery convention in LeRoy, New York. 29 January 1841. p.18, c5.

4296 J. S. GIBBONS AND THOS. VAN RENSSELAER *to* **THE MEMBERS OF THE AAS. n.d. n.p.** Discuss the society's financial condition. 29 January 1841. p.18, c6.

4297 NATHANIEL P. ROGERS *to* **THE CONGREGATIONAL CHURCH IN PLYMOUTH. 6 January 1840. Concord.** Opposes fellowship with slaveholders. 29 January 1841. p.19, c1,

4298 REV. NATHANIEL COLVER *to* **n.n. [extract] 30 November 1840. Boston.** States that Garrison has just held an "infidel" convention in order to call into question the validity of the Sabbath, the Church and the ministry. 29 January 1841. p.19, c2.

4299 REV. NATHANIEL COLVER *to* **n.n. [extract] 1 December 1840. Boston.** Denounces Garrison's "infidel fanaticism." 29 January 1841. p.19, c2.

4300 J. C. JACKSON *to* **W. L. GARRISON. 15 January 1841. Peterboro'.** Reports on the anti-slavery convention in LeRoy, New York. 29 January 1841. p.19, c5.

4301 GEO. W. SIMONDS *to* **THE EDITOR [W. L. GARRISON]. 18 January 1841. East Lexington.** Favors formation of a third [abolitionist] political party. 29 January 1841. p.19, c5.

4302 M. *to* **W. L. GARRISON. n.d. n.p.** Denounces the racial restrictions in the pre-emption bill before Congress. 29 January 1841. p.19, c5.

4303 LORRIN WHITING *to* **W. L. GARRISON. 14 January 1841. New Marlboro'.** Forwards [unprinted] petition; discusses Abby Kelley's lectures in New Marlboro' and new [abolitionist] organization activities. 29 January 1841. p.19, c6.

4304 THOS. FOWELL BUXTON *to* **REV. R. R. GURLEY. 9 October 1840. Aylsham, England.** Believes the ACS, which he once supported, has become an agent for the oppression of free blacks. 5 February 1841. p.21, c2.

4305 ALFRED WELLS *to* **INHABITANTS OF PULASKI. 28 December 1840. Colosse.** Reports on sectarianism in a "protracted" meeting in Colosse. 5 February 1841. p.21, c3.

4306 JAMES C. JACKSON *to* **FRANCIS JACKSON. 26 January 1841. Peterboro'.** Urges renewed action by abolitionists; opposes the formation of a political party. 5 February 1841. p.22, c3.

4307 JAMES C. FULLER *to* **W. L. GARRISON. 28 January 1841. Skaneateles.** Denounces Nathaniel Colver's attacks on John Collins. 5 February 1841. p.23, c5.

4308 THOS. CLARKSON *to* **LORD PALMERSTON. n.d. n.p.** Recommends that the British government use its influence to end slavery in the Ottoman Empire. 12 February 1841. p.25, c3.

4309 THOS. CLARKSON *to* **MAHOMET ALI PACHA, VICEROY OF EGYPT. n.d. n.p.** Begs the Egyptian viceroy to end slavery. 12 February 1841. p.25, c3.

4310 N. P. ROGERS *to* **BROTHER JOHNSON. 25 January 1841. Concord.** Regrets he cannot attend the annual meeting of the Massachusetts AS; reports on anti-slavery struggles in New Hampshire. 12 February 1841. p.27, c1.

4311 n.n. *to* **W. L. GARRISON. 1 February 1841. New Ipswich.** Reports opposition evoked by H. C. Wright's non-resistance lectures in New Hampshire. 12 February 1841. p.27, c1.

4312 H. COWDREY *to* **W. L. GARRISON. 26 January 1841. Acton.** Discusses an anti-slavery meeting in Acton which condemned the churches. 12 February 1841. p.27, c3.

4313 GERRIT SMITH *to* **WM. GOODELL. 21 January 1841. Peterboro'.** Criticizes abolitionists who support pro-slavery candidates and ministers; calls for harmony in the anti-slavery movement. 19 February 1841. p.29, c1.

4314 A. BROOKE *to* **W. L. GARRISON. 28 January 1841. Oakland, Oh.** Agrees that existing human governments err in theory and practice, but declares he is not an anarchist. 19 February 1841. p.30, c5.

4315 ABEL BROWN *to* **W. L. GARRISON. 8 February 1841. Northampton.** Reports on the Hampshire County anti-slavery convention. 18 February 1841. p.30, c6.

4316 n.n. *to* **W. L. GARRISON. 15 February 1841. Danvers.** Applauds W. L. Garrison's recent speech in Danvers. 19 February 1841. p.31, c2.

4317 n.n. *to* **W.L. GARRISON. n.d. Western New York.** Declares that Nathaniel Colver is unscrupulous. 19 February 1841, p.31, c3.

4318 H. C. WRIGHT *to* **BROTHER [W. L. GARRISON]. 23 January 1841. New Ipswich, N.H.** Reports he has left his church because of its position on slavery; encloses letter to the congregation. 19 February 1841. p.32, c2.

4319 H. C. WRIGHT *to* **THE FIRST CHURCH IN WEST NEWBURY, MA. 25 September 1840. Boston.** Renounces his position in the church because of its silence on the subject of slavery. 19 February 1841. p.32, c2.

4320 AMOS A. PHELPS *to* **W. L. GARRISON. 17 February 1841. Boston.** Opposes the assumption of public duties by women. 26 February 1841. p.34, c3.

4321 AMOS A. PHELPS *to* **SARAH M. AND ANGELINA E. GRIMKE. 29 July 1837. n.p.** Declares he is against allowing women to preach. 26 February 1841. p.34, c5.

4322 A. E. GRIMKE *to* **A. A. PHELPS. n.d. n.p.** Does not wish the AS to be blamed for their "promiscuous" meetings [at which she and her sister preached]. 26 February 1841. p.38, c5.

4323 H. S. FOX *to* **JOHN FORSYTH. 20 January 1840. Washington.** Forwards information from Her Majesty's government concerning the *Amistad* captives and their disposition according to international law. 26 February 1841. p.38, c6.

4324 JOHN FORSYTH *to* **H. S. FOX. 1 February 1840. Washington, D.C.** Replies to Mr. Fox, informing him of the capabilities of the United States government to act in the case of the Negroes captured from the *Amistad*. 26 February 1841. p.38, c6.

4325 H. C. WRIGHT *to* **BROTHER [W. L. GARRISON]. 22 January 1841. Peterboro', N.H.** Encloses letter from J. Blanchard for publication. 26 February 1841. p.36, c2.

4326 J. BLANCHARD *to* **n.n. 1840. Cincinnati, Oh.** Criticizes Garrison and his followers. 26 February 1841. p.36, c2.

4327 J. A. COLLINS *to* **J. H. TREDGOLD. 10 December 1840. London.** Requests financial aid from the British and Foreign AS on behalf of the AAS. 5 March 1841. p.37, c2.

4328 JOSEPH MARRIAGE, JR. *to* **THE COMMITTEE OF THE BRITISH AND FOREIGN AS. 30 December 1840. Chelmsford, Eng.** States that John A. Collins was questioned about the split among the American abolitionists while in Chelmsford; feels that a committee should be formed to decide which wing of the American abolitionists to support. 5 March 1841. p.37, c2.

4329 J. H. TREDGOLD *to* **J. A. COLLINS. 2 January 1841. London.** Refuses request to aid the AAS because it has alienated the British and Foreign AS. 5 March 1841. p.37, c3.

4330 N. *to* **n.n. [extract from the** *Hampshire Gazette***] 4 January 1841. Jamaica.** Describes new conditions since emancipation: provisions dear; "Negro labor" to be had for thirty-five cents per day. 5 March 1841. p.38, c4.

4331 N. H. WHITING *to* **W. L. GARRISON. 28 February 1841. Marshfield.** Endorses the plan for a "fraternal communion," Adin Ballou's utopian plan. 5 March 1841. p.38, c6.

4332 WM. MYERS, JOSEPH GRANETSTONE, THOS. E. LONGSHORE, BENJ. F. DAVIS, JAS. BARNABY, JR., OWEN THOMAS, MARY F. THOMAS AND HANNAH E. MYERS *to* **W. L. GARRISON. 17 February 1841. New Lisbon, Oh.** Describe the attributes of a model community. 5 March 1841. p.39, c1.

4333 X. *to* **MR. EDITOR [W. L. GARRISON]. 2 March 1841. Dorchester.** Reports the proscription of an anti-slavery lecturer in Dorchester. 5 March 1841. p.39, c2.

4334 H. C. WRIGHT *to* **n.n. [from the** *Herald of Freedom***] 8 February 1841. Concord.** Denounces sectarianism among the Congregational and Presbyterian clergy of New Hampshire. 5 March 1841. p.40, c2.

4335 P. PILLSBURY *to* **SUFFOLK NORTH ASSOCIATION. [extract] n.d. n.p.** Denounces Christians who maintain fellowship with slaveholding churches. 12 March 1841. p.41, c4.

4336 J. A. COLLINS *to* **J. H. TREDGOLD. 5 January 1841. London.** Wishes to know the circumstances which have "alienated" the AAS from the British and Foreign AS; believes their differences arise from a misunderstanding. 12 March 1841. p.42, c6.

4337 J. A. COLLINS *to* **J. H. TREDGOLD. 8 January 1841. London.** Requests further assurance that a committee of the British and Foreign AS will meet to reply to his previous letter. 12 March 1841. p.42, c6.

4338 J. H. TREDGOLD *to* **J. A. COLLINS. 8 January 1841. London.** Replies that he will submit Collins' letter to the Executive Committee of the British and Foreign AS. 12 March 1841. p.43, c1.

4339 J. H. TREDGOLD *to* **J. A. COLLINS. 16 January 1841. London.** Informs Collins that the division within the AAS has alienated the confidence of the British and Foreign AS, which now recognizes the American and Foreign AS as the true representative of the cause in America. 12 March 1841. p.43, c1.

4340 NATHANIEL COLVER *to* **W. L. GARRISON. 8 March 1841. Boston.** Requests reprinting of an article by A. A. Phelps. 12 March 1841. p.43, c3.

4341 RICHARD ALLEN *to* **FRIEND [W. L. GARRISON]. 2 February 1841. Dublin, Ireland.** Discusses the importance of temperance; foresees continued anti-slavery fervor in Ireland. 12 March 1841. p.43, c3.

4342 WILLIAM SMEAL *to* **W. L. GARRISON. 1 February 1841. Glasgow, Scotland.** Encourages Garrison in his efforts. 12 March 1841. p.43, c4.

4343 JAS. B. ROGERS AND JOHN R. MORSE *to* **W. L. GARRISON. n.d. n.p.** Report on meeting of the Walpole AS. 12 March 1841. p.43, c4.

4344 W. H. CHANNING, JOHN R. CHILD, THOS. MAYLIN, WM. GREENE, CHAS. FISHER, JNO. C. VAUGHAN, T. WALKER, JOHN B. RUSSELL, JOHN LEA, THOS. BAKEWELL, W. T. JONES, CHAS. D. DANA, CALVIN FLETCHER, LEWIS HUNT, T. NEWELL, E. PHELPS, E. P. GRANCH, NATHAN GUILFORD, GEORGE CARLISLE, JOS. S. SAMPSON, WM. GOODMAN, GEO. S. STEARNS, ROBT. HOGUE, E. GREENE, ROLAND ELLIS, JNO. W. HARTWELL, E. CHANNING, E. ALLEN, WM. P. RICE, AND S. R. COOLIDGE *to* **REV. AND DEAR SIR. 1 January 1841. Cincinnati, Oh.** Members of the Committee of the Unitarian Society request reconsideration of a minister's decision to withdraw from the Young Men's Bible Society because of its acceptance of Unitarians. 12 March 1841. p.44, c2.

4345 JOSHUA L. WILSON, JOHN BURTT, J. T. BROOKE, HENRY V. D. JOHNS, E. W. SEHON, WM. HERR, THORNTON A. MILLS, JOHN C. STEELE, J. L. GROVER, MAXWELL P. GRADDIS, ISAAC EBBERT, SAMUEL W. LYND, L. L. HAMLINE, CHARLES ELLIOTT, AND LEROY SWORMSTEDT *to* **MESSRS. W. H. CHANNING, AND OTHERS. 12 January 1841. Cincinnati, Oh.** Maintain their refusal to associate with Unitarians. 12 March 1841. p.44, c3.

4346 J. L. WILSON, J. T. BROOKE, HENRY D. V. JOHNS, E. W. SEHON, S. W. LYND, AND JOHN BURTT *to* **S. P. CHASE. n.d. Cincinnati, Oh.** Condemn the Young Men's Bible Society's practice of allowing Unitarians to hold office and speak. 12 March 1841. p.44, c3.

4347 S. P. CHASE, JNO. S. MERRILL AND F. A. WALDO *to* **REV. AND DEAR SIR. 30 November 1840. Cincinnati, Oh.** State that the Young Men's Bible Society resolves not to excommunicate Unitarians. 12 March 1841. p.44, c3.

4348 JOSHUA L. WILSON, J. T. BROOKE, H. V. D. JOHNS, S. W. LYND, E. W. SEHON, AND J. BURTT *to* **S. P. CHASE AND OTHERS. n.d. Cincinnati, Oh.** Believe that Unitarians should be excommunicated from the Young Men's Bible Society. 12 March 1841. p.44, c6.

4349 C. *to* **BROTHER MURRAY. 30 July 1840. Rutland, Vt.** Maintains that neither the Old nor the New Testament sanctions the right or duty of women to public action. 19 March 1841. p.45, c2.

4350 B. FOSTER PRATT *to* **PRESBYTERY OF RIPLEY, OHIO. 15 February 1841. Prattsburg.** Condemns slavery. 19 March 1841. p.46, c5.

4351 JOHN O. BURLEIGH *to* **W. L. GARRISON. 15 March 1841. Oxford.** Reports on anti-slavery activity in Oxford. 19 March 1841. p.46, c6.

4352 R. C. *to* **THE EDITOR [W. L. GARRISON]. 2 March 1841. Dorchester.** Concerning the proscription of an anti-slavery lecturer in Dorchester. 19 March 1841. p.46, c6.

4353 EDMUND QUINCY *to* **W. L. GARRISON. 15 March 1841. Dedham.** Claims that the Church, Ministry and Sabbath Convention was originally conceived by participants in the Union Convention at Groton, and not by Garrison, as popularly believed. 19 March 1841. p.47, c3.

4354 G. BRADBURN *to* **W. L. GARRISON. n.d. n.p.** Sends a report of the Massachusetts Legislature on abolitionist petitions. 19 March 1841. p.47, c4.

4355 RICHARD ALLEN *to* **FRIEND [W. L. GARRISON]. 2 February 1841. Dublin, Ireland.** Writes that Jamaican planters recruit Irishmen to work their estates. 19 March 1841. p.47, c4.

4356 S. L. L. *to* **THE CHRISTIAN CHURCHES IN NEWPORT, R.I. n.d. n.p.** Exhorts them to embrace the true spirit of Jesus. 19 March 1841. p.47, c5.

4357 LEWIS TAPPAN *to* **THE COMMITTEE ACTING FOR THE AFRICANS OF THE** *AMISTAD.* **19 March 1841. Long Island Sound.** Reports on interviews with the Africans; discusses their case. 26 March 1841. p.50, c2.

4358 RICHARD ALLEN *to* **THE** *DUBLIN MORNING REGISTER.* **n.d. Dublin, Ireland.** Forwards a communication of the Hibernian AS concerning the recognition of Texas. 26 March 1841. p.50, c4.

4359 RICHARD ALLEN *to* **LORD PALMERSTON. 15 January 1841. Dublin, Ireland.** Discusses Britain's recognition of Texas. 26 March 1841. p.50, c4.

4360 HARRIET MARTINEAU *to* **FRIEND [W. L. GARRISON]. 27 February 1841. Tynemouth, Northumberland, England.** Regrets the schism in the American anti-slavery movement ranks; urges conciliation on both sides. 26 March 1841. p.51, c2.

4361 WM. A. TWEED DALE *to* **W. L. GARRISON. 19 March 1841. Albany.** Hopes the *Liberator* will devote ample space to discussion of the questions considered at the Sabbath Convention. 26 March 1841. p.51, c4.

4362 JAMES L. SMITH *to* **W. L. GARRISON. n.d. n.p.** A "Self-Emancipated Bondman" expresses heartfelt appreciation of Garrison's efforts. 26 March 1841. p.51, c5.

4363 WM. STILLMAN *to* **MR. EDITOR [W. L. GARRISON]. 14 March 1841. Westerly, R.I.** Discusses the Sabbath Convention. 26 March 1841. p.52, c2.

4364 W. R. JOHNSON *to* **DELEGATES FROM THE SLAVEHOLDING STATES WHO SHALL ATTEND THE BAPTIST TRIENNIAL MISSIONARY CONVENTION IN APRIL NEXT. 20 February 1841. n.p.** Informs them that the meetinghouse in Baltimore in which they planned to assemble before the convention is closed to them. 26 March 1841. p.52, c3.

4365 KA-LE *to* **JOHN Q. ADAMS. 4 January 1841. New Haven, Ct.** An *Amistad* prisoner insists on his and his fellow Mendis' right to freedom. 2 April 1841. p.54, c4.

4366 JAMES HAUGHTON *to* **THE** *DUBLIN MORNING REGISTER.* **2 March 1841. Dublin, Ireland.** On the need to end slavery. 2 April 1841. p.54, c5.

4367 JAMES HAUGHTON *to* **THE EDITOR OF THE** *FRIEND OF AFRICA.* **4 January 1841. Dublin, Ireland.** Wishes to know if a member of its society, W. E. Gladstone, was once a British slaveholder; criticizes compensation of British West Indian slaveholders for emancipation, since they have already been compensated by the increase in land values. 2 April 1841. p.54, c5.

4368 GEO. THOMPSON *to* **n.n. [extract] 3 March 1841. Manchester, England.** Sends his regards. 2 April 1841. p.55, c1.

4369 H. HOBART BRIGHAM *to* **SIR. 25 March 1841. Abington.** Asserts the need to regenerate the churches. 2 April 1841. p.55, c2.

4370 GEORGE BRADBURN *to* **W. L. GARRISON. 27 March 1841. Nantucket.** An abolitionist legislator reports his rebuke of the Eastern Railroad for race discrimination. 2 April 1841. p.55, c4.

4371 JOHN GORDEN *to* **FRIEND [W. L. GARRISON]. 5 March 1841. Washington, Pa.** Praises Garrison and defends him from his enemies. 2 April 1841. p.55, c4.

4372 H. C. WRIGHT *to* **BROTHER [W. L. GARRISON]. 1 February 1841. Milford, N.H.** Describes reactions to his non-resistance lectures in New Hampshire. 2 April 1841. p.56, c2.

4373 ABBY KELLEY *to* **W. L. GARRISON. 24 March 1841. Hebron.** Rebukes the editor of the *Congregational Observer* for abolitionist backsliding. 9 April 1841. p.58, c4.

4374 H. G. AND M. W. CHAPMAN *to* **FRIEND GARRISON. 16 February 1841. Cape Haytien.** Report they are pleased with the "benevolence" of the Haitians; enclose translation of article from the *Feuille de Commerce*. 9 April 1841. p.58, c4.

4375 J. C. JACKSON *to* **W. L. GARRISON. 2 April 1841. New York.** Discusses Isaac T. Hopper's indictment for his association with the *Standard*. 9 April 1841. p.58, c5.

4376 ABEL BROWN *to* **REV. C. W. DENNISON. 2 April 1841. Northampton.** Rebukes him for opposing the discussion of slavery at the Baptist Triennial Convention. 9 April 1841. p.58, c5.

4377 THOS. CLARRSON [*sic*] *to* **THE CONVENTION. 9 February 1841. Playford Hall.** Discusses the divinity of the Sabbath. 9 April 1841. p.59, c1.

4378 A. *to* **THE EDITOR [W. L. GARRISON]. n.d. n.p.** Inquires whether Nathaniel Colver was once the pastor of a church which proclaimed that the Sabbath was merely a civil institution. 9 April 1841. p.59, c2.

4379 J. S. *to* **THE** *NON-RESISTANT.* **n.d. n.p.** Encloses his letter to the *Boston Recorder.* 9 April 1841. p.60, c2.

4380 J. S. *to* **THE** *BOSTON RECORDER.* **[from the** *Non-Resistant***] n.d. n.p.** Argues that non-resistants are not infidels. 9 April 1841. p.60, c2.

4381 C. K. W. *to* **THE** *BOSTON RECORDER.* **n.d. n.p.** Elaborates differences between non-resistance and infidelity. 9 April 1841. p.60, c2.

4382 P. D. HATHAWAY *to* **N. P. ROGERS. 11 March 1841. Peterboro'.** Bears testimony to the honesty and integrity of J. C. Jackson. 16 April 1841. p.61, c2.

4383 DANIEL P. PIKE AND DUDLEY D. TILTON *to* **RESPECTED BROTHER [W. L. GARRISON]. n.d. Newburyport.** Forward anti-slavery resolutions of a new church in Newburyport. 16 April 1841. p.62, c2.

4384 S. F. S. *to* **W. L. GARRISON. 28 March 1841. West Brattleboro.** Encloses extract of a sermon given before the House of Commons by Ralph Cudworth in 1647, which claimed that faith leads one to act and to serve God, and not merely to "speculate." 16 April 1841. p.62, c2.

4385 REV. DANIEL SHARP *to* **REV. OTIS SMITH. [from the** *Christian Index***] 21 January 1841. Boston.** Relates that the Boston Baptist Association is opposed to the efforts of abolitionists, and denies the legitimacy of the church's intervention in the controversy. 23 April 1841. p.65, c1.

4386 J. PIERPONT *to* **N. P. ROGERS. 20 March 1841. Boston.** Sends words of praise and encouragement; congratulates Rogers on his excommunication by the Plymouth Church. 23 April 1841. p.65, c4.

4387 N. P. ROGERS *to* **J. PIERPONT. 25 March 1841. Concord.** Thanks him for his kind words. 23 April 1841. p.65, c4.

4388 J. PIERPONT *to* **N. P. ROGERS. 5 April 1841. Boston.** Congratulates Rogers further on his excommunication from the Plymouth Church. 23 April 1841. p.65, c4.

4389 WILLIAM LADD *to* **n.n. 19 March 1841. Rochester.** Reports on his experiences in Rochester. 23 April 1841. p.66, c2.

4390 JESSE WHEELER *to* **THE** *CHRISTIAN REFLECTOR***. n.d. n.p.** Forwards resolutions of the Baptist church in Watertown denying fellowship to slaveholders. 23 April 1841. p.66, c3.

4391 VOICE FROM THE MINORITY [REV. MEDBURY] *to* **THE EDITOR. [from the** *Christian Reflector***] 17 February 1841. Watertown.** Relates the division of the congregation over the question of denial of fellowship to supporters of slavery. 23 April 1841. p.66, c3.

4392 R. B. *to* **THE** *CHRISTIAN REFLECTOR***. n.d. n.p.** Believes that withdrawal of fellowship from slaveholding brethren is not morally justifiable. 23 April 1841. p.66, c3.

4393 n.n. *to* **THE EDITOR [W. L. GARRISON]. n.d. n.p.** Objects to letter from R. B. to the *Christian Reflector*; affirms one's Christian duty to deny fellowship to slaveholders. 23 April 1841. p.66, c4.

4394 A BAPTIST LAYMAN *to* **BROTHER [W. L. GARRISON]. 17 April 1841. Abington.** Condemns Rev. Dr. Sharp's propitiation of Southern Baptists. 23 April 1841. p.66, c5.

4395 C. W. DENISON *to* **ABEL BROWN. 19 April 1841. Boston.** Defends his participation in the Baptist Triennial Convention. 23 April 1841. p.66, c5.

4396 H. C. WRIGHT *to* **BROTHER [W. L. GARRISON]. 16 April 1841. Philadelphia.** Denounces the "Artists' Fund Society" of Philadelphia for refusing to display a portrait of Cinque [one of the *Amistad* captives]. 23 April 1841. p.66, c6.

4397 J. NEAGLE *to* **MR. PURVIS. 14 April 1841. Philadelphia.** Refuses to exhibit a portrait of Cinque [one of the African prisoners of the *Amistad*]. 23 April 1841. p.66, c6.

4398 JOHN BARLEY AND N. A. BORDEN *to* **W. L. GARRISON. 14 April 1841. New Bedford, Ma.** Report on the Bristol County AS convention. 23 April 1841. p.66, c6.

4399 LUCINDA WILMARTH *to* **n.n. 12 April 1841. Attleboro'.** Affirms that no Christian church can, even by its silence, apologize for slavery. 23 April 1841. p.67, c1.

4400 J. C. JACKSON *to* **W. L. GARRISON. 22 April 1841. Boston.** Discusses the forthcoming AAS meeting and his speaking itinerary. 23 April 1841. p.67, c4.

4401 THOMAS MORRIS *to* **THE MAYOR OF DAYTON. [extract] n.d. n.p.** Reports an anti-abolitionist mob in Dayton. 30 April 1841. p.69, c4.

4402 ABBY KELLEY *to* **C. W. DENISON AND ICHABOD CODDING. [from the** *National Anti-Slavery Standard*] **13 April 1841. Bozrahville, Ct.** Criticizes their joining the American and Foreign AS, which denies women's rights. 30 April 1841. p.69, c6.

4403 JAS. C. WHITE, J. BLANCHARD AND THOS. E. THOMAS *to* **BRETHREN AND FRIENDS. 1 March 1841. Cincinnati, Oh.** Discuss the raising of funds for E. Lovejoy's widow. 30 April 1841. p.70, c2.

4404 JOHN BURDEN *to* **W. L. GARRISON. 20 April 1841. Salisbury, N.H.** Writes to correct an error in an article from the *Lynn Record*. 30 April 1841. p.71, c3.

4405 HENRY W. WILLIAMS *to* **W. L. GARRISON. 19 April 1841. Boston.** Sends correspondence relating to his renunciation of a "pro-slavery" church in Salem. 30 April 1841. p72. c2.

4406 HENRY W. WILLIAMS *to* **THE TABERNACLE CHURCH OF SALEM. 17 September 1840. Boston.** Declares that the church is a "serious hindrance to the progress of the gospel," in refusing to condemn "popular vices of the community." 30 April 1841. p.72, c2.

4407 SAMUEL M. WORCESTER *to* **H. W. WILLIAMS. 19 March 1841. Salem.** Informs him of the congregation's decision to excommunicate him. 30 April 1841. p.72, c2.

4408 J. T. *to* **MESSRS. EDITORS. [from the** *New York Observer*] **3 April 1841. Boston.** Discusses the Sabbath Convention held in Boston. 30 April 1841. p.72. c3.

4409 ASHER BLISS *to* **THE EDITOR OF THE** *AMERICAN CITIZEN*. **15 February 1841. Cattaraugus Mission.** Sends anti-slavery resolution adopted by a meeting of the Congregational Association in western New York. 7 May 1841. p.73, c1.

4410 ASHER BLISS, JOS. S. EMERY, AND HIRAM S. EDDY *to* **RALPH WARDLAW, DAVID RUSSELL, AND JAMES R. CAMPBELL. n.d. n.p** Congregationalists condemn slavery, in compliance with the wishes of their Scottish brethren. 7 May 1841. p.73, c1.

4411 J. N. T. TUCKER *to* **BRO. HOUGH. [from the** *Friend of Man*] **16 April 1841. Apulia.** Renounces politics in favor of moral agitation. 7 May 1841. p.73, c2.

4412 n.n. *to* **GERRIT SMITH. [from the** *Friend of Man*] **n.d. Tennessee.** Feels that abolitionists' influence has caused a reduction of the more barbarous forms of punishment of slaves. 7 May 1841. p.73, c6.

4413 H. C. WRIGHT *to* **A. A. PHELPS. 24 April 1841. Philadelphia.** Declares that the Presbyterian Church and clergy are a confederacy of manstealers. 7 May 1841. p.74, c2.

4414 A. BROOKE *to* **W. L. GARRISON. 26 February 1841. Oakland, Oh.** Forwards communication from citizens of Oakland who wish to form an ideal community. 7 May 1841. p.74, c6.

4415 J. C. C. *to* **THE EDITOR [W. L. GARRISON]. n.d. n.p.** Advocates exclusive consumption of products of free labor. 7 May 1841. p.74, c6.

4416 N. P. ROGERS *to* **W. L. GARRISON. 5 May 1841. Boston.** Explains the position of the *National Anti-Slavery Standard* toward non-resistance. 7 May 1841. p.75, c3.

4417 J. N. BUFFUM *to* **W. L. GARRISON. 3 May 1841. Lynn.** Discusses J. C. Jackson's lectures in Lynn. 7 May 1841. p.75, c4.

4418 REV. JACOB WESTON *to* **n.n. [extract] 19 February 1841. Jamaica.** Reports on the results of emancipation in the West Indies. 14 May 1841. p.77, c5.

4419 J. HOLCOMB *to* **THE** *VERMONT TELEGRAPH.* **n.d. n.p.** Believes a fast of atonement for the nation's wickedness would be more appropriate than that proposed by Pres. Tyler to mourn Mr. Harrison. 14 May 1841. p.78, c5.

4420 D. JENKINS, H. JOHNSON, AND J. BENNETT *to* **J. Q. ADAMS. [from the** *Philanthropist*] **n.d. Columbus, Oh.** Black citizens thank him for his efforts in behalf of the *Amistad* captives. 14 May 1841. p.78, c6.

4421 J. Q. ADAMS *to* **D. JENKINS, W. JOHNSON, AND J. BENNETT. [from the** *Philanthropist*] **15 April 1841. Washington, D.C.** Hopes the day is near when justice will know no color. 14 May 1841. p.78, c6.

4422 THEODORE SEDGEWICK *to* **D. JENKINS. 4 April 1841. New York.** Acknowledges their thanks for his efforts in the case of the African captives of the *Amistad*. 14 May 1841. p.78, c6.

4423 JAS. TURNER AND FIFTY-EIGHT OTHERS *to* **THE COMMITTEE OF THE GLASGOW EMANCIPATION SOCIETY. n.d. Scotland.** Members of the society urge the Committee to hear out J. A. Collins. 14 May 1841. p.79, c1.

4424 SAMUEL D. COCHRAN *to* **DR. BAILEY. 27 February 1841. Oberlin.** Reports an attempt by slavehunters from Kentucky to kidnap a colored man and his wife. 21 May 1841. p.81, c5.

4425 GEO. WHIPPLE, R. E. GILLETT, A. D. BARBER, H. E. TAYLOR AND L. HOLSTAND *to* **DR. BAILEY. March 1841. Cincinnati.** Attest to the truthfulness of S. Cochran's account of a kidnapping in Oberlin. 21 May 1841. p.81, c6.

4426 B. GREEN *to* **ELIZUR WRIGHT, JR. [from the** *Friend of Man*] **April 1841. Whitesboro'.** Denies that a Christian church can practice opposition to abolition. 21 May 1841. p.82, c1.

4427 MARY CLARK *to* **ROGERS. n.d. n.p.** On her death-bed, pleads to churches to cleanse themselves of guilt and take up the cause of slavery. 21 May 1841. p.82, c3.

4428 RICHARD ALLEN *to* **THE** *MORNING REGISTER.* **3 April 1841. Dublin, Ireland.** States that the Hibernian AS opposes the plan of the African Civilization Society, in the belief that only the abolition of slavery can end the slave trade. 21 May 1841. p.82, c6.

4429 ELIZABETH PEASE *to* **THE COMMITTEE OF THE BRITISH AND FOREIGN AS. 25 March 1841. Darlington.** Forwards [unprinted] letter of J. C. Fuller vindicating W. L. Garrison and J. A. Collins from Colver's previous charges. 21 May 1841. p.83, c4.

4430 JOHN SCOBLE *to* **ELIZABETH PEASE. 20 April 1841. n.p.** Denies that the British and Foreign AS circulated Colver's letters among its members. 21 May 1841. p.83, c4.

4431 ELIZABETH PEASE *to* **JOHN SCOBLE. 27 April 1841. Darlington.** Politely questions his denial that the British and Foreign AS circulated N. Colver's letters. 21 May 1841. p.83, c4.

4432 ELIZABETH PEASE *to* **FRIEND [W. L. GARRISON]. 2 May 1841. Darlington.** Defends him against the aspersions of his enemies. 21 May 1841. p.83, c4.

4433 CHARLES L. REMOND *to* **W. L. GARRISON. 7 March 1841. Newcastle-on-Tyne.** Reports anti-slavery affairs in England. 21 May 1841. p.83, c5.

4434 n.n. *to* **GERRIT SMITH. [from the** *Friend of Man***] n.d. Tennessee.** Expresses optimism about the influence of Northern abolitionists and the demise of slavery. 21 May 1841. p.84, c4.

4435 C. C. STILLMAN *to* **PRES. JOHN TYLER. 14 April [1841]. New London.** Contradicts Tyler's inaugural address, which had asserted that all individuals were guaranteed their rights under American institutions. 28 May 1841. p.85, c2.

4436 WM. PATISON, MALCOLM M'FARLANE AND CHARLES M'EWEN *to* **JOHN A. COLLINS. [from the** *Glasgow Post***] 26 April 1841. Glasgow, Scotland.** Workingmen of Glasgow hail his arrival. 28 May 1841. p.85, c3.

4437 BENJ. C. BACON *to* **W. L. GARRISON. 3 May 1841. Philadelphia.** Sympathizes with Garrison's struggles with enemies. 28 May 1841. p.87, c3.

4438 WENDELL PHILLIPS *to* **W. L.GARRISON. 12 April 1841. Naples.** Discusses his "melancholy tour" through Europe; affirms his eagerness to resume anti-slavery work. 28 May 1841. p.87, c4.

4439 ABEL BROWN *to* **W. L. GARRISON. 8 May 1841. Albany.** Returns to the "old organization," the Massachusetts AS, after being convinced that the Massachusetts Abolition Society was a less effective organization. 28 May 1841. p.87, c5.

4440 OLIVER JOHNSON *to* **W. L. GARRISON. 18 May 1841. New York.** Resigns as general agent of the *Liberator* in order to work for the *Standard*. 4 June 1841. p.91, c2.

4441 HENRIETTA SARGENT *to* **W. L. GARRISON. 23 May 1841. Boston.** Encloses letter addressed to her from the late Mary Clark. 4 June 1841. p.91, c4.

4442 MARY CLARK *to* **HENRIETTA SARGENT. 21 February and 26 March 1840. Concord.** Thanks her for remembrances and gifts. 4 June 1841. p.91, c4.

4443 E. W. GOODWIN *to* **BROTHER LEAVITT. [from the** *Emancipator***] 25 May 1841. Albany, N.Y.** Reports the recent abolition of the New York slave law. 11 June 1841. p.93, c2.

4444 THOMAS JINNINGS, JR. *to* **THE EDITOR. 31 May 1841. Boston.** A colored man reports an outrage against him on a local railroad. 11 June 1841. p.94, c6.

4445 G. ADAMS *to* **W. L. GARRISON. 1 June 1841. Boston.** Resigns from Board of Managers of Massachusetts AS because of sectarianism in the society. 11 June 1841. p.95, c1.

4446 ALMIRA *to* **DR. D. M. REESE. 29 March 1841. n.p.** Encloses poems for publication. 11 June 1841. p.96, c1.

4447 T. STOCKS *to* **THE BAPTIST CHURCHES OF CHRIST IN THE SOUTH AND SOUTH-WESTERN STATES OF THE UNITED STATES. [from the** *Christian Index***] n.d. n.p.** Describes agreeable intercourse with the Northern brethren at the South Carolina Baptist State Convention. 18 June 1841. p.97, c1.

4448 E. MACK *to* **BRO. BURR. n.d. n.p.** Reports on a meeting of the New Hampshire AS. 18 June 1841. p.97, c2.

4449 H. C. WRIGHT *to* **BROTHER [W. L. GARRISON]. 4 June 1841. Concord.** Discusses the New Hampshire AS; denounces American clergy and the Baptist Triennial Convention. 18 June 1841. p.98, c4.

4450 CHARLES STEARNS *to* **BROTHER GARRISON. 25 April 1841. Oberlin.** Upholds Garrison; discusses pro-slavery spirit in Detroit and the treatment of colored brethren in Detroit and Canada; relates that he has been helping fugitive slaves escape. 18 June 1841. p.98, c5.

4451 REV. SAMUEL OSGOOD *to* **W. L. GARRISON. n.d. n.p.** The president of the Massachusetts Abolitionist Society denies Garrison's allegation that he had closed his meeting-house to anti-slavery lectures. 18 June 1841. p.99, c1.

4452 J. C. JACKSON *to* **W. L. GARRISON. 8 June 1841. Peterboro'.** Writes of his poor health. 18 June 1841. p.99, c3.

4453 G. ADAMS *to* **W. L. GARRISON. 13 June 1841. Boston.** Refutes Garrison's interpretation of his letter of resignation from the Massachusetts AS. 18 June 1841. p.99, c3.

4454 OLIVE BEARSE *to* **n.n. [W. L. GARRISON]. 18 May 1841. Centreville.** Discusses the corrupting influence of money. 18 June 1841. p.100, c2.

4455 CHARLES T. TORREY *to* **THE GRAND JURY OF SUFFOLK COUNTY. 10 June 1841. Boston.** On the case of John Torrence, a fugitive slave. 18 June 1841. p.100, c5.

4456 RICHARD ALLEN *to* **THE *DUBLIN FREEMAN'S JOURNAL*. 2 June 1840. Dublin.** Exposes a Jamaican emigration scheme. 25 June 1841. p.101, c2.

4457 A. L. PALMER *to* **RICHARD ALLEN. 19 April 1841. Spanish Town, Jamaica.** Denounces scheme to bring European emigrants to Jamaica. 25 June 1841. p.101, c2.

4458 GEO. THOMPSON *to* **WM. SMEAL. 17 May 1841. Manchester.** Commends the AAS to the Glasgow Emancipation Society. 25 June 1841. p.101, c3.

4459 JOHN A. COLLINS *to* **THE EDITOR OF THE *GLASGOW ARGUS*. 24 April 1841. n.p.** Defends his earlier criticism of the Committee of the Glasgow Emancipation Society for its "ungenerous course" in regard to Collins' attempt to explain the views of the AAS. 25 June 1841. p.102, c5.

4460 J. C. JACKSON *to* **W. L. GARRISON. 15 June 1841. Peterboro'.** Laments willingness of people of Madison, New York, to hear lectures given by a visiting Georgian. 25 June 1841. p.103, c4.

4461 Q. IN A CORNER *to* **W. L. GARRISON. 20 May 1841. Rochester, N.Y.** Reports abolitionist backsliding in Rochester; upholds Garrison. 25 June 1841. p.103, c4.

4462 SAMUEL DYER *to* **W. L. GARRISON. 19 June 1841. Abington.** Sends resolution adopted by the AS in Abington. 25 June 1841. p.103, c5.

4463 ROBT. F. WALLCUTT *to* **CHARLOTTE AUSTIN. 25 March 1841. Dennis.** Denounces the Christian ministry for its "worthless instrumentality in regenerating the world." 25 June 1841. p.104, c2.

4464 ROBT. F. WALLCUTT *to* **GEO. BRADBURN. 5 May 1841. Dennis.** Discusses the schism among abolitionists. 25 June 1841. p.104, c2.

4465 CYRUS P. GROSVENOR *to* **WM. HENRY BRISBANE. 2 June 1841. Worcester.** Relates accusations made by Mr. Davis of Georgia that Brisbane supports slavery. 2 July 1841. p.105, c4.

4466 WM. HENRY BRISBANE *to* **CYRUS GROSVENOR. 9 June 1841. Cincinnati.** Replies to Davis' charges; states that he is an abolitionist and that he has given up all he ever earned from his previous holding of slaves. 2 July 1841. p.105, c4.

4467 ALEX. H. H. STUART *to* **GALES AND SEATON. [from the** *National Intelligencer***] n.d. n.p.** A Virginia congressman explains his opposition to the gag law. 2 July 1841. p.106, c1.

4468 X. *to* **n.n. [from the** *New York Evangelist***] 10 April 1841. Boston.** Assails [unnamed] convention which rejected the Bible as paramount authority; lists several participants. 2 July 1841. p.108, c2.

4469 R. FULLER *to* **BROTHER. [from the** *Raleigh Recorder and Watchman***] 1 June 1841. Beaufort, S.C.** On the Baptist Triennial Convention in Baltimore. 9 July 1841. p.109, c1.

4470 ISAAC T. HOPPER *to* **N. P. ROGERS. 16 June 1841. New York.** Discusses the meaning of Quakerism and the nature of the Society of Friends. 9 July 1841. p.110, c5.

4471 DAVID RUGGLES *to* **THE** *NEW BEDFORD DAILY REPORTER.* **23 June 1841. New Bedford.** Relates being assaulted by a steamboat captain who refused to sell him first class passage. 9 July 1841. p.110, c5.

4472 N. H. WHITING *to* **W. L. GARRISON. 6 July 1841. New London, Ct.** Reports on the state of the anti-slavery movement in New London. 9 July 1841. p.111, c2.

4473 SAVILION HALEY *to* **W. L. GARRISON. 5 July 1841. New London, Ct.** Forwards resolutions adopted by the AS of New London; reports on N. H. Whiting's lectures. 9 July 1841. p.111, c2.

4474 THOMAS EARLE *to* **RICHARD M. JOHNSON, VICE PRESIDENT OF THE UNITED STATES. 4 February 1841. n.p.** Objects to Johnson's refusal to submit an anti-slavery petition to Congress. 16 July 1841. p.113, c2.

4475 EDWARD BALDWIN *to* **RICHARD ALLEN. 17 February 1841. London.** Defends W. L. Garrison's criticisms of the ministry. 16 July 1841. p.115, c1.

4476 PUBICOLA *to* **W. L. GARRISON. n.d. Philadelphia.** Decries slavery as the moral evil of the times; affirms the ability of righteousness to triumph. 16 July 1841. p.115, c1.

4477 H. C. WRIGHT *to* **BROTHER [W. L. GARRISON]. 18 June 1841. East Bethel, Vt.** Discusses the proposed world's convention for human rights. 16 July 1841. p.115, c2.

4478 P. D. HATHAWAY *to* **W. L. GARRISON. 2 July 1841. Oberlin.** Praises the enlightened policies of Oberlin College, which welcomes women as students. 16 July 1841. p.115, c3.

4479 W. C. N. *to* **THE EDITOR [W. L. GARRISON]. n.d. n.p.** On the emancipation in New Bedford of Lucy Faggins, a slave who accompanied a Virginian to Massachusetts. 16 July 1841. p.115, c4.

4480 CHARLES MCLEOD *to* **THE INHABITANTS OF JONES VALLEY. n.d. n.p.** Claims that two letters signed "A Baptist" incorrectly attributed statements to him. 16 July 1841. p.116, c3.

4481 JOSEPH STURGE *to* **HOPE H. SLAUGHTER. 30 June 1841. New York.** Urges a Baltimore slave trader, whose establishment Sturge visited, to abandon his wicked occupation. 23 July 1841. p.118, c3.

4482 B. INGINAC *to* **W. L. GARRISON. 9 April 1841. Port-Au-Prince, Hayti.** Informs Garrison that Haiti's president sends his support and regrets that Henry S. Chapman could not visit the island. 23 July 1841. p.119, c2.

4483 JESSE P. HARRIMAN, JOHN HOOD, AND ASENATH S. HOOD *to* **THE BAPTIST CHURCH. 30 June 1841. Danvers (New Mills).** Renounce their affiliation with the church. 23 July 1841. p.119, c3.

4484 A. P. BLACK *to* **J. P. HARRIMAN. 2 July 1841. Danvers.** The Baptist Church clerk informs Harriman that he is excommunicated. 23 July 1841. p.119, c3.

4485 RICHARD ALLEN *to* **FRIEND [W. L. GARRISON]. 2 July 1841. Dublin, Ireland.** Reports on slavery in the British East Indies. 23 July 1841. p.119, c3.

4486 ELIAS RICHARDS *to* **W. L. GARRISON. 13 July 1841. Weymouth.** Encloses a letter from a minister in Braintree who failed to announce a temperance lecture to his congregation. 23 July 1841. p.119, c4.

4487 R. S. STORRS *to* **ELIAS RICHARDS. 12 July 1841. Braintree.** A minister explains his refusal to announce a temperance lecture to the congregation. 23 July 1841. p.119, c4.

4488 H. C. WRIGHT *to* **BROTHER [W. L. GARRISON]. [from the** *Non-Resistant***] 28 June 1841. Stafford.** Discusses the propagation of non-resistance principles in Vermont. 23 July 1841. p.120, c2.

4489 RICHARD D. ALEXANDER *to* **J. A. COLLINS. [extract from the** *Ipswich Express***] n.d. n.p.** Attempts to dissuade the recipient from paying Thomas Clarkson a visit. 30 July 1841. p.121, c2.

4490 J. A. COLLINS *to* **RICHARD D. ALEXANDER. [extract from the** *Ipswich Express***] 28 December 1840. Great White Horse.** Requests the use of Temperance Hall, owned by Alexander, to present views of the AAS to the community. 30 July 1841. p.121, c2.

4491 RD. D. ALEXANDER *to* **J. A. COLLINS. [extract from the** *Ipswich Express***] n.d. Ipswich.** Refuses the use of Temperance Hall "for the sole object of exposing the horrors of American slavery." 30 July 1841. p.121, c2.

4492 J. A. COLLINS AND C. L. REMOND *to* **RD. D. ALEXANDER. [extract from the** *Ipswich Express***] 30 December 1840. Ipswich.** Request the pleasure of his attendance at a public meeting to be held at the Town Hall that evening. 30 July 1841. p.121, c2.

4493 RD. D. ALEXANDER *to* **FRIENDS. [from the** *Ipswich Express***] 30 December 1840. Ipswich.** States he will not attend the evening's meeting; criticizes their publication of his private correspondence. 30 July 1841. p.121, c2.

4494 J. WATTS *to* **THE EDITOR OF THE** *GUIANA CHRONICLE***. n.d. n.p.** Describes the improved condition of his countrymen who have emigrated to Guiana. 30 July 1841. p.121, c6.

4495 JONATHAN DAVIS *to* **A. JAMES. June 1841. Albany, N.Y.** A Georgian gives his impressions of New England and Northern abolitionism. 30 July 1841. p.122, c3.

4496 RODRIGO DA FONSECA MAGALHAENS *to* **THOS. CLARKSON. 15 May 1841. Portugese Office for Foreign Affairs.** The Queen of Portugal expresses her desire for an end to the African slave trade. 30 July 1841. p.122, c3.

4497 L. T. *to* **THE EDITOR OF THE** *EMANCIPATOR*. **n.d. n.p.** Corrects misinterpretations of the Ohio Supreme Court's ruling that slaves brought into the state by their masters became free. 30 July 1841. p.122, c3.

4498 L. BODINE, WM. A. TYSON, S. HARDENBURGH, W. W. BEDFORD, AND REUBEN RUBY *to* **n.n. 1 May 1841. New York.** Discuss the purposes of the American Reformed Board of Disfranchised Commissioners. 30 July 1841. p.122, c4.

4499 EDITOR *to* **THE** *MIRROR OF LIBERTY*. **8 July 1841. New Bedford.** Cites discrimination against him by steamboat and railroad officials; reports an attempt to bring a slave into New Bedford. 30 July 1841. p.122, c4.

4500 CHARLES CORKRAN *to* **BROTHER [W. L. GARRISON]. 4 June 1841. Paris, France.** Upholds Garrison's views. 30 July 1841. p.122, c6.

4501 ELIZABETH PEASE *to* **n.n. [extract] n.d. Darlington, England.** Reports on English support of Garrison. 30 July 1841. p.123, c3.

4502 n.n. *to* **n.n. [extract] n.d. New Bedford.** Details the discovery of a slave girl in New Bedford. 30 July 1841. p.123, c4.

4503 NOAH JACKMAN *to* **W. L. GARRISON. 10 June 1841. Newbury, Belleville.** Announces that he has resigned from the Church of Christ in Newbury. 30 July 1841. p.124, c2.

4504 NOAH JACKMAN *to* **THE SECOND CHURCH OF CHRIST. n.d. Newbury, Ma.** Gives his reasons for leaving the church. 30 July 1841. p.124, c2.

4505 SALLY B. JACKMAN AND PERSIS SEAVEY *to* **THE CONGREGATIONAL CHURCH. 30 May 1841. London.** State the reasons for renouncing their affiliation with the church. 30 July 1841. p.124, c2.

4506 SETH M. GATES *to* **SIR. [from the** *Albany Evening Journal***] 20 June 1840. Washington.** Discusses the controversy in Congress concerning the right of petition. 6 August 1841. p.125, c5.

4507 RICHARD ALLEN *to* **FRIEND [W. L. GARRISON]. 16 July 1841. Dublin, Ireland.** Reports on a spirited city election there. 6 August 1841. p.127, c1.

4508 DAVID RUGGLES *to* **THE EDITOR [W. L. GARRISON]. 24 July 1841. Fall River.** Discusses the trial of his assailants in New Bedford. 6 August 1841. p.127, c2.

4509 FRANCIS JACKSON *to* **HARRIS COWDREY. 23 July 1841. Boston.** Regrets he cannot attend the Middlesex County AS meeting. 6 August 1841. p.127, c3.

4510 GEO. ROPES *to* **THE EDITOR. [from the** *Portland* **(Me.)** *Advocate and Baptist***] n.d. n.p.** Reports on Jonathan Davis' pro-slavery lecture in Portland. 6 August 1841. p.128, c2.

4511 M. N. C. *to* **W. L. GARRISON. n.d. n.p** Forwards a sermon given by William H. Furness. 13 August 1841. p.129, c2.

4512 JUSTICE *to* **MR. EDITOR [W. L. GARRISON]. n.d. n.p** Contradicts Henry Clay's statement to Senate that he is indebted to none, for he has never paid wages to his slaves. 13 August 1841. p.129, c3.

4513 JONATHAN DAVIS *to* **A. JAMES. 22 June 1841. Philadelphia.** A Georgia Baptist gives his impressions of the North. 13 August 1841. p.129, c4.

4514 MANSFIELD *to* **BROTHER MURRAY. 27 July 1841. Grafton.** On Jonathan Davis' pro-slavery lectures. 13 August 1841. p.129, c5.

4515 ELLIS G. LORING *to* **THE EDITOR OF THE** *TIMES.* **n.d. n.p.** Corrects a misrepresentation of his speech reported in the paper. 13 August 1841. p.129, c6.

4516 JOSEPH STURGE *to* **THE SOCIETY OF FRIENDS IN THE UNITED STATES OF AMERICA. 17 July 1841. New York.** On the importance of abolitionism among English and American Friends and the need to bear constant testimony against slavery. 13 August 1841. p.130, c1.

4517 H. C. WRIGHT *to* **THE METHODIST EPISCOPAL CHURCH AND CLERGY IN THE UNITED STATES. 1 May 1841. Philadelphia.** Labels them a "Brotherhood of Manstealers." 13 August 1841. p.130, c3.

4518 DAVID RUGGLES *to* **COLORED AMERICANS. n.d. n.p.** Notifies delegates to the Convention of the American Reform Board of Disfranchised Commissioners of the information and statistics they should bring with them. 13 August 1841. p.131, c2.

4519 EDMUND A. GRATTAN *to* **THE EDITOR [W. L. GARRISON]. n.d. Boston.** Informs the colored inhabitants of Boston of the benefits to be derived from emigration to Jamaica. 13 August 1841. p.131, c3.

4520 A. WARD *to* **FRIEND GARRISON. 8 August 1841. Ashburnham.** On Abby Kelley's lectures in Ashburnham. 13 August 1841. p.131, c4.

4521 WM. ENDICOTT *to* **W. L. GARRISON. 8 August 1841. Danvers.** Reports on Parker Pillsbury's activities in Danvers. 13 August 1841. p.131, c4.

4522 I. N. *to* **W. L. GARRISON. 1 August 1841. Abington.** On anti-slavery spirit in Abington. 13 August 1841. p.131, c5.

4523 JAMES HAUGHTON *to* **THE IRISH PEOPLE. June 1841. Dublin.** "On the use of articles produced by the labor of slaves, particularly tobacco and cotton." 20 August 1841. p.133, c2.

4524 J. Q. ADAMS *to* **EDITORS OF THE** *OLD COLONY MEMORIAL,* **THE** *HINGHAM PATRIOT,* **AND THE** *QUINCY PATRIOT.* **23 July 1841. Washington.** Discloses that the 1840 census reported one slave in residence in Massachusetts. 20 August 1841. p.134, c1.

4525 WM. A. WEAVER *to* **J. Q. ADAMS. 19 July 1841. Washington.** States that the report of a slave in the Massachusetts census of 1840 was erroneous, and that the mistake has been corrected. 20 August 1841. p.134, c2.

4526 SOLOMON LINCOLN *to* **WM. A. WEAVER. 12 July 1841. Boston.** Informs Weaver that there are no slaves, but free colored persons, residing in George Worth's district. 20 August 1841. p.134, c2.

4527 GEO. F. WORTH *to* **S. LINCOLN. 8 July 1841. Nantucket.** States that a reference to a free colored female as a slave caused an error in the state census of 1840. 20 August 1841. p.134, c2.

4528 A. B. CHAMBERS *to* **GERRIT SMITH. 16 July 1841. St. Louis, Mo.** Forwards a letter from James Seward. 20 August 1841. p.134, c3.

4529 GERRIT SMITH *to* **THE EDITOR OF THE** *FRIEND OF MAN.* **4 August 1841. Peterboro'.** Blames prejudice for the downfall of James W. Seward, one of the colored men executed in St. Louis for murder and arson. 20 August 1841. p.134, c3.

4530 JAMES SEWARD *to* **GERRIT SMITH. 7 July 1841. St. Louis, Mo.** A black prisoner, awaiting execution, remembers Smith's past kindnesses and regrets his own errors. 20 August 1841. p.134, c3.

4531 N. P. ROGERS *to* **J. R. F. 9 August 1841. Plymouth.** Reports on a speech condemning slavery and criticizing the ministry given by Rev. Beach in Campton. 20 August 1841. p.134, c4.

4532 JOSEPH BATES *to* **THE EDITOR [W. L. GARRISON]. n.d. n.p.** Forwards antislavery resolutions adopted by a church in Fairhaven, Massachusetts. 20 August 1841. p.135, c5.

4533 HENRY L. GRAVES *to* **THE EDITOR. [from the** *Raleigh* **(N.C.)** *Biblical Recorder***] 22 July 1841. Hamilton, N.Y.** Reports on Jonathan Davis' pro-slavery lectures in Utica and his debates with abolitionists. 27 August 1841. p.137, c1.

4534 J. D. BRIDGE *to* **THE EDITOR. [from the** *New England Christian Advocate***] July 1841. Saujus.** Reproaches abolitionists for raising the woman question. 27 August 1841. p.137, c1.

4535 ALANSON ST. CLAIR, JAMES BURR, AND GEORGE THOMPSON *to* **THE MISSION INSTITUTE. [extract from the** *St. Louis Republican***] 19 June 1841. Palmyra.** Send tidings from prison as they await trial for kidnapping slaves. 27 August 1841. p.137, c3.

4536 W. *to* **THE EDITOR [W. L. GARRISON]. n.d. n.p.** Notes the appearance of a new religious journal, the *Disciple.* 27 August 1841. p.138, c5.

4537 RICHARD HOOD *to* **THE BAPTIST CHURCH IN DANVERS. 3 July 1841. Danvers (New Mills).** Renounces his affiliation with the church. 27 August 1841. p.138, c6.

4538 H. C. WRIGHT *to* **BROTHER [W. L. GARRISON]. 18 August 1841. Millbury.** Discusses the quarterly meeting of the Massachusetts AS in Millbury. 27 August 1841. p.139, c4.

4539 B. GREEN *to* **THE EDITOR OF THE** *FRIEND OF MAN.* **n.d. n.p.** Assails Jonathan Davis, a known slaveholder who had dared to criticize Mr. Green's deficiencies. 3 September 1841. p.142, c1.

4540 ELIZA J. AND MARY P. KENNY *to* **W. L. GARRISON. 30 August 1841. Salem.** Forward correspondence concerning their renunciation of the Tabernacle Church in Salem. 3 September 1841. p.142, c5.

4541 ELIZA J. AND MARY P. KENNY *to* **THE MEMBERS OF THE TABERNACLE CHURCH. 23 April 1841. Salem.** Renounce their affiliation with the Tabernacle Church in Salem. 3 September 1841. p.142, c5.

4542 H. C. WRIGHT *to* **BROTHER [W. L. GARRISON]. 30 August 1841. Boston.** Denounces Dr. Francis Wayland of Brown University, who claimed that a Christian could also be a slaveholder, "provided he has the spirit of Christ." 3 September 1841. p.143, c2.

4543 W. *to* **THE EDITOR [W. L. GARRISON]. 24 August 1841. Salem.** Discusses Wendell Phillips' lectures here. 3 September 1841. p.143, c3.

4544 L. D. GRAY *to* **THE EDITOR [W. L. GARRISON]. 20 August 1841. Walpole.** Corrects the account of the Norfolk County AS meeting. 3 September 1841. p.143, c5.

4545 B. *to* **THE EDITOR OF THE *PHILANTHROPIST*. n.d. n.p.** Reports the burning of a slave in Kentucky. 3 September 1841. p.144, c4.

4546 RICHARD ALLEN *to* **FRIEND. 16 August 1841. Dublin, Ireland.** Reports on Charles L. Remond's anti-slavery efforts in Dublin. 10 September 1841. p.147, c3.

4547 G. W. F. MELLEN *to* **MR. EDITOR [W. L. GARRISON]. n.d. n.p.** Objects to the *Boston Post*'s criticisms of an anti-slavery pamphlet he wrote. 10 September 1841. p.147, c3.

4548 ABBY KELLEY *to* **W. L. GARRISON. 31 August 1841. Millville.** On the uproar caused by S. S. Foster's denunciations of a church in Millville. 10 September 1841. p.147, c4.

4549 D. M. *to* **W. L. GARRISON. n.d. n.p.** Asks whether the *Liberator* endorses D. L. Child's criticisms of third party candidates. 10 September 1841. p.147, c5.

4550 WM. M. CHACE *to* **W. L. GARRISON. 21 August 1841. Providence.** Discusses his views of sectarianism within the abolition movement. 10 September 1841. p.147, c5.

4551 JOSEPH R. ENGLEY *to* **W. L. GARRISON. 23 August 1841. Walpole.** Announces his rejection of a pro-slavery church. 17 September 1841. p.149, c6.

4552 JOSEPH R. ENGLEY *to* **THE ORTHODOX CONGREGATIONAL CHURCH. 2 May 1841. Walpole.** Renounces his affiliation with the church. 17 September 1841. p.149, c6.

4553 JOHN ORVIS *to* **W. L. GARRISON. 24 August 1841. Ferrisburgh.** Defends the Catholic principles of the early abolitionists who sought to unite opponents of slavery, regardless of their views on other issues. 17 September 1841. p.150, c1.

4554 n.n. *to* **THE EDITOR OF THE *NEW ERA*. 4 September 1841. Cincinnati.** Reports on current race riots in Cincinnati. 17 September 1841. p.150, c3.

4555 JAMES FORTEN *to* **W. L. GARRISON. 31 August 1841. Philadelphia.** Praises the *Liberator*; renews his subscription. 17 September 1841. p.151, c3.

4556 NANCY PRINCE *to* **W. L. GARRISON. 12 September 1841. Boston.** A colored Bostonian, currently teaching school in Jamaica, relates the mistreatment she received while traveling on a steamboat from New York to Providence. 17 September 1841. p.151, c3.

4557 GEO. W. HAYWOOD *to* **C. C. BATTLE. 30 November 1840. Raleigh.** Relates his attempts to buy his family out of slavery in North Carolina. 17 September 1841. p.151, c4.

4558 F. H. PETTIS *to* **JNO. R. FRENCH. 28 July 1841. New York.** An attorney charges the *Herald of Freedom* with false reporting of an incident in which he was falsely accused of beating a "black rascal." 17 September 1841. p.152, c2.

4559 STILLMAN LOTHROP *to* **W. L. GARRISON. n.d. n.p.** Forwards correspondence concerning his renunciation of his church and subsequent excommunication. 24 September 1841. p.153, c2.

4560 S[TILLMAN] LOTHROP *to* **THE THIRD BAPTIST CHURCH. 15 July 1841. Cambridgeport.** Renounces his affiliation with the church. 24 September 1841. p.153, c2.

4561 S. G. BOWDLEAR *to* **S[TILLMAN] LOTHROP. 7 September 1841. Boston.** Informs him that he has been excommunicated from the Third Baptist Church. 24 September 1841. p.153, c2.

4562 J. C. JACKSON *to* **W. L. GARRISON. 17 July 1841. Peterboro'.** Proposes the establishment of an abolitionist committee in New York City or Philadelphia to handle the forwarding of anti-slavery petitions to Congress. 24 September 1841. p.153, c3.

4563 C. STEARNS *to* **W. L. GARRISON. 4 August 1841. Oberlin.** Reproaches the Christian Church for forsaking its founding principles; announces his conversion to non-resistance principles. 24 September 1841. p.153, c4.

4564 SAMUEL DYER *to* **W. L. GARRISON. 6 September 1841. Abington.** Reports that anti-slavery interest has been renewed in Abington by Frederick Douglass' speeches. 24 September 1841. p.153, c5.

4565 B. BROWN, JR. AND A. P. JAQUES *to* **W. L. GARRISON. 6 September 1841. West Newbury.** Forward resolutions adopted by the West Newbury AS. 24 September 1841. p.153, c6.

4566 G. H. *to* **MR. EDITOR [W. L. GARRISON]. 9 September 1841. New York.** Reports on the Convention of the American Reform Board of Disfranchised Commissioners. 24 September 1841. p.154, c1.

4567 RICHARD D. WEBB *to* **W. L. GARRISON. 28 August 1841. Kilhee, Ireland.** Discusses Charles L. Remond's anti-slavery efforts in Ireland, and Irish reactions. 24 September 1841. p.155, c1.

4568 DANIEL P. PIKE *to* **W. L. GARRISON. 20 September 1841. Newburyport.** Forwards resolutions of the Rockingham Christian Conference. 24 September 1841. p.155, c4.

4569 JONATHAN WHIPPLE *to* **n.n. 20 June 1841. Ledyard, Ct.** Debates the distinction between paying military fines and taxes to the government. 24 September 1841. p.156, c4.

4570 A. F. JONES *to* **THE EDITOR OF THE** *CINCINNATI GAZETTE.* **7 September 1841. Cincinnati, Oh.** Reports that the Warsaw Guards were called to suppress a mob of abolitionists and Negroes in Cincinnati. 1 October 1841. p.157, c2.

4571 R. WALLACE *to* **MESSRS. BROUGH. [from the** *Cincinnati Enquirer***] 6 September 1841. Covington, Ky.** Denies that he led a Kentucky mob which aided the removal of "abolitionist nuisances" from Cincinnati. 1 October 1841. p.157, c2.

4572 ISAAC BASSETT *to* **THE EDITOR OF THE** *LYNN RECORD.* **13 September 1841. Lynn, Ma.** Relates the barring of a colored woman from travelling with white passengers on the Eastern Railroad. 1 October 1841. p.157, c4.

4573 T. P. BEACH *to* **WOOD. 2 August 1841. Campton.** Announces that he has abdicated the pulpit of the Congregational church, which he charges with sanctioning slavery. 1 October 1841. p.158, c2.

4574 LEWIS FORD *to* **BROTHER [W. L. GARRISON]. 2 September 1841. North Abington.** Believes that the time has arrived for abolitionists to renounce pro-slavery churches. 1 October 1841. p.158, c4.

4575 LEWIS FORD *to* **THE FOURTH CONGREGATIONAL CHURCH IN ABINGTON. 24 August 1841. North Abington.** Renounces his affiliation with the church. 1 October 1841. p.158, c4.

4576 ABEL BROWN *to* **W. L. GARRISON. 23 August 1841. Albany, N.Y.** Forwards information concerning the sanctioning of slavery by religious missionaries to the Cherokee and Choctaws. 1 October 1841. p.158, c5.

4577 PLAIN SPEAKER *to* **MR. GARRISON. n.d. n.p.** Criticizes the Charles Street Baptist Church, which charged Dea. Stillman Lothrop with slander; declares that one should consider it an honor to be excommunicated from a pro-slavery church. 1 October 1841. p.158, c6.

4578 W. L. GARRISON AND WENDELL PHILLIPS *to* **DR. GAMALIEL BAILEY, JR. 27 September 1841. Boston.** Donate one hundred dollars to the *Philanthropist* to help replace its press, which was destroyed by a Cincinnati mob. 1 October 1841. p.159, c2.

4579 GERRIT SMITH *to* **W. L. GARRISON. 24 September 1841. Peterboro'.** Sends donation to aid Lunsford Lane. 1 October 1841. p.159, c2.

4580 THOMAS PAUL *to* **THE PUBLIC. 29 September 1841. Boston.** Announces he intends to open a school for colored people in Boston. 1 October 1841. p.159, c6.

4581 D. *to* **MR. EDITOR. [from the** *Boston Courier***] n.d. n.p.** Discusses the manner in which slavery was abolished in Massachusetts. 8 October 1841. p.161, c6.

4582 J. MILLER MCKIM *to* **n.n. [extract] 26 August 1841. Bellforte, Pa.** Comments on the growing number of fugitive slaves. 8 October 1841. p.161, c6.

4583 EDITOR OF THE *CINCINNATI PHILANTHROPIST to* **n.n. 21 September 1841. Cincinnati, Oh.** Relates the destruction of the *Philanthropist*'s press by an anti-abolitionist mob. 8 October 1841. p.162, c4.

4584 EPSILON *to* **WORTH. [from the** *New Hampshire Baptist Register***] n.d. n.p.** On the use of the Bible by Southerners to sanction slavery. 8 October 1841. p.162, c6.

4585 ABBY KELLEY *to* **W. L. GARRISON. 20 September 1841. Westerly, R.I.** Discusses her renunciation of the Society of Friends. 8 October 1841. p.163, c3.

4586 ABBY KELLEY *to* **UXBRIDGE MONTHLY MEETING OF FRIENDS. 22 March 1841. Hebron, Ct.** Renounces her affiliation with the society. 8 October 1841. p.163, c3.

4587 CINCINNATUS *to* **W. L. GARRISON. 29 September 1841. Marlboro'.** Defends Abby Kelley from a slanderous attack in the *Boston Morning Post*. 8 October 1841. p.163, c4.

4588 SARAH C. REDLON *to* **W. L. GARRISON. 24 September 1841. Boston.** Forwards correspondence concerning her renunciation of and excommunication by a Baptist church in Lowell. 8 October 1841. p.164, c2.

4589 LEMUEL PORTER *to* **SARAH C. SANBORN. 10 June 1841. Lowell.** Concerning her withdrawal from the Baptist church in Lowell. 8 October 1841. p.164, c2.

4590 SETH POOLER *to* **SARAH C. REDLON. 28 August 1841. Lowell.** Concerning her withdrawal from the Baptist church in Lowell. 8 October 1841. p.164, c2.

4591 S. GRAHAM *to* **E. TAYLOR. 1 September 1841. Northampton.** Discusses temperance; announces that he will soon publish a book on the authority of the Bible in the use of "wine and strong drink." 8 October 1841. p.164, c3.

4592 JOHN A. COLLINS *to* **W. L. GARRISON. 4 October 1841. Boston.** Gives a detailed account of the repeated removals of Frederick Douglass from first class cars of the Eastern Railroad, requiring in one instance the aid of several men to drag him away. 15 October 1841. p.165, c4.

4593 N. *to* **MR. EDITOR [W. L. GARRISON]. n.d. n.p.** The opening of a school for young ladies in Boston by a young colored lady. 15 October 1841. p.167, c4.

4594 J. H. S. *to* **W. L. GARRISON. 11 September 1841. Georgetown.** Reports that Messrs. Douglass and Collins lectured at the Baptist meetinghouse in Georgetown after the Congregational Church denied its facilities to them. 15 October 1841. p.168, c4.

4595 JOHN RANKIN *to* **MR. EDWARDS. 13 September 1841. Ripley.** Reports attacks made upon him by pro-slavery mobs. 22 October 1841. p.169, c6.

4596 E. G. *to* **W. L. GARRISON. 9 August 1841. Fitchburg.** On Abby Kelley's lectures in Fitchburg. 22 October 1841. p.170, c4.

4597 GOOLD BROWN *to* **n.n. 16 October 1841. Lynn.** An abolitionist reproves his fellows for undue concern with the Eastern Railroad, which he believes has a right to enforce even offensive rules. 22 October 1841. p.170, c4.

4598 THOS. J. DOWNING AND GEO. J. DOWNING *to* **MR. EDITOR [W. L. GARRISON]. 11 October 1841. New York.** Deny [unclarified] accusations against them by a correspondent of the *Liberator*. 22 October 1841. p.170, c5.

4599 JAMES MUNROE *to* **W. L. GARRISON. 5 October 1841. Canterbury, Ct.** On abolitionism in Westerly, Rhode Island and New London County, Connecticut. 22 October 1841. p.170, c5.

4600 CHARLES P. BOSSON *to* **THE EDITOR OF THE** *BOSTON TIMES*. **n.d. n.p.** On his harassment by agents of the Eastern Railroad. 22 October 1841. p.171, c2.

4601 A. FAIRBANKS *to* **BROTHER [W. L. GARRISON]. 13 October 1841. Providence.** Criticizes the ministry's disregard for the slave. 22 October 1841. p.172, c2.

4602 A. FAIRBANKS *to* **REV. A. H. VINTON. 12 September 1841. Providence.** Denounces the moral indifference of the church toward slavery. 22 October 1841. p.172, c2.

4603 DAN'L WEBSTER *to* **MR. HALE. 8 October 1841. Marshfield.** Encloses letter from Earl Spencer and forged letter by Munroe Edwards, as a warning to the public of the latter's character. 22 October 1841. p.172, c4.

4604 EARL SPENCER *to* **RT. HON. DAN'L WEBSTER. 12 September 1841. Wiseton.** Recounts Munroe Edward's use of a forged letter from Webster for the purpose of defrauding Spencer; encloses the forgery. 22 October 1841. p.172, c4.

4605 DAN'L WEBSTER *to* **RT. HON. EARL SPENCER. 29 October 1840. Marshfield.** Forged letter introduces Col. M. Edwards as Webster's "valued friend," requesting that Spencer render him all services within his power. 22 October 1841. p.172, c4.

4606 WM. H. ANDERSON *to* **PERSONS WHO HAVE BEEN SENDING THEIR SERVANTS TO BAPTIST MEETINGS HELD AT THE COURT HOUSE, ON SABBATH EVENINGS. [from the** *Natchez Courier***] n.d. n.p.** Informs them that services for the benefit of their servants will be discontinued. 29 October 1841. p.173, c1

4607 FLETCHER WEBSTER *to* **LEWIS TAPPAN, ESQ. 16 October 1841. Department of State, Washington.** Informs Tappan that there is no provision of the law allowing for the return of the *Amistad* captives to Africa. 29 October 1841. p.173, c5.

4608 CINQUE [ONE OF THE *AMISTAD* **PRISONERS]** *to* **n.n. 5 October 1841. Farmington, Ct.** Thanks Mr. Tappan and friends; will tell Mendi people about "Merica" upon returning home. 29 October 1841. p.173, c5.

4609 MARY WELSH *to* **SISTERS AND FRIENDS. 19 May 1841. Glasgow, Scot.** A female AS formed recently in Glasgow sends greetings and encouragement. 29 October 1841. p.174, c5.

4610 F. *to* **THE** *MASSACHUSETTS SPY***. n.d. n.p.** Denounces the Jim Crow policy and abusiveness of the Eastern Railroad. 5 November 1841. p.177, c5.

4611 GEO. THOMPSON *to* **BROTHER. [from the** *Oberlin Evangelist***] 15 September 1841. Palmyra Jail, Mo.** Reports that he, Alanson Work, and James E. Burr have been sentenced to twelve years' labor for attempting to help a slave escape. 5 November 1841. p.178, c2.

4612 LEWIS TAPPAN *to* **MESSRS. EDITORS. [from the** *Congregational Observer***] n.d. New York.** Announces that the *Amistad* captives are returning to Sierra Leone. 5 November 1841. p.178, c4.

4613 H. HOBART BRIGHAM *to* **THE EDITOR [W. L. GARRISON]. 23 October 1841. Abington.** Announces his withdrawal from the Baptist church at Abington; encloses letter to the congregation. 5 November 1841. p.178, c4.

4614 H. HOBART BRIGHAM *to* **THE MEMBERS OF THE BAPTIST CHURCH AT ABINGTON. n.d. n.p.** Renounces the church's position on slavery; withdraws from the congregation. 5 November 1841. p.178, c4.

4615 MARY MARTIN *to* **WM. L. GARRISON. 25 September 1841. Darlington, England.** Conveys her respects to Garrison. 5 November 1841. p.178, c6.

4616 CHARLES T. TORREY *to* **MR. GARRISON. n.d. n.p.** Objects to Garrison's having equated the Liberty Party to "new organization abolitionism." 5 November 1841. p.178, c6.

4617 MARY MARTIN *to* **MR. GARRISON. 25 September 1841. Darlington, England.** An English Quaker upholds Garrisonian doctrine. 5 November 1841. p.178, c6.

4618 CHARLES T. TORREY *to* **W. L. GARRISON. n.d. n.p.** Takes issue with the assumption that the new organization and the Liberty Party are one and the same. 5 November 1841. p.178, c6.

4619 EDMUND QUINCY *to* **MR. GARRISON. 2 November 1841. Dedham.** Suggests asking political candidates their views on repealing the marriage laws and reforming the Eastern Railroad Company. 5 November 1841. p.179, c3.

4620 S. S. SEWALL *to* **FRIEND GARRISON. n.d. n.p.** Sends list of Liberty Party candidates in Massachusetts. 5 November 1841. p.179, c3.

4621 Entry number not used.

4622 EDMUND QUINCY *to* **BROTHER GARRISON. 2 November 1841. Dedham.** Reports that senatorial candidates Howe, Robbins, Everett, and Pond favor legislation preventing racial discrimination by railroads and repeal of the Marriage Law. 5 November 1841. p.179, c3.

4623 CHARLES T. TORREY *to* **MR. EDITOR [W. L. GARRISON]. n.d. n.p.** Objects to *Liberator*'s statement that he "slunk away" from a convention when in fact illness prompted his early departure. 5 November 1841. p.179, c4.

4624 Entry number not used.

4625 SAMUEL G. MAY *to* **HENRY C. WRIGHT. 16 September 1841. South Scituate.** Opposes a call for a "World's Convention." 12 November 1841. p.181, c1.

4626 MARIA W. CHAPMAN *to* **HENRY C. WRIGHT. 19 September 1841. Weymouth.** Favors holding a "World's Convention." 12 November 1841. p.181, c1.

4627 LINDLEY COATES *to* **HENRY C. WRIGHT. 29 August 1841. Sadsbury, Pa.** Favors holding a "World's Convention." 12 November 1841. p.181, c2.

4628 WILLIAM H. JOHNSON. *to* **H. C. WRIGHT. 3 September 1841. Buckingham, Pa.** Favors having a "World's Convention." 12 November 1841. p.181, c3.

4629 PHILIP SCARBOROUGH *to* **BROTHER GARRISON. 2 November 1841. Brooklyn, Ct.** Refutes article which implied that he was of violent temperament. 12 November 1841. p.183, c4.

4630 JOHN HOUGH *to* **BROTHER GARRISON. 1 November 1841. Lowell.** Describes the position of his church on slavery and slaveholders. 19 November 1841. p.186, c6.

4631 n.n. *to* **FRIEND GARRISON. 11 November 1841. New Bedford.** Reports on meetings at Whig headquarters and lectures at Liberty Hall. 19 November 1841. p.187, c4.

4632 W. T. *to* **GARRISON. November 1841. Sipican.** Discusses the wickedness of slavery. 19 November 1841. p.187, c4.

4633 RICHARD ALLEN *to* **JAMES CAUGHEY. 8 October 1841. Dublin.** Replies to Caughey's views on slavery. 26 November 1841. p.190, c1.

4634 STILLMAN LOTHROP *to* **ELIZUR WRIGHT, JR. 30 October 1841. Cambridgeport.** Gives his reason for leaving the Charles Street Church. 26 November 1841. p.190, c2.

4635 WM. JAY *to* **THE** *PHILANTHROPIST.* **26 October 1841. n.p.** Sends fifty dollar contribution toward replacement of printing press destroyed by mob. 26 November 1841. p.190, c3.

4636 JNO. MC KIM *to* **DR. BAILEY. 7 October 1841. Philadelphia.** Sends one hundred dollar contribution to *Philanthropist.* 26 November 1841. p.190, c3.

4637 J. TAYLOR, S. ALLEN AND OTHERS *to* **DR. BAILEY. 20 October 1841. Walpole, Ma.** Send ten dollar contribution to *Philanthropist.* 26 November 1841. p.190, c3.

4638 JOHN HOUGH *to* **BROTHER GARRISON. 1 November 1841. Lowell.** Discusses refusal of pastor and brethren to introduce the subject of slavery into a monthly missionary concert. 26 November 1841. p.190, c3.

4639 WM. LLOYD GARRISON *to* **SUMNER LINCOLN. 8 November 1841. Boston.** Rejects an invitation to attend a meeting in Gardner. 26 November 1841. p.191, c4.

4640 RICHARD ALLEN *to* **FRIEND GARRISON. 3 November 1841. Dublin.** Discusses anti-slavery activities in Dublin. 26 November 1841. p.191, c5.

4641 EDMUND QUINCY *to* **GARRISON. n.d. Medfield.** Lists officers of Medfield AS. 26 November 1841. p.191, c5.

4642 WM. WEST *to* **THE EDITOR OF THE** *NEW ENGLAND CHRISTIAN AD-VOCATE.* **21 November 1841. n.p.** Refutes article maligning the Sabbath, Ministry and Church Convention. 3 December 1841. p.196, c4.

4643 GEORGE BRADBURN *to* **GARRISON. 2 December 1841. Nantucket.** Explains why he was not elected to the legislature. 10 December 1841. p.198, c3.

4644 JOSEPH BRYANT *to* **MRS. JOSEPH BRYANT. 10 November 1841. n.p.** Describes conditions in jail and tries to console his wife. 10 December 1841. p.199, c4.

4645 HIRAM WILSON *to* **n.n. [extract] 2 November 1841. Toronto.** Describes welcoming fugitive slaves to Canada. 10 December 1841. p.200, c3.

4646 JAMES D. BLACK *to* **DR. BAILEY. 4 October 1841. Danvers, Ma.** Informs that the Essex County AS voted to send a contribution to the Ohio AS to aid in reestablishing the *Philanthropist* in Cincinnati. 17 December 1841. p.202, c4.

4647 RICHARD ALLEN *to* **FRIEND GARRISON. 17 November 1841. Dublin.** Describes events in Ireland. 17 December 1841. p.203, c3.

4648 WM. H. STOWELL *to* **MESSRS. WM. BERRY AND THOS. JINNINGS, JR. 22 November 1841. New Bedford.** Solicits help in obtaining abolitionist votes in the forthcoming election. 24 December 1841. p.205, c2.

4649 J. MONROE *to* **WM. L. GARRISON. 17 December 1841. Canterbury, Ct.** Discusses prospects for a third party. 24 December 1841. p.207, c4.

4650 WM. ENDICOTT *to* **FRIEND GARRISON. 9 December 1841. New Mills.** Considers the use of schoolhouse for meetings of "religious and moral" purposes. 24 December 1841. p.207, c5.

4651 ELKANAH NICKERSON *to* **BRO. GARRISON. 29 October 1841. Boston.** Affirms Scripture as the foundation of the true Church. 24 December 1841. p.208, c3.

4652 WILLIAM WEST *to* **WILLIAM LLOYD GARRISON. 6 December 1841. Boston.** Corrects article concerning his views on Christianity, citing numerous typographical and grammatical errors. 24 December 1841. p.208, c3.

4653 WILLIAM WEST *to* **WILLIAM LLOYD GARRISON. 13 December 1841. Boston.** Corrects article concerning his views on infidels. 24 December 1841. p.208, c3.

4654 ROBERT JOHNSTON *to* **REV. JAMES CAUGHEY. 16 September 1841. Dublin.** Discusses participation of the American Methodist Church in the sin of slavery. 31 December 1841. p.209, c3.

4655 JOSHUA COFFIN *to* **GARRISON. 2 November 1841. Philadelphia.** Discusses his discharge from his position as letter-carrier. 31 December 1841. p.211, c2.

4656 WENDELL PHILLIPS *to* **FRIEND GARRISON. 2 December 1841. Boston.** Regrets that he cannot attend a meeting. 31 December 1841. p.211, c4.

4657 NOAH JACKMAN *to* **GARRISON. 15 December 1841. Newbury, Ma.** Questions the purpose of a resolution passed by the Women's AS regarding Rev. Luther F. Dimmick. 31 December 1841. p.211, c4.

[1842]

4658 ROBERT JOHNSTON *to* **REV. JAMES CAUGHEY. 4 October 1841. Dublin.** Discusses the participation of the American Methodist Episcopal Church in the sin of American slavery. 7 January 1842. p.1, c2.

4659 REV. A. A. DAVIS *to* **EDITOR OF THE** *CHRISTIAN FREEMAN.* **[extract] n.d. Kingston, Jamaica.** Reports on the West Indies. 7 January 1842. p.2, c4.

4660 FRANCIS JACKSON *to* **FRIEND GARRISON. 27 December 1841. Boston.** Denies holding membership in the third party. 7 January 1842. p.3, c2.

4661 WENDELL PHILLIPS *to* **FRIEND GARRISON. 25 December 1841. Boston.** Supports third party. 7 January 1842. p.3, c2.

4662 CYRUS PEIRCE *to* **FRIEND GARRISON. 1 January 1842. Lexington.** Expresses his disapproval of some of the resolutions passed by various abolitionist societies. 7 January 1842. p.3, c3.

4663 JOHN ROBE *to* **WM. L. GARRISON. 25 November 1841. St. Croix.** Describes slavery in Dutch West Indies under the Danish power. 7 January 1842. p.3, c3.

4664 C. B. PECKHAM *to* **FRIEND GARRISON. 28 December 1841. Newport, R.I.** Reports that Pearce led a mob which disrupted an AS meeting. 7 January 1842. p.3, c4.

4665 A MEMBER OF THE CONFERENCE *to* **BROTHER GARRISON. 3 January 1842. Georgetown.** Discusses why Luther Dimmick was honored at the Woman's Anti-Slavery Conference in Georgetown. 7 January 1842. p.3, c4.

4666 CANNING *to* **GENTLEMEN. n.d. n.p.** Asserts that the British government wanted a safe return for the Mendians. 7 January 1842. p.3, c5.

4667 ROBERT JOHNSTON *to* **REV. JAMES CAUGHEY. 6 October 1841. Dublin.** Discusses the participation of the American Methodist Episcopal Church in the sin of slavery. 14 January 1842. p.5, c1.

4668 CHARLES CARROLL TAPPAN *to* **MR. ROGERS, EDITOR OF THE** *HERALD OF FREEDOM.* **2 December 1841. Bradford, N.H.** Thirteen-year-old youth reports that he enjoys reading the *Herald.* 14 January 1842. p.5, c4.

4669 SAMUEL HENRY *to* **SUNDERLAND. 15 March 1841. South Wilbraham.** Attacks Methodist Episcopal Church as autocratic, pro-war, and pro-slavery. 14 January 1842. p.6, c1.

4670 RICHARD ALLEN *to* **FRIEND GARRISON. 1 December 1841. Dublin.** Comments on a group of Irishmen in America who are thought to have instigated a riot. 14 January 1842. p.6, c2.

4671 LEWIS FORD *to* **GARRISON. 26 December 1841. Abington.** Gives account of conflict between pro- and anti-slavery factions of Abington Church. 21 January 1842. p.9, c6.

4672 CINCINNATUS *to* **BRO. GARRISON. 10 January 1842. Sutton.** Describes growth of anti-slavery sentiments in Millbury. 21 January 1842. p.10, c1.

4673 ABBY KELLEY *to* **THE** *NATIONAL ANTI-SLAVERY STANDARD.* **5 January 1842. Millbury.** Relates events at the Providence and Newport conventions. 21 January 1842. p.10, c5.

4674 GEORGE BRADBURN *to* **JOHN P. TARBELL. 8 January 1842. n.p.** Rejoices over the election of a strong democrat. 21 January 1842. p.10, c5.

4675 J. A. COLLINS *to* **GARRISON. 18 January 1842. Boston.** General agent of the Massachusetts AS gives an account of his proceedings during the past five months. 21 January 1842. p.11, c2.

4676 GEORGE FOSTER *to* **FRIEND GARRISON. 14 January 1842. Andover.** Describes an encouraging AS meeting held at Rockport. 21 January 1842. p.11, c4.

4677 D. M. *to* **GARRISON. n.d. n.p.** Questions Mr. Jackson's nomination as Liberty Party candidate. 21 January 1842. p.11, c5.

4678 H. C. WRIGHT *to* **n.n. 15 November 1841. Peru, N.Y.** Reports on non-resistance conventions held in Vermont. 21 January 1842. p.12, c2.

4679 JEAN PIERRE BOYER, PRESIDENT OF HAYTI *to* **MR. DODGE. 16 August 1821. Port-au-Prince.** Discusses commercial importance of Haiti. 21 January 1842. p.12, c4.

4680 H. C. WRIGHT *to* **BROTHER GARRISON. 16 December 1841. Ferrisburg, Vt.** Continues his account of his non-resistance conventions. 4 February 1842. p.20, c2.

4681 FRANCIS JACKSON *to* **THE EDITOR OF THE** *EMANCIPATOR AND FREE AMERICAN.* **n.d. n.p.** Explains the injustice done him in a letter written by A. B. Merrill which appeared in the *Emancipator and Free American.* 11 February 1842. p.22, c3.

4682 JOHN WHITE *to* **GARRISON. 25 JANUARY 1842. Acton.** Discusses resolution passed by Acton citizens denouncing the imprisonment of C. T. Torrey and three younger men in Missouri. 11 February 1842. p.22, c4.

4683 ROBERT BABB *to* **WM. LLOYD GARRISON. 23 January 1842. Bath.** Invites Garrison to lecture at the Bath AS. 11 February 1842. p.22, c5.

4684 M. W. C. *to* **W. L. GARRISON. n.d. n.p.** Gives account of the Massachusetts AS Annual Meeting and summary of a reply made by Frederick Douglass at the meeting regarding the Liberty Party. 11 February 1842. p.22, c6.

4685 HENRY A. WISE *to* **A. P. UPSHUR. n.d. n.p.** Discusses conflict between Judge Upshur and Mr. Botts. 18 February 1842. p.25, c3.

4686 HON. A. P. UPSHUR *to* **H. A. WISE. 29 January 1842. Navy Dept.** Describes conflict with Mr. Botts. 18 February 1842. p.25, c3.

4687 JOHN M. BOTTS *to* **THE EDITORS OF THE** *NATIONAL INTELLIGENCER.* **n.d. n.p.** Relates conflict with Judge Upshur. 18 February 1842. p.25, c4.

4688 O. P. Q. *to* **JAMES G. BENNETT. 29 January 1842. Boston.** Discusses abolitionists and Irish in the United States; describes a scene in Faneuil Hall. 18 February 1842. p.25, c5.

4689 D. L. CHILD *to* **FRIENDS. 23 January 1842. Northampton.** Reports he is unable to attend the annual meeting of the New England AS. 18 February 1842. p.27, c4.

4690 H. C. WRIGHT *to* **n.n. n.d. n.p.** Reports on his lectures in New England; describes non-resistance as consistent with Christianity. 18 February 1842. p.28, c2.

4691 J. P. B. *to* **MR. EDITOR [W. L. GARRISON]. 7 February 1842. n.p.** Questions a resolution passed by the Massachusetts AS condoning any attempt by the slaves to regain their freedom through the use of arms. 18 February 1842. p.28, c2.

4692 PATTEN DAVIS *to* **BROTHER GARRISON. 28 January 1842. East Bethel, Vt.** Discusses governmental violence in collecting debts. 18 February 1842. p.28, c4.

4693 JAMES C. JACKSON *to* **FRANCIS JACKSON, ESQ. 23 January 1842. Cazenovia.** Reports he is unable to attend the Massachusetts AS meeting. 25 February 1842. p.31, c5.

4694 THEODORE P. LOCKE *to* **BROTHER GARRISON. 14 February 1842. Barre.** Accepts position as one of the twenty-five vice-presidents of the Massachusetts AS. 25 February 1842. p.31, c5.

4695 W. *to* **MR. GARRISON. 17 February 1842. n.p.** Reports on proceedings at Liberty Party Convention. 25 February 1842. p.31, c5.

4696 SAMUEL FESSENDEN *to* **JOHN QUINCY ADAMS. n.d. n.p.** Discusses letter adopted by the Maine AS lauding Adams. 4 March 1842. p.33, c6.

4697 MR. WEBSTER *to* **MR. EVERETT. 29 January 1842. Dept. of State.** Discusses mutiny by slaves aboard the brig *Creole.* 4 March 1842. p.34, c3.

4698 EDITORS OF THE *NEW ENGLAND PURITAN to* **W. L. GARRISON. 25 February 1842. Boston.** Forward communications deemed appropriate for *Liberator* publication. 4 March 1842. p.35, c2.

4699 TRUTH *to* **MR. GARRISON. n.d. n.p.** Declares that he holds little respect for the *Post.* 4 March 1842. p.35, c5.

4700 GERRIT SMITH *to* **BRO. GARRISON. n.d. n.p.** Clarifies an address about which Garrison had commented negatively. 4 March 1842. p.35, c5.

4701 D. M. *to* **MR. GARRISON. n.d. n.p.** Reports on proceedings at Liberty Party Convention. 4 March 1842. p.35, c5.

4702 W. *to* **GARRISON. n.d. n.p.** Advises on best route to take when travelling North. 4 March 1842. p.35, c5.

4703 JOHN ALLEN *to* **MR. EDITOR [W. L. GARRISON]. n.d. n.p.** Charges that the *Liberator* did not give Mr. Taylor of Manchester his due. 4 March 1842. p.35, c5.

4704 C. LENOX REMOND *to* **MR. GARRISON. 5 March 1842. Salem.** Reports on a meeting in South Scituate where he noted new anti-slavery feelings. 11 March 1842. p.38, c5.

4705 WILLIAM HARLOW *to* **MR. GARRISON. 8 February 1842. Wrentham.** Reports resolutions adopted by the First Congregational Church in Wrentham. 11 March 1842. p.38, c6.

4706 DANIEL O'CONNELL, THEOBALD MATHEW, AND 60,000 OTHER INHABITANTS OF IRELAND *to* **THEIR COUNTRYMEN AND COUNTRYWOMEN IN AMERICA. n.d. n.p.** Urge the Irish-Americans to unite with the abolitionists. 11 March 1842. p.39, c3.

4707 H. C. WRIGHT *to* **BROTHER GARRISON. 6 March 1842. Philadelphia.** Eulogizes James Forten. 11 March 1842. p.39, c5.

4708 W. *to* **FRIEND GARRISON. 9 March 1842. Boston.** Reports proceedings at Liberty Party Convention. 11 March 1842. p.39, c5.

4709 JOSEPH BARROWSCALE *to* **MR. EDITOR [W. L. GARRISON]. 2 February 1842. n.p.** Commends Dr. Watson's curing ability. 11 March 1842. p.40, c6.

4710 N. P. FORD *to* **BROTHER GARRISON. 4 February 1842. Abington.** Refutes claims by Lewis Ford in an earlier edition [24 January] of the *Liberator*. 18 March 1842. p.41, c5.

4711 J. G. ADAMS *to* **OFFICERS OF A MEETING HELD IN ROCHESTER. 16 February 1842. Washington.** Replies to a letter requesting his interpretation of the Constitution. 18 March 1842. p.42, c2.

4712 JAMES HAUGHTON *to* **THE FRIENDS OF HUMAN FREEDOM [FROM THE** *DUBLIN MORNING REGISTER*]. **8 February 1842. Dublin.** Urges courage and perseverance in the fight against slavery. 18 March 1842. p.42, c6.

4713 RICHARD ALLEN *to* **GARRISON. 2 February 1842. Dublin.** Discusses American slavery and Irish sentiments toward slavery. 18 March 1842. p.43, c1.

4714 OBSERVER *to* **THE EDITOR OF THE** *LIBERATOR* **[W. L. GARRISON]. 11 March 1842. Washington.** Claims that the Irish address which appeared in the 11 March edition of the *Liberator* was "creating a sensation" among the political Irish. 18 March 1842. p.43, c3.

4715 H. C. WRIGHT *to* **BROTHER GARRISON. 11 March 1842. Philadelphia.** On the death of Grace Douglas. 18 March 1842. p.43, c4.

4716 CHARLES MARRIOTT *to* **N. B. 22 January 1842. New York.** Relates his being summoned to serve on a jury and the consequences of his refusal to do so. 18 March 1842. p.44, c3.

4717 JAMES HAUGHTON *to* **JOHN O'CONNELL. [extract] 26 January 1842. Dublin.** Introduces letter from George Bradburn. 25 March 1842. p.45, c1.

4718 GEORGE BRADBURN *to* **n.n. n.d. n.p.** Rejoices in the election of the "Lion of Derrynane" to the mayoralty of Dublin. 25 March 1842. p.45, c1.

4719 JOHN O'CONNELL *to* **JAMES HAUGHTON. 27 January 1842. Merrion-Square.** Emphasizes need to stress cause of Negro slavery in the United States, along with that of Irish oppression by British. 25 March 1842. p.45, c1.

4720 DANIEL O'CONNELL, THEOBALD MATTHEW, AND 60,000 OTHER IRISHMEN *to* **THEIR COUNTRYMEN AND COUNTRYWOMEN IN AMERICA. n.d. n.p.** Call for Irish in the United States to unite with abolitionists. 25 March 1842. p.45, c2.

4721 J. R. GIDDINGS *to* **MEMBERS OF OHIO SENATE AND HOUSE OF REPRESENTATIVES. 5 March 1842. n.p.** Expresses his disapproval of a resolution passed by the Ohio legislature censuring Adams's statements as "treasonable." 1 April 1842. p.49, c3.

4722 W. KNIBB *to* **EDITOR OF THE** *BAPTIST HERALD.* **n.d. n.p.** Discusses European and American emigrants in Jamaica. 1 April 1842. p.50, c1.

4723 JOHN CLARK *to* **THE EDITOR OF THE** *BAPTIST HERALD.* **24 November 1841. St. Ann.** Comments on European and American emigrants in Jamaica. 1 April 1842. p.50, c1.

4724 J. A. COLLINS *to* **BRO. GARRISON. n.d. n.p.** Encloses Massachusetts lecture schedule, which included as speakers Frederick Douglass, George Bradburn, Abel Tanner, George C. Leach, and Jeremiah B. Sanderson. 1 April 1842. p.51, c1.

4725 J. N. T. TUCKER *to* **FRIEND GARRISON. 13 March 1842. Groton.** Renounces the Liberty Party. 1 April 1842. p.51, c2.

4726 SAMUEL J. MAY *to* **GARRISON. n.d. n.p.** Reports on resolutions passed by the Old Colony AS. 1 April 1842. p.51, c3.

4727 PELEG CLARKE *to* **WM. REYNOLDS. 10 November 1841. Coventry.** Requests a letter from Reynolds. 1 April 1842. p.52, c2.

4728 SOLOMON, LYDIA, LUCY AND LEWIS FORD AND WM. JONES *to* **GARRISON. 18 March 1842. North Abington.** Write about weekly prayer meetings for the slaves. 1 April 1842. p.52, c3.

4729 JUSTICE *to* **MR. GARRISON. 22 March 1842. Kingston.** Reports that sectarianism in the Old Colony is a hindrance to abolition. 1 April 1842. p.52, c3.

4730 LEWIS FORD *to* **FRIEND GARRISON. 20 March 1842. North Abington.** Responds to a letter of N. P. Ford of 18 March. 1 April 1842. p.52, c3.

4731 BERNARD E. BEE *to* **GEN. SANTA ANNA. 27 December 1841. New Orleans.** Warns Mexico of dire consequences if Texas is invaded. 8 April 1842. p.53, c1.

4732 ANTONIO LOPEZ DE SANTA ANNA *to* **BERNARD E. BEE. 6 February 1842. Mexico.** Calls Texans "ungrateful"; counters Bee's warning with threat of war. 8 April 1842. p.53, c1.

4733 GEN. J. HAMILTON *to* **GEN. SANTA ANNA. 13 January 1842. At sea.** Offers peace treaty in exchange for five million dollars. 8 April 1842. p.53, c2.

4734 GEN. SANTA ANNA *to* **JAMES HAMILTON. 13 January 1842. Mexico.** Considers Hamilton's proposed sale of peace treaty "contemptible." 8 April 1842. p.53, c3.

4735 WM. LLOYD GARRISON *to* **BRO. BROWN. 18 March 1842. Boston.** Remarks favorably on Brown's Irish address on American slavery. 8 April 1842. p.54, c2.

4736 JAMES CANNINGS FULLER *to* **THE EMIGRANTS FROM IRELAND AND THEIR DESCENDANTS. 4 April 1842. Skaneateles.** Urges Irish-Americans to continue struggle for abolition and Irish independence. 8 April 1842. p.54, c3.

4737 A COLORED CITIZEN OF SALEM *to* **W. L. GARRISON. 28 March 1842. Eastern Rail-Road, Salem.** Expresses satisfaction with indefinite postponement of vote on the marriage law bill. 8 April 1842. p.54, c5.

4738 A COLORED CITIZEN OF SALEM *to* **W. L. GARRISON. 23 March 1842. Salem.** Discusses the repeal of the marriage law, and security for colored persons using the Eastern Railroad. 8 April 1842. p.54, c5.

4739 JAMES MONROE *to* **BRO. GARRISON. 25 February 1842. Canterbury, Ct.** Clergyman in eastern Connecticut gives a defense of slavery. 8 April 1842. p.55, c4.

4740 C. M. BURLEIGH *to* **BRO. GARRISON. February 1842. Brookline.** Discusses his lecture tour in Medfield. 8 April 1842. p.55, c4.

4741 J. A. COLLINS *to* **GARRISON. 6 April 1842. Boston.** Reports that Frederick Douglass took ill and was unable to keep an appointment to lecture at Bridgewater. 8 April 1842. p.55, c6.

4742 C. T. TORREY *to* **REV. SAMUEL J. MAY. 17 March 1842. Washington, D.C.** Traces the economic and political origins of slavery. 15 April 1842. p.57, c5.

4743 J. M. F. *to* **FRIEND GARRISON. 4 April 1842. West Brookfield.** States that as soon as the women of West Brookfield proclaimed that they opposed slavery, the church ordered that they be kept in subjection. 15 April 1842. p.58, c1.

4744 H. C. WRIGHT *to* **BROTHER GARRISON. 2 April 1842. Philadelphia.** Believes that the South would go to war with England and Mexico if it would help to perpetuate slavery. 15 April 1842. p.58, c3.

4745 J. A. COLLINS *to* **GARRISON. 6 April 1842. Boston.** Confirms arrangements for George Bradburn's lectures. 15 April 1842. p.58, c4.

4746 J. N. T. TUCKER *to* **GARRISON. 2 April 1842. Groton.** Addresses Liberty Party regarding reliance on "mechanical" religion in politics. 15 April 1842. p.58, c4.

4747 ADDISON DAVIS *to* **MR. COBB. 21 March 1842. Anisquam.** States reasons for condemning the Universalist minister Brother Newell. 15 April 1842. p.59, c3.

4748 JUSTUS HARLOW *to* **MR. GARRISON. 13 April 1842. Kingston.** Replies to 1 April letter of "Justice" which addressed the controversy over communion with slaveholders. 22 April 1842. p.62, c5.

4749 N. P. FORD *to* **MR. GARRISON. 11 April 1842. Abington.** Corrects misstatements Lewis Ford and others wrote concerning the proceeds of anti-slavery meetings. 22 April 1842. p.62, c6.

4750 H. C. WRIGHT *to* **BROTHER GARRISON. n.d. n.p.** Comments on the desperate condition of slaveholders. 22 April 1842. p.63, c5.

4751 JONATHAN WHIPPLE *to* **BRO. GARRISON. 2 March 1842. Ledyard, Ct.** Opposes governmental violence in collecting debts. 22 April 1842. p.64, c3.

4752 B. INGINAC *to* **GARRISON. 1 April 1842. Port-au-Prince.** Secretary of the Haitian Republic relates the Haitian president's high regard for the anti-slavery cause. 29 April 1842. p.67, c1.

4753 J. A. COLLINS *to* **THE ABOLITIONISTS OF NEW ENGLAND. 27 April 1842. Boston.** Urges abolitionists to attend the AAS meeting to be held in New York on 10 May. 29 April 1842. p.67, c2.

4754 H. C. WRIGHT *to* **GARRISON. 15 April 1842. Philadelphia.** Asserts that the Union has only two alternatives: dissolution of the Union or the abolition of slavery. 29 April 1842. p.67, c3.

4755 S - - - *to* **MR. EDITOR [W. L. GARRISON]. 7 March 1842. n.p.** Disapproves of John C. Park's description of the Creoles. 29 April 1842. p.67, c4.

4756 LIBERTE TOUTE ENTIERE *to* **MR. EDITOR [W. L. GARRISON]. 9 April 1842. Salem.** Denounces discrimination by the Eastern Railroad authorities. 29 April 1842. p.67, c5.

4757 J. R. GIDDINGS *to* **n.n. [extract] 5 April 1842. Jefferson.** Informs constituents of congressional action concerning his dispute with Mr. Botts. 6 May 1842. p.69, c2.

4758 H. HOBART BRIGHAM *to* **THE EDITOR OF THE** *LIBERATOR* **[W. L. GARRISON]. 13 April 1842. Abington.** Reports that the church urges that its members separate themselves from politics. 6 May 1842. p.70, c3.

4759 ADDISON DAVIS *to* **GARRISON. 26 April 1842. Sandisfield.** Declares that third partyism is the force which is making emancipation of slaves so difficult to achieve. 6 May 1842. p.70, c4.

4760 THOMAS BICKNELL *to* **GARRISON. 28 April 1842. Kingston.** Criticizes the Baptist Church in Kingston for giving communion to a slaveholder. 6 May 1842. p.70, c4.

4761 V. W. B. *to* **MR. GARRISON. 4 February 1842. New Orleans.** Expresses his grief over having seen a group of wretched slaves. 6 May 1842. p.70, c5.

4762 J. A. DUGDALE *to* **GARRISON. n.d. n.p.** Reports on resolutions passed by the Green Plain AS in Ohio on 2 April 1842. 6 May 1842. p.70, c5.

4763 C. M. BURLEIGH *to* **BROTHER GARRISON. 21 April 1842. Plainfield, Ct.** Explains his arrest. 6 May 1842. p.70, c6.

4764 THOS. JEFFERSON *to* **SAMUEL ADAMS. 8 September 1799. Monticello.** Believes that slavery is not sanctioned by the Constitution. [Letter not authenticated] 6 May 1842. p.71, c4.

4765 LEWIS FORD *to* **BROTHER GARRISON. 2 May 1842. S.S.** Reports that Foster denied him the opportunity to speak in Nashua. 6 May 1842. p.71, c5.

4766 JASON MESSINGER *to* **THE FIRST CONGREGATIONAL CHURCH IN DEDHAM, MA. 7 March 1842. Dedham.** Comments on the union between the church and the institution of slavery. 13 May 1842. p.73, c1.

4767 NATHANIEL BARNEY *to* **THE PROPRIETORS OF THE NEW BEDFORD AND TAUNTON RAILROAD. 14 April 1842. Nantucket.** A stockholder of the New Bedford and Taunton Railroad Company disapproves of the treatment accorded to the colored passengers. 13 May 1842. p.73, c2.

4768 J. N. T. TUCKER *to* **GERRIT SMITH. 3 May 1842. Groton.** Fears that the Liberty Party might attract a large number of abolitionists. 13 May 1842. p.74, c5.

4769 JESSE TORREY *to* **MR. GARRISON. 4 May 1842. Abington.** Discusses the North Church in Abington and its refusal to allow anti-slavery meetings. 13 May 1842. p.74, c6.

4770 OLIVER JOHNSON *to* **FRIEND GARRISON. 10 May 1842. New York.** Reports the proceedings of the anniversary meeting of the AAS. 13 May 1842. p.75, c1.

4771 J. A. COLLINS *to* **GARRISON. 20 May 1842. Boston.** Discusses AAS meeting. 20 May 1842. p.79, c3.

4772 H. C. WRIGHT *to* **BROTHER GARRISON. 12 May 1842. New York.** Discusses a resolution passed by the AAS in favor of dissolution. 20 May 1842. p.79, c3.

4773 J. N. T. TUCKER *to* **GARRISON. 18 May 1842. Groton.** Comments on dissolution of the Union. 20 May 1842. p.79, c4.

4774 SARAH PUGH *to* **FRIEND GARRISON. 20 January 1842. Philadelphia.** Forwards an extract of a letter from Elizabeth Pease on non-resistance. 20 May 1842. p.79, c5.

4775 ELIZABETH PEASE *to* **SARAH PUGH. [extract] n.d. n.p.** Expresses surprise that many people uphold the principles of non-resistance without knowing that a society of non-resistance exists. 20 May 1842. p.79, c5.

4776 ISAAC STEARNS *to* **MR. EDITOR [W. L. GARRISON]. 23 May 1842. Mansfield.** Advocates the dissolution of the Union. 27 May 1842. p.82, c5.

4777 F. *to* **MR. GARRISON. n.d. n.p.** Forwards a copy of letter to women in the South from Essex County Anti-Slavery Conference. 27 May 1842. p.82, c6.

4778 ESSEX COUNTY WOMEN'S ANTI-SLAVERY CONFERENCE *to* **MADAM. n.d. n.p.** Warns of the dangers of slavery. 27 May 1842. p.82, c6.

4779 RICHARD ALLEN *to* **FRIEND GARRISON. 3 May 1842. Dublin.** Discusses pro-slavery Irishmen in America. 27 May 1842. p.83, c4.

4780 GEORGE FOSTER *to* **FRIEND GARRISON. 30 May 1842. Andover.** Reports that Rev. R. R. Gurley and Rev. Mr. Harris were in Andover speaking on colonization. 3 June 1842. p.87, c4.

4781 n.n. *to* **W. L. GARRISON. 13 May 1842. Port-au-Prince.** Describes earthquake in Haiti. 3 June 1842. p.87, c5.

4782 GEO. THOMPSON *to* **GARRISON. 1 March 1842. Manchester.** Encloses a brief note with some books and pamphlets. 3 June 1842. p.87, c5.

4783 J. N. T. TUCKER *to* **FRIEND GARRISON. n.d. n.p.** Asserts that popular religion and true abolition are irreconcilably at war. 10 June 1842. p.90, c5.

4784 PATRONUS *to* **MR. EDITOR [W. L. GARRISON]. n.d. n.p.** Account of Masssachusetts CS meeting held 30 May at the Masonic Temple. 10 June 1842. p.91, c5.

4785 GEO. GERRY *to* **FRIEND GARRISON. n.d. n.p.** Reports on resolutions adopted by the Leominster AS. 10 June 1842. p.91, c5.

4786 JAMES HAUGHTON *to* **MY BROTHER REPEALERS. 7 April 1842. Dublin.** Discusses Irish repeal and American slavery. 17 June 1842. p.94, c1.

4787 M. *to* **MR. GARRISON. n.d. n.p.** Describes the arguments of Rev. Jonathan Davis, a Georgia slaveholder, who had visited the North denouncing the abolitionists. 17 June 1842. p.94, c2.

4788 LEWIS FORD *to* **GARRISON. 23 May 1842. Nashua.** Discusses a violent scene which took place at his church in which S. S. Foster was forcibly denied the opportunity to speak. 17 June 1842. p.94, c3.

4789 A. W. P. *to* **MR. GARRISON. 8 June 1842. Northbridge.** Describes the eloquence, intellect, and zeal of Frederick Douglass. 17 june 1842. p.94, c4.

4790 VIGILIUS *to* **MR. GARRISON. n.d. n.p.** Reports on a meeting of Orthodox, Evangelical, and Congregational ministers. 17 June 1842. p.94, c4.

4791 n.n. *to* **GARRISON. n.d. n.p.** Encloses resolutions passed by the Evangelical Union Church of Sudbury. 17 June 1842. p.94, c4.

4792 H. W. W. MILLER *to* **THE EDITORS OF THE** *PEOPLE'S ADVOCATE.* **14 May 1842. Hardwick.** Accuses the *Liberator* of treason because of its advocacy of dissolution. 24 June 1842. p.97, c1.

4793 JOHN A. COLLINS *to* **THE ABOLITIONISTS OF MASSACHUSETTS. 20 June 1842. Boston.** Discusses plans for the celebration of the anniversary of West Indies Emancipation. 24 June 1842. p.99, c1.

4794 SAMUEL J. MAY *to* **BRO. GARRISON. 15 June 1842. South Scituate.** Describes plans for the celebration of the anniversary of West Indies Emancipation. 24 June 1842. p.99, c1.

4795 J. A. COLLINS *to* **GARRISON. 21 June 1842. Boston.** Gives an account of the Ohio AS anniversary held in Mount Vernon. 24 June 1842. p.99, c2.

4796 CHARLES LOFTUS CORKRAN *to* **FRIEND GARRISON. 5 May 1842. Paris.** Congratulates Garrison on the progress he has made in the anti-slavery movement. 24 June 1842. p.99, c3.

4797 THOMAS DAVIS *to* **GARRISON. 19 May 1842. Dumfries, Scotland.** Discusses reform, anti-slavery, and Chartism. 24 June 1842. p.99, c4.

4798 B. *to* **MR. GARRISON. 14 May 1842. New Orleans.** Sends copy of two new Louisiana laws concerning slaves and free Negroes. 1 July 1842. p.102, c3.

4799 RICHARD ALLEN *to* **GARRISON. 2 June 1842. Dublin.** Comments on American slavery and Irish independence. 1 July 1842. p.103, c1.

4800 JOSHUA T. EVERETT *to* **MR. EDITOR [W. L. GARRISON]. 24 June 1842. Princeton, Ma.** Reflects upon Christianity and its role in a Boston woman's conversion to the abolitionist cause. 8 July 1842. p.105, c4.

4801 H. HOBART BRIGHAM *to* **FRIEND GARRISON. 23 June 1842. Abington.** Reports that anti-slavery is making gains in Abington. 8 July 1842. p.105, c5.

4802 B. *to* **THE EDITOR OF THE** *LIBERATOR* **[W. L. GARRISON]. n.d. n.p.** Condemns the *Christian Reflector.* 8 July 1842. p.105, c6.

4803 E. D. HUDSON *to* **FRIEND GARRISON. 24 June 1842. Wayne, Me.** Discusses antislavery in Maine. 8 July 1842. p.105, c6.

4804 WM. P. GRIFFIN *to* **MRS. MARIA W. CHAPMAN. 30 April 1842. Porto Plata.** Discusses the West Indies and the anti-slavery cause in Haiti. 8 July 1842. p.106, c2.

4805 HENRY PURDAY *to* **MRS. MARIA W. CHAPMAN. 17 March 1842. Porto Plata.** Comments on anti-slavery in Haiti. 8 July 1842. p.106, c2.

4806 J. HOLCOMB *to* **BROTHER MURRAY. n.d. n.p.** Comments that "Dutch Justice" often mitigates against abolitionists. 8 July 1842. p.106, c2.

4807 OTHELLO *to* **THE** *NANTUCKET ISLANDER.* **n.d. n.p.** Reports on Douglass' outstanding ability as an orator. 8 July 1842. p.106, c6.

4808 GEORGE THOMPSON *to* **GARRISON. 18 June 1842. Manchester.** Describes disturbances in Great Britain. 8 July 1842. p.107, c2.

4809 W. H. ASHURST *to* **WM. LLOYD GARRISON. 30 April 1842. Muswell Hill, Hornsey, England.** Compares slavery in America with labor in England. 15 July 1842. p.110, c4.

4810 ABEL TANNER *to* **BROTHER GARRISON. 12 July 1842. Raynham.** Discusses the lectures he had given in his town. 22 July 1842. p.114, c3.

4811 DANIEL WEBSTER *to* **WADDY THOMPSON. 13 July 1842. Washington.** Gives instructions to Thompson on how to reply to a letter from Mr. de Bocanegra. 22 July 1842. p.114, c5.

4812 ALETHES *to* **FRIEND GARRISON. n.d. n.p.** Comments on William Goodell's repudiation of Garrisonianism. 22 July 1842. p.115, c4.

4813 A. WILLEY *to* **THE EDITOR OF THE** *LIBERTY STANDARD.* **n.d. n.p.** Discusses Henry Clay's candidacy for president on the Whig ticket. 29 July 1842. p.117, c5.

4814 Q. E. D. *to* **THE EDITOR OF THE** *ALBANY TOCSIN OF LIBERTY.* **n.d. n.p.** Discusses Abby Kelley's unfavorable reception in Albany while on a lecture tour. 29 July 1842. p.118, c1.

4815 JOHN M. SPEAR *to* **BRO. GARRISON. 22 July 1842. Weymouth.** Refers to lecture where colored people were not admitted. 29 July 1842. p.118, c6.

4816 RICHARD ALLEN *to* **FRIEND GARRISON. 2 July 1842. Dublin.** Reports on Father Mathew, the Irish address and Peace Convention, and non-resistance. 29 July 1842. p.119, c3.

4817 GERRIT SMITH *to* **EDITOR OF THE** *CAZENOVIA ABOLITIONIST.* **12 July 1842. Peterboro'.** Favorably describes New York State abolition. 5 August 1842. p.121, c6.

4818 GERRIT SMITH *to* **THE EDITOR OF THE** *CAZENOVIA ABOLITIONIST.* **18 July 1842. Peterboro'.** Comments on the "mobocratic" conduct of certain abolitionists in the East. 5 August 1842. p.121, c6.

4819 AN EMINENT LAWYER OF JAMAICA *to* **A MERCHANT IN BOSTON. [extract from the** *Journal of Commerce***] n.d. n.p.** Reports frequent intermarriage between white men and women of color since emancipation. 5 August 1842. p.122, c1.

4820 GEORGE THOMPSON *to* **GARRISON. 13 June 1842. Liverpool.** Wishes Garrison the best of luck with the paper and the cause. 5 August 1842. p.122, c6.

4821 G. F. *to* **FRIEND GARRISON. 20 July 1842. Nantucket.** Comments on Lucretia Mott's visit to Nantucket. 5 August 1842. p.123, c2.

4822 AN OBSERVER *to* **BRO. GARRISON. 25 July 1842. Boston.** Describes the performance of the Republican Artillery, a military drill team from Albany. 5 August 1842. p.124, c2.

4823 P. F. *to* **FRIEND GARRISON. 20 July 1842. Nantucket.** Opposes capital punishment. 5 August 1842. p.124, c2.

4824 FORDYCE RUE *to* **MR. JACKSON. 28 July 1842. n.p.** Accuses Jackson and Gerrit Smith of "misrepresenting" Miss Kelley's speech. 12 August 1842. p.125, c6.

4825 ABBY KELLEY *to* **FRIEND JACKSON. 22 July 1842. Skaneateles.** Defends a speech she made which was misinterpreted by many. 12 August 1842. p.126, c6.

4826 H. C. WRIGHT *to* **GARRISON. 1 August 1842. Quincy.** Asks if brute force is necessarily the only means of moral and social reform. 12 August 1842. p.127, c3.

4827 AMASA WALKER *to* **GARRISON. 30 July 1842. Oberlin.** Refutes notion that Quakers are not allowed at Oberlin. 12 August 1842. p.127, c4.

4828 WM. BASSETT *to* **GARRISON. 2 August 1842. Lynn.** Gives account of the Lynn celebration of the First of August. 12 August 1842. p.127, c5.

4829 EDMUND QUINCY *to* **GARRISON. 6 August 1842. Dedham.** Describes the First of August jubilee at Dedham. 12 August 1842. p.127, c5.

4830 A BRISTOL COUNTY ABOLITIONIST *to* **MR. GARRISON. 6 August 1842. Fall River.** Applauds youth bands which performed at the First of August celebration. 12 August 1842. p.127, c5.

4831 JAS. MONROE *to* **MR. GARRISON. n.d. n.p.** Urges people to attend the meeting at Windham County, Connecticut. 12 August 1842. p.127, c6.

4832 A. FAIRBANKS *to* **BROTHER GARRISON. 7 August 1842. Providence.** Discusses the "civil war" in Rhode Island; challenges the accounts given thus far by a professed anti-slavery man. 19 August 1842. p.131, c3.

4833 J. J. *to* **FRIEND GARRISON. 6 August 1842. New York.** Comments on "civil war" in Rhode Island. 19 August 1842. p.131, c3.

4834 JOHN M. FISK *to* **THE EDITOR [W. L. GARRISON]. 15 August 1842. West Brookfield.** Disapproves of mob scenes by abolitionists in a Congregational meeting-house. 26 August 1842. p.134, c5.

4835 JOHN M. FISK *to* **MR. EDITOR [W. L. GARRISON]. 15 August 1842. West Brookfield.** Comments on article concerning mobocracy. 26 August 1842. p.134, c5.

4836 H. C. WRIGHT *to* **BROTHER GARRISON. n.d. n.p.** Sends an extract from a letter which contains a dialogue depicting the racist attitudes of a clergyman, Rev. Jacob Sandborn. 26 August 1842. p.134, c6.

4837 n.n. *to* **H. C. WRIGHT [extract] 11 August 1842. Lynn.** Exposes comments by Rev. Jacob Sandborn denouncing those who associate closely with colored people. 26 August 1842. p.134, c6.

4838 GEORGE W. SIMONDS *to* **GARRISON. 19 August 1842. East Lexington.** Discloses that Thomas W. Dorr once opposed clause which excluded black suffrage. 26 August 1842. p.135, c2.

4839 RICHARD ALLEN *to* **FRIEND GARRISON. 3 August 1842. Dublin.** Discusses the progress of anti-slavery sentiment in Ireland; reports on a meeting on temperance and anti-slavery. 26 August 1842. p.135, c3.

4840 J. M. F. *to* **MR. EDITOR [W. L. GARRISON]. 4 August 1842. W.B.** Supports Haitian independence. 26 August 1842. p.135, c4.

4841 G. *to* **GARRISON. 19 August 1842. New York.** Describes mob violence in Nantucket. 26 August 1842. p.135, c4.

4842 HIRAM WILSON *to* **WM. L. GARRISON. 23 August 1842. Boston.** Discusses aid for fugitives in Canada. 26 August 1842. p.135, c4.

4843 JUSTICE *to* **W. L. GARRISON. 23 August 1842. Philadelphia.** Reports on riots in Philadelphia. 2 September 1842. p.138, c5.

4844 TRUTH *to* **MR. GARRISON. 23 August 1842. Philadelphia.** Reports further on Philadelphia riots. 2 September 1842. p.138, c6.

4845 A. BROOKE *to* **MRS. MARIA W. CHAPMAN ET AL. 8 August 1842. Oakland, Oh.** Sends encouragement for their anti-slavery fair. 2 September 1842. p.139, c3.

4846 H. C. WRIGHT *to* **GARRISON. 28 August 1842. Boston.** Comments on Rev. Sandborn. 2 September 1842. p.139, c3.

4847 JUSTICE *to* **GARRISON. 20 August 1842. Boston.** Comments on an exhibition held at the Smith School for colored youths. 2 September 1842. p.139, c4.

4848 CLOTHER GIFFORD *to* **GARRISON. n.d. n.p.** Discusses the building of a manual labor school. 2 September 1842. p.139, c5.

4849 GARRISON *to* **EDITOR OF *ZION'S HERALD*. 27 August 1842. Boston.** Defends his views against misrepresentation by the *Zion's Herald*. 9 September 1842. p.141, c2.

4850 H. C. WRIGHT *to* **GARRISON. 31 August 1842. Boston.** Sends an extract from a letter which includes an account of the riot in Philadelphia. 9 September 1842. p.142, c3.

4851 n.n. *to* **H. C. WRIGHT. 22 August 1842. Philadelphia.** Claims that he is unqualified to answer for the "bloody-spirited mobs." 9 September 1842. p.142, c3.

4852 WILLIAM ENDICOTT *to* **GARRISON. 7 August 1842. Danvers.** Reports that many people in Danvers have left the church because of pro-slavery priests. 9 September 1842. p.142, c3.

4853 THERON E. HALL *to* **W. L. GARRISON. 18 August 1842. Sutton.** Describes the effectiveness of Frederick Douglass' oratory. 9 September 1842. p.142, c5.

4854 H. C. WRIGHT *to* **GARRISON. 15 August 1842. Salem.** Reports that the so-called "First Free School" was not a free school because colored people were denied admission. 9 September 1842. p.142, c6.

4855 PLUCK *to* **GARRISON. n.d. n.p.** Discusses Christianity and war. 9 September 1842. p.144, c2.

4856 JOHN LEEDS KERR *to* **GARRISON. 23 July 1842. Washington.** A slaveholder returns a copy of the *Liberator* which was sent to him by Garrison along with a note requesting that no more copies of the paper be sent to him. 16 September 1842. p.145, c1.

4857 OLD DOMINION *to* **MR. EDITOR [W. L. GARRISON]. n.d. n.p.** Compares slaves' position favorably to that of Northern industrial laborers. 16 September 1842. p.145, c1.

4858 LORD ASHBURTON *to* **DANIEL WEBSTER. 9 August 1842. Washington.** Deals with suppression of the slave trade. 16 September 1842. p.146, c1.

4859 MR. PAINE *to* **MR. WEBSTER. 2 May 1842. Washington.** Encloses a copy of the agreement between Commander William Tucker of the British Navy and himself. 16 September 1842. p.146, c1.

4860 J. K. PAULDING *to* **SIR. 4 June 1841. n.p.** Clarifies his previous instructions for the ship *Wolverine*. 16 September 1842. p.146, c1.

4861 J. S. PAINE *to* **CAPTAIN TUCKER. 27 April 1842. n.p.** Makes known the United States government's views of the agreement signed and exchanged at Sierra Leone. 16 September 1842. p.146, c1.

4862 J. S. PAINE *to* **n.n. 17 June 1841. Sierra Leone.** Discusses his arrangement with Commander Tucker. 16 September 1842. p.146, c1.

4863 J. S. PAINE *to* **n.n. n.d. n.p.** Queries whether any explanation or defense of Mr. Paulding's letter is necessary. 16 September 1842. p.146, c2.

4864 n.n. *to* **GARRISON. 4 September 1842. Bath.** Describes anti-slavery sentiment in Bath. 16 September 1842. p.147, c4.

4865 DANIEL WEBSTER *to* **LORD ASHBURTON. 1 August 1842. Washington.** Discusses the case of the *Creole*. 23 September 1842. p.149, c6.

4866 LORD ASHBURTON *to* **MR. WEBSTER. 6 August 1842. Washington.** Discusses British refusal to return slaves to the United States. 23 September 1842. p.150, c2.

4867 MR. WEBSTER *to* **LORD ASHBURTON. 8 August 1842. Washington.** Favors a treaty defining maritime laws. 23 September 1842. p.150, c3.

4868 ABEL TANNER *to* **GARRISON. 12 September 1842. Hanover.** Reveals the hypocrisy of pro-slavery ministers. 23 September 1842. p.150, c5.

4869 HARVY HURD *to* **GARRISON. 19 September 1842. New Bedford.** Reports on an incident of Jim Crowism which took place on the New Bedford and Taunton branch railroad. 23 September 1842. p.150, c6.

4870 H. C. WRIGHT *to* **W. L. GARRISON. 16 September 1842. Philadelphia.** Describes the treatment of colored people in Philadelphia. 23 September 1842. p.150, c6.

4871 A MEMBER OF THE SMITH SCHOOL BOARD *to* **GARRISON. 1 October 1842. Boston.** Defends the Smith School against charges made by correspondents of the *Liberator*. 7 October 1842. p.158, c2.

4872 ROBERT BABB *to* **GARRISON. 21 September 1842. Bath.** Discusses the disgraceful proceedings in Bath, where meeting halls do not allow anti-slavery gatherings. 7 October 1842. p.158, c3.

4873 HENRY HURD *to* **GARRISON. 26 September 1842. New Bedford.** Relates the treatment of Mr. Richard Johnson and his daughter by the New Bedford and Taunton Railroad. 7 October 1842. p.158, c4.

4874 T. P. BEACH *to* **GARRISON. Thursday. Newburyport Jail.** Affirms his interest in the anti-slavery cause, even though imprisoned. 7 October 1842. p.158, c5.

4875 C. L. REMOND *to* **WEST NEWBURY AS. 16 September 1842. Salem.** Regrets not having been able to attend a meeting of the Essex County AS. 7 October 1842. p.158, c5.

4876 J. N. T. TUCKER *to* **W. L. GARRISON. 13 September 1842. Sennett, N.Y.** Describes and praises Frederick Douglass. 7 October 1842. p.158, c5.

4877 RICHARD ALLEN *to* **GARRISON. 18 September 1842. Dublin.** Condemns Irish-Americans for having participated in the Philadelphia riots against the colored people. 7 October 1842. p.159, c3.

4878 H. C. WRIGHT *to* **GARRISON. 26 September 1842. New York.** Discusses "Popular Revivals and Sectarian Organizations." 14 October 1842. p.162, c3.

4879 J. N. T. TUCKER *to* **GARRISON. 20 September 1842. Sennett, N.Y.** Informs him that the American Board of Commissioners for Foreign Missions received $100,000 from missionaries in Ceylon. 14 October 1842. p.162, c4.

4880 EDWARD SEARCH *to* **GARRISON. 19 September 1842. London.** Discusses the struggle for equal rights in England against classism. 14 October 1842. p.162, c5.

4881 JAMES HAUGHTON *to* **GARRISON. 15 September 1842. Dublin.** Describes bigotry in England. 14 October 1842. p.162, c6.

4882 WM. GOODELL *to* **GARRISON. 3 October 1842. n.p.** Comments on free suffrage in Rhode Island. 14 October 1842. p.163, c1.

4883 PHILANTHROPIST *to* **EDITOR OF THE** *BOSTON MEDICAL JOURNAL.* **n.d. n.p.** Discusses vital statistics of Negroes and mulattoes; concludes that Africans live longer than mulattoes. 21 October 1842. p.165, c5.

4884 COLORED INHABITANTS OF UPPER CANADA *to* **SIR ALLEN MCNAB. n.d. n.p.** Hail McNab's anti-slavery efforts. 21 October 1842. p.166, c5.

4885 SIR ALLEN MCNAB *to* **COLORED INHABITANTS OF UPPER CANADA. n.d. n.p.** Laments case of Nelson Hacket, an abducted Negro. 21 October 1842. p.166, c5.

4886 THOMAS P. BEACH *to* **GARRISON. 10 October 1842. Newburyport Jail.** Discusses his reasons for becoming a clergyman. 21 October 1842. p.167, c2.

4887 S. LOVELL *to* **MR. GARRISON. 15 October 1842. Boston.** Denies responsibility for articles in the *Olive Branch*. 21 October 1842. p.167, c4.

4888 H. W. B. *to* **BROTHER GARRISON. n.d. Neponset Village.** Condemns "slumbering" anti-slavery movement. 21 October 1842. p.167, c5.

4889 GEORGE BRADBURN *to* **JAMES HAUGHTON. July 1842. Nantucket.** Comments on American slavery, O'Connell, and Irish repeal. 28 October 1842. p.169, c5.

4890 J. N. T. TUCKER *to* **GARRISON. 17 October 1842. Sennett.** Discusses Liberty Party politics. 28 October 1842. p.170, c3.

4891 SETH SPRAGUE *to* **GARRISON. 24 October 1842. Duxbury.** Comments on the Methodist Church and slavery. 28 October 1842. p.170, c4.

4892 H. C. WRIGHT *to* **GARRISON. 5 August 1842. Boston.** Describes A. A. Phelps' views of the American church and clergy in 1836. 28 October 1842. p.170, c5.

4893 H. H. BRIGHAM *to* **GARRISON. 15 October 1842. Abington.** Explains inconsistency of Liberty Party abolitionists. 4 November 1842. p.174, c4.

4894 D. S. GRANDIN *to* **GARRISON. 26 October 1842. Bath.** Reports on activities of R. R. Gurley in Bath. 4 November 1842. p.174, c4.

4895 BARON STOW *to* **GENTLEMEN. 28 October. Portland.** Informs that he is unable to attend meeting. 11 November 1842. p.177, c3.

4896 GEORGE BANCROFT *to* **GENTLEMEN. 27 October 1842. Boston.** Reports that he is unable to attend meeting. 11 November 1842. p.177, c3.

4897 W. B. CALHOUN *to* **JACKSON, LORING, MERRILL, AND SEWALL. 27 October 1842. Springfield.** Explains that bronchitis prevents his attendance at meeting. 11 November 1842. p.177, c3.

4898 SAMUEL HOAR *to* **GENTLEMEN. 27 October 1842. Concord.** Reports that he is unable to attend meeting. 11 November 1842. p.177, c3.

4899 JOHN QUINCY ADAMS *to* **S. E. SEWALL AND AMOS BINNEY. 24 October 1842. Quincy.** Comments on constitutional aspects of fugitive slave case. 11 November 1842. p.177, c3.

4900 J. DAVIS *to* **THE WORCESTER AS. 19 September 1842. Worcester.** Sends resolutions regarding the execution of any abolitionist found in the state of South Carolina. 11 November 1842. p.177, c4.

4901 W. C. PRESTON *to* **SIR. December 1839. Washington City.** Denies that he ever said that any abolitionist found in South Carolina would be hanged. 11 November 1842. p.177, c4.

4902 J. N. T. TUCKER *to* **GARRISON. n.d. n.p.** Comments on New York Liberty Party. 11 November 1842. p.177, c5.

4903 E. D. HUDSON *to* **GARRISON. 20 October 1842. Northampton.** Declares that the spirit of third partyism is unmasked. 11 November 1842. p.178, c1.

4904 W. *to* **GARRISON. 6 November 1842. Boston.** Discusses Rev. Dr. Jenks and slavery. 11 November 1842. p.178, c5.

4905 HIRAM WILSON *to* **GARRISON. 31 October 1842. Detroit.** Describes the fugitives in Upper Canada. 11 November 1842. p.178, c6.

4906 A SUBSCRIBER *to* **MR. EDITOR [W. L. GARRISON]. 6 November 1842. n.p.** Views constitutional arguments as valid in the Latimer case, despite moral issues. 18 November 1842. p.182, c4.

4907 FREDERICK DOUGLASS *to* **W. L. GARRISON. 8 November 1842. Lynn.** Describes efforts in behalf of George Latimer. 18 November 1842. p.182, c5.

4908 N. BARNEY *to* **GARRISON. 14 November 1842. Nantucket.** Reports on resolution concerning George Latimer. 18 November 1842. p.183, c6.

4909 REV. JOHN ROBE *to* **THE** *NEW YORK WATCHMAN.* **10 September 1842. West End, St. Croix.** Informs that slave rebellion is expected. 18 November 1842. p.184, c4.

4910 A. W. QUIMBY *to* **MR. EDITOR [W. L. GARRISON]. n.d. n.p.** Accuses the North of belligerence; urges self-defense in the South. 25 November 1842. p.185, c1.

4911 T. P. BEACH *to* **GARRISON. 30 October 1842. Newburyport Jail.** Discusses his imprisonment and feelings toward anti-slavery. 25 November 1842. p.185, c2.

4912 JOHN QUINCY ADAMS *to* **EDITORS OF THE** *BOSTON ATLAS.* **18 November 1842. Quincy.** Asserts that disproportionate power is held by Southern states. 25 November 1842. p.186, c3.

4913 ELIAS SMITH *to* **GARRISON. n.d. n.p.** Sends an extract from a letter of someone involved in the slave trade. 2 December 1842. p.190, c2.

4914 THEO. FREEMAN *to* **MESSRS. OVERLY AND SAUNDERS. [extract] 21 September 1839. Richmond.** Discusses the prices of Negroes. 2 December 1842. p.190, c2.

4915 C. LENOX REMOND *to* **W. L. GARRISON. n.d. n.p.** Discusses an article which appeared in the *Daily Bee* of 24 November 1842 regarding a rivalry between Douglass and Remond. 2 December 1842. p.191, c5.

4916 EDWARD NEEDLES *to* **WM. LLOYD GARRISON. 11 November 1842. Philadelphia.** Opposes Garrisonians' attacks on the Church. 9 December 1842. p.194, c2.

4917 E. W. C. *to* **FRIEND GARRISON. 28 October 1842. Walworth, N.Y.** Reports on proceedings of the Farmington Monthly Meeting of Hicksite Friends. 9 December 1842. p.194, c2.

4918 ELLIS GRAY LORING *to* **FRIEND GARRISON. 5 December 1842. Boston.** Comments on the Van Dyke painting presented to him by a Mr. Gore. 9 December 1842. p.195, c5.

4919 E. G. LORING *to* **GARRISON. 5 December 1842. Boston.** Remarks upon stylistic aspects of contrast in Van Dyke's paintings. 16 December 1842. p.199, c6.

4920 ALONZO P. JAQUES *to* **GARRISON. 4 December 1842. West Newbury.** Criticizes any religion which denounces abolitionists as infidels. 23 December 1842. p.202, c2.

4921 S. K. LOTHROP *to* **THE EDITOR OF THE** *LIBERATOR* **[W. L. GARRISON]. 7 December 1842. Boston.** Refutes an article entitled "New Notions about Prayer," which appeared in an earlier edition of the *Liberator*. 23 December 1842. p.203, c3.

4922 J. A. C. *to* **n.n. 22 December 1842. Washington.** Reports on proceedings of the Senate and the House of Representatives in Washington, D.C. 30 December 1842. p.206, c6.

[1843]

4923 H. H. BRIGHAM *to* **GARRISON. 16 December 1842. Abington.** Replies to Mr. Leavitt that the conflict in the Liberty Party is between acting politically and acting morally. 6 January 1843. p.1, c2.

4924 C. P. *to* **FRIEND GARRISON. 20 December 1842. Nantucket.** Poses a legal question relative to the Latimer case. 6 January 1843. p.3, c2.

4925 DAVID L. CHILD *to* **n.n. 26 December 1842. Washington.** Discusses the purpose of the National Institute; comments on divisions in the country over slavery. 6 January 1843. p.3, c3.

4926 DAVID L. CHILD *to* **n.n. 31 December 1841. Washington.** Discusses the United States government's confiscation of citizens' property. 6 January 1843. p.3, c3.

4927 WATCHMAN *to* **GARRISON. 14 December 1842. Philadelphia.** Relates an incident in which a freeman was forced to leave his hometown in North Carolina because of his brother's association with the Rhode Island AS. 6 January 1843. p.4, c2.

4928 ELIAS SMITH *to* **FRIEND GARRISON. 16 December 1842. Bath, Me.** Reports on anti-slavery in Maine. 13 January 1843. p.5, c5.

4929 MATILDA G. WEBSTER *to* **MR. GARRISON. 26 December 1842. Haverhill.** Encloses resolutions passed at the women's anti-slavery conference. 13 January 1843. p.5, c6.

4930 E. WRIGHT, JR. *to* **HENRY B. STANTON. 12 October 1839. Dorchester.** Relates the origins of the Liberty Party. 13 January 1843. p.6, c4.

4931 DAVID L. CHILD *to* **THE** *LIBERATOR.* **3 January 1843. Washington.** Discusses congressional vote to allow slave trade in the District of Columbia. 13 January 1843. p.7, c1.

4932 H. C. WRIGHT *to* **GARRISON. 16 November 1842. Dublin.** Describes his stay in London. 13 January 1843. p.7, c4.

4933 J. H. *to* **THE EDITORS (PRO TEM) OF THE** *LIBERATOR.* **8 January 1843. Lynn.** Accuses the *Liberator* of giving a false report of a meeting held in Lynn. 13 January 1843. p.7, c5.

4934 JOHN ORVIS *to* **BROTHER BEACH. 12 December 1842. Newburyport.** Reports that Brother Allen was denied the chance to speak at a church in Newburyport. 13 January 1843. p.8, c2.

4935 JOHN M. FISK *to* **REV. MOSES CHASE. 2 November 1842. n.p.** Wishes to discuss the reading of notices for meetings held on the Sabbath. 20 January 1843. p.9, c3.

4936 M. CHASE *to* **COL. JOHN M. FISK. 26 November 1846. West Brookfield.** Agrees to attend prayer meeting; outlines agenda for service. 20 January 1843. p.9, c3.

4937 JOHN M. FISK *to* **REV. MOSES CHASE. 20 November 1843. n.p.** Notes confusion in their correspondence caused by delay in mail. 20 January 1843. p.9, c3.

4938 H. F. *to* **WM. SCHOULER. [from the** *Lowell Journal*] **28 December 1842. Lowell.** Describes the anti-slavery fair in Boston. 20 January 1843. p.9, c6.

4939 JOHN TYLER *to* **THE SENATE OF THE UNITED STATES. 9 January 1842. Washington.** Forwards resolutions of the Senate on the quintuple treaty for suppression of the slave trade. 20 January 1843. p.10, c1.

4940 ELIZABETH PEASE *to* **FRIEND GARRISON. 31 October. Darlington.** Reports on the visit of George Thompson to India. 20 January 1843. p.10, c6.

4941 DAVID L. CHILD *to* **THE** *LIBERATOR*. **7 January 1843. n.p.** Gives account of congressional proceedings. 20 January 1843. p.11, c1.

4942 T. *to* **THE EDITOR OF THE** *HERALD OF FREEDOM*. **30 December 1842. Bradford, N.H.** Discusses the tragedy on board the U.S. brig *Somers.* 20 January 1843. p.12, c3.

4943 ENOCH MACH *to* **T. P. BEACH. 13 October 1842. Salem.** Consoles Beach for his imprisonment. 27 January 1843. p.13, c6.

4944 LORD MORPETH *to* **MRS. CHAPMAN. 28 October 1842. Castle Howard.** Gives reasons for not contributing to Chapman's annual publication, the *Liberty Bell.* 27 January 1843. p.14, c4.

4945 E. Q. *to* **THE** *COURIER*. **n.d. n.p.** Comments on Lord Morpeth's letter in which Morpeth states reasons for not submitting an article to the *Liberty Bell.* 27 January 1843. p.14, c5.

4946 J. C. CALHOUN *to* **REV. ALEXANDER MCCAIN. 3 August 1842. Washington.** Congratulates McCain on his pamphlet entltled "Slavery Defended from Scripture, Against the Attacks of the Abolitionists." 27 January 1843. p.14, c6.

4947 DAVID L. CHILD *to* **THE** *LIBERATOR*. **16 January 1843. Washington.** Describes annual debate on colonization. 27 January 1843. p.15, c4.

4948 C. L. *to* **GARRISON. 16 January 1843. Concord, Ma.** States that A. Bronson Alcott went to prison for refusing to pay taxes to a state which he felt supported the immoral practice of slavery. 27 January 1843. p.16, c3.

4949 E. A. WEBB *to* **BROTHER GARRISON. 14 January 1843. Keene, N.H.** Encloses contribution of fifty dollars to Garrison. 27 January 1843. p.16, c4.

4950 DAVID L. CHILD *to* **THE** *LIBERATOR*. **21 January 1843. Washington.** Describes congressional debate on annexation of Texas. 3 February 1843. p.17, c5.

4951 WM. ENDICOTT *to* **GARRISON. 23 January 1843. Danvers.** Encloses resolution commending the *Liberator* as an efficient instrument for the redemption of the slave. 3 February 1843. p.19, c1.

4952 THOMAS W. GILMER *to* **THE EDITOR OF THE** *MADISONIAN.* **10 January 1843. Washington.** Supports the annexation of Texas. 10 February 1843. p.21, c5.

4953 E. SMITH *to* **GARRISON. 25 January 1843. Hallowell.** Describes the anti-slavery cause in Maine. 10 February 1843. p.22, c1.

4954 E. W. CAPRON *to* **GARRISON. 21 January 1842. Rochester, N.Y.** Discusses pro-slavery sentiments in Society of Friends. 10 February 1843. p.22, c1.

4955 JAMES MUNROE *to* **EAST GREENWICH MONTHLY MEETING OF FRIENDS. 20 January 1843. Providence, R.I.** Withdraws from the Society of Friends because of their support of slavery. 10 February 1843. p.22, c2.

4956 DAVID RUGGLES *to* **GARRISON. 23 January 1843. Northampton.** Discusses inalienable rights; reports on the resolutions passed at the Latimer Convention in Northampton. 10 February 1843. p.22, c2.

4957 C. L. *to* **GARRISON. 28 January 1843. Concord, Ma.** Calls for a voluntary state government. 10 February 1843. p.22, c2.

4958 THOMAS HASKELL *to* **BROTHER GARRISON. 29 January 1843. Gloucester.** Protests employment of armed men to protect anti-slavery meetings held in Faneuil Hall. 10 February 1843. p.22, c3.

4959 AN ADVOCATE FOR EQUALITY *to* **MR. GARRISON. 24 January 1843. Dorchester.** Discusses the exclusion of females from voting at the Latimer Convention. 10 February 1843. p.22, c3.

4960 JOHN LEWIS RUSSELL *to* **THE EDITOR [W. L. GARRISON]. 28 January 1843. South Hingham.** Corrects a report of the Plymouth AS Convention. 10 February 1843. p.22, c3.

4961 G. N. BRIGGS, CHAS. HUDSON, ROBT. C. WINTHROP, BARKER BURNELL, OSMYN BAKER, AND LEVERETT SALTONSTALL *to* **JOHN QUINCY ADAMS. 13 January 1843. Washington.** Denounce vote censuring Adams as unjust. 10 February 1843. p.22, c4.

4962 JOHN QUINCY ADAMS *to* **MESSRS. BRIGGS, HUDSON, BURNELL, WINTHROP, BAKER, AND SALTONSTALL. 16 January 1843. Washington.** Thanks his colleagues for opposing his censure. 10 February 1843. p.22, c5.

4963 DAVID L. CHILD *to* **THE** *LIBERATOR.* **29 January 1843. Washington.** Discusses a vote against pending congressional reports. 10 February 1843. p.22, c5.

4964 A. M. B. *to* **MR. GARRISON. 1 February 1843. Boston.** Comments on Dickens' visit to the United States and slavery in ancient Greece. 17 February 1843. p.25, c4.

4965 STEPHEN S. FOSTER *to* **GARRISON. n.d. n.p.** Describes the disruption of his lecture by a mob in Portland. 17 February 1843. p.25, c5.

4966 HENRY WILSON *to* **THE EDITOR OF THE** *COURIER.* **6 February 1843. Natick.** Submits correspondence concerning Leverett Saltonstall and John Q. Adams. 17 February 1843. p.26, c5.

4967 HENRY WILSON *to* **LEVERETT SALTONSTALL. 27 January 1843. Natick.** Inquires whether he wrote to the Massachusetts legislature to ask that resolutions sustaining Mr. Adams be defeated. 17 February 1843. p.26, c5.

4968 LEVERETT SALTONSTALL *to* **HENRY WILSON. 31 January 1843. Washington.** Replies that he never wrote a letter to the Massachusetts legislature opposing resolutions sustaining Mr. Adams. 17 February 1843. p.26, c5.

4969 H. I. BOWDITCH *to* **THE** *BOSTON COURIER.* **n.d. n.p.** Attacks Mr. Saltonstall, a member of the Massachusetts legislature, for his support of resolutions against John Quincy Adams. 17 February 1843. p.26, c6.

4970 J. A. COLLINS *to* **W. L. GARRISON. 9 February 1843. Boston.** Discusses proceedings of a special meeting of the Society of Universal Inquiry and Reform; notes that Douglass was a member of the executive committee. 17 February 1843. p.28, c2.

4971 DAVID L. CHILD *to* **THE** *LIBERATOR.* **11 February 1843. Washington.** Condemns the conspiracy between Southern slaveholders and Northern ''slavedemocrats.'' 24 February 1843. p.29, c2.

4972 H. I. BOWDITCH *to* **FRIEND GARRISON. 9 February 1843. Boston.** Submits copies of the correspondence between himself and another physician, Lawrence M. Ricaud. 24 February 1843. p.30, c2.

4973 LAURENCE M. RICAUD *to* **GEO. VICKER. 21 January 1843. Chestertown.** Comments on a letter he received from Dr. H. I. Bowditch; warns of the dangers of abolitionism. 24 February 1843. p.30, c2.

4974 DR. H. I. BOWDITCH *to* **DR. LAURENCE M. RICAUD. 6 January 1843. Boston.** States that he will not sell a respirator to anyone connected with slavery. 24 February 1843. p.30, c2.

4975 SIDNEY HOWARD GAY *to* **MR. GARRISON. 14 February 1843. Hingham.** Replies to Mr. Russell regarding the report of the last Plymouth County AS. 24 February 1843. p.30, c4.

4976 W. ADAM *to* **W. L. GARRISON. 11 February 1843. Northampton.** Comments on ''An Advocate for Equality'' who had stated in an earlier letter that women were not allowed to vote at the Latimer Convention. 24 February 1843. p.30, c5.

4977 JOSHUA H. WARD *to* **THE EDITOR OF THE** *COURIER.* **15 February 1843. Salem.** Discusses the case of Leverett Saltonstall. 24 February 1843. p.30, c5.

4978 DAVID L. CHILD *to* **THE** *LIBERATOR.* **13 December 1842. Washington.** Describes congressional proceedings. 24 February 1843. p.30, c6.

4979 XENOS *to* **EDITOR OF THE** *MAINE CULTIVATOR.* **13 February. n.p.** Denounces Garrisonianism, claiming that the movement advocated rebellion against all authority. 3 March 1843. p.33, c1.

4980 A FRIEND OF THE COUNTRY *to* **THE** *RICHMOND WHIG.* **n.d. n.p.** Denounces Boston as hotbed of abolitionist fanaticism. 3 March 1843. p.33, c1.

4981 H. C. WRIGHT *to* **BRO. GARRISON. 29 January 1843. Dublin.** Describes his journey to Ireland; discusses meetings he has attended in Dublin. 3 March 1843. p.33, c2.

4982 EDWARD SEARCH *to* **GARRISON. 26 November 1842. Muswell Hill.** Condemns English and American laws preventing the exchange of food and manufactured goods; condemns slavery. 3 March 1843. p.33, c3.

4983 SOPHIA *to* **THE EDITOR OF THE** *BOSTON LIBERATOR* **[W. L. GARRISON]. 6 January 1843. Birmingham.** Discusses political struggle in England. 3 March 1843. p.33, c5.

4984 DAVID L. CHILD *to* **THE** *LIBERATOR*. **24 February 1843. Washington.** Describes passage of appropriations bill. 3 March 1843. p.35, c3.

4985 C. L. *to* **GARRISON. 21 February 1843. Concord, Ma.** Prefers a voluntary system of political government to republicanism. 3 March 1843. p.36, c2.

4986 F. WRIGHT *to* **W. L. GARRISON. 17 February 1843. Little Falls, N.Y.** Reports on an anti-slavery meeting which was disrupted by a mob. 10 March 1843. p.38, c4.

4987 E. SEARCH *to* **GARRISON. 27 January 1843. Muswell Hill (near London).** Describes political division in England. 10 March 1843. p.39, c3.

4988 DAVID L. CHILD *to* **THE** *LIBERATOR*. **4 March 1843. Washington.** Discusses congressional proceedings. 10 March 1843. p.39, c4.

4989 JOSEPH BARKER *to* **WM. L. GARRISON. 25 December 1842. Newcastle.** Affirms that slavery can imprison the body, but not the soul. 10 March 1843. p.40, c2.

4990 JACOB FERRIS *to* **THE EDITOR OF THE** *PRESBYTERIAN*. **n.d. n.p.** Refers to a slave whom the Synod of Alabama wished to send to Liberia as a missionary. 17 March 1843. p.42, c2.

4991 n.n. *to* **FRIEND GARRISON. 7 March 1843. West Brookfield.** Charges Deacon Henshaw with subversive and slanderous activities. 17 March 1843. p.42, c5.

4992 M. B. *to* **BRO. GARRISON. 13 March 1843. Concord.** Reports on 8 March AS Convention. 17 March 1843. p.42, c6.

4993 N. S. *to* **GARRISON. 1 March 1843. At sea, off Cape Fear River.** Describes a slave auction he witnessed in Charleston. 17 March 1843. p.42, c6.

4994 DAVID L. CHILD *to* **THE** *LIBERATOR*. **11 March 1843. Washington.** Discusses ambassadorial appointments. 17 March 1843. p.43, c4.

4995 FAIR PLAY *to* **GARRISON. 6 March 1843. Boston.** Reports that Liberty Party delegates voted the Democrat ticket. 17 March 1843. p.43, c6.

4996 RICHARD YEADON *to* **DR. DIONYSIUS LARDNER. 7 January 1843. Charleston.** Describes slaves as trusted, befriended members of the family; asks Lardner to shed his anti-slavery prejudice. 24 March 1843. p.45, c1.

4997 DR. A. BROOKE *to* **BROTHER GARRISON. 4 March 1843. Oakland, Oh.** Discusses anti-slavery activity in Ohio. 24 March 1843. p.46, c3.

4998 FREDERICK DOUGLASS *to* **FRIEND GARRISON. 27 February 1843. Providence.** Reports on a series of lectures in Providence at the request of the Rhode Island AS. 24 March 1843. p.46, c6.

4999 C. L. *to* **GARRISON. 7 March 1843. Concord, Ma.** Discusses a voluntary political government as a practical reform. 24 March 1843. p.48, c2.

5000 LEONARD CHASE *to* **FRIEND GARRISON. n.d. n.p.** Reports on an Andover AS meeting. 31 March 1843. p.50, c5.

5001 JOHN M. SPEAR *to* **BRO. GARRISON. 23 March 1843. Weymouth.** Remarks on the meeting held at Andover on 15 March. 31 March 1843. p.50, c6.

5002 RICHARD ALLEN *to* **GARRISON. 3 February 1843. Dublin.** Describes the political situation in Ireland. 31 March 1843. p.51, c4.

5003 SOLOMON WEST *to* **THE** *TRUE WESLEYAN.* **28 February 1843. South Wilbraham.** Believes Christ's teachings oppose war, imprisonment, and capital punishment. 31 March 1843. p.52, c3.

5004 WINFIELD SCOTT *to* **T. P. ATKINSON. 9 February 1843. Washington.** Discusses the subject of domestic slavery in connection with the presidency; favors a bill to provide gradual emancipation of slaves. 7 April 1843. p.53, c2.

5005 THOMAS JONES *to* **BAILEY. n.d. n.p. [from the** *Cincinnati Philanthropist*] Reports that a free black was kidnapped in Jefferson, Indiana. 7 April 1843. p.53, c6.

5006 D. S. G. *to* **BROTHER GARRISON. n.d. Bath, Me.** Examines John McDonogh, a slaveholder who professed to be a Christian and a philanthropist. 7 April 1843. p.54, c2.

5007 STEPHEN S. HARDING *to* **WM. LLOYD GARRISON. 16 March 1843. Milan, In.** Comments on anti-slavery in the far West, where people are beginning to feel the impact of slavery. 7 April 1843. p.54, c4.

5008 RICHARD ALLEN *to* **FRIEND GARRISON. 15 October 1842. Dublin.** Remarks with sadness the pre-eminence of Christian Britain in the skill of destroying lives in war. 7 April 1843. p.55, c3.

5009 C. L. *to* **GARRISON. 27 March 1843. Concord, Ma.** Argues in favor of a voluntary political government. 7 April 1843. p.56, c2.

5010 H. C. WRIGHT *to* **GARRISON. [extract] 27 February 1843. Manchester.** Describes his travels in England. 7 April 1843. p.56, c3.

5011 J. M. F. *to* **GARRISON. 27 March 1843. West Brookfield.** Reviews the case of Deacon Henshaw. 7 April 1843. p.56, c4.

5012 D. S. GRANDIN *to* **RICHARD YEADON. 1 April 1843. Brunswick.** Replies to Yeadon's characterization of slavery as paternalistic in letter to Dionysius Lardner. 14 April 1843. p.58, c3.

5013 PRENTICE H. EVANS *to* **BROTHER GARRISON. 20 March 1843. Angola, In.** Decries dormant anti-slavery feelings in Indiana. 14 April 1843. p.58, c4.

5014 L. S. I. *to* **BROTHER GARRISON. 2 February 1843. Delaware County, Pa.** Admonishes prominent Massachusetts abolitionists for lack of efforts to encourage the labor of freemen rather than that of slaves. 14 April 1843. p.58, c5.

5015 DAVID L. CHILD *to* **FRIEND GARRISON. 7 April 1843. Washington.** Reports on the refusal of the United States to suppress the slave trade. 14 April 1843. p.59, c3.

5016 J. A. COLLINS *to* **GARRISON. 10 April 1843. Lowell.** Complains of conflicting schedules of anti-slavery and social reform meetings. 14 April 1843. p.59, c4.

5017 GERRIT SMITH *to* **BRO. GARRISON. 11 April 1843. Peterboro'.** Informs Garrison of an error in the *Liberator*. 21 April 1843. p.62, c5.

5018 H. *to* **WM. LLOYD GARRISON. 11 February 1843. Syracuse.** Argues against the use of the term "colored person"; favors "Negro" as more respectable. 21 April 1843. p.62, c5.

5019 AMASA WALKER *to* **FRANCIS JACKSON. 13 March 1843. Oberlin.** Sends a twenty-five dollar contribution to the *Liberator*. 21 April 1843. p.63, c5.

5020 DANIEL O'CONNELL *to* **MR. BARRETT. 23 March 1843. Marrion Square.** Denies having corresponded with the editor of the *Baltimore Hibernian Advocate* or with any other American editor. 28 April 1843. p.65, c6.

5021 MARCUS MORTON *to* **GOV. JAMES M'DOWELL. 10 March 1843. Boston.** Comments on extradition in the Latimer case. 18 April 1843. p.65, c6.

5022 GERRIT SMITH *to* **DANIEL O'CONNELL. 2 July 1842. Peterboro'.** Criticizes O'Connell for discouraging abolitionists by no longer participating in the movement. 28 April 1843. p.66, c4.

5023 WILLIAM COMSTOCK *to* **NEIGHBOR GARRISON. n.d. n.p.** Denounces Daniel O'Connell for holding a Catholic view of observing the Sabbath. 28 April 1843. p.66, c5.

5024 HENRY C. WRIGHT *to* **GARRISON. 26 March 1843. Manchester.** Witnesses growth of anti-war sentiment in England. 28 April 1843. p.66, c5.

5025 JABEZ P. CAMPBELL *to* **FRIEND GARRISON. 18 April 1843. Providence.** Reports that he was forced into the "Jim Crow" car of a train. 28 April 1843. p.66, c6.

5026 C. LENOX REMOND *to* **FRIEND GARRISON. 25 April 1843. Salem.** Advocates anti-discrimination petitions to oppose discriminatory practices of the Eastern Railroad. 28 April 1843. p.67, c4.

5027 R. D. MADDEN *to* **GARRISON. 3 March 1843. Chelsea.** Laments apathy toward the anti-slavery cause in England. 28 April 1843. p.67, c4.

5028 J. A. COLLINS *to* **GARRISON. 24 April 1843. Boston.** Asserts that a property convention held recently in Worcester won over many who were at first hostile to their sentiments. 28 April 1843. p.67, c4.

5029 C. L. *to* **GARRISON. 17 April 1843. Concord, Ma.** Criticizes the present system of government; advocates voluntary associations to control education and "all establishments of a moral nature." 28 April 1843. p.68, c2.

5030 JAMES HAUGHTON *to* **THE EDITOR OF THE** *DUBLIN EVENING POST*. **25 March 1843. n.p.** Encourages "moral interference" on the issue of American slavery. 5 May 1843. p.69, c2.

5031 ABBY KELLEY *to* **THE** *NATIONAL ANTI-SLAVERY STANDARD*. **10 April 1843. Exeter, N.Y.** Describes anti-slavery in the Empire State. 5 May 1843. p.69, c3.

5032 H. C. WRIGHT *to* **GARRISON. 18 March 1843. Manchester.** Gives account of his speaking tour in England. 5 May 1843. p.70, c1.

5033 ELIZABETH PEASE *to* **GARRISON. 24 March 1843. Darlington, England.** Expresses concern for the health of H. C. Wright; reports on the Manchester Peace Society. 5 May 1843. p.70, c2.

5034 H. H. BRIGHAM *to* **WM. L. GARRISON. 22 April 1843. Abington.** Reports on the quarterly meeting of the Plymouth County AS. 5 May 1843. p.70, c3.

5035 LUTHER BOUTELLE *to* **BRO. GARRISON. 17 April 1843. Groton.** Believes that the Second Advent will destroy slavery. 5 May 1843. p.70, c5.

5036 W. O. DUVALL *to* **GARRISON. 14 April 1843. Port Byron, N.Y.** Observes that anti-slavery sentiment is on the wane in Port Byron. 5 May 1843. p.70, c5.

5037 G. W. *to* **FRIEND GARRISON. n.d. n.p.** Decries hypocritical ministers involved in anti-slavery in Lowell. 5 May 1843. p.70, c6.

5038 JAMES H. SWETT *to* **BRO. GARRISON. 28 March 1842. Salem Jail.** Condemns the clergy for supporting the slave system. 5 May 1843. p.70, c6.

5039 GERRIT SMITH *to* **WM. LLOYD GARRISON. 28 April 1843. Peterboro'.** Demands fair representation of his views in the columns of the *Liberator*. 5 May 1843. p.71, c2.

5040 NELSON BOSTWICK *to* **GARRISON. 19 February 1843. Rochester.** Submits a letter from S. Stanley for publication in the *Liberator*. 5 May 1843. p.72, c2.

5041 S. STANLEY *to* **FRIEND. 13 February 1843. Leroy.** Defends himself against complaints that he has pursued a course contrary to the advice of his friends, and retired to the humble condition of manufacturing washing machines since his suspension from the Presbytery. 5 May 1843. p.72, c2.

5042 NATHANIAL BRUCE *to* **REV. WOOD. 11 April 1843. Mr. Vernon.** Fears anti-slavery efforts may anger Southern churches. 12 May 1843. p.73, c3.

5043 NOAH JACKMAN *to* **BRO. GARRISON. 18 April 1843. North Attleboro.** Charges that the Baptist Church in North Attleboro sustains slavery by its connection with pro-slavery churches. 12 May 1843. p.74, c6.

5044 E. B. WORTHEN *to* **FRIEND GARRISON. 23 April 1843. Danvers.** Reports that Abner Sanger refuses to permit an anti-slavery meeting to be held in Union Hall. 12 May 1843. p.74, c6.

5045 H. W. FOSTER *to* **GARRISON. 4 May 1843. Lowell.** Notes that Frederick Douglass was present at a meeting in Lowell in April. 12 May 1843. p.75, c5.

5046 C. L. *to* **GARRISON. 4 May 1843. Concord, Ma.** Advocates voluntary political government; cites injustices of the present system. 12 May 1843. p.76, c2.

5047 SYLVANUS BROWN *to* **N. P. ROGERS. 3 April 1843. Salem Jail.** Recounts circumstances of his arrest. 19 May 1843. p.77, c2.

5048 I. C. RAY *to* **JOHN C. CALHOUN. 18 January 1843. Nantucket.** Discusses slavery and its effects on the forthcoming election. 19 May 1843.p.77, c6.

5049 AMOS H. WILLIS *to* **THE *LIBERATOR*. 18 April 1848. Freeport, Oh.** Notes hypocrisy at "protracted" meeting of the Methodists of Freeport. 19 May 1843. p.78, c1.

5050 EDWARD SEARCH *to* **FRIEND GARRISON. 28 April 1843. London.** Shares conviction that a "compact between North and South is a 'covenant with death—an agreement with Hell.' " 19 May 1843. p.78, c6.

5051 GERRIT SMITH *to* **WILLIAM LLOYD GARRISON. 8 May 1843. Peterboro'.** Explains his belief that abolitionists cannot be members of pro-slavery parties. 19 May 1843. p.79, c2.

5052 SYDNEY HOWARD GAY *to* **W. L. GARRISON. 22 May 1843. Hingham.** Reports that the Connecticut AS was unable to obtain a place of assembly. 26 May 1843. p.82, c4.

5053 GEORGE L. HARDING *to* **WM. LLOYD GARRISON. 10 May 1843. Milan, In.** Corrects an error; lauds judicial courage in sentencing the kidnapper of a runaway. 26 May 1843. p.82, c6.

5054 ELIZABETH PEASE *to* **GARRISON. 1 May 1843. Darlington.** Awaits arrival of H. C. Wright; notes that the Chartist movement supports women's rights. 26 May 1843. p.83, c4.

5055 C. L. *to* **GARRISON. 17 May 1843. Concord, Ma.** Opposes prisons as breeders of crime. 26 May 1843. p.84, c2.

5056 L. N. RANSOM *to* **BROTHER GARRISON. April 1843. Springfield, Il.** Fears growth of pro-slavery sentiment in Illinois. 26 May 1843. p.84, c4.

5057 JOSEPH STURGE *to* **THE EDITORS OF THE** *GLASGOW FRIEND.* **n.d. n.p.** Cautions readers on the Society of Friends in the United States who adhere to colonization and condemn anti-slavery. 2 June 1843. p.87, c5.

5058 H. C. HOWELLS *to* **GARRISON. 31 March 1843. Hay Breconshire, England.** Comments on the English attitude toward slavery. 2 June 1843. p.89, c5.

5059 W. [WATSON] *to* **GARRISON. n.d. n.p.** Refutes previous letter from "E." concerning the Church's role in reform. 2 June 1843. p.89, c5.

5060 WILLIAM M'KIM *to* **GARRISON. 21 May 1843. New York.** Discusses beliefs of Menonnites of Lancaster County, Pennsylvania. 2 June 1843. p.88[90], c2.

5061 WM. C. BLOSS *to* **C. T. TORREY. 18 April 1843. Rochester.** Declines his invitation to become an agent of the *Liberator* because of its allegiance to a political party. 2 June 1843. p.88[90], c2.

5062 JAMES CANNINGS FULLER *to* **EDITOR OF** *LONDON FRIEND.* **19 April 1843. Skaneateles, N.Y.** Pleads with English Quakers to urge their American counterparts to denounce slavery. 9 June 1843. p.91, c4.

5063 LIGHT *to* **GARRISON. n.d. n.p.** Opposes the Masons and Odd Fellows. 9 June 1843. p.98[93], c4.

5064 DR. JAMES HAUGHTON *to* **THOMAS STEELE. 5 May 1843. 35 Eccles-Street.** Clarifies his earlier statement which advised against visiting slave states. 16 June 1843. p.93*, c6.

5065 BETA *to* **GARRISON. n.d. n.p.** Submits a letter from "Gamma." 16 June 1843. p.94, c5.

5066 GAMMA *to* **MR. EDITOR [W. L. GARRISON]. 3 May 1843. Boston.** Refutes reasoning of "Delta," who had argued that maintaining fellowship with sinners did not make one a sinner as well. 16 June 1843. p.94, c5.

5067 RUFUS ROCKWOOD *to* **W. L. GARRISON. 15 May 1843. Leicester, Ma.** Bemoans the lack of anti-slavery activity in the First Congregational Church in Leicester. 16 June 1843. p.94, c5.

5068 WARREN ALLEN *to* **FRIEND GARRISON AND OTHERS. 29 May 1843. Walpole.** Remonstrates with Garrison for not having corrected errors in his paper. 16 June 1843. p.94, c5.

5069 Y. *to* **MR. EDITOR [W. L. GARRISON]. n.d. n.p.** Hopes the abolitionist cause can attract those who would disagree on other issues. 16 June 1843. p.94, c6.

5070 MELITO *to* **WILLIAM LLOYD GARRISON. n.d. n.p.** Supports Garrison in his protest against the new policies of the *Christian Reflector.* 16 June 1843. p.94, c6.

5071 C. L. *to* **GARRISON. 3 June 1843. Haward, Ma.** Favors a voluntary political government based on moral rather than political strength. 16 June 1843. p.96, c2.

5072 UTICA *to* **GARRISON. 9 June 1843. Utica.** Reports on the Wesleyan Convention of seceding Methodists. 23 June 1843. p.97, c3.

5073 P.C. *to* **THE EDITOR OF THE** *BOSTON CHRISTIAN WORLD.* **26 August 1842. England.** Gives account of H. C. Wright's efforts in England. 23 June 1843. p.98, c2.

5074 BENJAMIN WYMAN *to* **BROTHER GARRISON. 15 June 1843. Westminister.** Encloses resolutions passed at anti-slavery meetings in Lunenburg. 23 June 1843. p.98, c5.

5075 D. S. GRANDIN *to* **BROTHER GARRISON. 17 June 1843. Boston.** Views the colonization movement as an "abominable deformity." 23 June 1843. p.98, c5.

5076 ELIZABETH PEASE *to* **n.n. [extract] n.d. n.p.** Expresses her admiration of Henry C. Wright. 23 June 1843. p.99, c1.

5077 H. C. WRIGHT *to* **GARRISON. 31 May 1843. Darlington.** Describes the countryside in England. 23 June 1843. p.99, c2.

5078 LEWIS FORD *to* **FRIEND GARRISON. n.d. North Abington.** Disputes Rev. Willard Pierce's contention that killing is justified in defense of another's life. 30 June 1843. p.104, c2.

5079 JOHN RANKIN *to* **DR. BAILEY. 3 June 1843. Ripley.** Urges all anti-slavery Presbyterians to withdraw from the present branches of the Presbyterian Church. 7 July 1843. p.105, c5.

5080 WM. T. ALLAN *to* **NATIONAL ANTI-SLAVERY STANDARD. 10 May 1843. Peoria, Il.** Recounts that pro-slavery is bitter in Illinois. 7 July 1843. p.105, c6.

5081 J. N. T. TUCKER *to* **GARRISON. 24 June 1843. Massachusetts.** Condemns Methodist Episcopal Church for supporting slavery. 7 July 1843. p.106, c5.

5082 RICHARD ALLEN *to* **GARRISON. 18 June 1843. Dublin.** Predicts that the abolition of slavery will take place within ten years; reports growth of anti-slavery in Ireland. 7 July 1843. p.107, c5.

5083 JONATHAN DYMOND *to* **SAMUEL J. MAY. 5 September 1834. Exeter, England.** Expresses gratitude for his condolences on the death of his son. 7 July 1843. p.108, c2.

5084 WM. WISNER *to* **THE EDITORS OF THE** *NEW YORK OBSERVER*. **23 June 1843. Ithaca, N.Y.** Denounces Rev. George Duffield, who claimed that Wisner quoted Scripture to support slavery. 14 July 1843. p.109, c1.

5085 A. J. YATES *to* **MR. S. CONVERSE. 19 March 1842. Galveston.** Proposes limitation of slavery in Texas. 14 July 1843. p.109, c6.

5086 EDWARD SEARCH *to* **FRIEND GARRISON. May 1843. London.** Discusses the Peace Convention Society. 14 July 1843. p.111, c4.

5087 JOHN M. SPEAR *to* **BROTHER GARRISON. 11 July 1842. Weymouth.** Reports the exclusion of colored people from visiting the menagerie. 14 July 1843. p.111, c5.

5088 JOHN LEVY *to* **FRIEND GARRISON. 5 July 1843. Lowell.** Reports on the Fourth of July celebration in Lowell. 21 July 1843. p.114, c5.

5089 R. *to* **GARRISON. 13 July 1843. Nantucket.** Reports results of anti-slavery convention. 21 July 1843. p.115, c3.

5090 WM. P. POWELL *to* **MR. EDITOR [W. L. GARRISON]. 14 July 1843. Boston.** Describes the murder of a slave in Petersburg, Virginia. 21 July 1843. p.115, c3.

5091 SAMUEL BOWER *to* **WILLIAM L. GARRISON. 9 July 1843. n.p.** Defines two classes of reformers, social and spiritual. 21 July 1843. p.116, c2.

5092 THOMAS CLARKSON AND RICHARD COBDEN *to* **JOSEPH PEASE, SEN. 26 June 1843. London.** Hail the end of slavery in British India. 28 July 1843. p.117, c2.

5093 WILLIAM LLOYD GARRISON *to* **THE** *LIBERATOR*. **14 July 1843. Northampton.** Describes Northampton anti-slavery efforts. 28 July 1843. p.118, c2.

5094 RICHARD D. WEBB *to* **GARRISON. 30 June 1843. Liverpool.** Gives account of his travels in England. 28 July 1843. p.118, c5.

5095 H. C. WRIGHT *to* **WILLIAM [L. GARRISON]. 30 June 1843. London.** Discusses the second World's Anti-Slavery Convention and the first World's Peace Convention. 28 July 1843. p.119, c2.

5096 F. JOHNSON *to* **MR. EDITOR [W. L. GARRISON]. 18 July 1843. Broughton Meadows, Ma.** Calls for a "national convention among free people of color" to consider topics of importance. 28 July 1843. p.119, c5.

5097 H. C. WRIGHT *to* **GARRISON. 22 April 1843. Warrington.** Notes that he has spoken in England on free trade and the repeal of corn laws. 28 July 1843. p.120, c2.

5098 FRANCIS BISHOP *to* **GARRISON. 27 April 1843. Warrington.** Reports on the fine impression made by H. C. Wright in England. 28 July 1843. p.120, c3.

5099 H. C. WRIGHT *to* **GARRISON. 24 April 1843. Rochdale.** Likens English anti-alcohol movement to American anti-slavery; everyone opposes the evil yet it increases. 28 July 1843. p.120, c3.

5100 ABBY KELLEY *to* **THE EDITOR OF THE** *LIBERTY PRESS.* **12 July 1843. Vernon.** Attacks Alvan Stewart for urging the presidents of western and central New York societies to attend the conventions planned for the summer. 4 August 1843. p.122, c1.

5101 FRANCIS JACKSON *to* **GARRISON. 22 July 1843. Boston.** Encloses a letter written by M. W. C. 4 August 1843. p.122, c5.

5102 M. W. C. [MARIA WESTON CHAPMAN] *to* **ESTEEMED FRIEND. 22 July 1843. Boston.** Expresses gratitude for his support of the cause; outlines some of the grounds on which she believes anti-slavery efforts are based. 4 August 1843. p.122, c5.

5103 W. A. WHITE *to* **FRIEND GARRISON. 20 July 1843. Utica.** Reports on the western anti-slavery conventions. 4 August 1843. p.123, c3.

5104 A. B. *to* **MR. EDITOR [W. L. GARRISON]. 17 June 1843. East Stoughton.** Compares progress of the temperance cause in Massachusetts and Washington. 4 August 1843. p.124, c2.

5105 JAMES H. LINSLEY *to* **THE EDITORS OF THE** *NEW YORK OBSERVER.* **n.d. n.p.** Seeks to remove erroneous impressions which had been made abroad respecting his course in a slavery discussion in Philadelphia. 11 August 1843. p.125, c1.

5106 SAMUEL BOWER *to* **WILLIAM LLOYD GARRISON. 31 July 1843. Harvard, Ma.** Foresees an extensive change in the social, political, and religious aspects of society. 11 August 1843. p.128, c2.

5107 SURIMSAC *to* **THE EDITORS OF THE** *BOSTON PILOT.* **19 July 1843. Norfolk, Va.** Opposes speech made by O'Connell in the South attacking slavery. 18 August 1843. p.131, c1.

5108 JOHN QUINCY ADAMS *to* **CITIZENS OF BANGOR. 4 July 1843. Quincy.** Regrets not having been able to attend the First of August celebration at Bangor. 18 August 1843. p.131, c2.

5109 HON. WM. JAY *to* **MESSRS. WALKER, STACKPOLE, AND SABINE. 15 July 1843. Bedford.** Believes West Indies emancipation has succeeded in creating a multi-racial society. 25 August 1843. p.133, c2.

5110 THOMAS CLARKSON *to* **LORD ABERDEEN. 7 July 1843. 17, New Broad-Street.** Reports that the British and Foreign AS opposes American annexation of the Republic of Texas. 25 August 1843. p.134, c1.

5111 NATH'L CROCKER, G. L. CROCKER, JOHN MAYELL, W. GOODWIN, ALFRED MAYELL, T. WRIGHTSON, WM. CRAPO, C. P. WILLIAMS, JAS. MC-CLURE, HIRAM FANNING, WM. TILLINGHAST, STEVEN PAUL, J. F. MURRAY, N. COLBURN, JR., TAPPAN TOWNSHEND, SAMUEL H. HAMMOND, J. H. TOWNSHEND, JAMES TAYLOR, WM. MAYELL, GEORGE HEPINSTALL, C. A. PUGSLEY, CHARLES T. TORREY, JEFFERSON MAYELL, NATH'L SAFFORD, SELAH BELDEN, JAMES ROYCE, GEO. VANCE, JOSEPH PLADWELL, GEO. T. HILL, HOMER MARTIN, W. A. TWEED DALE, E. P. FREEMAN, B. LATTIMORE, STEPHEN TOWNSHEND, C. HEPINSTALL, D. CHRISTIAN, E. M. TEALL, AND JOSEPH STRAIN *to* **HON. WM. JAY. 18 July 1843. Albany.** Request that he visit Albany at his convenience, for the purpose of holding a public discussion of slavery. 25 August 1843. p.134, c2.

5112 JUDGE WM. JAY *to* **E. W. GOODWIN. 31 July 1843. U. S. Hotel, Saratoga Springs.** Replies to the petition against slavery, voicing his opposition to slavery. 25 August 1843. p.134, c2.

5113 GERRIT SMITH *to* **DANIEL O'CONNELL. 28 July 1843. Peterboro'.** Explains that the reason O'Connell was receiving little money from American abolitionists is because they are poor. 25 August 1843. p.134, c4.

5114 WM. T. ALLEN *to* **BRO. GARRISON. 18 May 1843. Peoria, Il.** Son of a slaveholder lauds the *Liberator*. 25 August 1843. p.134, c5.

5115 JOHN NOYES, JR. *to* **BRO. GARRISON. 1 August 1843. Abington.** Accuses Congregational ministers of supporting theft, robbery, adultery, and murder. 25 August 1843. p.134, c5.

5116 J. R. *to* **FRIEND GARRISON. 8 August 1843. Weymouth Landing.** Opposes discrimination in transportation. 25 August 1843. p.134, c6.

5117 R. *to* **FRIEND GARRISON. 14 September 1843. Nantucket.** Reports on 1 August celebration at New Bedford. 1 September 1843. p.138, c4.

5118 SYDNEY HOWARD GAY *to* **FRIEND GARRISON. 13 August 1843. Jefferson, Oh.** Comments on the Hundred Conventions against slavery. 1 September 1843. p.139, c2.

5119 C. LENOX REMOND *to* **FRIEND GARRISON. 12 August 1843. Buffalo.** Reports on his speaking engagements with Frederick Douglass. 1 September 1843. p.139, c3.

5120 ELIZABETH PEASE *to* **FRIEND GARRISON. 30 June 1843. London.** Expresses disappointment with the World's Convention. 1 September 1843. p.139, c4.

5121 HENRY C. WRIGHT *to* **GARRISON. 26 July 1843. Liverpool.** Comments on his ill health. 1 September 1843. p.139, c5.

5122 SAMUEL BOWER *to* **WILLIAM LLOYD GARRISON. 9 August 1843. Leominster.** Expects the reform of American society to take place by moral and intellectual means rather than by force. 1 September 1843. p.140, c2.

5123 MARY CAROLINE HINKLEY *to* **MR. GARRISON. 27 July 1843. Hallowell, Me.** Describes anti-slavery in Maine. 8 September 1843. p.141, c5.

5124 E. A. MARSH *to* **n.n. 24 August 1843. Buffalo.** Describes proceedings of the 15 August National Convention of Colored Men in Buffalo. 8 September 1843. p.142, c1.

5125 WM. P. POWELL *to* **[W. L. GARRISON]. n.d. n.p.** Gives account of the arrival of two fugitives in Gotham. 8 September 1843. p.142, c3.

5126 AMASA WALKER *to* **FRIEND GARRISON. 9 August 1843. Dublin.** Reports on growth of the repeal movement in Ireland. 8 September 1843. p.143, c3.

5127 H. C. HOWELLS *to* **BRO GARRISON. 15 July 1843. Hay Breconshire, England.** Forwards account of the anti-slavery and peace conventions held in London. 8 September 1843. p.143, c3.

5128 ROGERS *to* **J. R. F. 11 August 1843. Northampton.** Describes Northampton. 8 September 1843. p.144, c2.

5129 NATHANIEL RARNEY *to* **THE** *NATIONAL ANTI-SLAVERY STANDARD.* **20 August 1843. Nantucket.** Forwards contribution to the *National Anti-Slavery Standard.* 15 September 1843. p.146, c2.

5130 ABEL TANNER *to* **ROGERS. 11 August 1843. Bath.** Cites fraudulent practices by the pro-slavery agents in Bath. 15 September 1843. p.148, c2.

5131 WM. JACKSON *to* **GARRISON. 12 September 1843. Hubardston.** Comments on the fundamental principles which sway the destiny of the human race. 22 September 1843. p.150, c4.

5132 JESSE P. HARRIMAN *to* **BRO. GARRISON. 3 September 1843. Danvers New Mills.** Calls for farmers and mechanics to take part in the anti-slavery movement. 22 September 1843. p.150, c4.

5133 WM. A. WHITE *to* **FRIEND GARRISON. 6 September 1843. Oakland, Oh.** Contrasts AS meetings in Ohio and New York. 22 September 1843. p.151, c3.

5134 C. LENOX REMOND *to* **GARRISON. 30 August 1843. Buffalo.** Reports on large audiences which gathered to hear Frederick Douglass and himself. 22 September 1843. p.151, c4.

5135 CHARLES LANE AND A. BRONSON ALCOTT *to* **A. BROOKE. August 1843. Harvard, Ma.** Advocate vegetarian diet and abstinence from alcohol. 22 September 1843. p.152, c2.

5136 WM. LLOYD GARRISON *to* **THE** *LIBERATOR.* **17 September 1843. Northampton.** Explains his absence from his editorial chair due to his wife's accident. 29 September 1843. p.154, c5.

5137 SAMUEL MAY, JR. *to* **FRIEND GARRISON. 26 August 1843. Dublin.** Reports rise of anti-slavery sentiment in Ireland. [partially illegible] 6 October 1843. p.159, c2.

5138 WM. HENRY BRISBANE *to* **FRIEND GARRISON. 7 September 1843. Cheviot, Oh.** Commends Garrison for his devotion to the cause of anti-slavery. 6 October 1843. p.159, c3.

5139 ELIJAH RICHMOND *to* **GARRISON. 11 September 1843. Abington, Ma.** Claims the clergy has opposed every attempt to reform and improve the condition of the people. [mostly illegible] 13 October 1843. p.161, c5.

5140 SALEM *to* **n.n.** [illegible] 13 October 1843. p.161, c6.

5141 D. W. RUGGLES AND HENRY JOHNSON *to* **n.n. 29 August 1843.** [illegible] 13 October 1843. p.161, c6.

5142 HUMANITY *to* **EDITOR OF THE** *CLINTON* **[OHIO]** *REPUBLICAN.* **7 September 1843. Clinton County, Oh.** [illegible] 13 October 1843. p.162, c1.

5143 A. BROOKE *to* **BRO. GARRISON. 22 September 1843. Oakland, Oh.** Clarifies misrepresentations of abolitionism and the Liberty Party in Ohio. [partially illegible] 13 October 1843. p.162, c1.

5144 WILLIAM A. WHITE *to* **W. L. GARRISON. 23 September 1843. Newcastle, In.** Comments on the Hundred Conventions and the 14 September speech by Frederick Douglass at Pendleton. 13 October 1843. p.163, c3.

5145 AMASA WALKER *to* **FRIEND GARRISON. 15 September 1843. London.** Recounts his travels in Britain. 13 October 1843. p.163, c4.

5146 P. M. COMFORD *to* **GARRISON. 10 July 1843. Montego Bay, Jamaica.** Reports that Rev. Mr. Knibb will represent the Baptist Union at the forthcoming convention in Boston; requests subscription to the *Liberator*. [partially illegible] 13 October 1843. p.163, c4.

5147 J. JOSLYN *to* **THE EDITOR OF THE** *ONONDAGA STANDARD*. **16 August 1843. Cicero.** Lauds the Northampton Association, a self-sufficient community. 13 October 1843. p.164, c2.

5148 HAMMOND *to* **W. L. GARRISON. 30 September 1843. Abington.** Comments on a meeting of the Norfolk Association of Ministers and Churches. 20 October 1843. p.167, c4.

5149 WENDELL PHILLIPS *to* **FRIEND [W. L. GARRISON]. 15 October 1843. Farmington.** Suggests an abolitionist ticket for the coming elections. 20 October 1843. p.168, c1.

5150 SIDNEY HOWARD GAY *to* **W. L. GARRISON. 5 October 1843. Milan, In.** Reports on riots at abolitionist meetings. 20 October 1843. p.168, c3.

5151 WM. LLOYD GARRISON *to* **THE** *LIBERATOR*. **13 October 1843. Franklin, Ct.** Reports on his visit with Mrs. Garrison to Franklin, Connecticut to seek out the services of Dr. Sweet. 27 October 1843. p.171, c2.

5152 COMMITTEE OF EVANGELICAL CHURCH IN SHELBURNE, MA. *to* **J. R. MORSE. 7 April 1843. Shelburne.** Requests an explanation of his withdrawal from church affairs. 27 October 1843. p.172, c2.

5153 JOHN R. MORSE *to* **EVANGELICAL CHURCH OF SHELBURNE, MA. n.d. n.p.** Declares that hypocrisy in the church is his reason for leaving it. 27 October 1843. p.172, c2.

5154 JOS. T. RUCKINGHAM *to* **HON. GEO. N. BRIGGS. 17 October 1843. Boston.** Asks Briggs, the Whig candidate for governor of his state, to explain his views on slavery. 3 November 1843. p.174, c2.

5155 HON. GEO. N. BRIGGS *to* **JOS. T. RUCKINGHAM. 20 October 1843. Pittsfield.** Answers inquiries put to him relating to slavery. 3 November 1843. p.174, c2.

5156 H. *to* **MR. GARRISON. n.d. n.p.** Explains Massachusetts politics and its importance to abolitionists. 3 November 1843. p.175, c1.

5157 S. S. FOSTER *to* **GARRISON. n.d. n.p.** Comments on the National Liberty Party Convention. 3 November 1843. p.175, c1.

5158 A NEW BEDFORD ABOLITIONIST *to* **FRIEND GARRISON. 9 September 1843. New Bedford.** Urges the nomination of men who will take up the cause of human rights for the coming elections. 3 November 1843. p.175, c3.

5159 ADDISON DAVIS *to* **GARRISON. 30 October 1843. Lynn.** Questions the fraudulent transfer of editorship of the *Emancipator*. 3 November 1843. p.175, c3.

5160 JONATHAN LEONARD *to* **FRIEND GARRISON. 24 October 1843. Meriden, Ct.** Thanks Garrison for allowing the "communitymen" to introduce their questions to the readers of the *Liberator*. 3 November 1843. p.175, c4.

5161 HENRY C. WRIGHT *to* **GARRISON. 1 October 1843. Llangallen, North Wales.** Compares New England's industry, finances, and government with that of old England. 3 November 1843. p.176, c2.

5162 JAMES HAUGHTON *to* **GARRISON. 25 September 1843. Dublin.** Offers to buy a subscription to the *Liberator* for Wm. T. Allen of Peoria. 3 November 1843. p.176, c3.

5163 H. H. BRIGHAM *to* **FRIEND GARRISON. 14 October 1843. Abington.** Denies having made accusations against the church in Abington. 3 November 1843. p.176, c3.

5164 H. H. BRIGHAM *to* **REV. H. A. GRAVES. 11 September 1843. Abington.** Defends himself against charges made by the Baptist Church in Abington. 3 November 1843. p.176, c4.

5165 VINDEX *to* **THE EDITOR OF THE** *EMANCIPATOR.* **24 October 1843. n.p.** Inquires whether the Liberty Party is anti-church. 10 November 1843. p.177, c1.

5166 E. RICHMOND *to* **GARRISON. 28 October 1843. Abington.** Denounces money, trade, and "priestcraft" as systems of oppression. 10 November 1843. p.178, c2.

5167 E. W. CAPRON *to* **BRO. GARRISON. 1 November 1843. Walworth, N.Y.** Discusses the cowardice of the *Northern Advocate,* which refused to publish one of his anti-slavery letters. 10 November 1843. p.178, c2.

5168 FRANCIS JACKSON *to* **GEORGE N. BRIGGS. 10 July 1843. Boston.** Solicits Briggs's views on American slavery. 10 November 1843. p.179, c1.

5169 D. S. GRANDIN *to* **FRIEND [W. L. GARRISON]. 4 November 1843. Saccrappa, Me.** Laments the complacency of anti-slavery people in Saccrappa, Maine. 17 November 1843. p.182, c1.

5170 HAMMOND *to* **BROTHER GARRISON. 4 November 1843. Abington.** Cites inconsistency of Liberty Party in opposing two parties while participating in slave churches. 17 November 1843. p.182, c2.

5171 JAMES BOYLE *to* **BROTHER GARRISON. 2 November 1843. Northampton.** Expresses dismay with anti-slavery apathy in Connecticut. 24 November 1843. p.186, c3.

5172 B. *to* **W. L. GARRISON. 30 October 1843. Seneca Falls, N.Y.** Reports that Abby Kelley has tried to revive anti-slavery in Seneca Falls but needs assistance. 24 November 1843. p.186, c4.

5173 NATHANIEL BARNEY *to* **FRANCIS JACKSON. 10 November 1843. Nantucket.** Reports that the New Bedford and Taunton Railroad is no longer "proscriptive" in terms of abolitionist patronage. 1 December 1843. p.190, c3.

5174 AN ABOLITIONIST *to* **FRIEND GARRISON. 8 November 1843. Greenville, Ct.** Comments on the "moral tornado" caused by a speech given by Garrison in the area of Greenville, Connecticut. 1 December 1843. p.190, c3.

5175 HENRY HIGHLAND GARNET *to* **MARIA W. CHAPMAN. 17 November 1843. Troy, N.Y.** An ex-slave charges that abolitionists had been enslaving free colored persons by imposing their values on them and by not allowing them to think freely. 8 December 1843. p.193, c4.

5176 WILLIAM JAY *to* **GERRIT SMITH. 20–21 October 1843. Bedford.** En route to Egypt; states he favors dissolution of the Union if Texas is to be annexed. 8 December 1843. p.193, c5.

5177 MILO A. TOWNSEND *to* **GARRISON. 10 November 1843. New Brighton, Pa.** Gives account of lecture by Frederick Douglass on "prejudice against color." 8 December 1843. p.194, c3.

5178 WILLIAM LLOYD GARRISON *to* **DANIEL O'CONNELL. n.d. n.p.** Contends that O'Connell had no sound basis for the attacks he made on Garrison at a meeting in Ireland. 8 December 1843. p.194, c6.

5179 SAMUEL BOWER *to* **WILLIAM LLOYD GARRISON. 9 October 1843. North Chelmsford, Ma.** Outlines a scheme of government in accordance with the principles of liberty in the American Constitution. 8 December 1843. p.196, c2.

5180 E. W. CAPRON *to* **THE EDITOR OF THE** *LIBERATOR* **[W. L. GARRISON]. 20 November 1843. Walworth, N.Y.** Criticizes the Society of Odd Fellows. 8 December 1843. p.196, c3.

5181 L. D. Y. *to* **FRIEND GARRISON. 30 November 1843. Providence.** Reports that the despised Dr. Lardner of Providence is accused of adultery. 8 December 1843. p.196, c3.

5182 C. M. CLAY *to* **THE EDITOR OF THE** *NEW YORK TRIBUNE.* **November 1843. Lexington, Ky.** Describes slavery, the evil and the remedy; favors voluntary emancipation. 15 December 1843. p.198, c1.

5183 RICHARD ALLEN *to* **GARRISON. 18 November 1843. Dublin.** Reports that H. C. Wright is in good health in Ireland. 15 December 1843. p.198, c5.

5184 C. *to* **GARRISON. n.d. n.p.** Attacks the unwillingness of the clergy to speak out on slavery. 15 December 1843. p.200, c2.

5185 W. *to* **THE EDITOR OF THE** *BOSTON CHRISTIAN WATCHMAN.* **31 October 1843. Dedham.** Ridicules a parade held in honor of the ex-president. 22 December 1843. p.201, c1.

5186 F. *to* **THE EDITOR OF THE** *MASSACHUSETTS SPY.* **n.d. n.p.** Comments on the two classes of Irish repeal advocates. 22 December 1843. p.201, c6.

5187 E. D. HUDSON *to* **FRIEND GARRISON. November 1843. Northampton.** Finds hypocrisy at Middletown Ecclesiastical Convention amusing. 22 December 1843. p.202, c3.

5188 THOMAS HILL *to* **FRIEND GARRISON. 3 December 1843. Northampton.** Describes anti-slavery meetings in Northampton. 22 December 1843. p.202, c4.

5189 GEORGE THOMPSON *to* **THE GLASGOW EMANCIPATION SOCIETY. 8 August 1843. Delhi.** Reports that his labors are not wholly without fruit; notes repeal of a law on registration. 29 December 1843. p.205, c3.

5190 GEORGE THOMPSON *to* **THE GLASGOW EMANCIPATION SOCIETY. 10 August 1843. Begum's Palace, Delhi.** Describes his impressions of Delhi; reports that he has been appointed by the Landholder's Society of Calcutta to be their agent in England. 29 December 1843. p.205, c4.

5191 GEORGE THOMPSON *to* **THE GLASGOW EMANCIPATION SOCIETY. 12 August 1843. Delhi.** Describes his audience with His Majesty the King at the Court of Mogul. 29 December 1843. p.205, c5.

5192 GEORGE THOMPSON *to* **THE GLASGOW EMANCIPATION SOCIETY. 16 August 1843. Delhi.** Notes that H. C. Wright's peace lectures and recent numbers of the *British Friend* have arrived, and that he has discussed abolition with the American missionary in Delhi. 29 December 1843. p.205, c6.

5193 PARKER PILLSBURY *to* **FRIEND ROGERS. n.d. n.p.** Objects to the transfer of the editorship of the *Emancipator*. 29 December 1843. p.206, c1.

5194 AN OLD SUBSCRIBER *to* **MR. EDITOR [W. L. GARRISON]. n.d. n.p.** Criticizes the middle-of-the-road course of the *Christian Reflector*. 29 December 1843. p.206, c3.

5195 R. *to* **FRIEND GARRISON. 19 December 1843. New Bedford.** Lauds lectures by Charles C. Burleigh in New Bedford. 29 December 1843. p.206, c3.

5196 C. LENOX REMOND *to* **FRIEND GARRISON. 24 December 1843. Salem.** Reports that Frederick Douglass was expected to attend the next meeting in Essex. 29 December 1843. p.107[207], c5.

5197 ROBERT F. WALLCUT *to* **JOSEPH A. DAVIS. 29 November 1843. Boston.** Discusses ideals of brotherhood and equality. 29 December 1843. p.208, c3.

[1844]

5198 J. C. MARTIN *to* **FRIEND GARRISON. 17 December 1843. Chaplin, Ct.** Agrees with James Boyle that Connecticut is "heathenish, inhuman and priest-ridden." 5 January 1844. p.2, c5.

5199 J. BAILEY *to* **FRIEND GARRISON. 24 December 1843. New Bedford.** Reports on the lectures of C. C. Burleigh. 12 January 1844. p.5, c2.

5200 COMMITTEE OF PEWHOLDERS *to* **J. F. EMERSON AND WM. C. COFFIN. 8 December 1843. New Bedford.** Enumerates reasons for not permitting an anti-slavery meeting to be held in the church. 12 January 1844. p.5, c2.

5201 WM. LLOYD GARRISON *to* **THE *LIBERATOR*. 8 January 1844. Milford, N.H.** Observes strongest New Hampshire anti-slavery sentiments in Milford. 12 January 1844. p.6, c5.

5202 AMASA WALKER *to* **WILLIAM LLOYD GARRISON. 29 December 1843. North Brookfield.** Notes the health of Henry C. Wright is improving. 12 January 1844. p.7, c5.

5203 A. K. *to* **FRIEND GARRISON. n.d. Russellville, Pa.** Complains that the *Standard* will not print his letters. 12 January 1844. p.7, c5.

5204 SAMUEL BOWER *to* **WM. LLOYD GARRISON. 31 December 1843. Boston.** Proposes abolition of private property as a social reform. 12 January 1844. p.8, c4.

5205 SAMUEL SELLERS, JR. *to* **GARRISON. 26 December 1843. Delaware County, Pa.** Describes a series of meetings held in Pennsylvania and Delaware to promote social reorganization. 12 January 1844. p.8, c4.

5206 HON. WM. SLADE *to* **n.n. [extract] n.d. Middlebury, Vt.** Justifies his use of the franking privilege for any publication—in this case, an address by Dr. Lafon—which he considers to contain valuable information. 19 January 1844. p.10, c2.

5207 HON. SETH M. GATES *to* **SIR. 16 November 1843. Warsaw, N.Y.** Approves of Dr. Lafon's address condemning immorality of missionaries abroad. 19 January 1844. p.10, c2.

5208 MARY P. KENNY *to* **WM. LLOYD GARRISON. 9 January 1844. Salem.** Notes disappointment of the Essex County AS in Frederick Douglass' failure to appear on 5 January. 19 January 1844. p.10, c5.

5209 WM. LLOYD GARRISON *to* **THE** *LIBERATOR.* **15 January 1844. New Ipswich, N.H.** Reports on his lecture tour. 19 January 1844. p.11, c1.

5210 S. H. GAY *to* **THE EDITOR OF THE** *LIBERATOR* **[W. L. GARRISON]. n.d. n.p.** Reports on the Hundred Conventions against slavery. 19 January 1844. p.11, c2.

5211 SAMUEL BOWER *to* **MR. GARRISON. 13 January 1844. Boston.** Corrects a mistake which occurred in his last letter. 19 January 1844. p.11, c5.

5212 SYRACUSE CONVENTION *to* **ARTHUR O'NEIL. n.d. n.p.** Admires him for exemplifying the doctrine he taught. 19 January 1844. p.12, c2.

5213 ABBY KELLEY *to* **THE** *NATIONAL ANTI-SLAVERY STANDARD.* **2 January 1844. Utica.** Corrects an error which appeared in the *Liberty Press.* 26 January 1844. p.14, c3.

5214 EDWARD SEARCH *to* **GARRISON. 7 December 1843. Muswell Hill, England.** Comments on the aristocratic principles at work in England. 26 January 1844. p.14, c5.

5215 EDWARD SEARCH *to* **GARRISON. 7 December 1843. Muswell Hill, England.** Compliments American women involved in the cause of anti-slavery. 26 January 1844. p.14, c6.

5216 EDWARD SEARCH *to* **GARRISON. 7 December 1843. Muswell Hill, England.** Foresees abolition of the Corn Laws. 26 January 1844. p.15, c1.

5217 RICHARD ALLEN *to* **GARRISON. 17 December 1843. Dublin.** Reports on H. C. Wright's health; regrets apathetic view of his "unfortunate countrymen" toward slavery. 26 January 1844. p.15, c2.

5218 S. H. GAY *to* **THE EDITOR OF THE** *LIBERATOR* **[W. L. GARRISON]. [continued from 19 January 1844] n.d. n.p.** Reports on the Hundred Conventions. 26 January 1844. p.15, c5.

5219 C. P. WILLIAMS *to* **JAMES C. JACKSON. n.d. n.p.** Questions whether John Quincy Adams was disclaimed by the abolitionists. 2 February 1844. p.17, c1.

5220 JAMES C. JACKSON *to* **C. P. WILLIAMS. 11 January 1844. Utica.** Declares that John Quincy Adams was not disclaimed by the abolitionists. 2 February 1844. p.17, c1.

5221 JOHN F. A. CALDER *to* **THE EDITOR OF THE** *LIBERATOR* **[W. L. GARRISON]. n.d. n.p.** Relates his ill treatment and eventual imprisonment as an abolitionist for having revived a drowned Negro man. 2 February 1844. p.18, c1.

5222 C. GLADDING *to* **GARRISON. n.d. n.p.** Forwards account of the Upton Anti-Slavery Fair. 2 February 1844. p.18, c3.

5223 ELIZABETH PEASE *to* **FRIEND GARRISON. 28 December 1843. Darlington.** Observes that peace advocates are carefully scrutinized for their theological beliefs. 2 February 1844. p.20, c2.

5224 H. H. KELLOGG *to* **REV. H. C. WRIGHT. 4 December 1843. Edinburgh.** Wishes to know Wright's views on certain topics discussed in a preceding letter. 2 February 1844. p.20, c2.

5225 H. C. WRIGHT *to* **HIRAM H. KELLOGG. 9 December 1843. Dublin.** Presents views on the scheme of man's redemption by Christ. 2 February 1844. p.20, c2.

5226 H. H. KELLOGG *to* **BROTHER WRIGHT. 14 December 1843. Edinburgh.** Supports the death penalty for murder. 2 February 1844. p.20, c3.

5227 CHARLES SPEAR *to* **GARRISON. n.d. n.p.** Reports that he had begun teaching Sunday school in the prison near his town. 2 February 1844. p.20, c4.

5228 RICHARD D. WEBB *to* **GARRISON. 31 December 1843. Dublin.** Notes poor health of H. C. Wright; suggests the cold water cure. 9 February 1844. p.21, c5.

5229 HENRY C. WRIGHT *to* **AMASA WALKER. 17 December 1843. Dublin.** Discusses the justification of military power. 9 February 1844. p.22, c2.

5230 C. A. WHEATON *to* **GARRISON. 5 January 1844. Syracuse.** Pleads for reconciliation of the old and new school abolitionists. 9 February 1844. p.22, c3.

5231 SARAH D. FISH *to* **FRIEND GARRISON. 11 January 1844. Rochester.** Contends that the party spirit of abolitionists is poor. 9 February 1844. p.22, c4.

5232 LEWIS FORD *to* **BROTHER GARRISON. 21 January 1844. Abington.** Reports that Lunsford Lane, a fugitive, was denied access to the pulpit at the North Church. 9 February 1844. p.24, c2.

5233 JAMES MCCUNE SMITH *to* **REV. ORVILLE DEWEY, D.D. 11 January 1844. New York.** Attacks a statement made by Rev. Dewey regarding the condition of free colored people in relation to slaves; contends that slaves are more wretched than the freemen. 16 February 1844. p.25, c3.

5234 NOAH JACKMAN *to* **GARRISON. 6 February 1844. North Attleboro, Ma.** Gives account of a three-day meeting at North Attleboro. 16 February 1844. p.25, c4.

5235 n.n. *to* **REV. ORVILLE DEWEY. 29 January 1844. New Bedford.** Expresses disappointment over a speech made by Dewey. 16 February 1844. p.25, c6.

5236 PHILO C. PETTIBONE *to* **GARRISON. February 1844. n.p.** Discusses non-fellowship with pro-slavery bodies. 16 February 1844. p.26, c2.

5237 GEO. W. STACY *to* **W. L. GARRISON. 6 February 1844. Milford, Hopedale.** Reports that the citizens of Milford were aroused by the lectures of anti-slavery agents; Frederick Douglass was one of those who spoke there. 16 February 1844. p.26, c2.

5238 H. M. *to* **MR. GARRISON. 11 February 1844. Concord, Ma.** Reports that Concord had been stirred by the lectures of Phillips and Burleigh. 16 February 1844. p.26, c3.

5239 D. S. GRANDIN *to* **BROTHER GARRISON. n.d. n.p.** Regrets not having been able to attend a meeting of the Massachusetts AS. 16 February 1844. p.26, c4.

5240 C. M. BURLEIGH *to* **BROTHER GARRISON. 6 February 1844. Killingly, Ct.** Reports on an anti-slavery meeting in Windham County. 16 February 1844. p.26, c4.

5241 D. P. LIVERMORE *to* **MR. GARRISON. n.d. Duxbury, Ma.** Alleges that John Tyler is a slave owner. 16 February 1844. p.26, c4.

5242 C. M. BURLEIGH *to* **ABEL BROWN. 6 February 1844. Kilingly, Ct.** Requests that Brown supply evidence for statements he had made concerning slaveholding Baptist missionaries. 16 February 1844. p.26, c5.

5243 n.n. *to* **BRO. GARRISON. 19 January 1844. Newburyport.** States that members of the Newburyport Women's AS were disappointed that several members did not appear for their 3 January meeting. 16 February 1844. p.26, c5.

5244 D. L. C. *to* **THE** *NATIONAL ANTI-SLAVERY STANDARD.* **27 January 1844. Boston.** Reports the proceedings of the eleventh annual meeting of the Massachusetts AS. 16 February 1844. p.16, c5.

5245 S. W. W. *to* **THE EDITOR OF THE** *PROVIDENCE HERALD.* **n.d. n.p.** Reports that a statute forbidding any "black or colored unmarried woman" to charge a white man with begetting her with child narrowly escaped re-enactment by the state legislature; lists representatives who favored re-enactment. 23 February 1844. p.30, c1.

5246 n.n. *to* **REV. ORVILLE DEWEY. 4 February 1844. n.p.** Attacks Dewey's "Tabernacle speech" for upholding the favorable condition of slaves in relation to freemen. 23 February 1844. p.30, c4.

5247 J. C. R. *to* **FRIEND GARRISON. 17 February 1844. New Bedford.** Remarks on the speech of Cassius M. Clay against the annexation of Texas. 23 February 1844. p.30, c6.

5248 D. L. CHILD *to* **GARRISON. 16 February 1844. Washington.** Describes congressional debate on slavery. 23 February 1844. p.31, c2.

5249 GEO. THOMPSON *to* **SECRETARY OF THE GLASGOW EMANCIPATION SOCIETY. 21 September 1843. Delhi.** Foresees the advent of important political changes in India. 1 March 1844. p.33, c2.

5250 GEO. THOMPSON *to* **A SECRETARY OF THE GLASGOW EMANCIPATION SOCIETY. 13 October 1843. Begum's Palace, Delhi.** Reports on his travels in India. 1 March 1844. p.33, c2.

5251 A FRIEND *to* **THE EDITOR OF THE** *LIBERATOR* **[W. L. GARRISON]. n.d. n.p.** Reports on slavery in British Guiana. 1 March 1844. p.33, c4.

5252 WM. HENRY BRISBANE *to* **MR. EDITOR. n.d. n.p.** Favors the old anti-slavery organizations over the new. 1 March 1844. p.33, c5.

5253 ABEL BROWN *to* **REV. BENJAMIN M. HILL. 19 February 1844. Albany.** Names slaveholding Baptist missionaries. 1 March 1844. p.33, c6.

5254 CASSIUS M. CLAY *to* **ELIHU BURRITT. 30 January 1844. Lexington, Ky.** Attributes New England philanthropy to the spirit of the Pilgrim forefathers. 1 March 1844. p.34, c5.

5255 MARY A. MARTIN *to* **W. L. GARRISON. 29 January 1844. Woolwich, England.** Discusses her views of religion and non-resistance; mentions her meeting with H. C. Wright. 1 March 1844. p.35, c3.

5256 M. *to* **MR. GARRISON. n.d. n.p.** Expresses disappointment with Mr. Phelps' speech in favor of the gallows. 1 March 1844. p.36, c2.

5257 W. B. *to* **THE EDITOR OF THE** *BOSTON CHRISTIAN WORLD.* **n.d. n.p.** Resents the proposed Military Ball, viewed as another attempt to keep alive the military spirit among Bostonians. 1 March 1844. p.36, c5.

5258 J. E. SNODGRASS *to* **DR. BRISBANE. 19 February 1844. Baltimore.** Favors the purchase of slaves in order to relocate and free them. 8 March 1844. p.37, c5.

5259 WM. HENRY BRISBANE *to* **DR. SNODGRASS. 20 February 1844. Baltimore.** A former slave-holder turns to Christ. 8 March 1844. p.37, c5.

5260 DAVID LEE CHILD *to* **GARRISON. 25 February 1844. Washington.** Reviews parliamentary steps used to avoid a vote on slavery. 8 March 1844. p.39, c2.

5261 DAVID LEE CHILD *to* **GARRISON. 2 March 1844. Washington.** Reports on congressional debate on war over Oregon and the annexation of Texas. 8 March 1844. p.39, c2.

5262 W. A. W. *to* **GARRISON. 1 March 1844. Watertown.** Reports proceedings from the convention at Reading. 8 March 1844. p.39, c4.

5263 N. *to* **THE EDITOR OF THE** *MASSACHUSETTS SPY.* **n.d. n.p.** Laments the withholding of religious books from prisons. 8 March 1844. p.40, c2.

5264 SYDNEY HOWARD GAY *to* **GARRISON. 5 March 1844. No. Brookfield.** Gives account of Worcester County convention at Waterford. 15 March 1844. p.42, c2.

5265 FREDERICK DOUGLASS *to* **FRIEND GARRISON. 6 March 1844. Sudbury.** Notes that he has spoken at conventions in Middlesex County. 15 March 1844. p.42, c4.

5266 L. H. *to* **MR. GARRISON. 10 March 1844. Bedford.** Reports on convention at Bedford held in March; notes Frederick Douglass was present. 15 March 1844. p.42, c5.

5267 ELIAB W. CAPRON *to* **FARMINGTON MONTHLY MEETING OF FRIENDS. 20 February 1844. Walworth.** Renounces membership in the Society of Friends because of the slavery issue. 15 March 1844. p.42, c6.

5268 PARKER PILLSBURY *to* **FRIEND GARRISON. 12 March 1844. Medford.** Gives account of conventions at Medford; notes that Frederick Douglass was present on 11 March. 15 March 1844. p.42, c6.

5269 D. L. C. *to* **GARRISON. 9 March 1844. Washington.** Discusses the treaty with Britain and the fixing of a date for choosing Presidential electors. 15 March 1844. p.43, c3.

5270 ELIZUR WRIGHT, JR. *to* **HENRY B. STANTON. 12 October 1839. Dorchester.** Favors a union between the Liberty Party and the new anti-slavery organization. 15 March 1844. p.43, c5.

5271 A LOOKER ON *to* **GARRISON. n.d. n.p.** Criticizes the "bold stand" which Mr. Phelps and others have taken in support of the gallows. 15 March 1844. p.44, c2.

5272 DRACO *to* **EDITOR OF THE** *NEW YORK TRIBUNE.* **n.d. n.p.** Suggests that the management and efficiency of the gallows could be improved by appointing clergymen as hangmen and holding executions in churches. 15 March 1844. p.44, c2.

5273 DANIEL WEBSTER *to* **CITIZENS OF WORCESTER COUNTY. 23 January 1844. Washington.** Opposes the annexation of Texas by the United States. 22 March 1844. p.45, c2.

5274 S. H. GAY *to* **GARRISON. 12 March 1844. Lancaster.** Details proceedings of a convention at Braintree. 22 March 1844. p.46, c3.

5275 H. HOBART BRIGHAM *to* **FRIEND GARRISON. 7 March 1844. Abington.** Sends proceedings from a convention in Abington which was part of the One Hundred Conventions campaign. 22 March 1844. p.46, c4.

5276 T. *to* **GARRISON. n.d. n.p.** Ridicules a clerical defense of the gallows. 22 March 1844. p.48, c2.

5277 J. M. F. *to* **WILLIAM L. GARRISON. 13 March 1844. West Brookfield.** Condemns the arrogance of the Rev. Mr. Packard of Spencer who attempted to refute statements which had been made by abolitionists. 29 March 1844. p.49, c4.

5278 C. LENOX REMOND *to* **MEMBERS AND FRIENDS OF THE MASSACHUETTS AS. 20 March 1844. Salem.** Reports on anti-slavery conventions in Plymouth and Bristol counties. 29 March 1844. p.50, c2.

5279 EDWARD SEARCH *to* **WM. LLOYD GARRISON. February 1844. Muswell Hill, England.** Comments on the One Hundred Conventions campaign, O'Connell, and the Corn Laws. 29 March 1844. p.50, c3.

5280 C. A. B. *to* **GARRISON. n.d. n.p.** Finds marriage an enslavement. 29 March 1844. p.52, c2.

5281 A LISTENER *to* **GARRISON. n.d. n.p.** Differentiates between pain and injury in the philosophy of non-resistance. 29 March 1844. p.52, c2.

5282 CASSIUS M. CLAY *to* **W. J. MCKINNEY, MAYOR OF DAYTON, OHIO. 20 March 1844. Lexington, Ky.** Explains why he planned to vote for Henry Clay for president. 5 April 1844. p.53, c2.

5283 JAMES HAUGHTON *to* **FRIEND GARRISON. 23 February 1844. Dublin.** Contradicts Rev. Dewey; finds the terms "Unitarian" and "pro-slavery" incongruous. 5 April 1844. p.54, c1.

5284 HENRY C. WRIGHT *to* **GARRISON. 25 December 1843. Dublin.** Reports growth of repeal efforts in Ireland. 5 April 1844. p.54, c3.

5285 SYDNEY HOWARD GAY *to* **FRIEND GARRISON. n.d. n.p.** Reports on an anti-slavery convention at Oxford, Ohio. 5 April 1844. p.54, c4.

5286 DAVID L. CHILD *to* **GARRISON. 31 March 1844. Washington.** Reports congressional debate on annexation of Texas. 5 April 1844. p.55, c1.

5287 A LISTENER *to* **MR. GARRISON. n.d. n.p.** Praises Wendell Phillips and John Pierpont for their eloquence and competence as demonstrated at a lecture on the topic of the annexation of Texas. 5 April 1844. p.55, c3.

5288 SAMUEL BOWER *to* **FRIEND GARRISON. 21 February 1844. Boston.** Supports "sacred socialism" as antecedent to reform. 5 April 1844. p.56, c2.

5289 H. C. WRIGHT *to* **GARRISON. 25 December 1843. Hull.** Relays decision of Methodist churches to forbid teetotalist meetings. 12 April 1844. p.57, c1.

5290 H. C. WRIGHT *to* **GARRISON. 30 December 1843. Hamburg.** Comments on German militarism, market places, and wine drinking in Hamburg. 12 April 1844. p.57, c1.

5291 H. C. WRIGHT *to* **GARRISON. 1 January 1844. Stadt Hamburg, Elbe.** Sends New Year's greetings. 12 April 1844. p.57, c2.

5292 JOHN M. SPEAR *to* **REV. MARK STAPLES. 3 April 1844. Weymouth.** Applauds AS conventions held throughout the state of Massachusetts. 12 April 1844. p.58, c5.

5293 HIRAM W. BLANCHARD *to* **REV. MARK STAPLES. 26 March 1844. Neponset Village.** Discusses extraneous points raised by Staples to discredit some of the anti-slavery men; adds that Staples' speech, which denounced the institution of slavery, was presented in response to a lecture by Frederick Douglass noting the pro-slavery character of the Methodist church. 12 April 1844. p.58, c5.

5294 HENRY C. WRIGHT *to* **GARRISON. 12 January 1844. Magdeburg.** Describes travels in Germany en route to Austria. 19 April 1844. p.61, c2.

5295 L. B. T. *to* **THE GOVERNOR OF SOUTH CAROLINA. 7 April 1844. Waltham.** Appeals for a reconsideration of the laws concerning slavery. 19 April 1844. p.62, c1.

5296 D. *to* **GARRISON. 24 March 1844. Hallowell, Me.** Describes the case of John L. Brown, a free citizen sentenced to death for aiding a female slave's escape; forwards resolutions of indignation adopted by citizens of Hallowell. 19 April 1844. p.62, c2.

5297 D. S. GODFREY and C. K. SCRIBNER *to* **GARRISON. 8 April 1844. Milford.** Challenge Garrisonians to a debate between one of them and a representative from the Liberty Party. 19 April 1844. p.62, c2.

5298 J. TAYLOR *to* **W. L. GARRISON. 31 March 1844. Walpole.** Notes interest in anti-slavery in Walpole; reports that Frederick Douglass spoke there on 24 March. 19 April 1844. p.62, c5.

5299 CITIZENS OF ABINGTON *to* **FRIEND GARRISON. 10 April 1844. Abington.** Encourage fasting to protest slavery; enclose contribution to *Liberator*. 19 April 1844. p.62, c5.

5300 EXECUTIVE COMMITTEE OF THE AMERICAN AND FOREIGN AS *to* **COMMISSIONERS OF THE FREE CHURCH OF SCOTLAND. 2 April 1844. New York.** Appeals to the Scottish delegation to decline donations from slaveholders. 26 April 1844. p.65, c2.

5301 HENRY C. WRIGHT *to* **GARRISON. 5 January 1844. Leipzig.** Discusses his travels in Austria. 26 April 1844. p.65, c5.

5302 DANIEL MITCHELL *to* **FRIEND GARRISON. n.d. n.p.** Forwards proceedings of the meeting held at Pawtucket, Massachusetts in March. 26 April 1844. p.67, c5.

5303 H. CLAY *to* **THE EDITORS OF THE** *NATIONAL INTELLIGENCER.* **17 April 1844. Raleigh.** Opposes annexation of Texas. 3 May 1844. p.71, c1.

5304 D. L. CHILD *to* **GARRISON. 21 April 1844. Washington.** Details debate on Texas annexation in Washington. 3 May 1844. p.71, c5.

5305 D. L. CHILD *to* **GARRISON. 28 April 1844. Washington.** Reports on the death of Mr. Bossier, Congressman from Louisiana. 10 May 1844. p.73, c1.

5306 ANNE WARREN WESTON *to* **MR. GARRISON. 23 April 1844. Weymouth.** Reports that the Weymouth Female AS was denied the use of a local church meetinghouse. 10 May 1844. p.73, c1.

5307 F. M. BAKER *to* **GARRISON. 24 March 1844. Canterbury.** Reports the formation of an AS in Canterbury, the reputed "hot-bed of pro-slaveryism." 10 May 1844. p.73, c3.

5308 D. L. CHILD *to* **GARRISON. 5 May 1844. Washington.** Views Texas annexation as an expansion of slavery. 10 May 1844. p.75, c1.

5309 GARRISON *to* **YERRINTON. 7 May 1844. New York.** Forwards summary of proceedings of an anti-slavery meeting. 10 May 1844. p.75, c1.

5310 EDWARD SEARCH *to* **GARRISON. 5 April 1844. London.** Discusses the controversy concerning the Corn Laws. 10 May 1844. p.75, c2.

5311 WM. R. SMALL *to* **FRIEND GARRISON. n.d. n.p.** Notes that Frederick Douglass attended an anti-slavery meeting in Northampton. 10 May 1844. p.75, c5.

5312 PORTIA *to* **MR. GARRISON. n.d. n.p.** Notes disruptions of the "Tyler Meeting" which was held in Faneuil Hall. 10 May 1844. p.75, c6.

5313 CHARLES SPEAR *to* **BR. GARRISON. n.d. n.p.** Forwards short account of his lecture tour to Salem, Newburyport, and Danvers. 10 May 1844. p.76, c2.

5314 TRUTH AND UNION *to* **GARRISON. n.d. n.p.** Regrets that reform meetings at Amory Hall were suspended. 10 May 1844. p.76, c3.

5315 JOHN M. SPEAR *to* **GARRISON. 14 May 1844. Weymouth.** Calls for a campaign to abolitionize New England. 17 May 1844. p.79, c4.

5316 EDWARD SEARCH *to* **GARRISON. 27 April 1844. London.** Foresees the triumph of reform in England and Ireland. 17 May 1844. p.79, c5.

5317 PETER *to* **FRIEND GARRISON. 29 April 1844. Boston.** Notes growth of "come-outism", a philosophy which rejects all human governments. 17 May 1844. p.80, c2.

5318 C. A. B. *to* **GARRISON. n.d. n.p.** Believes slavery originated in the marriage covenant. 17 May 1844. p.80, c3.

5319 MILO A. TOWNSEND *to* **BRO. GARRISON. 24 March 1844. New Brighton, Pa.** Sees conflict between humanity and religion in the United States. 17 May 1844. p.80, c4.

5320 H. C. WRIGHT *to* **GARRISON. 8 January 1844. Breslau.** Describes conditions in Austria and Prussia. 24 May 1844. p.83, c2.

5321 PRIVATUS *to* **BRO. GARRISON. n.d. n.p.** Condemns the abuses of married life. 24 May 1844. p.84, c2.

5322 WM. H. CHANNING *to* **GARRISON. 12 May 1844. New York.** Predicts that an address lately approved by the AAS will bring a storm of condemnation upon abolitionists. 24 May 1844. p.85, c3.

5323 ELIZABETH PEASE *to* **GARRISON. 26 April 1844. Darlington.** Discusses the John Brown case and the One Hundred Conventions campaign. 24 May 1844. p.85, c4.

5324 LEWIS CASS *to* **W. T. COLQUITT. 10 May 1844. Detroit.** Favors the annexation of Texas. 31 May 1844. p.85, c5.

5325 GEN. JACKSON *to* **THE EDITOR OF THE** *UNION.* **13 May 1844. Hermitage.** Supports the annexation of Texas. 31 May 1844. p.87, c2.

5326 EDWARD SEARCH *to* **GARRISON. 5 April 1844. London.** Expresses shock at the sentencing of John L. Brown. 31 May 1844. p.87, c5.

5327 JOHN M. FISK *to* **MR. EDITOR [W. L. GARRISON]. 9 May 1844. West Brookfield, Ma.** Gives account of a legal case between himself and a pro-slavery cleric. 31 May 1844. p.88, c3.

5328 HENRY C. WRIGHT *to* **FRIEND GARRISON. 13 March 1844. Graefenberg, Silesia, Austria.** Reports from Austria on the water cure. 31 May 1844. p.88, c5.

5329 SENATOR ALEXANDER BARROW *to* **CITIZENS OF LOUISIANA. 24 May 1844. Washington.** Enumerates his reasons for voting against the annexation of Texas. 7 June 1844. p.90, c1.

5330 COL. JAMES POLK *to* **MESSRS. S. P. CHASE AND THOMAS HEATON. 23 April 1844. Columbia, Tn.** Favors the immediate annexation of Texas. 7 June 1844. p.90, c3.

5331 CASSIUS M. CLAY *to* **EDMUND QUINCY. 14 May 1844. Lexington, Ky.** Urges unity in the anti-slavery movement. 7 June 1844. p.91, c4.

5332 THEODORE LOCKE *to* **GARRISON. 26 May 1844. Barre.** Welcomes the "No union with slaveholders" stance of the Garrisonians. 7 June 1844. p.91, c6.

5333 HENRY C. WRIGHT *to* **GARRISON. 27 March 1844. Graefenberg, Silesia, Austria.** Reports on travels in Silesia. 7 June 1844. p.92, c2.

5334 SAMUEL HENRY *to* **GARRISON. May 1844. Palmer.** Advocates teachings of St. Paul to "overcome evil with good". 7 June 1844. p.92, c3.

5335 JUDGE WM. JAY *to* **GERRIT SMITH. 15 February 1844. Malta.** Gives account of his visit to Egypt. 14 June 1844. p.93, c4.

5336 NOAH JACKMAN *to* **BRO. GARRISON. 2 June 1844. North Attleboro.** Opposes capital punishment. 14 June 1844. p.96, c4.

5337 JAMES KENT *to* **MR. H. J. RAYMOND. 21 May 1844. New York.** Calls for the impeachment of President Tyler. 14 June 1844. p.96, c5.

5338 WM. B. CARPENTER *to* **THE REV. E. S. GANNETT. 3 April 1844. Bristol.** An English physiologist refutes statements in the *Christian Examiner* that the colored race is separated by "impassable" physical and mental boundaries from whites. 21 June 1844. p.97, c5.

5339 J. C. RAY *to* **GARRISON. 17 June 1844. New Bedford.** Forwards an extract of a letter written by Cassius M. Clay concerning the emancipation of his nine slaves. 21 June 1844. p.98, c5.

5340 CASSIUS M. CLAY *to* **n.n. [extract] n.d. n.p.** Answers those who claimed that he did not emancipate his slaves, stating that he freed the nine slaves he owned, yet some slaves are still kept by others in his family. 21 June 1844. p.98, c5.

5341 J. T. EVERETT *to* **BRO. GARRISON. 16 June 1844. Princeton.** Favors the New England Society's advocacy of disunion. 21 June 1844. p.98, c6.

5342 NOAH JACKMAN *to* **BRO. GARRISON. 20 May 1844. North Attleboro, Ma.** Expresses his disappointment with clerical abolitionism. 21 June 1844. p.98, c6.

5343 THOMAS CLARKSON *to* **MARIA W. CHAPMAN. 28 March 1844. Playford Hall, Near Ipswich.** Sends a copy of his latest pamphlet on slavery. 21 June 1844. p.99, c1.

5344 SAPHIA *to* **THE EDITOR OF THE** *LIBERATOR* **[W. L. GARRISON]. 8 January 1844. Birmingham.** Outlines tenets of Chartism in England. 21 June 1844. p.99, c1.

5345 LUCINDA HOSMER *to* **W. L. GARRISON. 28 April 1844. Bedford, Ma.** Contends that anti-slavery in Bedford needs a champion. 21 June 1844. p.99, c2.

5346 G. W. F. MELLEN *to* **MR. GARRISON. n.d. n.p.** Protests the proceedings of the New England Anti-Slavery Convention. 21 June 1844. p.99, c3.

5347 WEARE TAPPAN *to* **MR. GARRISON. 6 June 1844. Bradford, N.H.** Withdraws his name from the list of officers of the AAS. 21 June 1844. p.99, c4.

5348 H. W. BLANCHARD *to* **BRO. GARRISON. 8 June 1844. Dorchester.** Stresses importance of mass meetings of abolitionists. 21 June 1844. p.99, c5.

5349 X. Y. *to* **THE EDITOR OF THE** *CONCORD BAPTIST REGISTER.* **n.d. n.p.** Refutes alleged biblical support for capital punishment. 21 June 1844. p.100, c2.

5350 JOHN M. SPEAR *to* **FRIEND GARRISON. 24 June 1844. Hallowell, Me.** Forwards account of an anti-slavery discussion in Portland, Maine on the disunion question. 28 June 1844. p.103, c2.

5351 A SUBSCRIBER *to* **FRIEND GARRISON. n.d. n.p.** Finds Article IV of the Constitution pertinent in the case of fugitive slaves. 28 June 1844. p.103, c2.

5352 GEO. M. DALLAS *to* **A VIRGINIAN. 29 August 1840. Philadelphia.** Cites constitutional objections to federalism. 5 July 1844. p.105, c1.

5353 CLARKSON *to* **THE EDITOR OF THE** *COURIER.* **n.d. n.p.** Criticizes an attempt by abolitionists to remove the master of the African School and force "intermixture" of colored and white pupils. 5 July 1844. p.105, c1.

5354 WEARE TAPPAN *to* **MR. GARRISON. 25 June 1844. Bradford, N.H.** Offers further explanation of his withdrawal from office in the AAS. 5 July 1844. p.107, c1.

5355 ABEL TANNER *to* **FRIEND GARRISON. 15 June 1844. Bozrahville, Ct.** Expresses gratitude to Mr. and Mrs. George R. Andrews for their hospitality. 5 July 1844. p.107, c4.

5356 THOS. VAN RENSSELAER *to* **FRIEND GARRISON. 14 June 1844. Rochester.** Expresses disappointment that the Liberty Party in Rochester is so concerned with fund-raising. 5 July 1844. p.107, c5.

5357 C. SPEAR *to* **BRO. GARRISON. n.d. n.p.** Finds the slave laws written by Judge Stroud in 1824 useful for abolitionists. 5 July 1844. p.107, c5.

5358 ELKANAH NICKERSON *to* **MR. GARRISON. 18 June 1844. Harwick.** Discusses shortcomings of the United States Constitution. 12 July 1844. p.112, c2.

5359 CHARLES SPEAR *to* **BRO. GARRISON. 19 June 1844. Middletown, Ct.** Angrily describes the execution of a man in Middletown; condemns capital punishment. 12 July 1844. p.112, c3.

5360 ANN PAGE *to* **MR. GARRISON. 18 June 1844. Providence.** Renounces faith in political action and human government. 12 July 1844. p.112, c2.

5361 J. M. ALDRICH *to* **BRO. GARRISON. 26 April 1844. Fall River.** Denounces anti-religious aspect of ablitionism. 19 July 1844. p.113, c6.

5362 R. *to* **FRIEND GARRISON. 7 July 1844. New Bedford.** Denounces those who are afraid to uphold "No Union with Slaveholders". 19 July 1844. p.114, c1.

5363 C. M. BURLEIGH *to* **BRO. GARRISON. 9 July 1844. Plainfield, Ct.** Report on anti-slavery celebration in Canterbury, Connecticut. 19 July 1844. p.114, c1.

5364 H. W. F. *to* **GARRISON. 10 July 1844. Lowell.** Reports on a stirring lecture by C. L. Remond in Lowell. 19 July 1844. p.114, c2.

5365 CHARLES SPEAR *to* **FRIEND GARRISON. n.d. n.p.** Affirms that Universalism is consistent with anti-slavery. 19 July 1844. p.114, c2.

5366 EDWARD H. NEVIN *to* **MR. GARRISON. 29 June 1844. New Athens, Oh.** Responds to sharp attack made on his character by the *Liberator*. 19 July 1844. p.115, c1.

5367 C. M. CLAY *to* **THE EDITOR OF THE** *CINCINNATI HERALD*. **25 June 1844. Lexington, Ky.** Explains why he acted as second in a duel. 19 July 1844. p.116, c3.

5368 EDWARD M. SEARCH *to* **GARRISON. 1844. Muswell Hill.** Condemns the split in the abolitionist movement in America; urges abolitionists to follow the example of the Anti-Corn Law League and unite on one issue. 26 July 1844. p.117, c1.

5369 WENDELL PHILLIPS *to* **FRIEND GAY. n.d. n.p.** Examines the no-voting theory. 26 July 1844. p.117, c2.

5370 J. M. FISKE *to* **FRIEND GARRISON. 7 July 1844. West Brookfield.** On the state of religion in West Brookfield. 26 July 1844. p.119, c4.

5371 CHARLES SPEAR *to* **FRIEND GARRISON. n.d. n.p.** Regrets state of the abolition cause in Worcester County. 2 August 1844. p.123, c2.

5372 AN OBSERVER *to* **MR. GARRISON. 20 July 1844. Andover.** Reports on the anti-slavery picnic in Andover. 2 August 1844. p.123, c2.

5373 DAVID RUGGLES *to* **GARRISON. 23 July 1844. Northampton.** Expresses gratitude to those who were considering holding a meeting to help sustain him financially through the water cure. 2 August 1844. p.123, c3.

5374 INCREASE S. SMITH *to* **FRIEND GARRISON. 25 June 1844. Dorchester.** Discusses the observance of the Sabbath. 2 August 1844. p.124, c2.

5375 T. *to* **REV. RICHARD FULLER. n.d. Aiken, S.C.** Requests that he make a public statement on his position toward slavery; it was rumored that he pronounced slavery a moral evil while in Philadelphia. 9 August 1844. p.125, c1.

5376 R. FULLER *to* **T. 26 June 1844. Beaufort, S.C.** Refutes rumor that he had pronounced slavery a moral evil. 9 August 1844. p.125, c1.

5377 FRANCIS JACKSON *to* **HIS EXCELLENCY GEORGE N. BRIGGS. 4 July 1844. Boston.** Resigns as Justice of the Peace because he could no longer carry out his solemn oath to support the Constitution of the United States. 9 August 1844. p.125, c6.

5378 FRANCIS JACKSON *to* **S. J. MAY. 25 November 1844. Boston.** Replies to May's thanks for the use of his home for an AS meeting. 9 August 1844. p.126, c2.

5379 WM. E. LUKINS *to* **GARRISON. 30 July 1844. Cadiz, Oh.** Defends Mr. Nevin, who attacked *Liberator*. 9 August 1844. p.126, c4.

5380 ANSEL H. HARLOW *to* **BRO. GARRISON. 30 July 1844. Plymouth.** Explains an ambiguous statement regarding views of R. Tomlinson expressed at a meeting in Plymouth. 9 August 1844. p.126, c6.

5381 E. RICHMOND *to* **FRIEND GARRISON. n.d. Abington.** Affirms motto, "No Union with Slaveholders." 9 August 1844. p.126, c6.

5382 CHARLES FRANCIS ADAM *to* **MISS ANN Q. THAXTER. 29 July 1844. Quincy.** Regrets he was unable to attend the Hingham celebration of the First of August. 9 August 1844. p.127, c3.

5383 JOHN QUINCY ADAMS *to* **MISS THAXTER. 29 July 1844. Quincy.** Declines an invitation to attend the First of August celebration at Hingham. 9 August 1844. p.127, c3.

5384 LORING MOODY *to* **LEAVITT. 2 August 1844. Harwich.** Laments the case of Jonathan Walker, a native of Harwich, who was "captured" by the police in Florida for helping slaves. 16 August 1844. p.129, c6.

5385 GEO. BRADBURN *to* **JOHN B. SWANTON. n.d. n.p.** Clarifies his anti-slavery position. 16 August 1844. p.130, c2.

5386 EDWARD Y. PERRY *to* **FRIEND GARRISON. 30 July 1844. Hanover.** Expresses optimism at anti-slavery in Hanover. 16 August 1844. p.131, c1.

5387 H. C. WRIGHT *to* **GARRISON. 23 May 1844. Graefenberg, Silesia, Austria.** Reports on the benefits of the water-cure. 16 August 1844. p.131, c2.

5388 EDWARD SEARCH *to* **SIR [W. L. GARRISON]. 18 June 1844. Muswell Hill, England.** Condemns imprisonment of O'Connell by the government. 16 August 1844. p.131, c4.

5389 W. RITCHIE *to* **FRIEND GARRISON. 5 August 1844. Needham.** States he is displeased with pro-slavery elements of the United States Constitution. 16 August 1844. p.131, c5.

5390 E. RICHMOND *to* **FRIEND GARRISON. 31 July 1844. Abington.** Upholds liberty and equality as the rights of man. 16 August 1844. p.131, c6.

5391 CHARLES SPEAR *to* **BRO. GARRISON. n.d. n.p.** Proposes the establishment of an anti-capital punishment society. 16 August 1844. p.132, c2.

5392 CASSIUS M. CLAY *to* **SIR [W. L. GARRISON]. 10 July 1844. Lexington, Ky.** Declines an invitation to come to Massachusetts. 23 August 1844. p.134, c1.

5393 D. S. GRANDIN *to* **BROTHER GARRISON. 21 July 1844. Lewiston Falls.** Reports on anti-slavery in Maine. 23 August 1844. p.134, c4.

5394 GEO. THOMPSON *to* **GARRISON. 1 August 1844. Glasgow.** Encloses a resolution passed by the Glasgow Emancipation Society. 23 August 1844. p.135, c2.

5395 EDWARD SEARCH *to* **GARRISON. 2 July 1844. Muswell Hill, England.** Comments on reform in England. 23 August 1844. p.135, c3.

5396 n.n. *to* **FRIEND GARRISON. 16 August 1844. Concord, Ma.** Comments on the First of August events in Concord. 23 August 1844. p.135, c4.

5397 C. SPEAR *to* **BRO. GARRISON. n.d. n.p.** Discusses the duty of non-resistants regarding voting. 23 August 1844. p.135, c6.

5398 GERRIT SMITH *to* **JOHN G. WHITTIER. 18 July 1844. Peterboro'.** Affirms the anti-slavery character of the federal Constitution. 30 August 1844. p.137, c4.

5399 J. M. MCKIM *to* **W. L. GARRISON. 15 August 1844. Philadelphia.** Reports that Frederick Douglass spoke in Philadelphia on 17 August; notes favorable response to Douglass' speech. 30 August 1844. p.138, c5.

5400 FREDERICK DOUGLASS *to* **FRIEND GARRISON. 17 August 1844. Philadelphia.** Explains why he was unable to attend the First of August celebration in Providence. 30 August 1844. p.138, c5.

5401 JOHN BAILEY *to* **H. W. WILLIAMS. 13 August 1844. New Bedford.** Warns abolitionists to be certain that individuals coming to them for financial help are truly in need before granting any favors. 30 August 1844. p.139, c1.

5402 HENRY C. WRIGHT *to* **GARRISON. 28 June 1844. Graefenberg, Austria.** Gives account of his travels in Austria. 30 August 1844. p.139, c2.

5403 C. K. W. *to* **GARRISON. n.d. n.p.** Sends a petition calling for the establishment of an institution for those discharged from prison. 30 August 1844. p.140, c2.

5404 CHARLES SPEAR *to* **BRO. GARRISON. n.d. n.p.** Forwards account of a debate on capital punishment in Foxborough. 30 August 1844. p.140, c2.

5405 S. *to* **GARRISON. 16 August 1844. Northampton Assoc.** Reports on the Amherst College Convention. 30 August 1844. p.140, c3.

5406 H. CLAY *to* **THE** *NORTH ALABAMIAN.* **27 July 1844. Ashland.** Believes that the question of Texas should be decided by public opinion and not by a debate on slavery. 6 September 1844. p.142, c2.

5407 WENDELL PHILLIPS *to* **GARRISON. 30 August 1844. Nahant.** Argues that it is a waste of time to review Gerrit Smith's last letter. 6 September 1844. p.143, c1.

5408 WHILOM, A LIBERTY PARTY MAN *to* **GARRISON. 2 September 1844. Abington.** Asserts that he was not convinced by Smith's letter, which argued that the Constitution was an anti-slavery document. 6 September 1844. p.143, c2.

5409 JAMES JACKSON *to* **FRANCIS JACKSON. 15 August 1844. New Orleans.** Objects to Jackson's resignation. 6 September 1844. p.143, c3.

5410 WM. M. MONROE *to* **FRANCIS JACKSON. 20 August 1844. Clinton, Ga.** Views denunciation of the Constitution as folly. 6 September 1844. p.143, c3.

5411 JAMES HAUGHTON *to* **GARRISON. 16 July 1844. Dublin.** Comments on the latest abolition-related topics in United States. 6 September 1844. p.143, c4.

5412 JAMES CANNINGS FULLER *to* **GARRISON. 27 August 1844. Skaneateles.** Abhors the injustice committed against advocates of anti-slavery. 6 September 1844. p.143, c4.

5413 JOHN BAILEY *to* **GARRISON. 28 August 1844. New Bedford.** Expresses his desire to do something for Jonathan Walker, an imprisoned abolitionist. 6 September 1844. p.143, c5.

5414 JONATHAN WALKER *to* **HIS WIFE AND CHILDREN. 29 July 1844. Pensacola.** Describes the deplorable conditions to which he is subjected in prison. 6 September 1844. p.144, c3.

5415 CASSIUS M. CLAY *to* **GENTLEMEN. 11 July 1844. Lexington, Ky.** Declines invitation to speak in the North. 13 September 1844. p.146, c3.

5416 SETH SPRAGUE, JR. *to* **SCOTT. 20 August 1844. Duxbury.** Opposes dissolution of the Union. 13 September 1844. p.146, c4.

5417 CHARLES T. TORREY *to* **ELIAS SMITH. 19 August 1844. Baltimore Jail.** Believes the split among the abolitionists is advantageous. 13 September 1844. p.147, c3.

5418 D. S. GRANDIN *to* **FRIEND. 6 September 1844. Boston.** Forwards account of a meeting held at Northampton to consider the cases of Charles Torrey and Jonathan Walker, who are imprisoned in the South for abolitionism. 13 September 1844. p.147, c3.

5419 ARGUS *to* **FRIEND GARRISON. 5 September 1844. Pawtucket.** Lauds the redemption of a slave by the Rhode Island AS. 13 September 1844. p.147, c4.

5420 A SUBSCRIBER *to* **GARRISON. 31 August 1844. Pensacola.** Describes the arrest of Jonathan Walker. 13 September 1844. p.147, c4.

5421 THOS. VAN RENSSELEAR *to* **GEORGE BRADBURN. 1 September 1844. New York.** Reports that a fugitive slave was redeemed at Pawtucket. 13 September 1844. p.147, c4.

5422 REUBEN SIMPSON *to* **REV. JOHN T. RAYMOND. n.d. n.p.** Disputes Raymond's objection to the use of the term "African" in referring to the writer's race. 13 September 1844. p.147, c5.

5423 JAMES C. SPRIGG *to* **THE EDITOR OF THE** *WASHINGTON GLOBE.* **23 August 1844. Shelbyville.** Comments on a letter written by C. M. Clay. 20 September 1844. p.150, c3.

5424 HENRY CLAY *to* **MR. WICKLIFFE. 2 September 1844. Ashland.** Regrets hypocritical stand of C. M. Clay. 20 September 1844. p.150, c4.

5425 HENRY C. WRIGHT *to* **GARRISON. 29 March 1844. Graefenberg, Austria.** Recounts dialogue on the Church between himself and patient at the hospital. 20 September 1844. p.151, c3.

5426 GEO. W. STACY *to* **GARRISON. 17 September 1844. Milford.** Donates a portion of the proceeds from the Milford picnic and fair to the *Liberator*. 20 September 1844. p.151, c4.

5427 E. J. *to* **FRIEND GARRISON. n.d. n.p.** Encloses advertisement from a Whig paper for runaway slaves. 20 September 1844. p.151, c5.

5428 WM. W. BROWN *to* **FRIEND GARRISON. 21 August 1844. Madison, Oh.** Remembers with regret his military training days in Ohio. 20 September 1844. p.152, c2.

5429 JOSEPH MASH *to* **BROTHER. 10 September 1844. Harwich.** Voices concern for the condition of Jonathan Walker's family. 27 September 1844. p.154, c3.

5430 H. C. WRIGHT *to* **GARRISON. 30 March 1844. Graefenberg, Austria.** Relates dialogue between himself and another patient on nationalism. 27 September 1844. p.155, c1.

5431 LEWIS FORD *to* **FRIEND GARRISON. 1 September 1844. North Abington.** Appeals to abolitionists to come out. 27 September 1844. p.155, c4.

5432 WM. ENDICOTT *to* **FRIEND GARRISON. 8 September 1844. Danvers.** Affirms the pro-slavery character of the Constitution. 27 September 1844. p.155, c5.

5433 HENRY C. WRIGHT *to* **GARRISON. 14 August 1844. London.** Sympathizes with the spirit of the London Missionary Society. 27 September 1844. p.156, c2.

5434 CEPHAS *to* **GARRISON. n.d. n.p.** Advocates come-outism as consistent with the tradition of Luther and the Apostles. 27 September 1844. p.156, c3.

5435 C. SPEAR *to* **FRIEND GARRISON. n.d. n.p.** Describes solitary confinement. 27 September 1844. p.156, c4.

5436 HENRY C. WRIGHT *to* **DAUGHTER MARY. 2 July 1844. Graefenberg, Austria.** Declares he is preparing to depart from Austria. 4 October 1844, p.159, c4.

5437 NOAH JACKMAN *to* **BRO. GARRISON. 22 September 1844. North Attleboro.** Reports that a member was expelled from the N. Attleboro Baptist Church for fornication. 4 October 1844. p.159, c4.

5438 R. *to* **FRIEND GARRISON. 5 September 1844. New Bedford.** Reports on lectures given on phrenology and physiology by O. S. and L. N. Fowler. 4 October 1844. p.160, c2.

5439 JAS. D. MAKERSON *to* **J. E. HOOD. [from the** *Granite Herald***]. 16 July 1844. Athens, Ga.** Demands that the *Liberator* cease to be sent South. 11 October 1844. p.161, c1.

5440 AURELIA A. WORK *to* **GARRISON. 13 August 1844. Theopolis.** Describes the unpleasant conditions under which she had lived since the incarceration of her husband. 11 October 1844. p.161, c2.

5441 THOMAS CLARKSON *to* **REV. J. W. C. PENNINGTON. n.d. Suffolk.** Comments on slavery. 11 October 1844. p.161, c6.

5442 H. CLAY *to* **THE** *NATIONAL INTELLIGENCER***. 23 September 1844. Ashland.** Doubts the propriety of giving a public response to political questions; prefers to be "open-minded." 11 October 1844. p.162, c1.

5443 H. CLAY *to* **CASSIUS M. CLAY. 18 September 1844. Ashland.** Reprimands C. M. Clay for his letter to the *New York Tribune.* 11 October 1844. p.162, c1.

5444 RICHARD ALLEN *to* **GARRISON. 17 September 1844. Dublin.** Reports that H. C. Wright is back in Ireland. 11 October 1844. p.163, c2.

5445 H. C. WRIGHT *to* **GARRISON. n.d. n.p.** Sends account from his travel journal. 11 October 1844. p.163, c3.

5446 S. DYER *to* **FRIEND GARRISON. 8 October 1844. South Abington.** Announces meetings to be held in Plymouth County on behalf of Jonathan Walker and others imprisoned in the South for abolitionism. 11 October 1844. p.163, c5.

5447 HIRAM STAFFORD *to* **GARRISON. 8 September 1844. Cummington.** Sees private property as the cause of slavery; favors abolition of both. 11 October 1844. p.164, c2.

5448 A. S. MITCHELL *to* **JOSHUA LEAVITT. September 1844. Danville, Ky.** Attacks the character of Mr. Birney. 18 October 1844. p.166, c2.

5449 H. C. WRIGHT *to* **THE** *LIBERATOR.* **3 July 1844. Mueglitz.** Describes his travels in Austria. 18 October 1844. p.167, c3.

5450 NANTUCKET *to* **MR. EDITOR [W. L. GARRISON]. 1 October 1844. Nantucket.** Describes his conversion to Garrisonianism. 18 October 1844. p.167, c5.

5451 S. S. ASHLEY *to* **FRIEND GARRISON. 5 October 1844. Providence.** Encloses account of the Ladies Anti-Slavery Fair in Providence. 18 October 1844. p.167, c5.

5452 n.n. *to* **FRIEND GARRISON. 20 August 1844. Liverpool.** Condemns private property as the cause of slavery. 18 October 1844. p.168, c2.

5453 ADIN BALLOU *to* **GERRIT SMITH. n.d. n.p.** Disputes the interpretation of nonresistance presented in one of Smith's letters. 18 October 1844. p.168, c3.

5454 WENDELL PHILLIPS *to* **MR. GAY. 26 September 1844. Nahant.** Defends the no-voting position he has held for five years. 25 October 1844. p.169, c5.

5455 H. C. WRIGHT *to* **HIS DAUGHTER, HANNAH. 4 July 1844. Olmutz.** Comments on conditions in Olmutz; adds that he is en route to Vienna. 25 October 1844. p.171, c1.

5456 JOHN M. FISKE *to* **FRIEND GARRISON. 20 October 1844. West Brookfield.** Expresses disappointment with the lack of support for Deacon Josiah Henshaw, who was expelled from his church for having presided over an anti-slavery meeting. 25 October 1844. p.171, c2.

5457 JOHN CUSHING *to* **GARRISON. 20 October 1844. South Hingham.** Criticizes Whig anti-slavery as hypocritical. 25 October 1844. p.171, c3.

5458 LORING MOODY *to* **H. W. WILLIAMS. 17 October 1844. Hanover.** Forwards comments on the meeting in Hingham. 25 October 1844. p.171, c4.

5459 S. H. LLOYD *to* **REV. REUBEN MOREY. 14 October 1844. North Attleboro, Ma.** Believes Christianity embodies the doctrine of non-resistance. 25 October 1844. p.172, c2.

5460 STEPHEN LOTHROP *to* **THE EDITOR OF THE** *CHRISTIAN REFLECTOR.* **October 1844. Cambridgeport.** Opposes position of the Baptist Triennial Convention in refusing to oppose slavery. 1 November 1844. p.173, c6.

5461 H. C. WRIGHT *to* **GARRISON. n.d. Vienna.** Forwards an account of his travels in Vienna. 1 November 1844. p.174, c4.

5462 FREDERICK DOUGLASS *to* **FRIEND GARRISON. 27 October 1844. Lynn.** Denounces attacks on himself by the Liberty Party and George Bradburn. 1 November 1844. p.174, c5.

5463 S. *to* **GARRISON. 15 October 1844. Syracuse, N.Y.** Comments on a mass meeting of pro-slavery Whigs at Rochester. 1 November 1844. p.175, c1.

5464 A GARRISONIAN ABOLITIONIST *to* **GARRISON. 26 October 1844. Lynn.** Plans to vote for Hon. Daniel P. King for Congress on the basis of his opposition to slavery and the annexation of Texas. 1 November 1844. p.175, c3.

5465 JOHN B. ALLEY *to* **DANIEL KING. 19 October 1844. Lynn.** Wishes to know King's views on slavery and Texas. 1 November 1844. p.175, c3.

5466 S. C. WHEELER *to* **FRIEND GARRISON. 29 October 1844. Groton.** Requests publication of the correspondence between the Whig and Democratic candidates and himself upon the subject of slavery. 1 November 1844. p.175, c3.

5467 GEO. S. BOUTWELL *to* **S. C. WHEELER. 25 October 1844. Groton.** Cites Constitutional clauses on the right of Congress to abolish slavery in Washington. 1 November 1844. p.175, c3.

5468 AMOS ABBOTT *to* **S. C. WHEELER. 25 October 1844. Andover.** Supports the right of Congress to abolish slavery. 1 November 1844. p.175, c4.

5469 JAMES D. HERRICK *to* **GARRISON. 14 October 1844. Methuen.** Requests that Mr. Abel C. Brown acknowledge receipt of a box of clothes for fugitives. 1 November 1844. p.175, c4.

5470 R. *to* **W. L. GARRISON. 27 October 1844. New Bedford.** Reports that Douglass and Remond spoke at a Liberty Party convention on 24 October. 1 November 1844. p.175, c5.

5471 HENRY B. GOODWIN *to* **STILLMAN SMITH. 10 October 1844. Norton.** Relates that his slaves, when freed, preferred to stay with him rather than to leave the state of Maryland. 8 November 1844. p.174[178], c5.

5472 JOHN NOYES, JR. *to* **FRIEND GARRISON. 29 October 1844. South Abington.** Objects to the indifference of the clergy toward the case of Jonathan Walker. 8 November 1844. p.174[178], c6.

5473 J. B. *to* **FRIEND GARRISON. 4 November 1844. New Bedford.** Notes resolution offered at the last convention held in New Bedford, which condemned abolitionists who continued to participate in political activities. 8 November 1844. p.174[178], c6.

5474 H. C. WRIGHT *to* **DAUGHTER, HANNAH. [extract] 4 July 1844. Vienna.** Forwards notes from his travel journal. 8 November 1844. p.175[179], c4.

5475 D. L. CHILD *to* **MR. HAWLEY. [from the** *Northampton Gazette***] 4 November 1844. Springfield.** Replies to Joshua Leavitt concerning the origin and character of the Liberty Party. 15 November 1844. p.181, c3.

5476 ANDREW JACKSON *to* **MR. BLAIR. 24 October 1844. Hermitage.** Comments on John Quincy Adams' views on annexation. 15 November 1844. p.181, c4.

5477 H. *to* **EDITORS OF THE** *BANGOR GAZETTE.* **9 October 1844. Portland.** Reports that "come-outers" were forbidden the use of the city hall in Portland. 15 November 1844. p.181, c5.

5478 HIRAM A. MORSE *to* **FRIENDS OF THE** *LIBERATOR* **AND THE CAUSE. 27 October 1844. Holliston.** Calls for an effort to increase the circulation of the *Liberator.* 15 November 1844. p.182, c6.

5479 H. C. WRIGHT *to* **GARRISON. [extract] 5 July 1844. Vienna.** Forwards notes from his travel log. 15 November 1844. p.183, c4.

5480 E. SMITH *to* **LEAVITT. 7 November 1844. Boston.** Discusses Daniel P. King's five dollar contribution to "the cause," which was misconstrued to represent a coalition between the Massachusetts AS and the Whig Party. 15 November 1844. p.183, c5.

5481 GEO. BRADBURN *to* **FRIEND GARRISON. 12 November 1844. Boston.** Claims that the New England Convention "gagged" him. 22 November 1844. p.185, c2.

5482 S. M. STRONG *to* **BENJ. B. SMITH. [from the** *Georgia Flag of the Union***] 25 October 1844. Macon.** Questions whether the rumor of the presence of abolitionists in Georgia is correct. 22 November 1844. p.186, c2.

5483 BENJ. B. SMITH *to* **S. M. STRONG. 25 October 1844. Macon.** Confirms Strong's fears; states he met a man who was bold enough to call himself an abolitionist, at which Smith "gave him several blows." 22 November 1844. p.186, c2.

5484 CHARLES LENOX REMOND *to* **GARRISON. 13 November 1844. Salem.** Charges the *Boston Morning Chronicle* with false reporting. 22 November 1844. p.187, c3.

5485 JANE ELIZABETH HITCHCOCK *to* **GARRISON. 10 November 1844. Marlboro', N.H.** Finds encouragement in anti-slavery progress in New Hampshire. 29 November 1844. p.189, c3.

5486 WM. RITCHIE *to* **GARRISON. 18 November 1844. Needham.** States that he was stirred and inspired by Edmund Quincy's lecture at Needham. 29 November 1844. p.189, c4.

5487 H. H. BRIGHAM *to* **GARRISON. 7 November 1844. South Abington.** Laments the imprisonment of Jonathan Walker. 29 November 1844. p.189, c5.

5488 AN ABOLITIONIST *to* **HENRY B. GOODWIN. 11 October 1844. New Bedford.** Asks Goodwin questions relating to the freeing of his slaves. 29 November 1844. p.189, c5.

5489 SAMUEL J. MAY, JR. *to* **REV. GEO. ARMSTRONG. 9 October 1843. Geneva.** Charges that American Unitarians have supported slavery. 29 November 1844. p.190, c1.

5490 CHARLES STEARNS *to* **GARRISON. 4 October 1844. Springfield, Ma.** Believes in the Second Advent of Jesus Christ. 29 November 1844. p.192, c2.

5491 YANKEE *to* **THE EDITOR OF THE** *COURIER.* **n.d. n.p.** Opposes publication of letters favoring emigration of white Northerners to Virginia. 6 December 1844. p.193, c2.

5492 YANKEE *to* **EDITOR OF** *NEW ENGLAND FARMER.* **n.d. n.p.** Opposes emigration of white Northerners to Virginia. 6 December 1844. p.193, c3.

5493 ISAAC STEARNS *to* **MESSRS. LEAVITT AND ALDEN. 18 November 1844. Franklin City, Ma.** Expresses his disappointment that the *Emancipator* and *Chronicle* were not more devoted to the anti-slavery cause. 6 December 1844. p.194, c4.

5494 AN EYE-WITNESS *to* **HENRY W. WILLIAMS. 17 November 1844. Escambia County.** Reports on the sentencing of Jonathan Walker; notes that Walker was also branded "SS" on the hand, presumably denoting "slave stealer." 6 December 1844. p.195, c3.

5495 GEORGE BRADBURN *to* **THE EDITOR OF THE *LIBERATOR* [W. L. GARRISON]. 26 November 1844. n.p.** Retracts his charge of having been "gagged" by the New England Convention. 6 December 1844. p.195, c4.

5496 AMASA WALKER *to* **FRIEND GARRISON. 2 December 1844. North Brookfield.** Reports that Father Mathew of Ireland was on the verge of being incarcerated as a debtor; urges philanthropists to help him. 6 December 1844. p.195, c4.

5497 H. CLAPP, JR. *to* **GARRISON. 27 November 1844. Lynn.** Reports that Frederick Douglass was present at the Rhode Island AS meeting, at which he rebuked the local colored voters for having supported Clay. 6 December 1844. p.195, c5.

5498 A DEEPLY INTERESTED MEMBER *to* **REV. J. F. CLARKE. 27 November 1844. Boston.** Opposes violence on ground of the sacredness of human life. 6 December 1844. p.196, c2.

5499 WEARE TAPPAN *to* **ROGERS. 7 October 1844. Bradford, N.H.** Forwards report of New Hampshire AS meeting. 13 December 1844. p.198, c5.

5500 HENRY C. WRIGHT *to* **GARRISON. 5 July 1844. Vienna.** Comments from his travel log. 13 December 1844. p.199, c5.

5501 S. W. W. *to* **BROTHER GARRISON. 2 December 1844. Providence, R.I.** Reports that Adin Ballou spoke at several churches in Providence. 13 December 1844. p.200, c3.

5502 H. H. B. *to* **WM. LLOYD GARRISON. 25 November 1844. South Abington.** Forwards an extract from a letter by Dr. Wayland concerning moral duties. 13 December 1844. p.200, c3.

5503 REV. DR. WAYLAND OF BROWN UNIVERSITY *to* **n.n. [extract] n.d. n.p.** Argues that slavery is against the teachings of Christ. 13 December 1844. p.200, c3.

5504 ASHLEY *to* **JAMES GORDON BENNETT. [from the *New York Herald*] 7 December 1844. Charleston.** Contends that a division in the Union is imminent. 20 December 1844. p.202, c3.

5505 HENRY C. WRIGHT *to* **HIS DAUGHTER, HANNA. 6 July 1844. Vienna.** Describes his travels in Vienna. 20 December 1844. p.203, c6.

5506 CHARLES SPEAR *to* **GARRISON. n.d. n.p.** Sends account of two meetings in Hingham on capital punishment. 20 December 1844. p.204, c2.

5507 CHARLES SPEAR *to* **GARRISON. n.d. n.p.** Discusses his recent speaking engagements in New Hampshire. 20 December 1844. p.204, c2.

5508 J. P. HARRIMAN *to* **BROTHER GARRISON. 16 December 1844. Danvers.** Disputes with Garrison the matter of ownership of the *Herald of Freedom*. 27 December 1844. p.207, c2.

5509 HENRY C. WRIGHT *to* **GARRISON. [extract] 6 July 1844. n.p.** Describes his travels in Austria. 27 December 1844. p.207, c5.

[1845]

5510 COL. SAMUEL HUNTER *to* **S. T. BAILEY. 30 September 1844. Macon.** Lauds Bailey's heroic effort to recapture a fugitive slave in Vermont. 3 January 1845. p.1, c1.

5511 C. K. WHIPPLE *to* **FRIEND GARRISON. 14 December 1844. Newburyport.** Calls for a convention of the free states to devise measures for a peaceful dissolution of Union. 3 January 1845. p.3, c4.

5512 R. C. *to* **MR. GARRISON. n.d. n.p.** Finds Southern publications absurd and ill-informed. 3 January 1845. p.3, c5.

5513 WM. C. BROWN *to* **HON. JOHN C. CALHOUN. 31 October 1844. Boston.** Advocates support for the Rev. Charles T. Torrey, who was imprisoned for aiding runaway slaves. 3 January 1845. p.4, c2.

5514 WILLIAM H. SEWARD *to* **GERRIT SMITH. [from the** *Albany Daily Advertiser***] 25 November 1844. Auburn.** Laments results of the election. 3 January 1845. p.4, c3.

5515 ALBERT GALLATIN *to* **DAVID FIELD. 14 December 1844. New York.** Cites constitutional arguments for the annexation of Texas. 3 January 1845. p.4, c3.

5516 D. A. WEBSTER *to* **REV. HARVEY F. LEAVITT. 12 October 1844. Lexington.** Discusses her imprisonment on charges that she came South to incite the slaves. 10 January 1845. p.5, c3.

5517 N. P. ROGERS *to* **HENRY CLAPP. [from the Essex County** *Washingtonian***] n.d. n.p.** Clarifies questions about the ownership of the *Herald of Freedom*. 10 January 1845. p.6, c5.

5518 NOAH JACKMAN *to* **BRO. GARRISON. 24 December 1844. North Attleboro.** Considers the controversy over the ownership of the *Herald* in New Hampshire to be of little importance. 10 January 1845. p.7, c3.

5519 JAIRUS LINCOLN *to* **MR. GARRISON. 1 January 1845. Northboro'.** Encloses the resolutions passed at a meeting held in Northboro' in support of Jonathan Walker. 10 January 1845. p.7, c3.

5520 A. WELLS *to* **C. A. WHEATON. 26 December 1844. Colosse, N.Y.** Opposes holding a Christian reform convention. 10 January 1845. p.8, c2.

5521 J. W. CUNNINGHAM *to* **FRIEND GARRISON. 28 December 1844. Colosse, N.Y.** Discusses the cruel treatment he is receiving in prison. 10 January 1845. p.8, c3.

5522 C. M. CLAY *to* **THE** *BOSTON ATLAS***. 6 January 1845. Lexington, Ky.** Opposes the annexation of Texas. 24 January 1845. p.14, c1.

5523 C. M. CLAY *to* **T. B. STEVENSON. 8 January 1845. Frankfort, Ky.** Opposes liberation of slaves by force. 31 January 1845. p.18, c1.

5524 W. A. WHITE *to* **GARRISON. 27 January 1845. Watertown.** Forwards account of a meeting held in Concord to consider the question of Texas. 31 January 1845. p.19, c5.

5525 SUMNER LINCOLN *to* **FRIEND GARRISON. 30 December 1844. Jamaica, Vt.** Opposes capital punishment. 31 January 1845. p.20, c2.

5526 H. C. WRIGHT *to* **GARRISON. 7 July 1844. On the Danube.** Forwards notes from his travel journal. 7 February 1845. p.21, c1.

5527 WM. P. POWELL *to* **BRETHREN. 21 January 1845. New York.** Opposes disunion in a letter to the Massachusetts AS. 7 February 1845. p.21, c3.

5528 A TEXAN *to* **THE** *TRIBUNE.* **6 January 1845. Galveston, Tx.** Believes prospects for the annexation of Texas are dubious. 7 February 1845. p.21, c6.

5529 WM. LLOYD GARRISON *to* **THE EDITOR OF THE** *DAILY MAIL.* **n.d. n.p.** Reacts to an article in the *Daily Mail* denouncing his proposition of disunion. 7 February 1845. p.23, c2.

5530 THOMAS HASKELL *to* **BRO. GARRISON. 8 February 1845. Gloucester.** Believes the Massachusetts AS has wrongfully denied him funds they owe him. 14 February 1845. p.27, c5.

5531 IGNATIUS SARGENT *to* **GEO. N. BRIGGS. 21 January 1845. Georgetown, Ma.** Declares that he can no longer support the United States Constitution. 14 February 1845. p.28, c2.

5532 JOHN HOOD *to* **BRO. GARRISON. 29 December 1844. Beverly.** Denounces hypocrisy in the Liberty Party and the Church. 14 February 1845. p.28, c2.

5533 ELIZABETH B. CHASE *to* **PROVIDENCE MONTHLY MEETING OF FRIENDS. 28 November 1843. Valley Falls.** Withdraws from the group. 14 February 1845. p.28, c3.

5534 N. P. ROGERS *to* **WILLIAM LLOYD GARRISON. 1 February 1845. Concord, N.H.** Denounces Garrison's "conservatism." 21 February 1845. p.29, c1.

5535 GILBERT RICKETSON *to* **THE** *NEW BEDFORD REGISTER.* **n.d. n.p.** Defends his attempt to return a fugitive slave. 21 February 1845. p.29, c6.

5536 A. W. W. *to* **MR. GARRISON. 15 February 1845. Boston.** Provides account of the convention and fair at Fitchburg. 21 February 1845. p.31, c3.

5537 JAMES CANNINGS FULLER *to* **THE** *EMANCIPATOR.* **13 January 1845. Skaneateles.** Urges support for the imprisoned abolitionists. 21 February 1845. p.31, c4.

5538 JOHN PIERPONT *to* **J. C. FULLER. 17 January 1845. Boston.** Favors aid to the families of martyrs for the cause. 21 February 1845. p.31, c5.

5539 C. M. BURLEIGH *to* **W. L. GARRISON. n.d. n.p.** Sends an acccount of his anti-slavery tour to Cape Cod. 21 February 1845. p.31, c5.

5540 R. M. SHEARIN *to* **JOHN M. MOREHEAD. 7 October 1844. Halifax.** Resigns from his position as Justice of the Peace in Halifax, North Carolina. 21 February 1845. p.32, c3.

5541 HENRY C. WRIGHT *to* **HIS DAUGHTER, MARY. 8 July 1844. Linz.** Relates excerpts from his travel journal. 28 February 1845. p.33, c1.

5542 N. P. ROGERS *to* **HENRY CLAPP, JR. 16 February 1845. Concord, N.H.** Expresses indignation at the suppression of the *Herald of Freedom*. 28 February 1845. p.33, c2.

5543 C. M. BURLEIGH *to* **FRIEND GARRISON. n.d. n.p.** Continues the account of his Cape Cod tour. 28 February 1845. p.35, c3.

5544 J. FULTON, JR. *to* **FRIEND GARRISON. 26 December 1844. Philadelphia.** Urges an end to fighting among abolitionist friends. 28 February 1845. p.35, c4.

5545 H. C. *to* **MR. GARRISON. 24 February 1845. Upton.** Reports on the outcome of the Upton fair. 28 February 1845. p.35, c5.

5546 N. P. ROGERS *to* **WILLIAM LLOYD GARRISON. 24 February 1845. Concord, N.H.** Corrects errors found in his last letter. 28 February 1845. p.35, c5.

5547 SAMUEL SELLERS *to* **FRIEND GARRISON. 12 February 1845. Mottville, N.Y.** Describes the Skaneateles community. 28 February 1845. p.36, c2.

5548 A. D. *to* **SPEAR. 28 January 1845. Troy, N.Y.** Expresses rage at the execution of a man who declared he was innocent of the charge of murder. 28 February 1845. p.36, c4.

5549 G. B. STEBBINS *to* **FRIEND GARRISON. 27 February 1845. Syracuse, N.Y.** Gives an account of the Western New York AS. 7 March 1845. p.39, c5.

5550 ALFRED WELLS *to* **FRIEND GARRISON. 16 February 1845. Colosse.** Gives an account of the proceedings of a reform convention at Syracuse. 7 March 1845. p.40, c2.

5551 EZEKIEL SHOWERS *to* **MR. WILLIAM STRICKLAND. 27 January 1845. Martinsburgh.** Virginia slaveholder demands the return of his slave from an abolitionist in western Pennsylvania. 14 March 1845. p.41, c1.

5552 n.n. *to* **JACOB H. ELA. [from the** *Herald of Freedom***] n.d. n.p.** Discontinues subscription to *Herald of Freedom* because he is tired of abolitionist writings. 14 March 1845. p.42, c4.

5553 N. P. ROGERS *to* **W. L. GARRISON. [from the** *Lynn Pioneer***] n.d. n.p.** Claims that a controversy grew out of an attempt to "rein in the bold-spirited *Herald of Freedom* and yoke it to a spiritless corporation." 14 March 1845. p.42, c4.

5554 WM. LLOYD GARRISON *to* **SIR [LEVI WOODBURY]. n.d. n.p.** Condemns Woodbury's views on the annexation of Texas. 14 March 1845. p.42, c6.

5555 GEO. THOMPSON *to* **[W. L.] GARRISON. 27 January 1845. London.** States his support for Garrison. 14 March 1845. p.43, c3.

5556 HENRY C. WRIGHT *to* **E. L. B. WRIGHT [WIFE]. 10 July 1844. Salzburg.** Claims that abolitionists are not Christians; their revengeful nature is from hell. 14 March 1845. p.43, c4.

5557 C. STEARNS *to* **[W. L.] GARRISON. 2 March 1845. Springfield.** Proclaims that Christian religion is opposed to slavery, war, and drink. 14 March 1845. p.44, c2.

5558 C. M. BURLEIGH *to* **FRIEND SPEAR. n.d. n.p.** Relates story about a judge in Rhode Island who proposes capital punishment as a means of controlling the people. 14 March 1845. p.44, c3.

5559 FRANCIS MASON *to* **LEWIS TAPPAN. 2 May 1844. Tavoy, Burmah.** A missionary asserts his anti-slavery views. 21 March 1845. p.46, c3.

5560 PARKER PILLSBURY *to* **n.n. [from the** *Herald of Freedom***] n.d. n.p.** Declares that he has not been appointed editor of the *Herald of Freedom*. 21 March 1845. p.46, c4.

5561 N. P. ROGERS *to* **FRIENDS BENJAMIN COMINGS AND AMOS WOOD. 12 December 1844. n.p.** States that he would only consent to edit a free anti-slavery paper, and the *Herald of Freedom* is not free. 21 March 1845. p.46, c4.

5562 JOHN R. FRENCH *to* **FRIENDS [BENJAMIN] COMINGS AND [AMOS] WOOD. 10 December 1844. Concord.** Refuses further connection with the *Herald of Freedom* because of its Executive Committee. 21 March 1845. p.46, c4.

5563 n.n. [HENRY C. WRIGHT] *to* **n.n. n.d. Melech, Bavaria.** Describes his travels in Bavaria. 21 March 1845. p.47, c3.

5564 HENRY C. WRIGHT *to* **n.n. n.d. Bavaria.** Describes the "magnificent" Salzburg Alps. 21 March 1845. p.47, c3.

5565 HENRY C. WRIGHT *to* **n.n. n.d. Unkin.** Proclaims his disgust with the Austrian police. 21 March 1845. p.47, c3.

5566 HENRY C. WRIGHT *to* **n.n. n.d. Pass Strub.** Gives a brief history of the Tyrolean Pass Strub. 21 March 1845. p.47, c3.

5567 HENRY C. WRIGHT *to* **n.n. n.d. Waidring.** Describes an instance of rudeness of one passenger in a coach to another. 21 March 1845. p.47, c3.

5568 HENRY C. WRIGHT *to* **n.n. n.d. St. Johanna.** Comments on the low cost of living in St. Johanna. 21 March 1845. p.47, c3.

5569 HENRY C. WRIGHT *to* **n.n. n.d. Sall.** Describes the village of Sall. 21 March 1845. p.47, c3.

5570 JOHN M. SPEAR *to* **FRIEND GARRISON. 10 March 1844. Weymouth.** Denounces mob attacks on abolitionists; notes anti-slavery conventions held in Maine. 21 March 1845. p.47, c4.

5571 PHEBE P. BLACKMER *to* **FRIEND GARRISON. 4 December 1844. Plymouth, Ma.** Explains he charged that the Second Congregational Church was pro-slavery and was consequently excommunicated. 21 March 1845. p.47, c4.

5572 H. H. BRIGHAM *to* **FRIEND [W. L. GARRISON]. 22 February 1845. South Abington.** Accuses the Baptist church in Abington of being pro-slavery. 21 March 1845. p.47, c5.

5573 C. K. W. [CHARLES K. WHIPPLE] *to* **FRIEND GARRISON. n.d. n.p.** Relates an incident in which his invitation to a church was withdrawn because he wanted to bring a colored man with him. 21 March 1845. p.48, c5.

5574 HENRY C. WRIGHT *to* **n.n. n.d. Hall.** Describes the town of Hall. 28 March 1845. p.49, c1.

5575 HENRY C. WRIGHT *to* **n.n. 11 July 1844. Rattenberg.** Describes the village and cathedral of Rattenberg. 28 March 1845. p.49, c1.

5576 HENRY C. WRIGHT *to* **n.n. n.d. Schwartz.** Compares the invasion and persecution which took place in the village of Schwartz in 1781 with the plight of the slaves in the United States. 28 March 1845. p.49, c1.

5577 H. W. CARTER *to* **MR. GARRISON. 10 March 1844. Hubbardston.** Reports on an anti-slavery fair sponsored by the Massachusetts AS and Worcester North AS. 28 March 1845. p.49, c2.

5578 EDWARD SEARCH *to* **W. L. GARRISON. 10 February 1845. London.** Quotes article from the *London Times* to demonstrate that American anti-slavery effort is attracting European attention; comments on problems of the poor in England. 28 March 1845. p.49, c4.

5579 HENRY C. WRIGHT *to* **JAMES M'HENRY. 1 February 1845. Glasgow.** Reasserts his claim that President Tyler sold his own children into slavery and is a slaveholder. 28 March 1845. p.50, c2.

5580 JAMES HAUGHTON *to* **THE EDITORS OF THE PRESS IN GREAT BRITAIN AND IRELAND. [from the** *Tipperary Free Press***] 6 February 1845. Dublin.** Urges that President Tyler, as a slaveholder, be barred from England and Ireland. 28 March 1845. p.50, c3.

5581 JAMES HAUGHTON *to* **ALDERMAN O'CONNELL, M.P. 22 January 1845. Eccles Street.** Urges that President Tyler be made unwelcome in Ireland. 28 March 1845. p.50, c3.

5582 DANIEL O'CONNELL *to* **JAMES HAUGHTON, ESQ. 4 February 1845. Ireland.** States that local interest is not concerned with American slavery. 28 March 1845. p.50, c3.

5583 JOHN BRANCH *to* **THE SENATE AND HOUSE OF REPRESENTATIVES OF FLORIDA. n.d. n.p.** Accuses the British and Foreign AS of interfering with domestic affairs in Florida. 28 March 1845. p.50, c4.

5584 JOHN SCOBLE *to* **CAPT. JONATHAN WALKER. 9 October 1844. London.** States that British abolitionists sympathize with Walker's efforts to help slaves escape. 28 March 1845. p.50, c4.

5585 n.n. *to* **MR. EDITOR [W. L. GARRISON]. 12 March 1845. Concord.** Praises Wendell Phillips. 28 March 1845. p.51, c3.

5586 H. C. WRIGHT *to* **E. L. B. WRIGHT [WIFE]. 11 July 1844. Innsbruck.** States that he is homesick for "Yankee land"; believes that governments are subordinate to the individual; rejoices that his heart is free from "this malignant prejudice against color." 4 April 1845. p.53, c2.

5587 SHERMAN C. BLODGET *to* **MR. PILLSBURY. [from the** *Herald of Freedom***] 23 March 1845. Georgetown.** Demands that the *Herald of Freedom* no longer be sent to him. 4 April 1845. p.54, c2.

5588 A MASSACHUSETTS CLERGYMAN *to* **THE EDITOR OF THE** *[BALTIMORE SATURDAY] VISITOR*. **n.d. n.p.** Informs that in many cases he thought slaves in Virginia were treated well, but is horrified by slave prisons and markets. 4 April 1845. p.54, c3.

5589 C. M. CLAY *to* **G. SMITH, ESQ. 18 February 1845. Lexington, Ky.** States his continued support of the anti-slavery cause. 4 April 1845. p.54, c6.

5590 DISUNION *to* **[W. L.] GARRISON. 5 March 1845. Springfield, Ma.** Believes that the Constitution and the government are pro-slavery; supports the division of country to free it from the curse of slavery. 4 April 1845. p.55, c4.

5591 H. C. WRIGHT *to* **[W. L.] GARRISON. 1 January 1845. Dublin.** Thanks people in Dublin for their kindness. 4 April 1845. p.55, c5.

5592 HENRY C. WRIGHT *to* **n.n. 12 July 1845. Innsbruck.** Describes the town of Innsbruck. 11 April 1845. p.57, c2.

5593 JASON BARTON *to* **MR. WM. L. GARRISON. 18 December 1844. Middle Haddam, Ct.** Suggests mottos for the peace crusade. 11 April 1845. p.57, c3.

5594 E. W. CAPRON *to* **FRIEND HUMPHREY. [from the** *Rochester Advertiser***] n.d. n.p.** Believes that the "American union is the bulwark of slavery" and that the North helps the South to maintain slavery. 11 April 1845. p.57, c4.

5595 n.n. [E. W. CAPRON] *to* **FRIEND GARRISON. 21 March 1845. Rochester, N.Y.** Explains that his preceding letter does not advocate dissolution as the only means of abolishing slavery, but as the most speedy. 11 April 1845. p.57, c4.

5596 H. I. BOWDITCH *to* **THE EDITORS OF THE [***BOSTON***]** *ATLAS***. n.d. n.p.** Believes that the duty of the North is to see that Texas is not annexed. 11 April 1845. p.58, c1.

5597 WILLIAM JAY *to* **H. I. BOWDITCH, M.D. n.d. n.p.** Advocates stopping all actions against slaves or freedmen, and the dissolution of the Union. 11 April 1845. p.58, c1.

5598 BENJ. COMINGS *to* **FRIEND PILLSBURY. [from the** *Herald of Freedom***] n.d. n.p.** Opposes turning the *Herald of Freedom* over to N. P. Rogers. 11 April 1845. p.58, c4.

5599 DANIEL WEBSTER *to* **CHARLES W. RIDGELY. 3 March 1845. Washington.** Expresses his gratitude for being elected to the Baltimore Sabbath Association. 11 April 1845. p.59, c4.

5600 HENRY CLAY *to* **n.n. 7 March 1845. Ashland.** Expresses his gratitude for his election to the Baltimore Sabbath Association. 11 April 1845. p.59, c4.

5601 I. C. RAY *to* **HENRY CLAY. 16 November 1844. New Bedford.** Urges Clay to become the leader of an anti-slavery campaign. 11 April 1845. p.59, c5.

5602 I. C. R[AY] *to* **FRIEND GARRISON. 31 March 1845. n.p.** Advocates that Northerners write anti-slavery letters to Southerners. 11 April 1845. p.59, c5.

5603 W. P. *to* **MR. EDITOR [W. L. GARRISON]. n.d. n.p.** Claims that the Liberty Party is not to be trusted. 11 April 1845. p.59, c5.

5604 G. W. F. M. *to* **MR. GARRISON. n.d. n.p.** Believes that the South would violate the Constitution to preserve slavery. 11 April 1845. p.59, c5.

5605 WILLIAM JAY *to* **MR. EDWARD M. DAVIS. [from the** *Pennsylvania Freeman***] n.d. n.p.** Declares that if Texas is annexed, the Union should be dissolved immediately. 18 April 1845. p.60, c3.

5606 CHRONICLE *to* **MR. LEAVITT. 24 February 1845. Lexington, Ky.** Relates story concerning Calvin Fairbanks, who was jailed on the charge of helping slaves to escape. 18 April 1845. p.60, c5.

5607 HENRY C. WRIGHT *to* **n.n. 12 July 1845. Innsbruck.** Describes the site of the battle with Napoleon; claims he is the enemy of any government that upholds slavery. 18 April 1845. p.61, c1.

5608 CHARLES LENOX REMOND *to* **FRIEND PHILLIPS. 5 April 1845. Philadelphia.** Reports on the anti-slavery crusade in Pennsylvania. 18 April 1845. p.61, c3.

5609 JOHN NOYES, JR. *to* **FRIEND GARRISON. 6 April 1845. South Abington.** Reports on the meeting of the Plymouth County AS. 18 April 1845. p.61, c3.

5610 DISUNION *to* **BRO. GARRISON. 12 April 1845. Springfield.** Proclaims that the Constitution is pro-slavery. 18 April 1845. p.61, c4.

5611 E. J. A. *to* **BRO. GARRISON. 13 April 1845. Lowell.** Describes the way Massachusetts treated a free colored woman. 18 April 1845. p.61, c4.

5612 WM. C. COFFIN *to* **n.n. [from the** *New Bedford Path-Finder***] 7 April 1845. County Jail.** Refuses to take an oath or affirmation in court. 18 April 1845. p.62, c2.

5613 HENRY F. HARRINGTON *to* **FRIEND [W. L. GARRISON]. n.d. n.p.** Relates account of a shipwreck on the North River. 18 April 1845. p.62, c4.

5614 R. HILDRETH *to* **GENTLEMEN ORESTES A. BROWNSON AND THE** *NORTH AMERICAN REVIEW***. 17 April 1844. Boston.** Defends his theory of morals. 25 April 1845. p.65, c1.

5615 RICHARD D. WEBB *to* **GARRISON. 4 April 1845. Dublin.** Discusses the possibility of the annexation of Texas; gives his views on who is to blame for the *Herald of Freedom* controversy. 25 April 1845. p.66, c5.

5616 ELIZABETH PEASE *to* **FRIEND [W. L. GARRISON]. 26 March 1845. Darlington.** Praises the work of the AAS. 25 April 1845. p.66, c5.

5617 CH. CUPIDON *to* **W. L. GARRISON. 21 March 1845. Hayti.** Asks Garrison to forward his address to any liberated slaves who wish to emigrate to Haiti. 25 April 1845. p.67, c1.

5618 n.n. [THE ORIGINAL IS NUMEROUSLY SIGNED] *to* **MEMBERS OF THE ANTI-SLAVERY SOCIETY [HAYTI]. 10 March 1845. Port Republican.** Reports that Haitians continue the fight against slavery. 25 April 1845. p.67, c2.

5619 SARAH CROSBY *to* **BRO. GARRISON. 21 March 1845. Groton, N.H.** Expresses hope for the death of slavery; asks Garrison's opinion on the *Herald of Freedom* controversy. 25 April 1845. p.67, c4.

5620 JAMES HAUGHTON *to* **MR. SPEAR. [from the** *Hangman***] 15 February 1845. Dublin.** Discusses his efforts in Ireland to rouse anti-slavery sentiments. 25 April 1845. p.68, c3.

5621 HIRAM A. MORSE *to* **S. H. GAY. [from the** *Anti-Slavery Standard***] 24 March 1845. Holliston.** Discontinues subscription to *Anti-Slavery Standard*. 2 May 1845. p.70, c3.

5622 C. L. REMOND *to* **FRIEND GARRISON. 19 April 1845. Philadelphia.** Relates an account of a colored man executed for murder. 2 May 1845. p.71, c1.

5623 C. T. CUPIDON *to* **WM. L. GARRISON. 9 April 1845. Hayti.** Condemns the efforts of the enemies of Haiti for trying to give "false color" to events taking place. 2 May 1845. p.71, c2.

5624 H[ENRY] C. WRIGHT *to* **MARY [DAUGHTER]. 12 July 1844. Innsbruck.** Gives a brief history of Innsbruck. 2 May 1845. p.71, c3.

5625 G. W. F. MELLEN *to* **MR. GARRISON. n.d. n.p.** Believes that the Constitution is not pro-slavery. 2 May 1845. p.71, c4.

5626 E. J. A. *to* **BRO. GARRISON. 22 April 1845. Lowell.** Expresses gratitude to those who have sent assistance to a widowed colored woman. 2 May 1845. p.71, c4.

5627 E. W. FARNHAM *to* **FRIEND [W. L. GARRISON]. 21 April 1845. Sing-Sing.** Reports that singers perform for prisoners. 2 May 1845. p.72, c5.

5628 HENRY C. WRIGHT *to* **REV. WM. CUNNINGHAM. 15 March 1845. Glasgow.** Believes that the Church's duty is to oppose slavery in any way possible. 9 May 1845. p.73, c3.

5629 C. K. W[HIPPLE] *to* **FRIEND [W. L. GARRISON]. 1 May 1845. Boston.** Urges that the Church recognize that slavery is the nation's worst sin. 9 May 1845. p.75, c3.

5630 HENRY C. WRIGHT *to* **[W. L.] GARRISON. 28 March 1845. Edinburgh.** Attacks British church's defense of slavery. 9 May 1845. p.75, c4.

5631 AMOS TUCK *to* **THE EDITORS OF THE** *NEW HAMPSHIRE PATRIOT.* **3 March 1845. Exeter.** Advocates patriotic rather than partisan politics. 16 May 1845. p.77, c4.

5632 HENRY CLAY *to* **n.n. April 1845. Ashland.** Expresses regret over possible division in the Methodist Episcopal Church. 16 May 1845. p.78, c2.

5633 WM. A. BOOTH *to* **MESSRS. EDITORS. [from the** *Sommerville* **(Tn.)** *Reporter*] **April 1845. Sommerville.** Declares that he is opposed to the advocacy of dissolution of the Union by the Methodist Episcopal Church. 16 May 1845. p.78, c2.

5634 HARRIET MARTINEAU *to* **FRIENDS. 1 April 1845. Birmingham.** Sends her thanks for gift from fellow abolitionists. 16 May 1845. p.78, c4.

5635 GEORGE THOMPSON *to* **n.n. [extract] 17 April 1845. London.** Reports on his efforts to fight oppression in England and India. 16 May 1845. p.78, c6.

5636 G. *to* **FRANCIS JACKSON. n.d. n.p.** Reports that the Baptist Convention resolved that no slaveholder may preach. 16 May 1845. p.79, c5.

5637 J. C. *to* **n.n. [extract from the** *Boston Christian Watchman*] **n.d. n.p.** Inveighs against abolitionists. 23 May 1845. p.81, c1.

5638 HENRY C. WRIGHT *to* **[W. L.] GARRISON. 12 April 1845. Kirkaldy.** Describes the pro-slavery spirit of Free Church of Scotland. 23 May 1845. p.81, c2.

5639 CASSIUS M. CLAY *to* **THE EDITORS OF THE** *CINCINNATI GAZETTE.* **2 May 1845. Lexington, Ky.** Relates that he liberated most of his slaves but sold those who committed a crime or wanted to be sold. 23 May 1845. p.82, c2.

5640 H. C. WRIGHT *to* **THE EDITORS OF THE** *STIRLING JOURNAL AND ADVER-TISER.* **n.d. n.p.** Asks that the enclosed article on the Free Church and slavery be printed. 23 May 1845. p.82, c3.

5641 H[ENRY] C. WRIGHT *to* **[W. L.] GARRISON. 2 May 1845. Bannockburn.** Reports on a meeting in Edinburgh which resolved that slaveholders should not be admitted into British churches. 23 May 1845. p.83, c1.

5642 GEORGE THOMPSON *to* **H. C. WRIGHT. 15 April 1845. London.** Supports Wright's work with the Free Church. 23 May 1845. p.83, c1.

5643 THOMAS CLARKSON *to* **H. C. WRIGHT. 23 April 1845. England.** Agrees that the Free Church of Scotland should not hold fellowship with slaveholders. 23 May 1845. p.83, c1.

5644 H. C. WRIGHT *to* **W. L. GARRISON. n.d. n.p.** Praises the work of George Thompson, which he believes may help bring about the dissolution of the East India Company. 23 May 1845. p.83, c1.

5645 WILLIAM C. BELL *to* **W. L. GARRISON. 17 May 1845. Philadelphia.** States his position on religion and anti-slavery. 23 May 1845. p.83, c4.

5646 PROGRESS *to* **MR. EDITOR [W. L. GARRISON]. n.d. n.p.** States that people are confusing "come-outism" with infidelity. 23 May 1845. p.83, c4.

5647 C. SPEAR *to* **FRIEND [WM. C. COFFIN]. n.d. n.p.** Praises Coffin for carrying out his principles. 23 May 1845. p.84, c3.

5648 BOYER [FORMER PRESIDENT OF HAYTI] *to* **THE HAYTIANS, MY COUNTRYMEN. 20 December 1844. Kingston.** Protests the violation of his rights and confiscation of his property. 30 May 1845. p.85, c5.

5649 H. C. WRIGHT *to* **n.n. 13 July 1845. Zirl.** Describes the scenery of Zirl; discusses local history. 30 May 1845. p.87, c5.

5650 C. S. *to* **GARRISON. 7 April 1845. Springfield.** Likens the present state of Christianity to the fall of the Roman Empire. 30 May 1845. p.88, c2.

5651 CONSISTENCY *to* **[W. L.] GARRISON. 11 April 1845. Springfield.** Opposes the "present manner of doing things on the Sabbath." 30 May 1845. p.88, c2.

5652 JAMES C. PERRY *to* **FRIENDS OF PEACE IN THE UNITED STATES OF AMERICA. 16 April 1845. Birmingham.** Warns that war should be avoided with Great Britain. 30 May 1845. p.88, c2.

5653 HENRY C. WRIGHT *to* **n.n. n.d. Landeck.** Describes the town and scenery of Landeck. 6 June 1845. p.89, c2.

5654 G. B. STEBBINS *to* **FRIEND GARRISON. 30 April 1845. Chittenango, N.Y.** Believes that the Church and politics stand in the way of anti-slavery work. 6 June 1845. p.89, c4.

5655 A. M. *to* **W. L. GARRISON. 24 May 1845. Albany.** Expresses his reaction to Frederick Douglass' narrative. 6 June 1845. p.89, c5.

5656 LINSTANT *to* **SIR [W. L. GARRISON]. 3 May 1845. Hayti.** Comments on the death of President Geurrier. 6 June 1845. p.91, c5.

5657 C. LENOX REMOND *to* **THE MEMBERS AND FRIENDS OF THE ESSEX COUNTY AS. 1 June 1845. Salem.** Appeals for attendance at the eleventh annual meeting of Essex County AS. 6 June 1845. p.91, c6.

5658 G. M. DALLAS *to* **CHARLES SPEAR. 24 May 1845. n.p.** Sends a detailed account of the execution of James Cowley. 6 June 1845. p.92, c2.

5659 REV. THOMAS CHALMERS *to* **THE EDITOR OF THE** *WITNESS.* **[from the** *Edinburgh Christian Witness***] 12 May 1845. Morningside.** Expresses his pro-slavery sentiments. 13 June 1845. p.93, c3.

5660 J[OHN] C. CALHOUN *to* **PERCY WALKER, THOMAS HOLLAND, THOMAS MCGRAN, WILLIAM R. HALLET AND J. A. CAMPBELL. [from the** *Charleston Mercury***] 15 May 1845. Fort Hill.** Discusses the annexation of Texas; expresses thanks for the invitation to Mobile. 13 June 1845. p.94, c1.

5661 WENDELL PHILLIPS *to* **[W. L.] GARRISON. 8 June 1845. Boston.** Sends his impressions of a recent New Hampshire AS meeting which discussed the *Herald of Freedom* controversy. 13 June 1845. p.94, c4.

5662 J. N. BUFFUM *to* **FRIEND GARRISON. 8 May 1845. Lynn.** Gives an account of hearings on the *Herald of Freedom* and New Hampshire AS controversy. 13 June 1845. p.94, c5.

5663 C. L. REMOND *to* **FRIEND GARRISON. 9 June 1845. Salem.** Reports on the New Hampshire AS meeting. 13 June 1845. p.94, c6.

5664 HENRY C. WRIGHT *to* **n.n. [W. L. GARRISON]. 15 July 1844. Feldkirk.** Describes the countryside of Feldkirk. 13 June 1845. p.95, c1.

5665 H. C. HOWELLS *to* **FRIEND [W. L. GARRISON]. n.d. England.** Declares he is anti-slavery and anti-war. 13 June 1845. p.95, c2.

5666 E. J. *to* **THE EDITOR OF THE** *COURIER.* **[from the** *Boston Courier***] n.d. n.p.** Criticizes newspapers for silence on the domestic slave trade. 13 June 1845. p.95, c4.

5667 HENRY C. WRIGHT *to* **DAUGHTER HANNAH. 14 July 1844. Feldkirk.** Condemns the Christian abuse of the Sabbath and condoning of slavery. 13 June 1845. p.96, c3.

5668 HENRY C. WRIGHT *to* **E.L.B. WRIGHT [WIFE]. 16 July 1844. Baden.** Criticizes the Council of Constance. 20 June 1845. p.97, c3.

5669 RICHARD D. WEBB *to* **n.n. [W. L. GARRISON]. [extract] n.d. Dublin.** Describes conditions in Ireland as quiet. 20 June 1845. p.97, c4.

5670 R. *to* **FRIEND GARRISON. 7 June 1845. New Bedford.** Reports on the pro-slavery meetings of the New England Methodist Episcopal Conference. 20 June 1845. p.97, c5.

5671 ADDISON DAVIS *to* **FRIEND CLAPP. [from the** *Lynn Pioneer***] 8 June 1845. Lynn.** Agrees with the New Hampshire AS that Rogers and French are to blame in the "New Hampshire controversy." 20 June 1845. p.98, c6.

5672 C. K. WHIPPLE *to* **MR. EDITOR. [from the** *Boston Atlas***] n.d. n.p.** Considers the evils implicit in a war with England over the Oregon Territory. 20 June 1845. p.99, c3.

5673 A GENTLEMAN OF BRISTOL, ENGLAND *to* **C. K. WHIPPLE. [extract] n.d. n.p.** States that war with the United States over Oregon would be greeted by England as a struggle against the world's slave power. 20 June 1845. p.99, c3.

5674 GEORGE WILSON MCCREE *to* **WM. LLOYD GARRISON. 5 May 1845. Durham, England.** Regards the pro-slavery position of the Free Church of Scotland as anti-Christian. 20 June 1845. p.99, c4.

5675 BENJ. S. JONES *to* **FRIEND. [from the** *Pennsylvania Freeman***] n.d. n.p.** Describes his journey up the Hudson River. 20 June 1845. p.100, c2.

5676 A MAN ABOUT TOWN *to* **MESSRS. EDITORS. [from the** *Boston Recorder***] n.d. n.p.** Reports on the New England AS convention. 27 June 1845. p.101, c3.

5677 MIDDLESEX *to* **THE EDITOR OF THE** *BOSTON COURIER***. n.d. n.p.** Believes that the Whig Party should take "anti-slavery ground." 27 June 1845. p.101, c5.

5678 H. I. BOWDITCH *to* **[W. L.] GARRISON. n.d. n.p.** Describes integration of primary schools. 27 June 1845. p.102, c5.

5679 H[ENRY] C. WRIGHT *to* **[W. L.] GARRISON. 25 May 1845. Stirling.** Claims that members of the "Free Kirk" are attacking Garrison's views on the Sabbath and the Church in order to divert attention from their own indefensible wrong-doings. 27 June 1845. p.103, c1.

5680 A. *to* **W. L. GARRISON. 29 May 1845. n.p.** Defends the Church and states that he is an anti-slavery minister. 27 June 1845. p.103, c2.

5681 H[ENRY] C. WRIGHT *to* **BROTHER. 31 May 1845. Stirling.** Describes the conditions in England. 27 June 1845. p.104, c2.

5682 WM. ANDERSON *to* **JOHN MURRAY AND WILLIAM SMEAL. 21 May 1845. Loanhead.** Requests wide circulation of the resolutions adopted by the Reformed Presbytery of Edinburgh. 4 July 1845. p.105, c3.

5683 JOHN MURRAY *to* **W. L. GARRISON. 1 June 1845. Bowling Bay.** Encloses and discusses resolutions of the Reformed Presbytery of Edinburgh. 4 July 1845. p.105, c3.

5684 JOHN MURRAY AND WILLIAM SMEAL *to* **n.n. 3 May 1845. Glasgow.** Request signature for the "Memorial and Remonstrance" adopted by the Glasgow Emancipation Society. 4 July 1845. p.105, c4.

5685 ANOTHER FREE CHURCHMAN *to* **THE EDITOR OF THE** *STIRLING JOURNAL AND ADVERTISER***. 8 May 1845. Stirling.** Discusses slavery in the United States; believes the Church should "remove the accursed thing from amongst them." 4 July 1845. p.105, c6.

5686 THE RECTOR OF ST. JAMES *to* **THE EDITORS OF THE** *WHIG***. n.d. n.p.** Gives reassurance that colored people will not be taught to read and write in Sunday School. 4 July 1845. p.105, c6.

5687 L. W. RYCKMAN *to* **WORKINGMEN OF NEW ENGLAND. n.d. n.p.** Discusses the problems involved in industrial reform. 4 July 1845. p.106, c3.

5688 [W. L. GARRISON] *to* **A. n.d. n.p.** Discusses his views on the American clergy and slavery. 4 July 1845. p.106, c4.

5689 SEWARD MITCHELL *to* **MR. EDITOR. [from the *Boston Recorder*] 4 June 1845. Boston.** Upholds the duty of Christian ministers to assail the sin of slavery. 4 July 1845. p.107, c3.

5690 SEWARD MITCHELL *to* **THE EDITOR OF THE *LIBERATOR* [W. L. GARRISON]. 4 June 1845. Boston.** Criticizes a man who calls himself "anti-slavery" while ridiculing other abolitionists; questions his views on the Church. 4 July 1845. p.107, c3.

5691 R. *to* **FRIEND [W. L. GARRISON]. 12 June 1845. New Bedford.** Praises the lectures on slavery and temperance by John Campbell Cluer. 4 July 1845. p.107, c4.

5692 LORING MOODY *to* **FRIEND [W. L. GARRISON]. 21 June 1845. Portland, Me.** Reports on anti-slavery activity in Maine. 4 July 1845. p.107, c4.

5693 ROBERT WESSELHOEFT *to* **HORACE GREELEY. n.d. n.p.** Promotes the benefits of the water cure. 4 July 1845. p.108, c2.

5694 CHARLES SPEAR *to* **n.n. [from the *Hangman*] n.d. n.p.** Praises the water cure. 4 July 1845. p.108, c4.

5695 NO FELLOWSHIP WITH DARKNESS *to* **[W. L.] GARRISON. n.d. n.p.** Advocates dissolution of the Union in order to abolish slavery. 11 July 1845. p.109, c3.

5696 E. J. *to* **JOHN SCOBLE. 17 April 1845. Tunis.** Relates a discussion on the abolition of slavery in Tunis. 11 July 1845. p.110, c3.

5697 ELIZA LEE FOLLEN *to* **WM. LLOYD GARRISON. n.d. n.p.** Gives a brief biography of the late Charles Follen. 11 July 1845. p.111, c1.

5698 HENRY C. WRIGHT *to* **BROTHER. 13 June 1845. Linlithgow.** Relates a conversation with British clergymen; expresses pessimistic views of both Europe's and America's institutions; describes scenery of Linlithgow. 11 July 1845. p.111, c1.

5699 J. M. F. *to* **FRIEND GARRISON. 16 June 1845. West Brookfield.** Discusses anti-slavery progress in the Church. 11 July 1845. p.111, c3.

5700 J. C. *to* **THE EDITOR OF THE *LIBERATOR* [W. L. GARRISON]. n.d. n.p.** Forwards article rejected by the *American Traveller*. 11 July 1845. p.112, c2.

5701 J. C. *to* **THE EDITORS OF THE *TRAVELLER*. n.d. n.p.** Expresses opposition to capital punishment. 11 July 1845. p.112, c2.

5702 ARGUS *to* **n.n. [W. L. GARRISON]. 5 July 1845. Portland, Me.** Gives an account of the Liberty Party convention. 18 July 1845. p.113, c3.

5703 WILLIAM H. SEWARD *to* **THE ANTI-SLAVERY CONVENTION AT CINCINNATI. 26 May 1845. Auburn.** Regrets that he cannot attend the convention, but urges moderation. 18 July 1845. p.113, c6.

5704 n.n. *to* **THE EDITOR OF THE *COURIER*. n.d. n.p.** On the death of Andrew Jackson. 18 July 1845. p.114, c1.

5705 WM. LLOYD GARRISON *to* **ELIHU BURRITT. 16 July 1845. Boston.** Argues with Burritt's stand against dissolution of the Union. 18 July 1845. p.114, c3.

5706 LORING MOODY *to* **SIR. 23 June 1845. Portland, Me.** Reports on anti-slavery activity in Maine. 18 July 1845. p.115, c1.

5707 ANTI-SLAVERY *to* **[W. L.] GARRISON. 17 June 1845. Springfield.** Explains that Dr. Osgood, a minister, may lose his position because of his abolitionist sentiments. 18 July 1845. p.115, c3.

5708 THOMAS HASKELL *to* **BRO. GARRISON. 6 July 1845. Gloucester.** Clarifies his own statements at the Essex County AS meeting. 18 July 1845. p.115, c3.

5709 ELIAS SMITH *to* **WM. LLOYD GARRISON. 12 July 1845. New York.** Announces the safe arrival of Jonathan Walker in New York. 18 July 1845. p.115, c4.

5710 n.n. *to* **MESSRS. EDITORS. [from the** *Salem Register***] n.d. n.p.** Objects to the treatment of women in a previous article. 18 July 1845. p.116, c4.

5711 G. B. STEBBINS *to* **FRIEND GARRISON. 9 July 1845. Unionville, Oh.** Describes the anti-slavery cause in Ohio. 25 July 1845. p.117, c2.

5712 JOHN M'COMB *to* **MR. EDITOR [W. L. GARRISON]. 15 July 1845. Dover, N.H.** Comments on anti-slavery activity in Dover, New Hampshire. 25 July 1845. p.117, c3.

5713 JONATHAN WALKER *to* **THE COMMITTEE OF BRITISH AND FOREIGN AS. 12 July 1845. New York.** Expresses gratitude for the sympathy of their organization. 25 July 1845. p.118, c1.

5714 JAMES HAUGHTON *to* **FRIEND [W. L. GARRISON]. 2 July 1845. Dublin.** Sends encouragement, and relates status of anti-slavery in Ireland. 25 July 1845. p.119, c2.

5715 JAMES M. HAUGHTON *to* **COMMITTEE OF THE ANTI-CORN LAW LEAGUE. 26 May 1845. Dublin.** Dissociates himself from the Anti-Corn Law League. 25 July 1845. p.119, c2.

5716 HENRY C. WRIGHT *to* **n.n. 17 July 1845. Zurich.** Describes Zurich; informs that he spoke there on the evils of American slavery. 25 July 1845. p.119, c3.

5717 N. J. *to* **BRO. GARRISON. 7 July 1845. North Attleboro, Ma.** Suspects that the Odd Fellows have a binding oath to each other. 25 July 1845. p.120, c4.

5718 M. WRIGHT *to* **BRO. GARRISON. 10 July 1845. Georgetown.** Explains the rudeness of people towards him after he spoke in defense of the "come-outers." 1 August 1845. p.121, c2.

5719 HENRY C. WRIGHT *to* **WM. LLOYD GARRISON. 28 June 1845. Brae-Head.** Accuses the Scottish Free Church of trying to sidestep criticisms of their stance on slavery. 1 August 1845. p.121, c3.

5720 JAMES STANDFIELD *to* **THE EDITOR OF THE** *BELFAST COMMERCIAL CHRONICLE.* **6 June 1845. Belfast.** Criticizes the Free Church's position on slavery; requests the printing of a letter from Henry C. Wright. 1 August 1845. p.121, c4.

5721 HENRY C. WRIGHT *to* **THE EDITOR OF THE [***BELFAST***]** *NEWS-LETTER.* **29 May 1845. Stirling.** Believes that holding slaves should be grounds for exclusion from the Church. 1 August 1845. p.121, c4.

5722 E. J. *to* **THE EDITOR OF THE [***BOSTON***]** *COURIER.* **n.d. n.p.** Believes that the Constitution commits people of the United States to protect slavery. 1 August 1845. p.122, c1.

5723 E. J. *to* **THE EDITOR OF THE [BOSTON] COURIER. n.d. n.p.** Argues that the Constitution's position on slavery forces individuals to choose between manhood and citizenship. 1 August 1845. p.122, c1.

5724 HENRY C. WRIGHT *to* **n.n. 19 July 1844. Berne.** Describes the scenery of Berne. 1 August 1845. p.123, c1.

5725 LORING MOODY *to* **FRIEND [W. L. GARRISON]. 22 July 1845. Portland, Me.** Notes the arrival of Jonathan Walker in New York; states his views on the annexation of Texas. 1 August 1845. p.123, c1.

5726 JONA. WALKER *to* **WILLIAM LLOYD GARRISON. 28 July 1845. Boston.** Reports that his return to Boston was welcomed. 1 August 1845. p.123, c2.

5727 AN ABOLITIONIST *to* **FRIEND GARRISON. 28 July 1845. Lynn, Ma.** Announces Jonathan Walker's arrival in Lynn. 1 August 1845. p.123, c2.

5728 R. *to* **FRIEND. 19 July 1845. New Bedford.** Discusses the visit of John Campbell Cluer to Manchester. 1 August 1845. p.123, c2.

5729 A. BRISBANE *to* **WILLIAM LLOYD GARRISON. n.d. n.p.** Discusses the question of universal social reform. 1 August 1845. p.124, c2.

5730 D. MACK *to* **n.n. 22 July 1845. Brattleboro, Vt.** States that the water cure cleanses and purifies the body. 1 August 1845. p.124, c3.

5731 ELIPHALET GREELEY *to* **OLIVER DENNIT. n.d. Portland, Me.** Informs him that the Portland AS cannot hold their convention in the public hall. 8 August 1845. p.125, c1.

5732 ISAAC S. FLINT *to* **FRIEND GAY. [from the *National Anti-Slavery Standard*] 9 July 1845. Coopertown.** Feels encouraged by the fact that the Church seems to be using its influence in regard to the slavery issue. 8 August 1845. p.126, c1.

5733 GEO. S. HILLARD *to* **CHAS. K. WHIPPLE. 28 July 1845. n.p.** Sympathizes with the anti-slavery cause. 8 August 1845. p.126, c4.

5734 S. C. PHILLIPS *to* **C. K. WHIPPLE. 30 July 1845. Salem.** Sympathizes with the anti-slavery cause. 8 August 1845. p.127, c1.

5735 J. N. BUFFUM *to* **FRIEND. n.d. n.p.** Describes the First of August celebration at Fall River. 8 August 1845. p.127, c2.

5736 R. *to* **FRIEND. 2 August 1845. New Bedford.** Describes the anti-slavery picnic at New Bedford. 8 August 1845. p.127, c3.

5737 F. *to* **THE *WORCESTER SPY.* n.d. n.p.** Describes the First of August celebration. 8 August 1845. p.127, c3.

5738 JONA. WALKER *to* **FRIEND WM. LLOYD GARRISON. 4 August 1845. Boston.** Comments on the First of August celebration in Waltham. 8 August 1845. p.127, c5.

5739 ALFRED WELLS *to* **FRIEND GARRISON. 26 July 1845. Colosse, N.Y.** Forwards his letter to American Tract Society. 8 August 1845. p.128, c2.

5740 ALFRED WELLS *to* **INHABITANTS OF COLOSSE [N.Y.]. n.d. n.p.** Discusses the idea of "sanctuary" in Christianity. 8 August 1845. p.128, c2.

5741 ISAAC PITMAN *to* **BERNARD BARTON. 14 May 1845. Ipswich.** Comments on the uses of phonography. 8 August 1845. p.128, c3.

5742 L. MOODY *to* **BROTHER [W. L. GARRISON]. 2 July 1845. Portland, Me.** Comments on the anti-slavery cause in Maine. 15 August 1845. p.129, c4.

5743 R. S. STEWART *to* **JOHN L. CAREY. 12 March 1845. Dodon, Md.** States that he is a Maryland slaveholder who supports gradual emancipation. 15 August 1845. p.130, c2.

5744 J. ORCUTT *to* **MESSRS. EDITORS. 3 March 1845. Uxbridge.** Forwards resolutions of the Evangelical church on slavery. 15 August 1845. p.130, c5.

5745 Z *to* **FRIEND GARRISON. 11 August 1845. Hingham.** Describes the First of August celebration. 15 August 1845. p.131, c3.

5746 A. *to* **THE EDITOR OF THE** *LIBERATOR* **[W. L. GARRISON]. n.d. n.p.** Clarifies statements that Dr. Follen does not yet belong to a profession. 15 August 1845. p.131, c3.

5747 A. BRISBANE *to* **WILLIAM LLOYD GARRISON. n.d. n.p.** Discusses the question of universal social reform. 15 August 1845. p.132, c2.

5748 E. S. A[BDY] *to* **MRS. CHAPMAN. [from the** *Anti-Slavery Standard***] 22 June 1845. London.** Discusses abolitionism, free trade, and the Anti-Corn Law League. 22 August 1845. p.133, c2.

5749 GEORGE MCDUFFIE *to* **GEORGE WILSON. 11 March 1845. Washington.** Declares his support for Anti-Corn Law League; expresses optimism for free trade. 22 August 1845. p.133, c3.

5750 JOHN C. CALHOUN *to* **GEORGE WILSON. 24 March 1845. Fort Hill.** Declares his support for free trade and Anti-Corn Law League. 22 August 1845. p.133, c3.

5751 G. W. CLARK *to* **MR. EDITOR. [from the** *Cincinnati Herald***] 19 June 1845. Cincinnati.** Relates accounts of slaves burned to death. 22 August 1845. p.133, c5.

5752 LIBRE *to* **THE EDITOR OF THE** *JOURNAL.* **[from the** *Providence Journal***] n.d. n.p.** Defends anti-slavery pledges. 22 August 1845. p.134, c1.

5753 J. C. *to* **THE EDITOR OF THE** *LIBERATOR* **[W. L. GARRISON]. n.d. n.p.** Discusses his position on the topics of bathing, diet, and marriage. 22 August 1845. p.134, c2.

5754 GARCIA CONDE *to* **MINISTER OF FOREIGN RELATIONS AND POLICE. n.d. n.p.** Warns that Mexico will have to sustain its rights by force. 22 August 1845. p.134, c4.

5755 HENRY C. WRIGHT *to* **[W. L.] GARRISON. 26 July 1845. Rosenheath.** Describes the scenery of Rosenheath; discusses writing a pamphlet on the Sabbath. 22 August 1845. p.135, c2.

5756 HENRY C. WRIGHT *to* **W. L. GARRISON. 5 August 1845. Glasgow.** Gives an account of the meeting of the Glasgow Emancipation Society. 22 August 1845. p.135, c3.

5757 EDWARD SEARCH *to* **SIR [W. L. GARRISON]. 27 July 1845. England.** States that Garrison's efforts are attracting attention in Europe. 22 August 1845. p.135, c3.

5758 R *to* **FRIEND. 14 August 1845. New Bedford.** Reports on a meeting at which everyone examined Jonathan Walker's branded hand. 22 August 1845. p.135, c4.

5759 CICERO *to* **MESSRS. EDITORS. [from the** *Philadelphia Ledger***] 11 August 1845. Philadelphia.** Criticizes Garrison. 29 August 1845. p.137, c1.

5760 J. CUSHING *to* **MR. GARRISON. 2 August 1845. Searsport, Me.** Gives an account of the celebration of West Indies Emancipation. 29 August 1845. p.137, c2.

5761 G. B. STEBBINS *to* **FRIEND GARRISON. 6 August 1845. Akron, Oh.** Describes anti-slavery activity in Ohio. 29 August 1845. p.137, c3.

5762 C. M. CLAY *to* **KENTUCKIANS. 12 August 1845. Lexington.** Appeals to those sympathetic to the slave to stand firm in the hour of trial. 29 August 1845. p.138, c1.

5763 THOS. H. WATERS, B. W. DUDLEY AND JOHN W. HUNT *to* **CASSIUS M. CLAY. 15 August 1845. Lexington.** Request that Clay discontinue publication of the *True American*. 29 August 1845. p.138, c1.

5764 CASSIUS M. CLAY *to* **B. W. DUDLEY, THOS. H. WATERS AND JOHN W. HUNT. 15 August 1845. Lexington.** Refuses to cease publication of the *True American*. 29 August 1845. p.138, c1.

5765 JONA. WALKER *to* **FRIEND W. L. GARRISON. 19 August 1845. Danvers.** Corrects errors in *Liberator* of 8 August. 29 August 1845. p.138, c6.

5766 WENDELL PHILLIPS *to* **[W.L.] GARRISON. 22 August 1845. Natick.** Criticizes Lysander Spooner's pamphlet on "Unconstitutionality of Slavery." 29 August 1845. p.139, c2.

5767 HENRY C. WRIGHT *to* **n.n. 24 July 1844. Lausanne.** Describes the scenery of Lausanne and other Swiss towns. 29 August 1845. p.139, c4.

5768 R. *to* **MR. GARRISON. 15 August 1845. Cleveland.** Reports on the lectures given by Abby Kelley and S. S. Foster in Cleveland. 29 August 1845. p.139, c5.

5769 ALFRED WELLS *to* **FRIEND GARRISON. n.d. n.p.** Relates a conversation he had with a "skeptic" on the subject of brotherly kindness. 29 August 1845. p.140, c2.

5770 E. B. *to* **MR. EDITOR [W. L. GARRISON]. 9 August 1845. Worcester.** Proclaims that war wastes money. 29 August 1845. p.140, c2.

5771 PUNGENT *to* **THE EDITOR OF THE** *NEW YORK TRIBUNE.* **n.d. n.p.** Claims that a forty-five minute opening prayer drove audience away from a temperance lecture. 29 August 1845. p.140, c3.

5772 n.n. *to* **SIR. [from the** *New Orleans Republican***] 6 August 1845. Compte, La.** Describes slaves' attempt to revolt. 29 August 1845. p.140, c4.

5773 R. M. *to* **THE EDITOR OF THE** *COURIER* **[from the** *Boston Courier***] n.d. n.p.** States that pupils at the black school in Boston are not receiving the same quality treatment as are children in white schools. 5 September 1845. p.142, c1.

5774 CHARLES K. WHIPPLE *to* **THE ANTI-SLAVERY MEETING AT WESTMINSTER. 29 August 1845. n.p.** Sends sympathy and encouragement for the anti-slavery cause; believes there is evidence that God is anti-slavery. 5 September 1845. p.142, c5.

5775 E. W. *to* **THE EDITORS OF THE** *BRITISH FRIEND.* **14 July 1845. Edinburgh.** Urges British women to take up the anti-slavery cause. 5 September 1845. p.143, c2.

5776 GLASGOW FEMALE ANTI-SLAVERY SOCIETY *to* **THE EDITORS OF THE** *BRITISH FRIEND.* **12 July 1845. Glasgow.** Wishes to aid in the American anti-slavery effort. 5 September 1845. p.143, c2.

5777 LYSANDER SPOONER *to* **MR. GARRISON. 1 September 1845. Boston.** Replies to a letter by Wendell Phillips and reasserts his own opinions on the Constitution and slavery. 5 September 1845. p.143, c4.

5778 HENRY C. WRIGHT *to* **n.n. n.d. n.p.** States that he does not want to see slavery abolished at the expense of the slaveholder's blood. 5 September 1845. p.143, c5.

5779 A. BRISBANE *to* **WILLIAM LLOYD GARRISON. n.d. n.p.** Discusses the question of social reform. 5 September 1845. p.144, c2.

5780 CONSISTENCY *to* **[W. L.] GARRISON. 11 August 1845. Providence.** Believes that social reform can only come about through the Church. 5 September 1845. p.144, c3.

5781 JAMES HAUGHTON *to* **T. M. RAY. 9 August 1845. n.p.** Expresses his admiration for John O'Connell. 12 September 1845. p.146, c1.

5782 JOHN G. PALFREY *to* **THE GOVERNOR OF FLORIDA. 2 October 1844. Boston.** Requests his attention in the case of Jonathan Walker. 12 September 1845. p.146, c3.

5783 JOHN BRANCH *to* **WALKER ANDERSON. 25 October 1844. n.p.** Forwards letter written by John Palfrey to John Branch on to Walker Anderson. 12 September 1845. p.146, c4.

5784 n.n. *to* **MR. GARRISON. 8 September 1845. Springfield.** States that E. D. Hudson was jailed on the charge of attempting to aid the escape of a slave. 12 September 1845. p.146, c6.

5785 JUSTICE *to* **SIR [W. L. GARRISON]. n.d. n.p.** Calls on the editor of the *Christian Reflector* to retract an article criticizing Garrison's position on religion. 12 September 1845. p.146, c6.

5786 DELIA WEBSTER *to* **MR. GARRISON. 30 August 1845. Ferrisburgh.** Defends herself against Garrison's charge that she is too moderate. 12 September 1845. p.147, c1.

5787 S. R. HARRIS *to* **FRIEND GARRISON. 1 September 1845. Providence.** Defends the anti-slavery effort in Rhode Island. 12 September 1845. p.147, c3.

5788 A WORKINGMAN *to* **[W. L.] GARRISON. n.d. n.p.** Believes there is an unfair distribution of wealth in the world. 12 September 1845. p.148, c2.

5789 HENRY H. BROWN *to* **FRIEND GARRISON. 27 August 1845. New Lebanon Springs, N.Y.** Praises the water cure. 12 September 1845. p.148, c2.

5790 ABIAL SMITH *to* **DARIUS PRIDE. 7 June 1845. Orange County, Vt.** Disapproves of working on Sunday. 12 September 1845. p.148, c3.

5791 DARIUS PRIDE *to* **ANY SHERIFF OR CONSTABLE IN THE STATE [OF VERMONT]. 9 June 1845. Vermont.** States that Plymon Seaver was jailed for not paying a fine. 12 September 1845. p.148, c3.

5792 n.n. *to* **MESSRS. EDITORS. [from the** *New York Evangelist***] 25 August 1845. Philadelphia.** Criticizes Garrison. 12 September 1845. p.148, c4.

5793 W. W. ADAMS *to* **MR. EDITOR [W. L. GARRISON]. n.d. Yarmouth Port.** Believes that Jonathan Walker was wrong in attempting to free slaves. 19 September 1845. p.149, c1.

5794 C. M. CLAY *to* **BENJAMIN URNER, JAMES S. GLASCOE, JACOB ERNST, OLIVER LOVELL, GEORGE W. PHILLIPS, R. G. MITCHELL AND JAMES CALHOUN. 4 September 1844. Lexington, Ky.** Thanks them for their support of him and the *True American.* 19 September 1845. p.150, c6.

5795 L. D. SMITH *to* **FRIEND GARRISON. 16 September 1845. Stoneham.** Reports on a lecture by Parker Pillsbury. 19 September 1845. p.151, c2.

5796 E. D. HUDSON *to* **FRIEND GARRISON. 9 September 1845. Springfield Jail.** Reports that he was jailed for trying to help a slave to free herself. 19 September 1845. p.151, c3.

5797 C. M. BURLEIGH *to* **FRIEND GARRISON. 8 September 1845. Plainfield, Ct.** Discusses abolitionism in Rhode Island. 19 September 1845. p.151, c4.

5798 MILO A. TOWNSEND *to* **BROTHER GARRISON. 8 September 1845. Mt. Pleasant, Oh.** Laments the violent treatment of Abby Kelley at the Orthodox Yearly Meeting. 19 September 1845. p.151, c4.

5799 A. BRISBANE *to* **WILLIAM LLOYD GARRISON. n.d. n.p.** Examines the institutions of industry and commerce. 19 September 1845. p.152, c2.

5800 JUNIUS *to* **MESSRS. EDITORS. [from the *Massillon Gazette*] n.d. n.p.** Criticizes anti-slavery disunionists. 26 September 1845. p.153, c1.

5801 JAMES HAUGHTON *to* **THE EDITOR OF THE *INQUIRER.* [from the *London Inquirer*] 15 August 1845. Dublin.** Discusses Rev. Dr. Parkman's position on slavery. 26 September 1845. p.154, c1.

5802 JOHN O'CONNELL *to* **JAMES HAUGHTON. 11 August 1845. Dublin.** Believes that the North is more cruel to blacks than is the South. 26 September 1845. p.154, c2.

5803 JAMES HAUGHTON *to* **JOHN O'CONNELL. 6 August 1845. Dublin.** Forwards resolutions of the Loyal National Repeal Association. 26 September 1845. p.154, c2.

5804 FREDERICK DOUGLASS *to* **FRIEND GARRISON. 1 September 1845. Dublin.** States that the slavery debate continues on board his ship bound for Europe, but a pro-slavery mob prevents him from speaking. 26 September 1845. p.155, c1.

5805 RICHARD D. WEBB *to* **[W. L.] GARRISON. n.d. n.p.** Believes that Frederick Douglass and James N. Buffum are perfect anti-slavery missionaries. 26 September 1845. p.155, c2.

5806 JAMES N. BUFFUM *to* **FRIEND GARRISON. 1 September 1845. Dublin.** Records his impressions of Ireland. 26 September 1845. p.155, c2.

5807 JAMES MURRAY *to* **FRIEND [W. L. GARRISON]. 31 August 1845. Glasgow.** Discusses the work of Henry C. Wright. 26 September 1845. p.155, c3.

5808 R. *to* **FRIEND [W. L. GARRISON]. 22 September 1845. New Bedford.** Reports on the monthly meeting of AS in Liberty Hall; lectures on science and literature for blacks. 26 September 1845. p.155, c5.

5809 C. S. *to* **FRIENDS OF THE ABOLITION OF CAPITAL PUNISHMENT. 21 September 1845. Boston.** Calls for support of the movement to abolish capital punishment. 26 September 1845. p.155, c5.

5810 HENRY CLAY *to* **THO. B. STEVENS. 13 August 1845. Ashland.** Praises Dr. Bascomb's *Review of the Manifesto of the Majority.* 3 October 1845. p.157, c1.

5811 GEORGE W. CLARK *to* **FRIEND LEAVITT. [from the** *Emancipator***] n.d. n.p.** Presents proof that slaves were put to death on suspicion of setting fire to their overseer's house. 3 October 1845. p.157, c6.

5812 CHARLES FRANCIS ADAMS *to* **HENRY WILSON. 15 September 1845. Quincy.** Emphasizes union of sentiment in the anti-slavery cause. 3 October 1845. p.158, c1.

5813 A CORRESPONDENT *to* **MR. EDITOR [W. L. GARRISON]. n.d. n.p.** Asks farmers to send produce to the anti-slavery fair. 3 October 1845. p.158, c6.

5814 E. D. HUDSON *to* **FRIEND GARRISON. 20 September 1845. Springfield.** Gives an account of his attempt to free Catherine Linda, a slave. 3 October 1845. p.159, c1.

5815 EDWARD SEARCH *to* **SIR [W. L. GARRISON]. August 1845. England.** Demonstrates that the post office slows the progress of reform. 3 October 1845. p.159, c2.

5816 D. S. GRANDIN *to* **BROTHER GARRISON. 24 September 1845. Winthrop, Me.** Reports on the Congregational County Conference. 3 October 1845. p.159, c4.

5817 ONE *to* **MR. EDITOR. [from the** *Atlas***] August 1845. Boston.** States that blacks are not allowed to ride inside a stagecoach. 3 October 1845. p.159, c5.

5818 J. M. L. *to* **MR. EDITOR [W. L. GARRISON]. 9 September 1845. Cambridgeport.** Calls on blacks to cease supporting newspapers harmful to their interests. 3 October 1845. p.159, c5.

5819 A. BRISBANE *to* **WM. LLOYD GARRISON. n.d. n.p.** Reports on social reform and the conflict between capital and labor. 3 October 1845. p.160, c2.

5820 H[ENRY] C. WRIGHT *to* **[W. L.] GARRISON. 24 August 1845. Rosenheath.** States his indifference to the Sabbath; describes Loch Lomond. 3 October 1845. p.160, c4.

5821 NORTHERN MINISTER OF METHODIST EPISCOPAL CHURCH *to* **BROTHER [A SOUTHERN FRIEND]. [from the** *Southern Christian Advocate***] n.d. n.p.** Charges that Northern abolitionists lack concern for the Union and for the slave. 10 October 1845. p.161, c1.

5822 J. R. GIDDINGS *to* **THE EDITOR OF THE [***OHIO***]** *REPUBLICAN AND WHIG.* **28 August 1845. Jefferson.** Discusses at length his views on the doctrines of the AAS. 10 October 1845. p.162, c1.

5823 FREDERICK DOUGLASS *to* **FRIEND GARRISON. 16 September 1845. Dublin.** Comments on C. M. Clay's paper; notes the success of Frederick Douglass and abolitionists in Europe. 10 October 1845. p.163, c3.

5824 n.n. *to* **BROTHER [W. L. GARRISON]. 21 September 1845. West Brookfield, Vt.** Proposes that Garrison visit Vermont. 10 October 1845. p.163, c3.

5825 HENRY C. WRIGHT *to* **n.n. 19 July 1844. n.p.** Describes his travels through Switzerland. 10 October 1845. p.163, c4.

5826 CHARLES B. STEARNS *to* **SIR [W. L. GARRISON]. n.d. n.p.** States that society is not radical enough; the world needs something startling and invigorating. 10 October 1845. p.164, c2.

5827 DARIUS P. LAWTON *to* **FRIEND GARRISON. 25 September 1845. North Scituate.** Asks that J. L. Clarke's letter to Friends appear in the *Liberator*. 10 October 1845. p.164, c3.

5828 JOHN L. CLARKE *to* **THE MONTHLY MEETING OF FRIENDS, TO BE HELD IN PROVIDENCE. 14 June 1845. North Scituate.** Announces that he is leaving the Quakers because he opposes their indifference toward anti-slavery and non-resistance. 10 October 1845. p.164, c3.

5829 A. *to* **W. L. GARRISON. 23 August 1845. n.p.** Discusses the relationship of Church and reform, particularly in regard to slavery. 17 October 1845. p.165, c3.

5830 ANONYMOUS *to* **[W. L.] GARRISON. n.d. n.p.** Opposes the annexation of Texas. 17 October 1845. p.166, c4.

5831 HENRY C. WRIGHT *to* **n.n. 21 July 1844. Geneva.** Describes the scenery in Geneva; comments on anti-slavery. 17 October 1845. p.167, c3.

5832 PETER LIBBY *to* **BRO. GARRISON. 21 September 1845. Buxton, Me.** Reports on the anti-slavery cause in Maine. 17 October 1845. p.167, c4.

5833 WARREN *to* **n.n. [from the** *Cleveland American***] September 1845. Ashtabula County, Oh.** States that churches are withdrawing from the presbytery because of its stand on abolitionism. 24 October 1845. p.169, c2.

5834 C. M. CLAY *to* **LYMAN CLARY. 18 September 1845. Lexington, Ky.** Demands the right of freedom of the press. 24 October 1845. p.169, c4.

5835 ONE OF THE PROSCRIBED *to* **MR. EDITOR. [from the** *Christrian Register***] n.d. n.p.** Comments on James Haughton's attack on the clergy; argues that one need not be an abolitionist to be a lover of liberty. 24 October 1845. p.170, c2.

5836 FREDERICK DOUGLASS *to* **FRIEND GARRISON. 29 September 1845. Dublin.** Notes differences in the treatment of Frederick Douglass by Europeans and by Americans; states that his narrative was published in Europe and praised in a speech given by John O'Connell. 24 October 1845. p.170, c4.

5837 R[ICHARD] D. WEBB *to* **[W. L.] GARRISON. 2 October 1845. Dublin.** Notes the impression Frederick Douglass has made in Dublin. 24 October 1845. p.170, c4.

5838 RICHARD D. WEBB AND THOMAS WEBB *to* **THE SOCIETY OF FRIENDS IN DUBLIN. 17 September 1845. Dublin.** Criticize the society for prohibiting the use of their meetinghouse for Frederick Douglass' lectures on slavery. 24 October 1845. p.170, c5.

5839 H. C. WRIGHT *to* **[W. L.] GARRISON. 27 September 1845. Arbroath.** Describes the scenery in Arbroath. 24 October 1845. p.170, c6.

5840 H. C. WRIGHT *to* **E. L. B. WRIGHT. 23 July 1844. Geneva.** Describes the scenery in Switzerland; declares that man must abide by God's authority, not man's. 24 October 1845. p.171, c2.

5841 ADDISON DAVIS *to* **FRIEND GARRISON. n.d. n.p.** Comments on Lysander Spooner's argument of the unconstitutionality of slavery. 24 October 1845. p.171, c4.

5842 A. BRISBANE *to* **WM. LLOYD GARRISON. n.d. n.p.** Believes that social reform necessitates a restructuring of the entire social system. 24 October 1845. p.172, c2.

5843 MOSES BRADLEE *to* **THE EDITOR OF THE** *LIBERATOR* **[W. L. GARRISON]. 15 October 1845. Baldwin.** Supports the *Liberator*; challenges C. H. Stearn's views on God and the New and Old Testament. 24 October 1845. p.172, c3.

5844 AN UNITARIAN *to* **MR. GARRISON. n.d. n.p.** Criticizes Unitarian intellectual leadership because it is not strongly anti-slavery. 31 October 1845. p.173, c4.

5845 EDWARD SEARCH *to* **SIR [W. L. GARRISON]. October 1845. England.** Reports on European response to American anti-slavery agitation. 31 October 1845. p.173, c4.

5846 AMERICAN *to* **THE EDITOR OF THE** *TIMES.* **[from the** *London Times***] 20 September 1845. London.** Imputes England with responsibility for American slavery; states that the American government cannot correct the evil of slavery. 31 October 1845. p.173, c5.

5847 HENRY C. WRIGHT *to* **n.n. 25 July 1844. Basle.** Describes his travels through Switzerland. 31 October 1845. p.175, c1.

5848 R. *to* **[W. L.] GARRISON. 27 October 1845. New Bedford.** Reports that the New Bedford Lyceum does not admit colored or poor people. 31 October 1845. p.175, c3.

5849 JUSTICE *to* **WM. LLOYD GARRISON. n.d. n.p.** Criticizes the *Christian Reflector* and *Boston Recorder* for their attacks on Garrison. 31 October 1845. p.175, c3.

5850 ALFRED WELLS *to* **ADIN BALLOU. 12 October 1845. Oswego County, N.Y.** Reports on the status of the non-resistance cause in New York. 31 October 1845. p.176, c3.

5851 JOHN SMITH *to* **THE NEW ENGLAND NON-RESISTANCE SOCIETY. 20 September 1845. Trumbull County, Oh.** Believes that non-resistance is "in the highest sense an embodying of Christianity." 31 October 1845. p.176, c3.

5852 C. B. STEARNS *to* **BROTHER GARRISON. 18 October 1845. Boston.** Believes that non-resistance allows use of force if it does not cause injury to another. 31 October 1845. p.176, c4.

5853 AHMED EL KORAH *to* **BROTHER OF MY SOUL. n.d. Salem-alik.** Condemns slavery and the annexation of Texas. 7 November 1845. p.177, c4.

5854 SAMUEL BROOKE AND STEPHEN S. FOSTER *to* **SIR. 25 September 1845. Cincinnati.** Request that the enclosed disunion ballots be distributed among abolitionists. 7 November 1845. p.177, c6.

5855 STEPHEN B. IVES *to* **H. W. WILLIAMS. 13 October 1845. Salem.** Demands that they deliver "the bundle of the *Liberator*" to someone else. 7 November 1845. p.178, c5.

5856 HENRY C. WRIGHT *to* **MARY. 26 July 1844. Basle.** Describes his travels through Switzerland. 7 November 1845. p.179, c1.

5857 HIRAM WILSON *to* **W. L. GARRISON. 24 October 1845. Cleveland.** Comments on the welfare of fugitive slaves in Canada. 7 November 1845. p.179, c2.

5858 D. S. GRANDIN *to* **BRO. GARRISON. 26 October 1845. Bridgton, Me.** Comments on abolition, the *Liberator*, and Jonathan Walker. 7 November 1845. p.179, c3.

5859 HENRY C. WRIGHT *to* **n.n. 26 July 1844. Between France and Switzerland.** Describes his European travels; comments on American religion. 14 November 1845. p.181, c2.

5860 BRITISH NAVAL OFFICER *to* **n.n. [extract from the** *London Nonconformist*] **26 July 1845. West Coast of Africa.** Reflects upon the practical impossibility of suppressing slave trade. 14 November 1845. p.181, c5.

5861 JAMES HAUGHTON *to* **THE EDITOR OF THE** [*DUBLIN*] *FREEMAN*. **26 September 1845. Dublin.** Praises Frederick Douglass' lectures in Dublin; denounces slavery in America. 14 November 1845. p.181, c5.

5862 PARKER PILLSBURY *to* **FRIEND ELA. 25 October 1845. Quincy, Ma.** Reports on the position of the American Board of Commissions for Foreign Missions on slavery. 14 November 1845. p.182, c1.

5863 WM. IVES *to* **MR. GARRISON. 10 November 1845. Salem.** Declares his support of the *Liberator*. 14 November 1845. p.182, c4.

5864 n.n. *to* **MR. GARRISON. n.d. n.p.** Answers criticism of Unitarian ministry. 14 November 1845. p.183, c1.

5865 D. S. GRANDIN *to* **BRO. GARRISON. 26 October 1865. Bridgton.** Criticizes Peter Libby's account of the Liberty Party convention; discusses the position of the Liberty Party on the constitutional authority to abolish slavery. 14 November 1845. p.183, c2.

5866 PARKER PILLSBURY *to* **FRIEND GARRISON. 4 November 1845. Hanover, N.H.** Views election returns as a good sign for the anti-slavery cause. 14 November 1845. p.183, c3.

5867 H. C. WRIGHT *to* **BROTHER [W. L. GARRISON]. 6 April 1839. Peterboro'.** Declares that the Constitution is in conflict with principles of Christianity. 14 November 1845. p.183, c3.

5868 GERRIT SMITH *to* **W. L. GARRISON, MARIA W. CHAPMAN, AND EDMUND QUINCY. 15 March 1839. Peterboro'.** Donates one hundred dollars to the *Non-Resistant*. 14 November 1845. p.183, c4.

5869 n.n. *to* **n.n. [from the** *Philadelphia U.S. Gazette*] **29 July 1845. Pernambuco.** Announces the first steam-powered slave ship. 14 November 1845. p.183, c5.

5870 J. M. *to* **WILLIAM LLOYD GARRISON. 3 October 1845. Boston.** Feels that American reformers should be more interested in the poor in Ireland and England. 14 November 1845. p.184, c2.

5871 D. S. GRANDIN *to* **BRO. GARRISON. 3 October 1845. Bridgeton, Me.** Reports on the Sabbath Convention. 14 November 1845. p.184, c2.

5872 HENRY C. WRIGHT *to* **n.n. 27 July 1844. Strasburg.** Describes the area of Strasburg. 21 November 1845. p.185, c2.

5873 JACOB DISCOMB *to* **THE MEMBERS OF THE WEST CHURCH. 14 August 1845. Andover.** Laments his failure to persuade James Hendy to withdraw his anti-slavery views. 21 November 1845. p.187, c3.

5874 JAMES HENDY *to* **BRETHREN. n.d. n.p.** Opposes religious communion with slaveholders. 21 November 1845. p.187, c3.

5875 DAVID MIDDLETON *to* **MR. EDITOR [W. L. GARRISON]. 5 October 1845. Andover.** Notes indifference to the anti-slavery cause in Andover. 21 November 1845. p.187, c3.

5876 SAMUEL C. JACKSON *to* **JAMES HENDY. 23 August 1845. Andover.** Excommunicates Hendy from the church for his anti-slavery stand. 21 November 1845. p.187, c3.

5877 H. *to* **FRIEND GARRISON. 3 November 1845. South Dartmouth.** Discusses the constitutionality of slavery. 21 November 1845. p.187, c4.

5878 JOHN L. CLARKE *to* **FRIEND GARRISON. 11 July 1845. North Scituate, R.I.** Criticizes Providence Quakers' position on reform. 21 November 1845. p.188, c2.

5879 JOHN QUINCY ADAMS *to* **REV. SAMUEL H. COX. 19 August 1845. Quincy, Ma.** Comments on the passion for tobacco. 21 November 1845. p.188, c4.

5880 ALFRED WELLS *to* **FRIEND GARRISON. n.d. n.p.** States a case for slavery under certain circumstances. 28 November 1845. p.189, c2.

5881 JAMES HAUGHTON *to* **THE EDITOR OF THE [*LONDON*] *INQUIRER*. 3 October 1845. Dublin.** Answers those who defend Dr. Parkman and other Unitarians who have not taken up the anti-slavery cause. 28 November 1845. p.190, c1.

5882 FREDERICK DOUGLASS *to* **FRIEND [W. L. GARRISON]. 28 October 1845. Cork.** States that he will speak both on abolition and on temperance. 28 November 1845. p.190, c4.

5883 JAMES HAUGHTON *to* **FRIEND GARRISON. 30 October 1845. Dublin.** Reports on reform and conditions in Ireland; comments on Frederick Douglass' lectures in Ireland. 28 November 1845. p.190, c6.

5884 JAMES HAUGHTON *to* **A. W. PAWLTON. 27 October 1845. Dublin.** Criticizes Pawlton's correspondence with Calhoun and McDuffie. 28 November 1845. p.190, c6.

5885 JAMES HAUGHTON *to* **RICHARD COBDEN. 22 October 1845. Dublin.** Criticizes Cobden's correspondence with Calhoun and McDuffie. 28 November 1845. p.191, c1.

5886 JAMES HAUGHTON *to* **JOHN BRIGHT. 24 October 1845. Dublin.** Advocates free trade; opposes monopolies and the purchase of articles produced by slave labor. 28 November 1845. p.191, c1.

5887 C. B. STEARNS *to* **BROTHER GARRISON. 13 November 1845. Wrentham.** Believes that God is accountable and does not have the right to take life. 28 November 1845. p.192, c3.

5888 RHODA *to* **FRIEND GARRISON. n.d. n.p.** Feels that non-resistance is the most important cause. 28 November 1845. p.192, c3.

5889 W. *to* **MR. EDITOR. [from the *Western Citizen*] 25 October 1845. Rock Island.** Reports that he witnessed an execution. 28 November 1845. p.192, c4.

5890 HENRY C. WRIGHT *to* **n.n. 28 July 1844. Strasburg.** Describes his travels in Europe. 5 December 1845. p.193, c3.

5891 JAMES HAUGHTON *to* **SIR. [from the *Bible Christian*] 6 October 1845. Dublin.** Discusses Rev. Dr. Dewey's statements on seamen; charges him with indifference toward slavery. 5 December 1845. p.193, c6.

5892 ABBOTT LAWRENCE *to* **C. F. ADAMS. 7 November 1845. Boston.** Maintains opposition to the annexation of Texas, but thinks that efforts to prevent it are futile. 5 December 1845. p.194, c1.

5893 NATHAN APPLETON *to* **CHARLES F. ADAMS, JOHN G. PALFREY, AND CHARLES SUMNER. 10 November 1845. Boston.** Opposes annexation, but considers further protest a lost cause. 5 December 1845. p.194, c2.

5894 JOHN MCCOMB *to* **W. L. GARRISON. 17 November 1845. Georgetown.** Believes that American slaves are worse off than the suffering poor in Britain. 5 December 1845. p.195, c3.

5895 J. C. *to* **MR. GARRISON. n.d. n.p.** States that clergymen are emphasizing needs of the poor of Europe in their sermons. 5 December 1845. p.195, c3.

5896 HENRY C. WRIGHT *to* **[W. L.] GARRISON. 5 October 1845. Aberdeen.** Describes his travels in Scotland. 5 December 1845. p.195, c4.

5897 JOHN QUINCY ADAMS *to* **ANTI-CAPITAL PUNISHMENT MEETING. 7 November 1845. Boston.** Expresses his support for the meeting. 5 December 1845. p.196, c2.

5898 A DEMOCRAT IN NEW HAMPSHIRE *to* **FRIEND H. [EDITOR OF THE** *LOWELL PATRIOT*]. **[extract] 27 October 1845. Concord.** Condemns Hale for his endeavors to continue suppression of the slave. 12 December 1845. p.197, c3.

5899 RALPH VARIAN *to* **WM. LLOYD GARRISON. 10 November 1845. Cork.** Praises Garrison, Frederick Douglass, and J. N. Buffum on behalf of abolitionists of Cork. 12 December 1845. p.198, c4.

5900 J. N. BUFFUM *to* **FRIEND [W. L. GARRISON]. 17 November 1845. Liverpool.** Discusses the state of the British economy and the enlightening effect of the free trade movement. 12 December 1845. p.198, c5.

5901 H. C. WRIGHT *to* **[W. L.] GARRISON. 12 November 1845. Glasgow.** Discusses his anti-nationalism pamphlet. 12 December 1845. p.198, c6.

5902 R. D. WEBB *to* **HENRY C. WRIGHT. 9 November 1845. Dublin.** Praises Wright's anti-slavery pamphlet. 12 December 1845. p.199, c1.

5903 PETER LIBBY *to* **BROTHER GARRISON. 21 November 1845. Buxton, Me.** Attacks priesthood as pro-slavery. 12 December 1845. p.199, c3.

5904 S. *to* **FRIEND GARRISON. 8 December 1845. Mansfield.** Reports that a free colored woman was sent back to slavery. 12 December 1845. p.199, c3.

5905 A. BRISBANE *to* **WILLIAM LLOYD GARRISON. n.d. n.p.** Asserts the need for fundamental social reform. 12 December 1845. p.200, c2.

5906 A DEMOCRAT *to* **FRIEND ANTHONY. [from the** *Bristol County Democrat*] **20 November 1845. Easton.** Criticizes anti-annexation Whigs. 19 December 1845. p.201, c1.

5907 H. C. WRIGHT *to* **DAUGHTER HANNAH. 28 July 1844. Rhine.** Believes that maintaining an appointed hour of worship is unchristian. 19 December 1845. p.201, c2.

5908 HENRY C. WRIGHT *to* **THE EDITOR OF THE** *GLASGOW ARGUS*. **15 August 1845. Rosenheath, Scotland.** States that the fundamental role of slavery in the United States is revealed by its attitude toward Haiti. 19 December 1845. p.201, c4.

5909 J. B. *to* **FRIEND GARRISON. 15 December 1845. New Bedford.** Relates the story of an emancipated slave who desired to return to her master. 19 December 1845. p.203, c2.

5910 JAMES MITCHELL *to* **WILLIAM LLOYD GARRISON. 8 December 1845. Nantucket.** Discusses the problems of the poor of England in relation to the slaves in America. 19 December 1845. p.203, c3.

5911 JONATHAN WALKER *to* **FRIEND GARRISON. n.d. n.p.** Sends a donation to the anti-slavery cause. 19 December 1845. p.203, c6.

5912 N. SOUTHARD *to* **FRIEND GARRISON. 1 December 1845. Walpole.** Comments on Stearns' views of the rights of God. 19 December 1845. p.204, c2.

5913 C. B. S. *to* **GARRISON. 29 November 1845. New Bedford.** Believes that it is everyone's duty to "turn the other cheek" rather than strike back. 19 December 1845. p.204, c3.

5914 JOHN REED *to* **SIR. [from the** *Free State Rally***] 8 November 1845. Yarmouth Port.** Opposes the annexation of Texas. 19 December 1845. p.204, c4.

5915 W. B. CALHOUN *to* **C. F. ADAMS. 28 November 1845. Springfield.** Supports the movement against annexation. 19 December 1845. p.204, c4.

5916 S. H. WALLEY, JR. *to* **MESSRS. F. JACKSON, W. PHILLIPS AND E. WRIGHT, JR. n.d. n.p.** Supports the anti-annexation movement. 19 December 1845. p.204, c4.

5917 NATH. B. BORDEN *to* **CHARLES F. ADAMS. [extract] 28 November 1845. Fall River.** Supports the anti-annexation movement. 19 December 1845. p.204, c4.

5918 SAMUEL WILLARD *to* **E. WRIGHT, JR. 1 December 1845. Deerfield.** Supports the anti-annexation movement. 19 December 1845. p.204, c5.

5919 H. C. WRIGHT *to* **W. L. GARRISON. [extract] n.d. Glasgow.** Quotes from George Thompson's letter on his activities in Europe. 19 December 1845. p.204, c6.

5920 THOMAS CLARKSON *to* **W. L. GARRISON. [extract] 24 October 1845. n.p.** Claims that he is still an anti-slavery reformer at the age of eighty-six. 19 December 1845. p.204, c6.

5921 JAMES HAUGHTON *to* **W. L. GARRISON. [extract] 27 October 1845. n.p.** Supports Garrison's call for the dissolution of all relations with slaveholders. 19 December 1845. p.204, c6.

5922 ELIZABETH PEASE *to* **W. L. GARRISON. [extract] n.d. n.p.** Believes it is one's Christian duty to oppose slavery. 19 December 1845. p.204, c6.

5923 H. C. WRIGHT *to* **n.n. 25 July 1844. Coblenz.** Describes his travels in Coblenz. 26 December 1845. p.205, c2.

5924 J. H. ELA *to* **FRIEND GARRISON. n.d. n.p.** Corrects Garrison's misconceptions concerning which paper supports Mr. Hale. 26 December 1845. p.206, c3.

5925 DAVID LYMAN *to* **WM. H. BURLEIGH. n.d. n.p.** Claims that Thompson Miller is not a fugitive slave but an impostor. 26 December 1845. p.206, c6.

5926 RICHARD D. WEBB *to* **[W. L.] GARRISON. 30 November 1845. Dublin.** Believes that the problems of the poor in England are not so great as those of the slaves in America. 26 December 1845. p.207, c1.

5927 JAMES N. BUFFUM *to* **BRO. GARRISON. 2 December 1845. London.** Describes his travels in London. 26 December 1845. p.207, c2.

Index of Correspondents

Gentleman in New York, a, 618, 691, 1028
Gentleman in North Carolina, a, 611
Gentleman in Pennsylvania, a, 7
Gentleman in Philadelphia, a, 765
Gentleman in Sandwich, a, 376
Gentleman in Vermont, 756
Gentleman of Bristol, England, a, 5673
Gentleman of High Respectability, a, 356
Gentleman of High Standing, a, 126, 169
Gentleman of New York, a, 373
Gentleman of the City of New York, a, 1754
Gentleman Residing in District of Columbia, a, 613
Gentleman Residing Near Londongrove, a, 478
Gentleman Traveling South, a, 1863
Gentlemen of the Committee to Form a Vermont Anti-Slavery Society, 1970
Gentlemen of the *Genius of Universal Emancipation*, 549
Georgia Courier, editors of, 510
Georgian, 2680
Gerould, M., 1716
Gerry, 2000
Gerry, George, 4785
Ghose, Ram Gopaul, 3972
Gibbs, W. A., 2916
Gibbens, Daniel, 2639
Gibbons, James S., 4032, 4044, 4089, 4296
Giddings, J. R., 4721, 4757, 5822
Gifford, Clother, 3680, 3708, 4266, 4848
Gifford, Josiah, 2207, 2304, 2553, 2971
Gill, Mrs. D. L., 2502
Gill, Perez, 3174
Gill, Richard, W., 582
Gill, William L., 497
Gillett, R. E., 4425
Gillmer, Rev. D. R., 2807
Gilmer, Thomas W., 4952
Ginress, Bidford, 2470
Gladding, C., 5222
Glascoe, James S., 5794
Glasgow Argus, editor of, 4175, 4459, 5908
Glasgow Emancipation Society, the, 5189, 5190, 5191, 5192
Glasgow Female Anti-Slavery Society, 5776
Glasgow Friend, editors of, 5057
Glover, R., 3894, 3895
Glover, S., 3894, 3895
Goderich, 628
Godfrey, D. S., 5297

Going, ____, 2591
Gooch, C. W., 2654
Goodell, William, 713, 740, 1208, 1275, 1276, 1277, 1348, 1352, 1438, 1598, 1655, 1890, 2209, 2363, 2589, 2657, 2671, 2677, 2945, 3104, 3195, 3278, 3392, 3681, 3769, 3807, 3889, 3999, 4001, 4035, 4079, 4091, 4100, 4103, 4126, 4127, 4147, 4153, 4194, 4225, 4241, 4243, 4249, 4262, 4313, 4882
Goodman, William, 4344
Goodrich, S. G., 2938
Goodwin, E. W., 4443, 5111, 5112
Goodwin, Henry B., 5471, 5488
Gorden, John, 4371
Gotham, 1779
Gould, Samuel L., 1881, 2202, 2396, 2731, 2732
Gourley, Hugh, 2107
Gouverneur, Samuel L., 2061
Gove, Simon, 1901
Governor of Florida, the, 5782
Governor of Maryland, 485
Governor of South Carolina, the, 5295
Gowdey, 920
Graddis, Maxwell P., 4345
Gradin, D. S., 5075
Graham, James B., 3641
Graham, S., 4027, 4591
Granch, E. P., 4344
Grand Jury of Suffolk County, the, 4455
Grandin, D. S., 4894, 5012, 5169, 5239, 5393, 5816, 5858, 5865, 5871
Granetstone, Joseph, 4332
Granite State, 1940
Grattan, Edmund A., 4519
Graves, Rev. Henry L., 2988, 4533
Gray, Mr., 3851
Gray, Ira, 3400
Gray, L. D., 4544
Gray, M., 2384
Greeley, Eliphalet, 5731
Greeley, Horace, 5693
Green, Gen., 646
Green, Mr., 2484
Green, Rev. Beriah, 1147, 1149, 1198, 1208, 1295, 1352, 1355, 2195, 2997, 4539
Green, Charles, 2844
Green, Rev. J. S., 3415, 3472
Green, Josiah, 1121
Greenborough (N. C.) *Patriot*, editor of, 547
Greene, Mr., 896
Greene, Charles, 1604
Greene, David, 378, 2611